THE TRAFALGAR COMPANION

THE

TRAFALGAR COMPANION

EDITOR

ALEXANDER STILWELL

First published in Great Britain in 2005 by Osprey Publishing,
Midland House, West Way, Botley, Oxford OX2 9LP, UK.
443 Park Avenue South, New York, NY 10016, USA
Email: info@ospreypublishing.com

A CIP catalogue record for this book is available from the British Library.

ISBN 1 84176 835 9

The authors, John B. Hattendorf, Peter Padfield, Edgar Vincent, Rémi Monaque, Nicholas Tracy, Peter Goodwin, Joseph Callo and Andrew Lambert have asserted their rights under the Copyright, Designs and Patents Act, 1988, to be identified as the Authors of this Work.

Page layout by Ken Vail Graphic Design, Cambridge, UK
Index: Tim Pearce
Originated by PPS Grasmere Ltd, Leeds, UK
Printed and bound in China through Worldprint Ltd

05 06 07 08 09 10 9 8 7 6 5 4 3 2 1

For a catalogue of all books published by Osprey Military and Aviation please contact:
Osprey Direct UK, PO Box 140, Wellingborough, Northants, NN8 2FA, UK
Email: info@ospreydirect.co.uk

North America
Osprey Direct, 2427 Bond Street, University Park, IL 60466, USA
Email: info@ospreydirect.co.uk

www.ospreypublishing.com

Front cover image: Detail from *The Panorama of the Battle of Trafalgar* by W. L. Wyllie RA (1851–1931), showing HMS *Victory* and HMS *Téméraire* engaging the *Redoutable*. (The Royal Naval Museum)

Title page image: The *Santísima Trinidad*. (The Albert and Roland Umhey Collection)

Acknowledgments: The Editor would like to thank Dr Campbell McMurray, Chris Arkell and Matthew Sheldon at the Royal Naval Museum, Portsmouth, for all their help with this project. Thanks must also go to The Society for Nautical Research and especially Alan Aberg. Further information about the society's work and 'The Save the Victory Fund' can be found at the society's website www.snr.org. Finally, thanks must go to Anita Hitchings, Rachel Cartwright, Ruth Sheppard and all at Osprey for their hard work.

CONTENTS

LIST OF CONTRIBUTORS

Professor John B. Hattendorf D.Phil. (Oxon.), F.R. Hist. S. is the Ernest J. King Professor of Maritime History and Chairman, Maritime History Department at the US Naval War College, Newport, Rhode Island. He was awarded the Caird Medal by the National Maritime Museum in 2000. His many publications include *The Anglo-French Naval Wars, 1689–1815* (2005); *Every Man Will Do His Duty: An Anthology of First Hand Accounts from the Age of Nelson 1793–1815* (2003); *War at Sea in the Middle Ages and the Renaissance* (2003); and *Naval Strategy and Policy in the Mediterranean: Past, Present and Future* (2000). He is Editor-in-Chief of the *Oxford Encyclopedia of Maritime History*, 4 vols (planned for 2006).

Peter Padfield trained for the sea as a cadet on HMS *Worcester* and subsequently sailed on the replica 17th-century bark *Mayflower II* when she recreated the Pilgrim Fathers' voyage across the Atlantic to Plymouth, Massachusetts. He made his name as a naval historian with works on naval gunnery and biographies of gunnery innovators. He is presently working on a trilogy of maritime histories with the aim of bringing naval history out of the specialists' closet to incorporate it as a major determinant and shaper of the modern world. Two volumes have so far been published: *Maritime Supremacy and the Opening of the Western Mind: Naval Campaigns that Shaped the Modern World, 1588–1782*, and *Maritime Power and the Struggle for Freedom: Naval Campaigns that Shaped the Modern World, 1788–1851*, which was awarded the Mountbatten Maritime Prize 2003.

Edgar Vincent served in the Royal Navy after graduating from Oxford and Nelson has been his lifelong passion. He worked for ICI, was Chairman of the Management Advisory Council of INSEAD Fontainebleau, and later a head-hunter and management consultant. He is a member of the Society of Nautical Research, the Navy Records Society, the 1805 Club and the Nelson Society. Edgar Vincent's *Nelson: Love and Fame* (2003), which was shortlisted for the Samuel Johnson Prize for non-fiction, has been acclaimed as the best modern biography of Horatio Nelson.

Admiral Rémi Monaque entered the French Naval School in 1955 and went on to command a hydrographic ship and three anti-submarine warfare vessels. He was appointed Director of Studies of the French Naval War College and was promoted to Rear-Admiral in 1992. He also served in the Office of the Secretary-General of Defence. His books include *Latouche-Tréville: l'amiral qui defiait Nelson* (2000) and *L'école de guerre navale 1896–1993* (1995).

Dr Nicholas Tracy is Adjunct Professor of History at the University of New Brunswick and is an acknowledged expert on naval tactics. His publications include *The Naval Chronicle: Contemporary Views of the War at Sea* (2003) and *Naval Warfare in the Age of Sail: The Evolution of Fighting Tactics 1650–1815* (2001).

Peter Goodwin MPhil. IEng. MIMarEST. is keeper and curator of HMS *Victory*. His publications include *Men O'War: Life in Nelson's Navy* (2003) and *In Which We Served: A Comprehensive History of Nelson's Ships* (2002).

Rear-Admiral Joseph Callo (US Naval Reserve, retired) is a full-time naval historian and writer. He has held senior posts in advertising agencies and was named Author of the Year 1998 by *Naval History Magazine* (US Naval Institute). His books include *Nelson Speaks: Admiral Lord Nelson in his own Words* (2001); *Legacy of Leadership: Lessons from Admiral Lord Nelson* (1999); and *Nelson in the Caribbean* (2003). He is the US editor of *Who's Who in Naval History* (2005).

Professor Andrew Lambert F.R. Hist. S. is Laughton Professor of Naval History at King's College, London. He presented the BBC 2 television series *War at Sea* (2004) and his books include *Nelson: Britannia's God of War* (2004), *War at Sea in the Age of Sail* (2000), and *The Last Sailing Battlefleet: Maintaining Naval Mastery 1815–1850* (1992).

I'll be no *Towpenny Customer at St Paul's!
This shall be poor Jack's Monument, in his
little Garden, to his Noble Companion _
first of all is my Sea Chest, in memory
of the many Voyages I hav had with
his Honor _ on it I have chalk'd a
Text from Scripture suitable to the
occasion _ then comes two Cags of
Grog in memory of his noble Spirit _
then two Hangers in memory of his
gallant bravery _ then his uniform Hat,
which reminds me of the Nile, Copenhagen, and, Trafalgar, _ and above all is
the figure of an Englishman's Heart,
hung with black Crape.
And a third part of
of their ships were destroyed,
Revelations Chap, 8. Verse, 9,
must pay Twopence!!

INTRODUCTION

PROFESSOR JOHN B. HATTENDORF

Throughout the period from the mid-seventeenth century to 1815, France was the most powerful single state in Europe. England came into fundamental opposition to France in 1689, through the change of foreign policy that was associated with the accession of William III and Mary II to the English throne. Following that event, England (from 1707 Great Britain; and from 1801 the United Kingdom) fought a series of seven different major wars against France, during which she usually aligned herself with a coalition of other European powers designed to balance France's superior forces. The last two of these wars merged together, but are usually separately named: the War of the French Revolution from 1792 to 1799 and the Napoleonic Wars from 1799 to 1815.[1]

A series of wars, beginning with the Russo-Turkish War in 1787 and followed by the War of the French Revolution and the first phases of the Napoleonic Wars up to 1812, marked the gradual collapse in the structure of international politics that had characterized European relations for a century and more. The phases of warfare which immediately followed, between 1812 and 1815, were clearly a continuation of those wars, but their effects were directed toward the construction of a new replacement structure for European affairs. In this broad and difficult process, the earlier system of balance-of-power politics among the major states, focused around their own separate interests, was eventually succeeded by a new system, based on a European-wide consensus that preserved the existence and independence of all the actors, including those that had been previously threatened by the earlier process. This new approach involved a shift in European mentality and outlook, whose origins preceded the wars and whose results went far beyond them, to create an alternative to warfare through the new international system that was created.[2]

The collapse of the international system between 1793 and 1812 during this series of wars was paralleled and eventually intertwined with the initial failure of some of the patriotic reform movements that were trying to improve the

OPPOSITE
The Sailor's Monument to the memory of Lord Nelson (London: Etching published by William Holland, December 1805). This caricature criticized the policy of charging two pence for the public to pay their respects to Nelson.
(Royal Naval Museum)

Northern Bears Brought to Dance (London, Etching published by S.W. Fores, 14 February 1801). This political cartoon followed the announcement that the fleet under Admiral Sir Hyde Parker and Vice-Admiral Lord Nelson would be ordered to the Baltic and that a state of war existed with The League of Armed Neutrality, involving Britain's embargo against Danish, Swedish and Russian shipping. This caricature anticipated the Royal Navy's victory at Copenhagen, 2 April 1801. (Anne S. K. Brown Military Collection, Brown University Library)

functioning of the Old Regime monarchical system, and with the subsequent failure to replace it with democratic and republic forms of government. These efforts to instill democratic forms of government in Europe resulted in civil war and widespread chaos that turned quickly to rule by despotic force. The collapse in the international system brought with it a change in the character of warfare, as leaders sought to use battle as a decisive political force, involving extremes in violence and destruction that went far beyond what had been experienced previously.

The Wars of the French Revolution had begun only in April 1792, as a response to the slowly deteriorating international situation surrounding and resulting from the developing internal revolution in France that had begun in 1789. At first, Britain stood aside and declined to join the First Coalition that was forming to fight France from 1792 onwards. Within the context of a variety of crosscurrents in domestic and international politics that either encouraged war or argued against it, Britain eventually entered the war against France in February 1793. In this, the critical factor was the French invasion of the Austrian Netherlands and the associated threat to the Dutch Republic that led to the break-up of Anglo-French diplomatic relations.[3] Historically, the presence of an enemy in the Low Countries has repeatedly been a matter of the greatest strategic concern for Britain as the most effective staging point for an invasion. It had been the critical issue at the time of the Armada, and William III's successful landing had been launched from there, a century later, in 1688. It was an issue in the world wars of the twentieth century as it was in the time of the French Revolution and Napoleon.[4]

Following Britain's entry into the war against France in 1793, the next 22 years saw a series of interrelated, successive, or overlapping phases of warfare that alternated with brief periods of peace, to which historians have given varying names and coalition numbers. The following provides a list, among several alternatives available, for the purposes of general orientation:

1792–1797: First Coalition, ending with the Treaty of Campo Formio.
1797–1801: Quasi-War between France and the United States, ending in the Convention of Mortefontaine.
1798–1802: Second Coalition, ending with the Peace of Amiens.
1805: Third Coalition, ending with the Treaty of Pressburg.
1806–1807: Fourth Coalition, ending with the Treaty of Tilsit.
1808–1814: The Peninsular War in Spain and Portugal.
1809: Fifth Coalition, ending in the Treaty of Schönbrunn.
1812–1815: The Anglo-American War of 1812, ending with the Peace of Ghent.
1812–1814: Sixth Coalition, ending in Napoleon's abdication and exile to Elba, Treaty of Fontainebleau, and the Congress of Vienna.
1815: Seventh Coalition: The One Hundred Days, ending in the battle of Waterloo and Napoleon's exile to St Helena.

THE FRAGILE PEACE, 1801–03

The battle of Trafalgar was an event that occurred in the context of the events involved in the breakdown of the Peace of Amiens, which had ended the War of the Second Coalition in March 1802, and the formation and conduct of the War of the Third Coalition between 1803 and 1805. The Peace of Amiens was a compromise peace and the result of the momentary general exhaustion of both France and Britain. In the face of the dissolution of the Second Coalition and strong public demands at home for peace with a worsening economic situation, British Prime Minister Henry Addington and his Cabinet colleagues, who had come to power following William Pitt's resignation in February 1801 over the Catholic relief issue, felt that they could live with the agreement and with France. This view, however, was based on the assumption that the French Revolution was over and the government in Paris would remain stable and resist the temptation for further expansion, either in Europe or overseas. Even if the war were to be resumed, the Peace had the clear advantage of providing a respite to both sides to recover their finances and regroup their resources and plans. The Peace was certainly advantageous for Bonaparte, who immediately used the opportunity to

Dido in Despair! (London: Etching produced by James Gillray, artist and engraver, and H. Humphrey, publisher, 6 Feb, 1801). In one of James Gillray's most virulent satires, this caricature ridicules Lady Hamilton at a point when Nelson was relatively unpopular. Published shortly after the news that Parker and Hamilton would sail to the Baltic, the verse reads:

Ah, where, & ah where is my gallant sailor gone?
He's gone to fight the Frenchmen, for George upon the throne
He's gone to fight the Frenchmen, t'loose t'other Arm & Eye,
And left me with the old Antique, to lay me down & Cry.

(Royal Naval Museum)

develop a concordat with Pope Pius VII, to reorganize the French government to affirm his personal rule, to organize the territories under his control in Germany and Italy, and to use his naval resources to support recovering control of Santo Domingo in the West Indies from the Afro-American leader Toussaint l'Ouverture.

The Anglo-French peace negotiations and the subsequent peace agreement avoided a number of issues that eventually proved to be irritants to maintaining a stable peace in the future. The Peace of Amiens contained no provision that either protected British commerce or prevented further French overseas colonial growth. Additionally, it made no attempt to confirm the European status quo, failing to reaffirm the French boundaries that had been recognized in the separate Treaty of Lunéville which Austria had concluded, omitting recognition of the independence of the new satellite republics in Holland, Switzerland, and Lombardy, or dealing with the reorganization of Italy and Germany under Napoleon's influence. All these would become future issues, but these matters were momentarily obscured by immediate satisfaction with an interlude of peace and an initial feeling in Britain and in other European countries that they could all find a way to live peacefully with France, at least for a time.[5]

The Rt. Hon. William Pitt (London: Engraving by John Chapman, 1796). As Prime Minister from 1783 to February 1801, Pitt was largely responsible for nurturing the development of the Royal Navy during the decade of peace following the War of American Independence. By the time of the Wars of the French Revolution, the Navy was prepared, although a number of the early military efforts under Pitt's government were badly planned and executed. In February 1801, he resigned over domestic political issues in favour of his follower, Henry Addington, who served as Prime Minister until Pitt returned in May 1804 and remained in power through the Trafalgar campaign. (Anne S. K. Brown Military Collection, Brown University Library)

The Peace of Amiens attempted to utilize the long-standing 18th-century ideas of European balance-of-power politics to divide Europe into three main power blocks that could have prevented any of the major powers – Russia, France and Britain – from either completely dominating or threatening each other. Yet, it was a balance of power based around acceptance of Napoleonic France's hegemony within large parts of continental Europe.

Despite the potential for the Amiens settlement to create a stable peace for a time, there were several areas in Europe that remained potential flash points for renewed conflict. Among these were the Mediterranean and Near East regions, which Amiens could well have stabilized, if the treaty provisions had been carried out so that France evacuated Naples and handed Egypt back to the Turks; Britain evacuated its forces from Egypt and Malta, but kept Gibraltar; and Russia withdrew its squadron from the Mediterranean, but maintained a base in the Ionian Islands and a peacekeeping garrison to uphold Malta's neutrality.[6] In other areas, France controlled the entire southern shore of the Channel and its approaches in the Low Countries including the mouths of the Scheldt and the Rhine. Continental European markets were closed to British trade, both in the North and in the South. Overseas, British forces had made 25 conquests during the War of the Second Coalition, but all these were given up at Amiens, including the return of the Cape of Good Hope to the Netherlands and Martinique to France. By 1802, after nine years of warfare against France, Britain was exhausted and had gained nothing through the war.[7]

The failure of the Peace of Amiens and the renewal of war, first with Britain in 1803, and then with the Third Coalition in 1805, was clearly caused by Bonaparte and other French leaders, who continued to expand French military power in Europe and to encourage overseas expansion. As expressions of this, Bonaparte and some of his representatives gave clear indications of their long term ambitions to return to Egypt and to expand into other areas in North Africa, although they had no specific plans for doing this. Also, France showed an interest in Florida and other Spanish territories about the same time that she was selling the Louisiana Territory to the United States. In India, Bonaparte appointed a noted Anglophone to govern the French colonies there, while also ordering Rear-Admiral Denis Decrès, his Naval Minister, to expand the French Navy, all of which caused some concern in Britain. Even more disturbing were Bonaparte's political interventions into continental European affairs.[8]

Representative of what lay ahead in Europe, on 1 October 1801, the very day that Britain had signed the preliminaries for the Peace of Amiens, a plebiscite was held in the Netherlands on a new constitution based on the French model. Of the 416,619 voters who turned out, 16,771 voted in favor, while 52,219 voted against it and a stunning 347,629 abstained. The government declared that the abstentions and missing votes were 'tacit affirmations' and declared the new constitution as 'the will of people.'[9]

While some of Bonaparte's innovations were progressive and appropriate improvements for individual countries that came under his control, he made them in ways that aggravated relations with other powers, particularly Britain. In Switzerland, he used the 1800 Act of Mediation to render it neutral under French control, building on this over the next few years to bring Swiss troops into the French Army and announcing these changes in ways made to show them as demonstrations of French independence of British opinion, allowing no British residents in the country.[10]

In Germany, Bonaparte created a territorial revolution between 1800 and 1803, by eliminating many political remnants of the Middle Ages, including 112 previously independent states, 41 free cities, and 66 ecclesiastical principalities.

While this was a major step toward the formation of modern Germany, the redistribution of lands for the benefit of Prussia, Bavaria and others was simultaneously an alteration to the European system that created a direct threat to Austria with associated indirect threats to Prussia, to Russia and to Britain. While Britain paid little immediate attention beyond her concern for Hanover, the new tsar of Russia, Alexander I, began to have broader concerns about finding ways to restrain his French ally from late 1802 onwards.

It Italy, Bonaparte's territorial innovations were very similar to what he had done in Germany, but, in contrast to Germany, the Italians clearly violated international agreements, particularly the recent 1801 Peace of Lunéville with Austria. Bonaparte's aggressive polices included the creation of the Italian Republic with himself as its president assuming direct control over the Ligurian Republic, transforming Tuscany into the Kingdom of Etruria, and annexing Elba and Piedmont into France. Immediately following this, Bonaparte ordered all these newly formed states to arms and to prepare for war.

In mid-1802, Bonaparte sent General Pierre-Louis Roederer on an intelligence mission to Austria and Hungary to gather information on the military situation

A Jig Round the Statue of Peace (London: Etching October 1801). This political cartoon shows opponents Nelson and Napoleon, Pitt and C.J. Fox, dancing in celebration of the recently concluded Peace of Amiens, with John Bull asking "Who shall pay the piper?" for all the unresolved difficulties it involved. (Royal Naval Museum)

there and to look for potential popular uprisings that might create an Austrian–Russian conflict in the Balkans. At the same time, Bonaparte urged the Italian Republic to form an army of Austrian deserters as a provocation to Austria and he also tried to use the Ionian Islands as a bone of contention between the two powers. In making these provocative moves, Bonaparte was trying to find ways that would distract Austria from opposing his moves in Germany and Italy, while also encouraging Russia to ally herself more closely with France.

Bonaparte's continual expansion of French military power created uneasiness, both in Britain and in Russia, but his actions by themselves fell short of starting a new war. In spite of aggressive behaviour, Bonaparte did not intend to start a war immediately and thought of waiting until 1805, when he anticipated that his alliance with Russia could result in supplying enough timber and naval stores to effectively rebuild the French Navy.[11] He was aware that both Russia and Britain were located on the periphery of Europe and that they shared the attitude that they could stand apart from continental quarrels, as long as they presented no immediate, direct, and intolerable threat to their own interests. This attitude was certainly a strong factor in the initial acceptance of the terms of the Peace of Amiens, but very quickly Russia began to sense a threat, although in a place in which Bonaparte had not yet consciously created one: along its southern borders and in the Near East. This was a traditional security concern for Russia, in which the recent acquisition and continuing retention of Georgia in the Caucasus played a part. Russia saw this broad region, with tribally dominated and weak powers such as the Persian and Ottoman empires, as its own sphere of influence. At the same time, some in Britain began to sense that Bonaparte's moves could become eventual threats to British interests in the West Indies and in the Indian subcontinent.

While such broad strategic and security issues were beginning to develop in reaction to French policy following the Peace of Amiens, Bonaparte was also involved in another effort: to control information, not only within France, but throughout Europe. Bonaparte had immediately imposed censorship in 1800, shortly after becoming First Consul, and entered on a major campaign to silence critical comment by limiting the number of periodicals. Going far beyond this and beyond any previous attempt at controlling information and political opinion, Bonaparte moved to control information across Europe through a triple approach. He organized an effort to control the opposition press that was being promoted outside France by French émigré journalists. Bonaparte targeted individual journalists, using bribery and coercion, to force publication of favourable opinion. As part of this, the French government made a special effort to observe the content and the circulation of these foreign journals. At the same time, Bonaparte orchestrated a diplomatic offensive against such journalists, attempting to have them either punished by foreign governments or extraditing them to France for libel proceedings.[12]

Between 1800 and 1803, the French government made repeated diplomatic complaints about the material that émigré journalists in Britain and the Channel

Islands were publishing. The initial reaction of the Addington government was to be conciliatory to these complaints, without going so far as to limit the freedom of the Press at home. The situation was exacerbated further on 9 August 1802, when the *Moniteur* in Paris published an article, thought to have been written by Napoleon himself, which accused the British government of bad faith in not controlling criticism of a peaceful, neighbouring state. The article went so far as to suggest that the British lacked a government with the capability to make its authority felt and, for that reason, should not even be considered a sovereign power.

Failing to understand the range of British sensitivities and outrage surrounding this matter, the French continued to press for stronger measures. The Addington government did some of the things that Bonaparte requested: removing the anti-Bonapartist Chouan plotters from Jersey in the Channel Islands, putting on trial the émigré journalist Peltier, and taking some informal steps to tell the proprietors of various pro-government British newspapers that it disapproved of them publishing criticism of Bonaparte. All this had some direct effect in meeting Bonaparte's demands, but it was not enough. Bonaparte thought that British government influence over newspaper opinion was the same as his own control of the press in France. In his eyes, British failures to obtain full and satisfactory results made them seem duplicitous. To British eyes, Bonaparte's demands went too far and became unreasonable intrusions.

The tensions and cultural misunderstandings between France and Britain over the press issue soon merged with the more conventional aspects of grand strategy, as the time came to execute portions of the Amiens agreement. Article 10 of the treaty required Britain to evacuate its forces from Malta and to return it to the Order of the Knights of St John of Jerusalem upon the election of a new grand master, whose control of the island would be guaranteed by the European powers. In March 1801, the previous grand master, Tsar Paul I, had been strangled by his courtiers, four of whom were Knights of Malta. His successor as Tsar, Alexander I, refused the office with the view that Malta and the Order of St John should return to local control. The Treaty of Amiens reflected the same aim and the British government made preparations to comply and withdraw its troops and control. In September 1802, Pope Pius VII attempted to confer the grand mastership on the Roman knight Bartolemeo Ruspoli. He refused to accept the appointment and it was not until February 1803 that a replacement was found in the Balì Giovanni Tommasi, who became the grand master through an irregular election procedure.[13]

The unsettled situation over the grand mastership created a delay in putting in place the provisions of the Peace of Amiens, but the delay was not the only issue that led to Malta becoming the spark that renewed war between France and Britain. Behind this, only Austria had offered to act as guarantors of Malta's independence; Malta's future was questionable, as Russia and the other major powers had declined to act as guarantors, but in August, British diplomats in Berlin were still trying to persuade Prussia to join in the guarantee so that the original settlement could proceed.

Eventually in November 1802, the Addington government made a formal diplomatic proposal to Bonaparte asking to adjust the terms of the Amiens agreement. In this, Britain proposed to accept French hegemony and acquisitions in Western Europe, including the territorial changes to Italy and Germany, but asked in return that Bonaparte withdraw his troops from both Switzerland and Holland while still maintaining political control over those countries, and that Britain retain Malta. At the same time, as a measure of good faith toward the general peace settlement, Britain ordered the evacuation of her troops from the Cape of Good Hope and the return of the colony to the Dutch.

Neither Addington's cabinet nor Bonaparte was willing to go to war immediately. Negotiations over the proposals continued for the next several months, while Bonaparte delayed and British representatives did not even mention such traditional British national interests as creating an 18th-century style balance of power in Europe, obtaining access to continental trading markets, or even objecting to the strategic threat created by French political and military control over the Southern Netherlands.

The British government was clearly attempting to appease Bonaparte, but at the same time asking to revise the Amiens settlement so that a more permanent arrangement could exist in Europe under Bonaparte's hegemony.[14] By mid-November 1802, British officials began to suspect that Russia and France were planning to join forces in dismembering the Ottoman Empire and the British ambassador in Paris was instructed not to make any agreement on evacuating Malta. In the British view, there were a number of accumulating indications that had slowly begun to cast doubt on Bonaparte's intentions.

Months earlier in June 1802, the British ambassador in Vienna had reported that Bonaparte had predicted that there would be a future war between France and Britain. In London, it was not clear why Russia was refusing to guarantee Malta's neutrality. In August, Bonaparte declared himself First Consul for life and, at the end of September, followed this with reports in the official French press that he had sent Colonel Horace-François Sébastiani on a special mission to Egypt. British observers were deeply concerned about a revival of French interest in the Near East and began to suspect some sort of connection between Russia's ambivalence over Malta and Sébastiani's mission. The French had, in fact, made some sort of proposal to Russia about a partition of interests in the area, but this found no acceptance in St Petersburg, where the Tsar and some of the senior ministers were slowly evolving an anti-French and pro-British viewpoint.[15]

However, it was in this context that the British ambassador in St Petersburg was among the first to advise London that Britain should retain Malta as a restraint against French and Russian encroachment into the Ottoman Empire. After a time, it began to be clear that Russia under its new Tsar was initially reacting against his father's earlier policies by trying to disengage from European politics and from the internal Russian political issues surrounding the Knights of Malta that had arisen during Tsar Paul's reign as grand master of the Order.

Meanwhile, on 16 November 1802, the government in London ordered the evacuation of British forces in Egypt, realizing that this was a necessary act to avoid risking war with Bonaparte over the failure to uphold this part of the Amiens agreement. The situation continued in this manner until the end of January 1803, with Britain showing gathering remorse, but still proceeding with the intention to honour its part of the Amiens agreement while hoping to modify it.

In Russia, on 1 February 1803, Tsar Alexander I told his ambassador to Britain, Simon Vorontsov: 'The wisest system for Russia is to remain at peace and concern itself with internal prosperity,' adding:

> One of the circumstances about which I could not remain indifferent would be an invasion of the Ottoman Empire by the French. It appears that the First Consul is continually preoccupied with this project... I am going to instruct Count Morkov [Russian Ambassador to France] to explain frankly to him that I would not in any case lend a hand to the dismemberment of the Ottoman Empire, which I believe to be an advantageous neighbour for Russia, and I desire to conserve it.[16]

This pattern of views was shattered both in London and in St Petersburg, when news arrived of the 30 January 1803 issue of the *Moniteur* in Paris, which

Neptune Introducing the Four Quarters of the World to Commerce (London: Mezzotint published by J. Hinton, March 1803). Illustrating the powerful sentiments in Britain for continuing peace with France, this print included the following verse:

Commerce & Traffic now receives increase
and Merchant's boldly venture not 'tis peace,
with Commerce fill'd they lofty cities shine,
and all the products of the Globe are thine.

(Anne S. K. Brown Military Collection, Brown University Library)

had published a report from Colonel Sébastiani on his mission to Egypt. In the open press, Sébastiani scoffed at the effectiveness of British forces in Egypt and reported that the North African states, Syria, and the Ionian Islands were all ripe fields for French military expansion, even going on to estimate that an army of 10,000 French troops would be sufficient to re-conquer Egypt.[17] This report, along with the concentration of French troops still in Italy (in itself a violation of the Treaty of Amiens) and with French persistence in continuing to have in its army organization an 'Army of Egypt', left deep suspicions among officials in London and St Petersburg.[18]

In light of these French moves and a report that the Tsar had advised the British not to evacuate Malta, although Russia did not openly break with France at this point, the British Foreign Secretary, Lord Hawkesbury, instructed Ambassador Whitworth in Paris to advise the French government that British forces would withdraw from Malta only when the government in London was satisfied that the French had no plans to return to Egypt. It is probable that Napoleon had intended the publication of Sébastiani's report in the *Moniteur* to intimidate and to bully the British, just as he continued, at the same time, to make diplomatic attacks on the British government over the press issue during the trial of the émigré journalist Peltier that was simultaneously taking place in London during February 1803. The immediate responses from French Foreign Minister Talleyrand to reassure British leaders about Bonaparte's honorable intentions, suggests that there were cooler heads in Paris, but First Consul Bonaparte continued to make provocative comments. On 18 February he personally told British Ambassador Lord Whitworth that he could have landed an army of 25,000 in Egypt and the 4,000-man British force would have been helpless to oppose it.[19] Although the French ambassador to London reported that the British government did not want to go to war, citing the conviction of the journalist Peltier as evidence of British good faith in maintaining peace, Addington's ministry decided that it was time for King George III to make a clear statement to Parliament about the growing crisis in early March in which the House of Commons was told:

> that, whilst they partake of his majesty's continuance of the peace, he may rely, with perfect confidence on their public spirit and liberality, to enable his majesty to adopt such measures as circumstances may appear to require for supporting the honour of his crown, and the essential interests of his people.[20]

Bonaparte reacted violently to this statement. During a reception for the foreign diplomatic corps in Paris, Bonaparte lashed out at the British ambassador for all to hear, leaving them all silent in astonishment. As he slammed the door on his way out of the reception room in the Tuileries, he told Lord Whitworth, 'We shall be fighting in two weeks. Malta – or war!'[21] British leaders replied cautiously and calmly to this, opening negotiations with the First Consul through his brother, Joseph Bonaparte, who, with Talleyrand, personally seemed to be interested in maintaining peace. These discussions were repeatedly rebuffed by Bonaparte. On 26 April, the British government gave an ultimatum to the French: 1: Malta must be controlled by Britain for 10 years; 2: Lampedusa Island must be ceded to Britain by Naples; 3: Holland must be evacuated within a month; 4: When France made suitable provisions for the King of Sardinia and the Helvetian Republic, then Britain would recognize the Italian and Ligurian Republics.

In response to this, Russia offered to mediate the Maltese question, but in a meeting of the Council of State at St Cloud on 11 May, both the Russian offer of mediation and the British demands were rejected and the decision was made for war. Only Talleyrand and Joseph Bonaparte supported the peace proposals. On the next day, British diplomats left Paris for England. En route, Talleyrand sent a proposal for Malta to come under Russia, Austria, or Prussia, but Whitworth rejected this as merely a delaying tactic. Whitworth arrived in England from Calais on 17 May and, on the following day, George III declared war on the French Republic.

The convergence of events in the context of mutual misunderstanding helped to drive both France and Britain toward a renewal of war that neither were fully prepared to conduct.[22] As one historian has concluded, it was not the traditional geo-strategic reasons that drove Britain and France to renew war in 1803. 'The British went to war simply because they could not stand being further challenged and humiliated by Bonaparte; France went to war because Bonaparte could not stop doing it.'[23]

THE GENERAL STRATEGIC SITUATION, 1803–05

In military and naval terms, neither Britain nor France was fully prepared for war. There was a serious shortage of muskets for the British Army and most of those available were needed for home defence. Starting from a point at which there were serious shortages, British arms production was immediately pushed forward at Birmingham, and, additionally, the Ordnance Board began to produce its own muskets at the Tower of London. These were but the beginnings of a huge arms production, but it would take several years to bear fruit. The Navy rapidly mobilized, jumping from 32 ships-of-the-line in service in the spring of 1803 to 72 in July. While the ships that lay in 'ordinary' (reserve) could be readily brought in to service, the first problem was finding enough men to man them quickly and secondly to repair and maintain them while in service. On average it took more than five months to repair a major warship in this period, supplies of timber and stores were scarce, and there were bureaucratic difficulties over the prices of supplies. At this point, the dockyards were unable to respond fully to the sudden demands on them that the renewal of war had imposed, a situation that demanded rapid reform in this area.[24]

At the outbreak of the war, Britain was largely isolated diplomatically, and operating only with increasing indications that Russia seemed to be turning against France. When Britain declared war, the government did so without any firm commitment of assistance from any other country. In broad terms, the British government seems to have entered the war on the assumption that Britain could win a prolonged war of attrition fought in the realm of naval and maritime commercial warfare. This would suggest that British leaders believed that, crippled by loss of its maritime trade and unable to invade the British Isles, France would eventually face financial collapse and this would engender internal revolt against Bonaparte. As these forces began to take effect on France, they anticipated Bonaparte would turn on the parts of Europe that France did not yet fully control. This, in turn, would create the basis for a new coalition against France that would ultimately defeat it. In 1803, such a strategy rested on much wishful thinking and high risks. It was undertaken, too, without regard to the thought that continental Europe might not react in the same way that the British did, and continental Europe might find reason to blame Britain for forcing Bonaparte back into a war that would bring more destruction on them than it would on Britain. The British government, however, paid little heed to such thoughts in its diplomacy and tended to ignore Austria and Prussia, which would naturally bear the direct military brunt of Bonaparte's attacks, and to focus instead on the periphery of Europe, looking more toward Sweden and on Russia for assistance.[25]

Bonaparte had enormous strategic and military advantages over Britain in the period 1803–05, despite the fact that he had yet to organize Europe fully for the renewal of war. He had, readily at hand, a large coalition of his own, in the form of the satellite countries that he had established and allies within his sphere of influence. Thus, the Italian and Batavian Republics were immediately brought in to the war. Switzerland quickly joined Bonaparte in September and Spain in October 1803. Those who wished to stand aside and remain, were simply invaded and occupied, such as General Mortier's invasion of Hanover in May 1803 with a corps of 25,000 troops and the nearly simultaneous occupation by General St Cyr's army of the southern Neapolitan ports of Taranto, Otranto and Brindisi, establishing the potential for a direct French threat to Sicily, Greece and Egypt. With such operational capacities, Bonaparte was able not only to strengthen his strategic position but also to force the costs of warfare on areas of Europe outside of France, thereby preserving his political base at home at the expense of others. His sale of the Louisiana territory to the United States, although leaving his commitments on its purchase from Spain incomplete, succeeded in raising money for the war effort against Britain, while it removed the need to use French resources to defend it.

Russia continued its attempt to remain on good terms with France, while at the same time attempting to broker mediation between Britain and Bonaparte over the Malta issue, it strove to remain beyond the conflict, not faced by any direct threat from Bonaparte. With some considerable insight, Alexander I and his advisors began to propose solutions that involved a fundamental new approach to European affairs in which it was no longer individual great power

Well come sit down and do as we do –
We never bear malice to a Frenchman
after we have thrash'd him.
Ah! Ah! Begar you fite dam vell – but no
vonder – you eat dam vel – and you drink
dam vel!
Woodward Del
THE FRENCH ADMIRAL ON BOARD THE EURYALUS.

The French Admiral on Board the Euryalus (London: Etching produced by George M. Woodward, artist, engraved by Thomas Rowlandson, and published by Rudolph Ackermann, 11 Dec 1803). In this caricature, the French admiral's comment to the British sailor that 'you fight dam vell and drink dam vell' suggests the widespread belief that British seaman had higher morale than their French counterparts. *Euryalus* , a 36-gun fifth rate, was just launched at Buckler's Hard in June 1803. (Anne S. K. Brown Military Collection, Brown University Library)

interests that provided the pivot, but rather a guarantee for the independence of both large and small states. Despite its foresight into the ultimate solution to the broadest European issues, both Britain and France rejected these ideas. At this point, Bonaparte was motivated by his burning desire to humiliate the British and to exclude them from Europe. Bonaparte rejected the Russian proposals since they failed to recognize his hegemony, while Britain rejected the Russian proposals because they were limited to the Maltese issue and did not deal with the additional questions that had arisen on other areas of concern to Britain.

While this was going on, Bonaparte ordered the establishment of encampments of the French Army, numbering between 90,000 and 130,000 along the coast to prepare to invade Britain from Holland, Ghent, St Omer, Compiègne, St-Malo and Bayonne, with smaller encampments elsewhere. At the same time, Bonaparte ordered the readying of some 2,000 craft to sail from Bolougne, Étaples and Ambelteuse by November 1803. In hindsight the plan had such little practicability to it that historians have debated whether or not it was entirely a ruse to mask a military move in Central Europe. Despite all the serious doubts that do arise from a careful consideration of Bonaparte's practical arrangements

The Admiralty from an engraving by J. Tingle after Thomas H. Shepherd. The Admiralty building in Whitehall housed the London offices of the Lords Commissioners of the Admiralty. The key officials located here, with the dates of appointment were:

First Lord:
19 February 1801:
John Jervis, Earl of St Vincent
15 May 1804:
Henry Dundas, Viscount Melville
2 May 1805:
Charles Middleton, Lord Barham

First Naval Lord
19 February 1801:
Sir Thomas Troubridge
15 May 1804:
James Gambier

Admiralty Secretary
3 March 1795:
Sir Evan Nepean
21 January 1804:
William Marsden

(Mary Evans Picture Library)

for the success of this enterprise, there is considerable evidence to suggest that Bonaparte was entirely serious about it.[26]

In the first months of the war, the Royal Navy took up blockading positions off the French coast to keep the French Navy in port, where it could not challenge British uses of the sea. In the Atlantic and Bay of Biscay, Admiral Sir William Cornwallis took up station off Brest; Rear-Admiral Sir Edward Pellew caught the French Santo Domingo Squadron in port at Ferrol; Rear-Admiral Cuthbert Collingwood patrolled off Rochefort, and, in the Mediterranean, Vice-Admiral Sir Horatio Nelson watched Toulon. Overseas, British forces moved quickly to make up for the positions that they had voluntarily given up at Amiens, taking St Lucia, Tobago, Berbice, Demara, and Esquibo in 1803.

The presence of the French Army in a position to launch an amphibious assault, whether it was practical or not, created a serious threat that required home defence, particularly in those areas that directly faced the French army on the opposite shores in Kent and Sussex. The British saw themselves as being encircled by French forces, who could choose a variety of approaches to attack, not only the obvious threat directly across the Channel, but anywhere that amphibious landing forces from Brest, Lorient, and elsewhere in the Bay of Biscay could be readily embarked for a landing in Britain or Ireland. This required a mass mobilization of militia and volunteers and transporting about one third of that entire force from places throughout the country to positions south of London, while at the same time providing adequately for the need to defend Ireland and to maintain an effective land defensive capability along the entire coast of the United Kingdom.[27]

The main strategic idea here was to maintain a defensive perimeter around the country that would prevent French forces from establishing a base of operations on British soil. In a thoughtful consideration of Bonaparte's new approach to military tactics, British leaders prepared to meet French mobility and tactical surprise by cutting off its lines of supply from France and preventing its easy movement, through establishing a numerical superiority over the invading force obtained through trained British army units operating with civilian militia and volunteer auxiliaries.

Yet, Britain still faced France alone. In the years between 1803 and 1805, Britain lacked the military resources to put an expeditionary army of her own on the continent. It would take deeply involved and tortuous diplomacy across developing events in Europe to create a Third Coalition that could effectively challenge Bonaparte's military might on the Continent. During 1803, Bonaparte had been successful in getting Portugal, and then Spain to provide subsidies to France. In the same period, none of the other European states were initially willing to join Britain in a war against France, but some important seeds had been sown. One of the major events that played a role in turning many countries against Napoleon occurred almost simultaneously with his proclamation as emperor: the abduction of the 32-year old royalist Duc d'Enghien, the sole heir of the ancient Bourbon-Condé family, from neutral Baden, and his subsequent execution at Vincennes on 20 March. This was followed soon afterwards by Bonaparte's proclamation of himself as the Emperor Napoleon in May 1804 and his spectacular self-coronation with the crown of Charlemagne at Notre Dame in Paris on 2 December 1804. On the surface, Austria and others stayed either quietly neutral or completely in Napoleon's thrall.[28]

This situation began to change only very slowly in late 1804. By then, the Addington government had been succeeded by William Pitt's return to power in May 1804. By October, Britain was still alone and facing a larger coalition after British warships captured Spanish ships carrying gold from the Americas, forcing a break in diplomatic relations between Spain and Britain. In January 1805, Spain declared war against Britain, bringing Spanish naval resources to join Napoleon's fleet.

Finally, after lengthy negotiations, Britain and Russia were able to come to an agreement and to sign an alliance in April 1805 as the first step in the new coalition. In effect, Britain and Russia agreed that, between them, they should direct the war in Europe, decide on the war aims and regulate the peace that followed, while Austria would be persuaded, within four months, to bear the brunt of the land fighting for the two allies and to provide more than half the troops for a coalition army. The two new allies disagreed over many of the details as well as in the broad issues of how, precisely, they would share the burdens and benefits of their alliance. These disputes nearly caused the alliance

Nelson's Chase of Villeneuve, 12 May–15 August 1805

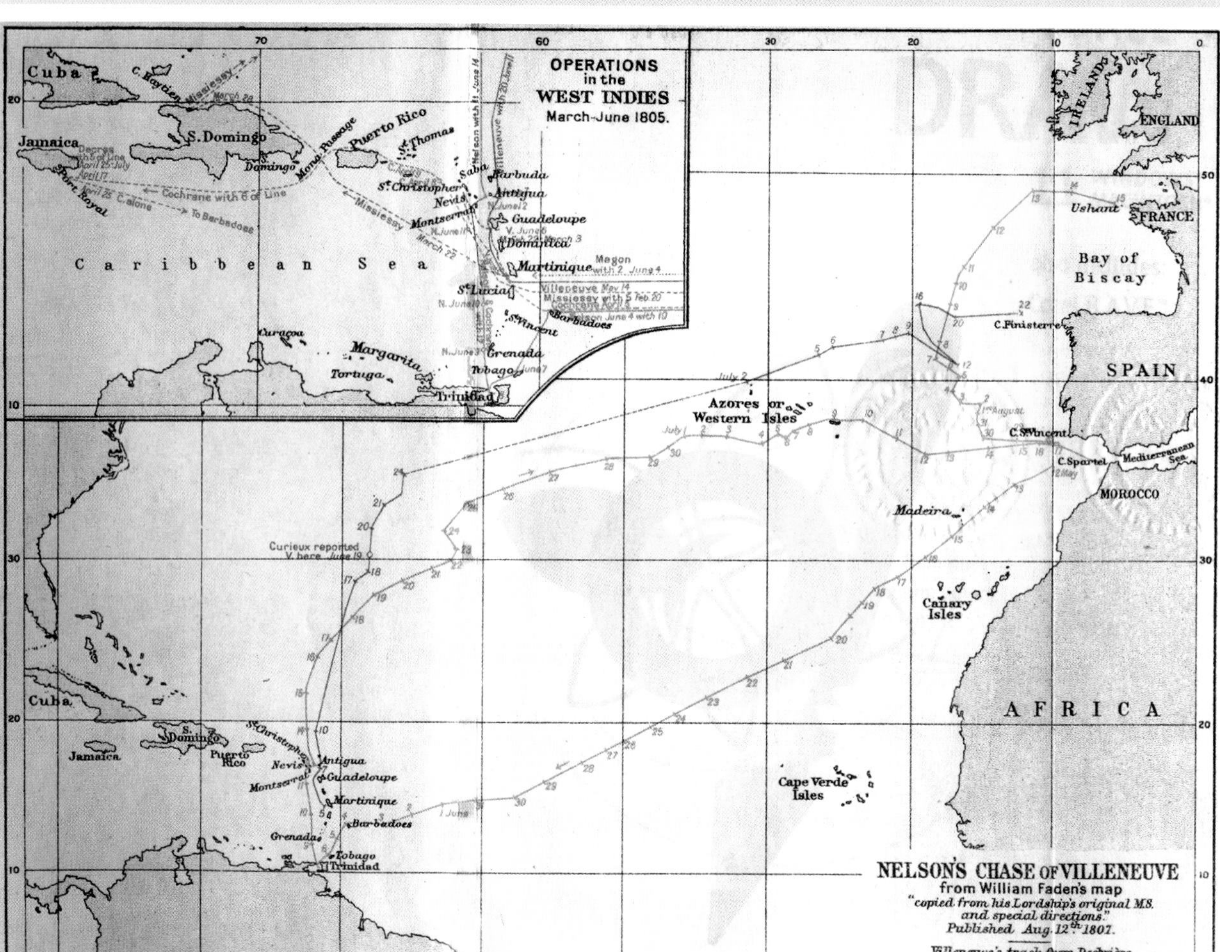

The opening of the Trafalgar Campaign was marked by Villeneuve's escape with the French fleet from under Nelson's blockade of Toulon to join with the Spanish squadron under Gravina at Cadiz, followed by Nelson's subsequent chase of the Franco-Spanish fleet to the West Indies and back. (Reproduced from Julian S. Corbett, *The Campaign of Trafalgar*, Longmans, Green, & Co., London [1910], facing p. 154)

to fail ratification, but Napoleon's transformation of the Republic of Italy into a Kingdom with himself as its hereditary king and his aggressive annexation of Genoa into metropolitan France saved the Anglo-Russian agreement, bringing the two allies back into concert with one another at the last moment, and causing Russia to break its relationship with France.

With the agreement between them made and ratified, Britain and Russia pushed together to get Austria to accede to their coalition. Some months earlier, in November 1804, Austria had signed a provisional, defensive alliance with Russia, but not with the idea of using it to attack France. In Austrian eyes, it was meant to protect Austria from French incursions and to provide assistance if France attacked her. Austria proceeded to try to involve Prussia in the Austro-Russian Alliance, but this attempt at allaying the long-standing Austro-Prussian rivalry failed. When the terms of the Anglo-Russian agreement

Calder's Action, 22 July and the Great Concentration at Ushant

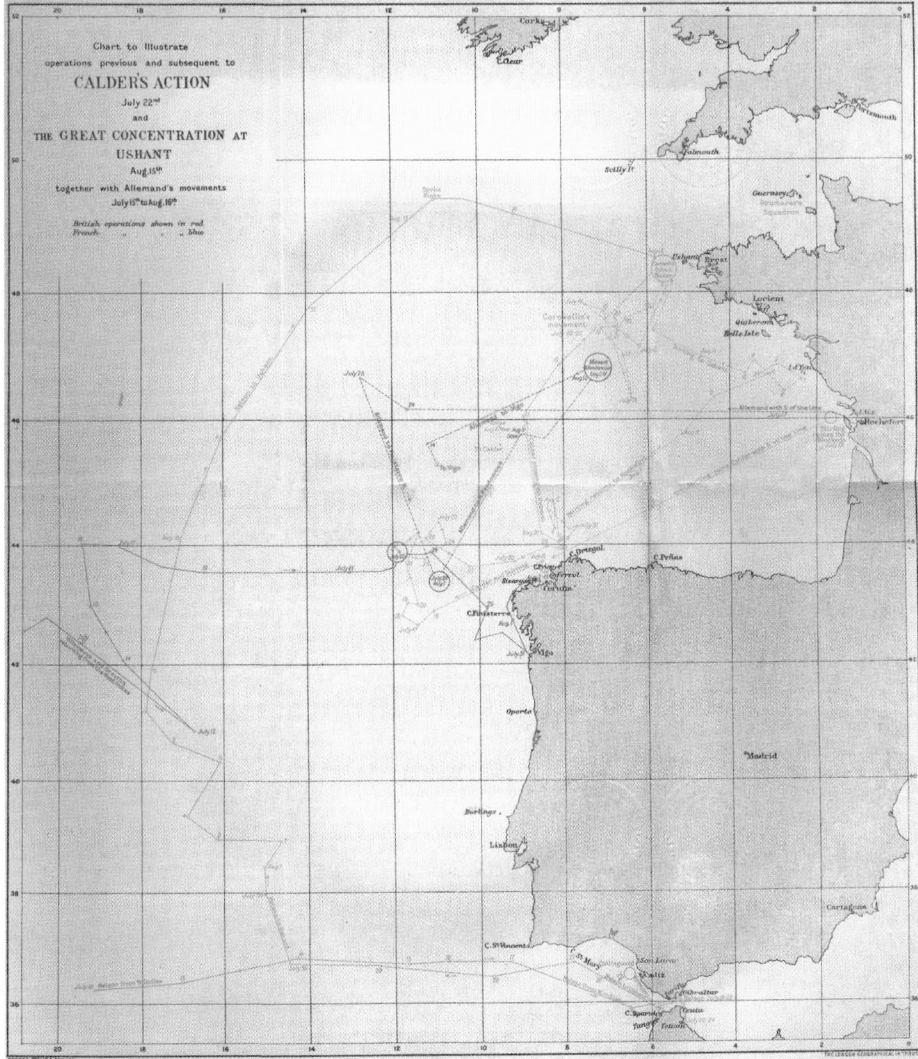

Vice-Admiral Sir Robert Calder with 15 ships of the line engaged Villeneuve and Gravina's 20 ships off Finisterre, as they returned from the West Indies. To support Calder, Rear-Admiral Charles Stirling raised his blockade of Rochefort, allowing Allemand to put to sea with five French ships of the line. After the inconclusive action with Calder, the Franco-Spanish forces gathered at Vigo and then moved to Ferrol and later, Coruña. Then, Nelson moved north from the Straits of Gibraltar to join Cornwallis and Calder off Brest, making a concentration of 36 ships to block the Franco-Spanish fleet from either joining Ganteaume's Brest squadron or entering the Channel. (Reproduced from Julian S. Corbett, *The Campaign of Trafalgar*, Longmans, Green, and Co., London [1910], facing p. 184)

were finally revealed to Austria, statesmen in Vienna were deeply shocked and a number of them thought the role that Russia and Britain had made for them to be disastrous. Yet, at the same time, nearly all agreed that if war with France were inevitable then it would have to be fought offensively. Finally, in the face of a French ultimatum to disarm and declare its neutrality, Austria saw that its only course of action if it wanted to remain independent was to opt to join the Third Coalition. On 8 August 1804, in reaction against Napoleon's continual threats and pressures, Austria finally stepped away from her neutral position and signed a modified form of the Anglo-Russian agreement to join the Third Coalition. It provided that Britain would pay an annual subsidy of £1,250,000 for every 100,000 troops that actually took the field, although Pitt's government indicated that there would be an approximately £5 million combined total limit for the military support of Austria and Russia. Following Austria's accession to the coalition, Sweden broke with both France and neutral Prussia and after a series of negotiations finally agreed on 3 October 1805 to join the Third Coalition. British subsidies supported the Swedish troops to be sent to join the proposed 400,000-man predominantly Austrian army and Sweden formally declared war against France on 31 October. [29]

Meanwhile, the slow growth of the Third Coalition had allowed Napoleon to gather even more allies. In a direct reaction to the threat created by Austria's entry in the coalition, Bavaria joined France in late August and she was soon joined at Napoleon's side by Baden in September and Württemberg in October, while Prussia's very effective army remained neutral despite calls from both sides. It was clearly in Napoleon's interest that Prussia was either on his side or remained neutral. To ensure it, French troops occupied neighbouring Cleves.

As war broke out on the Continent, Napoleon clearly continued to maintain his advantage over the Third Coalition. The alliance that Napoleon had forcefully created among the reluctant southern German states gave him full control of the Danube River and an open avenue to meet the threat from Austria. Meanwhile, Russia moved to support her own interests in the Near East and to directly replace Napoleon's influence in the region with the Tsar's. While expanding his own power in the Caucasus and in Iran, Tsar Alexander obtained promises of British military and naval support to protect the Ottoman Empire from the French.

THE OUTBREAK OF THE WAR OF THE THIRD COALITION

The outbreak of the war on the Continent in the late summer and autumn of 1805, although it had taken nearly three years to create, provided the grand strategic setting in which the battle of Trafalgar took place. The Coalition laid a plan of operations on the Continent that had three parts to it. First, an Anglo-Russian corps from Corfu and Malta would land in southern Italy, while a 90,000-man Austrian army under the Archduke Charles attacked French fortifications on the Mincio River to recapture parts of Italy that had formerly been under Habsburg control, and the Archduke John held Austrian positions in the Tyrol with 20,000 men. The second part of the plan was to take place simultaneously as the Archduke Ferdinand and General Mack invaded Bavaria and moved to hold a defensive position on the Inn River near Braunau. Here, Marshall Kutusov with 35,000 Russian troops would join up with them in mid-October 1805. After Archduke Charles defeated the French in Italy, the army under Ferdinand, Mack, and Kutusov would move north to the upper Rhine valley to defeat the French located there, while another Russian corps was to land in Pomerania, where it would be joined with the Swedish troops, and then march on Hanover.

Meanwhile, Napoleon was still concentrating on his plan to invade England, but this was stymied not only by its fundamental practical faults, but also by his need to have at least temporary naval supremacy in the Channel to allow his transports to sail. Napoleon went through a rapidly changing series of naval plans to bring this about. In terms of numbers, the total warships under his control would make a fleet that was superior to what Britain could put to sea. Napoleon's basic problem was that these ships were widely scattered in ports blockaded by the Royal Navy: Toulon, Cartagena, Cadiz, Ferrol, Rochefort, Brest and the Texel. The essential challenge was to unite them into a single force that could act together in battle. Napoleon repeatedly made the faulty assumption that when he ordered these ships to sail, they could do what he said and evade the blockading enemy ships in whatever conditions of weather, wind and tide that might exist.[30] In a confusing and rapidly changing series of orders and counter-orders, Napoleon repeatedly ordered his admirals to take their ships to sea in the summer and autumn of 1805. He had two objects in mind. One was, in conjunction with privateers, to attack and destroy British shipping around the world and so to damage the British war economy that was subsidizing military opposition. Here, two of Napoleon's admirals had some success. Missiessy had managed to sail to the West Indies, where his ships did some effective damage to British commerce. Then, Admiral Pierre de Villeneuve was able to slip out of

Equity or a Sailor's Prayer (London: Etching produced by Thomas Rowlandson, artist, and published by Thomas Tegg, 1806). This sailor's prayer that the enemy's shot be distributed like 'prize money, the greatest part among the officers,' suggests much about the views of the ordinary seaman. (Royal Naval Museum)

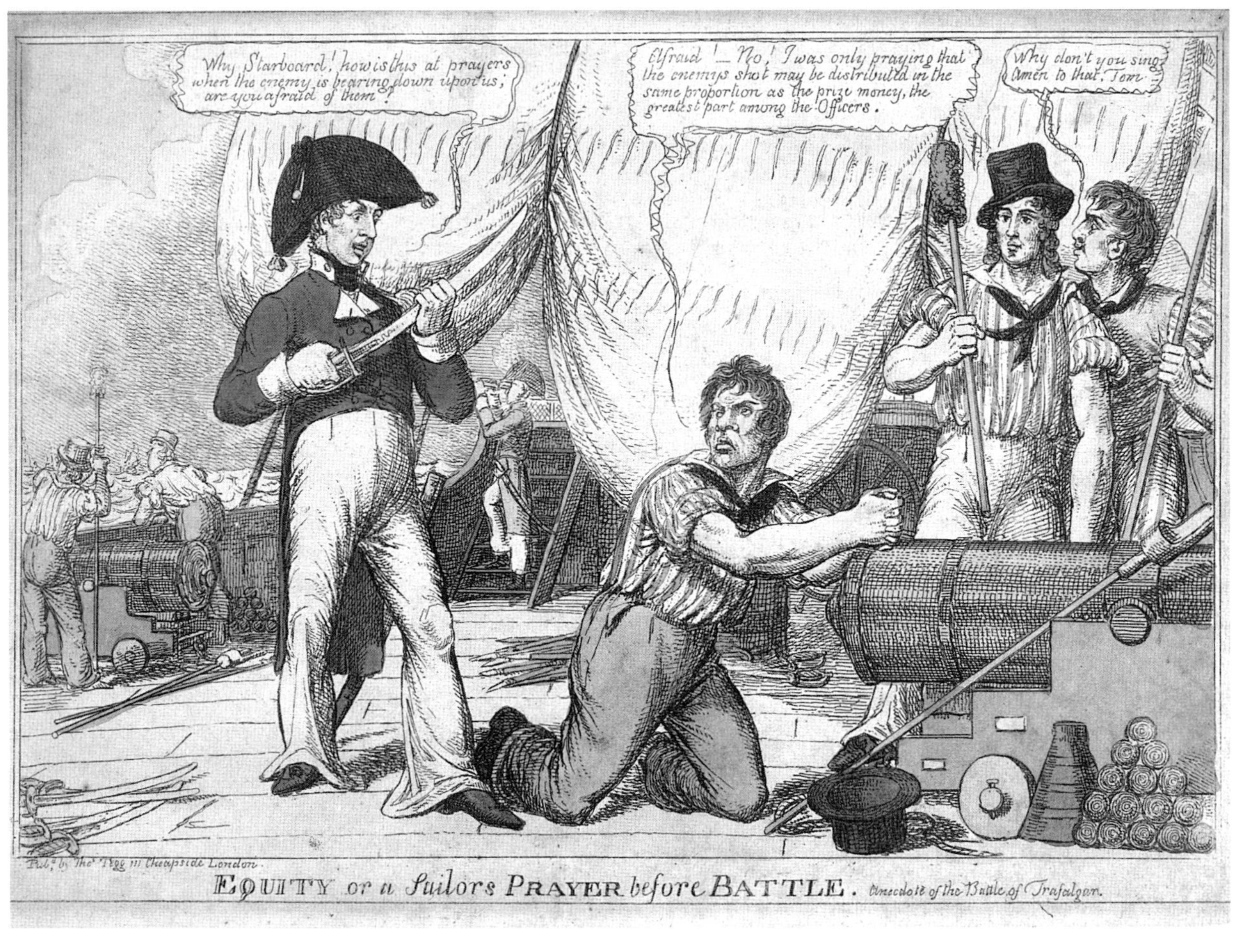

Calder's Retreat to Ushant and Return in Pursuit of Villeneuve

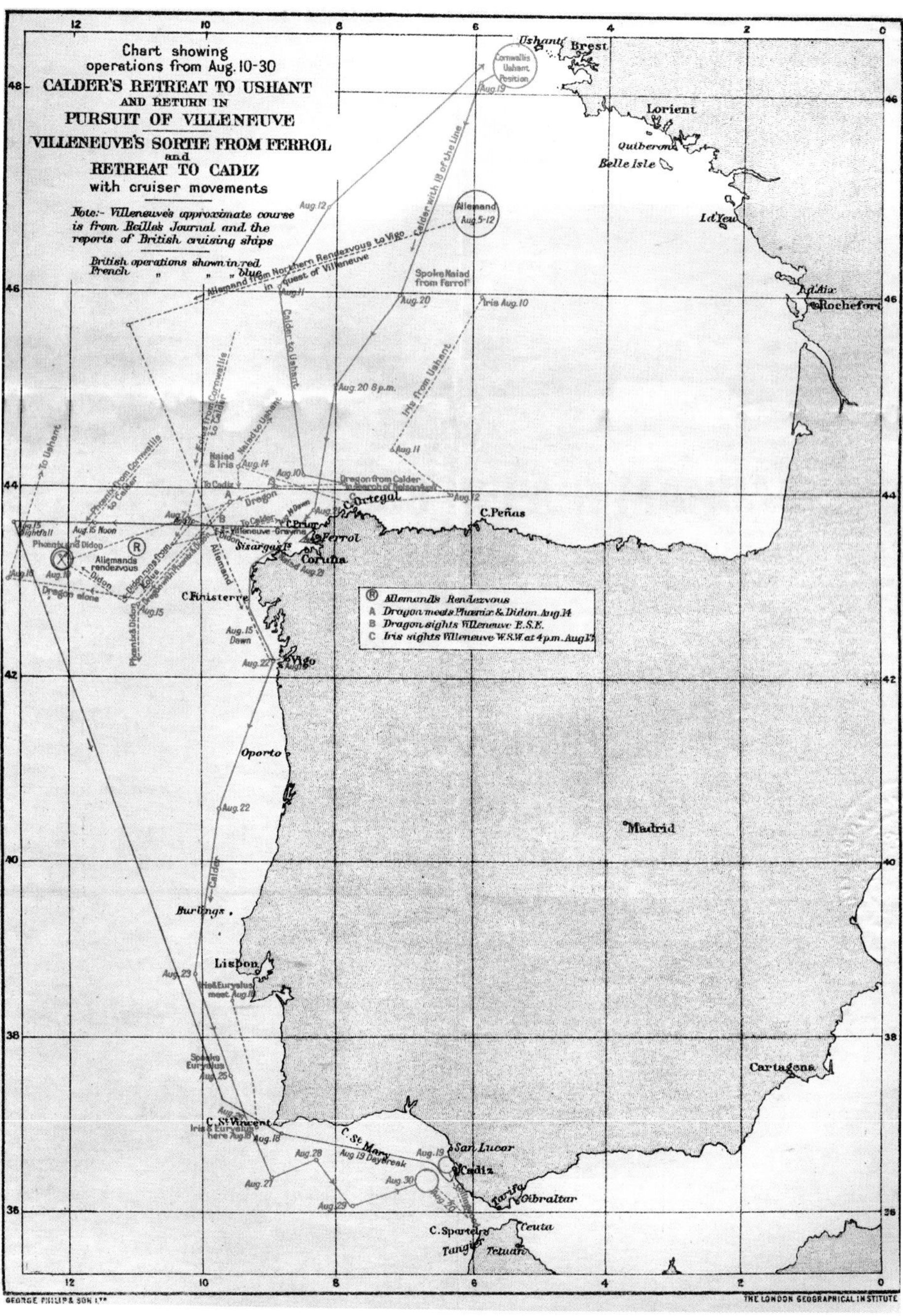

Napoleon waited in vain at the Headquarters of the Army of England at Boulogne for Villeneuve to join Ganteaume off Brest and to enter the Channel. On 10 August, Villeneuve left Ferrol, first sailing west as if initially reaching for Brest. Deciding this was not feasible, he fell back on contingency orders to concentrate his forces at Cadiz. Meanwhile, Allemand continued to try to find and join Villeneuve, while Calder pursued Villeneuve and joined Collingwood off Cadiz, blocking entry into the Mediterranean and any attempt of the French to interfere with Anglo-Russian military plans in Italy. (Reproduced from Julian S. Corbett, The *Campaign of Trafalgar*, Longmans, Green, and Co., London [1910], facing p. 254)

Toulon momentarily. Looking for more effective voyages, Napoleon ordered Villeneuve to sail to the West Indies in the hope that the Royal Navy would follow, leaving the Channel unguarded. Yet, this plan was not entirely successful, as Admiral Cornwallis kept the Brest squadron blockaded and Admiral Ganteaume was unable to lead Cornwallis's ships away to the West Indies or to

Chart to illustrate Operations to Intercept Allemand

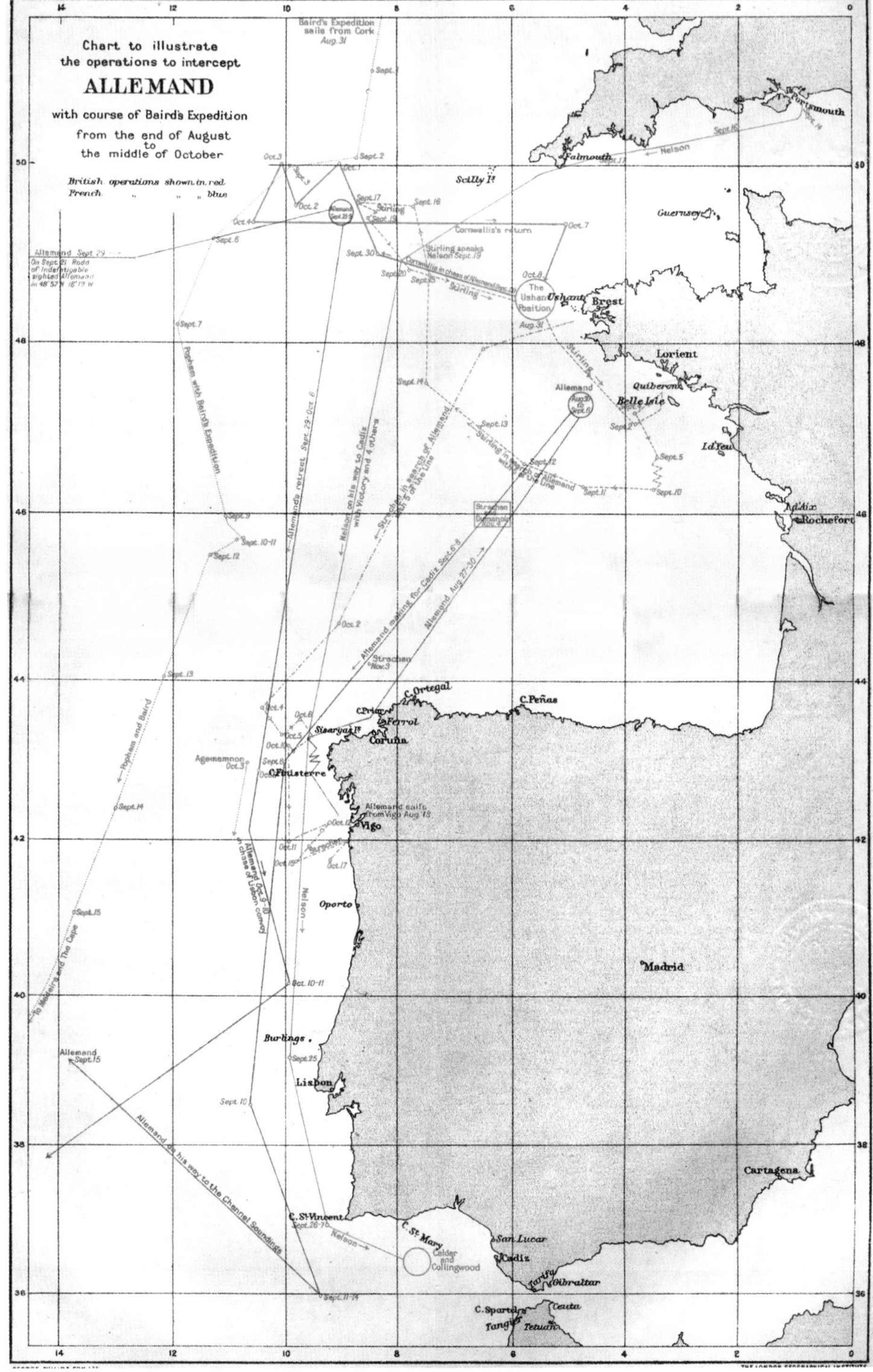

From mid-July through mid-October 1805, Commodore Allemand, with his formidable small squadron that included a 120-gun ship, four 74s, three frigates, and some sloops, had been attempting to rendezvous with Villeneuve in the Bay of Biscay, while, at the same time, evading battle and remaining a threat to British operations. The whereabouts of Allemand remained a continual uncertainty as General Sir David Baird's Expedition sailed from Ireland in mid-August to retake the Cape of Good Hope and, in early September, Nelson sailed from England to join Calder and Collingwood off Cadiz. (Reproduced from Julian S. Corbett, *The Campaign of Trafalgar*, Longmans, Green, and Co., London [1910], facing p. 302)

make his rendezvous with Villeneuve and the small squadron under Admiral Allemand. Napoleon grew increasingly irritated at the failure of his admirals to

Sir Richd. Strachan's Action with the French off Rochefort: Novr. 2. 1805 in which four French ships were taken. Ferrol 4th Nov 1805 (London: Aquatint published by Laurie and Whittle, 12 Dec 1805). Following the battle of Trafalgar, a number of the French and Spanish ships dispersed at sea. A fortnight after the battle, Captain Sir Richard Strachan in the 80-gun HMS *Caesar* with three 74s and four frigates, encountered four French warships under Rear-Admiral Dumanoir le Pelley in the Bay of Biscay, off Cape Ortegal, north-western Spain. Although the French initially declined to fight as they were making for French ports, Strachan pursued them and forced them to surrender in a series of sharp actions. The captured French flagship *Duguay-Trouin*, was taken into the Royal Navy and later became the boy's training ship *Implacable*, moored at Devonport from 1858 to 1949. (Anne S. K. Brown Military Collection, Brown University Library)

carry out his plans. In particular, he became increasingly and violently critical of Villeneuve for his failure to gather the scattered French and Spanish forces under his command and to move northward to cover the proposed cross-channel attack.

Meanwhile, during August 1805, Napoleon saw clear indications of the growing coalition army in Austria and Italy and realized that he needed to move quickly if he were to prevent it from becoming a major threat. Despairing of the French navy's ability to support his strategic plan to invade England – if, indeed, he had really ever thought it practicable – Napoleon gave up the plan or the pretence and disbanded the camps for the planned invasion army of England. While doing this, with characteristic acidity Napoleon wrote in early September to Naval Minister Admiral Decrès, 'Villeneuve is a villain to be ignominiously discharged. Without tactical ability, without courage, without general interest, he would sacrifice everything to save his own skin... Nothing is comparable to his ineptness.'[31]

Moving the French Army rapidly eastward from the encampments facing Britain to join those in northwest Germany, Napoleon moved quickly into southern Germany and on to Bavaria, where in the first week of October, he surprised, surrounded, and defeated General Mack's Austrian Army at Ulm, long before the Russian corps could come to join it. Napoleon's dramatic victory

Immortality – the Death of Admiral Lord Nelson – in the moment of Victory! – this Design for the Memorial intended by the City of London…humbly submitted to the…Lord Mayor…. (London: Etching produced by James Gillray, artist and engraver, and H. Humphrey, publisher, 23 December 1805.) James Gillray published this caricature on the day that Nelson's body was transferred from HMS *Victory* and delivered to Greenwich by HMS *Chatham*. (Royal Naval Museum)

marked the end of the Third Coalition's hopes for military victory on the Continent, although the Archduke Carl had a brief, initial success.

Occurring within days after battle of Ulm, the victory at Trafalgar clearly marked Britain's survival and made even the pretence of a French invasion an impotent threat. The main coalition partners were not so fortunate. By 13 November, Napoleon's cavalry entered Vienna while the main army pursued the retreating Austro-Russian Army into Moravia, where on 2 December 1805 the Coalition Army attacked Napoleon at Austerlitz and was decimated. The Third Coalition destroyed, at Pressburg on 29 December Austria agreed to peace, but it was one

Jack and Poll at Portsmouth after the Battle of Trafalgar. (London: Etching produced by Argus, artist & engraver, January 1806.) In contrast to the lavish formal and public spectacle of Nelson's funeral that was taking place in the first week of January 1806, this caricature emphasized the quiet remorse of the ordinary seaman. (Anne S. K. Brown Military Collection, Brown University Library)

that cost her heavily in Italian and southern German territory, virtually removing Austrian influence from these regions. At the same time, Napoleon's success in southern Germany let him control those states further by gifts of enemy territory. Among them, Prussia received Hanover, but found she had to pay dearly for the gift. British military expeditions in association with the allies in Northern Germany and in Italy had come to nothing. The Anglo-Russian alliance was not dead, even though the larger military coalition involving Austria had been defeated.

Nevertheless, the experience of the War of the Third Coalition demonstrated that, while Russia and Britain could survive in their geo-strategic positions on the periphery of Europe, they alone could neither defeat Napoleon nor, as the co-heads of a coalition, control the political future of Europe. Napoleon's military successes lured him on to wider and more ambitious dreams of empire.

CHAPTER ONE
THE RIVALS
PETER PADFIELD

Britain and France had fought each other throughout the 18th century, with intervals of mutual exhaustion. The initial trigger had been the accession to the English throne of William of Orange in 1689 after what was dubbed the 'Glorious Revolution' against James II for his arbitrary rule and perceived Popish preferences. The aims of William's English backers were to curtail the Royal prerogative by subordinating it to Parliament in most important areas, and to safeguard the established Protestant Church. William's aim when he accepted the Crown was to contain the expansionist ambitions of the 'Sun King', Louis XIV of France, by binding England into a great anti-French alliance. This chimed with his parliamentary supporters who had been watching anxiously as Louis built up a great navy in addition to his first class army. They perceived France as now the major naval, colonial and commercial rival. The position was described succinctly in a House of Commons debate some years before William's accession: 'The interest of the King of England is to keep France from being too great on the Continent, and the French interest is to keep us from being masters of the sea.'[1]

This could serve as a useful summary of the situation in 1789 when France erupted in Revolution against Louis XVI. The subsequent Revolutionary and Napoleonic Wars were the final desperate rounds in the struggle that had begun a hundred years before. This was not clear at the time. Nor was it clear that it was a struggle for world mastery, or that the victorious power would impose its own values and model of government on western Europe and large tracts of the globe over the following century – would, indeed, create the modern world.[2]

Historical speculation is deceptive; nonetheless it is useful to suggest, if only to stress the cosmic importance of the British–French struggle, that had France, not Britain, prevailed not only would French be the dominant world tongue today, but the government system of choice for rational men of goodwill would not be democracy, but top-down, centralized, rule-dominated bureaucracy – to which, it must be admitted, recent British governments and a sizeable proportion of the

OPPOSITE
Maximilien Robespierre (1758–94) was a leading member of the radical Jacobin Club and a disciple of Rousseau, whose major work, *The Social Contract*, he is said to have re-read every day. It is no accident that he was a chief architect of 'The Terror', to which he himself eventually fell victim. (Mary Evans Picture Library)

Edmund Burke (1729–97) penned the most lucid critique of the French Revolution in his *Reflections on the Revolution in France* (1790). The book spelled out the differences between the authentic freedoms enjoyed in Burke's view by the English, founded on order and moderation and hallowed by custom versus those grasped violently by the French revolutionaries. (Mary Evans Picture Library)

electorate have subscribed, despite our very different tradition. Similarly, concepts of freedom and the law would be state-centred: ideas of common law, residual freedoms – as opposed to statutory 'rights' – and trial by jury would be confined to a probably smaller, less dominant United States of America. What can scarcely be in doubt is that our mental and political worlds would be very different.

France did not win. She went down to humiliating defeat. This should be cause for wonder: on any rational calculation she appeared to hold the best cards. Her population at the time of the Revolution was perhaps three times that of Great Britain, her national product perhaps double. Her land was larger, spread across more diverse climatic regions, served by navigable rivers and she faced three major trading axes, the Mediterranean, the Atlantic and the Channel route to England and the Baltic. She maintained the greatest army in Europe; her colonies in the West Indies were at least as profitable as Britain's; she enjoyed a brilliant religious, cultural and intellectual life; as Edmund Burke, chief spokesman and prophet for the opposition to the French Revolution in Britain and abroad, wrote at the time:

> When I consider the face of the kingdom of France; the multitude and opulence of her cities; the useful magnificence of her spacious high roads and bridges; the opportunity of her artificial canals and navigations opening the convenience of maritime communications through a solid continent of so immense an extent; when I turn my eyes to the tremendous works of her ports and harbours, and to her whole naval apparatus, whether for war or trade ... when I reflect on the excellence of her manufactures and fabrics, second to none but our own, and in some particulars not second; when I contemplate the grand foundations of charity, public and private...the state of all the arts that beautify and polish life ... her able statesmen, the multitude of her profound lawyers and theologians, her philosophers, her critics, her historians and antiquaries, her poets and her orators ... I behold in all this something which awes and commands the imagination...[3]

France was a great power with a rich civilization. However, the splendid edifice was to a degree hollow and her institutions thoroughly outdated. In her constitutional and social arrangements, her financial practices, her agriculture and industry she was up to a century behind Great Britain – assuming progress, for better or for worse, flowed towards the modern world. And although she often built better warships than the British, her navy was far inferior. Admiral the Comte de Grasse, defeated by Admiral Sir George Rodney at the Saints in 1781 and brought aboard the British flagship said, after admiring the discipline, cleanliness and gunnery arrangements aboard, that the French service was a hundred years behind.[4]

The reason France lagged in so many fields, and one of the prime causes of the Revolution of 1789, was the rigidity of the regime and the social order. In common with other continental empires – unlike the major maritime powers, Great Britain and the Dutch Republic – the French people had traded in their ancient consultative forums for internal stability under a strong central government in which they had no say. The modern situation had begun in the seventeenth century when Louis XIV, after a miserable childhood in which he had seen his country torn apart by fractious nobles, had concentrated all power in his own hands, at the same time blunting the potency of the nobles by raising a new 'nobility of the robe' from the wealthy merchant class to be his ministers and administrators. Since these enjoyed the same considerable exemptions from taxes and the other prerogatives of the traditional 'nobility of the sword', this swelled the vested interest in preserving privilege. It was further swelled as Louis and his successors, needing vast sums to pay for wars, sold higher judicial and government offices which carried grants of nobility.

The Catholic Church and Church lands also enjoyed tax immunities, and the different regions of the country absorbed over centuries by conquest or dynastic inheritance preserved certain tax privileges. So, while in theory Louis' Bourbon successors ruled by divine right as absolute monarchs, they were in many respects as constrained by class, Church and provincial privilege, even public opinion and custom, as William's successors in Britain by Parliament and Statute, nowhere more than in the crucial area of tax. Paradoxically, while French taxes were still collected in traditional, often arbitrary ways by private consortia known as tax farmers, Britain had developed a centralized system of collection by permanent salaried officials which was far more efficient and above all transparent and manifestly fairer.

French finance ministers made repeated attempts over the years to reform the tax structure in order to tap more of the wealth of the nation, but they had been blocked by the privileged orders, in particular the hereditary nobles who sat as magistrates in the Paris and provincial parlements, the high courts of justice which retained as a vestige of their original function as a king's consultative council the right to register Royal decrees into law or to withhold registration and issue a 'remonstrance'. These provided the only constitutional checks on the king's power, although they could be overruled if the king appeared before the parlement in person.

The magistrates' arguments linked inequalities in the three 'Orders' of society, clergy, nobles and commoners, with divine law which had endowed men with unequal characteristics; they claimed that attempts to create an equality of duties between the classes would destroy the distinctions necessary to a harmonious society and provoke disorder. The different duties were spelled out by the Paris parlement in 1776 when Louis XVI's first Controller General of Finances proposed abolishing existing taxes and substituting a single tax on land, including noble and Church estates:

> The personal responsibility of the clergy is to fulfil all the functions relating to education and religion and to aid the unfortunate through alms. The noble devotes his life to the defence of the state and assists the sovereign by providing council. The last class of the nation [the Third Estate], which cannot render such distinguished service to the state, fulfils its obligations through taxes, industry and physical labour.[5]

This argument for duties and rights hallowed by time might have been penned by Edmund Burke; it was central to his philosophy. In *Reflections on the Revolution in France* (1790), Burke wrote, 'By a constitutional policy, working after the pattern of nature, we receive, we hold, we transmit our government and

Louis XVI (1755–93), King of France 1774–92. Although he was in principle in favour of reform, he lacked the strength of personality to engage successfully, let alone lead, France out of the political, financial and social morass and growing discontent that was eventually to spark the revolution. (Mary Evans Picture Library)

our privileges in the same manner in which we enjoy and transmit our property and our lives.'[6] But Burke never supposed tradition precluded change. He was a committed reformer, in the same work describing his ideal statesman as one with 'a disposition to preserve, and an ability to improve',[7] and asserting that 'A state without the means of change is without the means of its own conservation'.[8] Here was the nub of the French dilemma: the only independent organs of state, the parlements, lacking any elements representative of the bulk of the population, blocked all change that threatened noble or ecclesiastical privilege;

and viewing every national institution as a necessary link in the grand chain of state, shrank from loosening or abolishing any one. When Louis XVI's Controller General proposed abolishing the merchant and craft guilds which regulated production, quality, prices and wages in the commercial and industrial sectors, the Paris parlement remonstrated:

> Sire, because independence is a defect in the political constitution and men are always tempted to abuse liberty, the law has instituted corporations, created guilds, and established regulations. The law has wished to prevent frauds of all kinds and remedy all abuses ... to abolish the regulations ... is to destroy all the various means which commerce itself must want for its own preservation.[9]

Parlement, supported by the dominant noble interest at court, triumphed. Louis sacked his Controller General; the tax and guild reforms fell.

Nine years later in 1785 – four years before the Revolution – two young French noblemen, François and Alexandre de la Rochefoucauld, toured England on an informal spying expedition; there were any number of official French spies in the country attempting to probe the secrets of Britain's astonishing industrial and agricultural advances. At Sheffield the two were shown around a factory producing steel implements. François described the machine processes in detail in his journal, afterwards adding a general comment on English commerce and industry:

> there are no regulations at all, no restraints to hold them up; a merchant does well or badly as he pleases; these are his affairs and the buyer's, who is not taken in. There is nothing in England resembling all the commercial laws of France.[10]

Earlier, the brothers had been shown around a copper-button making factory. François noted that the greater part of the output went abroad: 'most goes to France. It is extraordinary that we [French] don't succeed in an art so simple.'[11]

Given the guild restrictions on enterprise, it was not so extraordinary; in addition the internal market in France was subject to tariff barriers between regions, another commercial handicap that successive finance ministers had been unable to break down. Of even greater significance was a national ethos derived from feudal chivalry. When remonstrating against the proposed single tax on land the Paris parlement had reminded Louis of 'the descendants of those ancient knights...who for so many centuries shed their blood for the extension and defence of the monarchy.'[12] In truth, by this date, while the nobility of the sword still provided the officers of both army and navy, the majority of noble families had commoner ancestors elevated, usually by purchase, within the past century.[13] This did not affect perceptions. The mental world inhabited by the nobility was constructed from national glory and personal honour and had a bias against trade. Nobles were not debarred from more 'respectable' enterprises such as overseas commerce or from membership of the more prestigious Paris guilds, and several did engage seriously in industrial enterprise, but in general the flow was in the opposite direction: successful merchants, craving nobility, spent fortunes purchasing government posts, thus tending to deprive the commercial sector of investment and effective leaders, and at the same time adding more tiers of officialdom to enforce the regulations which restricted Frenchmen in every economic activity.

The infiltration of the aristocracy by the wealthy bourgeoisie has been used to suggest that France and Great Britain were not dissimilar in terms of social mobility. Yet there was a vast difference. The elevated French man of business not only assumed the code, exclusivity and often it seems the hauteur of the order he had entered, but gained a different legal identity. That acute social analyst, Alexis de Tocqueville, summed up the difference with the words 'gentleman', in England applying to every well-educated man whatever his birth, and 'gentilhomme', applying only to a noble in France: 'The meaning of these two words of common origin has been so transformed by the different social climates of the two countries that today they simply cannot be translated.'[14]

In Britain the landed aristocracy had long been partners in or promoters of merchant enterprise. It was probably the result of Britain's island situation, the consequent commitment to oceanic discovery and trade. France produced great seamen explorers and traders, but for geographical reasons the focus of the French state had always been on the extension or defence of the land borders and internal harmonization of the different regions. Thus, while French nobles were in general dedicated to their estates, martial glory or government service, or fashion and amusement, disdaining trade, the British aristocracy was permeated by the habits and values of commercial exchange: in Britain alone of European nations, apart from the Dutch Republic, trade was accounted an honourable occupation fit for gentlemen.[15]

The commercial ethos had tended to break down received ideas and class barriers. With money a man could buy a landed estate and the social status that went with it. He might be resented by those of ancient lineage but would not, as in France, acquire a different legal status and an official post. It was the desire for self-improvement through trade, industry or agriculture unencumbered by government or guild regulations – since English craft guilds had fallen into decay – that had encouraged experiment and invention in every field. The la Rochefoucauld brothers were as astonished by the proportions of the cattle and sheep designed by selective breeding on Mr Bakewell's famous estate in Leicestershire as by the complexity and precision of the machines in the cotton mills of Derby or the unique bridge constructed entirely of iron over the Severn at Coalbrookdale in Shropshire; and they were awed by the number of steam engines they saw in use draining mines, lifting coal, pumping water, working the bellows of blast furnaces. 'We admired them [steam engines] as things simply unknown in our country',[16] François wrote.

The impression given by the journals of these inquiring and intelligent young Frenchmen is not only that Britain was technologically far ahead of France

Matthew Boulton (1728–1809) was a manufacturer of metal goods who saw the potential of steam engines for powering factory production lines and, in partnership with the inventor James Watt, produced the engines which revolutionized British industry. (Mary Evans Picture Library)

before the Revolution, but was well on the way to the economic transformation known as the Industrial Revolution: everything was in place, commercial agriculture, coal mines, ironworks, canals, water-powered textile mills, factory production lines, steam engines, engineers, inventors, driven entrepreneurs, local finance and, on the part of those managing the enterprises, confident assurance.

Apart from commercial character, the quality that most distinguished Britain from France was individual freedom. None were more aware of this than French intellectuals who were constrained by Royal or Church censorship in everything they wrote. Voltaire, forced into exile in England earlier in the century, had described his surprise at finding himself in a country where men were free to say or publish what they liked, there was no torture or arbitrary imprisonment, all religious beliefs were permitted and nobles and priests paid taxes like everyone else.[17] And Montesquieu described England as the freest country in the world: 'I call it free because the sovereign, whose person is controlled and limited, is unable to inflict any imaginable harm on anyone.'[18]

Integral to freedom of expression was the individual's freedom in law. The principle dated back at least to King John's Magna Carta of 1215, article 39 of which stated: 'No free man shall be arrested or imprisoned...or in any way victimized, neither will we attack him or send anyone to attack him, except by the lawful judgement of his peers or the law of the land.'[19] This was the basis of trial by jury. It was complemented by the common-law writ of habeas corpus, whose origins seem to have pre-dated Magna Carta, requiring a person held in custody to be produced before a court for judicial enquiry into the legality of his detention. These fundamental protections of individual liberty against arbitrary power stood at the opposite pole to the French system, where the king was the law and any of his subjects could be imprisoned indefinitely simply on the authority of a Royal warrant.

Voltaire and Montesquieu both observed that British freedoms were founded on common law, that is a body of individual court judgements arrived at by custom and precedent down the centuries rather more than from Royal decrees or statutes enacted by legislation; the English, Voltaire wrote, loved their laws 'because they are, or at least think themselves, the framers of them'.[20] Both also noted that ultimately freedom was preserved by the restraints placed on the king by Parliament. The principle of separating the powers of the executive – the king – and the legislature – Parliament – as a means of balancing one against the other and preventing either from arbitrary or tyrannical government had been propounded by the English philosopher, John Locke, in 1689 as William of Orange ascended the throne and, unlike his predecessors, showed no disposition to overstep the strict limits placed on his authority. From 1700 the judiciary also became separate in practice since judges could no longer be dismissed on purely political grounds.

Montesquieu worked up his observations of British constitutional practice into a volume, in English translation, *The Spirit of the Laws* (1750), which held the separation of the executive, legislature and judiciary as fundamental to liberty. The book became the cornerstone of political theory – not practice – in Europe, and after the revolt of Britain's north American colonies the principle of the separation of powers was enshrined in the constitution of the United States, ratified in 1788. The following year, as the French Revolution broke out, Congress passed ten amendments which gave US citizens practical rights the British had acquired down the centuries: freedom of religion, speech and the press; rights of peacable assembly; security against unreasonable searches; trial by jury; and the right not to be a witness against oneself or to be oppressed by excessive fines or 'cruel and unusual punishments'.

Another aspect of British freedom as first defined by Locke – also incorporated in the United States constitution – was the accountability of the government to the governed: should those in power neglect or miscarry in their duties, authority reverted to society, 'and the People have a Right to act as Supreme, and continue the Legislative in themselves, or place it in a new form, or new hands'.[21] This was not mere theory. Both the British and Americans had a fierce pride in their right and obligation to participate in local, even national affairs. This, again, was at the opposite pole to French society where decrees and

Thomas Paine (1737–1809) emigrated from England to Philadelphia in 1774, where he campaigned for independence from Britain. His *Rights of Man* (1791), a counterpoint to Burke's *Reflections* ..., supported the French Revolution and attacked the institution of monarchy. (Mary Evans Picture Library)

regulations handed down from Paris via the regional Intendant (governor) were administered by local state functionaries, depriving the populace of any degree of political initiative. In Britain central government was not involved in local matters. Lords Lieutenant, Sheriffs and Justices of the Peace in the counties and boroughs were notionally responsible to the Crown, but in practice administered their domains independently.

In their determination to keep central authority out of their lives the British, alone of European nations, had no disciplined bodies of police, and maintained the army at home in peacetime at the minimum strength necessary to quell civil disorder. No doubt in compensation for inadequate policing, punishments were savage. The death penalty was prescribed for over 150 crimes, including petty larceny and stealing sheep; and there were more executions in London than in Paris. These provided public spectacles catering to instincts otherwise indulged by bear-baiting, cock-fighting and similar degrading entertainments.

Nor were the British as a nation – with numerous honourable exceptions – more sensitive to the sufferings inflicted on negroes transported from Africa to the Caribbean and America to work as slaves in the growth industries of the day, sugar, cotton and tobacco. Liberal writers in Britain and France denounced the hideous traffic, but it still increased. Britain led in numbers of slaves transported, but France shipped substantial numbers in equally abominable conditions, and French West Indian planters were as capable of extreme cruelty to those they owned as personal property as their British counterparts. Nonetheless, consciences had been awakened and Britain's shame was about to provoke what must be accounted the most glorious episode in British Parliamentary history.

A campaign against the slave trade started by Quakers and other non-conformist Churches had won popular support throughout Britain and led to the establishment in London of a Committee for Effecting the Abolition of the Slave Trade – soon echoed in Paris by a Société des Amis des Noirs – and in May 1789, inaugural month of what was to become the French Revolution, a Member of Parliament, William Wilberforce, and the Prime Minister, William Pitt, supported by Edmund Burke and others, took the abolitionist cause to the House of Commons. Defeated initially by powerful West Indian and shipping interests, they persevered year after year and, aided by public agitation, won the argument: legislation outlawing the slave trade was passed by both Houses of Parliament in 1807; by coincidence, in the same month a similar law was passed in the United States Congress. They were victories for the first purely philanthropic public campaigns in history and triumphs of free speech and consultative government since they were moral decisions carried against huge commercial pressures and the countries' own self-interest, in Britain's case at the height of a life and death struggle against Napoleon. By contrast, one of Napoleon's first acts on taking power as military dictator was to reverse a decree passed earlier by the French Revolutionary Assembly for freeing slaves; and he restored government backing for the slave trade.

In practical terms the field in which British Parliamentary government under a constitutional monarch proved decisively superior to the absolutism of the Bourbons and successive Revolutionary and Napoleonic administrations was finance, in particular the ability to borrow money cheaply. Parliament's control of the national purse meant that loans taken out were guaranteed as a 'national debt', not the king's personal obligations. And the careful scrutiny of the public accounts in Parliament, the openness of the proceedings, together with the equally transparent tax system and a policy of funding loans with returns from specific taxes or duties, had given investors at home and abroad such confidence in the probity of the system that British governments were able to spread the huge costs of war far into the future with long-term borrowing at rates of interest scarcely above peacetime rates.

This was not an option available to absolute monarchical governments, whose borrowings were tied to the reputation of the king. In Bourbon France there was no public scrutiny of taxes raised or sums spent or borrowed in the national interest, nor even a ministerial audit. In war the resulting financial chaos was too often met by reneging on or renegotiating loans or inflating the currency by printing paper money; and the longer a war lasted, the more desperate the financial situation and the higher the rates of interest demanded by lenders. Moreover, the other expedients adopted to raise money with new or increased taxes and duties, forced levies and the sale of public offices had the effect of restraining economic activity and diverting investment. At some point in every war with Britain France was forced to make deep cuts in naval expenditure.

During negotiations to end the most recent War of American Independence, Louis XVI's foreign minister had implored France's ally, Spain, to endorse peace terms:

> The English have to some degree regenerated their navy while ours has been used up... Join to that the diminution of our financial means... That inconvenience is common, no doubt, also to England, but her constitution gives her in that regard advantages which our monarchical forms do not give us.[22]

When peace was signed after the American War, Britain's national debt had risen to three times its level at mid-century, yet she had been able to borrow throughout the war at peacetime rates of about three per cent, and was well able to service the debt. France had borrowed at up to ten per cent; her finances were again in chaos and it was more than ever clear to more intelligent observers that her whole constitution and social structure must undergo radical change.

The trigger for Revolution was national bankruptcy. Notwithstanding the accumulated debt from the American War, Louis XVI's government was preparing, as was customary, for the next war; the navy minister had embarked on construction of a fleet of 80 of the line, the largest in French history – far too large to man with available sailors – and a fantastical project to create an artificial harbour off Cherbourg, since France had no fleet base in the English Channel. It was a reaction to the threat posed to French trade and colonies by the dominant British navy and rapacious British merchants, but no doubt equally a positive drive to project French power and glory overseas. The programmes made a major contribution to economic disaster: with her incoherent fiscal and financial systems, France could not support both a first class army and a navy of a strength to challenge the British navy.

By 1888 accumulated debt in France had almost reached the size of the British national debt, but carrying higher interest, it cost twice as much to service; interest payments amounted to over half annual government expenditure and it had just been discovered that expenditure exceeded revenue by 130 million *livres* annually – about 20 per cent of the total budget. In addition, a substantial parcel of short-term debt was coming due for repayment.[23] The financial crisis was

Charles Maurice de Talleyrand (1754–1838) had been destined for the Catholic Church since a foot injury precluded his entry into the army. His ability to change colours to suit the moment was demonstrated when he sided with the revolutionaries to divest the Church of its lands. He was later excommunicated by the Pope. After a spell in the United States and England, where he became an admirer of parliamentary government, Talleyrand hitched his fortunes to Napoleon and he survived to engineer France's comparative success at the Congress of Vienna (1814–15). (Mary Evans Picture Library)

aggravated by escalating bread prices caused by a succession of poor harvests, an industrial depression and a deficit on the balance of trade with the outside world. The naval construction programme was sucking in raw materials from abroad, but the principal cause of the deficit was a trade treaty with Britain signed in 1786. William Pitt, a disciple of Adam Smith, was attempting to boost international commerce by freeing it from restrictions. Louis' ministers had agreed mutual reductions on import tariffs – most rashly since a large number of French manufacturers simply could not compete with the high-quality, low-cost products of Britain's nascent industrial revolution, and British goods flooded into the country with no reciprocal increase in the other direction.

After another vain attempt at tax reform, Louis bowed to popular pressure and convened an ancient representative forum which had long fallen into disuse, the Estates General. The deputies, elected from the three orders of society, assembled in their three orders at Versailles in May 1789 and immediately became locked in procedural dispute. In June the commoners of the Third Estate, claiming to represent 98 per cent of the nation, cut through argument by declaring themselves a 'National Assembly' with the right to consent to taxation. Louis shut them out of their meeting hall, whereupon they famously adjourned to a nearby Real Tennis court and vowed never to part until they had formed a new and just constitution. They were joined by many liberal representatives of the other two orders.

The Revolution thus begun had many currents. At one intellectual level it was concerned with the rationalist ideals of the 'Enlightenment', a new start for France and all mankind, written on a blank sheet from which all class distinction, stale custom and religious 'superstition' had been erased. Practical men of affairs, on the other hand, anticipated a French version of the 'Glorious Revolution', resulting in a constitutional monarchy, two-chamber legislature and separate judiciary after the British or American model; their aim was nationalistic: to enhance French power in financial, trading and industrial terms. Both groups had adherents among the nobles and clergy who had been infected over decades by Enlightenment ideas promulgated in salon discussion, banned books and circulated manuscripts, more recently with satirical and pornographic libels, chiefly against the Queen, Marie Antoinette. Beneath the outward show, the monarchy, nobility and particularly the Church had been fatally undermined.

At a more elemental level another Revolution had begun months earlier, born of hunger and unemployment among peasants, labourers and artisans, and manifest in rioting, looting and bloodshed in the cities, defiance of the game laws, attacks on grain transports and banditry in the countryside. Areas in the south were ungovernable. Everywhere, despair at high food prices found expression in rage against the system and the wealthy, supposed to be profiting at the expense of the poor. In April rioters in Paris had chanted 'Death to the rich! Death to aristocrats!' In July rampaging crowds overran customs posts and grain stores in the capital and stormed the Bastille prison, symbol of Royal power, cutting down the defenders and anyone suspected of being in the 'conspiracy' of wealth and privilege, parading their heads on pikes. Next day delegates from the different sections of the city formed an insurrectionary city government or 'commune' and adopted a blue and red (Parisian) and white (Bourbon) cockade as their symbol. *The Times* of London reported at the end of the month, 'There is neither law nor police at this moment in Paris. Our sovereign Lord the Mob govern the city at their pleasure.'[24]

The Paris commune and rioters throughout the country provided the dynamic of the Revolution. To stave off anarchy the National, renamed Constituent Assembly since it was to produce a new constitution, pulled down the differentiated orders of society at a stroke with a 'Declaration of the Rights of Man and of the Citizen', asserting that 'Men are born free and equal in rights', defining the rights as 'Liberty, Property, Safety and Resistance to Oppression'[25] – an indication of the anxiety felt by the entirely middle-class representatives of the Third Estate, as well as the nobles and clergy, for the safety of their property. In contrast to the practical prescriptions of the Bill of Rights accepted by William of Orange in 1689 or the recent constitution of the United States, the Declaration was rhetorical; yet the Assembly did take rapid, practical steps to address the people's grievances, reforming the tax structure, sweeping away internal customs dues and feudal rights and provincial administrative anomalies, achieving in a short space what Bourbon ministers had attempted without success for a century. And in a breathtaking resolution born of financial necessity they transferred all Church property to the state for use as security for new loans. They changed France for ever. Yet in administration and the constitution they produced the deputies showed themselves true heirs of the absolutist regime they had replaced.

One reason was the preponderance of lawyers among the delegates of the Third Estate and the number of these who held government office, 278 out of 648 deputies, or 43 per cent.[26] These men, who played a critical role in framing the constitution, had been raised within the centralized bureaucratic tradition; their concern was to smooth and rationalize administration, not to introduce checks and balances after the Anglo-American model. There was also a large measure of utopianism among the deputies. One form derived from the influential 'physiocrat' school of political philosophy; envisaging a transformation of government and society according to reason and natural law, as they defined it, physiocrats knew it would require absolute authority to force through the radical changes they desired. Openly contemptuous of the British system, they assumed abuse of power could be prevented by continuous public instruction in the essence of justice and the natural order – which de Tocqueville later described as 'trifling gibberish'.[27]

Undoubtedly the pervading influence on the Assembly was Jean-Jacques Rousseau's *Du contrat social* – The Social Contract – published in 1762. Rousseau initiated the shift away from Enlightenment reason towards the irrational, spontaneous, emotional and aesthetic areas of the mind termed the 'Romantic movement'; and his crucial contribution to Revolutionary theory lay in that zone. He proposed that individuals joining together in a 'Social Contract' to choose their own form of government and laws would be free since they shared sovereign authority in the constitution; at the same time they would be bound by their own free wills to obey the 'general will', famously concluding that individuals 'will be forced to be free'.[28] Belief in this paradox was another example of what de Tocqueville characterized as 'a kind of abstract and literary politics'[29] indulged by the French intelligentsia, since they had been excluded by the omnipresent state from real politics. It was also a rationalization for totalitarian government.

As such, it served the Revolutionaries. The new constitution presented to Louis XVI in 1791 reduced him to little more than a figurehead with certain

Marie Antoinette (1755–93), Louis XVI's Queen Consort, was widely rejected by the French people for her Austrian birth, extravagant and frivolous tastes and alleged sexual perversions as described in countless pornographic pamphlets which contributed to the downfall of the monarchy; she had little hope of mercy from the moral zealots of the Revolution. (Mary Evans Picture Library)

Jean Jacques Rousseau (1712–78) was the single most important influence on the course of the French Revolution; his theory of the 'general will', whereby an individual in society would 'be forced to be free', might be said to have laid the theoretical basis for 'the Terror'. (Mary Evans Picture Library)

powers to delay legislation. Real authority was reserved to an elected single-chamber Legislative Assembly, the repository of the 'general will' of the people – although the poorest were excluded from the vote. Already, the previous summer, two executive committees had been established, one to secure government control of political appointments in the regions, another to supervise state security with powers of search, arrest and imprisonment without trial as arbitrary as those of the Bourbon apparatus. This was in response to counter-revolutionary threats from nobles and priests and widespread unrest due to rising food prices. To save the Revolution, the old organs of control and repression had to be resurrected.

It was insufficient. The bonds of society had been severed, anarchy loosed. To unify the nation behind the Revolution the new government was impelled to find a foreign enemy. The emperor of Austria made a fitting target: he was supporting émigré noble factions on the French border and, together with the king of Prussia, had publicly denounced the Revolutionaries' rhetoric of equality and self determination for all peoples. In April 1792 the Revolutionary government declared war. The king of Prussia made common cause with the emperor to extirpate the Revolution, and the French army was forced into retreat. The army

Georges Danton (1759–94) was a leading Jacobin credited with a major share in the overthrow of the monarchy. Later, however, he attempted to moderate revolutionary excesses, in the course of which he himself was sentenced to the guillotine. (Mary Evans Picture Library)

had been a major casualty of Revolutionary doctrine: half the officers had emigrated, others distrusted their men who had been infected with the slogans of equal rights. The navy had been similarly affected.

The reverses suffered by the army provoked the people of Paris into a bloody uprising and demands for a new Assembly to be elected by universal male suffrage, together with a Revolutionary tribunal to weed out and condemn the aristocrats and wealthy 'traitors' deemed responsible for the enemies' successes. From the start the Revolution had been driven from ground level by popular resentment and atrocity. Now atrocity was formalized as state terror.

It was administered by a new National Convention elected by about 10 per cent of eligible voters – men over 25 – and 47 per cent of those elected were lawyers. Reflecting the radical mood on the streets, the Convention abolished the monarchy, declared a republic and pronounced the date of the inaugural session, 20 September 1792, the start of Year One of National Liberty. Afterwards, Louis XVI was placed on trial, found guilty of treason – to the Revolution – and sent to the guillotine. The army, meanwhile, had halted the enemy and pushed

ABOVE
Charlotte Corday (1768–93) was a 25-year-old supporter of moderate 'Girondin' elements driven from the National Convention by the Jacobin Cabal; determined to demonstrate her loathing for the direction these men were taking France, she stabbed Marat in his bath. She went to the guillotine. (Mary Evans Picture Library)

LEFT
Jean-Paul Marat (1743–93), another leading Jacobin, was a Swiss-born doctor whose speeches and articles inflamed the fears and hatreds of the populace and led directly to street riots and massacres. He justified 'the Terror' as 'the despotism of liberty', which was necessary to 'crush the despotism of kings'. (Mary Evans Picture Library)

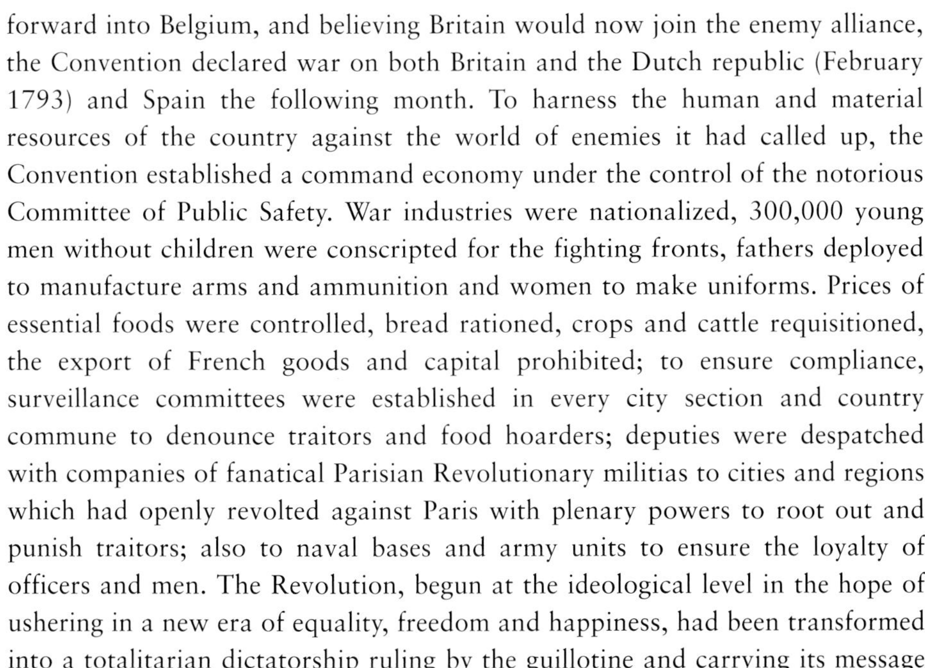

forward into Belgium, and believing Britain would now join the enemy alliance, the Convention declared war on both Britain and the Dutch republic (February 1793) and Spain the following month. To harness the human and material resources of the country against the world of enemies it had called up, the Convention established a command economy under the control of the notorious Committee of Public Safety. War industries were nationalized, 300,000 young men without children were conscripted for the fighting fronts, fathers deployed to manufacture arms and ammunition and women to make uniforms. Prices of essential foods were controlled, bread rationed, crops and cattle requisitioned, the export of French goods and capital prohibited; to ensure compliance, surveillance committees were established in every city section and country commune to denounce traitors and food hoarders; deputies were despatched with companies of fanatical Parisian Revolutionary militias to cities and regions which had openly revolted against Paris with plenary powers to root out and punish traitors; also to naval bases and army units to ensure the loyalty of officers and men. The Revolution, begun at the ideological level in the hope of ushering in a new era of equality, freedom and happiness, had been transformed into a totalitarian dictatorship ruling by the guillotine and carrying its message to Europe by war; as one of the chief ideologues in the Convention proclaimed, 'the moment has come for the temporary organization of the despotism of liberty in order to crush the despotism of kings'[30] – recalling Rousseau's paradox of the individual forced to be free.

Apologists for the Revolution claim that dictatorship and 'the Terror' were consequences of the desperate state of affairs in France; once the external enemies had been repulsed and the internal counter-revolutions suppressed – as they were by the most barbaric measures foreshadowing 20th-century mass atrocities – controls and 'Terror' were dismantled. Yet the move towards extreme centralization and uniformity, the use of surveillance, informers and arbitrary arrest had been apparent within months of the meeting of the Estates General. The true paradox of the Revolution is that, after erasing the old order, it had to re-erect the old institutions of control in monstrous form. It was entirely predictable. Edmund Burke did predict it; and as early as February 1790 warned the British people against imitating 'the excesses of an irrational, unprincipled, proscribing, confiscating, plundering, ferocious, bloody and tyrannical democracy'.[31]

In his *Reflections*, written in summer 1790, Burke provided a remarkably accurate forecast of the nature of the regime, known as the Directorate, which followed 'the Terror' in Year III (1795), composed of 'directors of assignats [government bonds originally issued for the purchase of nationalized Church property, subsequently used as paper money] and trustees for the sale of Church lands, attorneys, agents, money-jobbers, speculators and adventurers.'[32] And after this ruling oligarchy, he predicted the advent of a military dictatorship under a 'popular general':

> Armies will obey him on his personal account ... the moment in which that shall happen, the person who really commands the army is your master ... the master of your assembly, the master of your whole republic.[33]

Napoleon Bonaparte fulfilled this prediction precisely in Year VIII (1799), and five years later after a string of military victories, crowned himself emperor. Napoleon was the ultimate rationalizer and centralizer. He had every area of French life codified and enforced uniformly throughout France by *préfets*, each administering one of the *départements* into which the country had been divided, as in Bourbon times intendants had administered regions. This was in complete contrast to local government in Britain where each county, town and even parish looked after its own affairs largely ignored by the central administration. Napoleon's *préfets*, guided by increasingly detailed regulations, fed a mountainous correspondence with the Minister of the Interior.

Like the Bourbons, Napoleon appointed ministers, generals, senior civil servants and members of the Council of State through which he ruled. Retaining an elected legislative assembly as a symbolic gesture to the ideals of the Revolution,

The execution of Louis XVI on 20 January 1793 marked the real birth of the Republic. Rising at 5 a.m. on a cold, wet morning, he was escorted by a huge guard to the guillotine, accompanied by an English priest, Henry Edgeworth, with whom he recited psalms. His final address to the multitude of armed citizenry was, 'I die innocent of all the crimes laid to my charge; I pardon those who have occasioned my death; and I pray to God that the blood you are going to shed may never be visited upon France.' His bloody head was held up to cries of '*Vive la Republique!*' (Mary Evans Picture Library)

he emptied it of all power; and appointed safe men to a tame Senate. To restore values in the community, he brought back distinctions and created 18 Marshals of France as an emphatically military upper echelon of a new social hierarchy, endowing them with princely titles, lands and salaries. He strengthened the police, particularly the secret police, whose powers of arbitrary arrest, detention without trial, torture and even murder were used increasingly as opposition to his rule grew – assisted with British secret service funds – and imposed a rigorous press censorship. The result of Trafalgar was withheld for months, then reported as several ships lost after an imprudently delivered battle; the French commander-in-chief was expunged from the record. He was later found dead in an inn with several knife wounds and a suicide note. He was certainly murdered, possibly on the direct orders of Napoleon. As intellectual monitor, Napoleon established a University of France to supervise education throughout the empire and indoctrinate the young with the ideal of serving and dying for *la patrie*.

The Revolution had come full circle: from absolute monarchy, through the fiction of the 'general will' of the people to the absolute will of an emperor, always at the opposite pole to the British system; and it remained crucially inferior in the fields of finance, trade and industry. The National Convention had created a disastrous inflation of the *assignat* by printing it to excess. Napoleon stabilized the currency by tying the coinage to gold and silver and prohibiting the mass issue of paper money; but since he could not borrow on the security of the nation represented in open assembly, loans were tied to his reputation, as they had been for the Bourbons. At first military success enabled him to borrow at rates scarcely above those on British government debt, but when his star waned rates climbed. In any case, he distrusted borrowing, regarding it as an index of overspending. Instead the imperial budget was balanced with contributions from conquered enemies in the form of huge war indemnities, taxes, forced levies and simple theft. This necessarily produced diminishing returns, inducing further conquest.

The French Revolution turned full circle in December 1804 with General Bonaparte's self-elevation into the Emperor Napoleon - he literally seized the crown from the hands of the Pope and placed it on his own head. The position carried rights of succession for his heirs, and other trappings of the old order of nobility followed. (Mary Evans Picture Library)

Yet it was his determination to bring down Great Britain, the constant obstacle to his mastery in Europe, that drove him beyond his means. The obvious solution was invasion. When Trafalgar showed he could never hope to cross the Channel, he resolved to ruin the trade on which Britain's strength depended. He had already begun: British goods were banned from all ports under his control – the secondary consequence of which was a protected market for French goods which helped in the short term but ensured that French manufacturers would emerge from the war even less competitive with their British counterparts than before. However, it was his campaign to enforce a continent-wide blockade of British goods that led him to disaster. Attempting to stop British trade flowing into Europe through the Baltic ports, he encroached on the economic interests of the Tsar of Russia and was drawn into his fatal march ending in Moscow, humiliating retreat and the loss of his army. He never fully recovered.

In the decisive arena at sea, Horatio Nelson was the peerless champion of the British system. His was a conservative and intuitive rather than intellectual mind, and his patriotism was as instinctive as his belief in the God he had been taught to worship from his earliest days in his father's rectory. He hated the French and distrusted them. Naturally: they had been his country's enemy from before living memory; as he wrote once when refusing to take French Royalists aboard his ships, 'Forgive me; but my mother hated the French'.[34] As captain of the *Agamemnon* at the start of the Revolutionary War, he enjoined his midshipmen, first, that they must implicitly obey orders, 'secondly, you must consider every man your enemy who speaks ill of your king; thirdly, you must hate a Frenchman as you do the devil !'[35] By this time the ideologues in Paris had given him every reason for hating them by displaying fanatical atheism and executing their king.

Whatever the nature of his dislike, it fitted well with his overriding desire for personal distinction in action, although it never outweighed his concern for individuals. At the height of the battle of the Nile when the French flagship was ablaze and expected to blow apart, his first thought was to order boats to rescue her sailors. And in the last entry he made in his diary before action at Trafalgar when praying for 'a great and glorious victory', he added, 'may humanity after victory be the predominant feature in the British fleet'; after which he committed himself to his maker, together with 'the just cause which is entrusted to me to defend. Amen. Amen. Amen.'[36]

Napoleon had lost faith in his admirals and his navy long before Trafalgar. Nelson, when he defeated the Franco-Spanish fleet, was in a sense cashing the cheque won by the Royal Navy's operational superiority and constant vigilance. In terms of the war, Trafalgar was the final proof for Napoleon that he could neither invade Britain nor break out from continental Europe; nor could he prevent British military, commercial and political interference on the maritime fringes of his empire. His efforts to solve that punishing irregularity drew him into ever rasher adventures, and final disaster. In a more profound sense, his defeat at Waterloo in 1815 was the conclusion of over a century of Franco-British struggle. He was the ultimate expression of France's martial ethos, as Nelson was arguably the extreme example of Britain's will to rule the seas. The result of this final phase of the contest during which each side reverted to its naked character, the warrior horde against the ruthless merchant trader, proved, so far as any historical phenomenon is capable of scientific demonstration, that the French political system and culture formed from and dominated by land-holding values could not compete with the opposing merchant culture protected by and in command of the seas. Finally trade proved stronger than plunder. And after Napoleon's defeat Britain was able to project Pitt's goals of free trade, financial probity and liberal ideals on to France, western Europe and subsequently much of the rest of the world, which it transformed in its own image.

The most eloquent defence of the British system was mounted by Edmund Burke, its most precious value the freedom of the individual, which Burke claimed 'as an entailed inheritance derived to us from our forefathers, and to be transmitted to our posterity'.[37] Beside his organic view of the progress of society, the theories of the Revolutionaries appear in the light of history as dangerous fantasies.

CHAPTER TWO

NELSON THE MAN

EDGAR VINCENT

In the short space of eight years, 1797–1805, Nelson ascended from hero to living legend and then to icon of the nation. The crowds and public emotion at his funeral would not be equalled until those for Princess Diana in our own time. He died in the hour of victory, in a battle that released his country from imminent danger of invasion. Trafalgar was an episode as potent for the British as the Battle of Britain in 1940.

Hundreds of books have been written about Nelson, many of them hagiographic or hero worshipping, many derived from the books of others. Carola Oman began to rebuild on the primary sources available to her at the time, and in her *Nelson* (1947) produced a compelling narrative out of which emerged an engaging and likeable figure. More recently, new discoveries, wider and deeper research, more penetrating questions and less inhibited writers have enabled a badly needed warts-and-all approach, exemplified in particular by Tom Pocock's *Horatio Nelson* (1987), a realistic portrait balanced with recognition of Nelson's human weaknesses, Terry Coleman's revisionist *Nelson: The Man and the Legend* (2001) which portrays an even more flawed human being with few redeeming features, and Edgar Vincent's *Nelson: Love & Fame* (2003) which interweaves Nelson's professional and personal life and explores his motivations and the many contradictions and paradoxes in his charismatic character. But whatever the differing assessments of Nelson the man, his capacity to lead and inspire, to command great fleets and lead them to victory, is unassailable. And never did a fighting commander inspire such love, affection and emulation. His column in Trafalgar Square places him on a higher pedestal than any other hero or any king in the nation's history.

OPPOSITE
Nelson in 1800 by John Hoppner. According to Nelson's chaplain, Alexander Scott, this was Nelson's second best likeness after de Koster. (Royal Naval Museum)

MILESTONES IN NELSON'S LIFE

Horatio Nelson was born on 29 September 1758 at Burnham Thorpe in Norfolk where his father was Rector. He was the fourth of eight children who survived

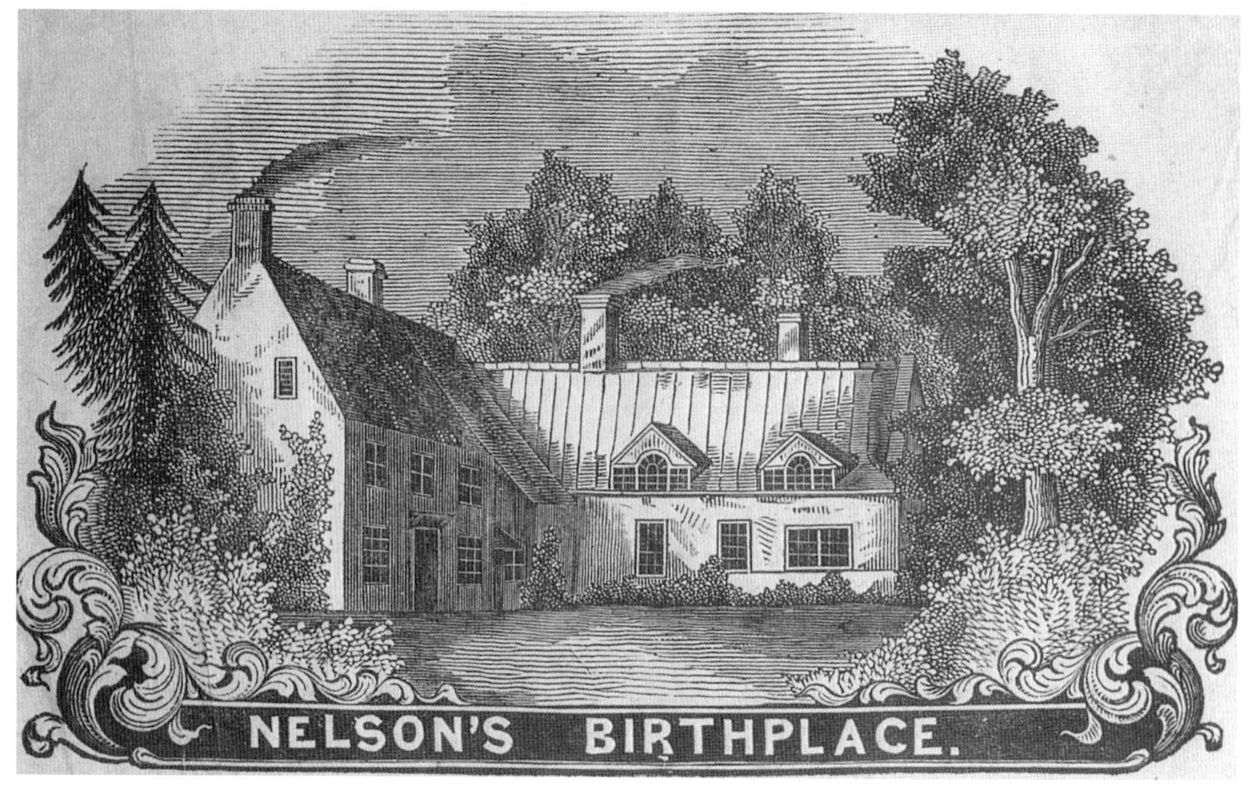

Nelson's birthplace. Burnham Thorpe parsonage where Nelson was born in September 1758, spent his early childhood and later spent the years 1788–93 as a newly wed and unemployed officer. (Royal Naval Museum)

infancy. He went to sea in 1771 at the age of 12½. All but 7½ of his remaining years were spent at sea.

Nelson married Frances (Fanny) Nisbet in the West Indies in 1787 when he was 28. On the outbreak of war with revolutionary France in 1793 he was appointed to the Mediterranean fleet under Admiral Hood but his star did not rise until 1797 when, aged 39, he was the hero of the battle of Cape St Vincent, for which he received a knighthood and his commander-in-chief Sir John Jervis an earldom. The next year (1798), his stupendous victory over the French at the battle of the Nile made him a living legend and a peer. Two years at Naples led to his involvement in Neapolitan politics and his entanglement with Emma Hamilton, wife of the British envoy Sir William Hamilton. He returned to England with the Hamiltons in July 1800. Separation from his wife, the birth of his illegitimate daughter Horatia (conceived in Naples), and the battle of Copenhagen, for which he was made Viscount, followed in 1801. The Peace of Amiens brought him on shore in late 1801 to his newly acquired house, Merton Place, where he lived with Emma until the final Trafalgar campaign which for him began in May 1803 and culminated in his death at Trafalgar on October 21 1805 aged 47.

WHAT SHAPED NELSON?

Nelson was a small boy, only 5 foot 6 inches as a man and slightly built; small men are frequently assertive and Nelson certainly was. It has been said that

Nelson's father (1722–1802). Edmund Nelson, good natured and rather whimsical, something of a hypochondriac, 'easily put in a fuss', 'tremulous over trifles.' Befriended by Nelson's wife. Not as significant a person in Nelson's life as other father figures Captain Locker and Admirals Hood and St Vincent. (Royal Naval Museum)

children of ministers of religion think of themselves as different and it is evident that Nelson always had a very high opinion of himself. He lost his mother when he was nine; there is ample evidence to suggest that early death of a parent provides a powerful motive force for a child who has the capacity and opportunity for great achievement.

On the other hand, Nelson's genetic inheritance seems to have been unremarkable. True, his mother's great-grandmother had been sister of Prime Minister Sir Robert Walpole, and his mother's brother was a naval captain destined to become Comptroller of the Navy, but his father was ineffectual and something of a hypochondriac, his brothers and sisters nothing out of the ordinary. He was a middle child in a large family, needing to compete for maternal attention and possibly perceiving a lack of it. This, together with his mother's

Nelson's uncle (1725–78). Captain Maurice Suckling took Nelson to sea in 1771, to help his widowed brother-in-law to provide for his family. He was a wonderful surrogate father to Nelson, using his influence to get him the right opportunities, especially when he became Comptroller of the Navy. (National Maritime Museum)

early death, may explain Nelson's constant craving for attention and his seemingly insatiable need to be liked and loved, both indicative of inner insecurities. Still a child when he went to sea, important formative years were spent in the Navy, an all-male hierarchic institution. From the beginning, Nelson seems to have fitted that mould. The Navy quickly became the centre of his life and remained so.

MOTIVATION AND GUIDING FORCES IN HIS LIFE

Nelson was always self-directed. He pushed himself forward to be taken to sea by his uncle Maurice Suckling. He pushed himself forward for a succession of new experiences, a polar expedition, a voyage to India and the Persian Gulf. True, his uncle, a captain in the Navy, had sufficient pull to enable the young

Nelson's mother (1725–67). Catherine Nelson died when Nelson was nine after bearing 11 children. He referred to her only twice in his voluminous correspondence, but her enthusiasm for the Navy and her captain brother probably provided the impetus for Nelson's career choice. Nelson said he had learned his hatred of the French at his mother's knee. (National Maritime Museum)

Nelson to achieve his ambitions, but he would always thrust himself forward. There was nothing of the shrinking violet in Nelson.

As a convalescent young man returning from India in 1776 he decided to be a hero. At least that is how he recounted his experience some 25 years later:

> I felt impressed with an idea that I should never rise in my profession. My mind was staggered with a view of the difficulties I had to surmount and the little interest I possessed. I could discover no means of reaching the object of my ambition. After a long and gloomy reverie, in which I almost wished myself overboard, a sudden glow of patriotism was kindled within me, and presented my king and country as my patron. My mind exulted in the idea. 'Well then, I exclaimed, I will be a hero, and confiding in Providence I will brave every danger.'

His huge latent ambition could now be focused and whatever the accuracy of his recollection the rest of his life was driven by a heroic search for fame and glory and his determination to be a man of destiny.

Much has been made of Nelson's Christian belief. God indeed seems to have been part of his military conviction, personally on his side and by definition against his enemy. He could cast himself in biblical proportions. In a letter to his father following victory at the Nile, the parson's son echoed the spirit of the Old Testament: 'The hand of God was visibly pressed on the French: it is not in the power of man to gain such a victory.' In 1793 his 64-gun *Agamemnon* chased and outfought a heavy French frigate only to be cornered by three more. Together his enemies had more than twice his firepower and four times his manpower; he escaped but it was a very close call. That night he entered in his journal the words, 'Though I know neither the time nor the manner of my death, I am not at all solicitous about it, because I am sure He knows them both, and that he will not fail to support and comfort me under them.' Here was the source of his legendary courage, his sense that death would come when it would come and that his God would enable him to bear it. When he left Merton for the last time he was still the trusting and believing fatalist:

> May the great God whom I adore enable me to fulfil the expectations of my country and if it is His good pleasure that I should return, my thanks will never cease being offered up to his Throne of Mercy. If it is his good providence to cut short my days upon earth, I bow with the greatest submission, relying that he will protect those so dear to me, that I may leave behind – His will be done Amen, Amen, Amen.

Just before the battle he went to his cabin and wrote his famous final prayer. Both prayers were exalted expressions of the way Nelson, throughout his life, steeled himself to meet the possibility of death.

During his affair with Emma Hamilton, Nelson persuaded himself that his motives were pure because he wanted to marry her. In September 1805 he took communion with Emma, declaring before the priest, 'Emma I have taken the Sacrament with you this day to prove to the world that our friendship is most pure and innocent, and of this I call God to witness.' As he lay dying he was heard to say, 'I have not been a great sinner,' even though he had broken at least three commandments. Nelson's religious feeling played an important and sustaining part in his military life but it was like that of many individuals, complex, selective, sometimes contradictory and tailored to meet his own psychological needs. At the scene of his death Nelson's final thoughts joined God and duty: 'Thank God I have done my duty.' Duty was a word that had resonated throughout his life from the time he had written to his complaining fiancée, 'duty is the great business of a sea officer. All private considerations must give way to it however painful it is.' Nelson always put duty and the Navy first. Neither in relation to wife, mistress nor daughter was there any 'All for Love' theme in Nelson's life.

APPEARANCES AND REALITY

The first portrait by John Francis Rigaud begun in May 1777 when Nelson was 19 reveals a charmingly boyish but confident young man. In 1797 when Nelson was 39, Lemuel Abbott painted a portrait which we all recognize with its compellingly serene, kind and resolute gaze. The strangest portrait is Guzzardi's painted in 1798 in Naples, a sad, weary Nelson, the personification of post-traumatic shock. On his way home in 1800 he was painted in Vienna by Heinrich Fuger, a portrait which seems to capture Nelson's ruthlessness; the lips are

Nelson in 1781 by J. F. Rigaud. The young post captain just back from the West Indies in a portrait commissioned by Captain Locker. (Royal Naval Museum)

thinner and the nose slightly more aquiline than is generally portrayed; he seems cool and distant. Nelson himself thought the best likeness was a profile sketch by Simon de Koster with its powerful, dominating face, straight nose, firm mouth and chin. His chaplain, the Revd Scott, thought the next best was Hoppner's oil sketch which brings out the softer feminine side of Nelson's personality. Significantly, Emma kept De Koster's miniature in her locket but she was also much moved by Catherine Andras' wax figure in Westminster Abbey, also notable for the power in his face. Nelson's nephew, George Matcham, said it was 'far more like him than any of the portraits.'

None of these artists appears to have seen quite the same man, hardly surprising in view of Nelson's many-sided character.

CONTRADICTIONS AND PARADOXES

Nelson's behaviour and personality were full of contradictions and paradoxes. He was in essence the most conciliatory, communicative and collaborative of men and yet his fund of aggression went beyond that required even for a successful fighting commander. He had an obsessive appetite for battle, possibly the by-product of his mission to be a hero or of inner insecurities which required him to prove himself time and time again. At the same time, he constantly aroused protective feelings in others. Sick in the West Indies, his friend Captain Cornwallis organized native nursing for him. His commander-in-chief's wife cared for him like a son. His captains Troubridge and Ball were worried and protective about his health and reputation at Palermo. During the Copenhagen campaign Captain Foley doctored him with a regimen of milk at four in the morning and his flag captain Murray dosed him with lozenges. In the earliest phase of his relationship with Emma she nursed and mothered the worn-out and injured little admiral. Maybe it was the combination of intrepid bravery, slight frame and willingness to appear vulnerable that was so potent. Certainly he aroused the mothering instincts of men and women alike.

Nelson demonstrated countless examples of kindness, generosity, thoughtfulness, empathy and sympathy but when he wanted something he was held back neither by diffidence, self respect, nor finer feelings; he was not above manipulating others (putting on quite a performance to wheedle out of Lady Spencer an extraordinary dinner invitation for his wife); emotional blackmail (when putting pressure on his uncle for a loan to enable him to marry); and a ruthless want of feelings (towards a wife he wanted to be rid of).

His inspiring self confidence and total self belief, so vital to his success, could on occasions metamorphose into self delusion, not least in his egocentric overestimate of the part he played in the sieges of Bastia and Calvi. There were other bouts of unreality, of sanctimonious grandiosity, referring to himself in the third person as Nelson, especially when somebody dared to question his motives or honesty, writing to the Victualling Board, 'Nelson is so far from doing a scandalous or mean action as the heavens are above the earth.' His sycophantic behaviour towards Prince William, later Duke of Clarence, 'Nothing is wanting

Nelson in 1797 by Lemuel Francis Abbott. The hero of the Nile. Nelson's wife wrote to Nelson 'The likeness is great' and 'our good father was delighted with the likeness.' (National Maritime Museum)

to make you the darling of the English nation,' and towards the King and Queen of Naples, showed a man willing to suspend his critical faculty when dazzled by royalty.

Nelson's constant desire for the limelight, his obsessive need to be first, and his flair for self publicity were all very real. Early experiences had persuaded him never to leave his reputation in the care of others. Thus he wrote his own spellbinding account of the battle of Cape St Vincent. But Nelson's reputation was not based on his own spin. His exploits at St Vincent were being celebrated in naval circles well before his own account reached home; there was nothing fictional about them. Subsequently he went to extraordinary lengths to ensure that his contribution as second-in-command at Copenhagen made its way back

Nelson in 1799 by Leonardo Guzzardi. The hero of the Nile showing the after effects of the cataclysmic battle. (National Maritime Museum)

Nelson in 1800 by Heinrich Fuger. On the way home in a triumphant progress with the Hamiltons. (Royal Naval Museum)

to Prime Minister Addington. In this he was very much his own man, held back neither by a conventional sense of loyalty nor inhibitions about indulging in organization politics.

Along with his love of the limelight went a streak of what is usually called vanity but perhaps ought to be described as exhibitionism, or a wish to singularize himself, an aspect of his need for attention. He liked his medals and stars (as indeed have many other military commanders). He told Colonel Drinkwater in the aftermath of the battle of Cape St Vincent that he would prefer a knighthood because it would provide visible evidence of his contribution (in its red sash). In July 1800 Sir John Moore, the future hero of Corunna (who had been seen by Nelson as an unconstructive army officer during the Corsica campaign) saw him at Leghorn, 'covered with stars, ribbons and medals, more like a prince of an opera than the conqueror of the Nile.' In 1801, when Nelson stopped off on his way to Plymouth to see St Vincent now first Lord of Admiralty, St Vincent wrote, 'Poor man he is devoured with vanity, weakness and folly, was strung with ribbons medals etc. and yet pretended that he wished to avoid the honour and ceremonies he met everywhere on the road.'(Perhaps St Vincent had become rather envious of Nelson and perhaps a little piqued at having lost their dispute over prize money.) In the same vein is the celebrated account by Wellington of their single meeting when at first he found Nelson to be 'a light and trivial character', that is until Nelson, according to Wellington, found out who Wellington was and changed his tune. (The patronizing tone of this account says as much about Wellington's snobbish arrogance as it does about Nelson's alleged behaviour.)

Nelson always put glory and fame, defeating the enemy, before prize money. One of the attractions of life in the navy was the opportunity for prize money, a kind of 18th-century incentive bonus. Nelson, like Hood, never put prize money first, although he could be jaundiced and envious of those who were more money-minded or luckier than he was, or seemed to have been put in the way of earning more than himself. There was in him a constant yearning for money. He could never get over the fact that St Vincent and Duncan both were awarded bigger pensions for their victories. Yet he was never mean, was generous towards his family, was a great giver of presents to all and sundry and could deny Emma nothing, even when his finances were at their most precarious and she was spending money like a drunken sailor.

NELSON'S PHYSICAL AND MENTAL HEALTH

Nelson's physical courage and mental energy coexisted with bouts of self pity, depression and intense preoccupation with his health. At times his behaviour suggests mental imbalance. His grandiose sense of self importance, unreasonable expectations of reward and recognition, attention-seeking theatricality, mood swings and emotionalism, may strike observers as abnormal, but like his physical symptoms, they neither impaired his social functioning nor his professional performance. Whatever his low mental state, the prospect of action instantly revived him. The idea that he developed a death wish and went into Trafalgar determined to be killed is singularly unlikely. He had too much to live for.

Nelson's medical history was remarkable. He lost the use of one eye at Calvi and later became worried by deterioration in his good eye. He suffered a blow to the belly at St Vincent and thereafter from a hernia. The amputation of his right arm without anaesthetic after the attack on Santa Cruz, bad enough in itself, led to prolonged painful after-effects. He suffered a head wound at the Nile and from time to time thereafter experienced a set of physically real symptoms, tentatively diagnosed by today's medical specialists as soldier's heart, angina, urinary tract infection and post-traumatic shock, some of his symptoms being of a psychosomatic nature. Given the immense burdens of command, the stress of battle and endless active service, it is not surprising that he frequently felt weaker and sicker than his doctors pronounced him to be. However, the autopsy done after Trafalgar by Dr Beatty showed that 'all the vital organs were so perfectly healthy in their appearance, and so small, that they resembled more those of a youth than a man who had attained his forty-seventh year; which state of the body, associated with habits of life favourable to health, gives every reason to believe that his Lordship might have lived to a great age,' a belief supported by the fact that his father survived till his 79th year and his sisters (Nelson's aunts) till they were 82 and 93 respectively.

FEELINGS AND FRIENDSHIPS

Nelson never bottled up his feelings. He wore his heart on his sleeve. If he was hurt, cast down, worried or depressed, he expressed it. He wrote to his commander-in chief: 'My heart would break to be near my Commander-in-Chief and not assisting him in such a time. What a state I am in!' To the First Lord he wrote: 'Do not my dear Lord let the Admiralty write harshly to me. My generous soul cannot bear it.' His words to Alexander Davison were typical: 'Believe me my only wish is to sink with honour into the grave and when that shall please God I shall meet death with a smile.' Such emotionalism was part and parcel of Nelson; it must have attracted some, repelled others and left others bemused. Occasionally his inner feelings could be unmanageable. His letters to Emma became hysterical when he suspected that the Prince of Wales was intent on seducing her. His so readily expressed feelings could, however, be shallow and temporary. He had the detachment and ruthlessness necessary in a commander; he seems generally to have shed no tears over his casualties, although later in life after the birth of his daughter, Horatia, he was untypically consumed with grief for Edward Parker, one of his young commanders who died of wounds sustained in the ill-fated raid on Boulogne. While he had gone to the funeral of his old 'sea daddy' Captain Locker, he was deterred by a vaguely described ailment from attending his own father's, which suggests a deep want of feeling.

It was in the nature of naval life that many friendships should be temporary and interrupted, others inhibited by competitive feelings and jealousies typical of any professional and organizational milieu. Because officers attached themselves to more senior officers in the hope of advancement, the stuff of much friendship was really self interest. Alexander Davison, a thrusting entrepreneurial government contractor, has traditionally been called Nelson's friend because he fulfilled a variety of functions as Nelson's agent, banker, public relations agent, confidant and go-between with his wife, in every sense his Mr Fixit. For Davison, Nelson's fame had economic potential and served also to support his energetic social climbing and wider political and commercial networks. On the other hand, his usefulness to Nelson was clearly immense, not least as a source of ready cash. But there were real and enduring friends, Locker, Sir Peter Parker and Collingwood, all dating from his early West Indies days, and Sir Gilbert Elliot, later Lord Minto, who had seen Nelson perform at close quarters when he was

Nelson in 1800 by Simon de Koster. The likeness Nelson preferred, a version of which was kept by Emma in a gold locket. (Royal Naval Museum)

viceroy of Corsica, witnessed the battle of Cape St Vincent, was fond of Emma and was with them at Merton the night before Nelson left for Trafalgar. Along the way Nelson made temporary friends with many officers irresistibly drawn to him by his charisma and reputation. And there were of course those who claimed to be his friend, but in the way of friends of celebrities, were more interested in reflected glory than friendship. On the other hand, Nelson was not greatly liked by officers of different personality and temperament. To imagine that a charismatic leader in a huge organization in the dangerous business of war will be universally admired is an illusion of Nelson worship. Nelson had his detractors on quarter decks and mess decks. His relationship with Emma divided him from some former friends, notably Troubridge, a long standing friend and protégé. Nelson became progressively disenchanted with St Vincent (who he had previously idealized and regarded as his father figure) seeing sides of him he did not like, his legal action over prize money (settled in Nelson's favour only after appeal) and what he perceived as St Vincent's lack of integrity. St Vincent, full of Nelson's praise to his face, never withdrew professional support but seems to have become progressively disillusioned and inclined to be pejorative to others about him. He did not attend Nelson's funeral.

INTELLECT, INTERESTS AND AMBITIONS

Nelson's native intelligence was of a very high order. In action he could rapidly process a multiplicity of variables, instantly decide on the best course of action and pursue it without hesitation. He had the mental energy to assemble arguments and persuade others that the option he was proposing was the best. He had the knack of being positively assertive. After the flag of truce incident at Copenhagen, he showed he was a natural negotiator, never getting himself into a corner, never exceeding his authority, never lost for a counter ploy.

He was a wonderful communicator. In his battle orders his general propositions were clear and compelling and could hardly have been better expressed. Detailed plans could be unclear in exposition and weak in analysis, notably his plan for opposing a French invasion in 1801. His preferred way of operating was face-to-face with his captains, communicating what he expected of them, in general but precise terms. His written instructions to individual captains on individual occasions, were always models of brevity, always clear in what was expected and suffused with a unique quality of confident trust which must have made them a pleasure to receive.

His friendship with Sir William Hamilton seems to have been the friendship of opposites; none of Hamilton's polymathic interests in arts or sciences seem to have rubbed off on Nelson. Uncritical devotees of Nelson make much of his use of Shakespeare but the clear fact is that in all his vast correspondence there are only a few half-remembered quotations. Nelson's wife, Fanny, played the piano but he shows no interest and refers to no favourite pieces. Apart from admiring the doge's palace at Genoa his visual senses are not greatly in evidence. He never managed to speak French and it has to be said that, unlike St Vincent, he showed little application or perseverance in trying to do so. Nelson preferred to act rather than reflect. His mental processes seem to have been governed by instinct and feelings and when those instincts were sound, as in battle, he prospered, but in general he was not overly analytical and not given to intellectualizing. Nelson was a sociable, communicative, well-informed action man of great native intelligence, practical common sense and outstanding professional talent. That he lacked wider cultural, intellectual and political interests made him less interesting as a person in some quarters but as a battle commander it was hardly germane.

Politically speaking, Nelson stood for the established order. Yet his heart was in the right place and he was moved by the hard facts of life as shown by his detailed account to the Duke of Clarence of the insufficiency of the meagre pay of Norfolk farm labourers. He was in all human respects a liberal at heart but he did not at all resonate to progressive political ideas or reformist politicians. Pitt and Wilberforce had opened the campaign for the abolition of slavery in the House of Commons in May 1789, but in his letters Nelson wrote against abolition as late as 1805. And he could be notably chauvinistic, dismissive and contemptuous of Neapolitans and prejudiced against his Portuguese allies. His ambition was narrowly focused. He did not have the grandiose political and personal ambition of a Napoleon. He did not have the political ambition of his contemporary Wellington, who would become Prime Minister. He did not even have the thirst for advancement and place of his mentor Admiral St Vincent, who succeeded Earl Spencer as First Lord of Admiralty. Time might well have produced a different outcome but during his lifetime Nelson cast himself as a hero, an instrument at the disposal of his king and country.

WOMEN, MARRIAGE AND LOVE

The early Nelson found it hard to be successful with women. He was infatuated with two women, Mary Simpson, the garrison commander's daughter in Quebec in 1782, and Elizabeth Andrews, a clergyman's daughter at St Omer in France in 1784. He seems to have been rejected by both. Then came his sentimental attachment to Mary Moutray, wife of the resident naval commissioner in Antigua which ended in 1785 when she returned to England. Two months later he met Frances Nisbet, a widow with a young son, Josiah, and rapidly reached an understanding with her, although they were not married until March 1787. Nelson's impetuous search for a wife had come to an end. Sentiments he expressed to his brother would have found favour with Jane Austen, his desire to be a good husband, his willingness to take responsibility for making the marriage work, his wholehearted acceptance of Fanny's child, the overall sense that he was looking for a companionable marriage based on mutual respect and affection. It is open to doubt whether he felt passionately about Fanny, or whether he was more in love with the idea of love. There was no indication in their voluminous correspondence of shared interests and time showed that their temperaments could not have been more diametrically opposed. Their early years of marriage were spent living with his father in cold Norfolk, bringing neither sign nor mention of a child of their own. When Nelson returned to sea in 1793, he left a wife who could not have been more unsuited to being a sailor's wife. Although parting on friendly terms, Nelson seems to have suffered no pangs at leaving Fanny behind. Within a year he was conducting an affair with Adelaide Correglia, an 'opera singer' in Leghorn.

When Nelson made his headquarters at Naples in 1798, he met Emma Hamilton. Her early background had been sensational, a blacksmith's daughter, giddy but ravishingly beautiful, living by her body, pregnant by Sir Harry Fetherstonhaugh, cast out, taken in by Charles Greville, a new lover and protector who subsequently passed her on to his uncle Sir William Hamilton, British envoy at Naples, who made her his mistress and subsequently married her when he was 60 and she still under 24. By the time Nelson met her she was established as a celebrated European beauty, famed for her performance of classical 'attitudes', welcomed at the Neapolitan court, a favourite of the Queen and accepted by visiting British aristocracy. Nelson and Emma were brought together in the complex political circumstances of the Neapolitan court, Nelson using Emma as his translator and go-between with the determinedly pro-British and deeply anti-French Queen. Being so alike in personality, having the same energy, decisiveness and theatrical personalities, Nelson and Emma were wonderfully suited as working partners. She brought Nelson the total unconditional approval and attention he sought, and when they became lovers in late 1799 or early 1800 she awoke and intoxicated his senses. In Nelson she encountered a man who loved her for herself and was not simply using her, as had so many men in her past. Each accepted the other uncritically. Each became entirely necessary to the other, whatever may have been the spiteful comments of onlookers about her increasing size, their mutual adoring dependence, or her dramatic and vulgar behaviour.

Nelson in 1805 by Catherine Andras. A waxwork still in Westminster Abbey. Emma said 'that it was impossible for anyone who had known him to doubt or mistake it.' (Westminster Abbey Historic Monuments)

Fanny had no hope of prevailing against this new alliance. Nelson began by naively behaving as though nothing needed to change, but the birth of his child, Emma's campaign against Fanny in the Nelson family and Nelson's inability to resist Emma's manipulations, led to Fanny's being ruled out of his life with utter insensitive ruthlessness, alleviated only by his financial generosity in giving her half his income and returning to her the capital she had brought with her on marriage. He was uncharacteristically cowardly, preferring to use Alexander Davison to convey messages to her rather than being open with her himself, no doubt trying to assuage his moral discomfort and guilt by being financially generous. Fanny always sought reconciliation and worked for it as far as she was able, but she and Nelson were an incompatible couple, their failing marriage finally destroyed by Nelson and Emma's overpowering mutual attraction. In the working out of this ordinary human drama, Nelson and Emma both displayed the worst and most unlikeable sides of their characters.

A STAIN ON NELSON'S REPUTATION

In February 1800 Charles James Fox, without actually naming Nelson, associated him by implication in the House of Commons with 'cruelties of every kind so abhorrent that the heart shudders at the recital.' He was referring to events during the restoration of the monarchy in Naples in 1799 when Nelson acted on behalf of King Ferdinand (an important British ally) at the overthrow of the French puppet Parthenopean Republic. It is alleged that Nelson lured collaborators and fellow travellers out of castles in which they had taken shelter and from which they had been granted safe conduct to France, before Nelson arrived on the scene. Two points are very clear. In treating with the 'rebels' Cardinal Ruffo, in command of the retaking of Naples, had totally disregarded orders from the king. Nelson, aware of these orders, never changed his position that surrender was the only option for those in the castles. Ruffo, realizing the

Nelson's wife Frances (Fanny) Nisbet (1761–1831), was a widow with a young child when Nelson met her in Nevis. Nelson may have married her on the rebound from his sentimental attachment to Mary Moutray wife of Antigua's dockyard commissioner and possibly because of her financial prospects. This turned out to be a marriage of opposite personalities, lacking the cement of passion, shared interests or children. (Royal Naval Museum)

dangerous position he was in with the king and having sole control of communication with the castles, had an urgent motive for getting the people out and it is most likely that to achieve his objective he misrepresented Nelson's position. Nelson himself never communicated directly with the forts. In the event 162 (4 per cent) of those from the castles were executed by order of the king (not Nelson). Retribution for traitors or collaborators seems unfortunately to be a deep human instinct and it is entirely illusory to think that Nelson could have had any control over inevitable blood letting by Neapolitans in Naples, let alone have prevented it. The horrendous atrocities that took place and to which Fox referred were committed on actual or suspected French sympathizers by the

Nelson's mistress Emma Hamilton (1765–1815). Daughter of a blacksmith in Cheshire who died when she was an infant, she subsequently made her way in the world on the strength of her beauty, personality, body and her capacity to learn and adapt. At times larger than life she went to pieces after Nelson's death. She died in reduced circumstances in Calais in 1815. (Royal Naval Museum)

Nelson's daughter with Emma Hamilton. Probably conceived on board the *Foudroyant* in spring 1800 and born secretly in London in early 1801 as Nelson was on his way to the battle of Copenhagen. Nelson doted on her and hung this portrait in his cabin. (Royal Naval Museum)

Neapolitan mob, much as in later times thousands would be killed by their own countrymen in France and Italy after liberation in the Second World War.

Much has also been made of the execution of Admiral Carracciolo who without a shadow of doubt had fired on the ships he had formerly commanded. He was tried by a Neapolitan court martial composed of Neapolitan officers which sentenced him to death. Nelson's function as the king's representative was to sign the death warrant and order execution. He ordered that Carracciolo be instantly hanged from the yardarm of the Neapolitan ship *Minerve* and resisted pleas for more time for Carracciolo to prepare himself and for execution by firing squad. This has cast Nelson as merciless and so he was, but them ashore there was near anarchy, order had to be quickly re-established and the lazzaroni who had remained loyal to the king at terrible cost to themselves were baying for blood. Under such circumstances Nelson decided that the best justice would be swift.

EPITAPHS

Freud holds that every man dies in a way true to himself. Nelson died gently, submissively, without histrionics, full of thought for those he loved, reassured that he had done his duty and had not let down others or himself. His death was not a case of 'shot so quick so clean an ending'. It took him three-and-a-quarter painful hours to die and from the beginning he knew he was a dead man. To the end he managed himself in character.

About his death itself, Mary Renault's words on Alexander the Great seem most apposite: 'One cannot suppose that Alexander would have wished it otherwise. He loved his fame. Like Achilles he had traded length of days for it.' George III said much the same thing in less fine language when he said bluntly to Nelson's brother William: 'He died as he would have wished.'

Lord Minto who had known Nelson for ten years told his wife after his last visit to Merton, 'He is in many points a really great man, in others a baby.' Alexander Scott, his chaplain and private secretary who had lived on board with him during the final two years of his life and for whom Nelson was, 'best beloved and most interesting of human beings,' put the same idea rather differently: 'That man possessed the wisdom of the serpent with the innocence of the dove.' Over the years his great commander St Vincent changed his view from 'There is but one Nelson' to 'Animal courage was the sole merit of Lord Nelson, his private character most disgraceful in every sense of the word.' Collingwood, a friend and fellow officer of Nelson since their early West Indian days, a fellow captain at the battle of Cape St Vincent and Nelson's second-in-command at Trafalgar, his 'dear Coll', described their friendship as 'a brotherhood of more than 30 years' and in everything he ever said about Nelson, revealed no trace of personal or professional jealousy.

Nelson was a kaleidoscopic character, many faceted, impossible to reduce to a single dimension. Blessed neither with a great physical presence nor fine and handsome looks, Nelson's persuasive mental energy, his capacity for empathy, his way with words in both public and private, the incongruity of his slight figure and heroic deeds, together invested him with charisma. His way of exercising authority was seductive yet so convincing that he was perceived as different, and very appealing in the rigid hierarchic service in which he worked. In private life, apart from his celebrity and achievements, Nelson might or might not have interested or appealed to us individually. However, had we had been serving in one of his fleets, we can be almost certain that we would have been among the majority swept along by his magic.

CHAPTER THREE

NELSON THE COMMANDER

EDGAR VINCENT

LEADER, MANAGER AND BATTLE COMMANDER

Judged against the concepts of today's most respected analysts of leadership, or against criteria laid down for today's naval officers, Nelson was a supreme leader.

If the competencies he displayed in managing fleets (huge logistical, administrative and managerial tasks), are judged against those required by today's senior naval officers and top business managers we find that he bears the hallmarks of a superb manager.

If Nelson's performance as a battle commander, his tactical insights and his command behaviour are compared with today's Maritime Doctrine of Naval Command we discover that his was a philosophy of command in tune with today and far ahead of his own time.

Two centuries on, Nelson is used as an exemplary case of leadership for today's officers. There could hardly be a more enduring monument. He was a complete combination of leader, manager and battle commander. He was motivated, talented, energetic and 'different'.

NELSON'S SUCCESS IN BATTLE

Success in battle is the ultimate measuring rod of a commander. Nelson's has never been more succinctly presented than by words on the plinth of the Nelson monument erected by public subscription in 1808 in the Place Jacques Cartier in Montreal, Canada.

On its right face the plinth reads:

> On the 1st and 2nd of August 1798 Rear-Admiral Sir Horatio Nelson KB with a British fleet of 12 sail of the line and a ship of 50 guns defeated in Aboukir Bay a French fleet of 19 sail of the line and 4 frigates under Admiral Brueys taking and destroying the

OPPOSITE
The Battle of Trafalgar. By George Chambers. Sandwiched between the three-decker *Victory* and Elias Harvey's 'fighting *Téméraire*' is the French *Redoutable* from whose tops sharpshooters fired on *Victory*'s decks and mortally wounded Nelson. (National Maritime Museum)

> whole except 2 sail of the line and 2 frigates without the loss of one British ship.

On its rear the plinth reads:

> On the 2nd April 1801 a British fleet of 10 sail of the line and 2 ships of 50 guns under the immediate command of the Right Honourable Vice-Admiral Lord Viscount Nelson Duke of Bronte attacked the Danish line moored for the defence of Copenhagen consisting of 6 sail of the line and 11 large ship batteries besides boat and gun vessels supported by the ground and land batteries when after a severe contest of 4 hours the whole line of defence was sunken taken or destroyed without the loss of a British ship.

On its left face the plinth reads:

> On the 21st October 1805 the British fleet of 27 sail of the line commanded by the Right Honourable Admiral Lord Viscount Nelson Duke of Bronte attacked off Trafalgar the combined fleet of France and Spain of 33 sail of the line commanded by the Admirals Villeneuve and Gravina when the latter were defeated with the loss of 19 sail of the line captured and destroyed. In this memorable action his country has to lament the loss of her greatest naval hero but not a single ship.

This terse arithmetic conveys the magnitude of Nelson's success as Britain's greatest ever naval commander. It explains how he enthused a nation in the darkest hours of its struggle against Napoleon and inspired succeeding generations.

THE ROAD TO COMMAND AND NELSON'S DEPTH OF EXPERIENCE

It is often said that great leaders are born not made, but whatever Nelson's inborn leadership qualities there is no doubt about the breadth of his professional knowledge.

The complexities of commanding a ship in battle, maintaining its edge in long wearisome blockade duty, creating an environment in which 500–600 men could live tolerably well together in close proximity for months on end, required knowledge and experience as well as aptitude. Nelson's early experience was directed at passing for lieutenant, the first step in commissioned rank. This he did in April 1777 when he was 18. He produced journals kept by himself in the five ships in which he had served and certificates from their captains. In essence they certified 'he can splice, knot, reef a sail & etc., and is qualified to do the duty of an Able seaman and Midshipman.' He was then orally examined by three captains on what he would do in such and such situations. Thus before he could

Captain William Locker. Nelson's first captain as a newly commissioned lieutenant in the frigate *Lowestoffe*. An ideal mentor and sea daddy for a young officer. Nelson reminded him after the Nile that it was he 'who always told me Lay a Frenchman close and you will always beat him.' (Royal Naval Museum)

take his first steps along the road to command Nelson had to prove that he could do the job of the men under him and that he possessed the basic skills required of an officer. This requirement to demonstrate competence made the British Navy the first comprehensively professional service in Europe. This was in sharp relief to the Army where for years it would still be possible to purchase the right to command.

While still a midshipman Nelson extended his horizons from rural Norfolk to the Arctic Ocean, the North Atlantic, the Carribean, the South Atlantic, the Southern Ocean, the Indian Ocean, the Arabian Sea and the Persian Gulf, thousands of miles of deep-sea sailing, six years' experience of men, of being commanded, of ships and weather. Then he worked his way through the officer ranks, third lieutenant of the frigate *Lowestoffe* sent to serve in the West Indies, first lieutenant in Sir Peter Parker's flagship, next Master & Commander of a smaller vessel, the *Badger,* his introduction to the demands and responsibilities of independent command. In 1779, three months before his 21st birthday, he was

Nelson's flagships. Right foreground *Victory* 100 guns, his Trafalgar flagship as vice-admiral of the white. Left foreground *Vanguard* 74 guns, his Nile flagship as rear admiral. Background from the left, *Agamemnon* 64 guns, his first post captain command during the Corsican and Italian-French riviera campaigns, *Elephant* 74 guns, his flagship at Copenhagen as vice-admiral, *Captain* 74 guns, which flew his commodore's broad red pendant at Cape St Vincent. An imaginary grouping by Nicholas Pocock painted in 1807. (National Maritime Museum)

'made', appointed post captain of a small frigate of 195 officers and men. It would be another 15 years before he was given command of a ship of the line, the 64-gun *Agamemnon* with a complement of 500 officers and men. Two years later, 36 years old and near the top of the captains list, Nelson took command of a small group of ships in operations off the Italian Riviera. Then came the battle of Cape St Vincent in 1797, and in the course of the next eight years he successively commanded three ships of the line and smaller ships in the attack on Tenerife, 13 ships at the Nile, 12 at Copenhagen and as Commander-in-Chief Mediterranean his fleet eventually increased to 35 ships of the line at Trafalgar.

Each of these phases placed different demands on him. As a post captain he was totally responsible for everything to do with his ship. As a flag officer (Commodore, Rear-Admiral and finally Vice-Admiral), he had a captain responsible for discipline and running the ship. He himself was primarily responsible for matters affecting the fleet as a whole and for directing the movements of the squadron or fleet under his command to meet the military, political, diplomatic and commercial objectives of the Government.

Nelson's apprenticeship was long, his accumulated experience deep. He was battle hardened, his exposure to battle unequalled by his contemporaries. At every level of command he displayed professional mastery, the *sine qua non* of the great commander.

PATRONS, MENTORS AND LUCK

Nelson was fortunate in his patrons, mentors and the circumstances of his time. His uncle, Captain Maurice Suckling, took him to sea, enabled all his early experience and, on becoming Comptroller of the Navy, was an important factor in his career progression and relatively early promotion to post captain. Nelson was again fortunate in his first, worldly wise and experienced captain, William Locker and subsequently to work for three powerful and influential admirals, Sir Peter Parker, Lord Hood and Sir John Jervis, later Earl St Vincent. They all respected Nelson's professional zeal, liked him and encouraged him. He admired and learned much from them. He was particularly fortunate in serving under the very demanding Jervis who quickly identified one of Nelson's strongest points,

Admiral Lord Hood, Commander-in-Chief Mediterranean Fleet 1793–95. Greatly admired by Nelson who served under him at the sieges of Bastia and Calvi in the campaign to take Corsica. Nelson was very disappointed that Hood did not give him sufficient credit for his contribution. (Royal Naval Museum)

the quality he most prized in a senior officer, capacity to bear the responsibility of command. Jervis quickly brought him to the attention of Lord Spencer, First Lord of Admiralty who was instrumental in choosing Nelson to take a squadron into the Mediterranean, a decision on which, in Spencer's words, the fate of Europe depended and which was to lead directly to the battle of the Nile. Spencer courageously dipped below more senior admirals and put his own political credibility at risk. Sir Gilbert Elliot, the former Viceroy of Corsica, had witnessed Nelson's impressive capacity to dominate people and events during the evacuation of Corsica. A spectator at the battle of Cape St Vincent, he had also seen Nelson's initiative and heroism and had made his views known to the Foreign Secretary, Lord Grenville. St Vincent selflessly equipped Nelson with a squadron of his finest ships. Thus Nelson earned the backing of powerful

Admiral Sir John Jervis, later Earl St Vincent, Commander-in-Chief Mediterranean Fleet 1759–99, First Lord of Admiralty 1801–1804. A disciplinarian who set new standards for officer performance and was chiefly responsible for making the Royal Navy such a formidable instrument. Nelson treated him as a father figure until their relationship later cooled. (Royal Naval Museum)

George Spencer, 2nd Earl Spencer, First Lord of Admiralty 1794–1801. He chose Nelson over the heads of more senior admirals to take a squadron into the Mediterranean in 1798 to find and destroy the French expedition which was carrying Bonaparte's army to Egypt. (Mary Evans Picture Library)

individuals who together provided him with the opportunity to establish his reputation. He was fortunate, too, in that continuous war from 1793 enabled him to be the right man in the right place at the right time, at St Vincent, the Nile, Copenhagen and Trafalgar. No other contemporary had such opportunities to distinguish himself.

LEADERSHIP ESSENTIALS

Courage was an absolute requirement of leadership. Officers had always to be alongside their men on the gun decks, on the exposed upper deck, or leading boarding parties. Nelson's personal courage, aggressive instincts, quick thinking and natural dominance made him the epitome of the leader. From his first charge at Spanish soldiers in an outpost of Fort San Juan in 1780 as a newly promoted

Nelson's boat action off Cadiz 4 July 1797. Nelson described this action as 'a hand-to-hand service with swords' and added 'It was during this period that perhaps my personal courage was more conspicuous than at any other part of my life.' A pen and wash drawing by William Bromley. (Royal Naval Museum)

post captain, Nelson displayed dash and courage and even as a commodore led his men over the side at the battle of Cape St Vincent (much to his wife's distress when she heard about it), to board the *San Nicolas*. During a subsequent bombardment of Cadiz when others were slow to respond to counterattack by Spanish gunboats, Nelson, now a Rear-Admiral, leaped into his barge and set his ten-man crew rowing furiously at the enemy. As has been said, 'His impulse to active leadership and his instinct to attack were phenomenal and while it was unwise of him to abandon all capacity to control the operation, it was a wonderfully inspiring sight to all those he needed to emulate him.' Paradoxically, failure at Tenerife in 1797 when he lost an arm and many of his men in a failed assault, confirmed his intrepid, aggressive, and some might say rash, leadership. It was not in his nature to be cautious or hesitating.

At the Nile Nelson's decision making was instantaneous, his mind processing all the key variables at lightning speed as he unhesitatingly sailed his fleet at the French line. At Copenhagen with ships aground and his battle plan virtually in tatters, he acted without pause or loss of confidence to reorganize his remaining ships.

Nelson's transcendent courage and aggression were such that men followed him. His brain power, self confidence, sheer mental energy, and persuasiveness gave him a natural dominance which caused others to turn to him. In the run up to Copenhagen these qualities were so effectively deployed that command, in effect, passed from Hyde Parker's irresolute hands into Nelson's.

MOTIVATION

Motivation is the fuel of achievement and success. Throughout his career Nelson was totally motivated. From his earliest days he was proactive, seeking new experiences and eagerly snatching at every opportunity that came his way. His professional enthusiasm impressed all he met and with it went professional optimism; everything was going to turn out well for him; his ships and crews were always the best; he never had doubts about winning. But he was also an organization man who instinctively worked with the grain of the Navy. He neither irritated nor alarmed the Admiralty with propositions for change and reform. Any differences between them were skilfully managed. He always knew when to give in gracefully and was unfailingly diplomatic. In fact he was never a maverick and his two great commanders-in-chiefs, Hood and St Vincent, both allowed and encouraged him to flower, cleverly realising that Nelson, self directed and capable of bearing any responsibility, could be managed on a very light rein and needed only encouragement. For them he was always an enthusiastic subordinate delivering without fail the results they wanted. But Nelson could be dismissive of admirals who were less commandingly professional, such as Hughes who did not have Nelson's sense of duty, Hotham who had not the same level of aggressive energy, Hyde Parker who tried to freeze him out of planning for Copenhagen and Keith who tried to treat him as a minion. On one famous occasion during his period at Naples, Nelson used his orders to protect Naples to disobey a direct order from Lord Keith to go to Minorca. He did this in a characteristically open way, keeping the Admiralty informed of his intention and rationale. For all that he believed in the importance of hierarchy and the necessity for obedience Nelson was not a yes man and always had the moral courage and self belief to deal openly with his political and naval masters, in this case to accept responsibility for making his own decision rather than taking the easy option of unthinking obedience.

For Nelson the Navy always came first, the cause was always great and it was to defeat the enemy.

ACHIEVING THE OBJECTIVE

As a post captain Nelson would know every man in his ship and excelled at creating a team out of his *Agamemnons* or his *Captains*. He remembered his Nile captains as 'a band of brothers.' But although he paid great attention to individuals and his team, he was always highly focused on meeting his objective.

Personal relationships were always a key part of his leadership. He was a great communicator and conciliator. When he suspected that his captain of the fleet Rear-Admiral Murray and Captain Keats of the *Superb* were at odds over the supply of hammocks, he wrote a private note to Keats, seeking to demonstrate that Murray, beset by demands from all ships, was not unfairly withholding supplies from him. Nelson had exerted himself personally to reinforce team spirit, had demonstrated quickness in picking up signals and shown unusual sensitivity in dealing with an apparently trivial inter-personal problem. It is not surprising that Nelson was an excellent diplomat and negotiator. He could assess the strength and weakness of his position, could deploy very forceful language but was always firm, clear and courteous, as in his negotiations with the Dey of Algiers, or at Copenhagen where detailed accounts of his negotiations with the Crown Prince of Denmark demonstrate the instincts of a born negotiator. And he seems to have been almost alone at the time in being able to collaborate with the Army in combined operations in which he was preeminently successful in the Corsican campaign and in the British retreat from the Mediterranean in 1797.

As Commander-in-Chief, he could not directly lead the thousands of men in his fleet. However much he walked the deck of his flagship, he could not get to know all his people intimately and so his symbolic acts became of the greatest importance. Nelson placed great emphasis on food and health and made these his managerial priorities and, not surprisingly, his captains felt encouraged to make them theirs too. Nelson knew that food was everything to sailors, the greatest single foundation of their health, happiness and morale. Evidence of his preoccupation with the quality as well as quantity of his men's food is everywhere. He showed infinite concern for health, especially care of the wounded. He was proud to say that the sick bays of his fleet were empty; he summed up his credo in the words, 'The great thing in all military service is health ... it is easier for an officer to keep men healthy, than the Physician to cure them.' Nelson was also concerned to transmit his values. In his fleet orders on desertion and in his personal actions in remitting sentences, he was hoping that his men would respond to his evident wish to be fair and merciful. He knew that a policy of warnings, of judging cases on their merits, of accepting pleas in mitigation on grounds of previous good conduct, would make severe punishment acceptable should the need for it arise. If men performed well they were forgiven. If officers blotted their copybook he was inclined to be merciful and give a second chance.

Nelson lived his values and modelled the behaviour he wished to see in his officers. Above all he kept his fingers on the pulse and mood of the fleet by attention to detail, endless communication and absorption of vast amounts of data. Together they ensured that he was a formidable but approachable and benign presence to his captains.

Yet Nelson was a hard-driving, demanding leader, always knowing exactly what he wanted, punctillious in things he regarded as important. He never complained about the harshness of the navy's discipline, nor sought to change it but tried in practice to find a balance between humanity, fairness and punishment to fit the crime. Brutality was endemic in Georgian society and was institutionalized in the Navy. Men accepted punishment as a fact of life, provided it was seen as fair and not sadistic. Behaviour that endangered the safety of the ship and the lives of others, or undermined discipline, had to be deterred. In *Agamemnon,* a happy and effective ship, men were flogged at a rate of two to three a month. Short sharp shocks of a few lashes were frequently administered and the logs of Nelson's early ships show that such men did not offend again, while heavier punishments were reserved for more serious crimes.

Nelson understood perfectly that a ship could not be managed effectively unless its captain and officers recognized the needs of their people for self respect, fairness and justice. To this end he tried to have around him officers who, if not gentlemen by birth, were gentlemen by nature, and knew how to behave in an acceptable way towards their fellow officers and men. This is what Nelson had in mind when he said, 'you must be a seaman to be an officer and also you cannot be a good officer without being a gentleman.'

INSPIRING AND ENTHUSING OTHERS

Commanders gain respect from their officers because they can do the business. Nelson additionally inspired affection for how he did things and became a model others wished to emulate. Riou, who commanded Nelson's frigates at Copenhagen, was completely won over and his last words, as he fatally obeyed Parker's signal to discontinue the action, were 'What will Nelson think of us?' Admiral Hoste, a great favourite of Nelson as a midshipman, flew a signal 'Remember Nelson' at the battle of Lissa. Blackwood, who commanded Nelson's frigates at Trafalgar became devoted to him, 'so kind, so good, so obliging a friend as never was.' Admiral Graves, who fought alongside him at Copenhagen referred to him as 'our gallant and enterprising little hero of the Nile.' Duff, captain of *Mars*, destined to die at Trafalgar, wrote to his wife, 'He is so good and pleasant a man, that we all wish to do what he likes, without any kind of orders.' In his ordinary transactions with subordinate officers Nelson always seemed to be confiding in them, trusting them. He very evidently made Blackwood feel how much really depended on him. He made individuals feel special and the centre of his attention. He had the knack of taking people into his confidence.

But it would be wrong to believe that everybody took to Nelson and his ways. Saumarez and Thompson were irritated by his self confidence and in their eyes, patronising behaviour, and there was a fellow captain who said to Nelson, 'You did just as you pleased in Lord Hood's time, the same in Admiral Hotham's and now again with Sir John Jervis. It makes no difference to you who is Commander-in Chief' – a not entirely admiring remark.

NELSON WAS DIFFERENT

Great leaders are often singular, stand out in a crowd and strike people as 'different'. The early Nelson had a kind of eccentric singularity of dress and appearance which Prince William remarked on in 1782, 'the old fashioned flaps of his waistcoat added to the general quaintness of his figure, and produced an appearence which particularly attracted my attention.' Nelson liked to deck himself out in his sash of the Order of the Bath, his gold medals and foreign decorations. Whether or not others approved is beside the point; his appearance made him memorable. His words could be equally singular. Churchill had his 'Never in the path of human conflict has so much been owed by so many to so few.' Nelson had 'England expects that every man will do his duty.' His gestures could be singularly theatrical and striking. He was given to putting his life on the line with expressions like, 'Westminster Abbey or glorious victory.' His reaction to Hyde Parker's potentially disastrous signal to break off the action at Copenhagen, 'I see no signal,' or his inspired truce message to the Danes, 'To the brothers of Englishmen the Danes...'; his reaction to the possibility of Hardy's being captured by the chasing French as his boat was being carried rapidly by the current towards the approaching enemy while attempting to rescue a seaman, 'By God I'll not lose Hardy; back the mizzen topsail'; his reaction to concerns about him as he was rowed for several hours in an open boat without an overcoat to join Hyde Parker's flagship in Kioge Bay, 'I have my duty to keep me warm.' It was always a case of the right gesture, or the right word, at the right time. He had the capacity to coin words that entered history. No wonder the little hero became increasingly larger in the hearts and minds of those who had to fight with him.

UNFAILING SUPPORT FOR HIS PEOPLE

All his life Nelson had a genius for self presentation. He was absolutely focused on getting the credit he felt due to him and resented being short-changed. As a very ambitious man he had also grasped that achievement is not its own reward but needs to be known about. However, it is safe to say that what mattered most to those who fought alongside him was that he never withheld credit from them, never took their credit and was assiduous in getting them rewards for their pains, an endearing and motivating characteristic. Reporting the capture by one of his ships of the *Guillaume Tell,* he wrote to Lord Spencer, 'I am sure your Lordship will not be sparing of promotion to the deserving. My friends wished me to be present. I have no such wish ... not for all the world would I rob any man of a sprig of laurel – much less my children of the *Foudroyant*.' Patronage and interest (capacity to ask for and grant favours) were an inescapable part of 18th-century life. Nelson did not abuse his patronage but exercised it to help many who were in no position to do him favours in return. He gave priority to sons of officers killed in action who he regarded as legacies to the Service, relatives of those who had helped him up the tree, and his own highly thought of young officers who he would push forward on their merits. He fought to get equal recognition for Troubridge following his misfortune in running aground at the Nile. He interceded with the First Lord of Admiralty on behalf of one of his bright stars, Layman, a young master and commander who had been court martialled for losing his ship. He put Gore, one of his most trusted frigate captains, in the way of prize money. Then there were older officers in unglamorous but essential shore jobs who were doing sterling work and merited his commendation and helping hand. And it was not just commissioned officers he supported. He went out of his way to commend the performance of Joseph King his boatswain in the *Boreas*, and Mr Morrisson the carpenter of the *Alexander* who played a major part in refitting *Vanguard* after she was almost wrecked in a storm. Like St Vincent he was interested in rewarding quality and merit. Like all commanders he liked to have tried and trusted men about him. All those who hitched themselves to his star wanted to feel that he would do his best for them; he unfailingly did, earning their gratitude and intensifying their motivation.

ATTITUDES AND PRINCIPLES AS A BATTLE COMMANDER

Nelson's single-minded aim was to find and beat the enemy and he allowed nothing to distract him. The importance of this cannot be overestimated. He had a particular horror of unfinished business. After Hotham's indecisive action of 1795 and his unwillingness to pursue the enemy, Nelson's reaction was, 'Had we taken ten sail and allowed the eleventh to escape when it had been possible to have got at her, I could never had called it well done,' – as Hotham had. In the aftermath of the Nile he was regretful that two surviving French ships had managed to escape. Even as he lay dying he was dissatisfied with the scale of his Trafalgar victory.

His fundamental principles were simple. He was convinced that one Englishman was worth three Frenchmen and that the way to beat a Frenchman was to get alongside him, hence his drive for close action. He understood that time and speed were always of the essence. He preferred a headlong and immediate attack, seizing the initiative, giving his own force the psychological upper hand. He would seek to concentrate force on one or two parts of his enemy, deliver a knock-out blow and then deal with the rest. Because he understood that chance and uncertainty were the two most important elements in war, Nelson seems to have spent little time pondering on what might happen or what might go wrong, hence his emphasis on speed of decision, speed of action and tactical simplicity. Nelson always had the knack of increasing his own chances, making his own luck and multiplying the enemy's uncertainties.

TACTICAL GENIUS

Nelson's tactical genius cannot be summed up in a technical way, for example that he broke the enemy's line in one or even two places. Howe had broken the line at The Glorious First of June in 1794, Jervis broke the line at the battle of Cape St Vincent in Nelson's presence in 1797 and Duncan broke the Dutch line in two places at Camperdown later in 1797. Howe had also ordered all his ships to break the line in order to foment a mêlée because that favoured British gunnery and seamanship. His officers were 'at liberty to act as circumstances require,' but did not reap the full reward because his captains had not understood so clearly what he was driving at.

Nelson genius was to implant his principles of battle in his captains' minds and to be adaptable. He would have fully appreciated the words of today's military doctrine: 'commanders who are in each others minds and who share a common approach to the conduct of operations are more likely to act in concert.' Nelson's realization that this was the key to commanding fleet operations might well have crystallized at the battle of Cape St Vincent in 1797. Admiral Jervis was conducting the action by signal. Nelson read the action as it unfolded and Admiral Jervis's signals in a way none of the others did. He alone used his initiative and wore out of the line, directly to attack the enemy. The others felt obliged to wait until told what to do. At the Nile his instinctive reading of the enemy's disposition and vulnerabilities produced a brilliant and rapid concentration of force on the French van and centre and presented a subsequent opportunity to roll up the rest of the French line. But Foley's initiative in going round to the other side of the French line, and the skill and discipline of four following captains, compounded Nelson's master stroke and brought an astounding team victory. Nelson seems to have intended Copenhagen to follow somewhat the Nile pattern, in other words, crush one segment of the fixed Danish line and move the concentration of force up the line to dispose of the rest, but misfortune struck. Ships went aground and he had to extemporize in placing his remaining ships. This time there was no scope for captains to exercise initiative. It had to be a hard slogging match between stationary sides, lined up facing each other at short range. It was a battle exemplifying above all Nelson's resolution and judgement as a fighting commander, keeping his nerve, pressing on with his attack while behind him his commander-in-chief wavered. At Trafalgar Nelson had again to extemporize. His plan for a third, fast-sailing, reserve squadron, had to be abandoned and he was at first unable to locate Villeneuve's flagship, the point of aim for his own line.

What was so striking about each of his victories was not only his capacity to adapt to circumstances but the huge risks he habitually ran, attacking a French fleet in Aboukir bay with night about to fall, attacking a resolute Danish defence line, sandwiched between shallow water and the Danish guns with no room to manoeuvre and no escape if the wind turned against him, and Trafalgar where his chosen mode of attack would expose his ships to a long, slow approach during which time his enemy could rake him but he could not reply. These were risks that probably no other admiral of his generation would have taken, but they paid off and Nelson's boldness provided unanswerable problems for his opponents.

The capture of the *Ca Ira* by the *Agamemnon*. A picture painted at the scene by Nicholas Pocock in 1795 when Nelson, serving under Admiral Hotham, was disappointed by Hotham's unwillingness to pursue the enemy fleet after the *Ca Ira* and *Censeur* had been captured. (National Maritime Museum)

CLARITY OF COMMUNICATION

In the run up-to the Nile, Nelson began to develop a process for face-to-face communication of the principles on which he would fight. Whatever the conditions of the day, minds would be prepared; there would be no scope for inertia or indecision. The Nile result was an unhesitating and wonderful team effort. At Copenhagen his broad method was the same. His journal entry for 26 March 1801 says, 'All day employed in arguing and convincing to [sic] the different officers the mode of attack.' Freemantle records how he succeeded. 'Lord Nelson is quite sanguine, but as you may well imagine there is a great diversity of opinion. In the mode of attack intended to be adopted and which is planned by Lord Nelson there is but one.' It was never a process of 'what do you think we should do?' or of group decision making, or of reaching consensus. It was always Nelson's plan, which stood or fell by his powers of communication, persuasion and inspiration. By the time of Trafalgar all this had become very clear, 'I laid before them the Plan I had previously arranged for attacking the enemy; and it was not only my pleasure to find it generally approved but clearly perceived and understood.' His delegation of complete control of one of his columns to Collingwood was within the context of his plan, not a modification of it and by no means an abdication of responsibility but a realistic judgement

Nelson explaining the Plan of Attack before the Battle of Trafalgar. Nelson made sure that his captains knew what he intended and what was expected of them. In this he was a precursor of today's military doctrine of Mission Command. An engraving by W. A. M. Craig, published by Edward Orme on the day of Nelson's funeral, 9 January 1806. (Royal Naval Museum)

that there needed to be a focus for leadership relatively close at hand in each of his two columns of attack. The level of confident trust and prominence thereby conferred on Collingwood evidently inspired him and others. A further master stroke was to direct any ship in doubt to get alongside an enemy. He defined what he wanted to happen, not in abstract terms such as 'use your initiative', but unambiguously: 'No captain can do very wrong if he places his ship alongside that of an enemy.' Nelson wanted all his ships to fight. Battle had to be swiftly set up and swiftly taken to close quarters and resolutely fought to a conclusion.

Once his opening gambit had been made they would not need to look to him for guidance. Nelson was anticipating Mission Command, the idea that a commander conveys what he intends, and what he expects of those under him, to the extent that all share in their commander's mind and are empowered to deal with the contingencies of battle without losing their sense of the plot. The supreme test of Mission Command is what happens if the commander is disabled or killed. At the Nile, Nelson was on deck for only an hour and a half in a battle that lasted till midday the following day and at Trafalgar for less than an hour. They were the two greatest naval victories in British history.

THE ESSENTIAL SPARK OF LEADERSHIP

Nelson's victories have been ascribed to many causes. The underlying confidence, commercial power and constitutional coherence of England, although not the cause of victory, was an underlying foundation. Other more direct causes included superior gunnery and the technological edge of better quality powder, use of carronades or 'smashers', and flintlock firing; better seamanship, the fact that a British crew could tack in five as opposed to 15 minutes and were sea-hardened, used to being at sea as opposed to being blockaded in harbours;

the character and morale of British sailors, comparatively better trained, better fed, fitter and better led, roused by the threat of invasion, compared with the politically purged and frequently alienated French officer cadre, and weaknesses in naval organization and practice in terms of health, food and pay in both the French and Spanish navies; the weakness of Franco-Spanish combinations, generally uneasy alliances, fraught with the endemic problems of coalitions; and finally Napoleon's centralist belief in controlling everything but in fact understanding nothing of the realities of marine warfare. There is some truth in all these contentions which, taken together, prompt the notion that Britain's professional navy, with its culture of competence, was an instrument at the peak of its powers and virtually irresistible.

But it has to be said that none of this actually guaranteed success. For example, in early 1799 the French fleet under Bruix escaped the blockade at Brest, entered the Mediterranean where the Commander-in-Chief was Lord St Vincent at Minorca and his second-in-command Vice-Admiral Lord Keith off Cadiz. The enemy evaded Keith, the Spaniards got out of Cadiz and linked with the French to create a combined fleet of more than 40 ships which eventually some months later escaped again, this time from the Mediterranean and was followed by Keith back to Brest The inability of either St Vincent, or Keith, who twice had the enemy in his sights, to initiate offensive action against Bruix tells its own story. Later in 1805, Admiral Calder encountered off Ferrol the combined fleet Nelson was then chasing from the West Indies, Calder's 15 ships against their 24. No greater contrast with Nelson could have been found. Calder,

The death of Nelson. A painting by A.W. Devis done in 1805 from sketches made on board *Victory*. Those present on the day are authentically represented. Captain Hardy (centre right), may have been caught just before or after he bent in response to Nelson's 'Kiss me Hardy.' (Royal Naval Museum)

inhibited by superior opposing numbers and cautious in spirit, settled for an abortive action for which he was subsequently reprimanded by a court of inquiry.

The fact that St Vincent, Keith and Calder could have made more of their opportunities with the same instruments and men under their command underlines that Nelson's genius as a commander was the vital spark enabling the British fleet to reach its full potential.

CHAPTER FOUR

THE FRENCH AND SPANISH PERSPECTIVE

ADMIRAL RÉMI MONAQUE

For a Frenchman, the word Trafalgar has a muted and sinister resonance and re-opens wounds that time has not entirely healed. The French still say nowadays, when speaking of an unjust, unforeseen and disastrous event, '*C'est un coup de Trafalgar*' ('It's a Trafalgar-like blow'). Also, it was not without apprehension that in the run-up to the 200th anniversary I began research on the battle that put an end to a naval rivalry which had lasted more than 100 years between France and Great Britain.[1] I take this step with the hope of making a modest contribution to a renewed history, where national prejudices fade to make way for a better understanding of the points of view of these old adversaries. Europe is on the move and it needs to build a common history for itself, capable of being equally adhered to in London, Paris and Madrid.

In the lines that follow, which have been written particularly for a British reader, my aim is to stress those points that have appeared to me to be little known or badly interpreted by English authors. I will also try to shed light on the main differences in the composition, organization, operation and mentalities of the three naval forces concerned. At the request of the editor of this work, I will take into account the point of view of our Spanish ally, which is, as you will see, extremely different from our own, and I hope to be as objective as possible in presenting it.

OPPOSITE
Admiral Decrès (1761–1820) by René Théodore Berthon. The son of a cavalry officer, Decrès fought at the Battle of the Saintes and later became Minister of the Navy. He successfully built up the French Navy, turning a purged, directionless and demoralized force into a well equipped fighting arm capable of giving the Royal Navy a run for its money. (Photo RMN Paris / © Gerard Blot)

REMINDER OF PREVIOUS INCIDENTS

In the long confrontation between France and Great Britain that began in 1688 with the fall of the Stuart allies of Louis XIV and ended in 1815, France was only able to stand up to its rival at sea on two occasions: during the reign of Louis XIV, when France was at the time so powerful it was able to fight most of Europe on the ground whilst also maintining a strong naval force; and under Louis XVI, during the American War of Independence, when French diplomacy was able to spare the country any involvement on the ground and had even obtained the support of significant allies such as Spain and Holland at sea. In every other case, France, bogged down in conflicts on the ground, had been forced to relinquish its efforts at sea little by little and had tasted the full force of British power. It had lost its colonies and saw its nautical trade ruined. Its squadrons, blocked in ports and having suffered heavy losses, were unable to act. Turning to a trade as a last resort produced disappointing results. The French governors, mostly possessed of a landsman mentality, quickly became resigned to being paralysed at sea and concentrated all their energies on countering the main threat, which had come from the north-east and which no maritime effort could see off.

This traditional scenario was replayed in 1793 with the same effects as during the Seven Years War. The situation was even worse because, in addition to the international restrictions, there was the disorder brought about by the French Revolution: a lack of organization, poor work at the naval dockyards and, even more serious, the emigration of nearly all the noble officers who had made up most of the staff officers of the old royal navy. Also, the setbacks experienced by the French naval forces during the first years of the conflict were particularly serious. In just a few years, more than 50 ships of the line had been lost. At the end of 1793, the Toulon affair, in which French royalists handed over the port to the British, cost 13 vessels. In 1794, the Prairial Battles, known in English as 'The Battle of the Glorious First of June', ended in the loss of seven ships. The great winter campaign of 1795 saw the disappearance of five ships due to the perils of the sea. Finally, at the battle of the Nile, Nelson destroyed a further 11 extra ships in August 1798. The human losses accompanying these misfortunes, even more serious because they were harder to replace, amounted to thousands of seamen, either killed in combat, death from illness or held prisoner in England. When the Trafalgar campaign began, despite a significant construction effort, France only had a fleet of around 45 vessels, and had the greatest difficulty in supplying them with qualified crews.

As for Spain, recent history had also been tragic. Placed in the camp of monarchies hostile to the French Revolution at the beginning of the war, it suffered heavy defeats on the ground and was forced to make a French alliance in the hope of avoiding an invasion of its territory. The sea battle against its ancient ally, Great Britain, cost it four vessels in 1797 with the severe defeat of Cape St Vincent. It had to hand over a further six to France and did not have sufficient finances to build new ones. Desperately trying to remain neutral after the Peace of Amiens was broken in May 1803, Spain thought it could buy its neutrality by paying France a monthly subsidy of four million francs. But it was easy for Great Britain to declare that this financial aid was nothing more than a rupture of the claimed neutrality. It used this as a pretext for the brutal aggression against four Spanish frigates off Portugal on 5 October 1804, which were carrying gold and silver from Peru. One of the ships exploded, the other three were seized and taken to England. Nevertheless, the joint pressure of Paris and indignant public opinion was needed to force the Spanish government, after several weeks of hesitation, to declare war on Great Britain. The naval potential which Spain provided to its ally was far from negligible. It still had around 30 vessels capable of being quickly rearmed in its arsenals at Ferrol, Cadiz and Cartagena. But these ships, which had not sailed for many years, were severely lacking in crew. The chronic shortage of seamen from which Spain was suffering had recently been further aggravated by a terrible yellow fever epidemic that had ravaged the sea-going population of Andalucia.

THE EMPEROR'S GRAND PLAN

The Peace of Amiens had been nothing more than a sort of truce, doomed to rupture because of the second thoughts of the two parties involved and their mutual unwillingness when the treaty was drawn up. When the conflict resumed, each of the two adversaries believed it could justify its hegemonic quest with noble ideals. The English presented themselves as the defenders of the European states against the aggression of an insatiable tyrant, whilst supporting and protecting the most retrograde and liberticidal regimes on the continent. The French claimed to be freeing the seas and oceans from the tentacles of the British. Everywhere they spread generous ideas about the Revolution, modernized worm-eaten societies and regimes, but behaved too often like pillagers, enslaving the people they claimed to emancipate. As for the Spanish, embarked on this adventure in spite of themselves, they were only concerned about preserving their declining empire, hoping without really believing that their alliance with the French would spare their home territory from being invaded, and would protect their colonies from the appetite of the British. They renewed the family pact established in 1761 between the Bourbons of France and Spain, which had served their interests well.

At the dawn of what was to be the last set-to between France and Great Britain, Napoleon decided to put an end to his most persistent enemy by striking at its heart through the invasion of its territory. For two years he devoted all his energies to and used all his imagination on this project. Some historians, however, claim that all this agitation was nothing more than a bluff aimed at dulling the vigilance of France's continental enemies in order to be able to take them more by surprise. This hypothesis does not seem acceptable to me. The immense material and financial means devoted to the undertaking, and perhaps even more the passion sparkling in the Emperor's correspondence, does not leave in any doubt the fact that he wanted to land in England.

Invasion plans had flourished in all the previous conflicts without ever getting off the ground. All the plans elaborated under the *Ancien Régime* involved gaining control of the Channel, at least temporarily, with an ocean-going fleet, and the embarkation of troops on transport ships. With the Revolution, a new idea came to light, that of the construction of a fleet built specifically for landing, comprising numerous flat-bottomed boats equipped with sails and oars that could land troops directly on enemy coastlines. The main promoter of this idea,

Admiral Louis René Levassor de Latouche-Tréville was one of the few French naval officers who had a successful record against Nelson. He died unexpectedly at Toulon and was replaced by Villeneuve. There has been inevitable speculation as to the likely outcome of the Battle of Trafalgar had he remained in command of the Combined Fleet. (© Musée National de la Marine/Latouche-Tréville)

the engineer Forfait,[2] had been inspired by the flotillas used by the Swedish and the Russians in the Baltic, without understanding that the hydrographical and meteorological conditions present in this sea were vastly different from those in the Pas de Calais. Forfait, who had placed heavy pieces of artillery at the front and back of the barges, even thought that a flotilla constituted in this way would be able to cross the strait without the help of a protective fleet. The campaign of 1801 demonstrated that this hope was an illusion. True, Latouche-Tréville had defended the light flotilla anchored at Boulogne against Nelson gloriously on two occasions, but this admiral, despite preferring small craft, had become aware of their very low military value and of their inability to operate in bad weather. When Napoleon drew up his plans for the invasion of England in 1803, although he envisaged an armada of around 2,000 small flat-bottomed craft to transport his army, he also provided for the intervention of a high seas fleet in the Channel to pave the way.

As the Emperor had such a fertile imagination and such a large capacity to multiply orders and counter-orders, there could have been an infinite number of solutions. What was the nature of the problem? In the vast operating theatre that was the Channel, the north Atlantic and the Mediterranean, the British had around 80 vessels that were armed[3] and more than ready for operation as they spent most of their time at sea. Napoleon could theoretically deploy 45 French vessels supported by around 30 Spanish vessels and approximately ten Dutch vessels against these forces. English authors never fail to observe that the two sides were very evenly matched from a numerical point of view, in fact that the odds were even in favour of the allies. However, a closer examination suggests a very different conclusion. The allies' vessels had been closed up in their ports for many months, and had therefore been deprived of any operational training. The main French squadron, comprising 21 vessels and based at Brest, was subject to a particularly tight blockade. The remaining French units were spread out between Rochefort and Toulon, but also Cadiz and Ferrol, where they found refuge when the war resumed. The Spanish forces were distributed between Cartagena, Cadiz and Ferrol. A very delicate problem concerning the concentration of forces, preceding any operation, had to be resolved. Napoleon understood that the Toulon squadron, comprising around ten vessels and far less severely blockaded than the other allied forces, should appear first and give the signal to begin the campaign.

Before Spain entered the war, the Emperor had planned to bring out the Toulon squadron, avoiding any contact with the enemy, reinforce it in the Atlantic by unblocking either the Ferrol squadron or the Rochefort squadron, and slip this fleet of around 15 vessels through to Boulogne incognito. This plan, based as it was on the avoidance of any confrontation with enemy squadrons, depended on surprise. It had a small chance of succeeding, notably by skirting around the north of the British Isles, if the mission were confined to a squadron of modest dimensions, made up of fast and well manned ships. Unfortunately, accustomed as he was to dealing with ground forces, Napoleon believed in the virtue of large armies and neglected the qualitative aspects. He always compelled his admirals to line up as many ships as possible, without understanding that a bad sailing ship or a vessel without qualified personnel constituted a hindrance rather than reinforcement for a squadron.

Once he had gained the support of the Spanish navy, Napoleon thought up new and ever more audacious plans which, while not specifically designed to provoke hostilities certainly did not exclude the possibility either, in view of the new force available. In the grandiose plan drawn up at the beginning of March 1805, the merged allied forces were to operate in the Antilles. The Rochefort squadron in the Antilles was to combine with the Toulon squadron, now reinforced by a Spanish squadron from Cadiz, and the Brest squadron, which in turn was to have freed the Franco-Spanish forces blockaded in Ferrol. This enormous fleet of nearly 60 vessels was to make a dash for the entrance to the Channel, where it would find nothing but inferior enemy forces. The British were expected to disperse and then pursue or seek out the allied squadrons. Their ships remaining in the Ushant region would be swept aside, and the triumphant combined fleet would gather outside Boulogne between 10 June and 10 July, allowing the 130,000 men in the Boulogne army to cross the strait and seal England's fate in a few days. 'We will then be the masters of the world,' Napoleon concluded.

THE ALLIED NAVAL HIGH COMMAND

As we have just seen, it was Napoleon, and him alone, who drew up and led the naval operations. His Minister for the Navy, Admiral Decrès, confined to the role of manager of his ministry's human, material and financial resources, performed this task very well, but did not intervene in the area of operations other than to advise the Emperor or pass on orders. Moreover, following the fall of the *Ancien Régime*, the ministry no longer had the small operational cell made up of ship's officers that drew up campaign plans and followed their execution. Napoleon did not think it was a good idea to re-establish this small group of competent seamen in its private staff office, despite the fact that they would have been able to translate his strategic plans into realistic methods of action, taking into account the constraints of the naval environment. Rather, when he had a new idea, he preferred to consult admirals such as Ganteaume, Bruix or Latouche-Tréville, in whom he had a certain confidence. These officer generals, often far away from him, were required to give him an opinion despite not being in possession of all the facts, and of which he would not take the slightest notice. Thus it was that the Emperor, used to seeing everything bend to his will, would dictate his instructions from the solitude of his cabinet at St-Cloud or a town in Germany or Italy. He gave orders that were too detailed, often irrelevant, and which did not take into account weather conditions, the possible opposition of the enemy, transmission delays or the uncertainness of whether his messages would be received. He wanted to be able to control everything and alter everything at sea as he pleased, as he did on the ground. But while three horsemen can reorientate the march of a division in a few hours on the battlefield, at sea a frigate needs several weeks to find the squadron in the Antilles that is to have its mission modified.

Moreover, when it came to naval strategy and tactics, Napoleon had surprisingly traditional, if not retrograde, ideas. While he revolutionized the rules of combat on the ground, when it came to the navy his ideas were based on those that had been around in France under the *Ancien Régime*. Thus respect for the mission as commanded was above any other consideration and this precluded, for example, seizing the opportunity to destroy any enemy forces that might be encountered. Combat was never an end in itself, and was only accepted if it was the only way to accomplish the mission. This was very different from Nelson's attitude, which could be summed up in his oft-repeated orders to: 'annihilate the enemy'. Little by little, however, the Emperor came to understand the disadvantages of his method. Manipulating his admirals like pawns from a distance of thousands of miles

OPPOSITE
Admiral Villeneuve (1763–1806), although of aristocratic birth, survived the purges due to his revolutionary sympathies. Following the death of Admiral Latouche-Tréville at Toulon in 1804, Villeneuve was tasked with breaking through the British blockade, along with his Spanish allies. Although criticised for negative thinking, Villeneuve organized the Combined Fleet to constitute a significant foe. It exploded into disorder, however, following the two arrow strikes by the British fleet. After a spell of captivity in England, the demoralized Villeneuve is said to have committed suicide on his return to France. (© Musée National de la Marine/Amiral Villeneuve)

and through orders given several weeks earlier led to serious setbacks. It would have been better to explain the objective and to encourage them to use their own initiative so they would act for the best in whatever circumstances they encountered. It was also necessary to take any opportunity to destroy the enemy, and the last orders passed on by his minister called for a 'battle of extermination' without regard for the losses incurred. But this new stance came too late to change the course of the campaign. Moreover, it was received by admirals who were traumatized and paralysed by the Emperor's often unfair criticism.

Who were these people charged with carrying out their master's fluctuating but always imperious directives? In the French navy, three admirals came to play

an important role in the Trafalgar campaign. It is important to note that these three men were all survivors of the battle of the Nile, and, fuelled by a bitter memory of this tragic event, they had developed a form of inferiority complex with regard to Nelson.

Decrès, minister for the navy from October 1801, was to stay in this position until the end of the Empire. A determined, energetic and intelligent worker with great professional competence, he proved his worth fighting a glorious battle against vastly superior forces on board the *Guillaume Tell*, shortly before the British took Malta. He was weakened unfortunately by a profound cynicism and an exaggerated concern for his career. He was afraid of being replaced and took care to keep all potential rivals away from positions of responsibility. He tended to favour his friends and all those from whom he had nothing to fear over chiefs with ambition and character. He made a major mistake by keeping his comrade Villeneuve at the head of the Toulon squadron, who, after an initial unfortunate sortie attempt in January 1805, asked to be relieved of his command. Decrès, who was also an excellent courtier, nevertheless forced himself, and not without courage, to educate Napoleon in naval matters, and to explain to him the constraints of the maritime environment.

At Brest, Ganteaume was in command of the largest and most powerful French squadron. He was a friend of the Emperor and the latter's most solicited advisor, all the more so for having brought him back from Egypt on board the frigate *Muiron*. The most faithful of the faithful, wild with admiration for Napoleon, Ganteaume was nevertheless described as a 'useless sailor without intellect' in *Mémorial de Sainte-Hélène*. On 24 March 1805, he sent a telegram proposing casting off at Brest with his 21 ships and entering into battle with the blockade force that was limited at the time to 15 ships. The Emperor's immediate response dissuaded him: 'A naval victory in such circumstances would not take me anywhere. Retire without engaging the enemy.' This absurd command was a serious blow to the admiral's morale.

Villeneuve owed his command to the premature disappearance of Latouche-Tréville, who died in Toulon harbour on board his flagship in August 1804. He never aspired to this responsibility and was completely surprised when he learned he had been given the main role in accomplishing the grand plan. Decrès had convinced Napoleon that from the list, albeit limited, of potential candidates, he was the best choice. He was a courageous and competent man, courteous and of agreeable demeanour. The British could not stop praising him, being surprised – a little naïvely – at having a real gentleman for a prisoner, when they had expected an uncouth and uncultured representative of the revolutionary navy. Villeneuve belonged to one of the oldest families in the Provence nobility and began his career as a midshipman in the navy of Louis XVI. This young admiral of 42 nevertheless had character traits that were incompatible with the exercise of great command. Very lucid, he analysed the factors leading to the superiority of the British navy at great length. His profound pessimism and chronic melancholy made him despair of being able to confront his adversaries successfully and even prevented him from trying. Extreme passiveness, which he had already demonstrated at the battle of the Nile,[4] led him to be resigned in the face of all the constraints put upon him and to accept the command of a mission of which he thought himself incapable. Several accounts show that, after he took command at Toulon, the morale of the squadron, which was at its highest under Latouche-Tréville, crumbled in just a few weeks. While his predecessor was extremely keen to square up again to the man he jokingly called 'his colleague Nelson', Villeneuve's one concern was how to avoid meeting a force that he considered to be superior to his own.

On the Spanish side, bearing in mind the unequal nature of the Franco-Spanish alliance, only one character really needs to be taken into account: Admiral Gravina, commander of the Spanish component of the combined fleet. This

Admiral Gravina (1756–1806) was the son of a Sicilian nobleman who had a distinguished career in the Spanish navy, and on one occasion worked alongside the British on an attack on Toulon. He fought against the British at the Siege of Gibraltar and again at Trafalgar. He was wounded on his flagship, *Príncipe de Asturias*, and rallied the remains of the fleet after the battle to lead them back to Cadiz. He died of his wounds the following year. (Museo Naval de Madrid)

49-year-old officer general belonged to the upper nobility and had benefited from a dazzling career, no doubt justified by his great merits but also helped by the very strong support he had in the Spanish court. In previous years he had already collaborated with the French on a number of occasions. After having participated in a Franco-Spanish campaign in the Mediterranean in 1799, he commanded the Spanish squadron at Brest – where it was blockaded in the port – for two years. In 1802, he participated in the St-Domingue expedition, transporting part of the expedition corps into this French colony. Finally, he had most recently been fulfilling the important role of Spanish ambassador in Paris for several months. On all these occasions, he had been able to earn the sympathy and often the friendship of those French with whom he came into contact. Latouche-Tréville said he was united to Gravina intellectually and emotionally. Decrès and even Napoleon held him in high esteem. During the whole of the Trafalgar campaign, Gravina was to Villeneuve a loyal and warm collaborator, providing him with real reassurance. This attitude irritates Spanish historians somewhat, who regret at times that another Spanish admiral was not chosen in place of this character, too Francophile for their taste. The names of Mazarredo and Grandallana are often quoted, both of whom had unquestionable professional qualities. But the former had greatly displeased Napoleon by his outspokenness and lack of flexibility when he was Spanish ambassador in Paris. As for the latter, his notorious francophobia meant he was unlikely to gain such a position. Incidentally Gravina, whilst being loyal and faithful to his allies, never forgot his own country's interests. Far from encouraging Villeneuve to lead the combined fleet to the Channel, he was able when the time came to use all his influence to reassure the latter in his decision not to carry out to the end a mission which did not serve Spanish interests in any way.

WEAKNESSES OF THE COMBINED FLEET

When one weighs the strengths and weaknesses of the fleets present at Trafalgar, it is surprisingly difficult to identify the advantages of the allied squadrons. Although the 27 British vessels capable of firing in a single shot around 24 tonnes of cannon balls were faced with 33 enemies in possession of a total of more than 32 tonnes of projectiles i.e. projectiles, as we shall see, the apparent advantage of the Franco-Spanish was an illusion. An analysis of the effective strength of a squadron should take numerous factors into account. Regarding materials, quantity is not everything: qualitative aspects are often determining factors. In the case of personnel, training and morale play a dominant role. Finally, intellectual strength should not be neglected, such as the combat doctrine shared by the commanders and the admirals' tactical ideas.

MATERIAL FACTORS

Historians from the three nations display a great deal of chauvinism when discussing the quality of their ships. The French believe they constructed the largest vessels – which is true[5] – but also the fastest and the most elegant. The Spanish consider that they succeeded in developing a happy synthesis between the French and British designs at the end of the 18th century, producing vessels that were both robust and fast. The English boast, and not without reason, of the solidity, simplicity and distinctly sea-going nature of their ships. Nevertheless, they did not hesitate to incorporate captured ships into their fleet, and even went as far as to copy their designs. Is the British reader aware that seven of Nelson's vessels at Trafalgar were of French design? Three were taken from the enemy, the *Tonnant*, the *Spartiate* and the *Belleisle*, while four were directly inspired by French designs, the *Achilles*, the *Ajax*, the *Leviathan* and the *Minotaur*. For their part, the French deployed two English vessels captured in combat, the *Swiftsure* and the *Berwick*. An impartial observer would probably conclude that the three fleets present at Trafalgar comprized for the most part high quality ships. The British units were very robust and also included security mechanisms such as drainage pumps. The Spanish vessels' weak point was their masts, which were somewhat over-proportioned and very fragile. This fault was also shared by the French ships, but to a lesser degree. Regarding the strength of the vessels, it can be seen that it was the British who had the advantage with seven triple-deck ships, while the allies deployed just four, all Spanish, two of which were excellent – the *Principe de Asturias* and the *Santa Ana* – and two very mediocre, the *Santísima Trinidad* and the *Rayo*.

With regard to artillery, the British advantage is much clearer. For their heaviest projectile, the English adopted the 32lb cannon ball (14.5kg), while the Franco-Spanish stuck with the 36lb calibre (17.6kg).[6] This difference in weight, of which the chargers were very sensitive, made Nelson's sailors' work easier, and helped facilitate a faster rate of fire. Moreover, the recent progress in English metallurgy meant that, with an equal calibre, the British pieces were lighter than those of their adversaries. Here, too, the result was greater convenience and speed in loading and firing the cannons, not to mention the reduced strain on the structure of the ship. But the most decisive advantage the British had was the possession of a particularly fearsome weapon: the carronade. In service since the American War of Independence, these short and light large-calibre cannons allowed large volleys of shot to be fired from a short distance. The French, who knew this weapon well, had been reluctant to use it for a long time because they were critical of its weak range and imprecision. Napoleon and Decrès nevertheless understood the interest in the weapon. They ordered large-scale production of the carronade without managing to equip the ships with it before Trafalgar. As for the Spanish, they had a few rare models of this type of weapon, which was to show its worth in the close combat which Nelson sought.

THE MEN

While the Royal Navy still used the barbarous system of the press gang to form crews for its warships, France and Spain had the more humane and rational naval subscription and '*matrícula de mar*', organizations charged with levying the seamen necessary for equipping the State's ships. This situation gave the two nations a significant theoretical advantage, notably at the beginning of a conflict, for the rapid establishment of competent crews. But in France, where war had been practically incessant since 1793, the relatively limited 'stock' of available professional seamen was nearly exhausted. Battles, illness and imprisonment in England had done their work, while the collapse of the commercial fleet compromised the training of new seamen. The recruitment drives carried out in 1804 to equip the newly constructed units were ineffective, and it was necessary to resort to expedients to form the crews: drawing on already bloodless local units, turning to black prisoners evacuated from St Domingue and hiring foreign sailors. All these steps having proved insufficient, the land army was forced to contribute men, either to complement the crews or garrisons[7] or to provide passenger troops. In total, the French vessels at Trafalgar were significantly overmanned as a result of the heavy presence of soldiers. On some ships, the proportion of men belonging to the ground forces was 48 per cent, although it should not have passed 15 per cent according to the standards in force. The lack of real sailors meant the vessels were less able to carry out manoeuvres. The over-population of the ships led to a worsening of hygiene conditions and a reduction in self-sufficiency in terms of supplies. On the other hand, the numerous soldiers provided significant help servicing cannons, sharpshooters and assault teams.

On the Spanish vessels, the situation was to a great extent comparable. The '*matrícula de mar*' was only able to provide one quarter of the necessary seamen, and it was necessary to resort to regrettable measures such as the forced embarkation of vagabonds, beggars or criminals charged with light penalties. Ground troops also made a large contribution.

The British navy also had serious difficulties recruiting its crews. It was very far from having at its disposal all the good sailors it would have liked. Nevertheless, it made arrangements for putting a few dozen excellent sailors (topmen) on each ship to assure safe and rapid sailing. Moreover, the statutory crews of the English ships were less numerous, but with the same strength as their adversaries. However, the determining factor in favour of the British was the training of the men. The English squadrons, comprising ships that had been at sea for months, were pitted against units that had been anchored since the war had resumed in May 1803, prisoners of the blockading forces. The situation was particularly dramatic for certain Spanish vessels, armed at Cadiz with improvised crews, who were to be thrown into the blaze of a terrible battle the day after they cast off for the first time. The Spanish command judged them barely able to sail, and certainly not able to fight.

THE ADMIRALS' TACTICAL IDEAS

Nelson's tactical genius is often lauded as if the great man had invented original methods and then put them into practice at Trafalgar. This is not the case at all. Line rupturing and the concentration of attacking forces on a portion of the enemy formation had already been practiced on many occasions, notably in 1782 at the battle of the Saintes won by Rodney against de Grasse, and, more recently, on 1 June 1794 , the Glorious First of June,[8] when Admiral Howe, dividing his fleet into four columns, cut the French line at various points. In France, Suffren demonstrated plenty of spirit and aggressiveness in the attack on the British squadrons at the time of his famous campaign in India, but failed to obtain the collaboration from his captains which would have been necessary for the full success of his undertakings. Nelson's merit lay in his having spent a long time considering the method to use to obtain the most complete destruction possible of his adversary, and having ardently researched the ways to achieve this end. His thoughts, undoubtedly spurred on by his hatred of the French,[9] marked a turning point in naval history. Before him, admirals did not have the annihilation of the enemy as their main objective, but rather gave preponderant weight to accomplishing the mission with which they had been charged. With Nelson, like Napoleon in the case of ground conflicts for that matter, we were entering into the era of wars of great destruction, where ideology played a dominant role. The British admiral was persuaded to fight, with God's help, against the enemies of order, legitimate sovereigns and the one true religion.

The tactic of breaking the opposing line, systematized by Nelson, presented serious disadvantages. It would have led to heavy setbacks if it had been used against an enemy possessing the same capabilities of manoeuvre and a comparably effective artillery. The vessels placed at the head of columns, subjected to the concentrated fire of numerous enemy units without being able to respond for a long time, ran the risk of arriving at the enemy line in a crippled state and of being overpowered there by forces in possession of all their faculties. With audacity, even temerity according to some, Nelson decided that it was worth running the risk and he won his bet. But the genius of the British admiral lay not so much in his aggressive tactics as in the enthusiasm he was able to create in his captains and the manner in which battle was led. With hindsight, these are the exceptional leadership qualities of the greatest English admiral that deserve the most admiration.

Villeneuve, for his part, had also thought long and hard on an encounter that he feared with the victor of the Nile. Many months before, he had guessed and described precisely the tactics his adversary would adopt. 'The enemy,' he began writing in December 1804, 'will not stop at creating a battle line parallel to ours and at delivering an artillery battle, often won by the most cunning, but always by the luckiest. He will seek to surround our rear guard, to cross us and to carry his own squadrons upon those vessels of ours that he will have separated, in order to surround and reduce them.' This pertinent analysis, this extraordinary lucidity was nevertheless accompanied by pessimism and passiveness which prevented him from devising an original disposition of forces and from giving his fleet the benefit of the effect of surprise, on which his adversary was – wrongly – counting. The allied vessels, he thought, could not do anything other than deploy in the tightest line possible against the attacks of the enemy. The adopted course of action – to alternate the French and Spanish units in order to demonstrate better the solidarity between the two countries – undoubtedly reduced even further the manoeuvring capacity of the mixed divisions. How was one to demand highly complicated manoeuvres from formations in which the units did not know one another and who certainly had not had the least bit of training? At Gravina's suggestion, an 'observation' squadron had nevertheless been made up and placed under the orders of the Spanish admiral. This formation, which was destined to remain to windward of the battle corps, could have attempted to impede the assault from the British columns. We shall soon see that this was not the case.

THE COLLAPSE OF THE GRAND PLAN

A series of events were to, either directly or indirectly, put the Emperor's dream in check. Missiessy, the admiral commanding Rochefort's squadron, did not receive the order to stay in the Antilles in time, and came back to Rochefort according to instructions. Ganteaume, commander of the Brest squadron, was never allowed to cast off without fighting, according to orders of the most imperative nature. Villeneuve, in charge of the Toulon squadron, succeeded in leaving his base, and reinforced himself with seven vessels at Cadiz, one French and six Spanish ships, to arrive without hindrance at Fort-de-France on 15 May. After a vain attempt and the arrival of new instructions, the combined fleet, reinforced with two ships from Rochefort, departed again for Europe on 10 June, not to deploy at the entrance to the Channel, but to remove the blockade facing the forces trapped at El Ferrol. Far from 'flying', the Franco-Spanish fleet, hindered by slow ships and burdened with sick crew members, did not appear off Cape Finisterre until 22 July, only to run into Admiral Calder's squadron. After an indecisive battle fought in fog, during which two Spanish ships were lost after falling into the English line, Villeneuve disembarked the sick and injured at Vigo, where he also got rid of three of the worst ships, one French and two Spanish, which were slowing down the fleet. He then went to El Ferrol where he was able to call five French and nine Spanish ships to his flag. Finally, on 13 August, he cast off for Brest in order to unblock Ganteaume's squadron there. He was already very late.

During this time the British squadrons, contrary to Naploean's predictions, had not dispersed. Nelson, however, in accord with the Emperor's wishes, had lost one month in the Mediterranean where he was protecting Egypt and the kingdom of Naples which he believed to be under attack, before hurrying to the Antilles where he only just missed the allied forces. The other admirals, obeying an unwritten order known by all, had gathered in the region of Ushant following the loss of contact with the forces they should have been surveying. Nelson himself ended up taking the same course of action. On 14 August, 39 British ships barred entrance to the Channel on the orders of Admiral Cornwallis. This was much more than was necessary to stop the 29 ships that now formed the combined fleet. Villeneuve on the other hand, aware that superior forces were awaiting him, and eaten up by an almost pathological pessimism which made him see all the very real weaknesses of his fleet in a much worse light, ceased to continue his journey north on 15 August, and retreated to Cadiz.

THE BATTLE: A DISASTER ACCEPTED FOR HONOUR

Among the numerous myths inspired by the battle of Trafalgar, one of the most tenacious is that Nelson's victory saved Great Britain from invasion by the French. On 23 August 1805, even before he learned of Villeneuve's retreat, the Emperor had taken the decision to take down the camp at Boulogne and to launch the Grande Armée into the famous campaign that was to lead to the crushing of the Austrians and the Russians at Austerlitz. When Villeneuve cast off from Cadiz on 20 October, he directed his fleet not towards the Channel, but towards Gibraltar and the Mediterranean, where he was to fulfil a completely secondary mission to support the French forces fighting in the kingdom of Naples. Napoleon, exasperated by his admiral's behaviour, had decided to replace him several weeks earlier. But working on the ridiculous assumption that Villeneuve, being far too fainthearted, would not carry out the last orders he had received, he had sent Admiral Rosily to Cadiz to take command of the combined fleet without having informed the disgraced captain. An extraordinary combination of circumstances, notably Rosily's delay, having been immobilized in Madrid following a broken carriage axle, meant that Villeneuve got wind of

Le Redoutable *a la bataille de Trafalgar* by Auguste-Etienne-Francois Mayer. The *Redoutable* was at the thick of the action in the Battle of Trafalgar. Coming to the aid of *Bucentaure*, she became locked with Nelson's flagship, *Victory*. The three-hour battle that ensued resulted in the death of Nelson while *Victory* herself only narrowly escaped capture by *Redoutable*'s highly trained assault teams due to the timely arrival of HMS *Téméraire*. (Photo RMN / © Bulloz)

his disgrace and replacement. Not having been informed officially, he believed – and what's more this contained something of the truth – that his friend Decrès had wanted to provide an opportunity for him to redeem himself and to avenge his outraged honour. It was with the energy of despair that the admiral, using as a pretext favourable wind conditions and a momentary and unrecognized weakness in the blockading forces, ordered the cast off. He was able, on this occasion, to convince his Spanish allies. The latter, however, had been more than reticent at the time of a war council held on 8 October where a joint agreement had been reached that the superiority of the English fleet was such that it would be necessary to await favourable circumstances. It is not easy to explain Gravina's change in attitude: should one see it as a demonstration of his faultless loyalty and Spanish honour, or as the result of pressure exercised by the Madrid court, so completely subordinated to the Emperor?

We will not attempt to repeat a detailed account of the battle here, as this would duplicate other chapters in this work. Our only aim is to provide the British reader with a Franco-Spanish point of view on the battle, and to suggest a few reasons allowing for a better comprehension of the allies' behaviour.

One initial comment is necessary. The battle was indecisive for a long time, and the resistance of the combined fleet was much more dogged than one would have thought given its weaknesses. It would not have taken much to tip the battle into a completely different scenario.

The British hoped, to a greater or lesser degree, to see their adversaries flee with the wind behind them in the face of their attacking columns. They found before them determined men waiting in a long line, doubled in numerous places, in a crescent shape with the points advancing. Some took this arrangement to be an elaborate tactic[10]: the tips of the crescent could close on the attackers who, after having crossed the first line, would find themselves trapped between two lines of fire. However, only chance and the difficulties encountered by the allies in obtaining correct formation were behind this supposedly shrewd plan of action.

All the allied witnesses agree on the disorder of the two English columns, divided into numerous platoons, which rushed towards the enemy cramming on sail. However, behind this apparent anarchy were Nelson's elaborate tactics. The north column, which he was leading himself, threatened the allied rear guard first, before falling back on the centre and breaking through the corner in the middle of the battle corps formed by the three triple-deckers placed at the head. The south column, under the direction of Collingwood, was deployed on his right as planned, and, formed as a rough relief line, surrounded the whole of the allied rear guard. The greatest shock was in the centre. *Victory*, *Téméraire* and *Neptune*, which had only suffered minor losses and damage in their approach, met the wall formed by the immense *Santísima Trinidad* followed by the *Bucentaure*, the French flagship, and the *Redoutable*. Nelson, one of whose great merits had been his confidence in his subordinates, allowed Hardy, his flag captain, to choose the point of impact. Hardy chose the *Redoutable*, a 74-cannon ship, the most feeble-looking of the three adversaries. He thought he would be able to see it off easily.

Captain Lucas was largely responsible for salvaging French honour in the Battle of Trafalgar. Having trained sharpshooters and assault teams to a make up for the superiority of British gunnery, he was on the verge of capturing HMS *Victory* herself, had it not been for the timely arrival of HMS *Téméraire*. Although *Victory* survived, Nelson himself succumbed to his worthy foe. (© Musée National de la Marine/Lucas, Lithographie de Maurin, 1837)

The battle fought by the *Redoutable* remains in the annals as one of the greatest feats of arms of the French navy. Lucas, who was commanding this ship, nevertheless did not benefit from favourable circumstances. His ship had just undergone a great deal of repairs. He had been manned at El Ferrol with an improvised crew, made up for the large part of personnel taken from other ships. The ship had only had six days to get used to the sea, the length of the crossing between El Ferrol and Cadiz. Its commander nevertheless succeeded in making it a splendid battle instrument. Lucas, who came from Marennes near Rochefort, was 41 years old. He began his career as a ship's boy in the French navy, and distinguished himself during the American War of Independence. A petty officer specialising as a pilot, he was one of those junior officers who had experienced lightning promotion thanks to the Revolution, in his case completely justified. Aware like other French commanders of the superiority of the British artillery, Lucas banked to a great extent on the use of sharpshooters and on assault. He constantly trained his men and communicated his enthusiasm and confidence. The rigorous organization of his ship and the proficiency of his soldiers and sailors were marvellous. In spite of the difference in rank separating the two vessels, the *Redoutable*, which had its bowsprit on the stern of the *Bucentaure*, faced the attack of the *Victory* without flinching, launching all its grapnels at the

Cayetano Valdés (1767–1835) was a Spanish naval officer and hydrographer who carried out extensive surveys of the north-west coast of North America. He fought against Admiral Howe's squadron in 1782. As captain of the *Neptuno*, he received a serious wound at Trafalgar. He was later to be exiled from Spain, seeking refuge in England, but returned to become Captain-General of the Spanish fleet. (Museo Naval de Madrid)

latter. With a tight hold on each other, the two ships began a fight to the death. Bit by bit, David gained the upper hand on Goliath. From the topmasts of the *Redoutable* there fell a hail of gunfire and grenades. The British ship's gunners were fired upon through the scuttles at point-blank range by the French soldiers stationed in the batteries. The death of Nelson[11] provoked a moment of stupor and Lucas saw that the moment had come to attempt the attack that his whole crew was waiting for. At the trumpet signal, the attacking divisions jumped on the forecastles. 'They climbed aboard in such an orderly fashion,' Lucas wrote, 'the officers and midshipmen at the head of their companies, that one could have

Trafalgar tableau showing the action between the Spanish ship *Santa Ana*, under Vice-Admiral Alava, and the British *Royal Sovereign*, under Vice-Admiral Collingwood. (Oil on cloth by Angel Cortellini Sánchez c. 1903) (Museo Naval de Madrid)

believed it to be nothing more than a training session.' The main yard was brought to serve as a deck as the wall of the triple-decker was much larger than that of its adversary. Some men were already aboard the *Victory* and the attacking teams were about to rush forward when the *Téméraire* appeared and, with a great volley of all its artillery, swept away the decks and the forecastles of the *Redoutable*. The *Victory* was saved, but Nelson had come across a worthy adversary for his final battle.

After very difficult battles, the three powerful British ships placed at the head of the column led by Nelson succeeded in beating their opponents. *Santísima Trinidad* and *Bucentaure*, completely dismasted, suffered heavy losses and were gradually rendered powerless. They received little help from the allied ships that had fallen to leeward, while the English column continued to feed their adversaries with fresh units. Villeneuve, who had sought death in vain and acknowledged the impossibility of leaving his ship, was forced to resolve to strike his flag at around 3:30p.m. Lucas, whose ship was completely devastated, was forced to do the same, but not without having inflicted painful losses on the *Téméraire*. This ship, like the *Victory*, was in any case unable to continue to fight effectively.

Bucentaure was the 80-gun flagship of Admiral Villeneuve and before that of Admiral Latouche-Tréville. She was widely admired for her balanced and elegant lines. *Bucentaure* was on the receiving end of the battering ram of the first English column, led by Nelson, and, although she received assistance from the *Santísima Trinidad* (140), *Neptuno* (80) and *Redoutable*, she gradually succumbed to consecutive British attacks. *Bucentaure* was later washed on to the rocks of the Spanish coast and wrecked. (© Musée National de la Marine/Le Vaisseau Bucentaure)

A large-scale and rapid intervention on the part of the allied rear guard, which was barely engaged in the first phase of the battle, could have reversed this situation. But Dumanoir, the young French admiral commanding this force, lacked initiative and decisiveness. When he did finally decide to give the order to tack, following a request from Villeneuve, his main preoccupation was to rectify the alignment of his ships and to ensure they kept to the regulation distances. Thus there appeared the bizarre spectacle of the *Formidable* followed by three other French ships, all impeccably aligned, crossing the entire battlefield windward of the combat zone, shelling the British units from long range. Several ships did not follow Dumanoir's orders. Two of these, the French *Intrépide* and the Spanish *Neptuno*, made straight for the *Bucentaure* and the *Santísima Trinidad*. Soon overwhelmed by far superior forces, they succumbed after an heroic resistance. Others which had fallen leeward left the battle and headed for Cadiz.

Collingwood fulfilled his pledges perfectly by taking on the best of the allies' 15 rear guard ships, in battles that were often fierce. The pattern followed was always the same. The British ships placed at the head of the different platoons which made up the attacking column attacked the allied line in several places. They experienced some very difficult moments before receiving help from the ships following them, as each individual vessel had to face numerous adversaries. But the enemy's shots were too slow and ill-adjusted to prevent them crossing the line. In close combat, the carronades played a decisive role by neutralising the allies' superiority in muskets and assault teams with their devastating anti-personnel fire.

With the exception of the *Principe de Asturias*, a flagship whose crew had been formed with particular care, the Spanish ships were difficult to manoeuvre. Placed in the front line, they fought with great courage, like the *Santa Ana*, the crew of which was nevertheless completely untrained. Those ships that fell to leeward did not in general succeed in participating effectively in the combat. When the battle turned in favour of the attacking force, some managed to escape, while others were caught and taken.

Several French ships, like the *Pluton* and the *Argonaute,* distinguished themselves by good manoeuvrability, which enabled them to avoid being captured after having fought vigorously. Many succumbed after heroic combat, such as the *Fougueux*, the *Aigle* and the *Achille,* which exploded towards the end of the battle.

THE CONSEQUENCES OF TRAFALGAR

The strategic consequences of Trafalgar were quite limited. The hopes of the British combatants of a glorious peace if they won were decidedly in vain. Undoubtedly the threat of a French invasion was ruled out definitively, and Great Britain, from then on the undisputed mistress of the seas, would be able to seize her adversaries' colonies and ruin the little that remained of their commercial traffic. But the war was to last another ten years, and it would be the coalition ground forces which would put an end to it at Waterloo.

On a psychological level, on the other hand, the fallout from the battle was immense. For the British the event was the most glorious peak in the history of the Royal Navy, a sort of apotheosis from which Nelson, the hero, emerged as a demi-god.[12] The entire nation drew pride and confidence in its destiny from Trafalgar. The French, scarred by the scale of the disaster, felt that their maritime activities were being struck by a kind of bad omen. The landsman mentality of the nation, which is strongly rooted in its history, was justified and reinforced. The French sailors themselves were resigned to never being more than second best at sea. For the Spanish, the event had a completely different resonance. Having fought for honour, for the benefit of an ungrateful ally, the only thing that resonates with them from the whole affair is the heroism of their fighters and the glory that they acquired. In Madrid there is a square, an avenue and even an entire district named after Trafalgar!

CHAPTER FIVE

NAVAL TACTICS IN THE AGE OF SAIL

DR NICHOLAS TRACY

Naval tactics are dominated by the limitations of ship design, the technologies of naval armament, and by the age old limitations of human courage and strength. Square rigged sailing ships were unable to hold any course closer than 6 points, or 67 degrees from the direction the wind was blowing. The ship of the line was the only weapon system ever developed which could deploy its weapons only at right-angles to its line of advance. And the capacity of admirals to develop tactics to deal with those restrictions was severely restrained by the limitation of signalling systems. Nelson was a unique naval leader, but his tactics at Trafalgar were a product of two-and-a-quarter centuries of experience in the Royal Navy of warfare by fleets of great sailing ships armed with batteries of heavy guns.

When cannons were first mounted on sailing vessels, the heaviest guns were the chase guns firing over the bow. This practice was copied from the oared galleys which had dominated naval warfare until the mid-16th century, but unlike galleys, sailing vessels could not count on being able to steer a course which would permit the laying of the bow guns against the enemy. On the other hand, sailing vessels were built heavily enough, and with enough beams, that great guns could be mounted along the decks to permit firing at right angles to the keel. Accordingly, the smaller guns were disposed so as to ensure that at least one weapon could be brought to bear on any relative bearing. A ship lying-to could defend itself against galleys attacking from any direction. But while this arrangement served the needs of the armed traders who first made use of great sailing ships, it was less useful for a ship of war pressing home an attack under sail. To employ its full gun power it was necessary for a 16th-century galleon to tack or wear about to open the firing arc of each gun in turn. Not only did this sequence limit the rate at which a single ship could bring fire against its enemy, but the turning movement also made close cooperation with a squadron difficult. It was impossible to concentrate enough weight of shot at any point to achieve decisive results, and naval battles continued to be decided by boarding. In order

OPPOSITE
Detail from *The Panorama of the Battle of Trafalgar* by W. K. Wyllie RA. HMS *Neptune* (right) engages the 130-gun Santísima Trinidad, which later sank. (Royal Naval Museum)

to accommodate larger batteries, ships began to be built longer, which also increased their speed, but reduced their tactical manoeuverability. This both made it possible, and necessary, that ships work together in fleets.

By the end of the 18th century the principal batteries of great ships were armed with smooth bore cannons weighing 6,000 pounds, mounted on a truck with four wheels so that they could recoil, and capable of firing a 32lb (14.5kg) shot. To fire it, the gun loader rammed a flannel bag of black gunpowder down the barrel, followed by the spherical iron ball and a wad to keep it in place, an awl was then driven down through the touch hole at the butt, breaking a hole in the charge bag, and a goose quill filled with fine gunpowder was inserted. By the end of the century the actual firing would be done by a flint-lock which was triggered by a long cord tugged by the gun captain when he considered that the gun would lay on its target. For close action, it was the practice to load two, or even three, balls for the first discharge. Once engaged, however, the confusion of action made it usual to stick to the simplest possible routine to reduce the risk of accidents. The gun was elevated by a wedge, or quoin, placed under the butt, which needed to be hove into position by men employing handspikes. Handspikes were also used to squew the gun truck across the deck to aim it properly through the port. The recoil was stopped by a heavy, and elastic, rope which was fastened to ring bolts at each end and passed round the butt of the gun. The gun would then be sponged out to ensure there was no lingering scrap of the powder bag which might prematurely ignite the next charge, and then it would be reloaded and run back out the gun port by its 13-man crew. Lighter 24-pounder guns were used on the middle and upper gun decks, but they had considerably less penetrating ability. Eighteen-pounder and 9-pounder guns were used as chase guns, and on lighter warships. In the 1770s light-weight, low calibre carronades were introduced into the fleet. Using a smaller charge, these guns could fire the same weight of shot but to a shorter range.

It was possible for a fully worked-up British crew at the end of the 18th century to sustain a rate of independent fire of one round every minute. In 1805 Collingwood's *Dreadnought* was able to deliver three full broadsides every three-and-a-half minutes. When in 1793 Admiral Don Frederico Gravina, briefly an ally of the British, visited Portsmouth dockyard he concluded that British superiority in gunnery was a result of the superiority of the British gun carriage, and the use of the flint-lock for firing. British propellant was also better, due to the East India Company's control of sources of saltpetre. But most important was good gun drill, constant practice and high morale. Victory depended on sustaining an effective rate of fire until the enemy gunners were killed or their weapons disabled. Shot from a 32-pounder could penetrate the heaviest ship timbers at close range, destroy guns, and produce showers of splinters which killed or maimed the men. Guns could be elevated so that shot would burst upwards through the upper decks of the enemy ship. It required a high degree of training to ensure that a gun-crew could continue to work their weapon when subjected to such attack, and to do so safely. The recoil of the guns could kill their own crews if they were not well drilled, and if the rammer failed to sponge out the gun, or lost count and rammed in two charges, premature discharge, or the bursting of the guns, was a real danger.

By the time Nelson first went to sea in 1770, the great ships, which had become known as ships of the line because of the tactical formations in which they were employed, had evolved into several distinct classes distinguished by their number of guns. The largest, with 100 guns or more on three gun decks, were considered First Rate ships. The most famous of all was HMS *Victory*, which had been launched in 1765 and was to be Nelson's flagship at Trafalgar. She was 186ft (nearly 57m) long on the gun deck, and displaced 2,142 tons. Her armament at the time of Trafalgar was 30 × 32-pounders, 28 × 24-pounders, 30 × 12-pounders, and 8 × 6-pounders, delivering a broadside of 1,020lb of shot (460kg). Second Rates were three-decked ships with less than 100 guns. By the end of the century they were nearly all armed with 98 guns. The *Prince of Wales* which was launched in 1794, displaced 2010 tons, and threw a broadside of 958lb of shot (453kg). Third Rates at the time of Trafalgar were all two-decked ships, armed with 64, 74 or 80 guns, of which the most numerous were the 74s. The *Centaur* launched in 1797 was rated at 1,842 tons, and had an armament of 28 × 32-pounders, 30 × 24-pounders and 16 × 9-pounders, throwing a broadside of 880lb (400kg).

Before the development of the ship of the line, tactical organization had largely consisted of mutual support, and the earliest fighting instructions were concerned with fleet discipline. Captains had to be restrained from abandoning tactical formations in order to make prizes. They had to be instructed to hold their fire until they were within effective range. And at their peril they were never to fire on the enemy over, or through, a friendly ship. By the mid-17th century, once ships had been developed which mounted batteries capable of defeating an enemy by its firepower alone, it became a matter of necessity to develop fleet tactics which not only would guard against 'friendly fire' mistakes, but would ensure that ships were provided with open arcs so that fleets could deploy their full fire power. From the time of the Second Dutch War the standard tactical formation for the fleets of sailing warships became a close order line of battle ahead. The Battle of Malaga in 1704 established in British and in French tactical thinking the absolute importance of maintaining the defensive strength of a well ordered line of battle. In the Admiralty's signal book of 1799, the advantages of linear tactics were stated to be 'that the ships may be able to assist and support each other in action; that they may not be exposed to the fire of the enemy's ships greater in number than themselves; and that every ship may be able to fire on the enemy without risk of firing into the ships of her own fleet.'[1]

The line of battle, however, had more advantages for the defence than it had for offense. A fleet of ships mounting heavy batteries on their sides, drawn up in close order line-ahead, presented a tremendous weight of fire against the lead ship or ships in an approaching fleet, and could direct their fire at the structurally weak, and lightly armed bows of the leading ships. The attacking fleet could only return fire if ships swung away from the line of advance to present their broadsides. In consequence, the central tactical problem in every battle of the sailing ship era was that of manoeuvring the ships of the line into firing range of the enemy. If the attack were made with line-ahead formation there was a danger that the lead ship would be disabled, and block the advance of the remainder of the line. If the attackers adopted a line-abreast formation and steered directly for the enemy they would cover the distance more rapidly, but all their ships would be highly vulnerable during the approach, and differences in the speed of individual ships could destroy the tactical formation when finally the fleet turned on a course parallel to the enemy.

The tactical problem of how to bring an enemy to action was further complicated by the need for an admiral, who was determined to press home an attack, to bring his fleet onto the same heading as the enemy fleet. If fleets passed each other in opposite directions there was little chance of decisive results. Only by prolonged firing at very close range, no more than a few hundred yards and ultimately at ranges so close that there was a danger of muzzle blast setting both ships on fire, could the heavy sides of a first or second rate ship of the line be subjected to a truly destructive force.

The development of systems of tactical manoeuvre to enable fleets of ships of the line to force decisive battle on their enemies was a result of experience, and

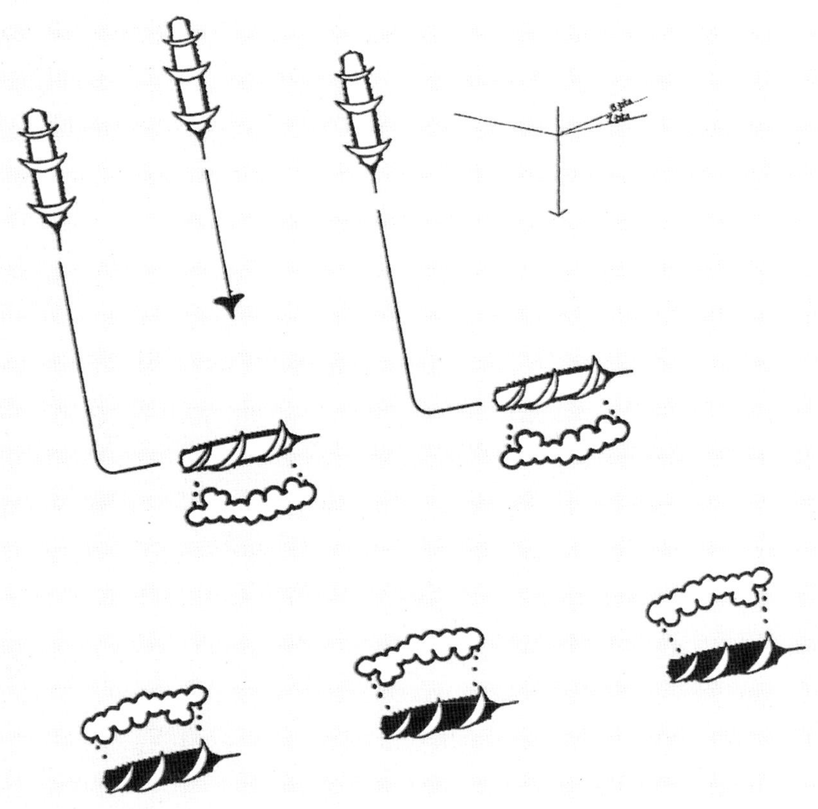

Approaching an enemy line of battle in line abreast exposed the heads of the ships to a fire they could not return. It had the additional problem that ships running before the wind were less able to control their speed because they could not back a sail. When the leading ships turned to fire on the enemy, they would mask the slower ships and break up the tactical formation. (Sarah Petite)

theoretical analysis, over the century and a half from the Second Dutch War beginning in 1664 to the wars of the French Revolution and Empire. Successive admirals drafted Sailing and Fighting Instructions, and added to them with 'Additional Instructions', setting out their intended method of making the dangerous approach, and of responding to moves of the enemy. These were consolidated in 1672 or 1673 when a volume was published under the name of James Duke of York containing all the standard signals and instructions.[2] In 1691 Admiral Russell put his name to a reissue of the Fighting Instructions, with a few additions, and his name continued to be attached to what became in fact, but not in law, an official Admiralty publication.

Almost as basic to naval tactics as the line of battle was the practice in the Royal Navy of meeting the enemy in a close hauled line to windward, because an admiral who kept his fleet in line ahead to windward was more likely to be able to control the subsequent encounter with the enemy. This practice was established, virtually as a legal requirement which admirals ignored only at very great risk of serious consequences, in Article 4 of the Fighting Instructions. It was only possible to keep formation seven points (79°) off the wind, or at best for a well-drilled French fleet of the mid-18th century, six points (67°). This limitation restricted the options open to both admirals, and each could seek to exploit the other's mistakes.

Article 7 instructed the fleet to endeavour to keep to windward of the enemy. A windward position had several advantages, not the least of which was that when the admiral judged it time to close with the enemy the dangerous approach could be made more quickly. Because of the direction of heel imparted by a windward position, gunnery against the enemy hull was more effective for the windward fleet, while the leeward position favoured gunnery against the enemy rigging. In any case, the leeward fleet was more likely to seek to disable the enemy's mobility. The leeward position had defensive advantages, because disabled ships would tend to drift into safety behind their own line, but for that very reason the windward position had psychological value because it gave 'shy' captains little chance to shirk their duty.

Article 8 instructed the leading squadron to steer for the leading ships of the enemy fleet. Should it be necessary to reverse the fleet to bring the enemy to action on the same tack, Article 1 established the principle that the rear ships of the line should be the first to begin the deployment.[3]

Attack from the windward was not without difficulties. When Lord Dartmouth issued instructions to the fleet assembled in 1688 to prevent a landing by William of Orange he planned to make a long approach at an oblique angle to the enemy wake. The idea was to expose his ships' heads as little as possible to a fire they could not return. Progress was to be controlled by the captains conforming to the movements of the flagship. From time to time, as appeared necessary, the ships were to swing round so that they could open fire on the enemy ships ahead of them. Then the admiral would bear down again with his ships taking their cue from his movements. When nearly within gunshot

RIGHT

The leeward position had the defensive advantage that damaged ships would tend to drift behind their own line and into safety. The windward line was more vulnerable, but was better able to force action on the enemy. (Sarah Petite)

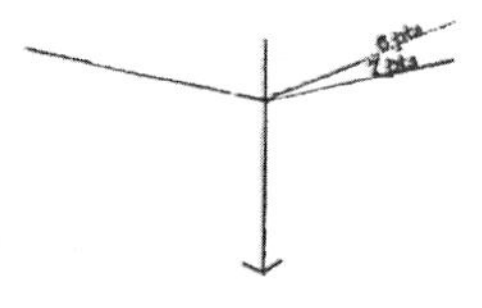

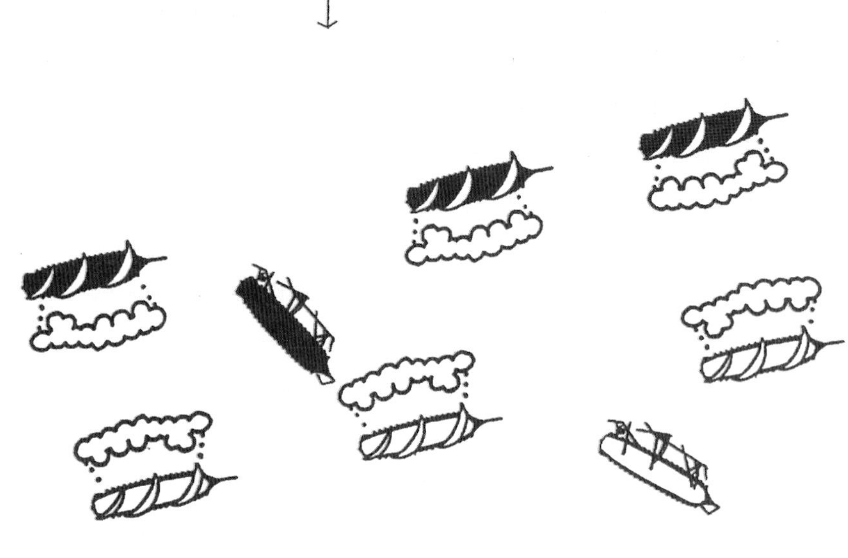

BELOW

Decisive action depended on protracted firing, for which fleets needed to be on nearly the same course. It was standard British practice in the event of successfully winning a race for the windward position, to sail the length of the enemy, and then to tack onto its course, with the last ship turning first to avoid the complex procedure of tacking disrupting tactical formation. (Sarah Petite)

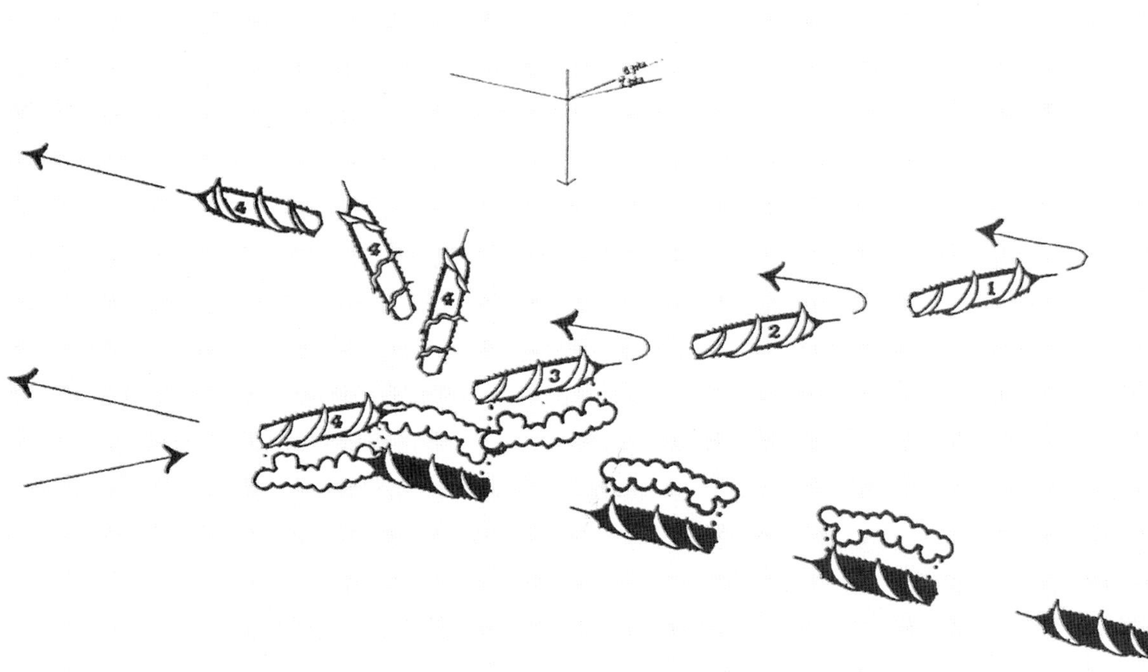

An oblique approach from windward required skilful ship handling if ships were to fire on the enemy without impeding the progress of the ships in their wakes. (Sarah Petite)

of the enemy, the ships were to 'lask away,' taking the wind on their quarters and steering courses to intercept their opposite number. At no point were they to head directly for the enemy when they would be exposed head-on to a raking fire.[4] Given the disparate nature of the English fleet at the time, this tactical plan may have been somewhat fanciful. It was to be attempted by Admiral Byng in 1756 at the Battle of Minorca, but he failed because his leading captain did not understand what was expected of him. Unless the attacking fleet had a useful speed advantage over the enemy it was inevitable that the approach would degrade into a stern chase.

The admiral's task was not finished by getting his fleet into firing range. Decisive victory depended upon concentration of the fire on a part of the enemy line. British 32-pounder long guns were capable of a range of 2,900yds (about 2650m), but battles were not fought at that range because the kinetic energy of the shot would be so diminished that its capacity to penetrate heavy timbering would be greatly reduced. Furthermore, too much of the shot would be wasted by falling into the sea, because of the inaccuracy of the gun, and because its elevation system did not permit continuous laying of the guns to compensate for the rolling of the ship. It was necessary for gunners to judge the precise point in the ship's roll to pull the firing cord, and the difficulty was greatly increased if the gun were elevated. Point-blank range of 350yds (about 320m), when no elevation was required, was considered maximum battle range, and the effectiveness of fire

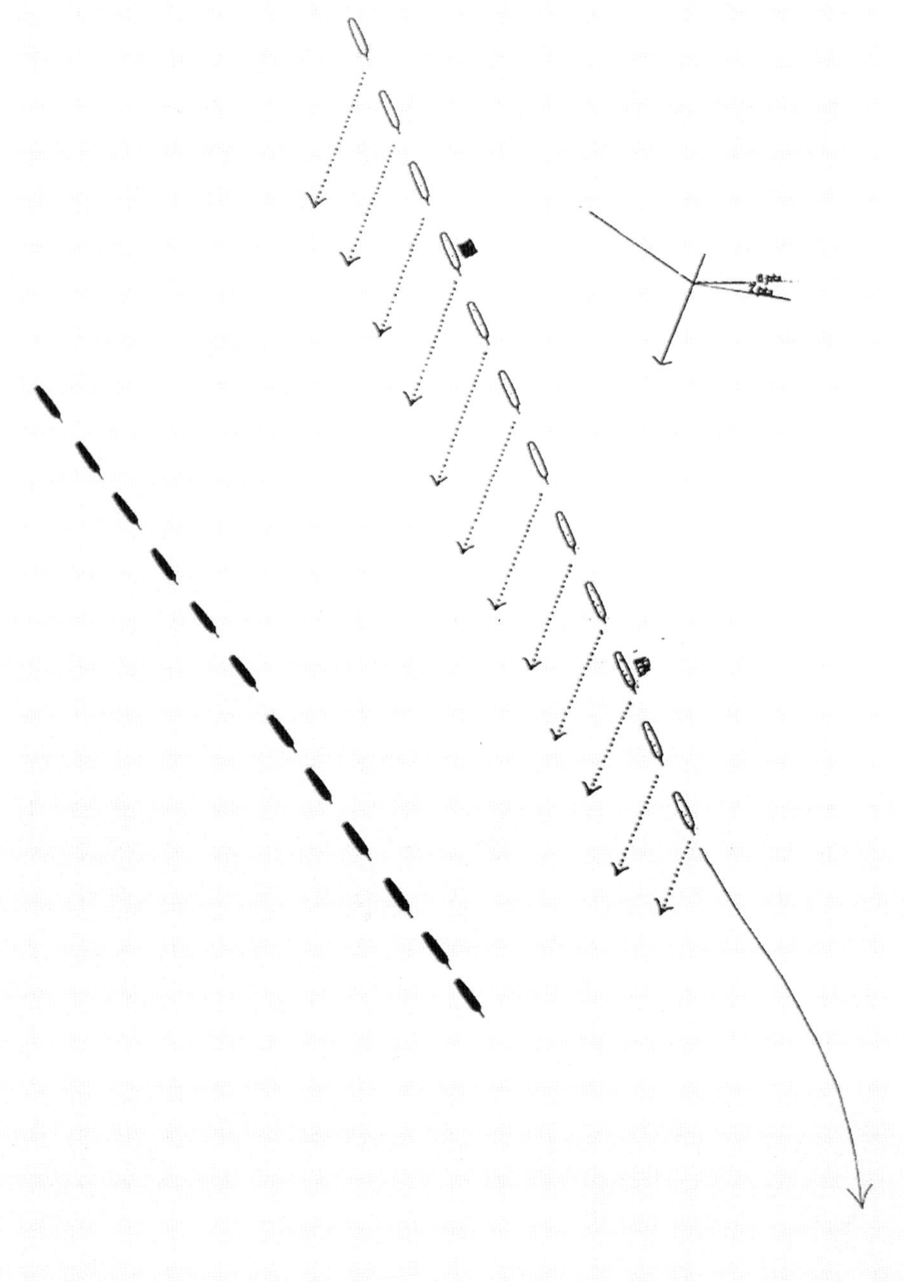

At the battle of Minorca Admiral Byng ordered his fleet to 'lask' down on the enemy line, but the leading ship mistook his order and sailed to intercept the leading ship of the enemy. (Sarah Petite)

could be increased by using double shot at a range of only 100yds (about 91m).[5] As was demonstrated in 1782 by the first British civilian student of tactics, John Clerk of Eldin, in *An Essay on Naval Tactics*, ships moving in line-ahead and a cable from each other, unless one of them swung out of line, could only fire on the same target if the enemy were over 720 yards away. With the longer-range guns which came into service in the late 19th century, concentration could be achieved by directing the fire of widely separated ships onto a single target. That

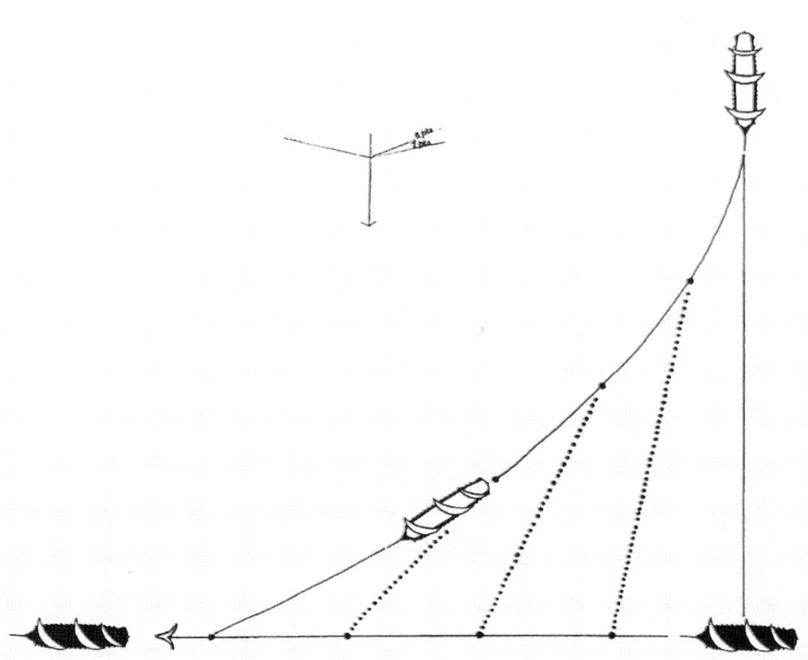

As John Clerk of Eldin demonstrated in 1782, a head on attack from windward tended to become a stern chase. (Sarah Petite)

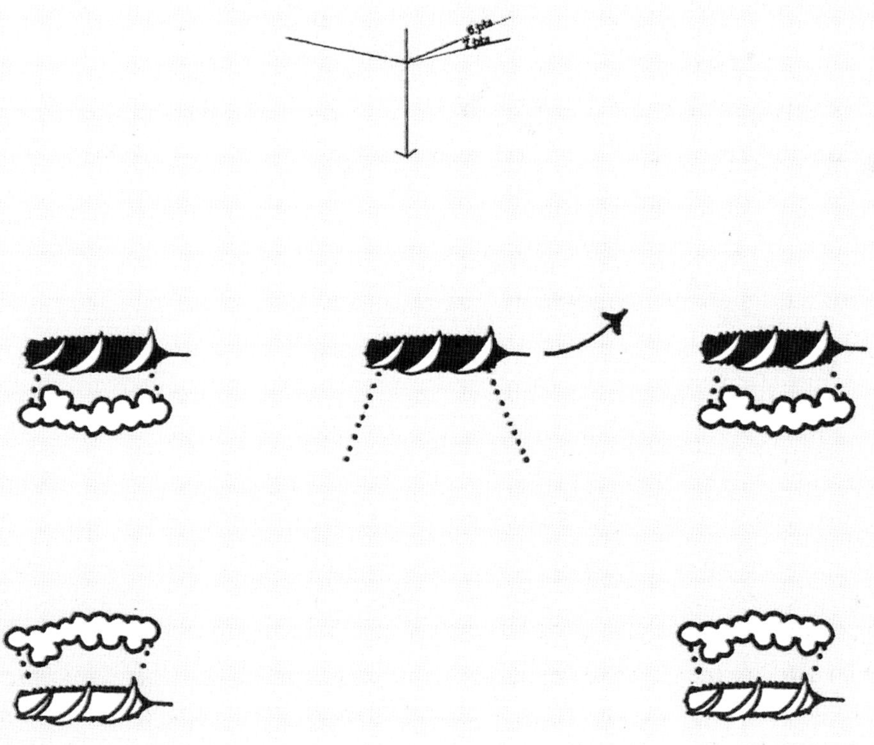

Clerk of Eldin also showed that ships in a fleet making way could only fire on the next ahead or astern in the enemy line while holding its course if the fleets were over 750 yards apart. Inside that range, if a ship in the windward fleet had no opposite number, it could only fire on the enemy by bearing up, which could put it 'in irons' making stern way, and disrupting the tactical formation. (Sarah Petite)

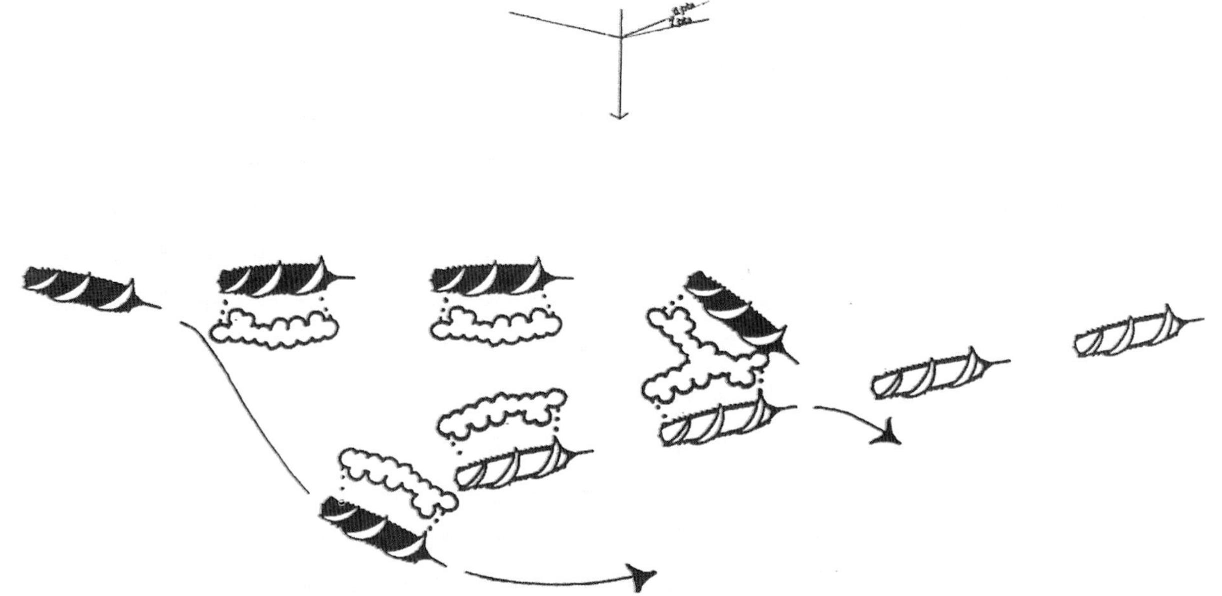

Crushing firepower could only be managed by 'doubling' the enemy line, from the rear or van, or by cutting the enemy line. (Sarah Petite)

was not possible with the short-range weapons available to Nelson. The only way an admiral could hope to bring concentrated fire against a part of the enemy line at ranges as short as 350 to 100 yards was to bring the enemy line between two fires, by 'doubling' the enemy line in the van or rear by detaching ships to pass around the van or rear of the enemy, or by cutting through the line.

To do so, without compromising the defensive strength of his own line, it would be necessary for an admiral confronting an enemy of equal strength to space out his own line so as to release forces for the enveloping movement. The thinned line might be able to contain the enemy because of the difficulty the latter would experience in employing its unengaged ships without disrupting his tactical movement.

So difficult was it to conform to best tactical practice and still force battle on a reluctant foe that there was a strong 'go at'em' school in the Royal Navy which thought it better to throw away the book, take your knocks, and close with the enemy. Admiral Vernon wrote in 1739: 'Our sea officers despise theory ... and by trusting only to their genius at the instant they are to act, have neither time, nor foundation whereby to proceed.' Vernon did not wholly disapprove of the anti-intellectual approach. 'Where officers are determined to fight in great fleets, 'tis much of the least of the matter what order they fight in... All formality ... only tends to keep the main point out of the question, and to give knaves and fools an opportunity to justify themselves on the credit of jargon and nonsense.'[6] Nelson's mentor, Admiral John Jervis, Earl St Vincent, was to observe that 'two fleets of equal strength can never produce decisive events, unless they are equally determined to fight it out or the Commander-in-chief of one of them so bitches it as to misconduct his line.'[7] And he expostulated that 'Lord Hawke when he ran out of the line [at the Battle of Toulon] and took the *Poder* sickened me of tactics.'[8] Part of Nelson's genius lay in his ability to judge just how far he could depart from tactical conventions in order to get decisive, yet successful, action.

Admirals continued to struggle to draft Additional Instructions but these began to change in character by the end of the 18th century, because the need for tactical flexibility and delegation of responsibility was increasingly recognized. During his brief period in command of the Channel Fleet during the Seven Years' War, Admiral Anson issued an instruction that, should he find that not enough of his ships were able to engage the enemy while maintaining line discipline, he would haul down the signal for the line. Every ship was then to engage the ship opposite it in the enemy line.[9] The next year Rear-Admiral Hawke amplified the same instruction when he took over command.[10] In 1747 Hawke issued a set of additional instructions which were intended to increase the flexibility of line tactics by giving the admiral more control over manoeuvre, and also by trusting individual captains to make appropriate decisions.[11] Hawke's Article 8 instructed the captains of the smaller ships, if the fleet were in action with a less numerous enemy force, to fall out of the line on their own initiative and manoeuvre to rake the enemy van or rear. His Articles 9 and 10 permitted more initiative to individual captains, in the particular circumstance of the pursuit of an enemy fleet which was unwilling to give battle.

It was recognized practice to give each ship a pre-assigned position in each squadron's line of battle.[12] This was necessary because fleets were made up of ships with differing weight of timber and gun, and commanded by officers with different degrees of capacity. No navy could afford to build all its ships of the largest rate, because they had to be constructed from the largest trees, which were relatively scarce. Furthermore, admirals needed battle-lines with roughly the same number of ships as those of their enemy so as to limit the danger of being overwhelmed by concentrations of force. These numbers could only be achieved by compromising on ship size and made it necessary for admirals to organize their lines so as to ensure the most capable ships with the most reliable captains were put where they would do most good. But deployment from order of sailing to order of battle could take so long that the enemy would have time to retreat. And the line of battle once formed could only advance at the speed of the slowest of the ships from which it was composed. The signal ordering 'general chase,' which permitted ships to leave the order of battle to pursue the enemy, was only suitable if the enemy force were disorganized. To address these problems, Hawke, or Anson, introduced the idea of an emergency line of battle which would be formed by the captains of the faster ships as they came up with the enemy, the furthest advanced taking the lead without regard to seniority. This *ad hoc* line was to engage the rearward ships of the enemy, and try to pass on to the enemy van.

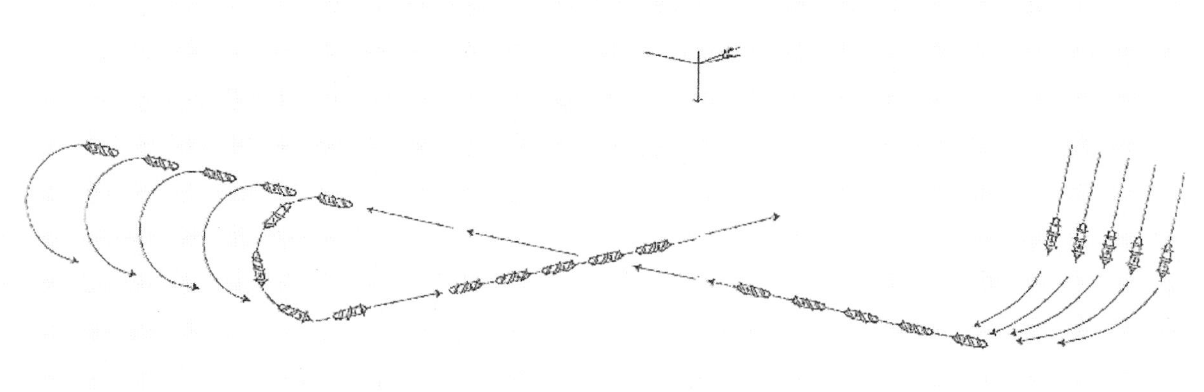

The fleet on the right is in 'Bow and Quarter' formation, with its axis seven points off the wind, allowing it to turn together into a close hauled line ahead on the starboard tack. Subsequently the ships wear, beginning with the rearmost, and form a close hauled line on the port tack. (Sarah Petite)

Anson also introduced into British tactics the Line of Bearing Formation, or the 'Bow and Quarter Line.' This was identical to the 'First Order of Sailing' which the French mathematician Pierre Paul Hoste had devized from abstract thinking about tactical problems, and published in 1697 in one of the great books of naval tactics, *L'Art des Armées Navales ou Traité des Evolutions Navales*. As with the later versions of Hoste's order, the axis of the formation could be any bearing ordered by the admiral, but the usual practice was to have the axis seven points off the wind, so that on the order being given the fleet could turn together into a close-hauled line ahead. The term 'Starboard' or 'Larboard (Port) Line of Bearing' was used to indicate lines of bearing which could be made into a close-hauled line to windward on the starboard or port tack by ordering the ships to change course. Until that order was given, the course set for the fleet could be anything the wind permitted. If it was wanted to change the line of bearing, as opposed to the ships heading, it was usually necessary to deploy into line ahead, and pay off on the new bearing, before returning to the intended heading.

The process of tactical reform was accelerated during the American Revolutionary war, notably by Lord Howe when he arrived in New York in 1776 to assume command of the North American Station. Howe's fleet was engaged in operations against the American rebels, but he took the opportunity to organize it for battle, and provided it with a *Signal Book For Ships of War* which was such an important development on standard British practice that it eventually became the model for official publication.[13] He believed strongly in the importance of a well ordered line of battle, and he renewed the ban on individual captains breaking the line to pursue individual ships of the enemy. His conservatism is revealed in his direction to his subordinate flag officers to engage their opposite numbers in the enemy line. But he also instructed the captains of ships which found that they could not keep up with the fleet to drop out of the line: 'The Captains of such ships will not be thereby left in a situation less at liberty to distinguish themselves; as they will have an opportunity to render essential service, by placing their ships to advantage when arrived up with the enemy, already engaged with the other part of the fleet.' To place such trust in individual captains was most innovative, and gives Howe a strong claim to have sewn the seeds which, under Jervis, and then Nelson, transformed the navy into 'the band of brothers' that won the battle of the Nile, and went on to win the battles of Copenhagen and Trafalgar.

Howe made provision for the eventuality that irregularities in the enemy line might make it desirable to permit his captains greater latitude in their station keeping. On the signal being made, individual captains were to continue to steer for those ships which in the sequence of the line ought to be their lot, making as little change of course as possible so that they would gradually work into position to engage without either exposing their own ship too greatly, or creating difficulties for the ships astern of them. They were free to engage from windward or leeward as they thought fit. He also issued instructions for two tactical deployments against the rearmost ships of a fleeing fleet, designed to force the enemy admiral to come about to protect his rear. In one variant the British leading ships were to turn away after firing so that the succeeding ships could take their place, and in the other the leading British ship was to lay along side the rearmost ship of the enemy, while the second British ship was to pass on the disengaged side and lay alongside the enemy second from the rear. In this way, the British line would be gradually inverted.

At the same time that Howe, and Rear-Admiral Richard Kempenfelt, were groping their way towards a new system of signals and tactics for the Royal Navy, other British admirals were continuing to issue additional instructions. In 1780 Admiral Rodney issued *Signals and Instructions in Addition* which included a signal ordering 'all the three-decked and heavy ships [to] draw out of their places in the line of battle and form in the van [or rear] of the fleet.'[14] It may have been the origin of Nelson's decision when planning for Trafalgar to place his flag-officers at the head of the columns where the heavier timbering of their first rate flag ships could absorb the punishment the leading ships would inevitably suffer. At the head of his column, Nelson was also in the best position to direct the attack. Most important of all, however, was the psychological necessity that he place himself in the position of most danger.

In April 1782 Rodney and de Grasse fought the last great battle of the American Revolutionary War, near the islets known as the Saints north of Dominica. The battle was technically interesting because the British fleet, for the first time since the Dutch Wars in a major fleet action, cut the enemy line. The tactical movement which effected this, Rodney taking the Centre squadron through a gap in the French line, was probably unpremeditated, and led to captains ahead and astern of the flag taking similar action. St Vincent was convinced that 'Lord Rodney passed through the enemy's line by accident.'[15] Rodney was presented with the opportunity to undertake the action because the enemy fleet had become disorganized in the gun smoke, and he could take

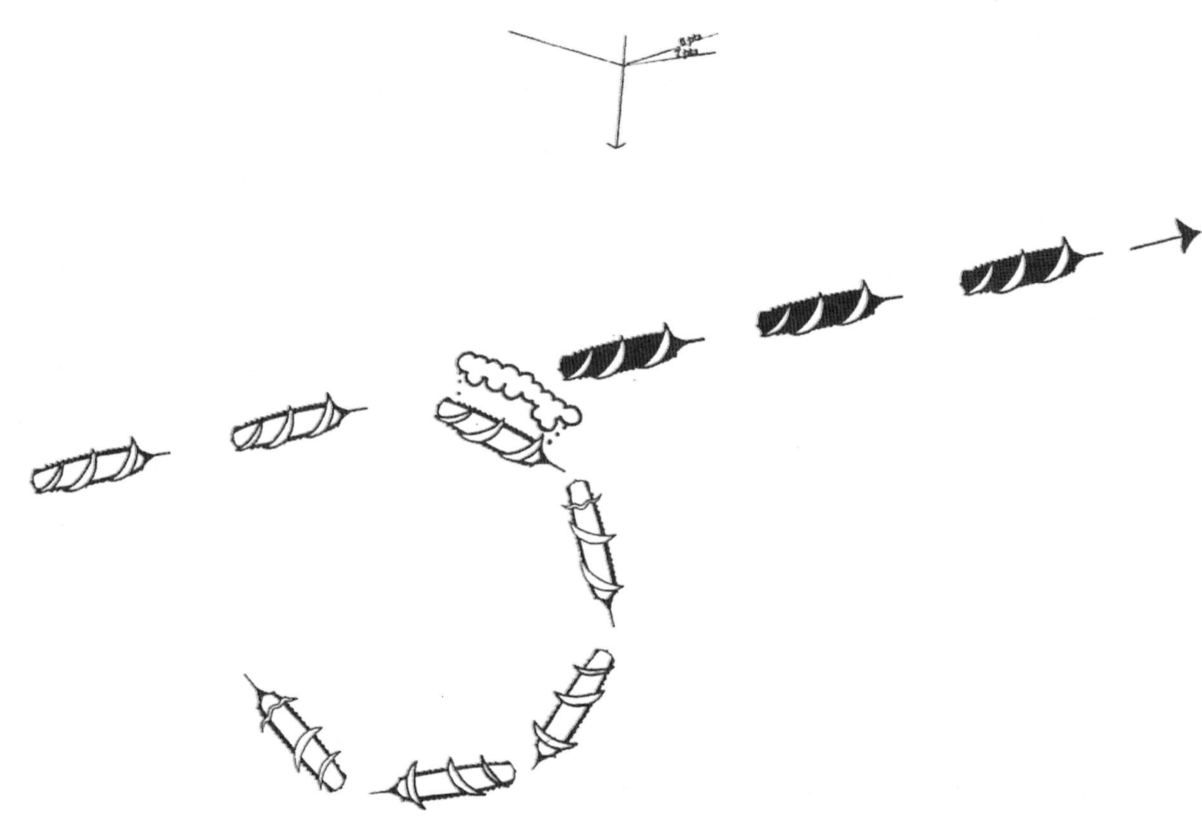

Admiral Howe's methods of attacking the rear of a fleeing enemy fleet, by firing in succession and turning away, or **(OPPOSITE)** by inverting the order of the line as each ship engages the rearmost disengaged ship of the enemy. (Sarah Petite)

advantage of the accident without undue risk because he was conscious of the moral ascendence the British fleet had already gained. As they passed through the French, their gunners were ready to fire into the vulnerable bows and sterns of the ships on either side of the break, and then they were able to hold some of the French between two fires. Their success was a valuable lesson for the future.

Article 3 of the Fighting Instructions had long since established that, if a fleet were forced into the leeward position, it was to attempt to cut the enemy line and so pass through to the windward side. But this had been considered almost as an act of desperation, and as late as the mid-18th century there was no signal in the Fighting Instructions which called for it. The notion that it could be easier to force a general action from the leeward position, and that the best way to do so was by cutting through the enemy line, was published by Clerk of Eldin in 1782. Rodney evidently thought that Clerk had got it right when he emphasized the importance of concentrating force against a part of the enemy line, noting in his own copy of Clerk's *An Essay on Naval Tactics* that 'during all the commands Lord Rodney has been intrusted with he made it a rule to bring his whole force against part of the enemy's and never was so absurd as to bring ship against ship, when the enemy gave him an opportunity of acting otherwise.'[16] The difficulty of forcing a general action from leeward, however, was greater than Clerk acknowledged. As soon as the leeward fleet bore up to close the enemy line it was bound to lose

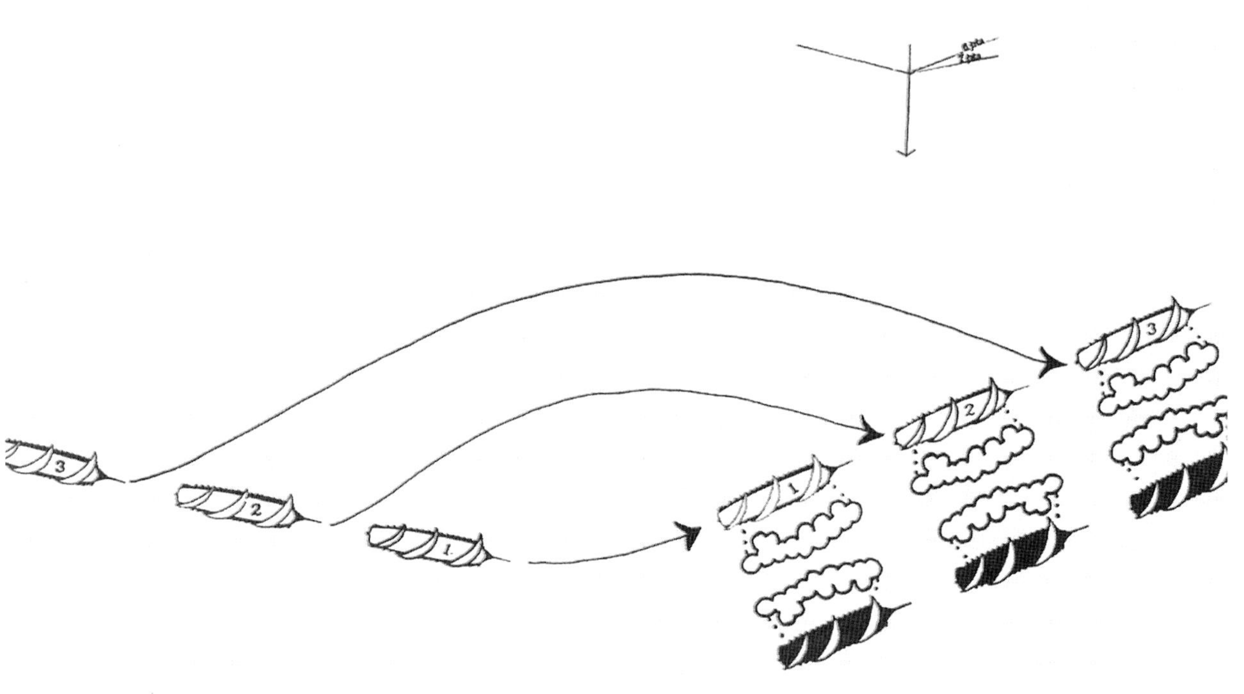

speed. Its exposure to raking fire would be protracted, and there was great probability that by the time it reached the position once occupied by the enemy fleet, it would find itself passing ineffectually across its rear. In a crossing movement such as had happened at the Saints, close action could be less problematic, but in fact it had only occurred as a result of de Grasse's clumsy handling of his fleet. In any case, crossing actions rarely produced decisive results.

Howe's tactical instructions for the Nootka Sound crisis of 1790 were little changed from those he had issued to the American station early in the American War, but he addressed the problem of bring the French to close action, and holding them, by issuing a new signal, number 34, which was to be used 'If when having the Weather Gage of the Enemy the Admiral means to pass between the ships in their line for engaging them to leeward.' This manoeuvre would combine the advantages of the windward position for forcing action on the enemy, and the leeward for preventing them escaping once engaged. It is unclear whether Howe's intent was to make the approach in line of bearing, and so break the enemy line in more than one place. That was what he attempted to do at the battle of The Glorious First of June in 1794, but he tried then to convey his meaning by employing another signal, number 36, indicating that every ship was to steer for her opposite number and engage her. The result confused his fleet, and when the Admiralty reissued the signal in 1799 as its new number 27 it

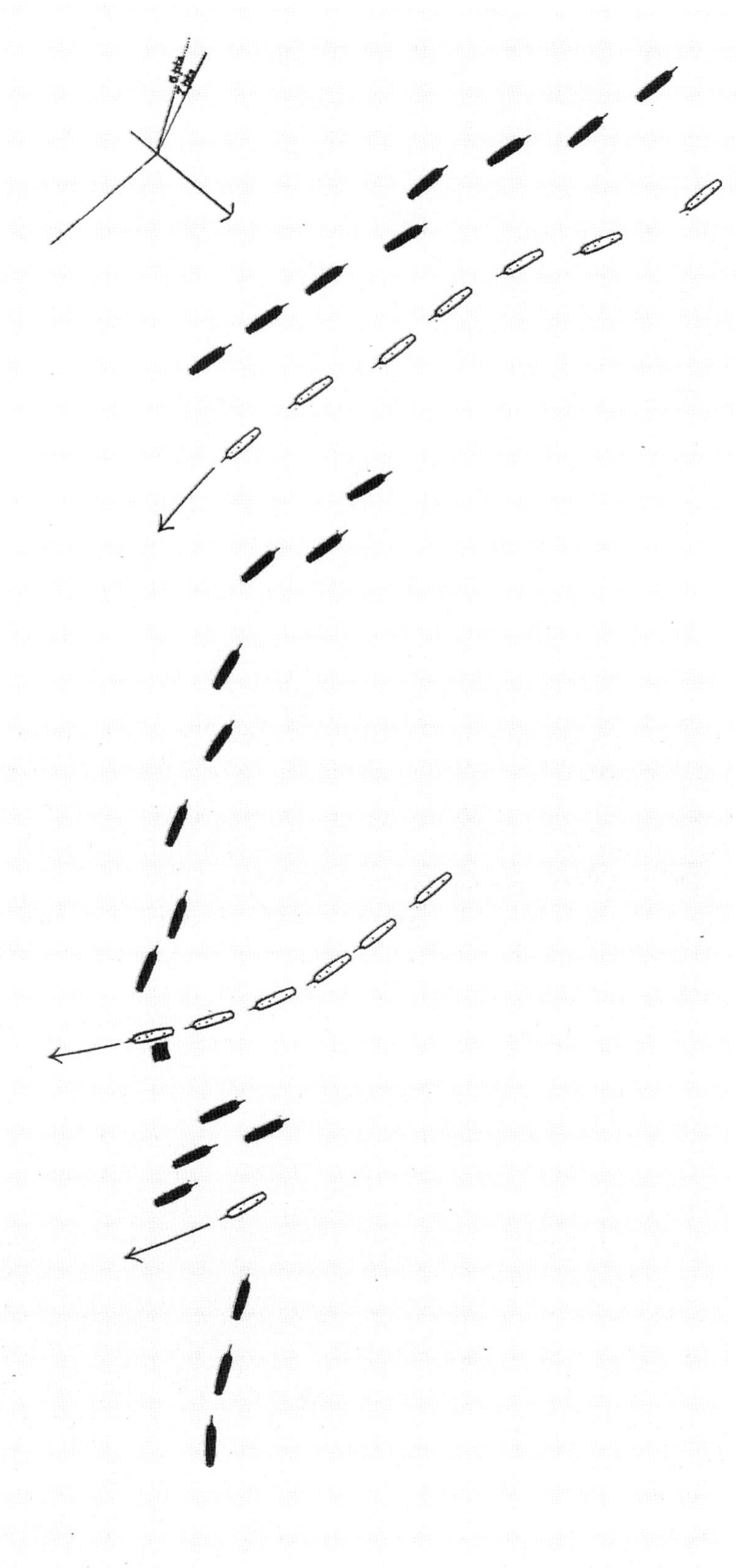

Admiral Rodney's cutting the enemy line from the leeward at the Battle of the Saints in 1782. (Sarah Petite)

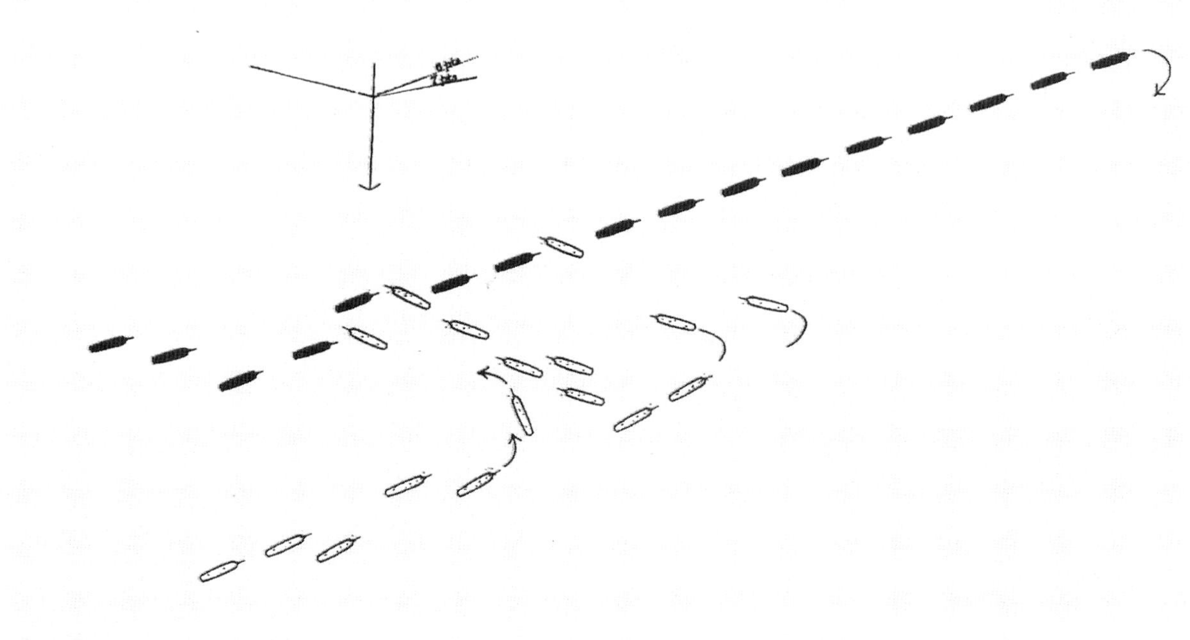

Admiral Howe's cutting the enemy line from the leeward at the Battle of the Glorious First of June, in 1794. (Sarah Petite)

specifically directed captains to 'Break through the enemy's line in all parts where it is practicable, and engage on the other side.' Unfortunately, the Admiralty then contributed its own confusion by using the same signal, with the addition of a blue pendant, to order the fleet in close order line-ahead to cut through the enemy in one place only, and presumably from the leeward.[17]

The latitude Howe permitted his captains certainly had its limits, and the numerical signalling system he introduced, which enabled the fleet to employ more sophisticated tactics, also enabled admirals to exert more control.[18] It employed a hoist of two flags to signify digits and tens, with a pendant for the hundreds. Ten numerical flags were required, and substitute pendants for repeating numbers, as well as for the hundreds. The use of pendants overcame the problem of distinguishing a hoist of three flags. In this way most three-digit numbers could be signalled, using flags and pendants flown from whatever position in the rigging they could best be seen. Each paragraph in the sailing and fighting instructions was numbered. The great advantages of converting signals into numbers were the speed with which they could be read, and the ease with which new signals could be incorporated. It was also easier to change signals if there was a risk that the enemy had obtained a copy of the signal book. The adoption of a signalling system which enabled the flags and pendants to be flown from the best position for them to be seen, rather than the older system which required flags to be flown from particular parts of the rigging, had obvious tactical advantages. On the other hand, the three-flag hoists were relatively difficult to distinguish at a distance. A supplementary system of 'distance signals' had to be devised. These used a limited number of flags and shapes which were flown from the fore, main, and mizzen mastheads. They were slower to use, but could be read at ranges which made it difficult to distinguish colours. It was by this method that Nelson received the signal that the enemy were leaving Cadiz on the eve of Trafalgar. Nelson was also able to make use of a supplementary signalling system devised by Admiral Popham following his experience off Copenhagen in 1800 when he used numerical signals to refer to words in a dictionary. This, for the first time, enabled an admiral to send signals in plain language which he had not previously issued in writing.

Earlier, during the American War, Howe had provided the fleet with a system of night signals for frigates on reconnaissance which gave Nelson the means of maintaining a continuous observation of the enemy in Cadiz in the days before Trafalgar.[19] The frigates engaged in the service were to carry distinguishing lights so placed that they could be seen by the fleet off-shore, but not by the enemy. They were to be especially careful to display their lights if the enemy were seen to be drawing towards or away from the fleet. This set of signals was reissued when Howe assumed command of the Channel Fleet in 1782, and became a permanent feature of all his future additional instructions.

The tactics Nelson used at Trafalgar benefited from the experience of Rodney and Howe, and from the use made of the new ideas by Admiral Jervis, Earl St Vincent, and by Admiral Duncan. When Jervis encountered the Spanish fleet on St Valentines day 1797 off Cape St Vincent, he profited by the new ideas in tactics when he did deliberately what Rodney had done accidentally, and steered to divide the Spanish line from to leeward. And when the manoeuvre orders he gave his fleet proved inadequate to prevent the Spaniards reuniting their line, Nelson as a senior captain broke with the older tradition of slavish obedience in a manner Howe might have approved and which Jervis did later endorse, using his initiative to wear out of line and block the Spanish movement. When in October of the same year Duncan met the Dutch fleet, he ordered his fleet to attack in line abreast, pass through the Dutch line, and prevent their escape to leeward, the tactic Howe had attempted at the First of June. Nelson's attack in two columns at Trafalgar to punch through the Franco-Spanish line from to windward and prevent their escape to leeward was no more than a variant on the tactics used by his brother admirals, tactics which were intended to overcome the limitations inherent in ships of the line, armed with short-ranged smooth-bore cannon.

Nevertheless, although the evolving tactical tradition of the Royal Navy was implicit in the tactics Nelson employed for the battle off Cape Trafalgar, it can also be said that he was building on his own tactical experience, even though Trafalgar was the first battle Nelson commanded in which his enemy was free to manoeuvre. At the battle of the Nile in 1798 his major contribution to the victory was the moral confidence he had imparted to his captains in the months he had known them, which inspired the initiative they showed in carrying out a ruthless and precipitant action in the gathering darkness close to shoals and the Egyptian coast. At Copenhagen in 1801 Nelson was able to provide his captains with detailed written orders for a more methodical action against the moored

Danish fleet, but he also set his captains a standard of complete commitment to the task which inspired their devoted support. Central to this conception was the belief that close mutual support, efficient ship handling, and good gunnery, were more important than good station keeping and fleet manoeuvre. His tactics emphasized momentum and morale in precisely the same way as was seen in the infantry tactics of the French Revolutionary army under the command of Napoleon's marshals. Napoleon won battle after battle in this way, until his columns came up against a well disciplined line of British regular infantry. Nelson's tactics would similarly have been defeated by a skilful French admiral commanding a fleet of the pre-revolutionary Marine, but that was not the enemy Nelson faced at Trafalgar. His tactics were suited to the occasion; especially to his knowledge of the professional abilities and morale of his fleet and that of his enemy. Had he realized, however, that Admiral Villeneuve was determined to fight if he could not get clean away, he might have given his fleet more time to get into order for mutual support. The battle was bitterly fought, and technically his tactics proved less than perfect, but at their heart was the inspiration of a determined leader who trusted and consulted with his captains, and it was that which carried the day.

CHAPTER SIX

HMS *VICTORY*

PETER GOODWIN

Preserved at Portsmouth today, the *Victory* is the only surviving warship that fought during the French Revolutionary and Napoleonic Wars. As a first rate 100-gun ship of the line, *Victory* was, in her day, the most formidable fighting machine, encompassing all the technical advances of the developing industrial age. Primarily a manoeuvrable floating gun battery, she could deliver a single broadside weight of over half a ton of iron at an opponent.

Victory's story starts in December 1758 when Parliament voted funding to build more ships to supplement the fleet during the Seven Years' War (1756–63). A formal order to build 12 ships was submitted by the Navy Board on 6 June 1759.[1]

Yet unnamed, this 100-gun ship was designed by Sir Thomas Slade, Surveyor of the Navy 1755–71. Perhaps the most notable warship designer of the 18th century, Slade was an innovative man who introduced vast improvements in ship design. Ignoring the conservative views of the Navy Board and working directly in collaboration with Admiral Lord Anson, Slade with his kinsman, Benjamin Slade, assistant master shipwright at Plymouth, based much of his improvements on the careful analysis of captured French ships.

Under the supervision of Master Shipwright John Lock, her keel was laid down in the Old Single Dock at the Royal Dockyard at Chatham, Kent, 23 July 1759. The year 1759, the *Annus Mirabilis*, or 'marvellous year', was the turning point of the war for Britain: victories had been won at Quebec, Minden, Lagos and Quiberon Bay. These facts may well have been instrumental to the Admiralty officially authorizing that Lock's ship be named *Victory* on 30 October 1760. When Lock died in 1762, construction work was completed by his successor, Edward Allin. Although it was intended to complete the ship within 30 months, in 1763 the Treaty of Paris ended the war, thus the rate of work on *Victory* was reduced. Completed after six years, *Victory* was launched 7 May 1765. Her overall cost was £63,176. 3s. 0d, amounting to £4,524,665 at the time of writing.[2]

OPPOSITE
HMS *Victory*'s mainmast soars into the sky. The quality of her restoration and her status as a serving warship testifies to the fact that something of Trafalgar remains very much alive. (By kind permission of the Commanding Officer of HMS *Victory*)

In all, some 6,000 trees had been expended in her construction which at 50 cubic feet per load, or tree, relates to 300,000 cubic feet of timber before conversion into specific ship components. Collectively these 6,000 trees, many aged between 80 and 120 years, would have been cut down from 100 acres of land. Ninety per cent of this quantity of timber was oak; the selected curved or 'compass' oak being used for her stempost, futtocks, frames, knees, breasthooks and deckhooks and so on. Because of her size, the sternpost was made from one single oak tree. While most of this oak was taken from the Wealden forests of Kent and Sussex, some of the straight oak used for her beams, external planking and internal longitudinal strengtheners, may have been imported from Dantzig, modern Gdansk. Sussex oak was considered the best wood for shipbuilding. Oak was also used for the planking of the main, or lower gun deck. Six baulks of elm some 25ft long and 21in. square in cross section were bolted and scarphed together to form her keel, and because of its properties elm was also used for the lower hull planking. Fir, lighter in weight, was used for the planking of the upper decks and bulkheads – the walls that divided the ship into compartments.[3]

As the Seven Years' War, for which she had been built, ended in 1763, *Victory* was laid up in 'ordinary' (reserve) for 13 years before she was commissioned for active sea service in 1778 to fight in the War of American Independence.[4]

Commissioned in February 1778, *Victory* became the flagship of Admiral Keppel. On 23 July Keppel fought an indecisive battle against D'Orvillier's French fleet off Ushant. For the next three years she served as flagship for Admirals Hardy, Geary, Drake and Parker.[5]

To comply with new legislation, the *Victory* was docked in March 1780 and sheathed with copper plating to combat ship-worm, *teredo navalis*, and marine growth. This innovation also improved her speed. In all, the hull was sheathed with approximately 3,923 copper plates, each measuring 4ft (1.22m) in length and 14in. (35.56cm) in width. Plating came in two sizes according to where it was applied: 28oz (0.79kg) and 32oz (0.91kg) per square foot. In all, each of the thinner plates weighed in total a little over 8lb (3.5kg) each, while the heavier plates weighed 9⅓lb (4.2kg). The sheathing plates were nailed to the hull planking with copper nails 1in. (3.8cm) long and quarter of an inch (6.4mm) in diameter. On average each plate was held with 140 nails, thus the total used was approximately 549,220.[6]

The year 1781 saw the *Victory* under the flag of Admiral Kempenfelt who, on 13 December fell in with a French fleet off Ushant. The French, bound from Brest to the West Indies, were escorting a convoy of troopships. Though Kempenfelt's squadron was numerically inferior, he captured the entire convoy from under the escort's noses. Flying the flag of Admiral Howe, in October 1782, *Victory* was in action off Cape Spartel and the Relief of Gibraltar. After the war, the ship was refitted in March 1783 at a cost of £15,372, 19s. 9d. At this stage her quarter-deck armament was modified, the 6-pounder guns being replaced with 12-pounders. Her sides, previously painted 'bright' with rosin above the lower-deck ports were now painted a dull yellow ochre. The area below remained painted black. In 1787

ITEM	IMP. TONS	METRIC TONNES
Estimated total weight of 3923 copper plates	15.30	15.05
Estimated weight of nails @ 0.16 oz (4.5 g) each	2.43	2.39
Total weight	17.73	17.45

she underwent a 'large repair' costing £37,523. 17s. 1d. Re-commissioned under Howe in 1789, she became the flagship of Lord Hood the following year.[7]

Storm clouds brewed over Europe. As a result of supporting the American cause, France herself was hurled into her own bloody revolution in 1789. The outcome was to have a devastating effect on Europe as a whole. With the opening of the French Revolutionary War in 1793, *Victory* became the flagship of Lord Hood who was appointed Commander-in-Chief of the Mediterranean fleet. While blockading Toulon, the ship was engaged in capturing the French vessels within this port and in July took part in the siege of San Fiorenzo, Calvi and Bastia on the Island of Corsica. It was during these actions that a young captain, Horatio Nelson, made his name.

In 1794 *Victory* returned to Plymouth and Hood, his health shattered, lowered his flag. After another refit in 1795, the ship returned to the Mediterranean under Admiral Man. That July *Victory* led the offensive in the unsuccessful action off Hyères where Admiral Hotham failed to fully engage the Toulon fleet. The consequences of his withdrawal were disastrous as Britain abandoned the Mediterranean. Nelson played a minor role at this battle commanding the 64-gun *Agamemnon*. After a brief command under Linzee, Admiral Sir John Jervis, later Earl St Vincent, hoisted his broad pendant on *Victory* the following December. On 14 February 1797, off Cape St Vincent, he led *Victory* with 14 ships of the line against a Spanish Squadron comprising 27 ships under Córdoba. A decisive victory was won. Much was due to Nelson's intuition who, now a Commodore in the 74-gun *Captain*, quitting the line of battle, strategically cut off the enemy's escape. Nelson engaged and boarded the 112-gun *San Josef*, then, using this ship as a 'patent boarding bridge', captured the neighbouring 80-gun *San Nicholas*. This action earned Nelson a knighthood, and promotion to rear-admiral.[8]

In October 1797 *Victory* returned to England and was surveyed at Portsmouth. Now 32 years old and battle weary the ship was sent to Chatham to await her fate. On 8 December, considered unfit for service, *Victory* was ordered to be converted to a hospital ship, and ultimate disposal. Fortune intervened when the First Rate *Impregnable* was lost near Chichester on 8 October 1799, creating an urgent need for an additional three-decked ship within the Channel fleet. Consequently, *Victory* was given a new lease of life. The survey revealed that she was 'in want of a middling repair' at an estimate of £23,500.[9]

Thomas Hardy was the Captain of HMS *Victory* at the fateful moment when the battle was won and when the hero Nelson died.

Refitting commenced at Chatham in 1800. A second survey highlighted considerable disorder: various parts of the hull required rebuilding, over 60 per cent of her knees needed refastening or replacing and many port lids needed refitting. To comply with recent improvements, her open stern galleries were removed and the entire stern was closed in. Two extra ports were cut on her lower gun deck and the magazines were lined in copper, conforming to current practice. The heavy ornate figurehead, now very rotten, was substituted with a simpler, lighter design. This, together with reduced ornate work on the stern, corresponded to contemporary restrictions on carving expenses. Composite masts, furnished with iron hoops, replaced her pole masts. The ship was also repainted with the black and yellow livery as seen today, albeit the port lids remained yellow. These were later painted black, producing the much-imitated 'Nelson chequer' pattern.

By March 1801, war had exhausted Britain and France and under the new administration of Henry Addington Britain negotiated a short-lived peace with France, ratified by the Peace of Amiens, signed on 27 March 1802. Now less urgent, work on *Victory* continued until she was finally undocked on 11 April 1803. The cost of this 'great repair' had now amounted to £70,933, some 66 per cent higher than originally estimated. In anticipation that hostilities would inevitably reopen with France, orders had been sent on 15 March to fit *Victory* for service. Ready for sea, all her heavy lower-deck 42-pounder guns had been replaced with lighter and more manageable 32-pounders.[10]

Re-commissioned under Captain Samuel Sutton on 9 April 1803, *Victory* sailed for Portsmouth on 14 May. Hostilities with France reopened on 16 May 1803, with an immediate threat of invasion. As the newly appointed Commander-in-Chief of the Mediterranean fleet, Vice-Admiral Lord Nelson hoisted his flag in the *Victory* at Portsmouth on 18 May but as the ship was not yet ready Nelson lowered his flag two days later and sailed for the Mediterranean in the frigate *Amphion* commanded by Captain Thomas Masterman Hardy. Provisionally appointed as flagship for Admiral Cornwallis stationed off Ushant, *Victory* sailed later. Finding that Cornwallis did not require the ship, Sutton continued into the Mediterranean, where, on 31 July, Nelson joined the *Victory* taking Captain Hardy with him in command, Sutton transferring into the *Amphion*.[11]

For the next year, Nelson blockaded the French fleet in Toulon to prevent them escaping to join forces with other squadrons based in France's Atlantic arsenals. Periodically ships of Nelson's squadron would retreat to repair at a safe anchorage of Agincourt Sound, Corsica. It was on such an occasion, 19 May 1805, that frigates, Nelson's 'eyes of the fleet', suddenly approached, signalling that the Toulon fleet under Villeneuve had sailed. *Victory* weighed anchor immediately and the 'great chase' began that was to lead the *Victory* first eastward to Alexandria, then across to the Atlantic and back. With no news, Nelson quit the Mediterranean, passing the Straits of Gibraltar on 4 May. Napoleon's invasion plan was beginning to unfold, with Villeneuve sailing to the West Indies to draw the English from the Channel. Nelson followed in hot pursuit and foiled Napoleon's intentions. He finally ran the enemy to ground at Cadiz where the combined French and Spanish fleet was blockaded. *Victory*, with a fatigued Nelson, dropped anchor at Spithead on 18 August. After brief respite the *Victory* sailed with Nelson from Portsmouth on 15 September and joined the blockading fleet under Collingwood off Cadiz on the 28th.[12]

Much damaged, the *Victory* was towed to Gibraltar and finally returned to Portsmouth, arriving on 4 December bearing her fallen hero. After repairs at Chatham costing £9,936, the *Victory* was re-commissioned in March 1808 as flagship of Admiral Saumarez, undertaking operations supporting the Swedes in the Baltic campaign. Next she was sent to Spain to evacuate the remnants of Sir John Moore's army from Corunna, returning on 23 January 1809. April saw her back in the Baltic for the blockade of Kronstadt, and later Karlscrona. The year 1811 saw the ship under Yorke transporting reinforcements to Lisbon for Wellington's army in the Peninsular War. Finally, after further campaigning in the Baltic, and now 47 years old, she finally returned to Portsmouth on 4 December 1812 and 'paid off' 16 days later.[13]

King George V visits HMS *Victory* in 1922 at the beginning of her restoration.

Between 1814 and 1816 *Victory* was rebuilt with much alteration. The ornate beakhead bulkhead had been replaced with a more practical round bow, her bulwarks were built up higher and her sides were painted with black and white horizontal stripes. As war with France had finally ended, she was placed back into 'ordinary' (reserve) until 1824 when she took on a new role as flagship for the Port Admiral and later tender to the Duke of Wellington. In 1831 the ship was listed for disposal but Hardy, now First Sea Lord, at his wife's request refused to sign and gave *Victory* her second reprieve. Refitted in 1888, she was re-coppered for the fifteenth and last time. The following year she became flagship for the Commander-in-Chief Naval Home Command.

Disaster struck in 1903 when *Victory* was accidentally rammed by *Neptune* which was under tow to the breakers. After emergency docking she went back to her familiar moorings. This event, together with the ensuing Centenary of Trafalgar, raised questions about her future, though the subject was put on hold for the duration of the First World War. Finally, through a national appeal raised by the Society for Nautical Research, *Victory* was put into her current dock on 12 January 1922 and restored to her 1805 appearance as a living monument to the Royal Navy. Final restoration, together with a highly integrated interpretation programme, commenced in 1991, made the ship ready for the Bicentennial of the battle of Trafalgar in 2005. As the world's longest serving ship in commission, she continued to serve as the flagship for the Second Sea Lord/Commander-in Chief Naval Home Command as well as a public attraction.[14]

To operate a ship of this magnitude required a crew of some 850 men including marines. Fully armed, stored and provisioned, *Victory* displaced a weight 3,500 tons. With a sail area equal to one and a third the size of a football pitch, under certain wind conditions she could attain a speed of 11 knots, about 12.5mph.[15]

VICTORY'S STATISTICS AT TRAFALGAR

Length overall (figurehead to taffrail)	227ft 6in.	69.34m
Length on the gun deck	186ft	56.70m
Length of the keel for tonnage	152ft 3 5/8in.	46.43m
Moulded breadth	51ft 6in.	69.34m
Extreme breadth	51ft 10in.	56.70m
Depth in hold *	21ft 6in. *	19.65m
Burthen	2,162 tons	2,196.60 tonnes
Displacement	3,500 tons	3,556.00 tonnes
Draught afore	23ft 9in.	7.24m
Draught abaft	24ft 5in.	7.44m
Average Speed	8 knots	9mph
Highest Speed Recorded	11 knots	12.5mph
Complement	850	
Complement (at Trafalgar)	820 (excluding Nelson)	

*This internal measurement, taken from the underside of the lower gun deck planking to the inner planking near the centre of the hold excludes the orlop deck, the orlop not being classified as a proper deck in the true sense.[16]

The quarterdeck of HMS *Victory* includes a brass plate marking the point where Nelson fell. (By kind permission of the Commanding Officer of HMS *Victory*)

Victory's masts were made from fir, pine or spruce, this type of wood being both light in weight and flexible. Mast timber was imported from the Baltic States and Norway. When she was first built, each lower mast was made from a single tree 3ft in diameter. This form of mast was called a 'pole mast'. Timber for pole masts was imported from New England but with the American War of Independence this supply was stopped. This was resolved by introducing an alternative system of mast-making which had already been adopted by the French. Known as a 'composite mast', the lower masts (main and fore) were manufactured using between seven and nine smaller trees, carefully shaped and joined together to form the required diameter.[17]

When *Victory* sailed from Portsmouth in September 1805 she was rigged with approximately 22,880 fathoms (26 miles or 41.83km) of hemp running and standing rigging, operated using 768 blocks, the largest being 26in. long, the smallest 6in. Additional blocks were used for a variety of functions throughout the ship; anchors and their associated gear, ship's boats, and storing ship. Besides carrying a good quantity of spares, a further 628 were used for the ropes operating the guns.[18]

Cleanliness and order on the upper gun deck: efficiency and high standards of training were to give the English the edge over their opponents at Trafalgar. (By kind permission of the Commanding Officer of HMS *Victory*)

The maximum number of sails *Victory* could be set was 37, including her staysails and studding sails. This vast amount of canvas gave her a sail area of 6,510 square yards (5,468.4 square metres). However, it was very unlikely that all her sails were set at the same time. According to the Boatswain's stores muster for March 1805, a total of 59 sails (including spares) were carried on the ship. Sails were made from canvas, most of which was manufactured in mills in Dundee, Scotland, Northern Ireland and Dorset. The canvas was made up by hand at the Royal Dockyards. *Victory's* sails were made at the sail loft at Chatham Dockyard and would have taken about 20 men 83 days to produce. Her original shot-riddled fore topsail from the battle of Trafalgar is now exhibited at Portsmouth.[19]

ARMAMENT: AT THE BATTLE OF TRAFALGAR *VICTORY* CARRIED THE FOLLOWING GUNS:

Lower Gun Deck	30 × 32-pounders
Middle Gun Deck	28 × 24-pounders
Upper Gun Deck	30 × long 12-pounders
Quarter Deck	12 × short 12-pounders
Forecastle	2 × medium 12-pounders 2 × 68-pounder carronades
Other	1 × 18-pounder carronade*

*Carried in storage for use in the launch.

The overall weight of a broadside fired by *Victory* was 1,148lb (522kg). When the *Victory* first opened fire at the Battle of Trafalgar, all of the guns, with the exception of the carronades on the port side, were treble-shotted. This gave her an opening broadside weight of 3,240lb (1473kg) – nearly 1.5 tons (1.6 tonnes) of iron. The velocity that this mass of iron left the ship was approximately 1,600ft (487.7m) per second.[20]

To reiterate, *Victory* needed a crew of 850 to operate the ship safely; however, at the battle of Trafalgar the total complement, excluding Admiral Nelson, was only 820. As admiral, Nelson lived in quarters comprising four separate compartments – day cabin, dining cabin, bed place and steerage, colloquially called the great cabin, which occupied one quarter the length of the upper gun deck. There were 10 commissioned naval officers of which most lived in the wardroom at the after end of the middle gun deck, while Captain Hardy had a day cabin, dining cabin and bed place at the after end of the quarter deck under the poop. On board were also four commissioned marine officers who lived in the wardroom.

Two views of the Great Cabin show the ample quarters that were provided for Admiral Nelson. (By kind permission of the Commanding Officer of HMS *Victory*)

Victory was also served by 44 non-commissioned (warrant) officers, the senior of which was the ship's Master, Thomas Atkinson, who was responsible for the sailing and navigation of the ship. The rest of this number was made up of the Boatswain, Gunner, Carpenter, Purser, Chaplain, Surgeon, Assistant Surgeon, Surgeon's Mate, seven Master's Mates, Admiral's Secretary, Captain's Secretary, Secretary's Clerk, the Agent Victualler and his Clerk, 22 midshipmen and the Ship's Cook (lowest warrant officer status). While half of these men had individual cabins and others shared the gun room at the after end of the lower gun deck, the midshipmen lived together in the after cockpit of the orlop deck.

The captain of the ship was provided with a day cabin and dining cabin as well as a bed space under the poop. (By kind permission of the Commanding Officer of HMS *Victory*)

The main body of the *Victory*'s ship's company, 604 personnel in all, comprised 80 petty officers, 204 able seamen, 195 ordinary seamen, 90 landsmen, four servants and 31 boys. Among this group were the sailmakers, ropemakers, carpenter's crew, coopers, armourers and many other specialists that were necessary for the maintenance of the ship. Most of these people lived and slept on the lower gun deck, divided into groups directed by their watch or station within the ship. Albeit that hanging space per hammock in the navy varied from 14 to 18 depending on the ship, in *Victory* it was set at 16in.; this gave room for some 470 hammocks, the remainder finding space elsewhere. While most of the boys were 14 years old, the younger ones (the youngest being 12) lived under the watchful eye of the gunner in the gun room. Meals were taken at tables slung from the beams between the guns and at every other available space throughout the lower gun deck, each table comprising two individual messes of four or six men.[21]

Also in *Victory* was a company of 149 marines from the Chatham Division, comprising four sergeants, seven corporals and 138 privates. These men messed and slept separately on the middle gun deck. Their four marine officers, comprising a Captain, two lieutenants, and one second lieutenant, all lived in the wardroom.[22]

Whether seaman or marine, each man ate reasonably well, receiving three meals per day. Although the quality of the food varied, especially when a ship had been at sea for a long period, there was generally plenty of it. Irrespective of general conceptions, on average each seaman received a daily ration containing

Hammocks arranged in the lower gun deck. The arrangement of watches meant that adjacent hammocks were not all used at the same time. (By kind permission of the Commanding Officer of HMS *Victory*)

Eating utensils on tables adjacent to the guns underline the importance of good nutrition for a hard-working crew. In addition to a high carbohydrate diet of 'hard tack', the men were given generous quantities of beer and wine. (By kind permission of the Commanding Officer of HMS *Victory*)

between 4,000 and 5,000 calories. This was important, as most of the work on a man-of-war was very labour-intensive. Bread, which came in the form of a very hard biscuit, called 'hard tack', had to be softened with water before eating. Although the basic diet comprised salted meat, peas, oatmeal, cheese and butter, supplemented with raisins and molasses, every opportunity was made to procure fresh vegetables and meat from the victualling ships or from land. Equally important, the ship carried large quantities of lemons or limes, which, high in vitamin C, were used to combat scurvy. Extant ship's logbooks record that fresh foodstuff and livestock was frequently embarked.[23]

The main drink supplied was water, beer, rum and wine. In addition, brandy, Madeira and sometimes port would have been carried for the officers, but usually at their own expense. The ship could carry up to 355 tons (360.6 tonnes) of water. Water was kept in large casks called leaguers stored in the lower level of the hold. As water did not keep well at sea, and deteriorated after a month or so, fresh water was embarked at every opportunity. This was done by conveying empty casks in boats ashore for refilling. The most common drink was beer, each man receiving one gallon (4.5lit) per day. The maximum capacity of beer carried was

50 tons (50.8 tonnes). The alternative ration to beer was either 2 pints (1.12lit) of wine or half a pint (0.28lit) of rum or brandy. Rum was watered down with two parts water to one part rum: this was known as 'grog'.[24]

Victory was equipped with a designated sick berth, or 'bay', sited on the starboard side of the upper gun deck underneath the forecastle. This area, comprising a ward and dispensary, was divided off with canvas and wooden screens. Here, men suffering from disease or injury could be isolated from the cramped confines of the lower deck, and more importantly, from the rest of the crew to prevent contagion. For practical reasons there were many advantages for placing the sick berth up on this deck: these were fresh air, nearby toilet facilities, warmth and ready supply of hot water from the galley.[25]

VICTORY AT THE BATTLE OF TRAFALGAR

Once the order had been given to clear the ship for action, all bulkheads subdividing the ship were taken down or hinged up to the beams out of the way and the ship was stripped of all superfluous gear. While most items such as mess equipment, tables and other furniture, sea chests and so on were struck down into the ship's hold, some items were jettisoned overboard including, according to the records, eight hen coops and one turkey coop.[26]

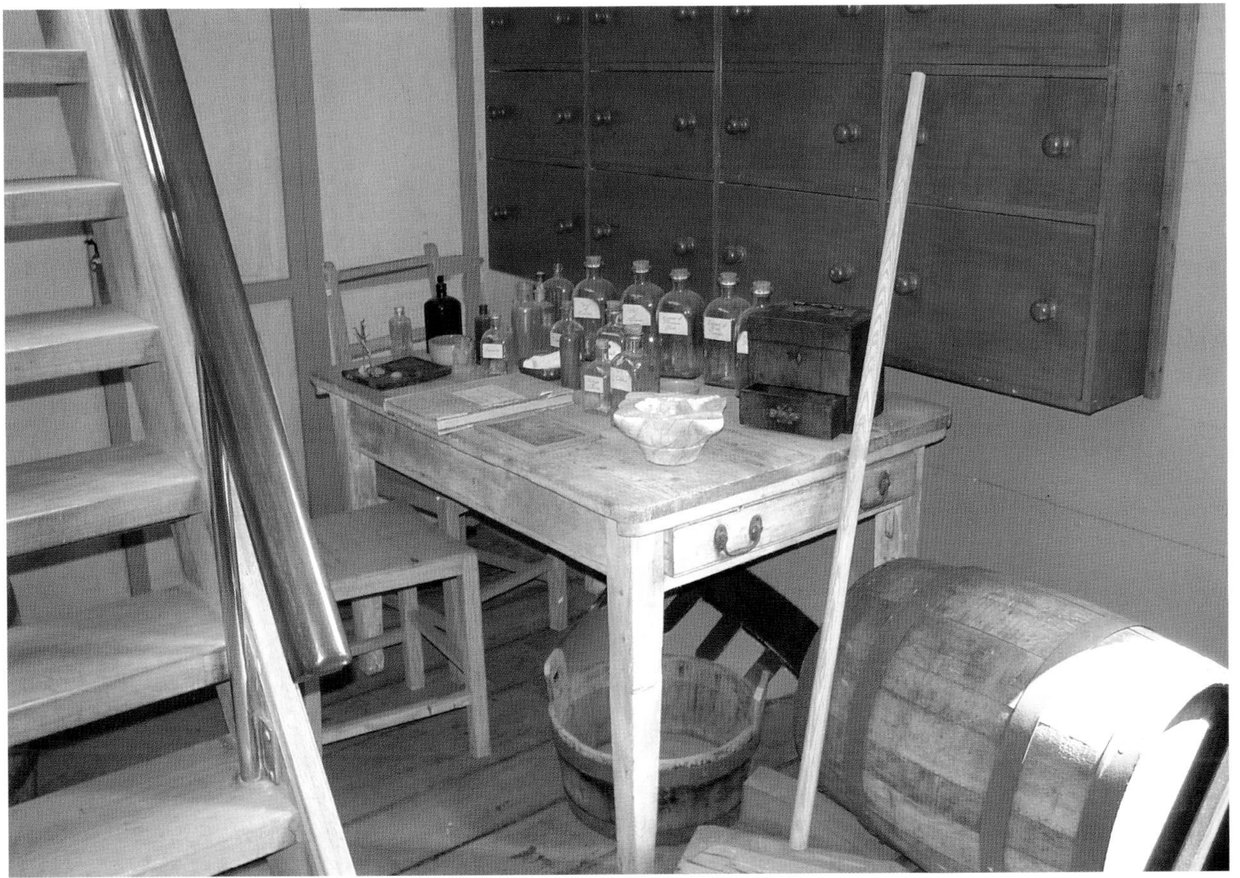

The dispensary under the forecastle was adjacent to hammocks made up with fresh sheets. Sun and fresh air would have contributed to a speedy recovery. (By kind permission of the Commanding Officer of HMS *Victory*)

DECK OR LOCATION	OFFICERS	SEAMEN AND MARINES	TOTAL
Poop	1 signal lieutenant, 4 marine officers, 1 midshipman	3 yeoman signallers, 1 sergeant, 8 marines	18
Quarter deck	Admiral, Captain, Master, First Lieutenant, 4 midshipmen, Admiral's secretary	7 quartermasters, 4 quartermaster's mates, 6 gun captains, 54 guns' crew (seamen and marines), 4 boys	84
Aloft in the main, fore, & mizzen tops		3 captains of the tops, 14 topmen	17
Forecastle	1 lieutenant, Boatswain, 2 midshipmen	2 gun captains, 13 guns' crew (seamen), 1 boy	20
Upper gun deck	2 lieutenants, 5 midshipmen	1 mate, 4 quarter gunners, 15 gun captains, 135 guns' crew (seamen & marines), 9 boys	171
Middle gun deck	2 lieutenants, 5 midshipmen	2 mates, 4 quarter gunners, 14 gun captains, 154 guns' crew (seamen & marines), 9 boys	190
Lower gun deck	2 lieutenants, 5 midshipmen	2 mates, 4 quarter gunners, 15 gun captains, 210 guns crew (seamen & marines), 9 boys	247
Orlop – after-Cockpit and wings	Surgeon, Assistant surgeon, Purser, Chaplain	6, including Loblolly boys, clerks and so on	10
Orlop – after-hanging magazine		1 yeoman of the powder room, 1 landsman	2
Orlop – fore-hanging magazine		1 yeoman of the powder room, 1 landsman	2
Grand Magazine		1 Gunner's mate, 1 Cooper, 4 Seamen	6
Grand magazine light room		Cook, Master at Arms	2
Ammunition train		72 Misc. landsmen, supply and secretariat ratings	52
TOTAL			**821**

When going to 'quarters', each man had a specific task and place of duty within the ship during battle; this was written up in the ship's Watch and Station

Bill. As *Victory* sailed towards the Combined Fleet, her men were stationed at quarters throughout as shown in the table on page 158.

Including Lord Nelson, *Victory* sustained 19.4 per cent casualties during the battle, comprising 54 killed and 102 wounded. Within four days, three more had died, one of which was a boy, bringing the toll to 57 dead. These figures equate to 6.9 and 12.42 per cent of *Victory's* crew.

During the battle *Victory* expended 7.67 tons of gunpowder and 27.87 tons of round shot, the latter amounting to 2,669 rounds. These quantities represented 12.91 per cent of the 35 tons of gunpowder she carried when fully stored and 23.23 per cent of the 120 tons of shot generally carried. In addition her crew fired off 186 grape shot and just 35 bar shot, most of these items being fired from her 12-pounders.[27]

Besides personnel, *Victory* was severely damaged, suffering considerable loss in masts and rigging. In all she lost her entire mizzen mast together with its various topmasts and yards, gaff and driver booms. She also lost a fore yard, both spritsail yards and flying jib booms. Although retained till after the battle,

The magazine was lined with copper to prevent rats getting in, while the powder barrels themselves were rested on leather skins to prevent chafing or sparks. (By kind permission of the Commanding Officer of HMS *Victory*)

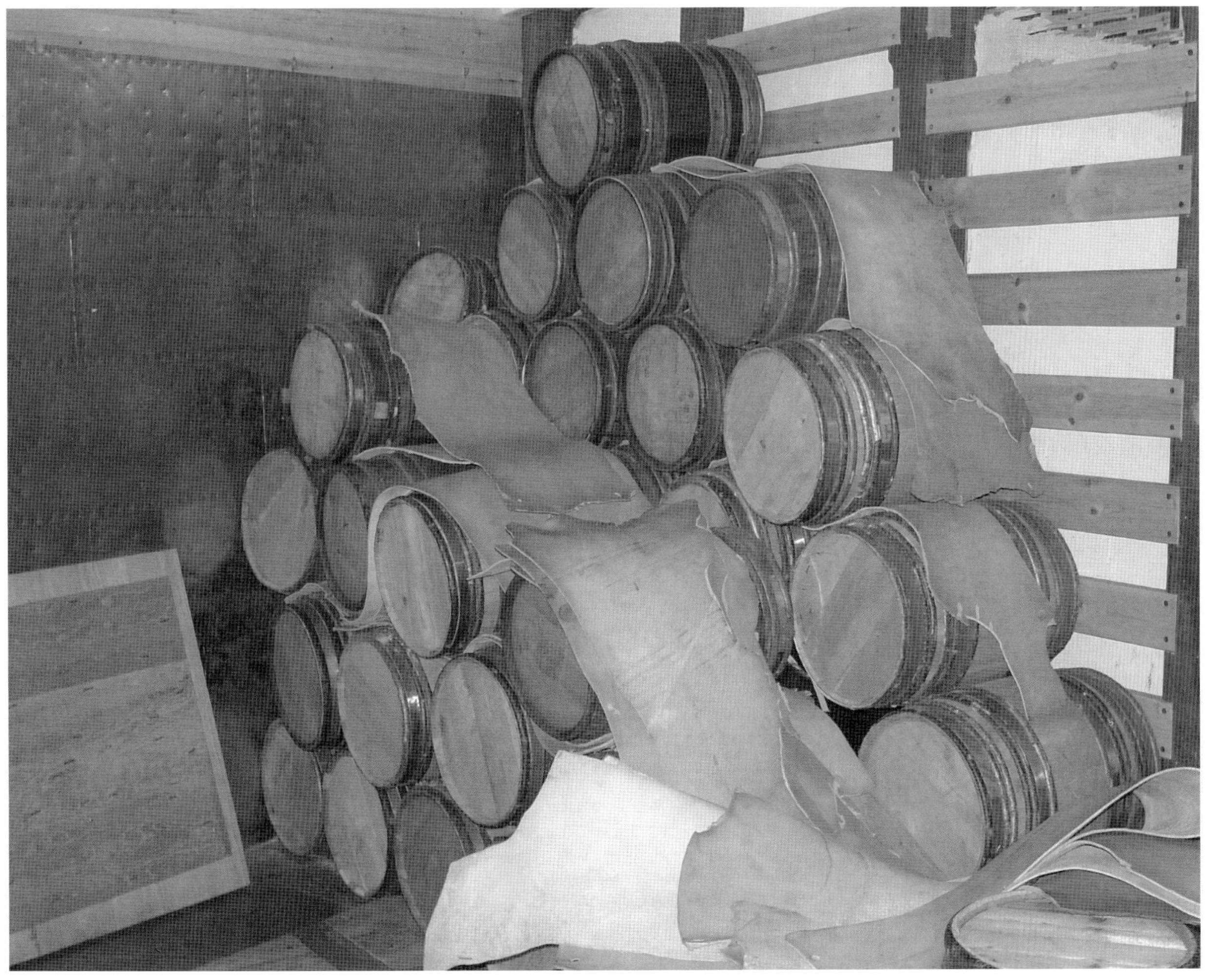

her fore topmast and yard had to be sent down as both were much injured with shot. It was at this point her fore topsail was unbent from its yard and sent down on deck to be stowed in the sail room. This initial act was one of many that allowed the battle-torn sail to survive for posterity. All of her boats were damaged as they stood on the booms in the waist of the ships, together with their respective masts and sails. Two cupids forming part of *Victory's* figurehead were also damaged, the larboard figure with its red sash having its arm shot away, the starboard figure with its blue sash losing its leg.

Shoring had to be set up under the starboard side of the forecastle where beams were near collapse and her starboard cathead had completely gone. The open upper decks were very much scored with shot and grenade explosions and blackened where fires had briefly started and the flat beakhead bulkhead at the head of the ship was completely riddled with round shot. So weak was this always-vulnerable part of the ship that it had been penetrated by grape shot. When she was later inspected it was found that there were some 300 shot embedded in her hull which had not penetrated enough to cause serious damage or injury.

During the storm following the battle, remaining mast and spar were adapted to provide *Victory* with a jury rig to prevent her running into danger on the treacherous lee shores around Cape Trafalgar. Her jib boom was removed and set up as a jury mizzen mast to balance her rig. This was supported by making a step using 10ft of three-inch oak plank and 15ft of elm four inches thick. Spare timber carried in the form of 48ft of four-inch thick oak plank and 40ft of three-inch oak plank were expended to 'fish' the shot riddled main mast: in effect, the mast was given splints.

As if the ship was not already in poor shape, the ensuing storm further took its toll, during which she lost her main yard. In his accounts, Mr Bunce, the ship's carpenter, also lists what items were 'Shot away, thrown overboard with the Bulk Heads in Clearing Ship and Missing after the Action'. Such equipment included two marine's arms chests, two armourers' benches, one airing stove, one anvil, five poop lanthorns 14 canvas births (cabins) and one grinding stone. Bunce also lists innumerable quantities of materials: lead and copper sheathing, nails, bolts and so on, as well as timber that was consumed making the necessary repairs while the ship made her way, on occasion under tow, first from the *Polyphemus* (64) and then by the *Neptune* (98), and her short refitting at Gibraltar.

In the Boatswain's accounts compiled by William Wilmet, some 20 sails are listed as damaged or lost and nearly 40 boats' oars, boat hooks and 283 hammocks, which served as splinter barricades in their nettings, were also damaged beyond repair. Losses also included 15 leather buckets, 51 wooden buckets, seven hatchets and two junk axes. His records also show that the hammock cloths, used to protect the hammocks from weather when stowed in the nettings, were used for enveloping the dead before being committed to overboard. This makes sense as hammocks were too necessary a commodity to be used as coffins, as generally believed.

After refitting to get her seaworthy and receiving a spare anchor to replace that which was 'wounded as unserviceable', *Victory* finally sailed from Gibraltar on Monday 4 November to carry Nelson's body home. Contrary winds delayed her homecoming to Portsmouth until Wednesday 4 December.

Gun charges line in racks at the back, while on the left a lamp lies behind thick glass windows. The lamps could only be accessed from behind to obviate the danger of a spark making contact with the gunpowder. (By kind permission of the Commanding Officer of HMS *Victory*)

THE BRITISH FLEET AT TRAFALGAR

The British fleet that was present with the *Victory* at the battle of Trafalgar comprised 33 ships in total, of which 27 were line-of-battle-ships, four frigates, the remaining vessels being the armed schooner *Pickle* and the cutter *Entreprenante.* Moreover, the ships in Nelson's fleet were not all British built: the 80-gun *Tonnant,* the 74-gun ships *Belleisle* and *Spartiate* and the 10-gun cutter *Entreprenante* were all French-built vessels that had been captured at some point in time. Unlike the French and Spanish ships present, most of which were identical in class and designer, the ships in the British fleet varied considerably in design and age as shown in the tables on the following pages, *Victory* herself being 40 years old.

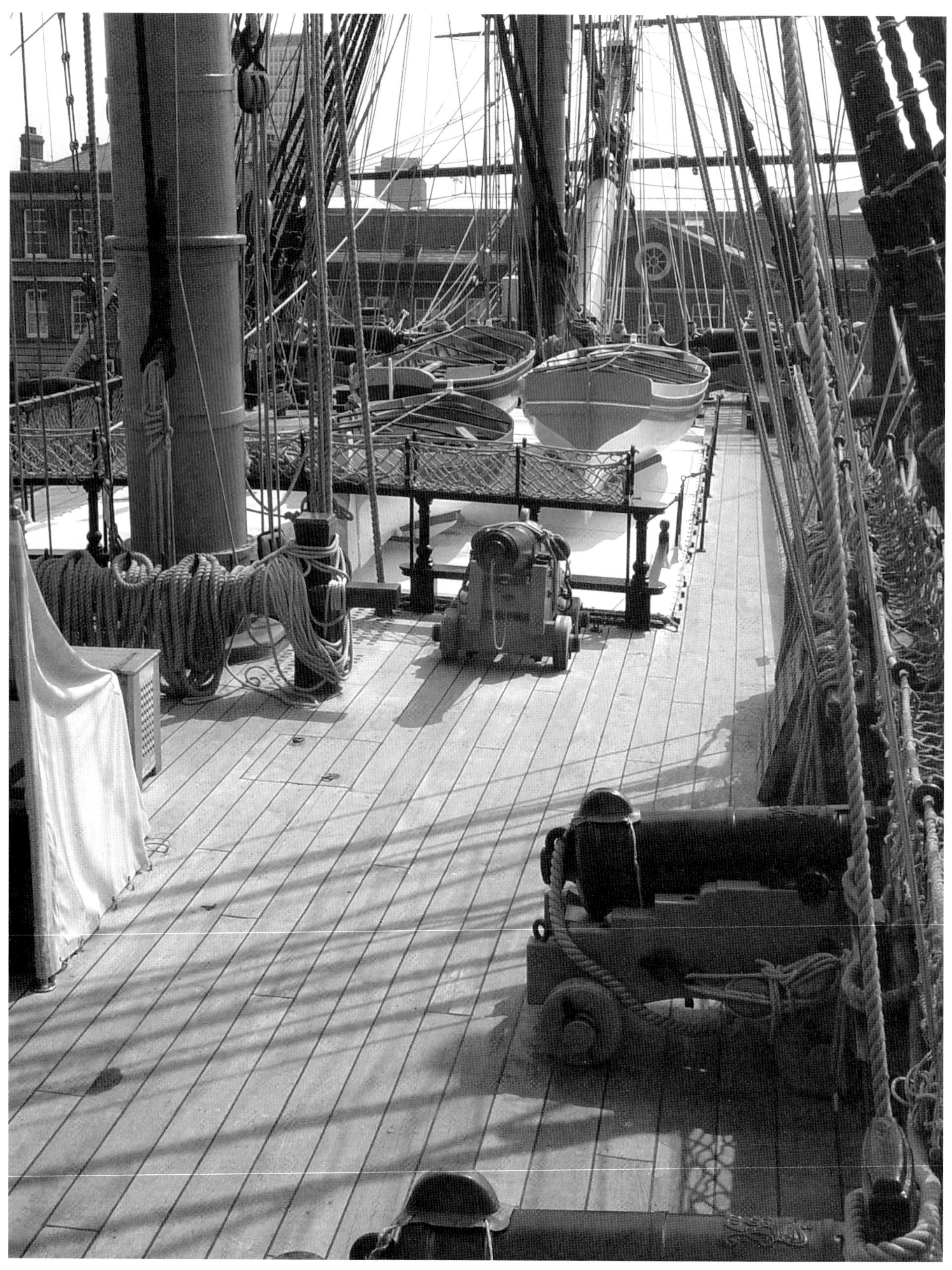

With the exception of *Britannia*, which was designed under the old 1745 Establishment, specifications authorized under the committee of the Navy Board, seven of the ships were designed by Thomas Slade, nine by John Henslow and three by John Williams, each of these men holding the post of Surveyor of the Navy. Sixty-eight per cent of the British built ships were constructed within the Royal dockyards of Chatham, Deptford, Plymouth, Portsmouth, Sheerness and Woolwich, with the majority being built in Deptford (eight) and Chatham (five, including the *Victory*). Only two were built in Portsmouth, three in Plymouth and one at Sheerness and Woolwich respectively. The remainder were built in various yards under private contract, three of which were constructed by Henry Adams at the Buckler's Hard on the River Beaulieu, Hampshire. Here timber was supplied direct from the New Forest.

While each of the ships are specified by rate, carrying a specific number of guns; in other words, 100, 80, 74 and so on, quite a number of the ships were actually carrying additional ordnance in the form of carronades mounted on their uppermost decks, forecastle and poop. By analysis it is found that the 33 ships forming the entire battle fleet and the 27 line-of-battle ships that actually fought were carrying armament as detailed on pages 164–65.

By comparison, Wellington's allied forces at the battle of Waterloo in 1815 had only 163 guns comprising 60 9-pounders, 70 6-pounders, and 31 24-pounder howitzers providing an overall weight of fire of 1,704lb, which is only 32.6 per cent greater than one broadside from the *Victory*. The overall weight of firepower of the 33 British ships at Trafalgar amounted to 51,962lb. The total firepower of the 27 British line-of-battle ships was 48,010lb. This amounted to 75.26 per cent of the combined firepower of the 2,971 guns carried on the 18 French and 15 Spanish ships of the line, which totalled 63,794lb.

While it is generally conceived that the predominant gun carried in the British ship was the 24- and 32-pounder as shown above, the most predominant gun was in fact the 18-pounder carriage gun which, proportional to its weight and calibre, fired a weighty shot. It also required fewer gun crew. This misconception probably derives from the fact that the *Victory*, which is visited by many people today, was armed with 32-, 24- and 12-pounders. The 18-pounder gun was equally predominant in the French fleet at Trafalgar, whereas the 24-pounder was the common-most gun carried in the Spanish ships.

The 27 British line of battle ships were manned with some 17,000 men, which equates to 57 per cent of the 30,000 men manning the combined Franco-Spanish fleet. Overall British casualties comprised 449 dead and 1,214 wounded. Casualties within the combined fleet were considerably higher: 4,408 dead and 2,545 wounded. That the dead outnumber the wounded related to several factors; the consistency and overwhelming weight of British firepower, which came from 25 per cent fewer guns, it was the sheer rate and consistency of fire that created such casualties. Moreover, French ships were less heavily built therefore were more easily penetrated by shot. The other factor relates to the point that the ships of the Combined Fleet, especially the Spanish ships, were far more heavily manned, thus it was inevitable that casualties were higher.

OPPOSITE
A view from the poop deck shows the complexity of rigging. The boat on the right is the Admiral's barge. (By kind permission of the Commanding Officer of HMS Victory)

STATISTICS OF THE BRITISH SHIPS AT TRAFALGAR

Ship's Name	Rate	Guns	Designer	Launch Date[1]	Age in 1805[2]	Fate	Date	Total years in service
Britannia	1st	100	1745 Establishment	1762	43	Prison Ship – Broken up	1825	63
Royal Sovereign	1st	100	John Williams	1786	19	Broken up	1841	55
Victory	1st	100	Thomas Slade	**1765**	**40**	Preserved	2005	240
Dreadnought	2nd	98	John Henslow	1801	4	Hospital – Broken up	1857	56
Neptune	2nd	98	John Henslow	1797	8	Prison Ship – Broken up	1818	21
Téméraire	2nd	98	John Henslow	1798	7	Broken up	1838	40
Prince	2nd	98	Thomas Slade	1788	17	Prison Ship – Broken up	1837	49
Tonnant	2nd	80	Noel Sane - French	**1798**	**7**	Broken up	1821	23
Achille	3rd	74	Copy French lines	1798	7	Sold & broken up	1865	67
Ajax	3rd	74	Thomas Slade	1798	7	Accidentally burnt	1807	9
Belleisle	3rd	74	Thomas Slade	**1795**	**10**	Broken up	1841	46
Bellerophon	3rd	74	Thomas Slade	1786	19	Prison Ship – Broken up	1836	50
Colossus	3rd	74	John Henslow	1803	6	Broken up	1826	23
Conqueror	3rd	74	John Henslow	1801	4	Broken up	1822	21
Defence	3rd	74	John Henslow	1763	42	Wrecked	1811	48
Defiance	3rd	74	Thomas Slade	1783	22	Prison Ship – Broken up	1817	34
Leviathan	3rd	74	Copy French lines	1790	15	Prison Ship – Broken up	1848	58
Mars	3rd	74	John Henslow	1794	11	Broken up	1823	29
Minotaur	3rd	74	Copy French lines	1793	12	Wrecked	1810	17

STATISTICS OF THE BRITISH SHIPS AT TRAFALGAR (Continued)

Ship's Name	Rate	Guns	Designer	Launch Date[1]	Age in 1805[2]	Fate	Date	Total years in service
Orion	3rd	74	William Bately	1787	18	Broken up	1814	27
Revenge	3rd	74	John Henslow	1805	6 mnths	Broken up	1849	44
Spartiate	3rd	74	Noel Sane - French	**1798**	7	Sheer Hulk – Broken up	1857	59
Swiftsure	3rd	74	John Henslow	1804	1	Receiving Ship – Broken up	1841	37
Thunderer	3rd	74	Thomas Slade	1783	22	Broken up	1814	31
Africa	3rd	64	John Williams	1781	24	Broken up	1814	33
Agamemnon	3rd	64	Thomas Slade	1781	24	Wrecked	1807	26
Polyphemus	3rd	64	John Williams	1782	23	Powder ship - Broken up	1827	45
Naiad	5th	38	William Rule	1797	8	Coal Ship in Peru	1866	69
Euryalus	5th	36	William Rule	1803	2	Prison Ship – Broken up	1860	57
Phoebe	5th	36	Edward Hunt	1795	10	Slop Ship – Broken up	1841	46
Sirius	5th	36	Copy French lines	1797	10	Grounded & burnt to prevent capture	1810	13
Pickle	Schooner	12	William Rule	1802	5	Lost – Foundered	1808	6
Entreprenante	Cutter	10	Unknown	**1798**	7	Broken up	1812	14

1 Launch dates denoted in bold type indicate date French prize ships entered into British navy.
2 Ages in 1805 denoted in bold type relate to time that prize ships are in service to that date.

While many of the British ships sustained considerable damage, many having lost masts, none were lost in battle or the storm afterwards and slowly but surely each either refitted at sea or, like *Victory*, got into Rosio Bay, Gibraltar to effect their repairs. The *Victory* was refitted at Chatham in 1806 and went back into service in 1808. Other ships actively continued to serve on the Mediterranean station while others were re-deployed in various theatres of war.

ORDNANCE OF THE BRITISH TRAFALGAR FLEET

Gun Type & Calibre (Weight of shot)	Total No. of Guns in fleet of 33 misc. ships	Total No. of Guns in the 60 line-of-battle ships
32-pounder carriage gun	624	624
24-pounder carriage gun	374	374
18-pounder carriage gun	756	624
12-pounder carriage gun	162	162
9-pounder carriage gun	238	222
6-pounder carriage gun	32	32
68-pounder carronade	2	2
32-pounder carriage gun	128	90
24-pounder carriage gun	6	6
18-pounder carriage gun	30	30
12-pounder carriage gun	18	0
TOTAL No. OF GUNS	**2,370**	**2,166**

Ironically a number of Nelson's Trafalgar ships were unfortunately wrecked or destroyed in some manner or other. The *Agamemnon* grounded and sank in Maldonado Bay on the River Plate while serving on the South American station in 1807 but with no loss of life, whereas the *Minotaur* was lost off the coast of Denmark and, more tragically, the *Defence* was also lost off Denmark the following year with few survivors. While serving in the East Indies in 1810 the frigate *Sirius* ran aground while in action and had to be burnt to prevent her falling into French hands, and the *Ajax* was accidentally lost by fire. *Pickle,* the armed schooner that brought the first news of Trafalgar and loss of Nelson back to England in November 1805, was lost at sea with all hands in 1808.

When the war against Napoleon finally ended on the Field of Waterloo in 1815 many of the Trafalgar ships were decommissioned and laid up, awaiting their fate. Some were used as receiving ships for men entering the navy, others used as powder hulks. Of the other surviving ships, seven were converted and served as prison ships for standard convict or French prisoners of war before finally being broken up. These comprised the *Britannia, Neptune, Prince, Bellerophon, Defiance, Leviathan* and Captain Blackwood's renowned frigate *Euryalus*. The three 98-gun ships,

Dreadnought, *Neptune* and *Téméraire*, all of the same design, proved to be poorly built and saw little service afterwards.

The *Victory* is the only surviving Trafalgar ship preserved in dry dock at Portsmouth today. Still in commission, she is manned by serving officers and ratings of the Royal Navy flying the white ensign and flagship of the Second Sea Lord/Commander-in-Chief Naval Home Command. Equally served by her Victory Corps of Guides, she operates as a public museum attracting national and international visitors.

CHAPTER SEVEN

'ENGAGE THE ENEMY MORE CLOSELY'

REAR-ADMIRAL JOSEPH CALLO

As dawn broke at Cape Trafalgar on 21 October 1805, the sky was overcast but not ominous; a gentle west-northwest breeze rippled the surface of the swells rolling in rhythmically from the west. The soft daybreak gave no hint of the carnage to come.

As the morning light grew over the southernmost tip of Spain, however, two slowly moving fleets of powerful ships of the line – 27 British plus 33 French and Spanish in the Combined Fleet – were gradually illuminated. The ships' sails gradually turned from darkest gray to a shade that harmonized with the morning light. The water through which the ships eased also changed colour, from pitch black to cobalt. Vessels smaller than the ships of the line manoeuvred among the main fleets.

The 27 British ships of the line were led by the 100-gun HMS *Victory,* with Vice-Admiral Lord Nelson embarked as commander-in-chief. The British fleet also included: the 100-gun ships *Britannia* and *Royal Sovereign* – with second in command Vice-Admiral Cuthbert Collingwood embarked; the 98-gun ships *Dreadnought, Neptune, Prince,* and *Téméraire*; the 80-gun ship *Tonnant*; the 74-gun ships *Achilles, Ajax, Belleisle, Bellerophon, Colossus, Conqueror, Defence, Defiance, Leviathan, Mars, Minotaur, Orion, Revenge, Spartiate, Swiftsure* and *Thunderer.* The smallest units among the British ships of the line were the 64-gun ships *Africa, Agamemnon* and *Polyphemus.* Along with the British main fleet were the frigates *Euryalus, Naïad, Phoebe* and *Sirius,* plus the schooner *Pickle* and the cutter *Entreprenante.*

The 18 French ships of the line in the Combined Fleet included the 80-gun ships *Bucentaure* – with Vice-Admiral Pierre Villeneuve embarked as commander-in-chief – *Formidable, Indomptable* and *Neptune*; the 74-gun ships *Achille, Aigle, Algeçiras, Argonaute, Berwick, Duguay Trouin, Fougueux, Héros, Intrépide, Mont Blanc, Pluton, Redoutable, Scipion* and *Swiftsure.* The 15 Spanish ships of the line included the largest known ship of its class at the time the 130-gun

OPPOSITE
Sir William Beechey's portrait shows a battle-worn Nelson in full regalia. (Getty Images/Bridgeman Art Library)

Santísima Trinidad; the 120-gun *Santa Ana*; the 112-gun *Príncipe de Asturias* – with second-in-command of the Combined Fleet Admiral don Federico Gravina embarked; the 84-gun *Argonauta*; the 80-gun *Neptuno*; the 74-gun ships *Bahama, Monarca, Montañes, Rayo, San Augustín, San Francisco de Assisi, San Ildefonso, San Juan Nepomuceno* and *San Justo*. The smallest among the Combined Fleet's ships of the line was the 64-gun *San Leandro*. The Combined Fleet also included the French frigates *Cornélie, Hermoine, Hortance, Rhin* and *Thémis* and the French brigs *Argus* and *Furet*.

FIREPOWER COMPARISON BETWEEN THE SHIPS OF THE LINE OF BRITISH AND COMBINED FLEETS

BRITISH NO. OF GUNS	NO. OF SHIPS	COMBINED FLEET NO. OF GUNS	NO. OF SHIPS
100	3	130	1
98	4	120	1
80	1	112	1
74	16	100	1
64	3	84	1
		80	4
		74	23
		64	1

The total number of guns of the British ships of the line was 2,148, compared to 2,632 guns for the ships of the line of the Combined Fleet.

The two fleets were approximately nine miles apart according to *Victory's* log, and they occupied nearly 50 square miles of the Cape. The ships seemed to move in slow motion, rising and falling on the large Atlantic Ocean swells rolling under them from the west. Signal officers in the ships of both fleets strained to pick up signals at the instant the flags would begin rising from the deck. The sense of anticipation in each of the ships was palpable.

The British maintained a relatively disciplined line-ahead formation while moving towards the north during the night. The exception was *Africa*, which had missed a signal for a fleet course change in the dark and was, by dawn, six miles to the north of the other British ships. A little after six, Nelson signalled from *Victory* to 'Form the order of sailing.'[1] As signal flags hung limply in the light breeze, they would have been difficult for many of the British ships to quickly decipher. But Nelson's tactical signal required little of his captains, other than tidying up their formation. Nelson's next signal was 'Prepare for battle,' followed quickly by 'Bear up in succession on the course set by the Admiral.' The eventual result was two columns of ships about a mile apart, one headed by Nelson, one headed by Collingwood; both columns were bearing straight down on the Combined Fleet.

Initially, the Combined Fleet was sailing south, and was to the east and downwind from the British. In that downwind position, Villeneuve had somewhat less tactical leverage than Nelson. And to make tactical matters worse for Villeneuve, he was between the proverbial hammer and anvil, with the British to windward and the rough coast of southern Spain to leeward. During the previous day and night, the Combined Fleet had been sailing mostly in five parallel columns, since it was easier to control a fleet from the centre of such a formation than from the centre of a single line. And at dawn on the 21st, Villeneuve's ships were in irregular clusters stretching almost five miles along the axis of their course.

At about 6:20am, Villeneuve signaled for his ships to form a single line of battle in a predetermined sequence. As was usual for the commander-in-chief in such a formation, he positioned himself at the centre. Villeneuve also ordered his captains to wear ship, reversing the fleet's direction and heading it towards the north. Villeneuve's turn to the north was a clear acceptance of the challenge being thrust forward by Nelson. With the light winds and large swells, however, the French and Spanish ships rolled heavily, dumping the wind from their sails as they manoeuvred. It was a slow process under the circumstances, and it took several hours for the Combined Fleet to carry out Villeneuve's signal. The eventual result was a line-ahead with considerable overlapping at points.

As the morning wore on, the maneuverings of the two fleets continued at a slow pace, at midday a roughly formed French line heading generally north and two roughly formed British lines heading generally east were about to meet. The farthest north of the two British lines was headed by Nelson and was heading for a point about one-third from the Combined Fleet's van. The British line to the south of Nelson that was headed by Collingwood was steering for a point about two-thirds from the Combined Fleet's van. As events would develop, the British ships would initially be in close and violent contact with approximately two-thirds of the Combined Fleet. And because of the state and direction of the wind and the sea conditions, it would take a significant amount of time for the Combined Fleet's van to reverse course and join the close combat.

THE MOOD IN THE COMBINED FLEET

Things were not well in the Combined Fleet. For one thing, a basic part of France's naval strategy had for years been to generally avoid fleet encounters with the British. The objective was to preserve its fleets for support of selective military land campaigns. The goal of seizing naval control of the English Channel to facilitate an invasion of Britain was an important ongoing element of that land-oriented

Cape Trafalgar is located between Cadiz to the northwest and the Strait of Gibraltar to the southeast. As the Battle of Trafalgar approached, Nelson feared that the French-Spanish Combined Fleet would escape to Cadiz or into the Mediterranean. (The National Archives)

strategy. Largely because of this French strategy, major elements of her navy were often blockaded, frequently in its main Atlantic port of Brest and its principal Mediterranean base of Toulon. Thus, the French Navy lacked the operational tempo of the British Navy, which was hardened by its long and arduous at-sea deployments. Nelson alluded to this in a letter to Lord Melville written from *Victory* in February 1805: 'Those gentlemen [the French] are not used to a Gulph of Lyons gale, which we have buffeted for 21 months and not carried away a Spar.'[2]

The lack of at-sea toughening for the French Navy was compounded by purges of the French naval officer ranks following the French Revolution. Many of its best officers were driven from the service, and their replacements, although possessing properly egalitarian backgrounds, were not up to the professional standards of their predecessors. This had inevitably eroded morale and combat effectiveness in the French Navy of the time.

Additional factors contributed to the less than optimistic mood in the Combined Fleet. One of those factors was the Battle of the Nile in 1798, a highly visible and

NELSON'S BAND OF BROTHERS AT THE BATTLE OF TRAFALGAR

- Vice-Admiral Cuthbert Collingwood, second-in-command: HMS *Royal Sovereign*
- Rear-Admiral William Earl of Northesk, third-in-command: HMS *Britannia*
- Captain Thomas Hardy, Flag Captain to Admiral Lord Nelson: HMS *Victory*
- Captain Edward Rotherham, Flag Captain to Vice-Admiral Cuthbert Collingwood: HMS *Royal Sovereign*
- Captain Charles Bullen, Flag Captain to Rear-Admiral William Earl of Northesk: HMS *Britannia*
- Captain Eliab Harvey: HMS *Téméraire*
- Captain Thomas Fremantle: HMS *Neptune*
- Captain John Conn: HMS *Dreadnought*
- Captain Richard Grindall: HMS *Prince*
- Captain Charles Tyler: HMS *Tonnant*
- Captain William Hargood: HMS *Belleisle*
- Captain Robert Moorsom (wounded): HMS *Revenge*
- Captain Sir Francis Laforey: HMS *Spartiate*
- Captain George Duff (killed): HMS *Mars*
- Captain Philip Durham (wounded): HMS *Defiance*
- Captain Charles Mansfield: HMS *Minotaur*
- Captain Israel Pellew: HMS *Conqueror*
- Captain Richard King: HMS *Achilles*
- Captain James Morris (wounded): HMS *Colossus*
- Captain George Hope: HMS *Defence*
- Captain Henry Bayntun: HMS *Leviathan*
- Captain John Cooke (killed): HMS *Bellerophon*
- Captain Edward Codrington: HMS *Orion*
- Captain William Rutherford: HMS *Swiftsure*
  Captain (acting) Lieutenant John Pilford: HMS *Ajax*
- Captain (acting) Lieutenant John Stockham: HMS *Thunderer*
- Captain Robert Redmill: HMS *Polyphemus*
- Captain Henry Digby: HMS *Africa*
- Captain Sir Edward Berry: HMS *Agamemnon*
- Captain the Honourable Henry Blackwood: HMS *Euryalus*
- Captain the Honourable Thomas Capel: HMS *Phoebe*
- Captain Thomas Dundas: HMS *Naïad*
- Captain William Prowse: HMS *Sirius*
- Lieutenant John Lapenotière: HMS *Pickle*
- Lieutenant Robert Young: HMS *Entreprenante*

strategically important defeat by Nelson of a fleet supporting Napoleon's invasion of Egypt. Then there was the matter of the on-again-off-again characteristic of the alliance with Spain. Although Spain's Navy was professional and possessed good ships and men, her intermittent political alliances with France did not translate into efficient joint fleet operations. Finally, there was the matter of Admiral Villeneuve's state of mind, which differed sharply with Nelson's attitude. The French admiral was an able leader, and he even had a pretty good idea of the tactics Nelson would employ. But he was in disfavour with Napoleon and had been virtually forced to put to sea with the Combined Fleet because his replacement as commander-in-chief in the Mediterranean was imminent. Villeneuve saw the impending battle as a slim chance to salvage his career or at least his honor, and his basic instructions to his captains revealed his lack of total commitment to battle. At one point, he wrote:

> 'I by no means propose to seek out the enemy; I even wish to avoid him in order to proceed to my destination. But should we encounter him, let there be no ignominious manoeuvring ... any captain who is not under fire will not be at his post.'[3]

The spirits of the senior Spanish admiral in the Combined Fleet, Federico Gravina, and the three other Spanish flag officers in the Fleet were no more sanguine than that of their French commander-in-chief. For one thing, their enthusiasm for serving in one of Napoleon's fleets was dampened by the emperor's lack of understanding of naval operations. In addition, there had been only intermittent joint operations with the French, and some preliminary training in basic fleet maneuvers with Villeneuve and his captains before the battle could have smoothed out the differences with their French counterparts. But there were none.

THE MOOD IN THE BRITISH FLEET

Nelson had full confidence in his captains and their crews. In a letter to Sir John Acton in April 1805, he was unequivocal: 'Nothing could be finer than the fleet I command.'[4] And because they had maintained arduous deployments during the months leading up to the fateful confrontation off the Spanish coast, they were finely honed. For them, the forthcoming battle would be a release. It was clear to all that Nelson eagerly sought combat with the Combined Fleet. In fact, his main initial worry was that Villeneuve would somehow avoid battle and escape to the northwest into Cadiz or to the southeast into the Mediterranean. There was, in addition, a 'corporate culture' of confidence that had been built up throughout the entire British Navy of the time.

Of particular significance, Nelson had communicated the importance of their mission, his confidence in their abilities, and a sense of optimism concerning the approaching battle to his captains. In turn, his 'band of brothers' communicated their enthusiasm about the outcome of the approaching battle to their crews. Arguably the best example of Nelson's ability to communicate with exceptional effectiveness with his captains was his Memorandum of 9 October.[5] In that message, he laid out his basic tactics, which involved three separate lines of British ships. Two of the lines would concentrate overwhelming force at separate points in the Combined Fleet's line, while a third squadron would be held in reserve. Nelson anticipated that a general mêlée would follow his first actions, and that he would then rely heavily on the individual judgment of his captains and the superior gunnery of the British seamen. In Nelson's words: 'The whole impression of the British Fleet must be to overpower from two or three Ships a-head of the Commander-in-Chief, supposed to be in the Centre, to the rear of their Fleet.' The only later change in the initial tactics outlined on 9 October was the use of two lines in his initial attack, rather than three.[6] It was a change driven by the fact that he had fewer ships than anticipated for the battle.

BEYOND TACTICS

One of the most important elements of Nelson's Memorandum of 9 October was that it established a clear combat doctrine – defined as the overarching attitude that determines how the battle is to be fought minute by minute, notwithstanding the inevitably changing circumstances and difficulty of communicating between ships during the chaos of battle. In fact, Nelson's Memorandum included what is one of the best expressions of a naval combat doctrine in history. He wrote at one point:

> Something must be left to chance; nothing is sure in a Sea Fight beyond all others. Shot will carry away the masts and yards of friends as well as foes....Captains are to look to their particular Line as their rallying point. But, in case Signals can neither be seen or perfectly understood, no Captain can do very wrong if he places his Ship alongside that of an Enemy.

The combat doctrine inherent in Nelson's Memorandum included, among other principles, the importance of seizing the initiative. And that importance of gaining the initiative in Battle was established in Nelson's mind well before the Battle of Trafalgar. In June of 1798, for example, he wrote to his commander-in-chief Admiral the Earl St Vincent before the Battle of the Nile: 'You may be assured I will fight them [the French] the moment I can reach their Fleet, be they at anchor, or under sail.'[7] And before the Battle of Copenhagen in March of 1801, he wrote to his commander-in-chief Admiral Sir Hyde Parker: '[T]he boldest measures are the safest.'[8] Closely linked with Nelson's aggressive combat doctrine was his strong reliance on the initiative of his subordinates. This was never better expressed than in his message to Collingwood, sent on the same day of his Memorandum to his captains:

> I send you my Plan of Attack, as far as a man dare venture to guess at the uncertain position the Enemy may be found in. But, my dear friend, it is to place you perfectly at ease respecting my intentions, and to give full scope to your judgment for carrying them into effect. We can, my dear Coll., have no little jealousies. We have only one object in view, that of annihilating our Enemies, and getting a glorious Peace for our Country. No man has more confidence in another man than I have in you: and no man will render your services more justice than your very old friend...[9]

The aggressive combat doctrine exuded from Nelson's Memorandums also reflected his understanding of what his leadership at Whitehall and the Admiralty, as well as the British public, needed. He wrote to Sir George Rose from *Victory* in early October 1805: '[I]t is, as Mr. Pitt knows, annihilation that the Country wants.'[10]

With all of its brilliance, there has been an enduring mystery associated with Nelson's battle plan. The mystery springs from a letter written to Lady Hamilton on 1 October from *Victory*:

> I believe my arrival was most welcome, not only to the Commander of the Fleet, but also to every individual in it; and, when I came to explain to them the *'Nelson touch,'* it was like an electric shock. Some shed tears, all approved – 'It was new – it was singular – it was simple!'...[11]

'The Nelson touch' was not actually defined by Nelson in his letter, and other references to it by him were also nonspecific. In recent years, after considerable past speculation, students of Nelson's career have generally come to believe that it was the total plan encompassed in the Memorandum of 9 October to his captains that Nelson had labelled 'the Nelson Touch.' Respected Nelson author Colin White, for example, recently wrote: 'Nelson devised a comprehensive battle plan based on his own long experience of war, and on the tactical experiments of his predecessors, which he called 'The Nelson Touch'.[12]

FINAL THOUGHTS BEFORE BATTLE

As the morning wore on, there doubtless was considerable letter writing in both fleets. One of Nelson's captains, George Duff, whose hurried note surely was typical of many others written that morning, wrote from *Mars* to his wife:

> 'My dear Sophia, I have just time to tell you that we are just going into action with the Combined [Fleet]. I hope and trust in God that we shall all behave as becomes us, and that I may have the happiness of taking my beloved wife and children in my arms.'[13]

Duff was killed during the ensuing battle. His son Norwich, listed as a Volunteer 1st Class in *Mars's* crew, did survive, however, and he had the unhappy task of writing to his mother with the news of his father's death.

In *Victory*, Nelson took time to write to his paramour, Lady Emma Hamilton. It was a letter he never finished, and when the uncompleted letter was delivered to Lady Hamilton, she scrawled at the end: 'Oh miserable wretched Emma – Oh glorious & happy Nelson.' Nelson also wrote a tender letter to his and Lady Hamilton's daughter Horatia. At another point, Nelson addressed a wider audience when he made a particularly significant entry in his diary on the morning of the impending battle. Those words became an enduring element of his historical legacy:

Nelson is portrayed at his writing table in *Victory's* great cabin on the morning of the Battle of Trafalgar in a painting Charles Lucy created in 1853. (Royal Naval Museum)

> May the Great God, whom I worship, grant to my Country, and for the benefit of Europe in general, a great and glorious Victory; and may no misconduct in anyone tarnish it; and may humanity after Victory be the predominant feature in the British Fleet. For myself, individually, I commit my life to Him who made me, and may his blessing light upon my endeavours for serving my country faithfully. To Him I resign myself and the just cause which is entrusted to me to defend. Amen. Amen. Amen.[14]

As the morning wore on, there was considerable discussion among the officers in *Victory* about the safety of their commander-in-chief. Some thought Nelson should remove the conspicuous awards he was wearing on his uniform jacket. Some thought he should direct the battle from a frigate, separated from the main action. Nelson had made it abundantly clear, however, that he understood his importance as an example to his captains and their crews, and the concerns of others about the need to protect his person went mostly unexpressed. One of the more interesting footnotes on Nelson's personal preparations for battle was that, for the first time in his career, he did not wear his sword.

As noon approached, with the bands in his various ships playing *Britons Strike Home*, *Rule Britannia*, and *Heart of Oak*, it was time for Nelson's final general signals to his fleet. One signal was 'Prepare to anchor after the close of day.' Since swells created by a storm invariably outrace the storm itself, Nelson knew that the swells from the west signalled the approach of a dangerous storm. He was, as commander-in-chief, thinking even beyond the coming combat.

Nelson also sent a signal to, as he said, 'amuse the fleet.' At first, he ordered, 'Nelson confides that every man will do his duty.' His signal officer Lieutenant Pasco suggested some word changes to reduce the number of signal flags required. The message that was agreed upon and hoisted into the breeze was: 'England expects that every man will do his duty.' Although Collingwood in *Royal Sovereign* was not amused and complained rather gruffly to those on *Royal Sovereign's* quarterdeck that Nelson should stop his signalling, Nelson's nine-word admonition has survived for two centuries as one of the memorable features of the battle of Trafalgar.

NELSON'S GENERAL SIGNALS OF 21 OCTOBER 1805

SIGNAL	ESTIMATED TIME
Form the order of sailing in two columns	0600
When lying-to, or sailing by the wind, to bear up and sail large on the course steered by the Admiral or that pointed out by signal	0600
Prepare for battle	0630
Prepare for battle	1000
England expects that every man will do his duty	1145
Make all sail possible with safety to the masts	1155
Prepare to anchor after the close of day	1200
Engage the enemy more closely	1215

Finally, Nelson ordered his last general signal to the fleet: 'Engage the Enemy More Closely.' It was the final reinforcement of his combat doctrine; no further fleet-wide instructions to his captains would be needed during the battle.

FOCUSED CHAOS

A few minutes after Nelson's last signal, *Royal Sovereign,* with a newly coppered bottom and greater speed than most of the other British ships, closed to about a half-mile of the Combined Fleet's line. By that time the French–Spanish fleet was in the shape of a sweeping curve, with the concave side towards the British. Their line was irregular, and at some points there were ships in the line virtually side by side. They were sailing slowly, at a speed of about three knots (about 3.5mph).

Roughly 15 minutes before noon, the French *Fougueux* fired what is believed to have been the first broadside from the Combined Fleet. For the next 30–45 minutes *Royal Sovereign* was exposed to the broadsides of several of the enemy ships she was approaching, while being able to return fire with only a few bow guns. First there would have been harmless splashes; then holes would have begun appearing in *Royal Sovereign's* sails; then, *Fougueux's* shot began parting *Royal Sovereign's* rigging and tearing at her hull and spars. That early damage to *Royal Sovereign, Victory* and the other ships in the van of the two British lines was a price Nelson paid to carry out his tactical plan. That price was fortunately reduced somewhat, however, by the heavy swells that significantly degraded the accuracy of the French gunners.

Finally, *Royal Sovereign* drove through the French-Spanish formation behind the 120-gun Spanish *Santa Ana,* the seventeenth ship in the enemy's line. At a range of approximately 30 yards, *Royal Sovereign* unleashed a double-shotted broadside from her port guns that ripped through the Spaniard's stern. The 100 cannon balls swept the length of the *Santa Ana* in a raking shot, killing or wounding an estimated 400 men. *Royal Sovereign* then turned to port and came alongside *Santa Ana.* With their yardarms touching, the two ships began pounding one another at point blank range.

Nelson and *Victory* in the van of the British line to the north arrived at the Combined Fleet line roughly 30 minutes after Collingwood. After suffering the same pounding as *Royal Sovereign* as they approached, *Victory* broke through the enemy's line behind the twelfth ship in the Combined Fleet's line, Villeneuve's flagship the French 80-gun *Bucentaure.* In this instance, the British ship fired a 68-pounder carronade loaded with round shot and a keg of 500 musket balls through *Bucentaure's* stern. The point blank raking shot had an effect similar to *Royal Sovereign's* opening broadside, sweeping along the axis of the enemy ship with incredibly lethal effect.

The carronade blast was followed almost immediately by a broadside fired in sequence from *Victory's* port side, with each of her port guns firing double- and in some cases triple-shotted blasts as it came to bear directly on the French ship's shattered stern. After taking a punishing broadside from the French 80-gun *Neptune, Victory* pulled away from *Bucentaure.* At this point, *Victory's* captain Thomas Hardy turned his attention to the nearby French 74-gun *Redoutable,* with a full broadside from his starboard guns.

After initial contact, Collingwood's line continued to fall one by one on the rear of the Combined Fleet, and Nelson's line similarly enveloped the centre of Villeneuve's force, leaving the French admiral's van to be dealt with in the following stages of the battle. What then ensued was the series of numerous individual, extremely violent, 'pell-mell' struggles Nelson had envisioned in his planning.

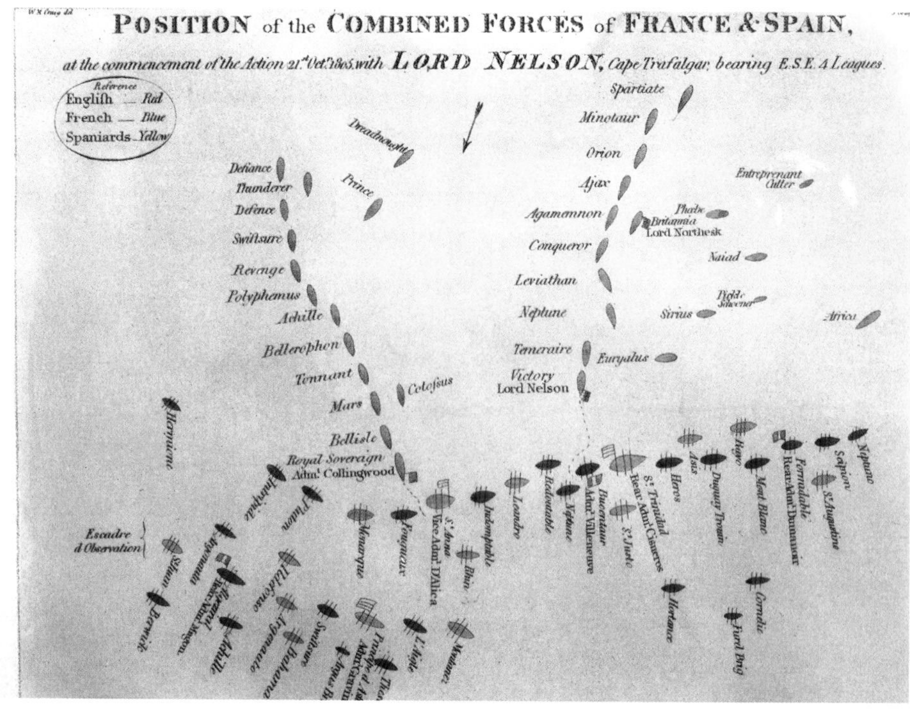

An engraving by W.M. Craig and published in 1806 by Edward Orme shows an interpretation of how the British and Combined Fleets were positioned at the beginning of the battle of Trafalgar. (National Maritime Museum)

A SERIES OF HELLISH CONFLICTS

After the opening attacks of the British lines, the scene at Trafalgar rapidly evolved into a series of life and death struggles between individual ships and between small clusters of ships. The slow motion ship movements resulting from the light winds added a surrealistic aspect to the mounting violence.

The action that the 74-gun *Achilles* was involved in was one of the numerous individual and overlapping dramas within the overall battle. Her captain Richard King was in the middle of Collingwood's line as it attacked. He broke through the Combined Fleet's formation under the stern of the 74-gun Spanish ship *Montañes,* the twenty-first ship in the initial, roughly formed Combined Fleet line. By this time any semblance of the original British and Combined Fleet formations had dissolved into pockets of violence. Smoke swirled around the ships, making it difficult to maintain any sense of the battle as a whole. The sound of the cannon fire, shot smashing through planking, and yards and masts crashing onto decks was deafening. The screams of the wounded pierced the seamless roar.

As *Achilles* passed under the stern of *Montañes,* King turned to port, and fired a devastating port broadside into the Spanish ship's starboard quarter. King then brought his ship alongside his enemy and the two ships traded point blank broadsides. Within half an hour the Spanish captain was dead and only a junior officer was left alive on the quarterdeck.

Seeing that *Montañes* was virtually out of action, King turned his attention to the 80-gun Spanish *Argonauta* on his starboard beam. For another 30 minutes King exchanged broadside with his new adversary, with a result similar to his

An early 19th-century engraving by J. Fitler from a painting by Nicholas Pocock recreates the scene at the beginning of the battle of Trafalgar. (National Martime Museum)

encounter with *Montañes*. *Argonauta*'s captain was wounded and most of her guns were out of action. With *Argonauta* at the point of surrendering and after a brief encounter with another French ship, King and *Achilles* were attacked by the 74-gun French *Berwick*. *Berwick's* fate was the same as King's first two antagonists. Within two hours, *Achilles* had defeated two Spaniards and one Frenchman. Such were the advantages of Nelson's tactics and doctrine, combined with his aggressive captains, and the more rapid rates of fire of the British gunners.

NELSON IS STRUCK DOWN

The decision of Nelson's flag captain Thomas Hardy to engage the French *Redoutable* was fateful. As *Victory* crashed into *Redoutable*, with her port side to their enemy's starboard side, the yards and rigging of the two ships became entangled, locking them in a deadly embrace. The two ships pounded one another with their cannons literally muzzle to muzzle. Because of the danger of the sails catching fire, sharpshooters had not been deployed aloft in *Victory*. Captain Jean-Jacques Lucas of *Redoutable*, in contrast, had positioned sharpshooters in his ship's rigging and on her tops, and they were firing down on the officers and crew on *Victory's* exposed decks with deadly effect.

One shot, believed to be from *Redoutable's* mizzen topmast, had historic impact. *Victory's* log reported it tersely: 'About 1.15 the Right Honourable Lord Viscount Nelson RB and Commander-in-chief was wounded in the shoulder.'[15]

When Hardy turned and saw the sergeant-major of marines and two seamen lifting Nelson from the deck, he expressed his hope that the admiral was not badly wounded. His commander-in-chief's reply was unequivocal: 'They have done for me at last Hardy.'[16] After Hardy said that he hoped it was not so, Nelson was specific: 'My backbone is shot through.'

Nelson was carried down to the ship's cockpit, deep below the main deck. There, in a small, poorly lit space, the ship's surgeon and his assistants tended to the wounded. It was a gruesome scene; gaping wounds were hurriedly stitched up, and mangled limbs were amputated with cold steel; there were no anaesthetics. The deck in the cockpit was painted red – for good reason. By the time the surgeon got to many of the wounded, they had died. In *Victory*'s cockpit, the roar of battle vibrated violently. At one point even the wounded Nelson reacted to the concussions of his flagship's gunfire: 'Oh Victory, Victory, how you distract my poor brain.'[17] The situation in *Victory*'s cockpit was described by a first-hand witness, the ship's chaplain Dr. John Scott: '[I]t was like a butcher's shambles.'[18]

Nelson had no illusions about surviving. From the time he fell to the deck until his death four hours later, he repeated that he would not live out the battle, making his other words at the time uniquely revealing. He was, of course, concerned with the progress of the battle, and he was also concerned with the condition of *Victory*. On several occasions when Hardy visited him in the cockpit, he urged him to be sure to anchor *Victory* at the end of the Battle. In a more personal perspective, he expressed concern for his paramour, Lady Hamilton, and for their daughter, Horatia. As his death neared, he also indicated that he had come to terms with his God, and he remarked to Dr Scott: 'I have not been a great sinner.' Then, with his last words, Nelson dealt with both 'Him who made me' and what was arguably the major preoccupation of his life. His final words were: 'Thank God I have done my duty.'[19]

A COMBINED FLEET PERSPECTIVE

One of the best of the Combined Fleet's captains was Jean Jacques Lucas, captain of the French *Redoutable*. His view from the deck of his doomed ship provides a valuable reminder of the courage and skill that was present in the Combined Fleet at the Battle of Trafalgar.

Lucas's ship was thirteenth in the Combined Fleet line as the battle began, immediately astern of the Combined Fleet commandeer-in-chief in *Bucentaure*. As *Victory* broke through the enemy's line, *Redoutable* was one of the ships that engaged her most aggressively. During their portion of the pell-mell battle, Lucas and his men took on not only the British flagship but the 98-gun *Téméraire* and a third British ship, identified by Lucas only as a two-decker.

After taking a heavy broadside from *Victory*, Lucas succeeded in crossing the British ship's bow, bringing his port guns to bear and pouring raking broadsides into that vulnerable part of Nelson's flagship. As the mêlée continued, one of *Victory's* topmasts was shot away, her wheel was shattered, and her mainmast and mizzenmast were heavily damaged. Nelson is reported to have remarked at this stage of the battle: 'This is too warm work, Hardy, to last long.'

In his after-action report, Lucas reported grappling on to *Victory* and attempting to board her after his enemy's exposed decks had been swept clear. Those attempts were thwarted, however, and as *Victory's* situation became perilous, the 98-gun *Téméraire* joined the fray in her support. Lucas described the result of *Téméraire's* broadsides:

> It is impossible to describe the carnage produced by the murderous broadsides of this ship. More than two hundred of our brave men were killed or wounded by it. I was wounded also at the same time, but not so seriously as to make me abandon my post. Not being able to undertake anything on the side of the *Victory*, I now ordered the rest of the crew to man the batteries on the other side and fire at the *Téméraire* with what guns the collision ... had not dismounted.[20]

Lucas's report places the end of his part of the combat at 3:30pm, when *Redoutable* was so badly damaged that she no longer had the means to resist. At that point the 74-gun British *Swiftsure* took his ship in tow, and a different battle began: the struggle to keep *Redoutable* afloat. That battle went on through the night and into the following day. Finally, around seven in the evening and in the midst of the post-battle storm, *Redoutable* sank, taking a considerable number of her wounded with her. Lucas's opinion of her crew was brief and unreserved: '[T]he whole history of our navy can show nothing like them.'[21]

Benjamin West's painting shows Nelson struck down on the deck of his flagship. The significance of the moment is such that the battle itself seems of secondary importance as the stunned audience regard their fallen leader. (Royal Naval Museum)

THE CARNAGE ENDS

The 74-gun French ship *Achille*, sometimes confused with the British *Achilles*, played a special role in the battle of Trafalgar. Initially, the French *Achille* was the thirtieth ship in the Combined Fleet's line. As the battle unfolded, she had engaged the 74-gun *Revenge*, the 74-gun *Defiance*, the 74-gun *Swiftsure*, and the 64-gun *Polyphemus*. In the action, *Revenge* inflicted fatal damage to *Achille* with repeated raking fire into the Frenchman's bow.

As the afternoon wore on, the French *Achille's* officers and crew were decimated, and she was under the command of a junior officer. Finally, one of the last ships in Collingwood's line, the 98-gun *Prince*, fired two broadsides into the stricken ship's stern, bringing down her mainmast and mizzenmast and starting an uncontrollable fire. Late in the afternoon she blew up, providing the final, violent punctuation to the day's carnage.

It was approximately five in the afternoon when the firing stopped, and a post-battle silence settled over the scene. Smoke and the smell of burned gunpowder lingered. Bodies and debris from shattered ships floated in the water. Eighteen ships of the Combined Fleet had been sunk or captured; many of those were subsequently wrecked in the storm that immediately followed the battle. No British ships were sunk or captured.

Two of the ships captured by the British later escaped. The French 74-gun *Algeçiras* was taken over by a British prize crew during the battle, but when the storm struck, the prisoners were released to help save the ship. With great skill the British-French crew managed to struggle into Cadiz, where roles were reversed; the British became the prisoners. The Spanish 120-gun *Santa Ana* and the 80-gun *Neptuno* were retaken two days after the battle by a French-Spanish squadron that ventured out of Cadiz to counterattack against the battle-damaged and storm-battered British ships nearby, but *Neptuno* was subsequently wrecked. Fifteen French and Spanish ships escaped, most with considerable damage, but within slightly more than a month after the battle, Captain Sir Richard Strachan captured four French ships that had been among the 15 that escaped from the Battle.

After the Battle, *Victory* eventually reached Gibraltar, where she was refitted. On 3 November she sailed for England with Nelson's body, which was interred under the Great Dome of St Paul's Cathedral, after one of the most memorable state funerals in history.

The toll in human suffering was immense. British estimates of casualties published in the *London Gazette* were 449 killed and 1,214 wounded. The Combined Fleet suffered much heavier casualties; more than 4,400 were killed, and more than 2,500 were wounded. In addition, almost 4,800 officers and men from the French-Spanish Fleet were captured. One of the indicators of the human toll within the Combined Fleet can be established by extrapolating the fate of its six admirals. The commander-in-chief French Admiral Villeneuve, was captured, and his second in command Spanish Admiral Gravina was grievously wounded and escaped to Cadiz. Spanish Vice-Admiral D'Alva was seriously wounded but

FATE OF THE COMBINED FLEET

Captured	*San Ildefonso* (Sp.) *San Juan Nepomuceno* (Sp.) *Bahama* (Sp.) *Swiftsure* (Fr.)
Captured, then wrecked	*Monarca* (Sp.) *Fougueux* (Fr.) *Bucentaure* (Fr.) *Berwick* (Fr.)
Captured, then burned	*Aigle* (Fr.) *Intrépide* (Fr.) *San Augustín* (Sp.)
Captured, then sank	*Santísima Trinidad* (Sp.) *Redoutable* (Fr.)
Captured, then scuttled	*Argonauta* (Sp.)
Captured, then escaped	*Algésiras* (Sp.)
Captured, then re-taken	*Santa Ana* (Sp.)
Captured, re-taken, then wrecked	*Neptuno* (Sp.)
Sunk in action	*Achille* (Fr.)
Escaped	*Argonaute* (Sp.) *Pluton* (Fr.) *San Justo* (Sp.) *San Leandro* (Sp.) *Neptune* (Fr.) *Héros* (Fr.) *Príncipe de Asturias* (Sp.) *Montañes* (Sp.)
Escaped, then wrecked	*El Rayo* (Sp.) *San Francisco de Asisi* (Sp.) *Indomptable* (Fr.)
Escaped, then captured *(captured in action by Sir Richard Strachan on 4 November in the Bay of Biscay off the Spanish coast)*	*Formidable* (Fr.) *Mont-Blanc* (Fr.) *Scipion* (Fr.) *Duguay-Trouin* (Fr.)

also escaped to Cadiz, and Spanish Rear-Admiral Cisneros was captured. French Rear-Admiral Magón was killed, and French Rear-Admiral Dumanoir escaped.

IMMEDIATE AFTERMATH

One might wonder why Collingwood did not anchor at the end of the day. Nelson's signal to 'Prepare to Anchor after the close of day' was meant for the entire fleet, and Collingwood would have been inclined to carry out the intentions of his fallen leader and good friend. Collingwood, as Nelson, knew what the heavy swells that had been rolling in from the west meant; a very serious storm was headed in his direction. Yet, for the most part, he did not follow Nelson's order to anchor the fleet. Why?

The answer to that question lies in the circumstances of the post-battle storm. When confronted by a serious storm, there are two basic reactions to evaluate. The first involves anchoring as securely as possible in as protected an area as possible and hoping you can ride out the storm. The problem with this alternative is that your fate hangs on how well protected your anchorage is, your anchor holding, and your ground tackle standing up. The second alternative involves getting as far out to sea as possible and taking advantage of the sea room to manoeuvre your ship through the storm. The danger of the second approach is that your ship can be simply overwhelmed by the elements and sunk.

Collingwood, who had no well-protected port to flee to, chose, in general, to try to get his ships as far off the land as possible. One of the determining factors was the poor condition of many of his ships and virtually all of the prizes. During the battle anchors were smashed and ground tackle was obliterated in many of the ships, making it simply impossible to anchor at all, let alone anchor securely. Further supporting his decision was the proximity of a dangerous lee shore towards which the storm was driving him. On the 22 October, Collingwood wrote to the secretary of the Board of Admiralty William Marsden:

> [I]t having blown a gale of wind ever since the Action, I have not yet had it in my power to collect any reports from the Ships.... After the Action I shifted my flag to her [the frigate *Euryalus*], that I might more easily communicate my orders to, and collect the Ships, and towed the Royal Sovereign out to seaward. The whole fleet was now in a very perilous situation. Many ships were dismasted; all shattered; in thirteen fathoms water, off the shoals of Trafalgar; and when I made the signal to prepare to anchor, few of the ships had an Anchor to let go, their cables being shot; but the same good Providence which aided us through such a day preserved us in the night, by the wind shifting a few points, and drifting the ships off the land, except four of the captured dismasted Ships, which are now at anchor off Trafalgar, and I hope will ride safe until those gales are over.[22]

THE FINAL PERSPECTIVE

By 26 October, Collingwood was able to detach the sloop HMS *Pickle*, commanded by Lieutenant John Lapenotière, from the fleet with the report of the battle to government in London. Lapenotière and his tiny ship fought their way through gales and heavy seas and arrived at Falmouth on 4 November. From there, the young officer raced to London by coach. He arrived at Whitehall in the early hours of 6 November and turned his dispatches over to the Secretary to the Board of the Admiralty with a sailor's blunt report: 'Sir, we have gained a great victory. But we have lost Lord Nelson.'

History has established a much more far-reaching evaluation of the battle of Trafalgar than Lapenotière. And none is more accurate than that of American sea power prophet A. T. Mahan. In 1897, then-Captain Mahan concluded his biography *The Life of Nelson* with a chapter on the Battle of Trafralgar, in which he wrote:

> There were, indeed, consequences momentous and stupendous yet to flow from the decisive supremacy of Great Britain's sea-power, the establishment of which, beyond all question or competition, was Nelson's great achievement; but his part was done when Trafalgar was fought. The coincidence of this death with the moment of completed success has impressed upon that superb battle a stamp of finality, an immortality of fame, which even its own grandeur scarcely could have insured.[23]

TRAFALGAR
NILE
COPENHA

CHAPTER EIGHT

NELSON AND TRAFALGAR: THE LEGACY

PROFESSOR ANDREW LAMBERT

Although it was a truly decisive battle, the consequences and significance of Trafalgar, and the meaning of the hero who died in the moment of victory, have been hotly debated. Trafalgar would give Britain command of the oceans for the next hundred years and was immediately marked out as the ideal naval victory. Yet for most this was simply a matter of how many ships were taken, rather than a demonstration of the highest intellectual and professional qualities. Admiral Sir Robert Calder was judged to have botched his action with Villeneuve off Cape Finisterre on 22 July 1805, not because of a failure to take more enemy ships, but because he did not transform his initial success into strategically significant results. This failure to identify the true meaning of Trafalgar was part of the process that saw Nelson portrayed as hero or god, rather than naval genius.

Because he succeeded so completely, and then died at the moment of victory, Nelson closed an era in world history and made Trafalgar magical. Trafalgar transcended the details of what happened to become the talisman of the nation, and a standard of success to which all must aspire. It gave the Royal Navy a unique status, closer to religion than reason, one that would be contested, but not countermanded.

STRATEGIC CONSEQUENCES

The morning after Trafalgar the world was a different place. The art of war at sea had been raised to a level of insight, leadership, daring and commitment that can never be excelled. Trafalgar was the ultimate expression of war at sea under sail, distilling and refining everything that had gone before into an irresistible compound. By his inspirational leadership, and genius for communicating Nelson had enabled a fleet, many of whose captains he hardly knew, to adopt radically new tactics, and use them to decide the hardest-fought naval battle of

OPPOSITE
The Immortality of Nelson by Benjamin West. This painting used classical imagery to mark the elevation of the hero to an imaginary pantheon of the gods. Although this jarred with Nelson's own simple Christian faith, it suited the national mood. (National Maritime Museum).

the age. He had focused his eye on the decisive point, leading the attack that destroyed the enemy's command and control, smashed their formation, and set up the battle of annihilation he had sought.

But this was only the tactical perspective. The purpose of Nelson's tactics had been, as ever, to advance the strategic needs of the theatre and the conflict. He did not restrict his horizons to winning battles: rather he was concerned to translate battle victories into successful campaigns and wars. Villeneuve had made a serious mistake coming out to sea, he had exposed a key French strategic asset, the combined fleet that could attack British trade and possessions, her Mediterranean ally Naples, or simply remain 'in being' to sustain the almost unbearable tension and pressure of the invasion scare. Once the enemy was at sea Nelson had to annihilate them, to make them pay for their temerity. The final complication to be addressed in his planning was the knowledge that a storm would break that night, an insight based on his assessment of the meteorological evidence. He had to finish the job in an afternoon.

Nelson's achievement, reinforced by the subsequent allied sortie, Strachan's capture of Dumanoir's four fugitives, and Duckworth's annihilation of Lessigue's squadron, destroyed the naval power that gave credence to Napoleon's invasion threat. Britain's command of the sea had been placed beyond doubt. Nelson knew that, once the British Empire and its trade was safe, it could prosper and expand, creating wealth and funding the war. It was time to translate naval power into strategic success.

However, the fruits of Trafalgar would take a decade to harvest. Within weeks Napoleon had transformed the European balance of power by smashing the Austro-Russian army at Austerlitz, within a year he had repeated the process at Jena/Auerstadt and Eylau. With Austria and Prussia cowed into submission and Russia a reluctant ally, Napoleon set up his Continental System, an economic blockade of Britain, excluding British trade from the Continent. With his fleet gone, Napoleon looked to extend his empire across the Continent, his gaze still fixed on the east. When Naples, the destination of Villeneuve's ill-fated sortie, fell to a French army it seemed that Bonaparte was invincible. Yet his power had been circumscribed, his ultimate fate already mapped out.

The British responded to Napoleon's Continental System with their own blockade of Europe, the 'Orders in Council', which, as Nelson had stressed, made the Continent suffer the cost of French occupation, and prompted rebellion. To sustain absolute naval command, any flickering naval threats were swiftly crushed, the Danish and Portuguese navies were removed from the board by British action in 1807, the still numerous Spanish fleet by a French invasion of their country. Bounded by naval might, Napoleon was unable to escape the confines of Europe, or sustain his empire of plunder and conquest. British aid, financial and military, revived the downtrodden peoples in Spain, Portugal, Italy and Germany. British trade, secured by Nelson's victory, funded the war that destroyed the French Empire, and the Industrial Revolution that fuelled the next century of British power.

Having destroyed the French fleet, the Royal Navy was reconfigured for a new war. With the residue of French seapower tightly blockaded in Brest, Toulon and Antwerp, British task forces swept up the last remnants of the French and Dutch overseas empires, boosting trade and ending the threat to shipping. Insurance rates fell. British cruisers shifted to the offensive: offshore islands and convoys were swept up, coastal towns attacked and the Spanish rising against the French sustained and reinforced. As Napoleon observed, while a prisoner on board HMS *Bellerophon*: 'If it had not been for you English, I should have been Emperor of the East. But wherever there is water to float a ship, we are sure to find you in our way.'[1] The French could only respond by pouring treasure and manpower into coastal defences and telegraph systems to counter the omnipotent Royal Navy. Emboldened by their success, the British became ever more aggressive, pushing their attacks to the point of foolhardiness, relying on reputation to make up for impossible odds. In 1813 Nelson's protégé William Hoste, not content with a superb naval victory at Lissa, used his sailors to haul heavy cannons to the top of Dalmatian mountains, to capture key fortresses!

In 1814, Napoleon, the military colossus, would be beaten by the armies of the European states, by Russia, Prussia and Austria, with the support of the British, Spanish and Portuguese effort in the Iberian Peninsula, but this was only possible because Britain never gave up the conflict, never allowed Napoleon the opportunity to consolidate his power and rebuild the Continent in his own image. Trafalgar was the beginning of the end.

TACTICS

Trafalgar completed a decade of remarkable change in naval tactical thinking. With Nelson at the forefront of the process, the old ideas based on the rigid linear thinking of the 17th century were abandoned. Nelson did not abandon the old tactics because they were wrong, but because against unskilled foes anxious to avoid battle they were unnecessary, and risked losing scarce opportunities to impose combat. The old systems remained enshrined in the formal tactical orders, but they were largely ignored for the duration of the war. However, the revolution was not one of fixed ideas, but of flexible, responsive tactics, meeting each situation with the best approach. As if to prove the point, the only officer to copy Nelson's Trafalgar tactics was Commodore Dubordieu, leading a Franco-Venetian squadron at the battle of Lissa in 1811. His bold two-column attack was shattered by the accurate and sustained gunnery of William Hoste's far smaller British force. In an action between fleets of equal ability, the Trafalgar tactics would always fail, Nelson or no. Nelson's genius was to know when to take such risks.

With the old tactical order changing, ships were modified to fight in the new mêlée battles. When the *Victory* arrived at Chatham for repairs, Master Shipwright Robert Seppings recognized the need to build stronger bows, to protect the crew from the terrible raking fire. His answer was to carry the same heavy structural timbers and planking right round the bow up to the upper deck,

In his painting of *The Battle of Trafalgar*, J. M. W. Turner invested the battle with an intensity of meaning that few others have equalled. (National Maritime Museum)

with acutely angled gun ports to facilitate ahead fire. Later he would apply the same logic to the stern, replacing the vast, flimsy glazed structure with solid timber. After Trafalgar the wooden warship was re-engineered for all-round combat, and re-painted Nelson-fashion, with the chequer-board design his ships had adopted before the battle.

THE NATIONAL HERO

However, the astonishing victory that saved Britain from economic ruin and invasion, while laying the foundations of ultimate victory, was not celebrated: instead there was a day of national mourning on 5 December 1805. While the final destruction of the invasion threat was a relief for many, the cost had been too high. The triumph was dimmed by the death of the hero. In life Nelson had become the embodiment of the newly focused British national identity, an 'immortal' who gave his countrymen the courage to resist a continent in arms, and confidence in their ultimate success. He was the icon of the age, and as Lord Byron noted, 'Britannia's god of War'. No other hero has matched Nelson's engagement with his public. As the only man to stand between Britain and a French invasion, his death was greeted with shock and grief. Little wonder he was mourned. As society hostess Lady Bessborough explained:

> How glorious if it was not so cruelly damped by Nelson's death! How truly he has accomplished his prediction that when they meet it must be to extermination. To a man like him he could not have picked out a finer close to such a life. But what an irreparable loss to England! ... Courage and perseverance like his cannot be too highly honoured, and it will encourage others to follow his noble career of glory. I can think of nothing else, and hardly imagined it possible to feel so much grief for a Man I did not know... Think of being mourned by a whole Nation, and having my name carried down with gratitude and praise to the latest generations.[2]

A few days later, Lady Bessborough realized the feeling was universal. 'Almost everybody wears a black crape scarf or cockade with Nelson written on it – this is almost general, high and low; indeed the enthusiasm is general beyond anything I ever saw.'[3] This was the first occasion for national grief, the first time that news had touched the newly created British consciousness. It would leave an indelible mark.

Because the nation had no one to replace the dead hero, he was buried in a way that captured his name and his indomitable spirit for the war effort. Hitherto naval heroes had been tucked away in dusty corners of Westminster Abbey, mixed up with poets and prelates: Nelson would be the first and greatest hero to be buried in St Pauls, cathedral of the City of London that so valued his work in securing global trade. He would be placed in the crypt, directly under the crossing, the central figure in a new national pantheon to ensure his name lived on and his example inspired future generations. His interment would be the most lavish and spectacular ever staged in Britain, because his country still needed him. This was no farewell, only translation to a new national role. A two-day funerary pageant on 8–9 January 1806 took his body by river from the Royal Naval Hospital at Greenwich to the Admiralty, and then on to St Paul's through immense crowds, who took off their hats and stood in silence as his mortal remains passed – unbidden, but eloquent testimony from the masses. By the time his coffin had been lowered into place, he had been deified, the war god of the British nation, the ultimate expression of the national effort.

His passing excited a massive artistic response. Arthur Devis, who took a passage on *Victory* when she left Spithead for Chatham presented the ship as a shrine, and the crew as disciples. His *The Death of Nelson* captured the moment when the mortal hero was transfigured into a divine being, it also secured Joshua Boydell's 500 guinea prize for the best death scene.[4] The series of 'death' paintings closed with Benjamin *West's The Immortality of Nelson* of 1807, with Nelson, posed as the dead Christ carried in arms of victory to a mourning Minerva, while Neptune watches. The signal 'England expects', gives the picture a motto.[5] The combination of sacred and profane imagery, Christ, Roman deities and a mortal man was irreligious, if not blasphemous. There were some in the Church who recognized the danger. The new secular faith, the cult of the hero, was a real threat to organized religion.

A national response required a truly great artist. J. M. W. Turner went on board the *Victory* at Chatham, beginning a lifelong attempt to explain the meaning of Trafalgar. Few artists have had such a strongly developed sense of their national role, or lived in an era that had such need of them. Turner had already recognized in Nelson the genius that would make him the national hero.[6] Trafalgar took the subject and the artist to new levels, using the sea and the great warships to define British resistance. His first picture of 1806 took an unconventional perspective, viewing the moment the fatal shot was fired from high in the *Victory's* rigging.[7] Trafalgar was a subject Turner would return to in the 1820s, before achieving his own immortality with *The Fighting Téméraire* of 1837. His pictures are the ultimate expression of Nelson's impact on his age, romantic hero, national symbol and war god. Beside Turner's compositions all other Trafalgar pictures appear pale, literal and short of meaning.

By 1815 naval officers had become popular heroes, in life and fiction. The men who fought alongside Nelson were lionized, while their fictional alter egos, in the new literary genre created by Captain Frederick Marryat, were used to teach moral lessons. While the impulse was romantic, the underlying idea reflected the rising power of the professional classes. The Reform Act of 1832 gave political power to middle-class men, and changed the nature of leadership. The new leaders were professionals, their status based on competence, not birth. They were part of a new culture of service, and their patron saint would be the apparently self-made hero Nelson.[8] Contemporary heroes were consciously compared to those from medieval literature,[9] and throughout the 19th century this would be the ultimate accolade for any warrior. Unfortunately this trend was also profoundly anti-intellectual, valuing character over ability.[10] This may explain the lack of any worthwhile attempt to analyze Nelson's professional legacy, as distinct from his personal life and character. The great Nelson debates of the century were about morality, character and honour, it simply did not matter that he was a genius. The new age did not appreciate vainglorious display: the Victorians found something vulgar in Nelson's public appearances, and the pleasure he took in his celebrity. They judged him by their standards, and not those of his own era. The origins of his behaviour were too complex for an age that preferred simple narrative to analytical insight. The nation needed a hero, the Navy an example, and no one needed to trouble their heads to think,

While Nelson was placed, god-like on his column, his ship, the *Victory*, so aptly named, would be accorded the ultimate accolade not only of preservation for posterity but to continue as the oldest serving ship in the Royal Navy. (Royal Naval Museum)

they could simply repeat the mantra. Thus Nelson, in whose brilliant mind the complex and demanding business of war was made simple for his followers, was reduced to the level of a parody, spouting nonsensical platitudes like: 'never mind tactics, always go at them'.

This anti-intellectual, idealized approach dominated the gallery at the Royal Naval Hospital, Greenwich that became the artistic shrine to the immortal memory. Begun in 1823, the collection consciously attempted to cover Britain's rise to naval glory.[11] In 1829 George IV handed over Turner's overwhelming *Trafalgar*. Later Prince Albert donated the bloodstained coat. Responses to the collection varied. Most read the history lesson in a conventional manner, as a shrine recording their rise to world-empire. Seen in this light, a preference for the literal was only to be expected. The nation knew exactly what Nelson meant. He had given them the empire of the world, its trade flowed past the building. However, that much-travelled seaman and storyteller Herman Melville visited

The significance of the victory at Trafalgar for a seafaring nation is exemplified by the fact that a British admiral was elevated on a monument that made even royal monuments pale in comparison. (Mary Evans Picture Library)

the Painted Hall in 1849 and, fascinated by the blood-stained coat,[12] Melville caught the meaning of the man, and Nelson became a powerful presence in his later work. He stood out against the Victorian tendency to treat Nelson literally, where a concern with fact and form invited unthinking responses.

The process of establishing Nelson as the national deity was completed by the erection of a monument in central London. Although the House of Commons had discussed the issue in 1816, nothing was done. Clearing away the slums, stables and warren of lanes between Charing Cross, St Martin in the Fields, Whitehall and St James's provided a suitable space, and the addition of the National Gallery in the early 1830s provided a focal point, but it was only in 1835 that the space was named Trafalgar Square. The King, Nelson's old friend William, accepted the inevitable. After William's death in 1837, Wellington, Hardy and Cockburn led a committee to collect money for a memorial. William Railton's design used a column from Augustus' Temple of Mars Ultor (Mars the Avenger, or he who has the last word). Taken from a temple built at the heart of Imperial Rome to celebrate the deification of Julius Caesar and the avenging of his death, it linked him with the god of war and established an Imperial regime that would last forever.[13] The meaning was obvious: Nelson had become the national god of war, and the nation had avenged his death by defeating Napoleon. By the 1840s it was clear that Trafalgar had set the seal on Britain's naval mastery for all time, Nelson and an Augustan column provided the ultimate expression of global maritime power. The column and statue were in place by November 1843, 24 years later Landseer's bronze lions completed the design.[14] The impact of the column was, and remains, immense. Hitler saw it as the 'symbol of British naval might and world domination': he planned to take it back to Berlin if his invasion project had been more successful than Bonaparte's. However, British naval might was far more than a symbol, and he did not make the attempt.[15]

NAVAL LEGACY

Although Nelson was a unique genius, of unequalled penetration, judgement and insight, his professional legacy was immense. The Mediterranean command was taken up by his life-long friend Collingwood, who shared many of his finer qualities, if not his talent for communication, or his good fortune. Among the men of the next generation, few escaped the impact of Nelson. Among his many talented followers, William Hoste, another Norfolk parson's son, won a brilliant frigate battle off Lissa in 1811, flying the signal 'Remember Nelson'. Edward Codrington commanded the last sailing ship fleet battle, at Navarino on 20 October 1827. The solid, reliable Thomas Hardy went on to command fleets, and to serve as First Sea Lord, while George Cockburn orchestrated the capture of Washington in 1814 and ran the navy for many years after 1815. The last of Nelson's followers was Sir William Parker, twice Commander-in-Chief in the Mediterranean, who died an Admiral of the Fleet in 1866. They were only the best known among many, and the service continued to bear Nelson's stamp long into the 19th century. It was only with the coming of new technology, and the waning of the threat from France that Nelson began to lose his immediate relevance, gradually becoming an ideal to be followed and no longer an inspiration.

In the Crimean War (1854–56) the Russians were so frightened of the Royal Navy that they stayed in harbour, deceived by Admiral Lyons, a slight, grey-haired officer who fancied he looked like Nelson, and persuaded *The Times* that he was suitably energetic. In truth the only character trait Lyons shared with Nelson was vanity.[16] Fortunately Britain did not need a real Nelson to deal with Russia. Thereafter the constant demands posed by shifting technology and the uncertainty surrounding the future of war at sea deprived officers of the opportunity to reflect on the intellectual demands of their profession. With few and small wars, the route to promotion lay through mastery of the new guns, torpedoes and engineering systems. Nelson was slowly transformed from an example into a mantra, his incisive and sophisticated tactical concepts, invariably determined by strategic circumstances, and grand strategic objectives, were boiled down into mindless aggression. Little wonder the real meaning of Trafalgar was lost, and so many naval leaders of the late 19th and early 20th centuries failed to meet the demands of war.

By the 1890s steam ships and sophisticated flag signalling systems allowed Admirals to control the detailed movements of their fleets, an opportunity which most exploited to reduce their captains to unthinking ship drivers. In 1893 Admiral Sir George Tryon, who ironically had attempted to break this vicious system, became its victim after he had issued a mistaken order. Because the second-in-command lacked the confidence or common sense to question the order, Tryon's flagship, *Victoria*, was rammed and sunk and Sir George's last words were said to have been 'It is all my fault'.

THE FRENCH PERSPECTIVE

While the Spanish accepted the judgement of Trafalgar, and celebrated the glory earned by Gravina and his heroic followers, Imperial France was anxious to suppress the news from the south. With Bonaparte still halfway between Ulm and Austerlitz, and Prussia pressing his flank, he dared not show any sign of weakness. Consequently Trafalgar passed without comment in the official press, but Bonaparte would never forgive Villeneuve. After a brief captivity in England, among men who admired his dignity, courage and lack of bombast, Villeneuve returned to France. He was murdered at Rennes, to remove an embarrassing reminder of Bonaparte's failure.

After the downfall of Bonaparte, the restored Bourbon government was prepared to ask why the French navy had been beaten so often and what it was that made Nelson the ideal commander. In an attempt to comprehend the basis of Britain's success in war, industry and trade, the French Government commissioned an official study from leading academician Charles Dupin. The second instalment of Dupin's *Voyages dans la Grand-Bretagne*, published in 1821, was devoted to the Royal Navy. Dupin stressed that the French did not use their naval forces in the same way as the British. For the French, strategic objectives invariably took precedence over tactical considerations, consequently battle did not occupy the central place that it was accorded by the British. Dupin offered a priceless insight into the greatness of Nelson. He recognized the vital role of 'mission-analysis', and argued that Nelson:

> ought to be held up as a pattern for admirals, by the extreme pains he took to impress upon his flag-officers and captains, the spirit of

Admiral Lord Lyons could call on the spirit of Nelson to cow his enemies during the Crimean War. There would come a time, however, when the Navy's failure to turn the spirit of Nelson's navy into practical action would lead it into dangerous waters. (Royal Naval Museum)

the enterprises which he resolved to undertake. He unfolded to them his general plan of operations, and the modifications with which the weather, or the manoeuvres of the enemy, might force him to qualify his original design. When once he had explained his system to the flag and superior officers of his fleet, he confided to them the charge of acting according to circumstances, so as to lead, in the most favourable manner, to the consummation of the enterprise thus planned. And Nelson, who was allowed to choose the companions of his glory, possessed the talent and the happiness to find men worthy of his instruction and confidence; they learnt, in action, to supply what had escaped his forethought, and in success, to surpass even his hopes.[17]

The fighting spirit of Nelson was embodied by several of his successors, not least William Hoste, another son of Norfolk, who won a brilliant victory at the battle of Lissa in 1811. (National Maritime Museum)

There is no better appreciation of Nelson's genius in contemporary literature, nor one so close to the modern understanding of 'mission-analysis' as the basis of tactical excellence.

Twenty-five years later, another Frenchman examined the professional side of Nelson's life. As a sea officer and the son of a Napoleonic Admiral, Captain Jurien de la Gravière found a rich haul of evidence in the Nicolas edition of

Nelson's correspondence. He emphasized Nelson's prodigious energy and uncommon valour, placing his astonishing seamanship above military daring. It was the combination of professional enthusiasm, exemplified by Nelson, with political commitment to sustained and ample funding that gave Britain victory in the long war at sea.[18] That de la Gravière's analysis was, like Dupin's, worthy of translation, reveals much about the relative poverty of British attempts to analyze Nelson's intellectual legacy. It was as if the very idea of an intellectual warrior was unacceptable, and the task should be left to foreign writers. The standard naval history of the Revolutionary and Napoleonic wars, by the lawyer-turned-historian William James, was content to cite Dupin.[19] Nor did things improve thereafter; whole volumes examined Nelson's character, attributing his success to energy, enthusiasm and patriotism. The tendency in British literature was always to explain the success by studying the man. It was so much easier than trying to fathom the depths of a remarkable intellect, and a unique naval mind. By focusing on the humdrum and the human, British Nelson studies demeaned the subject by treating him as popular literature: there was very little professional study. The French, by contrast, wanted to understand and took the trouble to think about underlying principles.

IN PRIVATE

Because Nelson was so much more than an admiral, his private life was a fit subject for comment even in his lifetime. That he chose an unconventional existence added a frisson of scandal to his celebrity, and opened a line of attack on his character as the moral climate of succeeding generations hardened. In the 20th century a different construction, the 'romantic' Nelson, was built, and much of his fame reflected his relationship with Emma Hamilton.

REVIVAL

The high Victorian decades of peace and prosperity, in which the very name of Nelson withered away, could not last The growth of rival fleets ended the long career of Prime Minister William Ewart Gladstone, who resigned in 1894 rather than accept increased naval spending. In 1893, anticipating this seismic shift in political opinion, naval historian Professor John Knox Laughton and the Director of Naval Intelligence, Captain Cyprian Bridge, founded the Navy Records Society. Their purpose was to publish critical material from the naval past to help develop doctrine and education for the modern Navy. Their target audience included statesmen, princes, newspaper writers and creators of popular culture. Through the Records Society, the Navy moved away from the amateurish, careless attitude to the past that had characterized the preceding 70 years, and began to draw on the wealth of hard-won experience that lay in Admiralty archives and private collections. Much of the intellectual force behind the development of war-planning and tactics was historical. Nelson was everywhere: his 'Trafalgar Memorandum' the key paper in a compilation distributed to the fleet to encourage modern officers to think about the next war.

Laughton also worked with American naval officer and theorist Captain Alfred Thayer Mahan, who used Nelson as 'the embodiment of the Sea Power of Great Britain', to teach naval strategy by example. Mahan's 1897 *Life of Nelson* showed how Nelson used 'Sea Power' to decisive effect. The book was large, and written in a ponderous, stately style that found a welcome audience in an era without television, radio or other distractions for long dark evenings. Having commanded sailing warships, and seen active service in the American Civil War, Mahan combined his theoretical ideas with practical experience. Mahan's book also prompted a revival of the hostile comments on Nelson's conduct at Naples in 1799.[20] Using the methods of the newly professional study of naval history, Laughton and Mahan defeated these attacks.

By 1900 Laughton had made the Royal Navy historically aware, and taken the past into the core of naval thinking. In the process he had created a discipline, and a professional body, brought together the new profession of historian and the old one of sea-service, assembling the great and good, the able and the industrious.

No sooner had Nelson's name been cleared of calumnies than the centenary of Trafalgar sparked a new debate on Nelson's tactics. Laughton passed the subject to his friend Julian Corbett, who provided masterful analyses of the Trafalgar campaign, British naval tactics and the application of maritime power in national strategy in the decade before the First World War. This was the culmination of the work begun back in the early 1890s, it gave the Navy a Nelson they could understand, and in *The Campaign of Trafalgar* a well-nigh perfect historical monograph and teaching text. Corbett's book linked the events of 1805 to current needs. Corbett was also a key member of John Fisher's Admiralty team, working on educational reforms and war planning.[21]

Just how much Corbett's work was needed became obvious during the 1907 discussion of the invasion threat, by politicians, admirals and generals. Their historical understanding was so weak that both the army and the navy accepted that Nelson had been 'decoyed' to the West Indies by Villeneuve.[22] Little wonder the Navy was happy to accept the simplest of pasts, in which Nelson always attacked: this avoided the need to do as he had done, to think, reflect and analyze the demands of war at sea in the broadest context. Few bothered to ask any questions of their history. It was easier to follow orders, and as the systems for sending such orders improved, so the space in which Nelson had operated at Cape St Vincent, of anticipation, insight and judgement, was restricted by the ability of the commander-in-chief to issue precise instructions.[23] Nelson's legacy had been frittered away.

As the 20th century opened, Nelson mattered. Yet a sudden shift in Britain's international position crippled the commemoration of the centenary of Trafalgar. In 1904 Britain signed an Entente with France, an agreement to settle the squabbles of the past 30 years, allowing the two powers to co-operate in the face of growing German power. The Foreign Office was so concerned to avoid upsetting French sensitivities that official celebrations were effectively stifled, and the Admiralty ordered the fleet not to make any special display. The Fleet review was more Entente celebration than Trafalgar commemoration. Exactly who came up with the idea that we should forget our past merely to avoid upsetting the sensitivities of our current friends is unknown, but such feeble, apologetic nonsense did not show the country in a particularly positive light. Trafalgar is a matter of fact, the outcome is not contested.

The nation was still content to attribute Trafalgar to character and courage. It was his self-sacrifice that the Victorians and Edwardians found so ennobling about Nelson. His devotion to 'duty' chimed with the service ethic of the age, his Christian values were modernized to suit current tastes, quietly disposing of Emma in favour of more pious pronouncements. It helped that he was a popular hero, above class or clique, without a significant political role, and of course the sea was Britain's element.[24]

It was a mark of the failure of the Royal Navy to examine the past that the tactics used at Trafalgar were only formally studied in 1911. This process was stimulated by Corbett's work on the famous Trafalgar Memorandum of 9 October. The meaning of this paper has been much debated, and the Admiralty's minute investigation was published less than a year before the First World War broke out.[25] However, most analysts have missed the key point. The memorandum was not a free-standing document: it completed a process begun with verbal discussions in the Great Cabin of the *Victory*, on 29 and 30 September, when Nelson explained the 'Nelson Touch' to his captains. His concept was, as ever, to reduce the complex, demanding problem of arranging a fleet for battle, forcing the enemy to fight and securing a complete victory into a set of basic ideas that could be easily understood. The written version contained the intellectual fruits of a career dedicated to the pursuit and destruction of the enemy. It distilled the history, techniques and possibilities of sailing-fleet tactics through the prism of personal experience, and applied them to the situation he anticipated. It was not prescriptive: Nelson was the last admiral to preclude the effects of chance, initiative, individual impulse, human error or enemy action. As the philosopher of war Carl von Clausewitz stressed, no plans survive first contact with the enemy. Instead Nelson had given his captains a priceless insight into his intellectual process, a guide to the way he thought and the objects at which he aimed, together with the core concept of breaking the enemy formation in two places, to destroy two thirds of their fleet. Finally he reminded them that 'something must be left to chance' and added 'in case Signals can neither be seen nor perfectly understood, no Captain can do very wrong if he places his Ship alongside that of an Enemy.'[26] This last was the fall-back position for the 'blockheads', without the wit to think for themselves. It was the least he expected, not a mantra for success in battle. Experience had taught him that not all captains were equal, and he did not know enough of his new team to rely on them all. This was why he chose the ships that would be close to him in battle, all were commanded by men he knew and trusted.[27]

In rebuilding the Royal Navy in the Edwardian era, Admiral Sir John Fisher consciously re-used the names of ships that fought at Trafalgar. Consequently the fleet that fought at Jutland in 1916 sounded remarkably familiar, although the leadership lacked the genius and professionalism of the original. Fisher was consciously preparing for a second Trafalgar, although he preferred to use the magic of these great names to deter war, rather than having to defend the legacy on the field of battle.

THE FIRST WORLD WAR

In 1914 the Royal Navy went to war with more ships, men and guns than the enemy, their confidence heightened by the knowledge that they were the heirs of Nelson. By contrast the magic of Trafalgar still oppressed the Germans, they would have to beat a bigger fleet, and Nelson too. It proved to be a burden the Kaiser's admirals could not shoulder. Buoyed up by an almost sublime

Admiral Lord Fisher rebuilt the navy and used the ship's names that were redolent of the Trafalgar era. The spell remained but British naval predominance now owed more to sheer numbers and size than to dash and daring. (Royal Naval Museum)

HMS *Dreadnought*, named for a ship that fought at Trafalgar, ushered in a new battleship era, making everything else afloat obsolete. The advance in ship technology, however, was not accompanied by fresh and innovative thinking. (Royal Naval Museum)

self-confidence, the British accepted risks, made mistakes, and in almost all cases escaped punishment. The only admirals to be censured were those who passed up an opportunity to engage the enemy more closely. Brave men like Christopher Cradock, who went to his death well aware that he could not win, were following a false and dangerous distortion of the Nelson tradition, one that esteemed courage above intellect. Throughout the war the Navy was desperate to find something heroic to celebrate.

The public expected a second Trafalgar, entirely unaware of the very different situation pertaining in 1914. In Nelson's day the British had to pin the French fleets in harbour, to secure their ocean communications. In 1914 they had only to wait and watch, if the Germans wanted to go anywhere other than the Baltic, they would have to come right past the main British base at Scapa Flow. Nelson took risks and operated on the offensive because he commanded, the second or, in 1801, the third fleet. If he lost it would not be fatal. In 1914 –18 the defeat of the Grand Fleet would have been the end of the war for Britain, and her allies. Admiral Sir John Jellicoe, as Winston Churchill pointed out, was the one man who could have lost the war in an afternoon. Furthermore Jellicoe did not have a 'band of brothers' to work with, he had a collection of solid fellows who would do their duty, but lacked the wit and the confidence to function in the fast-moving and complex situations of modern war. Unlike Nelson they had gown up in a

HMS *Nelson* was the most powerful ship in the world when she was built, but the Nelson image had taken a severe dent at Jutland and would only be restored when threats such as the U-boats called for the familiar inventiveness and initiative. (Royal Naval Museum)

peace-time navy of neatness, drill and good order. Men past 40 found it was too late to be learning about war. Without experience to fall back on, they needed clear instructions, and solid routines.

Consequently at Jutland on 31 May 1916, Jellicoe hammered the High Seas Fleet, but rather than take risks late on a gloomy afternoon he preferred to complete the task the next morning. This was judicious, but it allowed the Germans to scuttle home. Jellicoe had missed his moment. His report reflected the profound gloom that this unsatisfactory result produced in the fleet. The Battlecruiser fleet under Admiral Beatty had been more aggressive, but Beatty lacked Jellicoe's calm professionalism. His reckless pursuit of battle cost two ships, and 2,000 sailors. After he took over the Grand Fleet Beatty relaxed the restrictive tactical systems imposed by Jellicoe, and curbed his own enthusiasm. While he proved an effective First Sea Lord in the 1920s, Beatty's failed attempt to be a 'Nelsonic' leader in wartime reflected a comprehensive misunderstanding of the man. Beatty looked the part, and took big decisions with confidence, but he lacked the reflective mind and professional dedication that informed Nelson's judgments.

The morning after Jutland the Kaiser had boasted 'The Magic of Trafalgar is broken!' He could not have been more wrong. His commander-in-chief Admiral Scheer, well aware of what had really happened, reported that the fleet must never again face the British. The only weapon left to the German Navy was the

U-boat, used in a manner that was both unprecedented and illegal. Among the heirs of Nelson were men with the education, technical knowledge and ability to defeat this novel menace. Old methods, like the escorted convoy, new weapons, sensors and platforms, depth charges, hydrophones and aircraft all played their part. So did sophisticated intelligence-gathering and processing of a type that Nelson would have recognized. Finally, the response was national, involving increased shipbuilding, shipping companies, insurance markets, inland transport and food rationing. The submarine attack on merchant shipping in the two World Wars would be the 20th century equivalent of the 1805 invasion threat, the greatest challenge to Britain's survival. It was defeated by a national effort, spearheaded by the Royal Navy. The Great War at sea was won by sound, reliable officers, men who would have found Earl St Vincent a suitable model. For more than four years they blockaded Germany, and Germany collapsed.

The lack of a great sea battle left many dissatisfied with the Navy's performance. There was little sacrifice to set against the massive cost of victory on land. This mood spilled over into the post-war analysis. Without a smashing battle victory, a second Trafalgar, the whole myth of Nelson and the Navy seemed to be diminished. Post-war the *Victory* was restored, while the new HMS *Nelson* was the most powerful ship in the world, but there were cracks in the Nelson façade. Were navies and heroes, battleships and history the best preparation for the future?

CHURCHILLIAN RHETORIC

The over-centralized, stiff tactical instructions the Royal Navy used during the First World War were neither in the tradition set by Nelson, nor particularly successful. Having learned this lesson in the hard school of battle, the officers who lead the Royal Navy in the Second World War were better prepared. They were also given far better doctrine. Officers were enjoined to seek close-range engagement, where the outcome would be decisive, at lower fighting ranges than rival fleets. The 1939 Fighting Instructions opened with a truly Nelsonic injunction:

> Captains, whenever they find themselves without specific directions during an action or are faced with unforeseen circumstances which render previous orders inapplicable, must act as their judgement dictates to further their Admiral's wishes. Care should be taken when framing instructions that these are not of too rigid a nature.[28]

With such a clear brief the Royal Navy recovered the initiative, élan and aggression that had made Nelson's fleets so effective. New leaders exploited these instructions to the full. Admiral Sir Andrew Cunningham led the Mediterranean Fleet from 1940 to 1943 against seemingly insurmountable odds, his ceaseless determination to impose battle on a less willing Italian fleet gave the British a moral ascendancy that compensated for numerical inferiority. His

Admiral Cunningham's offensive spirit, particularly in the Mediterranean, was very much in the Nelson mould. Although many ships were sunk, he successfully upheld a centuries-old tradition. (Royal Naval Museum)

ultimate trial came off Crete in 1941, where the Navy had to evacuate a defeated British army under incessant attack by highly proficient Luftwaffe bombers. The fleet was decimated. Even the Army chiefs told Cunningham that he had done enough, and must not risk any more ships. Cunningham disagreed; 'It takes three years to build a ship', he observed, 'but it takes three hundred years to build a tradition.' Like Nelson he rose to every challenge, including those that lay outside his professional experience. Cunningham ended the war as First Sea Lord, and like Nelson, became a Viscount. His bust rightly stands on the north wall of Trafalgar Square, alongside Jellicoe and Beatty. Nor was he alone; like Nelson he was supported by outstanding officers in all ranks, Captain, later Admiral Sir Phillip Vian was one such. He began the war commanding a destroyer flotilla, progressed to escorting Malta convoys, commanded British naval forces at the D-Day landings, and ended the war in command of the British Pacific Fleet's Aircraft carrier Task Force. His tactical genius was only equalled by his willingness to act on his own initiative. Cunningham's finest moment came when, having sent Vian to escort a vital Malta convoy, he left him to control a major battle, in which his force was heavily outnumbered. He knew that the man on the spot was best placed to make decisions, and that Vian had earned his trust. A lesser man would have interfered.

At the outbreak of the Second World War the Navy found itself once more under the political direction of Winston Churchill. This time it would be his finest qualities that were most in evidence. In the darkest period of the war, from the fall of France in May 1940 to the German invasion of the Soviet Union in June 1941 Churchill's belief in ultimate victory, his confidence in the Navy, and his constant references to Nelson imbued his leadership and his speeches with a conviction that no one else in British public life could match. His radio broadcasts exploited the new medium to perfection, using well known phrases and historical examples to reinforce his argument. He called Nelson to aid the war effort with far more skill than had been the case a generation earlier. It was perhaps fortunate that his *The History of the English Speaking Peoples* had reached Trafalgar in early September 1939,[29] leaving the subject fresh in his mind. The connection was reinforced when he spent a day on board the Home Fleet flagship, HMS *Nelson*. By February 1940 he was ready to speak:

> The warrior heroes of the past may look down, as Nelson's monument looks down upon us now, without any feeling that the island race has lost its daring or that the examples which they set in bygone centuries have faded as the generations have succeeded to one another.

On becoming Prime Minister Churchill faced the gravest crisis since 1805, France was about to surrender, Italy had joined the war and Japan was increasingly hostile. By any rational calculation Britain could not survive. But Churchill, adopting a Nelson motto, went for 'the boldest measures'. His first decision was to take, sink, burn or otherwise destroy as much of the powerful French fleet as the Navy could reach. At Mers el Kebir the British opened fire on ships that had, but scant days before, been serving at their side. The French fleet was crippled, more than 1,500 men died and the event left a bitter legacy. But it also impressed upon Hitler, Stalin and Roosevelt the conviction that Britain would not surrender, and thereby changed the history of world. With no hope of a compromise peace, Hitler was forced to show his hand, and while the Luftwaffe held its own over southern Britain, Germany had nothing to counter the Royal Navy. As in 1805, any attempt to cross the Channel would have ended in disaster. While invasion threatened, Nelson was never far from Churchill's thoughts. He used Nelson's line about the want of frigates as the basis for his plea to Roosevelt to supply old destroyers, and told the Houses of Commons that the government was acting on good precepts in attacking enemy invasion harbours. 'As in Nelson's day, the maxim holds, 'our First line of Defence is the enemy's ports.' He compared the crisis to 'when Nelson stood between us and Napoleon's Grand Army at Boulogne.'[30]

Nelson's front line service in this war ended with the German invasion of the

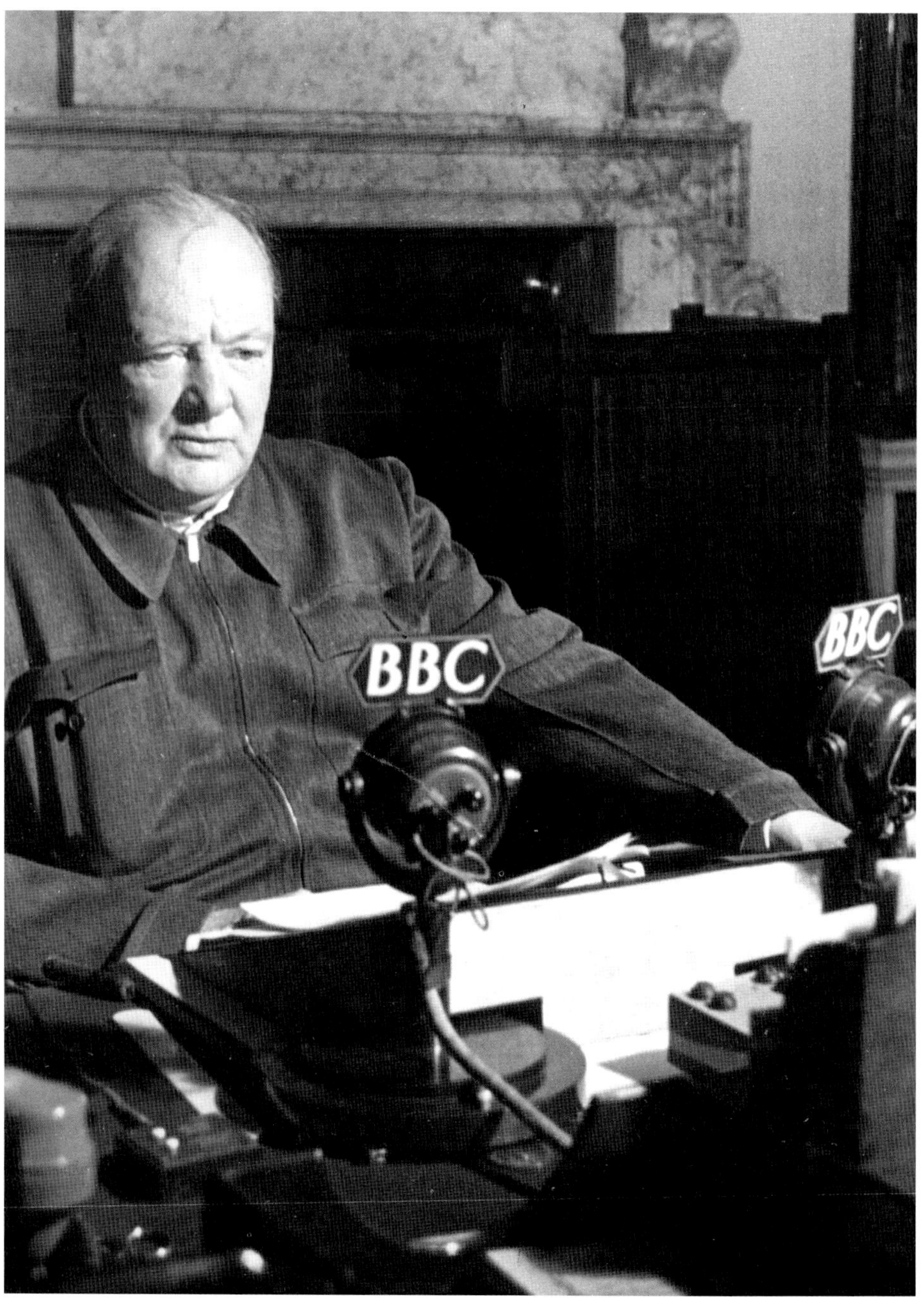

Winston Churchill made full use of Nelson and Trafalgar imagery in conjuring up a spirit of resistance in the dark days of the Second World War. (BBC Photo Library)

Soviet Union. In the darkest hour, when the nation needed more than facts, Churchill employed the ultimate expression of British resistance to continental threat, the magic of Nelson and Trafalgar. In the process he created his own legend. He also helped Alexander Korda script his film *Lady Hamilton*. Laurence Olivier gave Nelson a pronunciation quite unlike his thin nasal Norfolk drawl, but his Nelson stood for Britain, the Britain of the Blitz, defying the tyrant. Like the original, he had a dry humor, but unlike the hero of 1805 he was fashionably understated and reserved, his upper lip inappropriately stiff. [31] Churchill never tired of hearing Olivier deliver the portentous line: 'You can't make peace with dictators'. This was not surprising, he had written it! The film was shown many times at Chequers, to the consternation of his staff, who found the experience a trifle wearing. He would then dictate suitably Nelsonian missives to unfortunate senior officers, for whom 'No Captain can do very wrong....' may not have been the most welcome advice.[32]

Throughout the war, Trafalgar Square was used as a national point of reference, filled with images and artefacts for Warship Week, and events for the other services. Then it became the focal point for suitably enthusiastic celebrations of peace, civilians mixing with servicemen and women from many nations. Victory in Europe and Victory over Japan Day passed off under the empty gaze of a silent statue, the man it recalled passing out of the national consciousness as the country turned from war to peace, from danger to opportunity. New heroes were required: the old ones were no longer relevant.

POST-IMPERIAL MALAISE

Post-war the glory faded, the threat passed, replaced by new menaces in the shape of the hydrogen bomb. What use was Nelson now? The last ship to bear the greatest name in naval history, HMS *Nelson*, a mighty battleship with a proud war record, was used to test bombs before being scrapped. She was replaced by an accommodation block at Portsmouth. No other navy in the world would waste such a potent talisman of glory, success and power on something so banal. Fortunately there is a nuclear powered submarine bearing the name HMS *Trafalgar.* Attitudes to Nelson still mirrored the national mood, and the national need. As the empire passed, and the historians of decline argued that it was all over for Britain, Nelson was tarnished with the sins of his age, and the fatal curse of a celebrity personal life. He could be set aside, reduced to a cartoon caricature, more famous for loving Lady Hamilton than winning battles.

INTO THE MODERN AGE

Then it all turned around. In 1982, with the Royal Navy on the verge of politically disastrous cuts, the Argentine junta invaded the Falkland Islands. The Navy was saved, and the values of the greatest naval hero of them all came to fore – decisive leadership, commitment and professionalism. Since then the revival of the nation, the navy and the hero of Trafalgar has gone apace. The Royal Navy enshrined what Nelson meant in their doctrine in 1996, and has kept those ideas refreshed in the years that followed. It is a mark of the confidence of the modern service that it is ready to assume the mantle of genius, rather than relying on simplistic formulae.

Nelson's standing as the greatest British warrior hero is unquestioned, his name, image and memorials are central to the British identity. Even in times of profound peace he remains one of the best known names from the British past For the rest of the world he is equally iconic, and irresistible. When other navies choose their own ultimate hero he becomes their Nelson, as if his name had

HMS *Sheffield*. In the face of cuts, real and threatened, by its own Government, the Royal Navy succeeded in deploying thousands of miles away from home for a hazardous invasion of the Falkland Islands. In doing so, it amply justified its existence. (Royal Naval Museum)

become the noun for naval genius. All those navies with a soul would send a ship to join the bicentenary fleet review at Spithead, when all would recall the triumph and tragedy of Trafalgar. Two hundred years later, Nelson and Trafalgar remain a matchless combination of talismanic names, the ultimate achievement of war at sea.

ENDNOTES

Introduction

1 The first five wars were: The Nine Years' War, 1689–97; The War of the Spanish Succession, 1702–12; The War of 1739–48; The Seven Years' War, 1756–63; the War for America, 1778–83.

2 Schroeder, Paul W., *The Transformation of European Politics, 1763–1848*, Clarendon Press, Oxford (1994), pp. vii–viii.

3 Ibid., pp. 112–13.

4 See, for example, Bindoff, S.T., *The Scheldt Question to 1839; with a foreword by G.J. Renier,* Allen and Unwin, London (1945).

5 Mackesy, Piers, *War Without Victory: The Downfall of Pitt, 1799–1802,* Clarendon Press, Oxford (1984), pp. 217–19.

6 Saul, Norman E., *Russia and the Mediterranean, 1797–1801* , University of Chicago Press, Chicago (1970), pp. 160–64.

7 Mackesy, op. cit., p.225.

8 Schroeder, op. cit., pp. 231–32.

9 Schama, Simon, *Patriots and Liberators: Revolution in the Netherlands, 1780–1813,* Alfred A. Knopf, New York (1977), p. 418.

10 This and the following paragraphs are based on Schroeder, op. cit., pp. 233–45.

11 Gill, Conrad, 'The Relations between England and France in 1802', *English Historical Review,* xxiv (1909), pp. 61–78 at p. 66.

12 This and the following paragraphs are based on Burrows, Simon, *French Exile Journalism and European Politics, 1792–1814*: The Royal Historical Society, London (2000), pp. 106–28. See also, Burrows, Simon, 'Culture and Misperception: The Law and the Press in the Outbreak of War in 1803,' *International History Review,* xviii (1996), pp. 793–818.

13 Sire, H. J. A., *The Knights of Malta,* Yale University Press, New Haven (1994), p.245.

14 Schroeder, op. cit., p. 243.

15 Saul, op. cit., pp. 172–76.

16 Translated and quoted in Saul, Ibid., p. 176, from *Arkhiv Kniazia Voronstova.* (Moscow, Universitetskaia tipografiia) (1870–1895), vol. 28 of 40, pp.464–65.

17 Published in Britain in *Cobbett's Annual Register,* vol. 3 (January–June 1803), pp. 215–24; 245–47.

18 Rodger, A.B., *The War of the Second Coalition: A Strategic Commentary,* Clarendon Press, Oxford (1964), p. 293.

19 Flayhart III, William Henry, *Counterpoint to Trafalgar: The Anglo-Russian Invasion of Naples, 1805–1806,* University of South Carolina Press, Columbia (1992), pp.13–14.

20 Quoted in *Cobbett's Annual Register* (1803), p. 17, p. 646.

21 Quoted in Ibid., p. 18.

22 Burrows, *French Exile Journalism,* pp. 121–27.

23 Schroeder, op. cit., p. 243.

24 Christopher D. Hall, *British Strategy in the Napoleonic War, 1803–1815,* Manchester University Press, Manchester (1992), pp. 29–31; Morriss, Roger, *The Royal Dockyards during the Revolutionary and Napoleonic War,* Leicester University Press, Leicester (1983), pp. 18–25, 44

25 This and the following paragraphs are based on Schroeder, op. cit., pp. 244–51.

26 Asprey, Robert B., *The Rise of Napoleon Bonaparte,*: Basic Books, New York, (2000), Chapter 41: The Invasion of England – I, June 1803–February 1804, pp. 454–68.

27 This and the following paragraph is based on Cookson, J. E., *The British Armed Nation, 1793–1815,* Clarendon Press, Oxford (1997), pp. 40–65.

28 This and the following paragraphs are based on Schroeder, op. cit., pp. 257–76.

29 Carlsson, Sten, *Den Svenska Utrikes Politikens Historia, Del III: 1 1792–1810,* P.A. Norstedts & Söner Förlag, Stockholm (1954), pp. 92–99.

30 Rodger, N.A.M., *The Command of the Ocean: A Naval History of Britain, 1649–1815,* Penguin Allen Lane, London (2004), p.532.

31 Quoted in Asprey, p. 516, from *Correspondence de Napoléon I*, Plon/Dumaine, Paris (1858 ff), vol. XI, nr. 9179, Malmaison, 4 September 1804.

Chapter 1

1 Grey, A., *Debates in the House of Commons,* London (1763–69), vol. ii, p.213.

2 See, for instance, Niall Ferguson, *Empire*, Allen Lane, London (2003); his sub-title is *How Britain Made the Modern World.*

3 Burke, Edmund, *Reflections on the Revolution in France…,* London (1790), pp.194–95; see J.C.D.Clark's critical edition published by Stanford University Press (2001), pp.298–99.

4 Rodney to his wife, cited C.L.Lewis, *Admiral de Grasse and American Independence*, U.S.Naval Institute Press, Annapolis (1945), p.254.

5 Jules Flammermont, *Remonstrances du parlement de Paris au XVIIIe siècle*, Paris, vol. iii, 27592; cited internet http://chnm.gmv.edu/revolution/ – (text documents 31–60).

6 Burke, op. cit. (ref. 3 above), p.48.

7 Ibid., p.231.

8 Ibid., p.29.

9 Flammermont, op. cit. (ref. 5 above), 34454.

10 Scarfe, Norman, *Innocent Espionage: The La Rochefoucauld Brothers' Tour of England in 1785,* The Boydell Press, Suffolk (1995), p.56.

11 Ibid., p.54.

12 Flammermont, op. cit. (ref. 5 above), 27592.

13 See Schama, Simon, *Citizens: A Chronicle of the French Revolution*, Knopf, N.Y. (1989), pp.116–17.

14 A. de Tocqueville, *Journeys to England and Ireland*, trans. G. Lawrence and K. P. Mayer, Faber & Faber (1958), p.67.

15 See Basil Williams, *The Whig Supremacy, 1714–1760*, Oxford, revised edn. (1962), p.146.

16 Scarfe, op. cit. (ref. 10 above), p.100.

17 Cited H. A. L. Fisher, *A History of Europe*, London (1936), p.697.

18 Cited ibid.

19 *Encyclopedia Britannica*, vol. vii, p.675.

20 Cited I. Buruma, *Voltaire's Coconuts; or Anglomania in Europe*, Weidenfeld & Nicolson, London (1999), p.38.

21 Cited Williams, op. cit. (ref. 15 above), p.5.

22 Vergennes to Montmorin, 1 Nov. 1782; cited J. Dull, *The French Navy and American Independence*, Princeton University Press (1975), p.316; see also ibid., p.304.

23 See Jacques Godechot, *France and the Atlantic Revolution of the Eighteenth Century, 1770–1799*, The Free Press, N.Y. (1965), p.72.

24 Cited Clark, op. cit. (ref. 3 above), p.52, n.89.

25 *Encyclopedia Britannica*, vol. x, p.71.

26 Palmer, R.R., *The Age of Democratic Revolution*, Princeton University Press (1959), p.478.

27 De Tocqueville, A., *L'Ancien Régime* (originally *L'Ancien Régime et la Révolution*, 1856) (trans. Patterson, M.W.), Blackwell, Oxford (1947), p.148.

28 See Russell, B., *History of Western Philosophy*, Allen & Unwin (1946), pp.724ff.

29 De Tocqueville, op. cit. (ref. 27 above), p.148.

30 Marat, Jean-Paul, cited Soboul, A., *The French Revolution, 1787–1799*, trans. Forrest A. and Jones C., New Left Books (1974), p.305.

31 Speech on the Army Estimates, House of Commons, 9 Feb. 1790; cited Clark, op. cit. (ref. 3 above), p.66; and see Ibid., p.77.

32 Burke, op. cit. (ref. 3 above), p.283.

33 Ibid., p. 318.

34 To Elliot, H., 8 Oct. 1803; cited N.H. Nicolas, *The Dispatches and Letters of Vice Admiral Lord Viscount Nelson*, London (1846), vol. v, p.237.

35 Cited Mahan, A.T. , *The Life of Nelson: the Embodiment of the Sea Power of Great Britain*, London (1899), p.86.

36 Nicolas, op. cit. (ref. 34 above), vol. vii, p.199.

37 Burke, op. cit. (ref. 3 above), p.47.

Chapter 4

1 My previous work which was dedicated to Latouche-Tréville, the only French admiral who held Nelson in check, prepared me for this task. The absence of recent French works, and above all the useful contacts I was able to make with British and Spanish historians, strengthened my resolve.

2 Minister for the Navy in 1800 and 1801, then inspector of the Channel fleet.

3 They also had a reserve of 40 vessels in British ports which could be armed quickly and which would serve to replace units lost in battle.

4 Commander of the rear guard and kept out of the combat by Nelson, Villeneuve did not attempt to come to the aid of the remainder of the French squadron.

5 At Trafalgar, the largest vessel present was the *Santísima Trinidad* (61.3m long), but certain French triple-deck ships, absent from the battle, measured 63.6m. The French 80 cannon vessels, such as the *Bucentaure* (59.3m), were clearly longer than the *Victory* (56.7m).

6 The French pound is heavier than the English pound.

7 The garrisons correspond to Royal Marine contingents aboard British ships.

8 The British call this 'The Battle of the Glorious First of June'.

9 This fierce hatred, which bordered on the irrational, had something disturbing about it. It contrasted sharply with the attitudes of the other admirals, Nelson's contemporaries, who respected their adversaries and could maintain friendly relations with them once a conflict was over. This was the case with Keith, Elphinstone, Duckworth and Latouche-Tréville.

10 This was the case, notably, for William Stanhope Lovell, midshipman on board the *Neptune*.

11 I have shown that Robert Guillemard, the sergeant on board the *Redoutable* purported to have killed Nelson from the top of the mizzenmast, was a fictional character invented by the author of his supposed memoirs.

12 The famous painting by Benjamin West entitled *The Immortality of Nelson*, which is kept in the National Maritime Museum, represents a real ascension of the hero.

Chapter 5

1 National Maritime Museum [NMM], TUN/18 and 19; SIG/B/16, 74, 75 smf 78; HOL/51; DUN/32.

2 NMM, SIG/A/1, and NM/104.

3 In the 1690 *Sailing and Fighting Instructions*, this instruction was re-numbered as Article 17.

4 Sloane MS 3560, printed in *Fighting Instructions*, pp. 168–72.

5 Robert Gardiner, *The Line of Battle, The Sailing Warship 1650–1840*, Conway's History of the Ship, Conway Maritime Press, London (1992), pp.146–63.

6 *An Enquiry into the Conduct of Captain Savage Mostyn*, London (1754).

7 Tunstall, Brian and Tracy, Nicholas, *Naval Warfare in the Age of Sail*, Conway Maritime Press, London (1990), pp. 6–7.

8 Tunstall/Tracy, op. cit., p. 213.

9 30 August 1758, *in:* Bonner Smith, D., ed., *Letters and Papers of Admiral the Hon. Charles Barrington* (vol. I), Navy Records Society, London, vol. 77, pp. 231–32.

10 *Barrington*, op. cit., I, pp. 259–60.

11 NMM, CLE/2/19.

12 NMM, WYN/12/1,5,8 and WYN/13/1.
13 NMM, HOL/21.
14 NMM, Rodney 15 and 19; NM/83. *See:* Corbett, Julian, *Signals and Instructions, 1776–1794*, Navy Records Society, London Vol. 35 (1908), pp. 180–234.
15 Tucker, J.S., (Jervis's secretary), *Memoirs of Admiral the Rt. Hon. the Earl of St. Vincent*, London (1844), II pp. 281–83.
16 John Clerk of Eldin, *An Essay on Naval Tactics*, 3rd edn. (1827) p.18.
17 Creswell, John, *British Admirals in the 18th Century*, London (1972), pp. 187–88.
18 NMM, MKH/A/n/4. Tunstall/Tracy, op. cit., p. 194.
19 NMM, *Signals for the Frigates or other Ships of War appointed to observe the motions of a strange fleet discovered or enemy's fleet, during the night*, NM/34.

Chapter 6

1 Bugler, A.R., *HMS. Building Restoration and Repair*, HMSO (1966), pp.2-3.
2 Ibid., pp.3-5.
3 Goodwin, P., *The Influence of Industrial Technology and Material Procurement on the Design, Construction and Development of HMS* Victory, M. Phil. Dissertation, University of St Andrews, pp.25-26.
4 Goodwin, P., *Nelson's Ships: A History of the Vessels in Which He Served*, London (2002), pp.234-35.
5 Ibid.
6 Goodwin, P., *The Influence of Industrial Technology ...*, op. cit., pp.44-45.
7 Goodwin, P., *Nelson's Ships*, op. cit., pp.236-41.
8 Ibid., pp.245-47,
9 Ibid.
10 Bugler, op. cit., pp.25-29.
11 Goodwin, P., *Nelson's Ships*, op. cit., pp.249-50.
12 Pope, Dudley, *England Expects*, London (1959), passim, and Schom, A., *Trafalgar: Count Down to Battle 1803-1805*, London (199), passim.
13 Goodwin, P., *Nelson's* Victory*: 101 Questions and Answers About HMS* Victory, London (2004), p.81.
14 Ibid.
15 National Archives, Kew, ADM 95/76.
16 Goodwin, P., *Nelson's* Victory, op. cit., p.12.
17 Ibid., p.15.
18 Ibid.
19 Ibid., pp.15-16.
20 Ibid., p.20.
21 Ibid., pp.43-45.
22 Ibid., p.55.
23 Ibid., pp.61-63.
24 Ibid., pp.61-65.
25 Ibid., p.67.
26 RNM (Royal Naval Museum), MSS 1064/83 2376 *Record of the Carpenter's & Boatswain's Stores ad Expenses for* Victory, Britannia *and* Africa *for the year 1805*.
27 Goodwin, P., *HMS* Victory, Andover (2005).

Chapter 7

1 Consistently establishing exact times for events at Trafalgar is difficult. Many of the times recorded in accounts of the battle, even eye-witness accounts by the participants and the ships' logs, were estimates. Establishing a precise timeline for events is virtually impossible; it is only with cross-referencing of accounts that a general sequence of principal events can be established.
2 From a recently discovered Nelson letter included in *Nelson – The New Letters*, Colin White, Boydell & Brewer, London (2005).
3 Pope, Dudley, *Decision at Trafalgar*, J.B. Lippencott Company, Philadelphia & New York (1959), p.188.
4 White, op. cit (ref. 2 above).
5 Sir Nicolas, Nicholas Harris, ed., *The Dispatches and Letters of Vice Admiral Lord Viscount Nelson*, Vol. VII, Henry Colburn, London (1846), republished by Chatham Publishing, London (1998), pp.89–92.
6 The naval tactic of concentrating one's force to break the enemy's line ahead had been employed previously by other British admirals, including Admiral Lord Duncan at the British victory at Camperdown in 1797 and Admiral Sir George Rodney over the French at the Battle of the Saintes in 1782.
7 Sir Nicholas, Nicolas Harris, op. cit.., vol. III, p.28.
8 Ibid., Vol. IV, p.297.
9 Ibid., Vol. VII, p.95.
10 Ibid., p.80.
11 Ibid., p.60.
12 White, Colin, *The Nelson Encyclopaedia*, Chatham Publishing, London (2002), p.235.
13 Pope, Dudley, op. cit., p.217.
14 *Nelson's Last Diary and the Prayer Before Trafalgar*, ed. Warner, Oliver, The Kent State University Press, Kent, Ohio (1971), p.28.
15 The exact spot where Nelson fell on *Victory's* deck is marked with a brass plaque and can be viewed by visitors during conducted public tours of HMS *Victory* in Portsmouth's Historic Dockyard. Nelson's uniform jacket with the musket ball hole and the musket ball removed from Nelson's body are part of an extensive Nelson exhibition at the National Maritime Museum in Greenwich.
16 Sir Nicholas, Nicolas Harris, op. cit., p.244.
17 Ibid., p. 248.
18 Ibid., p.245.
19 Ibid., p.252.
20 Internet site for *War Times Journal* (www.wtj.com/archives/lucas_01.htm), p3.
21 Ibid., p.5.
22 Ibid., p.214.
23 Mahan, Captain A. T., *The Life of Nelson*, Sampson Low, Marston & Company (1897), pp.397, 398.

Chapter 8

1 Maitland, F., *Narrative of the Surrender of Bonaparte*, London (1826), p.99.

2 Lady Bessborough – Granville Leveson Gower 6.11.1805: Granville, Countess, ed. *Lord Granville Leveson Gower, Private Correspondence 1781–1821,* London (1916), Vol. II, p.132.

3 Ibid. (10.11.1805), p.133.

4 Walker, R., *The Nelson Portrait,* Portsmouth (1998), p.159.

5 Noszlopy, G. T., 'A Note on West's *Apotheosis of Nelson*', *Burlington Magazine* (December 1970), vol. 112, pp.813–17 is the best analysis of this piece.

6 Wilton, A. *Painting and Poetry: Turner's Verse Book and his work of 1804–1812,* London (1990), p.48.

7 Butlin, M. & Joll, E., *The Paintings of J. M. W. Turner,* Vol. I,Yale (1977), p.39.

8 Fulford, T., "Romanticising the Empire" the Naval Heroes of Southey, Coleridge, Austen and Marryat', *Modern Language Quarterly* 60 (1999), pp.193–94. It is important to stress how far Nelson's career had been massaged by him and by his brother, mistress and biographers into this mould. It was, in truth, based on patronage.

9 Girouard, M., *The Return to Camelot,* pp.40–2.

10 Ibid.. p.64.

11 Russett, A., *George Chambers, 1803–1840,* London (2000), pp.125–27.

12 Parker, H., *Herman Melville, 1819–1851,* Baltimore (1996), p.677.

13 Ramage, N. H. & Ramage, A., *Roman Art: Romulus to Constantine,* 2nd edn. Cornell (1995), pp. 88–90.

14 Crook & Port, *The King's Works:* Vol. VI, London (1973), pp. 491–94.

15 Mace, R. *Trafalgar Square: Emblem of Empire,* London (1976) provides a history of this important public space, and other major monuments it contains. See pp. 48–133 for the Column.

16 Lambert, A. D., *The Crimean War: British Grand Strategy against Russia, 1853 –1856,* Manchester (1990).

17 Dupin, C., *Voyages dans la Grand-Bretagne, Vol. IV,* Paris (1821), p.66.

18 De la Gravière, Capt. E. Jurien, *Sketches of the Late Naval War,* trans. Capt. Plunkett RN, London (1848), vol. II, p.298–300.

19 James, W., *The Naval History of Great Britain,* 2nd edn., London (1826), 6 vols.

20 Lambert, A.D., *The Foundations of Naval History: John Knox Laughton, the Royal Navy and the Historical Profession,* London (1998), pp.173–93.

21 Schurman D., *Julian S. Corbett 1854–1922,* London (1981).

22 Marder, A.J., *From the Dreadnought to Scapa Flow. Vol. I, 1904–1914,* Oxford (1961), p.348.

23 Gordon, G. A.H., *The Rules of the Game: Jutland and British Naval Command,* London (1996) addresses this question, and shows how Nelson's legacy was frittered away.

24 Behrman, C.F., *Victorian Myths of the Sea,* Athens, Ohio (1977), pp.93–107.

25 Corbett, J. S., *The Campaign of Trafalgar,.* London 191, .pp.342–59. *Report of a Committee appointed by the Admiralty to consider the tactics employed at Trafalgar,* HMSO, London (1913).

26 Nelson Memorandum 9.10.1805: Nicolas, H. ed. *Letters and Dispatches of Vice Admiral Lord Viscount Nelson.* Vol. VII London 1846 89–92. & Corbett, op. cit., pp..447–49.

27 Blackwood, Captain Henry – Wife 23.10.1805: Nicolas VII, p.226.

28 ADM 239/262, quoted in Levy, J., *The Royal Navy's Home Fleet in World War II,* London (2003), p.26.

29 Ramsden, J., *Man of the Century: Winston Churchill and his Legend since 1945,* London (2002), pp.57–78. Churchill – G. M. Young (10.9.1939): Gilbert, M. ed., *The Churchill War Papers I: The Admiralty,* London (1993), pp.69–71. Young was one of the historians who drafted much of the book for Churchill.

30 John Colville 10.8.1940 re destroyers; Speech of 20.8.1940: Broadcast of 11.9.1940.Gilbert II (1994) pp. 644, 691, 802.

31 Richards, J., *Films and British Identity: From Dickens to Dad's Army,* Manchester (1997), p.87.

32 Churchill – Korda (15.6.1941 & 1.7.1941). Memoirs of Oliver Harvey and Hastings Ismay (2.8.1941): Gilbert vol. III, pp.807, 882, 1027–28.

BIBLIOGRAPHY

Chapter 2

Primary sources

Gutteridge, H. C., *Nelson and the Neapolitan Jacobins: Documents relating to the suppression of the Jacobin Revolution at Naples, June 1799*, London (1903)

Naish, G. P. B., *Nelson's Letters to His Wife and Other Documents 1785–1831*, Navy Records Society, London (1958)

Nicolas, N. H., *The Dispatches and Letters of Vice-Admiral Lord Viscount Nelson*, London (1846)

White, C., *Nelson: The New Letters*, London (2005)

Secondary sources

Coleman, T., *Nelson The Man and the Legend*, London (2001)

Hayward, J., *For God and Glory*, Annapolis (2003)

Morriss, R., *Nelson: The Life and Letters of a Hero*, London (1996)

Oman, C., *Nelson*, London (1947)

Pocock, T., *Horatio Nelson*, London (1987)

Russell, J., *Nelson and the Hamiltons*, New York (1969)

Vincent, E. W., *Nelson Love & Fame*, London and New Haven (2003)

White, C., *The Nelson Encyclopaedia*, London (2002)

Chapter 3

Primary sources

British Maritime Doctrine BR1806, HM Stationery Office London, 1999

Secondary sources

Adair, J., *Inspiring Leadership*, London (2002)

Keegan, J., *The Mask of Command*, London (1987)

Lambert, A., *Nelson: Britannia's God of War*, London (2004)

Lavery, B., *Nelson's Navy: The Ships, Men and Organization 1793–5*, London (1989)

Mahan, A.T., *The Life of Nelson; The Embodiment of the Sea Power of Great Britain*, 2 vols, London (1897)

Rodger, N.A.M., *The Wooden World; An Anatomy of the Georgian Navy*, London (1986)

Padfield, P., *Maritime Power and the Struggle for Freedom*, London (2003)

Vincent, E.W., *Nelson; Love & Fame*, London (2003)

Chapter 6

Blane, Sir Gilbert, *Observations on the Diseases of Seamen*, 3rd edn (1798)

Buglar, A.R., *HMS* Victory: *Building Restoration & Repair* HMSO (1966)

Callander, G., *The Story of HMS* Victory, London (1914)

Goodwin, P., *Nelson's Ships: A History of the Vessels in Which He Served*, London (2002)

Goodwin, P., *Nelson's* Victory: *101 Questions & Answers About HMS* Victory, London (2004)

Goodwin, P., *The Ships at Trafalgar: A History of the British, French and Spanish Ships that Fought in the Battle*, London (2005)

Goodwin, P., *The Influence of Industrial Technology and Material Procurement on the Design, Construction and Developmen of HMS* Victory, M.Phil. Dissertation, University of St Andrews (1998)

McGowan, A., *HMS* Victory: *Her Construction, Career & Restoration*, London (1999)

Pope, Dudley, *England Expects*, London (1959)

Schom, A., *Trafalgar: Countdown to Battle 1803-1805*, London (1990)

Frazer, E., 'Sir Thomas Slade', *The Mariner's Mirror* Vol. 63 (1977)

INDEX

References to illustrations are shown in **bold**
Ships in *italic* are British unless otherwise indicated

1391
Athwin Foundation
801 Nicollet Mall, Suite 1420
Minneapolis 55402 (612) 340-3618

Trust established in 1956 in MN.
Donor(s): Atherton Bean, Winifred W. Bean.
Financial data (yr. ended 12/31/87): Assets, $4,402,361 (M); gifts received, $31,500; expenditures, $358,818, including $306,032 for 47 grants (high: $50,000; low: $33; average: $1,000-$5,000).
Purpose and activities: Support for educational, cultural, religious, and community welfare programs.
Types of support: Operating budgets, special projects.
Limitations: Giving primarily in the Minneapolis-St. Paul, MN, area; some giving also in Phoenix, AZ, and Claremont, CA. No grants to individuals, or for scholarships or fellowships; no loans.
Publications: Annual report.
Application information:
Initial approach: Proposal
Copies of proposal: 5
Deadline(s): None
Board meeting date(s): Quarterly
Final notification: 60 days
Write: Henry H. Nowicki, Managing Dir.
Trustees: Atherton Bean, Bruce W. Bean, Mary F. Bean, Winifred W. Bean, Eleanor Nolan.
Managing Director: Henry H. Nowicki.
Number of staff: 1 part-time support.
Employer Identification Number: 416021773

1392
Baker Foundation
4900 IDS Center
Minneapolis 55402 (612) 332-7479

Trust established in 1947; incorporated in 1954 in MN.
Donor(s): Morris T. Baker.†
Financial data (yr. ended 12/31/87): Assets, $3,234,883 (M); expenditures, $195,705, including $170,700 for 42 grants (high: $25,000; low: $50).
Purpose and activities: Emphasis on medical research, higher education, community funds, conservation, youth agencies, and music.
Types of support: Annual campaigns, building funds, capital campaigns, general purposes, operating budgets.
Limitations: Giving primarily in MN. No grants to individuals.
Application information:
Initial approach: Letter
Copies of proposal: 1
Deadline(s): None
Board meeting date(s): As required
Write: William M. Baker, Pres., or James W. Peter, Secy.
Officers and Directors: William M. Baker, Pres.; Roger L. Baker, V.P.; David C. Sherman, V.P.; James W. Peter, Secy.-Treas.; Morris T. Baker III, Doris G. Baker, Nancy W. Baker, Mary Baker-Philbin, Tobias R. Philbin, Charles C. Pineo III, Linda Baker Pineo, Sandra B. Sherman.
Employer Identification Number: 416022591

1393
James F. Bell Foundation
10000 Hwy. 55 West, Suite 450
Minneapolis 55441

Trust established in 1955 in MN.
Donor(s): James Ford Bell.†
Financial data (yr. ended 12/31/87): Assets, $7,929,125 (M); expenditures, $465,712, including $368,566 for 46 grants (high: $75,000; low: $500).
Purpose and activities: Emphasis on a local university library and cultural programs; support also for wildlife preservation and conservation, and youth agencies.
Limitations: Giving primarily in MN.
Application information:
Initial approach: Proposal
Deadline(s): None
Write: Robert O. Mathson, Exec. Secy.
Officer: Robert O. Mathson, Exec. Secy.
Trustees: Charles H. Bell, Ford W. Bell, Samuel H. Bell, Jr.
Employer Identification Number: 341018779

1394
Bemis Company Foundation
800 Northstar Center
Minneapolis 55402 (612) 340-6018

Trust established in 1959 in MO.
Donor(s): Bemis Co., Inc.
Financial data (yr. ended 12/31/87): Assets, $2,461,936 (M); expenditures, $563,740, including $474,665 for 185 grants (high: $80,000; low: $25) and $84,677 for 208 employee matching gifts.
Purpose and activities: Grants largely for scholarship programs for children of employees, state associations of independent colleges, an educational institution matching gift program, community funds, hospitals, and cultural and civic affairs programs.
Types of support: Annual campaigns, building funds, employee-related scholarships, employee matching gifts, continuing support.
Limitations: No support for religious or political purposes. No grants to individuals, or for endowment funds, research, educational capital programs, or trips or tours; no loans.
Publications: Corporate giving report, application guidelines.
Application information:
Initial approach: Proposal
Copies of proposal: 1
Deadline(s): None
Board meeting date(s): Mar., June, Sept., and Dec.
Officer and Trustees: Edward J. Dougherty, Exec. Dir.; Benjamin R. Field, L.E. Schwanke.
Number of staff: 2
Employer Identification Number: 416038616

1395
F. R. Bigelow Foundation
1120 Norwest Center
St. Paul 55101 (612) 224-5463

Trust established in 1934; incorporated in 1946 in MN.
Donor(s): Frederick Russell Bigelow,† Eileen Bigelow.
Financial data (yr. ended 12/31/87): Assets, $57,518,425 (M); expenditures, $2,884,555, including $2,502,272 for 97 grants (high: $220,000; low: $1,500; average: $10,000-$100,000).
Purpose and activities: Support for higher and secondary education, social services, including a community fund, arts and humanities, and health.
Types of support: Seed money, emergency funds, equipment, land acquisition, building funds, scholarship funds, matching funds, special projects, continuing support, renovation projects.
Limitations: Giving limited to the greater St. Paul, MN, metropolitan area. No grants to individuals, or for endowment funds; giving rarely for operating budgets; no loans.
Publications: Annual report (including application guidelines), application guidelines.
Application information: Application form required.
Initial approach: Telephone, letter, or proposal
Copies of proposal: 1
Deadline(s): 3 months prior to board meetings
Board meeting date(s): June, Aug., and Dec.
Final notification: 3 to 4 months
Write: Paul A. Verret, Secy.
Officer: Paul A. Verret, Secy.-Treas.
Trustees: Carl B. Drake, Jr., Chair.; Robert S. Davis, Malcolm W. McDonald, Eileen Bigelow McMillan, Kathleen Culman Ridder, Roger B. Shepard, Jr.
Number of staff: None.
Employer Identification Number: 363463945

1396
The Blandin Foundation
(Formerly Charles K. Blandin Foundation)
100 Pokegama Ave. N.
Grand Rapids 55744 (218) 326-0523

Incorporated in 1941 in MN.
Donor(s): Charles K. Blandin.†
Financial data (yr. ended 12/31/88): Assets, $25,099,017 (M); expenditures, $8,835,674, including $6,900,351 for 144 grants (high: $800,000; low: $700; average: $5,000-$50,000), $286,711 for 474 grants to individuals, $746,608 for 16 foundation-administered programs and $45,000 for loans.
Purpose and activities: Giving in three priority areas for the five year period of 1985-1990: 1) leadership development; 2) economic development; and 3) educational opportunities, including scholarships for undergraduates and vocational study for recent graduates under the age of 22 who attended an Itasca County, Hill City, or Remer, MN, high school. While the majority of funding will be directed toward these priority interest areas, consideration will also be given to projects in the fields of arts and humanities and health/human services.
Types of support: Seed money, matching funds, scholarship funds, program-related investments, special projects, consulting services, technical assistance, student aid.
Limitations: Giving limited to MN, with emphasis on rural areas; scholarships limited to graduates of an Itasca County, Hill City, or Remer high school. No support for religious

activities, camping programs, medical research, or travel. No grants to individuals (other than for scholarships), or for operating budgets, continuing support, annual campaigns, deficit financing, capital funds (outside home community), endowments, publications, conferences, or seminars.
Publications: Annual report, application guidelines, program policy statement.
Application information: Scholarship applicants should call or write to the foundation for deadlines and other information.
Initial approach: Letter or visit
Copies of proposal: 1
Deadline(s): Feb. 1, May. 1, Aug. 1, and Nov. 1
Board meeting date(s): 2nd week of Feb., May, Aug., and Nov.
Final notification: 2 weeks after board meeting
Write: Paul M. Olson, Pres.
Officers: Margaret Matalamaki,* Chair.; Bruce Stender, Vice-Chair.; Paul M. Olson, Pres.; Kathryn Jensen, V.P.; Mary Jo Jess,* Secy.; Russell E. Virden,* Treas.
Trustees:* Warren H. Anderson, Robert L. Bullard, Robert L. Comstock, Jr., Henry Doerr, Peter A. Heegaard, James R. Oppenheimer, Steve Shaler, Brian Vergin.
Number of staff: 5 full-time professional; 4 full-time support; 4 part-time support.
Employer Identification Number: 416038619
Recent arts and culture grants:
Childrens Theater Company and School, Minneapolis, MN, $10,000. To bring their national touring performances to rural Minnesota communities during 1988-89. 11/87.
Community Programs in the Arts and Sciences (COMPAS), Saint Paul, MN, $20,000. For 1988 Literary Post Project for seniors throughout MN who are interested in writing and wish professional assistance. 11/87.
COMPAS, Saint Paul, MN, $394,000. To initiate Young Audiences, Artists-in-the-Schools program for rural Minnesota communities. 5/88.
Grand Rapids Performing Arts Council, Grand Rapids, MN, $8,500. 2/12/88.
Guthrie Theater, Minneapolis, MN, $11,000. 2/12/88.
Illusion Theater and School, Minneapolis, MN, $35,000. To sponsor ten performances of Illusion Theater's AIDS prevention/education play. 5/88.
Iron Range Interpretive Center, Friends of the, Chisholm, MN, $5,000. To sponsor Fourth of July concert by Duluth Symphony Orchestra at Ironworld in Hibbing. 2/12/88.
Minneapolis Society of Fine Arts, Minneapolis, MN, $6,000. 2/12/88.
Minnesota Alliance for Arts in Education, Minneapolis, MN, $10,000. 2/12/88.
Minnesota Opera Company, Saint Paul, MN, $10,000. 2/12/88.
Minnesota Orchestral Association, Minneapolis, MN, $15,000. 2/12/88.
Northern Community Radio, Grand Rapids, MN, $19,200. For scientific survey of population of region to be served by new proposed radio network, Superior Radio Network. 2/12/88.
Northern Community Radio, Grand Rapids, MN, $5,000. 2/12/88.
Northern Minnesota Public Television, Bemidji, MN, $5,000. 2/12/88.
Reif Center, Grand Rapids, MN, $5,000. To conduct strategic planning sessions for Board and four other arts organizations. 2/12/88.
Saint Paul Chamber Orchestra, Saint Paul, MN, $11,500. 2/12/88.
Walker Art Center, Minneapolis, MN, $10,000. 2/12/88.

1397
Otto Bremer Foundation
55 East Fifth St., Suite 700
St. Paul 55101 (612) 227-8036

Trust established in 1944 in MN.
Donor(s): Otto Bremer.†
Financial data (yr. ended 12/31/87): Assets, $62,800,000 (M); expenditures, $3,915,141, including $3,359,055 for 461 grants (high: $75,000; low: $5; average: $1,000-$25,000) and $17,500 for 2 loans.
Purpose and activities: Emphasis on rural poverty, youth opportunities, early childhood education, rural and agricultural programs, post-secondary education, human services, health, religion, and community affairs; support also for conservation, peace, civil rights, women, the aged, the handicapped, and child welfare.
Types of support: Seed money, emergency funds, building funds, equipment, land acquisition, special projects, matching funds, scholarship funds, conferences and seminars, employee-related scholarships, publications, technical assistance, program-related investments, fellowships, internships, continuing support, employee matching gifts, loans.
Limitations: Giving limited to MN, ND, and WI where there are Bremer Bank affiliates, and to organizations addressing poverty in the city of St. Paul. No support for national health organizations. No grants to individuals, or for endowment funds, medical research, or professorships.
Publications: Annual report (including application guidelines).
Application information:
Initial approach: Letter or telephone
Copies of proposal: 1
Deadline(s): Submit proposal at least 3 months before funding decision is desired
Board meeting date(s): Monthly
Final notification: 3 months
Write: John Kostishack, Exec. Dir.
Officer: John Kostishack, Exec. Dir.
Trustees: William H. Lipschultz, Robert J. Reardon, Gordon Shepard.
Number of staff: 4 full-time professional.
Employer Identification Number: 416019050
Recent arts and culture grants:
CONNECT/US-USSR, Minneapolis, MN, $12,000. To support tour to Bremer bank communities of Minnesota-Moscow Youth Photography Exhibit. 10/1/87.
Pioneer Public Television, Appleton, MN, $10,000. To support television program highlighting exemplary young people involved in athletics in southwestern Minnesota. 11/25/87.
Saint Croix Tribal Council, Hertel, WI, $15,000. To further intercultural educational and historical work by Burnett County Historical Society. 11/25/87.
Wisconsin Cooperative Development Council, Woodland Indian Craft Cooperative, Madison, WI, $13,500. To develop Woodland Indian Craft Cooperative which will provide employment for American Indian artisans of northwestern Wisconsin. 3/3/88.

1398
The Bush Foundation
East 900 First National Bank Bldg.
332 Minnesota St.
St. Paul 55101 (612) 227-0891

Incorporated in 1953 in MN.
Donor(s): Archibald Bush,† Mrs. Archibald Bush.†
Financial data (yr. ended 11/30/88): Assets, $360,476,000 (M); expenditures, $15,132,167, including $11,724,291 for 189 grants (high: $750,000; low: $3,000; average: $20,000-$500,000) and $1,646,876 for 163 grants to individuals.
Purpose and activities: Support largely for education, arts and humanities, delivery of health care, and social service and welfare agencies. Also operates the Bush Leadership Fellows Program in MN, ND, SD, and western WI, the Bush Fellowships for Artists in MN, ND, and SD, and the Bush Clinical Fellows program in rural areas of MN, ND, and SD.
Types of support: Fellowships, matching funds, endowment funds, special projects, seed money, continuing support, capital campaigns, renovation projects.
Limitations: Giving primarily in MN, ND, and SD. No support for other private foundations, research in biomedical and health sciences, or for hospital construction. No grants to individuals (except for fellowships), or for deficit financing; generally no grants for continuing operating support; no loans.
Publications: Annual report, application guidelines, program policy statement, financial statement.
Application information:
Initial approach: Letter or telephone
Copies of proposal: 2
Deadline(s): 3 1/2 months before board meetings
Board meeting date(s): Feb., Apr. (odd-numbered years only), June, and Oct.
Final notification: 10 days after board meetings
Write: Humphrey Doermann, Pres.
Officers: Diana E. Murphy,* Chair.; Beatrix A. Hamburg,* 1st Vice-Chair.; Merlin E. Dewing,* 2nd Vice-Chair.; Humphrey Doermann, Pres.; Hess Kline,* Secy.; Anita M. Pampusch,* Treas.
Directors:* Thomas J. Clifford, Phyllis B. France, Ellen Z. Green, Thomas E. Holloran, John A. McHugh, John F. Nash, Kennon V. Rothchild, James P. Shannon, Frank B. Wilderson, Jr.
Number of staff: 7 full-time professional; 4 full-time support; 2 part-time support.
Employer Identification Number: 416017815
Recent arts and culture grants:
Actors Theater of Saint Paul, Saint Paul, MN, $50,000. To support completion of renovation and to pay off loans resulting from 1985 renovation campaign. 6/29/88.

Artspace Projects, Minneapolis, MN, $27,700. To support three part planning effort: artists' survey, building renovation feasibility study, and Metro Arts Tour for Greater Minnesota. 10/19/88.
Belcourt School District No. 7, KEYA Public Radio, Belcourt, ND, $30,000. To support start-up expenses of development office at KEYA Public Radio. 10/19/88.
Coffee House Press, Minneapolis, MN, $21,000. To support hiring of marketing/promotions director. 6/29/88.
COMPAS, Saint Paul, MN, $38,050. To support planning of development of Native American Cultural Arts fund. 10/19/88.
Graywolf Press, Saint Paul, MN, $75,000. To support memoir series. 10/19/88.
Guthrie Theater Foundation, Minneapolis, MN, $184,000. For operating expenses in 1988-89 season. 6/29/88.
Illusion Theater and School, Minneapolis, MN, $70,000. To support development of AIDS prevention play. 6/29/88.
Independent Feature Project/North, Minneapolis, MN, $15,000. To hire managing director. 10/19/88.
Intermedia Arts Minnesota, Minneapolis, MN, $35,000. For operating expenses in 1988-1990. 6/29/88.
Loft, The, Minneapolis, MN, $14,000. To hire fundraising consultant, and for $10,000 as matching grant. 6/29/88.
Minnesota Dance Alliance, Minneapolis, MN, $14,275. To support non-Twin Cities dance activities in Minnesota. 2/16/88.
Minnesota Historical Society, Saint Paul, MN, $750,000. To support Minnesota History Center project. 10/19/88.
Minnesota Opera Company, Saint Paul, MN, $75,000. To support 1987-88 season. 2/16/88.
Minnesota Orchestral Association, Minneapolis, MN, $200,000. To support 1987-88 season. 6/29/88.
Minnesota Public Radio, Collegeville, MN, $82,000. To support KSJR's capital campaign to start second station. 6/29/88.
Minnesota Public Radio, Saint Paul, MN, $150,000. For membership challenge grant. 10/19/88.
Mixed Blood Theater Company, Minneapolis, MN, $24,000. To hire fundraising consultant and as matching grant. 2/16/88.
Nancy Hauser Dance Company and School, Minneapolis, MN, $16,000. To support building renovation. 6/29/88.
Northern Minnesota Public Television, Bemidji, MN, $68,000. To support marketing activities. 10/19/88.
Northern Minnesota Public Television, Bemidji, MN, $13,000. Toward market research. 2/16/88.
Saint Paul Chamber Orchestra, Saint Paul, MN, $385,000. To support 1988-89 and 1989-90 seasons. 10/19/88.
Saint Paul Chamber Orchestra Society, Saint Paul, MN, $1,000,000. Toward endowment campaign. 2/16/88.
Saint Paul-Ramsey United Arts Council, Saint Paul, MN, $45,000. Toward Resources and Counseling's Arts Management Initiative. 2/16/88.
South Dakota Friends of Public Broadcasting, Vermillion, SD, $45,000. To support long-range planning project. 10/19/88.
Southern Theater Foundation, Minneapolis, MN, $50,000. To support marketing and public relations activities and establishment of box office. 10/19/88.
Theater de la Jeune Lune, Minneapolis, MN, $24,240. To support marketing activities in 1988-89 season. 6/29/88.
Twin Cities Public Television, Saint Paul, MN, $180,000. Toward operating expenses in 1987-88 and 1988-89. 2/16/88.
Visual Arts Information Service, Minneapolis, MN, $16,000. Toward visual arts publication called Artpaper in 1987-88. 2/16/88.
Visual Arts Information Service, Artpaper, Minneapolis, MN, $14,000. To support Artpaper. 10/19/88.

1399
Patrick and Aimee Butler Family Foundation

West 1380 First National Bank Bldg.
St. Paul 55101 (612) 222-2565

Incorporated in 1951 in MN.
Donor(s): Patrick Butler, and family.
Financial data (yr. ended 12/31/87): Assets, $7,296,631 (M); gifts received, $450,000; expenditures, $662,239, including $652,750 for 130 grants (high: $40,000; low: $350; average: $1,500).
Purpose and activities: Support for Catholic institutions outside the U.S., higher education, chemical dependency, visual arts, cultural institutions, health, women, social services, and human services.
Types of support: Continuing support, annual campaigns, building funds, matching funds, special projects, endowment funds.
Limitations: Giving primarily in the St. Paul and Minneapolis, MN, area; and to Catholic missions outside the U.S. No support for criminal justice, secondary and elementary education, medical research, performing arts, employment, vocational programs, or economic education. No grants to individuals; no loans.
Publications: Financial statement, annual report, informational brochure (including application guidelines).
Application information:
Initial approach: Letter
Copies of proposal: 1
Deadline(s): May 1 and Nov. 1
Board meeting date(s): June and as required
Final notification: July 1 and Dec. 30
Write: Sandra K. Butler, Prog. Officer
Officers: Patrick Butler,* Pres.; Peter M. Butler,* V.P. and Treas.; Terence N. Doyle, Secy.
Trustees:* Patrick Butler, Jr., Sandra K. Butler, Kate B. Peterson.
Number of staff: 1 part-time support.
Employer Identification Number: 416009902

1400
Cargill Corporate Contributions Committee

P.O. Box 9300
Minneapolis 55440 (612) 475-6213

Financial data (yr. ended 5/31/87): $2,141,400 for grants.
Purpose and activities: Support for a broad spectrum of programs that help achieve a better informed, healthier, more productive and prosperous citizenry, in the areas of education, social services, culture, civic affairs, and health; special emphasis is placed on educational and social service programs that help individuals in becoming more self-reliant and on organizations that involve company volunteers. Also donates products. Grants amount reflects giving by headquarters and the divisions and subsidiaries.
Types of support: In-kind gifts, annual campaigns, capital campaigns, continuing support, equipment, operating budgets, professorships, program-related investments, scholarship funds, employee-related scholarships, special projects, building funds.
Limitations: Giving primarily in the Twin Cities, greater MN area, and other areas in the U.S. where company has facilities.
Publications: Corporate giving report.
Application information: Application form required.
Initial approach: Write letter with supporting document
Copies of proposal: 1
Deadline(s): Grant requests reviewed year-round
Board meeting date(s): Every 6-8 weeks
Final notification: Immediately following committee meetings
Write: James S. Hield, Secy., Contribs. Comm.
Administrator: William R. Pearce, Chair., Contribs. Comm.
Number of staff: 1 full-time professional; 1 full-time support.

1401
The Cargill Foundation

P.O. Box 9300
Minneapolis 55440 (612) 475-6122

Incorporated in 1952 in MN.
Donor(s): Cargill Charitable Trust, Cargill, Inc.
Financial data (yr. ended 12/31/88): Assets, $30,236,098 (M); expenditures, $2,522,307, including $2,383,879 for 128 grants (high: $290,000; low: $1,000; average: $1,000-$5,000).
Purpose and activities: Emphasis on education, social service and youth programs, with limited support for health, cultural programs, and civic affairs.
Types of support: Operating budgets, continuing support, general purposes, special projects, capital campaigns.
Limitations: Giving primarily in the seven-county Minneapolis-St. Paul, MN, metropolitan area. No support for religious organizations for religious purposes. No grants to individuals, or for equipment and materials, land acquisition, endowment funds, matching gifts, research, demonstration projects, publications, films or

videos, travel, conferences, or fellowships; no loans.
Publications: Informational brochure (including application guidelines).
Application information: Application form required.
Initial approach: Telephone
Copies of proposal: 1
Deadline(s): Feb. 1 for educational grants; Mar. 15 for health grants; June 1 for social programs; Oct. 15 for cultural programs
Board meeting date(s): Apr., June, Sept., and Dec.
Final notification: 2 weeks to 1 month after board meetings
Write: Audrey Tulberg, Prog. Officer
Officers and Directors:* James R. Cargill,* V.P.; Peter Dorsey,* V.P.; Henry S. Kingman, Jr., V.P.; Cargill MacMillan, Jr.,* V.P.; Calvin J. Anderson, Secy.-Treas. and Exec. Dir.
Number of staff: 1 part-time professional; 1 full-time support; 1 part-time support.
Employer Identification Number: 416020221

1402
The Curtis L. Carlson Foundation
12755 State Hwy. 55
Minneapolis 55441

Incorporated in 1959 in MN.
Donor(s): Curtis L. Carlson.
Financial data (yr. ended 12/31/87): Assets, $254,737 (M); gifts received, $2,000; expenditures, $6,243,973, including $6,122,797 for 64 grants (high: $5,501,818; low: $25).
Purpose and activities: Giving for music and the arts, social agencies, higher education and schools, and Scandinavian intercultural organizations.
Limitations: Giving primarily in MN. No grants to individuals, or for endowment funds, conferences, travel, or athletic events.
Application information:
Initial approach: Proposal
Deadline(s): Sept. 1 for end of calendar year
Final notification: 2 to 4 months
Officers: Curtis L. Carlson, Pres. and Treas.; Arleen E. Carlson, V.P.; Rodney M. Wilson, Secy.
Employer Identification Number: 416028973

1403
Carolyn Foundation
1120 First Bank Place West
Minneapolis 55402 (612) 339-7101

Trust established in 1964 in MN.
Donor(s): Carolyn McKnight Christian.†
Financial data (yr. ended 12/31/88): Assets, $17,543,411 (M); expenditures, $998,444, including $834,140 for 42 grants (high: $150,000; low: $3,000; average: $4-$20,000).
Purpose and activities: Priorities include education, culture, health and welfare, including child welfare, the environment, and the disadvantaged.
Types of support: General purposes.
Limitations: Giving primarily in the metropolitan areas of New Haven, CT, and Minneapolis-St. Paul, MN. No support for political or veterans' groups, fraternal societies, or religious organizations for religious purposes. No grants to individuals, or for endowment funds, annual fund drives, deficit funding, costs of litigation, or continuing support; no loans.
Publications: Annual report (including application guidelines).
Application information:
Initial approach: Letter
Copies of proposal: 1
Deadline(s): Submit proposal between Jan. and Mar. for minor grants (under $10,000) and between Jan. and June for major grants ($10,000 and larger); board awards major grants at Dec. meeting; deadlines Mar. 1 for minor grants; July 1 for major grants
Board meeting date(s): June and Dec.
Write: Carol J. Fetzer, Exec. Dir.
Officers and Trustees: Lucy C. Mitchell, Chair.; Guido Calabresi, Vice-Chair.; Carol J. Fetzer, Secy. and Exec. Dir.; Edwin L. Crosby, Treas.; Beatrice C. Booth, Franklin M. Crosby III, G. Christian Crosby, Sumner McK. Crosby, Jr., Thomas M. Crosby, Jr., Carolyn C. Graham.
Number of staff: None.
Employer Identification Number: 416044416

1404
Chadwick Foundation
4122 IDS Center
Minneapolis 55402

Established in 1967 in MN.
Donor(s): Members of the Dayton family.
Financial data (yr. ended 12/31/87): Assets, $5,048,565 (M); expenditures, $164,168, including $157,250 for 65 grants (high: $15,000; low: $250).
Purpose and activities: Emphasis on secondary and higher education, community services, cultural programs, conservation, hospitals and medical research, the arts, and Protestant church support.
Types of support: Research, general purposes.
Limitations: Giving primarily in MN.
Application information: Contributes only to pre-selected organizations. Applications not accepted.
Officers and Directors: Donald C. Dayton, Pres. and Treas.; Edward N. Dayton, V.P.; John W. Dayton, V.P.; Robert J. Dayton, V.P.; Lucy J. Dayton, Secy.
Employer Identification Number: 416080619

1405
Conwed Foundation
620 Taft St., N.E.
Minneapolis 55413

Established in 1952.
Donor(s): Conwed Corp.
Financial data (yr. ended 11/30/87): Assets, $330,389 (M); expenditures, $13,009, including $12,652 for grants to individuals and $25 for employee matching gifts.
Purpose and activities: Giving primarily for community funds, business education, cultural programs, higher education, youth agencies, a scholarship program for children of employees, and an employee matching gifts program.
Types of support: Operating budgets, continuing support, annual campaigns, seed money, building funds, employee matching gifts, employee-related scholarships, special projects, equipment.
Limitations: Giving primarily in areas where there are major Conwed facilities. No support for religious organizations or member agencies of United Way. No grants to individuals, (except for scholarships for children of company employees), or for research, publications, endowment funds, travel, benefits, or conferences; no loans.
Publications: Program policy statement, application guidelines.
Application information: Contributes only to preselected organizations. Applications not accepted.
Officers and Directors: Frederick T. Weyerhaeuser, Pres.; B.J. Haacke, Secy.; L.A. Anderson, Treas.; W.G. Cowler, Jr., Don Q. Harayda, T.E. Mara.
Number of staff: None.
Employer Identification Number: 416038506

1406
Cowles Media Company Giving Program
329 Portland Ave.
Minneapolis 55415 (612) 375-7051

Financial data (yr. ended 04/02/88): Total giving, $737,500, including $666,200 for 134 grants and $71,300 for 105 employee matching gifts.
Purpose and activities: Support for the arts, early childhood education, family services, literacy, media and communications, and youth; employee matching gifts for art and education.
Types of support: Annual campaigns, capital campaigns, continuing support, employee matching gifts, endowment funds.
Limitations: Giving primarily in Minneapolis, MN.
Application information:
Initial approach: Letter and proposal
Copies of proposal: 1
Deadline(s): None
Board meeting date(s): Calendar quarters
Write: Jan Schwichtenberg

1407
Dain Bosworth/IFG Foundation
(Formerly Inter-Regional Financial Group, Inc., Foundation)
100 Dain Tower
Minneapolis 55402 (612) 371-7750

Incorporated in 1961 in MN.
Donor(s): Dain, Kalman and Quail, Inc., Inter-Regional Financial Group, Inc.
Financial data (yr. ended 12/31/87): Assets, $237,813 (M); gifts received, $256,145; expenditures, $280,723, including $150,448 for 392 grants (high: $46,000; low: $25) and $130,263 for 115 employee matching gifts.
Purpose and activities: Giving for economic development, community funds, cultural and civic affairs, health, education, and social services.

Types of support: Employee matching gifts, general purposes, continuing support, annual campaigns, seed money, building funds.
Limitations: Giving primarily in areas of company operations in MN. No grants to individuals, or for endowment funds, research, scholarships, or fellowships; no loans.
Publications: Program policy statement, application guidelines.
Application information:
Initial approach: Letter
Copies of proposal: 1
Deadline(s): None
Write: Carole Christianson, Exec. Dir.
Officers: L. Pape, Secy.-Treas.; Carole Christianson, Exec. Dir.
Directors: T. Dale, Paul D. Gubrud, Richard D. McFarland, J. Tracy.
Number of staff: 2 part-time professional; 2 part-time support.
Employer Identification Number: 416030639

1408
Edwin W. and Catherine M. Davis Foundation
2100 First National Bank Bldg.
St. Paul 55101 (612) 228-0935

Incorporated in 1956 in MN.
Donor(s): Samuel S. Davis,† Edwin W. Davis,† Frederick W. Davis.
Financial data (yr. ended 12/31/86): Assets, $6,871,442 (M); gifts received, $304,800; expenditures, $643,087, including $613,105 for 81 grants (high: $75,000; low: $200; average: $5,000-$20,000).
Purpose and activities: Concerned with "the amelioration of social problems and increasing the opportunities available to disadvantaged people," with particular interest in the fields of education, social welfare, mental health, the arts, and environmental problems. Educational grants primarily for colleges and universities; support also for religious youth groups.
Types of support: Annual campaigns, continuing support, operating budgets, scholarship funds, endowment funds, fellowships, research.
Limitations: No grants to individuals, or for emergency funds, capital outlay, building and equipment, or endowments; no loans.
Publications: Annual report (including application guidelines).
Application information:
Initial approach: Letter
Copies of proposal: 1
Deadline(s): None
Board meeting date(s): May or June and as required
Final notification: 4 to 6 weeks
Write: Frederick W. Davis, Pres.
Officers and Directors: Frederick W. Davis, Pres.; Bette D. Moorman, V.P.; Mary E. Davis, Secy.; Albert J. Moorman, Treas.; Joseph S. Micallef.
Number of staff: None.
Employer Identification Number: 416012064

1409
Dayton Hudson Corporation Charitable Giving Program
c/o Dayton Hudson Foundation
777 Nicollet Mall
Minneapolis 55402-2055 (612) 370-6555

Financial data (yr. ended 1/31/89): $791,319 for grants.
Purpose and activities: Dayton Hudson Corporation giving has three areas of emphasis: 1) Social Action--for the economic and social progress of individuals; and/or the development of community and neighborhood strategies that respond effectively to critical community social and economic concerns; 2) Arts--for artistic excellence and stronger artistic leadership in communities; and/or increased access to, and use of, the arts as a means of community expression; 3) Miscellaneous--to projects outside Social Action and the Arts that result in company responsiveness to special community needs and opportunities; and/or innovative partnerships with other community leaders. Half of giving is in the Twin Cities area and half is national.
Limitations: No support for religious groups for religious purposes. No grants to individuals, or for fund-raising dinners.
Publications: Corporate giving report.
Application information: All proposals from the Twin Cities area are reviewed by the Dayton Hudson Foundation.
Initial approach: Write or call for application procedures
Write: Cynthia Mayeda, Managing Dir.

1410
Dayton Hudson Department Store Corporate Giving Program
c/o Dayton Hudson Department Store Co. (Dayton's)
700 On The Mall
Minneapolis 55402 (612) 375-2836
Address in MI: Susan Kelly, Dir., Dayton Hudson Dept. Store Co. (Hudson's), 21500 Northwestern Hwy., Southfield, MI 48075; Tel.: (313) 443-6220

Financial data (yr. ended 1/31/89): $1,462,144 for grants.
Purpose and activities: Support for Social Action--for the economic and social progress of individuals; and/or the development of community and neighborhood strategies that respond effectively to critical community social and economic concerns. Arts--for artistic excellence and stronger artistic leadership in communities; and/or increased access to, and use of, the arts as a means of community expression. Miscellaneous--for projects outside Social Action and the Arts that result in our responsiveness to special community needs and opportunities; and/or innovative partnerships with other community leaders; also gives through the Dayton Hudson Foundation.
Types of support: Capital campaigns, endowment funds.
Limitations: Giving limited to areas of company operations in the Twin Cities areas, MN, and in the Southfield, MI, area. No support for religious groups for religious purposes. No grants to individuals, or for fund-raising dinners.
Publications: Corporate giving report.
Application information: Applicant should indicate an application to more than one Dayton Hudson Company when making a formal grant request, because each company has its own priorities and review process.
Initial approach: Write or call for application procedures
Write: Marcia K. Townley, Dir., Public Affairs

1411
Dayton Hudson Foundation
777 Nicollet Mall
Minneapolis 55402 (612) 370-6555

Incorporated in 1918 in MN.
Donor(s): Dayton Hudson Corp., and operating companies.
Financial data (yr. ended 1/31/89): Assets, $14,800,000 (M); gifts received, $10,300,000; expenditures, $9,277,140, including $9,247,354 for 364 grants (high: $1,189,065; low: $1,000; average: $5,000-$100,000).
Purpose and activities: Giving to social action programs that result in the economic and social progress of individuals, and that develop community strategies that respond effectively to community economic and social concerns; support also for arts programs that result in artistic excellence, community leadership in the arts, and increased access to the arts as a means of community expression. The Foundation also manages a small program of grants to national projects on behalf of Target Stores, Mervyn's, Dayton Hudson Department Store Company, Lechmere, and the Dayton Hudson Corporation, and reviews all Twin Cities-area proposals, and approves grants on behalf of Target Stores, Dayton Hudson Department Store Company, and Dayton Hudson Corporation.
Types of support: Operating budgets, continuing support, annual campaigns, matching funds, consulting services, technical assistance, special projects, publications, general purposes.
Limitations: Giving primarily in areas of company operations including MN, especially the Twin Cities metropolitan area, MI, MA, CA, IN, and TX; grants rarely for national organizations or programs. No support for religious organizations for religious purposes; grants rarely made to health organizations, educational institutions, or tax-supported activities. No grants to individuals, or for seed money, emergency funds, land acquisition, scholarships, fellowships, research, or conferences; grants rarely for endowment funds; no loans.
Publications: Corporate giving report, informational brochure, program policy statement, application guidelines, annual report, grants list.
Application information: Organizations located outside of MN should apply to a Dayton Hudson operating company. The Grant Application Guide explains how and where to apply.
Initial approach: Letter with proposal
Copies of proposal: 1
Deadline(s): None

Board meeting date(s): Mar., June, and Nov.
Final notification: Usually within 60 days, although decisions are generally not made between Jan. 31 and Apr. 15
Write: Cynthia Mayeda, Managing Dir.
Officers: Peter C. Hutchinson,* Chair.; Willard C. Shull III,* V.P. and Treas.; William E. Harder, Secy.; Cynthia Mayeda, Managing Dir.
Trustees:* Bruce G. Allbright, Kenneth A. Macke, Walter T. Rossi, C. George Scala, Robert J. Ulrich, Stephen E. Watson.
Number of staff: 4 full-time professional; 2 full-time support; 1 part-time support.
Employer Identification Number: 416017088
Recent arts and culture grants:
Actors Theater of Saint Paul, Saint Paul, MN, $33,000. For general support. 1988.
American Association of Museums, DC, $10,000. To establish Technical Assistance Information Services. 1988.
American Center for Students and Artists, Paris, France, $9,400. For New Dance Ensemble performance fee. 1988.
American Council for the Arts, NYC, NY, $5,000. For general support. 1988.
American Repertory Theater, Cambridge, MA, $35,000. For endowment campaign. 1988.
American Symphony Orchestra League, DC, $12,000. For general support. 1988.
American Variety Theater, Minneapolis, MN, $12,000. For general support for youth development program. 1988.
Arts Clayton, Jonesboro, GA, $10,000. For implementation of Get Your Hands On The Arts program. 1988.
Artspace Projects, Minneapolis, MN, $15,000. For general support to develop living/working space for artists. 1988.
At the Foot of the Mountain, Minneapolis, MN, $17,000. For capital improvements. 1988.
At the Foot of the Mountain, Minneapolis, MN, $15,000. For general support for season of multi-racial women's theater. 1988.
Bilingual Foundation of the Arts, Los Angeles, CA, $41,000. For Arts & Children Initiative-Create Professional Theater for Children. 1988.
Brass Tacks Theater, Minneapolis, MN, $8,500. For general support for season of new plays. 1988.
Brass Tacks Theater, Minneapolis, MN, $8,000. For production support for Cleveland, by Mac Wellman. 1988.
Business Committee for the Arts, NYC, NY, $5,000. For general support and for membership. 1988.
California Poets in the Schools, San Francisco, CA, $15,000. For Arts & Children Initiative-Poetry Residency Program. 1988.
Childrens Theater Company and School, Minneapolis, MN, $49,200. To sponsor production of Dracula. 1988.
Childrens Theater Company and School, Minneapolis, MN, $49,200. For general support. 1988.
Cobb County Arts Council, Marietta, GA, $10,000. Toward implementation of Get Your Hands In The Arts program. 1988.
Coffee House Press, Minneapolis, MN, $6,500. For spring publishing season. 1988.
Colorado Council on Arts and Humanities, Denver, CO, $20,000. For Arts Stabilization Program. 1988.
Columbia University, NYC, NY, $15,000. For Information on Artists project. 1988.
Como Conservatory Restoration Fund, Saint Paul, MN, $35,000. Toward renovation of Como Park Conservatory. 1988.
Cricket Theater, Minneapolis, MN, $15,000. For co-sponsorship of Suzuki Company residency. 1988.
Cricket Theater, Minneapolis, MN, $10,000. For general support. 1988.
Cultural Education Collaborative, Boston, MA, $25,000. For evaluation and documentation of initiatives in arts and children. 1988.
Dance USA, DC, $5,000. For general support for national dance organization. 1988.
DeKalb Council for the Arts, Decatur, GA, $10,000. For implementation of Get Your Hands In The Arts program. 1988.
Denver Art Museum, Denver, CO, $25,000. To sponsor exhibit, Hollywood: Legend and Reality. 1988.
Film in the Cities, Saint Paul, MN, $44,000. For general support for regional media arts center. 1988.
Film in the Cities, Saint Paul, MN, $37,720. For Arts and Children Initiative-Media Arts Education Project. 1988.
Film in the Cities, Saint Paul, MN, $30,000. For equipment needed to offer college accredited courses. 1988.
Foundation for the Extension and Development of the American Professional Theater, NYC, NY, $10,000. For support for moving costs. 1988.
Foundation for the Extension and Development of the American Professional Theater, NYC, NY, $7,500. For general support for technical assistance for theater and dance. 1988.
Graywolf Press, Saint Paul, MN, $15,000. For support for organizational development plan. 1988.
Graywolf Press, Saint Paul, MN, $10,000. For general support for small press activities. 1988.
Great Midwestern Bookshow, Minneapolis, MN, $8,500. For Bookshow. 1988.
Guthrie Theater, Minneapolis, MN, $500,000. For capital and endowment campaign. 1988.
Guthrie Theater, Minneapolis, MN, $123,000. For general support. 1988.
Guthrie Theater, Minneapolis, MN, $65,000. For production of The Bacchae. 1988.
Gwinnett Council for the Arts, Lawrenceville, GA, $10,000. For implementation of Get Your Hands On The Arts program. 1988.
Heart of the Beast Theater, Minneapolis, MN, $76,666. For Arts and Children Initiative to teach various artistic skills. 1988.
Illusion Theater and School, Minneapolis, MN, $25,000. For special grant toward current financial problems. 1988.
Illusion Theater and School, Minneapolis, MN, $18,000. For general support. 1988.
K T C A Twin Cities Public Television, Saint Paul, MN, $250,000. Capital grant for new building. 1988.
K T C A Twin Cities Public Television, Saint Paul, MN, $140,000. For arts programming. 1988.
Life After Performing, Lexington, MA, $6,000. Toward support for dancer and career development programs. 1988.
Loft, The, Minneapolis, MN, $17,500. For general support. 1988.
Meet the Composer, NYC, NY, $8,500. For general support. 1988.
Milkweed Chronicle, Minneapolis, MN, $22,000. For general support for small press publication. 1988.
Minneapolis American Indian Center, Minneapolis, MN, $11,000. For American Indian Art Gallery visual art exhibit program. 1988.
Minneapolis Chamber Symphony, Minneapolis, MN, $5,000. For concert support. 1988.
Minneapolis Public Schools, Minneapolis, MN, $25,000. For support for student opportunities in the arts. 1988.
Minneapolis Society of Fine Arts, Minneapolis, MN, $121,900. For general support for programs. 1988.
Minneapolis Society of Fine Arts, Minneapolis, MN, $55,000. For project support for exhibits. 1988.
Minnesota Alliance for Arts in Education, Minneapolis, MN, $8,000. For general support to promote arts in education. 1988.
Minnesota Alliance for Arts in Education, Minneapolis, MN, $5,000. For Phase II of capital improvement project. 1988.
Minnesota Center for Book Arts, Minneapolis, MN, $17,500. For general support for center to preserve and promote the book. 1988.
Minnesota Center for Book Arts, Minneapolis, MN, $9,500. For membership campaign materials and matching grants. 1988.
Minnesota Chorale, Minneapolis, MN, $10,000. For support for Chorale singers' salaries. 1988.
Minnesota Composers Forum, Saint Paul, MN, $19,000. For general support for service organization for composers. 1988.
Minnesota Dance Alliance, Minneapolis, MN, $15,000. For general support for choreographers' organization. 1988.
Minnesota Dance Alliance, Minneapolis, MN, $14,000. For Summer Dance Festival. 1988.
Minnesota Dance Theater and School, Minneapolis, MN, $15,000. For general support. 1988.
Minnesota Dance Theater and School, Minneapolis, MN, $10,000. For Pointe Drive. 1988.
Minnesota Dance Theater and School, Minneapolis, MN, $5,000. For artistic director search process. 1988.
Minnesota Jazz Dance Company, Minneapolis, MN, $5,000. For dancers' salaries for season. 1988.
Minnesota Motion Picture and Television Board, Minneapolis, MN, $10,000. For general support to promote film and video activity in Minnesota. 1988.
Minnesota Museum of Art, Saint Paul, MN, $30,000. For general support for programs. 1988.
Minnesota Opera Company, Saint Paul, MN, $34,300. For project support for Ariadne Auf Naxos. 1988.
Minnesota Opera Company, Saint Paul, MN, $34,300. For general support for season. 1988.
Minnesota Orchestral Association, Minneapolis, MN, $176,200. For general support for season. 1988.

Minnesota Orchestral Association, Minneapolis, MN, $65,000. For project support for Das Rheingold. 1988.
Minnesota Public Radio, Saint Paul, MN, $90,000. For cultural programming. 1988.
Minnesota Public Radio, Saint Paul, MN, $25,000. Toward renovation of World Theater. 1988.
Mixed Blood Theater Company, Minneapolis, MN, $23,000. For general support for season. 1988.
National Endowment for the Arts, DC, $13,000. For travel expenses for on-site reporters meeting. 1988.
Network, The, Minneapolis, MN, $15,000. For general support for season. 1988.
Network, The, Minneapolis, MN, $10,000. For capital grant to build permanent Tickets to Go kiosk. 1988.
New Dance Ensemble, Minneapolis, MN, $16,500. For general support for programs. 1988.
New Dramatists, Literary Managers and Dramaturgs Program, NYC, NY, $6,000. Toward support for national conference. 1988.
New Rivers Press, Saint Paul, MN, $5,000. For publication of Minnesota Voices project. 1988.
Opera America, DC, $8,500. For general support. 1988.
Penumbra Theater Company, Saint Paul, MN, $8,000. For general support for season of theater about black experience. 1988.
Playwrights Center, Minneapolis, MN, $44,335. For playwriting and theater arts program for Arts and Children Initiative. 1988.
Playwrights Center, Minneapolis, MN, $22,500. For general support for service organization for playwrights. 1988.
Plymouth Music Series, Minneapolis, MN, $18,000. To produce Britten's Paul Bunyan. 1988.
Poets and Writers, NYC, NY, $9,000. For general support. 1988.
Red Eye Collaboration, Minneapolis, MN, $9,000. For general support for season of experimental work. 1988.
Red Eye Collaboration, Minneapolis, MN, $5,000. For artists' salaries. 1988.
Saint Paul Chamber Orchestra, Saint Paul, MN, $50,100. For guest artists. 1988.
Saint Paul Chamber Orchestra, Saint Paul, MN, $50,100. For general support. 1988.
Schubert Club, Saint Paul, MN, $20,000. For Live from Landmark concert series. 1988.
Schubert Club, Saint Paul, MN, $10,000. For Benita Valente performance. 1988.
Southern Theater Foundation, Minneapolis, MN, $23,120. For general support for theater space. 1988.
Sylmar Chamber Ensemble, Minneapolis, MN, $5,500. For general support for season of chamber music. 1988.
Theater Communications Group, NYC, NY, $18,000. For general support. 1988.
Theater Communications Group, NYC, NY, $10,000. For national artistic agenda activity. 1988.
Theater de la Jeune Lune, Minneapolis, MN, $17,000. For general support for season. 1988.
United Arts, Saint Paul, MN, $27,500. For technical assistance for artists and arts groups. 1988.
University Community Video, Minneapolis, MN, $25,000. For general support for service organization for video artists. 1988.
University Community Video, Minneapolis, MN, $23,282. To videotape co-production with Brass Tacks/Bruce Charlesworth. 1988.
University of Minnesota, Minneapolis, MN, $8,000. For Mid-America Arts Association Conference. 1988.
University of Minnesota, Northrup Dance Series, Minneapolis, MN, $50,000. For new multi-disciplinary series presented with Walker Art Center. 1988.
Visual Arts Information Service, Minneapolis, MN, $10,000. For Artpaper, statewide visual arts newspaper. 1988.
Walker Art Center, Minneapolis, MN, $200,000. For educational programs in new Minneapolis sculpture garden. 1988.
Walker Art Center, Minneapolis, MN, $76,000. For general support. 1988.
West Bank School of Music, Minneapolis, MN, $5,415. For Spring Jazz Composer Series Concerts. 1988.
Womens Art Registry of Minnesota (WARM), Minneapolis, MN, $13,000. For general support and for juried exhibition. 1988.
Womens Theater Project, Saint Paul, MN, $5,500. For general support. 1988.
Zenon Dance Company and School, Minneapolis, MN, $6,000. For dancers' salaries. 1988.

1412
Roger L. and Agnes C. Dell Charitable Trust II

c/o First Trust National Association
Two South First Natl. Bank Bldg., P.O. Box 64704
St. Paul 55164-0704 (612) 291-5132

Established in 1970 in MN.
Financial data (yr. ended 7/31/87): Assets, $1,533,646 (M); expenditures, $78,249, including $65,950 for 20 grants (high: $10,250; low: $500; average: $500-$5,000).
Purpose and activities: Giving primarily for youth, education, and cultural programs.
Types of support: General purposes.
Limitations: Giving limited to Fergus Falls, MN, and the surrounding area.
Application information:
Initial approach: Letter
Write: Gerald S. Rufer, Trustee
Trustees: Richard C. Hefte, Gerald S. Rufer, Stephen Rufer, First Trust Co., Inc.
Employer Identification Number: 416059730

1413
Dellwood Foundation, Inc.

1000 Pioneer Bldg.
St. Paul 55101 (612) 224-1841

Established in 1958 in MN.
Financial data (yr. ended 12/31/88): Assets, $1,601,784 (M); expenditures, $123,842, including $112,500 for 30 grants (high: $17,500; low: $1,000).
Purpose and activities: Giving to the United Way, and for the arts, education, and the environment.
Types of support: Annual campaigns, building funds, capital campaigns, continuing support, endowment funds, general purposes, land acquisition, operating budgets, program-related investments, research.
Limitations: Giving primarily in the Twin Cities, MN, area. No grants to individuals.
Application information:
Initial approach: Proposal
Copies of proposal: 1
Deadline(s): None
Board meeting date(s): Varies
Final notification: None given
Write: J.G. Ordway, Jr., Pres. and Treas.
Officers and Directors: John G. Ordway, Jr., Pres. and Treas.; Margaret M. Ordway, V.P.; J.C. Foote, Secy.; John G. Ordway III, P.W. Ordway.
Number of staff: None.
Employer Identification Number: 416019244

1414
Deluxe Corporation Foundation

(Formerly Deluxe Check Printers Foundation)
1080 West County Rd. "F"
P.O. Box 64399
St. Paul 55164-0399 (612) 483-7842

Incorporated in 1952 in MN.
Donor(s): Deluxe Corp.
Financial data (yr. ended 12/31/88): Assets, $2,048,072 (M); gifts received, $2,900,000; expenditures, $3,316,044, including $3,060,995 for 679 grants (high: $100,000; low: $1,000; average: $1,000-$10,000) and $229,119 for 1,151 employee matching gifts.
Purpose and activities: Giving for private higher education, particularly independent college funds, and for youth organizations, social welfare agencies, and cultural organizations; grants largely for capital purposes, including buildings, renovations, or equipment, and for operations, programs, special projects, and an employee matching gifts program.
Types of support: Building funds, equipment, operating budgets, special projects, employee matching gifts, renovation projects.
Limitations: Giving primarily in areas of company operations. No support for primary or secondary schools, or for religious or political organizations. No grants to individuals, or for annual campaigns or research; no loans.
Publications: Annual report (including application guidelines).
Application information: Application form required.
Initial approach: Letter or telephone
Copies of proposal: 1
Deadline(s): None
Board meeting date(s): Feb.; regional meetings at least twice a year
Final notification: 3 months
Write: Jennifer Anderson, Grants Admin.
Officers and Trustees: Michael J. Welch, Pres.; Francis H. Cloutier, Treas.; Mark T. Gritton, Harold V. Haverty, James T. Nichols,

William J. Oliver, Charles M. Osborne, Bernard L. Sponsel, Jerry K. Twogood.
Number of staff: 2 full-time professional; 1 part-time professional; 1 part-time support.
Employer Identification Number: 416034786

1415
The Donaldson Foundation
c/o Donaldson Co., Inc.
P.O. Box 1299
Minneapolis 55440 (612) 887-3010

Established in 1966 in MN.
Donor(s): Donaldson Co., Inc.
Financial data (yr. ended 7/31/88): Assets, $495,656 (M); gifts received, $100,000; expenditures, $348,386, including $338,875 for 98 grants (high: $38,400; low: $300) and $6,850 for 12 employee matching gifts.
Purpose and activities: Support for community funds, youth agencies, arts and cultural organizations, vocational schools, and higher education; grants also for educational associations, environmental protection, community development, and health services.
Types of support: Employee matching gifts.
Limitations: Giving primarily in areas of company operations, including MN, WI, IL, IN, IA, MO, and KY. No support for religious organizations. No grants to individuals.
Publications: Application guidelines, annual report (including application guidelines).
Application information:
Initial approach: Letter
Copies of proposal: 1
Deadline(s): May 1 and Aug. 1
Board meeting date(s): Aug. and May
Write: Raymond Vodovnik, Secy.
Officers: John R. Schweers, Pres. and Treas.; Raymond Vodovnik,* Secy.
Trustees:* F.A. Donaldson, Sandy Donaldson, Sue Gentilini, Gloria Gordon, Dennis Grigal, Rudy Molck-Ude, Robert Schweitzer, William S. West.
Number of staff: None.
Employer Identification Number: 416052950

1416
Driscoll Foundation
2100 First National Bank Bldg.
St. Paul 55101 (612) 228-0935

Incorporated in 1962 in MN.
Donor(s): Members of the Driscoll family.
Financial data (yr. ended 2/28/87): Assets, $3,929,371 (M); gifts received, $648,920; expenditures, $318,818, including $294,218 for 32 grants (high: $50,000; low: $500; average: $5,000).
Purpose and activities: Emphasis on higher and secondary education, hospitals, the arts, Protestant church support, conservation, and community funds.
Limitations: Giving primarily in the metropolitan areas of St. Paul-Minneapolis, MN and San Francisco, CA. No grants to individuals, or for conferences, travel, publications, or films.
Publications: Annual report, application guidelines.
Application information:
Initial approach: Letter
Copies of proposal: 1
Deadline(s): None
Board meeting date(s): Annually and as required
Final notification: 3 to 4 weeks
Write: W. John Driscoll, Pres.
Officers: W. John Driscoll,* Pres.; Rudolph W. Driscoll,* V.P.; Joseph S. Micallef, Secy.; Gordon E. Hed, Treas.
Directors:* Elizabeth S. Driscoll, Margot H. Driscoll.
Number of staff: None.
Employer Identification Number: 416012065

1417
The Dyco Foundation
1100 Interchange Tower
Minneapolis 55426 (612) 545-4021

Established in 1977 in MN.
Donor(s): Dyco Petroleum Corp.
Financial data (yr. ended 12/31/87): Assets, $1,001,192 (M); gifts received, $11,600; expenditures, $134,630, including $105,775 for 57 grants (high: $15,000; low: $250; average: $1,000-$2,000) and $8,500 for 5 grants to individuals.
Purpose and activities: Support for medicine and health, social service agencies, the arts and cultural programs, community development, and youth organizations; primary focus: self sufficiency through employment programs targeting the handicapped, minority teens, and long term unemployed; support also for scholarships for the children of company employees.
Types of support: General purposes, special projects, employee-related scholarships, employee matching gifts, matching funds, program-related investments, technical assistance, emergency funds.
Limitations: Giving primarily in areas of company operations in the Minneapolis, MN, area, and Tulsa and Elk City, OK. No support for sectarian organizations for religious purposes. No grants to individuals (except for employee-related scholarships), or for operating budgets, seed money, capital drives, endowment funds, publications, advertising, tickets, or banquets.
Publications: Corporate giving report (including application guidelines).
Application information:
Initial approach: Telephone
Deadline(s): Mar. 1, June 15, Sept. 15, and Dec. 1; Mar. 30 for scholarships
Board meeting date(s): Quarterly
Write: Alicia E. Ringstad, Secy.
Officers and Directors: Jaye F. Dyer, Pres.; Lendell Z. Williams, V.P.; Alicia E. Ringstad, Secy.; Jack E. Hill, Treas.; James Rodger, Betty Shovelin, John F. West.
Number of staff: 1 part-time professional; 1 part-time support.
Employer Identification Number: 411390020

1418
Ecolab Foundation
Ecolab Ctr., 10th Fl.
St. Paul 55102 (612) 293-2222

Established in 1982 in MN.
Financial data (yr. ended 12/31/87): Assets, $3,243,963 (M); gifts received, $2,764,272; expenditures, $406,951, including $254,740 for 133 grants (high: $42,000; low: $25), $77,700 for 79 grants to individuals and $48,550 for 43 loans to individuals.
Purpose and activities: Gives one-year scholarships for tuition and academic fees at accredited colleges or universities, and also at technical community colleges and nursing schools; only for dependents of an employee or retiree; support also for higher education, social service organizations and the arts.
Types of support: Employee-related scholarships, loans.
Limitations: Giving primarily in Garland, TX; Beloit, WI; Minneapolis and St. Paul, MN; Woodbridge, NJ; Joliet, IL; and Columbus, OH.
Publications: Corporate giving report.
Application information: Application form required.
Initial approach: Letter
Copies of proposal: 1
Deadline(s): July 1
Board meeting date(s): Quarterly
Final notification: Mar.
Write: Kristie L. Greve, Dir. Communications and Commun. Relations
Officers and Directors: Jon R. Grunseth, Pres.; D.A. Grocholski, Secy.; Toni L. Hengesteg, Treas.; G.W. Leimer, S.L. Olson, Allan L. Schuman, M.E. Shannon.
Number of staff: None.
Employer Identification Number: 411372157

1419
Ferndale Foundation, Inc.
c/o First Trust National Association
First National Bank Bldg., P.O. Box 64704
St. Paul 55164

Incorporated in 1966 in MN.
Donor(s): William H. Lang, Mrs. William H. Lang, Lang-Ferndale Trusts.
Financial data (yr. ended 10/31/87): Assets, $36,532 (M); gifts received, $140,714; expenditures, $138,482, including $135,900 for 24 grants (high: $50,000; low: $400).
Purpose and activities: Emphasis on hospitals, cultural programs, and a community fund.
Types of support: General purposes, annual campaigns, building funds, scholarship funds, capital campaigns.
Limitations: Giving primarily in MN.
Application information:
Initial approach: Letter or proposal
Deadline(s): None
Write: Paul J. Kelly, Secy.
Officers: Theodora H. Lang, Pres.; A. Scheffer Lang, V.P.; Paul J. Kelly, Secy.-Treas.
Director: Barbara Lang Cochran, Andrew Scott.
Employer Identification Number: 416084166

1420
First Bank System Corporate Giving Program
P.O. Box 522
Minneapolis 55480 (612) 370-4359

Financial data (yr. ended 12/31/88): Total giving, $5,103,625, including $5,103,625 for grants and $489,253,685 for loans.
Purpose and activities: First Bank System makes financial contributions to its communities through both the FBS Foundation and individual FBS banks and subsidiaries. FBS provides corporate giving through charitable contributions in the areas of human services, education, and arts and culture; leadership in community development, economic development, neighborhood and housing programs, small business and job resources, and volunteerism; also makes program-related investments. The First Bank Neighborhood Lending Partnership Program makes low-interest loans for small businesses, and low- and moderate-income housing.
Limitations: Giving primarily in areas where First Bank System operates.
Application information: Application form required.
Initial approach: Request for guidelines; write to headquarters, foundation, or nearest branch
Copies of proposal: 1
Deadline(s): None
Board meeting date(s): Quarterly and unannounced
Final notification: One month after meeting
Write: John D. Taylor, Pres., First Bank System Fdn.

1421
First Bank System Foundation
P.O. Box 522, MPM2 0101
Minneapolis 55480 (612) 370-4359

Established about 1979.
Donor(s): First Bank System, First Bank Minneapolis Office, First Bank St. Paul Office, and other First Bank offices and trust, leasing, insurance, and mortgage companies.
Financial data (yr. ended 12/31/88): Assets, $1,780,302 (M); gifts received, $5,358,369; expenditures, $7,438,448, including $6,410,161 for grants (high: $735,800; low: $100; average: $2,000-$30,000) and $451,982 for 3,334 employee matching gifts.
Purpose and activities: Support for higher and other education, cultural programs, community funds, social services, and youth organizations.
Types of support: Operating budgets, continuing support, annual campaigns, emergency funds, employee matching gifts, employee-related scholarships, special projects, renovation projects, matching funds.
Limitations: Giving primarily in trade areas in MN, MT, ND, SD, WI, and WA. No support for religious organizations for religious purposes, camps, medical facilities, or drug or alcohol abuse prevention treatment. No grants to individuals, or for seed money, deficit financing, land acquisition, endowment funds, publications, conferences, trips, tours, or research; no loans.
Publications: Annual report, application guidelines.
Application information: Application form required.
Initial approach: Letter or telephone
Copies of proposal: 1
Deadline(s): 3 months before committee meetings
Board meeting date(s): Quarterly
Final notification: 1 month after committee meetings
Write: John D. Taylor, Pres.
Officers: John D. Taylor,* Pres.; Charles E. Riesenberg, V.P.; Sally A. Sumner, Secy.; Eugene R. Mason, Treas.
Directors:* DeWalt Ankeny, Jr., Chair.; D.S. Hanson, D.G. Knudson, R.W. Schoenke, M.W. Sheffert, J.B. Walters.
Number of staff: 5 full-time professional; 4 full-time support.
Employer Identification Number: 411359579

1422
Frenzel Foundation
c/o Norwest Bank St. Paul, N.A.
55 East Fifth St.
St. Paul 55101-2701

Established in 1959 in MN.
Financial data (yr. ended 12/31/87): Assets, $1,111,980 (M); expenditures, $224,773, including $186,700 for 22 grants (high: $125,000; low: $1,000).
Purpose and activities: Support primarily for education and culture.
Types of support: Scholarship funds.
Application information: Applications not accepted.
Trustees: Peter M. Frenzel, Robert P. Frenzel, William E. Frenzel.
Employer Identification Number: 416018060

1423
H. B. Fuller Community Affairs Program
2400 Energy Park Dr.
St. Paul 55108 (612) 647-3617

Financial data (yr. ended 12/31/88): $409,540 for 64 grants.
Purpose and activities: Support for social services/human relations, education, health and welfare, community development, environmental issues, and arts and humanities. Emphasizes youth development programs in the areas of literacy and crisis prevention. Encourages employee volunteerism through corporate community service projects, community service leave, and community affairs councils throughout the U.S., Latin America, and Europe.
Types of support: General purposes.
Limitations: Giving primarily in operating locations nationwide and in Argentina, Brazil, Chile, Costa Rica, Dominican Republic, El Salvador, Guatemala, Honduras, Mexico, Panama, Puerto Rico, West Germany, Austria, Belgium, France, Netherlands, Spain, Sweden, United Kingdom, Canada, and Japan. No support for religious, political, fraternal or veterans' organizations, except those which benefit the community, or to lobbying groups, national or local disease associations. No grants to individuals, or for capital or endowment drives, fund-raising campaigns, courtesy advertising, travel, or basic or applied research.
Publications: Corporate giving report (including application guidelines).
Application information: Include description of organization, amount requested, tax-exempt status, and current budget information.
Initial approach: Letter or proposal
Board meeting date(s): Community Affairs Councils meet monthly
Final notification: Within 6 weeks
Write: Karen Muller, Exec. Dir.
Council Chairpersons: Shirley Draft, Lewis Flanagan, Beverly Krebs, Diane Strickland.

1424
H. B. Fuller Company Foundation
2400 Energy Park Dr.
St. Paul 55108 (612) 647-3617

Established in 1986 in MN.
Donor(s): H.B. Fuller Company.
Financial data (yr. ended 11/30/87): Assets, $627,016 (M); gifts received, $894,175; expenditures, $276,854, including $251,162 for 200 grants (high: $80,000; low: $25; average: $1,000-$5,000) and $25,270 for 112 employee matching gifts.
Purpose and activities: Support for arts and humanities, education, the environment, youth, social services, and the United Way; support for higher education mainly through employee matching gifts. Youth grants have two thrusts: to develop self-esteem and literacy and to prevent drug abuse, teen pregnancy, and domestic violence in families.
Types of support: Annual campaigns, emergency funds, employee matching gifts, general purposes, operating budgets.
Limitations: Giving primarily in areas of company operations in MN, NJ, FL, MA, KY, TN, CA, GA, IL, OH, OR, NY, NC, WA, TX, MO. No support for religious, political, fraternal, or veterans' organizations. No grants to individuals, or for travel, basic or applied research, advertising, fund-raising campaigns, or capital or endowment drives; multiple year grants; grants are made for current year programs.
Publications: Corporate giving report (including application guidelines).
Application information:
Initial approach: Telephone or mail
Copies of proposal: 1
Deadline(s): First day of preceding month in which a committee meeting is held
Board meeting date(s): Mar., June, and Oct. for Contributions Committee; Community Affairs Councils meet monthly
Final notification: 2 weeks following committee meetings; Community Affairs Councils will respond within 6 weeks
Write: Karen Muller
Officers and Directors: Anthony L. Anderson, Pres.; Reatha Clark King, Walter Kissling, Robert Odom, Gregory Palen, John Ray, David Stanley, Ann Wynia.
Number of staff: 2 full-time professional; 1 full-time support.
Employer Identification Number: 363500811

1425
The B. C. Gamble and P. W. Skogmo Foundation
821 Marquette Ave., 500 Foshay Tower
Minneapolis 55402 (612) 339-7343

B.C. Gamble Foundation incorporated in MN in 1948; P.W. Skogmo Foundation also incorporated in 1948 in MN and merged with P.W. Skogmo Charitable Trust in 1962; B.C. Gamble Foundation merged with P.W. Skogmo Foundation in 1982 and became supporting organization of The Minneapolis Foundation.
Donor(s): P.W. Skogmo,† B.C. Gamble.†
Financial data (yr. ended 3/31/88): Assets, $19,455,272 (M); expenditures, $1,539,355, including $1,420,675 for 124 grants (high: $175,000; low: $500; average: $5,000-$20,000).
Purpose and activities: Giving for disadvantaged youth and their families, the handicapped, programs for low income senior citizens; health care, including research and education, and higher and secondary educational institutions.
Types of support: Building funds, capital campaigns, equipment, general purposes, seed money, operating budgets, special projects.
Limitations: Giving limited to the Minneapolis-St. Paul, MN, metropolitan area. No support for political organizations, veterans' organizations, fraternal societies, national fundraising campaigns, religious organizations for religious purposes, or for membership in civic or trade organizations. No grants to individuals, or for endowment funds, courtesy advertising, conferences, deficit financing, telephone solicitations or general fundraising expenses, tickets for benefits.
Publications: Annual report (including application guidelines).
Application information: Only 1 copy of proposal is required for requests $10,000 or less for general operating support.
Initial approach: Proposal
Copies of proposal: 10
Deadline(s): Apr. 1 and Oct. 1
Board meeting date(s): June and Dec.
Final notification: As soon as possible following board meeting
Write: Patricia A. Cummings, Mgr. of Supporting Organizations
Officers: Philip B. Harris,* Pres.; Georgia S. Bartlett,* V.P.; Donald G. Dreblow,* V.P.; Marion G. Etzwiler, Secy.-Treas.
Trustees:* Robert H. Engels, Timothy G. Johnson, Raymond O. Mithun, Henry T. Rutledge.
Number of staff: 3
Employer Identification Number: 411410675
Recent arts and culture grants:
American Swedish Foundation, Minneapolis, MN, $25,000. For renovation of Gladys Gamble Room and for display and promotion of Doughty Birds Collection. 1988.
American Variety Theater Company, 4H Club, Minneapolis, MN, $5,000. For renovation projects within Theater. 1988.
Childrens Theater Company and School, Minneapolis, MN, $6,500. For general operating support. 1988.
Illusion Theater and School, Minneapolis, MN, $10,000. For development of general public education play on subject of AIDS awareness and prevention. 11/87.
Minneapolis Society of Fine Arts, Minneapolis, MN, $13,000. For programs for handicapped. 1988.
Minnesota Orchestral Association, Minneapolis, MN, $5,000. For general operating support. 11/87.
Saint Paul Chamber Orchestra, Saint Paul, MN, $5,000. For general operating support. 1988.

1426
The Gelco Foundation
One Gelco Dr.
Eden Prairie 55344 (612) 828-2614
Additional tel.: (612) 828-2979

Incorporated in 1973 in MN.
Donor(s): Gelco Corp.
Financial data (yr. ended 6/30/87): Assets, $1,374,963 (M); gifts received, $63,000; expenditures, $303,914, including $302,250 for 119 grants (high: $85,000; low: $275).
Purpose and activities: The foundation is inactive.
Types of support: Annual campaigns, operating budgets, general purposes, special projects.
Limitations: Giving primarily in MN, with emphasis on the Minneapolis-St. Paul area. No support for political or fraternal organizations, or for religious organizations for sectarian purposes. No grants to individuals, or for scholarships, fellowships, fundraising events, medical research, or matching gifts; no loans.
Publications: Annual report (including application guidelines).
Application information:
Initial approach: Letter
Copies of proposal: 1
Deadline(s): Submit proposal preferably by Feb.; deadline for consideration in fiscal year is Apr. 15
Board meeting date(s): Usually in Jan. and June
Write: James P. Johnson, Dir.
Officers: N. Bud Grossman,* Pres.; Donald Herbert,* Secy.; Richard McFerran,* Treas.; James P. Johnson, Dir.
Directors:* Andrew Grossman, Kevin Mitchell, Lewis Rubin, Robert Ward.
Employer Identification Number: 237302799
Recent arts and culture grants:
Minneapolis Society of Fine Arts, Minneapolis, MN, $6,000. For annual campaign. 1987.
Minnesota Orchestral Association, Minneapolis, MN, $85,000. For New Dimensions II. 1987.
Minnesota Orchestral Association, Minneapolis, MN, $12,000. For Guaranty Fund. 1987.

1427
General Mills Corporate Giving Program
P.O. Box 1113
Minneapolis 55440 (612) 540-7890

Financial data (yr. ended 5/31/88): Total giving, $3,437,673, including $1,446,684 for grants (high: $360,000; low: $500; average: $1,000-$5,000) and $1,990,989 for in-kind gifts.
Purpose and activities: Supports fine arts and cultural institutes; elementary, secondary, continuing and vocational education; public and private colleges. Also supports civic and public affairs through community organizations, economic and job development, environmental affairs, welfare, youth service, and minority, urban, and political and legal advocacy programs. Community funding includes United Way. Non-monetary assistance through donations of company's primary goods or services and employee volunteer programs. The Foundation separately administers a budget for corporate giving which is a portion of total corporate giving by General Mills. The same staff handles Foundation and direct corporate giving.
Types of support: Conferences and seminars, publications, research, special projects.
Limitations: Giving primarily in headquarters city and major operating locations.
Publications: Application guidelines.
Application information: Proposal including project description and budget, financial report, list of board members and major donors, 501(c)(3).
Initial approach: Letter and proposal
Copies of proposal: 1
Board meeting date(s): Quarterly
Final notification: Soon after decision is made
Write: Reatha Clark King, Pres. and Exec. Dir., General Mills Foundation

1428
General Mills Foundation
P.O. Box 1113
Minneapolis 55440 (612) 540-7890

Incorporated in 1954 in MN.
Donor(s): General Mills, Inc.
Financial data (yr. ended 5/31/88): Assets, $20,359,413 (L); gifts received, $8,300,000; expenditures, $7,233,062, including $6,438,497 for 584 grants (high: $665,894) and $496,319 for 1,538 employee matching gifts.
Purpose and activities: Grants for higher and secondary education, social services, community funds, health, and civic and cultural activities.
Types of support: Operating budgets, employee matching gifts, scholarship funds, employee-related scholarships, special projects.
Limitations: Giving primarily in areas of major parent company operations, with emphasis on the Minneapolis, MN, area. No support for religious purposes, recreation, or national or local campaigns to eliminate or control specific diseases. No grants to individuals, or generally for endowment or capital funds, research, publications, films, conferences, seminars, advertising, athletic events, testimonial dinners, workshops, symposia, travel, fundraising events, or deficit financing; no loans.
Publications: Corporate giving report (including application guidelines).
Application information: Preliminary telephone calls or personal visits discouraged.
Initial approach: Proposal with brief cover letter
Copies of proposal: 1
Deadline(s): None
Board meeting date(s): 4 to 6 times a year and as required
Final notification: 4 weeks

Write: Reatha Clark King, Pres.
Officers: H. Brewster Atwater, Jr.,* Chair.; Reatha Clark King,* Pres. and Exec. Dir.; David Nasby, V.P.; Clifford L. Whitehill,* Secy.; Eugene P. Preiss, Treas.
Trustees:* F. Caleb Blodgett, T.P. Nelson, S.M. Rothschild, A.R. Schulze, Mark H. Willes.
Number of staff: 2 full-time professional; 2 full-time support; 1 part-time support.
Employer Identification Number: 416018495
Recent arts and culture grants:
Actors Theater of Saint Paul, Saint Paul, MN, $5,500. For operating support. 1987.
At the Foot of the Mountain, Minneapolis, MN, $5,000. For operating support. 1987.
Cedar Rapids Art Association, Cedar Rapids, IA, $10,000. For capital support. 1987.
Childrens Theater Company and School, Minneapolis, MN, $35,000. For operating support. 1987.
CLIMB, Saint Paul, MN, $6,000. For operating support. 1987.
Como Conservatory Restoration Fund, Saint Paul, MN, $15,000. For operating support. 1987.
Cricket Theater Corporation, Minneapolis, MN, $15,000. For operating support. 1987.
Dale Warland Singers, Saint Paul, MN, $5,000. For operating support. 1987.
Film in the Cities, Saint Paul, MN, $6,000. For operating support. 1987.
Guthrie Theater Foundation, Minneapolis, MN, $74,000. For operating support. 1987.
Illusion Theater and School, Minneapolis, MN, $5,500. For operating support. 1987.
Iowa Public Television Foundation, Johnston, IA, $5,000. For capital support. 1987.
K T C A Twin Cities Public Television, Minneapolis, MN, $150,000. For capital support. 1987.
K T C A Twin Cities Public Television, Minneapolis, MN, $120,000. For operating support. 1987.
Lincoln Center for the Performing Arts, NYC, NY, $5,000. For operating support. 1987.
Minneapolis Public Schools, Minneapolis, MN, $6,500. For Arts Partnership Funding Project. 1987.
Minneapolis Society of Fine Arts, Minneapolis, MN, $74,500. For operating support. 1987.
Minnesota Alliance for Arts in Education, Minneapolis, MN, $5,500. For operating support. 1987.
Minnesota Center for Book Arts, Minneapolis, MN, $7,000. For operating support. 1987.
Minnesota Composers Forum, Saint Paul, MN, $5,000. For operating support. 1987.
Minnesota Dance Theater and School, Minneapolis, MN, $5,000. For operating support. 1987.
Minnesota Museum of Art, Saint Paul, MN, $5,000. For operating support. 1987.
Minnesota Opera Company, Saint Paul, MN, $13,500. For operating support. 1987.
Minnesota Orchestral Association, Minneapolis, MN, $180,000. For New Dimensions II Program. 1987.
Minnesota Orchestral Association, Minneapolis, MN, $82,000. For operating support. 1987.
Minnesota Public Radio, Saint Paul, MN, $38,000. For operating support. 1987.
Minnesota Public Radio, Saint Paul, MN, $25,000. For capital/endowment campaign. 1987.
Mixed Blood Theater Company, Minneapolis, MN, $7,150. For operating support. 1987.
National Council for Families and Television, Princeton, NJ, $5,000. For operating support. 1987.
Paramount Arts Center Endowment, Aurora, IL, $5,000. For capital support. 1987.
Saint Paul Chamber Orchestra Society, Saint Paul, MN, $47,500. For operating support. 1987.
Science Museum of Minnesota, Saint Paul, MN, $35,000. For operating support. 1987.
United States Holocaust Memorial Council, U.S. Holocaust Memorial Museum, DC, $5,000. For capital support. 1987.
University of Minnesota Foundation, University Art Museum, Minneapolis, MN, $7,500. For Young Minnesota Artists Touring Exhibition. 1987.
Walker Art Center, Minneapolis, MN, $59,000. For general support. 1987.

1429
The Greystone Foundation
510 Baker Bldg.
Minneapolis 55402 (612) 332-2454

Established in 1948 in MN.
Donor(s): Members of the Paul A. Brooks family.
Financial data (yr. ended 12/31/87): Assets, $1,419,909 (M); gifts received, $104,742; expenditures, $469,983, including $439,491 for 113 grants (high: $235,000; low: $45; average: $1,000-$10,000).
Purpose and activities: Giving for health and medical research, community funds and a community foundation, private secondary education, animal care and preservation, and arts and cultural programs.
Types of support: Operating budgets, continuing support, annual campaigns, seed money, emergency funds, deficit financing, building funds, equipment, land acquisition, special projects, research, publications, conferences and seminars.
Limitations: Giving primarily in MN. No grants to individuals, or for endowment funds, matching gifts, scholarships, or fellowships; no loans.
Application information:
Initial approach: Proposal
Deadline(s): None
Board meeting date(s): As required
Write: John M. Hollern, Trustee
Trustees: John M. Hollern, Michael P. Hollern.
Number of staff: None.
Employer Identification Number: 416027765

1430
Mary Livingston Griggs and Mary Griggs Burke Foundation
1400 Norwest Center
55 East Fifth St.
St. Paul 55101 (612) 227-7683

Established in 1966 in MN.
Donor(s): Mary L. Griggs.†
Financial data (yr. ended 6/30/87): Assets, $16,031,799 (M); expenditures, $795,212, including $693,130 for 65 grants (high: $137,500; low: $1,000; average: $500-$50,000).
Purpose and activities: Support primarily for arts and culture, including museums and an Asian cultural society; support also for conservation, higher and secondary education, and social services.
Types of support: Fellowships, general purposes, operating budgets, annual campaigns, renovation projects, matching funds, building funds, endowment funds.
Limitations: Giving primarily in St. Paul, MN, and New York, NY. No grants to individuals, or for special projects or research.
Application information:
Initial approach: Letter
Copies of proposal: 1
Deadline(s): None
Board meeting date(s): Quarterly
Final notification: 10 days to 3 months
Write: Marvin J. Pertzik, Secy.
Officers and Directors: Mary Griggs Burke, Pres.; Richard A. Moore, V.P.; Marvin J. Pertzik, Secy.; Orley R. Taylor, Treas.; Eleanor Griggs, C.F. Bayliss Griggs.
Number of staff: None.
Employer Identification Number: 416052355

1431
Grotto Foundation, Inc.
West 1050 First National Bank Bldg.
332 Minnesota St.
St. Paul 55101 (612) 224-9431

Incorporated in 1964 in MN.
Donor(s): Louis W. Hill, Jr.
Financial data (yr. ended 4/30/88): Assets, $3,982,142 (M); gifts received, $150,000; expenditures, $334,833, including $293,922 for 55 grants (high: $50,000; low: $250; average: $3,000-$5,000).
Purpose and activities: Giving for education, especially higher education, cultural programs, welfare, and health; grants also for special projects relating to American Indians, recent American immigrants, and racially mixed families.
Types of support: Seed money, emergency funds, scholarship funds, internships, special projects, research.
Limitations: Giving limited to MN, adjoining Midwestern states, and, on a lesser basis, to AK. No support for writing projects, government projects, or art programs. No grants to individuals, or for capital or endowment funds, travel, continuing support, operating budgets (except to aid in initiating occasional programs), annual campaigns, deficit financing, student research, publications, or conferences; no loans.
Publications: Annual report (including application guidelines).
Application information: Application form required.
Initial approach: Letter or proposal
Copies of proposal: 2
Deadline(s): 60 days prior to months in which board meets
Board meeting date(s): Mar., June, Sept., and Dec., and as required
Final notification: 2 months
Write: A.A. Heckman, Exec. Dir.

Officers: Louis W. Hill, Jr.,* Pres.; Irving Clark,* V.P.; A.A. Heckman,* Secy. and Exec. Dir.; Jeffery T. Peterson, Treas.
Directors:* Cynthia Gehrig, John E. Diehl, Malcolm W. McDonald, William B. Randall.
Number of staff: 1 full-time professional; 1 part-time support.
Employer Identification Number: 416052604
Recent arts and culture grants:
Minnesota Museum of Art, Saint Paul, MN, $5,000. For Lost and Found Traditions, Native American Art 1965-85. 1988.
Minnesota Public Radio, Saint Paul, MN, $5,000. For public affairs program. 1988.
University of Iowa Foundation, Iowa City, IA, $6,000. For International Writing Program. 1988.

1432
Groves Foundation
10,000 Highway 55 West
P.O. Box 1267
Minneapolis 55440 (612) 546-6943

Incorporated in 1952 in MN.
Donor(s): S.J. Groves & Sons Co., Frank M. Groves.†
Financial data (yr. ended 9/30/87): Assets, $10,672,513 (M); expenditures, $244,247, including $149,746 for 32 grants (high: $58,420; low: $50) and $23,000 for 14 grants to individuals.
Purpose and activities: Giving for the arts, medical research, and social services; support for education includes employee-related scholarships for dependents of S.S. Groves & Sons Co. and its subsidiaries.
Types of support: Employee-related scholarships, annual campaigns.
Limitations: Giving primarily in the Minneapolis, MN, area. No grants to individuals (except for employee-related scholarships), or for capital or endowment funds, or matching gifts; no loans.
Application information:
Initial approach: Letter
Copies of proposal: 1
Deadline(s): None
Board meeting date(s): Nov. and as required
Write: Elfriede M. Lobeck, Exec. Dir.
Officers and Trustees: F.N. Groves, Pres.; C.T. Groves, V.P.; Elfriede M. Lobeck, Exec. Dir.
Number of staff: 1
Employer Identification Number: 416038512

1433
Hawthorne Foundation, Inc.
25 Peninsula Rd. Dellwood
White Bear Lake 55110 (612) 429-7683
Application address for Nov. thru May: P.O. Box 2383, Carefree, AZ 85377; Tel.: (602) 488-3459

Established in 1953.
Donor(s): Herbert R. Galloway.
Financial data (yr. ended 12/31/87): Assets, $288,542 (M); gifts received, $84,000; expenditures, $111,124, including $109,550 for 37 grants (high: $18,850; low: $100).
Purpose and activities: Support primarily for education, youth organizations, cultural programs, and community funds.
Types of support: General purposes.
Limitations: Giving primarily in the St. Paul, MN, area.
Application information:
Deadline(s): None
Write: Herbert R. Galloway, Pres.
Officers: Herbert R. Galloway, Pres. and Treas.; Janice T. Galloway, V.P.; Victoria G. Holmen,* Secy. .
Members:* Richard B. Galloway.
Employer Identification Number: 416038264

1434
Menahem Heilicher Charitable Foundation
850 Decatur Ave. North
Minneapolis 55427

Incorporated in 1963 in MN.
Donor(s): Amos Heilicher, Daniel Heilicher, Advance Carter Co.
Financial data (yr. ended 9/30/87): Assets, $1,918,228 (M); gifts received, $100,000; expenditures, $76,653, including $71,880 for 26 grants (high: $50,475; low: $25).
Purpose and activities: Emphasis on Jewish welfare funds and religious education, health services, the arts, and support for a hospital.
Limitations: Giving primarily in MN.
Application information: Contributes only to pre-selected organizations. Applications not accepted.
Officers: Amos Heilicher, Pres.; Daniel Heilicher, V.P. and Treas.; Marvin Borman, Secy.; Elisa Kane, Secy.
Employer Identification Number: 416043457

1435
Hersey Foundation
408 St. Peter St., Rm. 440
St. Paul 55102

Established about 1968 in MN.
Donor(s): William Hamm, Jr.†
Financial data (yr. ended 12/31/86): Assets, $4,904,840 (M); expenditures, $173,037, including $161,025 for 20 grants (high: $39,000; low: $25).
Purpose and activities: Emphasis on historic preservation, youth agencies, and urban affairs.
Limitations: Giving primarily in MN.
Officers: Edward H. Hamm, Pres. and Treas.; Austin Chapman, V.P.; Joseph A. Maun, Secy.
Employer Identification Number: 237001771

1436
Honeywell Corporate Giving Program
Honeywell Plaza
Minneapolis 55408 (612) 870-6821

Financial data (yr. ended 12/31/88): $2,000,000 for grants (high: $500,000; low: $250; average: $5,000-$10,000).
Purpose and activities: Supports a wide variety of local organizations through a giving program that is one fourth of company's total contributions. Gives to elementary, secondary, business, engineering, computer science, continuing education, public and private colleges, and performing and general arts. Also supports hospitals, hospices, and programs for the handicapped, the disabled, the aged, minorities, women, refugees, economic and job development, United Way, and civic programs. Non-monetary support through an employee volunteer program, volunteer recruitment, and in-kind services.
Types of support: Employee matching gifts, matching funds, scholarship funds, building funds, matching funds, operating budgets, scholarship funds, seed money, in-kind gifts.
Limitations: Giving primarily in headquarters city and major operating locations in MN, AZ, FL and WA.
Application information: Approach nearest facility; no formal process for applications.
Initial approach: Proposal
Copies of proposal: 1
Deadline(s): None
Board meeting date(s): Quarterly
Write: M. Patricia Hoven, Dir., Honeywell Fdn.

1437
Honeywell Foundation
Honeywell Plaza
Minneapolis 55408 (612) 870-6821
Grant application address for local agencies: send proposals to nearest company manufacturing facility

Incorporated in 1958 in MN.
Donor(s): Honeywell, Inc.
Financial data (yr. ended 12/31/87): Assets, $19,562,569 (M); gifts received, $7,400,000; expenditures, $5,603,747, including $4,903,888 for 571 grants (high: $578,813; low: $160; average: $1,500-$35,000) and $583,844 for 983 employee matching gifts.
Purpose and activities: Grants primarily for higher education, community funds, cultural programs, and youth agencies. Additional charitable support through direct corporate contributions.
Types of support: Operating budgets, continuing support, annual campaigns, seed money, building funds, employee matching gifts, scholarship funds, fellowships, special projects.
Limitations: Giving limited to cities where company has major facilities, with emphasis on Minneapolis, MN; support also in AZ, FL, WA, CO, CA, and MA. No grants to individuals, or for general endowment funds, deficit financing, land acquisition, matching or challenge grants, research, demonstration projects, or conferences; no loans.
Publications: Corporate giving report, application guidelines.
Application information:
Initial approach: Proposal
Copies of proposal: 1
Deadline(s): 15th of month preceding board meetings
Board meeting date(s): Jan., Apr., July, and Oct.
Final notification: 2 to 3 weeks
Write: M. Patricia Hoven, Dir.
Officers: Ronald K. Speed,* Pres.; Sigurd Ueland, Jr., Secy.; Louis E. Navin, Treas.

Foundation Board:* M. Patricia Hoven, Dir.; Karen Bachman, M. Bonsignore, Richard J. Boyle, J.E. Chenoweth, W.W. George, Kenneth J. Jenson, Charles W. Johnson, W.F. Wheaton.
Number of staff: 1 full-time professional; 1 full-time support.
Employer Identification Number: 416023933

1438
The Hubbard Foundation
3415 University Ave.
St. Paul 55114

Incorporated in 1958 in MN.
Donor(s): Stanley E. Hubbard, KSTP, Inc., Hubbard Broadcasting, Inc.
Financial data (yr. ended 11/30/88): Assets, $6,384,601 (M); gifts received, $108,069; expenditures, $103,052, including $103,052 for 29 grants (high: $35,000; low: $100).
Purpose and activities: Emphasis on youth agencies, recreation, community funds, hospitals, higher and secondary education, cultural programs, and health associations.
Types of support: Operating budgets, building funds.
Limitations: Giving primarily in MN.
Application information: Contributes only to preselected organizations. Applications not accepted.
Officers: Stanley E. Hubbard,* Pres.; Stanley S. Hubbard,* V.P. and Treas.; Karen H. Hubbard,* V.P.; Gerald D. Deeney, Secy.
Trustees:* Phillip A. Dufrene, Constance L. Eckert.
Employer Identification Number: 416022291

1439
Ingram Foundation
c/o First Trust Co., Inc.
W-555 First National Bank Bldg., P.O. Box 64704
St. Paul 55164-0367

Established in 1955 in MN.
Financial data (yr. ended 10/31/87): Assets, $1,073,639 (M); expenditures, $59,076, including $53,350 for 34 grants (high: $5,000; low: $100).
Purpose and activities: Support primarily for private secondary schools and colleges, cultural programs, and health.
Types of support: General purposes.
Limitations: Giving primarily in FL and TN.
Application information:
Initial approach: Letter
Deadline(s): None
Final notification: Within 3 months of receipt of request
Write: E. Bronson Ingram, Chair.
Officers and Trustees: E. Bronson Ingram, Chair.; Frederic B. Ingram, Vice-Chair.; Martha R. Ingram, Secy.; John L. Jerry, J.R. Oppenheimer.
Employer Identification Number: 416011520

1440
International Multifoods Charitable Foundation
Multifoods Tower, Box 2942
Minneapolis 55402 (612) 340-3485

Incorporated in 1970 in DE.
Donor(s): International Multifoods.
Financial data (yr. ended 2/28/89): Assets, $222,300 (M); gifts received, $282,900; expenditures, $278,000, including $217,774 for 53 grants (high: $18,000; low: $500; average: $1,000-$3,000) and $60,626 for 73 employee matching gifts.
Purpose and activities: Support for higher education and programs for minorities; welfare and youth agencies; health programs for nutrition; community and rural development; and the arts, including museums.
Types of support: Operating budgets, annual campaigns, employee matching gifts, capital campaigns, program-related investments, special projects.
Limitations: Giving primarily to programs and agencies operating in or directly benefiting communities in which company facilities are located. No support for religious purposes or political campaigns. No grants to individuals, or for deficit financing, equipment, fundraising drives, land acquisition, endowment funds, scholarships, fellowships, research, demonstration projects, publications, advertisements, or conferences.
Publications: Annual report, application guidelines.
Application information: Application form required.
Initial approach: Letter
Copies of proposal: 1
Deadline(s): None
Board meeting date(s): Quarterly or as required
Final notification: Within 90 days
Write: Sayre Carlson, Mgr. Community Afairs, V.P., Corp. Comm.
Officers and Directors: Andre Gillet, Chair.; Anthony Luiso, Pres.; K. Marvin Eberts, Jr.
Number of staff: None.
Employer Identification Number: 237064628

1441
International Multifoods Corporate Giving Program
Multifoods Tower
Multifoods Tower, Box 2942
Minneapolis 55402 (612) 340-3300

Financial data (yr. ended 02/28/88): $399,000 for grants.
Purpose and activities: "We want to use our resources to help address important issues and meet community needs. We consider our contributions of dollars and time to quality non-profit organizations as investments in our future. Our contributions are directed at four areas of community service: education, health and welfare, civic, and culture and the arts. Priority is given to programs in which employees and retirees are involved, and we want to recognize those who generously volunteered their time to community service projects during the year. We continue to support federated drives, such as the United Way, in all our plant communities." In fiscal 1988, contributions focused on specific community issues where Multifoods could make a difference--where the company could offer skills and expertise, as well as charitable dollars. About 20 percent of the company's total contributions budget is now targeted at focus issues, which include: Minority and higher education--in higher education, priority is given to programs which fit the company's business and knowledge base, such as baking and agriculture; Hunger--Multifoods has skills and resources to help with this community concern. Store to Door, in which Multifoods retirees are active, offers elderly and disabled Twin Cities citizens grocery shopping and delivery services. Multifoods and its employees also are involved in local and national foodshare drives, contributing food, money, and time to help stock community foodshelves. Other focus issues are: Community development and revitalization, where the company gives priority to rural and smaller communities with fewer resources to draw upon; also gives priority to touring cultural and arts education programs, including those which reach people outside metropolitan areas.
Types of support: Capital campaigns, general purposes, in-kind gifts.
Limitations: Giving primarily in Minneapolis, MN. No support for political or religious organizations. No grants to individuals, or for dinners, fundraisers, or special events.
Publications: Application guidelines, corporate giving report.
Application information: Proposal including organization history, project description and budget, list of board members and major donors, grant amount and objective, recent financial statement, 501 (c)(3) status letter. If accepted, organization must provide progress reports.
Initial approach: Letter and proposal
Copies of proposal: 1
Deadline(s): None
Board meeting date(s): Committee meets quarterly to review requests of $1000 or more
Final notification: Within 90 days
Write: Deborah Nelson, Commun. Coord.
Number of staff: 1

1442
J.N.M. 1966 Gift Trust
c/o Norwest Bank Duluth, Trust Dept.
Duluth 55802

Trust established in 1966 in MN as successor to J.N.M. Gift Trust established in 1949.
Donor(s): Newell Marshall.
Financial data (yr. ended 12/31/86): Assets, $986,036 (M); gifts received, $91,510; expenditures, $327,106, including $320,292 for 15 grants (high: $72,000; low: $120).
Purpose and activities: Emphasis on higher education and cultural programs; support also for international cooperation and conservation.
Limitations: Giving primarily in MN.
Application information:
Initial approach: Proposal
Deadline(s): None
Trustees: Caroline Marshall, Newell Marshall.
Employer Identification Number: 416050249

1443
Jerome Foundation

West 1050 First National Bank Bldg.
332 Minnesota St.
St. Paul 55101 (612) 224-9431

Incorporated in 1964 in MN.
Donor(s): J. Jerome Hill.†
Financial data (yr. ended 4/30/88): Assets, $32,454,945 (M); gifts received, $65,000; expenditures, $2,072,795, including $1,562,459 for 116 grants (high: $110,091; low: $200; average: $200-$130,000), $112,545 for 21 grants to individuals and $105,303 for 3 foundation-administered programs.
Purpose and activities: Support for arts and humanities programs only, including dance, film and video, literature, music, theater, performance art, visual arts, and selected areas of the humanities, especially arts criticism. The foundation is concerned primarily with providing financial assistance to emerging creative artists of promise, including choreographers, film and video artists, composers, literary and visual artists, and playwrights through the Film and Video Program and the Travel and Study Grant Program.
Types of support: Special projects, general purposes, fellowships, operating budgets, grants to individuals.
Limitations: Giving limited to New York, NY, and MN. Generally no support for crafts or for educational programs in the arts and humanities. No grants to individuals (except for New York City Film and Video Program and Twin Cities Travel and Study Grant Program), or for undergraduate or graduate student research projects, capital or endowment funds, equipment, scholarships, or matching gifts.
Publications: Annual report, informational brochure (including application guidelines).
Application information:
Initial approach: Letter or proposal
Copies of proposal: 1
Deadline(s): Apr. 1 and Oct. 1 for travel and study grants; none for other grants
Board meeting date(s): Bimonthly
Final notification: 3 to 4 months
Write: Cynthia Gehrig, Pres.
Officers: A.A. Heckman,* Chair. and Treas.; Irving Clark,* Vice-Chair.; Cynthia Gehrig, Pres. and Secy.
Directors:* Patricia Bratnober, John B. Davis, Thelma E. Hunter, Archibald Leyasmeyer.
Number of staff: 2 full-time professional; 2 full-time support.
Employer Identification Number: 416035163
Recent arts and culture grants:
Actors Theater of Saint Paul, Saint Paul, MN, $10,500. For 1986-87 First Stage Program, to develop and produce new writers and new works. 1987.
Alternative Museum, NYC, NY, $5,000. For 1986-87 Exhibition Series. 1987.
American Composers Orchestra, NYC, NY, $5,000. For composer commission. 1987.
American Craft Council, NYC, NY, $15,000. For 1988 Young Americans exhibition. 1987.
American Dance Festival, NYC, NY, $15,000. For Young Choreographers and Composers in Residence Program. 1987.
American Music Center, NYC, NY, $8,000. For Copying Assistance Program for emerging composers. 1987.
Ballet Harren, Minneapolis, MN, $6,000. For 1986-87 Season. 1987.
Brass Tacks Theater, Minneapolis, MN, $13,000. For 1986-87 Season. 1987.
Committee for the Visual Arts, Artists Space, NYC, NY, $16,000. For exhibitions serving emerging artists. 1987.
COMPAS, Saint Paul, MN, $8,000. For Writers-in-the-Schools Program. 1987.
Composers Forum, NYC, NY, $10,000. For New Music/New Composers Program. 1987.
Creation Company, NYC, NY, $10,000. For 1986-87 Season of this experimental theater/performance art company. 1987.
Creative Time, NYC, NY, $10,000. For 1987 Art on the Beach Program. 1987.
E. Monte Motion Dance Company, NYC, NY, $9,000. For 1986-87 Season. 1987.
Ensemble Studio Theater, NYC, NY, $26,000. For Playwright Development Program. 1987.
Eugene ONeill Memorial Theater Center, NYC, NY, $36,000. For National Playwrights Conference. 1987.
Film in the Cities, Saint Paul, MN, $156,000. For Regional Film/Video Grants Program. 1987.
Film in the Cities, Saint Paul, MN, $20,000. For general support. 1987.
Forecast Public Artspace Productions, Minneapolis, MN, $15,000. For Sculpture '87 Exhibition. 1987.
Franklin Furnace Archive, NYC, NY, $20,000. For fund for performance art. 1987.
Franklin Furnace Archive, NYC, NY, $10,000. For Performance Art Season. 1987.
Frederick Douglass Creative Arts Center, NYC, NY, $10,000. For developmental program for emerging playwrights. 1987.
Great Midwestern Bookshow, Minneapolis, MN, $10,000. For 1986 Bookshow. 1987.
Gregg Smith Singers, NYC, NY, $12,000. For performance and recording of choral music by emerging composers. 1987.
Haleakala, The Kitchen, NYC, NY, $15,000. For 1987 Contemporary Music Series. 1987.
Harvestworks, NYC, NY, $5,000. For Artists-in-residence Program at PASS, allowing artists access to equipment for electronic music and audio production. 1987.
Illusion Theater and School, Minneapolis, MN, $8,000. For development of new works by emerging playwrights. 1987.
International Arts Relations (INTAR), NYC, NY, $11,000. For Hispanic Playwrights Laboratory. 1987.
International Center of Photography, NYC, NY, $22,230. For NEW DIRECTIONS Exhibition Series. 1987.
Jacobs Pillow, NYC, NY, $6,000. For 1987 Choreographers-in-Residence Program. 1987.
Jacobs Pillow, NYC, NY, $6,000. For 1986 Artists-in-Residence Program. 1987.
Jacobs Pillow, NYC, NY, $5,000. For 1986-87 Season of Ralph Lemon and Dancers. 1987.
Kala Institute, San Francisco, CA, $9,000. For fellowships for emerging printmakers. 1987.
Kenneth Rinker Dance Company, NYC, NY, $7,000. For 1986-87 Season. 1987.
Kronos Quartet, San Francisco, CA, $12,000. For commissioning and performance of new works by emerging composers. 1987.
La Mama Experimental Theater Club, NYC, NY, $12,000. For production of new works by emerging playwrights. 1987.
Lark Quartet, Minneapolis, MN, $5,000. For second performances of works by emerging composers. 1987.
Loft, The, Minneapolis, MN, $7,800. For creative nonfiction program. 1987.
Mabou Mines, NYC, NY, $13,000. For collaborative project with emerging composer. 1987.
Mankato State University, Mankato, MN, $8,400. For Good Thunder Writing Series. 1987.
Marta Renzi and Dancers, NYC, NY, $8,000. For 1986-87 Season. 1987.
Minneapolis Artists Ensemble, Minneapolis, MN, $10,000. For commissioning and performance of new works by emerging composers. 1987.
Minneapolis College of Art and Design, Minneapolis, MN, $55,650. For Jerome Artists Fellowship Program. 1987.
Minnesota Composers Forum, Saint Paul, MN, $11,250. For debut concert of IMP ORK. 1987.
Minnesota Dance Alliance, Minneapolis, MN, $25,350. For Dancer Pool, Professional Enrichment Program, Choreographers Commissioning Program. 1987.
Minnesota Dance Alliance, Minneapolis, MN, $6,000. For New York Concert of Georgia Stephens and Dancers. 1987.
Minnesota Dance Alliance, Minneapolis, MN, $5,000. For Twin Cities and New York Seasons of Maria Cheng and Dancers. 1987.
Minnesota Jazz Dance Company, Minneapolis, MN, $12,000. For 1986 Jazz Dance Festival. 1987.
Minnesota Opera Company, Saint Paul, MN, $15,000. For 1987 Music-Theater Ensemble Program. 1987.
Minnesota Orchestral Association, Minneapolis, MN, $12,000. For 1987 Sommerfest commission. 1987.
Minnesota Public Radio, Saint Paul, MN, $10,000. For Music in Minnesota series. 1987.
Minnesota State Arts Board, Saint Paul, MN, $10,000. For Midwest CRAFTFAIR awards. 1987.
New Dance Ensemble, Minneapolis, MN, $15,000. For new works by emerging choreographers. 1987.
New Dance Ensemble, Minneapolis, MN, $5,000. For New York Concert of works by Wil Swanson. 1987.
New Rivers Press, Saint Paul, MN, $15,000. For 1986 Minnesota Voices Project. 1987.
New York City Film/Video Project, NYC, NY, $162,000. For production grants to emerging film and video artists living and working in NYC. 1987.
New York City Film/Video Project, NYC, NY, $14,300. For travel and study grant program. 1987.
Performance Space 122, NYC, NY, $14,500. For performance commissions to emerging dance and performance artists. 1987.
Playwrights Center, Minneapolis, MN, $93,000. For fellowships for emerging playwrights, development of scripts and general support. 1987.

Playwrights Center, Minneapolis, MN, $31,050. For Midwest Playlabs. 1987.
Playwrights Unlimited, Mill Valley, CA, $5,000. For Opera/Musical Theater Workshop. 1987.
Plymouth Music Series, Minneapolis, MN, $6,000. For commissions of new works by emerging composers. 1987.
Poetry Project, NYC, NY, $10,000. For 1986-87 Writing Workshops. 1987.
Red Eye Collaboration, Minneapolis, MN, $12,000. For 1986 Season. 1987.
Ringside Dance Company, NYC, NY, $6,000. For 1987 Spring Season. 1987.
Roulette Intermedium, NYC, NY, $9,000. For 1986-87 Performance Season. 1987.
Saint Louis County Heritage and Arts Center, Duluth, MN, $10,000. For Lake Superior Contemporary Writers Series. 1987.
Saint Paul Chamber Orchestra, Saint Paul, MN, $32,250. For commissioning and performance of works by emerging composers in Sunday Minnesota Series. 1987.
Sculpture Center, NYC, NY, $8,500. For Emerging Sculptors 1986 Exhibit. 1987.
Sing Heavenly Muse, Minneapolis, MN, $7,400. For Mentor Publication Program for this journal of women's poetry and prose. 1987.
Theater de la Jeune Lune, Minneapolis, MN, $10,000. For development of new work in 1986-87 Season. 1987.
University Community Video, Minneapolis, MN, $20,000. For Media arts installations. 1987.
Walker Art Center, Minneapolis, MN, $32,000. For purchase fund for emerging artists. 1987.
Walker Art Center, Minneapolis, MN, $15,000. For FORWARD MOTION Series, a program of dance residencies. 1987.
Walker Art Center, Minneapolis, MN, $10,000. For Video Viewpoints Exhibition and Conference. 1987.
West Bank School of Music, Minneapolis, MN, $10,000. For Jazz Composer Series. 1987.
YWCA, West Side, NYC, NY, $6,250. For The Writers Community Workshops sponsored by The Writer's Voice. 1987.
Zorongo Flamenco Dance Group, Minneapolis, MN, $6,000. For development and performance of GERNIKA. 1987.

1444
E. F. Johnson Company Foundation

299 Johnson Ave.
Waseca 56093 (507) 835-6201
Mailing address: c/o Norwest Bank Trust, Tax Div., Eighth & Marquette, Minneapolis, MN 55479-0063

Established in 1964 in MN.
Financial data (yr. ended 12/31/87): Assets, $1,131,254 (M); expenditures, $74,977, including $73,500 for 30 grants (high: $10,000; low: $200) and $1,477 for 24 employee matching gifts.
Purpose and activities: Giving primarily for higher education, including programs with scientific and technological focus and career awareness. Support also for arts and culture, social services, welfare, rehabilitation, and recreation.
Types of support: Operating budgets, scholarship funds, special projects, employee matching gifts, continuing support, emergency funds.
Limitations: Giving primarily in MN. No support for religious organizations for religious purposes. No grants to individuals, health fund drives (except as part of United Way), national fundraising campaigns, ticket sales, or fundraising dinners.
Publications: Annual report (including application guidelines).
Application information:
Initial approach: Letter
Copies of proposal: 1
Deadline(s): Dec. 1, Mar. 1, June 1, and Sept. 1
Board meeting date(s): Feb., May, Aug., and Nov.
Write: Joyce A. Thompsen, Secy.
Officers and Directors: John D. Somrock, Pres.; Robert E. Cavins, V.P.; Joyce A. Thompsen, Secy-Treas.
Number of staff: None.
Employer Identification Number: 416043126

1445
The Jostens Foundation, Inc.

5501 Norman Center Dr.
Minneapolis 55437 (612) 830-8461
Scholarship application address: Citizens' Scholarship Fdn. of America, P.O. Box 297, St. Peter, MN 56082; Tel.: (507) 931-1682

Established in 1976 in MN.
Donor(s): Jostens, Inc.
Financial data (yr. ended 6/30/88): Assets, $870,128 (M); gifts received, $1,303,000; expenditures, $1,072,997, including $498,610 for 194 grants (high: $51,130; low: $125; average: $500-$5,000), $350,000 for grants to individuals and $144,841 for 478 employee matching gifts.
Purpose and activities: Emphasis on organizations primarily serving and benefitting youth; support also for cultural programs, a scholarship program conducted by Citizens' Scholarship Foundation of America, and an employee matching gift program.
Types of support: Employee matching gifts, employee-related scholarships, capital campaigns, general purposes, operating budgets, special projects.
Limitations: Giving primarily in MN, particularly the Twin Cities area and other Jostens manufacturing locations; matching gift programs have a national scope. No support for religious or political organizations, public or private educational institutions, school districts, or organizations covered by the United Way. No grants to individuals, or for endowment funds; no loans.
Publications: Annual report (including application guidelines), program policy statement, application guidelines.
Application information:
Initial approach: Telephone or proposal
Copies of proposal: 1
Deadline(s): Last day of the month preceding board meeting; Nov. 15 for Leader Scholarship Program
Board meeting date(s): Bimonthly beginning in Jan.
Final notification: Within 10 days of board meeting
Write: Ellis F. Bullock, Jr., Exec. Dir.
Officers and Directors: H. William Lurton, Chair.; Don C. Lein, Pres.; Orville E. Fisher, Jr., Secy.; Barbara Thompson, Treas.; Ellis F. Bullock, Jr., Exec. Dir.
Number of staff: 2 part-time professional; 1 full-time support.
Employer Identification Number: 411280587

1446
Margaret H. and James E. Kelley Foundation Inc.

425 Hamm Bldg.
St. Paul 55102

Established in 1982 in MN.
Financial data (yr. ended 11/30/87): Assets, $1,449,927 (M); expenditures, $80,355, including $65,425 for 28 grants (high: $24,000; low: $100).
Purpose and activities: Support for education, the arts, health and social services.
Limitations: Giving primarily in MN.
Application information:
Initial approach: Letter
Write: James E. Kelley, Treas.
Officer: James E. Kelley, Treas.
Employer Identification Number: 416017973

1447
Land O'Lakes Corporate Giving Program

4001 Lexington Ave., N.
Arden Hills 55126 (612) 481-2222

Financial data (yr. ended 12/31/88): Total giving, $700,000, including $390,000 for 600 grants (high: $15,000; low: $1,000; average: $1,000-$5,000), $10,000 for 60 employee matching gifts and $300,000 for in-kind gifts.
Purpose and activities: Supports the hungry, the disadvantaged, United Way, business, economic and cooperative education programs, leadership development for rural and minority youth, community affairs, programs for the preservation and management of water and soil resources, and performing arts and touring programs to company-based areas. Rural and agricultural programs receive special consideration. Types of support include product donations and employee matching gifts for postsecondary education.
Types of support: General purposes, special projects, employee matching gifts, in-kind gifts.
Limitations: Giving primarily in the upper midwest and areas where the company has facilities. No support for national groups, except those related to agriculture; lobbying, political or religious organizations; veterans', labor, or fraternal organizations. No grants to individuals; fundraising events; advertising; capital campaigns for education.
Publications: Application guidelines.
Application information: For requests of $1,000 or more include: brief organization history, including objectives and current activities; program description with verification of need; method of evaluation; amount requested, including other sources of funding; financial report; current and proposed budget; list of Board members and their affiliations; brief resume of the administrator; and 501(c)(3).

Initial approach: Letter
Copies of proposal: 1
Deadline(s): None
Final notification: 3 months
Write: Bonnie Neuenfeldt, Mgr., Community Relations
Number of staff: 1 full-time professional; 1 part-time support.

1448
Richard Coyle Lilly Foundation
c/o First Trust Co., Inc.
W-555 First National Bank Bldg.
St. Paul 55164 (612) 291-5114

Incorporated in 1941 in MN.
Donor(s): Richard C. Lilly.†
Financial data (yr. ended 12/31/86): Assets, $4,188,348 (M); expenditures, $391,581, including $337,200 for grants.
Purpose and activities: Emphasis on higher and environmental education, culture, youth, and social services.
Types of support: General purposes, continuing support, annual campaigns, seed money, building funds, equipment, land acquisition, endowment funds, research, special projects, publications, matching funds.
Limitations: Giving primarily in St. Paul, MN. No grants to individuals, or for fellowships or scholarships; no loans.
Publications: 990-PF.
Application information:
Initial approach: Proposal or letter
Copies of proposal: 2
Deadline(s): None
Board meeting date(s): Dec.
Final notification: 6 weeks
Write: Jeffrey T. Peterson
Officers and Directors: David M. Lilly, Pres.; Elizabeth M. Lilly, V.P.; David M. Lilly, Jr., Secy.; Susanne Lilly Hutcheson, Bruce A. Lilly.
Employer Identification Number: 416038717

1449
The Mahadh Foundation
c/o Baywood Corp.
287 Central Ave.
Bayport 55003 (612) 439-1557

Established in 1962.
Donor(s): Mary Andersen Hulings, Fred C. Andersen,† Katherine B. Andersen.
Financial data (yr. ended 2/28/89): Assets, $7,232,291 (M); expenditures, $2,524,810, including $2,468,731 for 112 grants (average: $1,000-$20,000).
Purpose and activities: Emphasis on education, the arts, youth and social service agencies, medical research and health agencies, and civic activities.
Types of support: General purposes, operating budgets, seed money, research, capital campaigns, equipment, special projects.
Limitations: Giving primarily in MN, with emphasis on the Bayport area and St. Paul, and in western WI. No grants to individuals, or for scholarships or fellowships,; no loans.
Publications: Annual report (including application guidelines).
Application information: Application form required.
Initial approach: Letter or proposal
Copies of proposal: 1
Deadline(s): Submit proposal preferably in Mar., June, Sept., or Dec.; no set deadline
Board meeting date(s): May, Aug., Nov., and Jan.
Final notification: 3 months
Write: Mary Andersen Hulings, Pres.
Officers and Directors: Mary Andersen Hulings, Pres.; Albert D. Hulings, V.P.; Martha H. Kaemmer, V. P. ; Mary H. Rice, V.P. ; Kathleen R. Conley, Secy.; William J. Begin, Treas.
Number of staff: 2
Employer Identification Number: 416020911

1450
Marbrook Foundation
400 Baker Bldg.
Minneapolis 55402 (612) 332-2454

Trust established in 1948 in MN.
Donor(s): Edward Brooks,† Markell C. Brooks,† Markell C. Brooks Charitable Trust.
Financial data (yr. ended 12/31/88): Assets, $5,147,483 (M); expenditures, $305,505, including $250,000 for 56 grants (high: $24,000; low: $500).
Purpose and activities: Support for education, visual and performing arts, social welfare, health and medicine, and conservation and recreation.
Types of support: Operating budgets, continuing support, annual campaigns, seed money, emergency funds, building funds, endowment funds, matching funds, professorships, internships, research, conferences and seminars, special projects.
Limitations: Giving primarily in the Minneapolis-St. Paul, MN, area. No support for religious purposes. No grants to individuals, or for deficit financing, equipment, land acquisition, scholarships, fellowships, demonstration projects, or publications; no loans.
Publications: Annual report (including application guidelines).
Application information:
Initial approach: Proposal
Copies of proposal: 1
Deadline(s): Submit proposal preferably in Mar. or Sept.; deadlines May 15 and Oct. 15
Board meeting date(s): May and Nov.
Final notification: 3 weeks after meeting
Write: Conley Brooks, Jr., Exec. Dir.
Trustees: Conley Brooks, Jr., Exec. Dir.; John E. Andrus III, Conley Brooks, William R. Humphrey, Jr.
Number of staff: None.
Employer Identification Number: 416019899
Recent arts and culture grants:
Minnesota Orchestral Association, Minneapolis, MN, $24,000. 1987.
Minnesota Public Radio, Saint Paul, MN, $6,000. 1987.
Saint Paul Chamber Orchestra, Saint Paul, MN, $6,000. 1987.

1451
Mardag Foundation
1120 Norwest Center
St. Paul 55101 (612) 224-5463

Trust established in 1969 in MN.
Donor(s): Agnes E. Ober.†
Financial data (yr. ended 12/31/87): Assets, $21,035,433 (M); expenditures, $1,118,269, including $814,365 for 78 grants (high: $75,000; low: $1,500).
Purpose and activities: Giving for social service agencies, conservation, programs to benefit senior citizens, arts and cultural programs, and education.
Types of support: Special projects, building funds, research, seed money, deficit financing, matching funds, equipment, emergency funds, general purposes, renovation projects.
Limitations: Giving limited to MN. No support for sectarian religious programs. No grants to individuals, or for annual campaigns, endowment funds, scholarships, fellowships, or generally for continuing support.
Publications: Annual report, 990-PF, program policy statement, application guidelines.
Application information:
Initial approach: Letter or proposal
Copies of proposal: 1
Deadline(s): None
Board meeting date(s): Quarterly and as required
Final notification: 90 days
Write: Paul A. Verret, Secy.
Officers: Thomas G. Mairs,* Principal Officer; Stephen S. Ober,* Financial Officer; Paul A. Verret, Secy.
Trustees:* James E. Davidson, Virginia G. Davidson, Constance M. Levi, Gayle M. Ober, James C. Otis.
Number of staff: None.
Employer Identification Number: 237022429
Recent arts and culture grants:
Como Conservatory Restoration Fund, Saint Paul, MN, $15,000. To help finance restoration of Como Park Conservatory. 1987.
Hallie Q. Brown Community Center, Saint Paul, MN, $7,000. To help finance initiation of Penumbra Theater's Young and Emerging Actors Program. 1987.
Minnesota Public Radio, Saint Paul, MN, $10,000. To support Program Endowment Fund. 1987.
Ramsey County Historical Society, Saint Paul, MN, $5,000. To help finance new Development Director position. 1987.
Saint Paul Chamber Orchestra, Saint Paul, MN, $50,000. To Bridge Fund/Endowment Campaign. 1987.
Saint Paul, City of, Saint Paul, MN, $10,000. For COMPAS Community Art Fund. 1987.
World Theater Corporation, Saint Paul, MN, $5,000. For renovation of World Theater. 1987.

1452
The McKnight Foundation
410 Peavey Bldg.
Minneapolis 55402 (612) 333-4220

Incorporated in 1953 in MN.

Donor(s): William L. McKnight,† Maude L. McKnight,† Virginia M. Binger, James H. Binger.
Financial data (yr. ended 12/31/88): Assets, $793,402,592 (M); expenditures, $38,840,564, including $33,470,000 for 182 grants (high: $6,000,000; low: $1,500; average: $5,000-$500,000) and $50,000 for 10 grants to individuals.
Purpose and activities: Emphasis on grantmaking in the areas of human and social services; has multi-year comprehensive program in the arts, housing, and aid to families in poverty; has multi-year program for support of projects in non-metropolitan areas of MN; supports nationwide scientific research programs in areas of (1) neuroscience, particularly for research in memory and diseases affecting memory, and (2) basic plant biology (applications for these programs are solicited periodically through announcements in scientific journals and directly to institutions carrying out research programs).
Types of support: Research, operating budgets, building funds, seed money, emergency funds, equipment, matching funds, continuing support, capital campaigns, general purposes, renovation projects, special projects, grants to individuals.
Limitations: Giving limited to organizations in MN, especially the seven county Twin Cities , MN, area, except for special programs initiated by the board of directors. No support for religious organizations for religious purposes, or biomedical research (except for grants to the McKnight Endowment Fund for Neuroscience). No grants to individuals (except for the Human Service Awards), or for endowment funds, scholarships, fellowships, or national fundraising campaigns; no loans.
Publications: Annual report (including application guidelines), informational brochure (including application guidelines), grants list.
Application information: Human Service Awards are by nomination only and restricted to MN residents.
Initial approach: Letter
Copies of proposal: 7
Deadline(s): Mar. 1, June 1, Sept. 1, and Dec. 1
Board meeting date(s): May, Aug., Nov., and Feb.
Final notification: 2 and 1/2 months
Write: Michael O'Keefe, Exec. V.P.
Officers: Cynthia Boynton,* Pres.; Michael O'Keefe, Exec. V.P.; James M. Binger,* V.P. and Treas.; Marilyn Pidany, Secy.
Directors:* James H. Binger, Patricia S. Binger, Virginia M. Binger.
Number of staff: 3 full-time professional; 1 part-time professional; 4 full-time support.
Employer Identification Number: 410754835
Recent arts and culture grants:
Bigfork Center for the Performing Arts Foundation, Bigfork, MT, $10,000. For capital campaign to build center for performing arts. 12/5/87.
City, The, Minneapolis, MN, $5,000. For expenses for Leo Johnson Drum Corps to appear at Martin Luther King Day celebration in Atlanta, Georgia. 2/27/88.

1453
The Sumner T. McKnight Foundation
c/o Norwest Bank Minneapolis, Trust Dept.
Eighth and Marquette Ave.
Minneapolis 55479
Application address: 1108 Village Rd., 13C, Chaska, MN, 55318; Tel: (612) 448-3035

Incorporated in 1956 in MN.
Donor(s): Sumner T. McKnight,† H. Turney McKnight.
Financial data (yr. ended 12/31/86): Assets, $4,387,903 (M); gifts received, $30,221; expenditures, $340,886, including $279,500 for 26 grants (high: $50,000; low: $1,000).
Purpose and activities: Emphasis on music, fine arts, conservation and recreation, historical societies, higher and secondary education, inner-city programs, and community funds.
Limitations: Giving primarily in MN; some support also in MD. No support for religion. No grants to individuals, or for endowment funds.
Application information:
Initial approach: Proposal
Board meeting date(s): Jan. and mid-year
Write: Iva Kroeger
Officers and Directors: H. Turney McKnight, Pres.; Sumner T. McKnight II, V.P.; John T. Westrom, Secy.-Treas.; Christina M. Kippen.
Employer Identification Number: 416022360

1454
McVay Foundation
10201 Wayzata Blvd.
Minnetonka 55343

Established in 1984 in MN.
Donor(s): M.D. McVay.
Financial data (yr. ended 12/31/87): Assets, $2,796,930 (M); expenditures, $154,996, including $134,650 for 61 grants (high: $10,000; low: $50).
Purpose and activities: Support for education, particularly higher education, cultural programs, and youth and social service agencies.
Types of support: General purposes.
Application information: Applications not accepted.
Officers: M.D. McVay, Pres.; Danita Greene, V.P.; R. Thomas Green, Secy.; Mary McVay, Treas.
Number of staff: None.
Employer Identification Number: 363311833

1455
Meadowood Foundation
4122 IDS Center
Minneapolis 55402

Established in 1968.
Financial data (yr. ended 12/31/86): Assets, $3,889,730 (M); gifts received, $2,495; expenditures, $238,084, including $215,000 for 7 grants (high: $90,200; low: $2,500).
Purpose and activities: Giving for education, cultural programs, conservation, and youth.
Types of support: General purposes, building funds.
Limitations: Giving primarily in MN.
Application information: Contributes only to pre-selected organizations. Applications not accepted.
Officers and Directors: Douglas J. Dayton, Pres. and Treas.; Shirley D. Dayton, V.P.; Ronald N. Gross, Secy.; Bruce C. Dayton, David D. Dayton, Steven J. Melander-Dayton.
Employer Identification Number: 410943749

1456
The Medtronic Foundation
7000 Central Ave., N.E.
Minneapolis 55432 (612) 574-3024

Established in 1979 in MN.
Donor(s): Medtronic, Inc.
Financial data (yr. ended 4/30/88): Assets, $2,005,231 (M); expenditures, $993,374, including $913,037 for 74 grants (high: $240,775; low: $500; average: $1,000-$15,000) and $72,002 for 203 employee matching gifts.
Purpose and activities: Emphasis on physical health promotion, the elderly, education, arts and culture, social service agencies, and community funds.
Types of support: Operating budgets, continuing support, annual campaigns, seed money, matching funds, scholarship funds, fellowships, special projects, employee matching gifts.
Limitations: Giving primarily in areas of company operations, including Phoenix, AZ; Minneapolis, MN; Orange County, CA; and PR, or to national organizations having an effect on these areas. No support for United Way member agencies, primarily social organizations, religious, political, or fraternal activities, primary health care, or health research. No grants to individuals, or for deficit financing, capital funds, research, travel, fundraising events, or advertising; generally no grants for endowment funds, conferences, operating support for smaller arts groups, or multiple-year commitments.
Publications: Annual report, application guidelines.
Application information: Requests from the Twin Cities to be sent to MN address; requests from other Medtronic communities to be sent to local manager who will forward them to headquarters with an assessment of the request.
Initial approach: Proposal with letter
Copies of proposal: 1
Deadline(s): Submit proposal between Aug. and Mar.; no set deadline; most decisions made in Oct., Dec., and Apr.
Board meeting date(s): June, Aug., Oct., Dec., and Apr.
Final notification: At least 60 days
Write: Jan Schwarz, Mgr.
Officers and Directors: Paul Citron, Chair.; William W. Chorske, Vice-Chair.; Celia Barnes, Secy.; Lester J. Swenson, Treas.; Daniel R. Luthringshauser, Stephen H. Mahle, Glen D. Nelson, M.D., Richard F. Sauter.
Number of staff: 1 part-time professional; 1 part-time support.
Employer Identification Number: 411306950
Recent arts and culture grants:
Actors Theater of Saint Paul, Saint Paul, MN, $5,800. For senior outreach program. 1988.

Childrens Theater Company and School, Minneapolis, MN, $13,000. For general operating support. 1988.
Cricket Theater, Minneapolis, MN, $5,000. For marketing of productions. 1988.
Duck Soup Players, Saint Paul, MN, $5,600. For traveling theater production for elderly and hospital patients. 1988.
Film in the Cities, Saint Paul, MN, $5,000. For general support. 1988.
Guthrie Theater, Minneapolis, MN, $10,000. For general support. 1988.
K T C A Twin Cities Public Television, Saint Paul, MN, $20,000. Toward month-long programming focus on older Minnesotans. 1988.
K T C A Twin Cities Public Television, Saint Paul, MN, $12,000. Toward Tuesday evening prime time programming. 1988.
Minneapolis Society of Fine Arts, Minneapolis, MN, $8,000. For general support. 1988.
Minnesota Opera Company, Saint Paul, MN, $7,500. For general support. 1988.
Minnesota Orchestral Association, Minneapolis, MN, $142,000. For Sommerfest concert, and special audiences endowment. 1988.
Minnesota Public Radio, Saint Paul, MN, $10,000. For AM radio series of interviews with creative and active elderly people. 1988.
Minnesota Public Radio, Saint Paul, MN, $9,000. Toward Friday's All Things Considered program on AM radio, and programming focused on aging on AM and FM radio. 1988.
Minnesota Zoological Garden, Apple Valley, MN, $7,500. For two senior citizen days. 1988.
Ordway Music Theater, Saint Paul, MN, $20,000. Toward construction of multi-purpose facility. 1988.
Saint Paul Chamber Orchestra, Landmark Center, Saint Paul, MN, $85,000. For three daytime concerts and one-time grant to endowment to promote concerts to senior citizens. 1988.
Science Museum of Minnesota, Saint Paul, MN, $12,500. For general support. 1988.
Walker Art Center, Minneapolis, MN, $10,000. For general support. 1988.

1457
The Melamed Foundation
100 Washington Square, Suite 1650
Minneapolis 55401 (612) 473-2588
Application address: 2445 M St., N.W., Washington, D.C. 20037; Tel.: (202) 663-6736

Incorporated in 1947 in MN.
Donor(s): Members of the Melamed family.
Financial data (yr. ended 12/31/87): Assets, $540,118 (M); expenditures, $222,485, including $215,080 for 21 grants (high: $119,843; low: $22).
Purpose and activities: Emphasis on Jewish welfare funds; grants also for higher education, cultural organizations, temple support, and hospitals.
Application information:
Deadline(s): None
Write: Arthur Douglas Melamed, V.P.
Officers and Trustees: Ruth H. Melamed, Pres. and Secy.; Arthur D. Melamed, V.P. and Treas.; Barbara McConagha, V.P.; Robert L. Melamed, V.P.; William L. Melamed, V.P.
Employer Identification Number: 416019581

1458
The Gladys and Rudolph Miller Foundation
5112 IDS Center
Minneapolis 55402 (612) 332-9147

Established in 1980.
Donor(s): Rudolph W. Miller, Miller Felpa Corp.
Financial data (yr. ended 11/30/87): Assets, $831,784 (M); gifts received, $35,000; expenditures, $192,963, including $180,665 for 4 grants (high: $157,165; low: $500; average: $8,000).
Purpose and activities: Grants primarily as continuing support for medical organizations, Jewish giving, and the performing arts.
Types of support: Annual campaigns, continuing support, research, special projects.
Limitations: Giving primarily in MN, with emphasis on the Twin Cities.
Application information: Grants largely at the initiative of the donor.
Initial approach: Letter
Deadline(s): None
Write: Rudolph W. Miller, Pres.
Officers and Directors: Rudolph W. Miller, Pres. and Treas.; Sidney Loyber, V.P. and Secy.; Sidney Barrows.
Employer Identification Number: 411388774

1459
The Minneapolis Foundation
500 Foshay Tower
821 Marquette Ave.
Minneapolis 55402 (612) 339-7343
Application address for the Minnesota Nonprofits Assistance Fund: Susan Kenny Stevens, Admin., Colonial Office Park Bldg., 2700 University Ave. West, Suite 70, St. Paul, MN 55114; Tel.: (612) 647-0013

Community foundation incorporated in 1915 in MN.
Financial data (yr. ended 3/31/88): Assets, $106,455,326 (M); gifts received, $9,514,082; expenditures, $10,678,544, including $8,663,489 for 1,224 grants (high: $75,000; low: $500; average: $7,500-$35,000).
Purpose and activities: "To promote equality of opportunity for the citizens of MN, so that each individual, family and community can have access to the human and financial resources needed to reach full potential. The Foundation carries forward this mission in the following ways: As Grantmaker, providing direct financial resources to programs that target immediate or emerging community issues; as a Catalyst, mobilizing community leaders and constituencies; as a Community Resource, providing services to donors, nonprofit organizations, and the community at large; as a Resource Developer, building a permanent unrestricted endowment; and as a Steward, receiving and distributing community resources."
Types of support: Seed money, emergency funds, equipment, technical assistance, loans, special projects, continuing support, general purposes, operating budgets.
Limitations: Giving primarily in MN, with emphasis on the Minneapolis-St. Paul, seven-county metropolitan area. No support for national campaigns, religious organizations for religious purposes, veterans or fraternal organizations, or to organizations within umbrella organizations. No grants for annual campaigns, deficit financing, building or endowment funds, land acquisition, matching gifts, scholarships and fellowships, research, publications, conferences, courtesy advertising, benefit tickets, telephone solicitations, or memberships.
Publications: Annual report, newsletter, 990-PF, application guidelines.
Application information: Undesignated funds considered in May and Nov.; requests to the McKnight-Neighborhood Self-Help Initiatives Program and Emma P. House Memorial Fdn. reviewed in Mar. and Sept.; Minnesota Women's Fund considered in July and Jan.; B.C. Gamble and P.W. Skogmo Fdn., June and Dec. Application form required.
Initial approach: Applicant should request guidelines for the appropriate fund
Copies of proposal: 17
Deadline(s): Undesignated grants, Mar. 1 and Sept. 1; MNSHIP and Emma B. Howe Memorial Fdn. grants, Jan. 15 and July 15; Minnesota Women's Fund, May 15 and Nov. 15; B.C. Gamble and P.W. Skogmo Fdn., Apr. 1 and Oct. 1
Board meeting date(s): Quarterly; distribution committee meets 8 times a year
Write: Marion G. Etzwiler, Pres.
Officers and Trustees:* Mary Lee Dayton,* Chair.; Jean Burhardt Keffeler,* Vice-Chair.; Richard W. Schoenke, Vice-Chair.; C. Angus Wurtele,* Vice-Chair.; Marion G. Etzwiler, Pres.; Patricia M. Holloran,* Secy.; Clinton A. Schroeder,* Treas.; and 23 additional trustees.
Trustee Banks: First Bank Minneapolis, Norwest Bank Minneapolis.
Number of staff: 10 full-time professional; 8 full-time support.
Employer Identification Number: 416029402
Recent arts and culture grants:
Artspace Projects, Minneapolis, MN, $15,000. For salary of site development manager to oversee selection, acquisition and renovation of buildings to house low-income artists and their families. 5/25/88.
El Teatro Latino de Minnesota, Minneapolis, MN, $7,740. For purchase of administrative services to compliment artistic productions of theater group serving Hispanic community. 5/25/88.
Illusion Theater and School, Minneapolis, MN, $20,000. To develop theatrical production along with printed material and forums to provide public education on AIDS epidemic and prevention techniques. 11/87.
In the Heart of the Beast Puppet and Mask Theater, Minneapolis, MN, $20,000. For planning and management to facilitate growth and establishment of permanent home of theater featuring productions for children. 5/25/88.

1460
Minnegasco, Inc. Charitable Contributions Program

201 South Seventh St.
Minneapolis 55402 (612) 342-4821

Financial data (yr. ended 12/31/87): $587,363 for grants.
Purpose and activities: Giving for human services, education, arts, and the environment; also support through employee volunteer programs and employee matching gifts to education. HeatShare, a joint program of the Salvation Army and the company, provides energy bill payments and weatherization assistance to senior citizens, the disabled, and others in emergency situations.
Limitations: Giving primarily in communities served by company in MN, NE, and SD. No support for national fund drives, organizations supported by the United Way, organizations less than one year old that do not have broad community support, religious or political organizations, travel, or strictly administrative costs, athletic programs, fundraising dinners, pledges for miles run. No grants to individuals, or for national or local campaigns to eliminate or control specific diseases, product donations for fundraising events, or tickets or tables for conferences.
Publications: Corporate giving report, application guidelines.
Application information:
Initial approach: Request a copy of Minnegasco's application for corporate contribution or grant
Deadline(s): No set deadlines. Requests should be received no later than July of the year preceding the time of funding
Write: Kimberly M. Roden, Admin., Community Relations

1461
Minnesota Foundation

1120 Norwest Center
St. Paul 55101 (612) 224-5463

Incorporated in 1949 in MN; in 1984 became a supporting organization of the Saint Paul Foundation.
Financial data (yr. ended 12/31/87): Assets, $8,025,244 (M); gifts received, $1,042,675; expenditures, $793,056, including $558,192 for grants (high: $160,000; low: $500; average: $600-$20,000), $2,240 for 1 grant to an individual and $10,093 for 7 foundation-administered programs.
Purpose and activities: Giving primarily for the humanities and social services.
Types of support: Grants to individuals, operating budgets, continuing support, scholarship funds.
Limitations: Giving primarily in MN.
Publications: Annual report, occasional report.
Application information:
Deadline(s): Varies
Board meeting date(s): Quarterly or as required
Final notification: Varies
Write: Judith K. Healey, Pres.
Officers: Judith K. Healey, Pres.; Paul A. Verret, Secy.; Robert S. Davis,* Treas.
Trustees:* Frank Hammond, Chair.; Emily Anne Staples, Vice-Chair.; Robert L. Bullard, Richard A. Moore, Nancy N. Weyerhaeuser, Leonard H. Wilkening.
Number of staff: 2
Employer Identification Number: 410832480

1462
Minnesota Mining and Manufacturing Company Contributions Program

(also known as 3M Contributions Program)
c/o Community Affairs
Bldg. 521-11-01, 3M Ctr.
St. Paul 55144-1000 (612) 736-3781

Financial data (yr. ended 12/31/88): Total giving, $19,679,362, including $3,886,201 for grants and $15,793,161 for in-kind gifts.
Purpose and activities: Emphasis on projects which meet one or more of the following guidelines: projects which address specific needs of the community and suggest solutions; offer opportunities for enriched life, and provide communities with the skills to accomplish positive social goals; and seek self-support or broad-based community support as their ultimate goal. Support for educational institutions and organizations, civic and community organizations, the arts, media, culture, social services, health care, federated campaigns, and special projects/international activities. 3M requests that organizations seeking grants be in existence for at least one year. Also gives through in-kind gifts, employee volunteerism, and matching gifts for educational institutions and public radio and television. Programs reflect combined foundation and direct-giving and in-kind support.
Types of support: Employee matching gifts, fellowships, matching funds, operating budgets, research, scholarship funds.
Limitations: Giving limited to communities where 3M manufacturing, sales, and service activities exist in AL, AK, AZ, AR, CA, CO, CT, DC, FL, GA, HI, IL, IA, KY, MD, MA, MI, MN, MS, NE, NJ, NY, NC, ND, OH, OK, OR, PA, SC, SD, TN, TX, UT, VA, WA, WV, WI. No support for political, fraternal, social, veterans, or military organizations, religious organizations for religious purposes, cause-related marketing programs, media promotion or sponsorship, elementary or secondary schools, both public and private (though special programs relating to science, mathematics, economics, business, or vocational education may receive consideration), or subsidization of books, magazines, newspapers, or articles in professional journals (though publications related to 3M-supported projects may be given consideration). No grants to individuals, or for capital or endowment funds, emergency operating support, conferences, seminars, workshops, symposia, publication of conference-related proceedings, athletic events or associations, fund-raising and testimonial events/dinners, travel, advertising (though public service announcements may be considered), or for purchase of equipment not of 3M manufacture; 3M will not normally fund a program or project beyond 3 years.
Publications: Corporate giving report (including application guidelines).
Application information: If further consideration is to be given after the initial review, a grant application will be forwarded to the organization; multiple or repeat proposals from one organization in less than a 12-month period are discouraged. Application form required.
Initial approach: Letter of inquiry including brief organizational history, project description, amount requested, timetable, and listing of directors and officers and their affiliations
Deadline(s): Grant applications must be received at least 6 weeks prior to the month in which the request is to be reviewed
Board meeting date(s): Mar., Aug., and Dec.
Final notification: The requesting organization will receive notification of the results
Write: Eugene W. Steele, Mgr., 3M Contrib. Prog. and Secy., 3M Foundation
Corporate Contribution Committee: A.F. Jacobson, Chair. and C.E.O.; Donald W. Larson, Chair.; Kenneth A. Schoen, Exec. V.P.; Ralph D. Ebbott, V.P. and Treas.; William E. Coyne, Group V.P., Medical Products Group; Livio D. DeSimone, Exec. V.P., Info. and Imaging Technologies Sector; H.A. Hammerly, Exec. V.P., Industrial and Electronics Sector; Lester C. Krogh, Sr. V.P., Research and Development; M.J. Monteiro, Exec. V.P., International Operations; James Schoenwetter, V.P. and Cont.; T.P. Skoog, Group V.P., Advertising Services; Eugene W. Steele, Mgr., 3M Contrib. Prog.; Stanley W. Thiele, Sr. V.P., Admin. Services; Christopher J. Wheeler, V.P., Human Resources.

1463
Minnesota Mining and Manufacturing Foundation, Inc.

(also known as 3M Foundation, Inc.)
3M Center, Bldg. 521-11-01
St. Paul 55144-1000 (612) 736-3781

Incorporated in 1953 in MN.
Donor(s): Minnesota Mining & Manufacturing Co.
Financial data (yr. ended 12/31/87): Assets, $48,866,596 (M); gifts received, $42,900,000; expenditures, $6,586,863, including $5,747,614 for grants (high: $750,000; low: $50; average: $25-$10,000) and $756,506 for employee matching gifts.
Purpose and activities: Support for community funds, higher education, the arts, human services, youth agencies, civic involvement and preventive health care.
Types of support: Operating budgets, continuing support, annual campaigns, emergency funds, matching funds, employee matching gifts, scholarship funds, professorships, internships, fellowships, special projects, research.
Limitations: Giving primarily in areas where the company has facilities in AL, AK, CA, CO, FL, GA, HI, IL, IN, IA, KY, MD, MA, MI, MN, MS, MO, NE, NJ, NY, NC, ND, OH, OK, OR, PA, SC, SD, TX, UT, VA, WA, WV, WI. No support for projects of specific religious denominations or sects, athletic events, or conduit agencies. No grants to individuals, or

for capital or endowment funds, loans or investments, propaganda and lobbying efforts, fundraising events and associated advertising, travel, publications unrelated to foundation-funded projects, seed money, deficit financing, or conferences; no loans.
Publications: Annual report (including application guidelines).
Application information: Application form required.
Initial approach: Letter or personal visit by appointment
Copies of proposal: 1
Deadline(s): At least 6 months prior to month in which board meets
Board meeting date(s): Mar., Aug., and Dec.
Final notification: 3 months
Write: Eugene W. Steele, Secy.
Officers and Directors: Donald W. Larson, Pres.; Stanley W. Thiele, V.P.; Eugene W. Steele, Secy.; Ralph D. Ebbott, Treas.; William E. Coyne, Livio D. DeSimone, Allan J. Huber, Allen F. Jacobson, Lester C. Krogh, Manuel J. Monteiro, Thomas J. Scheuerman, Kenneth A. Schoen, James Schoenwetter, Christopher J. Wheeler.
Number of staff: 3 full-time professional; 2 full-time support.
Employer Identification Number: 416038262

1464
MWVE Fund
807 Lonsdale Bldg.
Duluth 55802 (218) 722-4757

Established in 1968 in MN.
Donor(s): Mary C. Van Evera, William P. Van Evera, other members of the Van Evera family.
Financial data (yr. ended 12/31/87): Assets, $121,474 (M); gifts received, $142,444; expenditures, $129,531, including $125,484 for grants.
Purpose and activities: Aid to indigent persons, higher education, fine arts, public health and medical research, churches, public information, and public policy organizations.
Types of support: General purposes.
Limitations: Giving primarily in northeastern MN, with emphasis on the city of Duluth. No grants to individuals.
Application information:
Initial approach: Proposal
Deadline(s): None
Final notification: Within 1 month
Write: William P. Van Evera or Mary C. Van Evera, Trustees
Trustees: Mary C. Van Evera, William P. Van Evera.
Employer Identification Number: 416081875

1465
Nash Foundation
c/o Norwest Capital Advisers
3444 IDS Center
Minneapolis 55402-2049

Established in 1922 in MN.
Financial data (yr. ended 12/31/87): Assets, $1,807,877 (M); expenditures, $94,279, including $63,350 for 56 grants (high: $10,000; low: $500).
Purpose and activities: Support for education, particularly higher education, social service and youth agencies, and cultural programs.
Types of support: Annual campaigns, capital campaigns, continuing support, general purposes, special projects.
Limitations: Giving primarily in the midwestern states, with emphasis on MN.
Publications: Application guidelines.
Application information: Foundation is not actively seeking additional requests for contributions.
Deadline(s): Jan. 15
Board meeting date(s): May
Final notification: June
Write: John M. Nash, Pres.
Officers and Trustees: John M. Nash, Pres.; Nicholas Nash, V.P.; Nanette D. Schoeder, Secy.; Charles H. Nash, Treas.; Henry K. Atwood, Mary Anna Dyar, Kathleen L. Nash, Mary A. Nash, Jeffrey Norton.
Number of staff: 1 part-time professional.
Employer Identification Number: 416019142

1466
George W. Neilson Foundation
625 Second Ave. S., No. 404
Minneapolis 55402 (612) 339-8101

Trust established in 1962 in MN.
Donor(s): George W. Neilson.†
Financial data (yr. ended 12/31/88): Assets, $2,253,611 (M); gifts received, $2,500; expenditures, $68,221, including $49,175 for grants.
Purpose and activities: Emphasis on matching funds for community needs, leadership, and economic development.
Types of support: Annual campaigns, conferences and seminars, matching funds.
Limitations: Giving primarily in the Bemidji, MN, area. No support for religious activities or governmental services. No grants to individuals, or for endowment funds, scholarships, fellowships, or basic research.
Application information:
Initial approach: Letter
Copies of proposal: 1
Deadline(s): May 1
Board meeting date(s): July or Aug.
Write: Henry Doerr, Treas.
Officers: Katharine Neilson Cram, Pres.; Edward M. Arundel, Secy.; Henry Doerr, Treas.
Number of staff: None.
Employer Identification Number: 416022186

1467
Northern Star Foundation
440 Hamm Bldg.
408 St. Peter St.
St. Paul 55102

Incorporated in 1960 in MN.
Donor(s): Members of the Hamm family.
Financial data (yr. ended 10/31/87): Assets, $3,017,876 (M); expenditures, $148,331, including $140,000 for grants.
Purpose and activities: Emphasis on secondary and higher education, including scholarship funds, cultural programs, youth agencies, and a community fund.
Types of support: Scholarship funds.
Limitations: Giving primarily in MN and CA.
Application information: Contributes only to pre-selected organizations. Applications not accepted.
Write: William H. Hamm, Pres.
Officers and Directors:* William H. Hamm,* Pres.; Edward H. Hamm,* V.P. and Treas.; Candace S. Hamm, V.P.; Joseph A. Mann, Secy.
Employer Identification Number: 416030832

1468
Northern States Power Corporate Contributions
414 Nicollet Mall
Minneapolis 55401 (612) 330-6026
Additional tel.: (612) 330-7701

Financial data (yr. ended 12/31/87): Total giving, $3,191,047, including $3,114,656 for 841 grants (high: $75,000; low: $25; average: $25-$75,000) and $76,391 for 413 employee matching gifts.
Purpose and activities: Supports community services, including United Way, social services, crisis assistance, housing, employment, childcare and youth programs. Also supports education, civic affairs, arts and culture, mental health, Native Americans, the homeless, elderly, disabled, women, minorities, volunteerism, the disavantaged, literacy, and health programs, including chemical dependency treatment and prevention.
Types of support: Building funds, general purposes, capital campaigns, employee matching gifts, continuing support, emergency funds, operating budgets, special projects, scholarship funds.
Limitations: Giving limited to applicants within service area of Northern States Power; no support for national groups. No support for fraternal or athletic organizations. No grants to individuals, or for endowments, research programs, conferences, advertising, fundraising, or travel.
Publications: Program policy statement, corporate giving report, application guidelines.
Application information: Request application and funding guidelines. Application form required.
Initial approach: Letter
Copies of proposal: 1
Deadline(s): None
Board meeting date(s): Bimonthly
Write: Linda J. Granoien, Consultant, Corp. Contribs. or Bruce A. Palmer, Mgr., Corp. Contribs.
Corporate Contributions Committee: Bruce A. Palmer, Mgr.; Linda J. Granoien, Consultant.
Number of staff: 2 full-time professional; 1 full-time support.

1469
Northwest Area Foundation
West 975 First National Bank Bldg.
St. Paul 55101-1373 (612) 224-9635

Incorporated in 1934 in MN as Lexington Foundation; name changed to Louis W. and Maud Hill Family Foundation in 1950; present name adopted 1975.
Donor(s): Louis W. Hill, Sr.,† and other members of the Hill family.

Financial data (yr. ended 2/28/87): Assets, $194,439,842 (M); expenditures, $10,400,793, including $7,486,860 for 251 grants (average: $40,000-$75,000) and $500,000 for loans.
Purpose and activities: Program directions include 1)regional economic vitality; 2)responsibly meeting basic human needs; 3)enhancing and conserving natural resources; and 4)access to the arts.
Types of support: Special projects, research, consulting services, technical assistance, program-related investments, seed money.
Limitations: Giving primarily in ID, IA, MN, MT, ND, OR, SD, and WA. No support for religious programs or propaganda. No grants to individuals, or for scholarships, fellowships, endowment or capital funds, films, travel, overhead, physical plants, equipment, publications, operating budgets, continuing support, annual campaigns, emergency funds, deficit financing, building funds, land acquisition, renovation projects, or conferences.
Publications: Annual report, newsletter, application guidelines.
Application information: Must include tax-exempt letter. Application form required.
Initial approach: Letter
Copies of proposal: 1
Deadline(s): None
Board meeting date(s): Bimonthly beginning in Feb.
Final notification: 3 to 4 months
Write: Terry Tinson Saario, Pres.
Officers: W. John Driscoll,* Chair. and Treas.; Irving Clark,* Vice-Chair.; Terry Tinson Saario, Pres. and Secy.; Karl N. Stauber, V.P.
Trustees: Sheila ffolliot, Louis W. Hill, Jr., Maud Hill Schroll.
Directors:* Steven L. Belton, Worth Bruntjen, Marcia J. Bystrom, Shirley M. Clark, Roger R. Conant, David A. Lanegran, Norman M. Lorentzsen, Carlos Luis, Francis B. Tiffany, M.D.
Number of staff: 6 full-time professional; 1 part-time professional; 7 full-time support; 1 part-time support.
Employer Identification Number: 410719221
Recent arts and culture grants:
Alaska Public Radio Network, Anchorage, AK, $150,000. For first daily national radio newscast and feature service covering Native American issues and events. 10/27/87.
American Festival Ballet, Moscow, ID, $60,000. To support performances in eight rural communities in Idaho and eastern Oregon. 10/27/87.
Artspace Projects, Minneapolis, MN, $90,000. To expand Artspace's mission to include real estate development and other cooperative ventures for arts. 2/18/88.
Ballet Harren, Minneapolis, MN, $15,000. To help fund creation of touring dance concert. 10/27/87.
Brass Tacks Theater, Minneapolis, MN, $20,000. To support development and production of new play by Patty Lynch, The Wreck of the Hesperus. 10/27/87.
Childrens Theater Company and School, Minneapolis, MN, $35,000. To partially underwrite costs of touring Rumplestiltskin and Kalulu: Two African Tales to economically depressed communities in Northwest. 2/18/88.
Cricket Theater Corporation, Minneapolis, MN, $45,000. For general operating support. 10/27/87.
Festival at Sandpoint, Sandpoint, ID, $20,000. For general operating support for concerts and training programs in summer of 1988. 2/18/88.
Fox Theater Corporation, Billings, MT, $30,000. For support of programming at new cultural center. 10/27/87.
Graywolf Press, Saint Paul, MN, $20,000. To help support publication of work of mid-career writers in American Writers Series. 10/27/87.
Minneapolis College of Art and Design, Gallery Program, Minneapolis, MN, $50,000. To enable MCAD Gallery to provide more extensive catalogs, additional publications, and more complex installations. Grants made through Minneapolis Society of Fine Arts. 10/27/87.
Minnesota Museum of Art, Saint Paul, MN, $100,000. For operating support designed to increase audience and enhance internal management. 10/27/87.
Minnesota Opera Company, Saint Paul, MN, $35,000. To support creation, development, and production of new operas and other forms of music-theater. 2/18/88.
National Arts Stabilization Fund, Seattle, WA, $100,000. To help support arts stabilization program in Seattle area. 10/27/87.
Red Eye Collaboration, Minneapolis, MN, $8,000. To fund creation and production of new multimedia work. 10/27/87.
Saint Marys College, Winona, MN, $16,000. To support College's 1987-88 fine arts performing series. 10/27/87.
Saint Paul-Ramsey United Arts Council, Saint Paul, MN, $44,000. For operating support for technical services provided by Resources and Counseling Division. 10/27/87.
Southern Theater Foundation, Minneapolis, MN, $20,000. For presentation of trilogy based on Marcel Duchamp's, The Large Glass. 10/27/87.
UCVideo, Minneapolis, MN, $30,000. To strengthen quality of UCVideo's exhibition program. 10/27/87.

1470
Norwest Corporate Giving Program
Norwest Center
Seventh and Marquette
Minneapolis 55479 (612) 667-7860

Financial data (yr. ended 12/31/87): $988,123 for grants.
Purpose and activities: Norwest banks and affiliates which are found in nearly 200 communities in 7 states contribute to the communities in which they are located. Interests include education, including education for minorities, social services, civic and cultural activities, including performing arts, employment, and the disadvantaged; gifts over $500 are recommended to Norwest Foundation for funding and paid through the foundation; gifts of $500 or less are paid directly through the banks or affiliates.
Types of support: Annual campaigns, capital campaigns, employee matching gifts, equipment, operating budgets, employee-related scholarships, scholarship funds, special projects.
Limitations: Giving primarily in areas served by company and its subsidiaries in MN, IA, NE, ND, SD, MT, and WI; within each of these states focus is in communities where Norwest does business. No grants for conferences or seminars; United Way funded agencies have low priority.
Application information:
Initial approach: Contact nearest Norwest bank or affiliate
Copies of proposal: 1
Write: Carolyn H. Gabanski, Prog. Assoc.

1471
Norwest Foundation
Norwest Center
Seventh and Marquette
Minneapolis 55479-1055 (612) 667-7860

Established in 1979 in MN.
Donor(s): Norwest Corp., and affiliated banks.
Financial data (yr. ended 12/31/87): Assets, $99,003 (M); gifts received, $1,559,000; expenditures, $2,831,840, including $2,735,731 for 308 grants (high: $585,000; low: $250) and $91,075 for 464 employee matching gifts.
Purpose and activities: Giving for community funds, higher education, cultural programs (including performing arts and theater), social service and youth agencies, and economic development.
Types of support: Annual campaigns, building funds, capital campaigns, continuing support, employee matching gifts, equipment, operating budgets, employee-related scholarships, seed money, special projects.
Limitations: Giving primarily in areas of company operations, including MN, IA, NE, ND, SD, MT, and WI. No support for religious organizations for religious purposes, or for fraternal organizations. No grants to individuals, or for conferences, tickets, or travel; no loans.
Publications: Annual report (including application guidelines).
Application information:
Initial approach: Letter
Copies of proposal: 1
Deadline(s): None
Board meeting date(s): Varies; usually every 2 months
Write: Diane P. Lilly, Pres.
Officers: Diane P. Lilly,* Pres.; Stanley S. Stroup, Secy.; Carolyn H. Gabanski, Treas.
Directors:* Lloyd P. Johnson, Richard M. Kovacevich.
Number of staff: 1 part-time professional; 2 full-time support.
Employer Identification Number: 411367441

1472
Alice M. O'Brien Foundation
324 Forest
Mahtomedi 55115 (612) 426-2143

Incorporated in 1951 in MN.
Donor(s): Miss Alice M. O'Brien.†
Financial data (yr. ended 12/31/86): Assets, $2,498,118 (M); expenditures, $161,861,

including $142,750 for 25 grants (high: $29,000; low: $150).
Purpose and activities: Emphasis on secondary and higher education, including medical education and research; some support for social services and cultural programs.
Types of support: Operating budgets, annual campaigns, seed money, building funds, equipment, research.
Limitations: Giving primarily in MN. No grants to individuals, or for endowment funds, scholarships, fellowships, or matching gifts; no loans.
Application information:
Initial approach: Proposal
Copies of proposal: 1
Deadline(s): May 1 and Nov. 15
Board meeting date(s): June and Dec.
Final notification: 6 months
Write: Julia O'Brien Wilcox, Pres.
Officers and Directors: Julia O'Brien Wilcox, Pres.; Richard S. Wilcox, Jr., V.P.; Thomond R. O'Brien, Treas.; Eleanor M. O'Brien, Terance G. O'Brien, William J. O'Brien.
Number of staff: None.
Employer Identification Number: 416018991

1473
I. A. O'Shaughnessy Foundation, Inc.
c/o First Trust Co., Inc.
P.O. Box 64704
St. Paul 55164 (612) 222-2323

Incorporated in 1941 in MN.
Donor(s): I.A. O'Shaughnessy,† John F. O'Shaughnessy, Globe Oil and Refining Companies, Lario Oil and Gas Co.
Financial data (yr. ended 12/31/86): Assets, $33,919,021 (M); gifts received, $5,255,159; expenditures, $1,653,776, including $1,551,588 for 47 grants (high: $200,000; low: $1,000; average: $5,000-$50,000).
Purpose and activities: Giving for cultural programs, secondary and higher education, social services, medical research, and Roman Catholic religious organizations.
Types of support: Annual campaigns, building funds, equipment, endowment funds, research, general purposes, continuing support.
Limitations: Giving limited to the U.S., with emphasis on MN, IL, KS, and TX. No support for religious missions or individual parishes. No grants to individuals; no loans.
Publications: Application guidelines.
Application information: Grants usually initiated by the directors.
Initial approach: Letter
Copies of proposal: 1
Deadline(s): None
Board meeting date(s): June and Nov.
Final notification: 6 months
Write: Paul J. Kelly, Secy.-Treas.
Officers and Directors:* John F. O'Shaughnessy,* Pres.; Charles E. Lyman IV,* V.P.; Donald E. O'Shaughnessy,* V.P.; Eileen O'Shaughnessy,* V.P.; Lawrence O'Shaughnessy,* V.P.; Paul J. Kelly, Secy.-Treas.
Employer Identification Number: 416011524

1474
Oakleaf Foundation
4122 IDS Center
Minneapolis 55402

Established in 1967 in MN.
Donor(s): K.N. Dayton, Julia W. Dayton.
Financial data (yr. ended 12/31/87): Assets, $1,715,225 (M); gifts received, $1,395,719; expenditures, $410,205, including $406,200 for 4 grants (high: $200,000; low: $1,200).
Purpose and activities: Emphasis on cultural programs; support also for philanthropic associations.
Types of support: General purposes.
Limitations: Giving primarily in the Minneapolis and St. Paul, MN, area.
Application information: Contributes only to pre-selected organizations. Applications not accepted.
Officers and Directors: K.N. Dayton, Pres. and Treas.; Julia W. Dayton, V.P. and Secy.; Duncan N. Dayton, Judson M. Dayton.
Employer Identification Number: 416080485

1475
Onan Family Foundation
310 Interchange Plaza West
435 Ford Rd.
Minneapolis 55426 (612) 544-4702

Incorporated in 1942 in MN.
Donor(s): Members of the Onan family.
Financial data (yr. ended 12/31/87): Assets, $4,257,322 (M); expenditures, $174,657, including $143,000 for 28 grants (high: $15,000; low: $1,500; average: $1,500-$10,000).
Purpose and activities: To improve the physical, cultural, and educational condition of mankind; emphasis on social welfare agencies, cultural and civic organizations, educational institutions, and church support.
Types of support: Continuing support, emergency funds, general purposes, operating budgets, seed money, special projects.
Limitations: Giving primarily in the Twin Cities, MN, metropolitan area. No grants to individuals, or for capital or endowment funds, research, scholarships, fellowships, trips, political campaigns, or matching gifts; no loans.
Publications: Annual report (including application guidelines).
Application information:
Initial approach: Letter
Copies of proposal: 1
Deadline(s): Submit proposal in Apr. or Sept.
Board meeting date(s): May and Nov.
Write: David W. Onan, II, Pres.
Officers and Trustees: David W. Onan II, Pres. and Treas.; Bruce R. Smith, Secy.; David W. Onan III, Lois C. Onan.
Staff: Susan J. Smith, Exec. Dir.
Number of staff: 1 part-time professional.
Employer Identification Number: 416033631
Recent arts and culture grants:
K T C A Twin Cities Public Television, Saint Paul, MN, $11,000. 1987.
Minnesota Historical Society, Saint Paul, MN, $5,000. 1987.
Minnesota Public Radio, Saint Paul, MN, $6,000. 1987.
Minnesota Transportation Museum, Saint Paul, MN, $11,000. 1987.

1476
Otter Tail Power Company Corporate Giving Program
215 South Cascade St.
Fergus Falls 56537 (218) 739-8200

Financial data (yr. ended 12/31/87): Total giving, $261,904, including $247,747 for grants, $2,540 for 39 employee matching gifts and $11,617 for in-kind gifts.
Purpose and activities: Giving for arts and culture, the elderly, child welfare, community development, the disadvantaged, the environment, the handicapped, mental health, volunteerism, recreation, minorities, health, including cancer, welfare, education, including secondary and business, and civic activities. Also gives through in-kind donations.
Types of support: In-kind gifts, annual campaigns, building funds, conferences and seminars, continuing support, employee matching gifts, endowment funds, equipment, matching funds, renovation projects.
Limitations: Giving primarily in home and field offices in MN, ND, and SD.
Application information: Include contributors list.
Initial approach: Letter
Final notification: 1-4 weeks
Write: John MacFarlane, Pres. and C.E.O.

1477
Pentair, Inc. Corporate Giving Program
1700 West Highway 36
St. Paul 55113 (612) 636-7920

Financial data (yr. ended 12/31/87): Total giving, $358,000, including $328,000 for grants (average: $1,000-$5,000) and $30,000 for 100 employee matching gifts.
Purpose and activities: Support for arts and culture, health and welfare, education, civic affairs and music.
Types of support: Annual campaigns, capital campaigns, continuing support, employee matching gifts, endowment funds, fellowships.
Application information:
Initial approach: Letter of inquiry
Copies of proposal: 1
Board meeting date(s): Quarterly
Final notification: 12 weeks
Write: Helen Hallstadt, Corp. Office Coord.
Administrators: H.A. Hollstadt, Corp. Office. Coord.; D. Eugene Nugent, Chair.

1478
The Jay and Rose Phillips Family Foundation
(Formerly The Phillips Foundation)
100 Washington Sq., Suite 1650
Minneapolis 55401
Mailing address: 2345 Northeast Kennedy St., Minneapolis, MN 55413; Tel.: (612) 331-6230

Incorporated in 1944 in MN.
Donor(s): Jay Phillips, and members of his family.
Financial data (yr. ended 12/31/86): Assets, $56,774,301 (M); expenditures, $2,494,290, including $2,173,337 for 231 grants (high: $537,967; low: $15; average: $1,000-$36,000).

Purpose and activities: Giving primarily for hospitals and medical research, Jewish religious organizations and welfare funds, higher education, social services, and cultural programs.
Types of support: Building funds, equipment, research, scholarship funds, fellowships, professorships, matching funds, loans, lectureships.
Limitations: Giving primarily in MN and the Midwest. No support for religious organizations for sectarian purposes. No grants to individuals, or for endowment funds.
Publications: Application guidelines.
Application information:
Initial approach: Letter
Copies of proposal: 1
Deadline(s): None
Board meeting date(s): As required
Final notification: 30 days
Write: Thomas P. Cook, Exec. Dir.
Officers and Trustees: Jay Phillips, Pres.; Rose Phillips, V.P.; Morton B. Phillips, Treas.; Thomas P. Cook, Exec. Dir.; Paula Bernstein, William Bernstein, Jack I. Levin, Pauline Phillips.
Number of staff: 3 full-time professional; 1 part-time professional.
Employer Identification Number: 416019578

1479
The Pillsbury Company Foundation
Mail Station 3775
200 South Sixth St.
Minneapolis 55402-1464 (612) 330-7230

Incorporated in 1957 in MN.
Donor(s): The Pillsbury Co.
Financial data (yr. ended 5/31/88): Assets, $10,700,787 (M); gifts received, $7,587,454; expenditures, $5,039,551, including $4,033,102 for grants and $310,324 for employee matching gifts.
Purpose and activities: The foundation has two emphases: 1)alleviation of hunger and malnutrition through cash grants, gifts in kind, technical assistance which uses food industry expertise domestically and internationally, and public awareness; 2)preparation of disadvantaged youth for employment through community service, career training, and pre-employment preparation. Support also for health and welfare, mainly through the United Way; job training; higher education, including employee-related scholarships through the Citizen's Scholarship Foundation of America, and matching gifts; culture and art; and civic affairs and community development; support for scholarship funds only at pre-selected institutions. In 1988, corporate giving, excluding product donations, amounted to $3 million. Product donations totalled $4.2 million.
Types of support: Continuing support, annual campaigns, conferences and seminars, scholarship funds, employee-related scholarships, matching funds, employee matching gifts, seed money, fellowships, technical assistance, operating budgets.
Limitations: Giving primarily in areas where the company has plants and subsidiaries in the U.S. No support for religious denominations or sects, or for health organizations. No grants to individuals, or for capital or endowment campaigns, fundraising, or travel; no loans; no product donations except through the Second Harvest Food Bank Network.
Publications: Annual report, corporate giving report (including application guidelines), informational brochure (including application guidelines).
Application information:
Initial approach: Letter
Copies of proposal: 1
Deadline(s): None
Board meeting date(s): Bimonthly
Final notification: 1-4 months
Write: Carol B. Truesdell, Secy.
Officers: Ian A. Martin,* Pres.; Carol B. Truesdell, Exec. Dir.
Contributions Committee:* James R. Behnke, N. Jean Fountain.
Number of staff: 2 full-time professional; 2 full-time support.
Employer Identification Number: 416021373
Recent arts and culture grants:
Childrens Theater Company and School, Minneapolis, MN, $15,000. For arts education program for young people. 1987.
Dallas Museum of Art, Dallas, TX, $5,000. 1987.
Dallas Symphony Orchestra, Dallas, TX, $5,000. For concert series. 1987.
Five Hundred, The, Dallas, TX, $20,000. 1987.
Guthrie Theater, Minneapolis, MN, $35,000. 1987.
K T C A Twin Cities Public Television, Saint Paul, MN, $105,000. To underwrite programming and construction of new broadcast facility. 1987.
Miami Youth Museum, Miami, FL, $5,000. 1987.
Minneapolis Society of Fine Arts, Minneapolis, MN, $35,000. For educational programs. 1987.
Minnesota Historical Society, Saint Paul, MN, $20,000. For general support. 1987.
Minnesota Opera Company, Saint Paul, MN, $8,000. 1987.
Minnesota Orchestral Association, Minneapolis, MN, $255,787. For general support. 1987.
Minnesota Public Radio, Saint Paul, MN, $40,000. For operating support. 1987.
Performing Arts Center and Theater, Ruth Eckerd Hall, Clearwater, FL, $10,000. For concert series. 1987.
Saint Paul Chamber Orchestra, Saint Paul, MN, $18,000. For general support. 1987.
Science Museum of Minnesota, Saint Paul, MN, $25,000. For educational programs. 1987.
United Arts, Saint Paul, MN, $15,000. 1987.
Walker Art Center, Minneapolis, MN, $25,000. For art education programs for young people. 1987.

1480
Piper, Jaffray & Hopwood Corporate Giving Program
Box 28
222 South Ninth Street
Minneapolis 55440 (612) 342-6000

Financial data (yr. ended 9/30/88): Total giving, $562,625, including $536,003 for grants (average: $100-$15,000) and $26,592 for employee matching gifts.
Purpose and activities: Support for social services, education, arts and culture, and civic affairs, with emphasis on organizations and programs in which there is a substantial employee involvement; lower priority for general operating support, public agencies, United Way, national fundraising expenses, health care, or hospitals.
Types of support: Capital campaigns, continuing support, emergency funds, employee matching gifts, endowment funds, general purposes, employee-related scholarships.
Limitations: Giving primarily in areas where company has branch offices in CO, ID, IL, IA, KS, MN, MO, MT, NE, NY, ND, OR, SD, UT, WA, WI, and WY. No support for religious organizations for direct religious activities, veterans organizations, fraternal societies or orders, political organizations or candidates, basic or applied research, campaigns for the elimination or control of specific diseases, and athletic teams or events. No grants to individuals, or for courtesy advertising or travel.
Publications: Corporate report, application guidelines.
Application information: Local branch offices are responsible for grants made in their own communities. Interested organizations should apply directly to the branch manager of the Piper Jaffray office in their city. Grants are made on a one year basis. Requests for second year support for the same program will be considered, given a positive review of the program. Application form required.
Initial approach: Formal application; proposal including organization description, project description, project budget, list of board of trustees and staff; list of funding sources and amounts; organization's current operating budget; and 501(c)(3)
Copies of proposal: 1
Board meeting date(s): Mar., May, Sept., and Dec.
Write: Karen M. Bohn, Chair., Corp. Contribs. Comm.
Corporate Contributions Committee: Karen M. Bohn, Chair.; Leslie A. Johnson, Secy.

1481
The Elizabeth C. Quinlan Foundation, Inc.
1205 Foshay Tower
Minneapolis 55402 (612) 333-8084

Incorporated in 1945 in MN.
Donor(s): Elizabeth C. Quinlan.†
Financial data (yr. ended 12/31/86): Assets, $2,294,811 (M); expenditures, $192,946, including $138,050 for 61 grants (high: $20,000; low: $100).
Purpose and activities: Grants largely for Roman Catholic institutions, higher and secondary education, cultural programs, health agencies, and social services.
Types of support: Operating budgets, continuing support, annual campaigns, seed money, emergency funds, deficit financing, building funds, equipment, land acquisition, endowment funds, research, scholarship funds, matching funds, general purposes, special projects.
Limitations: Giving limited to MN. No grants to individuals; no loans.

Publications: Annual report (including application guidelines).
Application information:
Initial approach: Letter
Copies of proposal: 1
Deadline(s): Submit proposal preferably in May or June; deadline Sept.
Board meeting date(s): Oct.
Final notification: Dec. 1
Write: Richard A. Klein, Pres.
Officers and Trustees: Richard A. Klein, Pres. and Treas.; Eugene P. McCahill, V.P.; Mary Elizabeth Lahiff, Secy.; Lucia L. Crane, Eileen L. Grundman, Anne L. Klein, Alice M. Lahiff.
Number of staff: 2 part-time support.
Employer Identification Number: 410706125

1482
The Regis Foundation
5000 Normandale Rd.
Minneapolis 55436

Established in 1981 in MN.
Financial data (yr. ended 6/30/88): Assets, $0 (M); gifts received, $572,085; expenditures, $572,085, including $572,025 for 14 grants (high: $233,425; low: $100).
Purpose and activities: Emphasis on Jewish welfare, culture and the arts, and education.
Application information:
Initial approach: Letter
Write: Myron Kunin, Pres.
Officers: Myron Kunin, Pres. and Treas.; Frank Evangelist, Secy.
Employer Identification Number: 411410790

1483
Margaret Rivers Fund
c/o First National Bank of Stillwater
213 East Chestnut St.
Stillwater 55082

Incorporated in 1948 in MN.
Donor(s): Robert E. Slaughter.†
Financial data (yr. ended 12/31/87): Assets, $14,573,453 (M); expenditures, $698,246, including $585,250 for 211 grants (high: $50,000; low: $300).
Purpose and activities: A private operating foundation; grants primarily for hospitals, church support, youth agencies, aid to the handicapped, and care of the aged; grants also for cultural programs and conservation.
Limitations: Giving primarily in MN.
Application information:
Initial approach: Letter
Deadline(s): None
Write: William Klapp, Pres.
Officers and Trustee:* David Pohl, William D. Klapp,* Pres.; Helen Moelter, Secy.; Robert G. Briggs, Treas.
Employer Identification Number: 416017102

1484
RMT Foundation
12001 Technology Dr.
Eden Prairie 55344

Established in 1982 in MN.
Donor(s): Rosemount, Inc.
Financial data (yr. ended 11/30/87): Assets, $618,365 (M); gifts received, $360,440; expenditures, $179,867, including $179,280 for 42 grants (high: $54,500; low: $300).
Purpose and activities: Support for educational institutions, and cultural and social service organizations.
Limitations: Giving primarily in Saint Paul and Minneapolis, MN.
Officers: Vernon H. Heath, Pres.; John R. Duxbury, V.P.; Bonnie Smith, Secy.; Richard D. Royle, Treas.
Employer Identification Number: 411433607

1485
Rochester Area Foundation
First Bank Bldg., Suite 436
201 Southwest First Ave.
Rochester 55902 (507) 282-0203

Community foundation established in 1944 in MN by resolution of trust.
Financial data (yr. ended 12/31/87): Assets, $2,075,450 (M); gifts received, $34,055; expenditures, $102,798, including $59,525 for 14 grants (high: $10,000; low: $700).
Purpose and activities: To help launch new projects which represent innovative approaches to community needs, support special purposes of established organizations, promote volunteer and citizen involvement in community, respond to current human needs in community, and support projects without other sources of support; giving in areas of health, education, social services, and civic and cultural affairs.
Types of support: Seed money, emergency funds, building funds, equipment, matching funds, technical assistance, conferences and seminars, program-related investments.
Limitations: Giving limited to Olmsted County, MN. No support for religious organizations for sectarian purposes. No grants to individuals, or for endowment funds, annual campaigns, operating budgets, continuing support, land acquisition, deficit financing, consulting services, scholarships, fellowships, or research; no loans.
Publications: Annual report, program policy statement, application guidelines, newsletter, informational brochure.
Application information: Application form required.
Initial approach: Letter
Copies of proposal: 11
Deadline(s): Submit proposals in Jan., Apr., July, and Oct.; deadline 1st working day of the month
Board meeting date(s): Feb., May, Aug., and Nov.
Final notification: 1 week
Write: Chuck Hazama, Exec. Dir.
Trustees: James L. Talen, Chair.; Betty A. Beck, Vice-Chair.; Ann N. Ferguson, Vice-Chair.; Donald M. Sudor, Secy.; Jean Freeman, Treas.; William C. Boyne, Dorothy Callahan, Vera M. Elgin, Claude Glatzmaier, Isabel C. Huizenga, Jennings O. Johnson, Michael D. Klampe, Anna McGee, Sue M. Norris, Charles Pappas, Robert Smoldt, Herbert M. Stellner, Jr., Curtis L. Taylor, Charles R. Von Wald, Nedra Wicks, Barbara Withers.
Number of staff: 2 part-time support.
Employer Identification Number: 416017740

1486
The Rodman Foundation
2100 First National Bank Bldg.
St. Paul 55101 (612) 228-0935

Established in 1969 in MN.
Donor(s): Members of the Titcomb family.
Financial data (yr. ended 12/31/86): Assets, $1,313,126 (M); gifts received, $192,307; expenditures, $205,757, including $174,100 for 41 grants (high: $35,000; low: $250; average: $500-$3,000).
Purpose and activities: Emphasis on higher and secondary education, historic preservation, and a science museum; grants also for cultural programs, hospitals, community funds, and youth agencies.
Types of support: Operating budgets, building funds, scholarship funds.
Limitations: Giving primarily in MN. No grants to individuals.
Application information:
Initial approach: Letter
Copies of proposal: 1
Deadline(s): None
Board meeting date(s): As required
Final notification: 2 to 3 weeks
Write: E. Rodman Titcomb, Jr., Pres.
Officers: E. Rodman Titcomb, Jr.,* Pres.; Julie C. Titcomb,* V.P.; Joseph S. Micallef, Secy.; Gordon E. Hed, Treas.
Directors:* Edward R. Titcomb.
Number of staff: None.
Employer Identification Number: 237025570

1487
The Saint Paul Foundation
1120 Norwest Center
St. Paul 55101 (612) 224-5463

Community foundation established in 1940 in MN by adoption of a plan; incorporated in 1964.
Financial data (yr. ended 12/31/87): Assets, $104,131,705 (M); gifts received, $8,159,682; expenditures, $8,755,794, including $5,670,518 for 405 grants (high: $370,364; low: $11; average: $500-$50,000), $166,701 for 324 grants to individuals, $929,527 for 46 foundation-administered programs and $299,907 for loans.
Purpose and activities: Support for educational, charitable, cultural, or benevolent purposes of a public nature. Grants largely to cultural, educational, health, and welfare agencies.
Types of support: Seed money, emergency funds, building funds, equipment, research, matching funds, special projects, scholarship funds, fellowships, program-related investments, employee-related scholarships, renovation projects, loans, capital campaigns, technical assistance.
Limitations: Giving limited to Ramsey, Washington, and Dakota counties and to the St. Paul, MN, metropolitan area. No support for sectarian religious programs, except from designated funds. No grants for operating budgets, annual campaigns, deficit financing, endowment funds (except through designated funds) or generally, for continuing support; no student loans.

Publications: Annual report, application guidelines.
Application information:
Initial approach: Proposal
Copies of proposal: 1
Deadline(s): 3 months before next board meeting
Board meeting date(s): Quarterly
Final notification: Within 1 month
Write: Paul A. Verret, Pres.
Officers: Frederick T. Weyerhaeuser,* Chair.; Virginia D. Brooks,* Vice-Chair.; Paul A. Verret, Pres. and Secy.; Jean E. Hart, V.P.; John D. Healey, Jr.,* Treas.
Board of Directors:* David M. Craig, M.D., Patrick J. Donovan, Willis M. Forman, Marice L. Halper, Reatha Clark King, Joseph R. Kingman III, Richard H. Kyle, Thomas W. McKeown, Joseph T. O'Neill, Barbara B. Roy, Jon A. Theobald.
Corporate Trustees: American National Bank & Trust Co., First Trust Co., Inc., Norwest Bank St. Paul, N.A.
Number of staff: 9 full-time professional; 1 part-time professional; 10 full-time support; 2 part-time support.
Employer Identification Number: 416031510
Recent arts and culture grants:
Actors Theater of Saint Paul, Saint Paul, MN, $17,500. To hire coordinator for outreach and education programs. 8/19/87.
Como Conservatory Restoration Fund, Saint Paul, MN, $370,364. For grant of all funds received to date plus accumulated interest up to date of payment. 1/28/87.
Fairview Cemetery Association, Stillwater, MN, $10,000. To undertake beautification, preservation and maintenance projects at Fairview Cemetery. 3/17/87.
Film in the Cities, Saint Paul, MN, $7,000. Toward development of Saint Paul area audiences for Jerome Hill Theater. 6/17/87.
Goodhue County Historical Society, Red Wing, MN, $25,500. For preservation project. 9/14/87.
Goodhue County Historical Society, Red Wing, MN, $9,500. For preservation project. 8/17/87.
K T C A Twin Cities Public Television, Minneapolis, MN, $250,000. To help finance construction of Minnesota TeleCenter. 1/28/87.
Minnesota Museum of Art, Saint Paul, MN, $5,000. To finance presentation of International Art Show for the End of World Hunger. 8/19/87.
Minnesota Zoological Garden Foundation, Apple Valley, MN, $10,265. To support Captive Breeding Specialist Group Fund. 6/22/87.
Saint Paul Chamber Orchestra Society, Saint Paul, MN, $25,000. For general support for Bridge Fund Campaign. 6/29/87.
Saint Paul-Ramsey United Arts Council, Saint Paul, MN, $60,500. For 1987 United Arts Fund Campaign. 8/19/87.
Saint Paul, City of, Saint Paul, MN, $5,000. To support COMPAS Community Art Fund. 6/8/87.
Schubert Club, Saint Paul, MN, $13,287. For general operating support. 1/28/87.
Schubert Club, Saint Paul, MN, $12,040. For general operating support. 1/28/87.
United Way of the Saint Paul Area, Saint Paul, MN, $10,000. To United Way of the Saint Paul Area, Inc. for Chicanos/Latinos en Servicios, Inc. to finance cultural management project. 8/19/87.
University of Minnesota, Office of Research Administration, Saint Paul, MN, $6,000. Toward cataloging and conference presentation for Ellis Collection of Children's Literature Research Collection. 6/17/87.

1488
The Fred M. Seed Foundation
1235 Yale Pl., No. 1702
Minneapolis 55403

Established in 1960 in MN.
Donor(s): Fred M. Seed,† Fred M. Seed Living Trust.
Financial data (yr. ended 12/31/87): Assets, $1,117,800 (M); gifts received, $633,858; expenditures, $198,749, including $192,517 for 84 grants (high: $80,100; low: $15).
Purpose and activities: Support primarily for higher and secondary education; limited giving to cultural programs, social services, and civic affairs.
Application information: Contributes only to pre-selected organizations. Applications not accepted.
Officers: Grace M. Seed, Pres.; John C. Seed, V.P.; James M. Seed, Secy.
Employer Identification Number: 416029620

1489
Somerset Foundation, Inc.
322 Minnesota St.
P.O. Box 64704
St. Paul 55164-0704

Established in 1960 in MN.
Financial data (yr. ended 12/31/87): Assets, $1,427,444 (M); expenditures, $166,370, including $153,950 for 17 grants (high: $75,000; low: $250).
Purpose and activities: Support for cultural programs, including performing arts groups and arts councils.
Types of support: General purposes.
Limitations: Giving primarily in MN.
Application information:
Deadline(s): None
Write: Paul J. Kelly, Secy.
Officers and Trustees:* Hella L. Mears Hueg,* Pres.; William F. Hueg, Jr.,* V.P.; Paul Kelly, Secy.-Treas.
Employer Identification Number: 416029569

1490
The Southways Foundation
c/o Sargent Management Co.
1300 TCF Tower
Minneapolis 55402 (612) 338-3871

Incorporated in 1950 in MN.
Donor(s): John S. Pillsbury,† and family.
Financial data (yr. ended 12/31/86): Assets, $5,371,501 (M); gifts received, $114,118; expenditures, $313,455, including $287,333 for 106 grants (high: $50,000; low: $100; average: $1,500).
Purpose and activities: Emphasis on secondary and higher education, cultural activities, and community funds.
Limitations: Giving primarily in MN.
Application information:
Deadline(s): None
Write: Donald K. Morrison
Officers: John S. Pillsbury, Jr.,* Pres.; Donald K. Morrison, V.P.; John S. Pillsbury III,* V.P.; George S. Pillsbury,* Secy.-Treas.
Trustees:* Mrs. Thomas M. Crosby, Lucy C. Mitchell, Mrs. John S. Pillsbury.
Employer Identification Number: 416018502

1491
St. Croix Foundation
c/o First Trust Co., Inc.
W-555 First National Bank Bldg., P.O. Box 64706
St. Paul 55164 (612) 291-5114

Established in 1950 in MN.
Donor(s): Ianthe B. Hardenbergh, I. Hardenbergh Charitable Annuity Trust, Gabrielle Hardenbergh.
Financial data (yr. ended 12/31/87): Assets, $1,837,930 (M); gifts received, $336,502; expenditures, $243,707, including $205,876 for 55 grants (high: $35,000; low: $250).
Purpose and activities: Giving for health organizations and hospitals, cultural programs, social service and youth agencies, and education, particulary higher education; support also for churches.
Types of support: General purposes, operating budgets.
Limitations: Giving limited to the Stillwater and St. Paul, MN, areas.
Application information:
Initial approach: Letter
Write: Jeffrey T. Peterson
Officers and Directors: Robert S. Davis, Pres.; Quentin O. Heimerman, V.P.; Gabrielle Hardenbergh, Secy.; Edgerton Bronson, Treas.; Raymond A. Reister.
Employer Identification Number: 416011826

1492
The St. Paul Companies, Inc. Corporate Contributions Program
385 Washington St.
St. Paul 55102 (612) 221-7757

Financial data (yr. ended 12/31/88): $3,422,193 for 157 grants (high: $321,000; low: $500).
Purpose and activities: Support for economic development, cultural growth, nonprofit management, and programs which aid families. A Leadership Initiatives in Neighborhoods program makes grants to individuals with a demonstrated commitment to neighborhood development in the St. Paul area, particularly in the fields of housing, health care, crime prevention, child care, education, jobs, and economic development.
Types of support: Annual campaigns, continuing support, employee matching gifts, matching funds, employee-related scholarships, technical assistance.
Limitations: Giving primarily in the Twin Cities region of MN; service centers and subsidiaries

give in their locations in AR, GA, IL, MO, NJ, and NY. No support for religious organizations for sectarian purposes, veterans' organizations, or political or lobbying groups, or advertising.
Publications: Application guidelines.
Application information: In reviewing grant requests from nonprofit organizations, the company looks for: a clear program description, quality delivery of a needed service, the organization's willingness to cooperate with others in the community, broad-based community support, effective evaluation method, sound fiscal policies, full financial disclosure, reasonable administrative overhead, qualified staff, programs in which those being served are actively involved in decision-making and volunteer activities, and programs which could have broader application to the community, region, or county.
Initial approach: Obtain grant application materials from Community Affairs Dept.
Deadline(s): Completed application must be submitted at least 2 months prior to meeting dates
Board meeting date(s): Feb. 26, Mar. 26, May 14, July 23, Sept. 24, Oct. 30 (leadership program), and Nov. 12.
Final notification: 3 weeks after meetings
Write: Polly Nyberg, Community Affairs Mgr.
Number of staff: 3 full-time professional; 2 full-time support.

1493
The Harold W. Sweatt Foundation
1500 Bracketts Point Rd.
Wayzata 55391 (612) 473-9200

Trust established in 1968 in MN as successor in part to The Sweatt Foundation established in 1951.
Donor(s): Harold W. Sweatt.†
Financial data (yr. ended 2/28/87): Assets, $2,123,299 (M); expenditures, $110,211, including $87,800 for 98 grants (high: $8,000; low: $10).
Purpose and activities: Emphasis on higher and secondary education, health and social services, religious organizations, and the arts.
Application information:
Deadline(s): None
Write: Karen McGlynn
Trustees: A. Lachlan Reed, Harold S. Reed, Martha S. Reed, William S. Reed.
Employer Identification Number: 416075860

1494
Target Stores Corporate Giving Program
33 South 6th Street
P.O. Box 1392
Minneapolis 55440 (612) 370-6098

Financial data (yr. ended 1/31/89): $3,899,630 for grants.
Purpose and activities: Support for Social Action: 40 percent of community giving funds are contributed to programs and projects that result in the economic and social progress of individuals, and/or the development of community and neighborhood strategies that respond effectively to critical community, social, and economic concerns. Arts: 40 percent of community giving funds are contributed to programs and projects that result in artistic excellence and stronger artistic leadership in communities, and/or increased access to and use of the arts as a means of community expression. Miscellaneous: 20 percent of community giving funds are contributed to programs and projects outside Social Action and the Arts that result in our responsiveness to special community needs and opportunities, and/or innovative partnerships with other community leaders. Special emphasis has been on strengthening family life and making the arts affordable and accessible; also gives through the Dayton Hudson Foundation.
Types of support: General purposes, special projects.
Limitations: Giving primarily in AZ, AR, CA, CO, IL, IN, IA, KS, KY, LA, MI, MN, MO, MT, NE, NV, ND, OH, OK, SD, TN, TK, WA, WI, WY. No support for religious organizations for religious purposes, or for fundraising dinners. No grants to individuals.
Application information:
Initial approach: Contact store manager at nearest store
Write: Susan K. Anderson, Mgr., Community Affairs

1495
Tennant Company Foundation
701 North Lilac Dr.
P.O. Box 1452
Minneapolis 55440 (612) 540-1207

Established in 1973 in MN.
Donor(s): Tennant Co.
Financial data (yr. ended 12/31/88): Assets, $29,259 (M); expenditures, $398,210, including $365,719 for 137 grants (high: $10,000; low: $500) and $17,211 for 128 employee matching gifts.
Purpose and activities: Giving for community funds, social service and youth agencies, higher education, and cultural programs including the arts and public broadcasting; limited support for conservation and health; employee-related scholarships paid through the Citizen's Scholarship Foundation of America.
Types of support: Employee-related scholarships, employee matching gifts, capital campaigns, operating budgets.
Limitations: Giving primarily in areas where Tennant Company employees live and work; support depends on the extent to which the applicant offers its services to Tennant Company communities. No support for agencies funded through umbrella organizations, or for religious organizations for religious purposes. No grants to individuals, or for travel, benefit tickets, or courtesy advertising.
Publications: Annual report (including application guidelines).
Application information:
Initial approach: Proposal or telephone
Copies of proposal: 1
Deadline(s): 4 weeks prior to board meetings
Board meeting date(s): Feb., May, Sept., and Dec.
Final notification: 4 weeks
Write: Donna Anderson, Admin., or Paul E. Brunelle, Pres.
Officers: Paul E. Brunelle, Pres.; Donna W. Anderson, Secy.; Joseph A. Shaw,* Treas.
Directors:* Chandlee M. Barksdale, Roger L. Hale, George T. Pennock.
Number of staff: 1 part-time professional; 1 part-time support.
Employer Identification Number: 237297045

1496
James R. Thorpe Foundation
8085 Wayzata Blvd.
Minneapolis 55426 (612) 545-1111

Incorporated in 1974 in MN.
Donor(s): James R. Thorpe.†
Financial data (yr. ended 11/30/88): Assets, $6,393,030 (M); expenditures, $339,176, including $323,700 for 84 grants (high: $18,000; low: $1,000; average: $3,000-$5,000).
Purpose and activities: Giving primarily for social service agencies, especially those addressing the needs of youth, the elderly, and the disadvantaged; arts and cultural programs, and higher and secondary education; support also for community health care and medical research, and religious organizations.
Types of support: Operating budgets, annual campaigns, seed money, building funds, equipment, scholarship funds, capital campaigns, general purposes, internships, research, special projects.
Limitations: Giving primarily in MN, with emphasis on Minneapolis and St. Paul. No grants to individuals, or for continuing support, emergency or endowment funds, deficit financing, land acquisition, matching gifts, publications, seminars, benefits, or conferences; no loans.
Publications: Biennial report.
Application information:
Initial approach: Letter outlining proposal
Copies of proposal: 1
Deadline(s): Mar. 1 and Sept. 1
Board meeting date(s): May and Nov.
Final notification: 1 week
Write: Mrs. Edith D. Thorpe, Pres.
Officers and Directors: Edith D. Thorpe, Pres.; Leonard M. Addington, V.P.; Samuel A. Cote, V.P.; Elizabeth A. Kelly, V.P.; Mary C. Boos, Secy.; Samuel S. Thorpe III, Treas.
Number of staff: 1
Employer Identification Number: 416175293

1497
Tozer Foundation, Inc.
c/o First Trust National Assoc.
First National Bank Bldg., P.O. Box 64704
St. Paul 55164 (612) 291-5134

Incorporated in 1946 in MN.
Donor(s): David Tozer.†
Financial data (yr. ended 10/31/88): Assets, $14,578,994 (M); expenditures, $841,916, including $222,180 for 38 grants (high: $35,000; low: $100; average: $1,000-$20,000) and $487,200 for 537 grants to individuals.
Purpose and activities: Giving primarily for scholarships to graduating high school students as well as undergraduate scholarships in various colleges; support also for educational projects,

cultural programs, community funds, and aid to the handicapped.
Types of support: Student aid, general purposes.
Limitations: Giving primarily in MN.
Publications: 990-PF.
Application information: Candidates must apply for scholarships through selected high schools.
Initial approach: Letter
Copies of proposal: 1
Deadline(s): None
Board meeting date(s): Monthly
Final notification: Immediately after board meeting
Write: Grant T. Waldref, Pres.
Officers and Directors: Grant T. Waldref, Pres.; Robert S. Davis, V.P.; Harry L. Holtz, James R. Oppenheimer, J. Thomas Simonet, Earl C. Swanson, John F. Thoreen.
Number of staff: None.
Employer Identification Number: 416011518

1498
Dewitt Van Evera Foundation
29710 Kipper Rd.
St. Joseph 56374 (612) 363-8388

Established in 1959 in UT.
Donor(s): Dewitt Van Evera,† Caroline Irene Van Evera.†
Financial data (yr. ended 12/31/88): Assets, $2,131,753 (M); expenditures, $96,000 for 7 grants (high: $30,000; low: $1,000).
Purpose and activities: Grants for higher and secondary education, and for projects to aid youth, the arts, and the disadvantaged. Almost all funding distributed on a continuing basis to ongoing projects which have been selected by the Foundation's advisors.
Types of support: Continuing support, general purposes, building funds, endowment funds, scholarship funds, lectureships, operating budgets.
Limitations: Giving primarily in MN, WI, and UT. No grants to individuals, or for matching gifts; no loans.
Application information:
Initial approach: Letter
Copies of proposal: 1
Deadline(s): Submit proposal preferably in Sept. through Dec.
Board meeting date(s): Feb.
Write: Laura Jane V.E. La Fond, Advisor
Advisors: Laura Jane V.E. La Fond, Robert W. Van Evera, William P. Van Evera.
Trustee: First Interstate Bank of Utah.
Number of staff: None.
Employer Identification Number: 876117907

1499
Louis F. and Florence H. Weyand 1977 Charitable Trust
First Trust National Assoc.
Two South, First Natl. Bank Bldg., P.O. Box 64704
St. Paul 55164-0704 (612) 291-5132

Established in 1977.
Donor(s): Louis F. Weyand,† Florence H. Weyand.
Financial data (yr. ended 9/30/87): Assets, $1,531,723 (M); expenditures, $133,272, including $121,804 for 30 grants (high: $40,000; low: $100; average: $1,000-$10,000).
Purpose and activities: Giving primarily for the arts; support also for education.
Limitations: Giving limited to MI, FL, and CA.
Application information:
Initial approach: Letter
Write: Jeffrey T. Peterson
Trustees: Lois Bachman, Carolyn Yorston, First Trust Co., Inc.
Employer Identification Number: 942473421

1500
F.K. and Vivian O'Gara Weyerhaeuser Foundation
2100 First National Bank Bldg.
St. Paul 55101 (612) 228-0935

Established in 1966 in MN.
Donor(s): F.K. Weyerhaeuser, Lynn Weyerhaeuser Day, Stanley R. Day.
Financial data (yr. ended 12/31/87): Assets, $1,759,308 (M); gifts received, $42,250; expenditures, $321,258, including $286,650 for 7 grants (high: $218,000; low: $1,000).
Purpose and activities: Giving primarily for cultural programs, higher and secondary education, and conservation.
Application information: Applications considered throughout the year.
Initial approach: Proposal
Deadline(s): None
Write: Vivian W. Piasecki, Pres.
Officers and Directors: Vivian Weyerhaeuser Piasecki, Pres.; Lynn Weyerhaeuser Day, V.P.; Frank N. Piasecki, Secy.; Stanley R. Day, Treas.
Employer Identification Number: 416054303

1501
The Frederick and Margaret L. Weyerhaeuser Foundation
2100 First National Bank Bldg.
St. Paul 55101 (612) 228-0935

Incorporated in 1963 in MN.
Donor(s): Margaret Weyerhaeuser Harmon.
Financial data (yr. ended 6/30/88): Assets, $1,925,304 (M); gifts received, $189,033; expenditures, $581,154, including $561,200 for 24 grants (high: $200,000; low: $500; average: $1,000-$5,000).
Purpose and activities: Giving primarily for a local college library building fund, a theological seminary, and religious welfare; support also for cultural programs and higher education.
Types of support: Annual campaigns, renovation projects, special projects, general purposes, capital campaigns.
Limitations: Giving primarily in MN. No grants to individuals.
Publications: 990-PF.
Application information:
Initial approach: Letter
Copies of proposal: 1
Deadline(s): None
Board meeting date(s): June
Final notification: 4 to 5 weeks
Write: Frederick T. Weyerhaeuser, Pres.
Officers and Directors:* Frederick T. Weyerhaeuser,* Pres.; Charles L. Weyerhaeuser, V.P.; Joseph S. Micallef,* Secy.; Gordon E. Hed,* Treas.
Number of staff: None.
Employer Identification Number: 416029036

1502
The Charles A. Weyerhaeuser Memorial Foundation
2100 First National Bank Bldg.
St. Paul 55101 (612) 228-0935

Incorporated in 1959 in MN.
Donor(s): Carl A. Weyerhaeuser trusts, Sarah-Maud W. Sivertsen Trusts.
Financial data (yr. ended 2/28/87): Assets, $3,527,488 (M); gifts received, $498,774; expenditures, $233,338, including $111,000 for 16 grants (high: $50,000; low: $500; average: $1,000-$5,000).
Purpose and activities: Grants primarily for art, music, higher education, and community funds.
Types of support: Annual campaigns, continuing support, special projects.
Limitations: Giving primarily in MN. No grants to individuals.
Publications: 990-PF.
Application information:
Initial approach: Letter
Copies of proposal: 1
Deadline(s): None
Board meeting date(s): As required
Final notification: 5 to 6 weeks
Write: Walter S. Rosenberry, III, Pres.
Officers and Directors: Walter S. Rosenberry III, Pres.; Robert J. Sivertsen, V.P.; Joseph S. Micallef, Secy.-Treas.; Elise R. Donohue, Richard E. Kyle, Lucy R. McCarthy.
Employer Identification Number: 416012063

MISSISSIPPI

1503
H. C. Bailey Company Foundation
P.O. Box 27704
Jackson 39225-2704
Application address: P.O. Box 1389, Jackson, MS 39225; Tel.: (601) 949-8106

Financial data (yr. ended 12/31/87): Assets, $355,174 (M); gifts received, $385,000; expenditures, $57,986, including $53,444 for 22 grants (high: $12,000; low: $250).
Purpose and activities: Support for higher education, religion, civic affairs, the arts, social services and youth.
Application information:
Initial approach: Proposal
Deadline(s): None
Write: Lauren Shields
Officers and Directors: Joan B. Bailey, Pres.; Carol A. Bailey, V.P.; William C. Bailey, Secy.; H.C. Bailey, Jr.
Employer Identification Number: 640754593

1504
Deposit Guaranty Foundation
One Deposit Guaranty Plaza
P.O. Box 1200
Jackson 39215-1200 (601) 354-8114

Incorporated in 1962 in MS.
Donor(s): Deposit Guaranty National Bank.
Financial data (yr. ended 1/31/88): Assets, $14,896 (M); gifts received, $255,000; expenditures, $366,191, including $351,406 for 72 grants (high: $111,352; low: $10) and $14,500 for employee matching gifts.
Purpose and activities: Emphasis on higher education and a community fund; support also for youth and social service agencies, hospitals, and the arts.
Types of support: Annual campaigns, capital campaigns, employee matching gifts, operating budgets, program-related investments, employee-related scholarships, scholarship funds.
Limitations: Giving limited to MS. No grants to individuals.
Application information:
Initial approach: Letter
Copies of proposal: 1
Board meeting date(s): Annually
Write: William M. Jones, Sr. V.P., Deposit Guaranty National Bank
Officers and Directors: E.B. Robinson, Jr., Pres.; Robert G. Barnett, Secy.; Arlen McDonald, Treas.; Howard L. McMillan, Jr.
Employer Identification Number: 646026793

1505
First Mississippi Corporation Foundation, Inc.
700 North St.
P.O. Box 1249
Jackson 39215-1249 (601) 948-7550

Incorporated in 1975 in MS.
Donor(s): First Mississippi Corp.
Financial data (yr. ended 6/30/88): Assets, $638,327 (L); gifts received, $125,004; expenditures, $258,820, including $204,572 for 45 grants (high: $20,000; low: $100; average: $5,000-$6,000), $15,800 for 26 grants to individuals and $37,471 for 64 employee matching gifts.
Purpose and activities: Emphasis on higher education, including scholarships limited to valedictorians of local high schools, and employee matching gifts, community funds, excellence awards to workers (chosen by peer committee) in experimental agriculture programs, and youth agencies.
Types of support: Operating budgets, continuing support, annual campaigns, emergency funds, building funds, equipment, land acquisition, endowment funds, matching funds, employee matching gifts, scholarship funds, special projects, research, student aid.
Limitations: Giving primarily in MS, in areas of company operations. No support for health or church-related programs. No grants for seed money, deficit financing, publications, or conferences; no loans.
Application information:
Initial approach: Letter
Copies of proposal: 1
Deadline(s): Submit education proposals preferably between Feb. and July and all others between Aug. and Jan.; deadline 1 month prior to board meetings
Board meeting date(s): Feb. and Aug.
Final notification: 2 weeks after meetings
Write: Bonnie H. Kelley, Admin. Asst.
Officers: J. Kelley Williams,* Chair. and C.E.O.; Charles R. Gibson,* V.P.; C.M. McAuley, V.P.; R. Michael Summerford, V.P.
Trustees:* R.P. Anderson, Paul A. Becker, James W. Crook, Robert P. Guyton, Charles P. Moreton, Paul W. Murrill, William A. Percy II, Maurice T. Reed, Jr., Frank G. Smith, Jr., Leland R. Speed, R.G. Turner.
Number of staff: None.
Employer Identification Number: 510152783

1506
McRae Foundation, Inc.
P.O. Box 20080
Jackson 39209

Established in 1965 in MS.
Donor(s): McRae's.
Financial data (yr. ended 1/31/88): Assets, $6,012,024 (M); gifts received, $400,000; expenditures, $343,316, including $181,062 for 70 grants (high: $43,475; low: $20).
Purpose and activities: Grants primarily for social services, religion, and education, especially higher education; some support for cultural programs.
Officers: Richard D. McRae, Sr.,* Pres.; Jim Glasscock, Secy.; Vaughan W. McRae,* Treas.
Directors:* D. Carl Black, Richard D. McRae, Jr.
Employer Identification Number: 646026795

1507
W. E. Walker Foundation
1675 Lakeland Dr.
Riverhill Tower, Suite 400
Jackson 39216 (601) 362-9895

Established in 1972 in MS.
Donor(s): W.E. Walker, Jr., W.E. Walker Stores, Inc.
Financial data (yr. ended 12/31/87): Assets, $11,053,952 (M); gifts received, $190,000; expenditures, $314,548, including $218,922 for 74 grants (high: $50,000; low: $15; average: $100-$20,000) and $20,000 for 8 grants to individuals.
Purpose and activities: Giving for independent schools, Protestant churches, higher education, and youth agencies; grants also for cultural programs, health, and welfare agencies, and scholarships to local residents attending graduate school, with a focus on theology and human service.
Types of support: General purposes, student aid.
Limitations: Giving primarily in MS.
Application information: Application form required for scholarships.
Deadline(s): None
Board meeting date(s): As needed
Write: W.E. Walker, Jr., Trustee
Trustees: Edmund L. Brunini, Baker Duncan, Justina W. McClean, Gloria M. Walker, W.E. Walker, Jr.
Number of staff: 1
Employer Identification Number: 237279902

MISSOURI

1508
Anheuser-Busch Charitable Trust
c/o Anheuser-Busch Companies, Inc.
One Busch Place
St. Louis 63118 (314) 577-7368

Trust established in 1951 in MO.
Donor(s): August A. Busch, Jr., Alice Busch,† Anheuser-Busch, Inc., August A. Busch & Co. of Massachusetts, Inc.
Financial data (yr. ended 9/30/88): Assets, $4,512,038 (M); expenditures, $3,625,538, including $3,602,167 for 52 grants (high: $721,000; low: $2,000).
Purpose and activities: Support for higher education, cultural programs, programs for minorities and youth, health organizations and hospitals, and environmental protection groups.
Types of support: Building funds, equipment, professorships, capital campaigns, renovation projects.
Limitations: Giving primarily in areas of company operations, with emphasis on the St. Louis, MO, area. No support for political, religious, social, fraternal, or athletic organizations, or for hospital operating budgets. No grants to individuals; no loans.
Publications: Application guidelines.
Application information: Application form required.
Initial approach: Proposal
Copies of proposal: 1
Deadline(s): None
Board meeting date(s): As required
Final notification: 6 to 8 weeks
Write: Cynthia M. Garrone, Contrib. Admin.
Board of Control: August A. Busch, Jr., August A. Busch III, Jerry E. Ritter.
Trustee: Centerre Trust Co. of St. Louis.
Number of staff: None.
Employer Identification Number: 436023453

1509
Anheuser-Busch Corporate Contributions Program
One Busch Place
St. Louis 63118-1852 (314) 577-2425

Purpose and activities: Support for social service agencies, arts and cultural groups, health care institutions, colleges and universities, youth groups, and United Way; additional support for scientific research into the causes, treatment, and prevention of alcoholism, and minority educational/training programs.

Limitations: Giving primarily in headquarters city and cities in which company has manufacturing facilities. No support for political, religious, social, fraternal, athletic, and non tax-exempt organizations. No grants to individuals, or hospital operating budgets.
Publications: Application guidelines.
Application information: Include: application form; current audited financial statement; current operating budget; annual report; board list; 501(c)(3); donors list. Application form required.
Initial approach: Letter and proposal
Deadline(s): None
Board meeting date(s): Every 6-8 weeks
Final notification: 6-8 weeks
Write: Nancy Calcaterra, Contribs. Admin.

1510
Anheuser-Busch Foundation
c/o Anheuser-Busch Companies, Inc.
One Busch Place
St. Louis 63118 (314) 577-7368

Established in 1975 in MO.
Donor(s): Anheuser-Busch, Inc.
Financial data (yr. ended 12/31/87): Assets, $44,903,583 (M); gifts received, $14,000,025; expenditures, $3,518,149, including $3,288,853 for 138 grants (high: $665,600; low: $150; average: $3,500-$30,000) and $43,240 for 295 employee matching gifts.
Purpose and activities: Giving primarily for United Way agencies and for higher education; support also for youth, community development, the arts, and health agencies.
Types of support: Building funds, capital campaigns, continuing support, employee matching gifts, matching funds.
Limitations: Giving primarily in areas of company operations. No support for political organizations, organizations whose activities are primarily religious in nature, social or fraternal groups, or athletic organizations. No grants to individuals, or for hospital operating budgets.
Publications: Application guidelines.
Application information: Application form required.
Initial approach: Letter
Copies of proposal: 1
Deadline(s): None
Board meeting date(s): Approximately every 2 months
Final notification: Following board meetings
Write: Cynthia M. Garrone, Contribs. Admin.
Trustees: August A. Busch III, John L. Hayward, Jerry E. Ritter.
Trustee Bank: Boatmen's National Bank of St. Louis.
Employer Identification Number: 510168084

1511
The Henry W. and Marion H. Bloch Foundation
4410 Main St.
Kansas City 64111 (816) 753-6900

Established in 1983 in MO.
Donor(s): Henry W. Bloch, Marion H. Bloch.
Financial data (yr. ended 12/31/87): Assets, $6,565,560 (M); gifts received, $1,885,625; expenditures, $221,457, including $170,632 for 38 grants (high: $75,000; low: $15).
Purpose and activities: Emphasis on ballet, art and music, and hospitals; some support also for temples and community funds.
Types of support: Building funds, capital campaigns, special projects.
Limitations: Giving limited to the 50-mile area around Kansas City, MO, including KS. No grants to individuals.
Application information: Contributes only to pre-selected organizations. Applications not accepted.
Write: Terrence R. Ward, Admin.
Officers and Directors: Henry W. Bloch, Pres. and Treas.; Marion H. Bloch, V.P. and Secy.; Robert L. Bloch, Thomas M. Bloch, Mary Jo Brown, Edward A. Smith, Elizabeth Bloch Uhlmann.
Number of staff: 2 full-time professional.
Employer Identification Number: 431329803

1512
The H & R Block Foundation
4410 Main St.
Kansas City 64111 (816) 932-8424

Incorporated in 1974 in MO.
Donor(s): H & R Block, Inc.
Financial data (yr. ended 12/31/87): Assets, $11,480,902 (M); gifts received, $2,077,383; expenditures, $715,389, including $515,170 for 145 grants (high: $40,000; low: $50), $66,000 for 33 grants to individuals and $16,875 for 42 employee matching gifts.
Purpose and activities: Giving primarily for education, arts and culture, United Way, youth, elderly, neighborhood development, health and mental health, civic endeavors; scholarships for children of company employees only.
Types of support: General purposes, building funds, equipment, land acquisition, matching funds, employee matching gifts, program-related investments, employee-related scholarships, operating budgets, continuing support, annual campaigns, seed money, emergency funds, capital campaigns, special projects.
Limitations: Giving limited to the 50-mile area around Kansas City, MO, including KS. No support for religious purposes, single-disease agencies, or historic preservation projects. No grants to individuals (except for scholarships to children of company employees), or for endowment funds, travel, telethons, research, demonstration projects, publications, or conferences; no loans.
Publications: Informational brochure (including application guidelines), annual report.
Application information:
Initial approach: 1-2 page letter
Copies of proposal: 1
Deadline(s): 45 days prior to meetings
Board meeting date(s): Mar., June, Sept., and Dec.
Final notification: 2 weeks after board meeting
Write: Terrence R. Ward, Pres.
Officers and Directors:* Henry W. Block,* Chair. and Treas.; Edward A. Smith,* Vice-Chair.; Terrence R. Ward, Pres.; Barbara Allmon, Secy.; Charles E. Curran,* Morton I. Sosland.*
Number of staff: 3 full-time professional; 2 full-time support.
Employer Identification Number: 237378232

1513
Boatmen's Bancshares Charitable Trust
P.O. Box 7365
St. Louis 63177 (314) 425-7711

Financial data (yr. ended 12/31/87): Assets, $1,545,329 (M); gifts received, $1,181,440; expenditures, $1,436,536, including $1,420,145 for 179 grants (high: $245,640; low: $260; average: $1,000-$20,000).
Purpose and activities: Giving primarily for the arts, including museums; support also for community organizations, social services, and higher education.
Limitations: Giving primarily in MO.
Application information:
Deadline(s): None
Board meeting date(s): Monthly
Final notification: N
Write: John L. Phillips, Jr.
Trustee: Boatmen's National Bank of St. Louis.
Number of staff: 1
Employer Identification Number: 431363004

1514
Boone County Community Trust
c/o Boone County National Bank
P.O. Box 678
Columbia 65205 (314) 874-8100
Additional tel.: (314) 449-4576

Established in 1976 in MO.
Donor(s): R.B. Price, Jr.,† Noma S. Brown,† Sam Waiton.
Financial data (yr. ended 5/31/88): Assets, $1,312,137 (M); expenditures, $126,136, including $114,212 for 16 grants (high: $53,826; low: $250).
Purpose and activities: Giving for education, social services, and cultural programs.
Types of support: Equipment, general purposes, seed money, emergency funds, building funds, land acquisition, professorships, internships, scholarship funds, exchange programs, fellowships, special projects, research, publications, conferences and seminars.
Limitations: Giving limited to Boone County, MO. No grants to individuals, or for operating budgets, continuing support, annual campaigns, deficit financing, endowment funds, or matching gifts; no loans.
Publications: Application guidelines, program policy statement.
Application information:
Initial approach: Telephone or letter
Copies of proposal: 1
Deadline(s): None
Board meeting date(s): As needed
Final notification: 6 weeks
Write: Jerry Epple, Trust Admin.
Trustee: Boone County National Bank.
Selection Committee: W.H. Bates, John Epple, Jr., David Knight, A.M. Price, Hazel Riback.
Number of staff: None.
Employer Identification Number: 436182354

1515
Guy I. Bromley Residuary Trust
c/o Boatmen's First National Bank of Kansas City
14 West 10th St.
Kansas City 64183 (816) 234-7481

Established in 1964 in MO.
Donor(s): Guy I. Bromley.
Financial data (yr. ended 12/31/88): Assets, $2,454,000 (M); gifts received, $463,130; expenditures, $136,280, including $131,800 for 11 grants (high: $40,000; low: $100; average: $5,000-$10,000).
Purpose and activities: Giving primarily for education, with emphasis on higher education; support also for social service and youth agencies, and cultural programs.
Types of support: Seed money, special projects.
Limitations: Giving primarily in the metropolitan Kansas City, MO, area and KS.
Application information:
Initial approach: Letter not exceeding 3 pages
Deadline(s): None
Final notification: 2 months
Write: David Ross, Sr. V.P., Boatmen's First National Bank of Kansas City
Trustee: Boatmen's First National Bank of Kansas City.
Employer Identification Number: 436157236

1516
Maurice L. & Virginia L. Brown Foundation
5049 Wornall, Apt. 7AB
Kansas City 64112

Established in 1980 in MO.
Financial data (yr. ended 9/30/87): Assets, $1,383,418 (M); expenditures, $108,780, including $89,857 for 73 grants (high: $40,000; low: $10).
Purpose and activities: Support primarily for a hospital and health agencies, and for cultural programs.
Limitations: No grants to individuals.
Application information: Contributes only to pre-selected organizations. Applications not accepted.
Trustees: Maurice L. Brown, Virginia L. Brown.
Employer Identification Number: 431213063

1517
Brown Group, Inc. Charitable Trust
8400 Maryland Ave.
Clayton 63166 (314) 854-4120

Trust established in 1951 in MO.
Donor(s): Brown Group, Inc.
Financial data (yr. ended 10/28/88): Assets, $6,180,337 (M); gifts received, $800,000; expenditures, $1,329,603, including $1,134,284 for 106 grants (high: $300,000; low: $50; average: $100-$20,000), $145,082 for 469 employee matching gifts and $402,219 for in-kind gifts.
Purpose and activities: Giving primarily for community funds, hospitals, higher education, the arts, and youth agencies.
Types of support: General purposes, operating budgets, continuing support, annual campaigns, emergency funds, building funds, equipment, land acquisition, employee matching gifts, scholarship funds, renovation projects.
Limitations: Giving limited to areas of company's major operations, with emphasis on St. Louis, MO. No grants to individuals, or for endowment funds, special projects, research, publications, or conferences; no loans.
Application information:
Initial approach: Proposal
Copies of proposal: 1
Deadline(s): None
Board meeting date(s): As needed
Final notification: 1 to 3 months
Write: Harry E. Rich, C.F.O., Brown Group, Inc.
Control Committee: David L. Bowman, Secy.; Richard Lee Anderson,* B.A. Bridgewater, Jr., W.L. Hadley Griffin, Ben Peck, Harry E. Rich,* Richard W. Shomaker.*
Trustees:* Centerre Trust Co. of St. Louis.
Number of staff: 2
Employer Identification Number: 237443082

1518
Centerre Trust Company Charitable Trust Fund
510 Locust St.
P.O. Box 14737
St. Louis 63178 (314) 436-9228

Established in 1948 in MO.
Financial data (yr. ended 12/31/87): Assets, $410,064 (M); expenditures, $122,758, including $121,025 for 19 grants (high: $20,000; low: $150).
Purpose and activities: Support for the arts and social services; also awards scholarships to individuals.
Types of support: Student aid.
Limitations: Giving primarily in the greater St. Louis, MO, area.
Application information:
Initial approach: Letter
Deadline(s): None
Write: Martin E. Galt III, Exec. V.P.
Agent and Trustees: Centerre Trust Co. of St. Louis, John H. Biggs, Donald C. Danforth, Jr., Eugene F. Williams, Jr.
Employer Identification Number: 436023132

1519
The Commerce Foundation
P.O. Box 13686
Kansas City 64199

Incorporated in 1952 in MO.
Donor(s): Commerce Bank of Kansas City.
Financial data (yr. ended 12/31/87): Assets, $4,355,087 (M); gifts received, $2,914,929; expenditures, $547,296, including $523,458 for grants.
Purpose and activities: Emphasis on community funds, the performing arts, higher education, music, youth agencies, and hospitals.
Types of support: Continuing support, annual campaigns, seed money, building funds, endowment funds, special projects, professorships, general purposes.
Limitations: Giving primarily in MO. No grants to individuals, or for operating budgets or matching gifts; no loans.
Application information:
Initial approach: Letter
Copies of proposal: 1
Deadline(s): None
Board meeting date(s): As required
Write: Warren W. Weaver, Pres.
Officers: Warren W. Weaver,* Pres.; Charles E. Templer, V.P. and Treas.; T. Alan Peschka,* Secy.
Directors:* David W. Kemper, James M. Kemper, Jr.
Number of staff: None.
Employer Identification Number: 446012453

1520
CPI Corporate Giving Program
1706 Washington Ave.
St. Louis 63103 (314) 231-1575

Financial data (yr. ended 02/06/89): Total giving, $635,810, including $265,840 for 151 grants (high: $20,000; low: $100), $25,000 for 83 grants to individuals, $20,000 for 210 employee matching gifts and $324,970 for 72 in-kind gifts.
Purpose and activities: Support for culture and the arts, including museums, theater, and libraries; Jewish welfare; social services, including programs involving senior citizens, the handicapped, the disadvantaged, child welfare, and hunger; health, including AIDS, pharmacies, and hospitals; and education, including higher education, educational building funds, and minority education.
Types of support: Employee-related scholarships, employee matching gifts.
Limitations: Giving primarily in the metropolitan St. Louis, MO, area.
Publications: Corporate report, application guidelines, program policy statement.
Application information:
Initial approach: Letter
Copies of proposal: 1
Deadline(s): None
Board meeting date(s): As needed
Write: Stephen Glickman, Chair.
Administrator: Stephen Glickman, Asst. to the Pres.
Number of staff: 1 full-time professional.

1521
CPI Corporation Philanthropic Trust
1706 Washington Ave.
St. Louis 63103 (314) 231-1575

Established in 1984 in MO.
Donor(s): CPI Corp.
Financial data (yr. ended 1/31/88): Assets, $323,311 (M); gifts received, $409,184; expenditures, $314,914, including $314,814 for 77 grants (high: $80,000; low: $150).
Purpose and activities: Support primarily for cultural programs, higher education, social services, and Jewish giving.
Limitations: Giving limited to areas of company operations.
Application information: Application form required.
Deadline(s): Oct. 15
Write: Steve Glickman
Trustees: Sander Coovert, Alyn Essman.
Employer Identification Number: 431334012

1522
The Cross Foundation, Inc.
106 East 31 Terrace, Rm. 206
Kansas City 64111 (816) 753-7119

Incorporated in 1955 in MO.
Donor(s): Annette Cross Murphy.
Financial data (yr. ended 12/31/86): Assets, $1,307,960 (M); expenditures, $201,359, including $165,800 for 9 grants (high: $150,000; low: $200).
Purpose and activities: Grants largely for medical research, and health-related programs, and youth, and the arts.
Types of support: Operating budgets, research, building funds, endowment funds.
Application information:
Initial approach: Proposal
Deadline(s): Applications are reviewed between Apr. 1 and Dec. 31 for approval for the following year
Write: Mrs. Martha O. Lever, Exec. Dir.
Officers: Annette Cross Murphy, Pres.; Lyman Field,* V.P. and Secy.; Martha O. Lever, Exec. Dir.
Directors:* Robert R. Cross, George E. Murphy, M.D., David Oliver, Gertrude F. Oliver.
Employer Identification Number: 440613382

1523
The Danforth Foundation
231 South Bemiston Ave., Suite 580
St. Louis 63105-1903 (314) 862-6200

Incorporated in 1927 in MO.
Donor(s): William H. Danforth,† Mrs. William H. Danforth.†
Financial data (yr. ended 5/31/88): Assets, $132,573,011 (M); expenditures, $13,296,849, including $11,596,719 for 115 grants (high: $7,000,072; low: $230; average: $10,000-$50,000) and $813,904 for 7 foundation-administered programs.
Purpose and activities: Dedicated to enhancing the humane dimensions of life through activities which emphasize the theme of improving the quality of teaching and learning. Serves precollegiate education through grantmaking and program activities, particularly those in support of administrators and legislators who are formulating public policy on elementary and secondary public education.
Types of support: Consulting services, technical assistance, special projects.
Limitations: No support for colleges and universities (except for projects in elementary and secondary education). No grants to individuals, or for building or endowment funds, or operating budgets; no loans.
Publications: Annual report, informational brochure (including application guidelines), financial statement, grants list.
Application information: Grant proposals for higher education not accepted; fellowship applications available only through participating universities.
Initial approach: Letter
Copies of proposal: 1
Deadline(s): None
Board meeting date(s): May and Nov., and as required
Final notification: 4 weeks
Write: Gene L. Schwilck, Pres.
Officers: Katharyn Nelson, Prog. Dir.; William H. Danforth,* Chair.; James R. Compton,* Vice-Chair. and Secy.; Gene L. Schwilck,* Pres.; Bruce J. Anderson, V.P.; Donn William Gresso, V.P.; Melvin C. Bahle, Treas.
Trustees:* Virginia S. Brown, George H. Capps, Donald C. Danforth, Jr., Charles Guggenheim, George E. Pake, P. Roy Vagelos.
Number of staff: 4 full-time professional; 1 part-time professional; 4 full-time support.
Employer Identification Number: 430653297
Recent arts and culture grants:
Institute for the Study of the Humanities, Ogden, UT, $35,000. For Wasatch Front International Education Consortium. 11/9/87.
Springboard to Learning, Saint Louis, MO, $34,000. For multi-ethnic education program. 5/2/88.

1524
Mr. & Mrs. Barney A. Ebsworth Foundation
7711 Bonhomme Ave.
St. Louis 63105

Established in 1986 in MO.
Financial data (yr. ended 12/31/87): Assets, $3,049,025 (M); gifts received, $42,732; expenditures, $17,433, including $15,800 for 1 grant.
Purpose and activities: Support primarily for an exhibition at an art museum.
Types of support: Special projects.
Application information: Contributes only to pre-selected organizations.
Deadline(s): None
Officers: Barney A. Ebsworth, Pres.; Patricia A. Ebsworth, V.P.; Daniel A. Puricelli, Secy.-Treas.
Employer Identification Number: 431397651

1525
Edison Brothers Stores Foundation
501 North Broadway
St. Louis 63102

Incorporated in 1956 in MO.
Donor(s): Members of the Edison family, Edison Brothers Stores, Inc., and its subsidiaries.
Financial data (yr. ended 5/31/88): Assets, $1,957,112 (M); expenditures, $425,963, including $423,470 for 26 grants (high: $140,000; low: $120).
Purpose and activities: Support for community and Jewish welfare funds, higher education, and cultural organizations.
Limitations: Giving primarily in St. Louis, MO. No grants to individuals.
Officers and Directors: Bernard Edison, Pres.; Eric P. Newman, V.P. and Secy.; Lee G. Weeks, V.P. and Treas.; Julian Edison, V.P.; Andrew E. Newman, V.P.
Employer Identification Number: 436047207

1526
Harry Edison Foundation
501 North Broadway
St. Louis 63102 (314) 331-6540

Incorporated in 1949 in IL.
Donor(s): Harry Edison.†
Financial data (yr. ended 12/31/87): Assets, $22,509,365 (M); expenditures, $1,289,515, including $927,500 for 87 grants (high: $300,000; low: $100; average: $100-$10,000).
Purpose and activities: Emphasis on higher education, Jewish welfare funds, children's services, social services, cultural programs, hospitals, and medical research.
Types of support: Professorships, building funds, annual campaigns.
Limitations: Giving primarily in St. Louis, MO. No grants to individuals.
Application information: Contributes only to pre-selected organizations. Applications not accepted.
Board meeting date(s): As required
Write: Eric P. Newman, Pres.
Officers and Directors: Eric P. Newman, Pres.; Bernard Edison, V.P. and Secy.; Henry Kohn.
Number of staff: None.
Employer Identification Number: 436027017

1527
Emerson Charitable Trust
c/o Emerson Electric Co.
8000 West Florissant, P.O. Box 4100
St. Louis 63136 (314) 553-2000

Established in 1944 in MO as Emerson Electric Manufacturing Company Charitable Trust; present name adopted in 1981.
Donor(s): Emerson Electric Co.
Financial data (yr. ended 9/30/88): Assets, $7,411,012 (M); gifts received, $5,500,000; expenditures, $6,588,359, including $6,188,765 for 1,741 grants (high: $600,000; low: $25; average: $100-$10,000) and $131,875 for 211 grants to individuals.
Purpose and activities: Grants for community funds, higher education, cultural programs, hospitals and health agencies, public policy organizations, and youth agencies.
Types of support: Employee matching gifts, employee-related scholarships.
Limitations: Giving primarily in areas of company operations. No grants to individuals.
Application information: Application form required.
Initial approach: Letter
Deadline(s): None
Board meeting date(s): Distribution committee meets 3 times a year
Write: R.W. Staley, Chair.
Officer: R.W. Staley, Chair. and Exec. V.P.
Trustee: Centerre Trust Co. of St. Louis.
Number of staff: None.
Employer Identification Number: 526200123

1528
Milton W. Feld Charitable Trust
1000 United Missouri Bank Bldg.
Kansas City 64106

Established in 1980 in MO.
Donor(s): Milton W. Feld.†
Financial data (yr. ended 8/31/87): Assets, $2,033,892 (M); expenditures, $449,301, including $356,410 for 36 grants (high: $81,200; low: $1,000; average: $1,000-$50,000).
Purpose and activities: Emphasis on hospitals, higher education, Jewish welfare organizations, cultural programs, and social service agencies.
Types of support: Special projects.
Limitations: Giving primarily in Kansas City and St. Louis, MO. No grants to individuals.
Application information: Contributes only to pre-selected organizations. Applications not accepted.
Board meeting date(s): As necessary
Write: Abraham E. Margolin, Trustee
Trustees: Selma S. Feld, Abraham E. Margolin, Irving Selber.
Number of staff: None.
Employer Identification Number: 431155236

1529
Louis and Elizabeth Flarsheim Charitable Foundation
c/o Boatmen's First National Bank of Kansas City
14 West Tenth St.
Kansas City 64183 (816) 234-7481
Application address: Boatmen's First National Bank of Kansas City, P.O. Box 419038, Kansas City, MO 64183

Donor(s): Louis Flarsheim, Elizabeth Flarsheim.
Financial data (yr. ended 11/30/88): Assets, $2,333,000 (M); expenditures, $163,439, including $159,933 for 8 grants (high: $50,000; low: $5,000; average: $5,000-$50,000).
Purpose and activities: Grants primarily for the performing and visual arts; support also for youth agencies and for volunteer and welfare organizations.
Types of support: Seed money, special projects.
Limitations: Giving primarily in the Kansas City, MO, area.
Application information:
Initial approach: Letter of no more than 3 pages
Deadline(s): None
Write: David P. Ross, Sr. V.P., Boatmen's First National Bank of Kansas City
Trustee: Boatmen's First National Bank of Kansas City.
Number of staff: 1 full-time professional.
Employer Identification Number: 436223957

1530
Edward Chase Garvey Memorial Foundation
c/o Commerce Bank of St. Louis, N.A.
8000 Forsyth Blvd.
Clayton 63105 (314) 726-2255

Trust established in 1970 in MO.
Donor(s): Edward C. Garvey.†
Financial data (yr. ended 9/30/87): Assets, $2,429,805 (M); gifts received, $111,000; expenditures, $125,435, including $111,000 for 16 grants (high: $15,000; low: $1,000).
Purpose and activities: Giving for higher and secondary education, music, the performing arts, and youth agencies.
Limitations: Giving primarily in MO. No grants to individuals.
Application information:
Initial approach: Proposal
Copies of proposal: 1
Deadline(s): None
Board meeting date(s): Annually, in the summer
Write: Michael C. Erb, V.P., Commerce Bank of St. Louis, N.A.
Trustees: Bliss Lewis Shands, Commerce Bank of St. Louis, N.A.
Employer Identification Number: 436132744

1531
The Catherine Manley Gaylord Foundation
314 North Broadway, Rm. 1230
St. Louis 63102 (314) 421-0181

Trust established about 1959 in MO.
Donor(s): Catherine M. Gaylord.†
Financial data (yr. ended 6/30/88): Assets, $4,424,790 (M); expenditures, $354,898, including $261,898 for 74 grants (high: $54,000; low: $100; average: $3,000).
Purpose and activities: Emphasis on private higher education, Protestant and Roman Catholic church support, youth and child welfare agencies, civic affairs, social services, and music and art.
Types of support: Operating budgets, continuing support, annual campaigns, seed money, emergency funds, deficit financing, building funds, equipment, endowment funds, matching funds, scholarship funds, special projects, publications, conferences and seminars.
Limitations: Giving primarily in the St. Louis, MO, metropolitan community. No grants to individuals; no loans.
Publications: Annual report, program policy statement, application guidelines.
Application information:
Initial approach: Letter
Copies of proposal: 1
Deadline(s): None
Board meeting date(s): Monthly
Final notification: 30 days
Write: Donald E. Fahey, Trustee
Trustees: Donald E. Fahey, Leigh Gerdine, Glen K. Robbins II.
Number of staff: 1 full-time professional; 1 part-time support.
Employer Identification Number: 436029174

1532
Clifford Willard Gaylord Foundation
c/o Boatmen's National Bank of St. Louis
P.O. Box 7365, Main Post Office
St. Louis 63166 (314) 425-7714

Trust established in 1948 in MO.
Donor(s): Clifford W. Gaylord.†
Financial data (yr. ended 12/31/87): Assets, $6,057,843 (M); expenditures, $502,115, including $451,250 for 76 grants (high: $65,000; low: $1,000).
Purpose and activities: Giving for higher education, hospitals, social service and youth agencies, child welfare, health agencies, and cultural programs.
Limitations: Giving primarily in St. Louis, MO. No grants to individuals.
Application information:
Deadline(s): None
Write: George H. Halpin, Jr.
Trustees: H. Sam Priest, Pres.; Frances M. Barnes III, Clair S. Cullinbine, Gaylord Fauntleroy, Robert G.H. Hoester, Barbara P. Lawton.
Agent for Trustees: Boatmen's National Bank of St. Louis.
Employer Identification Number: 436027517

1533
Graybar Foundation
c/o Graybar Electric Co., Inc.
34 North Meramec Ave.
Clayton 63105 (314) 727-3900

Established in 1984 in MO.
Donor(s): Graybar Electric Co., Inc.
Financial data (yr. ended 10/31/88): Assets, $518,715 (M); expenditures, $184,730, including $169,833 for 55 grants (high: $15,000; low: $100) and $14,897 for employee matching gifts.
Purpose and activities: Support for social sciences, culture and performing arts.
Types of support: Employee matching gifts, annual campaigns, general purposes, special projects.
Limitations: Giving primarily in MO and in other areas of company operations all over the US.
Application information: Applications not accepted.
Officers and Directors: J.L. Hoagland, Pres.; E.A. McGrath, Exec. V.P.; L.C. Owen, Jr., V.P. and Treas.; G.H. Booth, J.R. Seaton, G.S. Tulloch, Jr., J.F. van Pelt, D.H. Whittington.
Trustee: Mercantile Trust Co.
Employer Identification Number: 431301419

1534
Allen P. & Josephine B. Green Foundation
P.O. Box 523
Mexico 65265 (314) 581-5568

Trust established in 1941 in MO.
Donor(s): Allen P. Green,† Mrs. Allen P. Green.†
Financial data (yr. ended 12/31/87): Assets, $3,985,559 (M); expenditures, $579,522, including $471,748 for 44 grants (high: $35,000; low: $500).
Purpose and activities: Giving for health care and educational programs for children, and cultural and preservation projects; giving also for the aged, higher education, and the environment.
Types of support: Continuing support, seed money, emergency funds, building funds, equipment, endowment funds, scholarship

funds, special projects, research, publications, conferences and seminars, land acquisition, matching funds, capital campaigns, fellowships, renovation projects.
Limitations: Giving primarily in the Mexico, MO, area. No grants to individuals, or for operating budgets; no loans.
Publications: Annual report.
Application information:
Initial approach: Letter
Copies of proposal: 1
Deadline(s): Apr. 1 or Oct. 1
Board meeting date(s): May and Nov.
Final notification: 1 month
Write: Walter G. Staley, Secy.
Officers and Directors: Homer E. Sayad, Pres.; Walter G. Staley, Secy.-Treas.; Christopher S. Bond, Robert R. Collins, Susan Green Foote, Susan K. Green, Martha S. Marks, James F. McHenry, Walter G. Staley, Jr., George C. Willson III, Robert A. Wood.
Number of staff: 1 part-time support.
Employer Identification Number: 436030135
Recent arts and culture grants:
Audrain County Historical Society, Mexico, MO, $30,000. Toward restoration of museum dining room. 1987.
Center for American Archeology, Kampsville, IL, $5,500. Toward relocation of center and construction of building. 1987.
Missouri Botanical Garden, Saint Louis, MO, $30,000. Toward renovation of Climatron. 1987.
Missouri Mansion Preservation, Jefferson City, MO, $10,000. Toward library revitalization and Missouri history curriculum enrichment program. 1987.
Missouri Symphony Society, Columbia, MO, $7,500. For promotional materials and equipment. 1987.
Opera Theater of Saint Louis, Saint Louis, MO, $10,000. Toward outstate presentations and residency in Mexico, Missouri. 1987.
Ozark Public Telecommunications, Springfield, MO, $10,000. Toward Save The Vision Campaign. 1987.
Repertory Theater of Saint Louis, Saint Louis, MO, $20,000. For van for Imaginary Theater Company. 1987.
Saint Louis Art Museum, Saint Louis, MO, $15,000. Toward Small World II Project. 1987.
Saint Louis Mercantile Library Association, Saint Louis, MO, $15,000. Toward Globe-Democrat preservation project. 1987.
Saint Louis Zoological Park, Saint Louis, MO, $10,000. For expansion of Zoo's educational outreach program. 1987.
Saint Louis Zoological Park, Saint Louis, MO, $7,500. To purchase mini-van. 1987.
Webster University, Saint Louis, MO, $10,000. For support for radio broadcasting curriculum. 1987.

1535
Hall Family Foundations
Charitable & Crown Investment - 323
P.O. Box 419580
Kansas City 64141-6580 (816) 274-5879

Hallmark Educational Foundation incorporated in 1943 in MO; Hallmark Education Foundation of KS incorporated in 1954 in KS; combined funds known as Hallmark Educational Foundations.
Donor(s): Hallmark Cards, Inc., Joyce C. Hall,† E.A. Hall,† R.B. Hall.†
Financial data (yr. ended 12/31/87): Assets, $223,786,008 (M); expenditures, $12,392,804, including $6,810,299 for 62 grants (high: $2,000,000; low: $2,000; average: $10,000-$50,000), $288,564 for 152 grants to individuals and $2,000,000 for 1 loan.
Purpose and activities: Giving within four main areas of interest: 1) the performing and visual arts; 2) youth, especially education, including student aid for the children of Hallmark employees, and programs that promote social welfare, health and character building of young people; 3) economic development; and 4) the elderly.
Types of support: Operating budgets, seed money, emergency funds, building funds, equipment, special projects, matching funds, general purposes, employee-related scholarships, renovation projects.
Limitations: Giving limited to MO and KS, in the Kansas City area. No support for international or religious organizations or for political purposes. No grants to individuals (except for emergency aid to Hallmark Cards employees, and scholarships for their children only), or for endowment funds, travel, operating deficits, conferences, scholarly research, or fundraising campaigns such as telethons.
Publications: Annual report, informational brochure (including application guidelines).
Application information: Scholarships are for the children of Hallmark Cards employees only. Only eligible applicants should apply.
Initial approach: Letter
Copies of proposal: 1
Deadline(s): 4 weeks before board meetings
Board meeting date(s): Mar., June, Sept., and Dec.
Final notification: 4 to 6 weeks
Write: Margaret H. Pence, Dir.; Wendy Burcham or Peggy Collins, Prog. Officers
Officers: William A. Hall, Pres.; John A. McDonald, V.P. and Treas.; Eleanor Angelbeck, Secy.
Directors: Donald J. Hall, Chair.; Irvine O. Hockaday, Jr., David H. Hughes, Robert A. Kipp, John P. Mascotte, Margaret H. Pence, Morton I. Sosland.
Number of staff: 3 full-time professional; 1 part-time professional.
Employer Identification Number: 446006291
Recent arts and culture grants:
Choral Arts Ensemble, Kansas City, MO, $7,500. For staff support. 1987.
Friends of Chamber Music, Kansas City, MO, $30,000. For Richard Goode concert series. 1987.
Genesis School, Kansas City, MO, $61,250. For Writers' Project. 1987.
Kansas City Art Institute, Kansas City, MO, $2,000,000. To support purchase of U.M.K.C. Conservatory. 1987.
Kansas City Symphony, Kansas City, MO, $200,000. For special operating support. 1987.
National Arts Stabilization Fund, NYC, NY, $766,667. To help implement financial stabilization strategy for five Kansas City arts institutions. 1987.
Nelson-Atkins Museum of Art, Kansas City, MO, $603,329. For Rozzelle kitchen renovation. 1987.
Nelson-Atkins Museum of Art, Kansas City, MO, $121,000. For Oriental Art acquisition. 1987.
Starlight Theater, Kansas City, MO, $23,300. For special operating support. 1987.
Unicorn Theater, Kansas City, MO, $10,000. For special operating support. 1987.
University of Missouri, Department of Theater, Kansas City, MO, $155,818. To promote excellence. 1987.
William Jewell College, Liberty, MO, $12,925. To strengthen management and financial stability of Fine Arts program. 1987.

1536
Hallmark Cards Corporate Contributions Program
P.O. Box 580
Kansas City 64141-6580 (816) 274-8515
Application address for products: Charitable Contribs. Mgr. Product, 160, Kansas City, MO 64141-6580

Financial data (yr. ended 12/31/88): Total giving, $2,000,000, including $1,500,000 for grants, $300,000 for employee matching gifts and $200,000 for loans.
Purpose and activities: Hallmark's Corporate Contribution Program serves as a general purpose fund in support of a broad range of programs in areas such as education, social welfare, arts and humanities, health care, and civic affairs; in the majority of cases, Hallmark Cards participates with others in funding programs of community concern. Hallmark Cards also makes charitable donations of its products to qualifying agencies.
Types of support: In-kind gifts, annual campaigns, building funds, capital campaigns, continuing support, employee matching gifts, internships, program-related investments, technical assistance, equipment, general purposes, matching funds, operating budgets, seed money, special projects.
Limitations: Giving limited to headquarters city and major operating locations in CT, GA, IL, KS, MO, NC, TX, and UT. No support for religious, fraternal, international or veterans' organizations, atheletic, labor, or social clubs. No grants to individuals, or for United Way recipients, endowment funds, for past operating deficits, travel, conferences, scholarly research, charitable advertisements, mass-media campaigns, and non tax-exempt organizations.
Publications: Application guidelines.
Application information: If the request falls within an area of company interest and meets the guidelines, applicants may be asked to submit a project description including the program goals and objectives, background information on the agency or organization, budget, information on the staff administering the program, list of current board members, information on the criteria for evaluating the program's effectiveness, financial plan, 501(C)(3). Requests are initially reviewed by the Plant Contribution Committee in non-Kansas City locations or the corporate contribution staff at headquaters.

Initial approach: Letter describing the need, purpose, and general activities of the requesting organizations
Copies of proposal: 1
Deadline(s): None
Board meeting date(s): Periodic
Final notification: 4 to 6 weeks
Write: Jeanne M. Bates, Community Development Mgr.
Contributions Committee: Jeanne M. Bates, Community Development Mgr.; Walt Richards, Mgr., Charitable Contribs. (products).
Number of staff: 3 full-time professional; 1 full-time support.

1537
Hallmark Corporate Foundation
P.O. Box 419580, Dept. 323
Kansas City 64141-6580 (816) 274-8515

Established in 1983 in MO.
Donor(s): Hallmark Cards, Inc.
Financial data (yr. ended 12/31/87): Assets, $31,820,124 (M); gifts received, $33,000,000; expenditures, $1,607,764, including $1,505,174 for 228 grants (high: $200,000; low: $25) and $20,393 for employee matching gifts.
Purpose and activities: Support for a wide range of programs, including AIDS, employment, journalism, literacy, urban affairs, youth (including the problem of delinquency), and higher and pre-college education; also provides in-kind giving.
Types of support: In-kind gifts, annual campaigns, building funds, continuing support, employee matching gifts, equipment, internships, matching funds, program-related investments, seed money, technical assistance, special projects.
Limitations: Giving limited to Kansas City, MO, and cities where Hallmark facilities are located.
Publications: Application guidelines.
Application information:
Initial approach: Written proposal
Copies of proposal: 1
Deadline(s): None
Board meeting date(s): Periodic
Final notification: Within 6 weeks
Write: Jeanne Bates, Secy.
Officers: Donald J. Hall,* Chair.; William A. Hall, Pres.; Jeanne Bates, Secy.-Treas.
Directors:* Irvine O. Hockaday, Jr., David H. Hughs, Robert L. Stark.
Number of staff: 2 full-time professional; 1 full-time support.
Employer Identification Number: 431303258

1538
Interco, Inc. Charitable Trust
P.O. Box 387
St. Louis 63166 (314) 863-1100
Application address: Interco, Inc., 101 South Hanley Rd., Clayton, MO 63105

Trust established in 1944 in MO.
Donor(s): Interco, Inc., and subsidiaries.
Financial data (yr. ended 12/31/87): Assets, $21,672,844 (M); gifts received, $512,072; expenditures, $1,367,030, including $1,175,333 for 76 grants (high: $305,000; low: $300; average: $1,000-$10,000).
Purpose and activities: Emphasis on a community fund, higher education, and cultural programs; support also for hospitals, and social service and youth agencies.
Limitations: Giving primarily in St. Louis, MO.
Application information:
Deadline(s): None
Board meeting date(s): As required
Write: Robert T. Hensley, Jr., Trustee
Trustees: Robert T. Hensley, Jr., Mercantile Bank, N.A.
Number of staff: None.
Employer Identification Number: 436020530

1539
The Jackes Foundation
c/o Centerre Trust Co. of St. Louis
510 Locust St., P.O. Box 14737
St. Louis 63178 (314) 436-9228

Established in 1967 in MO.
Donor(s): Dorothy J. Miller,† Stanley F. Jackes, Margaret F. Jackes.
Financial data (yr. ended 12/31/87): Assets, $1,547,413 (M); expenditures, $169,273, including $151,500 for 51 grants (high: $44,650; low: $50).
Purpose and activities: Support for education, cultural programs, social services, religious giving, health associations, and hospitals.
Limitations: Giving primarily in the St. Louis, MO, area.
Application information:
Deadline(s): None
Write: Martin E. Galt III, Trustee
Trustees: Martin E. Galt III, Margaret F. Jackes, Stanley F. Jackes.
Employer Identification Number: 436074447

1540
Mary Ranken Jordan and Ettie A. Jordan Charitable Foundation
c/o Mercantile Bank, N.A.
P.O. Box 387
St. Louis 63166 (314) 231-7626

Trust established in 1957 in MO.
Donor(s): Mrs. Mary Ranken Jordan.†
Financial data (yr. ended 12/31/87): Assets, $14,242,095 (M); expenditures, $779,951, including $623,090 for 63 grants (high: $75,000; low: $1,000).
Purpose and activities: Giving limited to charitable and eleemosynary institutions with emphasis on higher education and cultural programs; grants also for social services, secondary education, and hospitals and health services.
Types of support: Building funds, operating budgets, special projects, continuing support.
Limitations: Giving limited to MO, with emphasis on St. Louis. No grants to individuals, or for endowment funds.
Publications: Application guidelines.
Application information:
Initial approach: Letter
Copies of proposal: 3
Deadline(s): None
Board meeting date(s): Jan.
Final notification: After Jan. 15
Write: Jill Fivecoat, Asst. V.P., Mercantile Bank, N.A.
Trustee: Mercantile Bank, N.A.
Number of staff: None.
Employer Identification Number: 436020554

1541
The Greater Kansas City Community Foundation and Its Affiliated Trusts
127 West 10th St., Suite 406
Kansas City 64105 (816) 842-0944

Established in 1978 in MO.
Financial data (yr. ended 1/31/88): Assets, $27,764,289 (M); gifts received, $6,667,146; expenditures, $5,754,849, including $5,331,261 for grants.
Purpose and activities: Giving primarily to improve the quality of life in the metropolitan area in the fields of culture, health, welfare, community action, and education; giving also for matching and challenge grants.
Types of support: Seed money, operating budgets, consulting services, technical assistance, matching funds, general purposes, lectureships.
Limitations: Giving primarily in five county greater Kansas City, MO, area. No grants to individuals, or for deficit financing, endowments, or capital campaigns.
Publications: Annual report, application guidelines, newsletter, informational brochure.
Application information:
Initial approach: Proposal or letter
Deadline(s): None
Board meeting date(s): Nov.
Final notification: 4 to 6 months
Write: Dalene D. Bradford, V.P., Program
Officers and Directors:* Marjorie P. Allen,* Chair.; James P. Sunderland,* Vice-Chair.; Janice C. Kreamer,* Pres.; George S. Bittner, V.P., Finance; Dalene D. Bradford, V.P., Program; Edward A. Smith,* Secy.; Charles A. Duboc,* Treas.; and 22 additional directors.
Number of staff: 3 full-time professional; 2 full-time support; 1 part-time support.
Employer Identification Number: 431152398
Recent arts and culture grants:
American Arts Festival Fund, Kansas City, MO, $15,000. For Kansas City American Arts Festival 1988. 1987.
Good Neighbor Program, Kansas City, MO, $14,000. For sewing co-op. 1987.
Kansas City Public Television, Kansas City, MO, $40,000. For Holiday Concert Program. Grant shared with Kansas City Symphony. 1987.
Lyric Opera of Kansas City, Kansas City, MO, $25,000. For telemarketing campaign. 1987.
Mid-America Arts Alliance, Kansas City, MO, $75,000. For regional and visual touring arts support. 1987.
Music/Arts Institute of Independence, Independence, MO, $6,500. For Michelangelo Project/scholarship program. 1987.
State Ballet of Missouri, Kansas City, MO, $30,000. For production of Napoli. 1987.
Young Audiences, Kansas City, MO, $7,500. For transition staffing assistance. 1987.

1542
R. C. Kemper Charitable Trust & Foundation
c/o United Missouri Bank of Kansas City
Tenth & Grand Ave.
Kansas City 64141

Trust established in 1953 in MO.
Donor(s): R. Crosby Kemper, Sr.†
Financial data (yr. ended 12/31/86): Assets, $11,432,761 (M); expenditures, $499,057, including $432,500 for 11 grants (high: $250,000; low: $250).
Purpose and activities: Emphasis on cultural activities, higher education, including scholarship funds, and youth agencies.
Limitations: Giving primarily in MO.
Application information: Contributes only to pre-selected organizations. Applications not accepted.
Trustees: Mary S. Kemper, R. Crosby Kemper, Jr., United Missouri Bank of Kansas City, N.A.
Employer Identification Number: 446010318

1543
Enid and Crosby Kemper Foundation
c/o United Missouri Bank of Kansas City
Tenth St. and Grand Ave., P.O. Box 226
Kansas City 64141 (816) 556-7722

Established in 1972 in MO.
Donor(s): Enid J. Kemper, R. Crosby Kemper, Sr.†
Financial data (yr. ended 12/31/86): Assets, $28,394,777 (M); expenditures, $4,050,965, including $3,850,833 for 60 grants (high: $1,589,500; low: $50; average: $500-$5,000).
Purpose and activities: Emphasis on secondary education and cultural programs, including museums and performing arts; some support also for health and higher education.
Types of support: General purposes.
Limitations: Giving primarily in KS and MO. No support for medical institutions. No grants for capital funds.
Application information: Grants only to pre-selected organizations. Applications not accepted.
Board meeting date(s): Quarterly and as needed
Write: Melanie Alm
Trustees: Malcolm M. Aslin, Mary S. Kemper, R. Crosby Kemper, Jr., Richard C. King, United Missouri Bank of Kansas City, N.A.
Employer Identification Number: 237279896

1544
The David Woods Kemper Memorial Foundation
1800 Commerce Bank Bldg.
P.O. Box 419248
Kansas City 64199 (816) 234-2346

Incorporated in 1946 in MO.
Donor(s): James M. Kemper, James M. Kemper, Jr.
Financial data (yr. ended 12/31/87): Assets, $4,478,986 (M); expenditures, $377,877, including $357,901 for 108 grants (high: $200,000; low: $25).
Purpose and activities: Support for cultural programs, higher and secondary education, population control, Protestant church support, youth agencies, and community funds.
Limitations: Giving primarily in Kansas City, MO.
Application information:
Deadline(s): None
Write: James M. Kemper, Jr., Pres.
Officers and Directors: James M. Kemper, Jr., Pres.; Laura Kemper Fields, V.P. and Treas.
Number of staff: None.
Employer Identification Number: 446012535

1545
Laclede Gas Charitable Trust
720 Olive St., Rm. 1525
St. Louis 63101 (314) 342-0506

Trust established in 1966 in MO.
Donor(s): Laclede Gas Co.
Financial data (yr. ended 9/30/88): Assets, $5,851,376 (M); gifts received, $25,000; expenditures, $603,614, including $553,099 for 127 grants (high: $188,125; low: $10) and $24,465 for 62 employee matching gifts.
Purpose and activities: Support of public charitable organizations with emphasis on community funds, higher and secondary education, the arts, hospitals, family services, public policy, and youth agencies.
Types of support: Annual campaigns, endowment funds, general purposes, matching funds, employee-related scholarships, employee matching gifts, operating budgets, scholarship funds, building funds, equipment, emergency funds, conferences and seminars, special projects.
Limitations: Giving primarily in areas of company operations. No support for religious or sectarian organizations, political organizations, or veterans' groups. No grants to individuals.
Publications: Informational brochure.
Application information:
Initial approach: Proposal
Copies of proposal: 1
Deadline(s): None
Board meeting date(s): Mar., June, Sept., and Dec.
Write: David L. Gardner, Trustee
Trustees: David L. Gardner, Lee M. Liberman, D.A. Novatny.
Number of staff: None.
Employer Identification Number: 436068197

1546
The Lantz Welch Charitable Foundation
1200 Main St., Suite 3500
Kansas City 64105
Application address: P.O. Box 26250, Kansas City, MO 64196

Established in 1985 in MO.
Donor(s): Lantz Welch.
Financial data (yr. ended 12/31/87): Assets, $1,228,442 (M); gifts received, $21,955; expenditures, $106,159, including $99,309 for 40 grants (high: $15,000; low: $50).
Purpose and activities: Support primarily for health assocations, cultural programs, and youth agencies.
Application information:
Initial approach: Proposal
Deadline(s): Apr. 1 and Oct. 1
Board meeting date(s): Twice a year
Write: Lantz Welch, Pres.
Officers and Directors: Lantz Welch, Pres. and Treas.; James Bartimus, V.P.; Laura Gault, Secy.
Employer Identification Number: 431388861

1547
George A. and Dolly F. LaRue Trust
c/o Commerce Bank of Kansas City
P.O. Box 248
Kansas City 64141 (816) 234-2568
Application address: Kansas City Assn. of Trusts and Foundations, Board of Trade Bldg., Kansas City, MO 64105

Trust established in 1973 in MO.
Donor(s): George A. LaRue,† Dolly F. LaRue.†
Financial data (yr. ended 12/31/86): Assets, $2,402,771 (M); expenditures, $137,398, including $122,373 for 6 grants (high: $30,000; low: $2,000).
Purpose and activities: Grants for cultural organizations, education, social services, and conservation.
Limitations: Giving primarily in MO, with emphasis on Kansas City.
Trustee: Commerce Bank of Kansas City.
Number of staff: None.
Employer Identification Number: 436122865

1548
Lincoln Engineering Company Charitable Trust
One Lincoln Way
St. Louis 63120

Financial data (yr. ended 12/31/87): Assets, $55,650 (M); gifts received, $38,000; expenditures, $60,787, including $59,587 for 18 grants (high: $24,200; low: $100).
Purpose and activities: Support for community funds, youth, social services, education, the arts, and health services.
Limitations: Giving primarily in MO.
Application information:
Initial approach: Letter
Deadline(s): None
Write: Thomas L. Glover
Trustee: Centerre Trust Co. of St. Louis.
Board Members: Thomas L. Glover, James Lane, Jr., Kenneth P. Lockwood.
Employer Identification Number: 436023506

1549
Carrie J. Loose Trust
406 Board of Trade Bldg.
Tenth and Wyandotte Sts.
Kansas City 64105 (816) 842-0944

Trust established in 1927 in MO.
Donor(s): Harry Wilson Loose,† Carrie J. Loose.†
Financial data (yr. ended 12/31/87): Assets, $7,227,405 (M); expenditures, $528,725, including $414,500 for 22 grants (high: $50,000; low: $10,000).
Purpose and activities: Grants to established local educational, health, and welfare institutions; support for research into the

community's social and cultural needs and for experimental and demonstration projects. A member trust of the Kansas City Association of Trusts and Foundations.
Types of support: Research, special projects.
Limitations: Giving limited to Kansas City, MO. No grants to individuals, or for building funds, matching gifts, endowment funds, general support, scholarships, or fellowships; no loans.
Publications: Annual report, program policy statement, application guidelines.
Application information:
Initial approach: Letter or proposal
Copies of proposal: 1
Deadline(s): 6 weeks prior to board meetings
Board meeting date(s): Feb., May, Sept., and Dec.
Write: Janice C. Kreamer, Admin. Officer
Officer: Janice C. Kreamer, Admin. Officer.
Trustees: Taylor S. Abernathy, Boatmen's First National Bank of Kansas City.
Number of staff: 3 full-time professional; 2 full-time support; 1 part-time support.
Employer Identification Number: 446009246

1550
Harry Wilson Loose Trust
406 Board of Trade Bldg.
Tenth and Wyandotte Sts.
Kansas City 64105 (816) 842-0944

Trust established in 1927 in MO.
Donor(s): Harry Wilson Loose.†
Financial data (yr. ended 12/31/87): Assets, $2,937,646 (M); expenditures, $146,695, including $108,675 for 6 grants (high: $25,000; low: $1,175).
Purpose and activities: Emphasis on civic and community development in Kansas City, including grants for the arts and cultural programs. A member trust of the Kansas City Association of Trusts and Foundations.
Types of support: Research, special projects, conferences and seminars, professorships, internships, exchange programs.
Limitations: Giving primarily in Kansas City, MO. No grants to individuals, or for endowment funds, general support, building funds, matching gifts, scholarships, or fellowships; no loans.
Publications: Annual report, application guidelines, program policy statement.
Application information:
Initial approach: Letter or proposal
Copies of proposal: 1
Deadline(s): 3 months prior to full board meetings
Board meeting date(s): Feb., May, Sept., and Dec.
Final notification: Within 2 weeks of the full board meeting
Write: Dalene Bradford, V.P. or Terry Henrichs, Secy., Kansas City Assn. of Trusts and Fdns.
Trustees: Donald H. Chisholm, Robert T.H. Davidson, Boatmen's First National Bank of Kansas City.
Number of staff: 3 full-time professional; 2 full-time support; 1 part-time support.
Employer Identification Number: 446009245

1551
John Allan Love Charitable Foundation
c/o Edgar G. Buedecker, Ziercher & Hocker
130 South Bemiston, 4th Fl.
St. Louis 63105 (314) 863-6900

Established in 1966 in MO.
Donor(s): John Allan Love Trusts.
Financial data (yr. ended 12/31/86): Assets, $2,245,177 (M); expenditures, $117,941, including $95,300 for 25 grants (high: $15,000; low: $100).
Purpose and activities: Grants for medical research concerning the handicapped, cultural programs, education, community funds, and the promotion of good citizenship.
Limitations: Giving primarily in MO.
Officers: Rumsey Ewing, Pres.; William W. Boyd, V.P.; James G. Forsyth, Treas.
Directors: John McKinney, C. Venable Minor, W. Anderson Payne.
Employer Identification Number: 436066121

1552
The Mathews Foundation
c/o Boatmen's First National Bank
P.O. Box 419038
Kansas City 64183
Application addresses: M. Mathews Jenks, Trustee, P.O. Box 19769, Brentwood, MO 63144; Harry B. Mathews III, Trustee, c/o John D. Schaperkotter, Bryan, Cave, McPheeters, & McRoberts, 500 North Broadway, Suite 2000, St. Louis, MO 63102

Trust established in 1959 in IL.
Donor(s): Harry B. Mathews, Jr. Trust.
Financial data (yr. ended 11/30/87): Assets, $1,425,793 (M); expenditures, $74,825, including $62,000 for 6 grants (high: $15,000; low: $5,000).
Purpose and activities: Giving for Protestant church support, including church-related higher and secondary education; support also for cultural programs, including historic preservation, and for hospitals, the handicapped and social service agencies.
Types of support: Building funds, endowment funds, operating budgets, renovation projects, scholarship funds.
Limitations: Giving primarily in MO and AZ.
Publications: 990-PF.
Application information:
Initial approach: Proposal
Deadline(s): None
Trustees: M. Mathews Jenks, Harry B. Mathews III, Robert J. Wharton.
Employer Identification Number: 376040862

1553
The Morton J. May Foundation
c/o Frank J. Reilly
611 Olive St., Suite 2074
St. Louis 63101 (314) 342-8405

Trust established in 1959 in MO.
Donor(s): Morton J. May.†
Financial data (yr. ended 3/31/87): Assets, $7,609,751 (M); expenditures, $775,916, including $671,300 for 54 grants (high: $180,000; low: $150).
Purpose and activities: Emphasis on Jewish welfare funds, music and art, higher education, a community fund, hospitals, and social service agencies.
Limitations: Giving primarily in St. Louis, MO.
Application information:
Initial approach: Letter
Deadline(s): None
Write: Betty McNichols, Trustee
Trustees: Betty McNichols, Frank J. Reilly, Sarah Jane May Waldheim.
Employer Identification Number: 436027519

1554
The May Stores Foundation, Inc.
Sixth and Olive Sts.
St. Louis 63101

Incorporated in 1945 in NY.
Donor(s): May Department Stores Co.
Financial data (yr. ended 12/31/87): Assets, $22,271,987 (M); gifts received, $2,825,000; expenditures, $8,023,783, including $7,837,509 for grants.
Purpose and activities: Grants to charitable and educational institutions throughout the country, with emphasis on community funds in areas of company operations; support also for cultural programs, hospitals and health care, and civic affairs.
Limitations: Giving primarily in areas of company operations.
Application information: Contributes only to preselected organizations. Applications not accepted.
Officers and Directors: Jerome T. Loeb, Pres.; Jan R. Kniffen, V.P. and Secy.-Treas.; David C. Farrell, V.P.; Thomas A. Hays, V.P.; Robert F. Cerulli.
Number of staff: None.
Employer Identification Number: 436028949

1555
McDonnell Douglas Foundation
c/o McDonnell Douglas Corp.
P.O. Box 516, Mail Code 1001440
St. Louis 63166 (314) 232-8464

Incorporated in 1977 as successor to McDonnell Aerospace Foundation, a trust established in 1963 in MO.
Donor(s): McDonnell Douglas Corp.
Financial data (yr. ended 12/31/87): Assets, $54,198,853 (M); expenditures, $7,516,090, including $6,790,895 for 288 grants (high: $1,000,000; low: $25; average: $5,000-$10,000) and $637,690 for 3,401 employee matching gifts.
Purpose and activities: Emphasis on higher education and community funds; support also for aerospace and aviation organizations, social service and youth agencies, and public, civic, and cultural affairs.
Types of support: General purposes, special projects, employee matching gifts, annual campaigns, building funds, capital campaigns, operating budgets, employee-related scholarships.
Limitations: Giving primarily in AZ, CA, FL, MO, OK, and TX.
Application information:
Deadline(s): None

Board meeting date(s): Monthly
Write: Walter E. Diggs, Jr., Pres.
Officers: John F. McDonnell, Chair.; Walter E. Diggs, Jr., Pres.; Gerald A. Johnston,* V.P.; E.F. Doering, Jr., Secy.-Treas.
Directors:* R.L. Harmon, James S. McDonnell III.
Number of staff: None.
Employer Identification Number: 431128093
Recent arts and culture grants:
Air Force Armament Museum Foundation, Valparaiso, FL, $5,000. For general support. 1987.
Air Force Museum Foundation, Wright-Patterson A.F.B., OH, $60,000. For general support. 1987.
Aray Aviation Museum Foundation, Fort Rucker, AL, $15,000. For capital campaign. 1987.
Arts and Education Council of Greater Saint Louis, Saint Louis, MO, $73,000. For general support. 1987.
Association for Community Television, Houston, TX, $6,790. For general support. 1987.
California Museum Foundation, Los Angeles, CA, $12,500. To support aerospace component. 1987.
Craft and Folk Art Museum Incorporating the Egg and the Eye, Los Angeles, CA, $5,000. To support Saudi Arabia Exhibit. 1987.
K C E T Community Television of Southern California, Los Angeles, CA, $12,500. For general support. 1987.
Los Angeles County Museum of Art, Los Angeles, CA, $10,000. For general support. 1987.
Los Angeles County Museum of Natural History Foundation, Los Angeles, CA, $5,000. For general support. 1987.
Missouri Botanical Garden, Saint Louis, MO, $120,000. For capital campaign. 1987.
Missouri Historical Society, Saint Louis, MO, $38,000. For general support. 1987.
Municipal Theater Association of Saint Louis, Saint Louis, MO, $25,000. To sponsor production of Sound of Music. 1987.
Naval Aviation Museum Foundation, Pensacola, FL, $100,000. To sponsor Blue Angels exhibit. 1987.
Naval Aviation Museum Foundation, Pensacola, FL, $50,000. For capital campaign. 1987.
Pacific Symphony Association, Santa Ana, CA, $5,000. For general support. 1987.
Performing Arts Council of the Music Center, Los Angeles, CA, $25,000. For general support. 1987.
Saint Louis Art Museum, Saint Louis, MO, $200,000. For capital for West Wing project. 1987.
Saint Louis Regional Educational and Public Television Commission, Saint Louis, MO, $30,000. For general support. 1987.
Saint Louis Symphony Society, Saint Louis, MO, $100,000. For endowment drive and operating expenses. 1987.
Saint Louis Zoo, Great Education Center, Saint Louis, MO, $25,000. For general support. 1987.
Smithsonian Institution, ANA Fund, DC, $5,000. To renovate Sea-Air Gallery. 1987.
Statue of Liberty-Ellis Island Foundation, NYC, NY, $60,000. For capital campaign. 1987.

1556
James S. McDonnell Foundation
1034 South Brentwood Blvd., Suite 1610
St. Louis 63117 (314) 721-1532

Incorporated in 1950 in MO.
Donor(s): James S. McDonnell,† James S. McDonnell III, John F. McDonnell.
Financial data (yr. ended 12/31/88): Assets, $115,000,000 (M); expenditures, $12,300,000, including $11,970,199 for 49 grants (high: $2,000,000; low: $1,000).
Purpose and activities: Giving for biomedical research, research and innovation in education, and research on issues related to global understanding; support also for cultural and educational activities in the St. Louis metropolitan area.
Types of support: Special projects, research, conferences and seminars.
Limitations: Giving limited to the St. Louis, MO, area for cultural programs. No grants to individuals, or generally for endowment funds, capital campaigns, building funds, renovations, scholarships, or general purposes.
Publications: Informational brochure (including application guidelines), annual report.
Application information:
Initial approach: Letter
Deadline(s): None
Board meeting date(s): As needed
Final notification: Varies
Write: John T. Bruer, Pres.
Officers: John T. Bruer, Pres.; James S. McDonnell III,* V.P. and Secy.; John F. McDonnell,* Treas.
Directors:* Michael Witunski.
Number of staff: 1 full-time professional; 1 full-time support.
Employer Identification Number: 436030988
Recent arts and culture grants:
First Street Forum, Saint Louis, MO, $20,000. For unrestricted support for programs in the arts. 1987.
Greater Washington Educational Telecommunications Association, DC, $1,140,000. For Smithsonian World Program. 1987.
Municipal Theater Association of Saint Louis, Saint Louis, MO, $25,000. To sponsor Gentlemen Prefer Blondes. 1987.
Saint Louis Science Center, Saint Louis, MO, $100,000. For Phase III of Center's planning effort. 1987.

1557
Sanford N. McDonnell Foundation, Inc.
1034 South Brentwood, Suite 1620
St. Louis 63117

Established in 1977 in MO.
Financial data (yr. ended 12/31/87): Assets, $1,260,489 (M); gifts received, $405,563; expenditures, $115,457, including $109,710 for 54 grants (high: $25,100; low: $30).
Purpose and activities: Support for cultural organizations, education, and Christian organizations and churches.
Application information: Contributes only to pre-selected organizations. Applications not accepted.
Officers and Directors: Sanford N. McDonnell, Pres.; Priscilla R. McDonnell, V.P.; William R. McDonnell, Secy.-Treas.
Employer Identification Number: 431104889

1558
Mercantile Trust Company Charitable Trust
c/o Mercantile Bank, N.A.
P.O. Box 387
St. Louis 63166 (314) 425-2672

Trust established in 1952 in MO.
Donor(s): Mercantile Trust Co.
Financial data (yr. ended 2/28/87): Assets, $3,527,293 (M); expenditures, $486,067, including $477,067 for 45 grants (high: $80,000; low: $500; average: $1,000-$7,000).
Purpose and activities: Emphasis on higher education, hospitals, and cultural programs; support also for youth agencies, and community development.
Limitations: Giving primarily in MO.
Application information:
Initial approach: Letter
Copies of proposal: 1
Deadline(s): None
Write: H. Jill Fivecoat
Trustees: Neal J. Farrell, Donald E. Lasater, Mercantile Bank, N.A.
Employer Identification Number: 436020630

1559
Miller-Mellor Association
708 East 47th St.
Kansas City 64110 (816) 561-4307

Established in 1950 in MO.
Financial data (yr. ended 6/30/87): Assets, $1,725,319 (M); expenditures, $89,551, including $85,093 for 59 grants (high: $9,500; low: $50).
Purpose and activities: Grants for Catholic church support, higher education, cultural programs, and health services.
Limitations: Giving primarily in Kansas City, MO.
Application information:
Initial approach: Letter or proposal
Deadline(s): None
Write: James L. Miller, Secy.-Treas.
Officers: Jozach Miller IV, Pres.; Helena Miller Norquist, V.P.; James Ludlow Miller, Secy.-Treas.
Employer Identification Number: 446011906

1560
Monsanto Fund
800 North Lindbergh Blvd.
St. Louis 63167 (314) 694-4596

Incorporated in 1964 in MO as successor to Monsanto Charitable Trust.
Donor(s): Monsanto Co.
Financial data (yr. ended 12/31/88): Assets, $3,087,287 (M); expenditures, $9,356,571, including $8,285,748 for grants (high: $1,112,000; low: $100; average: $100-$5,000) and $1,019,417 for employee matching gifts.
Purpose and activities: Giving primarily for higher education, specifically science and

math, and community funds; support also for hospitals and health services, cultural programs and the arts, social services, and youth.
Types of support: General purposes, building funds, equipment, operating budgets, annual campaigns, seed money, fellowships, special projects, employee matching gifts, continuing support.
Limitations: Giving primarily in areas of company operations in AL, CA, FL, GA, ID, IL, MA, MI, MO, NJ, NC, OH, SC, TX, and WV, with emphasis on St. Louis, MO. No support for religious institutions. No grants to individuals, or for endowment funds.
Application information:
Initial approach: Proposal
Copies of proposal: 1
Deadline(s): None
Board meeting date(s): 4 to 6 times a year
Final notification: 2 to 4 months
Write: John L. Mason, Pres.
Officers: John L. Mason, Pres.; Richard W. Duesenberg,* V.P.; Juanita H. Hinshaw, Treas.
Directors:* Francis A. Stroble, Chair.; Peter Clarke, Norma J. Curby, Robert E. Flynn, Robert J. Mason, Daniel J. Mickelson, Michael E. Miller, Fred L. Thompson.
Number of staff: 2 full-time professional; 2 full-time support.
Employer Identification Number: 436044736

1561
Nichols Company Charitable Trust
310 Ward Pkwy.
Kansas City 64112

Trust established in 1952 in MO.
Donor(s): J.C. Nichols Co., members of the Nichols family.
Financial data (yr. ended 12/31/86): Assets, $767,728 (M); gifts received, $200,500; expenditures, $168,452, including $167,345 for 60 grants (high: $25,000; low: $100).
Purpose and activities: Emphasis on the performing arts and higher and secondary education; grants also for a community fund, youth agencies, and hospitals.
Types of support: Annual campaigns, building funds, capital campaigns, continuing support, endowment funds, general purposes, special projects.
Limitations: Giving primarily in MO.
Publications: Annual report.
Application information: Applications not accepted.
Trustees: Lee Fowler, Lynn L. McCarthy, Miller Nichols.
Employer Identification Number: 446015538

1562
Miller Nichols Foundation
310 Ward Pkwy.
Kansas City 64112

Established in 1960.
Donor(s): Miller Nichols.
Financial data (yr. ended 12/31/86): Assets, $1,878,460 (M); expenditures, $115,794, including $112,947 for 53 grants (high: $38,000; low: $10).
Purpose and activities: Emphasis on civic and cultural organizations and education.
Limitations: Giving primarily in Kansas City, MO.
Application information: Applications not accepted.
Trustees: Kay Nichols Callison, Walter C. Janes, Jeannette Nichols, Miller Nichols.
Employer Identification Number: 446015540

1563
John M. Olin Charitable Trust
c/o Centerre Trust Co. of St. Louis
P.O. 14737
St. Louis 63178 (314) 436-9263

Trust established in 1945 in MO.
Donor(s): John M. Olin.†
Financial data (yr. ended 12/31/87): Assets, $1,621,548 (M); expenditures, $126,364, including $115,000 for 13 grants (high: $20,000; low: $5,000).
Purpose and activities: Grants primarily for medical research, hospitals, museums, cultural programs, and youth agencies.
Limitations: No grants to individuals, or for building funds, endowment funds, or special projects.
Application information:
Initial approach: Letter
Deadline(s): None
Write: Robert Brummet, V.P., Centerre Trust Co.
Trustees: Constance B. Josse, Centerre Trust Co. of St. Louis.
Employer Identification Number: 436022769

1564
Spencer T. and Ann W. Olin Foundation
925 Pierre Laclede Bldg.
7701 Forsyth Blvd.
St. Louis 63105 (314) 727-6202

Incorporated in 1957 in DE.
Donor(s): Spencer T. Olin, Ann W. Olin.†
Financial data (yr. ended 12/31/87): Assets, $33,690,873 (M); gifts received, $698,510; expenditures, $9,531,544, including $9,531,544 for 31 grants (high: $3,000,000; low: $750; average: $1,000-$100,000).
Purpose and activities: Giving primarily for higher education, medical education, research, and health services; support also for community, cultural, and social service agencies.
Types of support: Annual campaigns, research, general purposes.
Limitations: Giving primarily in the St. Louis, MO, area. No support for national health or welfare organizations, religious groups, or generally for secondary education, or projects which are substantially financed by public tax funds. No grants to individuals, or for building or endowment funds, deficit financing, operating budgets, conferences, travel, exhibits, scholarships, fellowships, or matching gifts; no loans.
Publications: Annual report (including application guidelines).
Application information:
Initial approach: Letter
Copies of proposal: 1
Deadline(s): None
Board meeting date(s): Usually in Apr.
Final notification: 2 weeks
Write: Rolla J. Mottaz, Pres.
Trustees: Rolla J. Mottaz, Pres.; J. Lester Willemetz, Treas.; Eunice Olin Higgins, Mary Olin Pritzlaff, Barbara Olin Taylor.
Number of staff: 2 part-time professional; 1 part-time support.
Employer Identification Number: 376044148
Recent arts and culture grants:
Arts and Education Fund of Greater Saint Louis, Saint Louis, MO, $25,000. 1987.
Missouri Botanical Garden, Saint Louis, MO, $40,000. 1987.
Saint Louis Art Museum, Saint Louis, MO, $50,000. 1987.
Saint Louis Symphony Society, Saint Louis, MO, $25,000. 1987.

1565
Oppenstein Brothers Foundation
c/o Christopher G. Blair
P.O. Box 419248
Kansas City 64141-6248 (816) 753-6955

Trust established in 1975 in MO.
Donor(s): Michael Oppenstein.†
Financial data (yr. ended 3/31/88): Assets, $15,429,211 (M); expenditures, $915,687, including $711,627 for 77 grants (high: $100,000; low: $1,000; average: $2,500-$10,000).
Purpose and activities: Grants primarily for social services, education, and health care programs, emphasizing the prevention of illness and abuse, and programs which enhance the ability of individuals to remain or become self-sufficient; some support for community development and arts education.
Types of support: Operating budgets, general purposes, seed money, emergency funds, equipment, special projects, matching funds, renovation projects, consulting services, lectureships.
Limitations: Giving primarily in the Kansas City, MO, metropolitan area. No support for medical research. No grants to individuals, or for annual campaigns, building funds, scholarships, fellowships, technology, equipment, building expansion, or generally for endowment funds; limited operating funds for United Way or Jewish Federation supported agencies; no loans.
Publications: Multi-year report, informational brochure (including application guidelines).
Application information:
Initial approach: Telephone or letter
Copies of proposal: 2
Deadline(s): Submit proposal with complete information 2 weeks preceding board meetings; no set deadline
Board meeting date(s): Usually in Feb., Apr., June, Aug., Oct., and Dec.
Final notification: 2 to 4 months
Write: Karen M. Herman, Prog. Officer
Officers: Karen M. Herman, Prog. Officer; Candace Fowler, Prog. Associate.
Disbursement Committee: John Morgan, Chair.; Laura Fields, Roger Hurwitz, Estelle Sosland, Suzanne Statland.
Trustee: Commerce Bank of Kansas City.
Number of staff: 1 part-time professional; 1 part-time support.
Employer Identification Number: 436203035

Recent arts and culture grants:

Arts Partners Council, NYC, NY, $20,000. For arts curriculum coordination program for metropolitan school districts. 1988.

Immocolata Manor, Kansas City, MO, $6,800. To provide Fine Arts Program for mentally retarded women. 1988.

Nelson-Atkins Museum of Art, Kansas City, MO, $13,500. For expansion of adult education program. 1988.

Nelson-Atkins Museum of Art, Kansas City, MO, $10,000. For library acquisitions. 1988.

Young Audiences, Kansas City, MO, $7,700. To support school performance program and Learning Through the Arts. 1988.

1566
Orchard Foundation

1154 Reco Dr.
St. Louis 63126 (314) 822-3880

Established in 1962 in MO.
Donor(s): Orchard Corp. of America.
Financial data (yr. ended 12/31/87): Assets, $4,820 (M); gifts received, $213,488; expenditures, $214,118, including $198,480 for 33 grants (high: $100,000; low: $8).
Purpose and activities: Giving primarily for culture and education.
Limitations: No grants to individuals.
Application information:
Write: Robert H. Orchard, Trustee
Trustee: Robert H. Orchard.
Employer Identification Number: 436049376

1567
Pet Incorporated Community Support Foundation

400 South Fourth St.
St. Louis 63166 (314) 621-5400

Established in 1959.
Donor(s): Pet, Inc.
Financial data (yr. ended 12/31/87): Assets, $326,940 (M); gifts received, $232,850; expenditures, $295,016, including $294,550 for 33 grants.
Purpose and activities: Giving primarily for education, youth, and cultural programs; support also for a community fund.
Types of support: General purposes, operating budgets, equipment, scholarship funds.
Limitations: Giving primarily in MO.
Application information:
Initial approach: Letter and proposal
Deadline(s): None
Write: Thomas R. Pellett, Pres.
Officers: Thomas R. Pellett,* Pres. and Treas.; Anthony C. Knizel, V.P.; Myron W. Sheets, V.P.; James A. Wescott, V.P.; Phyllis P. Vogt, Secy.
Trustees:* A.J. Matson, Ray Morris, Larry D. Umlanf.
Employer Identification Number: 436046149

1568
Pitzman Fund

c/o Centerre Trust Co. of St. Louis
510 Locust St., P.O. Box 14737
St. Louis 63178 (314) 436-9042

Established in 1944.
Donor(s): Frederick Pitzman.†
Financial data (yr. ended 12/31/87): Assets, $2,012,000 (M); expenditures, $109,000, including $100,700 for 65 grants (high: $10,000; low: $500; average: $500-$1,500).
Purpose and activities: Giving for education, cultural programs, Protestant church support, social services, and youth agencies.
Types of support: Annual campaigns, continuing support, general purposes.
Limitations: Giving primarily in St. Louis, MO.
Application information:
Copies of proposal: 1
Deadline(s): None
Write: Roy T. Blair
Trustees: Pauline S. Eades, Robert H. McRoberts, Centerre Trust Co.
Number of staff: None.
Employer Identification Number: 436023901

1569
Pulitzer Publishing Company Foundation

900 North Tucker Blvd.
St. Louis 63101 (314) 622-7000

Incorporated in 1963 in MO.
Donor(s): The Pulitzer Publishing Co.
Financial data (yr. ended 12/31/87): Assets, $684,414 (M); gifts received, $544,405; expenditures, $541,236, including $540,315 for 90 grants (high: $100,000; low: $100).
Purpose and activities: Giving primarily for music, cultural programs, a community fund, and higher education, including a scholarship fund to the University of Missouri Journalism School for black students residing in the St. Louis area.
Types of support: Scholarship funds, annual campaigns, building funds, capital campaigns, endowment funds, equipment, general purposes, operating budgets, professorships, research.
Limitations: Giving primarily in MO, with emphasis on the St. Louis area.
Application information: Application form required.
Deadline(s): Mar. 1 for scholarships only
Board meeting date(s): Varies
Officers and Directors: Joseph Pulitzer, Jr., Chair.; Michael E. Pulitzer, Vice-Chair. and Pres.; Ronald H. Ridgway, Secy.-Treas.; David Lipman, Nicholas Penniman, William Woo.
Employer Identification Number: 436052854

1570
Ralston Purina Corporate Contributions

Checkerboard Square
St. Louis 63164 (314) 982-3230

Financial data (yr. ended 9/30/88): Total giving, $3,024,063, including $2,744,911 for grants (high: $620,000; low: $500) and $279,152 for 1,363 employee matching gifts.
Purpose and activities: Support for civic and community affairs, the United Way, social services and youth agencies, education, health, and arts and culture.
Types of support: Capital campaigns, general purposes, operating budgets, research, scholarship funds, employee matching gifts.
Limitations: Giving primarily in headquarters city and major operating locations. No support for religious or political groups, veterans' or fraternal organizations unless their activities will benefit the general public. No grants to individuals, or for investment funds, deficit underwriting, advertising, research, or individuals; no loans.
Publications: Application guidelines.
Application information: Include statement of problem/need, timetable for program, organization description, general plan for post-grant evaluation, amount request, budget, 501(c)(3), recently audited financial statement, list of board members, and annual report.
Initial approach: Letter and proposal
Deadline(s): None
Board meeting date(s): Monthly
Final notification: 6-8 weeks
Write: John L. Lenza, Jr., Mgr., Contribs. Progs.

1571
The J. B. Reynolds Foundation

3520 Broadway
Kansas City 64111 (816) 753-7000

Incorporated in 1961 in MO.
Donor(s): Walter Edwin Bixby, Sr., Pearl G. Reynolds.†
Financial data (yr. ended 12/31/87): Assets, $8,726,399 (M); expenditures, $449,529, including $407,300 for 73 grants (high: $30,000; low: $100; average: $1,000-$20,000).
Purpose and activities: Grants for higher education, medical research, social service and youth agencies, and community projects; support also for cultural programs.
Types of support: Annual campaigns, seed money, emergency funds, building funds, equipment, land acquisition, research, publications, conferences and seminars, continuing support.
Limitations: Giving primarily in a 150-mile radius of Kansas City, MO. No grants to individuals.
Application information: Applications not accepted.
Initial approach: Letter
Copies of proposal: 1
Board meeting date(s): Apr. and Dec.
Write: Walter E. Bixby, V.P.
Officers: Joseph Reynolds Bixby,* Pres.; Walter E. Bixby,* V.P. and Treas.; Richard L. Finn, Secy.
Trustees:* Kathryn Bixby, Ann Bixby Oxler.
Employer Identification Number: 446014359

1572
Sachs Fund

400 Chesterfield Ctr., Suite 600
Chesterfield 63017 (314) 537-1000

Trust established in 1957 in MO.

Donor(s): Samuel C. Sachs, Sachs Electric Corp., and others.
Financial data (yr. ended 4/30/87): Assets, $3,294,770 (M); gifts received, $50,000; expenditures, $370,713, including $360,200 for 31 grants (high: $202,500; low: $100).
Purpose and activities: Emphasis on Jewish welfare funds, community funds, higher education, cultural programs, and hospitals.
Limitations: Giving primarily in MO.
Application information: Contributes only to pre-selected organizations. Applications not accepted.
Write: Louis S. Sachs, Trustee
Trustees: Lewis H. Sachs, Louis S. Sachs, Jerome W. Sandweiss.
Employer Identification Number: 436032385

1573
Shoenberg Foundation, Inc.
200 North Broadway, Suite 1475
St. Louis 63102 (314) 421-2247

Incorporated in 1955 in MO.
Donor(s): Sydney M. Shoenberg.†
Financial data (yr. ended 12/31/87): Assets, $4,479,652 (M); expenditures, $494,808, including $485,741 for 26 grants (high: $140,000; low: $100).
Purpose and activities: Giving for hospitals, community funds, Jewish welfare funds, and the arts.
Types of support: Annual campaigns, capital campaigns, continuing support.
Limitations: Giving primarily in MO. No grants to individuals.
Application information:
Initial approach: Letter
Write: William W. Ross, Secy.-Treas.
Officers and Directors: Sydney M. Shoenberg, Jr., Chair.; Robert H. Shoenberg, Pres.; E.L. Langenberg, V.P.; William W. Ross, Secy.-Treas.
Number of staff: None.
Employer Identification Number: 436028764

1574
Lindon Q. Skidmore Charitable Foundation
c/o Boatmen's First National Bank of Kansas City
14 West 10th St.
Kansas City 64183 (816) 239-7481

Established in 1977 in MO.
Financial data (yr. ended 12/31/88): Assets, $1,446,000 (M); expenditures, $87,557, including $85,500 for 10 grants (high: $20,000; low: $2,000; average: $2,000-$20,000).
Purpose and activities: Support for youth organizations, historical societies and museums.
Limitations: Giving primarily in Henry county, MO.
Application information:
Initial approach: Letter
Deadline(s): None
Board meeting date(s): 2 months
Write: David P. Ross, Sr. V.P., Boatmen's First National Bank of Kansas City
Trustees: William V. Sisney, Boatmen's First National Bank of Kansas City.
Number of staff: 1
Employer Identification Number: 431119922

1575
Caro Sewall Holmes Smith Charitable Foundation
c/o Mercantile Bank, N.A.
P.O. Box 387
St. Louis 63166

Established in 1983 in MO.
Financial data (yr. ended 12/31/87): Assets, $746,703 (M); expenditures, $305,230, including $285,000 for 15 grants (high: $95,500; low: $500).
Purpose and activities: Support for the arts and educational institutions.
Limitations: Giving primarily in St. Louis, MO.
Application information: Applications not accepted.
Trustess: Caro S. Schneithorst, William Van Cleve, Mercantile Bank, N.A.
Employer Identification Number: 363229539

1576
Southwestern Bell Foundation
One Bell Center, Rm. 36-P-1
St. Louis 63101 (314) 235-7040

Established in 1984 in MO.
Donor(s): Southwestern Bell Corp.
Financial data (yr. ended 12/31/88): Assets, $33,903,516 (M); gifts received, $15,000,000; expenditures, $14,884,000, including $14,157,000 for 2,556 grants (high: $870,000; low: $100) and $727,000 for 5,400 employee matching gifts.
Purpose and activities: Giving largely for education; support also for health, welfare, the arts and civic affairs.
Types of support: Conferences and seminars, employee matching gifts, lectureships, matching funds, research, seed money, special projects, technical assistance.
Limitations: Giving primarily in KS, MO, DC, TX, AR, and NY. No support for political activities, religious organizations, fraternal, veterans' or labor groups. No grants to individuals, or for operating funds for hospitals, capital funds, operating funds for United Way-supported organizations, or special advertising, or ticket/dinner purchases.
Publications: Annual report (including application guidelines), informational brochure (including application guidelines).
Application information: Unsuccessful applicants may not reapply in same calendar year.
Initial approach: Letter
Copies of proposal: 1
Deadline(s): None
Final notification: Four to six weeks
Write: Charles DeRiemer, Exec. Dir.
Officers and Directors: Gerald Blatherwick, Pres.; Robert Pope, V.P. and Treas.; James Ellis, V.P. and Secy.; Charles DeRiemer, Exec. Dir.
Number of staff: 3 full-time professional; 2 full-time support.
Employer Identification Number: 431353948
Recent arts and culture grants:
Allied Arts Foundation, Oklahoma City, OK, $15,000. 1987.
American Council for the Arts, NYC, NY, $75,000. 1987.
Arkansas Arts Center Foundation, Little Rock, AR, $10,000. For continued support of Traveling Artmobile to travel throughout rural Arkansas, exhibiting original works of art from Arts Center's permanent collection. 1987.
Arkansas Repertory Theater Company, Little Rock, AR, $15,000. 1987.
Army Medical Department Museum Foundation, San Antonio, TX, $10,000. 1987.
Arts Council of Fort Worth and Tarrant County, Fort Worth, TX, $28,980. 1987.
Austin Lyric Opera, Austin, TX, $10,000. 1987.
Austin Symphony Orchestra Society, Austin, TX, $10,000. 1987.
Dallas Arboretum and Botanical Society, Dallas, TX, $13,333. 1987.
Dallas Arts Association, Dallas Museum of Arts, Dallas, TX, $10,000. 1987.
Dallas County Historical Foundation, Dallas, TX, $30,000. 1987.
Dallas Opera, Dallas, TX, $20,000. 1987.
Dallas Symphony Association, Dallas, TX, $35,000. 1987.
Dance Saint Louis, Saint Louis, MO, $165,000. 1987.
Greater Saint Louis Council for Arts and Education, Saint Louis, MO, $100,000. 1987.
Houston Lyric Theater Foundation, Houston, TX, $25,000. 1987.
Houston Museum of Natural Science, Houston, TX, $12,500. 1987.
Houston Symphony Society, Houston, TX, $70,000. 1987.
John F. Kennedy Center for the Performing Arts, DC, $10,000. 1987.
Kansas City Symphony, Kansas City, MO, $34,000. 1987.
Kansas City Symphony Foundation, Kansas City, MO, $10,000. 1987.
Marion Koogler McNay Art Museum, San Antonio, TX, $15,000. 1987.
Missouri Botanical Garden, Saint Louis, MO, $150,000. 1987.
Missouri Historical Society, New Dimensions Fund, Saint Louis, MO, $15,000. 1987.
National Gallery of Art, DC, $200,000. 1987.
Nelson Gallery Foundation, Kansas City, MO, $100,000. 1987.
Oklahoma Arts Institute, Oklahoma City, OK, $50,000. 1987.
Opera Theater of Saint Louis, Saint Louis, MO, $25,000. 1987.
Public Communication Foundation for North Texas, Dallas, TX, $60,000. 1987.
R G V Educational Broadcasting, Harlingen, TX, $15,000. 1987.
Saint Louis Art Museum, Saint Louis, MO, $25,000. 1987.
Saint Louis Regional Educational and Public Television Commission, Saint Louis, MO, $10,000. 1987.
Saint Louis Symphony Orchestra, Saint Louis, MO, $225,000. For orchestra tour. 1987.
Saint Louis Zoo Friends Association, Saint Louis, MO, $50,000. 1987.
San Antonio Art Institute, San Antonio, TX, $25,000. 1987.
Sons of the Republic of Texas, San Antonio, TX, $10,000. 1987.
State Historical Society of Missouri, Columbia, MO, $10,000. 1987.
Symphony Society of San Antonio, San Antonio, TX, $20,000. 1987.
Thomas Gilcrease Museum Association, Tulsa, OK, $20,000. 1987.

Topeka Civic Theater, Topeka, KS, $12,000. 1987.
Tulsa Philharmonic Society, Tulsa, OK, $10,000. 1987.
University of Arkansas Foundation, Little Rock, AR, $10,000. For support under Foundation's Grants to Culture and the Arts program. 1987.
Wichita State University Endowment Association, Wichita, KS, $10,000. For support under Foundation's Grants to Culture and the Arts program. 1987.
Zoological Society of Houston, Houston, TX, $10,000. 1987.

1577
St. Louis Community Foundation
818 Olive St., Suite 737
St. Louis 63101 (314) 241-2703

Community foundation established in 1915 in MO.
Financial data (yr. ended 12/31/87): Assets, $6,686,460 (M); gifts received, $233,538; expenditures, $416,024, including $355,424 for 175 grants (high: $20,000; low: $150; average: $5,000).
Purpose and activities: Purposes include, but are not limited to, the promotion of education, social and scientific research, the care of the sick, aged, infirm, and handicapped, the care of children, the improvement of living, working, recreation, and environmental conditions or facilities, cultural programs, and such other charitable, educational, and social purposes that will assist the betterment of the mental, moral, social, and physical conditions of the inhabitants of the St. Louis metropolitan area.
Types of support: Research, seed money, scholarship funds, operating budgets, emergency funds, special projects, renovation projects, equipment.
Limitations: Giving primarily in the St. Louis, MO, metropolitan area, and in IL. No support for sectarian religious programs, or private elementary or secondary schools. No grants to individuals, or for deficit financing, or endowment or building funds; grants for operating expenses only during an organization's start-up.
Publications: Annual report (including application guidelines), newsletter, informational brochure.
Application information:
Initial approach: Proposal
Copies of proposal: 1
Deadline(s): Jan. 15, Apr. 15, July 15, and Oct. 15
Board meeting date(s): Quarterly
Final notification: Usually within 1 week of board meetings
Write: Mary Brucker, Exec. Dir.
Officers: Henry O. Johnston,* Treas.; Mary Brucker, Exec. Dir.
Directors:* Walter F. Gray, Chair.; Nichola M. Gillis, Vice-Chair.; Marguerite Ross Barnett, John H. Biggs, Vincent J. Cannella, Sue Clancy, F.J. Cornwell, Jr., Mark A. Dow, W. Lynton Edwards III, Edwin S. Jones, Stanley L. Lopata, William S. McEwen, Susan B. Musgrave, Donald H. Streett, Ann Daly Tretter, Franklin F. Wallis.
Trustee Banks: Boatmen's National Bank of St. Louis, Centerre Trust Co. of St. Louis, Commerce Bank of St. Louis, N.A., Guaranty Trust Co. of Missouri, Mercantile Bank, N.A.
Number of staff: 1 full-time professional; 1 full-time support.
Employer Identification Number: 436023126

1578
Stupp Brothers Bridge & Iron Company Foundation
P.O. Box 6600
St. Louis 63125 (314) 638-5000

Trust established about 1952 in MO.
Donor(s): Stupp Bros. Bridge & Iron Co.
Financial data (yr. ended 10/31/88): Assets, $5,949,747 (M); expenditures, $321,039, including $309,605 for 171 grants (high: $44,000; low: $50).
Purpose and activities: Giving to hospitals, community funds, and higher education and educational associations; support also for cultural, health, and welfare programs.
Limitations: Giving primarily in MO.
Application information: Contributes only to pre-selected organizations. Applications not accepted.
Trustees: Erwin P. Stupp, Jr., John P. Stupp, Robert P. Stupp.
Employer Identification Number: 237412437

1579
Sverdrup and Parcel, Inc. Charitable Trust
c/o Centerre Trust Co. of St. Louis
510 Locust St., P.O. Box 14737
St. Louis 63178 (314) 436-7600
Application address: 801 North Eleventh, St. Louis, MO 63101

Established in 1951 in MO.
Donor(s): Sverdrup & Parcel, Inc., Aro, Inc.
Financial data (yr. ended 12/31/87): Assets, $1,008,967 (M); gifts received, $250,000; expenditures, $181,305, including $174,050 for 70 grants (high: $37,000; low: $50).
Purpose and activities: Support primarily for community funds, education, and culture; grants also for youth and social services.
Application information:
Initial approach: Proposal
Deadline(s): None
Write: Thomas E. Wehrle
Members: E.S. Davis, W.F. Knapp, B.R. Smith, Jr.
Trustee: Centerre Trust Co. of St. Louis.
Employer Identification Number: 436023499

1580
John S. Swift Company Charitable Trust, Inc.
c/o Mercantile Bank, N.A.
P.O. Box 387
St. Louis 63166
Application address: 1248 Research Dr., St. Louis, MO 63132; Tel.: (314) 991-4300

Trust established in 1952 in MO.
Donor(s): John S. Swift Co., Inc.
Financial data (yr. ended 12/31/87): Assets, $1,338,200 (M); expenditures, $81,806, including $73,555 for 53 grants (high: $37,500; low: $25).
Purpose and activities: Grants for higher and secondary education, cultural programs, including museums, and hospitals.
Limitations: Giving primarily in MO and IL.
Application information:
Initial approach: Letter
Deadline(s): None
Write: Ben Heckel, Trustee
Trustees: Ben Heckel, Hampden M. Swift, Mercantile Bank, N.A.
Employer Identification Number: 436020812

1581
Sycamore Tree Trust
P.O. Box 11264
Clayton 63105 (314) 725-8666
Application address: 7733 Forsyth Blvd., Suite 1050, St. Louis, MO 63105

Trust established about 1953 in MO.
Donor(s): Katherine M. Walsh, Dorothy M. Moore, Adelaide M. Schlafly, Thomas F. Schlafly, Daniel L. Schlafly, Jr.
Financial data (yr. ended 12/31/86): Assets, $950,363 (M); gifts received, $1,137,569; expenditures, $814,956, including $813,708 for 244 grants (high: $143,200; low: $10; average: $350-$10,000).
Purpose and activities: Giving for Roman Catholic church support and religious associations; support also for the arts and cultural programs, higher education, and a community fund; some support also for international affairs organizations.
Limitations: Giving primarily in MO. No grants to individuals.
Application information:
Initial approach: Letter
Deadline(s): None
Board meeting date(s): Monthly
Final notification: 1st week of month following submission date
Write: J. Morris
Trustee: The Commonwealth Trust Co.
Number of staff: None.
Employer Identification Number: 436026719

1582
Tension Envelope Foundation
819 East 19th St., 5th Fl.
Kansas City 64108 (816) 471-3800

Incorporated in 1954 in MO.
Donor(s): Tension Envelope Corp.
Financial data (yr. ended 11/30/88): Assets, $2,887,824 (M); gifts received, $100,000; expenditures, $301,581, including $268,834 for 153 grants (high: $30,094; low: $225).
Purpose and activities: Emphasis on Jewish welfare funds; support also for community funds, higher education, health, civic affairs, culture and the arts, and youth.
Limitations: Giving primarily in areas of company operations. No grants to individuals.
Application information:
Initial approach: Letter
Deadline(s): None
Write: Eliot S. Berkley, Secy.

Officers: Richard L. Berkley,* Pres.; Walter L. Hiersteiner, V.P.; Eliot S. Berkley,* Secy.; E. Bertram Berkley,* Treas.
Directors:* William Berkley, Abraham E. Margolin.
Employer Identification Number: 446012554

1583
Courtney S. Turner Charitable Trust
c/o Boatmen's First National Bank of Kansas City
P.O. Box 419038
Kansas City 64183 (816) 234-7481

Established in 1986 in MO.
Donor(s): Courtney S. Turner.
Financial data (yr. ended 12/31/88): Assets, $14,961,000 (M); gifts received, $361,000; expenditures, $958,312, including $944,469 for 24 grants (high: $188,000; low: $1,000; average: $500-$100,000).
Purpose and activities: Support for youth organizations, higher education, and cultural programs.
Types of support: Matching funds, seed money, special projects.
Limitations: Giving primarily in Atchison, KS.
Publications: 990-PF.
Application information:
Deadline(s): None
Write: David P. Ross, Trust Officer, Boatmen's First National Bank of Kansas City
Trustees: Daniel C. Weary, Boatmen's First National Bank of Kansas City.
Number of staff: 1
Employer Identification Number: 436316904

1584
Union Electric Company Charitable Trust
1901 Gratiot St.
P.O. Box 149
St. Louis 63166 (314) 621-3222

Trust established in 1944 in MO.
Donor(s): Union Electric Co.
Financial data (yr. ended 12/31/88): Assets, $3,149,286 (M); gifts received, $1,000,000; expenditures, $1,608,461, including $1,533,960 for 42 grants (high: $340,000; low: $3,000; average: $5,000-$25,000) and $51,808 for 631 employee matching gifts.
Purpose and activities: Giving largely for community funds and higher education; grants also for hospitals; employee-related scholarships administered by the National Merit Scholarship Corporation.
Types of support: Annual campaigns, building funds, emergency funds, employee matching gifts, equipment, general purposes, land acquisition, operating budgets, employee-related scholarships, scholarship funds, fellowships, capital campaigns, matching funds, renovation projects, special projects.
Limitations: Giving limited to company locations in IA, IL, and MO. No grants to individuals, or for endowment funds or research-related programs; no loans.
Publications: Application guidelines.
Application information:
Initial approach: Letter
Copies of proposal: 1
Deadline(s): None
Board meeting date(s): 2 or 3 times a year
Final notification: 60 to 90 days
Write: Ms. Patricia Barrett, Mgr., Community Services
Trustees: William E. Cornelius, Boatmen's Trust Co. of St. Louis.
Number of staff: 1 full-time professional; 2 part-time professional; 1 part-time support.
Employer Identification Number: 436022693

1585
Union Electric Company Corporate Giving Program
1901 Gratiot St.
P.O. Box 149
St. Louis 63166 (314) 621-3222

Financial data (yr. ended 12/31/87): $306,052 for grants (high: $2,500).
Purpose and activities: The company supports the following general areas: civic, cultural and arts organizations, educational institutions and programs, medical facilities, social services, urban affairs, and youth activities. Considered are programs for the elderly, business, child welfare, community development, conservation, the disadvantaged, the handicapped, health, the homeless, hunger, minorities, museums, public policy, rural development, science and technology, urban affairs, volunteerism, women, welfare, and economics. Types of support include employee matching gifts for education. The company also makes in-kind donations of its salvage/surplus and materials. The corporate contributions program is specifically designated to provide small gifts of less than $2,500.
Types of support: Capital campaigns, operating budgets, building funds, employee matching gifts, annual campaigns, continuing support, emergency funds, endowment funds, equipment, general purposes, matching funds, renovation projects, research, special projects, technical assistance, scholarship funds, in-kind gifts.
Limitations: Giving primarily in the St. Louis, MO, area and operating locations. No support for political organizations or candidates, or social, religious, fraternal, veterans', or similar organizations.
Publications: Informational brochure (including application guidelines).
Application information: Include: project description; organization purpose and services; the fundraising goal; amount requested; current status of fundraising efforts; current approved operating budget and audited financial statement; 501(c)(3); board list.
Initial approach: Proposal on organization letterhead
Copies of proposal: 1
Deadline(s): None
Board meeting date(s): Applications reviewed as received
Write: Patricia Barrett, Mgr., Community Services
Number of staff: 1 full-time professional; 2 part-time professional; 1 full-time support.

1586
Valley Line Company Charitable Trust
510 Locust St.
P.O. Box 14737
St. Louis 63178-4737 (314) 889-0100

Financial data (yr. ended 12/31/87): Assets, $216,577 (M); expenditures, $52,821, including $50,000 for 4 grants (high: $20,000; low: $5,000).
Purpose and activities: Support for a foundation, a children's hospital, and an art museum.
Application information:
Initial approach: Letter
Trustee: Centerre Trust Co. of St. Louis.
Employer Identification Number: 436023507

1587
Louis L. and Adelaide C. Ward Foundation
1000 Walnut
Kansas City 64106

Established in 1966 in MO.
Donor(s): Louis L. Ward, Adelaide C. Ward.
Financial data (yr. ended 12/31/87): Assets, $4,375,000 (M); gifts received, $1,500,000; expenditures, $160,000, including $160,000 for 50 grants (high: $100,000; low: $25; average: $5,000).
Purpose and activities: Support primarily for health and culture; some support for education.
Types of support: Annual campaigns, building funds, capital campaigns, general purposes, scholarship funds, endowment funds.
Limitations: Giving primarily in KS, MO, MT, and OH.
Application information:
Write: Louis L. Ward, Pres.
Officers: Louis L. Ward, Pres.; Adelaide C. Ward, V.P. and Secy.-Treas.
Employer Identification Number: 436064548

1588
Western Philanthropies, Inc.
c/o Commerce Tower, 911 Main St., Suite 1402
P.O. Box 13503
Kansas City 64199

Established in 1956 in MO.
Donor(s): Charles A. Duboc.
Financial data (yr. ended 12/31/87): Assets, $1,196,156 (M); gifts received, $246,733; expenditures, $64,010, including $60,000 for 6 grants (high: $31,750; low: $1,000).
Purpose and activities: Support primarily for higher education and cultural organizations.
Limitations: Giving primarily in KS and MO.
Application information: Applications not accepted.
Officers and Directors: Charles A. Duboc, Pres.; Charles M. Duboc, V.P.; Barbara D. Duboc, Secy.-Treas.; Robert M. Duboc.
Number of staff: None.
Employer Identification Number: 446011936

1589
Mr. and Mrs. Lyndon C. Whitaker Charitable Foundation
c/o Urban C. Bergbauer, Jr.
7711 Bonhomme Ave., Suite 201
St. Louis 63105 (314) 726-8534

Trust established in 1975 in MO.
Donor(s): Mae M. Whitaker.†
Financial data (yr. ended 4/30/88): Assets, $15,983,930 (M); expenditures, $1,230,711, including $993,377 for 65 grants (high: $73,600; low: $60; average: $2,000-$25,000).
Purpose and activities: Emphasis on handicapped children, medical research, cultural programs including music, historic preservation and hospitals; grants also for youth and social service agencies and education.
Limitations: Giving primarily in St. Louis, MO.
Application information:
Initial approach: Letter or proposal
Deadline(s): None
Trustee: Urban C. Bergbauer, Jr.
Advisory Board: Cyril J. Costello, James D. Cullen, George T. Guernsey, James C. Thompson, Jr., Anita D. Vincel.
Employer Identification Number: 510173108

1590
Kearney Wornall Charitable Trust & Foundation
Tenth & Grand
Kansas City 64141

Established in 1954 in MO.
Financial data (yr. ended 12/31/87): Assets, $3,162,858 (M); gifts received, $885,519; expenditures, $5,146, including $4,240 for 13 grants (high: $1,700; low: $100).
Purpose and activities: Support primarily to cultural programs, hospitals, historic societies,and religious welfare.
Types of support: General purposes.
Limitations: Giving primarily in the Kansas City, MO, area.
Application information: Contributes only to pre-selected organizations. Applications not accepted.
Trustee: United Missouri Bank of Kansas City, N.A.
Employer Identification Number: 446013874

MONTANA

1591
Dufresne Foundation
P.O. Box 1484
Great Falls 59403 (406) 761-7200

Established about 1958 in MT.
Donor(s): Fred Dufresne,† Bertha Dufresne.†
Financial data (yr. ended 12/31/88): Assets, $1,186,509 (M); expenditures, $71,670, including $47,769 for 47 grants (high: $4,556; low: $100; average: $1,000).
Purpose and activities: Giving primarily for education, especially higher education, and social service and youth agencies; some support for cultural programs.
Types of support: Scholarship funds, special projects, operating budgets.
Limitations: Giving primarily in MT, and the Great Falls Track area.
Publications: Program policy statement.
Application information:
Deadline(s): None
Write: Daniel C. Ewen, V.P.
Officers and Directors: Dan C. Ewen, V.P.; William M. Scott, Secy.; Clarence D. Misfeldt, Treas.; Milo F. Dean, S.F. Meyer.
Number of staff: None.
Employer Identification Number: 810301465

1592
First Interstate Banks of Billings Centennial Youth Foundation
(Formerly Security Banks Centennial Youth Foundation)
P.O. Box 30918
Billings 59116-0918 (406) 255-5016

Financial data (yr. ended 12/31/87): Assets, $126 (M); gifts received, $10,000; expenditures, $10,084, including $9,800 for 9 grants (high: $2,030; low: $525).
Purpose and activities: Support for youth organizations in the areas of arts, education, and health.
Types of support: Operating budgets.
Limitations: Giving limited to Yellowstone County, MT.
Application information: Forms may be obtained at any participating bank of First Interstate Bank of Billings. Application form required.
Deadline(s): July 15
Write: Willard Wallace, Secy.
Trustees: Roger Eble, Father Donald McKay, Lynn Montogne, Charles Rohrer, Marsh Sapulding.
Employer Identification Number: 742265711

1593
Sample Foundation, Inc.
14 North 24th St.
P.O. Box 279
Billings 59103 (406) 256-5667

Incorporated in 1956 in FL.
Donor(s): Helen S. Sample.
Financial data (yr. ended 10/31/88): Assets, $2,589,015 (M); gifts received, $132,817; expenditures, $144,441, including $130,830 for 23 grants (high: $50,000; low: $500).
Purpose and activities: Grants for higher education, museums, social services, youth agencies, hospitals, and community funds.
Limitations: Giving primarily in MT and Collier County, FL. No support for religious organizations or any group with political affiliations. No grants to individuals.
Publications: Application guidelines.
Application information:
Initial approach: Letter
Board meeting date(s): Oct. 1
Write: Miriam T. Sample, V.P.
Officers: Joseph S. Sample, Pres.; Michael S. Sample, V.P.; Miriam T. Sample, V.P.; T.A. Cox, Secy.-Treas.
Number of staff: None.
Employer Identification Number: 596138602

NEBRASKA

1594
Alan and Marcia Baer Foundation
11222 I St.
Omaha 68137 (402) 399-6973

Established in 1950 in NE.
Donor(s): E. John Brandeis.†
Financial data (yr. ended 6/30/87): Assets, $2,746,368 (M); expenditures, $159,156, including $134,118 for 182 grants (high: $12,303; low: $15).
Purpose and activities: Giving for health associations and services, youth, culture, and religious giving; substantial support for the Baer Indigent Fund which disburses grants to various charitable organizations.
Limitations: Giving primarily in Omaha, NE.
Application information:
Initial approach: Letter
Deadline(s): At least 30 days before grant is required
Write: Alan Baer, Pres.
Officers: Alan Baer, Pres.; Marcia Baer, V.P. and Secy.; George Krauss, V.P. and Treas.
Employer Identification Number: 476032560

1595
The Theodore G. Baldwin Foundation
2033 Central Ave.
Kearney 68847-6855 (308) 234-9889
Application address: P.O. Box 922, Kearny, NE 68848

Established in 1982 in NE.
Donor(s): Ellen W. Craig.
Financial data (yr. ended 12/31/87): Assets, $1,099,403 (M); gifts received, $100; expenditures, $49,584, including $45,000 for 6 grants (high: $24,000; low: $1,000).
Purpose and activities: Giving for an opera and a symphony; support also for local arts organization.
Types of support: General purposes, matching funds.
Limitations: Giving primarily in NE and Dallas, TX.
Publications: 990-PF, application guidelines.
Application information: Application form required.
Initial approach: Letter
Copies of proposal: 1
Deadline(s): Oct. 1
Board meeting date(s): 4th quarter of each calendar year
Final notification: Dec. 31
Write: Michael W. Baldwin, Treas.

Officers: Ellen W. Craig,* Pres.; Juli Baldwin Brown,* V.P.; Robert R. Craig, Secy.; Michael W. Baldwin,* Treas.
Directors:* Charles P. Curtiss, James A. McKenzie.
Number of staff: None.
Employer Identification Number: 470641432

1596
Blumkin Foundation, Inc.
7001 Farnam St.
Omaha 68132

Incorporated in 1956 in Omaha, NE.
Donor(s): Louie Blumkin, Rose Blumkin, Nebraska Furniture Mart, Inc.
Financial data (yr. ended 11/30/87): Assets, $1,304,000 (M); gifts received, $35,000; expenditures, $72,064, including $50,395 for 129 grants (high: $12,200; low: $25).
Purpose and activities: Giving primarily for Jewish religious groups and welfare funds, higher education, and cultural programs.
Limitations: Giving primarily in NE.
Application information:
Write: Norman B. Batt, V.P.
Officers: Rose Blumkin, Chair.; Louie Blumkin, Pres.; Norman B. Batt, V.P.; Ben F. Shrier, Secy.-Treas.
Employer Identification Number: 476030726

1597
ConAgra Charitable Foundation, Inc.
c/o ConAgra, Inc.
One Central Park Plaza
Omaha 68102 (402) 978-4160

Donor(s): ConAgra, Inc.
Financial data (yr. ended 5/25/88): Assets, $1,206,967 (M); gifts received, $500,000; expenditures, $822,761, including $821,722 for 196 grants (high: $73,025; low: $50).
Purpose and activities: Emphasis on higher education, youth agencies, community funds, and cultural programs.
Limitations: Giving primarily in Omaha, NE. No grants to individuals.
Application information: Grants are generally preselected.
Initial approach: Proposal
Deadline(s): None
Write: M.G. Colladay, V.P.
Officers: Charles M. Harper,* Pres.; M.G. Colladay,* V.P. and Secy.; J.P. O'Donnell, Treas.
Directors:* Robert B. Daugherty.
Employer Identification Number: 362899320

1598
Cooper Foundation
504 Cooper Plaza
12th and P Sts.
Lincoln 68508 (402) 476-7571

Incorporated in 1934 in NE.
Donor(s): Joseph H. Cooper.†
Financial data (yr. ended 12/31/88): Assets, $9,857,722 (M); expenditures, $704,003, including $392,310 for 128 grants (high: $30,000; low: $150; average: $500-$5,000).
Purpose and activities: Grants largely for programs benefiting children and young people, primarily in education, the arts, and social services.
Types of support: Annual campaigns, seed money, emergency funds, research, scholarship funds, matching funds.
Limitations: Giving primarily in NE, with emphasis on Lincoln and Lancaster County. No grants to individuals, or for endowment funds; no loans.
Publications: Biennial report (including application guidelines).
Application information: Application form required.
Initial approach: Proposal
Copies of proposal: 1
Deadline(s): None
Board meeting date(s): Monthly
Final notification: 1 month
Write: Elwood N. Thompson, Pres.
Officers and Trustees: Burnham Yates, Chair.; Elwood N. Thompson, Pres.; Jack Campbell, V.P.; Peg Huff, Secy.; W.W. Nuernberger, Treas.; Richard Knudsen, Counsel; Robert Dobson, Kathryn Druliner, E.J. Faulkner, Harold Hoppe, John Olsson, Bill Smith, E. Arthur Thompson, Norton E. Warner.
Number of staff: 3 full-time professional.
Employer Identification Number: 470401230

1599
Dr. C. C. and Mabel L. Criss Memorial Foundation
c/o Firstier Bank Omaha, N.A.
17 Farnham St.
Omaha 68102

Trust established in 1978 in NE.
Donor(s): C.C. Criss, M.D.,† Mabel L. Criss.†
Financial data (yr. ended 2/28/87): Assets, $30,016,676 (M); expenditures, $2,321,941, including $1,981,126 for 23 grants (high: $1,170,000; low: $1,000; average: $10,000-$100,000).
Purpose and activities: Educational and scientific purposes; primarily to meet the needs of Creighton University's medical center; support also for education, including higher education, cultural agencies, youth and social agencies, and a hospital.
Limitations: Giving primarily in NE.
Application information: Contributes only to pre-selected organizations. Applications not accepted.
Write: Joseph J. Vinardi, Trustee
Trustees: M. Thomas Crummer, Richard L. Daly, Gale E. Davis, Joseph J. Vinardi, The Omaha National Bank.
Employer Identification Number: 470601105

1600
Frank M. and Alice M. Farr Trust
1101 12th St.
Aurora 68818 (402) 694-3136

Established in 1985 in NE.
Financial data (yr. ended 12/31/87): Assets, $3,497,360 (M); expenditures, $315,680, including $200,792 for 7 grants (high: $100,000; low: $2,500).
Purpose and activities: Support for cultural programs and civic affairs.
Limitations: Giving limited to Hamilton County, NE.
Application information: Application form required.
Deadline(s): Feb. 1
Write: James E. Koepke, Trustee
Trustees: James E. Koepke, First National Bank and Trust Co.
Employer Identification Number: 476144457

1601
FirsTier Bank, N.A., Omaha Charitable Foundation
(Formerly Omaha National Bank Charitable Trust)
c/o FirsTier Bank Omaha
17th and Farnum St.
Omaha 68102

Trust established in 1962 in NE.
Donor(s): FirsTier Bank Omaha.
Financial data (yr. ended 12/31/87): Assets, $1,478,258 (M); gifts received, $47,420; expenditures, $571,891, including $566,146 for 91 grants (high: $100,500; low: $50).
Purpose and activities: Emphasis on a community fund, higher education, cultural programs, and youth agencies.
Limitations: Giving primarily in Omaha, NE.
Application information: Contributes only to preselected organizations. Applications not accepted.
Trustee: FirsTier Bank Omaha.
Employer Identification Number: 476020716

1602
Gifford Foundation
c/o First National Bank of Omaha, Trust Dept.
P.O. Box 3128
Omaha 68114 (402) 341-0500

Established in 1964 in NE.
Financial data (yr. ended 12/31/87): Assets, $998,529 (M); expenditures, $119,465, including $107,269 for 82 grants (high: $25,000; low: $10).
Purpose and activities: Support for cultural programs, higher education, and conservation.
Limitations: No grants to individuals.
Application information:
Deadline(s): None
Write: Harold Gifford, Pres.
Officers and Directors: Harold Gifford, Pres.; Mary Elizabeth Gifford, V.P. and Treas.; Alfred G. Ellick, Secy.; Charles A. Gifford, Harold M. Gifford, Glenn H. Le Dioyt, Jessica Shestack.
Employer Identification Number: 476025084

1603
Paul and Oscar Giger Foundation, Inc.
c/o Fraser, Stryker Law Firm
500 Electric Bldg.
Omaha 68102 (402) 341-6000

Established in 1985 in NE.
Donor(s): Ruth Giger.†
Financial data (yr. ended 12/31/87): Assets, $1,596,461 (M); gifts received, $198;

expenditures, $125,034, including $71,481 for 18 grants (high: $25,000; low: $500).
Purpose and activities: Support primarily for music, natural resources, Christian organizations, and the aged.
Limitations: Giving limited to the Omaha, NE, area. No grants to individuals.
Application information: Application form required.
Copies of proposal: 4
Deadline(s): May 15 and Oct. 1
Board meeting date(s): Quarterly
Write: Amy S. Bones
Officers: Frank A. Blazek, Pres.; Beverly Ingram, V.P.; Janet Acker, Secy.
Employer Identification Number: 470682708

1604
Gilbert M. and Martha H. Hitchcock Foundation
Kennedy Holland Bldg.
10306 Regency Pkwy. Dr.
Omaha 68114 (402) 397-0203

Incorporated in 1943 in NE.
Donor(s): Mrs. Martha H. Hitchcock.†
Financial data (yr. ended 12/31/88): Assets, $8,364,390 (M); expenditures, $691,546 for 33 grants (high: $200,000; low: $500; average: $1,000-$15,000).
Purpose and activities: Support for private secondary and higher education; support also for cultural programs and youth and social service agencies; sponsors scholarship program for newspaper carriers.
Types of support: Annual campaigns, building funds, endowment funds, matching funds, general purposes, scholarship funds.
Limitations: Giving limited to NE and western IA, with emphasis on Omaha. No grants to individuals, or for research-related programs.
Publications: Application guidelines.
Application information:
Initial approach: Proposal or letter
Copies of proposal: 4
Deadline(s): Dec. 1
Board meeting date(s): Jan. and as required
Final notification: After Jan. board meeting
Write: Thomas R. Burke, Secy.
Officers: Denman Kountze,* Pres.; Neely Kountze,* V.P.; Thomas R. Burke, Secy.; Tyler B. Gaines,* Treas.
Trustees:* Mary Jennings, Charles Kountze, Ronald R. Ruh, Paul Shirley, Jr.
Number of staff: None.
Employer Identification Number: 476025723

1605
Hazel R. Keene Trust
c/o Fremont National Bank Trust, Trust Dept.
152 East 6th St.
Fremont 68025 (402) 721-1050

Established in 1986 in NE.
Donor(s): Hazel Keene.
Financial data (yr. ended 12/31/87): Assets, $2,211,538 (M); expenditures, $137,482, including $40,000 for 5 grants (high: $20,000; low: $5,000).
Purpose and activities: Giving primarily for social services, including programs for the aged, child welfare, and youth; support also for education, health, the arts, and historic preservation.
Types of support: Building funds, capital campaigns, general purposes, lectureships, matching funds, scholarship funds.
Limitations: Giving primarily in Fremont, NE.
Application information: Application form required.
Copies of proposal: 2
Deadline(s): May 1
Final notification: June 30
Write: Joe Twidwell
Trustee: Fremont National Bank Trust.
Number of staff: None.
Employer Identification Number: 476144486

1606
Peter Kiewit Foundation
Woodmen Tower, Suite 900
Farnam at 17th
Omaha 68102 (402) 344-7890

Established in 1975 in NE.
Donor(s): Peter Kiewit.†
Financial data (yr. ended 6/30/88): Assets, $183,284,118 (M); gifts received, $2,001; expenditures, $11,489,188, including $8,798,296 for 81 grants (high: $850,000; low: $250; average: $10,000-$100,000) and $355,869 for 91 grants to individuals.
Purpose and activities: Giving primarily for cultural programs, civic affairs and community development, higher education, health and social service agencies, and youth programs. Contributions almost always made as challenge or matching grants.
Types of support: Matching funds, student aid, capital campaigns, equipment, general purposes, land acquisition, program-related investments, renovation projects, seed money, special projects.
Limitations: Giving limited to NE and western IA; Sheridan, WY; and Rancho Mirage, CA; college scholarships available to high school students in the Omaha, NE--Council Bluffs, IA, area only. No support for elementary or secondary education, churches, or religious groups. No grants to individuals (except for scholarships), or for endowment funds, or annual campaigns.
Publications: Annual report, informational brochure (including application guidelines), application guidelines.
Application information: For scholarships, request application form from high school principal who makes scholarship selection for his or her school. Application form required.
Initial approach: Letter or telephone
Copies of proposal: 3
Deadline(s): June 30, Sept. 30, Dec. 31, and Mar. 31 for organizations; Mar. 1 for scholarships
Board meeting date(s): Sept., Dec., Mar., and June
Final notification: Within 30 days of board meeting
Write: Lyn Wallin Ziegenbein, Exec. Dir.
Officer: Lyn Wallin Ziegenbein, Exec. Dir. and Secy.
Trustees: Ray L. Daniel, Jr., Chair.; Marjorie B. Kiewit, Vice-Chair.; Richard L. Coyne, Robert B. Daugherty, Peter Kiewit, Jr., FirsTier Bank Omaha.
Number of staff: 2 full-time professional; 1 part-time professional; 2 full-time support.
Employer Identification Number: 476098282

1607
The Peter Kiewit Sons, Inc. Foundation
1000 Kiewit Plaza
Omaha 68131 (402) 342-2052

Established in 1963 in NE.
Donor(s): Peter Kiewit Sons Co., Wytana, Inc., Big Horn Coal Co.
Financial data (yr. ended 12/31/87): Assets, $12,600,016 (M); gifts received, $1,000,000; expenditures, $1,628,620, including $1,581,711 for 136 grants (high: $250,000; low: $25; average: $500-$10,000).
Purpose and activities: Grants largely for higher education, the arts, community development, and social service agencies.
Limitations: Giving primarily in NE and the northwestern states, or in areas where the company has permanent operations; in education, preference given to areas where the company recruits. No support for elementary or secondary schools, individual churches or similar religious groups. No grants to individuals, or for endowment funds.
Application information:
Deadline(s): None
Board meeting date(s): As needed
Final notification: Varies
Write: Michael L. Faust
Trustee: FirsTier Bank Omaha.
Number of staff: None.
Employer Identification Number: 476029996

1608
Robert J. Kutak Foundation
1650 Farnam St.
Omaha 68102-2103

Established in 1983 in NE.
Donor(s): Kutak, Rock & Campbell.
Financial data (yr. ended 12/31/87): Assets, $811,715 (M); gifts received, $125,675; expenditures, $216,190, including $205,766 for grants.
Purpose and activities: Grants to organizations that foster, encourage, support, or maintain the fine arts.
Application information:
Initial approach: Proposal
Deadline(s): None
Final notification: Within 3 months
Write: Harold L. Rock, Pres.
Officers and Directors: Harold L. Rock, Pres.; William G. Campbell, V.P.; D. Dean Poblenz, Secy. and Exec. Dir.; Lamont R. Wallin, Treas.; Allan J. Garfinkle, Peter W. Hill.
Employer Identification Number: 470652086

1609
Lincoln Foundation, Inc.
215 Centennial Mall South
Lincoln 68508 (402) 474-2345

Community foundation incorporated in 1955 in NE.

Financial data (yr. ended 12/31/85): Assets, $12,946,228 (M); gifts received, $2,406,277; expenditures, $1,248,220, including $698,417 for grants.
Purpose and activities: To promote the mental, moral, intellectual, and physical improvement, assistance, and relief of the inhabitants of Lincoln and Lancaster County in particular, and elsewhere in the U.S. where funds are available; giving mainly in the areas of civic and community affairs, cultural programs, health and welfare, and higher education.
Types of support: Scholarship funds, seed money, emergency funds, research, matching funds, special projects.
Limitations: Giving primarily in Lincoln and Lancaster County, NE. No grants to individuals, or for building or endowment funds or operating budgets.
Publications: Annual report, program policy statement, application guidelines, newsletter.
Application information:
Initial approach: Telephone
Copies of proposal: 12
Board meeting date(s): Quarterly and as required
Write: Phil Heckman, Pres.
Officers: Charles C. Barton, Chair.; Stephen W. Carveth, Vice-Chair.; James F. Nissen, Vice-Chair.; Phil Heckman, Pres.; Glenn Clements, Secy.; Mrs. Lawrence Arth, Treas.
Number of staff: 3 full-time professional; 1 part-time professional; 2 full-time support; 1 part-time support.
Employer Identification Number: 470458128

1610
The Milton S. and Corinne N. Livingston Foundation, Inc.
300 Overland Wolf Center
6910 Pacific St.
Omaha 68106 (402) 558-1112

Incorporated in 1948 in NE.
Donor(s): Milton S. Livingston.†
Financial data (yr. ended 12/31/87): Assets, $3,096,766 (M); expenditures, $271,671, including $236,498 for 61 grants (high: $100,000; low: $100; average: $2,500).
Purpose and activities: Grants largely for local Jewish welfare funds, higher education, temple support, culture, and health services.
Types of support: Continuing support, building funds, general purposes.
Limitations: Giving primarily in NE. No grants to individuals.
Application information:
Initial approach: Letter
Copies of proposal: 1
Deadline(s): None
Board meeting date(s): May and Oct.
Write: Yale Richards, Exec. Dir.
Officers and Trustees: Jule M. Newman, Pres.; Morton A. Richards, V.P.; Robert I. Kully, Secy.; Stanley J. Slosburg, Treas.; Murray H. Newman.
Employer Identification Number: 476027670

1611
Mid-Nebraska Community Foundation, Inc.
117 North Dewey
P.O. Box 1321
North Platte 69103 (308) 534-3315

Established in 1978 in NE.
Financial data (yr. ended 5/31/88): Assets, $456,380 (M); gifts received, $142,049; expenditures, $125,443, including $103,218 for grants.
Purpose and activities: Support primarily for the arts, education, civic development, health, and welfare.
Types of support: Building funds, equipment, matching funds, program-related investments, publications, renovation projects, seed money, special projects.
Limitations: Giving primarily in Lincoln, Keith, McPherson, Logan, Custer, Dawson, Frontier, Hayes, and Perkins Counties, NE.
Publications: Annual report.
Application information: Application form required.
Initial approach: Letter or telephone
Copies of proposal: 1
Deadline(s): None
Board meeting date(s): Quarterly
Write: Ruby Coleman, Exec. Dir.
Executive Director: Ruby Coleman.
Number of staff: 1 part-time professional.
Employer Identification Number: 470604965

1612
Northwestern Bell Foundation
1314 Douglas-on-the-Mall, 5th Fl.
Omaha 68102 (402) 422-4242

Established in 1985 in NE.
Donor(s): Northwestern Bell Corp.
Financial data (yr. ended 12/31/87): Assets, $1,202,575 (M); gifts received, $2,520,000; expenditures, $2,650,100, including $2,436,782 for 529 grants (high: $50,000; low: $150; average: $250-$15,000) and $194,777 for employee matching gifts.
Purpose and activities: Grants primarily for education, with emphasis on higher education, youth and social service agencies, community funds, and cultural programs.
Types of support: Capital campaigns, employee matching gifts, general purposes, matching funds, special projects.
Limitations: Giving primarily in areas of company operations in IA, MN, NE, ND, and SD. No grants to individuals.
Publications: Annual report (including application guidelines), 990-PF.
Application information:
Initial approach: Letter
Deadline(s): None
Board meeting date(s): Quarterly
Write: J.W. Leuschen, Exec. Dir.
Officers and Directors: K.D. Power, Pres.; J.D. Aipperspach, V.P. and C.E.O. (IA); Peg R. Milford, V.P. and C.E.O. (SD); A.L. Grauer, V.P. and Secy.; J.W. Leuschen, Exec. Dir.; J. Hawes.
Number of staff: 1 full-time support.
Employer Identification Number: 363374437

1613
The Omaha World-Herald Foundation
c/o Omaha World-Herald Co.
14th and Dodge Sts.
Omaha 68102 (402) 444-1000

Trust established in 1968 in NE.
Donor(s): Omaha World-Herald Co.
Financial data (yr. ended 12/31/88): Assets, $1,376,179 (M); expenditures, $845,960, including $837,630 for grants.
Purpose and activities: Giving primarily for education, cultural programs including historic preservation, social service and youth agencies, community funds, civic affairs, the media, and conservation.
Types of support: Seed money, building funds, land acquisition, internships, scholarship funds, matching funds, special projects, continuing support, equipment.
Limitations: Giving limited to the Omaha, NE, area. No grants to individuals, or for operating endowments, research, seminars, or dinners.
Publications: 990-PF.
Application information:
Initial approach: Proposal
Copies of proposal: 1
Deadline(s): None
Board meeting date(s): As required
Final notification: 2 months
Write: John Gottschalk, Pres.
Distribution Committee: Harold W. Andersen, John Gottschalk, G. Woodson Howe.
Trustee: Norwest Capital Management and Trust Co. Nebraska.
Number of staff: None.
Employer Identification Number: 476058691

1614
The Owen Foundation
One Owen Pkwy.
2200 Abbott Dr.
Carter Lake 51510

Incorporated in 1959 in NE.
Donor(s): Paxton & Vierling Steel Co., Missouri Valley Steel Co., Northern Plains Steel Co.
Financial data (yr. ended 11/30/87): Assets, $89,661 (M); gifts received, $174,745; expenditures, $149,280, including $148,200 for 14 grants (high: $60,000; low: $250).
Purpose and activities: Primarily local giving, with emphasis on a zoological society and a state wildlife department; grants also for higher education, cultural programs, and social agencies.
Limitations: Giving primarily in NE.
Officers: Robert E. Owen, V.P.; Edward F. Owen, Pres.; Dolores C. Owen, V.P.; Robert K. Andersen, Secy.-Treas.
Employer Identification Number: 476025298

1615
Physicians Mutual Insurance Company Foundation
2600 Dodge St.
Omaha 68131 (402) 633-1000

Financial data (yr. ended 11/30/87): Assets, $775,052 (M); expenditures, $65,770, including $65,065 for 55 grants (high: $19,025; low: $25).

Purpose and activities: Support for the United Way, public and private education, medical research, the elderly, the disadvantaged, and the arts.
Limitations: Giving primarily in Omaha, NE.
Application information:
Initial approach: Written proposal
Write: Robert A. Reed, Pres.
Officers and Directors: Bill R. Benson, V.P.; Jerome J. Coon, Treas.; Robert A. Reed, Pres.
Employer Identification Number: 363424068

1616
Quivey-Bay State Foundation
1515 East 20th St.
Scottsbluff 69361 (308) 632-2168

Established in 1948 in NE.
Donor(s): M.B. Quivey, Mrs. M.B. Quivey.
Financial data (yr. ended 1/31/88): Assets, $2,039,899 (M); expenditures, $143,279, including $133,232 for 60 grants (high: $15,000; low: $100).
Purpose and activities: Emphasis on higher education, church support, and youth and child welfare agencies; support also for historic preservation.
Limitations: Giving primarily in NE. No grants to individuals, or for endowment funds.
Application information:
Initial approach: Letter
Copies of proposal: 1
Deadline(s): Submit proposal in Sept.; deadline Oct. 15
Board meeting date(s): Oct. and Nov.
Write: Ted Cannon, Secy.-Treas.
Officers and Trustees: Earl R. Cherry, Pres.; Ted Cannon, Secy.-Treas.
Employer Identification Number: 476024159

1617
Rogers Foundation
1311 M St., Suite A
Lincoln 68508 (402) 477-3725

Established in 1954 in NE.
Donor(s): Richard H. Rogers.†
Financial data (yr. ended 12/31/86): Assets, $4,736,326 (M); expenditures, $194,150, including $174,200 for 31 grants (high: $25,500; low: $100).
Purpose and activities: Emphasis on support for cultural programs, civic affairs, youth and health agencies, and education.
Limitations: Giving primarily in Lincoln and Lancaster County, NE. No support for religious activities, national organizations, or organizations supported by government agencies. No grants to individuals, or for fundraising benefits, program advertising, endowments, or continuing support; no loans.
Publications: Application guidelines.
Application information:
Initial approach: Proposal
Write: Richard W. Agee, Pres.
Officers and Directors: Richard W. Agee, Pres.; Eloise R. Agee, V.P.; Richard R. Agee.
Employer Identification Number: 476026897

1618
Robert Herman Storz Foundation
Eighth Fl., Kiewit Plaza
Omaha 68131

Established in 1957.
Donor(s): Robert Herman Storz.
Financial data (yr. ended 12/31/87): Assets, $5,645,509 (M); gifts received, $250,000; expenditures, $194,346, including $34,355 for 16 grants (high: $9,700; low: $100).
Purpose and activities: Support for hospitals, higher education, and cultural programs.
Limitations: Giving primarily in NE.
Application information: Contributions only to pre-selected organizations. Applications not accepted.
Trustees: Susan Storz Butler, Robert Herman Storz.
Employer Identification Number: 476025980

1619
The Valmont Foundation
c/o Valmont Industries, Inc.
Valley 68064

Established in 1976.
Donor(s): Valmont Industries, Inc.
Financial data (yr. ended 2/28/88): Assets, $22,585 (M); gifts received, $215,000; expenditures, $201,678, including $201,663 for 67 grants (high: $31,850; low: $100).
Purpose and activities: Giving primarily for higher education, youth agencies, community funds, and cultural programs.
Limitations: Giving primarily in NE.
Officers: Robert B. Daugherty, Pres.; Paul F. Linemann, Secy.; Terry J. McClain, Treas.
Director: Mel Bannister.
Employer Identification Number: 362895245

NEVADA

1620
Bing Fund Corporation
302 East Carson Ave., Suite 617
Las Vegas 89101 (702) 386-6183
Application address: 9700 West Pico Blvd., Los Angeles, CA 90035; Tel.: (213) 277-3222

Incorporated in 1977 in NV as partial successor to Bing Fund, Inc., incorporated in NY.
Donor(s): Leo S. Bing,† Mrs. Anna Bing Arnold, Peter S. Bing.
Financial data (yr. ended 5/31/88): Assets, $34,610,348 (M); gifts received, $225,000; expenditures, $1,110,952, including $1,030,350 for 127 grants (high: $155,000; low: $200).
Purpose and activities: Giving primarily for higher education, museums, the arts, secondary education, hospitals, and population control.
Limitations: Giving primarily in southern CA.
Application information:
Deadline(s): None
Write: Peter S. Bing, V.P.
Officers: Anna H. Bing, Pres.; Peter S. Bing, V.P. and Treas.; Robert D. Burch, Secy.
Employer Identification Number: 942476169

1621
First Interstate Bank of Nevada Foundation
One East First St.
P.O. Box 11007
Reno 89501 (702) 784-3844

Established in 1983 in NV.
Donor(s): First Interstate Bank of Nevada.
Financial data (yr. ended 12/31/88): Assets, $431,804 (M); gifts received, $480,000; expenditures, $447,277, including $446,527 for 51 grants (high: $100,000; low: $1,000; average: $8,000-$9,000) and $750 for 2 employee matching gifts.
Purpose and activities: Emphasis on community funds, higher education, arts and cultural programs and social service agencies.
Types of support: Capital campaigns, continuing support, employee matching gifts, equipment, general purposes, matching funds, operating budgets, renovation projects.
Limitations: Giving primarily in NV. No support for religious organizations or United Way recipients. No grants to individuals.
Publications: Informational brochure (including application guidelines).
Application information: Application form required.
Copies of proposal: 1
Deadline(s): 10th of each month
Board meeting date(s): 3rd Tuesday of each month
Final notification: Immediately after board meeting
Write: Kevin Day, Pres.
Officers: Kevin Day, Pres.; Larry Tuntland, V.P.; Ronald Zurek, Secy.; Kevin J. Sullivan, Treas.
Trustees: J.H. Bradshaw, Don Snyder.
Number of staff: 1 part-time professional.
Employer Identification Number: 942831988

1622
The Hall Family Foundation
P.O. Box 1479
Minden 89423-1479 (702) 782-5174

Established in 1983 in NV.
Donor(s): Joanne Hall.
Financial data (yr. ended 12/31/87): Assets, $1,816,644 (M); expenditures, $64,512, including $57,231 for 23 grants (high: $10,000; low: $50).
Purpose and activities: Giving primarily for higher education, conservation of wilderness areas, cancer research and a facility that provides temporary lodging for families of cancer patients on a cost-free basis, and a child welfare organization; support also for health, including medical education, and the biological sciences, and nursing.
Types of support: Matching funds, building funds, general purposes, operating budgets.
Limitations: Giving primarily in CA and NV.

Application information: Contributes only to pre-selected organizations. Applications not accepted.
Officers and Directors:* Arthur E. Hall,* Chair.; Joanne Hall, Secy.-Treas.; Christina Holloway.
Employer Identification Number: 880193741

1623
Robert Z. Hawkins Foundation
One East Liberty St., Suite 509
Reno 89505 (702) 786-4646

Established in 1980.
Financial data (yr. ended 12/31/87): Assets, $9,043,525 (M); expenditures, $663,121, including $519,365 for 70 grants (high: $89,427; low: $166).
Purpose and activities: Emphasis on education, including a university, youth agencies and child welfare, church support, and a museum.
Types of support: Special projects.
Limitations: Giving limited to NV. No grants to individuals.
Application information: Awards are limited to $20,000 a year per organization.
Deadline(s): None
Write: Paul O. Wiig, Chair.
Trustees: Paul O. Wiig, Chair.; Kathryn A. Hawkins, Robert M. Hawkins, Bill A. Ligon, Security Bank of Nevada.
Employer Identification Number: 880162645

1624
The Murray Petersen Foundation
2900 Las Vegas Blvd. South
Las Vegas 89109

Established in 1976 in NV.
Donor(s): Dean Petersen, Faye Petersen Johnson.
Financial data (yr. ended 12/31/87): Assets, $93,592 (M); gifts received, $107,707; expenditures, $113,691, including $113,637 for 21 grants (high: $25,000; low: $64).
Purpose and activities: Emphasis on higher education, educational broadcasting, youth agencies, recreation, social agencies, child welfare, and cultural programs. Support also for health agencies and medical research.
Limitations: Giving primarily in NV.
Application information: Contributes only to pre-selected organizations. Applications not accepted.
Trustees: Faye Petersen Johnson, Ralph Johnson, Dean Petersen, Mary Petersen.
Employer Identification Number: 880138035

1625
Porsche Foundation
c/o Edward Triolo, Public Relations
P.O. Box 30911
Reno 89520-3911

Established in 1986 in NV.
Financial data (yr. ended 12/31/87): Assets, $477,848 (M); gifts received, $100,000; expenditures, $105,328, including $104,951 for grants.
Purpose and activities: Support for environmental research, cultural programs, and general charities.
Officer: John A. Cook, Pres.
Employer Identification Number: 943024854

1626
Carol Buck Sells Foundation
P.O. Drawer CE
Incline Village 89450 (702) 831-6366

Foundation incorporated in 1979 in NV.
Donor(s): Carol B. Sells, John E. Sells.
Financial data (yr. ended 11/30/88): Assets, $5,393,174 (M); expenditures, $310,619, including $210,780 for 7 grants (high: $60,000; low: $6,000).
Purpose and activities: Support for the performing arts, especially music.
Types of support: Continuing support, annual campaigns, matching funds, endowment funds, special projects.
Limitations: Giving primarily in the western U.S. No grants to individuals, or for emergency funds, deficit financing, capital campaigns, equipment, land acquisition, renovations, scholarships, fellowships, research, publications, or conferences; no loans.
Application information:
Initial approach: Letter or telephone
Copies of proposal: 1
Deadline(s): Mar. 31 and Sept. 31
Board meeting date(s): Jan., Apr., July, and Oct.
Final notification: 3 months
Write: Marya A. Beam, Admin. Asst., or Carol B. Sells, Pres.
Officers and Trustees: Carol B. Sells, Pres. and Secy.; Christian P. Erdman, V.P. and Treas.; John M. Barry, Helen O'Hanlon.
Number of staff: 1 full-time professional; 1 part-time professional.
Employer Identification Number: 880163505
Recent arts and culture grants:
Arizona Opera Company, Phoenix, AZ, $35,000. For costume expenses for opera, Romeo and Juliet. 11/17/87.
Houston Grand Opera, Houston, TX, $25,000. Toward production costs of Ariadne auf Naxos. 11/17/87.
K U N R-FM Public Radio, Reno, NV, $7,280. For underwriting saturday morning opera broadcasts. 11/17/87.
Nevada Opera Association, Reno, NV, $12,500. For production costs of Joan of Arc. 11/17/87.
North Tahoe Fine Arts Council, Tahoe City, CA, $5,000. For Shakespeare Music Festivals at Sand Harbor. 11/17/87.
San Francisco Symphony, San Francisco, CA, $50,000. To support symphony's permanent fund campaign. 11/17/87.
Sierra Nevada Museum of Art, Reno, NV, $50,000. For matching grant to museum endowment fund. 11/17/87.
University of Nevada, Nightengale Concert Hall, Reno, NV, $13,000. For matching grant toward grand opening of Hall. 11/22/87.

1627
The Southwest Gas Foundation
5241 Spring Mountain Rd.
Las Vegas 89102 (702) 876-7222

Established in 1985 in NV.
Donor(s): Southwest Gas Corp.
Financial data (yr. ended 12/31/87): Assets, $680,036 (M); gifts received, $620,000; expenditures, $296,556, including $296,278 for 1,096 grants (high: $25,000; low: $125).
Purpose and activities: Emphasis on higher education; art associations and museums; United Way; health associations and services for the handicapped.
Types of support: General purposes, employee matching gifts.
Limitations: Giving primarily in NV, AZ, and San Bernardino County, CA.
Application information: Application form required.
Initial approach: Letter
Write: Dennis M. Hetherington, V.P., Corp. Communications (Fdn. Mgr.)
Officer: Dennis M. Hetherington, Mgr.
Directors: Fred W. Cover, Kenny C. Guinn, Micheal O. Maffie.
Number of staff: None.
Employer Identification Number: 942988564

1628
E. L. Wiegand Foundation
Wiegand Ctr.
165 West Liberty St.
Reno 89501 (702) 333-0310

Established in 1982 in NV.
Donor(s): Ann K. Wiegand,† Edwin L. Wiegand.†
Financial data (yr. ended 10/31/88): Assets, $73,147,880 (M); expenditures, $4,035,340, including $3,520,390 for 70 grants.
Purpose and activities: Grants primarily for education, health and medical research; also for public affairs, civic and community affairs, and arts and cultural affairs; emphasis on Roman Catholic institutions.
Types of support: Equipment, matching funds, special projects, renovation projects.
Limitations: Giving primarily in NV and adjoining western states, including CA, AZ, OR, ID, and UT. No support for organizations receiving significant support from public tax funds; organizations with beneficiaries of their own choosing; or federal, state, or local government agencies or institutions. No grants to individuals, or for endowment funds, fundraising campaigns, or operating funds.
Publications: Informational brochure (including application guidelines).
Application information: Application form required.
Initial approach: Letter
Copies of proposal: 1
Deadline(s): Feb. 15 and Aug. 15
Board meeting date(s): Oct. and Apr.
Write: Raymond C. Avansino, Jr., Chair. and Pres.
Officers: Raymond C. Avansino, Jr.,* Chair. and Pres.; Michael J. Melarkey, V.P. and Secy.-Treas.; Norbert F. Stanny,* V.P.
Trustees:* Harvey C. Fruehauf, Jr.
Employer Identification Number: 942839372

NEW HAMPSHIRE

1629
Norwin S. and Elizabeth N. Bean Foundation
c/o New Hampshire Charitable Fund
One South St., P.O. Box 1335
Concord 03302-1335 (603) 225-6641

Trust established in 1957 in NH; later became an affiliated trust of the New Hampshire Charitable Fund.
Donor(s): Norwin S. Bean,† Elizabeth N. Bean.†
Financial data (yr. ended 12/31/87): Assets, $5,811,392 (M); expenditures, $351,612, including $287,245 for 25 grants (high: $114,700; low: $600) and $12,000 for loans.
Purpose and activities: Grants primarily for health, education, welfare, and cultural activities.
Types of support: General purposes, seed money, emergency funds, building funds, equipment, land acquisition, special projects, conferences and seminars, matching funds, loans, program-related investments, consulting services.
Limitations: Giving limited to Amherst and Manchester, NH. No grants to individuals, or for scholarships, fellowships, operating budgets, deficit financing, or endowment funds.
Publications: Annual report, informational brochure (including application guidelines).
Application information:
Initial approach: Letter or telephone
Copies of proposal: 1
Deadline(s): Feb. 1, May 1, Aug. 1, and Nov. 1
Board meeting date(s): Mar., June, Sept., and Dec.
Write: Deborah Cowan, Prog. Dir.
Officers and Trustees: Charles A. DeGrandpre, Chair.; Elizabeth Lown, John R. McLane, Jr., Francis N. Perry, James A. Shanahan, Jr., Angie Whidden, R.S.M.
Number of staff: 5
Employer Identification Number: 026013381

1630
Cogswell Benevolent Trust
875 Elm St.
Manchester 03101 (603) 622-4013

Trust established in 1929 in NH.
Donor(s): Leander A. Cogswell.†
Financial data (yr. ended 12/31/86): Assets, $9,379,023 (M); expenditures, $364,441, including $287,165 for 55 grants (high: $40,000; low: $500), $14,900 for 36 grants to individuals and $11,525 for 37 loans to individuals.
Purpose and activities: Grants principally for higher education, youth agencies, performing arts, health associations, community funds, hospitals, and church support.
Limitations: Giving primarily in NH. No grants to individuals, or for endowment funds or operating budgets.
Application information: The foundation no longer gives scholarships or loans to individuals; scholarship funds have been donated to the New Hampshire Charitable Fund-Student Aid Program, One South St., Concord, NH 03301.
Initial approach: Letter
Copies of proposal: 1
Deadline(s): None
Board meeting date(s): Usually weekly and as required
Final notification: 30 days
Write: David P. Goodwin, Trustee
Officer: Mary Stimans, Secy.
Trustees: David P. Goodwin, Mark Northridge, Theodore Wadleigh.
Number of staff: 1
Employer Identification Number: 020235690

1631
Indian Head Banks Charitable Foundation
One Indian Head Plaza
Nashua 03060 (603) 880-5000

Donor(s): Indian Head National Bank.
Financial data (yr. ended 12/31/87): Assets, $75,524 (M); gifts received, $110,000; expenditures, $56,491, including $56,428 for 26 grants (high: $10,000; low: $250).
Purpose and activities: Support for conservation, youth, historical preservation, and education.
Application information:
Deadline(s): None
Write: Sheree Goldwin, Mgr.
Officer: Sheree Goldwin, Mgr.
Employer Identification Number: 222606775

1632
Oleonda Jameson Trust
One Eagle Square
P.O. Box 709
Concord 03301

Established in 1977 in NH.
Financial data (yr. ended 12/31/86): Assets, $2,320,000 (M); expenditures, $148,090, including $133,500 for 38 grants (high: $15,000; low: $100).
Purpose and activities: Giving primarily for higher education, community funds, social service agencies, hospitals, and cultural programs.
Limitations: Giving limited to NH, with emphasis in Concord. No grants for capital improvements, construction, or endowment funds.
Trustees: Malcolm McLane, Dudley W. Orr, Robert H. Reno.
Employer Identification Number: 026048930

1633
New Hampshire Ball Bearings Foundation
U.S. Route 202 South
Peterborough 03458-2106 (603) 924-3311

Financial data (yr. ended 12/31/87): Assets, $321,155 (L); expenditures, $27,743, including $26,915 for 10 grants (high: $15,000; low: $500).
Purpose and activities: Support for youth, education, arts, health services, and social services.
Limitations: Giving primarily in areas of company operations in Peterborough, Jaffrey, and Laconia, NH.
Application information:
Initial approach: Letter
Board meeting date(s): Usually early Feb.
Write: James C. Finch, Trustee
Trustees: Jerry G. Calvin, Chair.; James C. Finch, Michael R. Samide.
Employer Identification Number: 026005861

1634
The New Hampshire Charitable Fund
One South St.
P.O. Box 1335
Concord 03302-1335 (603) 225-6641

Community foundation incorporated in 1962 in NH.
Financial data (yr. ended 12/31/88): Assets, $39,601,937 (M); gifts received, $5,371,095; expenditures, $4,126,480, including $2,013,646 for 482 grants (high: $50,000; low: $100; average: $100-$5,000), $566,751 for 478 grants to individuals, $372,611 for loans to organizations and $274,234 for 203 loans to individuals.
Purpose and activities: Giving for charitable and educational purposes including the arts, humanities, the environment and conservation, health, and social and community services; grants primarily to inaugurate new programs and strengthen existing charitable organizations, with emphasis on programs rather than capital needs; support also for college scholarships.
Types of support: Seed money, loans, student aid, scholarship funds, general purposes, special projects, student loans, consulting services, technical assistance.
Limitations: Giving limited to NH. No grants to individuals (except for student aid); generally no grants for building funds, endowments, operating support, or deficit financing.
Publications: Annual report, program policy statement, informational brochure (including application guidelines).
Application information:
Initial approach: Telephone or letter
Copies of proposal: 1
Deadline(s): Feb. 1, May 1, Aug. 1, and Nov. 1; May 2 for student aid applicants for upcoming school year
Board meeting date(s): Mar., June, Sept., and Dec.
Final notification: 4 to 6 weeks
Write: Deborah Cowan, Assoc. Dir.
Officers: Aollis E. Harrington, Jr.,* Chair.; Lewis Feldstein,* Pres.; Linda McGoldrick,* Secy.; Robert H. Reno,* Treas.
Directors:* Ferris G. Bavicchi, Martin L. Gross, Hollis E. Harrington, Jr., J. Bonnie Newman, Walter Peterson, Kimon S. Zachos.
Number of staff: 6 full-time professional; 1 part-time professional; 4 full-time support; 1 part-time support.
Employer Identification Number: 026005625
Recent arts and culture grants:

Apple Hill Center for Chamber Music, East Sullivan, NH, $7,500. For initiation of program to secure corporate sponsorship of performances. 1987.
Monadnock Music, Peterborough, NH, $10,500. For final challenge grant and completed fundraising toward endowment. 1987.
New Hampshire Music Festival, Center Harbor, NH, $14,000. To begin endowment development effort. 1987.
New Hampshire Performing Arts Center, Manchester, NH, $5,960. For initiation of annual marketing program using broadcast media. 1987.
North Country Center, Lincoln, NH, $6,020. For consultancy and expenses to establish systems for membership and subscription sales. 1987.
Pontine Movement Theater, Portsmouth, NH, $15,000. To support major marketing initiative for performance series and educational programs. 1987.
Portsmouth Academy of Performing Arts, Portsmouth, NH, $7,044. For administrative support for newly established performance collaborative. 1987.
W E V O-Granite State Public Radio, Concord, NH, $9,000. To support ten candidate forums and statewide conference on how long term health care for aged and disabled issue impacts in New Hampshire. 1987.

1635
Ellis L. Phillips Foundation
13 Dartmouth College Hwy.
Lyme 03768 (603) 795-2790

Incorporated in 1930 in NY.
Donor(s): Ellis L. Phillips.†
Financial data (yr. ended 6/30/88): Assets, $5,025,728 (M); expenditures, $339,121, including $264,300 for 45 grants (high: $25,000; low: $600; average: $1,000-$10,000).
Purpose and activities: Grants to organizations emerging on the regional or national scene seeking to develop programs and attract wider suppport. Grants made for education on public issues, religion, education, the arts, preservation/conservation, social services and health care.
Types of support: Annual campaigns, conferences and seminars, continuing support, endowment funds, internships, seed money.
Limitations: Giving primarily in northern New England. No support for medical research. No grants to individuals, or for scholarships, fellowships, or matching gifts; no loans.
Publications: Annual report (including application guidelines).
Application information:
Initial approach: Letter of 1 to 3 pages
Copies of proposal: 1
Board meeting date(s): Oct., Feb., and May
Write: Patricia A. Cate, Exec. Dir.
Officers and Directors: Ellis L. Phillips, Jr., Pres.; Marion G. Phillips, V.P.; Ellis L. Phillips III, Secy.; George C. Thompson, Treas.; Patricia A. Cate, Exec. Dir.; David L. Grumman, George E. McCully, John W. Oelsner, Walter C. Paine, Elise Phillips Watts.
Number of staff: 1 part-time professional.
Employer Identification Number: 135677691
Recent arts and culture grants:
Governors Institutes of Vermont, Shaftsbury, VT, $5,000. Toward 1987 budget of summer programs in art, science and technology for high school students. 1987.
Greenwich Historical Society, Greenwich, CT, $5,000. Toward construction of Historical Archives building. 1987.
Penobscot Marine Museum, Searsport, ME, $7,500. Toward renovating barn to become Visitor Orientation Center. 1987.
Pentangle, Woodstock, VT, $5,000. To help support arts programs in local elementary and high schools. 1987.
Save Our Universalist Landmark (S.O.U.L), NYC, NY, $5,000. Toward restoration and preservation of 1897 English Gothic church on Central Park West. 1987.
Shelburne Farms, Shelburne, VT, $10,000. For The Stewardship Institute. 1987.
Vermont Historical Society, Montpelier, VT, $8,500. To continue cataloguing Rugg Collection of Vermontiana. 1987.
Weathersfield, Town of, Weatherfield, VT, $5,000. Toward renovation and relocation of Salmond Covered Bridge. 1987.

1636
Putnam Foundation
150 Congress St.
Keene 03431 (603) 352-2448
Additional address: P.O. Box 323, Keene, NH 03431

Trust established in 1952 in NH.
Financial data (yr. ended 10/31/87): Assets, $4,100,000 (M); expenditures, $280,000, including $260,000 for grants (high: $100,000; low: $100; average: $5,000).
Purpose and activities: Emphasis on civic affairs, cultural programs, historic preservation, ecological maintenance, youth agencies, education, and conservation.
Limitations: Giving primarily in NH.
Application information:
Initial approach: Letter
Deadline(s): None
Write: Thomas P. Putnam, Secy.
Officer: Thomas P. Putnam, Secy.
Trustees: David F. Putnam, James A. Putnam, Rosamond P. Putnam.
Employer Identification Number: 026011388

1637
Marion C. Smyth Trust
875 Elm St., Rm. 615
Manchester 03101 (603) 623-3420

Established in 1946 in NH.
Donor(s): Marion C. Smyth.†
Financial data (yr. ended 12/31/87): Assets, $3,759,034 (M); expenditures, $231,416, including $192,490 for 50 grants (high: $51,600; low: $200).
Purpose and activities: To establish and maintain the Frederick Smyth Institute of music; giving also for musical education, including scholarships in the city of Manchester (a) for the cultural benefit of the citizens of Manchester and the state of New Hampshire and (b) to aid and encourage deserving youth of Manchester and adjacent towns to increase their knowledge of the field of music.
Types of support: Continuing support, equipment, scholarship funds.
Limitations: Giving limited to NH, primarily Manchester.
Application information: Application form required for student scholarships.
Initial approach: Letter
Copies of proposal: 1
Board meeting date(s): As required
Write: Lyford B. MacEwen, Chair.
Trustees: John H. Giffin, Jr., Lyford B. MacEwen, Roger E. Sundeen.
Number of staff: 1 part-time support.
Employer Identification Number: 026005793

1638
Gilbert Verney Foundation
c/o Monadnock Paper Mills
Bennington 03442 (603) 588-3311

Donor(s): Monadnock Paper Mills, Inc.
Financial data (yr. ended 12/31/87): Assets, $883,777 (M); gifts received, $175,000; expenditures, $41,098, including $39,550 for 35 grants (high: $12,500; low: $50).
Purpose and activities: Support for youth, the arts, conservation, wildlife, women, and religion.
Limitations: Giving primarily in NH. No support for organizations trying to influence legislation.
Application information:
Initial approach: Letter
Deadline(s): None
Write: Richard G. Verney, Pres.
Officer: Richard G. Verney, Pres.
Trustees: Diane V. Greenway, E. Geoffrey Verney.
Employer Identification Number: 026007363

NEW JERSEY

1639
Allied-Signal Foundation
(Formerly Allied Corporation Foundation)
Columbia Rd. and Park Ave.
P.O. Box 2245R
Morristown 07962 (201) 455-5876

Incorporated in 1963 in NY; in 1982 absorbed Bunker Ramo Foundation; in 1984 absorbed Bendix Foundation; merged and incorporated in 1982 in NJ as Allied Corporation Foundation; in 1987 name changed to Allied-Signal Foundation.
Donor(s): Allied-Signal, Inc.
Financial data (yr. ended 12/31/88): Assets, $111,748 (M); gifts received, $9,085,956; expenditures, $7,363,725 for 600 grants (high: $500,000; low: $1,000; average: $2,000-$15,000) and $1,312,529 for 7,007 employee matching gifts.

Purpose and activities: Support primarily for higher education, including fellowship and scholarship programs, and community funds; grants also for health, aging, human services, youth agencies, urban affairs, and cultural programs.
Types of support: Operating budgets, continuing support, annual campaigns, seed money, building funds, equipment, employee matching gifts, fellowships, employee-related scholarships, scholarship funds, renovation projects.
Limitations: Giving primarily in areas of company operations. No support for church-related programs. No grants to individuals, or for endowment funds; no loans.
Application information:
Initial approach: Letter
Copies of proposal: 1
Deadline(s): Submit proposal preferably in July and Aug.; no set deadline
Board meeting date(s): Feb.
Final notification: Only if approved
Write: Alan S. Painter, V.P. and Exec. Dir.
Officers: David G. Powell,* Pres.; Alan S. Painter, V.P. and Exec. Dir.; Brian D. Forrow,* V.P.; Heather M. Mullett, Secy.; G. Peter D'Aloria, Treas.
Directors:* Edward L. Hennessy, Jr., Chair.; John W. Barter, Alan Belzer, John L. Day, Roy H. Ekrom, Mary L. Good, Robert L. Kirk, Edwin M. Halkyard, Fred M. Poses.
Number of staff: None.
Employer Identification Number: 222416651

1640
American Cyanamid Company Contributions Program
One Cyanamid Plaza
Wayne 07470 (201) 831-2714

Financial data (yr. ended 12/31/87): Total giving, $3,647,000, including $3,515,000 for grants (low: $25; average: $1,000-$5,000) and $132,000 for employee matching gifts.
Purpose and activities: Supports programs which benefit the company's business environment, and its employees. Support for education, the arts and humanities, sciences, business education, health, welfare, civic affairs, and the United Way. Grants to universities are made to strengthen the economics, business administration, chemistry, chemical engineering, and life sciences departments. Grants are unrestricted within these disciplines so that funds can be directed to where they are most needed. Support also for local cultural organizations which benefit the community as a whole. Support for hospital building funds and capital campaigns in plant communities only; employee matching gifts for higher education only.
Types of support: Building funds, capital campaigns, conferences and seminars, employee matching gifts, fellowships, general purposes, operating budgets, research, scholarship funds, special projects.
Limitations: Giving primarily in headquarters city and major operating areas in NJ, CT, NY, OH, LA, CA, FL, MI, MO, and MA. No support for sectarian, religious, political, veterans', special interest groups, or for organizations participating in the United Way. No grants to individuals.
Publications: Program policy statement.
Application information: Include description of organization and project, plan for future funding, and list of other funding sources; form letters are not accepted.
Initial approach: Letter
Deadline(s): No deadlines but large requests preferred in Aug. or Sept.
Final notification: 4-6 weeks for full review and decision
Write: Dolores Stortz, Contribs. Mgr.
Number of staff: 1 full-time professional; 1 part-time support.

1641
Armco Foundation
300 Interpace Pkwy.
Parsippany 07054-0324 (201) 316-5274

Incorporated in 1951 in OH.
Donor(s): Armco, Inc.
Financial data (yr. ended 12/31/87): Assets, $8,737,934 (M); expenditures, $595,165, including $422,166 for 25 grants (high: $100,000; low: $500; average: $100-$5,000) and $145,021 for 589 employee matching gifts.
Purpose and activities: Grants for health and welfare, including youth agencies, hospitals, education, including higher education and a scholarship for the children of active company employees administered by the College Scholarship Service; support also for civic and public affairs, cultural programs, and a matching grant program for higher educational and cultural institutions.
Types of support: Continuing support, annual campaigns, seed money, building funds, equipment, matching funds, consulting services, employee-related scholarships, employee matching gifts, special projects.
Limitations: Giving primarily in areas of company operations. No support for religious organizations. No grants to individuals (except for employee-related scholarships), or for operating budgets, deficit financing, land acquisition, endowment funds, fellowships, demonstration projects, or publications; no loans.
Application information: Funds presently committed. Applications not accepted.
Board meeting date(s): Mar. and Dec.
Write: Ms. Loyce A. Martin, Fdn. Admin.
Officers: Robert E. Boni,* Pres.; John M. Bilich, Exec. V.P.; Robert W. Kent, V.P. and Secy.; James L. Bertsch, Treas.
Trustees:* Frederick B. Dent, Chair.; Wallace B. Askins, Brage Golding, Harry Holiday, Jr., John W. Ladish, Robert L. Purdum.
Number of staff: 1 full-time professional; 1 full-time support.
Employer Identification Number: 316026565

1642
The Armour Family Foundation
c/o Schotz Simon Miller & Co.
One Mack Centre Dr.
Paramus 07652-3905

Established in 1981.
Donor(s): George and Frances Armour Foundation, Inc.
Financial data (yr. ended 3/31/87): Assets, $1,448,372 (M); expenditures, $101,646, including $57,300 for 21 grants (high: $10,700; low: $250; average: $2,500).
Purpose and activities: Emphasis on Jewish sociological areas, medical research and hospitals, cultural programs and higher education; some support also for social service agencies.
Application information: Contributes only to pre-selected organizations.
Officers and Directors: Robert N. Armour, Pres.; Joan Armour, Secy.; David Armour, Frederick Sudekum.
Number of staff: 1 part-time professional.
Employer Identification Number: 510257055

1643
The Edna & Jack Belasco Foundation
P.O. Box 100
135 High St.
Mount Holly 08060 (609) 234-8462
Application address: 139 East Main St., Moorestown, NJ 08057

Established in 1977 in NJ.
Donor(s): Edna R. Belasco.†
Financial data (yr. ended 3/31/88): Assets, $579,389 (M); expenditures, $246,487, including $235,889 for 77 grants (high: $10,000; low: $1,000; average: $2,500-$5,000).
Purpose and activities: Grants for social service and youth organizations, hospitals and health agencies, education, religious organizations, and cultural programs in the arts community.
Types of support: Special projects, scholarship funds, continuing support, seed money, emergency funds, equipment, matching funds, internships, scholarship funds, research, conferences and seminars, renovation projects, technical assistance.
Limitations: Giving primarily in the Delaware Valley (southern NJ and the greater Philadelphia, PA, area). No grants to individuals, or for operating budgets, annual campaigns, deficit financing, endowment funds, consulting services, exchange programs, fellowships, or publications; no loans.
Publications: Application guidelines, 990-PF.
Application information: Funds committed for 1989; no applications accepted until 1990.
Initial approach: Letter, telephone, or proposal
Copies of proposal: 1
Deadline(s): Submit proposal preferably in Jan. or Feb.; deadline Feb. 28
Board meeting date(s): Mar. and Sept.
Final notification: Within fiscal year
Write: Peggy Maitland Henry, Exec. Dir.
Officer: Peggy Maitland Henry, Exec. Dir.
Trustees: William H. Wells, Provident National Bank.
Number of staff: 1 part-time professional.
Employer Identification Number: 236656485

1644
Frank and Lydia Bergen Foundation
c/o First Fidelity Bank
55 Madison Ave.
Morristown 07960 (201) 829-7111

Incorporated in 1983 in NJ.
Donor(s): Charlotte V. Bergen.†
Financial data (yr. ended 12/31/88): Assets, $5,434,611 (M); expenditures, $378,040, including $298,971 for 36 grants (high: $41,275; low: $1,500).
Purpose and activities: For the benefit of the musical arts; support for educational out-reach activity of performing arts agencies; aid for worthy students of music through institutions; support for the development of music skills; and increased recognition, training, and conducting opportunities for American conductors.
Types of support: Conferences and seminars, consulting services, matching funds, scholarship funds, special projects, continuing support.
Limitations: Giving primarily in the NJ area, except for young American conductor projects of nationwide impact. No grants for annual campaigns, deficit financing, land acquisition, renovation projects; no loans.
Publications: Annual report, informational brochure (including application guidelines), application guidelines.
Application information:
Initial approach: Letter or telephone
Copies of proposal: 1
Deadline(s): 15th of Feb., May, Aug., and Nov.
Board meeting date(s): Apr., July, Oct., and Jan.
Write: Jane Donnelly, Exec. Dir.
Officers and Trustee Committee: Marie Carlone, Treas.; A. Daniel D'Ambrosio, Chair.; Peter T. Lillard, Vice-Chair.; Bryant K. Alford, Secy.; Jane Donnelly, Exec. Dir.
Trustee: First Fidelity Bank.
Number of staff: 1 full-time professional.
Employer Identification Number: 226359304

1645
The Russell Berrie Foundation
111 Bauer Dr.
Oakland 07436-3192

Established in 1985 in NJ.
Financial data (yr. ended 10/31/87): Assets, $2,030,621 (M); gifts received, $2,267,600; expenditures, $232,798, including $232,500 for 19 grants (high: $35,000; low: $5,000).
Purpose and activities: Giving primarily for Jewish welfare; support also for the arts and higher education.
Application information:
Initial approach: Letter
Deadline(s): None
Write: Russell Berrie, Pres.
Officers and Trustees: Russell Berrie, Pres.; Leslie Berrie, Uni Berrie, Myron Rosner.
Employer Identification Number: 222620908

1646
Adele & Leonard Block Foundation, Inc.
257 Cornelison Ave.
Jersey City 07302-3116

Established in 1945 in NJ.
Financial data (yr. ended 11/30/87): Assets, $5,112 (M); gifts received, $155,000; expenditures, $210,095, including $201,000 for 15 grants (high: $100,000; low: $300).
Purpose and activities: Giving primarily for the arts and higher education.
Officers: Leonard Block, Pres.; Thomas Block, V.P. and Treas.; Adele G. Block, V.P.; Peggy Danziger, V.P.; John E. Peters, Secy.
Employer Identification Number: 226026000

1647
James and Barbara Block Foundation, Inc.
257 Cornelison Ave.
Jersey City 07302

Established in 1975 in NJ.
Financial data (yr. ended 6/30/87): Assets, $335,386 (M); expenditures, $248,918, including $248,280 for 26 grants (high: $75,000; low: $25).
Purpose and activities: Support primarily for higher education and cultural programs; support also for a Jewish welfare fund.
Officers and Trustees: James A. Block, Pres.; Barbara Block, V.P.; Peter J. Repetti, Secy.-Treas.
Employer Identification Number: 510138517

1648
The Mary Owen Borden Memorial Foundation
160 Hodge Rd.
Princeton 08540 (609) 924-3637

Incorporated in 1934 in NJ.
Donor(s): Bertram H. Borden,† Victory Memorial Park Foundation.
Financial data (yr. ended 12/31/87): Assets, $7,292,211 (M); expenditures, $436,698, including $368,805 for 51 grants (high: $37,401; low: $100; average: $7,230).
Purpose and activities: Grants for programs focusing on special needs of youth which include: family planning counselling to teenagers; assistance to unwed, teenage mothers; day care centers for young, disadvantaged parents; assistance to families where instability prevails; assistance to institutions or programs aiding delinquent youth; and innovative or alternative forms of criminal justice for youthful offenders. Support also for human services, the arts, conservation and the environment, nuclear disarmament, and substance abuse. Emphasis on grants for new and innovative projects and preference for support to organizations that are new, or established organizations undertaking new projects.
Types of support: Seed money, matching funds, special projects, general purposes, operating budgets, publications.
Limitations: Giving primarily in particularly Monmouth and Mercer counties, NJ. No grants to individuals, or for scholarships (except to graduates of Rumson-Fair Haven New Jersey Regional High School) or fellowships; no loans.
Publications: Application guidelines.
Application information: Application form required.
Initial approach: Write for form if request meets foundation guidelines
Copies of proposal: 1
Deadline(s): Jan. 1, Apr. 1, and Sept. 1
Board meeting date(s): Feb., May, and Oct.
Final notification: 3 months
Write: John C. Borden, Jr., Exec. Dir.
Officers: Mrs. Q.A. Shaw McKean, Jr.,* Pres.; Mrs. Marvin Broder,* V.P.; Mary L. Miles, Secy.; Joseph Lord, Treas.; John C. Borden, Jr.,* Exec. Dir.
Trustees:* Rev. Daphne Hawkes, Dorothy Ransom, Stuart A. Young, Jr.
Number of staff: 1 part-time professional; 1 part-time support.
Employer Identification Number: 136137137

1649
Brady Foundation
P.O. Box 351
Gladstone 07934 (201) 234-1900

Incorporated in 1953 in NJ.
Donor(s): Helen M. Cutting,† Nicholas Brady.
Financial data (yr. ended 12/31/88): Assets, $3,509,000 (M); expenditures, $305,000, including $160,000 for 33 grants (high: $20,000; low: $1,000; average: $5,000).
Purpose and activities: Emphasis on hospitals, youth agencies, museums, and religious organizations.
Limitations: Giving primarily in NJ.
Application information:
Initial approach: Letter
Deadline(s): None
Board meeting date(s): Quarterly
Write: Joseph A. Gaunt, Secy.
Officers: James C. Brady, Jr.,* Pres. and Treas.; Joseph A. Gaunt, Secy.
Trustees:* N.F. Brady, Anderson Fowler.
Number of staff: 3 part-time professional; 2 part-time support.
Employer Identification Number: 136167209

1650
Charles E. and Edna T. Brundage Charitable, Scientific and Wild Life Conservation Foundation
c/o Thomas L. Morrissey, V.P.
100 Mulberry St.
Newark 07102

Established in 1955 in NJ.
Financial data (yr. ended 12/31/87): Assets, $1,388,436 (M); gifts received, $20,000; expenditures, $80,631, including $68,000 for 35 grants (high: $5,000; low: $500).
Purpose and activities: Giving for cultural activities, including historical preservation, and for social services.
Types of support: General purposes.
Limitations: Giving primarily in NJ.
Application information: Contributes only to pre-selected organizations. Applications not accepted.
Officers and Trustees: Samuel C. Williams, Jr., Pres.; Thomas L. Morrissey, V.P. and Secy.;

William B. Cater, V.P. and Treas.; Edna T. Brundage, Charles B. Cater, June B. Cater, William B. Cater, Jr., Susan Jukowsky.
Employer Identification Number: 226050185

1651
The Bunbury Company, Inc.
169 Nassau St.
Princeton 08542 (609) 683-1414

Incorporated in 1952 in NY.
Donor(s): Dean Mathey.†
Financial data (yr. ended 12/31/88): Assets, $10,970,065 (M); expenditures, $721,380, including $464,000 for 100 grants (high: $100,000; low: $50).
Purpose and activities: Grants primarily for higher and secondary education, youth agencies, health and family services, the fine arts and cultural organizations, environment and ecology, and organizations benefiting women.
Types of support: General purposes.
Limitations: Giving primarily in NJ. No grants to individuals, or for building funds, fellowships, or matching gifts; no loans.
Publications: Annual report.
Application information:
Initial approach: Proposal
Copies of proposal: 1
Deadline(s): 1 month before board meetings
Board meeting date(s): Feb., May, July, and Oct.
Final notification: 1 to 2 weeks after board meeting
Write: Samuel W. Lambert, III, Pres.; or Barbara L. Ruppert, Asst. Secy.
Officers and Directors: Howard W. Stepp, Chair. Emeritus; Samuel W. Lambert III, Pres.; Edward J. Toohey, V.P.; Charles B. Atwater, Secy.; James R. Cogan, Treas.; Charles B. Atwater, Stephan A. Morse, William B. Wright.
Number of staff: 7 part-time professional; 1 part-time support.
Employer Identification Number: 136066172

1652
Campbell Soup Fund
Campbell Place
Camden 08103 (609) 342-6431

Incorporated in 1953 in NJ.
Donor(s): Campbell Soup Co.
Financial data (yr. ended 6/30/88): Assets, $10,101,316 (M); gifts received, $1,700,000; expenditures, $1,531,507, including $1,474,989 for 104 grants (high: $75,000; low: $1,200; average: $5,000-$35,000).
Purpose and activities: Capital grants to private institutions of higher education, and to hospitals and other health care facilities; support also for cultural programs, social service and youth agencies, community funds, and public interest groups.
Types of support: Building funds, renovation projects, capital campaigns.
Limitations: Giving primarily in areas of company operations, with emphasis on the Camden, NJ, and Philadelphia, PA, areas. No grants to individuals, or for operating budgets, continuing support, annual campaigns, seed money, emergency funds, deficit financing, land acquisition, endowment funds, matching gifts, equipment, or scholarships or fellowships; no loans.
Application information:
Initial approach: Letter
Copies of proposal: 1
Deadline(s): None
Board meeting date(s): As required
Final notification: 4 to 8 weeks
Write: Frank G. Moore, Vice-Chair.
Officers: J.J. Furey, Secy.; D.H. Springer,* Treas.; R.J. Land, Cont.
Trustees:* R.L. Baker, Chair.; Frank G. Moore, Vice-Chair.; J.F. O'Brien, Vice-Chair.; A.A. Austin, J.J. Baldwin, R.S. Page, C.S. Rombach.
Number of staff: 2 part-time professional; 2 part-time support.
Employer Identification Number: 216019196

1653
Cape Branch Foundation
c/o Danser, Balaam & Frank
Five Independence Way
Princeton 08540 (609) 987-0300

Established in 1964 in NJ.
Financial data (yr. ended 12/31/87): Assets, $2,788,263 (M); expenditures, $370,547, including $319,000 for 12 grants (high: $175,000; low: $2,000; average: $40,000).
Purpose and activities: Support for secondary education, conservation, museums, and a university.
Types of support: Research, building funds, land acquisition, general purposes.
Limitations: Giving primarily in NJ. No grants to individuals.
Publications: 990-PF.
Application information:
Initial approach: Brief letter
Deadline(s): None
Board meeting date(s): Annually
Write: Dorothy Frank
Directors: Gretchen W. Johnson,* James L. Johnson.
Trustees:* G.O. Danser, John R. Wittenborn.
Number of staff: None.
Employer Identification Number: 226054886

1654
Capezio-Ballet Makers Dance Foundation, Inc.
One Campus Rd.
Totowa 07512 (201) 595-9000

Financial data (yr. ended 12/31/87): Assets, $61,921 (M); gifts received, $90,150; expenditures, $107,543, including $107,101 for grants.
Purpose and activities: Support primarily for service organizations which contribute to dance and to those that contribute to the public awareness of dance as an art form.
Application information:
Initial approach: Letter
Deadline(s): Apr. 1
Board meeting date(s): Annual
Final notification: June
Write: Jane Remel
Officers: Alfred Terlizzi, Pres.; Nick Terlizzi, V.P.; Anthony Giocoio, Secy.
Directors: Robert Carr, Donald Terlizzi.
Employer Identification Number: 136161198

1655
Liz Claiborne Foundation
One Claiborne Ave.
North Bergen 07047 (201) 662-6000

Established in 1981 in NY.
Donor(s): Liz Claiborne, Inc.
Financial data (yr. ended 12/31/87): Assets, $5,376,223 (M); gifts received, $2,500,000; expenditures, $942,567, including $936,851 for 94 grants (high: $263,050; low: $500).
Purpose and activities: Grants primarily for health, culture, education, including higher education, and Jewish community funds; support also for a public television station.
Application information:
Write: Melanie Lyons
Trustees: Leonard Boxer, Jerome A. Chazen, Arthur Ortenberg, Elisabeth Claiborne Ortenberg.
Employer Identification Number: 133060673

1656
Russell Colgate Fund, Inc.
15 Exchange Pl.
Jersey City 07302 (201) 434-7464

Established in 1943 in NJ.
Financial data (yr. ended 12/31/87): Assets, $1,702,645 (M); expenditures, $76,346, including $61,550 for 69 grants (high: $10,000; low: $50).
Purpose and activities: Support primarily for higher education, social services, and cultural programs.
Application information:
Initial approach: Letter
Deadline(s): None
Officers: John K. Colgate, Jr., Pres.; Josephine Wilkinson, V.P.
Employer Identification Number: 221713065

1657
Colton Family Foundation, Inc.
232 Hartshorn Dr.
Short Hills 07078 (201) 467-9360

Established in 1983 in NJ.
Donor(s): Judith S. Colton, Stewart M. Colton.
Financial data (yr. ended 11/30/87): Assets, $215,710 (M); gifts received, $215,200; expenditures, $544,735, including $541,280 for grants (high: $500,000).
Purpose and activities: Grants for higher education in the U.S. and Israel, cultural activities and a Jewish welfare fund.
Limitations: No support for private foundations. No grants to individuals.
Application information:
Initial approach: Letter and proposal
Deadline(s): None
Write: Stewart M. Colton, Mgr.
Managers: Judith S. Colton, Stewart M. Colton, Irving C. Marcus.
Employer Identification Number: 222520918

1658
CPC International Corporate Giving Program
International Plaza
P.O. Box 8000
Englewood Cliffs 07632 (201) 894-2336

Financial data (yr. ended 12/31/87): Total giving, $9,660,201, including $646,148 for grants (high: $22,000; low: $100), $628,053 for employee matching gifts and $8,386,000 for in-kind gifts.
Purpose and activities: Support for education, health and welfare, arts and culture, and civic and community programs, with emphasis on helping minorities, women, the handicapped, child welfare, the disadvantaged, law and justice, literacy, mental health, museums, race relations, drug abuse, and volunteerism. Regionally and nationally, company tends to focus on larger, well-established organizations; local giving sometimes goes to smaller, more innovative programs; support includes in-kind giving of surplus food products. Programs do not reflect in-kind support.
Types of support: Operating budgets, capital campaigns, employee matching gifts, general purposes, special projects.
Limitations: Giving primarily in headquarters city and major operating locations. No support for fraternal, political or religious organizations. No grants to individuals or fundraising projects.
Publications: Program policy statement.
Application information: Application form required.
Initial approach: Letter and proposal
Copies of proposal: 1
Deadline(s): Send proposal by July or Aug.; applications recommended between Sept. and Dec. for consideration in following years budget
Board meeting date(s): Quarterly: Mar., June, Sept., and Nov.
Final notification: Month following meeting
Write: Joseph R. Ellicott, Mgr., Community Relations
Number of staff: 2 full-time support.

1659
Crum and Forster Foundation, Inc.
211 Mt. Airy Rd.
Basking Ridge 07920 (201) 204-3577

Incorporated in 1953 in CA as the Industrial Indemnity Foundation; the foundation is registered in CA and NJ.
Donor(s): Crum and Forster Corp., and affiliated companies.
Financial data (yr. ended 12/31/87): Assets, $28,425 (L); gifts received, $741,101; expenditures, $712,676, including $650,766 for 454 grants (high: $40,200; low: $100; average: $500-$3,000) and $61,863 for 470 employee matching gifts.
Purpose and activities: Giving primarily for community funds, youth agencies, health agencies, higher and secondary education, hospitals, safety, culture and the arts, and civic affairs.
Types of support: Operating budgets, annual campaigns, seed money, emergency funds, equipment, building funds, endowment funds, scholarship funds, exchange programs, continuing support, capital campaigns, employee matching gifts.
Limitations: No support for political organizations or candidates, or religious organizations or activities. No grants to individuals; no loans.
Application information:
Initial approach: Letter or proposal
Deadline(s): Submit proposal preferably from Sept. through Nov.; deadline Nov. 30
Board meeting date(s): Mar. and as required
Write: Ruth G. Goodell, Contribs. Admin.
Officers: Robert J. Vairo,* Pres.; Robert A. Zito, V.P.; Antoinette C. Bentley,* Secy.; Dennis J. Hammer, Treas.
Directors:* Sidney F. Wentz, Chair. and C.E.O.; James J. Cutro, Melvin Howard, John J. McGinty, George J. Rachmiel.
Number of staff: 1 full-time professional.
Employer Identification Number: 946065476

1660
Geraldine R. Dodge Foundation, Inc.
95 Madison Ave.
P.O. Box 1239
Morristown 07962-1239 (201) 540-8442

Incorporated in 1974 in NJ.
Donor(s): Geraldine R. Dodge.†
Financial data (yr. ended 12/31/88): Assets, $133,725,919 (M); expenditures, $9,795,898, including $7,982,527 for 301 grants (high: $221,921; low: $500; average: $15,000-$25,000) and $290,000 for 2 foundation-administered programs.
Purpose and activities: Grant-making emphasis in NJ on secondary education, performing and visual arts and other cultural activities, projects in population, environment, energy, and other critical areas, and programs in the public interest, including development of volunteerism, communications, and public issues. Interest in independent secondary schools in New England and Middle Atlantic states and in projects on the national level that are likely to lead to significant advances in secondary education. Projects that have implications beyond the school itself are of special interest. Support also for projects in animal welfare on a national and local level which explore the human/animal bond, promote humane education, and address issues of cruelty, pet overpopulation, the protection of wildlife, farm animal abuse, and animal exploitation in the laboratories.
Types of support: Seed money, conferences and seminars, matching funds, special projects, publications, continuing support, employee matching gifts, research.
Limitations: Giving primarily in NJ, with support for local humane groups limited to NJ, and support for other local projects limited to the Morristown-Madison area; some giving in the other Middle Atlantic states and New England, and to national organizations. No support for religion, higher education, health, international programs, or conduit organizations. No grants to individuals, or for capital projects, endowment funds, deficit financing, scholarships, or fellowships.
Publications: Annual report (including application guidelines).
Application information:
Initial approach: Letter or proposal
Copies of proposal: 1
Deadline(s): Submit proposal preferably in Mar., June, Sept., or Dec.; deadlines Jan. 1 for animal welfare and local projects; Apr. 1 for secondary education; July 1 for the arts; and Oct. 1 for public issues
Board meeting date(s): Mar., June, Sept., and Dec.
Final notification: By the end of the months in which board meetings are held
Write: Scott McVay, Exec. Dir.
Officers: William Rockefeller,* Chair.; Robert H.B. Baldwin,* Pres.; Scott McVay, Exec. Dir.
Trustees:* Barbara Knowles Debs, Henry U. Harder, John Lloyd Huck, Robert LeBuhn, Nancy D. Lindsay, David Hunter McAlpin, Walter J. Neppl, Paul J. O'Donnell, Edwin J. Sayres.
Number of staff: 5 full-time professional; 5 full-time support; 1 part-time support.
Employer Identification Number: 237406010
Recent arts and culture grants:
Academy of Natural Sciences of Philadelphia, Philadelphia, PA, $15,000. For research by Dr. Sybil Seitzinger, examining natural purification processes in cedar swamp areas of Pinelands. Also, base of knowledge will be created to aid discussion with Pinelands Commission in implementing development plans founded on accurate scientific information. 1987.
American Council for the Arts, NYC, NY, $20,000. To assist preparatory phase of National Arts Convention to be held in New Brunswick, New Jersey, on October 5, 6, and 7, 1988. Convention will focus on arts agenda for the 1990s. 1987.
American Craft Museum, NYC, NY, $10,325. For Meet the Artist demonstrations for American Craft Museum's 1987 holiday exhibition, Quilts: The State of the Art. 1987.
American Stage Company, Teaneck, NJ, $30,000. For production of new plays for coming season and toward new play, Other People's Money, a humorous and trenchant exploration of the contemporary world of Wall Street. 1987.
Appel Farm Arts and Music Center, Elmer, NJ, $12,000. For renewed support of Community Outreach Program, schedule of art, music, dance and theater presentations by talented young people who study at Appel Farm each summer. 1987.
Arts Council of the Morris Area, Madison, NJ, $8,000. Toward Arts in Education Program and for general operating support. 1987.
Arts Foundation of New Jersey, New Brunswick, NJ, $70,000. For Summer Arts Institute at Rutgers University, five-week residency program offering talented high school students instruction in literary, visual and performing arts. 1987.
ArtsPower, Paramus, NJ, $15,000. To enable professional musicians of ArtsPower to present jazz, brass and musical theater productions in each of 30 schools in Bergen, Essex and Morris counties. 1987.
Autumn Stages, Upper Montclair, NJ, $9,000. For training programs and performances-on-tour for this company of elderly folk who entertain in nursing homes, nutrition centers and other senior citizen settings. 1987.

Carolyn Dorfman Dance Company, Summit, NJ, $10,000. To assist in-school instruction of students on elements of movement and choreography as well as production concerns shared by all of performing arts. 1987.

Center for Plant Conservation, Arnold Arboretum of Harvard University, Jamaica Plain, MA, $76,000. For program conserving endangered plant species of New Jersey and for research on their survival. 1987.

Chatham Community Players, Chatham, NJ, $7,500. Toward costs of membership development, programming for children, and salaries for professional directors and musicians. 1987.

City Without Walls, Newark, NJ, $15,000. For imaginative array of programs in 1987-88 involving diverse organizational collaboration. City Without Walls features work by professional artists as well as students. 1987.

Colonial Symphony, Madison, NJ, $10,000. For support when three lead candidates for conductor will be featured under continuing search, supported by AT&T and Schering-Plough as well as heightened response to annual giving. 1987.

Creative Glass Center of America, Millville, NJ, $15,000. For fellowship program, enabling eight glass artists to work for five months in restored 19th-century glass making plant at historic Wheaton Village. 1987.

Crossroads Theater Company, New Brunswick, NJ, $45,000. To assist production of new work, strengthen administrative efforts, and increase marketing and fundraising outreach. Crossroads is one of only three all-black companies in the nation. 1987.

DanceCompass, Montclair, NJ, $15,000. For artistic development of DanceCompass and aid for performance and choreography fees. 1987.

Festival of Music, Tenafly, NJ, $25,000. For school performances by Festival's 10 professional music groups, and for production of supplemental educational materials to distribute to teachers and students. 1987.

Foundation Theater, Pemberton, NJ, $20,000. For production of The Other Side of Newark by New Jersey playwright Enid Rudd. Play focuses on racial concerns and provides an outlook that runs counter to interracial hostilities featured on nightly news. 1987.

Garden State Ballet School, Newark, NJ, $25,000. For scholarship aid, enabling serious young students to study classical ballet and contemporary dance at School's locations in Newark, Rutherford and Morristown. 1987.

George Street Playhouse, New Brunswick, NJ, $41,050. For intern program, and to assist issue-oriented programming by Theater for Young audiences, which will address such concerns as drug abuse and teenage pregnancy. 1987.

Geraldine R. Dodge Poetry Program, Morristown, NJ, $77,181. To underwrite poets who work closely with individual teachers and their students in 60 New Jersey schools, to sponsor teacher workshops, and to mount Geraldine R. Dodge Poetry Festival at Waterloo Village on October 6, 7, and 8, 1988. 1987.

Greater Trenton Symphony Orchestra, Trenton, NJ, $7,800. For orchestra to expand Symphonies for Students program from two concerts to four, reaching more than 7,000 school children throughout central New Jersey. 1987.

Haddonfield Symphony Society, Haddonfield, NJ, $10,000. To aid Solo competition for Young Artists (7,500) and to contribute to recruitment of musicians from New Jersey colleges and universities to participate in Internship Program. 1987.

Historic Morven, Princeton, NJ, $10,000. For development of interpretive and educational tools for new role that Morven, once the stately mansion of New Jersey governors, will play as museum. 1987.

Historic Speedwell, Morristown, NJ, $10,000. For hiring of curator of collections and education at this National Historic Site, where Samuel Morse and Alfred Vail perfected telegraph in 1838. 1987.

Hoboken Chamber Orchestra, Hoboken, NJ, $20,000. For educational touring program in inner-city schools in 1988 reaching youth in Jersey City, Bayoone, Union City, Weehawken and Hoboken.. 1987.

Hollybush Festival Association, Glassboro, NJ, $20,000. For production of Offenbach's Bluebeard by Festival in 1988. 1987.

Inner City Ensemble, Paterson, NJ, $20,000. For scholarships for students without financial resources, attending theater and dance classes on regular basis at Ensemble in 1987-88. 1987.

International Foundation for Art Research, NYC, NY, $13,866. For public education efforts in New Jersey to directly and through publication and other media, address increasing problems of fraud and forgery. Programs will increase sophistication of wider public as well as museum staffs while enlarging a membership network to assist in identifying fraudulence and in securing retrieval of missing works. 1987.

Jersey City Museum, Jersey City, NJ, $10,700. To underwrite in part series of one-person shows by four Latin American artists. Teachers and students will be invited to artists' studios; schoolchildren in Jersey City are 90 percent Hispanic. 1987.

Lillo Way Dance Company, Upper Montclair, NJ, $11,895. For continuation of the Lillo Way statewide artists-in-the-schools program. Program provides a sophisticated understanding of modern dance. 1987.

Manomet Bird Observatory, Manomet, MA, $10,000. For Harbor Herons Project, research and education program focused on large urban colony of herons, egrets, and ibis. 1987.

McCarter Theater Company, Princeton, NJ, $65,000. For New Play Development Program, which includes series of staged readings (Playwrights-at-McCarter) and production of new play on Stage II leading to full production on Main Stage. 1987.

Metropolitan Opera Association, NYC, NY, $100,000. To assist New Jersey part of 1988 Met in the Parks concert series, open to public free of charge. 1987.

Metropolitan Opera Guild, NYC, NY, $30,000. For New Jersey/Met Opera Teacher Training workshop series and to assist new production of Gianni Schicchi. 1987.

Monmouth Museum, Lincroft, NJ, $20,000. For exhibit for children, entitled Westward Ho!, simulation of westward migration of mid-1880s. 1987.

Montclair Art Museum, Montclair, NJ, $30,000. For development and implementation of The Monclair Art Museum's Education program entitled Art Reflects Change. Program will train high school teachers in relating American art to social studies curriculum. 1987.

Morris Museum, Morristown, NJ, $37,665. For show of America Indian art, Theaterworks-USA's production of We the People, and Discovery 1988 Science Lecture Series on animal behavior and communication. 1987.

Museum of Early Trades and Crafts, Madison, NJ, $7,500. For staff support for Museum, whose exhibits of tools and craft techniques dating back to colonial times are viewed by 50,000 visitors yearly. 1987.

National Association for Young Writers, Belvidere, NJ, $7,000. For production of Shoe Tree: The Literary Magazine by and for Children, nationally distributed journal that inspires exceptionally good writing and artwork by very young children. 1987.

National Choral Council, NYC, NY, $15,000. For expanding New Jersy Festival of American Music Theater into major series of summer concerts featuring music of Broadway. 1987.

National Humanities Center, Research Triangle Park, NC, $9,700. For 1987 Institute, which is organized in response to widespread need among humanities teachers for continued scholarly discipline. 1987.

National Public Radio, DC, $137,000. For reporting on biological resource issues over acclaimed news programs, Morning Edition, All Things Considered, and Weekend Edition. 1987.

New Brunswick Cultural Center, New Brunswick, NJ, $21,400. For hiring Program Consultant and to present New Jersey Chamber Music Society in three international concerts. 1987.

New Jersey Ballet Company, West Orange, NJ, $20,000. For cost of series of lecture/demonstrations in Newark schools in spring 1988. 1987.

New Jersey Center for Visual Arts, Summit, NJ, $17,000. For month-long series of events during April 1988 nurturing connections between practicing artists, apprentice artists, and teachers of art. The major curated exhibit, The manipulated Print, will offer a vibrant environment for workshops with leading people in printmaking field. 1987.

New Jersey Chamber Music Society, Montclair, NJ, $33,000. For marketing development program by which Society is broadening its base of financial support from individuals, corporations, and other sources. 1987.

New Jersey Shakespeare Festival, Madison, NJ, $30,000. To assist intern scholarships, promotion and marketing, and colloquium weekend entitled The Infinite Variety of Shakespeare's Women. 1987.

New Jersey State Opera, Newark, NJ, $12,500. For production of Hans Krasa's Brundibar (The Evil Organ Grinder), a children's opera

scheduled for spring of 1988 at Garden State Arts Center, Stockton State College, and Montclair State College. 1987.
New Jersey State Teen Arts Program, New Brunswick, NJ, $7,500. For Young Playwrights Festival, which culminates in professionally staged readings of six outstanding plays written by New Jersey high school students. 1987.
New Jersey Symphony Orchestra, Newark, NJ, $50,000. To assist Young Artists Auditions in 1987-88. 1987.
New Jersey Theater Group, Teaneck, NJ, $25,000. To assist efforts to enrich theatrical presence in Garden State. 1987.
New York Center for Visual History, NYC, NY, $50,000. For pilot for adaptation of 13 Voices and Visions films on major American poets for high school use. Films convey life and work of American poets by combining visualizations of actual poetry with archival film and photographs. 1987.
New York Zoological Society, Bronx, NY, $20,000. For summer seminar program at Bronx Zoo, one of nation's premier zoological parks, for up to 60 elementary and high school teachers. 1987.
Newark Community School of the Arts, Newark, NJ, $175,000. For work of six composers-in-residence to assist production of And Still the Snowflakes Fall and provide gifted student scholarships. 1987.
Newark Public Radio, Newark, NJ, $50,000. For support of news and public affairs programming. 1987.
Passage Theater Company, Trenton, NJ, $10,000. To assist with fund raising, audience development and production costs for professional company committed to creating new works. 1987.
Pennsylvania Opera Theater, Philadelphia, PA, $7,500. For Pennsylvania Opera Theater in including additional New Jersey schools in educational program, In Every Way the Arts, that moves beyond music education to include drama, literature, dance, theater, and visual arts. Program has strong representation of black and Hispanic youngsters. 1987.
Playwrights Theater of New Jersey, Madison, NJ, $15,000. For high school student playwriting program. 1987.
Princeton Ballet, New Brunswick, NJ, $30,000. For Dance Power, residency program of dance instruction for third and fourth graders in New Brunswick Public Schools. 1987.
Princeton University, Art Museum, Princeton, NJ, $28,000. To aid development of materials for teachers' kits for visits of school children. Also, the Museum's docent effort will be upgraded and attuned to enlarged responsibilities. And for purchase of photography. 1987.
Printmaking Council of New Jersey, Somerville, NJ, $7,500. For Council's public education and traveling exhibition programs. 1987.
Rehabilitation Center for the Handicapped, Morris Plains, NJ, $7,300. To assist arts-in-education program for disabled children in Morris County sponsored by Center and Arts Council of the Morris Area. Also to include two-day seminar for teacher training. 1987.
Renegade Theater Company, Hoboken, NJ, $8,900. For premiere of The Ghostman by playwright Wendy Hammond, who gives insight into growing problem of domestic violence. 1987.
Rutgers, The State University of New Jersey, Stedman Art Gallery, Camden, NJ, $12,500. For Museum Enrichment Program reaching disadvantaged youngsters from minority backgrounds. 1987.
Saint Benedicts Preparatory School, Newark, NJ, $45,000. For support of salaries for two performing arts teachers and four minority teachers of math and science. 1987.
South Jersey Regional Theater, Somers Point, NJ, $26,280. For development of professional staff, addition of associate producing director, to enable theater to keep pace with impressive growth in its audience. 1987.
Theater Program for Teachers and Playwrights, Morristown, NJ, $7,608. For exploration and planning for initiative to link leading high school drama teachers with New Jersey regional theaters. Focus will feature development of new plays, culminating in conference in 1989 with playwrights of national note. 1987.
Theaterworks/USA, NYC, NY, $20,000. For inner-city tour of New Jersey schools of production Just Say No, an entertaining approach to sensitive subject of drug abuse. 1987.
Thomas A. Edison Black Maria Film Festival and Competition, West Orange, NJ, $10,000. For seventh international annual competition and traveling showcase. 1987.
Very Special Arts New Jersey, North Brunswick, NJ, $14,000. For VISIBILITY, program that helps disabled artists of established talent market their work and obtain transportation to exhibits and workshops. 1987.
Voices, Pennington, NJ, $10,000. For development and field testing of school programs and concerts to provide children, teachers, and parents a basic understanding of elements of musical composition and good vocal production. 1987.
W H Y Y-Radio 91 FM, Philadelphia, PA, $30,000. For increased New Jersey news coverage by Philadelphia Public Radio, one-fourth of whose listeners live in Garden State. 1987.
W N E T Channel 13, Newark, NJ, $125,000. For Currents, weekly program over 102 public television stations exploring in depth a wide range of current issues involving economy, education, environment, public health, and social problems. 1987.
Warp and Woof, New Brunswick, NJ, $10,000. For renewed support of administration salary costs for Shoestring Players, children's theater troupe that performs throughout New Jersey and in as many as 17 other states. 1987.
Waterloo Foundation for the Arts, Stanhope, NJ, $60,000. To assist Geraldine R. Dodge Guest Artist Series for 1987. The Series features world-renowned musicians. 1987.
Whole Theater Company, Montclair, NJ, $45,000. For new play development as spur to 15th anniversary season of The Whole Theater. 1987.
William Carlos Williams Center for the Performing Arts, Rutherford, NJ, $20,000. For expansion of Poets and Painters gallery exhibitions and to enable Center to increase its administrative staff in anticipation of major capital funds drive. 1987.
YMCA of Madison Area, Madison, NJ, $84,334. For development of computerized administrative capability, arts development study, continued development of the Children's Theater Workshop and Center for the Dance Arts, and to assist general operating costs during capital campaign. 1987.
Young Audiences of New Jersey and Eastern Pennsylvania, Princeton, NJ, $13,000. For support in bringing programs in performing arts-music, dance, and theater-to school children in Trenton and Camden. 1987.
Zoological Society of Philadelphia, Philadelphia, PA, $35,000. To develop valid methodology for assessing effect of zoo and individual exhibits upon the casual visitor, thus finding ways to make zoo more valuable educationally. 1987.

1661
The Doris Duke Foundation, Inc.

Duke Farms
P.O. Box 2030
Somerville 08876

Incorporated in 1934 in DE.
Donor(s): Doris Duke.
Financial data (yr. ended 12/31/87): Assets, $5,126,092 (M); expenditures, $253,166, including $82,850 for 14 grants (high: $20,000; low: $300).
Purpose and activities: Grants to charitable institutions on an annual basis, including support for social service programs, improved services for the aging, child welfare and aid to agencies giving relief and medical care; support also for cultural organizations.
Limitations: Giving primarily in NJ, NY, and CA. No support for religious organizations for sectarian purposes. No grants to individuals, or for building or capital funds, publications, or general operating expenses.
Application information: Contributes only to pre-selected organizations. Applications not accepted.
Officer and Directors: Doris Duke, Pres.; Lloyd A. Pantages.
Employer Identification Number: 131655241

1662
Charles Edison Fund

101 South Harrison St.
East Orange 07018 (201) 675-9000

Incorporated in 1948 in DE.
Donor(s): Charles Edison,† and others.
Financial data (yr. ended 12/31/87): Assets, $20,289,532 (M); gifts received, $1,322; expenditures, $970,853, including $358,135 for 38 grants (high: $60,000; low: $50) and $150,371 for foundation-administered programs.
Purpose and activities: Grants largely for historic preservation, with emphasis on the homes of Thomas Alva Edison, and for education, medical research, and hospitals. Support also for foundation-sponsored exhibits at over 80 museums throughout the U.S., for

science education teaching kits in over 20,000 classrooms, and for cassette re-recording of antique phonograph records for schools and museums.
Types of support: Operating budgets, continuing support, seed money, special projects, research, equipment.
Limitations: No grants to individuals, or for building or endowment funds, scholarships, fellowships, or matching gifts; no loans.
Publications: Informational brochure (including application guidelines).
Application information:
Initial approach: Letter or proposal
Copies of proposal: 1
Deadline(s): 30 days prior to board meetings
Board meeting date(s): Mar., June, Sept., and Dec.
Write: Paul J. Christiansen, Pres.
Officers and Trustees: Paul J. Christiansen, Pres.; John P. Keegan, V.P.; David O. Schantz, Secy.-Treas.; Willaim M. Henderson, James E. Howe, Nancy M. Milligan, Robert E. Murray, John N. Schullinger, M.D., J. Thomas Smoot, Jr., John D. Venable.
Number of staff: 2 full-time professional; 1 part-time professional; 1 full-time support; 2 part-time support.
Employer Identification Number: 221514861

1663
Elizabethtown Gas Company Corporate Giving Program
One Elizabethtown Plaza
Elizabeth 07207 (201) 289-5000

Purpose and activities: Educational giving includes gifts to colleges and universities, vocational training, and technical/engineering education in service areas. Civic donations include support of local economic development. Social service contributions go to local United Way agencies, local rescue squads, local youth organizations, and community funds. The company also supports local hospitals and various local cultural concerns.
Limitations: Giving limited to service areas of Union, Middlesex, Warren, and Hunterdon counties, NJ.
Application information:
Initial approach: Letter or telephone
Deadline(s): By end of Aug. for consideration
Write: Carol Sliker, Asst. Corp. Secy.
Number of staff: None.

1664
The Charles Engelhard Foundation
P.O. Box 427
Far Hills 07931 (212) 697-4410

Incorporated in 1940 in NJ.
Donor(s): Charles Engelhard,† Engelhard Hanovia, Inc., and others.
Financial data (yr. ended 12/31/87): Assets, $69,101,993 (M); expenditures, $5,685,400, including $5,197,523 for 167 grants (high: $891,000; low: $500; average: $1,000-$100,000).
Purpose and activities: Emphasis on higher and secondary education, and cultural, medical, religious, wildlife, and conservation organizations.
Types of support: General purposes, special projects, continuing support, operating budgets.
Limitations: No grants to individuals, or for building funds.
Publications: Application guidelines.
Application information: Giving only to organizations known to the trustees.
Initial approach: Proposal
Copies of proposal: 1
Deadline(s): None
Board meeting date(s): Quarterly
Final notification: Varies
Write: Elaine Catterall, Secy.
Officers: Jane B. Engelhard,* Pres.; Elaine Catterall, Secy.; Edward G. Beimfohr,* Treas.
Trustees:* Sophie Engelhard Craighead, Charlene B. Engelhard, Susan O'Connor, Sally E. Pingree, Anne E. Reed.
Number of staff: 1 full-time professional.
Employer Identification Number: 226063032

1665
Englehard Corporate Giving Program
Menlo Park, Cn 40
Edison 08818 (201) 632-6000

Purpose and activities: Maintains strong interest in technical programs, chemical engineering, and education, with most funds going for scholarships or general support. Health and welfare funding provided for diverse organizations, including United Way; giving also for cultural programs. Emphasis on projects that benefit customers, employees, or operating communities.
Types of support: Employee matching gifts, equipment, fellowships, matching funds, scholarship funds.
Limitations: Giving primarily in headquarters city and major operating locations. No support for political, religious, or veterans' organizations (except for programs which benefit the community at large). No grants to individuals.
Application information: Proposal including description of organization and project, amount requested, budget, 501(c)(3), budget and list of directors.
Initial approach: Letter and proposal
Copies of proposal: 1
Deadline(s): Oct. 1 for funding the following year
Board meeting date(s): As needed
Final notification: Response within 3 months
Write: Warren E. Smith, Dir. of Community Affairs
Number of staff: 1 full-time professional; 1 full-time support.

1666
Exxon Education Foundation
P.O. Box 101
Florham Park 07932 (201) 765-3004

Incorporated in 1955 in NJ as Esso Education Foundation; name changed in 1972.
Donor(s): Exxon Corp., and affiliated companies.
Financial data (yr. ended 12/31/88): Assets, $53,757,334 (M); gifts received, $9,921,619; expenditures, $21,128,780, including $10,746,357 for 415 grants (high: $400,000; low: $1,000; average: $25,895) and $8,503,735 for employee matching gifts.
Purpose and activities: To aid education in the U.S. through programs of general support that include (a) the matching of gifts made by Exxon employees and retirees to colleges and universities; (b) grants to college and university schools, programs, and departments making outstanding educational contributions in areas of science, technology, and business; (c) grants to organizations and associations serving significant segments of the educational community; (d) other educational interests including mathematics education from kindergarten through the post-doctoral level; undergraduate general education; undergraduate developmental (remedial) education; teacher education and the restructuring of elementary and secondary schooling; education of "at-risk" students and especially students from minority groups underrepresented among college degree-holders and in certain key professions.
Types of support: Employee matching gifts, general purposes, special projects.
Limitations: No grants to individuals, or for institutional scholarship or fellowship programs, capital or building funds, land acquisition, equipment, renovation projects, or endowment purposes; no loans.
Publications: Corporate giving report, application guidelines.
Application information: Prospective applicants should write to the foundation for detailed program information and guidelines.
Write: Dr. Arnold R. Shore, Exec. Dir.
Officers: Elliot R. Cattarulla,* Chair. and Pres.; J.K. Kansas, V.P.; C.G. Korshin, Secy.; J.E. Bayne, Treas.; Arnold R. Shore, Exec. Dir.; L.J. Brown, Controller.
Trustees:* R.J. Kruizenga, H.J. Lartigue, U.J. LeGrange, T.J. McDonagh, F.A. Risch, Edgar A. Robinson, F.B. Sprow.
Number of staff: 5 full-time professional; 3 full-time support.
Employer Identification Number: 136082357
Recent arts and culture grants:
American Academy of Arts and Sciences, Cambridge, MA, $5,000. Toward an issue of Daedalus on Philanthropy, Patronage, Politics. 1987.
American Antiquarian Society, Worcester, MA, $9,030. For conference, Teaching the History of the Book. 1987.
American Council of Learned Societies, NYC, NY, $20,000. For support as part of Foundation's Organizational and Institutional Support Program, which seeks to ensure the continued existence of educational institutions, associations and agencies. 1987.
Claremont University Center, Claremont, CA, $50,000. For center for the Humanities' Commission on Humanities and Public Affairs. 1987.
Lincoln Center for the Performing Arts, NYC, NY, $20,000. For general support of Lincoln Center Institute for the Arts in Education. 1987.
Modern Language Association of America, NYC, NY, $23,000. For National Conference on the Teaching of English. 1987.
National Humanities Center, Research Triangle Park, NC, $25,000. For support as part of

Foundation's Organizational and Institutional Support Program, which seeks to ensure the continued existence of educational institutions, associations and agencies. 1987.
National Humanities Center, Research Triangle Park, NC, $5,000. For 1987 conference series. 1987.
New York University, NYC, NY, $75,000. For activities of Humanities Council. 1987.
New York University, NYC, NY, $50,000. For Humanities Seminars for Visiting Scholars. 1987.
University of Iowa, International Writing Program, Iowa City, IA, $10,000. For support as part of Foundation's Organizational and Institutional Support Program, which seeks to ensure the continued existence of educational institutions, associations and agencies. 1987.

1667
Fanwood Foundation
c/o King, King & Goldsack
450 Somerset St., P.O. Box 1106
North Plainfield 07061-1106 (201) 756-7804

Trust established in 1940 in NJ.
Donor(s): Dorothy W. Stevens.
Financial data (yr. ended 12/31/88): Assets, $10,693,748 (M); expenditures, $473,094, including $470,200 for 87 grants (high: $100,000; low: $500).
Purpose and activities: Support primarily for education; some support for cultural programs, hospitals, and religion.
Types of support: Annual campaigns, endowment funds, operating budgets.
Application information: Contributes only to pre-selected organizations. Applications not accepted.
Deadline(s): None
Write: Victor R. King, Trustee
Manager and Trustees: Whitney Stevens, Mgr.; Victor R. King, Robert T. Stevens, Jr.
Number of staff: None.
Employer Identification Number: 136051922

1668
The Frelinghuysen Foundation
P.O. Box 726
Far Hills 07931 (201) 439-3499

Incorporated in 1950 in NJ.
Donor(s): Frelinghuysen family, The.
Financial data (yr. ended 12/31/87): Assets, $1,661,817 (M); gifts received, $70,000; expenditures, $185,390, including $160,600 for 42 grants (high: $15,000; low: $500).
Purpose and activities: Emphasis on higher and secondary education, cultural programs, and hospitals.
Types of support: General purposes, fellowships, internships, capital campaigns, equipment.
Limitations: Giving primarily in NJ and NY.
Application information:
Initial approach: Letter
Deadline(s): None
Write: Frederick Frelinghuysen, Pres.
Officers and Directors: Frederick Frelinghuysen, Pres.; Frank E. Carr, V.P.; George L.K. Frelinghuysen, V.P.; H.O.H. Frelinghuysen, V.P.; Peter Frelinghuysen, V.P.; John F. Szczepanski, Secy.; Barratt Frelinghuysen, Mrs. H.O.H. Frelinghuysen, Mrs. Peter H.B. Frelinghuysen, Rodney P. Frelinghuysen, Beatrice van Roijen.
Employer Identification Number: 221723755

1669
The Grand Marnier Foundation
Glenpointe Centre West
Teaneck 07666-6897 (201) 836-7799

Established in 1985 in NY.
Donor(s): Carillon Importers, Ltd.
Financial data (yr. ended 12/31/87): Assets, $5,323,461 (M); gifts received, $2,046,787; expenditures, $283,827, including $202,500 for 1 grant.
Purpose and activities: Support for a Jewish welfare fund, cultural programs, and education.
Application information:
Initial approach: Letter
Deadline(s): None
Write: Jerry Ciraulo, Treas.
Officers and Directors: Michel Roux, Pres.; Joel Buchman, Secy.; Jerry Ciraulo, Treas.
Employer Identification Number: 133258414

1670
The Grand Union Company Corporate Contributions Committee
201 Willowbrook Blvd.
Wayne 07470 (201) 890-6000

Financial data (yr. ended 4/2/88): $200,000 for grants.
Purpose and activities: Supports community arts and culture, film, fine arts institutes, general education, minority programs, music, private colleges, public broadcasting, theater, United Way, youth service, alcohol recovery programs, social services, programs for the disadvantaged, and conservation programs.
Types of support: Special projects, annual campaigns, emergency funds.
Limitations: Giving primarily in headquarters city and major operating locations in GA, NJ, NY, SC, and VA.
Application information: Applications not accepted.
Board meeting date(s): Monthly
Write: Donald C. Vailloncourt, Corp. V.P.
Number of staff: 1 full-time professional; 1 full-time support; 8 part-time support.

1671
E. J. Grassmann Trust
P.O. Box 4470
Warren 07060 (201) 753-2440

Trust established in 1979 in NJ.
Donor(s): Edward J. Grassmann.†
Financial data (yr. ended 12/31/87): Assets, $28,344,100 (M); gifts received, $3,755; expenditures, $2,430,603, including $2,187,199 for 106 grants (high: $140,000; low: $2,000).
Purpose and activities: Grants for higher and secondary education, hospitals and health organizations, historical associations, and social welfare organizations, particularly those helping children. Preference given to organizations with low administration costs, and which show efforts to achieve a broad funding base.
Types of support: Endowment funds, scholarship funds, building funds, equipment, land acquisition.
Limitations: Giving primarily in NJ, particularly Union County, and in GA. No grants to individuals, or for operating expenses.
Publications: Application guidelines.
Application information:
Initial approach: Letter
Deadline(s): June 15 and Nov. 15
Board meeting date(s): June or July and Dec.
Final notification: After June or July meeting by July 31; after Dec. meeting by Dec. 31
Write: William V. Engel, Exec. Dir.
Officer: William V. Engel, Exec. Dir.
Trustees: Charles Danzig, Edward G. Engel, Joseph G. Engel, John B. Harris, Haydn H. Murray.
Number of staff: None.
Employer Identification Number: 226326539

1672
Harbourton Foundation
33 Witherspoon St.
Princeton 08542-3298

Established in 1982 in NJ.
Financial data (yr. ended 6/30/87): Assets, $1,463,728 (M); expenditures, $36,218, including $24,000 for grants.
Purpose and activities: Support primarily for medical research and for a theatre.
Types of support: General purposes.
Application information: Contributes only to pre-selected organizations. Applications not accepted.
Officers and Directors: James S. Regan, Pres. and Treas.; Amy H. Regan, V.P.; Kathleen Dalzell.
Employer Identification Number: 223027014

1673
Hoechst Celanese Foundation, Inc.
Rt. 202-206 North
Somerville 08876 (201) 231-2000

Financial data (yr. ended 12/31/86): Assets, $501,067 (M); expenditures, $37,461, including $35,000 for grants.
Purpose and activities: Support for education, particularly in the sciences, health and welfare, hospitals, and youth organizations. Support also for civic and public affairs, culture, and the environment. Grants are based on an organization's influence on the community, its potential of increasing public awareness of Hoechst Celanese, and the level of Hoechst employee involvement. At times, in-kind donations of employee time and equipment may be given.
Types of support: Capital campaigns, operating budgets, research, special projects, in-kind gifts.
Limitations: Giving primarily in headquarters city and national operating locations; national organizations also considered. No support for religious organizations. No grants to individuals, or for operating expenses of United Way recipients; no commitments for more than

five years; special projects of hospitals have low priority.
Application information:
Initial approach: Letter
Deadline(s): None
Write: Lewis Alpaugh, Dir., Corp. Relations
Trustee: Harry R. Benz.
Employer Identification Number: 222577170

1674
Richard H. Holzer Memorial Foundation
120 Sylvan Ave.
Englewood Cliffs 07632 (201) 947-8810

Established in 1969 in NJ.
Donor(s): Erich Holzer.
Financial data (yr. ended 6/30/87): Assets, $2,073,709 (M); gifts received, $444,487; expenditures, $229,200, including $227,918 for 35 grants (high: $81,250; low: $100).
Purpose and activities: Giving primarily for Jewish organizations and welfare funds and for cultural activities, particularly music.
Application information:
Initial approach: Letter
Officers: Eva Holzer, Pres.; Erich Holzer, Secy.-Treas.
Employer Identification Number: 237014880

1675
The Hoyt Foundation
Half Acre Rd.
Cranbury 08512 (609) 655-6000

Incorporated in 1957 in DE.
Financial data (yr. ended 6/30/87): Assets, $3,059,866 (M); expenditures, $154,043, including $146,000 for 12 grants (high: $45,000; low: $1,000).
Purpose and activities: Grants primarily for higher and secondary education, with emphasis on medical education and research; support also for health agencies and hospitals, the handicapped, and music.
Limitations: Giving primarily in NJ and NY. No grants to individuals.
Application information:
Initial approach: Letter
Deadline(s): None
Write: Charles O. Hoyt, Secy.
Officers and Trustees: Henry H. Hoyt, Pres.; Frank M. Berger, M.D., V.P.; Charles O. Hoyt, Secy.; Henry H. Hoyt, Jr., Treas.
Employer Identification Number: 136110857

1676
The Hyde and Watson Foundation
437 Southern Blvd.
Chatham Township 07928 (201) 966-6024

The Lillia Babbitt Hyde Foundation incorporated in 1924 in NY; The John Jay and Eliza Jane Watson Foundation incorporated in 1949; consolidation of two foundations into Hyde and Watson Foundation in 1983.
Donor(s): Lillia Babbitt Hyde,† Eliza Jane Watson.†
Financial data (yr. ended 12/31/88): Assets, $47,660,913 (M); expenditures, $2,782,289, including $2,189,260 for 151 grants (high: $120,000; low: $1,000; average: $1,000-$20,000) and $25,000 for 1 loan to an individual.
Purpose and activities: Support primarily for facilities, equipment and other developmental capital needs and projects of educational and religious institutions, and of social and health agencies. Includes projects designed to increase the efficiency, quality, or capacity of important programs and services or to provide primarily capital seed money to establish new programs and services to meet important public needs. Priority on new grants authorized in 1988-1989 will be given to emergency needs, to satisfying previous indications of assistance, to certain ongoing capital projects of prior grantees, and to institutions serving the disadvantaged.
Types of support: Building funds, equipment, land acquisition, matching funds, research, seed money, emergency funds, renovation projects, capital campaigns.
Limitations: Giving primarily in the NY-NJ metropolitan area. No grants to individuals, or generally for operating budgets, continuing support, annual campaigns, general endowments, deficit financing, scholarships, or fellowships.
Publications: Annual report (including application guidelines).
Application information: Application format required if proposal is considered by grants committee. Application form required.
Initial approach: Letter
Copies of proposal: 1
Deadline(s): Submit preliminary letter of appeal by Feb. 15 for spring meeting and by Sept. 15 for fall meeting
Board meeting date(s): Apr./May and Nov./Dec.
Final notification: After board meeting
Write: Robert W. Parsons, Jr., Pres.
Officers and Trustees: John G. MacKechnie, Chair.; Robert W. Parsons, Jr., Pres. and Principal Officer; Roger B. Parsons, V.P. and Secy.; Hunter W. Corbin, V.P.; John W. Holman, Jr., Treas.; Joseph G. Engel, William V. Engel, David G. Ferguson, G. Morrison Hubbard, Jr., Richard W. KixMiller.
Number of staff: 7 full-time professional.
Employer Identification Number: 222425725
Recent arts and culture grants:
Hudson River Sloop Clearwater, Poughkeepsie, NY, $5,000. Toward purchase of equipment and tools to enable research vessel, Clearwater, to operate more safely and efficiently. 1987.
Lyric Opera of Chicago, Chicago, IL, $20,000. Toward purchase of special stage and theater equipment to improve and expand programs. 1987.
Morris Museum of Arts and Sciences, Morristown, NJ, $15,000. For expansion and modernization of facilities to increase capacity of programs and exhibitions. 1987.
New Jersey Ballet Company, West Orange, NJ, $5,800. Toward purchase of essential sound system to enhance quality of performances. 1987.
New Jersey Center for Visual Arts, Summit, NJ, $25,000. For essential alterations and improvements of grounds to comply with City requirements and provide increased parking. 1987.
New Jersey Historical Society, Newark, NJ, $20,000. For challenge grant toward purchase of computer and office equipment to increase effectiveness of administration and fund raising efforts. 1987.
New Jersey Shakespeare Festival, Madison, NJ, $6,000. Toward purchase of essential lighting equipment to improve quality of program. 1987.
New Jersey Symphony Orchestra, Newark, NJ, $10,000. Toward purchase of software for organization project. 1987.
Newark Community School of the Arts, Newark, NJ, $6,000. Toward purchase of grand piano to enhance effectiveness of programs. 1987.
Paper Mill Playhouse, Millburn, NJ, $50,000. For alteration and expansion of facilities to enhance programs. 1987.
Preservation New Jersey, Belle Mead, NJ, $5,000. Toward purchase of computer and office equipment to increase effectiveness of administration. 1987.
Suburban Community Music Center, Madison, NJ, $15,000. For establishment of essential revolving working capital fund. 1987.

1677
The International Foundation
c/o John D. Carrico & Associates
Ten Park Place, P.O. Box 88
Butler 07405 (201) 838-4664
Grant application office: Box 31, Downstate Medical Center, 450 Clarkson Ave., Brooklyn, NY 11203; Tel.: (718) 270-3106

Incorporated in 1948 in DE.
Financial data (yr. ended 12/31/87): Assets, $15,155,990 (M); expenditures, $1,066,388, including $800,000 for 45 grants (high: $50,000; low: $5,000; average: $5,000-$50,000).
Purpose and activities: To conduct and/or support medical, educational, humanitarian, scientific, technical, and cultural institutions which operate primarily in developing nations.
Types of support: Seed money, building funds, equipment, publications, conferences and seminars, emergency funds, special projects.
Limitations: No grants to individuals, or for endowment funds, operating budgets, scholarships, fellowships, or matching gifts; no loans.
Publications: Program policy statement, application guidelines.
Application information:
Initial approach: Letter
Copies of proposal: 2
Deadline(s): Submit proposal preferably from Nov. to Mar.
Board meeting date(s): Jan., Apr., July, and Oct.
Final notification: 6 months; grants awarded Nov. 30
Write: Chandler McC. Brooks, M.D., Chair., Grants Comm.
Officers: Wallace S. Jones,* Pres.; Frank Madden,* V.P.; John D. Carrico, Secy.-Treas.
Trustees:* David S. Bate, Chandler McC. Brooks, M.D., Duncan W. Clark, M.D., J. Carter Hammel, Edward Holmes.
Number of staff: 1 part-time support.
Employer Identification Number: 131962255

1678
The Jockey Hollow Foundation, Inc.
P.O. Box 462
Bernardsville 07924

Incorporated in 1960 in NJ.
Donor(s): Carl Shirley, Mrs. Carl Shirley.
Financial data (yr. ended 3/31/87): Assets, $9,662,091 (M); gifts received, $206,000; expenditures, $697,074, including $532,200 for 48 grants (high: $220,000; low: $1,000).
Purpose and activities: Support for scholarship funds, education, conservation, hospitals, and cultural programs.
Types of support: Scholarship funds.
Limitations: Giving primarily in NJ and MA. No grants to individuals.
Application information:
Write: Betsy S. Michel, Pres.
Officers and Trustees: Betsy S. Michel, Pres. and Secy.; Joanne S. Forkner, V.P.; Carl Shirley, V.P.; Clifford L. Michel, Treas.; Virginia L. Hartmann, Betsy B. Shirley.
Employer Identification Number: 221724138

1679
Johnson & Johnson Corporate Giving Program
One Johnson & Johnson Plaza
New Brunswick 08933 (201) 524-3255

Purpose and activities: Supports projects or organizations which advance the science of medicine. Also supports higher educaton, arts and cultural programs, civic affairs and public interest organizations, social welfare, including community funds and an employee matching gifts program.
Types of support: Operating budgets, continuing support, annual campaigns, emergency funds, matching funds, fellowships, research, technical assistance, operating budgets, employee matching gifts, special projects, general purposes, scholarship funds, equipment.
Limitations: Giving primarily in areas where company has facilities. No support for sectarian and religious organizations that do not serve the general public, political groups, groups receiving federated drive support, most preschool, elementary or secondary educational institutions. No grants to individuals, or for trips or tours, endowments of any kind, advertising for benefit purposes, deficit financing, capital funds, demonstration projects, publications, or loans.
Publications: Application guidelines.
Application information: Include statement of purpose; IRS 501(c)(3) status letter; annual budget; annual financial report; audit statement; donor list; board list; and IRS form 990, if available.
Initial approach: Telephone or letter; if interested company will request full proposal
Copies of proposal: 1
Deadline(s): Aug. and Sept.
Board meeting date(s): Trustees meet in Mar., June, Sept. and Dec.
Final notification: Response within three months
Write: Herbert T. Nelson, V.P.
Number of staff: 1 full-time professional; 3 full-time support.

1680
Johnson & Johnson Family of Companies Contribution Fund
One Johnson & Johnson Plaza
New Brunswick 08933 (201) 524-3255

Incorporated in 1953 in NJ.
Donor(s): Johnson and Johnson, and subsidiary companies.
Financial data (yr. ended 12/31/87): Assets, $129,676 (M); gifts received, $7,303,750; expenditures, $7,280,333, including $5,189,714 for 303 grants (high: $1,050,000; low: $300; average: $1,000-$25,000) and $2,031,248 for 3,500 employee matching gifts.
Purpose and activities: Grants for projects or organizations which advance the science of medicine. Support also for higher education, arts and cultural programs, civic affairs and public interest organizations, social welfare agencies, including community funds, and an employee matching gift program.
Types of support: Operating budgets, continuing support, annual campaigns, emergency funds, matching funds, fellowships, research, technical assistance, special projects, employee matching gifts, general purposes, scholarship funds.
Limitations: Giving primarily in areas where company has facilities, to both national and local organizations. No grants to individuals, or for deficit financing, capital or endowment funds, or publications; no loans.
Publications: Application guidelines, program policy statement.
Application information:
Initial approach: Telephone or letter
Copies of proposal: 1
Deadline(s): None
Board meeting date(s): Mar., June, Sept., and Dec.
Final notification: 2 months
Write: Herbert T. Nelson, V.P.
Officers and Trustees: John J. Heldrich, Pres.; F.A. Bolden, V.P. and Secy.; Herbert T. Nelson, V.P.; Andrew J. Markey, Treas.
Number of staff: 2 full-time professional; 2 full-time support.
Employer Identification Number: 226062811

1681
Barbara Piasecka Johnson Foundation
Eight Lawrenceville Rd.
Princeton 08540 (609) 921-1200

Established in 1976 in DE.
Donor(s): J. Seward Johnson, Sr.,† Barbara Piasecka Johnson.
Financial data (yr. ended 12/31/88): Assets, $2,544,060 (M); expenditures, $1,149,020, including $994,639 for 12 grants (high: $750,000; low: $2,000) and $154,381 for 22 grants to individuals.
Purpose and activities: To support institutions which promote human rights in Poland, promote institutions of Polish character in the U.S. and abroad, and support artists and scientists, primarily those who are Polish or of Polish extraction, and institutions which support such individuals.
Types of support: Grants to individuals, conferences and seminars, fellowships, publications, research, special projects, student aid.
Publications: Application guidelines.
Application information: Scholarships and fellowships are for graduate, Doctoral and post-graduate education only; no undergraduate program considered. Application form required.
Initial approach: Letter or telephone
Copies of proposal: 1
Deadline(s): Mar. 30 and Sept. 1; all considered within three-month basis
Board meeting date(s): July
Write: Beata P. Bulaj, Secy.
Officers and Trustees: Barbara Piasecka Johnson, Chair.; Beata Bulaj, Secy.; John M. Peach, Treas.; Gregory Gorzynski, Christopher Piasecki, Grzegorz Piasecki, Wojciech Piasecki.
Number of staff: 1 part-time professional; 1 part-time support.
Employer Identification Number: 510201795

1682
The Robert Wood Johnson Foundation
P.O. Box 2316
Princeton 08543-2316 (609) 452-8701

Incorporated in 1936 in NJ.
Donor(s): Robert Wood Johnson.†
Financial data (yr. ended 12/31/88): Assets, $2,054,534,000 (M); expenditures, $97,952,000, including $87,552,000 for grants and $1,414,000 for loans.
Purpose and activities: Improvement of health services in the U.S., with emphasis on projects to improve access to personal health care for the most underserved population groups; to make health care arrangements more effective and affordable; and to help people maintain or regain maximum attainable function in their everyday lives. Within these areas, support provided for the development and testing of previously untried approaches; demonstrations to assess objectively the operational effectiveness of approaches shown to be effective in more limited settings; and the broader diffusion of programs objectively shown to improve health status or make health care more affordable.
Types of support: Seed money, research, special projects, fellowships, continuing support.
Limitations: Giving limited to the U.S. No support for international activities; programs or institutions concerned solely with a specific disease; or basic biomedical research or broad public health problems, except as they might relate to the foundation's areas of interest. No grants to individuals, or for ongoing general operating expenses, endowment funds, construction, or equipment (except for local purchases).
Publications: Annual report, informational brochure, program policy statement, application guidelines, occasional report, newsletter.
Application information:
Initial approach: Letter
Copies of proposal: 1
Deadline(s): None
Board meeting date(s): Feb., May, July, Oct., and Dec.
Final notification: 6 to 12 months
Write: Edward H. Robbins, Proposal Mgr.

Officers: Leighton E. Cluff, M.D.,* Pres.; William R. Walsh, Jr.,* Exec. V.P. for Finance and Treas.; J. Warren Wood III, V.P. and Secy.; Thomas P. Gore, V.P. for Communications; Terrance Keenan, V.P. for Special Progs.; Alan B. Cohen, V.P.; Ruby P. Hearn, V.P.; Jeffrey C. Merrill, V.P.; Richard C. Reynolds, M.D., V.P.
Trustees:* Robert H. Myers, Chair.; Edward C. Andrews, Jr., M.D., Robert J. Dixson, Edward R. Eberle, Lawrence G. Foster, Leonard F. Hill, Frank J. Hoenemeyer, John J. Horan, Richard B. Ogilvie, Jack W. Owen, Norman Rosenberg, M.D., Ian M. Ross, Richard B. Sellars, Foster B. Whitlock.
Number of staff: 35 full-time professional; 55 full-time support; 2 part-time support.
Employer Identification Number: 226029397
Recent arts and culture grants:
Statue of Liberty-Ellis Island Foundation, NYC, NY, $150,000. For medical processing gallery in museum on Ellis Island. 1987.

1683
F. M. Kirby Foundation, Inc.
P.O. Box 151
Morristown 07963-0151 (201) 538-4800
IRS filing state: DE

Incorporated in 1931 in DE.
Donor(s): F.M. Kirby,† Allan P. Kirby, Sr.,† F.M. Kirby.
Financial data (yr. ended 12/31/88): Assets, $157,000,000 (M); expenditures, $8,300,000, including $7,500,000 for grants.
Purpose and activities: Support for higher and secondary education, health and hospitals, community funds, historic preservation, church support and church-related organizations, social services, conservation, public policy organizations, and population control. Grants almost entirely limited to organizations associated with personal interests of present or former foundation directors.
Types of support: Operating budgets, special projects, general purposes, equipment, renovation projects, research, scholarship funds, seed money, annual campaigns, continuing support.
Limitations: Giving primarily in NY, NJ, PA, and VA. No grants to individuals; no loans or pledges.
Publications: Informational brochure.
Application information:
Initial approach: Proposal with cover letter; no telephone solicitations accepted
Copies of proposal: 1
Deadline(s): Proposals considered throughout the year; deadline Oct. 31
Board meeting date(s): Quarterly; proposals are acted on in June and Dec.
Final notification: By Dec. 31 for positive responses only
Write: F.M. Kirby, Pres.
Officers and Director:* F.M. Kirby,* Pres.; Paul B. Mott, Jr., Exec. Dir.
Number of staff: 2 part-time professional; 2 part-time support.
Employer Identification Number: 516017929
Recent arts and culture grants:
American Boychoir School, Princeton, NJ, $10,000. 1987.
American Museum of Natural History, NYC, NY, $25,000. 1987.
Arts Council of the Morris Area, Madison, NJ, $8,000. 1987.
Big Apple Circus, NYC, NY, $22,000. For support for Clown Care Unit. 1987.
Carpenter Center for the Performing Arts, Richmond, VA, $15,000. 1987.
Chatham Community Players, Chatham, NJ, $6,000. 1987.
Clinton Historical Museum, Clinton, NJ, $25,000. 1987.
Colonial Little Symphony Society, Madison, NJ, $5,000. 1987.
Department of State Fine Arts Committee, DC, $10,000. 1987.
Educational Cable Consortium, Summit, NJ, $6,000. 1987.
F. M. Kirby Center for the Performing Arts, Wilkes-Barre, PA, $100,000. 1987.
Friday Evening Club, Morristown, NJ, $5,000. 1987.
Gill/Saint Bernards School, Bernardsville, NJ, $10,000. For Dramatic Arts Program for Timeless Tales. 1987.
Harding Township Historical Society, New Vernon, NJ, $5,000. 1987.
Heritage House, Wilkes-Barre, PA, $33,000. 1987.
Historic Richmond Foundation, Richmond, VA, $30,000. 1987.
Historic Speedwell, Morristown, NJ, $40,000. 1987.
Hugh Moore Historical Park and Museums, Easton, PA, $15,000. For Canal Museum. 1987.
Intrepid Museum Foundation, NYC, NY, $5,000. 1987.
Lafayette College, Easton, PA, $153,000. For Reserve for Future Decision, and John D. Raymond Music Fund. 1987.
Little Theater of Wilkes-Barre, Wilkes-Barre, PA, $6,000. 1987.
MacCulloch Hall Historical Museum, Morristown, NJ, $8,000. 1987.
Morris Museum of Arts and Sciences, Morristown, NJ, $106,000. 1987.
Museum of Early Trades and Crafts, Madison, NJ, $70,000. For cataloging system. 1987.
Museum of the Confederacy, Richmond, VA, $25,000. 1987.
National Football Foundation and Hall of Fame, Larchmont, NY, $25,000. 1987.
New Jersey Historical Society, Newark, NJ, $5,000. 1987.
New Jersey Shakespeare Festival, Madison, NJ, $7,000. 1987.
New York Botanical Garden, Bronx, NY, $5,000. 1987.
New York City Opera, NYC, NY, $7,500. 1987.
New York Zoological Society, Bronx, NY, $35,000. 1987.
Newark Boys Chorus School, Newark, NJ, $5,000. 1987.
Newark Museum, Newark, NJ, $155,000. 1987.
Norfolk and Norwich Genealogical Society, London, England, $45,000. 1987.
Old Sturbridge Village, Sturbridge, MA, $10,000. 1987.
Paper Mill Playhouse, Millburn, NJ, $6,500. 1987.
Rahway Historical Society, Rahway, NJ, $15,000. 1987.
Richard M. Nixon Presidential Archives Foundation, DC, $5,000. 1987.
Richmond Ballet, Richmond, VA, $17,000. 1987.
Richmond Symphony, Richmond, VA, $17,000. 1987.
School of American Ballet, NYC, NY, $5,000. 1987.
South Carolina Historical Society, Charleston, SC, $23,000. 1987.
State Theater, Easton, PA, $100,000. 1987.
Statue of Liberty-Ellis Island Foundation, NYC, NY, $5,500. 1987.
Theater Virginia, Richmond, VA, $17,000. 1987.
Tri-State Railway Historical Society, Clifton, NJ, $15,000. 1987.
Virginia Foundation for Archaeological Research, Spring Grove, VA, $97,000. 1987.
Virginia Historical Society, Richmond, VA, $5,000. 1987.
W N E T Channel 13, NYC, NY, $80,000. 1987.
Walter Cecil Rawls Library and Museum, Courtland, VA, $14,000. 1987.
War Memorial Museum of Virginia, Newport News, VA, $16,000. 1987.
Welsh Valley Preservation Society, Kulpsville, PA, $5,000. For Morgan Log House. 1987.

1684
Ernest Christian Klipstein Foundation
Village Rd.
New Vernon 07967

Established in 1954 in NJ.
Donor(s): Kenneth H. Klipstein.
Financial data (yr. ended 12/31/86): Assets, $1,593,296 (M); expenditures, $65,715, including $52,555 for 91 grants (high: $5,000; low: $25).
Purpose and activities: Grants for higher education, cultural programs, and conservation.
Officers: Kenneth H. Klipstein, Pres.; David H. Klipstein, V.P. and Treas.; Marion C. White, Secy.
Employer Identification Number: 226028529

1685
The Large Foundation
c/o Large, Scammell & Danziger
117 Main St.
Flemington 08822

Incorporated in 1957 in NJ.
Donor(s): George K. Large,† and members of the Large family.
Financial data (yr. ended 12/31/87): Assets, $6,829,407 (M); expenditures, $400,426, including $372,255 for 39 grants (high: $54,000; low: $500).
Purpose and activities: Emphasis on health agencies; grants also for social service and youth agencies, and historic preservation.
Limitations: Giving primarily in NJ, particularly Hunterdon County.
Officers and Trustees: Edwin K. Large, Jr., Pres.; Lloyd B. Wescott, V.P.; Robert F. Danziger, Secy.; Charles W. Fouts, Treas.; Alfred R. Dorf, Benjamin B. Kirkland, Catherine L. O'Shea, Deborah J. Scammell, H. Seely Thomas, Jr.
Employer Identification Number: 226049246

1686
Lasky Company Foundation
67 East Willow St.
Millburn 07041

Established in 1964 in NJ.
Donor(s): Lasky Co., Sherwood A. Barnhard, Seymour J. Weissman.
Financial data (yr. ended 09/30/88): Assets, $47,738 (M); gifts received, $188,850; expenditures, $178,404, including $177,359 for 79 grants (high: $126,550; low: $10).
Purpose and activities: Giving primarily for Jewish welfare funds and organizations; support also for hospitals, arts and culture, youth, and civic affairs.
Limitations: Giving primarily in NJ and NY.
Application information: Contributes only to preselected organizations. Applications not accepted.
Officers: Sherwood A. Barnhard, Pres.; Seymour J. Weissman, V.P. and Secy.
Employer Identification Number: 226059928

1687
The Lautenberg Foundation
P.O. Box 816
Newark 07102

Established in 1967 in NJ.
Donor(s): Frank R. Lautenberg Charitable Trusts.
Financial data (yr. ended 12/31/87): Assets, $3,354,170 (M); expenditures, $302,525, including $283,500 for 55 grants (high: $123,000; low: $100).
Purpose and activities: Grants largely for Jewish welfare funds, education, and cultural programs locally; support also for educational and cultural institutions in Israel.
Limitations: Giving primarily in the NJ and NY area, and Israel. No grants to individuals.
Application information: Contributes only to pre-selected organizations. Applications not accepted.
Officers: Frank R. Lautenberg, Pres.; Lois Lautenberg, V.P.; Fred S. Lafer, Secy.
Employer Identification Number: 226102734

1688
Alan Levin Foundation
70 Undercliff Terr.
West Orange 07052

Financial data (yr. ended 8/31/87): Assets, $1,043,326 (M); expenditures, $95,435, including $95,399 for 27 grants (high: $49,000; low: $39).
Purpose and activities: Support primarily for Jewish welfare organizations and art museums.
Officer: Martin Levin, Mgr.
Employer Identification Number: 221711646

1689
The Philip & Janice Levin Foundation
893 Route 22
North Plainfield 07060

Incorporated in 1963 in NJ.
Donor(s): Philip J. Levin.†
Financial data (yr. ended 8/31/87): Assets, $5,131,445 (M); gifts received, $520,000; expenditures, $415,963, including $395,500 for 24 grants (high: $120,000; low: $500).
Purpose and activities: Emphasis on higher education, Jewish welfare funds, and the arts.
Limitations: Giving primarily in NJ and New York, NY.
Officer: Janice H. Levin, Pres.
Employer Identification Number: 226075837

1690
Thomas J. Lipton Foundation, Inc.
c/o Thomas J. Lipton, Inc.
800 Sylvan Ave.
Englewood Cliffs 07632

Incorporated in 1952 in DE.
Donor(s): Thomas J. Lipton, Inc.
Financial data (yr. ended 12/31/87): Assets, $209,150 (M); gifts received, $817,249; qualifying distributions, $821,628, including $821,451 for 251 grants (high: $100,000; low: $100) and $14,225 for 4 employee matching gifts.
Purpose and activities: Emphasis on research in nutrition, community funds, higher education, including scholarship aid, hospitals, cultural programs, social services, and youth agencies.
Types of support: Research, scholarship funds, employee matching gifts.
Application information: Application form required.
Deadline(s): None
Write: Helen Siegle, Grant Coord.
Officers: H.M. Tibbetts, Pres.; D.W. St. Clair, V.P. and Secy.; D.E. Grein, Jr., V.P. and Treas.; J.N. Byrne, V.P.; C.B. Fuller, V.P.; W.K. Godfrey, V.P.; W.J. Sellitti, V.P.
Employer Identification Number: 226063094

1691
The Magowan Family Foundation, Inc.
c/o Merrill Lynch
100 Union Ave.
Cresskill 07626
Application address: c/o Mary Ann Chapin, 2100 Washington St., San Francisco, CA 94109; Tel.: (415) 563-5581

Incorporated in 1954 in NY.
Donor(s): Charles E. Merrill,† Robert A. Magowan,† Doris M. Magowan, Merrill L. Magowan, Robert A. Magowan, Jr.
Financial data (yr. ended 10/31/87): Assets, $5,158,269 (M); gifts received, $23,529; expenditures, $512,007, including $425,018 for 102 grants (high: $54,090; low: $500).
Purpose and activities: Grants for higher and secondary education, hospitals, church support, and cultural programs.
Limitations: Giving primarily in NY, CA, and FL.
Application information:
Initial approach: Letter
Deadline(s): None
Write: Rolando E. Fernandez, Asst. Treas.
Officers: Peter A. Magowan, Pres.; Doris M. Magowan, V.P.; Merrill L. Magowan, V.P.; Stephen C. Magowan, V.P.; Bernat Rosner, Secy.; Thomas J. Lombardi, Treas.
Employer Identification Number: 136085999

1692
Mercedes-Benz of North America Corporate Giving Program
One Mercedes Dr.
Montvale 07645 (201) 573-0600

Purpose and activities: Supports community development, family services, public affairs, volunteerism, education, adult education, business education, leadership development, humanities, minorities, Native Americans, welfare, youth, and historic preservation. Provides in-kind gifts.
Types of support: Annual campaigns, building funds, emergency funds, employee matching gifts, matching funds, publications, research, seed money, scholarship funds, technical assistance, in-kind gifts.
Limitations: Giving primarily in major markets and areas near company facilities. No grants for religious organizations (excluding religious education or welfare).
Publications: Corporate report.
Application information:
Initial approach: Letter
Copies of proposal: 1
Write: Frederick A. Chapman, Press Info. Mgr.
Number of staff: 1 part-time professional; 1 part-time support.

1693
Merck and Company Corporate Giving Program
P.O. Box 2000
Rahway 07065-0900 (201) 574-4375

Financial data (yr. ended 12/31/88): Total giving, $22,605,295, including $3,300,000 for grants and $22,305,295 for in-kind gifts.
Purpose and activities: "The business of Merck is improving the quality of life throughout the world." Main emphasis is the development of innovative products for the health and well-being of society. Support for medicine and science, health and social services, and civic and cultural activities. In addition to cash grants, Merck also donates products to meet the needs of the ill and the indigent, and for victims of natural disasters. Programs reflect combined foundation and corporate giving.
Types of support: In-kind gifts.
Limitations: Giving primarily in headquarters city and major operating locations. No support for political, labor, fraternal, or veterans' groups. No grants to individuals, or for endowments, publications, or media productions.
Application information: Proposal including complete budget, audited statement, 501(c)(3), and lists of board members and major contributors.
Initial approach: Letter; proposal
Deadline(s): None
Board meeting date(s): Semiannually and as required
Final notification: Two months required for full review and decision
Write: Charles R. Hogan, Jr., Dir.
Contributions Staff: Charles R. Hogen, Jr., Sr. Dir.; Larry W. Saufley, Mgr., Finance and Administration; Shuang Ruy Huang, Mgr.; Lois F. Schwartz, Coord.

1694
The Merck Company Foundation
P.O. Box 2000
Rahway 07065-0900 (201) 594-4375

Incorporated in 1957 in NJ.
Donor(s): Merck & Co., Inc.
Financial data (yr. ended 12/31/87): Assets, $7,467,288 (M); gifts received, $610,888; expenditures, $5,641,416, including $4,339,419 for 391 grants (high: $200,000; low: $100; average: $1,000-$10,000), $264,672 for 12 grants to individuals and $860,904 for 4,021 employee matching gifts.
Purpose and activities: Support of education, primarily medical and including the Merck Sharp & Dohme International Fellowships in Clinical Pharmacology; community programs, hospitals, health agencies, civic organizations, and colleges in localities where the company has major operations; and an employee matching gift program for colleges, secondary schools, hospitals, public broadcasting and public libraries.
Types of support: Seed money, building funds, equipment, employee matching gifts, fellowships.
Limitations: Giving primarily in areas of company operations. No grants to individuals (except for fellowships in clinical pharmacology), or for operating budgets, continuing support, annual campaigns, emergency or endowment funds, deficit financing, land acquisition, research, travel, or conferences; no loans.
Publications: Corporate giving report.
Application information: Grants usually made at the initiative of the foundation.
Initial approach: Proposal
Copies of proposal: 1
Deadline(s): Aug. 31 for fellowships in clinical pharmacology; no set deadline for other grants
Board meeting date(s): Semiannually and as required
Final notification: 2 months
Write: Charles R. Hogen, Jr., Exec. V.P.
Officers: Albert D. Angel,* Pres.; Charles R. Hogen, Jr., Exec. V.P.; Shuang Ruy Huang, V.P.; Clarence A. Abramson, Secy.; Larry W. Saufley, Treas.
Trustees:* P. Roy Vagelos, M.D., Chair.; H. Brewster Atwater, Jr., William G. Bowen, Frank T. Cary, Lloyd C. Elam, Charles E. Exley, Jr., Jacques Genest, Marian S. Heiskell, John J. Horan, John E. Lyons, John K. McKinley, Albert W. Merck, Ruben F. Mettler, Paul G. Rogers, Richard S. Ross, Dennis Weatherstone.
Number of staff: 3 full-time professional; 4 full-time support.
Employer Identification Number: 226028476
Recent arts and culture grants:
John F. Kennedy Center for the Performing Arts, DC, $15,000. 1987.
Lincoln Center for the Performing Arts, NYC, NY, $20,000. 1987.
McCarter Theater Company, Princeton, NJ, $11,000. 1987.
Metropolitan Opera Association, NYC, NY, $20,000. 1987.
New Jersey Ballet Company, West Orange, NJ, $10,000. 1987.
New Jersey State Opera, Newark, NJ, $10,000. 1987.
New Jersey Symphony Orchestra, Newark, NJ, $15,000. 1987.
New York City Opera, NYC, NY, $25,000. 1987.
Ponce Museum of Art, Puerto Rico, $12,000. 1987.
Rahway Historical Society, Rahway, NJ, $15,000. 1987.
Rahway Landmarks, Rahway, NJ, $50,000. 1987.

1695
Jay R. Monroe Memorial Foundation
44 Main St.
Millburn 07041-1399

Established in 1959 in NJ.
Donor(s): Malcolm Monroe,† Ethlyn Monroe.†
Financial data (yr. ended 12/31/87): Assets, $1,149,694 (M); gifts received, $25,000; expenditures, $83,410, including $75,950 for 155 grants (high: $8,000; low: $100).
Purpose and activities: Support for the arts and historic preservation, secondary and early childhood education, child welfare and youth programs, health organizations, community development, and associations concerned with environmental conservation and ecology.
Application information: Contributes only to pre-selected organizations. Applications not accepted.
Officers and Trustees: Jay R. Monroe IV, Pres.; D.W. Moore, V.P.; M.M. Morrow, V.P.; J.M. McEvoy, Secy.; C.M. Byrne, J.M. McEvoy.
Number of staff: None.
Employer Identification Number: 226050156

1696
Mutual Benefit Life Insurance Charitable Trust
520 Broad St., 1 RM A05N
Newark 07101 (201) 481-8107

Financial data (yr. ended 12/31/86): Expenditures, $876,000 for grants.
Purpose and activities: Support for human services, including AIDS programs, children and youth, health and hospitals, and culture.
Application information:
Initial approach: Letter
Deadline(s): July 31 for consideration in the next year's budget
Write: Betty Lee Hagerty, V.P., Public Affairs
Employer Identification Number: 221134800

1697
Mutual Benefit Life Insurance Company Giving Program
520 Broad St. 1 Rm. AO5N
Newark 07101 (201) 481-8441

Financial data (yr. ended 12/31/86): Total giving, $524,000, including $449,000 for grants and $75,000 for in-kind gifts.
Purpose and activities: Supports education, housing, recreation, and employment, AIDS programs, child development and youth, volunteerism, hospitals, health, and arts and culture, including museums, libraries, and public broadcasting. Organizations with employee involvement receive special consideration. Also supports programs concerning minorities, community development, environment and urban revitalization; support includes in-kind donations.
Types of support: General purposes, employee matching gifts, building funds, capital campaigns, special projects, operating budgets, technical assistance.
Limitations: Giving primarily in Newark, NJ and Kansas City, MO. No support for religious organizations for sectarian purposes or political organizations. No grants to individuals.
Application information: Include description of organization and project, list of officers and board members, budget, audited financial statement, tax-exempt status, and current and potential donors' list.
Initial approach: Brief letter and proposal
Deadline(s): Submit by July 31 for consideration in the next year's budget
Board meeting date(s): Quarterly
Final notification: 12 weeks
Write: Betty Lee Hagerty, V.P., Public Affairs
Administrators: Betty Lee Haggerty, Marilyn M. Jones.

1698
Nabisco Foundation
(also known as The National Biscuit Company Foundation Trust)
Nabisco Brands Plaza
Parsippany 07054

Incorporated in 1953 in NJ.
Donor(s): Nabisco Brands, Inc.
Financial data (yr. ended 12/31/87): Assets, $7,164,562 (M); expenditures, $1,204,570, including $270,133 for 37 grants (high: $50,000; low: $1,000; average: $1,000-$20,000) and $878,309 for employee matching gifts.
Purpose and activities: Giving largely for higher education and United Funds; support also for hospitals, youth agencies, and cultural programs.
Types of support: Building funds, scholarship funds, fellowships, employee matching gifts.
Limitations: No grants to individuals.
Application information:
Deadline(s): None
Board meeting date(s): As needed
Final notification: Varies
Write: Henry A. Sandbach, Dir. of Contribs.
Administrative Committee: Henry A. Sandbach, Dir. of Contributions; R.M. Schaeberle.
Trustee: Bankers Trust Co.
Employer Identification Number: 136042595

1699
Community Foundation of New Jersey
P.O. Box 317
Knox Hill Rd.
Morristown 07963-0317 (201) 267-5533

Community foundation incorporated in 1979 in NJ.
Financial data (yr. ended 6/30/88): Assets, $4,908,954 (M); gifts received, $1,288,052; expenditures, $968,228, including $726,142

for 95 grants (high: $62,896; low: $25) and $79,692 for 5 loans to individuals.
Purpose and activities: Support "for innovative programs which can exert a multiplier effect or which through research may contribute to the solution or easing of important community problems." Areas of interest include cultural programs, education, environment and conservation, health, religion, and social services.
Types of support: Seed money, matching funds, technical assistance, special projects, conferences and seminars, program-related investments.
Limitations: Giving limited to NJ. No support for sectarian religious programs. No grants for capital or endowment funds, operating budgets, continuing support, annual campaigns, emergency funds, deficit financing, or fellowships.
Publications: Annual report, application guidelines, newsletter, informational brochure.
Application information: Application form required.
Initial approach: Telephone
Copies of proposal: 1
Write: Sheila C. Williamson, Exec. Dir.
Officers: William Simon, Chair.; John L. Kidde,* Pres.; John D. Mack,* V.P.; Tilly-Jo B. Emerson,* Secy.; S. Jervis Brinton, Jr.,* Treas.; Sheila C. Williamson, Exec. Dir.
Trustees:* George L. Bielitz, Jr., Barbara M. Caspersen, Raymond G. Chambers, Robert P. Corman, Peter Dawkins, Adrian M. Foley, Jr., Robert M. Gardner, Henry Henderson, Hilda Hidalgo, Frederick G. Meissner, Jr., Herbert F. Moore, Robert B. O'Brien, Jr., Dillard H. Robinson, Richard W. Roper, E. Burke Ross, Jr., Christine T. Whitman.
Number of staff: 3 full-time professional; 2 part-time professional; 1 part-time support.
Employer Identification Number: 222281783

1700
The Charlotte W. Newcombe Foundation

35 Park Place
Princeton 08542 (609) 924-7022
Fellowship application address: Newcombe Fellowships, Woodrow Wilson National Fellowship Foundation, P.O. Box 642, Princeton, NJ 08542; Tel.: (609)924-4666

Trust established in 1979 in PA.
Donor(s): Charlotte W. Newcombe.†
Financial data (yr. ended 12/31/88): Assets, $29,928,467 (M); expenditures, $1,892,442, including $1,487,274 for 64 grants (high: $527,674; low: $1,000; average: $1,000-$40,000).
Purpose and activities: Grants available to colleges and universities for scholarship or fellowship aid only in four programs: 1) doctoral dissertation fellowships awarded annually for degree candidates in the humanities and social sciences whose work focus on ethics and religion (national selection process administered by Woodrow Wilson National Fellowship Foundation); 2) scholarships for physically disabled students, restricted to private four-year colleges and universities in PA, NJ, New York City, MD, DE, and Washington, DC; 3) scholarships for mature second-career women in the same states with no grants made in this program to two-year colleges, professional schools, or theological seminaries; 4) scholarships for economically disadvantaged or minority students attending colleges affiliated with the Presbyterian Church (U.S.A.). Scholarships for undergraduate and graduate students only; no aid available for post-doctoral fellowships. Selection of student recipients and scholarship administration are the responsibility of the academic institution.
Types of support: Scholarship funds, fellowships.
Limitations: No support for colleges except for scholarship and fellowship programs; within the scholarships for physically disabled students, no grants to publicly-supported two-year colleges. No grants to individuals, or for staffing, program development, or building funds; scholarships to institutions only; no loans.
Publications: Annual report, program policy statement, application guidelines.
Application information: Application materials available from mid-June through mid-Oct. for physically disabled students and mature women students; Presbyterian college scholarships have no application materials--colleges should inquire to the foundation regarding these scholarships; fellowship applicants should request applications by Dec. 15 from the Woodrow Wilson National Fellowship Foundation at address given above. Application form required.
Initial approach: Letter or telephone
Copies of proposal: 5
Deadline(s): Nov. 1 for scholarship programs; Nov. 15 for fellowships
Board meeting date(s): Feb., Apr., June, Sept., and Dec.
Final notification: Apr. for fellowships beginning in June; May for scholarships beginning in July
Write: Janet A. Fearon, Exec. Dir.
Trustees: Robert M. Adams, K. Roald Bergethon, Janet A. Fearon, Aaron E. Gast, Thomas P. Glassmoyer.
Number of staff: 2 full-time professional; 1 part-time support.
Employer Identification Number: 232120614
Recent arts and culture grants:
Woodrow Wilson National Fellowship Foundation, Princeton, NJ, $541,000. For 41 Charlotte W. Newcombe Fellowships in 1989 for doctoral dissertation work in humanities and social sciences concerned with ethical and religious values. 5/6/88.

1701
George A. Ohl, Jr. Trust

c/o First Fidelity Bank, N.A., N.J.
765 Broad St.
Newark 07101 (201) 430-4237

Trust established in 1947 in NJ.
Financial data (yr. ended 12/31/87): Assets, $3,427,378 (M); expenditures, $297,774, including $266,595 for 54 grants (high: $60,295; low: $150; average: $6,061).
Purpose and activities: Emphasis on higher and secondary education, health agencies, and a medical and dental school; support also for the handicapped and cultural programs.
Types of support: General purposes, continuing support, annual campaigns, seed money, equipment, research, publications, conferences and seminars, scholarship funds, matching funds.
Limitations: Giving limited to NJ. No grants to individuals; no loans.
Publications: 990-PF, application guidelines.
Application information:
Initial approach: Proposal or letter
Copies of proposal: 1
Board meeting date(s): Jan., Mar., June, Sept., and Dec.
Final notification: 1 month after board meets
Write: John C. Leeds, Exec. V.P., First Fidelity Bank, N.A., N.J.
Trustee: First Fidelity Bank, N.A., NJ.
Employer Identification Number: 226024900

1702
Albert Penick Fund

c/o Horizon Trust Co.
65 Madison Ave., CN 1969
Morristown 07960

Trust established in 1951 in NY.
Donor(s): A.D. Penick,† Mrs. Albert D. Penick.
Financial data (yr. ended 12/31/87): Assets, $1,691,709 (M); expenditures, $148,744, including $126,500 for 36 grants (high: $50,000; low: $1,000).
Purpose and activities: Grants largely for higher and secondary education, hospitals, animal welfare, conservation, youth programs, and cultural organizations.
Application information:
Initial approach: Letter
Deadline(s): None
Trustees: Nancy P. Corcoran, K. Philip Dresdner, V. Susan Penick, Horizon Trust Co.
Employer Identification Number: 136161137

1703
Howard Phipps Foundation

c/o Bessemer Trust Co.
100 Woodbridge Center Dr.
Woodbridge 07095-0903

Established in 1967 in NJ.
Donor(s): Harriet Phipps.†
Financial data (yr. ended 06/30/88): Assets, $5,927,759 (M); gifts received, $1,528,545; expenditures, $1,184,828, including $1,059,500 for 46 grants (high: $100,000; low: $5,000; average: $5,000-$50,000).
Purpose and activities: Support for conservation and cultural programs.
Limitations: Giving primarily in New York, NY.
Application information:
Initial approach: Letter
Deadline(s): None
Write: Austin J. Power, Jr.
Trustees: Howard Phipps, Jr., Anne P. Sidamon-Eristoff, Bessemer Trust Co.
Employer Identification Number: 226095226

1704
The Prudential Foundation
15 Prudential Plaza
Newark 07101 (201) 802-7354

Incorporated in 1977 in NJ.
Donor(s): Prudential Insurance Co. of America, Prudential Property & Casualty Co.
Financial data (yr. ended 12/31/88): Assets, $103,984,048 (M); expenditures, $13,526,298, including $11,625,138 for 750 grants (average: $5,000-$10,000) and $1,901,160 for employee matching gifts.
Purpose and activities: Program interests include education, public affairs, urban and community affairs, health and human services, culture, and conservation and ecology; support also for United Way drives in areas of company operations.
Types of support: Operating budgets, continuing support, annual campaigns, seed money, emergency funds, deficit financing, building funds, equipment, matching funds, employee matching gifts, consulting services, technical assistance, employee-related scholarships, research, special projects, capital campaigns, conferences and seminars, general purposes.
Limitations: Giving primarily in areas of company operations, especially Newark, NJ, and in CA, FL, MN, and PA. No support for labor, religious or athletic groups, or single-disease health organizations seeking funds independently of federated drives. No grants to individuals or for endowment funds; no loans.
Publications: Annual report (including application guidelines).
Application information: Additional information will be requested as needed.
Initial approach: Letter with brief description of program
Copies of proposal: 1
Deadline(s): None
Board meeting date(s): Apr., Aug., and Dec.
Final notification: 4 to 6 weeks
Write: Donald N. Treloar, Secy.
Officers: George V. Franks, V.P.; Paul G. O'Leary, V.P.; Donald N. Treloar, Secy.; Nancy R. Moscato, Treas.
Trustees: William H. Tremayne, Chair.; Adrian M. Foley, Jr., James R. Gillen, Donald E. Procknow, Robert C. Winters, Edward D. Zinbarg.
Number of staff: 11 full-time professional; 11 full-time support.
Employer Identification Number: 222175290
Recent arts and culture grants:
Affiliate Artists, NYC, NY, $22,000. For Artist-in-Residence Program. 1987.
Connie Goldman Productions, DC, $60,000. For National Public Radio series on aging. 1987.
Down Town Park Committee, Newark, NJ, $10,000. For restoration of monument in park. 1987.
John F. Kennedy Center for the Performing Arts, DC, $20,000. For general support. 1987.
Lincoln Center for the Performing Arts, NYC, NY, $25,000. For general support. 1987.
McCarter Theater Company, Princeton, NJ, $28,000. For building improvements. 1987.
Montclair State College Development Fund, Opera/Music Theater Institute of New Jersey, Upper Montclair, NJ, $10,000. For Adopt an Apprentice program. 1987.
New Brunswick Cultural Center, New Brunswick, NJ, $15,000. For Arts Guide project. 1987.
New Jersey State Opera, Newark, NJ, $20,000. For debt reduction challenge grant. 1987.
New Jersey Symphony Orchestra, Newark, NJ, $50,000. For general support. 1987.
Newark Community School of the Arts, Newark, NJ, $15,000. For computer-assisted music theory program. 1987.
Newark Public Radio, Newark, NJ, $20,000. For broadcasts and news coverage on AIDS. 1987.
Newark Symphony Hall Corporation, Newark, NJ, $56,000. For general support. 1987.
State Police Memorial Association, West Trenton, NJ, $25,000. For museum start-up funds. 1987.
United States Holocaust Memorial Museum, DC, $10,000. For museum and library start-up costs. 1987.
Young Audiences, NYC, NY, $55,000. For Arts Card program in Essex County, NJ. 1987.

1705
Public Service Electric and Gas Corporate Giving Program
80 Park Plaza
Newark 07101 (201) 430-8660

Financial data (yr. ended 12/31/88): Total giving, $2,500,000, including $2,330,000 for grants and $170,000 for 200 employee matching gifts.
Purpose and activities: Support for economic development, environmental issues, federated campaigns, arts, education, hospitals, minority programs, urban problems, welfare, youth, and civic affairs. Also support for in-kind giving.
Types of support: Building funds, special projects, capital campaigns, continuing support, emergency funds, employee matching gifts, operating budgets, research, scholarship funds.
Limitations: Giving primarily in areas of service territory.
Application information:
Initial approach: Proposal
Copies of proposal: 1
Deadline(s): None
Board meeting date(s): Irregular
Final notification: By letter or personal contact
Write: Maureen G. Resch, Corp. Contribs. Mgr.
Number of staff: 2 full-time professional; 9 part-time professional; 1 full-time support; 3 part-time support.

1706
The Sarah and Matthew Rosenhaus Peace Foundation, Inc.
Picatinny Rd.
Morristown 07960 (201) 267-6583

Incorporated in 1959 in NY.
Donor(s): Sarah Rosenhaus,† Matthew B. Rosenhaus.†
Financial data (yr. ended 7/31/87): Assets, $10,516,204 (M); gifts received, $235,447; expenditures, $781,117, including $678,000 for 39 grants (high: $100,000; low: $200; average: $1,000-$25,000).
Purpose and activities: To promote world peace and understanding, with emphasis on medical research and health services, Jewish organizations, higher education, including theological education and international peace organizations; some support for social service agencies and cultural programs.
Limitations: Giving primarily in NJ and NY. No grants to individuals.
Application information: Contributes only to pre-selected organizations. Applications not accepted.
Write: Irving Rosenhaus, Managing Dir.
Officers and Directors: Alice Fetro, Secy.; Robert Bobrow, Treas.; Irving R. Rosenhaus, Managing Dir.; Anetra Chester, Jerome Cossman, Harriet Grosc, Albert Rosenhaus, Lawrence Rosenhaus, Gila Rosenhaus Weiner.
Number of staff: 1
Employer Identification Number: 136136983

1707
Roxiticus Fund
P.O. Box 326
Mendham 07945 (201) 543-4833

Financial data (yr. ended 12/31/87): Assets, $1,167,982 (M); expenditures, $91,518, including $89,695 for 173 grants (high: $18,900; low: $2,700).
Purpose and activities: Support for education, health associations and hospitals, conservation, social service organizations, and the arts.
Limitations: Giving primarily in NJ and NY. No grants for scholarships or fellowships; no loans.
Application information:
Initial approach: Letter
Deadline(s): None
Write: Hugo De Neufville, Trustee
Trustees: Hugo De Neufville, Margaret Wade De Neufville.
Employer Identification Number: 226041443

1708
David and Eleanore Rukin Philanthropic Foundation
17 Franklin Tpke.
Mahwah 07430

Established in 1951 in NJ.
Donor(s): David Rukin.
Financial data (yr. ended 12/31/86): Assets, $2,352,309 (M); gifts received, $15,000; expenditures, $72,932, including $71,105 for 57 grants (high: $25,000; low: $10).
Purpose and activities: Giving primarily for Jewish welfare and education; some support also for other education, health and hospitals, and culture.
Application information:
Deadline(s): None
Write: Julius Eisen
Officer and Directors: David Rukin, Pres.; Julius Eisen, Susan Eisen, Barnett Rukin, Eleanore Rukin.
Employer Identification Number: 221715380

1709
L. P. Schenck Fund
c/o Midlantic National Bank, Trust Dept.
One Engle St.
Englewood 07631

Trust established in 1960 in NJ.
Donor(s): Lillian Pitkin Schenck.†
Financial data (yr. ended 8/31/88): Assets, $5,954,039 (M); expenditures, $440,472, including $402,220 for 33 grants (high: $35,000; low: $1,000).
Purpose and activities: Grants restricted to institutions in the immediate local area, including support for youth and social service agencies, and cultural programs.
Types of support: General purposes, operating budgets, special projects, building funds.
Limitations: Giving primarily in NJ. No grants to individuals, or for endowment funds.
Application information:
Initial approach: Proposal
Copies of proposal: 3
Deadline(s): Aug. 1
Board meeting date(s): Sept.
Write: Norman E. Smyth, V.P., Midlantic National Bank
Trustees: Mary P. Oenslager, Elizabeth N. Thatcher, Midlantic National Bank.
Employer Identification Number: 226040581

1710
Schering-Plough Corporate Giving Program
Schering Plough Corp.
Madison 07940-1000 (201) 822-7407

Financial data (yr. ended 12/31/87): $770,000 for grants.
Purpose and activities: Through active participation in local community programs and through the creation of partnerships with civic and non-profit organizations, Schering-Plough Corp. seeks to address emerging issues and community problems. Grants are for health and welfare, civic and cultural programs, educational activities, including scholarship programs, and the United Way. In addition to cash grants, the company also makes contributions through employee volunteerism, including providing tutorial support to community high school students, sponsoring cultural events (exhibitions and performances), health fairs and other health programs (child safety and drug abuse), offering management and technical support to small and minority businesses, and donating products and surplus equipment.
Types of support: In-kind gifts, employee-related scholarships.
Limitations: Giving primarily in areas where corporate sponsor has major facilities in AR, CA, FL, GA, IL, NE, NJ, PR, TN, and TX. No grants to individuals.
Publications: Corporate giving report.
Application information:
Initial approach: Letter
Deadline(s): None
Write: Joan Henderson, Community Affairs Admin.

1711
Schering-Plough Foundation, Inc.
One Giralda Farms
P.O. Box 1000
Madison 07940-1000 (201) 822-7412

Incorporated in 1955 in DE.
Donor(s): Schering Corp., The Plough Foundation, Schering-Plough Corp.
Financial data (yr. ended 12/31/88): Assets, $16,540,581 (M); expenditures, $2,413,986, including $2,003,419 for 94 grants (high: $1,000,000; low: $1,000; average: $20-$25,000) and $359,744 for 1,022 employee matching gifts.
Purpose and activities: Primary objective is support of institutional activities devoted to improving the quality and delivery of health care, through medical and allied education. Selective support to higher education, hospitals, health care programs, and cultural organizations in those communities where the corporation has major facilities. Grants made both directly and through national granting groups. Matching gift plan includes accredited higher and secondary educational institutions, and hospitals.
Types of support: Employee matching gifts, annual campaigns, seed money, building funds, equipment, research, internships, fellowships, general purposes, professorships, continuing support, operating budgets, scholarship funds, capital campaigns, endowment funds, renovation projects, employee-related scholarships, special projects.
Limitations: Giving primarily in areas where corporate sponsor has major facilities, especially NJ and TN. No grants to individuals, or for deficit financing, publications, or conferences; no loans.
Publications: Annual report (including application guidelines).
Application information:
Initial approach: Letter
Copies of proposal: 1
Deadline(s): Feb. 1 and Sept. 1
Board meeting date(s): Spring and Fall
Final notification: 6 months
Write: Rita Sacco, Asst. Secy.
Officers: Allan S. Kushen,* Pres.; Richard J. Kinney, Secy.; J. Martin Comey, Treas.
Trustees:* Donald R. Conklin, Hugh A. D'Andrade, Harold R. Hiser, Jr., R. Lee Jenkins, Richard J. Kogan, Robert P. Luciano.
Number of staff: 1 full-time professional; 1 part-time professional; 1 part-time support.
Employer Identification Number: 221711047
Recent arts and culture grants:
Arts in the Schools Endowment Fund, Memphis, TN, $30,000. To support Memphis Arts Council's program, Arts In The Schools. 1987.
Colonial Symphony, Madison, NJ, $20,000. To sponsor annual concert. 1987.
Dixon Gallery and Gardens, Memphis, TN, $50,000. To support building campaign, designated for Loan Exhibit Gallery in memory of Abe Plough. 1987.
Montclair State College, Opera/Music Theater Institute of New Jersey, Newark, NJ, $10,000. To support Schering-Plough Fellow in young artists program. 1987.
Morris Museum, Morristown, NJ, $25,000. To support campaign, Continue the Heritage-Preserve the Future, designated for Gift Shop. 1987.
Newark Museum, Newark, NJ, $10,000. To support Master Plan Campaign. 1987.
Sci-Tech Center at Liberty State Park, Morris Plains, NJ, $100,000. To support development campaign for construction of Center. 1987.
State Police Memorial Association, West Trenton, NJ, $5,000. To support New Jersey State Police Memorial Museum Campaign. 1987.
Statue of Liberty-Ellis Island Foundation, NYC, NY, $50,000. To support Liberty Centennial Campaign. 1987.
Waterloo Foundation for the Arts, Waterloo Village, Stanhope, NJ, $10,000. To support 1987 Festival and School of Music. 1987.

1712
The Florence and John Schumann Foundation
33 Park St.
Montclair 07042 (201) 783-6660

Incorporated in 1961 in NJ.
Donor(s): Florence F. Schumann, John J. Schumann, Jr.†
Financial data (yr. ended 12/31/87): Assets, $67,816,197 (M); expenditures, $3,878,841, including $3,162,390 for 112 grants (high: $250,000; low: $1,000; average: $10,000-$50,000).
Purpose and activities: Grants for education, community development programs, and health.
Types of support: Operating budgets, continuing support, seed money, emergency funds, matching funds.
Limitations: No grants to individuals, or for annual campaigns, deficit financing, equipment and materials, land acquisition, or endowment funds; no loans.
Publications: Annual report (including application guidelines).
Application information:
Initial approach: Letter
Copies of proposal: 1
Deadline(s): Jan. 15, Apr. 15, Aug. 15, and Oct. 15
Board meeting date(s): Feb., June, Sept., and Dec.
Final notification: 2 to 3 months
Write: William B. Mullins, Pres.
Officers and Trustees: Robert F. Schumann, Chair.; William B. Mullins, Pres. and Dir.; Howard D. Brundage, V.P., Finance; Caroline S. Mark, V.P.; W. Ford Schumann, V.P.; David S. Bate, Secy.-Treas.; Aubin Z. Ames, Robert D.B. Carlisle, Edwin D. Etherington, Charles B. Sanders.
Staff: Patricia A. McCarthy, Admin. Officer.
Number of staff: 2 full-time professional; 2 part-time support.
Employer Identification Number: 226044214
Recent arts and culture grants:
Lyme Historical Society, Old Lyme, CT, $20,000. Toward Campaign for Florence Griswold Museum. 12/87.
Montclair Art Museum, Montclair, NJ, $15,000. For general support. 12/87.
Montclair Art Museum, Montclair, NJ, $5,000. Toward 75th Anniversary Fund. 12/87.

Montclair Art Museum, Montclair, NJ, $5,000. For Acquisition Fund. 12/87.
National Gallery of Art, DC, $5,000. For Collectors Committee. 12/87.
New Jersey Historical Society, Newark, NJ, $5,000. Toward celebration of bicentennial of U.S. Constitution. 12/87.
Newark Public Radio, Newark, NJ, $15,000. For news and public affairs programming for WBGO-FM. 12/87.
W N E T Channel 13, NYC, NY, $300,000. To support activities of Public Affairs Television. 12/87.
W N E T Channel 13, NYC, NY, $50,000. To support proposal to explore feasibility of combining certain operations with New Jersey Network. 9/24/87.

1713
The South Branch Foundation

c/o Gillen & Johnson
P.O. Box 477
Somerville 08876 (201) 722-6400

Trust established in 1960 in NJ.
Donor(s): J. Seward Johnson, The J. Seward Johnson Charitable Trust.
Financial data (yr. ended 12/31/86): Assets, $8,091,178 (M); expenditures, $789,052, including $642,500 for 28 grants (high: $125,000; low: $1,000; average: $2,000-$100,000).
Purpose and activities: Emphasis on civil rights, education, conservation, protection of animals, cultural programs, social services, and health.
Types of support: Continuing support, fellowships, research, scholarship funds, special projects.
Limitations: No grants to individuals, or for building funds.
Application information:
Initial approach: Proposal
Copies of proposal: 1
Deadline(s): Submit proposal preferably in Nov. or Dec.; deadline Dec. 31
Board meeting date(s): Jan.
Final notification: 45 days
Write: Peter S. Johnson
Director: Jennifer U. Johnson.
Trustees: Esther U. Johnson, James L. Johnson, John D. Mack.
Number of staff: None.
Employer Identification Number: 226029434

1714
Leonard N. Stern Foundation

700 South Fourth St.
Harrison 07029

Donor(s): Leonard N. Stern.
Financial data (yr. ended 12/31/87): Assets, $1,041,806 (M); gifts received, $2,999,970; expenditures, $2,983,724, including $2,950,902 for 77 grants (high: $400,000; low: $150; average: $5,000-$70,000).
Purpose and activities: Grants for Jewish giving, including Jewish welfare funds, higher education, culture, and social services.
Application information: Contributes only to pre-selected organizations. Applications not accepted.
Officers and Directors: Leonard N. Stern, Pres.; Armand Lindenbaum, V.P.; Curtis Schwartz, Secy.-Treas.; Carol Kellermann, Exec. Dir.; Joseph A. Bardwil, Richard Stearn.
Employer Identification Number: 136149990

1715
Subaru of America Foundation

Subaru Plaza
P.O. Box 6000
Cherry Hill 08034-6000 (609) 488-5099

Established in 1984 in NJ.
Donor(s): Subaru of America, Inc.
Financial data (yr. ended 10/31/88): Assets, $1,436,911 (M); expenditures, $414,598, including $374,455 for 134 grants (high: $15,000; low: $50; average: $2,000-$3,000) and $40,143 for 319 employee matching gifts.
Purpose and activities: Giving for cultural programs, health and hospitals, social services, education, and civic organizations.
Types of support: Operating budgets, continuing support, annual campaigns, seed money, emergency funds, building funds, equipment, employee matching gifts, special projects, general purposes, matching funds, technical assistance.
Limitations: Giving limited to areas of company operations, primarily in the Cherry Hill, NJ, area, and immediate subsidiary communities in Addison, IL; Aurora, CO; Columbus, OH; Portland, OR; San Antonio, TX; Savage, MD; West Palm Beach, FL; and Garden Grove, Irvine, and West Sacramento, CA. No support for religious, fraternal, or veterans' groups. No grants to individuals, or for land acquisition, endowment funds, scholarships, fellowships, research, publications, conferences and seminars, or vehicle donations; no loans.
Publications: Annual report (including application guidelines).
Application information:
Initial approach: Letter, telephone, or proposal
Copies of proposal: 1
Deadline(s): Dec. 1, Mar. 1, June 1, and Sept. 1
Board meeting date(s): Jan., Apr., July, and Oct.
Final notification: Up to 5 months, depending on cycle
Write: Denise L. Schwartz, Mgr.
Officers and Trustees:* Thomas R. Gibson,* Pres.; Marvin S. Riesenbach,* Exec. V.P. and C.F.O.; Frank T. Aspell, V.P.; Harvey H. Lamm,* C.E.O.
Contributions Committee: Herman E. Berg, Chair.; R. Curtis Allen, David Bryson, Richard L. Crosson, Deborah D. Ritch, Leonard M. Romberg, Gary Sampson, Denise M. Wallace, Betty Y. Wenger.
Staff: Denise L. Schwartz, Mgr.
Number of staff: 1 full-time professional; 2 full-time support.
Employer Identification Number: 222531774

1716
Supermarkets General Corporate Giving Program

301 Blair Road
Woodbridge 07095 (201) 499-3000

Purpose and activities: Support for local organizations, including community funds, education, youth and civic organizations, minority programs, and cultural and fine arts institutes.
Types of support: Annual campaigns, emergency funds, program-related investments.
Limitations: Giving primarily in headquarters city and major operating locations in CT, DE, NJ, NY, and PA.
Application information: Include IRS 501 (c)(3) status letter.
Initial approach: Short letter of inquiry on organization's letterhead
Write: Robert Wunderle, V.P., Public Affairs
Number of staff: 1 part-time professional; 1 full-time support.

1717
Ann Earle Talcott Fund

c/o Fidelity Bank
765 Broad St.
Newark 07101 (201) 565-3751

Trust established in 1972 in NJ.
Donor(s): Ann Earle Talcott.†
Financial data (yr. ended 10/31/87): Assets, $1,396,864 (M); expenditures, $83,275, including $73,000 for 8 grants (high: $25,000; low: $2,000).
Purpose and activities: Giving primarily for youth activities and for mental health; some support for culture and education.
Application information:
Initial approach: Proposal
Copies of proposal: 1
Deadline(s): June 30
Board meeting date(s): Dec.
Write: Richard Reitmeyer
Trustee: First Fidelity Bank.
Employer Identification Number: 226203894

1718
W. Parsons Todd Foundation, Inc.

c/o Shanley & Fisher
131 Madison Ave.
Morristown 07960

Incorporated in 1949 in NJ.
Donor(s): W. Parsons Todd.
Financial data (yr. ended 12/31/87): Assets, $3,069,626 (M); expenditures, $122,121, including $107,417 for 8 grants (high: $99,609; low: $250).
Purpose and activities: Emphasis on an historical museum; grants also for church support.
Limitations: Giving limited to the Morris County, NJ, and Houghton County, MI, areas.
Application information: Contributes only to pre-selected organizations. Applications not accepted.
Officers and Trustees: Mortimer J. Propp, Pres.; H.T. Todd, V.P.; E.A. Deckenbach, Seymour Propp.
Employer Identification Number: 136116488

1719
Turrell Fund
33 Evergreen Place
East Orange 07018 (201) 678-8580

Incorporated in 1935 in NJ.
Donor(s): Herbert Turrell,† Margaret Turrell.†
Financial data (yr. ended 12/31/88): Assets, $73,668,720 (M); expenditures, $4,449,734, including $3,650,350 for 201 grants (high: $300,000; low: $750; average: $5,000-$50,000) and $275,504 for 1 foundation-administered program.
Purpose and activities: Grants to organizations dedicated to service to or care of children and youth under 18 years of age, with emphasis on the needy, the socially maladjusted, and the disadvantaged.
Types of support: Operating budgets, seed money, emergency funds, building funds, equipment, land acquisition, matching funds, scholarship funds, renovation projects, general purposes, special projects.
Limitations: Giving limited to NJ, particularly the northern urban areas centered in Essex County, and to VT. No support for advocacy work, most hospital work, or health delivery services; generally no support for cultural activities. No grants to individuals, or for endowment funds, publications, conferences, or research; no loans.
Publications: Annual report (including application guidelines).
Application information:
Initial approach: Letter
Copies of proposal: 1
Deadline(s): Submit proposal preferably in Jan. or Feb. or between June and Sept.; deadlines Feb. 14 and Sept. 15 for first-time applicants; Mar. 1 and Oct. 1 for others
Board meeting date(s): May and Nov. and/or Dec.
Final notification: 3 months after deadlines
Write: E. Belvin Williams, Exec. Dir.
Officers: S. Whitney Landon, Chair.; Frank J. Hoenemeyer, Pres.; Carl Fjellman,* Secy.-Treas.; E. Belvin Williams,* Exec. Dir.
Trustees:* Paul J. Christiansen, Ann G. Dinse, Robert H. Grasmere, Richard R. Hough, Frank A. Hutson, Jr., Vivian Shapiro.
Number of staff: 2 full-time professional; 1 part-time professional; 3 full-time support.
Employer Identification Number: 221551936
Recent arts and culture grants:
Fairbanks Museum and Planetarium, Saint Johnsbury, VT, $13,500. For equipment and materials for education program in area schools. 1987.
New Jersey Symphony Orchestra, Newark, NJ, $15,000. For educational concerts presented to school groups. 1987.
Newark Boys Chorus School, Newark, NJ, $12,000. For program support for this special alternative school. 1987.
Newark Community School of the Arts, Newark, NJ, $26,000. For scholarships for youngsters supplementing their public school with after-school and Saturday classes in the arts, and for employment training program. 1987.

1720
Union Camp Charitable Trust
c/o Union Camp Corp.
1600 Valley Rd.
Wayne 07470 (201) 628-2248

Trust established in 1951 in NY.
Donor(s): Union Camp Corp.
Financial data (yr. ended 12/31/87): Assets, $889,308 (M); gifts received, $2,000,000; expenditures, $1,234,294 for grants (high: $137,000; low: $10; average: $200-$5,000), $100,852 for 57 grants to individuals and $136,309 for 861 employee matching gifts.
Purpose and activities: Grants largely for community funds, higher education, including employee-related scholarships and matching gifts, hospitals and health services, social service and youth agencies, civic affairs and public interest, and cultural programs.
Types of support: Employee matching gifts, employee-related scholarships, operating budgets, continuing support, annual campaigns, building funds, equipment, special projects, research, capital campaigns.
Limitations: Giving primarily in areas of company operations and to national organizations. No grants to individuals (except employee-related scholarships); no loans.
Application information:
Initial approach: Proposal
Copies of proposal: 1
Deadline(s): Submit proposal preferably from Jan. through Aug.
Board meeting date(s): Nov.
Final notification: By Jan. 1
Write: Sydney N. Phin, Dir., Human Resources
Trustees: R.W. Boekenheide, R.E. Cartledge, J.M. Reed, Morgan Guaranty Trust Co. of New York.
Number of staff: 2 part-time professional; 1 part-time support.
Employer Identification Number: 136034666

1721
Union Foundation
31C Mountain Blvd.
P.O. Box 4470
Warren 07060 (201) 753-2440

Incorporated in 1951 in NJ.
Donor(s): Edward J. Grassmann,† and others.
Financial data (yr. ended 11/30/87): Assets, $8,904,647 (M); expenditures, $659,308, including $602,600 for 68 grants (high: $30,000; low: $600; average: $5,000-$25,000).
Purpose and activities: Grants largely for hospitals and health agencies, social service and youth agencies, privately-supported higher and secondary education, conservation, the humanities, and denominational giving.
Types of support: Endowment funds, building funds, equipment.
Limitations: Giving primarily in Union County, NJ. No grants to individuals, or for operating budgets.
Publications: Application guidelines.
Application information:
Initial approach: Proposal
Copies of proposal: 1
Deadline(s): Oct. 15
Board meeting date(s): Nov.
Final notification: Dec. 15
Write: William V. Engel, Secy.
Officers and Trustees: Joseph G. Engel, Pres.; Edward G. Engel, V.P.; William V. Engel, Secy.; Thomas H. Campbell, Treas.; Haydn H. Murray, Suzanne B. Richard, William O. Wuester, M.D.
Number of staff: 1 part-time professional.
Employer Identification Number: 226046454

1722
Lucy and Eleanor S. Upton Charitable Foundation
100 Mulberry St.
Newark 07102

Established in 1965.
Donor(s): Eleanor S. Upton.†
Financial data (yr. ended 12/31/86): Assets, $4,075,240 (M); expenditures, $263,603, including $220,500 for 14 grants (high: $60,000; low: $2,000).
Purpose and activities: Support primarily for an educational institution; giving also to hospitals and cultural programs.
Types of support: General purposes, research, fellowships.
Limitations: Giving primarily in NJ.
Application information: Contributes only to pre-selected organizations. Applications not accepted.
Trustees: William B. Cater, Thomas L. Morrissey, Samuel C. Williams, Jr.
Employer Identification Number: 226074947

1723
Van Pelt Foundation
P.O. Box 823
Westwood 07675

Established in 1977 in NJ.
Donor(s): Edwin Van Pelt.
Financial data (yr. ended 9/30/88): Assets, $4,200,277 (M); expenditures, $288,596, including $283,000 for 42 grants (high: $60,000; low: $250).
Purpose and activities: Support for smaller organizations who have been hurt by cutbacks in federal monies and/or individual contributions; support primarily for hospitals, social service and cultural organizations.
Types of support: Building funds, capital campaigns, continuing support, employee matching gifts, equipment, general purposes.
Application information:
Initial approach: Proposal
Copies of proposal: 5
Deadline(s): Before board meetings
Board meeting date(s): June 1, and Dec. 1
Officers and Trustees: Lawrence D. Bass, Pres.; Henry Gerke, V.P.; Robert DuBois, Secy.; Henry Bass, Treas.; Meredith Van Pelt.
Employer Identification Number: 222188191

1724
Victoria Foundation, Inc.
40 South Fullerton Ave.
Montclair 07042 (201) 783-4450

Incorporated in 1924 in NJ.
Donor(s): Hendon Chubb.†

Financial data (yr. ended 12/31/88): Assets, $74,206,000 (M); expenditures, $3,892,891, including $3,483,842 for 170 grants (high: $100,000; low: $5,000; average: $20,000-$45,000).
Purpose and activities: Grants primarily for welfare and education programs, including urban problems, neighborhood development, youth agencies, and behavioral rehabilitation; support also for certain statewide environmental projects.
Types of support: Operating budgets, continuing support, seed money, emergency funds, deficit financing, building funds, matching funds, scholarship funds, special projects, research, consulting services, technical assistance, general purposes, renovation projects.
Limitations: Giving primarily in Essex County, NJ, with emphasis on the greater Newark area. No support for organizations dealing with specific diseases or afflictions, geriatric needs, or day care. No grants to individuals, or for publications or conferences; no loans.
Publications: Annual report (including application guidelines).
Application information: Telephone followed by letter or proposal. Application form required.
Initial approach: Proposal
Copies of proposal: 1
Deadline(s): Submit proposal Jan. 1 through Mar. 15 or June 1 through Sept. 15
Board meeting date(s): May and Dec.
Final notification: Within 3 weeks after board meeting if accepted
Write: Catherine M. McFarland
Officers: Percy Chubb III,* Pres.; Margaret H. Parker,* V.P.; Howard E. Quirk, Secy.; Kevin Shanley,* Treas.
Trustees:* Matthew G. Carter, Charles Chapin, Corinne A. Chubb, Sally Chubb, Mary Coggeshall, Robert Curvin, Haliburton Fales II, Jean Felker, Gordon A. Millspaugh, Jr., Bernard M. Shanley, William Turnbull.
Number of staff: 2 full-time professional; 1 full-time support.
Employer Identification Number: 221554541
Recent arts and culture grants:
Arts Foundation of New Jersey, New Brunswick, NJ, $15,000. For scholarships for Newark students at Summer Arts Institute. 1987.
Carter G. Woodson Foundation, Newark, NJ, $10,000. For general support of agency which arranges and promotes Afro-American cultural productions. 1987.
Cathedral Concert Series, Newark, NJ, $20,000. For general support. 1987.
Leaguers, Newark, NJ, $20,000. Toward performing and fine arts program for elementary, middle and high school students. 1987.
New Jersey Chamber Music Society, Newark, NJ, $15,000. For presentations in Newark schools. 1987.
New Jersey Network, Trenton, NJ, $25,000. For operating support to Public Television station featuring programs for Hispanic population. 1987.
New Jersey Symphony Orchestra, Newark, NJ, $12,500. Toward endowment. 1987.
New Jersey Symphony Orchestra, Newark, NJ, $12,500. Toward programs for Newark youth. 1987.
New School for the Arts, Montclair, NJ, $44,000. For instruction in music and dance in four Newark schools. 1987.
Newark Boys Chorus School, Newark, NJ, $20,000. For general support. 1987.
Newark Community School of the Arts, Newark, NJ, $66,700. For scholarships, operating support, summer music camp and equipment. 1987.
Newark Museum, Newark, NJ, $100,000. For capital drive to increase gallery and exhibit space. 1987.
Newark Public Radio, Newark, NJ, $20,000. For local news programs. 1987.
Pushcart Players, Vernon, NJ, $10,000. For performances in Newark schools. 1987.
School of the Garden State Ballet, Newark, NJ, $20,000. For scholarships for Newark youth. 1987.
Theaterworks/USA, NYC, NY, $10,000. For performances in Newark schools. 1987.
Whole Theater Company, Montclair, NJ, $20,000. For Arts Alternative Program in Newark schools. 1987.

1725
Visceglia-Summit Associates Foundation
Raritan Plaza
Raritan Center
Edison 08818 (201) 225-2900

Incorporated in 1953 in NJ.
Donor(s): Vincent Visceglia, Diego R. Visceglia, John B. Visceglia.
Financial data (yr. ended 3/31/86): Assets, $2,155,920 (M); expenditures, $195,267, including $172,272 for 185 grants (high: $20,000; low: $25).
Purpose and activities: Support for hospitals, higher education, church support, and religious associations; some support also for community funds, music, opera, ballet, and other performing arts, and youth agencies.
Limitations: Giving primarily in Essex and Middlesex counties, NJ. No grants to individuals.
Publications: Financial statement.
Application information: Applications not accepted.
Officers: Diego R. Visceglia, Pres.; Vincent Visceglia, V.P.; John B. Visceglia, Secy.
Employer Identification Number: 226041608

1726
Woolley-Clifford Foundation
c/o Gerald A. Wolf
Two North Dean St.
Englewood 07631

Incorporated in 1953 in DE.
Donor(s): Stewart B. Clifford, Cornelia W. Clifford.
Financial data (yr. ended 12/31/87): Assets, $699,430 (M); gifts received, $135,893; expenditures, $265,385, including $257,550 for 30 grants (high: $103,250; low: $150).
Purpose and activities: Support primarily for higher education and private secondary schools; giving for social services and cultural programs; support also for a Protestant church.
Limitations: Giving primarily in NY.
Application information: Contributes only to pre-selected organizations. Applications not accepted.
Officers and Trustees: Stewart B. Clifford, Pres.; Cornelia W. Clifford, V.P.; C.L.C. Wareham, Treas.; J.L.C. Danner, Secy.
Employer Identification Number: 136100412

NEW MEXICO

1727
Albuquerque Community Foundation
P.O. Box 8847
Albuquerque 87198 (505) 883-6240
Additional address: 6400 Uptown Blvd., N.E., Suite 500 West, Albuquerque, NM 87110

Established in 1981 in NM.
Financial data (yr. ended 6/30/88): Assets, $1,136,506 (M); gifts received, $484,578; expenditures, $139,487, including $382,177 for 71 grants (high: $500; low: $100; average: $8,000-$10,000) and $1,000 for 2 grants to individuals.
Purpose and activities: Support for cultural programs, education, health, conservation and social services.
Types of support: Exchange programs, fellowships, publications, research, scholarship funds, seed money, special projects, student aid, technical assistance, consulting services, emergency funds, loans.
Limitations: Giving primarily in the greater Albuquerque, NM, area. No support for religious, political, or grant-making organizations. No grants to individuals; or for purchase of equipment, debt requirement, or interest or tax payments.
Publications: Annual report (including application guidelines), newsletter, occasional report, informational brochure (including application guidelines).
Application information: Selection is by invitation based on letter of intent.
Initial approach: Letter by Mar. 1; proposal by May 1
Copies of proposal: 1
Board meeting date(s): Quarterly
Final notification: annually in Sept.
Write: Laura E. Threet, Exec. Dir.
Officers and Trustees:* John T. Ackerman,* Pres.; Robert J. Stamm,* V.P.; Gloria G. Mallory,* Secy.; Ray Zimmer,* Treas.; Laura E. Threet, Exec. Dir.; and 15 other trustees.
Number of staff: 1 full-time professional; 2 part-time support.
Employer Identification Number: 850295444

1728
The Witter Bynner Foundation for Poetry, Inc.
660 East Garcia
P.O. Box 2188
Santa Fe 87504 (505) 983-4629

Incorporated in 1972 in NM.
Donor(s): Witter Bynner.†
Financial data (yr. ended 5/31/88): Assets, $2,526,272 (M); expenditures, $142,576, including $24,425 for 5 grants (high: $7,525; low: $2,000) and $27,850 for 5 grants to individuals.
Purpose and activities: To make grants, particularly as seed money, in support of poetry and poetry translation to nonprofit organizations and institutions.
Types of support: Seed money, matching funds, special projects, research, conferences and seminars.
Limitations: No support for poetry readings. No grants for building or endowment funds, publications, continuing support, or operating expenses; no loans.
Publications: Annual report, application guidelines, program policy statement, informational brochure, grants list.
Application information: Application form required.
Initial approach: Letter or telephone
Copies of proposal: 3
Deadline(s): Feb. 1
Board meeting date(s): Apr. or May
Final notification: 2 weeks after annual meeting
Write: Steven Schwartz, Exec. Dir.
Officers and Trustees: Douglas W. Schwartz, Pres.; Thomas B. Catron III, Art Gallaher, Jr., Vera Zorina Lieberson.
Number of staff: 3 part-time support.
Employer Identification Number: 237169999
Recent arts and culture grants:
Art.re.grup, San Francisco, CA, $7,525. For Third Wave Poets: Poems from Moscow's Emerging Avant-Garde. 1988.
Corporation of Yaddo, Saratoga Springs, NY, $7,500. For resident fellowships for poets. 1988.
Hambidge Center for Creative Arts & Sciences, Rabun Gap, GA, $5,000. For Letters From a Caribbean Island, to enable J.O. Cofer to concentrate on writing book length series of poems. 1988.
New York Center for Visual History, NYC, NY, $20,000. For Voices & Visions Secondary School Program, complete videotaped poetry curriculum that will be distributed to secondary schools across the country. 1988.
University of Colorado Foundation, Boulder, CO, $6,515. For Gender Poetics: A Discussion Model, to examine poetics of female gender in contemporary American society. 1988.
W G B H Educational Foundation, Boston, MA, $5,000. For Poetry Breaks, presenting poets and performers reading short poems in 1/2 to 2 minute spots. 1988.
Western Pennsylvania School for the Deaf, Pittsburgh, PA, $10,355. For The Deaf Poet: A Role Model in the Classroom, to aid development of poetic expression in young people who are severely and profoundly deaf. 1988.

1729
J. F. Maddox Foundation
P.O. Box 5410
Hobbs 88241 (505) 393-6338

Established in 1963 in NM.
Donor(s): J.F. Maddox,† Mabel S. Maddox.†
Financial data (yr. ended 6/30/88): Assets, $48,042,567 (M); gifts received, $2,100,243; expenditures, $1,333,084, including $1,231,005 for 101 grants (high: $325,000; low: $250; average: $1,000-$25,000) and $59,935 for loans to individuals.
Purpose and activities: Giving for community projects where self-help is evident, activities benefiting the elderly, youth education and development programs, the arts, and higher education, including student loans.
Types of support: Student loans, building funds, equipment, general purposes, matching funds, seed money, special projects, renovation projects.
Limitations: Giving primarily in NM and western TX. No support for private foundations. No grants to individuals, or for operating budgets, or endowment funds.
Publications: Application guidelines.
Application information: Application form required for student loans.
Initial approach: Letter
Copies of proposal: 1
Deadline(s): None
Board meeting date(s): As needed
Final notification: Varies
Write: Robert D. Socolofsky, Exec. Dir.
Officers and Directors: Donovan Maddox, Pres.; Don Maddox, V.P.; James M. Maddox, Secy.-Treas.; Harry H. Lynch.
Number of staff: 1 full-time professional; 2 part-time professional; 1 full-time support.
Employer Identification Number: 756023767

1730
Robert Moody Foundation, Inc.
P.O. Box 1705
Santa Fe 87504-1705

Established in 1945 in NM.
Financial data (yr. ended 12/31/87): Assets, $44,010 (M); gifts received, $22,200; expenditures, $112,121, including $109,245 for 49 grants (high: $30,000; low: $20).
Purpose and activities: Giving primarily for museums, higher education and general charitable giving.
Application information: Contributes only to pre-selected organizations. Applications not accepted.
Deadline(s): None
Officers and Directors: Robert McKinney, Chair.; Robert Martin, Pres.; Meade P. Martin, V.P.; Holly Field, Secy.-Treas.
Employer Identification Number: 856009504

1731
Waite and Genevieve Phillips Foundation
P.O. Box 5726
Santa Fe 87502

Established in 1986 in NM.
Donor(s): Waite and Genevieve Phillips Charitable Trust.
Financial data (yr. ended 5/31/87): Assets, $39,287,303 (M); expenditures, $758,018, including $650,125 for 31 grants (high: $452,625; low: $500).
Purpose and activities: Giving primarily to the arts, cultural organizations, and education.
Application information: Contributes only to pre-selected organizations. Applications not accepted.
Officers and Directors: Elliott W. Phillips, Pres.; John Phillips, V.P.; Julie Puckett, V.P.; Virginia Phillips, Secy.-Treas.
Employer Identification Number: 850335071

1732
Luther A. Sizemore Foundation
6010 Lomas Blvd., NE
Albuquerque 87110

Established in 1977.
Financial data (yr. ended 12/31/87): Assets, $1,087,079 (M); expenditures, $80,838, including $57,670 for 29 grants (high: $14,976; low: $240).
Purpose and activities: Giving for higher education, Christian religious organizations, and cultural programs, with emphasis on a natural history museum.
Limitations: Giving primarily in Albuquerque, NM.
Application information:
Deadline(s): None
Officers: Marcial Rey, Pres.; Wilfred Padilla, V.P.; Clinton Abel, Secy.-Treas.
Employer Identification Number: 510206540

1733
The Helene Wurlitzer Foundation of New Mexico
P.O. Box 545
Taos 87571 (505) 758-2413

Incorporated in 1956 in NM.
Donor(s): Mrs. Howard E. Wurlitzer.†
Financial data (yr. ended 3/31/88): Assets, $4,128,899 (M); gifts received, $1,025; expenditures, $102,093, including $1,378 for 13 grants (high: $250; low: $15) and $19,837 for 19 grants to individuals.
Purpose and activities: A private operating foundation established to encourage and stimulate creative work in the humanities, arts, and allied fields through the provision of rent-free and utilities-free housing in Taos, NM.
Types of support: Grants to individuals, internships.
Application information: Application form required.
Initial approach: Letter
Deadline(s): None
Board meeting date(s): As required
Final notification: Several weeks
Write: Henry A. Sauerwein, Jr., Pres.
Officers and Trustees: Mrs. Toni Tarleton, Henry A. Sauerwein, Jr., Pres. and Exec. Dir.; Burton Phillips, V.P. and Treas.; Kenneth Peterson, Secy.; Sumner S. Koch.
Number of staff: 1 part-time professional; 1 full-time support; 1 part-time support.
Employer Identification Number: 850128634

NEW YORK

1734
Joseph & Sophia Abeles Foundation, Inc.
1055 Bedford Rd.
Pleasantville 10570-3907 (914) 769-0781

Established in 1960 in NY.
Financial data (yr. ended 12/31/87): Assets, $1,833,630 (M); expenditures, $99,187, including $84,967 for 65 grants (high: $10,000; low: $100).
Purpose and activities: Giving primarily for higher education, including a scholarship fund, cultural programs, and social services.
Types of support: Scholarship funds.
Application information:
Initial approach: Letter
Deadline(s): None
Write: Sophia Abeles, Treas.
Officers: Joseph C. Abeles, Pres. and V.P.; David Teitelbaum, Secy.; Sophia Abeles, Treas.
Employer Identification Number: 136259577

1735
Benjamin and Elizabeth Abrams Foundation, Inc.
645 Madison Ave.
New York 10022

Incorporated in 1943 in NY.
Donor(s): Benjamin Abrams,† Elizabeth Abrams Kramer.
Financial data (yr. ended 12/31/87): Assets, $1,955,628 (M); expenditures, $105,332, including $63,650 for 40 grants (high: $14,000; low: $200).
Purpose and activities: Emphasis on higher education, including medical education, hospitals, Jewish welfare funds, and cultural programs.
Limitations: Giving primarily in NY and in Palm Beach County, FL.
Application information: Contributes only to pre-selected organizations. Applications not accepted.
Officers and Directors: Elizabeth Abrams Kramer, Pres. and Treas.; Marjorie A. Hyman, V.P.; Geraldine A. Kory, Secy.; Cynthia Bernstein.
Employer Identification Number: 136092960

1736
Louis and Anne Abrons Foundation, Inc.
c/o First Manhattan Co.
437 Madison Ave.
New York 10017 (212) 832-4376

Incorporated in 1950 in NY.
Donor(s): Anne S. Abrons,† Louis Abrons.†
Financial data (yr. ended 12/31/87): Assets, $30,000,000 (M); expenditures, $2,652,973, including $2,528,424 for 150 grants (high: $500,000; low: $500; average: $5,000-$50,000).
Purpose and activities: Giving primarily to social welfare agencies, Jewish charities, major New York City institutions, civic improvement programs, and environmental and cultural projects.
Types of support: Operating budgets, continuing support, annual campaigns, seed money, general purposes, special projects, scholarship funds, research, technical assistance, building funds, consulting services.
Limitations: Giving primarily in the New York, NY, metropolitan area. No grants to individuals.
Application information: Contributes primarily to pre-selected organizations.
Copies of proposal: 1
Board meeting date(s): Jan., Apr., June, and Sept.
Write: Richard Abrons, Pres.
Officers: Richard Abrons,* Pres.; Herbert L. Abrons,* V.P.; Rita Aranow,* V.P.; Edward Aranow, Secy.-Treas.
Directors:* Alix Abrons, Anne Abrons, Peter Abrons, Vicki Klein.
Number of staff: None.
Employer Identification Number: 136061329

1737
The Achelis Foundation
c/o Morris & McVeigh
767 Third Ave.
New York 10017 (212) 418-0588

Incorporated in 1940 in NY.
Donor(s): Elizabeth Achelis.†
Financial data (yr. ended 12/31/88): Assets, $17,127,220 (M); expenditures, $867,924, including $715,000 for 44 grants (high: $30,000; low: $10,000; average: $10,000-$25,000).
Purpose and activities: Support for youth and social service agencies, education, health and hospitals, the arts, and cultural programs.
Types of support: Building funds, general purposes, operating budgets, matching funds, equipment, land acquisition, annual campaigns, capital campaigns, endowment funds, renovation projects, research, fellowships.
Limitations: Giving primarily in the NY area. No grants to individuals, or for experimental projects, films, travel, publications, or conferences; no loans.
Publications: Biennial report (including application guidelines), financial statement.
Application information:
Initial approach: Letter or proposal
Copies of proposal: 1
Deadline(s): None
Board meeting date(s): Usually in Apr., July, and Dec.
Write: Mary E. Caslin, Secy. and Exec. Dir.
Officers and Trustees: Guy G. Rutherfurd, Pres.; Peter Frelinghuysen, V.P. and Treas.; Mary E. Caslin, Secy. and Exec. Dir.; Harry W. Albright, Jr., Mary B. Braga, Gordon S. Braislin, Walter J.P. Curley, Jr., Anthony Drexel Duke, John N. Irwin III, Marguerite Sykes Nichols, Peter S. Paine, Russel Pennoyer, Mary S. Phipps.
Number of staff: 2 full-time professional.
Employer Identification Number: 136022018

1738
The Acorn Foundation
620 Park Ave.
New York 10021

Etablished in 1955 in NY.
Donor(s): Anna Glen Butler Vietor.
Financial data (yr. ended 12/31/87): Assets, $1,347,855 (M); gifts received, $37,795; expenditures, $192,627, including $165,543 for 59 grants (high: $14,000; low: $200).
Purpose and activities: Support primarily for historic preservation, culture, and education.
Officers: Anna Glen Butler Vietor, Pres.; Pauline V. Sheehan, Robert W. Sheehan.
Employer Identification Number: 136098172

1739
Louis and Bessie Adler Foundation, Inc.
c/o Shea & Gould
330 Madison Ave.
New York 10017

Incorporated in 1946 in NY.
Donor(s): Louis Adler,† Louis Adler Realty Co., Inc.
Financial data (yr. ended 12/31/87): Assets, $3,899,069 (M); expenditures, $287,844, including $244,736 for 32 grants (high: $27,500; low: $500).
Purpose and activities: Support for Jewish welfare funds, higher and secondary education, hospitals, youth agencies, and museums.
Limitations: Giving primarily in NY.
Application information: Contributes only to pre-selected organizations. Applications not accepted.
Write: Seymour M. Klein, Chair.
Officers and Directors: Seymour M. Klein, Chair. and Pres.; Ruth Klein, V.P. and Secy.; Robert Liberman, Treas.
Employer Identification Number: 131880122

1740
The Aeroflex Foundation
c/o Berman and Hecht
10 East 40th St., Rm. 710
New York 10016 (212) 696-4235

Established in 1964 in NY.
Donor(s): The Aeroflex Corp.
Financial data (yr. ended 9/30/88): Assets, $3,421,341 (M); expenditures, $246,251, including $156,000 for 9 grants (high: $30,000; low: $5,000).
Purpose and activities: Emphasis on cultural programs and higher education.
Limitations: No grants to individuals.
Application information:
Initial approach: Letter
Copies of proposal: 1
Deadline(s): None
Board meeting date(s): Quarterly
Trustees: Kay Knight Clarke, Derrick Hussey, William A. Perlmuth.
Employer Identification Number: 136168635

1741
AKC Fund, Inc.
145 East 74th St., Suite 1C
New York 10021 (212) 737-1011

Incorporated in 1955 in NY.
Donor(s): Members of the Childs and Lawrence families.
Financial data (yr. ended 12/31/87): Assets, $2,518,857 (M); expenditures, $170,981, including $140,000 for 54 grants (high: $20,000; low: $500; average: $750-$5,000).
Purpose and activities: Grants largely for elementary, secondary, and higher education; support also for conservation, hospitals, and the arts.
Types of support: Annual campaigns, capital campaigns, continuing support, general purposes, lectureships, professorships.
Limitations: No grants to individuals.
Application information: Currently supporting trustee-sponsored projects only.
Write: Ann Brownell Sloane, Admin.
Officers and Directors: Barbara Childs Lawrence, Pres.; Edward C. Childs, V.P.; Richard S. Childs, Jr., V.P.; James Vinton Lawrence, Secy.; John W. Childs, Treas.; Anne C. Childs, Starling W. Childs, Timothy W. Childs, Barbara L. Garside.
Number of staff: 3
Employer Identification Number: 136091321

1742
Allade, Inc.
c/o Arthur D. Emil
599 Lexington Ave.
New York 10022

Established in 1956 in NY.
Donor(s): Kate S. Emil.
Financial data (yr. ended 12/31/87): Assets, $1,880,254 (M); gifts received, $9,000; expenditures, $182,907, including $146,182 for 89 grants (high: $50,000; low: $50).
Purpose and activities: Giving primarily for Jewish welfare, temple support, social services, and general charitable contributions.
Limitations: No grants to individuals.
Application information: Contributes only to pre-selected organizations. Applications not accepted.
Trustees: Arthur D. Emil, Kate S. Emil, Judy E. Tenney.
Employer Identification Number: 136097697

1743
The Allyn Foundation, Inc.
P.O. Box 22
Skaneateles 13152
Grant application address: RD No. 1, Cayuga, NY 13034; Tel.: (315) 252-7618

Incorporated in 1956 in NY.
Financial data (yr. ended 12/31/87): Assets, $2,961,668 (M); expenditures, $238,697, including $219,460 for 46 grants (high: $50,000; low: $150).
Purpose and activities: Emphasis on higher education, including medical education; support also for general charitable purposes, youth agencies, arts and culture, and hospitals.
Limitations: Giving primarily in Skaneateles and the Onondaga County, NY, area. No support for religious programs. No grants to individuals, or for endowment funds; no loans.
Publications: Application guidelines.
Application information:
Initial approach: Letter
Copies of proposal: 1
Deadline(s): None
Board meeting date(s): Quarterly
Write: Mrs. Marie Infanger, Exec. Dir.
Officers and Directors: William G. Allyn, Pres.; Lew F. Allyn, V.P.; William F. Allyn, V.P.; Donald G. Kreiger, V.P.; Marie Infanger, Secy.-Treas. and Exec. Dir.; Dawn Allyn, Janet J. Allyn, Sonya Allyn, Robert C. Heaviside, Rev. Stephen A. Kish, Ruth C. Penchoen, Elsa A. Soderberg, Peter Soderberg, Robert C. Soderberg.
Number of staff: 1 part-time professional.
Employer Identification Number: 156017723

1744
Altman Foundation
220 East 42nd St., Suite 411
New York 10017 (212) 682-0970

Incorporated in 1913 in NY.
Donor(s): Benjamin Altman,† Colonel Michael Friedsam.†
Financial data (yr. ended 12/31/88): Assets, $99,550,168 (M); expenditures, $5,226,306, including $4,034,725 for 117 grants (high: $300,000; low: $2,500; average: $5,000-$100,000).
Purpose and activities: Support primarily for education, particularly programs benefitting talented underprivileged youth; private voluntary hospitals and health centers to extend medical services to the underserved; artistic and cultural institutions for outreach projects; and social welfare programs providing long-term solutions for the needs of the disadvantaged.
Types of support: Special projects.
Limitations: Giving limited to NY, with emphasis on the New York City metropolitan area. No grants to individuals.
Publications: Application guidelines.
Application information:
Initial approach: Letter
Copies of proposal: 1
Deadline(s): None
Board meeting date(s): 5 times a year
Write: John S. Burke, Pres.
Officers: John S. Burke,* Pres.; Marion C. Baer, Secy.; Thomas C. Burke,* Treas.
Trustees:* Bernard Finkelstein, Jane B. O'Connell, Maurice A. Selinger, Jr., Martin F. Shea.
Number of staff: 2 full-time professional; 4 full-time support.
Employer Identification Number: 131623879
Recent arts and culture grants:
Alliance for the Arts, NYC, NY, $15,000. To continue support for pilot program linking schools and cultural organizations through computerized information access system. 1987.
Boys Choir of Harlem, NYC, NY, $20,000. To help expand Choir's Tutoring and Counseling Program for inner-city youngsters. 1987.
Bronx Museum of the Arts, Bronx, NY, $10,000. To help support educational outreach program of upcoming exhibition, The Latin American Presence in the United States: 1920-1970. 1987.
Brooklyn Museum, Brooklyn Institute of Arts and Sciences, Brooklyn, NY, $45,000. To help launch stipended internship program in museum education for New York City minority students. 1987.
Cultural Council Foundation, Center for Creative Collaboration, NYC, NY, $35,000. To help launch comprehensive arts program for at-risk youth. 1987.
Dance Theater of Harlem, NYC, NY, $20,000. To help present lecture demonstrations as part of Dance Theater of Harlem's Arts Exposure Program at Aaron Davis Hall. 1987.
Ensemble Studio Theater, NYC, NY, $25,000. To continue and expand intensive one-on-one workshop component for 52nd Street Project for disadvantaged children. 1987.
Metropolitan Museum of Art, NYC, NY, $100,000. To develop and produce multi-lingual brochures for non-English speaking visitors to Museum. 1987.
National Theater Workshop of the Handicapped, NYC, NY, $10,000. For general support. 1987.
New York School for Circus Arts, Big Apple Circus, NYC, NY, $25,000. To continue and expand the Emergency Clown Unit project for seriously ill children in New York hospitals. 1987.
Original Ballets Foundation, New Ballet School, NYC, NY, $35,000. To support New Ballet School's programs for disadvantaged youngsters. 1987.
Pierpont Morgan Library, NYC, NY, $10,000. For general support. 1987.
Pratt Institute, Brooklyn, NY, $30,000. To expand Project Display and Heritage Symphony programs for gifted children in Pratt's Youth Skills Discovery and Development Project. 1987.
YM-YWHA, 92nd Street, NYC, NY, $25,000. To continue development of Sidney A. Wolff New York Concert Program for chldren. 1987.

1745
American Academy & Institute of Arts and Letters
633 West 155th St.
New York 10032 (212) 368-5900

Established in 1976 as a result of a merger between the National Institute of Arts and Letters, founded in 1898, and the American Academy of Arts and Letters, founded in 1904.
Donor(s): Mildred B. Strauss,† Channing Pollock,† and others, Archer M. Huntington.
Financial data (yr. ended 12/31/87): Assets, $20,469,690 (M); gifts received, $251,720; expenditures, $1,482,776, including $89,520 for 21 grants (high: $14,400; low: $400), $394,881 for 68 grants to individuals and $437,307 for foundation-administered programs.
Purpose and activities: A private operating foundation; arts and letters awards, fellowships, and scholarships to individuals showing promise and/or achievement in literature,

music, and the arts. Childe Hassam Fund and Eugene Speicher awards for the purchase of works of contemporary art for distribution to museums.
Types of support: Grants to individuals, emergency funds, fellowships.
Limitations: No support for the performing arts, or for photography.
Publications: Informational brochure.
Application information: Applications for awards or financial assistance not accepted, with the exception of the Richard Rodgers Production Award for the Musical Theatre (for off-Broadway productions).
Write: Lydia Kaim, Asst. to the Exec. Dir.
Officers and Directors: Hortense Calisher, Pres.; Philip Pearlstein, V.P.; George Perle, V.P.; William Jay Smith, V.P.; Margaret M. Mills, Exec. Dir.; John Hollander, Secy.; John M. Johansen, Treas.; Milton Babbitt, Stanley Kunitz, Jacob Lawrence, John Updike.
Number of staff: 4 full-time professional; 2 full-time support.
Employer Identification Number: 130429640

1746
American Conservation Association, Inc.
30 Rockefeller Plaza, Rm. 5402
New York 10112 (212) 649-5822

Incorporated in 1958 in NY.
Donor(s): Laurance S. Rockefeller, Laurance Rockefeller, Rockefeller Brothers Fund, Jackson Hole Preserve, Inc.
Financial data (yr. ended 12/31/88): Assets, $1,790,994 (M); gifts received, $2,000,000; expenditures, $1,901,096, including $1,642,500 for 48 grants (high: $150,000; low: $3,000; average: $20,000-$50,000) and $78,445 for 4 foundation-administered programs.
Purpose and activities: A private operating foundation organized to advance knowledge and understanding of conservation; to preserve the beauty of the landscape and the natural and living resources in areas of the U.S. and elsewhere; and to educate the public in the proper use of such areas.
Types of support: Consulting services, continuing support, general purposes, operating budgets, publications, special projects, technical assistance.
Limitations: No grants to individuals, or for building funds, endowments, scholarships, or fellowships; no loans.
Application information:
Initial approach: Letter or proposal
Copies of proposal: 1
Deadline(s): Submit proposal preferably early in the spring
Board meeting date(s): Sept. or Oct.; executive committee meets as needed
Final notification: Varies
Write: George R. Lamb, Exec. V.P.
Officers: Laurance Rockefeller,* Chair.; George R. Lamb,* Exec. V.P.; Gene W. Setzer,* V.P.; Franklin E. Parker,* Secy.; Ruth C. Haupert, Treas.
Trustees:* John H. Adams, Frances G. Beinecke, Nash Castro, Charles H. Clusen, William G. Conway, Dana S. Creel, Henry L. Diamond, Mrs. Lyndon B. Johnson, Fred I. Kent III, W. Barnabas McHenry, Patrick F. Noonan, Story Clark Resor, Cathleen Douglas Stone, Russell E. Train, William H. Whyte, Jr., Conrad L. Wirth.
Number of staff: 2 part-time professional; 2 part-time support.
Employer Identification Number: 131874023

1747
American Express Foundation
c/o American Express Company
American Express Tower, World Financial Center
New York 10285-4710 (212) 640-5661

Incorporated in 1954 in NY.
Donor(s): American Express Co., and its subsidiaries.
Financial data (yr. ended 12/31/88): Assets, $487,816 (M); gifts received, $11,101,229; expenditures, $10,871,418, including $9,695,490 for grants (high: $300,000; low: $1,000; average: $10,000-$20,000) and $1,175,928 for employee matching gifts.
Purpose and activities: The foundation's philanthropic activities focus on three strategic themes: community service, education and employment, and cultural programs.
Types of support: Special projects, employee-related scholarships, employee matching gifts, seed money, general purposes.
Limitations: Giving primarily in AZ, CA, CO, FL, GA, IL, MN, NC, NE, NY, TX, UT, MA, PA AND DC. International Committees include Asia/Pacific, Canada, Europe, Latin America, and Japan. No support for religious, political or fraternal organizations; sporting events or athletic programs; legislative or lobbying efforts; umbrella organizations with active grantmaking programs; or professional, trade, or marketing associations. No grants to individuals, or for endowments; capital campaigns; advertising in journal or yearbooks; publication of books, magazines or articles in professional journals; or medical research.
Publications: Corporate giving report, biennial report, grants list, informational brochure (including application guidelines).
Application information:
Initial approach: Letter or proposal
Copies of proposal: 1
Deadline(s): None
Board meeting date(s): Biannually
Final notification: 3 to 4 months
Write: Mary Beth Salerno V.P., Domestic Prog., or Cornelia W. Higginson, V.P., Philanthropic Prog. (Intl. Prog.)
Senior Staff: Cornelia Higginson, V.P., Philanthropy Prog.; Mary Beth Salerno, V.P., Domestic Prog.
Trustees: Aldo Papone, James D. Robinson III, Robert F. Smith.
Number of staff: 7 full-time professional; 7 full-time support.
Employer Identification Number: 136123529
Recent arts and culture grants:
Allegheny Conference on Community Development, Pittsburgh, PA, $5,000. For City of Pittsburgh landmark proposal. 1987.
American Academy in Rome, NYC, NY, $12,500. For general support. 1987.
American Museum of Natural History, NYC, NY, $15,000. For general support. 1987.
Asia Society, NYC, NY, $15,000. For general support. 1987.
Associated Japan-America Societies of the United States, NYC, NY, $5,000. For general support. 1987.
Carnegie Hall Society, NYC, NY, $50,000. For Carnegie Hall restoration project. 1987.
Centre Europeen de Prospective et de Synthese, Paris, France, $20,000. For Promethee. 1987.
Choral Arts Society of Washington, DC, $5,000. For The Singers of All Seasons. 1987.
Colonial Williamsburg Foundation, Williamsburg, VA, $5,000. For general support. 1987.
Communaute Israelite De Geneve, Geneva, Switzerland, $50,000. For restoration of 1859 synagogue. 1987.
Council for the United States and Italy, NYC, NY, $25,000. For general operating support. 1987.
Dallas Theater Center, Dallas, TX, $10,000. For Project Discovery. 1987.
Dana-Thomas House Historic Site, Springfield, IL, $25,000. For restoration project. 1987.
DeMenil House Foundation, Saint Louis, MO, $5,000. For DeMenil Mansion Spring Painting. 1987.
Duke of Edinburghs Award Scheme, London, England, $15,000. 1987.
Edgewood, The San Francisco Protestant Orphanage, Edgewood Children's Center, San Francisco, CA, $5,000. For creative arts program. 1987.
Edison National Historic Site, Friends of, West Orange, NJ, $5,000. For The Invention Factory Video. 1987.
Educational Broadcasting Corporation, NYC, NY, $15,000. For annual operating fund. 1987.
Esalen Soviet-American Exchange Program, San Francisco, CA, $10,000. For Soviet-American Exchange Program. 1987.
Europa Nostra, London, England, $40,000. For annual heritage award. 1987.
Forecast Public Artspace Productions, Minneapolis, MN, $5,000. For Art of the Eye exhibit. 1987.
Foundation Cartier Pour L Art Contemporian, Jouy-en-Josas, France, $5,000. For general support. 1987.
French-American Foundation, NYC, NY, $28,000. For U.S. study tour for French mayors. 1987.
French-American Foundation, NYC, NY, $25,000. To fund staff support for Foundation Franco-Americaine. 1987.
Heard Museum, Phoenix, AZ, $5,000. For building fund. 1987.
John F. Kennedy Center for the Performing Arts, DC, $15,000. For corporate fund. 1987.
K C T S Association, Seattle, WA, $100,000. For Who Cares for the Children. 1987.
Lincoln Center for the Performing Arts, NYC, NY, $50,000. For Lincoln Center consolidated corporate fund. 1987.
Lower Manhattan Cultural Council, NYC, NY, $7,500. For general support. 1987.
Meridian House International, DC, $25,000. For capital campaign for Crescent Place. 1987.
Milwaukee Foundation for Guitar Studies, Milwaukee, WI, $23,200. For Nureyev and Friends. 1987.

Min-Jung Theater Group, Seoul, South Korea, $20,000. For performance sponsorship. 1987.
Montclair State College Development Fund, Upper Montclair, NJ, $10,000. For Opera/Music Theater Institute of New Jersey. 1987.
Monteverdi Choir and Orchestra, London, England, $7,500. For 1987 concert. 1987.
Musee Internationales de la Parfumerie, Grasse, France, $10,000. For enlarging museum collection. 1987.
National Arts Stabilization Fund, NYC, NY, $10,000. For Arizona Arts Stabilization. 1987.
National Corporate Theater Fund, NYC, NY, $8,000. For general support. 1987.
National Theater of the Deaf, Chester, CT, $5,000. For general support. 1987.
National Trust for Historic Preservation, DC, $10,000. For general support. 1987.
National Trust for Historical and Cultural Preservation of the Philippines, Manila, Philippines, $5,000. For historical and cultural preservation of Philippines. 1987.
New York Botanical Garden, NYC, NY, $10,000. For general support. 1987.
New York Landmarks Conservancy, NYC, NY, $5,000. For general operating support. 1987.
Orchestral Association, Chicago, IL, $15,000. For Sir Georg Solti Birthday Performance Program Book. 1987.
Philadelphia Festival Theater for New Plays, Philadelphia, PA, $10,000. For production grant. 1987.
Phillips Collection, DC, $5,000. For corporate membership. 1987.
Planned Parenthood of Central and Northern Arizona, Positive Force Players, Phoenix, AZ, $5,000. 1987.
Portland Civic Theater, Portland, OR, $10,000. For Peter Pan production. 1987.
Portland Opera Association, Portland, OR, $15,000. For Jerome Hines and Friends concert. 1987.
Royal Academy of Arts, Royal Academy Trust, London, England, $15,000. For restoration of heritage property. 1987.
School of American Ballet, NYC, NY, $5,000. For general operating support. 1987.
Scoula Teatro Dimitri, Ticino, Switzerland, $20,000. For theater restoration. 1987.
Snug Harbor Cultural Center, Staten Island, NY, $7,500. For 1988 Jazz Festival. 1987.
Solomon R. Guggenheim Foundation, NYC, NY, $50,000. For capital campaign. 1987.
Southwest Human Development, Phoenix Head Start, Phoenix, AZ, $10,000. For performing arts training and child development. 1987.
Stockholm Opera Special, Stockholm, Sweden, $15,000. For Scandinavian opera festival. 1987.
United States Department of Treasury, DC, $10,000. For preservation of treasury building. 1987.
United States-New Zealand Council, DC, $10,000. For general support. 1987.
United States/International Council on Monuments and Sites, DC, $27,000. For 8th General assembly, The American Mosaic. 1987.
Young Audiences, NYC, NY, $10,000. For general support. 1987.
Young Audiences, New York Committee, NYC, NY, $5,000. For general support. 1987.
Youth in Arts, San Rafael, CA, $5,000. For artist in residence program. 1987.
Youth Symphony Orchestra of New York, NYC, NY, $5,000. For performances for special audiences. 1987.

1748
American Express Philanthropic Program

American Express Tower, World Financial Center
200 Vesey St.
New York 10285-4710 (212) 640-2000

Financial data (yr. ended 12/31/88): $5,228,582 for grants.
Purpose and activities: "Our philanthropic activities focus on three strategic themes: community service; education and employment and culture." Education and employment giving supports public and private partnerships that help children and youth stay in school and prepare for careers. For cultural projects, the company may also undertake some promotional activities related to the grant. Programs reflect combined foundation and corporate giving, including gifts from IDS Financial Services and American Express Travel Related Services.
Types of support: Employee matching gifts, continuing support, seed money, special projects.
Limitations: No support for organizations funded by the United Way , with rare exceptions, economic development organizations, hospitals, medical research, university chairs, professional projects, scientific research, curriculum development outside area of focus, or individual day care centers or nursing homes. No grants to individuals, or for medical or scientific research, student or faculty scholarships, educational publications, television and film productions, travel stipends, or tours of large performing arts groups.
Publications: Informational brochure (including application guidelines), corporate giving report.
Application information: Include geographic area served by organization, history of previous support from American Express Foundation, the Philanthropic Program, or a subsidiary, description of project, budget; 501(c)(3) status, audited financial statement; list of board of directors, and annual report.
Initial approach: Letter of inquiry or proposal can be addressed to headquarters or local branch
Board meeting date(s): 2 meetings per year
Final notification: 3 to 4 months
Write: Cornelia W. Higginson, V.P., Philanthropic Prog. (International); Mary Beth Salerno, V.P., American Express Foundation (Domestic)
Administrators: Cornelia Higginson, V.P., Philanthropic Prog., International; Fran Kittredge, Sr. V.P., Shearson Lehman Hutton; Mary Beth Salerno, V.P., American Express Fdn., Domestic; Dee Topol, V.P., American Express Fdn., Educ. and Empt.
Number of staff: 7 full-time professional; 7 full-time support.

1749
American Philanthropic Foundation

122 East 42nd St., 24th Fl.
New York 10168 (212) 697-2420

Incorporated in 1929 in IL.
Donor(s): Nina Rosenwald.
Financial data (yr. ended 12/31/86): Assets, $1,157,404 (M); gifts received, $90,310; expenditures, $232,820, including $224,063 for 65 grants (high: $106,338; low: $100).
Purpose and activities: Support for Jewish organizations; grants also for higher education, hospitals, and cultural organizations.
Limitations: Giving primarily in New York, NY; support also in FL, CT, and Chicago, IL.
Application information:
Deadline(s): None
Write: David P. Steinmann, Secy.
Officers: William Rosenwald, Pres. and Treas.; Mary K. Rosenwald,* V.P.; Nina Rosenwald,* V.P.; Alice R. Sigelman,* V.P.; Elizabeth R. Varet,* V.P.; David P. Steinmann, Secy.
Directors:* Hulbert S. Aldrich, Bernard E. Brandes, Samuel Hoffman, Aniela T. McCool, Henry Z. Steinway, Frank D. Williams.
Employer Identification Number: 136088097

1750
American Society of the French Legion of Honor, Inc.

22 East 60th St.
New York 10022 (212) 751-8537

Financial data (yr. ended 12/31/87): Assets, $2,878,333 (M); gifts received, $21,318; expenditures, $164,547, including $67,500 for 6 grants (high: $40,000; low: $500) and $31,408 for 1 foundation-administered program.
Purpose and activities: Grants to promote friendship through education and literature between France and the U.S.A.. The society publishes a magazine.
Application information:
Deadline(s): None
Write: Raymond J. Picard
Officers: Raymond J. Picard, Pres. and Treas.; Alden K. Sibley, Exec. V.P.; George S. Blanchard, V.P.; Christian A. Chapman, V.P.; William Schieffelin III, V.P.
Employer Identification Number: 130434237

1751
American Stock Exchange Corporate Giving Program

86 Trinity Place
New York 10006 (212) 306-1205

Purpose and activities: Supports arts, culture, theater, dance, all levels of education, children's and youth services, women's issues, minority programs, international groups, rural concerns, and urban problems. Community funding includes economic aid and job development, community organizing, and civic affairs; employee gift matching for education. Provides use of company facilities and donations of company's primary goods or services.
Types of support: General purposes, special projects, technical assistance, in-kind gifts.

Limitations: Giving primarily in headquarters city.
Publications: Application guidelines.
Application information:
Initial approach: Proposal
Copies of proposal: 1
Board meeting date(s): End of each quarter
Final notification: Varies
Write: Yvonne Harris Jones, Asst. V.P.
Number of staff: 1 full-time professional; 1 full-time support.

1752
American Telephone & Telegraph Company Corporate Giving Program
550 Madison Ave., Rm. 2700
New York 10022

Financial data (yr. ended 12/31/88): $6,229,330 for 2,000 grants (high: $100,000; low: $25; average: $1,000-$10,000).
Purpose and activities: Support for "community needs which do not fit within the guidelines and mission of AT&T Foundation"; including general and higher education, health care, hospitals, social action, arts and culture, the United Way, and social services.
Limitations: Giving primarily in areas of company operations except for for national organizations.
Publications: Informational brochure.
Application information: National organizations, or universities, or organizations in New York City should write to NY office; local organizations should write for list of regional Contributions Coordinators.
Initial approach: Letter of inquiry no more than 3 pages
Deadline(s): None
Write: AT&T Contribs. Coord.
Number of staff: 12 full-time professional; 12 part-time support.

1753
Douglas G. Anderson - Leigh R. Evans Foundation
1420 College Ave.
Elmira 14902 (607) 734-2281

Incorporated in 1960 in NY.
Donor(s): Hardinge Brothers, Inc.
Financial data (yr. ended 10/31/87): Assets, $1,323,497 (M); gifts received, $62,000; expenditures, $181,560, including $175,200 for 23 grants (high: $50,000; low: $500).
Purpose and activities: Giving for higher education, hospitals, community funds, and the performing arts.
Types of support: General purposes, building funds, equipment.
Limitations: Giving primarily in Elmira, NY. No grants to individuals.
Application information:
Initial approach: Proposal
Copies of proposal: 1
Board meeting date(s): Semiannually and as required
Write: Robert G. Prochnow, Pres.
Officers: Robert G. Prochnow,* Pres.; Bertha A. Greenlee,* V.P.; Bela C. Tifft,* Secy.; Malcolm L. Gibson, Treas.
Trustees:* Robert E. Agan, James L. Flynn, E. Martin Gibson, Douglas A. Greenlee, Joseph C. Littleton, Boyd McDowell.
Employer Identification Number: 166024690

1754
The Anderson Foundation, Inc.
c/o Chemung Canal Trust Co.
P.O. Box 1522
Elmira 14902

Incorporated in 1960 in NY.
Donor(s): Jane G. Anderson, Douglas G. Anderson.†
Financial data (yr. ended 4/30/88): Assets, $2,469,905 (M); expenditures, $240,065, including $232,344 for 22 grants (high: $88,444; low: $1,820).
Purpose and activities: Emphasis on cultural programs and social service agencies.
Types of support: Scholarship funds, operating budgets, deficit financing, equipment, general purposes.
Limitations: Giving primarily in Elmira, NY.
Officers and Trustees: Bertha A. Greenlee, Pres. and Treas.; Charles A. Winding, V.P.; Ethel A. Whittaker, V.P.; Bela C. Tifft, Secy.; Robert T. Jones, Jane G. Joralemon, Charles M. Streetcar, E. William Whittaker.
Employer Identification Number: 166024689

1755
Adrian & Jessie Archbold Charitable Trust
Seven East 60th St.
New York 10022 (212) 371-1152

Trust established in 1976 in NY.
Donor(s): Mrs. Adrian Archbold.†
Financial data (yr. ended 11/30/87): Assets, $14,377,184 (M); expenditures, $795,625, including $666,000 for 54 grants (high: $200,000; low: $1,000; average: $5,000-$10,000).
Purpose and activities: Grants primarily for the medical sciences, especially biology; hospitals and health-related organizations, higher education, child welfare and youth programs, social service agencies, including Catholic and Protestant welfare programs, and the arts.
Types of support: General purposes, continuing support, program-related investments, publications, conferences and seminars, special projects.
Limitations: No grants to individuals, or for endowment funds, scholarships, fellowships, or building funds; no loans.
Publications: Program policy statement.
Application information:
Initial approach: Letter
Copies of proposal: 1
Deadline(s): None
Board meeting date(s): As required
Final notification: 3 to 6 months
Write: William G. O'Reilly, Dir.
Trustees: Arthur J. Mahon, Chemical Bank.
Director: William G. O'Reilly.
Number of staff: 1
Employer Identification Number: 510179829

1756
J. Aron Charitable Foundation, Inc.
126 East 56th St., Suite 2300
New York 10022 (212) 832-3405

Incorporated in 1934 in NY.
Donor(s): Members of the Aron family.
Financial data (yr. ended 12/31/87): Assets, $25,896,527 (M); expenditures, $2,093,427, including $1,810,437 for 46 grants (high: $300,000; low: $100).
Purpose and activities: Giving primarily for hospitals and health associations, cultural programs, social service and youth agencies, Jewish welfare funds, and education, including medical schools.
Types of support: Annual campaigns, building funds, capital campaigns, general purposes, research, special projects.
Limitations: Giving primarily in New York, NY, and New Orleans, LA. No grants to individuals.
Application information:
Initial approach: Proposal
Copies of proposal: 1
Deadline(s): None
Board meeting date(s): Apr., July, Sept., and Dec.
Write: Peter A. Aron, Exec. Dir.
Officers and Directors:* Jack R. Aron, Pres.; Robert Aron, V.P.; Hans P. Jepson, Secy.-Treas.; Peter A. Aron, V.P. and Exec. Dir.; Jacqueline A. Morrison, Ronald J. Stein.
Number of staff: 1 full-time support; 1 part-time support.
Employer Identification Number: 136068230

1757
Art Matters, Inc.
131 West 24th St.
New York 10011 (212) 929-7190
Application address: P.O. Box 1428, New York, NY 10011

Established in 1985 in NY.
Donor(s): Laura Donnelley.
Financial data (yr. ended 12/31/87): Assets, $1,510,575 (M); gifts received, $338,364; expenditures, $405,097, including $75,000 for 40 grants (high: $4,000; low: $1,000; average: $1,000-$4,000) and $275,000 for 200 grants to individuals.
Purpose and activities: Grants and fellowships to fund experimental work in the arts, including experimental theater, performance art, film, video, painting, and sculpture.
Types of support: Fellowships.
Limitations: No support for dance or music.
Publications: Grants list, application guidelines.
Application information: Art students, writers, dancers and musicians are ineligible to receive funding. Application form required.
Initial approach: Letter
Copies of proposal: 2
Deadline(s): Fall and spring
Board meeting date(s): 3 months after deadline
Write: Philip Yenawine, V.P. or Marianne Weems, Admin.
Officers: Laura Donnelley, Pres.; Philip Yenawine, V.P. and Secy.; Laurence Miller, Treas.

Directors: Mary Beebe, Cee Brown.
Number of staff: 1 full-time professional; 1 part-time support.
Employer Identification Number: 133271577

1758
ASARCO Foundation

180 Maiden Ln.
New York 10038 (212) 510-2000

Incorporated in 1956 in NY.
Donor(s): ASARCO, Inc.
Financial data (yr. ended 12/31/87): Assets, $414,957 (M); gifts received, $100,000; expenditures, $86,679, including $77,490 for 38 grants (high: $10,000; low: $200; average: $500-$1,000) and $7,500 for 1 employee matching gift.
Purpose and activities: A limited program, including support for community funds, scholarship programs of colleges and universities with emphasis on mineral technology and engineering, hospitals, and cultural activities.
Types of support: Scholarship funds, fellowships, general purposes, continuing support, employee matching gifts.
Limitations: Giving limited to areas of company operations. No grants to individuals, or for endowment funds, research, or operating budgets; no loans.
Publications: Program policy statement, application guidelines.
Application information:
Initial approach: Letter
Deadline(s): None
Board meeting date(s): As required
Final notification: 2 to 3 months
Write: Yvonne Lumsden, V.P.
Officers: Francis R. McAllister,* Pres.; J.R. Corbett,* V.P.; Yvonne M. Lumsden,* V.P.; K.A. Dockry, Secy.; Stephen P. McCandless,* Treas.
Directors:* George W. Anderson, Alexander J. Gillespie, Jr., Robert J. Muth, Richard J. Osborne, T.C. Osborne.
Number of staff: 1 part-time support.
Employer Identification Number: 136089860

1759
The Vincent Astor Foundation

405 Park Ave.
New York 10022 (212) 758-4110

Incorporated in 1948 in NY; reincorporated in 1974 in DE.
Donor(s): Vincent Astor.†
Financial data (yr. ended 12/31/87): Assets, $27,316,464 (M); expenditures, $4,039,803, including $3,493,772 for 95 grants (high: $250,000; low: $1,000; average: $1,000-$25,000).
Purpose and activities: Increased support for programs alleviating the problems of homelessness and illiteracy; support for programs which promote the preservation of open space and the thoughtful development of the urban environment; to a lesser extent support for certain cultural institutions, parks and landmark preservation, and neighborhood revitalization projects.
Types of support: Operating budgets, continuing support, seed money, building funds, equipment, endowment funds, matching funds, capital campaigns, general purposes, renovation projects, special projects.
Limitations: Giving primarily in New York City, NY. No support for performing arts, medicine, mental health, or private schools. No grants to individuals, or for annual campaigns, deficit financing, research, film production, publications, or conferences; no loans.
Publications: Annual report (including application guidelines).
Application information: Average range of grants will be reduced to $1,000-$25,000.
Initial approach: Letter or telephone
Copies of proposal: 1
Deadline(s): None
Board meeting date(s): May, Oct., and Dec.
Final notification: 6 months
Write: Linda L. Gillies, Dir.
Officers: Mrs. Vincent Astor,* Pres.; Anthony D. Marshall,* V.P.; Peter P. McN. Gates, Secy.; Fergus Reid III,* Treas.; Linda L. Gillies,* Dir.
Trustees:* Thomas R. Coolidge, Henry N. Ess III, Howard Phipps, Jr., John Pierrepont.
Advisory Trustees: Peter S. Paine, David W. Peck, Richard S. Perkins.
Number of staff: 1 full-time professional; 2 full-time support; 1 part-time support.
Employer Identification Number: 237167124
Recent arts and culture grants:
Brooklyn Museum, Brooklyn, NY, $5,000. For general support. 1/1/88.
City University of New York, Graduate School and University Center, NYC, NY, $25,000. Toward Vartan Gregorian Fellowship, to be awarded annually to student in Graduate School's humanities program. 12/3/87.
Dance Theater of Harlem, NYC, NY, $25,000. For general support. 5/26/88.
Duke Ellington Memorial Fund, NYC, NY, $25,000. Toward Duke Ellington Memorial, statue designed by Robert Graham, to be placed in Frawley Circle in Harlem. 10/8/87.
Erasmus Hall High School and Academy of the Arts Alumni, Brooklyn, NY, $25,000. Toward development of programs and exhibitions in the landmark Academy building and toward fundraising costs. 10/8/87.
General Theological Seminary of the Protestant Episcopal Church in the United States, NYC, NY, $25,000. Toward renovations undertaken on accasion of Dean Hoffman's Grand Design, exhibition about General Theological's campus in Chelsea. 10/8/87.
Metropolitan Museum of Art, NYC, NY, $20,000. Toward acquisition of storage cabinets for Photographic Department. 5/26/88.
Metropolitan Opera Association, NYC, NY, $5,000. For general support. 1/1/88.
Municipal Art Society, NYC, NY, $25,000. For general support for City's oldest landmark preservation and urban design advocacy organization. 10/8/87.
Museum of the City of New York, NYC, NY, $25,000. Toward exhibition On Being Homeless in New York: An Historical Perspective. 10/8/87.
New York Dance Center, NYC, NY, $50,000. Toward acquisition of 890 Broadway, which will house three dance companies. 12/3/87.
New York Landmarks Preservation Foundation, NYC, NY, $5,000. Toward Commission's program to identify landmark buildings by specially designed plaques. 1/1/87.
New York Public Library, NYC, NY, $25,000. Toward A Visual Testimony: Judaica from the Vatican Library, a loan exhibition to be held in fall of 1988. 12/3/87.
Saint Pauls Memorial Church, Staten Island, NY, $10,000. Toward renovation of landmark church on Staten Island. 5/26/88.
Snug Harbor Cultural Center, Staten Island, NY, $25,000. Toward endowment of Music Hall, which is currently undergoing renovation. 5/26/88.
South Street Seaport Museum, NYC, NY, $5,000. For general support. 1/1/87.
Staten Island Historical Society, Staten Island, NY, $20,000. Toward relocation and restoration of Jacob Crocheron House. 5/26/88.
Vivian Beaumont Theater, NYC, NY, $25,000. For general support. 5/26/88.
W N E T Channel 13, NYC, NY, $50,000. Toward production costs of Metroline, a weekly news program which concentrates on New York City. 10/8/87.

1760
AT&T Foundation

550 Madison Ave.
New York 10022-3297 (212) 605-6734

Established in 1984 in NY.
Donor(s): American Telephone & Telegraph Co., Western Electric Fund.
Financial data (yr. ended 12/31/88): Assets, $134,212,000 (M); expenditures, $30,303,350, including $26,757,236 for 951 grants (high: $400,000; low: $1,000; average: $2,000-$50,000) and $3,546,114 for 31,912 employee matching gifts.
Purpose and activities: Principal source of philanthropy for AT&T and its subsidiaries; scope is national, emphasizing support of private higher education, and institutions and projects in the areas of health care, social action, and the arts. Aid to local communities provided primarily through the United Way.
Types of support: Building funds, equipment, matching funds, employee matching gifts, special projects, research, annual campaigns, endowment funds, operating budgets, renovation projects, seed money, technical assistance.
Limitations: No support for religious organizations for sectarian purposes; local chapters of national organizations; elementary or secondary schools, social sciences or health sciences programs, medical or nursing schools, or junior and community colleges; industrial affiliate programs or technical trade associations; medical research projects, disease-related health associations, or for operating expenses or capital campaigns of local health or human service agencies other than hospitals; or sports, teams, or athletic competitions. No grants to individuals, or for emergency funds, deficit financing, land acquisition, fellowships, publications, or conferences; does not purchase advertisements or donate equipment.

Publications: Annual report, program policy statement, biennial report, informational brochure (including application guidelines).
Application information: Detailed program limitations provided in guidelines and addresses of regional Contributions Coordinators.
Initial approach: Letter and proposal
Copies of proposal: 1
Deadline(s): None
Board meeting date(s): Mar., June, Sept., and Dec.
Final notification: 90 days
Write: Sheila A. Connolly, Secy.
Officers: Reynold Levy,* Pres.; Jane Redfern, Sr. V.P.; Anne Alexander, V.P., Education Programs; Tim McClimon, V.P., Cultural Programs; Gina Warren, V.P., Health and Social Action Programs; Sheila A. Connolly, Secy.; Sarah Jepsen, Exec. Dir.
Trustees:* Marilyn Laurie, Chair.; John A. Blanchard, W. Frank Blount, John Bucter, Harold Burlingame, Richard Draper, M.J. Eisen, John Fischer, John C. Guerra, Jr., John W. Hahn, John A. Hinds, Reynold Levy, Judith A. Maynes, C. Kumar Patel, John C. Petrillo, N. Rhinehart, Jr., Marc Rosen, Frederic S. Topor.
Number of staff: 7 full-time professional; 4 part-time professional; 4 full-time support.
Employer Identification Number: 133166495
Recent arts and culture grants:
Academy of Natural Sciences of Philadelphia, Philadelphia, PA, $5,000. For eudcation programs. 1987.
Acting Company, NYC, NY, $10,000. For national tour. 1987.
Acting Company, NYC, NY, $5,000. For Kabuki Macbeth tour. 1987.
Alabama Shakespeare Festival, Montgomery, AL, $25,000. To sponsor musical. 1987.
Allied Arts Foundation, Oklahoma City, OK, $18,000. For operating support. 1987.
American Composers Orchestra, NYC, NY, $7,500. To fund recording. 1987.
American Council for the Arts, NYC, NY, $25,000. For operating support. 1987.
American Council for the Arts, NYC, NY, $25,000. For capital/development. 1987.
American Craft Council, NYC, NY, $7,500. For operating support. 1987.
American Dance Festival, NYC, NY, $12,500. To commission New Work-87. 1987.
American Dance Festival, NYC, NY, $12,500. To commission New Work-88. 1987.
American Federation of Arts, NYC, NY, $5,000. For operating support. 1987.
American Museum of Natural History, NYC, NY, $10,000. For operating support. 1987.
American Music Theater Festival, Philadelphia, PA, $20,000. To underwrite Let Freedom Sing. 1987.
American Symphony Orchestra League, DC, $25,000. For national conference. 1987.
Andover Endowment for the Arts, Andover, MA, $5,000. To support three programs. 1987.
Arena Stage, Washington Drama Society, DC, $20,000. For capital support. 1987.
Arkansas Arts Center Foundation, Little Rock, AR, $15,000. For national drawing invitational. 1987.
Arkansas Repertory Theater Company, Little Rock, AR, $10,000. For Second Stage series. 1987.
Art Institute of Chicago, Chicago, IL, $25,000. For series of forums. 1987.
Art Institute of Chicago, Chicago, IL, $10,000. For capital support. 1987.
Arts and Science Council, Charlotte, NC, $10,000. For operating support. 1987.
Arts Council, Winston-Salem, NC, $17,000. For operating support. 1987.
Arts Inc. of Central Florida, Orlando, FL, $16,000. For operating support. 1987.
Artsplosure, The Raleigh Arts Festival, Raleigh, NC, $5,000. To support 1988 spring festival. 1987.
Atlanta Arts Alliance, Atlanta, GA, $50,000. For operating support. 1987.
Austin Childrens Museum, Austin, TX, $7,500. For Oaxaca Village exhibit. 1987.
Austin Lyric Opera, Austin, TX, $15,000. To underwrite production. 1987.
Baltimore Symphony Orchestra Association, Baltimore, MD, $15,000. For regional touring program. 1987.
Berkeley Repertory Theater, Berkeley, CA, $15,000. To support Tale of Lear production. 1987.
Boston Ballet, Boston, MA, $25,000. For discovery series. 1987.
Boston Symphony Orchestra, Boston, MA, $5,000. To underwrite reference book. 1987.
Brattleboro Music Center, Friends of the, Brattleboro, VT, $25,000. For New England Bach Festival. 1987.
Brooklyn Academy of Music, Brooklyn, NY, $50,000. For Peter Brooke Project. 1987.
Brown University, Department of Computer Science, Providence, RI, $20,283. For Parallel VLSI Architecture. 1987.
Buffalo State College Foundation, Buffalo, NY, $7,500. For Killing Angels production. 1987.
Business Committee for the Arts, NYC, NY, $5,000. Toward operating support. 1987.
Chamber Music America, NYC, NY, $5,000. For Volunteer Chamber Music Fund. 1987.
Charlotte Symphony Orchestra Society, Charlotte, NC, $15,000. To sponsor Nureyev concert. 1987.
Cherokee National Historical Society, Tahlequah, OK, $7,500. For educational and cultural program. 1987.
Chicago Theater Company, Chicago, IL, $10,000. To sponsor one production. 1987.
Chicago Theater Group, Chicago, IL, $10,000. To sponsor Red Roses opening. 1987.
Childrens Museum, Boston, MA, $7,500. To expand activities. 1987.
Chrysler Museum, Norfolk, VA, $10,000. For capital expansion campaign. 1987.
Cincinnati Symphony Orchestra, Cincinnati, OH, $10,000. To support special concert. 1987.
City Center Ballet of San Jose, San Jose, CA, $10,000. To sponsor performance. 1987.
Colonial Williamsburg Foundation, Williamsburg, VA, $100,000. For history of 18th century blacks. 1987.
Commonwealth Players, Theater Virginia, Richmond, VA, $10,000. To sponsor Noises Off. 1987.
Community Arts Foundation, Chicago, IL, $10,000. To sponsor opening production. 1987.
Corcoran Gallery of Art, DC, $35,000. For Hispanic art exhibit. 1987.
Corcoran Gallery of Art, DC, $5,000. For Hispanic art project. 1987.
Corporate Council for the Arts, Seattle, WA, $10,000. For operating support. 1987.
Court Theater Fund, Chicago, IL, $10,000. To sponsor guest directors. 1987.
Crossroads Theater Company, New Brunswick, NJ, $15,000. Toward capital support. 1987.
Cultural Council of Richland and Lexington Counties, Columbia, SC, $5,000. Toward capital endowment. 1987.
Cunningham Dance Foundation, NYC, NY, $7,500. For dance tour. 1987.
Currier Gallery of Art, Manchester, NH, $25,000. For Contemporary New England Art Survey. 1987.
Dallas Black Dance Theater, Dallas, TX, $15,000. For Alvin Ailey work. 1987.
Dance Saint Louis, Saint Louis, MO, $10,000. Toward performance support. 1987.
Dance USA, DC, $5,000. For membership directory. 1987.
Denver Center for the Performing Arts, Denver, CO, $25,000. To sponsor Man of La Mancha. 1987.
Denver Museum of Natural History, Denver, CO, $16,500. For lecture series. 1987.
Denver Symphony Orchestra, Denver, CO, $12,500. For children's concert. 1987.
Detroit Institute of Arts, Founders Society, Detroit, MI, $15,000. For three exhibitions. 1987.
Detroit Symphony Orchestra, Detroit, MI, $25,000. For operating support. 1987.
Eastern Music Festival, Greensboro, NC, $5,000. To sponsor 1988 catalog. 1987.
Educational Broadcasting Corporation, NYC, NY, $10,000. For field study. 1987.
Exploratorium, San Francisco, CA, $20,000. To sponsor festival. 1987.
Fernbank Science Center, Atlanta, GA, $20,000. For capital support. 1987.
Flynn Theater for Performing Arts, Burlington, VT, $10,000. For modern jazz/dance collaboration. 1987.
Fort Mason Foundation, San Francisco, CA, $25,000. For capital support. 1987.
Friends of Puerto Rico, NYC, NY, $15,000. For exhibition. 1987.
Friends of the Arts, Locust Valley, NY, $5,000. For Saint Paul Chamber Orchestra. 1987.
Fund for Artists Colonies, NYC, NY, $10,000. To sponsor artists-in-residence. 1987.
Garden State Ballet Foundation, Metuchen, NJ, $10,000. To sponsor production. 1987.
George Street Playhouse, New Brunswick, NJ, $12,500. To sponsor new play. 1987.
Greater Miami Opera Association, Miami, FL, $25,000. To sponsor Bianca e Falliero. 1987.
Guadalupe Cultural Arts Center, San Antonio, TX, $10,000. For Media Arts Program. 1987.
Handel and Haydn Society, Boston, MA, $10,000. To support live performances. 1987.
Historical Society of Berks County, Reading, PA, $5,000. For capital support. 1987.
Honolulu Symphony Society, Honolulu, HI, $16,000. To sponsor two concerts. 1987.
Honolulu Symphony Society, Honolulu, HI, $10,000. To sponsor The Nutcracker. 1987.
Houston Ballet Foundation, Houston, TX, $50,000. For The Nutcracker. 1987.
Houston Lyric Theater Foundation, Houston, TX, $20,000. For capital support. 1987.

Illinois Theater Center, Park Forest, IL, $10,000. For post-play lecture series. 1987.
Immediate Theater Company, Chicago, IL, $10,000. To sponsor Chicago Premiere. 1987.
Institute of Contemporary Art, Boston, MA, $37,500. For German-American cultural exchange. 1987.
International Arts Relations (INTAR), NYC, NY, $25,000. For Tango Apasionado production. 1987.
International Museum of Photography at George Eastman House, Rochester, NY, $12,500. To sponsor traveling exhibit. 1987.
Jacobs Pillow Dance Festival, Lee, MA, $7,500. To sponsor performances. 1987.
Japan Society, NYC, NY, $25,000. For development project. 1987.
Japanese American Cultural and Community Center, Los Angeles, CA, $20,000. To sponsor production of Utamaro. 1987.
John F. Kennedy Center for the Performing Arts, DC, $50,000. For operating support. 1987.
Kansas City Symphony, Kansas City, MO, $10,000. For capital support. 1987.
Knoxville Civic Opera Company, Knoxville, TN, $5,000. To underwrite opera. 1987.
Lincoln Center for the Performing Arts, NYC, NY, $50,000. For operating support. 1987.
Los Angeles Festival, Valencia, CA, $37,500. To support various performances. 1987.
Los Angeles Philharmonic Association, Los Angeles, CA, $60,000. For American Encore Series. 1987.
Los Angeles Philharmonic Association, Los Angeles, CA, $40,000. For American Encore Series. 1987.
Louisville Orchestra, Louisville, KY, $10,000. To sponsor music festival. 1987.
Lyric Opera of Chicago, Chicago, IL, $50,000. For capital support. 1987.
Manhattan Theater Club, NYC, NY, $15,000. For project support. 1987.
Margaret Jenkins Dance Company, San Francisco, CA, $7,500. To choreograph Shelf Life. 1987.
McCarter Theater Company, Princeton, NJ, $30,000. For capital support. 1987.
Meet the Composer, NYC, NY, $10,000. For national expansion program. 1987.
Metropolitan Arts Council, United Arts Fund, Omaha, NE, $10,000. For operating support. 1987.
Mexican Museum, San Francisco, CA, $5,000. For exhibition. 1987.
Michigan Opera Theater, Detroit, MI, $8,000. To sponsor Man of La Mancha. 1987.
Morris Museum, Morristown, NJ, $25,000. For operating support. 1987.
Municipal Art Society, NYC, NY, $5,000. For operating support. 1987.
Museum of Art, Fort Lauderdale, FL, $20,000. For Wilfredo Lam Exhibition. 1987.
Museum of Contemporary Art, Los Angeles, CA, $25,000. For capital support. 1987.
Museum of Fine Arts of Houston, Houston, TX, $50,000. For operating support. 1987.
Museum of Flight Foundation, Seattle, WA, $25,000. Toward capital development. 1987.
Museum of Modern Art, NYC, NY, $10,000. For corporate membership. 1987.
Museum of Science and Industry, Chicago, IL, $30,000. Toward capital development. 1987.
Musical Theater Works, NYC, NY, $5,000. To sponsor production series. 1987.
National Arts Stabilization Fund, Seattle, WA, $10,000. For operating support. 1987.
National Corporate Fund for Dance, NYC, NY, $15,000. For outreach to dance community. 1987.
National Humanities Center, Research Triangle Park, NC, $25,000. For capital support. 1987.
National Institute for Music Theater, DC, $5,000. To underwrite international colloquium. 1987.
National Jazz Service Organization, DC, $5,000. For technical assistance program. 1987.
National Museum of American History, DC, $50,000. For Information Revolution. 1987.
National Museum of Women in the Arts, DC, $20,000. For operating support. 1987.
National Symphony Orchestra, DC, $20,000. For support for women musicians. 1987.
National Theater of the Deaf, NYC, NY, $5,000. To sponsor new dramatic work. 1987.
Nelson Atkins Museum of Art, Kansas City, MO, $25,000. For exhibition. 1987.
New Brunswick Cultural Center, New Brunswick, NJ, $15,000. For capital endowment. 1987.
New Dance Theater, Denver, CO, $5,000. For dance ensemble. 1987.
New England Foundation for the Arts, Cambridge, MA, $7,500. For Regional Dance Conference. 1987.
New Jersey Symphony Orchestra, Newark, NJ, $50,000. To sponsor production program. 1987.
New York City Ballet, NYC, NY, $50,000. For choreography project. 1987.
New York City Opera, NYC, NY, $25,000. For fund for directors and designers. 1987.
New York City Opera, NYC, NY, $25,000. For capital endowment. 1987.
New York Shakespeare Festival, NYC, NY, $5,000. For operating support. 1987.
Newark Museum Association, Newark, NJ, $30,000. For capital/development. 1987.
North Carolina School of the Arts Foundation, Winston-Salem, NC, $10,000. For guest artist program. 1987.
Northlight Theater, Evanston, IL, $10,000. To support residencies of artists. 1987.
Oakland Ballet Company and Guild, Oakland, CA, $7,000. For project support. 1987.
Oakland Museum Association, Oakland, CA, $10,000. For photography exhibition. 1987.
Opera America, DC, $6,000. For operating support. 1987.
Opera Company of Philadelphia, Philadelphia, PA, $15,000. To underwrite guest artist fees. 1987.
Opera Theater of Saint Louis, Saint Louis, MO, $25,000. For opera premieres. 1987.
Oregon Shakespearean Festival Association, Ashland, OR, $12,500. To underwrite Macbeth production. 1987.
Original Ballets Foundation, NYC, NY, $20,000. For dance tour. 1987.
Paul Taylor Dance Company, NYC, NY, $40,000. For dance tour. 1987.
Performing Arts Council of the Music Center, Los Angeles, CA, $15,000. For operating support. 1987.
Philadelphia Orchestra Association, Philadelphia, PA, $60,000. To sponsor American Encore Series. 1987.
Philadelphia Orchestra Association, Philadelphia, PA, $40,000. To sponsor American Encore Series. 1987.
Philharmonic Orchestra of Florida, Fort Lauderdale, FL, $25,000. For Marvin David Levy composition. 1987.
Philharmonic-Symphony Society of New York, NYC, NY, $60,000. For conference. 1987.
Phoenix Symphony, Phoenix, AZ, $15,000. To support concert series. 1987.
Pick Up Performance Company, NYC, NY, $5,000. For sponsor tour expansion. 1987.
Pioneer Courthouse Square of Portland, Portland, OR, $5,000. For weather machine program. 1987.
Pittsburgh Ballet Theater, Pittsburgh, PA, $10,000. To support mixed repertoire. 1987.
Pittsburgh Symphony Society, Pittsburgh, PA, $15,000. To underwrite performance. 1987.
Portland Opera Association, Portland, OR, $7,500. For Mozart production. 1987.
Princeton Ballet Society, Princeton, NJ, $10,000. Toward operating support. 1987.
Remains Theater, Chicago, IL, $10,000. To sponsor three new plays. 1987.
Repertory Theater of Saint Louis, Saint Louis, MO, $5,000. For operating support. 1987.
Ric-Charles Choral Ensemble, Plainfield, NJ, $7,500. For program expansion. 1987.
Saint Louis Science Center, Saint Louis, MO, $5,000. For sound demonstration project. 1987.
Saint Louis Symphony Society, Saint Louis, MO, $20,000. To underwrite orchestra series. 1987.
San Antonio Festival, San Antonio, TX, $10,000. To underwrite two performances. 1987.
San Antonio Museum Association, Witte Museum, San Antonio, TX, $12,500. For exhibition. 1987.
San Antonio Performing Arts Association, San Antonio, TX, $20,000. For Bolshoi Ballet Celebration. 1987.
San Antonio Performing Arts Association, San Antonio, TX, $10,000. To sponsor dance performances. 1987.
San Diego Opera, San Diego, CA, $15,000. To support Donizetti performance. 1987.
San Diego Symphony Orchestra, San Diego, CA, $15,000. For project support. 1987.
San Francisco Museum of Modern Art, San Francisco, CA, $25,000. For exhibition. 1987.
San Francisco Symphony, San Francisco, CA, $30,000. For Vienna Philharmonic Program. 1987.
Science Museum of Virginia Foundation, Richmond, VA, $25,000. For capital support. 1987.
Seattle Symphony Orchestra, Seattle, WA, $25,000. To sponsor new music series. 1987.
Shreveport Regional Arts Council, Shreveport, LA, $5,000. For Fair Park Culture series. 1987.
South Carolina State Museum, Columbia, SC, $25,000. For capital support. 1987.
South Coast Repertory, Costa Mesa, CA, $10,000. To fund production of new American plays. 1987.
Steppenwolf Theater, Chicago, IL, $10,000. To sponsor Little Egypt play. 1987.

Summit Art Center, Summit, NJ, $16,700. For exhibition. 1987.
Sundance Institute for Film and Television, Salt Lake City, UT, $10,000. To develop 1988-89 production. 1987.
Symphony Society of Greater Hartford, Hartford, CT, $10,000. To sponsor opening night concert. 1987.
Symphony Space, NYC, NY, $5,000. To sponsor music marathon. 1987.
Tampa Bay Performing Arts Center, Tampa, FL, $15,000. For operating support. 1987.
Theater Communications Group, NYC, NY, $17,500. To support literary projects. 1987.
Theater Project Company, Saint Louis, MO, $5,000. To sponsor The Mandrake. 1987.
Trinity Repertory Company, Providence, RI, $30,000. To sponsor All the King's Men. 1987.
Twyla Tharp Dance Foundation, NYC, NY, $30,000. For dance tour. 1987.
Twyla Tharp Dance Foundation, NYC, NY, $25,000. For dance tour. 1987.
United Arts Council of Greensboro, Greensboro, NC, $20,000. For capital support. 1987.
United Arts Council of Greensboro, Greensboro, NC, $15,000. For operating support. 1987.
United Arts Omaha, Omaha, NE, $20,000. For capital support. 1987.
University of Iowa Foundation, Iowa City, IA, $5,000. For International Writing Program. 1987.
University of Nebraska, Lied Center for the Performing Arts, Omaha, NE, $10,000. For capital support. 1987.
Victory Gardens Theater, Chicago, IL, $10,000. To sponsor Colored Museum play. 1987.
Vinnette Carroll Repertory Company, Fort Lauderdale, FL, $5,000. To sponsor Dark of the Moon. 1987.
Virginia Beach Arts Center, Virginia Beach, VA, $5,000. For capital support. 1987.
Virginia Museum Foundation, Richmond, VA, $12,000. For exhibition. 1987.
Virginia Stage Company, Norfolk, VA, $5,000. For capital support. 1987.
Walker Art Center, Minneapolis, MN, $25,000. For Sculpture Gardens Project. 1987.
Washington Performing Arts Society, DC, $25,000. To underwrite orchestra series. 1987.
Whitney Museum of American Art, NYC, NY, $10,000. For operating support. 1987.
Whole Theater Company, Montclair, NJ, $10,000. For operating support. 1987.
Williamstown Theater Festival, Williamstown, MA, $10,000. For capital support. 1987.
Wisdom Bridge Theater, Chicago, IL, $10,000. For new play reading series. 1987.
Wolf Trap Foundation for the Performing Arts, Vienna, VA, $30,000. For capital support. 1987.
Yale University, Yale Repertory Theater, New Haven, CT, $15,000. For administrative costs of Piano Player. 1987.
YM-YWHA, 92nd Street, NYC, NY, $25,000. To endow conductor's chair. 1987.
YM-YWHA, 92nd Street, NYC, NY, $10,000. To support festival. 1987.

1761
Atran Foundation, Inc.

23-25 East 21st St., 3rd Fl.
New York 10010 (212) 505-9677

Incorporated in 1945 in NY.
Donor(s): Frank Z. Atran.†
Financial data (yr. ended 11/30/88): Assets, $12,673,116 (M); expenditures, $885,625, including $573,550 for 51 grants (high: $100,000; low: $250).
Purpose and activities: Support for research relating to labor and labor relations, art, science, literature, economics, and sociology; support of publications furthering these purposes; and endowment for chairs of learning in these fields.
Types of support: Continuing support, annual campaigns, seed money, emergency funds, endowment funds, research, publications, conferences and seminars, scholarship funds, professorships, exchange programs, matching funds, special projects, fellowships, general purposes.
Limitations: No grants to individuals.
Publications: Application guidelines.
Application information:
Initial approach: Proposal
Copies of proposal: 4
Deadline(s): Sept. 30
Board meeting date(s): Between Nov. and Feb. and as required
Write: Diane Fischer, Corp. Secy.
Officers and Directors: Max Atran, Pres.; William Stern, V.P.; Diane Fischer, Corp. Secy.
Employer Identification Number: 135566548

1762
Avon Products Foundation, Inc.

Nine West 57th St.
New York 10019 (212) 546-6731

Incorporated in 1955 in NY.
Donor(s): Avon Products, Inc.
Financial data (yr. ended 12/31/87): Assets, $166,476 (M); gifts received, $1,926,000; expenditures, $1,927,233, including $1,643,995 for 322 grants (high: $100,000; low: $2,000; average: $2,000-$15,000), $160,277 for 67 grants to individuals and $85,784 for employee matching gifts.
Purpose and activities: Support for social services, including institutions and agencies whose main focus is on individuals, particularly youth, women, minorities and the disadvantaged; support also for hospitals, education (including employee-related scholarships and matching gifts), community funds, cultural organizations, urban programs, and civic projects.
Types of support: General purposes, operating budgets, employee-related scholarships, technical assistance, special projects, employee matching gifts, capital campaigns, scholarship funds, continuing support.
Limitations: Giving limited to areas immediately surrounding company operations in New York City, Rye, and Suffern, NY; Newark, DE; Atlanta, GA; Springdale, OH; Pasadena, CA; and Morton Grove, IL. No support for individual member agencies of United Way and United Fund, or national health and welfare organizations. No grants to individuals (except for scholarships for children of company employees), or for capital or endowment funds; no loans.
Publications: Application guidelines, informational brochure (including application guidelines).
Application information: Application form required for scholarships only. The foundation has declared a moratorium on active grantmaking activities for 1989 and 1990.
Initial approach: Letter
Copies of proposal: 1
Deadline(s): Sept. 15
Board meeting date(s): 3 times yearly
Final notification: Oct. 15
Write: Glenn S. Clarke, Pres.
Officers and Directors: Glenn S. Clarke, Pres.; Donna Blackwell, V.P.; Phyllis B. Davis, V.P.; James E. Preston, V.P.; John F. Cox, Secy.; Margro R. Long, Treas.
Number of staff: 1 full-time professional; 1 full-time support.
Employer Identification Number: 136128447
Recent arts and culture grants:
Alliance of New York Arts Councils, NYC, NY, $5,000. For operating support. 1987.
Ballet Hispanico of New York, NYC, NY, $5,000. For operating support. 1987.
El Museo del Barrio, NYC, NY, $5,000. For operating support. 1987.
Harlem School of the Arts, NYC, NY, $5,000. For operating support. 1987.
Lincoln Center for the Performing Arts, NYC, NY, $5,000. For operating support. 1987.
Metropolitan Museum of Art, NYC, NY, $7,000. For operating support. 1987.
National Museum of Women in the Arts, DC, $5,000. For operating support. 1987.
New York City Opera, NYC, NY, $5,000. For special project. 1987.
Plaza de la Raza, Los Angeles, CA, $5,000. For special project. 1987.
Studio Museum in Harlem, NYC, NY, $5,000. For operating support. 1987.

1763
Axe-Houghton Foundation

875 Third Ave., 23rd Fl.
New York 10022 (212) 866-0564

Incorporated in 1965 in NY.
Donor(s): Emerson W. Axe.†
Financial data (yr. ended 2/29/88): Assets, $4,286,772 (M); expenditures, $233,304, including $166,850 for 34 grants (high: $10,000; low: $1,000).
Purpose and activities: To encourage the improvement of spoken English in all its manifestations, including remedial speech, public speaking, and speaking as an art form.
Types of support: Seed money, research, special projects, conferences and seminars.
Limitations: No grants to individuals, or for operating budgets, general purposes, continuing support, annual campaigns, emergency funds, deficit financing, capital funds, endowment funds, matching gifts, scholarships, fellowships, or publications; no loans.
Publications: Program policy statement, application guidelines.
Application information:
Initial approach: Letter
Copies of proposal: 1

Deadline(s): Submit proposal preferably in Sept.; deadline Oct. 1
Board meeting date(s): May and Nov.
Final notification: 2 months
Write: Remington P. Patterson, Pres.
Officers: Remington P. Patterson,* Pres.; Robert B. von Mehren,* V.P.; Beth Ann Wahl, Secy.; Thomas J. McDonald, Treas.
Directors:* Alfred Berman, William A. Hance, John B. Oakes, Suzanne Schwartz.
Number of staff: 1 part-time professional.
Employer Identification Number: 136200200

1764
N. W. Ayer Foundation, Inc.
c/o N.W. Ayer, Inc.
1345 Ave. of the Americas
New York 10105 (212) 708-5000

Financial data (yr. ended 12/31/87): Assets, $1,008,593 (M); expenditures, $83,657, including $70,000 for 14 grants to individuals.
Purpose and activities: Scholarships awarded to unmarried children of current full-time regular employees of N.W. Ayers, Inc.
Types of support: Employee-related scholarships.
Application information: Application form required.
Initial approach: Letter
Deadline(s): Jan. 1
Write: Walter Lance, Secy.-Treas.
Officers: Neal W. O'Connor, Pres.; Louis T. Hagopian, V.P.; Walter Lance, Secy.-Treas.
Directors: George Eversman, Jerry Jordan, David Means, John B. Roedig, Marcella Rosen, Earl Shorris, Jerry J. Siano, Roger Smith.
Employer Identification Number: 236296499

1765
The B Fund
c/o Edward H.R. Blitzer
75 Central Park West
New York 10021

Established in 1958 in NY.
Financial data (yr. ended 12/31/87): Assets, $839,378 (M); expenditures, $118,082, including $104,000 for 13 grants (high: $20,000; low: $1,000).
Purpose and activities: Support for Jewish giving, education, and culture.
Application information: Contributes only to pre-selected organizations. Applications not accepted.
Officers: Edward H.R. Blitzer, Pres.; William F. Blitzer, V.P.; Adele Goldenberg, Secy.; Jeremiah Blitzer, Treas.
Employer Identification Number: 136082886

1766
Rose M. Badgeley Residual Charitable Trust
c/o Marine Midland Bank, N.A.
250 Park Ave.
New York 10177 (212) 503-2773

Trust established about 1977 in NY.
Donor(s): Rose Badgeley.†
Financial data (yr. ended 1/31/87): Assets, $11,578,409 (M); gifts received, $59,018; expenditures, $976,874, including $848,852 for 62 grants (high: $55,000; low: $2,000; average: $5,000-$25,000).
Purpose and activities: Emphasis on hospitals and health associations, particularly those concerned with medical research; higher education, cultural programs, and social service and youth agencies.
Types of support: Annual campaigns, building funds, equipment, general purposes, renovation projects, research, special projects, continuing support.
Limitations: Giving primarily in the five boroughs of New York City, NY, and in Westchester County. No grants to individuals.
Application information:
Initial approach: Full written proposal
Deadline(s): Submit proposal no earlier than Dec. 1 and no later than Mar. 15
Board meeting date(s): Apr.
Final notification: Within a month after grant committee meeting if approved
Write: Mr. Loren R. Sattinger, V.P., Marine Midland Bank, N.A.
Trustees: John J. Duffy, Marine Midland Bank, N.A.
Number of staff: None.
Employer Identification Number: 136744781

1767
The Bagby Foundation for the Musical Arts,, Inc.
501 Fifth Ave.
New York 10017

Established in 1925 in NY.
Donor(s): Rugene M. Grant, John H. Steinway.
Financial data (yr. ended 12/31/87): Assets, $1,095,897 (M); gifts received, $6,454; expenditures, $82,308, including $10,500 for 8 grants (high: $1,500; low: $1,000) and $23,155 for 19 grants to individuals.
Purpose and activities: Support primarily for aged, needy individuals who have aided the world of music and who are in need of financial support; some support for music schools, societies, and study grants.
Types of support: Grants to individuals, scholarship funds.
Application information:
Initial approach: Letter
Deadline(s): None
Write: Eleanor C. Mark, Exec. Dir.
Officers and Trustees: Rose Bampton, Chair.; F. Malcolm Graff, Jr., Pres.; Jarmila Packard, V.P. and Treas.; William Mayo Sullivan, V.P.; and 10 other trustees.
Employer Identification Number: 131873289

1768
Marie Baier Foundation, Inc.
Six East 87th St.
New York 10128 (212) 410-2130

Donor(s): John F. Baier.†
Financial data (yr. ended 1/31/88): Assets, $8,578,197 (M); expenditures, $534,446, including $464,000 for 21 grants (high: $55,000; low: $4,000).
Purpose and activities: Grants primarily for higher and secondary education, cultural programs, and youth agencies; support also for German-American organizations, and a home for the aged.
Limitations: No grants to individuals.
Application information:
Initial approach: Letter
Deadline(s): None
Write: Berteline Baier Dale, Pres.
Officers: Berteline Baier Dale,* Pres.; John F. Baier, Jr.,* V.P.; Ida Schuller, Secy.; Erich H. Markel,* Treas.
Directors:* Carl H. Ficke, Guenter F. Metsch, Sidney Sirkin.
Employer Identification Number: 136267032

1769
The Baird Foundation
122 Huntington Ct.
P.O. Box 514
Williamsville 14221 (716) 633-5588

Trust established in 1947 in NY.
Donor(s): Flora M. Baird,† Frank B. Baird, Jr.,† Cameron Baird,† William C. Baird.†
Financial data (yr. ended 12/31/88): Assets, $5,836,844 (M); expenditures, $202,287, including $178,287 for 72 grants (high: $14,000; low: $500; average: $1,000-$2,000).
Purpose and activities: Emphasis on higher education, church support, cultural programs, hospitals, medical research, and the environment.
Types of support: Research, matching funds, general purposes, capital campaigns.
Limitations: Giving primarily in Erie County, NY. No grants to individuals; no loans.
Application information:
Initial approach: Letter
Copies of proposal: 1
Deadline(s): None
Board meeting date(s): About 4 times a year
Final notification: 3 months
Write: Carl E. Gruber, Mgr.
Officer: Carl E. Gruber, Mgr.
Trustees: Arthur W. Cryer, Robert J.A. Irwin, William Baird Irwin.
Number of staff: 1 full-time professional; 1 part-time professional.
Employer Identification Number: 166023080

1770
The Cameron Baird Foundation
Box 564
Hamburg 14075

Trust established in 1960 in NY.
Donor(s): Members of the family of Cameron Baird.
Financial data (yr. ended 12/31/87): Assets, $11,301,145 (M); expenditures, $1,077,558, including $1,029,533 for 49 grants (high: $55,000; low: $133).
Purpose and activities: Emphasis on music and cultural programs, higher and secondary education, social services, population control, conservation, and civil rights.
Limitations: Giving primarily in the Buffalo, NY, area. No support for religious organizations. No grants to individuals.
Application information: Generally contributes to pre-selected organizations.
Initial approach: Letter
Copies of proposal: 1

Deadline(s): Submit proposal in the fall; most grants are made in Dec.
Board meeting date(s): Annually
Write: Brian D. Baird, Trustee
Trustees: Brian D. Baird, Bridget B. Baird, Bruce C. Baird, Jane D. Baird, Bronwyn Baird Clauson, Brenda Baird Senturia.
Number of staff: None.
Employer Identification Number: 166029481

1771
Bankers Trust Corporate Contributions Program
280 Park Ave.
New York 10017 (212) 850-3500

Financial data (yr. ended 12/31/88): $4,200,000 for 987 grants.
Purpose and activities: Supports social and public issues, education, minority education, community development, hospital building funds, libraries, urban development, volunteerism, economic development, environmental issues, historical preservation, arts and culture. Types of support include in-kind donations, media, foundation support, and loan of employees and executives.
Types of support: Capital campaigns, employee matching gifts, general purposes, operating budgets, publications, renovation projects.
Limitations: Giving primarily in New York City. No grants to individuals, United Way recipients or to political, religious, fraternal, or veterans' organizations.
Publications: Informational brochure.
Application information: Include description of organization and project, population served, budget, most recently audited financial statement, list of directors and donors, and proof of tax-exemption.
Initial approach: Letter
Copies of proposal: 1
Deadline(s): Applications accepted throughout the year
Write: Nancy S. Ticktin, V.P. and Secy., Contribs. Comm.
Number of staff: 1 full-time professional; 1 full-time support.

1772
J. M. R. Barker Foundation
630 Fifth Ave.
New York 10111 (212) 541-6970

Established in 1968 in NY.
Donor(s): James M. Barker,† Margaret R. Barker,† Robert R. Barker.
Financial data (yr. ended 12/31/88): Assets, $9,246,213 (M); expenditures, $412,609, including $289,000 for 45 grants (high: $30,000; low: $500).
Purpose and activities: Support primarily for organizations that are well known to one or more directors, with some emphasis on the areas of higher education, cultural programs, and scientific research.
Types of support: Operating budgets, continuing support, annual campaigns, seed money, general purposes, building funds, endowment funds, special projects, research.
Limitations: Giving primarily in the greater New York City, NY, area, and the greater Boston, MA, area. No grants to individuals, or for scholarships, fellowships, or matching gifts; no loans.
Application information:
Copies of proposal: 1
Deadline(s): Submit proposal in May or Oct.
Board meeting date(s): June and Dec.
Final notification: 3 months
Write: Robert R. Barker, Pres.
Officers: Robert R. Barker,* Pres.; Elizabeth S. Barker,* V.P.; James R. Barker,* V.P.; Dwight E. Lee,* V.P.; Maureen A. Hopkins, Secy.and Admin; Robert P. Connor,* Treas.
Directors:* Margaret W. Barker, W.B. Barker, John W. Holman, Jr., Richard D. Kahn, Ann B. Kolvig.
Number of staff: 1 part-time professional.
Employer Identification Number: 136268289

1773
The Barker Welfare Foundation
P.O. Box 2
Glen Head 11545 (516) 625-0465
Application address for Chicago agencies: c/o Philip D. Block III, One First National Plaza, Suite 2544, Chicago, IL 60603; Treasurer's Office: c/o Charles C. Hickox, 26 Broadway, New York, NY 10004

Incorporated in 1934 in IL.
Donor(s): Mrs. Charles C. Hickox.†
Financial data (yr. ended 9/30/87): Assets, $35,798,656 (M); expenditures, $1,875,649, including $1,362,750 for 182 grants (high: $100,000; low: $1,000; average: $3,000-$9,000).
Purpose and activities: Grants to established organizations and charitable institutions, with emphasis on arts and culture, youth agencies, health, welfare, aid to the handicapped, and recreation.
Types of support: Operating budgets, continuing support, building funds, equipment, land acquisition, matching funds, publications, special projects, renovation projects, annual campaigns.
Limitations: Giving primarily in Chicago, IL, Michigan City, IN, and New York, NY. No support for private elementary and secondary schools or for higher education. No grants to individuals, or for endowment funds, seed money, emergency funds, deficit financing, scholarships, fellowships, medical or scientific research, or conferences; no loans.
Publications: Program policy statement, application guidelines.
Application information:
Initial approach: Letter or telephone
Copies of proposal: 1
Deadline(s): Submit proposal preferably between Sept. and Dec.; deadline Feb. 1 for completed proposal
Board meeting date(s): May
Final notification: After annual meeting for positive response; from Sept. to May for negative response
Write: Mrs. Walter L. Ross, II, Pres. (NY and national agencies); Philip D. Block, III (Chicago agencies)
Officers: Mrs. Walter L. Ross II,* Pres.; Mrs. Charles Becker,* V.P. and Secy.; Mrs. John A. Garrettson,* V.P.; Charles C. Hickox, Treas.
Directors:* Philip D. Block III, Diane Curtis, James R. Donnelley, John A. Garrettson, Mrs. Edward A. Hansen, Mrs. Charles C. Hickox, John B. Hickox, Alline Matheson.
Number of staff: 1 part-time support.
Employer Identification Number: 366018526

1774
Chuck Barris Foundation
c/o Mason & Co.
400 Park Ave.
New York 10022 (213) 278-9550

Established in 1984 in CA.
Financial data (yr. ended 9/30/88): Assets, $1,043,436 (M); expenditures, $106,172, including $99,830 for 34 grants (high: $36,945; low: $10).
Purpose and activities: Support for cultural programs and social services, including child welfare.
Officers and Directors: Charles H. Barris, Pres.; David Gotterer, Secy.-Treas.; Robin Barris.
Employer Identification Number: 953954357

1775
The Theodore H. Barth Foundation, Inc.
1211 Ave. of the Americas
New York 10036 (212) 840-6000

Incorporated in 1953 in DE.
Donor(s): Theodore H. Barth.†
Financial data (yr. ended 12/31/87): Assets, $9,766,347 (M); expenditures, $640,995, including $478,700 for 51 grants (high: $75,000; low: $100; average: $1,000-$10,000) and $42,819 for 26 grants to individuals.
Purpose and activities: Grants for higher education, including scholarships, hospitals, religion, the arts and cultural organizations, health agencies, and social services; support also for civic affairs, aid to the handicapped, and conservation.
Types of support: Student aid.
Application information:
Initial approach: Letter
Deadline(s): None
Write: Irving P. Berelson, Pres.
Officers and Directors: Irving P. Berelson, Pres.; Charlton T. Barth, Thelma D. Berelson.
Employer Identification Number: 136103401

1776
Bat Hanadiv Foundation No. 3
c/o Carter, Ledyard & Milburn
Two Wall St.
New York 10005 (212) 732-3200
Application address outside Israel: Mr. M. Rowe, Trustee, 5 Rue Pedro Mevlan, Geneva, Switzerland; in Israel: Mr. A. Fried, 16 Ibn Gvirol St., Jerusalem 92430

Established in 1981.
Donor(s): Bat Hanadiv Foundation, Bat Hanadiv Foundation No. 2.
Financial data (yr. ended 12/31/87): Assets, $191,485,557 (M); expenditures, $5,945,109,

including $4,641,732 for 49 grants (high: $598,663; low: $2,822; average: $10,000-$85,000).
Purpose and activities: Grants primarily for higher and other education; support also for conservation, youth and social service agencies, and cultural programs.
Types of support: Operating budgets, equipment, special projects.
Limitations: Giving primarily in Israel. No grants to individuals.
Application information:
Initial approach: Letter
Deadline(s): None
Write: Jerome Caulfield
Trustee: Doder Trust Ltd.
Number of staff: None.
Employer Identification Number: 133091620

1777
The Bay Foundation, Inc.
(Formerly Charles Ulrick and Josephine Bay Foundation, Inc.)
14 Wall St., Suite 1600
New York 10005 (212) 815-7500

Incorporated in 1950 in NY.
Donor(s): Charles Ulrick Bay,† Josephine Bay.†
Financial data (yr. ended 12/31/87): Assets, $9,700,000 (M); expenditures, $1,074,282, including $782,000 for 79 grants (high: $200,000; low: $500; average: $2,000-$6,000).
Purpose and activities: Support primarily for art museum conservation, education, with emphasis on pre-college children's projects, and medical sciences, particularly veterinary medicine.
Types of support: Operating budgets, seed money, research, scholarship funds, matching funds, general purposes.
Limitations: No support for the performing arts, or for other than publicly supported charities. No grants to individuals, or for capital or endowment funds; no loans.
Publications: Annual report (including application guidelines), 990-PF.
Application information:
Initial approach: Proposal
Copies of proposal: 1
Deadline(s): Submit proposal preferably in Jan. or Aug.
Board meeting date(s): Mar. and Oct.
Final notification: 3 months
Write: Robert W. Ashton, Exec. Dir.
Officers and Directors: Frederick Bay, Chair.; Synnova B. Hayes, Pres.; Robert W. Ashton, Exec. Dir.; Daniel Demarest, Hans Ege.
Number of staff: 2 part-time professional.
Employer Identification Number: 135646283

1778
The Howard Bayne Fund
c/o Simpson Thacher & Bartlett
One Battery Park Plaza
New York 10004

Incorporated in 1960 in NY.
Donor(s): Louise Van Beuren Bayne Trust.
Financial data (yr. ended 12/31/87): Assets, $6,300,000 (M); expenditures, $350,000, including $320,000 for 79 grants (high: $20,000; low: $750; average: $750-$2,000).
Purpose and activities: Emphasis on music, cultural programs, education, conservation, and hospitals.
Types of support: Annual campaigns, building funds, endowment funds, equipment, general purposes, renovation projects, research, seed money.
Publications: 990-PF.
Application information: Applications not accepted.
Write: Kathy Foer
Officers: Gurdon B. Wattles,* Pres.; Elizabeth B. Shields,* V.P.; Thomas J. McGrath, Secy. and Treas.
Directors:* Daphne B. Shih, Diana de Vegh, Pierre J. de Vegh, Mrs. Gurdon B. Wattles.
Employer Identification Number: 136100680

1779
Beck Foundation
c/o T. Edmund Beck
Six East 43rd St.
New York 10017 (212) 661-2640

Established in 1954 in NY.
Donor(s): T. Edmund Beck.
Financial data (yr. ended 12/31/87): Assets, $2,395,163 (M); expenditures, $85,070, including $76,740 for 57 grants (high: $50,000; low: $10).
Purpose and activities: Grants primarily for education, social services, and religious giving.
Application information:
Initial approach: Letter
Deadline(s): None
Officers: T. Edmund Beck, Pres.; John C. Beck, Madeline C. Beck, T.E. Beck, Jr., Susan Beck Wasch.
Number of staff: None.
Employer Identification Number: 136082501

1780
The Bedminster Fund, Inc.
1270 Ave. of the Americas, Rm. 2300
New York 10020 (212) 315-8300

Incorporated in 1948 in NY.
Financial data (yr. ended 6/30/88): Assets, $3,694,838 (M); gifts received, $93,923; expenditures, $111,631, including $86,500 for 11 grants (high: $40,000; low: $500; average: $1,000-$3,000).
Purpose and activities: Emphasis on education, hospitals, the arts, and welfare agencies. Grants only to present beneficiary organizations and to special proposals developed by the directors; additional requests seldom considered.
Types of support: General purposes.
Limitations: No grants to individuals; no loans.
Application information: Applications not accepted.
Board meeting date(s): Nov. and as required
Officers: Dorothy Dillon Eweson,* Pres.; Philip D. Allen,* V.P.; David H. Peipers,* V.P.; Joan Waldron, Secy.; Robert F. Quick, Treas.
Directors:* Christine Allen, Douglas E. Allen, Judith S. Leonard, Anne D. Zetterberg.
Number of staff: None.
Employer Identification Number: 136083684

1781
Beefeater Foundation
134 East 40th St.
New York 10016 (212) 490-9300

Established in 1972.
Financial data (yr. ended 12/31/87): Assets, $857,277 (M); gifts received, $141,350; expenditures, $216,283, including $199,992 for grants (high: $146,902).
Purpose and activities: Giving for health and social service agencies, and for awards in recognition of outstanding works of literature relating to British or American culture; support also for education, religion, hospitals, and youth agencies.
Application information:
Write: Charles S. Mueller, Chair.
Officers and Directors: Charles S. Mueller, Chair.; Robert A. Aldridge, Pres.; Richard Reitman, V.P. and Treas.; Michael S. Insel, Secy.
Employer Identification Number: 237309965

1782
The Morris S. & Florence H. Bender Foundation, Inc.
c/o Summit Rovins & Feldesman
445 Park Ave.
New York 10022

Established in 1978 in NY.
Financial data (yr. ended 6/30/87): Assets, $1,185,282 (M); expenditures, $146,215, including $126,700 for 32 grants (high: $25,000; low: $1,000).
Purpose and activities: Giving primarily for Jewish welfare, hospitals and medicine, and cultural activities.
Limitations: No grants to individuals.
Application information:
Initial approach: Proposal
Deadline(s): None
Write: Howard L. Klein, Pres.
Officers and Directors: Howard L. Klein, Pres.; Lenore Klein, V.P.; Ralph M. Engel, Secy.; Stephen A. Goldstein, Treas.
Employer Identification Number: 132951469

1783
Frances & Benjamin Benenson Foundation, Inc.
708 Third Ave., 28th Fl.
New York 10017

Established in 1983 in NY.
Donor(s): Charles B. Benenson.
Financial data (yr. ended 11/30/87): Assets, $5,178,870 (M); gifts received, $1,118,916; expenditures, $241,203, including $237,785 for 12 grants (high: $150,000; low: $105).
Purpose and activities: Support primarily for Jewish welfare, secondary education and museums.
Application information: Contributes only to pre-selected organizations. Applications not accepted.
Officers: Charles B. Benenson, Pres.; Emanuel Labin, V.P.
Employer Identification Number: 133267113

1784
David & Minnie Berk Foundation, Inc.
315 West 70th St., Rm. 8I
New York 10023-3504
Application address: c/o 1055 Franklin Ave., Suite 300, Garden City, NY 11530

Established in 1961 in NY.
Donor(s): Members of the Berk family.
Financial data (yr. ended 10/31/86): Assets, $1,326,181 (M); gifts received, $4,914; expenditures, $85,301, including $70,687 for 8 grants (high: $28,000; low: $3,600).
Purpose and activities: Giving primarily for the aged and social services.
Types of support: General purposes.
Application information:
Initial approach: Letter
Copies of proposal: 10
Deadline(s): None
Write: David Green, Pres.
Officers: David Green, Pres.; Ronald Berk, 1st V.P.; Alan Grossman, 2nd V.P.; Joy Levien, Secy.; Nancy Goodman, Treas.
Number of staff: None.
Employer Identification Number: 116038062

1785
Irving Berlin Charitable Fund, Inc.
29 West 46th St.
New York 10036

Incorporated in 1947 in NY.
Donor(s): Irving Berlin.
Financial data (yr. ended 12/31/87): Assets, $18,322,484 (M); gifts received, $75,000; expenditures, $74,783, including $66,050 for 14 grants (high: $36,000; low: $300).
Purpose and activities: Giving primarily to a music school, an opera association, and to Jewish welfare funds.
Limitations: Giving primarily in NY.
Application information:
Initial approach: Letter
Deadline(s): None
Write: Irving Berlin, Pres.
Officers and Directors: Irving Berlin, Pres. and Treas.; Ellen Berlin, V.P.; Norman J. Stone.
Employer Identification Number: 136092592

1786
Rhonie & George Berlinger Foundation, Inc.
1120 Park Ave.
New York 10128

Incorporated in 1958 in NY.
Donor(s): George F. Berlinger, Rhonie H. Berlinger.
Financial data (yr. ended 5/31/87): Assets, $320,153 (M); gifts received, $174,975; expenditures, $114,758, including $111,653 for 98 grants (high: $60,000; low: $25).
Purpose and activities: Emphasis on health agencies, children, cultural programs, education, and Jewish welfare funds.
Application information:
Deadline(s): None
Write: Rhonie H. Berlinger, Pres.
Officers: Rhonie H. Berlinger, Pres.; Nancy K. Stone, Secy.-Treas.
Employer Identification Number: 136084411

1787
Bezalel Foundation, Inc.
The Clock Tower Bldg.
Two Madison Ave.
Larchmont 10538 (914) 833-0425

Incorporated in 1940 in MD; in 1981 merged with Ferdinand W. Breth Foundation.
Donor(s): Henry Sonneborn III, Rudolf G. Sonneborn,† Gustave Schindler.†
Financial data (yr. ended 6/30/88): Assets, $1,322,200 (M); gifts received, $18,868; expenditures, $253,465, including $238,495 for 107 grants (high: $58,400; low: $100).
Purpose and activities: Emphasis on Jewish welfare funds and higher education, including institutions in Israel; support also for hospitals, music, and museums.
Limitations: No grants to individuals.
Application information: Funds are fully committed. Applications not accepted.
Write: Henry Sonneborn III, Pres.
Officers and Directors: Henry Sonneborn III, Pres.; Clara L. Sonneborn, Secy.; Amalie S. Katz, Mark D. Neumann, Hans Schindler.
Employer Identification Number: 136066999

1788
The Siegfried & Josephine Bieber Foundation, Inc.
70 Pine St.
New York 10270

Incorporated in 1960 in NY.
Donor(s): Siegfried Bieber,† Josephine Bieber.†
Financial data (yr. ended 12/31/87): Assets, $729,755 (M); expenditures, $217,455, including $194,500 for 53 grants (high: $35,000; low: $500).
Purpose and activities: Emphasis on religious welfare funds, social services, hospitals and medical research, the performing arts, education, and museums.
Limitations: Giving primarily in NY.
Application information: Applications not accepted.
Write: Rene Loeb, Pres.
Officers and Directors: Rene Loeb, Pres.; Leonard Wacksman, Secy.; Stephen M. Kellen, Treas.; Stephen Connolly.
Employer Identification Number: 136162556

1789
Henry M. Blackmer Foundation, Inc.
c/o White & Case
1155 Ave. of the Americas
New York 10036

Incorporated in 1952 in DE.
Donor(s): Henry M. Blackmer.†
Financial data (yr. ended 12/31/87): Assets, $2,044,506 (M); expenditures, $187,665, including $143,500 for 30 grants (high: $15,000; low: $500).
Purpose and activities: Support for education, hospitals, cultural programs, and a zoological foundation; grants generally limited to a small list of institutional donees who have received grants from the Foundation in the past.
Application information: Contributes only to pre-selected organizations. Applications not accepted.
Officers and Trustees: Morton Moskin, Pres.; W. Perry Neff, V.P.; David W. Swanson, Secy.-Treas.; Henry M. Blackmer II.
Employer Identification Number: 136097357

1790
Blinken Foundation, Inc.
466 Lexington Ave.
New York 10017

Established in 1965 in NY.
Financial data (yr. ended 12/31/86): Assets, $2,193,314 (M); gifts received, $223,275; expenditures, $215,930, including $175,495 for 65 grants (high: $25,000; low: $50; average: $500-$5,000).
Purpose and activities: Giving for cultural activities, scientific research, and Jewish welfare funds.
Types of support: Annual campaigns, fellowships, general purposes, internships, scholarship funds.
Officers and Directors: Donald M. Blinken, Pres. and Treas.; Robert J. Blinken, V.P. and Secy.; Alan J. Blinken, V.P.; Ethel H. Blinken, V.P.
Number of staff: None.
Employer Identification Number: 136190153

1791
Cornelius N. Bliss Memorial Fund
c/o U.S. Trust Co. of NY, Tax Dept.
45 Wall St.
New York 10005

Incorporated in 1917 in NY.
Donor(s): Cornelius N. Bliss,† Elizabeth M. Bliss, Lizzie P. Bliss, William B. Markell.
Financial data (yr. ended 12/31/86): Assets, $1,419,965 (M); gifts received, $3,733; expenditures, $88,283, including $72,000 for 20 grants (high: $23,750; low: $250).
Purpose and activities: Giving primarily to cultural programs, hospitals, and secondary education.
Limitations: Giving primarily in NY.
Application information:
Initial approach: Letter
Deadline(s): None
Write: Cornelius N. Bliss, Jr., Pres.
Officers and Directors: Cornelius N. Bliss, Jr., Pres.; Elizabeth B. Parkinson, V.P.; Anthony A. Bliss, Secy.-Treas.; Cornelius N. Bliss III, John Parkinson.
Employer Identification Number: 136400075

1792
Charles G. & Yvette Bluhdorn Charitable Trust
c/o Jack H. Klein & Co.
220 East 42nd St., No. 3108
New York 10017 (212) 333-4300

Established in 1967 in NY.
Financial data (yr. ended 12/31/86): Assets, $4,852,137 (M); gifts received, $141,612; expenditures, $230,712, including $226,207 for 20 grants (high: $112,500; low: $100).
Purpose and activities: Giving for social services and culture.
Application information:

Initial approach: Letter
Deadline(s): None
Write: Dominique Bluhdorn, Trustee
Trustees: Dominique Bluhdorn, Paul Bluhdorn, Yvette Bluhdorn.
Employer Identification Number: 136256769

1793
Edith C. Blum Foundation
300 Park Ave.
New York 10022

Trust established in 1976 in NY.
Donor(s): Albert Blum,† Edith C. Blum.†
Financial data (yr. ended 9/30/87): Assets, $10,161,842 (M); expenditures, $671,693, including $529,828 for 160 grants (high: $95,000; low: $78).
Purpose and activities: Emphasis on higher education, including legal education; cultural programs, including the performing arts and museums; and public interest organizations.
Limitations: Giving primarily in New York, NY.
Application information:
Deadline(s): None
Write: Wilbur H. Friedman, Trustee
Trustees: Frances M. Friedman, Wilbur H. Friedman.
Employer Identification Number: 132871362

1794
The Elmer and Mamdouha Bobst Foundation, Inc.
c/o The Elmer Holmes Bobst Library, New York Univ.
70 Washington Square South
New York 10012

Incorporated in 1968 in NY.
Donor(s): Elmer H. Bobst.†
Financial data (yr. ended 12/31/86): Assets, $24,986,568 (M); expenditures, $1,057,897, including $921,075 for 30 grants (high: $600,000; low: $25; average: $350-$50,000).
Purpose and activities: Emphasis on the promotion of health and medical research services, higher education, cultural programs, and youth agencies, and Islamic organizations, nationally and internationally.
Publications: Annual report, informational brochure (including application guidelines).
Application information:
Initial approach: Letter
Deadline(s): None
Write: Mamdouha S. Bobst, Pres.
Officers: Mamdouha S. Bobst,* Pres. and Treas.; Arthur J. Mahon, Secy.
Directors:* Farouk as-Sayid, Raja Kabbani, Mary Rockefeller, Milton C. Rose.
Employer Identification Number: 132616114

1795
The Bodman Foundation
c/o Morris & McVeigh
767 Third Ave., 22nd Fl.
New York 10017-2023 (212) 418-0500

Incorporated in 1945 in NJ.
Donor(s): George M. Bodman,† Louise C. Bodman.†
Financial data (yr. ended 12/31/88): Assets, $31,727,000 (M); expenditures, $2,508,123, including $1,985,000 for 62 grants (high: $100,000; low: $10,000; average: $10,000-$75,000).
Purpose and activities: Support largely for youth and social service agencies, educational institutions, hospitals, and cultural programs.
Types of support: Building funds, equipment, annual campaigns, capital campaigns, general purposes, land acquisition, matching funds, operating budgets, research.
Limitations: Giving primarily in the New York City, NY, area. Generally, no support for colleges or universities, performing arts groups, museums, or national health or mental health organizations. No grants to individuals, or for conferences, publications, travel, or film; no loans.
Publications: Biennial report (including application guidelines), program policy statement.
Application information:
Initial approach: Letter and proposal
Copies of proposal: 1
Deadline(s): None
Board meeting date(s): Apr., Sept., Dec., and as needed
Final notification: Only when requested
Write: Mary E. Caslin, Secy.
Officers: Guy G. Rutherfurd,* Pres. and Treas.; Marguerite Sykes Nichols,* V.P.; Mary E. Caslin, Secy. and Exec. Dir.
Trustees:* Harry W. Albright, Jr., Mary B. Braga, Gordon S. Braislin, Walter J.P. Curley, Jr., Anthony Drexel Duke, Peter Frelinghuysen, John N. Irwin III, Peter S. Paine, Russel Pennoyer, Mary S. Phipps.
Number of staff: 2 full-time professional.
Employer Identification Number: 136022016

1796
Booth Ferris Foundation
30 Broad St.
New York 10004 (212) 269-3850

Trusts established in 1957 and 1958 in NY; merged in 1964.
Donor(s): Chancie Ferris Booth,† Willis H. Booth.†
Financial data (yr. ended 12/31/87): Assets, $100,984,048 (M); expenditures, $6,098,830, including $4,893,434 for 88 grants (high: $250,000; low: $5,000; average: $15,000-$100,000).
Purpose and activities: Grants primarily for private education, especially theological education, smaller colleges, and independent secondary schools; limited support also for urban programs, social service agencies, and cultural activities.
Types of support: Continuing support, annual campaigns, seed money, emergency funds, building funds, equipment, renovation projects, endowment funds, matching funds, capital campaigns, general purposes.
Limitations: Giving limited to the New York, NY, metropolitan area for social service agencies and cultural organizations. No support for federated campaigns, community chests, or for work with specific diseases or disabilities. No grants to individuals, or for research; generally no grants to educational institutions for scholarships, fellowships, or unrestricted endowments; no loans.
Publications: Annual report (including application guidelines).
Application information:
Initial approach: Telephone, letter, or proposal
Copies of proposal: 1
Deadline(s): None
Board meeting date(s): Bimonthly
Final notification: 4 months
Write: Robert J. Murtagh, Trustee
Trustees: Robert J. Murtagh, Morgan Guaranty Trust Co. of New York.
Number of staff: 3 part-time professional.
Employer Identification Number: 136170340
Recent arts and culture grants:
Alliance of Resident Theaters, NYC, NY, $20,000. For unrestricted support. 1987.
Brooklyn Academy of Music, Brooklyn, NY, $100,000. For Next Wave Festival. 1987.
Chamber Music Society of Lincoln Center, NYC, NY, $30,000. For Together with Chamber Music program. 1987.
Childrens Art Carnival, NYC, NY, $15,000. For unrestricted support. 1987.
Citizens to Save Saint Marks, NYC, NY, $15,000. For unrestricted support. 1987.
Columbia University, Teachers College, NYC, NY, $75,000. For development of literature-based writing program for NYC public schools. 1987.
David Gordon Pick Up Company, NYC, NY, $25,000. For unrestricted support. 1987.
Feld Ballet, NYC, NY, $150,000. For building acquisition. 1987.
Joffrey Ballet, NYC, NY, $60,000. For New Ballet Fund. 1987.
Joyce Theater, NYC, NY, $100,000. For program expansion. 1987.
Lincoln Center for the Performing Arts, NYC, NY, $250,000. For construction of new building. 1987.
Mannes College of Music, NYC, NY, $50,000. For unrestricted support. 1987.
New York City Ballet, NYC, NY, $100,000. For Dance Training Program and American Music Festival. 1987.
New York Foundation for the Arts, NYC, NY, $25,000. For education efforts to reach arts constituency of New York State, and for Artists in Residence program. 1987.
Paul Taylor Dance Company, NYC, NY, $50,000. For new office and rehearsal space. 1987.
Saint Lukes Performing Arts Ensemble, NYC, NY, $35,000. For unrestricted support. 1987.
Second Stage Theater, NYC, NY, $40,000. For Artist in Perspective Program. 1987.
Spanish Theater Repertory Company, NYC, NY, $40,000. For unrestricted support. 1987.
Trisha Brown Dance Company, NYC, NY, $25,000. For unrestricted support. 1987.
Twyla Tharp Dance Foundation, NYC, NY, $30,000. For construction of new ballet. 1987.
Westminster School, Simsbury, CT, $50,000. For new performing arts facility. 1987.

1797
Botwinick-Wolfensohn Foundation, Inc.
599 Lexington Ave.
New York 10022 (212) 909-8100

Established in 1952.
Donor(s): James D. Wolfensohn, Benjamin Botwinick, Edward Botwinick.
Financial data (yr. ended 12/31/87): Assets, $5,077,704 (M); gifts received, $1,907,011; expenditures, $1,064,294, including $1,044,187 for 206 grants (high: $230,500; low: $10; average: $1,000-$5,000).
Purpose and activities: Emphasis on Israeli and Jewish interests, music education, minority education, medical research, and the homeless.
Types of support: Annual campaigns, building funds, capital campaigns, continuing support, general purposes, research, scholarship funds, seed money.
Limitations: Giving primarily in New York, NY. No grants to individuals.
Publications: 990-PF.
Application information:
Initial approach: Letter or telephone
Deadline(s): None
Final notification: 3 to 6 months
Write: James D. Wolfensohn, Chair.
Officers: James D. Wolfensohn, Chair.; Benjamin Botwinick, Pres.; Edward Botwinick, V.P.; Elaine Wolfensohn, Secy.; Bessie Botwinick, Treas.; Florence M. Sterrett, Exec. Dir.
Number of staff: 1 full-time professional; 1 full-time support.
Employer Identification Number: 136111833

1798
Bowne & Company, Inc. Corporate Contributions Program
345 Hudson St.
New York 10014 (212) 924-5500

Purpose and activities: Supports education, including private colleges, literacy, culture, and legal services.
Types of support: Annual campaigns, capital campaigns, general purposes.
Publications: Corporate report.
Application information:
Write: Douglas F. Bauer, Corp. Secy.
Number of staff: 1

1799
Bozell, Inc. Corporate Contributions Program
40 West 23rd St.
New York 10010 (212) 206-5000
Address for applications: 10250 Regency Circle/Omaha, NE 68114

Purpose and activities: Interest in civic programs and the United Way, the arts, museums, fine arts institutes, dance and community arts, education, private colleges, health services, hospitals, medical research, race relations, and welfare.
Types of support: Annual campaigns, building funds, capital campaigns, continuing support, endowment funds, general purposes, operating budgets, scholarship funds.
Limitations: Giving primarily in headquarters city and major operating locations.
Publications: Program policy statement, application guidelines.
Application information:
Copies of proposal: 1
Deadline(s): Quarterly; week prior to Board meeting dates
Board meeting date(s): Apr., June, Sept., and Dec.
Write: Don Carlos, Dir., Contribs.
Number of staff: 3

1800
Branta Foundation, Inc.
c/o Perelson Johnson & Rones
560 Lexington Ave.
New York 10022

Established in 1955 in NY.
Donor(s): Harvey Picker.
Financial data (yr. ended 5/31/87): Assets, $1,620,176 (M); expenditures, $403,990, including $372,000 for 28 grants (high: $95,000; low: $1,000).
Purpose and activities: Support primarily for higher education, culture, and international affairs.
Application information: Contributes only to pre-selected organizations. Applications not accepted.
Officers and Directors: Jean Picker, Pres. and Treas.; Harvey Picker, V.P. and Secy.; Christine Beshar.
Employer Identification Number: 136130955

1801
Breyer Foundation, Inc.
800 Park Ave., Rm. 4
New York 10021 (212) 582-6232

Established in 1940 in NY and DE.
Donor(s): Henry W. Breyer III.
Financial data (yr. ended 12/31/87): Assets, $1,419,399 (M); gifts received, $300; expenditures, $128,872, including $125,275 for 50 grants (high: $30,000; low: $100).
Purpose and activities: Support for education, health organizations and hospitals, conservation, social services, religious organizations, culture and performing arts.
Application information:
Initial approach: Letter or proposal
Deadline(s): None
Write: Henry W. Breyer III, Pres.
Officers and Directors: Henry W. Breyer III, Pres.; Margaret McKee Breyer, Secy.; Joanne Breyer.
Employer Identification Number: 236295924

1802
Bristol-Myers Company Contributions Program
345 Park Ave., 43rd Fl.
New York 10154 (212) 546-4000

Purpose and activities: Supports medical, including AIDS, cancer, nutrition, orthopaedic, neuroscientific and pain research, and research for alternatives to animal testing; support also for education, community and job programs for women, minorities, and the handicapped, and cultural, civic and community programs.
Types of support: Research, scholarship funds, fellowships, conferences and seminars, internships.
Limitations: Giving primarily in operating areas nationally and internationally. No support for political, fraternal, social or veterans' organizations, religious or sectarian organizations, unless project will benefit the community as a whole. No grants to individuals, or for the United Way and other federated campaign funding recipients, endowments, courtesy advertising, non tax-exempt organizations; no loans.
Application information:
Initial approach: Letter outlining request
Write: Marilyn L. Gruber, Dir., Corp. Contribs.

1803
The Bristol-Myers Fund, Inc.
345 Park Ave., 43rd Fl.
New York 10154 (212) 546-4331

Trust established in 1953 in NY; successor fund incorporated in 1982 in FL as Bristol-Myers Fund, Inc.
Donor(s): Bristol-Myers Squibb Co., divisions and subsidiaries.
Financial data (yr. ended 12/31/87): Assets, $10,147,590 (M); gifts received, $6,407,500; expenditures, $4,804,693, including $4,804,607 for 400 grants (high: $330,000; low: $1,000; average: $5,000-$35,000) and $324,064 for 976 employee matching gifts.
Purpose and activities: Giving for medical research, community funds, higher education (including employee-related scholarships administered by the National Merit Scholarship Corporation and matching gifts), and health care; support also for civic affairs, minority and women's organizations, youth agencies, and the arts.
Types of support: Annual campaigns, research, employee-related scholarships, fellowships, scholarship funds, general purposes, employee matching gifts.
Limitations: Giving limited to areas of company operations, and to national organizations. No support for political, fraternal, social, or veterans' organizations; religious or sectarian organizations not engaged in a significant project benefiting the entire community; specific public broadcast programs or films; or organizations receiving support through federated campaigns. No grants to individuals, or for endowment funds; no loans.
Publications: Annual report, informational brochure.
Application information:
Initial approach: Proposal
Copies of proposal: 1
Deadline(s): Submit proposal preferably between Feb. and Sept.; deadline Oct. 1
Board meeting date(s): Dec. and as needed
Final notification: 2 to 3 months
Write: Marilyn L. Gruber, V.P.
Officers: Patrick F. Crossman,* Pres.; Marilyn L. Gruber, V.P.; J. Richard Edmondson, Secy.; Jonathan B. Morris, Treas.; Nancy Arnot Taussig, Mgr.

Directors:* Bruce S. Gelb, Richard L. Gelb, William R. Miller.
Number of staff: 2 full-time professional; 1 part-time professional; 2 full-time support.
Employer Identification Number: 133127947

1804
Kenneth D. Brody Foundation
c/o Goldman Sachs & Co.
85 Broad St., Tax Dept.
New York 10004-2408

Established in 1980 in NY.
Donor(s): Kenneth D. Brody.
Financial data (yr. ended 9/30/87): Assets, $474,070 (M); gifts received, $318,328; expenditures, $262,003, including $261,775 for 94 grants (high: $50,000; low: $15).
Purpose and activities: Support primarily for higher education, cultural programs, health services, and hospitals.
Limitations: Giving primarily in New York, NY. No grants to individuals.
Application information: Contributes only to pre-selected organizations. Applications not accepted.
Trustees: Kenneth D. Brody, Donald R. Gant, H. Frederick Krimendahl II.
Employer Identification Number: 133050750

1805
Ann L. Bronfman Foundation
c/o Main Hurdman
55 East 52nd St.
New York 10055

Established in 1958.
Donor(s): Ann L. Bronfman.
Financial data (yr. ended 7/31/86): Assets, $80,878 (M); expenditures, $102,975, including $100,342 for 10 grants (high: $30,000; low: $1,000).
Purpose and activities: Giving primarily for cultural programs and groups working to better international relations.
Types of support: General purposes.
Application information: Contributes only to pre-selected organizations. Applications not accepted.
Write: L. Foster
Officers: Ann L. Bronfman, Pres.; Alan M. Stroock, V.P.; Ronald J. Stein, Secy.; John L. Loeb, Treas.
Employer Identification Number: 136085595

1806
BT Foundation
280 Park Ave.
New York 10015 (212) 850-3500
Application address: P.O. Box 318, Church St. Station, New York, NY 10012

Established in 1986 in NY.
Donor(s): BT Capital Corp.
Financial data (yr. ended 11/30/87): Assets, $229,729 (M); gifts received, $1,140,000; expenditures, $4,583,940, including $3,780,840 for 257 grants (high: $845,000; low: $45; average: $3,000-$20,000) and $641,356 for 825 employee matching gifts.
Purpose and activities: Support for arts and culture, economic development, with emphasis on community development and housing, social and public services, and urban amenities.
Types of support: General purposes, operating budgets, employee matching gifts, capital campaigns, continuing support.
Limitations: Giving primarily in NY. No support for religious purposes, veterans' and fraternal organizations, or United Way agencies unless they provide a fundraising waiver. No grants to individuals.
Application information:
Initial approach: Proposal
Deadline(s): None
Write: Nancy S. Ticktin, Pres.
Officers and Directors: Nancy S. Ticktin, Pres.; Maureen S. Bateman, V.P.; James J. Baechle, Page Chapman, III.
Number of staff: 2 full-time professional; 3 full-time support.
Employer Identification Number: 133321736

1807
Buffalo Forge Company Giving Program
490 Broadway
Buffalo 14204 (716) 847-5121

Financial data (yr. ended 12/31/88): $35,000 for 10 grants (high: $5,000; low: $1,000).
Purpose and activities: Supports civic programs, the arts, education and private colleges.
Types of support: Equipment, operating budgets, capital campaigns.
Limitations: Giving primarily in Buffalo, NY.
Application information:
Initial approach: Letter of inquiry describing project
Copies of proposal: 1
Deadline(s): Applications accepted throughout the year
Board meeting date(s): Decisions made as needed
Final notification: 4-6 weeks
Write: J. Robert Adare, Pres.
Number of staff: None.

1808
The Buffalo Foundation
1601 Main-Seneca Bldg.
237 Main St.
Buffalo 14203-2780 (716) 852-2857

Community foundation established in 1919 in NY by resolution and declaration of trust.
Financial data (yr. ended 12/31/87): Assets, $23,973,370 (M); gifts received, $328,497; expenditures, $1,617,716, including $1,167,762 for 145 grants (high: $124,590; low: $60) and $258,026 for 429 grants to individuals.
Purpose and activities: To administer trust funds for charitable, educational, and civic purposes. Grants for educational institutions, scholarships, family and child welfare, health services and hospitals, the arts, and community development.
Types of support: Operating budgets, seed money, emergency funds, building funds, equipment, land acquisition, special projects, matching funds, consulting services, technical assistance, research, publications, conferences and seminars, general purposes, renovation projects, student aid.
Limitations: Giving primarily in Erie County, NY; scholarships awarded to local residents only. No grants for annual campaigns, deficit financing, or endowment funds; no loans.
Publications: Annual report (including application guidelines), application guidelines, informational brochure, newsletter.
Application information: Application forms required only for scholarships, and must be requested between Mar. 1 and May 10.
Initial approach: Proposal
Copies of proposal: 1
Deadline(s): Mar. 31, June 30, Sept. 30, or Dec. 31 for grants; May 25 for scholarships
Board meeting date(s): 1st Wednesday of Feb., May, Aug., and Nov.
Final notification: 1st meeting after submission
Write: William L. Van Schoonhoven, Dir.
Officers: Edwin Polokoff, Chair.; Richard B. McCormick, Vice-Chair.; William L. Van Schoonhoven, Dir. and Secy.
Governing Committee: Ronald J. Anthony, Mrs. Robert S. Grantham, Mrs. Warren W. Lane, John T. Smythe, Paul A. Willax.
Trustee Banks: Key Trust Co., Manufacturers and Traders Trust Co., Marine Bank West, Norstar Bank, N.A.
Number of staff: 2 full-time professional; 2 full-time support; 1 part-time support.
Employer Identification Number: 160743935
Recent arts and culture grants:
Albright-Knox Art Gallery, Buffalo, NY, $16,014. For development program. 1987.
Buffalo Lighthouse Association, Buffalo, NY, $5,000. For stone work repair. 1987.
Buffalo Philharmonic Orchestra Society, Buffalo, NY, $35,000. For annual fund drive. 1987.
Buffalo Philharmonic Orchestra Society, Buffalo, NY, $14,514. For unrestricted use, operating budget. 1987.
Buffalo Society of Natural Sciences, Buffalo, NY, $10,000. For video disc system. 1987.
Carousel Society of Niagara Frontier, Buffalo, NY, $5,000. For Roundhouse rehabilitation. 1987.
Greater Buffalo Development Foundation, Buffalo, NY, $5,000. For Cultural Arts Fiscal Study. 1987.
Sheas Buffalo Theater, Buffalo, NY, $7,500. For new phone system. 1987.
Studio Arena Theater, Buffalo, NY, $10,000. For capital fund drive. 1987.
Ujima Theater Company, Buffalo, NY, $5,680. For furniture and equipment. 1987.
Zoological Society of Buffalo, Buffalo, NY, $25,000. For Free the Cats Campaign. 1987.
Zoological Society of Buffalo, Buffalo, NY, $6,338. For Free the Cats Campaign. 1987.

1809
Charles E. Burchfield Foundation, Inc.
210 Convention Tower
Buffalo 14202 (716) 853-7338

Incorporated in 1966 in NY.
Donor(s): Charles E. Burchfield.†
Financial data (yr. ended 12/31/87): Assets, $2,356,522 (M); expenditures, $76,718,

including $32,000 for 11 grants (high: $15,000; low: $2,000; average: $2,500-$20,000) and $3 for grants to individuals.
Purpose and activities: Support for Lutheran religious and charitable organizations, including a local program for disadvantaged youth and international programs for relief and medical assistance.
Types of support: Operating budgets, continuing support, building funds, matching funds.
Publications: Annual report.
Application information:
Initial approach: Letter
Deadline(s): None
Board meeting date(s): Spring and fall
Write: Robert J. Schutrum, Sr., Treas.
Officers and Trustees: C. Arthur Burchfield, Pres.; Sally Hill, V.P.; Robert J. Schutrum, Sr., Secy.-Treas.; Violet Burchfield, George Hill.
Number of staff: 1 full-time professional; 2 part-time professional.
Employer Identification Number: 166073522
Recent arts and culture grants:
Columbus Museum of Art, Columbus, OH, $15,000. 11/30/87.

1810
Florence V. Burden Foundation
630 Fifth Ave., Suite 2900
New York 10111 (212) 489-1063

Incorporated in 1967 in NY.
Donor(s): Florence V. Burden,† and members of her family.
Financial data (yr. ended 12/31/87): Assets, $12,225,311 (M); expenditures, $1,090,546, including $758,405 for 59 grants (high: $57,000; low: $175; average: $5,000-$50,000).
Purpose and activities: Support primarily in two fields of concentration: aging and crime and justice; emphasis on practical approaches to solving problems, implementation, management improvement, and continuing research.
Types of support: Seed money, special projects, research.
Limitations: Giving primarily in the Eastern U.S. with an emphasis on New York, NY. No grants to individuals, or for capital or endowment funds, operating expenses, annual campaigns, emergency funds, deficit financing, scholarships, fellowships, or matching gifts; no loans.
Publications: Annual report (including application guidelines).
Application information: Proposals accepted for crime and justice and elderly programs only. Application form required.
Initial approach: Letter of intent
Copies of proposal: 1
Deadline(s): Submit letter of intent by Apr. 1, Aug. 1 or Dec. 1; deadlines for applications Jan. 1, May 1, and Sept. 1
Board meeting date(s): Feb., June, and Oct.
Final notification: 2 weeks after board meeting
Write: Barbara R. Greenberg, Exec. Dir.
Officers and Directors: Marvin Bower, Chair.; Shirley C. Burden, V.P.; William L. Musser, Jr., Treas.; Barbara R. Greenberg, Exec. Dir.; Robert R. Barker, Carter Burden, Margaret L. Burden, Ordway P. Burden, Susan L. Burden, Margaret B. Childs, Robert F. Higgins, John W. Holman, Jr., Stephen R. Petschek, John H. Watts III.
Number of staff: 2 full-time professional; 1 part-time support.
Employer Identification Number: 136224125
Recent arts and culture grants:
W G B H Educational Foundation, Boston, MA, $25,000. For Violence Prevention Television Project. 6/21/88.

1811
Jacob Burns Foundation, Inc.
c/o Jacob Burns
60 East 42nd St.
New York 10165 (212) 867-0949

Incorporated in 1957 in NY.
Donor(s): Mary Elizabeth Hood,† Jacob Burns, Rosalie A. Goldberg.
Financial data (yr. ended 12/31/87): Assets, $9,647,200 (M); gifts received, $122,780; expenditures, $940,369, including $863,009 for 72 grants (high: $273,500; low: $50).
Purpose and activities: Giving primarily for education, Jewish organizations, law and civil rights organizations, cultural programs, religious organizations, and hospitals and medical research.
Limitations: Giving primarily in NY. No grants to individuals.
Application information: Contributes only to pre-selected organizations. Applications not accepted.
Officers: Jacob Burns, Pres. and Treas.; Rosalie A. Goldberg, V.P. and Secy.
Employer Identification Number: 136114245

1812
The Bydale Foundation
299 Park Ave., 17th Fl.
New York 10171 (212) 207-1968

Incorporated in 1965 in DE.
Donor(s): James P. Warburg.†
Financial data (yr. ended 12/31/88): Assets, $8,721,881 (M); expenditures, $624,327, including $514,750 for 61 grants (high: $50,000; low: $500; average: $2,500-$15,000).
Purpose and activities: Emphasis on international understanding, public policy research, environmental quality, cultural programs, the law and civil rights, social services, higher education, and economics.
Types of support: Operating budgets, continuing support, seed money, matching funds, research, publications, conferences and seminars, special projects, general purposes.
Limitations: No grants to individuals, or for annual campaigns, emergency funds, deficit financing, endowment funds, demonstration projects, capital funds, scholarships, or fellowships; no loans.
Application information:
Initial approach: Letter or proposal
Copies of proposal: 1
Deadline(s): Submit proposal preferably in July or Aug.; deadline Nov. 1
Board meeting date(s): June, Nov., and Dec.
Final notification: 2 or 3 weeks
Write: Milton D. Solomon, V.P.
Officers: Joan M. Warburg,* Pres.; Milton D. Solomon,* V.P. and Secy.; Frank J. Kick, Treas.
Trustees:* Sarah W. Bliumis, James P. Warburg, Jr., Jenny Warburg, Philip N. Warburg.
Number of staff: 1 part-time professional.
Employer Identification Number: 136195286

1813
The Louis Calder Foundation
230 Park Ave., Rm. 1530
New York 10169 (212) 687-1680

Trust established in 1951 in NY.
Donor(s): Louis Calder.†
Financial data (yr. ended 10/31/88): Assets, $96,775,081 (M); expenditures, $5,446,703, including $4,383,060 for 165 grants (high: $200,000; low: $4,700; average: $15,000-$50,000).
Purpose and activities: To support mainly those programs deemed best calculated to promote health, education, and welfare of New York City residents through grants to established organizations. Current programs are designed to enhance the potential and increase self-sufficiency of children, youth, and their families.
Types of support: Operating budgets, equipment, special projects, research, scholarship funds, general purposes.
Limitations: Giving primarily in New York, NY. No support for publicly-operated educational or medical institutions, private foundations, or governmental organizations; cultural grants only to well-known and established institutions. No grants to individuals; generally no grants for building or endowment funds, capital development, or continuing support.
Publications: Annual report (including application guidelines).
Application information:
Initial approach: Letter to the attention of the Trustees
Copies of proposal: 1
Deadline(s): Submit proposal between Nov. 1 and Mar. 31; deadline Mar. 31
Board meeting date(s): As required
Final notification: July 31
Write: The Trustees
Trustees: Paul R. Brenner, Peter D. Calder, Manufacturers Hanover Trust Co.
Number of staff: 1 full-time support.
Employer Identification Number: 136015562
Recent arts and culture grants:
Affiliate Artists, NYC, NY, $50,000. To support general operations during 1987-88 program year and to augment cash reserves. 1987.
Arts Connection, NYC, NY, $30,000. To support enhancement of counseling and tutoring components of Young Talent program during 1987-88 program year. 1987.
Boys Choir of Harlem, NYC, NY, $15,000. To support tutoring and counseling service components of their programs. 1987.
Brooklyn Academy of Music, Brooklyn, NY, $57,000. To support Performing Arts for Young People program during 1986-87 and 1987-88 program years. 1987.
Brooklyn Childrens Museum, Brooklyn, NY, $20,000. To support educational programs for young people. 1987.

Brooklyn Conservatory of Music, Brooklyn, NY, $10,000. To support financial aid program and assist students enrolled in Childrens Division. 1987.
Carnegie Hall Society, NYC, NY, $30,000. To support Childrens Education Program. 1987.
Cathedral Church of Saint John the Divine, NYC, NY, $10,000. To support Cathedral Free Concert Series and other Great Space programs. 1987.
Childrens Art Carnival, NYC, NY, $5,000. To support current arts instruction and training programs. 1987.
Childrens Museum of Manhattan, NYC, NY, $15,000. To support current programs and projects of Education Department. 1987.
Church of Saint Joseph, Bronxville, NY, $50,000. To be used exclusively for purchase and installation, including preparation of church space, of new organ. 1987.
Council for the Arts in Westchester, White Plains, NY, $50,000. To support establishment of Teacher Training Center in Yonkers Public School System. 1987.
Educational Broadcasting Corporation, NYC, NY, $50,000. To support production of METROLINE documentary on youth unemployment. 1987.
Fifty-Fifth Street Dance Theater Foundation, NYC, NY, $25,000. To support services to performing arts organizations and general operations of City Center Theater. 1987.
Fools Company, NYC, NY, $5,000. To support citywide Artsworker Apprentices program. 1987.
Harlem School of the Arts, NYC, NY, $30,000. To support Release Time Program for students from New York City public schools. 1987.
Jamaica Center for the Performing and Visual Arts, Jamaica, NY, $15,000. To support Education and Family programs. 1987.
Joffrey Ballet, Foundation for the, NYC, NY, $20,000. To support Joffrey II Dancers during 1987-88 program year. 1987.
Lincoln Center for the Performing Arts, Lincoln Center Institute for Arts in Education, NYC, NY, $20,000. Toward elementary and secondary school educational programs. 1987.
Manhattan School of Music, NYC, NY, $10,000. To support Public Service Music Project during 1987-88 and 1988-89 academic years. 1987.
New York Botanical Garden, Bronx, NY, $10,000. To support Children's Education Program. 1987.
New York City Opera, NYC, NY, $25,000. To support current programs and projects of Education Department. 1987.
New York Zoological Society, Bronx, NY, $25,000. To support children's programs of Education Department. 1987.
Paper Bag Players, NYC, NY, $7,500. To support program providing free weekday performances for New York City public school children. 1987.
Saint Lukes Chamber Ensemble, NYC, NY, $5,000. To support Children's Free Opera and Dance program. 1987.
South Street Seaport Museum, NYC, NY, $20,000. To support Public School Project and expansion of programming for New York City public school students. 1987.
Staten Island Childrens Museum, Staten Island, NY, $15,000. To support educational programs. 1987.
Theater for the New City Foundation, NYC, NY, $25,000. To support community outreach programs including Summer Street Theater and Free Admission Program. 1987.
Town Hall Foundation, NYC, NY, $15,000. To support programs and activities for New York City school children. 1987.
Wave Hill, Bronx, NY, $15,000. To support environmental education programs for New York City school children and their teachers. 1987.
Whitney Museum of American Art, NYC, NY, $40,000. To support Artreach program for New York City public school children during 1987-88 and 1988-89 school years. 1987.

1814
The Ed Lee and Jean Campe Foundation, Inc.

c/o U.S. Trust Co. of NY
45 Wall St.
New York 10005 (212) 269-4310

Incorporated in 1944 in NY.
Donor(s): Ed Lee Campe,† Jean Campe.†
Financial data (yr. ended 12/31/86): Assets, $1,395,858 (M); expenditures, $136,398, including $123,260 for grants (high: $15,000; average: $100-$5,000).
Purpose and activities: Giving largely for higher education, including scholarship funds and musical education, community funds, Jewish welfare funds, and youth and social agencies.
Types of support: Scholarship funds, general purposes, continuing support, building funds, endowment funds, special projects.
Limitations: Giving primarily in NY. No grants to individuals, or for matching gifts; no loans.
Application information:
Initial approach: Letter
Copies of proposal: 1
Deadline(s): Submit proposal between Jan. and Mar.
Board meeting date(s): Apr.
Write: Henry Kohn, Pres.
Officers and Directors: Henry Kohn, Pres.; Anne F. Kohn, V.P.; Herbert A. Schneider, Secy.
Number of staff: None.
Employer Identification Number: 136123939

1815
B. G. Cantor Art Foundation

One World Trade Ctr., Suite 10500
New York 10048

Established in 1967 in NY.
Donor(s): B.G. Cantor.
Financial data (yr. ended 4/30/87): Assets, $5,034,338 (M); gifts received, $831,999; expenditures, $2,043,495, including $1,707,650 for 52 grants (high: $250,000; low: $125).
Purpose and activities: Support for exhibits and studies of the work of Rodin.
Application information: Contributes only to pre-selected organizations. Applications not accepted.
Officers: B.G. Cantor,* Pres. and Treas.; Harry Needleman, Secy.
Trustees:* Peter Bing, Iris Cantor, Rod Fisher, Michael Spero.
Employer Identification Number: 136227347

1816
Cantor, Fitzgerald Foundation

One World Trade Ctr., Suite 10500
New York 10048

Established in 1982 in NY.
Donor(s): Cantor Fitzgerald Securities Corp.
Financial data (yr. ended 12/31/87): Assets, $367,672 (M); gifts received, $250,000; expenditures, $169,385, including $169,113 for 51 grants (high: $100,000; low: $100).
Purpose and activities: Emphasis on Jewish organizations, including charities, cultural and community affairs, and the arts.
Limitations: Giving primarily in NY and CA.
Officers: B. Gerald Cantor,* Pres.; Harry Needleman, Secy.; Joel Rothstein, Treas.
Directors:* James M. Avena, Rod Fisher.
Employer Identification Number: 133117872

1817
Capital Cities/ABC Foundation, Inc.

77 West 66th St., Rm. 16-15
New York 10023 (212) 887-7498

Incorporated in 1974 in DE.
Donor(s): Capital Cities Communications, Inc.
Financial data (yr. ended 11/30/87): Assets, $1,696,255 (M); gifts received, $1,500,000; expenditures, $1,309,017, including $1,306,838 for 123 grants (high: $142,000; low: $50; average: $1,000-$20,000).
Purpose and activities: Grants for higher education, hospitals, health agencies, and local minority development; some support for social service agencies, civic affairs, communications, cultural programs, and youth agencies.
Limitations: Giving primarily in areas where company properties are located. No grants to individuals, or for building funds.
Application information: Contributes only to preselected organizations. Applications not accepted.
Board meeting date(s): Quarterly
Write: Bernadette Longford-Williams, Contribs. Admin.
Officers: Thomas S. Murphy, Pres.; Daniel B. Burke, V.P. and Treas.; Andrew E. Jackson, V.P.
Employer Identification Number: 237443020

1818
Carnegie Corporation of New York

437 Madison Ave.
New York 10022 (212) 371-3200

Incorporated in 1911 in NY.
Donor(s): Andrew Carnegie.†
Financial data (yr. ended 9/30/88): Assets, $803,404,682 (M); expenditures, $44,990,868, including $35,512,429 for 381 grants (high: $750,000; low: $975) and $1,503,127 for 8 foundation-administered programs.

Purpose and activities: The advancement and diffusion of knowledge and understanding among the peoples of the U.S. and of certain countries that are or have been members of the British overseas Commonwealth. In 1984 the foundation announced four program goals: 1) The avoidance of nuclear war and improvement in U.S.-Soviet relations through support for science-based analyses of ways in which the risk of nuclear war can be diminished and for efforts to ensure that the results of such analyses are widely known and understood. This program emphasizes the mobilization of the best possible intellectual, technical, and moral resources to work toward this objective. 2) The education of all Americans, especially youth, for a scientifically and technologically based economy, linking the movement for education reform to changes in society and the economy. This program draws upon the Corporation's past interests in the education of children, youth, and adults and particularly its commitment to equity for women and members of minority groups. 3) The prevention of damage to children from birth through early adolescence. This program focuses on ways to prevent the development of serious problems for children and young teenagers, primarily school failure and school-age pregnancy and secondarily childhood injury and substance abuse. It continues the foundation's interests in early education and child care. 4) Strengthening human resources in developing countries. This program aims to engage the scientific and scholarly communities in the U.S. and developing countries in this effort and to heighten American understanding of Third World development. Giving primarily to academic and research institutions.
Types of support: Operating budgets, continuing support, seed money, program-related investments, special projects, research, publications, conferences and seminars, exchange programs, general purposes, fellowships.
Limitations: Giving primarily in the U.S. Some grants in Sub-Saharan Africa, South Africa, and the Caribbean. No support for the arts, operating budgets of educational institutions or day care centers, or general support for social service agencies. No grants for annual campaigns, deficit financing, capital, building, or endowment funds, scholarships, or matching gifts.
Publications: Annual report, informational brochure, newsletter.
Application information:
Initial approach: Telephone or letter
Deadline(s): None
Board meeting date(s): Oct., Dec., Feb., Apr., and June
Final notification: 6 months
Write: Dorothy Knapp, Secy.
Officers: David A. Hamburg,* Pres.; Barbara D. Finberg, Exec. V.P. and Prog. Chair., Special Projects; Dorothy Knapp, Secy.; Jeanmarie C. Grisi, Treas.
Trustees:* Helene L. Kaplan, Chair.; Fred M. Hechinger, Vice-Chair.; Richard I. Beattie, Warren Christopher, Eugene H. Cota-Robles, Richard B. Fisher, James Lowell Gibbs, Jr., Joshua Lederberg, Ann R. Leven, Ray Marshall, Mary Patterson McPherson, Newton N. Minow, Laurence A. Tisch, Thomas A. Troyer, John C. Whitehead, Sheila E. Widnall.
Number of staff: 22 full-time professional; 3 part-time professional; 25 full-time support; 3 part-time support.
Employer Identification Number: 131628151
Recent arts and culture grants:
Action for Childrens Television, Cambridge, MA, $20,000. Toward projects to improve children's television. 4/21/88.
Childrens Television Workshop, NYC, NY, $300,000. Toward production of television series about mathematics for children. 10/8/87.
Childrens Television Workshop, NYC, NY, $250,000. Toward planning television series on reading and writing for children. 6/18/87.
Educational Broadcasting Corporation, NYC, NY, $250,000. Toward production of television series on U.S.-Soviet relations. 6/18/87.
National Humanities Center, Research Triangle Park, NC, $16,500. Toward radio programs on education. 2/18/88.
National Public Radio, DC, $200,000. Toward coverage of 1988 presidential campaign. 4/21/88.
Nebraskans for Public Television, Lincoln, NE, $150,000. Toward production of television science programs for primary school children. 10/8/87.
Science Museum of Connecticut, West Hartford, CT, $300,000. Toward program of elementary and secondary mathematics and science enrichment for minority students in Connecticut. 4/21/88.
W G B H Educational Foundation, Boston, MA, $400,000. Toward production, promotion, and educational research for television series for early adolescents. 12/10/87.
W G B H Educational Foundation, Boston, MA, $400,000. Toward support of educational television series and course on Latin America and the Caribbean. 4/21/88.
W G B H Educational Foundation, Boston, MA, $25,000. For symposium on children's television. 10/8/87.
W G B H Educational Foundation, Boston, MA, $25,000. Toward audience research and promotion for television series for early adolescents. 10/8/87.
Western New York Public Broadcasting, Buffalo, NY, $25,000. For production and evaluation of teacher's guides for instructional television broadcasts. 12/10/87.
Worldwide Documentaries, Rochester, NY, $25,000. Toward production and distribution of film on South African church leader. 10/8/87.

1819
Carrier Corporation Community Programs
Carrier Pkwy
P.O. Box 4808, ARC Bldg.
Syracuse 13221 (315) 433-4787

Financial data (yr. ended 12/31/88): Total giving, $850,000, including $650,000 for grants (average: $500-$5,000) and $200,000 for employee matching gifts.
Purpose and activities: Supports education, health, hospitals, social services, volunteerism, culture and civic groups.
Types of support: Matching funds, capital campaigns, general purposes, scholarship funds, employee matching gifts.
Limitations: Giving primarily in headquarters city and major operating locations.
Application information: Include organization description, amount requested, purpose for funding, recently audited financial statement, 501 (c)(3) status letter.
Initial approach: Brief letter or proposal
Copies of proposal: 1
Deadline(s): None
Board meeting date(s): Preliminary budget preparation-July through Sept. 15
Final notification: Feb.
Write: Patricia W. Gonzalez, Dir., Community Programs
Number of staff: 1 full-time professional; 1 full-time support.

1820
The Carter-Wallace Foundation
767 Fifth Ave.
New York 10153 (212) 758-4500

Established in 1986 in NY.
Donor(s): Carter-Wallace, Inc.
Financial data (yr. ended 3/31/87): Assets, $990,236 (M); gifts received, $900,000; expenditures, $844,952, including $822,220 for 140 grants (high: $45,000; low: $20).
Purpose and activities: Support primarily for arts, health, welfare and higher education.
Officers: Henry H. Hoyt, Jr., Pres.; Charles O. Hoyt, Secy.; Daniel J. Black, Treas.; James L. Wagar, Mgr.
Employer Identification Number: 133359226

1821
Mary Flagler Cary Charitable Trust
350 Fifth Ave., Rm. 6622
New York 10118 (212) 563-6860

Trust established in 1968 in NY.
Donor(s): Mary Flagler Cary.†
Financial data (yr. ended 6/30/88): Assets, $103,146,182 (M); expenditures, $7,697,215, including $6,538,874 for 88 grants (high: $3,025,000; low: $2,500; average: $15,000-$50,000).
Purpose and activities: The trust entertains grant proposals in two areas: for music in New York City (including institutional support for commissioning, recording and performance of contemporary music, and support for community music schools); and for the conservation of natural resources (restricted to the preservation of barrier islands and beaches along the eastern coastal states, with grant funds directed toward land acquisition and legal protection; and to the support of the urban environment in low-income neighborhoods of New York City). The balance of the trust's grant budget is devoted primarily to testamentary obligations or to established commitments; in particular, support for the collections established by the donor and for The Mary Flagler Cary Arboretum in Millbrook, NY.

Types of support: Operating budgets, continuing support, land acquisition, matching funds, special projects, program-related investments, general purposes.
Limitations: Giving limited to New York City, NY, for music and the eastern coastal states for conservation. No support for private foundations, hospitals, religious organizations, primary or secondary schools, or colleges and universities or libraries or museums (other than those with programs supported by family collections). No grants to individuals, or for scholarships, fellowships, capital funds, annual campaigns, seed money, emergency funds, deficit financing, or endowment funds; no loans to individuals.
Publications: Informational brochure (including application guidelines), grants list.
Application information:
Initial approach: Letter with brief proposal
Copies of proposal: 1
Deadline(s): None
Board meeting date(s): Monthly
Final notification: 2 months
Write: Edward A. Ames, Trustee
Trustees: Edward A. Ames, William R. Grant, Herbert J. Jacobi.
Number of staff: 2 full-time professional; 1 full-time support.
Employer Identification Number: 136266964
Recent arts and culture grants:
Alternative Center for International Arts, NYC, NY, $8,500. Toward 1987-88 music program. 12/1/87.
American Music Center, NYC, NY, $200,000. For support of live music for opera and dance. 8/3/88.
American Music Center, NYC, NY, $100,000. Toward Pocket Orchestra Project. 5/29/87.
American Music Center, NYC, NY, $25,000. Toward Margaret Fairbank Jory Copying Program. 1/6/88.
American Music Center, NYC, NY, $12,100. For administrative costs associated with live music for opera and dance. 8/3/88.
American Music Center, NYC, NY, $7,000. For administrative costs associated with Pocket Orchestra Project. 10/1/87.
Augustine Fine Arts, Bronx, NY, $10,000. For general support. 6/3/88.
Boys Choir of Harlem, NYC, NY, $7,500. For general support. 4/6/88.
Boys Harbor, NYC, NY, $12,500. Toward Harbor Performing Arts Center. 12/1/87.
Brooklyn Academy of Music, Brooklyn, NY, $35,000. Toward 1987 Next Wave Festival. 8/5/87.
Brooklyn Music School, Brooklyn, NY, $10,000. For general support. 12/1/87.
Bryant Park Restoration Corporation, NYC, NY, $10,000. For support of Bryant Park music and dance half-price tickets booth. 3/1/88.
Composers Forum, NYC, NY, $13,000. Toward New York concert series. 9/1/87.
Concert Artists Guild, NYC, NY, $250,000. Toward support for recording program. 5/10/88.
Concert Artists Guild, NYC, NY, $101,000. Toward support for commission program. 4/6/88.
Concert Artists Guild, NYC, NY, $100,000. Toward commissioning program for professional chamber, jazz and new music ensembles, orchestras, choral ensembles and presenting organizations based in New York City. 10/1/87.
Concert Artists Guild, NYC, NY, $12,500. For administrative costs associated with 1988 Recording Program. 5/10/88.
Concert Artists Guild, NYC, NY, $5,050. For administrative costs associated with 1988 commissioning program. 4/6/88.
Concert Artists Guild, NYC, NY, $5,000. For administrative costs associated with commissioning program. 10/1/87.
Dance Theater of Harlem, NYC, NY, $15,000. Toward Universal Symphony's participation in Dance Theater's 1988 City Center season. 6/29/88.
Dance Theater Workshop, NYC, NY, $10,000. Toward 1987-88 Economy Tires Music series. 11/4/87.
Elaine Summers Experimental Intermedia Foundation, NYC, NY, $6,000. Toward 1987-88 concert series, Concerts By Composers. 1/6/88.
Emigre Orchestra, NYC, NY, $5,000. Toward 1987-88 New York concert season. 9/1/87.
Greenwich House Music School, NYC, NY, $15,000. For general support. 10/1/87.
Greenwich House Music School, NYC, NY, $15,000. Toward refurbishment of roof on school building. 4/6/88.
Gregg Smith Singers, NYC, NY, $5,000. For support of 1987-88 New York concert season. 3/1/88.
Harlem School of the Arts, NYC, NY, $20,000. For general support of school's music program. 6/3/88.
Harlem School of the Arts, NYC, NY, $15,000. For general support of school's music program. 6/25/87.
Hebrew Arts School, NYC, NY, $12,500. For general support of Young People's Division. 10/1/87.
Hebrew Arts School, NYC, NY, $10,000. Toward Music Today series at Merkin Concert Hall. 9/1/87.
Henry Street Settlement, NYC, NY, $15,000. For general support of Music School. 11/4/87.
Jupiter Symphony of New York, NYC, NY, $23,500. Toward support for board and fundraising development project. 8/5/87.
Meet the Composer, NYC, NY, $25,000. To enable composers to collaborate with opera/music theater and dance companies in New York City. 2/3/88.
Musical Elements/Daniel Asia, NYC, NY, $5,000. Toward 1987-88 concert season. 5/10/88.
New York Botanical Garden, Bronx, NY, $1,600,000. For supplement to Cary Arboretum Endowment Fund. 6/25/87.
New York Botanical Garden, Bronx, NY, $1,300,000. Toward partial prepayment of operating expenses for Cary Arboretum. 8/3/88.
New York Botanical Garden, Bronx, NY, $600,000. Toward Cary Building Fund for repair of roof on Plant Science Building at Cary Arboretum. 8/3/88.
New York Botanical Garden, Bronx, NY, $98,140. Toward capital grant to strengthen and modernize library of Institute of Ecosystem Studies at Cary Arboretum. 12/1/87.
New York Botanical Garden, Bronx, NY, $70,000. For capital improvements at Cary Arboretum (growth chambers in Pole barn). 1/6/88.
New York Botanical Garden, Bronx, NY, $69,524. Toward supplementary grant for operations of Cary Arboretum. 1988.
New York Youth Symphony, NYC, NY, $15,000. Toward symphony's 1988-89 First Music program. 4/6/88.
New York Youth Symphony, NYC, NY, $5,000. For general support. 4/6/88.
Performers Committee, NYC, NY, $5,000. For 1987-88 New York concert season. 1/6/88.
Philharmania Virtuosi Corporation, NYC, NY, $25,000. Toward 1987-88 Town Hall concert series. 11/4/87.
Pierpont Morgan Library, NYC, NY, $68,000. Toward Mary Flagler Cary Music Collection 20th Anniversary exhibition. 1/6/88.
Pierpont Morgan Library, NYC, NY, $15,000. Toward cost of Stravinsky manuscript for addition to Mary Flagler Cary Music Collection. 2/88.
Queens Symphony Orchestra, Rego Park, NY, $6,000. Toward Orchestra's contemporary music series entitled Sounds from the Left Bank. 3/1/88.
Roosa School of Music, Brooklyn, NY, $15,000. For general support. 4/6/88.
Roulette Intermedium, NYC, NY, $10,000. Toward 1987-88 concert season. 9/1/87.
Society for the Preservation of Weeksville and Bedford Stuyvesant History, Brooklyn, NY, $15,000. For general support. 5/10/88.
Solisti New York, NYC, NY, $10,000. For support of 1987-88 New York concert season. 3/1/88.
Third Street Music School Settlement, Society of the, NYC, NY, $20,000. For general support. 4/6/88.
Turtle Bay Music School, NYC, NY, $15,000. For general support. 4/6/88.
World Music Institute, NYC, NY, $10,000. Toward 1988 Improvisations! Festival of Contemporary Music from American tradition. 2/3/88.
YM-YWHA, 92nd Street, NYC, NY, $15,000. For scholarship program of 92nd Street Y School of Music. 10/1/87.

1822
CBS Foundation, Inc.
51 West 52nd St.
New York 10019 (212) 975-5791

Incorporated in 1953 in NY.
Donor(s): CBS, Inc.
Financial data (yr. ended 12/31/87): Assets, $5,411,759 (M); gifts received, $638,908; expenditures, $272,790, including $257,316 for 3 grants (high: $204,316; low: $3,000; average: $10,000-$50,000).
Purpose and activities: Grants primarily for higher education, cultural affairs, the performing and fine arts, and civic affairs.
Types of support: Annual campaigns, continuing support, general purposes, operating budgets, research.
Limitations: Giving primarily in areas of company operations. No grants to individuals, or for building or endowment funds, or matching gifts; no loans.

Application information:
Initial approach: Letter
Copies of proposal: 1
Deadline(s): None
Board meeting date(s): Quarterly and as required
Final notification: 4 months
Write: Helen M. Brown, V.P. and Exec. Dir.
Officers: H.P. MacCowatt, Pres.; Helen M. Brown, V.P. and Exec. Dir.; Charles T. Bates, Secy.; Louis J. Rauchenberger, Treas.
Directors: Newton N. Minow, Chair.; Michel C. Bergerac, Walter L. Cronkite, Roswell L. Gilpatric, Franklin A. Thomas.
Number of staff: None.
Employer Identification Number: 136099759

1823
Centennial Foundation
c/o Joel E. Sammet & Co.
19 Rector St.
New York 10006

Incorporated in 1965 in NY.
Donor(s): Henry H. Arnhold, Arnold S. Bleienroeder, and others.
Financial data (yr. ended 12/31/87): Assets, $1,622,625 (M); gifts received, $219,989; expenditures, $194,575, including $187,410 for 125 grants (high: $25,000; low: $100).
Purpose and activities: Giving for hospitals and health agencies, international relations, community development, the performing arts, and education.
Limitations: Giving primarily in New York, NY.
Application information: Contributes only to pre-selected organizations. Applications not accepted.
Officers: Stephen M. Kellen, Chair.; Henry H. Arnhold,* Pres.
Trustees:* Michael Kellen, Gilbert Kerlin.
Employer Identification Number: 136189397

1824
Central New York Community Foundation, Inc.
500 South Salina St., Suite 428
Syracuse 13202 (315) 422-9538

Community foundation incorporated in 1927 in NY; reorganized in 1951.
Financial data (yr. ended 3/31/88): Assets, $13,667,747 (M); gifts received, $1,960,816; expenditures, $2,238,434, including $1,918,394 for 341 grants (high: $129,773; low: $25; average: $2,000-$12,000).
Purpose and activities: Grants primarily to existing agencies for health, welfare, educational, recreational, or cultural purposes.
Types of support: Continuing support, seed money, emergency funds, building funds, equipment, special projects, matching funds, capital campaigns, technical assistance, renovation projects.
Limitations: Giving limited to Onondaga and Madison counties, NY for general grants; giving in a wider area for donor-advised funds. No support for religious purposes. No grants to individuals, or for conferences and seminars, deficit financing, consulting services, endowment funds, scholarships, fellowships, land acquisition, operating budgets, publications, travel expenses, purchase of vehicles, or research; no loans.
Publications: Annual report, application guidelines.
Application information: Application form required.
Initial approach: Letter or telephone
Copies of proposal: 12
Deadline(s): 6 weeks before board meetings
Board meeting date(s): Mar., May, Sept., and Dec.
Final notification: Immediately following board meetings
Write: Margaret G. Ogden, Pres.
Officers: Margaret G. Ogden, Pres. and C.E.O.; Richard A. Russell,* Treas.
Directors:* N. Earle Evans, Chair.; Edward S. Green, 1st Vice-Chair.; Ernest L. Sarason, 2nd Vice-Chair.; Sara Barclay, David J. Connor, Maceo Felton, Burnett D. Haylor, H. Follett Hodgkins, Jr., Richard Horowitz, Robert J. Hughes, Clarence L. Jordan, Michael Rulison, Robert Salisbury, Miriam Swift, Jay W. Wason, Samuel W. Williams, Peggy Wood.
Number of staff: 2 full-time professional; 1 full-time support.
Employer Identification Number: 150626910

1825
Dorothy Jordan Chadwick Fund
c/o U.S. Trust Co. of New York
45 Wall St.
New York 10005 (212) 425-4500
Application address: Davidson Dawson & Clark, P.O. Box 298, New Canaan, CT 06840

Trust established in 1957 in NY.
Donor(s): Dorothy J. Chadwick,† Dorothy R. Kidder.
Financial data (yr. ended 5/31/87): Assets, $7,735,562 (M); gifts received, $100,000; expenditures, $299,925, including $236,000 for 30 grants (high: $50,000; low: $1,000).
Purpose and activities: Grants largely for the arts including the performing arts; support also for higher education.
Limitations: Giving primarily in New York City, NY, and Washington, DC.
Application information:
Initial approach: Proposal
Copies of proposal: 1
Deadline(s): None
Board meeting date(s): As required
Write: Berkeley D. Johnson, Jr., Trustee
Trustees: Berkeley D. Johnson, Jr., U.S. Trust Co. of New York.
Employer Identification Number: 136069950

1826
Charina Foundation, Inc.
85 Broad St.
New York 10004

Incorporated in 1980 in NY.
Donor(s): Richard L. Menschel, The Menschel Foundation.
Financial data (yr. ended 8/31/87): Assets, $9,147,287 (M); gifts received, $2,324,392; expenditures, $322,153, including $314,882 for 198 grants (high: $91,667; low: $100; average: $500-$2,500).
Purpose and activities: Emphasis on arts and culture; support also for health services, higher education, and Jewish organizations.
Limitations: Giving primarily in NY. No grants to individuals.
Application information: Foundation depends almost exclusively on self-initiated grants. Applications not accepted.
Write: Richard L. Menschel, Pres.
Officers and Directors: Richard L. Menschel, Pres. and Treas.; Ronay Menschel, Secy.; Eugene P. Polk.
Number of staff: None.
Employer Identification Number: 133050294

1827
Chase Manhattan Corporation Philanthropy Department
44 Wall St., 14th Fl.
New York 10005 (212) 676-5080
Applications from upper New York State: Government Relations, Philanthropic Activities, Chase Lincoln First Bank, N.A., 1 Lincoln First Sq., Rochester NY 14643

Financial data (yr. ended 12/31/88): Total giving, $10,711,710, including $9,879,069 for 1,608 grants, $67,185 for 25 grants to individuals and $765,456 for 3,465 employee matching gifts.
Purpose and activities: The corporate contributions program is directed by Chase Manhattan's Corporate Responsibility Committee, whose members also serve as trustees of the foundation. Support is for culture and the arts, education, AIDS, health and human services, the handicapped, international relief, literacy, urban development, women, housing development, neighborhood and economic development, and public policy and economic education. In addition, Chase donates equipment, supports fundraisers, and provides executive-on-loan services.
Types of support: Scholarship funds, employee-related scholarships, employee matching gifts, capital campaigns, general purposes, operating budgets, special projects, continuing support, in-kind gifts.
Limitations: Giving primarily in headquarters city and state and national operating locations. No support for religious, fraternal, or veterans' organizations; international organizations or programs (generally funded only through the Chase Manhattan Foundation). No grants to individuals, except for National Merit Scholarship Program; member organizations of the United Way(s), to which the company already contibutes; endowment funds.
Publications: Corporate giving report.
Application information: In proposal, include history, goals and accomplishments of organization, and a one-page description of present activities, purpose and amount requested for project,and current budget, including anticipated expenses and income; complete current donor list and amounts given; most recent audited financial statement, or last year's IRS form 990; annual report; number of professional and support staff, including name and title of highest paid staff member; and board list.
Initial approach: Two-page letter of inquiry; for Neighborhood Grants Program,

application form can be obtained from a Chase branch beginning in early Jan.
Copies of proposal: 1
Final notification: For Neighborhood Grants Program: June
Write: David Ford, V.P. and Dir. of Philanthropy

Number of staff: 6 full-time professional; 2 full-time support.

1828
Chautauqua Region Community Foundation, Inc.
812 Hotel Jamestown Bldg.
Jamestown 14701 (716) 661-3390

Incorporated in 1978 in NY.
Financial data (yr. ended 12/31/88): Assets, $8,247,217 (M); gifts received, $1,536,450; expenditures, $721,288, including $360,828 for 45 grants (high: $44,000; low: $370; average: $2,500-$8,000) and $200,543 for 239 grants to individuals.
Purpose and activities: Giving for cultural, educational, civic, and charitable projects; scholarships mainly for undergraduate study.
Types of support: Operating budgets, continuing support, seed money, emergency funds, equipment, publications, conferences and seminars, student aid, general purposes, renovation projects.
Limitations: Giving limited to the Chautauqua, NY, area. No support for religious or sectarian purposes. No grants to individuals (except for scholarship grants); no loans.
Publications: Annual report (including application guidelines), informational brochure, newsletter.
Application information: Application form required.
Initial approach: Letter
Copies of proposal: 11
Deadline(s): Feb. 28 for scholarships; Nov. 30 for other grants
Board meeting date(s): Feb. for grants; May for scholarships
Final notification: Late Feb. for grants; late May for scholarships
Write: Francis E. Wakely, Exec. Dir.

Officers: Craig P. Colburn,* Pres.; Marion Panzarella,* V.P.; Elizabeth S. Lenna,* Secy.; R. Michael Goldman,* Treas.; Francis E. Wakely, Exec. Dir.
Directors:* Betty Erickson, Marilyn Gruel, Frederick J.W. Heft, Gregory L. Peterson, Kenneth W. Strickler.
Number of staff: 1 full-time professional; 1 part-time professional; 5 part-time support.
Employer Identification Number: 161116837
Recent arts and culture grants:
Little Theater of Jamestown, Jamestown, NY, $7,500. For sprinkler system. 1987.
Reg Lenna Civic Center, Jamestown, NY, $10,000. For renovation fund campaign. 1987.

1829
Owen Cheatham Foundation
540 Madison Ave.
New York 10022 (212) 753-4733

Incorporated in 1957 in NY as successor to Owen R. Cheatham Foundation, a trust established in 1934 in GA.
Donor(s): Owen Robertson Cheatham,† Celeste W. Cheatham.†
Financial data (yr. ended 12/31/86): Assets, $6,062,904 (M); expenditures, $470,418, including $265,125 for 43 grants (high: $120,000; low: $25; average: $1,000-$5,000).
Purpose and activities: Support primarily to assist programs that might not otherwise be achieved; grants mainly for education, health, the arts, and welfare.
Officers and Directors:* Celeste C. Weisglass,* Pres.; Stephen S. Weisglass,* V.P. and Treas.; Thomas P. Ford, V.P.; Ilse C. Meckauer, Secy.
Employer Identification Number: 136097798

1830
Chemical Bank Corporate Contributions Program
380 Madison Ave., Rm. 1406
New York 10017 (212) 309-5851

Purpose and activities: Chemical Bank has long demonstrated an understanding of community needs. The Bank strives to be sensitive and responsive to the social and human needs of the diverse communities in its marketplace. The Contributions Program is divided into four distinct areas of giving: 1) Corporate Contributions Department, which accepts, reviews, and analyzes requests from larger, more traditional organizations having city-wide impact and broad-based support. The department acts as staff to the Corp. Contribs. Committee, administering the overall corporate budget for contributions; 2) Urban Affairs, which supports smaller grass-roots organizations, emphasizing community revitalization and programs serving the disenfranchised and disadvantaged; 3) Units of the Bank which involve grants to organizations of particular relevance to the vitality of the marketplaces of the bank's branches, districts, and divisions; and 4) An Employee Matching Gifts program for education, cultural organizations and voluntary hospitals. Grants are for education, including higher, business, economic, and minority education, health and human services, arts and culture, and civic improvement. In addition, the Bank coordinates and produces, in conjunction with nonprofit organizations, workshops and seminars for community-based organizations on topics relating to management, offers computers and information management seminars, and donates equipment. The Bank also works with public schools in New York City by sponsoring special programs, assisting in management administration, and offering scholarships to students. Support for nonprofit organizations also offered through an employee volunteer program.
Limitations: Giving primarily in the nine-county Metropolitan NY area; generally only one grant is made to any one organization per calendar year. No support for religious or veterans' organizations or fraternal organizations unless they are non-discriminatory, or organizations belonging to United Way of Tri-State. No grants to individuals, or for dinners, exhibits, sports events, conferences, and other short-term, one-time activities, journal advertisements, or ticket purchases.
Publications: Corporate giving report, application guidelines.
Application information:
Initial approach: Letter, no more than 4 typed pages; include summary paragraph, amount, purpose, time frame, population served, qualifications of those responsible for programs, plans for future funding, latest audited financial report, annual report, 501(c)(3), board list
Write: Kathleen Pavlick, Mgr., Community Programming

1831
The Chisholm Foundation
c/o United States Trust Company
45 Wall St.
New York 10005

Established in 1960 in MS.
Donor(s): A.F. Chisholm.†
Financial data (yr. ended 12/31/87): Assets, $5,474,519 (M); expenditures, $337,303, including $228,059 for 20 grants (high: $50,000; low: $481).
Purpose and activities: Giving for education and Protestant organizations; support also for health, cultural programs, youth, and community funds.
Types of support: General purposes.
Limitations: Giving primarily in MS and New York, NY.
Application information: Applications not accepted.
Officers: Jean C. Lindsey, Pres.; Cynthia C. Saint-Amand, Secy.; Margaret A. Chisholm, Treas.
Director: Nathan E. Saint-Amand.
Employer Identification Number: 646014272

1832
Cintas Foundation, Inc.
140 Broadway, Rm. 4500
New York 10005
Fellowship application address: Institute of International Education, 809 United Nations Plaza, New York, NY 10017; Tel.: (212) 883-8485

Incorporated in 1957 in NY as Cuban Art Foundation, Inc.
Donor(s): Oscar B. Cintas.†
Financial data (yr. ended 8/31/87): Assets, $2,375,500 (M); expenditures, $156,500, including $100,000 for 10 grants to individuals of $10,000 each.
Purpose and activities: To foster and encourage art within Cuba and art created by persons of Cuban citizenship or lineage within or outside of Cuba. Present activities restricted to fostering art and granting fellowships to those in the above categories living outside of Cuba who show professional achievement in

music, literature, or the arts; students pursuing academic programs are not eligible.
Types of support: Fellowships.
Limitations: No grants for building or endowment funds, operating budgets, or special projects.
Publications: Application guidelines.
Application information: Application form required.
Initial approach: Letter
Deadline(s): Mar. 1 for fellowships beginning Sept. 1
Board meeting date(s): May or June, late Oct. or Nov., and as required
Final notification: 4 to 5 months
Write: William B. Warren, Pres., Cintas Fellowship Program
Officers and Directors: William B. Warren, Pres.; Maria Heilbron Richter, Secy.; Hortensia Sampedro, Treas.; Margarita Cano, Riva Castleman, Ulises Giberga, Marta Gutierrez, Daniel Serra-Badue, Roger D. Stone.
Number of staff: None.
Employer Identification Number: 131980389

1833
Citicorp/Citibank Corporate Contributions Program
Citicorp/Citibank
399 Park Ave.
New York 10043 (212) 559-8182

Financial data (yr. ended 12/31/88): Total giving, $10,680,883, including $8,572,898 for grants (high: $1,000,000; low: $500) and $2,107,985 for 7,386 employee matching gifts.
Purpose and activities: Citibank operates a decentralized giving program consisting of 36 regional contributions committees run by regional business managers and international giving administered by Country Corporate Officers. Designed to meet local needs through local organizations/programs, the various committees may focus on specific areas in their giving and often have their own published guidelines, even though they operate under Citicorp's general Contributions Program guidelines. The company has designated six areas for giving: culture, education-research, health, community revitalization, United Way and international. The Company prefers to support through "target grants to specific one-year programs that closely match our priorities," but also will consider multi-year grants for capital campaigns and general support. The company also offers employee gift matching. The VIM (Volunteer Involvement Match) matches employee contributions to organizations to which the employee volunteers time and effort on a regular basis. Citicorp branches also "adopt" local public schools providing practical help and positive role models for students.
Types of support: Continuing support, research, special projects, technical assistance, capital campaigns, general purposes, employee matching gifts.
Limitations: Giving primarily in New York City and operating locations nationwide in AZ, CA, CO, CT, DE, DC, FL, GA, IL, TN, ME, MD, MA, MN, MO, NV, NJ, NM, NY, NC, OH, OR, PA, RI, SD, TX, UT, VA, WA, and internationally. No support for religious, fraternal or veterans' organizations "unless they are engaged in a significant project benefiting the entire community"; or national programs. No grants to individuals, or for fundraising dinners, benefits or events, courtesy advertising, or generally major public broadcast underwriting or films.
Publications: Corporate giving report (including application guidelines), grants list.
Application information: Include in request: amount requested; brief organization history, including goals and accomplishments to date; proposal objective statement; current annual report; 501(c)(3); current year's budget with anticipated expenses and income; IRS 990; donor list of current corporate and foundation funders, with amounts given within the last fiscal year or last 12 months; most recent audited financial statement; board list; where appropriate, list of accrediting agencies. Many of the programs require application forms.
Initial approach: "Contact the contributions committee representative in your area for the specific guidelines of that committee"
Copies of proposal: 1
Deadline(s): Generally review process is ongoing; certain areas have their own deadlines
Final notification: Within 60 to 90 days
Write: Donna Stiansen, Mgr., Corp. Contribs., Citibank N.A.
Number of staff: 3

1834
David C. Clapp Foundation
c/o Goldman, Sachs & Co.
85 Broad St., Tax Dept.
New York 10004

Established in 1985 in NY.
Donor(s): David C. Clapp.
Financial data (yr. ended 6/30/87): Assets, $92,396 (M); gifts received, $200,442; expenditures, $153,200, including $153,180 for 28 grants (high: $50,000; low: $100).
Purpose and activities: Giving primarily for higher and secondary education; support also for cultural programs, including museums.
Limitations: Giving primarily in NY. No grants to individuals.
Application information: Applications not accepted.
Trustees: David C. Clapp, Francis X. Coleman, Jr., Frederic B. Garonzik.
Employer Identification Number: 133318134

1835
The Clark Foundation
30 Wall St.
New York 10005 (212) 269-1833

Incorporated in 1931 in NY; merged with Scriven Foundation, Inc. in 1973.
Donor(s): Members of the Clark family.
Financial data (yr. ended 6/30/88): Assets, $212,933,562 (M); gifts received, $4,300,343; expenditures, $11,257,962, including $8,354,943 for 134 grants (high: $3,200,000; low: $1,000), $1,882,974 for grants to individuals and $736,533 for 1 foundation-administered program.
Purpose and activities: Support for a hospital and museums in Cooperstown, NY; grants also for charitable, welfare, and educational purposes, including undergraduate scholarships to students residing in the Cooperstown area. Support also for health, educational, youth, cultural, and community welfare organizations and institutions and for medical and convalescence care of needy individuals.
Types of support: Operating budgets, continuing support, annual campaigns, seed money, emergency funds, building funds, equipment, special projects, student aid, general purposes, grants to individuals, capital campaigns.
Limitations: Giving primarily in upstate NY and New York City. No grants for deficit financing or matching gifts; no loans.
Publications: Program policy statement, application guidelines.
Application information:
Initial approach: Letter
Copies of proposal: 1
Deadline(s): None
Board meeting date(s): Oct. and May
Final notification: 2 to 6 months
Write: Edward W. Stack, Secy.
Officers: Stephen C. Clark, Jr.,* Pres.; Michael A. Nicolais,* V.P.; Edward W. Stack, Secy.; John J. Burkly, Treas.
Directors:* Alfred C. Clark, Jane F. Clark II, William M. Evarts, Jr., Archie F. MacAllaster, Mrs. Edward B. McMenamin, A. Pennington Whitehead, Malcolm Wilson.
Number of staff: 4 full-time professional; 3 part-time professional; 43 full-time support; 20 part-time support.
Employer Identification Number: 135616528
Recent arts and culture grants:
American Museum of Natural History, NYC, NY, $50,000. For compact storage units. 6/88.
Boys Choir of Harlem, NYC, NY, $7,500. For general support. 6/88.
Educational Broadcasting Corporation, NYC, NY, $50,000. For cash reserve fund. 4/88.
Farmers Museum, Cooperstown, NY, $100,000. For budget deficit/working capital. 1/88.
Fine Arts Center of Kershaw County, Camden, SC, $25,000. For Circus Arts Foundation. 5/88.
Glimmerglass Opera Theater, Cooperstown, NY, $100,000. For capital campaign. 1987.
Glimmerglass Opera Theater, Cooperstown, NY, $100,000. For capital campaign. 1/88.
Harlem School of the Arts, NYC, NY, $15,000. For general support. 1987.
Hospital Audiences, NYC, NY, $10,000. For general support. 1987.
Hospital Audiences, NYC, NY, $5,000. For Art Cart Program. 1987.
Lincoln Center for the Performing Arts, NYC, NY, $10,000. For Lincoln Center Institute. 1987.
Mannes College of Music, NYC, NY, $15,000. For scholarship support. 6/88.
New York Philharmonic, NYC, NY, $5,000. For teachers seminars. 1987.
New York State Historical Association, Cooperstown, NY, $250,000. For budget deficit/working capital. 1/88.
New York Zoological Society, Bronx, NY, $15,000. For general support. 6/88.

1836
The Edna McConnell Clark Foundation
250 Park Ave., Rm. 900
New York 10017 (212) 986-7050

Incorporated in 1950 in NY and 1969 in DE; the NY corporation merged into the DE corporation in 1974.
Donor(s): Edna McConnell Clark,† W. Van Alan Clark.†
Financial data (yr. ended 9/30/88): Assets, $372,054,687 (M); gifts received, $2,030; expenditures, $23,257,094, including $18,471,486 for 170 grants (high: $855,000; low: $50; average: $78,500).
Purpose and activities: Programs presently narrowly defined and directed toward five specific areas: 1) reducing unnecessary removal of children from troubled families by establishing better family preservation policies and services; supporting courts, agencies, and advocates in implementation of specific foster care and adoption reforms; 2) improving the educational opportunities of disadvantaged young people by designing intervention programs for the middle school years; 3) seeking a more rational, humane, and effective criminal justice system by establishing constitutional conditions in adult and juvenile correctional institutions, encouraging community-based sanctions for adults as alternatives to incarceration, and helping to dismantle large state training schools in favor of community-based programs for juveniles; 4) reducing the debilitating and deadly burden of illness in the poorest countries of the developing world through a targeted research program aimed at controlling the tropical diseases schistosomiasis, trachoma, and onchocerciasis; 5) seeking to assist families in New York City to move out of emergency shelters and hotels into permanent housing by supporting projects to assess and plan for the needs of families before and immediately after they leave the shelters; supporting programs aimed at forming tenants associations and other mechanisms that give families a stake in their communties; and supporting efforts to create, improve, and expand public and social services in neighborhoods receiving large numbers of previously homeless families. The foundation also maintains a program of Special Projects which primarily focuses on projects serving the poor and disadvantaged in New York City outside the established program areas that reflect our basic mission.
Types of support: Consulting services, continuing support, research, seed money, technical assistance, special projects.
Limitations: Giving primarily in New York City, NY, for special projects; nationally for other programs. No grants to individuals, or for capital funds, construction and equipment, endowments, scholarships, fellowships, annual appeals, deficit financing, or matching gifts; no loans to individuals.
Publications: Annual report, informational brochure (including application guidelines), grants list, occasional report.
Application information: Action-oriented projects preferred; research support primarily in Tropical Disease Program.
Initial approach: Letter
Copies of proposal: 1
Deadline(s): None
Board meeting date(s): Feb., Apr., June, Sept., and Dec.
Final notification: 1 month for declination; 2-3 months for positive action
Write: Peter D. Bell, Pres.
Officers: James M. Clark,* Chair. and Treas.; Peter D. Bell,* Pres.; Peter W. Forsythe, V.P.; Patricia Carry Stewart, V.P. and Secy.
Trustees:* Hays Clark, Drew S. Days III, Eleanor T. Elliott, John M. Emery, Lucy H. Nesbeda, Walter N. Rothschild, Jr., Sidney J. Weinberg, Jr., O. Meredith Wilson.
Number of staff: 11 full-time professional; 9 full-time support; 3 part-time support.
Employer Identification Number: 237047034
Recent arts and culture grants:
Boys Choir of Harlem, NYC, NY, $18,000. To support counseling services for families of choir members and recruits to choir. 6/1/88.

1837
Robert Sterling Clark Foundation, Inc.
112 East 64th St.
New York 10021 (212) 308-0411

Incorporated in 1952 in NY.
Donor(s): Robert Sterling Clark.†
Financial data (yr. ended 10/31/87): Assets, $51,038,529 (M); expenditures, $2,511,185, including $1,716,815 for 76 grants (high: $60,000; low: $2,500; average: $25,000-$30,000).
Purpose and activities: The foundation supports projects that: 1) strengthen the management of cultural institutions in New York City and the greater metropolitan area; 2) ensure the effectiveness and accountability of public agencies in New York City and State; and 3) protect reproductive freedom and access to family planning services.
Types of support: Special projects, research, general purposes, consulting services, continuing support, general purposes, research, special projects.
Limitations: Giving primarily in NY, with emphasis on New York City; giving nationally for reproductive freedom projects. No grants to individuals, or for operating budgets, annual campaigns, seed money, emergency funds, deficit financing, capital or endowment funds, matching gifts, scholarships, fellowships, conferences, or films.
Publications: Annual report, application guidelines.
Application information:
Initial approach: Proposal
Copies of proposal: 1
Deadline(s): None
Board meeting date(s): Jan., Apr., July, and Oct.
Final notification: 1 to 6 months
Write: Margaret C. Ayers, Exec. Dir.
Officers: Winslow M. Lovejoy, Jr.,* Pres. and Treas.; Miner D. Crary, Jr.,* Secy.; Margaret C. Ayers, Exec. Dir.
Directors:* Lewis Mack, Charles G. Meyer, Jr., Winthrop R. Munyan, Richardson Pratt, Jr., Philip Svigals.
Number of staff: 3 full-time professional; 1 part-time professional; 1 full-time support.
Employer Identification Number: 131957792
Recent arts and culture grants:
Alliance of Resident Theaters, NYC, NY, $30,000. To support Real Estate Project, designed to assist theaters in locating and renovating needed space, and to develop long term cooperative solutions to space shortage. 1/18/88.
American Composers Orchestra, NYC, NY, $25,000. For general support. General program support for cultural institutions is not in response to requests, but at initiation of Foundation. 10/20/87.
Artists Space, NYC, NY, $25,000. For general support. General program support for cultural institutions is not in response to requests, but at initiation of Foundation. 10/20/87.
Composers Forum, NYC, NY, $15,000. To support marketing and visibility campaign designed to raise profile of organization and to attract ticket buyers to sponsored concerts. 1/18/88.
Dance Theater Workshop, NYC, NY, $15,000. For revision and publication of updated edition of Poor Dancer's Almanac, survival manual for choreographers, dancers and other artists. 7/19/88.
Early Music America, NYC, NY, $10,000. To support completion of comprehensive survey of scope and needs of early music field in America. 1/18/88.
ECF Management, NYC, NY, $15,000. To support study of needs and credit capacities of New York City's nonprofit cultural organizations in anticipation of creation of capital improvements loan fund. 1/18/88.
Electronic Arts Intermix, NYC, NY, $15,000. For publication and distribution of EAI's first major catalogue of artists and videotapes in its Distribution Collection. 7/19/88.
Mozartean Players, Bronx, NY, $12,000. To support marketing campaign designed to increase domestic touring. 1/18/88.
Orpheus Chamber Ensemble, NYC, NY, $20,000. To support marketing project to encourage new corporate support. 10/20/87.
Pentacle, NYC, NY, $25,000. For general support. General program support for cultural institutions is not in response to requests, but at the initiation of the Foundation. 10/20/87.
Poets and Writers, NYC, NY, $20,000. To support marketing campaign aimed at increasing subscribers to new magazine. 10/20/87.
Theater for the New City, NYC, NY, $25,000. For general support. General program support for cultural institutions is not in response to requests, but at the initiation of the Foundation. 10/20/87.
Trisha Brown Dance Company, NYC, NY, $25,000. For general support. General program support for cultural institutions is not in response to requests, but at the initiation of the Foundation. 10/20/87.
Vineyard Theater and Workshop Center, NYC, NY, $15,000. For comprehensive marketing campaign designed to increase ticket sales and lessen audience confusion as Vineyard makes transition to two theater operation. 7/19/88.

1838
The Phyllis and Lee Coffey Foundation, Inc.
355 Lexington Ave.
New York 10017-6603

Established in 1952 in NY.
Donor(s): Lee W. Coffey.
Financial data (yr. ended 12/31/87): Assets, $1,176,173 (M); gifts received, $3,000; expenditures, $57,407, including $53,910 for 16 grants (high: $25,000; low: $50).
Purpose and activities: Support for health services, social services, religious giving and cultural activities.
Limitations: Giving primarily in NY. No grants to individuals.
Application information: Contributes only to pre-selected organizations. Applications not accepted.
Officers: Lee W. Coffey, Pres. and Treas.; Phyllis C. Coffey, V.P. and Secy.
Director: Daniel Cowin.
Employer Identification Number: 116014056

1839
The Marilyn B. & Stanley L. Cohen Foundation, Inc.
c/o Oppenheim, Appel, Dixon & Co.
One New York Plaza
New York 10004

Established in 1977 in NY.
Donor(s): Stanley L. Cohen.
Financial data (yr. ended 6/30/87): Assets, $282,349 (M); gifts received, $300,000; expenditures, $153,354, including $150,274 for 122 grants (high: $50,000; low: $10).
Purpose and activities: Support for youth organizations, cultural programs, and Jewish organizations.
Limitations: Giving primarily in New York, NY. No grants to individuals.
Application information: Contributes only to pre-selected organizations. Applications not accepted.
Officers and Directors: Stanley L. Cohen, Pres. and Treas.; Marilyn B. Cohen, V.P. and Secy.; Jacob Cohen, Edward Small, William J. Voute.
Employer Identification Number: 132930968

1840
Herman & Terese Cohn Foundation
c/o Chase Lincoln First Bank, N.A.
P.O. Box 1412
Rochester 14603 (716) 258-5175

Trust established in 1954 in NY.
Donor(s): Herman M. Cohn.†
Financial data (yr. ended 12/31/87): Assets, $4,297,823 (M); gifts received, $5,000; expenditures, $488,557, including $453,000 for 12 grants (high: $200,000; low: $3,000).
Purpose and activities: Giving for a musuem, an educational fund, family and youth services, and educational television.
Limitations: Giving primarily in NY.
Application information:
Initial approach: Proposal
Deadline(s): None
Write: Patricia C. Bonawitz
Trustee: Chase Lincoln First Bank, N.A.
Employer Identification Number: 166015300

1841
Sylvan C. Coleman Foundation
c/o The Bank of New York, Tax Dept.
48 Wall St.
New York 10015 (212) 536-4703

Established about 1956.
Donor(s): Sylvan C. Coleman.
Financial data (yr. ended 11/30/86): Assets, $1,364,351 (M); expenditures, $61,039, including $44,500 for 21 grants (high: $12,000; low: $500).
Purpose and activities: Giving primarily for higher education, cultural programs, health, social services and Jewish welfare funds.
Application information:
Initial approach: Letter
Deadline(s): None
Write: Lloyd Evans
Trustees: Clarence B. Coleman, Joan F. Coleman.
Employer Identification Number: 136091160

1842
George E. Coleman, Jr. Foundation
c/o Neville, Rodie & Shaw, Inc.
200 Madison Ave.
New York 10016 (212) 725-1440

Established in 1979 in NY.
Donor(s): George E. Coleman, Jr.†
Financial data (yr. ended 12/31/87): Assets, $4,276,907 (M); expenditures, $318,889, including $233,675 for 35 grants (high: $37,000; low: $500).
Purpose and activities: Grants largely for educational institutions and associations, historic preservation, cultural organizations, and conservation.
Types of support: Research.
Application information:
Deadline(s): None
Write: Denis Loncto, Trustee
Trustees: Denis Loncto, Louise Oliver.
Employer Identification Number: 133025258

1843
The Coler Foundation
c/o ATC Co.
441 Fifth Ave.
New York 10016

Established in 1976 in NY.
Financial data (yr. ended 12/31/87): Assets, $230,951 (M); expenditures, $188,148, including $186,280 for 33 grants (high: $100,000; low: $75).
Purpose and activities: Grants for health, culture, and Jewish giving.
Application information: Contributes only to pre-selected organizations. Applications not accepted.
Trustee: Arthur Cohen.
Employer Identification Number: 133071235

1844
Coles Family Foundation
c/o Goldman, Sachs & Co.
85 Broad St.
New York 10004

Established in 1980 in NY.
Donor(s): Michael H. Coles, Joan C. Coles.
Financial data (yr. ended 3/31/87): Assets, $2,448,276 (M); gifts received, $1,105,156; expenditures, $225,896, including $221,423 for 106 grants (high: $25,000; low: $100).
Purpose and activities: Grants for Catholic giving, child welfare, higher and other education, and culture.
Types of support: Endowment funds, general purposes, matching funds.
Limitations: Giving primarily in NY. No grants to individuals.
Application information: Applications not accepted.
Trustees: Alison Aldredge, Isobel Coles, Joan C. Coles, Michael H. Coles, Richard Coles, Caroline Scudder, Roy C. Smith.
Number of staff: 1 part-time support.
Employer Identification Number: 133050747

1845
Colgate-Palmolive Corporate Giving Program
300 Park Avenue
New York 10022 (212) 310-2000

Purpose and activities: Supports a variety of areas, including education, arts and culture, health care and hospitals, youth and minorities, civic and community programs, welfare and social services, and United Way.
Limitations: Giving primarily in headquarters city and operating locations; national programs also considered.
Application information: Letter including project budget and 501(c)(3) status letter. Company considers unsolicited requests for funding.
Initial approach: Query letter
Deadline(s): Best time to apply is Aug.-Sept.
Final notification: Within 3 weeks; rejection sent if denied.
Write: Mary Lennor, Contribs. Admin.

1846
Colt Industries Charitable Foundation, Inc.
c/o Colt Industries, Inc.
430 Park Ave.
New York 10022 (212) 940-0410

Incorporated in 1963 in DE.
Donor(s): Colt Industries, Inc.
Financial data (yr. ended 6/30/87): Assets, $3,535 (M); expenditures, $118,702, including $118,271 for 48 grants (high: $20,000; low: $250; average: $2,000-$3,000).
Purpose and activities: Giving for community funds, higher education, hospitals, cultural programs, and youth agencies; support also for civic affairs and public interest groups.
Types of support: Building funds, operating budgets.
Limitations: Giving primarily in areas of company operations. No grants to individuals.

Application information:
Initial approach: Letter
Copies of proposal: 1
Deadline(s): Submit proposal preferably in Sept. or Oct.
Board meeting date(s): Quarterly
Final notification: 3 months
Write: Andrew C. Hilton, Exec. V.P.
Officers and Directors: David I. Margolis, Pres.; Anthony J. di Buono, V.P. and Secy.; Salvatore J. Cozzolino, V.P. and Treas.; Andrew C. Hilton, V.P.
Number of staff: 2 part-time support.
Employer Identification Number: 256057849

1847
Colt Industries Foundation, Inc.
c/o Colt Industries, Inc.
430 Park Ave.
New York 10022

Established in 1958 in IA.
Financial data (yr. ended 9/30/87): Assets, $28,909 (M); expenditures, $390,957, including $390,256 for 150 grants (high: $62,500; low: $100).
Purpose and activities: Support primarily for welfare, higher education and culture.
Limitations: Giving primarily in areas of company operations.
Application information:
Initial approach: Proposal
Deadline(s): During 4th quarter of calendar year
Write: John F. Campbell
Officers: David I. Margolis, Pres.; Anthony J. diBuono,* V.P. and Secy.; Salvatore J. Cozzolino,* V.P. and Treas.
Directors:* Andrew C. Hilton.
Employer Identification Number: 426067817

1848
Compton Foundation, Inc.
20 Exchange Place
New York 10005 (212) 510-5040

Incorporated in 1972 in NY as successor to The Compton Trust.
Donor(s): Members of the Compton family.
Financial data (yr. ended 12/31/86): Assets, $48,617,010 (M); gifts received, $10,466,526; expenditures, $2,582,824, including $2,165,756 for 436 grants (high: $135,000; low: $30; average: $200-$60,000).
Purpose and activities: To coordinate the family giving to community, national, and international programs in areas of its special interests, including higher education, peace and world order, population control, the arts, conservation, race relations, and welfare.
Types of support: Endowment funds, fellowships, general purposes, matching funds, scholarship funds, operating budgets, continuing support, annual campaigns, seed money, special projects, consulting services.
Limitations: No grants to individuals, or for capital or building funds; no loans.
Publications: Biennial report.
Application information:
Initial approach: Letter
Deadline(s): None
Board meeting date(s): May and Nov.
Final notification: 6 months, favorable replies only
Write: James R. Compton, Pres.
Officers and Directors: James R. Compton, Pres.; Ann C. Stephens, V.P. and Secy.; Arthur L. Bowen, Treas.; Jan H. Lewis, Kenneth W. Thompson, Michael P. Todaro.
Number of staff: 1 part-time support.
Employer Identification Number: 237262706

1849
Constans Culver Foundation
600 Fifth Ave.
New York 10020 (212) 957-1500

Trust established in 1965 in NY.
Donor(s): Erne Constans Culver.†
Financial data (yr. ended 12/31/87): Assets, $3,997,257 (M); expenditures, $278,982, including $220,250 for 86 grants (high: $22,500; low: $500; average: $1,000-$2,000).
Purpose and activities: Emphasis on church support, civic and cultural organizations, and higher education.
Types of support: Annual campaigns, continuing support, general purposes.
Limitations: Giving primarily in NY. No grants to individuals, or for endowment funds.
Application information:
Initial approach: Letter
Copies of proposal: 1
Deadline(s): Submit proposal preferably in Sept.
Board meeting date(s): Oct. and as required
Write: Robert Rosenthal, V.P., Manufacturers Hanover Trust Co.
Trustees: Pauline Hoffmann Herd, Pauline May Herd, Victoria Prescott Herd, Manufacturers Hanover Trust Co.
Number of staff: 5
Employer Identification Number: 136048059

1850
The Cook Foundation
85 Broad St.
New York 10004 (212) 902-6897

Established in 1981 in NY.
Donor(s): Daniel W. Cook III.
Financial data (yr. ended 1/31/87): Assets, $1,128,850 (M); gifts received, $645,739; expenditures, $346,479, including $345,960 for grants.
Purpose and activities: Support primarily for education, cultural programs, and social services.
Limitations: Giving primarily in Dallas, TX.
Managers: Daniel W. Cook III, Gail B. Cook, Stephen Friedman.
Employer Identification Number: 133102939

1851
Corning Glass Works Foundation
MP-LB-02-1
Corning 14831 (607) 974-8719

Incorporated in 1952 in NY.
Donor(s): Corning Glass Works.
Financial data (yr. ended 12/31/88): Assets, $2,567,571 (M); gifts received, $1,937,038; expenditures, $2,939,365, including $1,733,037 for 241 grants (high: $167,000; low: $100; average: $500-$2,500) and $499,118 for 4,155 employee matching gifts.
Purpose and activities: Support of educational, civic, cultural, health and social service institutions; scholarships and fellowships in selected educational fields at selected institutions.
Types of support: Seed money, equipment, employee matching gifts, scholarship funds, fellowships, special projects.
Limitations: Giving primarily in communities where Corning Glass works has manufacturing operations. No support for elementary or secondary schools outside of school systems in plant communities, or for veterans' organizations, political parties, labor groups, or religious organizations. No grants to individuals; no loans.
Publications: Annual report (including application guidelines).
Application information:
Initial approach: Letter
Copies of proposal: 1
Deadline(s): None
Board meeting date(s): Mar., June, Sept., and Dec.
Final notification: 2 months
Write: Kristin A. Swain, Exec. Dir.
Officers: David N. Van Allen,* Chair.; Richard B. Bessey,* Pres.; James L. Flynn,* V.P.; A. John Peck, Jr., Secy.; Richard B. Klein, Treas.
Trustees:* Roger G. Ackerman, Thomas S. Buechner, Van C. Campbell, David A. Duke, Richard Dulude, E. Martin Gibson, James R. Houghton, Richard E. Rahill, William C. Ughetta.
Number of staff: 2 full-time professional; 1 part-time professional; 2 full-time support.
Employer Identification Number: 166051394
Recent arts and culture grants:
Alfred University, Alfred, NY, $25,000. For McMahon Chair in Ceramics. 1987.
Arnot Art Museum, Elmira, NY, $5,000. For building expansion. 1987.
Buffalo Fine Arts Academy, Buffalo, NY, $5,000. For Albright-Knox Art Gallery. 1987.
Business Committee for the Arts, NYC, NY, $5,000. For program support. 1987.
Chamber Music Society of Lincoln Center, NYC, NY, $10,000. For concert series. 1987.
Chemung Valley Arts Council, Corning, NY, $6,500. For arts in education. 1987.
Corning Philharmonic Society, Corning, NY, $11,500. For concert series. 1987.
Corning-Painted Post Historical Society, Corning, NY, $10,000. For Benjamin Patterson Inn Museum. 1987.
Corning-Painted Post Historical Society, Corning, NY, $5,000. For educational programs. 1987.
Edison Institute, Henry Ford Museum and Greenfield Village, Dearborn, MI, $10,000. For exhibition. 1987.
Harvard University, Cambridge, MA, $5,000. For new Philip Hofer Curatorship of Printing and Graphic Arts. 1987.
Japan Society, NYC, NY, $10,000. For education programs. 1987.
Mark Twain Arts Council, Elmira, NY, $25,000. For historical drama. 1987.
Metropolitan Museum of Art, NYC, NY, $25,000. For Rembrandt Gallery. 1987.

Museum of Modern Art, NYC, NY, $5,000. For 50th anniversary campaign. 1987.
One Seventy One Cedar, Corning, NY, $19,500. For general support. 1987.
Pierpont Morgan Library, NYC, NY, $5,000. For public programs. 1987.
Southern Tier Educational Television Association, Binghamton, NY, $9,731. For program underwriting. 1987.
Southern Tier Educational Television Association, Binghamton, NY, $5,000. For relocation project. 1987.
Statue of Liberty-Ellis Island Foundation, NYC, NY, $5,000. For restoration project. 1987.

1852
The Cowles Charitable Trust
630 Fifth Ave., Suite 1612
New York 10111-0144 (212) 765-6262

Trust established in 1948 in NY.
Donor(s): Gardner Cowles.†
Financial data (yr. ended 12/31/87): Assets, $14,152,994 (M); gifts received, $1,119,621; expenditures, $899,657, including $633,057 for 439 grants.
Purpose and activities: Grants largely for cultural programs, higher and secondary education, hospitals, community funds, and social services.
Types of support: Operating budgets, continuing support, annual campaigns, seed money, emergency funds, building funds, equipment, endowment funds, matching funds, capital campaigns, general purposes, renovation projects, special projects, professorships.
Limitations: Giving primarily in NY and FL. No grants to individuals; no loans.
Publications: Annual report (including application guidelines), application guidelines.
Application information:
Initial approach: Proposal or letter
Copies of proposal: 7
Deadline(s): 4 weeks before board meeting
Board meeting date(s): Jan., Apr., July and Oct.
Write: Martha Roby Stephens, Secy.
Officers: Gardner Cowles III,* Pres.; Martha Roby Stephens,* Secy.; Mary Croft, Treas.
Trustees:* Charles Cowles, Jan Cowles, Gardner Cowles III, Lois Cowles Harrison, Virginia Cowles Kurtis, Kate Cowles Nichols, Martha Roby Stephens.
Number of staff: 2 part-time professional.
Employer Identification Number: 136090295
Recent arts and culture grants:
Brooklyn Museum, Brooklyn, NY, $5,250. 1987.
Center for the Fine Arts, Miami, FL, $10,000. 1987.
Cooper-Hewitt Museum, The Smithsonians National Museum of Design, NYC, NY, $5,000. 1987.
Florida Orchestra, Tampa, FL, $5,000. 1987.
Lincoln Center for the Performing Arts, NYC, NY, $5,000. 1987.
Miami City Ballet, Miami, FL, $5,000. 1987.
National Trust for Historic Preservation, DC, $5,000. 1987.
New York Philharmonic, NYC, NY, $5,000. 1987.
Polk Museum of Art, Lakeland, FL, $25,000. 1987.
Whitney Museum of American Art, NYC, NY, $5,000. 1987.

1853
Herbert and Jeanine Coyne Foundation
85 Broad St.
New York 10004

Established in 1983 in NY.
Donor(s): Herbert J. Coyne, Jeanine Coyne.
Financial data (yr. ended 12/31/87): Assets, $650,479 (M); gifts received, $20,000; expenditures, $199,720, including $194,898 for 39 grants (high: $37,000; low: $50).
Purpose and activities: Emphasis on arts and cultural institutions, including a crafts organization, museums, and dance; some support also for the aged, higher education, social services and hospitals.
Limitations: Giving primarily in FL, New York City, NY, and MA. No grants to individuals.
Application information: Contributes only to pre-selected organizations. Applications not accepted.
Officers: Herbert J. Coyne, Pres. and Treas.; Jeanine Coyne, V.P. and Secy.
Director: Robert Pelz.
Employer Identification Number: 133206423

1854
The Crane Foundation
(Formerly UniDynamics Foundation, Inc.)
c/o Crane Co.
757 Third Ave.
New York 10017 (212) 415-7275

Incorporated in 1937 in DE; in 1951 in MO.
Donor(s): UMC Industries, Inc.
Financial data (yr. ended 12/31/86): Assets, $2,070,824 (M); expenditures, $71,018, including $60,825 for 19 grants (high: $15,400; low: $100).
Purpose and activities: Emphasis on community funds, higher education, performing arts, youth agencies, and hospitals.
Types of support: General purposes, continuing support, annual campaigns, scholarship funds.
Limitations: No grants to individuals, or for endowment funds, capital funds, or research; no loans.
Application information:
Initial approach: Letter
Deadline(s): None
Board meeting date(s): As required
Write: R.K. Whitley, V.P.
Officers and Directors: R.R. Evans, Pres.; R. Kenneth Whitley, V.P.; P.R. Hundt, Secy.; T.J. Ungerland, Treas.
Employer Identification Number: 436051752

1855
Josephine B. Crane Foundation
781 Fifth Ave.
New York 10022

Incorporated in 1955 in NY.
Donor(s): Josephine B. Crane.†
Financial data (yr. ended 12/31/87): Assets, $1,640,080 (M); expenditures, $48,326, including $43,000 for 8 grants (high: $10,000; low: $2,500).
Purpose and activities: Emphasis on social and cultural advancement.
Limitations: Giving primarily in NY and MA.
Application information: Contributes only to pre-selected organizations. Applications not accepted.
Write: Lawrence E. Brinn, V.P.
Officers and Directors: Louise B. Crane, Pres.; Lawrence E. Brinn, V.P. and Treas.; Peter F. De Gaetano, Secy.
Employer Identification Number: 136156264

1856
Crosswicks Foundation, Ltd.
924 West End Ave.
New York 10025 (203) 491-3676

Established in 1972 in NY.
Financial data (yr. ended 11/30/87): Assets, $1,535,869 (M); expenditures, $107,496, including $80,000 for 23 grants (high: $10,000; low: $1,000).
Purpose and activities: Grants for church support, social services, cultural organizations, hospitals, and education.
Types of support: Continuing support, scholarship funds.
Application information:
Initial approach: Letter
Deadline(s): Nov. 1
Officers: M.L. Franklin, Pres.; Josephine Jones, V.P.; J. Franklin Laurie, Secy.; Bion B. Franklin, Treas.
Employer Identification Number: 132732197

1857
Lewis B. & Dorothy Cullman Foundation, Inc.
c/o Lewis B. Cullman
767 Third Ave.
New York 10017

Established in 1958 in NY.
Donor(s): Lewis B. Cullman.
Financial data (yr. ended 11/30/87): Assets, $64,591 (M); gifts received, $6,530; expenditures, $239,249, including $231,635 for 84 grants (high: $30,000; low: $25).
Purpose and activities: Emphasis on cultural programs; support also for a Jewish welfare organization.
Limitations: Giving primarily in New York, NY. No grants to individuals.
Application information: Contributes only to pre-selected organizations. Applications not accepted.
Officers and Directors: Dorothy F. Cullman, Pres. and Treas.; Mordecai Rochlin, V.P.; Mildred F. Eisermayer, Secy.
Employer Identification Number: 510243747

1858
Louise B. & Edgar M. Cullman Foundation
641 Lexington Ave., 29th Fl.
New York 10022-4599 (212) 838-0211

Established in 1956 in NY.
Financial data (yr. ended 12/31/88): Assets, $708,162 (M); gifts received, $343,463; expenditures, $243,870, including $234,800 for 25 grants (average: $25-$80,000).
Purpose and activities: Support for education, including medical education, health, the performing arts and other cultural programs, and wildlife preservation.
Types of support: Annual campaigns, building funds, endowment funds.
Application information: Application form required.
Copies of proposal: 1
Deadline(s): None
Board meeting date(s): Dec.
Write: Edgar M. Cullman, Pres.
Officers: Edgar M. Cullman, Pres.; Louise B. Cullman, V.P.; John C. Emmert, Secy.
Number of staff: 1 part-time professional; 1 part-time support.
Employer Identification Number: 136100041

1859
Charles E. Culpeper Foundation, Inc.
866 United Nations Plaza, Rm. 408
New York 10017 (212) 755-9188

Incorporated in 1940 in CT; in 1955 in NY.
Donor(s): Charles E. Culpeper.†
Financial data (yr. ended 12/31/87): Assets, $114,954,121 (M); gifts received, $1,587; expenditures, $6,710,750, including $5,141,450 for 184 grants (high: $250,000; low: $500; average: $2,500-$75,000).
Purpose and activities: Grants to organizations concerned with health, education, science and technology, arts and letters, youth programs, and administration of justice.
Types of support: Research, fellowships, general purposes, special projects.
Limitations: No grants to individuals, or for conferences, conduit organizations, operating budgets, or travel; no loans. Limited support only for endowment or building funds.
Publications: Informational brochure, program policy statement, application guidelines, multi-year report.
Application information:
Initial approach: Proposal
Copies of proposal: 1
Deadline(s): Submit proposal preferably between Feb. and Sept.; no set deadline
Board meeting date(s): Usually in Mar., May, Sept., and Dec.
Final notification: 3 weeks
Write: Helen D. Johnson, Pres.
Officers and Directors: Francis J. McNamara, Jr., Chair.; Helen D. Johnson, Pres.; Philip M. Drake, Secy.-Treas.; Colin G. Campbell, Joseph F. Fahey, Jr., John A. Huston, John C. Rose.
Number of staff: 4
Employer Identification Number: 131956297
Recent arts and culture grants:
AFS International-Intercultural Programs, NYC, NY, $5,000. Toward American-Soviet Youth Orchestra. 5/88.
Ballet Theater Foundation, NYC, NY, $5,000. For general support. 12/87.
Beth Israel Medical Center, NYC, NY, $42,220. Toward Music Therapy program of Jacob Perlow Hospice Program. 12/15/87.
Boston Symphony Orchestra, Boston, MA, $200,000. To Charles E. Culpeper Library in new Tanglewood Music Center. 6/22/88.
Boys Choir of Harlem, NYC, NY, $5,000. For scholarship aid. 4/87.
Caramoor Center for Music and the Arts, Katonah, NY, $10,000. Toward 1987 program. 4/87.
Childrens Museum of Indianapolis, Indianapolis, IN, $75,000. Toward Center for Exploration. 12/15/87.
Council for the Arts in Westchester, White Plains, NY, $50,000. For program entitled: The Arts and the Aging. 3/5/87.
Fairfield University, Fairfield, CT, $250,000. Toward Center for the Performing and Visual Arts. 12/15/87.
Florence Griswold Museum, Old Lyme, CT, $50,000. 12/15/87.
Georgetown University, DC, $25,000. For Intercultural Festival of Performing Arts. 12/87.
Lincoln Center for the Performing Arts, NYC, NY, $300,000. To technical workshop of Lincoln Center Institute. 12/15/87.
Marlboro School of Music, Marlboro, VT, $35,000. For endowment program. 3/5/87.
Massachusetts Historical Society, Boston, MA, $50,000. Toward endowment fund. 6/23/87.
Musica Sacra, NYC, NY, $125,000. Toward producing record of choral music. 12/15/87.
National Museum of Women in the Arts, DC, $30,000. For audiovisual display room. 3/30/88.
National Theater of the Deaf, NYC, NY, $10,000. Toward Professional School. 4/15/88.
New York Philharmonic, NYC, NY, $75,000. Toward Young People's Concerts. 9/16/87.
Newberry Library, Chicago, IL, $50,000. Toward cataloguing fund. 3/30/88.
Opera/Music Theater Institute of New Jersey, Upper Montclair, NJ, $15,000. Toward stipend for Charles E. Culpeper Foundation Artist. 9/16/87.
Oregon Shakespearean Festival, Ashland, OR, $10,000. Toward meeting NEA challenge grant. 6/15/88.
Saratoga Springs Performing Arts Center, Saratoga Springs, NY, $10,000. Toward special choreography project of School of American Ballet. 4/87.
Valentine Museum, Richmond, VA, $10,000. For preservation program. 12/10/86.
Young Audiences, NYC, NY, $35,000. Toward meeting and NEA challenge grant. 3/30/88.

1860
The Nathan Cummings Foundation, Inc.
885 Third Ave., Suite 3160
New York 10022 (212) 230-3377

Established in 1949 in NY.
Donor(s): Nathan Cummings.†
Financial data (yr. ended 12/31/88): Assets, $49,455,000 (M); expenditures, $3,022,500, including $2,566,000 for 53 grants (high: $1,000,000; low: $1,000).
Purpose and activities: Grants primarily for Jewish giving, cultural programs, higher education, and hospitals.
Types of support: Annual campaigns, building funds, capital campaigns, consulting services, general purposes, lectureships, special projects.
Application information: Applications not accepted.
Board meeting date(s): 4 times a year
Officers and Directors: Mrs. Robert Mayer, Chair.; Herbert Cummings, Vice-Chair.; Mrs. R.C. Sorensen, Vice-Chair.; Daniel G. Ross, Secy.; Jay Levy, Treas.
Number of staff: 1 part-time support.
Employer Identification Number: 237093201

1861
D.C. Foundation, Inc.
c/o Meyer Handelman Co.
2500 Westchester Ave.
Purchase 10577-2515

Established in 1959 in NY.
Donor(s): Nedenia H. Robertson.
Financial data (yr. ended 8/31/88): Assets, $2,210,983 (M); gifts received, $138,000; expenditures, $121,270, including $115,650 for 31 grants (high: $25,000; low: $250).
Purpose and activities: Support for youth and child welfare, higher education, medical research, and the arts.
Limitations: Giving primarily in NY, CT, and MA. No grants to individuals.
Application information: Contributes only to pre-selected organizations. Applications not accepted.
Officers: Nedenia H. Robertson, Pres.; Donald E. Handelman, V.P. and Secy.-Treas.
Trustees: Nedenia R. Craig, Joseph W. Handelman, Heather M. Robertson, Stanley H. Rumbough.
Employer Identification Number: 136113272

1862
Daily News Foundation, Inc.
220 East 42nd St.
New York 10017 (212) 210-6320

Incorporated in 1958 in NY.
Donor(s): New York News, Inc.
Financial data (yr. ended 12/31/87): Assets, $3,401,130 (M); gifts received, $2,000; expenditures, $170,952, including $102,148 for 48 grants (high: $10,000; low: $218).
Purpose and activities: Emphasis on a community fund, higher education, urban affairs, cultural activities, and youth agencies.
Limitations: Giving primarily in the five boroughs of New York City.
Application information:
Initial approach: Letter
Deadline(s): No later than the 1st of the month preceding the month meeting is held
Board meeting date(s): Quarterly
Write: Lucius P. Gregg, Asst. Secy.
Officers and Directors: James F. Hoge, Pres.; F. Gilman Spencer, V.P.; J.C. Mason, Secy.; L. Bloom, Treas.; J. Campi, J. Dunleavy, R. Herbert, M. Pankenham.
Employer Identification Number: 136161525

1863
Eleanor Naylor Dana Charitable Trust
375 Park Ave., 38th Fl.
New York 10152 (212) 754-2890

Established in CT in 1979.
Donor(s): Eleanor Naylor Dana.†
Financial data (yr. ended 5/31/88): Assets, $10,651,701 (M); expenditures, $4,911,255, including $4,476,446 for 102 grants (high: $200,000; low: $888; average: $5,000-$100,000).
Purpose and activities: Grants are given mainly to foster and finance progress and the pursuit of excellence in two areas: (1) biomedical research, "to support clinical investigations by established scientists in qualified institutions in the U.S., to pursue innovative projects designed to improve medical practice or prevent disease," and (2) the performing arts, to assist the various performing arts fields in ways that could be of substantial import to the grantees and the artists and the publics which they serve.
Types of support: Research, special projects.
Limitations: Giving primarily in areas east of the Mississippi River. No grants to individuals, or for instrumentation other than that required for a specific project, large scale field studies of a therapeutic or epidemiological nature, or conferences (in biomedical research); or for deficit financing, exhibits, publications, or conclaves (in the arts).
Publications: Informational brochure.
Application information:
Initial approach: Letter under 1,000 words
Deadline(s): None
Board meeting date(s): Quarterly
Final notification: After meetings
Write: Carol Bartos, Exec. Asst.
Officers: David Mahoney,* Chair.; Edward F. Rover, V.P.; Wallace L. Cook, Secy.; A.J. Signorile,* Treas.
Trustees:* Robert A. Good, M.D., Carlos Moseley, Robert E. Wise, M.D.
Number of staff: 1 full-time professional; 1 full-time support.
Employer Identification Number: 132992855

1864
The Charles A. Dana Foundation, Inc.
150 East 52nd St., 23rd Fl.
New York 10022 (212) 223-4040

Incorporated in 1950 in CT.
Donor(s): Charles A. Dana,† Eleanor Naylor Dana.†
Financial data (yr. ended 12/31/88): Assets, $160,735,525 (M); expenditures, $11,835,239, including $9,237,032 for 102 grants (high: $2,500,000; low: $2,000; average: $50,000-$200,000) and $377,876 for grants to individuals.
Purpose and activities: Principal interests in private higher education at four-year liberal arts colleges and the protection of human health and prevention of disease through grants to major academic medical centers, as well as a program instituted in 1986, the Charles A. Dana Awards for Pioneering Achievements in Health and Higher Education; support also for cultural and civic programs and the Dana-Farber Cancer Institute.
Types of support: Seed money, matching funds, scholarship funds, professorships, internships, fellowships, research, grants to individuals.
Limitations: Giving primarily in the eastern U.S.; support of cultural and civic programs principally in the greater New York, NY area. No support for professional organizations. No grants to individuals (except for the Charles A. Dana Awards), or for capital or endowment funds, operating budgets, continuing support, annual campaigns, building or emergency funds, deficit financing, publications, conferences, demonstration projects, or colloquia; no loans.
Publications: Annual report (including application guidelines), newsletter.
Application information: Applications for the Charles A. Dana Awards by nomination only; guidelines available.
Initial approach: Letter
Deadline(s): None
Board meeting date(s): Apr., June, Oct., and Dec.
Final notification: 2 to 3 months
Write: Robert N. Kreidler, Pres.; Marilyn A. Baldwin, Prog. Officer (higher education); or Stephen A. Foster, Prog. Officer (health)
Officers and Directors: David J. Mahoney, Chair.; Robert N. Kreidler, Pres.; Walter G. Corcoran, V.P.; Clark M. Whittemore, Jr., Secy.-Treas.; Edward C. Andrews, Jr., Wallace L. Cook, Charles A. Dana, Jr., Donald B. Marron, Carlos Moseley, L. Guy Palmer II, Donald C. Platten.
Number of staff: 6 full-time professional; 1 part-time professional; 3 full-time support.
Employer Identification Number: 066036761
Recent arts and culture grants:
Emory University, Atlanta, GA, $475,000. For partnership between 14 private colleges and Emory University to develop new interdisciplinary courses in humanities. 6/15/88.

1865
Gerard & Ruth Daniel Foundation, Inc.
Polly Park Rd.
Rye 10580

Donor(s): Gerard Daniel & Co.
Financial data (yr. ended 12/31/87): Assets, $2,938,618 (M); expenditures, $89,623, including $80,300 for 19 grants (high: $13,070; low: $400).
Purpose and activities: Grants primarily for Jewish welfare funds, cultural and educational organizations, and temple support; support also for museums.
Application information: Contributes only to pre-selected organizations. Applications not accepted.
Officers and Directors: Gerard Daniel, Pres.; Ruth Daniel, V.P.
Employer Identification Number: 136207879

1866
The Michel David-Weill Foundation
c/o Lazard Freres and Co.
One Rockefeller Plaza
New York 10020 (212) 489-6600

Established in 1984 in NY.
Donor(s): Michel David-Weill.
Financial data (yr. ended 6/30/87): Assets, $3,086,604 (M); gifts received, $2,492,240; expenditures, $2,283,386, including $2,282,000 for 14 grants (high: $1,500,000; low: $10,000; average: $30,000-$100,000).
Purpose and activities: Support for cultural programs and Jewish welfare funds.
Limitations: Giving primarily in the New York, NY, area.
Application information:
Initial approach: Letter
Deadline(s): None
Write: Thomas R.X. Mullarkey, Secy.
Officers: Michel David-Weill, Pres.; Eliane David-Weill, V.P.; Thomas F.X. Mullarkey, Secy.-Treas.
Number of staff: 2
Employer Identification Number: 133240809

1867
Harry De Jur Foundation, Inc.
c/o Pavia & Harcourt
600 Madison Ave.
New York 10022 (212) 980-3500

Incorporated in 1958 in NY.
Donor(s): Harry De Jur.†
Financial data (yr. ended 11/30/86): Assets, $1,439,579 (M); gifts received, $3,490; expenditures, $163,033, including $149,473 for 68 grants (high: $30,850; low: $50).
Purpose and activities: Emphasis on education, both in Israel and the U.S., social and health agencies, Jewish social and charitable organizations and cultural programs.
Limitations: Giving primarily in NY.
Application information:
Deadline(s): None
Write: David Botwinick, Secy.
Officers: Robert Greenberg, Pres.; Marian De Jur, V.P.; Benjamin Neuwirth, V.P.; David Botwinik, Secy.
Employer Identification Number: 136110844

1868
The Edmond de Rothschild Foundation
c/o Proskauer, Rose, Goetz & Mendelsohn
300 Park Ave., Rm. 2100
New York 10022 (212) 909-7724

Incorporated in 1963 in NY.
Donor(s): Edmond de Rothschild.
Financial data (yr. ended 2/28/87): Assets, $23,384,522 (M); gifts received, $1,400,000; expenditures, $829,545, including $673,601 for 43 grants (high: $89,241; low: $500).
Purpose and activities: Grants largely for Jewish welfare funds, higher education, and organizations concerned with Israeli affairs in the U.S. and abroad; support also for cultural programs, hospitals, and scientific research.
Types of support: General purposes.

Limitations: Giving primarily in New York City, NY, and in France; some giving in Israel. No grants to individuals.
Application information:
Initial approach: Letter
Copies of proposal: 1
Deadline(s): None
Board meeting date(s): As required
Final notification: Varies
Write: Paul H. Epstein, Secy.
Officers and Directors: Edmond de Rothschild, Chair.; George M. Shapiro, Pres.; George C. Karlweis, V.P.; Paul H. Epstein, Secy.-Treas.; Benjamin de Rothschild, Bernard Esambert, Stanley Komaroff.
Number of staff: None.
Employer Identification Number: 136119422

1869
The Dewar Foundation, Inc.
c/o Rutson R. Henderson
45 Dietz St.
Oneonta 13820 (607) 432-1811

Incorporated in 1947 in NY.
Donor(s): Jessie Smith Dewar.†
Financial data (yr. ended 12/31/87): Assets, $13,739,502 (M); expenditures, $1,203,031, including $1,144,600 for 64 grants (high: $381,500; low: $500).
Purpose and activities: Giving for civic and charitable organizations, including support for cultural organizations, youth agencies, Protestant churches, education, and child welfare.
Limitations: Giving primarily in Oneonta, NY. No grants to individuals.
Application information:
Initial approach: Letter
Deadline(s): None
Officer and Trustees: Rutson R. Henderson, Pres.; Richard Applebaugh, V.P.; Frank W. Getman, Secy.; Nancy A. Lynch, Treas.
Employer Identification Number: 166054329

1870
The Aaron Diamond Foundation, Inc.
1270 Ave. of the Americas, Suite 2624
New York 10020 (212) 757-7680

Established in 1955 in NY.
Donor(s): Aaron Diamond.†
Financial data (yr. ended 12/31/88): Assets, $119,311,770 (M); gifts received, $14,449,045; expenditures, $17,778,882, including $18,625,812 for 255 grants (high: $500,000; low: $500; average: $10,000-$100,000).
Purpose and activities: Grants primarily for medical research, minority education, and cultural programs.
Types of support: General purposes, research, continuing support, operating budgets, special projects.
Limitations: Giving limited to New York City, NY. No support for theatre projects. No grants to individuals, or for building funds, endowments, or other capital expenditures; no loans.
Publications: Annual report (including application guidelines), informational brochure (including application guidelines).
Application information:
Initial approach: Letter and proposal
Deadline(s): None
Board meeting date(s): Quarterly
Write: Vincent McGee, Exec. Dir.
Officers and Directors: Irene Diamond, Pres.; Robert L. Bernstein, V.P.; Charles L. Mandelstam, Secy.; Peter Kimmelman, Treas.; Vincent McGee, Exec. Dir.; Adrian W. DeWind, Peggy Dulany, Alfred Gellhorn, Lewis Thomas.
Number of staff: 4 full-time professional; 3 part-time professional; 4 full-time support; 1 part-time support.
Employer Identification Number: 132678431
Recent arts and culture grants:
American Composers Orchestra, NYC, NY, $15,000. For general support. 1987.
American Museum of Natural History, NYC, NY, $5,000. For general support. 1987.
American Music Center, NYC, NY, $25,000. For general support. 1987.
Arts Connection, NYC, NY, $25,000. For general support. 1987.
Asia Society, NYC, NY, $5,000. For general support. 1987.
Ballet Hispanico of New York, NYC, NY, $25,000. For general support for training and education programs. 1987.
Bargemusic, Brooklyn, NY, $20,000. For general support. 1987.
Bargemusic, Brooklyn, NY, $10,000. For one-time support for development consultant. 1987.
Bread and Roses Cultural Project, NYC, NY, $10,000. For general support. 1987.
Brooklyn Academy of Music, Brooklyn, NY, $50,000. For general support. 1987.
Brooklyn Childrens Museum, Brooklyn, NY, $30,000. For development of science programming. 1987.
Brooklyn Childrens Museum, Brooklyn, NY, $5,000. For general support. 1987.
Brooklyn Museum, Brooklyn, NY, $25,000. For educational programs. 1987.
Brooklyn Museum, Brooklyn, NY, $5,000. For general support. 1987.
Carnegie Hall, NYC, NY, $10,000. For children's concerts in Weill Recital Hall for special education students. 1987.
Chamber Music Society of Lincoln Center, NYC, NY, $25,000. For general support. 1987.
Childrens Book Council, Newark, DE, $10,000. For U.S. participation in 1990 World Congress on Children's Books. 1987.
Childrens Museum of Manhattan, NYC, NY, $5,000. For general support. 1987.
City Center of Music and Drama, NYC, NY, $5,000. For general support. 1987.
Concert Association of Greater Miami, Miami Beach, FL, $20,000. For matching grant for general support. 1987.
Concert Association of Greater Miami, Miami Beach, FL, $10,000. For supplemental grant to assist with deficit incurred in presentation of National Ballet of Canada. 1987.
Dance Theater Foundation, Alvin Ailey American Dance Theater, NYC, NY, $25,000. For scholarships for gifted minority youth in New York City. 1987.
Dance Theater of Harlem, NYC, NY, $200,000. For matching grant for scholarship/endowment development. 1987.
Feld Ballet, NYC, NY, $25,000. For scholarships for disadvantaged public school children from five boroughs of New York City. 1987.
Film Society of Lincoln Center, NYC, NY, $25,000. For New Directors Program. 1987.
Harlem School of the Arts, NYC, NY, $25,000. For general support. 1987.
Independent Curators, NYC, NY, $10,000. For general support. 1987.
Institute of Jazz Studies, Newark, NJ, $25,000. For project to transcribe and disseminate classic arrangements of works for jazz orchestra. 1987.
Joffrey Ballet, NYC, NY, $25,000. For general support. 1987.
Juilliard School, NYC, NY, $75,000. For project support for recruitment of minority/low-income students. 1987.
La Mama Experimental Theater Club, NYC, NY, $25,000. For training program for minority students of dance, drama and music. 1987.
Learning to Read Through the Arts Program, NYC, NY, $5,000. For general support. 1987.
Lincoln Center for the Performing Arts, NYC, NY, $50,000. For special projects. 1987.
Lincoln Center for the Performing Arts, Lincoln Center Institute, NYC, NY, $50,000. 1987.
Little Orchestra Society, NYC, NY, $20,000. For Chance for Children Program. 1987.
MacDowell Colony, NYC, NY, $25,000. For general support. 1987.
Metropolitan Museum of Art, NYC, NY, $5,000. For general support. 1987.
Metropolitan Opera Association, NYC, NY, $6,000. For general support. 1987.
Metropolitan Opera Guild, NYC, NY, $10,000. For In-School Residency Program. 1987.
Museum of Modern Art, NYC, NY, $5,000. For general support. 1987.
Museum of the City of New York, NYC, NY, $5,000. For general support. 1987.
National Dance Institute, NYC, NY, $25,000. For project support for special classes. 1987.
New School Concerts, NYC, NY, $10,000. For New York String Orchestra 1987 Seminar. 1987.
New York City Ballet, NYC, NY, $50,000. For Education Department and Apprentice/Dancer Training Program. 1987.
New York City Ballet, NYC, NY, $5,000. For general support. 1987.
New York City Opera, NYC, NY, $50,000. For general support and for Donald Gramm Fund. 1987.
New York Dance Center, NYC, NY, $100,000. For start-up operating costs. 1987.
New York Foundation for the Arts, NYC, NY, $5,000. For general support and one-time project support. 1987.
New York Hall of Science, Corona, NY, $25,000. For Explainers Program. 1987.
New York International Festival of the Arts, NYC, NY, $250,000. For general support. 1987.
New York Philharmonic, NYC, NY, $100,000. For MAX Program and minority and disadvantaged audience development. 1987.
New York Philharmonic, NYC, NY, $5,000. For general support. 1987.
New York Public Library, Schomburg Center for the Research in Black Culture, NYC, NY, $50,000. For special project support for

Black History and Culture collections and programs. 1987.
Saint Augustine School of the Arts, Bronx, NY, $50,000. For general support. 1987.
Saint Lukes Chamber Ensemble, NYC, NY, $10,000. For expansion of educational program. 1987.
Solomon R. Guggenheim Museum, NYC, NY, $5,000. For general support. 1987.
Studio in a School Association, NYC, NY, $50,000. For general support of agency bringing arts to public schools. 1987.
Studio Museum in Harlem, NYC, NY, $20,000. For artists in residence program. 1987.
Sundance Institute for Film and Television, Salt Lake City, UT, $50,000. For general support. 1987.
Symphony Space, NYC, NY, $15,000. Support for Wall to Wall Mozart. 1987.
Symphony Space, NYC, NY, $10,000. For project support for Wall to Wall Schubert and Selected Shorts. 1987.
Third Street Music School Settlement, NYC, NY, $10,000. For general support. 1987.
Tides Foundation, Film and Theater Diplomacy, San Francisco, CA, $10,000. To support Film and Theater Diplomacy, sponsored project of Tides Foundation. 1987.
W N E T Channel 13, NYC, NY, $75,000. For program development of Global Rivals. 1987.
W N E T Channel 13, NYC, NY, $50,000. For supplemental grant for Global Rivals. 1987.
W N E T Channel 13, NYC, NY, $10,000. For general support. 1987.
Westchester Community College Foundation, Valhalla, NY, $5,000. For Third Annual Literary Symposium. 1987.
Whitney Museum of American Art, NYC, NY, $5,000. For general support. 1987.
Yaddo, Corporation of, Saratoga Springs, NY, $25,000. For general support. 1987.
YM-YWHA, 92nd Street, NYC, NY, $50,000. For cultural and arts programming and for general support of New York Chamber Symphony. 1987.
Young Audiences, NYC, NY, $25,000. For general support of New York Program. 1987.
Young Concert Artists, NYC, NY, $50,000. For general support. 1987.

1871
Clarence and Anne Dillon Dunwalke Trust

1270 Ave. of the Americas, Rm. 2300
New York 10020 (212) 315-8343

Trust established in 1969 in NY.
Donor(s): Clarence Dillon.†
Financial data (yr. ended 6/30/88): Assets, $14,596,077 (M); expenditures, $793,797, including $680,976 for 28 grants (high: $250,000; low: $1,000).
Purpose and activities: Emphasis on hospitals, education, public affairs, the arts, and community funds. Grants primarily to present beneficiary organizations and for special proposals developed by the trustees.
Types of support: Fellowships, endowment funds, equipment, research, annual campaigns, operating budgets, building funds, special projects, general purposes.
Limitations: Giving primarily in NJ and NY. No grants to individuals; no loans.
Application information: New requests seldom considered.
Deadline(s): None
Board meeting date(s): Nov. and as required
Write: Crosby R. Smith, Trustee
Trustees: Christine Allen, Philip D. Allen, Joan M. Bryan, Mark M. Collins, Jr., Phyllis Dillon Collins, C. Douglas Dillon, Dorothy Dillon Eweson, David H. Peipers, Crosby R. Smith, Frances C. Stillman.
Number of staff: 1 part-time professional.
Employer Identification Number: 237043773

1872
The Dillon Fund

1270 Ave. of the Americas, Rm. 2300
New York 10020 (212) 315-8343

Incorporated in 1922 in NY.
Donor(s): Clarence Dillon,† C. Douglas Dillon.
Financial data (yr. ended 12/31/87): Assets, $616,353 (M); gifts received, $3,541,517; expenditures, $3,297,620, including $3,250,227 for 84 grants (high: $766,875; low: $1,000; average: $1,000-$50,000).
Purpose and activities: Emphasis on education and the arts.
Types of support: Continuing support, annual campaigns, building funds, operating budgets, publications, endowment funds, general purposes, renovation projects.
Limitations: No grants to individuals; no loans.
Application information: New applications seldom considered; giving only to present beneficiaries and for special proposals developed by the directors.
Deadline(s): None
Board meeting date(s): May and as required
Write: Crosby R. Smith, Pres.
Officers: Crosby R. Smith,* Pres.; Robert F. Quick, V.P. and Treas.; Alan Comrie, V.P.; Shirley Ondrick, Secy.
Directors:* Joan M. Bryan, Mark M. Collins, Jr., Phyllis Dillon Collins, Susan S. Dillon.
Number of staff: 1 part-time professional.
Employer Identification Number: 136400226

1873
The Dobson Foundation, Inc.

Four East 66th St., Suite 1E
New York 10021

Incorporated in 1961 in NY.
Donor(s): Walter M. Jeffords, Jr.
Financial data (yr. ended 12/31/87): Assets, $4,082,751 (M); expenditures, $185,090, including $165,810 for 45 grants (high: $89,000; low: $50).
Purpose and activities: Emphasis on conservation; support also for hospitals, higher education, sports museums and Catholic church support.
Limitations: Giving primarily in NY and ME.
Application information: Contributes only to pre-selected organizations. Applications not accepted.
Officers: Walter M. Jeffords, Jr., Pres.; Kathleen McL. Jeffords, V.P. and Secy.-Treas.
Employer Identification Number: 136168259

1874
Cleveland H. Dodge Foundation, Inc.

670 West 247th St.
Riverdale 10471 (212) 543-1220

Incorporated in 1917 in NY.
Donor(s): Cleveland H. Dodge.†
Financial data (yr. ended 12/31/88): Assets, $20,209,310 (M); expenditures, $1,030,947, including $802,930 for grants (high: $125,000).
Purpose and activities: "To promote the well-being of mankind throughout the world." Grants for a selected list of international organizations in the Near East; grants also to a selected few national agencies in the U.S. The balance directed to organizations located in New York City. Most grants in the U.S. for higher and secondary education, youth agencies and child welfare and cultural programs.
Types of support: Building funds, equipment, endowment funds, matching funds.
Limitations: Giving primarily in New York, NY, the Near East, and national organizations. No support for health care or medical research. No grants to individuals, or for general purposes, research, scholarships, or fellowships; no loans.
Publications: Annual report, program policy statement.
Application information:
Initial approach: Letter
Copies of proposal: 1
Deadline(s): Submit letter prior to the 15th of Jan., Apr., or Oct.
Board meeting date(s): 3 times a year
Final notification: Within 3 months of submitting the proposal
Write: Phyllis M. Criscuoli, Admin. Dir.
Officers: Cleveland E. Dodge, Jr.,* Pres.; Alfred H. Howell,* V.P.; Gilbert Kerlin,* Secy.; Phyllis M. Criscuoli, Admin. Dir. and Treas.
Directors:* David S. Dodge, Margaret Dodge Garrett, Robert Garrett, William Dodge Rueckert, Ingrid R. Warren, Mary Rea Weidlein.
Number of staff: 1 full-time professional.
Employer Identification Number: 136015087
Recent arts and culture grants:
Fort Ligonier Association, Ligonier, PA, $5,000. For education and curatorial programs. 1987.
Silver City Museum, Silver City, NM, $5,000. Toward Building Fund. 1987.
Wave Hill, Bronx, NY, $50,000. For Lower Hudson Valley Project. 1987.
Wave Hill, Bronx, NY, $15,000. For operating expenses. 1987.

1875
Henri & Eugenia Doll Foundation, Inc.

Four East 66th St.
New York 10021-6548

Established in 1954 in TX.
Financial data (yr. ended 12/31/87): Assets, $133,014 (M); gifts received, $338,082; expenditures, $329,056, including $324,250 for 79 grants (high: $50,000; low: $250).
Purpose and activities: Grants primarily to cultural organizations and the performing arts.
Limitations: No grants to individuals.

Application information: Contributes only to pre-selected organizations. Applications not accepted.
Officer: Henri G. Doll, Pres.
Employer Identification Number: 746036663

1876
Jean and Louis Dreyfus Foundation, Inc.
c/o Decker, Hubbard and Welden
30 Rockefeller Plaza
New York 10112 (212) 581-7575

Incorporated about 1978 in NY.
Donor(s): Louis Dreyfus.†
Financial data (yr. ended 12/31/87): Assets, $11,440,181 (M); expenditures, $672,526, including $525,600 for 52 grants (high: $100,000; low: $1,000; average: $5,000-$10,000).
Purpose and activities: Grants primarily to established institutions of the arts and medical research; some support also for hospitals and social services.
Limitations: Giving primarily in New York, NY, area.
Application information:
Initial approach: Proposal
Copies of proposal: 2
Board meeting date(s): Spring and Fall
Write: Edmee de Montmollin, Prog. Dir.
Officers: Valli V. Dreyfus Firth, Pres.; Thomas J. Sweeney, V.P. and Treas.; Nicholas L.D. Firth, V.P.; Thomas J. Hubbard, Secy.
Number of staff: 1 part-time professional.
Employer Identification Number: 132947180

1877
The Max and Victoria Dreyfus Foundation, Inc.
575 Madison Ave.
New York 10022 (212) 605-0354

Incorporated in 1965 in NY.
Donor(s): Victoria Dreyfus,† Max Dreyfus.†
Financial data (yr. ended 12/31/87): Assets, $35,894,885 (M); expenditures, $1,781,317, including $1,276,975 for 170 grants (high: $30,000; low: $500; average: $1,000-$25,000).
Purpose and activities: Support for hospitals, medical research, education, health and social services, with emphasis on youth and aid to the aged and handicapped, and cultural programs.
Types of support: Research, special projects.
Limitations: No grants to individuals.
Application information: Submit proposal upon request of the foundation only.
Initial approach: Letter
Deadline(s): 10 weeks prior to board meeting dates
Board meeting date(s): Usually in mid-Feb., June, and Oct.
Final notification: 2 weeks following board meetings
Write: Ms. Lucy Gioia, Admin. Asst.
Officers and Directors: David J. Oppenheim, Pres.; Nancy E. Oddo, V.P.; Norman S. Portenoy, V.P.; Winifred Riggs Portenoy, Secy.-Treas.
Number of staff: 1 full-time support; 1 part-time support.
Employer Identification Number: 131687573

1878
The Caleb C. and Julia W. Dula Educational and Charitable Foundation
c/o Manufacturers Hanover Trust Co.
600 Fifth Ave.
New York 10020 (212) 957-1615

Trust established in 1939 in NY.
Donor(s): Julia W. Dula.†
Financial data (yr. ended 12/31/88): Assets, $19,200,000 (M); expenditures, $811,000 for 85 grants (high: $100,000; low: $1,000).
Purpose and activities: Grants to charities which the Dulas supported during their lifetime, with emphasis on higher and secondary education, hospitals, libraries, social service agencies, child welfare, church support, cultural programs, and historic preservation.
Types of support: Operating budgets.
Limitations: No grants to individuals; no loans.
Application information:
Deadline(s): None
Board meeting date(s): Usually spring and fall
Write: Sarita A. Albertson, Trust Officer, Manufacturers Hanover Trust Co.
Trustees: Margaret C. Taylor, Julia P. Wightman, Orrin S. Wightman III, Manufacturers Hanover Trust Co.
Employer Identification Number: 136045790

1879
The Dun & Bradstreet Corporation Foundation
299 Park Ave.
New York 10171 (212) 593-6746

Incorporated in 1953 in DE.
Donor(s): The Dun & Bradstreet Group.
Financial data (yr. ended 12/31/87): Assets, $15,651,410 (M); expenditures, $2,992,379, including $938,769 for 309 grants (high: $187,688; low: $25; average: $500-$10,000) and $1,957,005 for 2,080 employee matching gifts.
Purpose and activities: To assist charitable and educational institutions, with emphasis on cultural programs, community funds, higher education, health and welfare, and youth agencies.
Types of support: Operating budgets, continuing support, annual campaigns, general purposes, employee-related scholarships, employee matching gifts.
Limitations: No grants to individuals (except for employee-related scholarships), or for building or endowment funds, or research; no loans.
Application information:
Initial approach: Letter or proposal
Copies of proposal: 1
Deadline(s): Submit proposal preferably in Sept. or Oct.; no set deadline
Board meeting date(s): Semiannually
Final notification: 4 weeks
Write: Juliann Gill, Admin.
Officers: Charles W. Moritz,* Pres.; William O. Frohlich, V.P.; N. Eugene Harden, V.P.; Robert G. Wallace, Secy.; Steven G. Klein, Treas.; Juliann Gill, Admin.
Trustees:* Edwin A. Bescherer, Jr., Robert E. Weissman.
Number of staff: 2
Employer Identification Number: 136148188

1880
Dyson Foundation
230 Park Ave., Rm. 659
New York 10169 (212) 661-4600

Trust established in 1949 in NY; incorporated in 1958 in DE.
Donor(s): Charles H. Dyson, Margaret M. Dyson, The Dyson-Kissner-Moran Corp.
Financial data (yr. ended 12/31/87): Assets, $646,649 (M); gifts received, $1,560,100; expenditures, $1,418,320, including $1,415,875 for 97 grants (high: $100,000; low: $100; average: $1,000-$50,000).
Purpose and activities: Grants primarily for civic and cultural affairs, and for medical research, with emphasis on pediatrics; support also for higher education and social service agencies.
Types of support: Building funds, general purposes, research.
Limitations: Giving primarily in NY; but no stated limitations. No grants to individuals.
Application information:
Initial approach: Proposal
Deadline(s): None
Board meeting date(s): Quarterly
Write: Anne E. Dyson, M.D., Pres.
Officers: Anne E. Dyson, M.D.,* Pres.; Charles H. Dyson,* V.P.; Margaret M. Dyson,* V.P.; Robert R. Dyson,* V.P.; John A. Moran,* V.P.; John H. FitzSimons, Secy.
Directors:* Ernest H. Lorch, Joseph V. Mariner, Jr.
Number of staff: 1 part-time professional; 1 part-time support.
Employer Identification Number: 136084888

1881
Eastman Kodak Charitable Trust
c/o Eastman Kodak Company
343 State St.
Rochester 14650 (716) 724-2434

Trust established in 1952 in NY.
Donor(s): Eastman Kodak Co.
Financial data (yr. ended 12/31/88): Assets, $13,023,318 (M); gifts received, $8,373,229; expenditures, $8,373,229, including $8,337,201 for 235 grants (high: $3,200,000; low: $150).
Purpose and activities: Support for community funds, higher education, health, human services, civic affairs, community activities, arts and culture, and conservation and environmental affairs.
Types of support: Annual campaigns, general purposes, continuing support.
Limitations: Giving primarily in high employment locations, including Rochester, NY; Kingsport, TN; Windsor, CO; Columbia, SC; and Longview, TX; giving nationally only for higher education. No grants to individuals, or for matching gifts; no loans; low priority given to building or endowment funds.
Publications: Corporate giving report.
Application information: Contributes only to pre-selected organizations. Applications not accepted.
Board meeting date(s): Monthly
Write: Stanley C. Wright, Dir., Corp. Contribs. Prog.
Trustee: Chase Lincoln First Bank, N.A.

Number of staff: None.
Employer Identification Number: 166015274
Recent arts and culture grants:
Bucket Dance Theater, Rochester, NY, $10,000. 1987.
Cultural Council of Richland and Lexington Counties, Columbia, SC, $8,000. 1987.
Genesee Country Museum, Mumford, NY, $11,800. 1987.
Genesee Valley Arts Foundation, Rochester, NY, $25,585. 1987.
Genesee Valley Arts Foundation, Rochester, NY, $24,000. 1987.
Genesee Valley Arts Foundation, Rochester, NY, $24,000. 1987.
Genesee Valley Arts Foundation, Rochester, NY, $6,000. 1987.
Genesee Valley Arts Foundation, Rochester, NY, $6,000. 1987.
Hands-On Museum, Ann Arbor, MI, $7,000. 1987.
International Museum of Photography at George Eastman House, Rochester, NY, $221,166. 1987.
International Museum of Photography at George Eastman House, Rochester, NY, $221,166. 1987.
International Museum of Photography at George Eastman House, Rochester, NY, $221,166. 1987.
International Museum of Photography at George Eastman House, Rochester, NY, $220,500. 1987.
International Museum of Photography at George Eastman House, Rochester, NY, $100,000. 1987.
Kingsport Fine Arts Center, Kingsport, TN, $12,000. For partnership. 1987.
Lincoln Center for the Performing Arts, NYC, NY, $5,000. 1987.
Margaret Woodbury Strong Museum, Rochester, NY, $5,000. 1987.
Memorial Art Gallery of the University of Rochester, Rochester, NY, $55,000. 1987.
Memorial Art Gallery of the University of Rochester, Rochester, NY, $50,000. 1987.
Northern Colorado Foundation for the Arts, Greeley, CO, $25,000. 1987.
Permanent Charities Committee of the Entertainment Industry, Los Angeles, CA, $5,000. 1987.
Rochester Area Educational Television Association, Rochester, NY, $7,000. 1987.
Rochester Museum and Science Center, Rochester, NY, $150,000. 1987.
Rochester Museum and Science Center, Rochester, NY, $50,000. 1987.
Rochester Philharmonic Orchestra, Rochester, NY, $120,000. 1987.
Rochester Philharmonic Orchestra, Rochester, NY, $100,000. 1987.
Rochester Philharmonic Orchestra, Rochester, NY, $100,000. 1987.
Sonnenberg Gardens, Canandaigua, NY, $5,000. 1987.
South Carolina State Museum, Columbia, SC, $9,500. 1987.

1882
Dean S. Edmonds Foundation
c/o The Bank of New York
48 Wall St.
New York 10015 (212) 536-4828

Established in 1959 in NY.
Financial data (yr. ended 12/31/87): Assets, $1,609,334 (M); expenditures, $101,521, including $73,000 for 44 grants (high: $6,000; low: $500) and $1,000 for 1 grant to an individual.
Purpose and activities: Giving for higher and secondary education, and cultural programs.
Application information:
Initial approach: Letter
Deadline(s): None
Write: Marjorie Thompson
Trustees: Dean S. Edmonds III, The Bank of New York.
Employer Identification Number: 136161381

1883
Seymour Eisenberg Memorial Foundation
c/o Goldman, Sachs & Co., Tax Dept.
85 Broad St.
New York 10004-2408

Established in 1979 in NY.
Donor(s): Lewis M. Eisenberg.
Financial data (yr. ended 7/31/88): Assets, $1,374,062 (M); gifts received, $630,658; expenditures, $224,474, including $224,015 for 82 grants (high: $40,000; low: $55).
Purpose and activities: Giving primarily for Jewish welfare funds and other Jewish organizations; support also for health associations, youth, medical research, and higher education.
Limitations: Giving primarily in New York, NY. No grants to individuals.
Application information: Applications not accepted.
Trustees: Judith Ann Eisenberg, Lewis M. Eisenberg, Eugene Mercy, Jr.
Employer Identification Number: 133001003

1884
Elsmere Foundation, Inc.
c/o L.T. Rothschild
222 Broadway, 10th Fl.
New York 10038

Incorporated in 1955 in NY.
Donor(s): Kate S. Heming, Henry L. Heming, Henry A. Cohn, Abraham S. Platt, Richard H. Baer, Walter W. Hess, Jr., Herbert H. Weitsman,† Chester Viale, Stephen Kovacs.
Financial data (yr. ended 12/31/87): Assets, $739,424 (M); gifts received, $40,556; expenditures, $265,158, including $253,995 for 119 grants (high: $55,000; low: $10).
Purpose and activities: Giving for Jewish welfare funds, social service agencies, cultural programs, and hospitals.
Limitations: Giving primarily in NY. No grants to individuals.
Application information: Contributes only to pre-selected organizations. Applications not accepted.
Write: Walter W. Hess, Jr., Pres.
Officers and Directors: Walter W. Hess, Jr., Pres.; Stephen Kovacs, 1st V.P.; Alexander Bing III, 2nd V.P.; Robert Schoenthal, Treas.; Anny M. Baer, Helen Cohn, Daniel Kampel, Chester Viale.
Employer Identification Number: 136061343

1885
Fred L. Emerson Foundation, Inc.
63 Genesee St.
P.O. Box 276
Auburn 13021 (315) 253-9621

Incorporated in 1932 in DE.
Donor(s): Fred L. Emerson.†
Financial data (yr. ended 12/31/87): Assets, $41,177,397 (M); expenditures, $2,241,430, including $1,824,961 for 41 grants (high: $306,400; low: $100).
Purpose and activities: Giving to private colleges and universities (primarily for scholarships or building funds), community funds, and a library building fund; grants also for youth and social service agencies and cultural programs.
Types of support: Building funds, matching funds, annual campaigns, emergency funds, equipment, endowment funds, scholarship funds, special projects, research, renovation projects, capital campaigns.
Limitations: Giving primarily in the central NY area. No grants to individuals, or for deficit financing; no loans. Support for operating budgets is discouraged.
Publications: Program policy statement, application guidelines.
Application information:
Initial approach: Letter, telephone, or proposal
Copies of proposal: 1
Deadline(s): 2 months prior to board meetings
Board meeting date(s): June and Dec.
Final notification: 2 to 3 weeks after board meetings (positive replies only)
Write: Ronald D. West, Exec. Dir.
Officers and Directors: William V. Emerson, Pres.; Peter J. Emerson, V.P.; Ronald D. West, Exec. Dir. and Secy.; Thomas S. Tallman, Treas.; William F. Allyn, David L. Emerson, W. Gary Emerson, E. Paul Flynn, J. David Hammond, Richard B. Secrest.
Number of staff: 1 full-time professional; 1 full-time support.
Employer Identification Number: 156017650

1886
EMSA Fund, Inc.
147 East 48th St.
New York 10017

Incorporated in 1962 in GA.
Donor(s): Phoebe Weil Lundeen,† and members of the Franklin family.
Financial data (yr. ended 12/31/86): Assets, $1,633,398 (M); expenditures, $81,481, including $67,560 for 58 grants.
Purpose and activities: Giving primarily for social services, cultural, health, and educational programs, particularly for those who have been neglected or hard to reach in the provision of

such programs; some support for environmental programs.
Types of support: General purposes, operating budgets, continuing support, annual campaigns, seed money, emergency funds, building funds, endowment funds, special projects, research.
Limitations: Giving primarily in GA, particularly the Atlanta area, and in CO. No grants to individuals, or for scholarships, fellowships, or matching gifts; no loans.
Publications: Application guidelines.
Application information:
Initial approach: Letter
Copies of proposal: 1
Deadline(s): None
Board meeting date(s): Annually
Final notification: 2 to 4 weeks
Write: Alice Franklin, Pres.
Officers and Trustees: Andrew D. Franklin, Chair.; Alice Franklin, Pres.
Number of staff: 1 part-time professional.
Employer Identification Number: 586043282

1887
The Equitable Foundation, Inc.
787 Seventh Ave., 7th Fl.
New York 10019 (212) 554-3475

Established in 1986 in New York.
Donor(s): The Equitable Financial Cos.
Financial data (yr. ended 9/30/88): Assets, $683,715 (M); gifts received, $4,594,546; expenditures, $5,351,816, including $1,238,400 for 54 grants (high: $125,000; low: $3,000; average: $5,000-$25,000), $78,000 for 37 grants to individuals and $3,751,775 for employee matching gifts.
Purpose and activities: Giving primarily for minority education, arts and community services, AIDS, and equal opportunity programs.
Types of support: Employee matching gifts, continuing support, general purposes, operating budgets, employee matching gifts, scholarship funds, special projects.
Limitations: Giving primarily in New York City, NY. No support for political, religious, or international purposes. No grants to individuals (other than employee-related scholarships).
Publications: Application guidelines.
Application information:
Initial approach: Letter
Copies of proposal: 1
Deadline(s): None
Board meeting date(s): Quarterly
Write: Nancy H. Green, Pres.
Officers: Nancy H. Green,* Pres.; William T. McCaffrey, V.P.; Patricia A. Kelly, Secy.; Paul H. Olsavsky, Treas.
Directors:* Robert W. Barth, David H. Harris, Benjamin D. Holloway, Eleanor Sheldon.
Number of staff: 4 full-time professional; 3 full-time support.
Employer Identification Number: 133340512

1888
The Armand G. Erpf Fund, Inc.
c/o Main Hurdman
640 Park Ave.
New York 10021

Incorporated in 1951 in NY.
Donor(s): Armand G. Erpf.†
Financial data (yr. ended 11/30/87): Assets, $4,893,018 (M); gifts received, $126,069; expenditures, $550,732, including $444,217 for 120 grants (high: $71,750; low: $20).
Purpose and activities: Support for environment and conservation, education, and cultural programs.
Limitations: Giving primarily in NY. No grants to individuals, or for endowment funds.
Application information:
Initial approach: Proposal
Copies of proposal: 1
Board meeting date(s): Quarterly
Write: Gerrit P. Van de Bovenkamp, Pres.
Officers and Trustees: Sue Erpf Van de Bovenkamp, Pres.; Gerrit P. Van de Bovenkamp, Exec. V.P.; John G. Clancy, Secy.; Carl Kempner, Treas.; Douglas Campbell, Henry B. Hyde, Roger D. Stone.
Employer Identification Number: 136085594

1889
The T. M. Evans Foundation, Inc.
300 Park Ave.
New York 10022 (212) 735-1217

Incorporated in 1951 in DE.
Donor(s): Thomas Mellon Evans.
Financial data (yr. ended 12/31/87): Assets, $5,245,366 (M); expenditures, $376,827, including $313,640 for 41 grants (high: $75,000; low: $100; average: $1,000).
Purpose and activities: Grants primarily for museums and historic preservation, higher education, hospitals, medical research, music, religion, youth guidance services, and literary activities.
Types of support: Annual campaigns, building funds, capital campaigns, continuing support, emergency funds, equipment, general purposes, matching funds, operating budgets, renovation projects, research.
Limitations: No grants to individuals, or for scholarships or fellowships; no loans.
Application information:
Initial approach: Proposal
Copies of proposal: 1
Board meeting date(s): Dec.
Write: L.F. Cerrone, Asst. Secy.
Officers and Trustees: Thomas Mellon Evans, Pres.; James H. Fraser, Secy.-Treas.; Betty B. Evans, Edward P. Evans, Thomas M. Evans, Jr.
Employer Identification Number: 256012086

1890
The David Everett Foundation, Inc.
150 East 69th St.
New York 10021

Incorporated in 1957 in NY.
Donor(s): Henry Everett, Edith B. Everett.†
Financial data (yr. ended 12/31/87): Assets, $3,398,917 (M); gifts received, $1,003,496; expenditures, $80,246, including $58,783 for 77 grants (high: $15,000; low: $7).
Purpose and activities: Giving primarily for Jewish welfare organizations, including those in Israel; some support for cultural programs and higher education, and the disadvantaged.
Limitations: Giving primarily in the New York, NY, metropolitan area. No grants to individuals.
Application information: Application form required.
Initial approach: Letter
Copies of proposal: 1
Write: Edith B. Everett, V.P.
Officers: Henry Everett, Pres. and Treas.; Edith B. Everett, V.P. and Secy.
Employer Identification Number: 116038040

1891
Exxon Corporate Giving Program
1251 Avenue of the Americas
New York 10020-1198 (212) 333-6346

Financial data (yr. ended 12/31/88): $29,735,000 for grants.
Purpose and activities: Supports arts and culture, civic and community service, United Appeals and federated drives, public information and policy research, education, environmental research, minority programs, health and welfare. Funding available for publications and media; also makes in-kind donations.
Types of support: Capital campaigns, employee matching gifts, equipment, general purposes, renovation projects, research, scholarship funds, special projects, employee-related scholarships.
Limitations: Giving primarily in areas of company operations. No grants to individuals.
Application information:
Initial approach: Initial contact by letter to the local Exxon facility or to headquarters
Deadline(s): None
Write: Leonard Fleischer, Mgr., Contribs. Coordination

1892
Fay's Drug Company Foundation, Inc.
7245 Henry Clay Blvd.
Liverpool 13088 (315) 451-8000

Established in 1981 in NY.
Donor(s): Fay's Drug Co., Inc.
Financial data (yr. ended 1/31/88): Assets, $533,896 (M); gifts received, $80,000; expenditures, $152,204, including $145,662 for 230 grants (high: $20,000; low: $10).
Purpose and activities: Grants for hospitals and health services, community funds, culture, social services, and community development.
Types of support: General purposes.
Limitations: Giving primarily in the Northeast, with emphasis on NY and PA.
Application information:
Initial approach: Proposal
Copies of proposal: 1
Deadline(s): None
Board meeting date(s): 1st Fri. of each month
Write: Gillian M. McAuliffe, Pres.
Officers and Directors: Gillian M. McAuliffe, Pres.; Donald R. Bregande, V.P.; David Panasci, V.P.; Allan Travis, V.P.; Warren D. Wolfson, Secy.-Treas.
Number of staff: None.
Employer Identification Number: 222353455

1893
Federated Foundations, Inc.
c/o Theodore Present
450 Seventh Ave.
New York 10001

Incorporated in 1961 in NY.
Donor(s): Harry Keiser, Edward Netter, and others.
Financial data (yr. ended 12/31/87): Assets, $287,249 (M); expenditures, $253,052, including $252,229 for 56 grants (high: $170,000; low: $25).
Purpose and activities: Grants primarily for education, cultural programs, hospitals, and Jewish welfare funds.
Limitations: Giving primarily in New York City, NY, and Greenwich, CT.
Officer: Richard Netter, Pres.
Employer Identification Number: 136143973

1894
The Donald M. Feuerstein Foundation
(Formerly The Feuerstein-Dryfoos Foundation, Inc.)
c/o Salomon Brothers, Inc.
One New York Plaza
New York 10004 (212) 747-7843

Established in 1975 in NY.
Donor(s): Donald M. Feuerstein.
Financial data (yr. ended 6/30/87): Assets, $78,489 (M); gifts received, $201,000; expenditures, $191,138, including $190,063 for 45 grants (high: $50,000; low: $96).
Purpose and activities: Giving for cultural programs, secondary and higher education, and health agencies.
Limitations: Giving primarily in the New York, NY, metropolitan area.
Application information: Contributes only to pre-selected organizations. Applications not accepted.
Officers: Donald M. Feuerstein, Pres. and Treas.; Richard G. Rosenthal, V.P. and Secy.
Employer Identification Number: 132838464

1895
Elias and Bertha Fife Foundation, Inc.
Standard Motor Products, Inc.
37-18 Northern Blvd.
Long Island City 11101 (718) 392-0200

Incorporated in 1959 in NY.
Donor(s): Members of the Fife family, Standard Motor Products, Inc.
Financial data (yr. ended 4/30/87): Assets, $4,460,381 (M); gifts received, $120,000; expenditures, $191,975, including $189,925 for 121 grants (high: $90,450; low: $100).
Purpose and activities: Support for Jewish welfare funds, health and welfare agencies, and cultural programs.
Application information:
Write: Bernard Fife, Pres.
Officers and Directors: Bernard Fife, Pres.; Nathaniel L. Sills, Secy.-Treas.; Arlene Fife, Ruth Sills.
Employer Identification Number: 116035634

1896
The First Boston Foundation Trust
c/o Maria Lilly
12 East 49th St.
New York 10017 (212) 909-4575

Trust established in 1959 in MA.
Donor(s): The First Boston Corp.
Financial data (yr. ended 12/31/87): Assets, $283,991 (M); gifts received, $671,750; expenditures, $1,842,794, including $1,012,850 for 128 grants (high: $200,000; low: $200) and $826,544 for 361 employee matching gifts.
Purpose and activities: Emphasis on community funds and higher education; support also for cultural programs, community development, and groups seeking to improve international relations.
Types of support: Employee matching gifts.
Limitations: No grants to individuals.
Application information:
Initial approach: Proposal
Deadline(s): None
Write: William W. Galvin, III, Trustee
Officers: Michael Raoul-Duval,* Chair.; Kerry Arnold, Secy.
Trustees:* Robert K. deVeer, Jr., William W. Galvin III, William E. Mayer, Michael G. Zeiss.
Employer Identification Number: 046059692

1897
Vain and Harry Fish Foundation, Inc.
225 West 34th St., Rm. 1617
New York 10122

Incorporated in 1972 in NY.
Donor(s): Vain B. Fish,† Harry Fish.†
Financial data (yr. ended 12/31/86): Assets, $3,395,696 (M); expenditures, $250,579, including $190,700 for 54 grants (high: $25,000; low: $500).
Purpose and activities: Grants for higher education and hospitals; grants also for cultural activities, youth agencies, the handicapped, and church support.
Limitations: Giving primarily in NY.
Application information:
Write: Alexander W. Gentleman, Pres.
Officers: Alexander W. Gentleman, Pres.; Vivian F. Gentleman, V.P. and Secy.; Bernard Leegant, Treas.
Employer Identification Number: 132723211

1898
The Fisher Fund
85 Broad St., Tax Dept.
New York 10004

Established in 1985 in NY.
Donor(s): Pieter A. Fisher.
Financial data (yr. ended 5/31/88): Assets, $1,544,287 (M); expenditures, $160,717, including $156,000 for 16 grants (high: $25,000; low: $1,000).
Purpose and activities: Grants for higher education, health, culture, and international affairs.
Types of support: General purposes.
Limitations: No grants to individuals, or for scholarships; no loans.
Application information: Applications not accepted.
Trustees: Geoffrey T. Boisi, M. Helen Fisher, Pieter A. Fisher.
Employer Identification Number: 133318154

1899
Forbes Foundation
60 Fifth Ave.
New York 10011 (212) 620-2248

Established in 1979 in NJ.
Donor(s): Forbes, Inc.
Financial data (yr. ended 12/31/87): Assets, $1,946,489 (M); gifts received, $3,700,000; expenditures, $2,680,805, including $2,678,488 for 507 grants (high: $1,000,000; low: $20; average: $100-$10,000).
Purpose and activities: Support for higher and secondary education, hospitals, cultural programs, museums, and welfare funds.
Types of support: General purposes, building funds, endowment funds.
Limitations: No grants to individuals, or for matching gifts; no loans.
Publications: 990-PF.
Application information: Contributes only to preselected organizations. Applications not accepted.
Board meeting date(s): As required
Write: Leonard H. Yablon, Secy.-Treas.
Officers: Malcolm S. Forbes, Pres.; Malcolm S. Forbes, Jr., V.P.; Leonard H. Yablon, Secy.-Treas.
Number of staff: None.
Employer Identification Number: 237037319

1900
The Forchheimer Foundation
c/o Weitzner, Levine, Hamburg & Walzer
230 Park Ave.
New York 10169 (212) 661-3140

Established in NY.
Donor(s): Leo Forchheimer.†
Financial data (yr. ended 12/31/87): Assets, $7,607,097 (M); expenditures, $1,150,794, including $1,065,000 for 16 grants (high: $500,000; low: $5,000; average: $10,000-$50,000).
Purpose and activities: Giving primarily for hospitals, health agencies, higher education, including medical and technical education, Jewish welfare funds, museums, and social services.
Limitations: Giving primarily in New York, NY, and Israel.
Application information:
Deadline(s): None
Officers: Julia Forchheimer, Pres.; Ludwig Jesselson, V.P. and Treas.; Rudolph Forchheimer, Secy.
Employer Identification Number: 136075112

1901
The Ford Foundation
320 East 43rd St.
New York 10017 (212) 573-5000

Incorporated in 1936 in MI.
Donor(s): Henry Ford,† Edsel Ford.†

Financial data (yr. ended 9/30/88): Assets, $5,037,728,000 (M); expenditures, $267,566,000, including $178,136,980 for 1,453 grants (high: $4,228,250; low: $451; average: $50,000-$1,000,000), $5,988,805 for 557 grants to individuals, $2,099,436 for 20 foundation-administered programs and $17,851,854 for loans.
Purpose and activities: To advance the public well-being by identifying and contributing to the solution of problems of national and international importance. Grants primarily to institutions for experimental, demonstration, and developmental efforts that are likely to produce significant advances within the Foundation's six major fields of interest: urban poverty and the disadvantaged--including community and neighborhood self-help initiatives, housing rehabilitation, educational and employment programs for disadvantaged youth and for welfare recipients, early childhood education, maternal and child health and nutrition, and research on urban problems; rural poverty and resources--including community-based rural development national policy planning, income-generating projects, improvement of opportunities for women, the landless, and migrants, and management of land and water resources; human rights and social justice--including civil rights, sex discrimination, and the rights of refugees and migrants; governance and public policy--including projects to strengthen democratic processes and institutions, to promote civic participation, improve state and local governments, and to enhance the vitality of the nonprofit sector; education and culture--support for excellence and equity in urban and rural public schools and in higher education, artistic creativity, and cultural preservation in developing countries; international affairs--analysis, research, dialogue, and public education on international peace, security and arms control, international economics, international refugees and migration, international organizations and law, and foreign-area studies.
Types of support: Conferences and seminars, consulting services, exchange programs, general purposes, matching funds, professorships, program-related investments, publications, research, seed money, special projects, technical assistance, continuing support, endowment funds, fellowships, grants to individuals.
Limitations: No support for programs for which substantial support from government or other sources is readily available, or for religious activities. No grants for routine operating costs, construction or maintenance of buildings, or undergraduate scholarships; graduate fellowships generally channeled through grants to universities or other organizations; no grants for purely personal or local needs.
Publications: Annual report, newsletter, program policy statement (including application guidelines), occasional report.
Application information: Foreign applicants should contact foundation for addresses of its overseas offices, through which they must apply.
Initial approach: Letter, proposal or telephone
Copies of proposal: 1
Deadline(s): None
Board meeting date(s): Dec., Mar., June, and Sept.
Final notification: Initial indication as to whether proposal falls within program interests within 1 month
Write: Barron M. Tenny, Secy.
Officers: Franklin A. Thomas,* Pres.; Barron M. Tenny, V.P., General Counsel, and Secy.; Susan V. Berresford, V.P.; William D. Carmichael, V.P.; John W. English, V.P.; John Koprowski, Treas.; Barry D. Gaberman, Deputy V.P.; John D. Gerhart, Deputy V.P.; Diane Galloway, Asst. Secy.
Trustees:* Edson W. Spencer, Chair.; Rodrigo Botero, Yvonne Braithwaite Burke, Nina G. Garsoian, Sir Christopher Hogg, Vernon E. Jordan, Jr., Donald F. McHenry, Paul F. Miller, Jr., William G. Milliken, General Olusegun Obasanjo, Donald S. Perkins, Barbara Scott Preiskel, Harriet S. Rabb, Henry B. Schacht, M.S. Swaminathan, Thomas H. Wyman.
Number of staff: 218 full-time professional; 3 part-time professional; 339 full-time support; 8 part-time support.
Employer Identification Number: 131684331
Recent arts and culture grants:
African Research and Communications, DC, $50,000. For international book fair and writers' conference on South Africa and preparation of scholarly writings by black South Africans on history of anti-apartheid struggle. 10/87.
Akademi Seni Karawitan Indonesia, Indonesia, $40,000. For ethnomusicology program. 10/87.
Alternate ROOTS (Regional Organization of Theaters South), Atlanta, GA, $33,215. To celebrate ROOTS's tenth anniversary with festival of performances and conference on impact of culture on racial attitudes in Southeast. 10/87.
American Composers Orchestra, NYC, NY, $200,000. For supplement, for further institutional development. Repertoire emphasizes twentieth-century American orchestral music. 6/88.
American Dance Festival, NYC, NY, $200,000. For supplement to complete project preserving modern dance classics created by black American choreographers. 11/88.
American Museum of the Moving Image, Astoria, NY, $35,350. For oral history project on films produced by blacks for black audiences during 1920s and 1930s. 2/88.
American Music Theater Festival, Philadelphia, PA, $250,000. For supplement for Music Theater Production Partnership, through which festival works with regional theaters to create and produce new music theater. 11/88.
American Music Theater Festival, Music Theater Production Partnership, Philadelphia, PA, $250,000. To continue national network of 9 resident theaters who jointly develop and produce contemporary music theater. 10/87.
American Repertory Theater, Cambridge, MA, $100,000. To develop new works in music theater through collaboration by composers, writers, choreographers, directors, and other creative artists. 12/87.
American Research Center in Egypt, NYC, NY, $15,000. To train Egyptian museum curators at Metropolitan Museum of Art in New York. 10/87.
American Symphony Orchestra League, NYC, NY, $25,000. To develop ways to provide more employment opportunities for black classical musicians. 11/88.
Arizona State University, Tempe, AZ, $100,000. To carry out comprehensive program of writing instruction. 10/87.
Arts Midwest, Minneapolis, MN, $300,000. For minority arts administration fellowship program. 6/88.
Astro Artz, Los Angeles, CA, $20,000. For subscription campaign for arts journal High Performance. 2/88.
At the Foot of the Mountain, Minneapolis, MN, $225,000. To help maintain multiracial performing ensemble recently established by this experimental women's theater. 6/88.
Bethune Museum and Archives, DC, $150,000. For exhibit and film on role of black women in civil rights movement. 6/88.
Birzeit University, Jordan, $5,000. For publication of collection of Palestinian folk tales. 6/88.
Boston University, Boston, MA, $338,328. For video archive of senior American artists and cultural figures who have made vital contributions to twentieth-century art and literature. 10/87.
Center for Andean Rural Studies, Peru, $40,000. For archive of Andean historical photographs. 2/88.
Central and East European Publishing Project, England, $400,000. For publication of important writings in Central and East European languages and their translations into Western languages. 6/88.
Central Pennsylvania Youth Ballet, Carlisle, PA, $400,000. For supplement for Carlisle Project, program of residencies and workshops to train emerging choreographers. 6/88.
Chinese Academy of Social Sciences, Beijing, China, $250,000. For U.S.-China scholarly exchanges in social sciences and humanities. 6/88.
Cine-Mujer, Bogota, Colombia, $31,000. To distribute videos and films that seek to change public images of women in gender roles. 2/88.
Civil Rights Project, Boston, MA, $1,000,000. For second part of documentary film series, Eyes on the Prize, on black civil rights movement from 1965 to 1980. 10/87.
Clarity Educational Productions, Berkeley, CA, $25,000. For planning of One Summer in Mississippi, film based on 1964 civil rights marches in South. 10/87.
Columbia University, NYC, NY, $29,000. To enable delegation from university's Center on U.S.-China Arts Exchange to travel to China. 6/88.
Corisco Films, Brazil, $27,500. For survey of films about blacks in Brazil. 10/87.
Dance Theater of Harlem, NYC, NY, $350,000. To strengthen administrative structure. 10/87.
Dance Theater Workshop, NYC, NY, $330,000. For supplement, for general support of National Performance Network, which provides subsidies for presentation of new work in dance, theater, and music. 6/88.

Emilio Goeldi Museum of Para, Brazil, $49,434. For ethnobiological research on Kayapo Indians of Brazil. 12/87.
Feminist Press, NYC, NY, $30,420. For review of university programs in developing countries that address women's studies and development. 6/88.
Friends of the Barrio Museum, NYC, NY, $50,000. For outreach activities aimed at increasing membership and support of Hispanic arts institution. 12/87.
Future Educational Films, San Francisco, CA, $30,000. For production and distribution of documentary film on women who have risen from poverty to self-sufficiency. 6/88.
Gambia, Government of, Ministry of Education, Youth, and Sports, Gambia, $32,000. To develop national cultural policy and establish small grants program. 10/87.
Gambia, Government of, Monuments and Relics Commission, Gambia, $28,000. For training in management of collections. 10/87.
George Balanchine Foundation, NYC, NY, $50,000. For series of videotapes demonstrating Balanchine's choreographic techniques. 11/88.
Group I Acting Company, NYC, NY, $75,000. For 1988-89 season. Company is only national U.S. professional touring repertory theater. 6/88.
Group Theater Company, Seattle, WA, $162,725. To strengthen administration of multiracial company, which produces contemporary American plays. 6/88.
Guadalupe Cultural Arts Center, San Antonio, TX, $215,000. For staff development and for 1988 TENAZ festival of Latino-Chicano theater. 6/88.
Harvard University, W.E.B. DuBois Institute for Afro-American Research, Cambridge, MA, $336,000. For supplement, for visiting scholars and collaborative research. 6/88.
Historical Society of Nigeria, Nigeria, $11,000. For workshop on Nigerian oral traditions. 10/87.
Hudson River Film and Video Company, Garrison, NY, $40,000. For documentary film on status of American agriculture and effects of change on rural community. 8/88.
Independent Broadcasting Associates, Littleton, MA, $50,000. For radio series on Third World hunger, poverty, and chronic underdevelopment. 6/88.
Independent Broadcasting Associates, Littleton, MA, $50,000. For educational radio series, Living on Edge, to examine problems of hunger, poverty, and chronic underdevelopment in parts of Third World. 11/88.
Independent Committee on Arts Policy, NYC, NY, $15,000. For general support of forum of artists, critics, and funders. 2/88.
Institute for Schools of the Future, NYC, NY, $49,500. To develop instructional materials that use music and computers to teach mathematics and science to junior and senior high school students. 11/88.
International African Institute, London, England, $334,000. For supplement to secure new director for West African Museums Project and to open office in Dakar, Senegal. 11/88.
International Association of the Pan African Festival of Arts and Culture, Senegal, $25,000. To organize festival and do pilot television program on cultures of participating countries. 10/87.
International Center for the Study of the Preservation and the Restoration of Cultural Property, Italy, $72,000. For supplement to enable three West African museum technicians to participate in specialized course on methods of conserving African collections. 11/88.
International Center for the Study of the Preservation and the Restoration of Cultural Property, Italy, $30,000. For first issue of International Conservation Research Index, which will list all ongoing research projects in conservation. 10/87.
International Council of Museums, France, $10,000. For travel expenses for West African museum professionals. 10/87.
International Theater Institute of the United States, NYC, NY, $23,280. To catalogue recently acquired collection of Latin American theater materials. 6/88.
Jacobs Pillow Dance Festival, Lee, MA, $30,000. For Roots of Creole, celebration of Portuguese and African influences on Brazilian and North American dance. 8/88.
John Snow International Research and Training Institute, Boston, MA, $115,000. For drama and music festivals in Kenya promoting family-planning themes. 2/88.
Jose Bonifacio University, Brazil, $21,000. For research on relationship between gender and culture. 2/88.
K C T S/9 Public Television, Seattle, WA, $50,000. For community outreach activities related to documentary film showing innovative ways to provide quality child care. 8/88.
K Q E D, San Francisco, CA, $50,000. For screenings and promotional activities for Hispanic musical drama Corridos. 12/87.
Kidsnet, DC, $20,000. To add information on programming for minorities to its clearinghous on radio and television programs for children. 2/88.
La Mama Experimental Theater Club, NYC, NY, $500,000. To stabilize operations and to support residency of Great Jones Repertory Company. 11/88.
League for the Humanities, DC, $250,000. To help community colleges redesign and strengthen their humanities curricula. Six regional institutes will be established, drawing faculty from two- and four-year colleges to develop core liberal arts curriculum. 12/87.
Library of Congress, DC, $100,000. For review of library's mission, strategies, and management practices. 8/88.
Library of Tibetan Works and Archives, India, $40,000. For preservation and interpretation of Tibetan culture. 10/87.
Lincoln Center for the Performing Arts, NYC, NY, $50,000. For documentary on South African musical, Sarafina. 8/88.
Makerere University, Kampala, Uganda, $5,000. For restoration of modern East African art collection at Makerere Art Gallery. 11/88.
Maryland Institute College of Art, Baltimore, MD, $321,000. For supplement for minority scholarship program in visual arts at five professional art colleges. 2/88.
Meet the Composer, NYC, NY, $900,000. For program for joint commissions in all musical and dance idioms, to encourage collaborations between American composers and choreographers. 2/88.
Mid-America Arts Alliance, Kansas City, MO, $120,900. To organize six-state tour by Bilingual Foundation of the Arts of its production of Orinocol, contemporary Mexican play. 2/88.
Mozambique, Government of, Ministry of Culture, Mozambique, $140,000. For staff training and publications for national cultural archive. 6/88.
Music-Theater Performing Group, NYC, NY, $100,000. To develop new works in music theater through collaboration by composers, writers, choreographers, directors, and other creative artists. 12/87.
Music-Theater Performing Group, NYC, NY, $10,000. To replace stage sets, costumes and properties lost in warehouse fire. 2/88.
National Academy of History, Peru, $60,000. For equipment and supplies for academy's conservation laboratory and for training of archivists. 12/87.
National Archives Trust Fund Board, DC, $50,000. To publish papers of Margaret Sanger, pioneer and influential champion of birth control in America. 10/87.
National Gallery of Art, DC, $20,000. For travel and living expenses of participants in symposium on urban studies in South Asia. 10/87.
National Museum, Philippines, $11,500. To document architectural and historical heritage of town of Vigan in Ilocos Sur. 10/87.
National Public Radio, DC, $375,000. For supplement, for continued news coverage on Latin America and to develop reportage on Eastern Europe. 6/88.
National Temple Non-Profit Corporation, Philadelphia, PA, $100,000. To establish fund to help finance restoration and conversion of two historic buildings in north central Philadelphia into apartments for low-income families. 12/87.
Negro Ensemble Company, NYC, NY, $100,000. For general operating expenses and to launch subscription drive. 11/88.
Negro Ensemble Company, NYC, NY, $10,000. For preparation of audit reports and restructuring of financial records. 12/87.
New York University, Tisch School of the Arts, NYC, NY, $32,000. For scholarships to two minority students enrolled in Musical Theater program. 6/88.
Northern Arizona University, Flagstaff, AZ, $100,000. For coordinated program of writing in arts and sciences, with initial focus on multicultural civilization of U.S. Southwest. 10/87.
Nucleus for Indigenous Culture, Brazil, $49,000. To prepare radio programs on Indian culture and related topics, as part of freedom of expression awards. 11/88.
Old Globe Theater, Teatro Meta, San Diego, CA, $280,000. To continue support to pilot project established to provide training and employment to Hispanic actors and to produce plays by Hispanic playwrights. Funds will also support new Master of Fine

Arts program for young Hispanic performers. 10/87.
Opera de Camara, Santurce, Puerto Rico, $164,881. To strengthen administration and increase income to professional Puerto Rican opera company. 10/87.
Padatik, Calcutta, India, $50,000. For international symposium on relationship of Asian martial arts to contemporary performance arts. 8/88.
Pan Asian Repertory Theater, NYC, NY, $240,000. For senior artists ensemble. Pan Asian is country's major Asian-American theater company. 6/88.
Paraphrase, Bronx, NY, $50,000. To establish Black Heritage Trail on New York's Lower East Side and produce guidebook documenting experiences of nineteenth-century blacks in area. 8/88.
Playwrights Horizons, NYC, NY, $100,000. To develop new works in music theater through collaboration by composers, writers, choreographers, directors, and other creative artists. 12/87.
Pontifical Catholic University of Peru, Lima, Peru, $90,000. For archival preservation of traditional Andean music by University's Riva Aguero Institute. 10/87.
Princeton University, Princeton, NJ, $42,000. For supplement to microfilm selected items from Saint-Louis de Gonzague collection of Haitian historical and cultural materials in Port-au-Prince. 10/87.
Public Television Playhouse, NYC, NY, $50,000. For film about Hispanic immigrant's teaching successes at East Los Angeles high school. 12/87.
Radio Free Europe, DC, $40,000. For summer internship program concerned with Eastern Europe and ethnic nationalities in Soviet Union, at radio's headquarters in Munich. 10/87.
Seagull Foundation for the Arts, India, $79,000. For publication of English translations of contemporary plays and performance texts. 2/88.
Shanghai Academy of Social Sciences, China, $100,000. For U.S.-China scholarly exchanges in social sciences and humanities. 6/88.
Shri Ram Centre for Art and Culture, India, $31,000. For workshops on Hindi playwriting. 10/87.
Smithsonian Institution, DC, $40,000. For publications and video conference on role of Afro-Americans in Constitutional history. 6/88.
Society for the Preservation of Weeksville and Bedford Stuyvesant History, Brooklyn, NY, $50,000. For efforts to restore historic black neighborhood of Weeksville. 6/88.
South Africa Committee for Higher Education Development Trust (SACHED), Johannesburg, South Africa, $86,000. For educational publications and African literature program. 2/88.
South Coast Repertory, Costa Mesa, CA, $50,000. For expansion of Hispanic Playwrights Project. 6/88.
Space for Living Science, Rio de Janeiro, Brazil, $5,000. For science museum in Rio de Janeiro. 10/87.
Sri Lanka, Government of, Ministry of Cultural Affairs, Colombo, Sri Lanka, $50,000. For training and technical assistance in conservation of mural paintings. 8/88.
Statue of Liberty-Ellis Island Foundation, NYC, NY, $500,000. For Peopling of America Exhibit in Ellis Island Immigration Museum. With help of scholars in American history, immigration, and ethnicity, exhibit has been organized to emphasize continuity between past and present in ongoing story of immigration. 8/88.
Sumatera Utara University, Indonesia, $98,000. For ethnomusicology program. 10/87.
Task Force for Historic Preservation and the Minority Community, Richmond, VA, $250,000. For housing revitalization and counseling programs. 8/88.
Teatro Avante, Key Biscayne, FL, $25,000. For Miami's third Hispanic Theater Festival. 8/88.
Telugu University, India, $140,000. For postgraduate training workshops in folklore theory and archival techiques. 6/88.
Thailand, Government of, Thailand, $24,000. For laboratory equipment for archaeology division of government's fine arts department. 10/87.
University of Colorado, Boulder, CO, $50,000. To establish series of courses on ethical problems in writing. 10/87.
University of Khartoum, Khartoum, Sudan, $150,000. For staff training and technical assistance to collect, record, and perform traditional Sudanese music. 6/88.
University of Mississippi, University, MS, $50,000. To complete and computerize annotated bibliography and abstracts of Afro-American novels from 1853 to 1986. 6/88.
University of New Mexico, Albuquerque, NM, $50,000. To develop seminars on thinking and writing in undergraduate liberal arts curriculum. 10/87.
University of Oklahoma, Norman, OK, $53,000. To test ways of integrating writing instruction into state-mandated core curriculum in American history, American government, and English. 10/87.
University of Sao Paulo, Sao Paulo, Brazil, $100,000. For four visiting fellowships in humanities at university's Institute of Advanced Studies. 2/88.
University of Texas, Austin, TX, $53,000. To develop models of argumentation and teaching techniques to guide students' writing in various disciplines, and for demonstration project that will integrate writing into required courses in American government. 10/87.
University of Texas, El Paso, TX, $90,000. To revise writing composition courses to include liberal arts content, and to develop writing components in liberal arts courses. 10/87.
Vanderbilt University, Nashville, TN, $21,836. For review of plan to publish critical text of Old Ethiopic Bible. 6/88.
Visions Foundation, DC, $50,000. For conference on Afro-American art. 2/88.
W G B H Educational Foundation, Boston, MA, $200,000. For outreach activities associated with Degrassi Junior High, television series aimed at promoting responsible adolescent behavior, as part of Foundation's teen pregnancy grants. 8/88.
W N E T Channel 13, NYC, NY, $200,000. For Metroline 1987-88 TV series, which focuses on urban problems. 8/88.
Worldview Productions, NYC, NY, $60,000. To edit film on poor, self-employed women in India. 2/88.
Worldwide Documentaries, Rochester, NY, $40,000. To complete film on life of Beyers Naud, Afrikaner church leader and proponent of social justice in South Africa. 2/88.
Worldwide Documentaries, Rochester, NY, $10,000. To complete film on life of Beyers Naude, Afrikaner churchman and leading proponent of social justice in South Africa. 6/88.
Writers and Scholars Educational Trust, London, England, $120,000. For research and publications on censorship. 11/88.
Yayasan Nusantara Jaya, Indonesia, $80,000. To enable Indonesian museum staff to study in American institutions and for American museum experts to conduct workshops in Indonesia. 10/87.

1902
Max & Clara Fortunoff Foundation, Inc.

1300 Old Country Rd.
Westbury 11590-5102

Established in 1959 in NY.
Donor(s): Max Fortunoff, Alan Fortunoff.
Financial data (yr. ended 12/31/87): Assets, $43,669 (M); gifts received, $166,429; expenditures, $217,919, including $217,820 for 18 grants (high: $65,000; low: $100).
Purpose and activities: Support primarily for Jewish giving, higher education, hospitals, and social services.
Application information:
Initial approach: Letter
Deadline(s): None
Write: Alan Fortunoff, Pres.
Officers: Alan Fortunoff, Pres.; Helene Fortunoff, V.P.
Employer Identification Number: 116036903

1903
Foundation for the Needs of Others, Inc.

c/o Patterson, Belknap, Webb & Tyler
30 Rockefeller Plaza, Suite 3500
New York 10112 (212) 541-4000

Incorporated in 1953 in NY.
Donor(s): Helen W. Buckner, Walker G. Buckner, Thomas W. Buckner.
Financial data (yr. ended 12/31/87): Assets, $4,771,142 (M); expenditures, $339,200, including $306,500 for 32 grants (high: $40,000; low: $1,000).
Purpose and activities: Emphasis on conservation, higher and elementary education, and cultural programs; grants also for social service agencies and international relief.
Limitations: Giving primarily in New York, NY. No grants to individuals.
Publications: 990-PF.
Application information:
Initial approach: Letter
Deadline(s): None
Write: Mimi Kaplansky

Officers and Trustees: Helen W. Buckner, Pres.; Elizabeth B. Buckner, V.P.; Walker G. Buckner, Jr., V.P.; Thomas W. Buckner, Secy.-Treas.
Employer Identification Number: 136119874

1904
Ernst & Elfriede Frank Foundation
85-19 Abingdon Rd.
Kew Gardens 11415

Financial data (yr. ended 8/31/87): Assets, $4,072,649 (M); expenditures, $170,943, including $153,065 for 107 grants (high: $12,000; low: $50).
Purpose and activities: Giving for social services and cultural programs.
Limitations: Giving primarily in NY.
Application information: Contributes only to pre-selected organizations. Applications not accepted.
Officers: Ernest L. Frank, Pres.; Sybil Ann Brennan, V.P.; Ernest H. Frank, V.P.; Eva Maria Tausig, V.P.
Employer Identification Number: 136106471

1905
Franklin Fund
345 East 46th St.
New York 10017

Financial data (yr. ended 6/30/88): Assets, $866,245 (M); expenditures, $184,609, including $163,822 for grants.
Purpose and activities: Support primarily for international affairs and foreign policy organizations; support also for the arts.
Application information:
Initial approach: Letter
Deadline(s): None
Write: George S. Franklin, Trustee
Trustees: George S. Franklin, Helena Franklin.
Employer Identification Number: 136160092

1906
Samuel Freeman Charitable Trust
c/o U.S. Trust Co. of New York
45 Wall St.
New York 10005 (212) 806-4316

Established in 1981 in NY.
Donor(s): Samuel Freeman.†
Financial data (yr. ended 12/31/87): Assets, $19,298,716 (M); gifts received, $23,195; expenditures, $1,169,013, including $954,748 for 87 grants (high: $100,000; low: $103).
Purpose and activities: Giving primarily for health and education.
Limitations: Giving primarily in New York, NY.
Application information:
Initial approach: Proposal of not more than 2 pages
Deadline(s): None
Write: Anne L. Smith Ganey
Trustees: U.S. Trust Co. of New York, William E. Murray.
Employer Identification Number: 136803465

1907
Arnold D. Frese Foundation, Inc.
30 Rockefeller Plaza, Suite 1938
New York 10112

Established in 1966.
Donor(s): Arnold D. Frese.†
Financial data (yr. ended 12/31/87): Assets, $12,190,000 (M); expenditures, $1,700,000, including $1,275,000 for 40 grants (high: $425,000; low: $1,000; average: $1,000-$35,000).
Purpose and activities: Support for hospitals, cultural programs, especially an opera company, and higher education.
Limitations: Giving primarily in New York, NY, and Greenwich, CT.
Application information:
Deadline(s): None
Board meeting date(s): Quarterly
Final notification: 3 to 4 months
Write: E. Gayle Fisher, Exec. Dir.
Officers: James S. Smith, Pres. and Treas.; Hector G. Dowd, Secy.; E. Gayle Fisher, Exec. Dir.
Trustees: Ines Frese, Chair.; Henry D. Mercer, Jr., Emil Mosbacher, Jr.
Number of staff: 1 full-time professional.
Employer Identification Number: 136212507

1908
Fribourg Foundation, Inc.
277 Park Ave., 50th Fl.
New York 10172 (212) 207-5571

Incorporated in 1953 in NY.
Donor(s): Michel Fribourg, Lucienne Fribourg, Arrow Steamship Co., Inc., Continental Grain Co.
Financial data (yr. ended 12/31/87): Assets, $1,953,955 (M); expenditures, $314,992, including $288,450 for 122 grants (high: $50,000; low: $100).
Purpose and activities: Emphasis on higher and secondary education, cultural relations with France and Israel, and Jewish welfare funds; some support for community funds and the performing arts.
Limitations: Giving primarily in New York, NY.
Application information:
Initial approach: Letter
Deadline(s): None
Write: Dwight C. Coffin, Secy.
Officers: Michel Fribourg,* Pres.; Sheldon L. Berens,* V.P.; Dwight C. Coffin, Secy.; Hendrick J. Laverge, Treas.
Directors:* Mary Ann Fribourg, Bernard Steinweg.
Employer Identification Number: 136159195

1909
Eugen Friedlaender Foundation, Inc.
c/o Bernard E. Brandes
Seven Hanover Sq.
New York 10004

Established in 1953 in NY.
Donor(s): Helmut N. Friedlaender, Edith S.E. Bondi.
Financial data (yr. ended 12/31/87): Assets, $1,255,175 (M); expenditures, $120,130, including $94,263 for 52 grants (high: $5,250; low: $50).
Purpose and activities: Emphasis on cultural programs, health, higher education, and ecology programs; support also for law and justice programs.
Types of support: General purposes.
Limitations: Giving primarily in NY. No grants to individuals.
Application information:
Deadline(s): None
Officers and Directors: Helmut N. Friedlaender, Pres.; Judith G. Friedlaender, Secy.; Jane Lury, Treas.; Edith S.E. Bondi, Bernard E. Brandes, John R. Menke, Ronald J. Stein.
Employer Identification Number: 136077311

1910
Stephen & Barbara Friedman Foundation
c/o Goldman, Sachs & Co.
85 Broad St.
New York 10004

Established in 1979 in NY.
Donor(s): Stephen Friedman.
Financial data (yr. ended 7/31/87): Assets, $1,419,576 (M); gifts received, $139,299; expenditures, $578,882, including $578,082 for 105 grants (high: $50,000; low: $72).
Purpose and activities: Giving for Jewish organizations, cultural programs, and higher education.
Limitations: Giving primarily in New York, NY.
Application information: Contributes only to pre-selected organizations. Applications not accepted.
Trustees: H. Corbin Day, Barbara Friedman, Stephen Friedman.
Employer Identification Number: 133025979

1911
Ludwig W. Frohlich Charitable Trust
c/o Chadbourne & Parke
30 Rockefeller Plaza
New York 10112

Trust established in 1969 in NY.
Donor(s): Ludwig W. Frohlich.†
Financial data (yr. ended 12/31/87): Assets, $6,840,482 (M); expenditures, $605,258, including $458,950 for 34 grants (high: $100,000; low: $500).
Purpose and activities: Giving for hospitals, medical research, cultural programs, and social and youth agencies.
Limitations: Giving primarily in New York, NY.
Application information: Contributes only to pre-selected organizations. Applications not accepted.
Trustees: Kathleen B. Buddenhagen, Ingrid Lilly Burns, Thomas R. Burns, Richard B. Leather.
Employer Identification Number: 136288404

1912
Charles A. Frueauff Foundation, Inc.
70 Pine St.
New York 10270 (212) 422-4799

Incorporated in 1950 in NY.
Donor(s): Charles A. Frueauff.†
Financial data (yr. ended 12/31/87): Assets, $52,573,176 (M); expenditures, $3,041,928, including $2,783,865 for 214 grants (high: $50,000; low: $1,000).
Purpose and activities: Support for health, including hospitals, mental health, and other health services; welfare purposes, including services to children, the indigent, and the handicapped; and higher education, including student aid.
Types of support: Operating budgets, annual campaigns, emergency funds, building funds, equipment, endowment funds, scholarship funds, matching funds, general purposes, continuing support, capital campaigns, renovation projects.
Limitations: No grants to individuals, or for research; no loans.
Publications: Program policy statement, annual report.
Application information:
Initial approach: Proposal, telephone, or letter
Copies of proposal: 1
Deadline(s): Submit proposal between Sept. and Mar.; deadline Mar. 31
Board meeting date(s): May
Final notification: After annual meeting
Write: Katherine R. Pawson, Secy.-Treas.
Officers: Harry D. Frueauff,* Pres.; Charles T. Klein,* V.P.; Katherine R. Pawson, Secy.-Treas.
Trustees:* James P. Fallon, Margaret Perry Fanning, A.C. McCully.
Number of staff: 1 full-time support; 3 part-time support.
Employer Identification Number: 135605371
Recent arts and culture grants:
Boys Choir of Harlem, NYC, NY, $5,000. For artistic, tutoring and counseling services. 1987.
Metropolitan Museum of Art, NYC, NY, $5,000. For education programs. 1987.
W N E T Channel 13, NYC, NY, $15,000. For program ventures. 1987.

1913
Fund for the City of New York, Inc.
121 Ave. of the Americas
New York 10013 (212) 925-6675

Incorporated in 1968 in NY.
Donor(s): The Ford Foundation, The Aaron Diamond Foundation, Inc., Helena Rubinstein Foundation, Inc.
Financial data (yr. ended 9/30/88): Assets, $4,091,300 (M); gifts received, $3,999,471; expenditures, $4,008,672, including $299,200 for 39 grants (high: $50,000; low: $800; average: $5,000-$10,000), $35,000 for 7 grants to individuals, $3,484,081 for foundation-administered programs and $2,300,000 for loans.
Purpose and activities: An operating foundation and public charity supporting public and private projects designed to improve the management and effectiveness of government and the quality of life in New York City, with particular emphasis on public service productivity, accountability, performance monitoring, and computer assistance; operates a program of assistance to public and nonprofit managers; also runs a cash flow loan program against governmental grants and contracts.
Types of support: Technical assistance, loans, exchange programs, consulting services, special projects, grants to individuals.
Limitations: Giving limited to New York City. No grants to individuals (except for public service awards), or for ongoing service programs, academic research, building or endowment funds, scholarships, fellowships, matching gifts, or studies that do not show promise of leading directly to policy or program improvement.
Publications: Multi-year report (including application guidelines), financial statement, grants list, informational brochure.
Application information:
Initial approach: Proposal
Copies of proposal: 1
Deadline(s): None
Board meeting date(s): Approximately 5 times a year in Feb., Apr., June, Oct., and Dec.
Write: Anita Nager, Grants Admin.
Officers: Frederick A.O. Schwarz, Jr.,* Chair.; Stephen Lefkowitz,* Vice-Chair.; R. Palmer Baker,* Secy.; Paul Gibson,* Treas.; Gregory R. Farrell, Exec. Dir.
Directors:* Roscoe Brown, Jr., Carolyn Chin, Peggy Davis, Nathan Quinones, Suzanne Schwerin, Vaughn Williams.
Number of staff: 19 full-time professional; 3 part-time professional; 8 full-time support; 2 part-time support.
Employer Identification Number: 132612524
Recent arts and culture grants:
ODN Productions, NYC, NY, $5,000. For supporting materials for Dropping In...A Film About Dropping Out. 10/6/87.

1914
Gebbie Foundation, Inc.
Hotel Jamestown Bldg., Rm. 308
Jamestown 14701 (716) 487-1062

Incorporated in 1963 in NY.
Donor(s): Marion B. Gebbie,† Geraldine G. Bellinger.†
Financial data (yr. ended 9/30/88): Assets, $51,702,693 (M); expenditures, $3,048,603, including $2,661,509 for 53 grants (high: $475,000; low: $1,000) and $100,400 for loans.
Purpose and activities: Grants primarily for local organizations such as hospitals, libraries, youth agencies, cultural programs, social agencies, and the United Way. Giving also to organizations that have shown an interest in medical and scientific research related to metabolic diseases of the bone and in detection of deafness in children and their education.
Types of support: Annual campaigns, seed money, building funds, equipment, matching funds, general purposes, loans.
Limitations: Giving primarily in Chautauqua County and, secondly, in neighboring areas of western NY; giving in other areas only when the project is consonant with program objectives that cannot be developed locally. No support for sectarian or religious organizations or for higher education, except to institutions that were recipients of lifetime contributions of the donor. No grants to individuals, or for endowment funds.
Application information:
Initial approach: Letter
Copies of proposal: 10
Deadline(s): Mar. 1, Aug. 1, and Oct. 1
Board meeting date(s): Apr., Sept., and Nov.
Final notification: 1 to 4 months
Write: John D. Hamilton, Pres.
Officers and Directors: John D. Hamilton, Pres.; Myron B. Franks, V.P.; William I. Parker, Secy.; Carol Lorene, Treas.; Gerald E. Hunt, Charles T. Hall, Robert E. Halsted, Geraldine Parker, Paul W. Sandberg, Jennie Vimmerstedt.
Number of staff: 1 full-time professional; 2 part-time professional; 1 part-time support.
Employer Identification Number: 166050287
Recent arts and culture grants:
Albright-Knox Art Gallery, Buffalo, NY, $5,000. For capital campaign. 1987.
Arts Fund for Chautauqua County, Jamestown, NY, $60,000. For annual support. 1987.
Chautauqua County Historical Society, Westfield, NY, $7,197. For PATRIOTS Vol. II. 1987.
Chautauqua Institution, Chautauqua, NY, $40,500. For scholarships and annual support. 1987.
Reg Lenna Civic Center, Jamestown, NY, $250,000. For capital campaign. 1987.
Roger Tory Peterson Institute for the Study of Natural History, Jamestown, NY, $750,000. For capital campaign. 1987.

1915
Lawrence M. Gelb Foundation, Inc.
300 Park Ave., Rm. 2100
New York 10022
Application address: 345 Park Ave., New York, NY 10022

Established in 1957 in NY.
Donor(s): Lawrence M. Gelb.†
Financial data (yr. ended 12/31/87): Assets, $6,248,057 (M); gifts received, $309,063; expenditures, $493,287, including $447,500 for 38 grants (high: $64,000; low: $1,000).
Purpose and activities: Support primarily for private secondary and higher education; some support also for cultural programs.
Application information:
Initial approach: Letter
Deadline(s): None
Write: Richard L. Gelb, Chair.
Officers and Directors: Richard L. Gelb, Chair. and Treas.; Bruce S. Gelb, Pres.; Wilbur M. Friedman, Secy.; John T. Gelb, Lawrence N. Gelb, Robert M. Kaufman.
Employer Identification Number: 136113586

1916
General Railway Signal Foundation, Inc.
c/o General Motors Signal Co.
801 West Ave.
Rochester 14611-2413 (716) 783-2000

Established in 1952 in NY.

Donor(s): General Railway Signal Div. of General Signal Corp.
Financial data (yr. ended 9/28/88): Assets, $892,159 (M); gifts received, $5,644; expenditures, $56,594, including $54,977 for 34 grants (high: $21,000; low: $50).
Purpose and activities: Support for institutions of higher education in NY, museums and historical societies, social science and development, hospitals, United Way, and civic affairs.
Types of support: Annual campaigns, building funds.
Limitations: Giving primarily in Rochester, NY.
Application information:
Initial approach: Letter
Deadline(s): None
Write: Thomas A. Yaeger, Secy.-Treas.
Officers: G.E. Collins, Pres.; Thomas A. Yaeger, Secy.-Treas.
Directors: T.T. Balog, James J. Cole.
Number of staff: None.
Employer Identification Number: 237447593

1917
The Laurent and Alberta Gerschel Foundation, Inc.
c/o Campus Network
114 Fifth Ave., 12th Fl.
New York 10011

Donor(s): Laurent Gerschel.
Financial data (yr. ended 12/31/87): Assets, $6,852,589 (M); gifts received, $1,000; expenditures, $107,730, including $77,045 for 22 grants (high: $15,000; low: $75).
Purpose and activities: Support primarily for education, health, and the arts.
Application information:
Initial approach: Proposal
Deadline(s): None
Write: Laurent Gerschel, Pres.
Officer: Laurent Gerschel, Pres.; Alberta Gerschel, V.P.; Monica Hoffman, Secy.-Treas.
Employer Identification Number: 133098507

1918
Patrick A. Gerschel Foundation
122 East 42nd St.
New York 10168 (212) 490-4995

Established in 1986 in NY.
Financial data (yr. ended 12/31/87): Assets, $6,645,139 (M); expenditures, $510,055, including $405,911 for 29 grants (high: $250,000; low: $100).
Purpose and activities: Support primarily for an Asian cultural institution; support also for the arts, medical research, community development and for higher and secondary education.
Types of support: Grants to individuals, research.
Limitations: Giving primarily in NY.
Application information:
Write: Patrick A. Gerschel, Pres.
Officers: Patrick A. Gerschel, Chair. and Pres.; Geoffrey Handler, Secy.; Charles H. Richter, Treas.
Employer Identification Number: 133317180

1919
GFI/Knoll International Foundation
230 Park Ave., Suite 416
New York 10162 (212) 490-8080

Established in New York around 1983.
Donor(s): General Felt Industries, Inc.
Financial data (yr. ended 12/31/86): Assets, $97,353 (M); gifts received, $377,000; expenditures, $711,605, including $711,605 for 73 grants (high: $80,000; low: $500).
Purpose and activities: Giving for higher education with emphasis on government, and for cultural affairs, Jewish welfare, organizations in Israel, and secondary education.
Types of support: General purposes.
Limitations: Giving primarily in New York City, NY. No grants to individuals.
Application information:
Initial approach: Proposal
Deadline(s): None
Write: Gary A. Schonwald, Secy.
Officers: Rocco A. Barbieri, Pres.; Robert Condon, Jr., V.P.; Gary A. Schonwald, Secy.
Director: Marshall S. Cogan.
Employer Identification Number: 222518739

1920
Gibbs Brothers Foundation
c/o Morgan Guaranty Trust Co. of New York
Nine West 57th St.
New York 10019 (212) 826-7615

Trust established in 1957 in NY.
Donor(s): Gibbs & Cox, Inc.
Financial data (yr. ended 12/31/86): Assets, $3,029,645 (M); gifts received, $146,296; expenditures, $346,260, including $319,250 for 56 grants (high: $40,000; low: $500).
Purpose and activities: Grants largely for continuing support of organizations including maritime museums and seamen's institutes, hospitals, colleges and universities, naval engineering societies, and legal organizations.
Types of support: Operating budgets, research.
Limitations: No grants to individuals, or for annual campaigns, seed money, emergency funds, deficit financing, capital and endowment funds, matching gifts, scholarships, fellowships, program support, demonstration projects, publications, or conferences; no loans.
Application information:
Initial approach: Letter with financial information
Copies of proposal: 1
Deadline(s): None
Board meeting date(s): May
Write: Richard Ehrlich
Advisory Committee: M. Bernard Aidinoff, Richard M. Ehrlich, Walter Malmstrom, Edward J. Willi.
Trustee: Morgan Guaranty Trust Co. of New York.
Number of staff: None.
Employer Identification Number: 136037653

1921
Gibraltar Foundation
2545 Walden Ave.
Buffalo 14225-4737 (716) 684-1020

Donor(s): Gibraltar Steel.
Financial data (yr. ended 12/31/88): Assets, $631,349 (M); expenditures, $59,704, including $56,967 for 32 grants (high: $25,000; low: $50).
Purpose and activities: Support for historical preservation, civic affairs, culture, religious charities, and higher education.
Limitations: Giving primarily in Buffalo, NY. No grants to individuals.
Application information: Contributes only to preselected organizations. Applications not accepted.
Write: Ken Lipke
Trustee: Ken E. Lipke.
Employer Identification Number: 510176074

1922
The Rosamond Gifford Charitable Corporation
731 James St., Rm. 404
Syracuse 13203 (315) 474-2489

Incorporated in 1954 in NY.
Donor(s): Rosamond Gifford.†
Financial data (yr. ended 12/31/87): Assets, $12,811,279 (M); expenditures, $879,860, including $705,485 for 34 grants (high: $120,000; low: $3,845; average: $4,000-$40,000).
Purpose and activities: Emphasis on urban problems, higher and secondary education, health research, hospital construction and equipment, youth agencies, rehabilitation of alcoholics, the aged, general welfare, a community fund, and cultural programs.
Types of support: Operating budgets, annual campaigns, seed money, emergency funds, building funds, equipment, research, renovation projects.
Limitations: Giving limited to organizations serving the residents of Syracuse and Onondaga County, NY. No grants to individuals, or for endowment funds, continuing support, deficit financing, land aquisition, special projects, matching gifts, scholarships, or fellowships; no loans.
Publications: Program policy statement, application guidelines, multi-year report.
Application information:
Initial approach: Letter or telephone
Copies of proposal: 2
Deadline(s): None
Board meeting date(s): Monthly
Final notification: 2 months
Write: Dean A. Lesinski, Exec. Dir.
Officers: Virginia Z. Lynch,* Pres.; Roger L. MacDonald,* V.P. and Treas.; Charles J. Miller,* Secy.; Dean A. Lesinski, Exec. Dir.
Directors:* John H. Lynch, Donald M. Mills.
Number of staff: 2 full-time professional; 1 part-time support.
Employer Identification Number: 150572881

1923
The Howard Gilman Foundation, Inc.
111 West 50th St.
New York 10020 (212) 246-3300

Incorporated in 1982 in NY.
Donor(s): Gilman Foundation, Inc.
Financial data (yr. ended 4/30/87): Assets, $12,772,590 (M); expenditures, $521,174, including $342,315 for 54 grants (high: $50,000; low: $30).
Purpose and activities: Giving for hospitals, higher education, music, cultural programs, social services, and for wildlife preservation.
Limitations: Giving primarily in New York, NY.
Application information:
Deadline(s): None
Write: Howard Gilman, Pres.
Officers and Directors: Howard Gilman, Pres.; Bernard D. Bergreen, Sylvia P. Gilman.
Employer Identification Number: 133097486

1924
Sondra & Charles Gilman, Jr. Foundation, Inc.
109 East 64th St.
New York 10021 (212) 734-8011

Established in NY in 1981 as a successor to the Gilman Foundation.
Financial data (yr. ended 4/30/87): Assets, $10,939,351 (M); expenditures, $812,082, including $302,971 for 106 grants (high: $25,000; low: $25).
Purpose and activities: Support for health organizations, education (especially secondary education), museums, music, and environmental organizations.
Application information:
Initial approach: Letter
Deadline(s): None
Write: Sondra Gilman, Pres.
Officers and Directors: Sondra Gilman, Chair. and Pres.; Celso M. Gonzalez, V.P.; John Mosler, Secy.; Walter Baur, Treas.; Jack Friedland, Hadley R. Gilman, Sylvia P. Gilman, Myrna Schatz.
Employer Identification Number: 133097485

1925
Gleason Memorial Fund, Inc.
30 Corporate Woods
P.O. Box 22856
Rochester 14692-2856 (716) 272-6000

Incorporated in 1959 in NY.
Donor(s): Miriam B. Gleason.†
Financial data (yr. ended 12/31/86): Assets, $37,517,373 (M); gifts received, $445,000; expenditures, $2,818,110, including $2,317,137 for grants (high: $300,000; low: $25).
Purpose and activities: Emphasis on higher education, including research and technology; support also for community funds, youth and social service agencies, public interest and civic affairs groups, and cultural activities.
Types of support: Operating budgets.
Limitations: Giving primarily in the Rochester, NY, metropolitan area. No support for United Way-supported agencies. No grants to individuals.
Publications: Application guidelines.
Application information:
Initial approach: Proposal
Deadline(s): None
Board meeting date(s): Quarterly
Final notification: After board meetings
Write: Calvin A. Miller, V.P. for Administration
Officers: Sterling L. Weaver,* Chair.; James S. Gleason,* Pres.; Calvin A. Miller,* V.P. for Administration; Morton A. Polster, Secy.; James E. Thomas, Treas.
Directors:* Louis A. Langie, Jr., Albert W. Moore.
Employer Identification Number: 166023235

1926
Edward and Marjorie Goldberger Foundation
126 East 56th Street
New York 10022 (212) 371-8077

Established in 1957 in NY.
Financial data (yr. ended 12/31/87): Assets, $1,512,778 (M); expenditures, $61,011, including $53,200 for 97 grants (high: $7,500; low: $10).
Purpose and activities: Support primarily for Jewish giving, education, and culture.
Application information: Contributes only to pre-selected organizations. Applications not accepted.
Officers and Directors: Edward Goldberger, Pres.; Marjorie Goldberger, Secy.-Treas.; Susan Jacoby, Ann Jurdem, Sarah Siegel.
Employer Identification Number: 136084528

1927
Golden Family Foundation
40 Wall St., Rm. 4201
New York 10005 (212) 425-0333

Incorporated in 1952 in NY.
Donor(s): William T. Golden, Sibyl R. Golden.†
Financial data (yr. ended 12/31/88): Assets, $26,855,822 (M); gifts received, $1,750,033; expenditures, $1,028,895, including $862,715 for 141 grants (high: $250,000; low: $100; average: $100-$7,000) and $200,000 for loans.
Purpose and activities: Support for a broad range of programs in higher education, science, public affairs, and cultural areas.
Types of support: General purposes, building funds.
Limitations: No grants to individuals.
Application information: Contributes only to pre-selected organizations. Applications not accepted.
Board meeting date(s): Jan. and as required
Write: William T. Golden, Pres.
Officers and Directors: William T. Golden, Pres.; Sibyl R. Golden, V.P.; Helene L. Kaplan, Secy.; Ralph E. Hansmann, Treas.; Pamela P. Golden.
Number of staff: None.
Employer Identification Number: 237423802

1928
John Golden Fund, Inc.
36 West 44th St., Suite 707
New York 10036-8102

Incorporated in 1944 in NY.
Donor(s): John Golden.†
Financial data (yr. ended 12/31/86): Assets, $1,235,300 (M); expenditures, $101,700, including $94,500 for 27 grants (high: $15,000; low: $500; average: $2,000).
Purpose and activities: For the advancement of playwriting for the American legitimate theater or of the individuals in any way associated with it, through improvement of the teaching of drama in universities and colleges, and through other organizations and workshops, prize awards to playwrights engaged in, or in training for, dramatic playwriting in colleges, and promotion of theatrical productions for young people; all grants through organizations only.
Types of support: Special projects.
Limitations: Giving primarily in CT, MA, and NY. No grants to individuals, or for building or endowment funds, research programs, or matching gifts.
Application information:
Initial approach: Proposal
Copies of proposal: 1
Deadline(s): Apr. 30 and Oct. 31
Board meeting date(s): May and Nov.
Write: Mrs. Zilla Lippmann, Pres.
Officers and Directors: Zilla Lippmann, Pres.; Norman J. Stone, Treas.; Jean Dalrymple, John Houseman, John Lippman, Edwin Wilson.
Number of staff: None.
Employer Identification Number: 136065978

1929
Faith Golding Foundation, Inc.
900 Third Ave., 35th Fl.
New York 10022

Established in 1984 in NY.
Donor(s): Faith & Ronald Perelman Foundation, First Sterling Corp.
Financial data (yr. ended 11/30/87): Assets, $594,025 (M); gifts received, $620,000; expenditures, $242,074, including $240,981 for 47 grants (high: $73,100; low: $50).
Purpose and activities: Support for education, cultural organizations, and general charitable giving.
Trustees: Bernard Creene, Faith Golding, Ira W. Krauss.
Employer Identification Number: 133260491

1930
Jerrold R. & Shirley Golding Foundation, Inc.
1290 Ave. of the Americas, Suite 960
New York 10104

Established in 1969 in NY.
Donor(s): Montvale Imperial, Inc.
Financial data (yr. ended 12/31/87): Assets, $657,907 (M); gifts received, $350,000; expenditures, $197,959, including $195,750 for 18 grants (high: $100,000; low: $200).

Purpose and activities: Support primarily for higher education, health services, and cultural organizations.
Limitations: Giving primarily in NY.
Application information: Contributes only to pre-selected organizations. Applications not accepted.
Officers: Joseph J. Marcheso, Pres. and Treas.; Harriet G. Levy, V.P.; Morton J. Schlossberg, Secy.
Employer Identification Number: 237046427

1931
Herman Goldman Foundation

61 Broadway, 18th Fl.
New York 10006 (212) 797-9090

Incorporated in 1943 in NY.
Donor(s): Herman Goldman.†
Financial data (yr. ended 2/29/88): Assets, $27,503,286 (M); expenditures, $2,610,942, including $2,061,495 for 111 grants (high: $160,000; low: $500; average: $5,000-$50,000).
Purpose and activities: Emphasis on aiding economically and socially deprived persons through innovative grants in four main areas: Health - to achieve effective delivery of physical and mental health care services; Social Justice - to develop organizational, social, and legal approaches to aid deprived or handicapped people; Education - for new or improved counseling for effective pre-school, vocational and paraprofessional training; and the Arts - to increase opportunities for talented youth to receive training and for less affluent individuals to attend quality presentations; some aid for programs relating to nation-wide problems.
Limitations: Giving primarily in the New York, NY, metropolitan area. No support for religious organizations. No grants to individuals.
Publications: Annual report (including application guidelines).
Application information:
Initial approach: Proposal
Copies of proposal: 1
Deadline(s): Middle of month preceding board meeting
Board meeting date(s): Monthly; grants considered every other month beginning in Apr.
Final notification: 1 to 2 months
Write: Richard K. Baron, Exec. Dir.
Officers and Directors: Michael L. Goldstein, Pres.; Stanley M. Klein, V.P.; David A. Brauner, Secy. and Treas.; Jules M. Baron, Raymond S. Baron, Paul Bauman, Robert N. Davies, Emanuel Goldstein, Seymour Kligler, Elias Rosenzweig, Howard A. Scribner, Jr., Norman Sparber.
Number of staff: 3 full-time professional; 1 part-time professional.
Employer Identification Number: 136066039

1932
Goldome Foundation

c/o Goldome Tax Dept.
One Fountain Plaza
Buffalo 14203 (716) 847-5800

Established in 1969 in NY.
Donor(s): Goldome F.S.B.
Financial data (yr. ended 12/31/87): Assets, $1,156,757 (M); gifts received, $321,170; expenditures, $419,728, including $403,282 for 287 grants (high: $19,350; low: $10) and $16,121 for 190 employee matching gifts.
Purpose and activities: Support for urban affairs, youth agencies, hospitals, educational organizations, social services, community development, culture and the arts; also sponsors an employee matching gift program primarily for higher education.
Types of support: Operating budgets, continuing support, annual campaigns, building funds, employee matching gifts.
Limitations: Giving limited to NY state, with emphasis on western NY (Buffalo, Syracuse, and Rochester); some support also in the New York metropolitan area. No grants to individuals, or for seed money, emergency funds, deficit financing, equipment, land acquisition, renovations, endowment funds, scholarships, fellowships, special projects, research, publications, or conferences; no loans.
Application information: Contributes only to preselected organizations. Applications not accepted.
Officers: Robert C. Carroll, Pres.; James J. Batt, V.P.; Mary Ellen Beres, V.P.; Peter Bevins, V.P.; Maureen A. Owens, V.P.; Terry L. Poppleton, V.P.; Jeanette Shaw, V.P.; Robert M. Edwards, Secy.; Richard M. Hessinger, Treas.
Directors: Thomas Bilbao, Edward K. Duch, Jr., Ross B. Kenzie, H. Eugene Richards, E. Peter Ruddy, Jr.
Number of staff: None.
Employer Identification Number: 237029266

1933
The Joseph G. Goldring Foundation

100 Crossways Park West, Rm. 306
Woodbury 11797

Established about 1970 in NY.
Donor(s): Overseas Military Sales Corp., Military Car Sales, Inc., Chrysler Military Sales Corp.
Financial data (yr. ended 6/30/87): Assets, $42,153 (M); gifts received, $200,000; expenditures, $169,685, including $169,628 for 86 grants (high: $500,000; low: $25).
Purpose and activities: Giving primarily to Jewish welfare funds, museums, and a medical center.
Limitations: Giving primarily in the New York, NY, metropolitan area, including the North Shore of Long Island.
Officers: Allen A. Goldring, Pres.; Lola A. Goldring, V.P.; Bernard Frey, Secy.; Rita G. Frey, Treas.
Employer Identification Number: 116084103

1934
Horace W. Goldsmith Foundation

c/o White & Case
1155 Ave. of the Americas
New York 10036 (212) 819-8580

Incorporated in 1955 in NY.
Donor(s): Horace Goldsmith.†
Financial data (yr. ended 12/31/87): Assets, $213,771,189 (M); gifts received, $10,183; expenditures, $12,742,980, including $9,225,140 for 166 grants (high: $500,000; low: $7,350; average: $25,000-$100,000).
Purpose and activities: Support for cultural programs, including the performing arts and museums; Jewish welfare funds and temple support; hospitals and a geriatric center; and education, especially higher education.
Types of support: Operating budgets, endowment funds, building funds, matching funds, general purposes.
Limitations: Giving primarily in New York City, NY, and in MA and AZ. No grants to individuals.
Application information: Foundation depends virtually exclusively on self-initiated grants. Applications not accepted.
Board meeting date(s): 8 times a year
Write: Robert R. Slaughter, Chief Exec.
Officers and Directors: Grace R. Goldsmith, Chair. (Emeritus); Robert R. Slaughter, Chief Exec.; Richard Menschel, Robert B. Menschel, James C. Slaughter, William A. Slaughter.
Employer Identification Number: 136107758

1935
Goldsmith-Perry Philanthropies, Inc.

c/o Yohalem Gillman & Co.
477 Madison Ave.
New York 10022-5802

Established in 1969 in NY.
Donor(s): Barbara Lubin Perry Charitable Trust, Joseph I. Lubin.†
Financial data (yr. ended 12/31/87): Assets, $5,667,481 (M); gifts received, $915,000; expenditures, $685,300, including $574,755 for grants.
Purpose and activities: Support primarily for Jewish giving, higher education, and cultural programs.
Limitations: Giving primarily in New York, NY.
Officers and Directors: Barbara L. Goldsmith, Pres.; Frank Perry, Secy.
Employer Identification Number: 237031986

1936
The Golub Foundation

501 Duanesburg Rd.
Schenectady 12306 (518) 356-9450
Scholarship application address: c/o Golub Corp., Scholarship Comm., P.O. Box 1074, Schenectady, NY 12301

Established in 1981 in NY.
Donor(s): Golub Corp., Jane Golub, Neil M. Golub.
Financial data (yr. ended 3/31/88): Assets, $12,196 (M); gifts received, $401,200; qualifying distributions, $432,818, including $407,853 for 361 grants (high: $34,000; low: $25) and $148,082 for 17 grants to individuals.
Purpose and activities: Support for the United Way, arts, health, and higher education; and scholarship awards to high school graduates in areas served by the company.
Types of support: Student aid.
Limitations: Giving limited to the Price Chopper Supermarket marketing area: the counties of Berkshire, Hampden, and Hampshire, MA; Lackawanna, Luzerne, Susquehanna, Wayne, and Wyoming, PA;

Bennington, VT; and Albany, Broom, Clinton, Columbia, Delaware, Essex, Franklin, Fulton, Greene, Hamilton, Herkimer, Jefferson, Madison, Montgomery, Oneida, Onondaga, Oswego, Otsego, Rensselaer, Saratoga, Schenectady, Schoharie, Warren, and Washington, NY.
Publications: Informational brochure.
Application information: Application form required for scholarships.
Deadline(s): Mar. 14 for full application packet for scholarships
Write: Mary Lou Sennes, Admin. Golub Foundation
Trustees: A. Susan Gabriel, Frank Lorch, Sue Ann Ritchko.
Employer Identification Number: 222341421

1937
Good Neighbor Foundation, Inc.
777 Third Ave.
New York 10017 (212) 546-2424

Incorporated in 1952 in NY.
Financial data (yr. ended 12/31/88): Assets, $421,907 (M); expenditures, $166,475, including $166,475 for 80 grants (high: $25,000; low: $50).
Purpose and activities: Giving primarily to Jewish welfare funds, community funds, cultural institutions, health associations, and higher education.
Types of support: General purposes, operating budgets.
Limitations: Giving primarily in New York City, NY, and in CA.
Application information:
Write: Lucille Caserio
Officers: Edward H. Meyer, Pres.; Robert L. Berenson, V.P.; Alan B. Fendrick, Treas.; Lucille Caserio, Secy.
Number of staff: None.
Employer Identification Number: 136161259

1938
The Goodman Family Foundation
c/o Roy M. Goodman
1035 Fifth Ave.
New York 10028

Trust established in 1970 in NY as one of two successor trusts to the Matz Foundation.
Donor(s): Israel Matz.†
Financial data (yr. ended 6/30/87): Assets, $2,879,012 (M); expenditures, $172,896, including $124,644 for 101 grants (high: $20,000; low: $50).
Purpose and activities: Giving for higher education and Jewish welfare funds; grants also for temple and church support, social service agencies, and arts organizations.
Limitations: Giving primarily in NY.
Trustees: Barbara F. Goodman, Roy M. Goodman.
Employer Identification Number: 136355553

1939
Adolph and Esther Gottlieb Foundation, Inc.
380 West Broadway
New York 10012 (212) 226-0581

Established in 1976 in NY.
Donor(s): Adolph Gottlieb,† Esther Gottlieb.†
Financial data (yr. ended 6/30/88): Assets, $2,751,521 (M); expenditures, $263,493, including $133,400 for 21 grants to individuals (high: $10,000; low: $1,700; average: $1,700-$10,000).
Purpose and activities: Two separate grant programs: 1. Individual support program for painters, sculptors, and printmakers who have at least 20 years in a mature phase of their art, and are in current financial need. 2. Emergency assistance program for painters, sculptors, and printmakers who have at least 10 years in a mature phase of their art and are in current financial need in excess of and unrelated to their normal economic situation, and which is the result of a recent emergency occurence such as a fire, flood or medical emergency.
Types of support: Grants to individuals.
Limitations: No support for support organizations, educational institutions, projects, or those working in crafts.
Publications: Informational brochure, application guidelines.
Application information: Emergency grant applications may be submitted and reviewed year round. Application form required.
Initial approach: Letter
Copies of proposal: 1
Deadline(s): Dec. 15 for individual support program
Board meeting date(s): Quarterly
Final notification: Early Mar.
Officers and Directors: Dick Netzer, Pres.; Lawrence Alloway, V.P.; Sanford Hirsch, Secy.-Treas.; Charlotte Kotik, Robert Mangold.
Number of staff: 2 full-time professional; 1 part-time support.
Employer Identification Number: 132853957

1940
The Florence J. Gould Foundation
c/o Cahill Gordon and Reindel
80 Pine St.
New York 10005 (212) 701-3400

Incorporated in 1957 in NY.
Donor(s): Florence J. Gould.†
Financial data (yr. ended 12/31/88): Assets, $57,894,637 (M); gifts received, $3,865,249; expenditures, $4,954,654, including $4,119,878 for 59 grants (high: $750,000; low: $1,500; average: $1,500-$750,000) and $300,000 for in-kind gifts.
Purpose and activities: Established "to promote French-American amity and understanding" and for general charitable giving; support for museums, higher education, and the arts in the U.S. and France, and for a hospital in Paris.
Application information:
Deadline(s): None
Write: John R. Young, Pres.
Officers and Directors: John R. Young, Pres.; William E. Hegarty, V.P. and Secy.; Daniel Davison, V.P. and Treas.; Daniel Wildenstein, V.P.; Walter C. Cliff.
Employer Identification Number: 136176855

1941
Grace Foundation, Inc.
1114 Ave. of the Americas
New York 10036-7794 (212) 819-6640

Incorporated in 1961 in NY.
Donor(s): W.R. Grace & Co.
Financial data (yr. ended 12/31/88): Assets, $500,000 (M); gifts received, $2,500,000; expenditures, $1,923,696, including $1,739,909 for 270 grants (high: $100,000; low: $1,000; average: $1,000-$20,000) and $356,629 for 1,700 employee matching gifts.
Purpose and activities: Grants primarily to organizations in communities in which the corporation does business, for education (including employee matching gifts), urban and minority affairs, cultural programs, including performing arts, community funds, and hospitals.
Types of support: Operating budgets, continuing support, annual campaigns, building funds, equipment, matching funds, employee matching gifts, scholarship funds, employee-related scholarships, fellowships.
Limitations: No support for secondary schools(other than employee matching gifts). No grants to individuals, or for endowment funds, seed money, emergency funds, deficit financing, land acquisition, publications, demonstration projects, conferences, or specific research projects.
Application information:
Initial approach: Letter
Copies of proposal: 1
Deadline(s): None
Board meeting date(s): As required
Final notification: 2 to 3 months
Write: Brian J. Smith, Pres.
Officers and Directors: Paul D. Paganucci, Chair.; Brian J. Smith, Pres.; Francis J. Brennan, V.P. and Treas.; Thomas M. Doyle, V.P.; Robert B. Lamm, Secy.; J.P. Bolduc, James W. Frick, Charles W. Miller, Eben W. Pyne, Harold A. Stevens, John R. Young.
Number of staff: None.
Employer Identification Number: 136153305

1942
The Gramercy Park Foundation, Inc.
c/o Zemlock, Levy, Bick & Karnbad
225 Broadway
New York 10007 (212) 964-4140

Incorporated in 1952 in NY.
Donor(s): Benjamin Sonnenberg, Helen Sonnenberg Tucker.
Financial data (yr. ended 12/31/88): Assets, $1,546,571 (M); expenditures, $104,695, including $77,985 for 60 grants (high: $25,000; low: $50).
Purpose and activities: Grants for arts and cultural programs, with emphasis on libraries and the performing arts; support also for higher education, including music education.

Limitations: Giving primarily in the New York City metropolitan area. No grants to individuals.
Application information:
Write: Norman Motechin
Officers: Helen Sonnenberg Tucker, Pres. and Treas.; Steven Tucker, Secy.; William Spears.
Number of staff: 1 part-time support.
Employer Identification Number: 132507282

1943
William T. Grant Foundation
515 Madison Ave., 6th Fl.
New York 10022-5403 (212) 752-0071

Incorporated in 1936 in DE.
Donor(s): William T. Grant.†
Financial data (yr. ended 12/31/88): Assets, $130,800,000 (M); expenditures, $6,775,217 for 98 grants (high: $500,000; low: $1,000; average: $75,000-$100,000) and $875,000 for 5 grants to individuals.
Purpose and activities: Support nationally and internationally for research, professional training, and social policy and advocacy projects concerned with the healthy psychological and social development of children and youth. Current emphasis on research projects dealing with stress and coping of school-age children. The foundation is especially interested in projects which examine the connections between several problem behaviors and clusters of causes common to those problems. Preference given to projects involving multiple disciplines as well. Preference given to the support of new programs in their initial stages of development. Support is channeled through three mechanisms: Investigator-initiated projects, Faculty Scholars Program, and the Action Research Program. Awards limited number of small one-time grants for small-scale research, training, and service projects in the New York City metropolitan area.
Types of support: Continuing support, seed money, research, special projects, fellowships.
Limitations: No grants to individuals (except Faculty Scholars Program), or for annual fundraising campaigns, deficit financing, equipment and materials, land acquisition, renovation projects, capital funds, operating budgets of on-going service agencies or educational institutions, or matching gifts; no loans.
Publications: Annual report, informational brochure (including application guidelines), newsletter.
Application information: Application to Faculty Scholars Program by nomination only.
Initial approach: Letter
Copies of proposal: 10
Deadline(s): July 1 for Faculty Scholars Program nominations; no set deadline for grants
Board meeting date(s): Feb., May, Sept., and Dec.
Final notification: Immediately following board meeting
Write: Robert Johns Haggerty, M.D., Pres.
Officers: Robert Johns Haggerty, M.D.,* Pres.; Lonnie Sherrod, V.P. for Prog.; William H. Chisholm,* Treas.; Eileen Dorann, Controller.
Trustees:* Robert P. Patterson, Jr., Chair.; William Bevan, Ellis T. Gravette, Jr., Beatrix A. Hamburg, M.D., Martha L. Minow, Henry W. Riecken, Kenneth S. Rolland, Rivington R. Winant.
Number of staff: 4 full-time professional; 10 full-time support.
Employer Identification Number: 131624021
Recent arts and culture grants:
Boys Choir of Harlem, NYC, NY, $5,000. For tutoring and counseling program for youth members of Choir. 6/3/88.
National Public Radio, DC, $225,000. For coverage of issues affecting children and youth. 6/3/88.
University of Maine, Orono, ME, $175,000. For Faculty Scholars Program in Mental Health of Children: Peer Relations and Adjustment, A longitudinal study of outcomes and processes in school age children. 2/24/88.
Veritas Therapeutic Community, NYC, NY, $10,000. For Recreation-Cultural-Arts-Family Therapy program. 2/24/88.
W G B H Educational Foundation, Boston, MA, $63,915. For DeGrassi Junior High School mental health research project. 12/7/88.
W G B H Educational Foundation, Boston, MA, $10,000. For DeGrassi Jr. High School project, to evaluate impact of television series on early adolescents' social attitudes, emotional well-being, and stress/coping skills. 9/28/88.

1944
Graphic Controls Corporate Giving Program
P.O. Box 1271
Buffalo 14240 (716) 853-7500
Mailing Address: P.O. Box 1271, Buffalo, NY 14240

Financial data (yr. ended 12/31/88): Total giving, $150,000, including $141,703 for grants (high: $25,000; low: $100; average: $2,500-$5,000) and $8,297 for 11 employee matching gifts.
Purpose and activities: Support for human services, including the elderly, child welfare, drug abuse, the handicapped, education, including minority, business, and early childhood education, health, including AIDS, and medical research, and the arts and humanities. Company also has employee volunteer programs.
Types of support: Annual campaigns, building funds, capital campaigns, conferences and seminars, continuing support, emergency funds, employee matching gifts, internships, lectureships, matching funds, operating budgets, publications, renovation projects, research, employee-related scholarships, scholarship funds, seed money, special projects, technical assistance.
Limitations: Giving primarily in Buffalo, Clayton, and other parts of western NY; Cherry Hill, NJ; and Wilmerding, PA.
Publications: Program policy statement, application guidelines.
Application information:
Initial approach: Request letter with financial information
Deadline(s): Nov. 1
Board meeting date(s): Approx. Nov. 15
Write: May C. Randazzo, APR, Mgr., Public Affairs and Communication
Administrators: Patricia Baubonis, Mgr., Legal Services; Rosanne Dee, Sr. Human Resource Rep.; James Menchette, Quality Control Technician; John Neuretuer, Sr. Inventory Planner.
Number of staff: 1 part-time professional; 1 part-time support.

1945
The Green Fund, Inc.
501 Fifth Ave., Suite 1615
New York 10017 (212) 697-9531

Incorporated in 1947 in NY.
Donor(s): Evelyn Green Davis,† Louis A. Green.†
Financial data (yr. ended 1/31/88): Assets, $25,497,379 (M); gifts received, $656,400; expenditures, $1,656,036, including $1,334,503 for 201 grants (high: $407,000; low: $25; average: $250-$15,000).
Purpose and activities: Giving primarily for Jewish welfare funds, hospitals within the Jewish Federation network, services to the aged and mentally handicapped, higher and secondary education, the performing arts, social services, and youth agencies.
Limitations: Giving primarily in the New York, NY, metropolitan area. No grants to individuals.
Application information: Grants initiated by the fund's members. Applications not accepted.
Write: Cynthia Green Colin, Pres.
Officers and Directors: Cynthia Green Colin, Pres.; S. William Green, Treas.
Number of staff: 1 part-time support.
Employer Identification Number: 136160950

1946
The Alan C. Greenberg Foundation, Inc.
c/o Bear Stearns & Co.
55 Water St.
New York 10041 (212) 272-2000

Established in 1964.
Donor(s): Alan C. Greenberg.
Financial data (yr. ended 12/31/86): Assets, $1,026,183 (M); gifts received, $2,139,600; expenditures, $1,985,809, including $1,983,861 for 81 grants (high: $1,100,550; low: $18; average: $500-$20,000).
Purpose and activities: Emphasis on Jewish organizations, higher education, medical research, and cultural programs.
Limitations: Giving primarily in NY and Israel.
Application information: Contributes only to pre-selected organizations. Applications not accepted.
Board meeting date(s): As necessary
Write: Alan C. Greenberg, Pres.
Officers and Directors: Alan C. Greenberg, Pres. and Treas.; Maynard Greenberg, V.P. and Secy.
Number of staff: None.
Employer Identification Number: 136271740

1947
The David J. Greene Foundation, Inc.
c/o Ms. Florence B. Weingart
30 Wall St.
New York 10005 (212) 344-5180

Incorporated in 1966 in NY.
Donor(s): David J Greene,† and members of the Greene family.
Financial data (yr. ended 12/31/88): Assets, $5,918,096 (M); gifts received, $10,000; expenditures, $400,105, including $366,487 for 259 grants.
Purpose and activities: Grants largely for hospitals, higher and secondary education, social service and youth agencies, and Jewish welfare funds.
Types of support: General purposes.
Limitations: Giving primarily in the New York, NY, metropolitan area. No grants to individuals.
Application information:
Initial approach: Letter
Board meeting date(s): Mar., June, Sept., and Dec.
Officers and Directors: Alan I. Greene, Pres.; Robert J. Ravitz, V.P.; Florence B. Weingart, Secy.; James R. Greene, Treas.; Michael Greene.
Number of staff: None.
Employer Identification Number: 136209280

1948
The Jerome L. Greene Foundation, Inc.
450 Park Ave.
New York 10022

Established in 1978.
Donor(s): Jerome L. Greene.
Financial data (yr. ended 11/30/86): Assets, $2,823,020 (M); gifts received, $2,133,000; expenditures, $282,352, including $271,818 for 45 grants (high: $125,035; low: $25).
Purpose and activities: Grants primarily for cultural programs and Jewish welfare funds.
Application information:
Deadline(s): None
Officer and Directors: Jerome L. Greene, Pres.; Dawn Greene.
Employer Identification Number: 132960852

1949
Greentree Foundation
110 West 51st St., Rm. 4600
New York 10020

Established in NY in 1982.
Financial data (yr. ended 12/31/86): Assets, $7,399,884 (M); expenditures, $493,385, including $443,500 for 29 grants (high: $100,000; low: $2,500).
Purpose and activities: Giving to reduce educational, social and cultural deficiencies in urban areas, preferably through programs initiated by local communities.
Limitations: Giving primarily in the New York metropolitan area.
Officers: Betsey C. Whitney, Pres.; Sara R. Wilford, V.P. and Treas.; Kate R. Whitney, V.P. and Secy.; Kathryn A. Richie, Secy.
Employer Identification Number: 133132117

1950
The Greenwall Foundation
370 Lexington Ave., Rm. 310
New York 10017 (212) 661-0831

Incorporated in 1949 in NY.
Donor(s): Anna A. Greenwall,† Frank K. Greenwall.†
Financial data (yr. ended 12/31/88): Assets, $48,197,059 (M); expenditures, $2,953,613, including $2,130,711 for 56 grants (high: $245,810; low: $500; average: $2,500-$100,000).
Purpose and activities: Giving primarily for medical research, especially in bone cancer, diabetes, immunology, molecular biology, and dementia; education, especially scholarships through institutions; and the arts and humanities. The foundation expects to expand its efforts in arts and education.
Types of support: Continuing support, seed money, emergency funds, equipment, matching funds, scholarship funds, professorships, fellowships, research, special projects.
Limitations: Giving primarily in New York, NY for arts and humanities; giving nationally for medical research and education. No support for state or religious schools, or private foundations. No grants to individuals, or for building or endowment funds, operating budgets, annual campaigns, deficit financing, publications, or conferences; no loans.
Publications: Annual report (including application guidelines).
Application information:
Initial approach: Letter
Copies of proposal: 1
Deadline(s): Submit proposal preferably in Jan. or Aug.; deadlines Feb. 1 and Aug. 1
Board meeting date(s): May and Nov.
Final notification: After next board meeting
Write: John L. Dugan, Jr., Pres.
Officers: Oscar M. Ruebhausen,* Chair.; Donald J. Donahue,* Vice-Chair.; John L. Dugan, Jr., Pres.; Richard L. Salzer,* V.P.; William S. Vaun, M.D.,* V.P.; Edith Levett, Corp. Secy.; C. Richard MacGrath,* Treas.
Directors:* Chester Billings, Jr., George Bugliarello, George F. Cahill, Jr., M.D., Beatrix A. Hamburg, M.D., Edward M. Kresky, Andrew A. MacGrath, Francis F. MacGrath, Susan A. MacGrath, Carl B. Menges, Richard L. Salzer, Jr., M.D.
Number of staff: 2 full-time professional; 1 part-time professional; 1 full-time support.
Employer Identification Number: 136082277
Recent arts and culture grants:
American Museum of Natural History, NYC, NY, $10,000. For undergraduate and graduate research program. 1987.
Brooklyn Academy of Music, Brooklyn, NY, $25,000. For performing arts program for young people. 1987.
Brooklyn Conservatory of Music, Brooklyn, NY, $5,000. For scholarships. 1987.
Brooklyn Museum, Brooklyn, NY, $24,000. For internships for museum management. 1987.
Chamber Music Society of Lincoln Center, NYC, NY, $10,000. For general purposes. 1987.
Dance Theater Foundation, NYC, NY, $10,000. For Alvin Ailey Repertory Ensemble. 1987.
Gallery Association of New York State, Hamilton, NY, $20,000. For general purposes. 1987.
Harlem School of the Arts, NYC, NY, $10,000. For general purposes. 1987.
Joffrey Ballet, NYC, NY, $7,560. For Joffrey II apprentice dancers. 1987.
Lincoln Center for the Performing Arts, NYC, NY, $10,000. For educational programs. 1987.
Manhattan School of Music, NYC, NY, $5,000. For scholarships. 1987.
Metropolitan Opera Association, NYC, NY, $33,000. For general purposes. 1987.
Metropolitan Opera Association, NYC, NY, $25,000. For Young Singers Development program. 1987.
Mirror Repertory Company, NYC, NY, $5,000. For Arts in Education programs. 1987.
Museum of Modern Art, NYC, NY, $10,000. For general purposes. 1987.
New York City Opera, NYC, NY, $10,000. For Donald Gramm Fund for American Artists. 1987.
New York Landmarks Conservancy, NYC, NY, $5,000. For general purposes. 1987.
New York Shakespeare Festival, NYC, NY, $12,500. For Playwriting in the Schools arts-in-education program. 1987.
New York Zoological Society, NYC, NY, $10,000. For marine research at Aquarium. 1987.
Skowhegan School of Painting and Sculpture, Skowhegan, ME, $8,334. For faculty endowment fund. 1987.
Skowhegan School of Painting and Sculpture, Skowhegan, ME, $5,000. For general purposes. 1987.
Studio Museum in Harlem, NYC, NY, $10,000. For general purposes. 1987.

1951
The William and Mary Greve Foundation, Inc.
630 Fifth Ave., No. 1750
New York 10111 (212) 758-8032

Incorporated in 1964 in NY.
Donor(s): Mary P. Greve.†
Financial data (yr. ended 12/31/86): Assets, $17,704,370 (M); expenditures, $1,131,429, including $713,746 for 101 grants (high: $67,277; low: $500; average: $1,000-$5,000).
Purpose and activities: Grants largely for education and related fields, including U.S.-Eastern Bloc relations and the performing arts.
Types of support: Seed money, endowment funds, matching funds, general purposes, continuing support.
Limitations: No grants to individuals, or for scholarships or fellowships; no loans.
Publications: Program policy statement, application guidelines.
Application information:
Initial approach: Letter
Copies of proposal: 1
Deadline(s): None
Board meeting date(s): Variable
Final notification: 2 months
Officers and Directors: John W. Kiser III, Chair.; Anthony C.M. Kiser, Pres.; John J.

Tommaney, Secy.; John A. Buckbee, James W. Sykes, Jr.
Number of staff: 1 full-time support; 2 part-time support.
Employer Identification Number: 136020724

1952
The Griffis Foundation, Inc.
101 West 57th St., Rm. 9F
New York 10019 (212) 759-8693

Incorporated in 1943 in NY.
Donor(s): Stanton Griffis,† Nixon Griffis.
Financial data (yr. ended 12/31/87): Assets, $7,252,675 (M); expenditures, $780,804, including $476,170 for 64 grants (high: $235,905; low: $30; average: $250-$3,000).
Purpose and activities: Emphasis on continuing projects in conservation, education, the humanities, health, and research in oceanographic fields; support also for religious purposes and social services.
Types of support: Operating budgets, continuing support, seed money, deficit financing, professorships, fellowships, research, publications.
Limitations: Giving primarily in NY and CT. No grants to individuals, or for capital or endowment funds, annual campaigns, emergency funds, matching gifts, or conferences; no loans.
Publications: Program policy statement, application guidelines.
Application information:
Deadline(s): None
Board meeting date(s): 10 months per year
Final notification: 2 months
Write: Nixon Griffis, Pres.
Officers and Directors: Nixon Griffis, Pres.; Heather Nye, V.P.; Hughes Griffis, Secy.-Treas.; William G. Conway.
Number of staff: 1 full-time support.
Employer Identification Number: 135678764

1953
The Martin D. Gruss Foundation
(Formerly The Martin and Agneta Gruss Foundation)
900 Third Ave.
New York 10022 (212) 688-1500

Established in 1982 in NY.
Donor(s): Gruss Petroleum Corp.
Financial data (yr. ended 8/31/87): Assets, $546,725 (M); expenditures, $275,052, including $264,000 for 23 grants (high: $100,000; low: $100).
Purpose and activities: Giving primarily for secondary education, museums, and Jewish organizations, including welfare funds; some support also for hospitals.
Limitations: Giving primarily in the New York City metropolitan area.
Application information:
Write: Martin D. Gruss, Trustee
Trustee: Martin D. Gruss.
Employer Identification Number: 133132987

1954
John Simon Guggenheim Memorial Foundation
90 Park Ave.
New York 10016 (212) 687-4470

Incorporated in 1925 in NY.
Donor(s): Simon Guggenheim,† Mrs. Simon Guggenheim.†
Financial data (yr. ended 12/31/88): Assets, $120,804,356 (M); expenditures, $9,162,470, including $6,997,500 for 290 grants to individuals (high: $27,000; low: $6,000; average: $24,000).
Purpose and activities: Fellowships offered to further the development of scholars and artists by assisting them to engage in research in any field of knowledge and creation in any of the arts, under the freest possible conditions and irrespective of race, color, or creed. Fellowships are awarded by the trustees upon nomination by a Committee of Selection. Awards are made to citizens and permanent residents of the U.S. and Canada, and Latin America and the Caribbean. Guggenheim fellowships may not be held concurrently with other fellowships.
Types of support: Fellowships.
Limitations: No grants for building or endowment funds, operating budgets, or special projects.
Publications: Annual report, informational brochure (including application guidelines).
Application information: Grants are awarded to individuals rather than institutions. Application form required.
Initial approach: Letter
Deadline(s): Oct. 1 for U.S. and Canada; Dec. 1 for Latin America and the Caribbean
Board meeting date(s): Apr. and June and as required
Final notification: Approximately 6 months
Write: Joel Conarroe, Pres.
Officers: Joel Conarroe,* Pres.; G. Thomas Tanselle, V.P. and Secy.; Coleen P. Higgins-Jacob, Treas.
Trustees:* W. Clarke Wescoe, Chair.; Richard W. Couper, Edward E. David, Jr., Helene L. Kaplan, Robert V. Lindsay, Joseph A. Rice, Charles Andrew Ryskamp, Malcolm B. Smith, Roger W. Straus, Jr., Jean Strouse.
Number of staff: 8 full-time professional; 16 full-time support.
Employer Identification Number: 135673173

1955
Guilden Foundation, Inc.
c/o Richard A. Eisner & Co.
575 Madison Ave.
New York 10022

Established in 1984 in NY.
Financial data (yr. ended 05/31/87): Assets, $1,078,233 (M); expenditures, $38,096, including $30,150 for 9 grants (high: $16,000; low: $1,000).
Purpose and activities: Support for higher education, civic affairs, Jewish concerns, and the performing arts.
Limitations: Giving primarily in New York, NY.
Application information: Contributes only to pre-selected organizations. Applications not accepted.
Write: Paul Guilden, Pres.
Officers: Paul Guilden, Pres.; Daniel Saltzer, V.P.; Harold Perlman, Secy.
Employer Identification Number: 133185270

1956
The Guinzburg Fund
Three West 29th St.
New York 10001

Incorporated in 1955 in NY.
Donor(s): Harold K. Guinzburg.†
Financial data (yr. ended 12/31/87): Assets, $1,500,000 (M); expenditures, $455,694, including $407,807 for 130 grants (high: $300,000; low: $20; average: $1,000).
Purpose and activities: Giving for hospitals, higher education, cultural activities, and community development.
Types of support: Annual campaigns, research, special projects.
Limitations: Giving primarily in NY.
Officer and Director: Thomas H. Guinzburg, Pres. and Treas.
Number of staff: 1 part-time support.
Employer Identification Number: 136108425

1957
Gumpel-Lury Foundation
c/o Stroock & Stroock & Lavan
Seven Hanover Sq.
New York 10004

Established in 1977 in NY.
Financial data (yr. ended 10/31/87): Assets, $524,695 (M); gifts received, $500; expenditures, $129,312, including $113,390 for 57 grants (high: $14,300; low: $50).
Purpose and activities: Grants to organizations that promote peace among nations, or benefit the New York City metropolitan community or the Jewish community in the U.S. and abroad; areas of interest include higher education, art, and culture.
Types of support: General purposes.
Limitations: Giving primarily in the New York City area. No grants to individuals.
Application information:
Deadline(s): None
Write: Bernard E. Brandes
Officers & Directors: Judith G. Friedlaender, Pres.; Thomas M. Franck, V.P.; Edgar J. Nathan, V.P.; Marie S. Neuberger, V.P.; Jane Lury, Treas.
Employer Identification Number: 132915655

1958
The Gutfreund Foundation, Inc.
John Gutfreund, Salomon Brothers Inc.
One New York Plaza
New York 10004 (212) 627-7710
Application address: c/o Joint Foundation Support, Inc., 40 West 20th St., New York, NY 10011

Incorporated in 1967 in NY.
Donor(s): John H. Gutfreund.

Financial data (yr. ended 4/30/87): Assets, $1,834,587 (M); expenditures, $171,052, including $143,500 for 12 grants (high: $25,000; low: $6,000; average: $7,500-$15,000).
Purpose and activities: Small grants (averaging $10,000) to support projects designed to ensure civil rights and civil liberties, encourage self-help, and promote equality of opportunity for the urban and rural poor; giving also to promote appreciation for the arts; grants to groups organizing for change at the community level, as well as to organizations seeking new ways to deliver services. Grants sometimes made outside the New York City area to organizations that do not have access to larger sources of funding. Occasional larger grants to projects or institutions of personal interest to the trustees.
Types of support: Operating budgets, seed money, general purposes, matching funds, special projects.
Limitations: Giving primarily in New York, NY. No grants to individuals, or for building or endowment funds, scholarships, or fellowships; no loans.
Publications: Annual report, application guidelines.
Application information: Contributes only to pre-selected organizations. Applications not accepted.
Copies of proposal: 1
Deadline(s): Spring and fall
Board meeting date(s): Spring and fall
Write: Nanette Falkenberg, Pres.
Officers and Trustees: John H. Gutfreund, Pres.; Lawrence B. Buttenwieser, Secy.-Treas.
Number of staff: 3 full-time professional; 3 full-time support.
Employer Identification Number: 136227515

1959
Stella and Charles Guttman Foundation, Inc.
595 Madison Ave., Suite 1604
New York 10022 (212) 371-7082

Incorporated in 1959 in NY.
Donor(s): Charles Guttman,† Stella Guttman.†
Financial data (yr. ended 12/31/87): Assets, $20,595,097 (M); expenditures, $1,191,863, including $957,500 for 108 grants (high: $300,000; low: $500; average: $1,000-$10,000).
Purpose and activities: Support for organizations providing social, physical, medical, mental health, cultural and educational services. The foundation has also supported ongoing programs, such as its college scholarship program which provides annual grants to 20 liberal arts colleges. Support also for a limited number of charities that conduct activities in the state of Israel.
Types of support: Scholarship funds.
Limitations: Giving primarily in the New York, NY, metropolitan area for health and welfare; nationally for education. No support for religious organizations for religious purposes, public interest litigation, or anti-vivisectionist causes. No grants to individuals, or for foreign trade or foreign study.
Publications: Program policy statement.
Application information:
Initial approach: Letter
Deadline(s): None
Board meeting date(s): As required
Write: Elizabeth Olofson, Exec. Dir.
Officers and Directors: Abraham Rosenberg, Pres.; Edgar H. Brenner, V.P.; Sonia Rosenberg, Secy.; Robert S. Gassman, Treas.; Elizabeth Olofson, Exec. Dir.; Charles S. Brenner, Peter A. Herbert, Ernest Rubenstein.
Employer Identification Number: 136103039

1960
Hagedorn Fund
600 Fifth Ave.
New York 10020 (212) 957-1500

Trust established in 1953 in NY.
Donor(s): William Hagedorn.†
Financial data (yr. ended 12/31/88): Assets, $19,981,244 (M); expenditures, $1,169,847, including $1,040,950 for 108 grants (high: $85,000; low: $1,000; average: $5,000-$10,000).
Purpose and activities: Support for higher and secondary education, and church support; grants also for hospitals and health agencies, the aged, youth agencies, social welfare, and cultural organizations.
Types of support: Operating budgets, annual campaigns, building funds, capital campaigns, general purposes.
Limitations: Giving limited to the New York, NY, metropolitan area, including NJ and CT. No grants to individuals, or for continuing support, seed money, emergency funds, deficit financing, endowment funds, matching gifts, scholarships, fellowships, research, special projects, publications, or conferences; no loans.
Application information:
Initial approach: Proposal
Copies of proposal: 1
Deadline(s): Submit proposal preferably in Nov.; deadline Nov. 15
Board meeting date(s): Dec.
Final notification: 1 month
Write: Robert Rosenthal, V.P., Manufacturers Hanover Trust Co.
Trustees: William J. Fischer, Jr., Charles B. Lauren, Manufacturers Hanover Trust Co.
Number of staff: 5
Employer Identification Number: 136048718

1961
The Hanes Foundation
460 Park Ave.
New York 10022 (212) 486-7229

Incorporated in 1952 in NY.
Donor(s): John W. Hanes, Sr.
Financial data (yr. ended 12/31/87): Assets, $279,078 (M); gifts received, $20,861; expenditures, $299,436.
Purpose and activities: Contributes to cultural organizations, conservation programs, and educational institutions.
Application information:
Initial approach: Proposal
Deadline(s): None
Write: John W. Hanes, Sr.
Officers and Directors: John W. Hanes, Jr., Pres.; John W. Hanes, Sr., V.P. and Treas.; David G. Hanes, Secy.; Mrs. John W. Hanes, Mrs. Ormsby H. Matthiessen, Agnes H. McKnight.
Employer Identification Number: 136087828

1962
William Hale Harkness Foundation, Inc.
145 East 48th St., Suite 26C
New York 10017 (212) 755-5540

Established in 1936 in NY.
Financial data (yr. ended 12/31/87): Assets, $8,000,000 (M); expenditures, $300,000, including $250,000 for 50 grants.
Purpose and activities: Emphasis on the the performing arts and medicine.
Limitations: No grants to individuals.
Application information:
Initial approach: In writing; no telephone calls
Deadline(s): None
Write: Theodore S. Bartwink, Exec. Dir.
Officers and Directors: Barnett G. Kriesberg, Pres.; William A. Perlmuth, V.P.; Theodore S. Bartwink, Exec. Dir.; Bernard Brandes.
Employer Identification Number: 131790755

1963
Mary W. Harriman Foundation
63 Wall St., 23rd Fl.
New York 10005 (212) 493-8182

Trust established in 1925 in NY; incorporated in 1973.
Donor(s): Mary W. Harriman.†
Financial data (yr. ended 12/31/87): Assets, $15,565,720 (M); expenditures, $965,778, including $735,500 for 89 grants (high: $50,000; low: $1,000; average: $1,000-$10,000).
Purpose and activities: Emphasis on higher and secondary education, hospitals and health agencies, cultural programs, public policy, civic affairs, and social service and youth agencies.
Types of support: Annual campaigns, capital campaigns, general purposes, operating budgets.
Limitations: Giving primarily in the New York, NY, metropolitan area. No grants to individuals.
Publications: 990-PF.
Application information:
Initial approach: Proposal
Copies of proposal: 1
Deadline(s): Sept. 15
Board meeting date(s): Dec.
Final notification: 1 month
Write: William F. Hibberd, Secy.
Officers: Kathleen N. Mortimer,* Pres.; William Rich III, V.P.; William F. Hibberd, Secy.; William J. Corcoran, Treas.
Directors:* Mary A. Fisk, Elbridge T. Gerry, Sr., Pamela C. Harriman, John B. Madden, Edward H. Northrop.
Number of staff: 2 full-time professional; 2 full-time support.
Employer Identification Number: 237356000

1964
W. Averell and Pamela C. Harriman Foundation
63 Wall St., 23rd Fl.
New York 10005

Established in 1969 in NY.
Donor(s): W. Averell Harriman.†
Financial data (yr. ended 12/31/87): Assets, $1,838,369 (M); gifts received, $379,300; expenditures, $177,172, including $107,500 for 24 grants (high: $20,000; low: $500).
Purpose and activities: Giving for general charitable purposes, including to cultural orgainzations and for international affairs.
Application information:
Initial approach: Proposal
Deadline(s): None
Write: William F. Hibberd, Secy.
Officers: Pamela C. Harriman,* Pres.; William Rich III, V.P.; William F. Hibberd, Secy.; William J. Corcoran, Treas.
Directors:* Kathleen L.H. Mortimer, Mary A. Fisk, Elbridge T. Gerry, John B. Madden.
Employer Identification Number: 510193921

1965
Jesse and Dorothy Hartman Foundation
c/o Proskauer, Rose, Goetz and Mendelsohn
300 Park Ave.
New York 10022

Established in 1954 in NY.
Donor(s): Jesse Hartman.†
Financial data (yr. ended 12/31/86): Assets, $2,281,643 (M); expenditures, $129,616, including $119,600 for 7 grants (high: $50,000; low: $1,000).
Purpose and activities: Grants for philanthropic and cultural programs.
Application information: Contributes only to pre-selected organizations. Applications not accepted.
Officers: Margot H. Tenney,* Pres.; Charles Looker,* V.P.; Milton Mann, Secy.-Treas.
Trustees:* Delbert Tenney.
Employer Identification Number: 066044501

1966
Merrill G. and Emita E. Hastings Foundation
c/o Conceptual Planning, Inc.
245 Fifth Ave.
New York 10016 (212) 779-1300

Trust established in 1966 in NY.
Donor(s): Emita E. Hastings.†
Financial data (yr. ended 2/28/88): Assets, $2,579,809 (M); expenditures, $124,214, including $58,900 for 36 grants (high: $15,000; low: $100; average: $2,000).
Purpose and activities: Giving for cultural programs, including museums, and for education and conservation.
Limitations: Giving primarily in the New York, NY, area. No grants to individuals, or for endowment funds.
Publications: 990-PF.
Application information:
Initial approach: Letter
Copies of proposal: 1
Deadline(s): None
Board meeting date(s): As required
Write: Lee R. Robins, Accountant
Trustees: Elizabeth H. Peterfreund, Janis Peterfreund, Joshua Peterfreund, Liza Peterfreund.
Employer Identification Number: 136203465

1967
Charles Hayden Foundation
One Bankers Trust Plaza
130 Liberty St.
New York 10006 (212) 938-0790

Incorporated in 1937 in NY.
Donor(s): Charles Hayden.†
Financial data (yr. ended 9/30/88): Assets, $132,251,000 (M); expenditures, $7,514,889, including $6,331,889 for 140 grants (high: $500,000; low: $2,126; average: $5,000-$100,000).
Purpose and activities: To assist young people; emphasis on helping to provide physical facilities and equipment for organizations primarily concerned with the mental, moral, and physical development of youth; some limited program support available for experimental projects with well-defined goals and the potential for replication by others.
Types of support: Building funds, equipment, land acquisition, matching funds, renovation projects, scholarship funds, special projects.
Limitations: Giving limited to the New York, NY (including northern NJ), and Boston, MA, metropolitan areas. No support for fraternal groups, religious organizations for other than community youth-related projects, or hospitals, hospices, and projects essentially medical in nature. No grants to individuals, or for endowment funds, operating budgets, general support, continuing support, fellowships, annual campaigns, emergency funds, deficit financing, publications, or conferences; no loans.
Publications: Annual report.
Application information:
Initial approach: Proposal
Copies of proposal: 1
Deadline(s): None
Board meeting date(s): Monthly
Final notification: 4 to 6 weeks
Write: William T. Wachenfeld, Pres.
Officers and Trustees: William T. Wachenfeld, Pres.; David B. Stone, V.P.; Howard F. Cerny, Secy.; John L. Kidde, Treas.; Andrew Ardito.
Number of staff: 3 full-time professional; 5 part-time professional; 1 full-time support.
Employer Identification Number: 135562237
Recent arts and culture grants:
American Museum of Natural History, Hayden Planetarium, NYC, NY, $260,000. Toward modernization of various sections of planetarium. 9/87.
Audubon Society of Massachusetts, Lincoln, MA, $15,000. Toward renovation of Blue Hills Trailside Museum. 10/87.
Belmont Hill School, Belmont, MA, $50,000. Toward conversion of space into arts center. 7/88.
Brooklyn Childrens Museum, Brooklyn, NY, $40,000. Toward exhibition development. 1/88.
Greenburgh Nature Center, Scarsdale, NY, $30,000. Toward construction of greenhouse. 1/88.
Longy School of Music, Cambridge, MA, $8,000. Toward installation of facilities for handicapped. 11/87.
Milton Academy, Milton, MA, $75,000. Toward construction of Performing Arts Center. 9/87.
New England Aquarium, Boston, MA, $200,000. Toward construction of new Gallery. 10/86.
New York School for Circus Arts, NYC, NY, $37,500. Toward purchase of new state-of-the-art bleacher system. 9/87.
Sci-Tech Center at Liberty State Park, Morris Plains, NJ, $300,000. Toward construction of Sci-Tech Center at Liberty State Park. 2/88.
Staten Island Historical Society, Staten Island, NY, $7,500. Toward completion of interior furnishings for Voorlezer's House. 3/88.

1968
The Edward W. Hazen Foundation, Inc.
505 Eighth Ave., Rm. 2300
New York 10018 (212) 967-5920

Incorporated in 1925 in CT.
Donor(s): Edward Warriner Hazen,† Helen Russell Hazen,† Lucy Abigail Hazen,† Mary Hazen Arnold.†
Financial data (yr. ended 12/31/87): Assets, $9,000,000 (M); expenditures, $767,976, including $451,716 for 61 grants (high: $30,000; low: $100; average: $18,000).
Purpose and activities: Support focused on young people and their values, primarily in community agencies and educational programs at the secondary level that include action and/or research in: the quality of education of adolescents in general and of at-risk youngsters, especially from disadvantaged minorities; youth development through community institutions; and community service by young people and by adult volunteers who serve youth. Exploratory fields include improvement of writing, juvenile justice, and youth in the armed forces.
Types of support: Seed money, matching funds, special projects.
Limitations: No support for programs or projects in medicine or health sciences, engineering, law, or public and business administration. No grants to individuals, or for operating budgets, continuing support, annual campaigns, deficit financing, capital or endowment funds, scholarships, fellowships, publications, or conferences; no loans.
Publications: Biennial report, informational brochure (including application guidelines), grants list.
Application information: Request guidelines for detailed program and support limitations. Application form required.
Initial approach: Letter
Copies of proposal: 2
Deadline(s): Jan. 15 and July 15
Board meeting date(s): Apr. and Oct.
Final notification: 10 days
Write: Sharon B. King, Pres.
Officers and Trustees: Manuel P. Guerrero, Chair.; Sharon B. King, Pres.; Vilma S. Martinez, V.P.; Carol Anastasio, Secy.; Harry Wugalter, Treas.; Alyson J. Tufts, Grants Admin.; Adrienne Y. Bailey, Edward E. Booher, Mary L. Bundy, Lewis Feldstein, Claire

Guadiani, Richard Green, Edward M. Harris, Jr., Barbara K. Hatton, Richard Schall.
Number of staff: 1 full-time professional; 1 full-time support; 1 part-time support.
Employer Identification Number: 060646671
Recent arts and culture grants:
Detroit Center for the Performing Arts, Detroit, MI, $5,000. For professional theater training for low income, juvenile offenders and otherwise disadvantaged artists in exchange for volunteer work. 1988.
Metropolitan Arts Council, Omaha, NE, $20,000. For first part of three year project to help black, Hispanic and Native American youth develop life management skills through arts. 1988.
Teaching Through Theater, Anchorage, AK, $10,000. For grant to use theater techniques to help troubled teenagers, especially those with drug and alcohol problems, increase their self-esteem and ability to communicate. 1988.
Youth Initiative Project, Brunswick, GA, $15,000. For social, cultural, educational and employment programs for disadvantaged black youth. 1988.

1969
Joseph H. Hazen Foundation
645 Madison Ave.
New York 10022

Incorporated in 1957 in NY.
Donor(s): Joseph H. Hazen.
Financial data (yr. ended 12/31/86): Assets, $1,140,408 (M); gifts received, $5,000; expenditures, $308,474, including $305,028 for 23 grants (high: $100,000; low: $100).
Purpose and activities: Emphasis on Jewish welfare funds, cultural organizations, and educational institutions; support also for museums and hospitals.
Limitations: Giving primarily in New York, NY, and Israel.
Application information: Contributes only to pre-selected organizations. Applications not accepted.
Officers and Directors: Joseph H. Hazen, Pres.; Cynthia H. Polsky, V.P.; Robert Anthoine, Secy.; Lita A. Hazen.
Employer Identification Number: 136161536

1970
The Hearst Foundation, Inc.
888 Seventh Ave.
New York 10106-0057 (212) 586-5404
Address for applicants from west of the Mississippi River: Thomas Eastham, V.P. and Western Dir., 90 New Montgomery St., Suite 1212, San Francisco, CA 94105; Tel.: (415) 543-0400

Incorporated in 1945 in NY.
Donor(s): William Randolph Hearst.†
Financial data (yr. ended 12/31/88): Assets, $117,832,000 (M); expenditures, $5,584,000, including $5,157,000 for 276 grants (high: $100,000; low: $5,000; average: $10,000-$25,000).
Purpose and activities: Giving for programs to aid poverty-level and minority groups, educational programs with emphasis on private secondary and higher education, health-delivery systems and medical research, and cultural programs with records of public support. Organizations serving larger geographic areas generally favored over those of a narrow community nature.
Types of support: Special projects, scholarship funds, research, endowment funds, general purposes, matching funds, operating budgets.
Limitations: Giving limited to the U.S. and its territories. No support for political purposes. No grants to individuals; no loans.
Publications: Program policy statement, application guidelines.
Application information:
Initial approach: Letter or proposal
Copies of proposal: 1
Deadline(s): None
Board meeting date(s): Mar., June, Sept., and Dec.
Final notification: 4 to 6 weeks
Write: Robert M. Frehse, Jr., Exec. Dir. (east of the Mississippi River); Thomas Eastham, V.P. and Western Dir. (west of the Mississippi River)
Officers and Directors:* George R. Hearst, Jr.,* Pres.; Thomas Eastham, V.P. and Western Dir.; Robert M. Frehse, Jr., V.P. and Exec. Dir.; Harvey L. Lipton,* V.P. and Secy.; Frank A. Bennack, Jr.,* V.P.; Millicent H. Boudjakdji,* V.P.; Richard E. Deems,* V.P.; John R. Hearst, Jr.,* V.P.; Randolph A. Hearst, V.P.; William R. Hearst, Jr.,* V.P.; J. Kingsbury-Smith,* V.P.; Frank Massi,* V.P.; Gilbert C. Maurer,* V.P.; Raymond J. Petersen,* V.P.; Franklin C. Snyder,* V.P.; Ralph J. Cuomo, Treas.
Number of staff: 11 full-time professional; 3 full-time support; 1 part-time support.
Employer Identification Number: 136161746
Recent arts and culture grants:
American Composers Orchestra, NYC, NY, $25,000. To meet National Endowment for the Arts Challenge Grant. 6/88.
Art Museum of Southeast Texas, Beaumont, TX, $35,000. For newly built Museum facility (Formerly Beaumont Art Museum). 6/88.
Arts Connection, NYC, NY, $10,000. For expansion of Young Talent program for inner city elementary-school youngsters and to meet National Endowment for Arts Challenge Grant. 3/88.
Billings Studio Theater, Billings, MT, $25,000. Toward general operating expenses. 9/87.
Boston Youth Theater, Cambridge, MA, $10,000. Toward general support. 12/87.
California Museum Foundation, Los Angeles, CA, $50,000. For Mark Taper Hall of Economics. 6/88.
Cooper-Hewitt Museum, The Smithsonians National Museum of Design, NYC, NY, $25,000. To meet Andrew W. Mellon Foundation challenge grant for endowment funds in support of research projects. 6/88.
Corporate Council for the Arts, Seattle, WA, $50,000. For general support. 6/88.
East Woods School, Oyster Bay, NY, $25,000. Toward capital campaign to build music center. 6/88.
Feld Ballet, NYC, NY, $15,000. Toward New Ballet School. 12/87.
Friends of the Arts, Locust Valley, NY, $15,000. Toward relocation of Children and Dance Series. 12/87.
Helena Film Society, Helena, MT, $30,000. Toward cultural education programs in schools. 6/88.
Independent Curators, NYC, NY, $10,000. Toward Tenth Anniversary Endowment Fund. 9/87.
International Visitors Center of the Bay Area, San Francisco, CA, $5,000. Toward program support. 12/87.
Learning Through Education in the Arts Project (LEAP), San Francisco, CA, $12,500. For stipends for resident artists who work side by side with children to enhance their educational experience. 3/88.
Lincoln Center for the Performing Arts, NYC, NY, $100,000. Toward Consolidated Corporate Fund Drive. 6/88.
Los Angeles Chamber Orchestra, Pasadena, CA, $15,000. Toward general operating support. 9/87.
Luther Burbank Memorial Foundation, Luther Burbank Center for the Arts, Santa Rosa, CA, $15,000. Toward capital campaign. 9/87.
Museum of Fine Arts, School of the Museum of Fine Arts, Boston, MA, $25,000. Toward scholarship aid for students. 9/87.
Music Center of Los Angeles County, Los Angeles, CA, $25,000. For educational programs and to meet National Endowment for the Arts challenge grant. 6/88.
National Choral Council, NYC, NY, $10,000. For general support. 6/88.
National Dance Institute, NYC, NY, $25,000. Toward National Program to bring performing arts to children across country. 6/88.
Nevada Opera Association, Reno, NV, $10,000. Toward general support. 12/87.
Newark Community School of the Arts, Newark, NJ, $30,000. For scholarship aid for economically disadvantaged youngsters. 6/88.
Nicolaysen Art Museum, Casper, WY, $10,000. For general endowment fund targeted for Children's Center, artist-in-residence program providing lectures, concerts, films and plays for children in Wyoming. 3/88.
Oakland Festival of the Arts, Oakland, CA, $10,000. For general support of art educational program to make highest quality of art available to widest possible audience. 3/88.
Oberlin College, Oberlin, OH, $35,000. For establishment of William Randolph Hearst Endowed Scholarship in the Conservatory of Music. 3/88.
Parrish Art Museum, Southampton, NY, $10,000. For educational outreach programs for minority youngsters in Bridgehampton School District. 3/88.
Performing Arts Workshop, San Francisco, CA, $5,000. Toward matching California Arts Council grant for Artists in School program. 12/87.
Performing Tree, Los Angeles, CA, $10,000. For National Endowment for the Arts Challenge Grant and development of multi-cultural and multi-language educational and art programs to students in Los Angeles area. 3/88.
Professional Childrens School, NYC, NY, $15,000. Toward renovation of multi-purpose facility. 9/87.

Reno Philharmonic Association, Reno, NV, $25,000. For general support. 6/88.
Saint Louis Conservatory of Music, Saint Louis, MO, $25,000. Toward scholarship assistance. 6/88.
San Francisco Chanticleer, San Francisco, CA, $10,000. For multi-school residency vocal music program designed to serve students and teachers in four middle and high schools by providing classes, workshops and coaching. 3/88.
San Francisco Museum of Modern Art, San Francisco, CA, $20,000. Toward matching challenge grant from National Endowment for the Arts. 9/87.
Science Museum of Long Island, North Shore Junior Science Museum, Plandome, NY, $10,000. Toward development of science center at Castlegould in Sands Point, Long Island. 12/87.
Seattle Art Museum, Seattle, WA, $35,000. For support of educational programs. 6/88.
Sleepy Hollow Restorations, Tarrytown, NY, $10,000. Toward restoration of Sunnyside, home of Washington Irving. 9/87.
Southern California Conservatory of Music, Sun Valley, CA, $7,000. Toward scholarship assistance for Hispanic students. 6/88.
Symphony Space, NYC, NY, $10,000. Toward expansion of Curriculum Arts Project. 9/87.
Theater for a New Audience, NYC, NY, $5,000. Toward general support. 12/87.
University of California, Friends of the Bancroft Library, Berkeley, CA, $15,000. Toward Mark Twain papers. 12/87.
University of California, Pacific Film Archive, Berkeley, CA, $25,000. To complete William Randolph Hearst Endowment. 6/88.
Valley Institute of Theater Arts, Saratoga, CA, $20,000. For support of educational programs. 6/88.
Wave Hill, Bronx, NY, $15,000. For renovation of exhibits in Learning Center on archaeological excavations and Forest Management Project in order to increase visitors, most of whom are school children and their families from New York City area. 3/88.
West End Symphony, NYC, NY, $15,000. Toward support for Marketing/Development Specialist. 9/87.
Whole Theater Company Foundation, Montclair, NJ, $10,000. For general support. 6/88.
Wolf Trap Foundation for the Performing Arts, Vienna, VA, $5,000. For general support to maintain low ticket prices and insure performances benefit general public. 3/88.
Young Audiences, Kansas City Chapter, Kansas City, MO, $10,000. For Arts Partners - The Arts in Education Resource in Kansas City, program enabling six to eight thousand school children and their families to see professional performers. 3/88.

1971
William Randolph Hearst Foundation

888 Seventh Ave., 27th Fl.
New York 10106-0057 (212) 586-5404
Address for applicants from west of the Mississippi River: Thomas Eastham, V.P. and Western Dir., 90 New Montgomery St., Suite 1212, San Francisco, CA 94105; Tel.: (415) 543-0400

Incorporated in 1948 in CA.
Donor(s): William Randolph Hearst.†
Financial data (yr. ended 12/31/88): Assets, $259,556,000 (M); expenditures, $12,994,000, including $8,654,000 for 271 grants (high: $1,000,000; low: $6,000; average: $15,000-$35,000).
Purpose and activities: Programs to aid poverty-level and minority groups, educational programs with emphasis on private secondary and higher education, health delivery systems and medical research, programs affiliated with religious institutions, and cultural programs with records of public support. Organizations serving larger geographic areas are generally favored over those of a narrow community nature. Support also through two independent scholarship programs: Journalism Awards Program and United States Senate Youth Program.
Types of support: Endowment funds, research, scholarship funds, matching funds, general purposes, special projects, student aid, operating budgets.
Limitations: Giving limited to the U.S. and its territories. No support for political purposes. No grants to individuals (except scholarships through the Journalism Awards and United States Senate programs); no loans.
Publications: Program policy statement, application guidelines.
Application information:
Initial approach: Letter or proposal
Copies of proposal: 1
Deadline(s): None
Board meeting date(s): Mar., June, Sept., and Dec.
Final notification: 4 to 6 weeks
Write: Robert M. Frehse, Jr., Exec. Dir. (east of the Mississippi River); Thomas Eastham, V.P. and Western Dir. (west of the Mississippi River)
Officers and Directors:* Randolph A. Hearst,* Pres.; Thomas Eastham, V.P. and Western Dir.; Robert M. Frehse, Jr., V.P. and Exec. Dir.; Harvey L. Lipton,* V.P. and Secy.; Frank A. Bennack, Jr.,* V.P.; Millicent H. Boudjakdji,* V.P.; Richard E. Deems,* V.P.; George R. Hearst, Jr.,* V.P.; John R. Hearst, Jr.,* V.P.; William R. Hearst, Jr.,* V.P.; J. Kingsbury-Smith,* V.P.; Frank Massi,* V.P.; Gilbert C. Maurer,* V.P.; Raymond J. Petersen,* V.P.; Franklin C. Snyder,* V.P.; Ralph J. Cuomo, Treas.
Number of staff: 11 full-time professional; 3 full-time support; 1 part-time support.
Employer Identification Number: 136019226
Recent arts and culture grants:
American Conservatory Theater, San Francisco, CA, $15,000. To further development of American theater and outstanding artists in west coast area. 3/88.
American Symphony Orchestra League, DC, $10,000. Toward general support. 9/87.
Berkeley Repertory Theater, Berkeley, CA, $20,000. For Teaching Artists Program, in which actors visit classrooms and conduct participatory workshops for students in order to enhance students' understanding of skills involved in theatrical productions. 3/88.
Bethel College, Kauffman Museum, North Newton, KS, $25,000. Toward matching NEH Challenge Grant. 9/87.
Big Apple Circus, New York School for Circus Arts, NYC, NY, $10,000. Toward general support. 9/87.
Bilingual Foundation of the Arts, Los Angeles, CA, $10,000. Toward general support. 12/87.
Boston Ballet, Boston, MA, $35,000. For South End Community Dance Project which provides free introductory dance courses to grade school students and scholarships to students who continue their dance education. Students come from minority backgrounds. 3/88.
Brooklyn Museum, Brooklyn, NY, $25,000. For exhibition, Fin de Siecle: The Couture Houses of Worth, Doucet and Pingat. 3/88.
California State Summer School Arts Foundation, Encino, CA, $25,000. Toward establishment of Hearst Scholarship Endowment. 9/87.
Casper Civic Symphony, Casper, WY, $20,000. To strengthen orchestra's educational outreach programs to increase audiences. About 1200 individuals attend each concert and music demonstrations, including Kinder Concerts, which are played throughout season to Casper's school children. 3/88.
Center for Creative Studies: College of Art and Design, Institute of Music and Dance, Detroit, MI, $15,000. Toward general support. 9/87.
Cooper Union for the Advancement of Science and Art, NYC, NY, $40,000. To complete William Randolph Hearst Scholarship Endowment Fund. 6/88.
Dayton Philharmonic Orchestra Association, Dayton, OH, $5,000. Toward educational programs. 9/87.
Folger Shakespeare Library, DC, $25,000. Toward fellowship endowment in support of predoctoral studies. Grant made through Trustees of Amherst College. 12/87.
Interlochen Center for the Arts, Interlochen, MI, $25,000. Toward WRH Endowed Scholarship Fund. 12/87.
Jewish Museum, NYC, NY, $20,000. Toward curriculum project based on The Dreyfus Affair: Art, Truth and Justice. 12/87.
Juilliard School, NYC, NY, $250,000. Toward William Randolph Hearst Endowed Fund for Scholarships. 6/88.
Lincoln Center for the Performing Arts, NYC, NY, $200,000. Toward new building endowment fund as part of major capital campaign. 6/88.
Los Angeles Childrens Museum, Los Angeles, CA, $10,000. Toward general support for From Africa to Los Angeles exhibit. 9/87.
Marlboro School of Music, Philadelphia, PA, $25,000. To support endowment campaign to meet National Endowment for the arts challenge grant. 6/88.
Metropolitan Museum of Art, NYC, NY, $250,000. Toward Hearst Endowment Fund to provide seed monies for special exhibitions. 9/87.
Metropolitan Opera Association, NYC, NY, $400,000. To William Randolph Hearst Endowed Young Artist Development Program. 6/88.

Milwaukee Public Museum, Milwaukee, WI, $30,000. For conservation of three sixteenth century Brussels tapestries given to Museum by Hearst Foundation. 3/88.
Museum of Modern Art, NYC, NY, $40,000. Toward William Randolph Hearst Endowment Fund for Department of Education's School Programs. 6/88.
National Trust for Historic Preservation, DC, $25,000. Toward Inner-City Ventures Fund. 9/87.
New York Committee for Young Audiences, NYC, NY, $20,000. For expanding to six more schools, THE MAX - The Musical Arts Experience project, developed with New York Philharmonic, Carnegie Hall and New York City Ballet. THE MAX brings performing artists to high schools with high dropout rate. 3/88.
New York School of Academic Art, NYC, NY, $25,000. For Graduate School Transition Fund. Academy plans to recast and expand art program into graduate degree program and establish Graduate School of Figurative Art. 3/88.
Oakland Museum Association, Oakland, CA, $10,000. Toward educational programs. 9/87.
Opera Colorado, Denver, CO, $15,000. For general support. 6/88.
Oregon Art Institute, Portland, OR, $20,000. Toward Native American Art Collection Exhibition. 12/87.
Philharmonic-Symphony Society of New York, NYC, NY, $400,000. To William Randolph Hearst Endowed Education Fund. 6/88.
San Antonio Art Institute, San Antonio, TX, $50,000. Toward scholarship endowment for qualified needy students. 3/88.
San Diego Opera Association, San Diego, CA, $15,000. Toward music education programs. 12/87.
San Francisco Ballet Association, San Francisco, CA, $250,000. To William Randolph Hearst Endowment Fund for Educational Programs. 6/88.
San Francisco Opera Association, San Francisco, CA, $250,000. To William Randolph Hearst Endowment Fund for Young Artists. 6/88.
San Francisco Symphony, San Francisco, CA, $250,000. To William Randolph Hearst Endowed Scholarship for Young Artists. 6/88.
Santa Barbara Museum of Art, Santa Barbara, CA, $20,000. Toward William Randolph Hearst Endowment for educational programs. 6/88.
Save Orchestra Hall, Detroit, MI, $25,000. Toward capital campaign to renovate hall and to meet Kresge challenge grant. 12/87.
Seattle Repertory Theater, Seattle, WA, $20,000. Toward outreach programs. 12/87.
Sioux Falls Community Playhouse, Sioux Falls, SD, $20,000. For expansion of educational outreach programs in surrounding rural areas of South Dakota.. 3/88.
Skowhegan School of Painting and Sculpture, Skowhegan, ME, $25,000. Toward capital campaign, endowment for scholarship money and to help meet NEA challenge grant. 12/87.
Smith College, Northampton, MA, $25,000. Toward William Randolph Hearst Emergency Financial Aid Fund to aid fully qualified women with adverse family and financial circumstances. 3/88.
Spanish Theater Repertory Company, NYC, NY, $20,000. For funding to add Educational Coordinator in order to allow Theater to respond to increased requests from schools. Theater currently offers matinee performances to 7,500 students. 3/88.
Tanglewood Music Center, Boston, MA, $25,000. Toward establishment of William Randolph Hearst Endowed Fellowship for talented young musicians. Income would be used to support residency of one talented young musician with the Boston Symphony Orchestra. 3/88.
Whitney Museum of American Art, NYC, NY, $250,000. Toward funding to endow Artreach Program. 9/87.

1972
The Heckscher Foundation for Children

17 East 47th St.
New York 10017 (212) 371-7775

Incorporated in 1921 in NY.
Donor(s): August Heckscher.†
Financial data (yr. ended 12/31/87): Assets, $22,163,000 (M); expenditures, $1,822,547, including $1,688,498 for 119 grants (high: $166,667; low: $1,000; average: $100-$25,000).
Purpose and activities: To promote the welfare of children; grants particularly for child welfare and family service agencies, education, recreation, performing arts, music, hospitals, summer youth programs and camps, and aid to the handicapped.
Types of support: Seed money, emergency funds, building funds, equipment, land acquisition, renovation projects, special projects, scholarship funds.
Limitations: Giving primarily in the greater New York, NY, area. No grants to individuals, or for operating budgets, annual campaigns, deficit financing, fellowships, or endowment funds; no loans.
Publications: Application guidelines.
Application information:
Initial approach: Letter or proposal
Copies of proposal: 1
Deadline(s): None
Board meeting date(s): Monthly except July and Aug.
Final notification: 1 month
Write: Virginia Sloane, Pres.
Officers and Trustees: Louis Smadbeck, Chair.; Virginia Sloane, Pres.; Howard G. Sloane, V.P. and Treas.; William D. Hart, Jr., Secy.; Mrs. J. Clarence Davis, Jr., Richard N. Kerst, John D. MacNeary, Gail Meyers, John M. O'Mara, Howard Grant Sloane, Arthur J. Smadbeck, Mina Smadbeck, Paul Smadbeck, Florence Wallach.
Number of staff: 1 full-time professional; 1 part-time professional; 1 part-time support.
Employer Identification Number: 131820170

1973
Heineman Foundation for Research, Educational, Charitable and Scientific Purposes, Inc.

c/o Brown Brothers Harriman & Co.
59 Wall St.
New York 10005

Incorporated in 1947 in DE.
Donor(s): Dannie N. Heineman.†
Financial data (yr. ended 12/31/87): Assets, $6,642,478 (M); expenditures, $397,631, including $355,000 for 17 grants (high: $125,000; low: $5,000).
Purpose and activities: Support for research programs in mathematical sciences and medicine; grants for higher education, Jewish giving, specialized libraries (including the Heineman Library of Rare Books and Manuscripts given to The Pierpont Morgan Library, New York), music schools and two annual physics awards.
Application information: Contributes only to pre-selected organizations. Applications not accepted.
Board meeting date(s): Sept.-Oct.
Officer: David Rose, Pres.; Agnes Gautier, Esq., V.P.; Ann R. Podlipny, Secy.; Simon M.D. Rose, Treas.
Directors: Sibylle Evelt, Robert O. Fehr, James H. Heineman, Marian Rose, Hans Tauber, M.D.
Employer Identification Number: 136082899

1974
Hellman Family Foundation

c/o Barry M. Strauss Assoc.
875 Ave. of the Americas, Suite 1001
New York 10001-3580

Established in 1983 in CA.
Financial data (yr. ended 11/30/87): Assets, $219 (L); gifts received, $434,500; expenditures, $433,412, including $431,750 for 29 grants (high: $80,000; low: $1,750).
Purpose and activities: Support for higher education and cultural programs, social services and Jewish organizations.
Application information:
Deadline(s): None
Write: F. Warren Hellman
Officers and Directors*: Patricia C. Hellman,* Pres.; Marco Hellman, V.P.; Maureen Cantor, Secy.-Treas.; Patricia Hellman Gibbs, Richard Dwight Gibbs, F. Warren Hellman, Frances Hellman, Judith Hellman, Sabrina Hellman.
Employer Identification Number: 942880118

1975
The Victor Herbert Foundation

c/o Burns, Summit, Rovins & Feldesman
445 Park Ave.
New York 10022

Established in 1969 in NY.
Financial data (yr. ended 4/30/87): Assets, $1,485,675 (M); expenditures, $107,494, including $83,750 for 67 grants (high: $12,500; low: $25).
Purpose and activities: Emphasis on music organizations, and higher education in music and the arts.

Limitations: Giving primarily in New York City, NY. No grants to individuals.
Application information:
Deadline(s): None
Write: Herbert P. Jacoby, Pres.
Officers and Directors: Herbert P. Jacoby, Pres.; Arthur H. Schwartz, V.P.; Carolyn B. Jacoby, Secy.; Lois C. Schwartz.
Employer Identification Number: 237044623

1976
Harry Herskowitz Foundation, Inc.
c/o Ruth Skydell
975 Park Ave.
New York 10028

Established in 1958 in NY.
Financial data (yr. ended 11/30/87): Assets, $902,833 (M); expenditures, $119,871, including $111,110 for grants.
Purpose and activities: Support for education, Jewish welfare, hospitals, Israel, libraries, museums, and social services.
Types of support: Continuing support.
Officers: Ruth H. Skydell, Pres. and Treas.; Adrian Skydell, V.P.; Laurie S. Goldberg, Secy.
Employer Identification Number: 136115242

1977
Hess Foundation, Inc.
1185 Ave. of the Americas
New York 10036 (212) 997-8500

Incorporated in 1954 in DE.
Donor(s): Leon Hess.
Financial data (yr. ended 11/30/86): Assets, $51,445,218 (M); gifts received, $651,420; expenditures, $3,541,144, including $3,481,762 for 57 grants (high: $640,750; low: $500; average: $1,000-$100,000).
Purpose and activities: Emphasis on higher education, a disaster relief fund, and hospitals; grants also for a football foundation, performing arts organizations, synagogues, and social welfare agencies.
Limitations: No grants to individuals.
Application information:
Initial approach: Letter of request
Deadline(s): None
Board meeting date(s): As required
Final notification: Varies
Write: Leon Hess, Pres.
Officers and Directors: Leon Hess, Pres.; Steve Gutman, V.P. and Secy.; Norma Hess, V.P. and Treas.; John B. Hess, V.P.
Number of staff: 1 full-time professional.
Employer Identification Number: 221713046

1978
Hilliard Foundation, Inc.
100 West Fourth St.
Elmira 14901-2190 (607) 733-7121

Donor(s): The Hilliard Corp.
Financial data (yr. ended 4/30/88): Assets, $219,332 (M); gifts received, $50,000; expenditures, $26,034, including $24,963 for 17 grants (high: $8,163; low: $100).
Purpose and activities: Support for arts, culture, and youth.
Limitations: Giving primarily in Elmira, NY.
Application information:
Initial approach: Letter
Deadline(s): None
Write: Mary A. Van Horn, Treas.
Officers: Nelson M. van den Blink, Pres.; Mary Welles Smith, V.P.; John R. Alexander, Secy.; Mary A. Van Horn, Treas.
Trustees: Clement N. Cranoff, John H. Fassett, George L. Howell, Ralph H. Roberts, Jr., Gerald F. Schichtel, Paul H. Schweizer, Finley M. Steele.
Employer Identification Number: 161176159

1979
The Alex Hillman Family Foundation
630 Fifth Ave.
New York 10111 (212) 265-3115

Incorporated in 1966 in NY.
Donor(s): Alex L. Hillman,† Rita K. Hillman.
Financial data (yr. ended 12/31/87): Assets, $17,002,008 (M); expenditures, $118,237, including $74,700 for 20 grants (high: $23,500; low: $100).
Purpose and activities: Educational purposes, including encouragement of the arts; primarily local grants for higher education, art museums, and music.
Types of support: Operating budgets.
Limitations: Giving primarily in NY. No grants to individuals, or for continuing support.
Publications: Annual report.
Application information:
Initial approach: Letter
Copies of proposal: 1
Deadline(s): None
Board meeting date(s): Semiannually
Final notification: 2 months
Write: Mrs. Rita K. Hillman, Pres.
Officers and Directors: Rita K. Hillman, Pres.; William M. Griffin, V.P.; Harold Schiff, Secy.
Number of staff: None.
Employer Identification Number: 132560546

1980
Hilson Fund, Inc.
c/o Rochlin, Lipsky, Goodkin, Stoler & Co.
510 Fifth Ave.
New York 10036
Application address: c/o Wertheim & Co., Inc., 200 Park Ave., New York, NY 10166; Tel.: (212) 578-0200

Established in 1947 in NY.
Donor(s): John S. Hilson, Mildred S. Hilson.
Financial data (yr. ended 11/30/87): Assets, $1,530,632 (M); expenditures, $136,780, including $127,773 for 56 grants (high: $33,333; low: $50).
Purpose and activities: Emphasis on the arts and hospitals, including medical research.
Limitations: Giving primarily in New York City, NY.
Application information:
Initial approach: Letter
Deadline(s): None
Write: John S. Hilson, V.P.
Officers and Trustees: Mildred S. Hilson, Pres.; John S. Hilson, V.P.; Peter J. Repetti, Secy.; Howard D. Taylor, Treas.
Employer Identification Number: 136028783

1981
A. W. Hoernle Foundation
630 Central Park Ave.
Yonkers 10704

Established in 1978 in NY.
Donor(s): Adolph W. Hoernle.
Financial data (yr. ended 5/31/87): Assets, $5,578,092 (M); expenditures, $332,757, including $267,685 for 24 grants (high: $150,150; low: $200).
Purpose and activities: Support primarily for hospitals and health agencies, cultural programs, education, and social service agencies.
Limitations: Giving limited to NY and FL. No grants to individuals.
Application information:
Board meeting date(s): Annually
Write: Fred W. Lessing, Secy.-Treas.
Officers: Adolph W. Hoernle, Pres.; Fred W. Lessing, Secy.-Treas.
Number of staff: None.
Employer Identification Number: 132945331

1982
Marion O. & Maximilian Hoffman Foundation
277 Northern Blvd., Suite 200
Great Neck 11021-4796

Financial data (yr. ended 06/30/87): Assets, $105,665 (M); expenditures, $386,476, including $375,000 for 7 grants (high: $250,000; low: $10,000).
Purpose and activities: Giving primarily to an animal medical center; support also for the arts, public television and social services.
Limitations: Giving primarily in New York City, NY.
Application information: Contributes only to pre-selected organizations. Applications not accepted.
Write: Ursula Niarakis, Pres.
Officer: Ursula C. Niarakis, Pres.
Employer Identification Number: 112697957

1983
The Home Group Foundation
59 Maiden Ln.
New York 10038
Scholarship application address: Bob Wood Endowment Fund, 55 Madison St., Suite 800, Denver, CO 80206

Incorporated in 1963 in MO.
Donor(s): World Color Press, Inc., City Investing Co., and related companies.
Financial data (yr. ended 12/31/87): Assets, $3,956,575 (M); gifts received, $318,325; expenditures, $580,089, including $539,450 for 44 grants (high: $50,000; low: $500).
Purpose and activities: Support primarily for higher education, including employee-related scholarships, hospitals, medical research; youth and civic agencies, cultural programs, and health associations.
Types of support: Employee-related scholarships.
Application information: Application form required for employee-related scholarships. Application form required.

Initial approach: Letter
Deadline(s): May
Officers: George T. Scharffenberger,* Chair.; Marshall Manley,* Pres.; Robert L. Woodrum, V.P.; Bruce W. Bean, Secy.
Directors:* Eben W. Pyne.
Employer Identification Number: 133246657

1984
Hooper Foundation
5590 Camp Rd.
Hamburg 14075-3702 (716) 649-5590

Donor(s): Hooper Handling, Inc.
Financial data (yr. ended 9/30/88): Assets, $293,314 (M); gifts received, $5,000; expenditures, $14,701, including $12,900 for 9 grants (high: $6,500; low: $50).
Purpose and activities: Support for music, youth, and health services.
Types of support: Operating budgets, capital campaigns.
Limitations: Giving primarily in Buffalo, NY. No grants to individuals.
Application information: Contributes only to preselected organizations. Applications not accepted.
Trustees: Harold M. Finger, Lois A. Hooper, W. Stanley Hooper.
Employer Identification Number: 237045144

1985
Josephine Lawrence Hopkins Foundation
61 Broadway, Suite 2912
New York 10006

Incorporated in 1968 in NY.
Donor(s): Josephine H. Graeber.†
Financial data (yr. ended 12/31/86): Assets, $3,577,011 (M); expenditures, $294,395, including $225,000 for 29 grants (high: $45,000; low: $500).
Purpose and activities: Emphasis on hospitals and medical research, Roman Catholic church support, animal welfare, youth agencies, and cultural programs including the performing arts.
Limitations: Giving primarily in NY. No grants to individuals; no loans.
Application information: Contributes only to pre-selected organizations. Applications not accepted.
Board meeting date(s): Once a year, usually in Oct.
Officers and Directors: Ivan Obolensky, Pres. and Treas.; Lawrence X. Cusack, V.P. and Secy.; Vera Colage, V.P.; Meredith N. Stiles, Jr., V.P.; Susan H. Whitmore, V.P.
Employer Identification Number: 136277593

1986
Horncrest Foundation, Inc.
Six Sleator Dr.
Ossining 10502 (914) 941-5533

Established in 1960 in NY.
Financial data (yr. ended 9/30/87): Assets, $2,178,862 (M); gifts received, $8,417; expenditures, $190,732, including $179,000 for 10 grants (high: $25,000; low: $1,000).
Purpose and activities: Grants for education, with emphasis on a university loan program; support for social services, cultural programs, medical education, and organizations that develop interest in governmental issues.
Types of support: General purposes, matching funds, scholarship funds.
Publications: Annual report.
Application information:
Deadline(s): None
Write: Lawrence Blau, Pres.
Officer and Director: Lawrence Blau, Pres.
Employer Identification Number: 136021261

1987
Gedale B. and Barbara S. Horowitz Foundation
c/o Solomon Brothers, Inc.
One New York Plaza
New York 10004

Established in 1970 in NY.
Donor(s): Gedale B. Horowitz, Gedale B. Horowitz Charitable Lead Trust.
Financial data (yr. ended 6/30/87): Assets, $3,091,768 (M); gifts received, $1,367,167; expenditures, $433,312, including $426,820 for 55 grants (high: $180,000; low: $50).
Purpose and activities: Grants primarly for Jewish giving, including welfare and temple support; support also for education and culture.
Types of support: General purposes.
Limitations: Giving primarily in New York City, NY, and Nassau County.
Application information: Contributes only to pre-selected organizations. Applications not accepted.
Officers and Directors: Gedale B. Horowitz, Pres.; David Horowitz, V.P.; William Donovan, Secy.; Barbara Horowitz, Treas.
Employer Identification Number: 237101730

1988
Stewart W. & Willma C. Hoyt Foundation
300 Security Mutual Bldg.
80 Exchange St.
Binghamton 13901 (607) 722-6706

Established in 1970 in NY.
Donor(s): Willma C. Hoyt.†
Financial data (yr. ended 12/31/87): Assets, $10,578,872 (M); expenditures, $685,194, including $525,044 for 32 grants (high: $75,000; low: $1,000; average: $1,500-$30,000).
Purpose and activities: Giving for the arts and humanities, education, health, and social and human services, with preference for capital campaigns, special projects, seed money, and operating expenses.
Types of support: General purposes, building funds, matching funds, seed money, special projects, operating budgets, continuing support, emergency funds, equipment, technical assistance, consulting services, scholarship funds, conferences and seminars, capital campaigns.
Limitations: Giving limited to Broome County, NY. No support for religious purposes. No grants to individuals, or for annual campaigns, deficit financing, land acquisition, general endowments, research, or publications; no loans.
Publications: Informational brochure (including application guidelines).
Application information: No grants considered at Jan. meeting.
Initial approach: Telephone or letter
Copies of proposal: 1
Deadline(s): The 1st of months prior to board meetings
Board meeting date(s): Bimonthly, beginning in Jan.; no grants awarded in Jan.
Final notification: 1 to 3 days following board meetings
Write: Judith C. Peckham, Exec. Dir.
Officers and Directors: John F. Russell, Chair.; Shirley W. Keller, Vice-Chair.; William Rincker, Secy.-Treas.; William S. Chittenden, John M. Keeler, Stuart McCarty, Jane M. Park.
Trustee: Chase Lincoln First Bank, N.A.
Number of staff: 1 full-time professional; 1 part-time support.
Employer Identification Number: 237072539
Recent arts and culture grants:
BC Pops, Binghamton, NY, $12,000. For general operating support for 1986-87. 1987.
Binghamton Symphony Orchestra, Binghamton, NY, $8,000. For expanding computer capabilities. 1987.
Binghamton Symphony Orchestra, Binghamton, NY, $5,000. For matching support for Morris & Deborah Gitlitz concerts for young people. 1987.
Broome County Arts Council, Binghamton, NY, $55,000. Toward operating expenses of organizations served by United Cultural Fund. 1987.
Community Music Center of Broome County, Binghamton, NY, $5,000. Toward general operating support for 1986-87. 1987.
Discovery Center of the Southern Tier, Binghamton, NY, $75,000. Toward relocation and renovation. 1987.
Imagination Celebration, Binghamton, NY, $8,075. For series of workshops for children to increase their drawing skills, their enthusiasm for art; to provide videotaped lessons for permanent library. 1987.
Roberson Center for the Arts and Sciences, Binghamton, NY, $20,000. Toward construction of Broome County History Gallery. 1987.
Southern Tier Institute for Arts in Education, Binghamton, NY, $10,000. For operating summer session, and for transitional funding. 1987.

1989
Graham Hunter Foundation, Inc.
c/o Rusconi, Cahill & Larkin
521 Fifth Ave.
New York 10175
Application address: One East 42nd St., New York, NY 10017

Established in 1946 in NY.
Donor(s): Graham Hunter.†
Financial data (yr. ended 12/31/87): Assets, $1,342,946 (M); expenditures, $66,074, including $43,782 for 11 grants (high: $31,382; low: $200).

Purpose and activities: Grants primarily for higher education, including medical education; support also for cultural programs.
Application information:
Deadline(s): None
Write: Thomas G. Burke, V.P.
Officer and Trustees: Carol Hunter Kelley, Pres.; William McClarence, V.P. and Secy.; Thomas G. Burke, V.P. and Treas.
Employer Identification Number: 136161726

1990
IBM Corporate Contributions Program
2000 Purchase St.
Purchase 10577 (914) 765-5284

Purpose and activities: For IBM, corporate contributions are a way of strengthening its partnership with the communities in which IBM employees and customers live and work. Most of IBM's contributions support education, both nationally and internationally. The emphasis in this area is on assisting students to pursue professional and technical studies. IBM supports education in an effort to "foster new ideas; to ensure that tomorrow's managers, professionals and leaders are up-to-date on the latest technology; to support technical and business education in communities in which IBM facilities are located; to assist women, minority and handicapped students; and to strengthen academic research and curricula in high technology areas." IBM also lends executives to school systems to set up programs. Company also supports efforts in the areas of health, welfare, civic affairs, culture, and the arts.
Types of support: Fellowships, scholarship funds, capital campaigns, operating budgets, special projects, matching funds, equipment.
Limitations: Giving primarily in headquarters city and company operating locations; company also gives nationally and internationally. No support for political or religious organizations. No grants to individuals.
Publications: Application guidelines, corporate giving report.
Application information: Include description of organization, proposed project, objectives and goals, current annual report, latest audited financial statements, form 990, 501(c)(3) status letter, list of directors, and support levels of other companies.
Initial approach: Query letter and complete proposal. Local community organizations should contact the branch office within their area; all others submit proposal to headquarters
Deadline(s): None
Board meeting date(s): Decisions made as needed by senior officials and directors
Final notification: Decision time varies, averaging 2 to 3 months
Write: A.N. Scallon, Dir., Corp. Support Programs

1991
Carl C. Icahn Foundation
100 South Bedford Rd.
Mount Kisco 10549 (914) 242-4010

Established in 1980 in NY and DE.
Donor(s): Carl C. Icahn.
Financial data (yr. ended 11/30/86): Assets, $11,415,755 (M); gifts received, $596,351; expenditures, $1,815,265, including $796,800 for 50 grants (high: $500,000; low: $100; average: $750-$20,000).
Purpose and activities: Giving for cultural programs, hospitals, and for child welfare, including a child abuse prevention clinic.
Limitations: Giving primarily in New York, NY. No grants to individuals.
Application information:
Initial approach: Letter
Deadline(s): None
Board meeting date(s): As necessary
Write: Gail Golden
Officers: Carl C. Icahn, Pres.; Leba Icahn, Secy.-Treas.
Number of staff: 1
Employer Identification Number: 133091588

1992
The IFF Foundation, Inc.
521 West 57th St.
New York 10019 (212) 765-5500

Incorporated in 1963 in NY.
Donor(s): International Flavors & Fragrances, Inc.
Financial data (yr. ended 12/31/87): Assets, $646,994 (M); gifts received, $600,000; expenditures, $224,836, including $224,080 for 72 grants (high: $80,000; low: $100).
Purpose and activities: Grants primarily for higher education, including medical education and matching gifts; support also for research in chemistry and international affairs, for hospitals and mental health services, civic affairs agencies, and cultural activities.
Types of support: Research, employee matching gifts.
Application information:
Write: John P. Winandy, Treas.
Officers: Eugene P. Grisanti, Pres.; W. Dempsey, Secy.; John P. Winandy, Treas.
Employer Identification Number: 136159094

1993
Institute for Aegean Prehistory
c/o The Millburn Corp.
1211 Ave. of the Americas
New York 10036

Established in 1983 in NY.
Donor(s): Malcolm H. Wiener.
Financial data (yr. ended 6/30/88): Assets, $4,449,580 (M); gifts received, $1,040,500; expenditures, $466,170, including $232,085 for 13 grants (high: $75,500; low: $2,000) and $215,152 for 35 grants to individuals.
Purpose and activities: A private operating foundation; opportunities to participate in the organization's activities are given only for the purpose of allowing and encouraging persons to study Aegean prehistory with expectation of research publication under the direct supervision of the institute.
Types of support: Grants to individuals.
Application information:
Initial approach: Letter
Deadline(s): None
Write: Malcolm H. Wiener, Pres.
Officers and Trustees: Malcolm H. Wiener, Pres. and Treas.; Harvey Beker, V.P.; George E. Crapple, V.P.; Thomas R. Moore, Secy.; Martin J. Whitman.
Employer Identification Number: 133137391

1994
International Paper Company Charitable Giving Program
Two Manhattanville Rd.
Purchase 10577 (914) 397-1500

Purpose and activities: Support for health and welfare, community development, engineering and economics programs, culture, and education. The corporate giving program is decentralized and more industry-related than the International Paper Company Foundation. The two programs contribute nearly the same dollar amounts.
Types of support: Building funds, capital campaigns, employee matching gifts, matching funds, publications, research, special projects, annual campaigns, continuing support, fellowships, operating budgets, program-related investments, seed money.
Limitations: Giving primarily in communities where company facilities are located; national organizations are considered for funding; no support for foreign organizations or those whose funds go outside the U.S. No support for religious, veterans', labor, political, or fraternal organizations, or for sports groups. No grants to individuals, or for operating expenses, endowments, courtesy advertising, or charitable functions; grants for capital campaigns are limited to youth or health care organizations in communities with company facilities.
Application information: Include concise description of program and objectives, IRS 501(c)(3) status letter, funding sources and specific amounts, current annual report, program budget, and amount requested.
Initial approach: Letter, telephone, or proposal; organizations in company communities write to the local company mill
Deadline(s): Submit by Oct. for next calendar year
Final notification: Normally final decision forthcoming within 6-8 weeks
Write: Patricia Freda-Chan, V.P.

1995
International Paper Company Foundation
Two Manhattanville Rd.
Purchase 10577 (914) 397-1581

Incorporated in 1952 in NY.
Donor(s): International Paper Co.
Financial data (yr. ended 12/31/87): Assets, $21,265,985 (M); gifts received, $4,000,000; expenditures, $1,535,000, including

$1,119,186 for 170 grants (high: $116,500; low: $1,000; average: $2,500-$5,000) and $225,594 for 349 employee matching gifts.
Purpose and activities: Grants primarily for model projects in company communities and selected programs with potental national impact, with focus on pre-college levels of economic and career education, programs for minorities and women in engineering, health and welfare, and community and cultural affairs. Operates own program EDCORE (Education and Community Resource Program) in selected International Paper communities for public schools.
Types of support: Seed money, special projects, annual campaigns, research, publications, matching funds, employee matching gifts, continuing support, fellowships, operating budgets, capital campaigns, program-related investments.
Limitations: Giving primarily in communities where there are company plants and mills in AL, AR, LA, ME, MS, NY, OR, SC, TN, and TX. No support for athletic organizations or religious groups. No grants to individuals, or for endowment funds, capital expenses (except in company communities), or general operating expenses of health and welfare agencies or higher educational institutions; no loans.
Publications: Occasional report, informational brochure (including application guidelines).
Application information: Address requests from organizations in company communities to the local company mill or plant manager; no applications accepted for EDCORE (Education and Community Resource Program) or for fellowships.
Initial approach: Letter, telephone, or proposal
Copies of proposal: 1
Deadline(s): Previous summer for next calendar year
Board meeting date(s): Jan.
Final notification: 6 to 8 weeks
Write: Patricia Freda-Chan, V.P.
Officers: Arthur Wallace, Pres.; Patricia Freda-Chan, V.P.; Tracy Doolittle, Secy.; Myra Drucker, Treas.
Directors: John A. Georges, W. Craig McClelland, James P. Melican, Jr., David W. Oskin.
Trustee: State Street Bank and Trust Co.
Number of staff: 1 full-time professional; 1 full-time support; 1 part-time support.
Employer Identification Number: 136155080

1996
O'Donnell Iselin Foundation, Inc.
40 Wall St.
New York 10005 (212) 425-0105
IRS filing state: DE

Donor(s): Peter Iselin, Emilie I. Wiggin.
Financial data (yr. ended 12/31/86): Assets, $1,438,005 (M); gifts received, $100,000; expenditures, $105,497, including $90,250 for 34 grants (high: $20,000; low: $250).
Purpose and activities: Support for secondary education, cultural programs, and health associations.
Limitations: Giving primarily in NY.
Application information:
Deadline(s): None
Write: Peter Iselin, Pres.
Officers: Peter Iselin, Pres. and Treas.; Emilie I. Wiggin, V.P.; John F. Walsh, Secy.
Employer Identification Number: 516016471

1997
Ittleson Foundation, Inc.
645 Madison Ave., 16th Fl.
New York 10022 (212) 838-5010

Trust established in 1932 in NY.
Donor(s): Henry Ittleson,† Blanche F. Ittleson,† Henry Ittleson, Jr.,† Lee F. Ittleson,† Nancy S. Ittleson.
Financial data (yr. ended 12/31/87): Assets, $14,879,558 (M); expenditures, $1,593,803, including $1,141,149 for 50 grants.
Purpose and activities: For the promotion of the well-being of mankind throughout the world, including research, publication, and the establishment, maintenance, and aid of charitable activities and institutions; interests include health, welfare, and education for health and welfare, with special emphasis on mental health, psychiatric research, and behavioral science research.
Types of support: Operating budgets, seed money, matching funds, professorships, special projects, research, publications, technical assistance.
Limitations: No support for the humanities or cultural projects, general education, or to social service agencies offering direct service to people in local communities. No grants to individuals, or for continuing support, scholarships, fellowships, annual campaigns, travel, emergency, capital, or endowment funds, or deficit financing; no loans.
Publications: Informational brochure, program policy statement, application guidelines.
Application information:
Initial approach: Letter
Copies of proposal: 1
Deadline(s): None
Board meeting date(s): May and Dec.
Final notification: 3 weeks to 3 months
Write: David M. Nee, Exec. Dir.
Officers: H. Anthony Ittleson,* Chair. and Pres.; Mrs. Henry Ittleson, Jr.,* V.P.; Pamela Lee Syrmis,* V.P.; Bernard W. Schwartz, Treas.; David M. Nee, Exec. Dir.
Directors:* Mrs. H. Anthony Ittleson, Lionel I. Pincus, Victor Syrmis, M.D.
Number of staff: 1 part-time professional; 1 part-time support.
Employer Identification Number: 510172757
Recent arts and culture grants:
K C T S/9 Public Television, Seattle, WA, $26,000. To produce national public television documentary about domestic elder abuse and neglect entitled, The Golden Years. 12/15/87.
W G B H Educational Foundation, Boston, MA, $25,000. To distribute one hour television documentary to help educate public about prevention of violence. 6/13/88.
W N E T Channel 13, NYC, NY, $40,000. To assist in production of public broadcast documentary dealing with health care concerns of elderly, entitled When I'm 65. 12/15/87.

1998
The J.M. Foundation
60 East 42nd St., Rm. 1651
New York 10165 (212) 687-7735

Incorporated in 1924 in NY.
Donor(s): Jeremiah Milbank,† Katharine S. Milbank.†
Financial data (yr. ended 12/31/88): Assets, $23,946,130 (M); expenditures, $4,045,829, including $2,814,155 for 115 grants (high: $1,000,000; low: $1,000; average: $15,000-$35,000), $74,155 for 50 employee matching gifts and $150,000 for 2 foundation-administered programs.
Purpose and activities: Giving primarily for rehabilitation of the physically handicapped; prevention and wellness, with an emphasis on individual responsibility for health; education, prevention, and early intervention in alcohol and other drug abuse; expansion of effective extramural care; health-related public policy research; and selected projects in biomedical research and medical education. The foundation also has a strong interest in educational activities which strengthen America's pluralistic system of free markets, individualism, entrepreneurship, voluntarism, and private enterprise. It also supports organizations that enhance the quality of family life, and provide today's youth with meaningful life experiences, productive employment opportunities, healthy lifestyles, and positive character development. Support also for two in-house operating projects: the Medical Student Scholarship Program in Alcohol and Other Drug Dependencies and National Awards for Excellence in Vocational Programs. The foundation also sponsors a matching gift program for its board members and full-time staff.
Types of support: Research, special projects, publications, internships, scholarship funds, matching funds, conferences and seminars, technical assistance, seed money, employee matching gifts, general purposes.
Limitations: No support for the arts. No grants to individuals, or for operating expenses, international activities, annual fundraising campaigns, capital campaigns, or endowment funds; no loans.
Publications: Annual report (including application guidelines), program policy statement, application guidelines, occasional report.
Application information:
Initial approach: Summary letter accompanied by proposal
Copies of proposal: 1
Deadline(s): Submit proposal preferably in Feb., July, or Oct.; deadline 45 days prior to meetings
Board meeting date(s): Jan., May, Sept., and Dec.
Final notification: Preliminary response within 20 working days
Write: Jack Brauntuch, Exec. Dir.
Officers: Jeremiah Milbank, Jr.,* Pres.; Mrs. H. Lawrence Bogert,* V.P.; Daniel G. Tenney, Jr.,* Secy.; William Lee Hanley, Jr.,* Treas.; Jack Brauntuch, Exec. Dir.
Directors:* Mary E. Caslin, Peter C. Morse.
Number of staff: 3 full-time professional; 3 full-time support; 1 part-time support.

Employer Identification Number: 136068340
Recent arts and culture grants:
Cold Spring Harbor Laboratory, Cold Spring Harbor, NY, $25,000. To establish DNA Learning Center and open Smithsonian's Search for Life Exhibit. 4/27/88.
Free Congress Research and Education Foundation, DC, $15,000. To support Institute for Cultural Conservatism. 9/15/87.
Video Information Network, NYC, NY, $17,500. To produce news stories on public policy issues for television news programs and cable systems. 4/27/88.

1999
JCT Foundation
145 Central Park West, Apt. 25 C
New York 10023

Established in 1984 in NY.
Donor(s): Jeff C. Tarr.
Financial data (yr. ended 12/31/86): Assets, $7,826,090 (M); gifts received, $3,756,967; expenditures, $105,010, including $103,550 for 49 grants (high: $2,000; low: $250).
Purpose and activities: Support primarily for cultural programs, the performing arts, and museums; some support for higher education and a fund for Israel.
Limitations: Giving primarily in the New York, NY, area.
Application information: Contributes only to pre-selected organizations. Applications not accepted.
Directors: Jeff C. Tarr, Patricia C. Tarr.
Employer Identification Number: 133237111

2000
The JDR 3rd Fund, Inc.
30 Rockefeller Plaza, Rm. 5600
New York 10112 (212) 247-3700

Incorporated in 1963 in NY.
Donor(s): John D. Rockefeller, 3rd.†
Financial data (yr. ended 8/31/87): Assets, $3,447,734 (M); gifts received, $2,685,752; expenditures, $3,780,738, including $2,422,907 for 17 grants (high: $1,000,000; low: $500).
Purpose and activities: Support primarily for Asian cultural institutions; support for the arts and performing arts.
Types of support: Exchange programs, endowment funds, operating budgets.
Limitations: No grants to individuals.
Application information: Contributes only to pre-selected organizations. Applications not accepted.
Officers: Mrs. John D. Rockefeller, 3rd, Pres. and Chair; Elizabeth J. McCormack, V.P.; Paulette Walther, Secy.; David G. Fernald, Treas.
Trustees: Hope Aldrich, Alida Rockefeller Dayton, Donal C. O'Brien, Jr.
Number of staff: 3 full-time professional.
Employer Identification Number: 131988876

2001
Richard Hampton Jenrette Foundation, Inc.
c/o Wood, Struthers & Winthrop
P.O. Box 18
New York 10005

Established in 1967 in NY.
Donor(s): Richard H. Jenrette.
Financial data (yr. ended 11/30/87): Assets, $968,813 (M); expenditures, $272,748, including $249,897 for 35 grants (high: $100,000; low: $100) and $3,293 for 1 grant to an individual.
Purpose and activities: Emphasis on giving for the arts, historical preservation, and higher education; contributes also to an educational foundation.
Types of support: General purposes.
Limitations: Giving primarily in SC.
Application information: Contributes only to pre-selected oganizations. Applications not accepted.
Officers and Directors: Richard H. Jenrette, Pres.; Joseph M. Jenrette III, V.P.; Thomas E. Siegler, Secy.-Treas.; Warren Haight, William L. Thompson.
Employer Identification Number: 136271770

2002
Jesselson Foundation
1221 Ave. of the Americas
New York 10020

Incorporated in 1955 in NY.
Donor(s): Ludwig Jesselson.
Financial data (yr. ended 4/30/87): Assets, $22,379,841 (M); gifts received, $34,991; expenditures, $2,167,984, including $2,104,541 for 341 grants (high: $587,850; low: $20; average: $100-$10,000) and $400 for 6 grants to individuals.
Purpose and activities: Grants largely for higher and Jewish education, welfare funds, health agencies, and synagogues; some support for cultural programs.
Application information: Contributes only to pre-selected organizations. Applications not accepted.
Officers: Ludwig Jesselson, Pres. and Treas.; Erica Jesselson, V.P. and Secy.; Michael Jesselson, 2nd V.P.
Employer Identification Number: 136075098

2003
Johnson & Higgins Corporate Responsibility
125 Broad St.
New York 10004 (212) 574-7000

Purpose and activities: Company considers dance, libraries, museums, fine arts, music, theater, economic development, civic affairs, international groups, minority programs, private colleges, scholarships, secondary and insurance education, science, health and hospitals, urban development, and youth service.
Types of support: Scholarship funds.
Limitations: Giving primarily in headquarters city and major operating locations; company will consider national programs for funding.
Application information:
Write: F.H. Kingsbury III, V.P. and Corp. Responsibility Officer

2004
Axel Johnson Corporate Giving Program
110 East 59th St.
New York 10022 (212) 758-3200

Purpose and activities: Support for fine and performing arts, education, and wildlife.
Types of support: Employee matching gifts.
Application information: All gifts are given on merit basis, as judged by corporate giving program administrators.
Write: Vernon Anderson, Pres. and C.E.O.

2005
Christian A. Johnson Endeavor Foundation
1060 Park Ave.
New York 10128 (212) 534-6620

Incorporated in 1952 in NY.
Donor(s): Christian A. Johnson.†
Financial data (yr. ended 9/30/88): Assets, $58,879,136 (M); expenditures, $3,740,658, including $2,591,925 for 43 grants (high: $750,000; low: $500; average: $5,000-$25,000) and $488,146 for 1 foundation-administered program.
Purpose and activities: Concentrates on the improvement of the cultural and intellectual environments of American society; emphasis on education, particularly liberal arts at the baccalaureate level; primary concern in the arts for developing new talent and bringing the arts to young people.
Types of support: Operating budgets, seed money, building funds, equipment, matching funds, professorships, scholarship funds, renovation projects.
Limitations: Giving limited to the eastern U.S. No support for government agencies, or for community or neighborhood projects, religious institutions, or for health care. No grants to individuals, or for continuing support, annual campaigns, emergency funds, deficit financing, land acquisitions, medical research, demonstration projects, publications, or conferences; no loans.
Publications: Annual report (including application guidelines), financial statement, program policy statement, application guidelines.
Application information: Proposals by invitation only. Applications not accepted.
Initial approach: Letter of inquiry
Deadline(s): Submit proposal upon foundation's request
Board meeting date(s): Fall, winter, spring, and early summer
Final notification: 8 months
Write: Mrs. Wilmot H. Kidd, Pres.
Officers and Trustees: Mrs. Christian A. Johnson, Chair. and Treas.; Julie Kidd, Pres.;

Marie Jordan, Secy.; Charles H. Harff, Donald Kersting.
Number of staff: 1 full-time professional; 2 part-time professional; 3 full-time support.
Employer Identification Number: 136147952

2006
Willard T. C. Johnson Foundation, Inc.
c/o Shea & Gould
1251 Ave. of the Americas
New York 10020

Incorporated in 1979 in NY.
Donor(s): Willard T.C. Johnson.†
Financial data (yr. ended 12/31/87): Assets, $23,957,283 (M); expenditures, $1,379,285, including $1,116,000 for 5 grants (high: $125,000; low: $70,000).
Purpose and activities: Emphasis on culture and social services.
Application information:
Deadline(s): None
Write: Seymour M. Klein, Pres.
Officers and Directors: Betty W. Johnson, Chair.; Seymour M. Klein, Pres.; Robert J. Mortimer, V.P. and Secy.-Treas.
Employer Identification Number: 132993310

2007
Daisy Marquis Jones Foundation
620 Granite Bldg.
130 East Main St.
Rochester 14604 (716) 263-3331

Established in 1968 in NY.
Donor(s): Daisy Marquis Jones.†
Financial data (yr. ended 12/31/87): Assets, $17,287,656 (M); gifts received, $26,340; expenditures, $1,524,397, including $1,331,214 for 105 grants (high: $62,500; low: $200; average: $500-$25,000) and $105,530 for loans.
Purpose and activities: Grants primarily to improve the quality of health care for local residents; support also for services for senior citizens, women and youth, with special emphasis on the disadvantaged; support also toward improving the administration of justice. Special attention to preventive programs.
Types of support: Operating budgets, seed money, emergency funds, building funds, equipment, land acquisition, matching funds, technical assistance, special projects, publications, renovation projects.
Limitations: Giving limited to Monroe and Yates counties, NY. No support for the arts or for religious purposes. No grants to individuals, or for endowment funds, research, continuing support, scholarships, fellowships, annual campaigns, or deficit financing; no loans.
Publications: Annual report, application guidelines.
Application information: Application form required.
Initial approach: Letter
Copies of proposal: 1
Deadline(s): None
Board meeting date(s): Monthly (except summer)
Final notification: 2 to 3 months
Write: Pearl W. Rubin, Pres.
Trustees: Leo M. Lyons, Chair.; Pearl W. Rubin, Pres.; Helen G. Whitney, Vice-Chair.; Sydney R. Rubin, Gen. Counsel; Marine Midland Bank, N.A.
Number of staff: 2 full-time professional; 2 part-time professional; 1 part-time support.
Employer Identification Number: 237000227
Recent arts and culture grants:
Arts for Greater Rochester, Arts Reach, Rochester, NY, $7,000. To continue support for a program which provides enrichment opportunities for people traditionally deprived of access to resources, kprimarily the elderly and the chronically ill. 1987.
Garth Fagans Bucket Dance Theater, Rochester, NY, $5,000. To sponsor fully subsidized dance performances and workshops for minority, handicapped and disadvantaged students who ordinarily would not have these opportunities and who can be positively influenced by role models that group represents. 1987.
International Museum of Photography at George Eastman House, Rochester, NY, $15,000. To provide additional support for construction of new archives building to keep museum in Rochester. 1987.
Rochester Area Educational Television Association, Rochester, NY, $29,700. To provide local underwriting for programs within Foundation's area of interest. 1987.
Rochester Museum and Science Center, Rochester, NY, $30,000. To help purchase and install two elevators which will provide handicapped direct access to expanded museum. 1987.
University of Rochester, Memorial Art Gallery, Rochester, NY, $25,000. To help make new and expanded facilities handicapped accessible. 1987.

2008
Julia R. and Estelle L. Foundation, Inc.
817 Washington St.
Buffalo 14203 (716) 857-3325

Incorporated in 1941 in NY.
Donor(s): Peter C. Cornell Trust, R. John Oishei.†
Financial data (yr. ended 12/31/87): Assets, $17,285,369 (M); gifts received, $897,755; expenditures, $1,564,779, including $1,525,248 for 103 grants (high: $83,000; low: $150; average: $5,000-$10,000).
Purpose and activities: Emphasis on hospitals and medical research, higher and secondary education, and social services, including programs for the aged and youth; some support for health agencies and cultural programs.
Types of support: General purposes, research, building funds.
Limitations: Giving primarily in Buffalo, NY.
Application information:
Deadline(s): None
Write: Richard L. Wolf
Officers and Directors: R. John Oishei, Pres.; Rupert Warren, V.P. and Secy.-Treas.; Carl E. Larson, V.P.
Members: Patricia O. Colby, Julian R. Oishei.
Number of staff: None.
Employer Identification Number: 160874319

2009
Alfred Jurzykowski Foundation, Inc.
21 East 40th St.
New York 10016 (212) 689-2460
Address for award nominations by scholarly and cultural institutions: Cultural Advisory Comm., 15 East 65th St., New York, NY 10021

Incorporated in 1960 in NY.
Donor(s): Alfred Jurzykowski.†
Financial data (yr. ended 12/31/87): Assets, $16,447,058 (M); expenditures, $898,473, including $698,346 for 68 grants (high: $100,000; low: $1,200; average: $5,000-$15,000) and $56,000 for 16 grants to individuals.
Purpose and activities: Grants primarily for projects in the fields of culture and education. Annual awards, by nomination only, for achievement in science, the arts, medicine, and literary translations by scholars, writers, and artists of Polish ethnic background regardless of their residence or citizenship.
Types of support: Operating budgets, annual campaigns, special projects, general purposes, publications, exchange programs, matching funds, continuing support.
Limitations: Giving primarily in the New York, NY, metropolitan area. No grants to individuals (except for awards made by nomination only), or for endowment funds; no loans.
Publications: Application guidelines.
Application information:
Initial approach: Proposal
Copies of proposal: 1
Deadline(s): 1 month before board meetings
Board meeting date(s): Jan., May, and Sept.
Final notification: 2 weeks after board meeting
Write: Mrs. Bluma D. Cohen, V.P.
Officers and Trustees: Yolande L. Jurzykowski, Exec. V.P.; Bluma D. Cohen, V.P. and Exec. Dir.; M. Christine Jurzykowski, Secy.-Treas.; Karin Falencki, William Pyka, M.D.
Number of staff: None.
Employer Identification Number: 136192256

2010
Kane Lodge Foundation, Inc.
P.O. Box 12446, Church St. Station
New York 10249

Established in 1960 in NY.
Financial data (yr. ended 9/30/87): Assets, $1,223,303 (M); expenditures, $81,239, including $63,000 for 13 grants (high: $13,500; low: $1,000).
Purpose and activities: Support primarily for a museum, education and social services.
Limitations: Giving primarily in New York, NY.
Application information:
Initial approach: Letter
Deadline(s): None
Write: John Stitcher, Pres.
Officers: John Stitcher, Pres.; Herman E. Muller, Jr., V.P.; John R. Ahlgren, Secy.; John Campbell Henry, Treas.
Directors: Albert C. Valentine, Rodney I. Woods.
Employer Identification Number: 136105390

2011
Rita J. and Stanley H. Kaplan Foundation, Inc.

866 U.N. Plaza
New York 10017 (212) 688-1047

Incorporated in 1984 in NY.
Donor(s): Stanley H. Kaplan.
Financial data (yr. ended 12/31/86): Assets, $8,084,615 (M); gifts received, $100,676; expenditures, $297,684, including $239,471 for 138 grants (high: $50,000; low: $20).
Purpose and activities: Emphasis on Jewish welfare organizations; support also for performing arts organizations and higher education.
Application information: Contributes only to pre-selected organizations. Applications not accepted.
Officers and Directors: Stanley H. Kaplan, Pres.; Rita J. Kaplan, Secy.; Nancy Kaplan Belsky, Paul Alan Kaplan, Susan Beth Kaplan.
Number of staff: None.
Employer Identification Number: 133221298

2012
The J. M. Kaplan Fund, Inc.

330 Madison Ave.
New York 10017 (212) 661-8485

Incorporated in 1948 in NY as Faigel Leah Foundation, Inc.; The J.M. Kaplan Fund, Inc., a DE corporation, merged with it in 1975 and was renamed The J.M. Kaplan Fund, Inc.
Donor(s): Members of the J.M. Kaplan family.
Financial data (yr. ended 11/30/88): Assets, $78,000,000 (M); gifts received, $100; expenditures, $8,130,642, including $6,147,000 for 180 grants (high: $430,000; low: $1,000; average: $5,000-$50,000).
Purpose and activities: Giving for Land Use: conservation, architecture, historic preservation, and strong neighborhoods; enhancement of natural resources, public gardens, parks, farmlands, and open space; and rational planning by government; Civil Liberties and Human Needs: to end prejudice and ensure First Amendment rights and other legal protections, basic public services, and worldwide human rights; Arts: libraries, writers' organizations, special publications, poetry, exhibitions, catalogues, and music groups of a high order.
Types of support: Continuing support, seed money, special projects, publications, technical assistance, general purposes, operating budgets, land acquisition.
Limitations: Giving primarily in NY, with emphasis on New York City; and for rural open space and farmland preservation programs in NY State, with emphasis on the Hudson River Valley. No support for education, medicine, or science; or for theater or dance. No grants to individuals; films or video; building, operating, or endowment funds; annual campaigns; deficit financing; equipment and materials; renovation projects; or scholarships, fellowships, conferences, research, prizes, study, or travel; no loans.
Publications: Annual report (including application guidelines).
Application information: Application form required.
Initial approach: Telephone or letter
Copies of proposal: 1
Deadline(s): Submit proposal only from Mar. 1 to Oct. 15; Music proposals in Sept. only
Board meeting date(s): As required
Final notification: 2 months
Write: Joan K. Davidson, Pres.
Officers: Joan K. Davidson,* Pres.; Elizabeth K. Fonseca,* V.P.; Mary E. Kaplan,* V.P.; Richard D. Kaplan,* V.P.; John Matthew Davidson,* Secy.; Lothar Stiefel,* Treas.; Suzanne Davis, Exec. Dir.
Trustees:* Maurice Austin, Betsy Davidson, Bradford Davidson, Peter Davidson, Bruno Fonseca, Caio Fonseca, Isabel Fonseca, Quina Fonseca, Maurice C. Kaplan.
Number of staff: 5 full-time professional; 4 full-time support; 1 part-time support.
Employer Identification Number: 136090286
Recent arts and culture grants:

Alliance for the Arts, NYC, NY, $10,000. To produce third edition of A Guide to New York City Museums, covering over 220 cultural institutions in five boroughs. 1987.
American Composers Orchestra, NYC, NY, $25,000. For general support. 1987.
American Music Center, NYC, NY, $10,000. For general support. 1987.
Architectural League of New York, NYC, NY, $15,000. For public programs about architecture, design and arts, including publication about building New York; exhibition on vacant lots. 1987.
Artists Space, NYC, NY, $10,000. Toward London Project, series of collaborative works by architects from New York and London at contemporary Soho art gallery that assists young artists. 1987.
Boston Preservation Alliance, Boston, MA, $5,000. For role in movement to preserve historic religious properties, particularly at upcoming Philadelphia National Trust conference. 1987.
British American Arts Association, London, England, $10,000. Toward restoration of Charleston, Sussex home of Vanessa Bell, Duncan Grant and other members of Bloomsbury group, sponsored by bi-national organization that exchanges cultural programs between U.S. and U.K.. 1987.
Brooklyn Academy of Music, Local Development Corporation, Brooklyn, NY, $100,000. For special grant to acquire theatrical equipment for Majestic Theater, for use of local, national and international groups performing in renovated turn-of-the-century theater in newly-designated Brooklyn Acdemy District. 1987.
Brooklyn Historic Railway Association, Brooklyn, NY, $5,000. To help preserve historic abandoned subway tunnel beneath Atlantic Avenue and develop it as railway museum and eventually as trolley link to Brooklyn waterfront and Fulton Landing. 1987.
Brooklyn Historical Society, Brooklyn, NY, $50,000. For permanent exhibition about Brooklyn Bridge in Society's new Gallery of Brooklyn History, in research library and museum housed in landmark building in Brooklyn Heights. 1987.
Brooklyn Institute of Arts and Sciences, Brooklyn, NY, $100,000. For major exhibition of Cleopatra's Egypt, era Brooklyn Museum believes to be particularly rich in historical interest as well as in masterworks of great beauty. Works of distinction and rarity will be assembled from great museums of Europe, North America, and elsewhere. 1987.
Brooklyn Philharmonic Symphony Orchestra, Brooklyn, NY, $10,000. For general support. 1987.
Center for Book Arts, NYC, NY, $25,000. For exhibition program of organization that encourages art of book, both historical and contemporary. 1987.
City College of the City University of New York, Fiction Magazine, NYC, NY, $15,000. For literary magazine housed in English Department. 1987.
City Gallery of the NYC Department of Cultural Affairs, Department of Cultural Affairs, NYC, NY, $10,000. For exhibition of drawings and models of works for art commissioned through City's Percent for Art program, which requires that City agencies spend at leat 1% of construction budget on public art for buildings. 1987.
Committee to Oppose the Sale of Saint Bartholomews Church, NYC, NY, $20,000. Toward legal costs in fight to prevent landmark St. Bartholomew's Church on Park Avenue from turning its Community House into base of skycraper. 1987.
Cooper-Hewitt Museum, The Smithsonians National Museum of Design, NYC, NY, $20,000. For retrospective of drawings of idiosyncratic and important architect Erich Mendelsohn (1887-1953), following Fund's sponorship of last year's exhibition of work of Louis Sullivan. 1987.
Cultural Council Foundation, NYC, NY, $5,000. For new institutional brochure describing services for nonprofit community. 1987.
DaCapo Chamber Players, NYC, NY, $5,000. For general support. 1987.
Drawing Center, NYC, NY, $25,000. For Viewing Program that helps young artists by providing curator to view and discuss work on or of paper submitted by some 2,500 artist; also for shows, slide registry and educational programs. 1987.
Duke Ellington Memorial Fund, NYC, NY, $25,000. For general support. 1987.
Franklin Furnace Archive, NYC, NY, $5,000. For general support for Soho museum that collects, exhibits, and interprets art created by 20th century artists in book form, performance art, and temporary installations. 1987.
Frederick Law Olmsted Association, NYC, NY, $60,000. For work in cause of Olmsted's vision of American landscape, including book on Olmsted's partner Calvert Vaux and for Riverside Park Fund to enhance and restore somewhat neglected park in Manhattan. 1987.
Friends of Terra Cotta, San Francisco, CA, $10,000. For exhibition, brochure and related programs on new Terra Cotta Designs--to develop contemporary uses for traditional building material. 1987.
Friends of the Seventh Regiment, NYC, NY, $12,000. For education materials for visitors to Regiment's landmark headquarters on Park Avenue, first true armory built in NYC and toward restoration of interior. 1987.

Friends of the Upper East Side Historic Districts, NYC, NY, $20,000. For general support for dedicated neighborhood watchdog group that monitors five Historic Districts; includes funds to produce Historic Preservation Manual for owners of landmark properties, explaining rights and responsibilities. 1987.

General Society of Mechanics and Tradesmen of the City of New York, NYC, NY, $5,000. To assist Library's Small Press Center to publicize, through brochure and mailing, conference on Local History and Travel Books issued by small presses. 1987.

Greenwich Village Society for Historic Preservation, NYC, NY, $13,000. For study to document Greenwich Village waterfront, to encourage Landmarks Preservation Commission to include area in Historic District to ensure that Village not be cut off from major historical boundary and amenity, Hudson River. 1987.

Guggenheim Neighbors, NYC, NY, $10,000. To assist efforts to protect architectural integrity of Guggenheim Museum, Frank Lloyd Wright's only major building in NYC and masterpiece of his later years. Grant made through Cultural Council Foundation. 1987.

Historic Districts Council, NYC, NY, $5,000. For advocacy for City's 51 Historic Districts, and many historic neighborhoods actively seeking such official designation. 1987.

Historic Preservation Education Foundation, DC, $11,250. To prepare traveling exhibition, publication and workshops on Historic American Windows, to promote public awareness of standards and techniques of design and preservation of windows, and of significance and distinctive qualities of historic windows. 1987.

Hudson River Sloop Clearwater, Poughkeepsie, NY, $25,000. For floating environmental center that seeks to protect and clean up Hudson River, as well as spread word about historic and cultural treasures of Hudson Valley. 1987.

Institute for Art and Urban Resources, Long Island City, NY, $35,000. For catalogue of comprehensive exhibition of contemporary art to be largest ever assembled in U.S., titled Out of Site. Works will be commissioned specifically for unique spaces of their gallery at PS 1, a Romanesque former school in Long Island City, Queens, and for Artist Emergency Fund. 1987.

International Council on Monuments and Sites, DC, $15,000. To produce 2,000 copies of book, The American Mosaic: Preserving the Cultural Heritage of the United States--to educate public on history and benefits of distinguished urban design. 1987.

Landmark West!, NYC, NY, $20,000. To preserve best of Upper West Side through appropriate landmark designation of individual buildings and historic districts. 1987.

Lower Manhattan Cultural Council, NYC, NY, $25,000. For exhibition on architectural history of lower Manhattan, to increase public awareness of fragile nature of rich architectural heritage of downtown Manhattan, to help preserve it. 1987.

Manitoga, Garrison, NY, $10,000. For general support to help maintain house and landscape in Garrison, NY, and to expand public programming. 1987.

Martha Graham Center of Contemporary Dance, NYC, NY, $50,000. For production of new works by Martha Graham. 1987.

Meet the Composer, NYC, NY, $20,000. For general support. 1987.

Metropolitan Historic Structures Association, NYC, NY, $5,000. For general support for association of historic house museums in all five boroughs, which provides support services for membership, produces newsletter, exhibitions, tours, and publications. 1987.

Metropolitan Museum of Art, NYC, NY, $15,000. To promote exhibitions about Book Arts held in Watson Library of the Museum, through posters and catalogues. 1987.

National Building Museum, DC, $35,000. Toward Blueprints, well-written and attractively designed quarterly publication of unique institution dedicated to American building arts. 1987.

National Center for Preservation Law, DC, $25,000. To prepare and publish series of Preservation Law Updates summarizing important court decisions of concern to preservationists, and distributing them to 1,200 local Landmark Preservation Commissions across country, including 120 in New York State. 1987.

National Trust for Historic Preservation, Department of Maritime Preservation, DC, $30,000. To protect ships and small craft, historic waterfronts, lighthouses and canals of historic significance. 1987.

New Music Consort, NYC, NY, $10,000. For general support. 1987.

New York Landmarks Conservancy, NYC, NY, $135,000. For Sacred Sites and Properties Fund to aid in repair and restoration of architecturally significant houses of worship and related sites in New York State; and for Technical Preservation Services Center to provide professional preservation advice to owners of landmark properties. 1987.

New York Opera Repertory Theater, NYC, NY, $10,000. For general support. 1987.

New York Philomusica Chamber Ensemble, NYC, NY, $5,000. For general support. 1987.

New York Public Library, Astor, Lenox and Tilden Foundations, NYC, NY, $100,000. For Schomburg Center for Research in Black Culture, for branch libraries, and for public programs in Bartos Forum of 42nd Street Research Library. 1987.

New York Shakespeare Festival, NYC, NY, $125,000. For general support for productive arts institution that enhances intellectual and cultural life of New York and nation. 1987.

New York State Historical Association, Cooperstown, NY, $10,000. For institute that promotes study of history and collects and preserves artifacts of New York State; for general programs, and for special issue of Heritage Magazine on Hudson River. 1987.

Opera Orchestra of New York, NYC, NY, $10,000. For general support. 1987.

Partisan Review, Boston, MA, $30,000. For general support to increase writers' fees and otherwise maintain quality of established literary journal. 1987.

PEN American Center, NYC, NY, $25,000. For Writer's Fund that gives discreet emergency grants to writers in temporary financial difficulty; and for Freedom-to-Write Committee which defends freedom of expression and is active on behalf of imprisoned writers around world. 1987.

Philadelphia Historic Preservation Corporation, Philadelphia, PA, $25,000. For exhibition on America's historic churches and synagogues at April 1988 Restoring Faith conference in Philadelphia, co-sponsored by National Trust for Historic Preservation. 1987.

Pierpont Morgan Library, NYC, NY, $26,000. For new lighting system in Cloister gallery. 1987.

Poets House, NYC, NY, $10,000. For general support for poetry center and library on West 18th Street in Manhattan, a gathering place and reference center for poets and general public. 1987.

Preservation League of New York State, Albany, NY, $150,000. For general support and start-up funds for Preservation League Assistance Center to provide technical services and advice to owners of historic properties. 1987.

Preservation League of Staten Island, Staten Island, NY, $25,000. To help move landmark Ichabod Crane House to wildlife refuge in Staten Island Greenbelt to save it from demolition. House will be restored and used as visitors' center, classroom, and exhibition space. 1987.

Public Art Fund, NYC, NY, $20,000. To create three design prototypes for newsstands, secure Art Commission approval of them, and then circulate architectural plans to newsstand license applicants--as means of upgrading character and appeal of these essential urban fixtures. 1987.

Publishing Center for Cultural Resources, NYC, NY, $125,000. To enable unique service organization concerned with improvement of nonprofit publishing to reorganize and achieve firm financial footing. 1987.

Queens Historical Society, Flushing, NY, $5,000. For publications program of group that works to survey, document, preserve and restore architectural treasures of Queens County. 1987.

Restore, NYC, NY, $10,000. To purchase books to establish Masonry Restoration Library for use of public and students in restoration skills training program for people in building industry. 1987.

Saint Lukes Chamber Ensemble, NYC, NY, $25,000. For general support. 1987.

Saint Peters Church, Midtown Arts Common, NYC, NY, $8,000. For general support for various cultural programs within versatile performance spaces at Saint Peters Church in midtown Manhattan's Citicorp Center. 1987.

Save the Theaters, NYC, NY, $10,000. For general support for work to promote preservation of historic theaters, including public education, advocacy and testimony before City agencies; newsletter; providing information on theater history, planning and design issues. 1987.

Scenic Hudson, Poughkeepsie, NY, $55,000. For general support for watchdog organization in Hudson River Valley that preserves land, monitors riverfront development, and guards against pollution, includes funds to help protect from commercial development key land parcel adjacent to Franklin Delano Roosevelt home. 1987.

Sculpture Center, NYC, NY, $5,000. For Upper East Side gallery and school that assists contemporary sculptors through exhibitions, studio space, and workshops. 1987.

Society for the Preservation of New England Antiquities, Boston, MA, $15,000. For preservation, conservation, research and advocacy work in New York State. 1987.

Speculum Musicae, NYC, NY, $10,000. For general support. 1987.

Staten Island Historical Society, Staten Island, NY, $25,000. To relocate Woodrow Wilson Road Farmhouse, important historic Staten Island building, to Richmondtown Restoration, Society's outdoor museum and village complex of 25 buildings dating from 17th to early 20th Century. 1987.

Storefront for Art and Architecture, NYC, NY, $5,000. For general support for Soho galley which believes that art and architecture are inseparable from public issues, and whose exhibitions reflect public concerns and proposed solutions. 1987.

Tribeca Community Association, NYC, NY, $5,000. To produce publication as advocacy tool to preserve special commercial neighborhood below Canal Street and west of Broadway by having it designated Historic District. 1987.

Union Settlement Association, NYC, NY, $5,000. For exhibition of paintings on East Harlem people and street scenes by children of community, to be on display at 96th Street and Lexington subway station in conjunction with MTA. 1987.

United Jewish Appeal-Federation of Jewish Philanthropies Campaign, Eldridge Street Project, NYC, NY, $25,000. Toward preservation and restoration of Eldridge Street Synagogue, key element of immigrant experience in America. 1987.

W N E T Channel 13, NYC, NY, $50,000. For third season of Metroline program covering local news, problems and suggested solutions in areas of education, work, safety, community and government. 1987.

W N Y C Foundation, NYC, NY, $45,000. For The Radio Stage, major series of modern American radio dramas produced in collaboration with several NYC theater, to bring live theater to flexible and intimate medium of radio. 1987.

YM-YWHA, 92nd Street, NYC, NY, $25,000. For general support of music programs. 1987.

Young Concert Artists, NYC, NY, $5,000. For general support. 1987.

2013
The Harvey L. Karp Foundation, Inc.

P.O. Box 30
East Hampton 11937

Established in 1968 in NY.
Financial data (yr. ended 6/30/87): Assets, $1,743,994 (M); expenditures, $76,880, including $66,519 for 36 grants (high: $33,334; low: $50).
Purpose and activities: Emphasis on the arts, higher education, medical research, and Jewish giving.
Limitations: Giving primarily in New York, NY.
Application information: Contributes only to pre-selected organizations. Applications not accepted.
Officers: Harvey L. Karp, Pres. and Treas.; Robert B. Hodes, Secy.
Employer Identification Number: 132621240

2014
Howard & Holly Katz Foundation

Goldman, Sachs & Co.
85 Broad St., Tax Dept.
New York 10004-2408

Established in 1983 in NY.
Donor(s): Howard C. Katz.
Financial data (yr. ended 8/31/88): Assets, $201,526 (M); gifts received, $125,000; expenditures, $202,964, including $202,607 for 46 grants (high: $50,000; low: $100).
Purpose and activities: Support for Jewish welfare, health services, cultural organizations and educational institutions.
Limitations: Giving primarily in New York, NY. No grants to individuals; or for scholarships; no loans.
Application information: Contributes only to pre-selected organizations. Applications not accepted.
Trustees: Holly M. Katz, Howard C. Katz, Ronald S. Tauber.
Employer Identification Number: 133199938

2015
The Katzenberger Foundation, Inc.

c/o Golieb & Golieb
Six East 43rd St.
New York 10017 (212) 687-3340

Incorporated in 1952 in NY.
Donor(s): Walter B. Katzenberger,† Helen Katherine Katzenberger,† The Advertising Checking Bureau, Inc.
Financial data (yr. ended 11/30/87): Assets, $9,590,193 (M); expenditures, $571,058, including $500,000 for 42 grants (high: $125,000; low: $1,000).
Purpose and activities: Grants for church support, welfare, higher and secondary education, the performing arts, and youth agencies.
Limitations: No grants to individuals; no scholarships.
Application information:
Initial approach: Letter
Copies of proposal: 2
Deadline(s): Submit proposal preferably between July and Oct.; deadline Oct. 31
Board meeting date(s): Nov. and May
Write: Abner J. Golieb, Pres.
Officers and Directors: Abner J. Golieb, Pres.; Edward Davis, Secy.; Richard Eason, Warren Grieb, Jon McIntyre, Earl Swanson.
Employer Identification Number: 136094434

2016
Henry Kaufmann Foundation

300 Park Ave.
New York 10022 (212) 909-5951

Incorporated in 1928 in NY.
Donor(s): Henry Kaufmann.†
Financial data (yr. ended 12/31/87): Assets, $7,684,589 (M); expenditures, $1,484,496, including $1,380,800 for 18 grants (high: $400,000; low: $2,500; average: $5,000-$160,000).
Purpose and activities: Capital grants principally for geriatric care facilities, arts and educational institutions, and camping and community centers.
Types of support: Building funds, equipment, general purposes, capital campaigns, land acquisition, professorships, renovation projects.
Limitations: Giving primarily in the New York, NY, and Pittsburgh, PA, metropolitan areas. No grants to individuals, or for endowment funds, operating budgets, scholarships, fellowships, or matching gifts; no loans.
Publications: 990-PF, annual report.
Application information:
Initial approach: Written proposal
Copies of proposal: 2
Deadline(s): Submit written proposal preferably 1 or 2 months before board meeting dates; no set deadline
Board meeting date(s): May and Nov.
Final notification: After board meetings
Write: Jeffrey A. Horwitz, Asst. Secy.
Officers: Walter Mendelsohn,* Chair. and Pres.; Maurice B. Hexter,* V.P. and Treas.; Daniel D. Mielnicki, Secy.
Directors:* Leonard N. Block, William T. Golden, Charles Looker, Frederick Rose, John M. Wolf, Sr.
Number of staff: None.
Employer Identification Number: 136034179

2017
Hagop Kevorkian Fund

1411 Third Ave.
New York 10028 (212) 988-9304

Trust established in 1950; incorporated in 1951 in NY.
Donor(s): Hagop Kevorkian.†
Financial data (yr. ended 12/31/87): Assets, $83,277,783 (M); expenditures, $1,406,161, including $1,195,243 for 10 grants (high: $668,950; low: $6,700; average: $6,700-$79,000).
Purpose and activities: To promote interest in Near and Middle Eastern art through exhibitions and through fellowships administered by the recipient institutions for research and study in this field.
Types of support: Fellowships, research.
Application information: Contributes only to pre-selected organizations. Applications not accepted.
Write: Ralph D. Minasian, Secy.-Treas.
Officers and Trustees: Stephen Chan, Chair. and Exec. V.P.; Marjorie Kevorkian, Pres. and Curator; Ralph D. Minasian, Secy.-Treas.; Miriam Chan, Martin D. Polevoy.
Employer Identification Number: 131839686

2018
KeyCorp Corporate Contributions Program
P.O. Box 88
Albany 12201 (518) 486-8500

Purpose and activities: Support for the United Way, education, with emphasis on banking, finance, business management, economics, and vocational training; support also for arts and humanities, and economic health and revitalization.
Limitations: Giving primarily in areas where Key Banks are located; parent company handles national funding requests.
Application information:
Initial approach: Write to nearest KeyBank; national requests to headquarters
Write: Nancy Herron, V.P., Public Relations

2019
The Kidder Peabody Foundation
c/o Kidder, Peabody & Co., Inc.
20 Exchange Pl.
New York 10005 (212) 510-5502

Incorporated in 1959 in NY.
Donor(s): Kidder, Peabody & Co., Inc.
Financial data (yr. ended 12/31/87): Assets, $3,299,233 (M); expenditures, $372,898, including $355,050 for 73 grants.
Purpose and activities: Emphasis on higher and secondary education; support also for arts, culture, and hospitals.
Limitations: Giving primarily in NY and areas where company maintains offices. No support for religious organizations. No grants to individuals; no loans.
Application information:
Initial approach: Letter
Deadline(s): None
Board meeting date(s): Annually
Write: Helen B. Platt, V.P.
Officers and Directors: Silas S. Cathcart, Chair.; Max C. Chapman, Jr., Pres.; Helen B. Platt, V.P.; John Liftin, Secy.; Joseph Martorella, Treas.
Number of staff: None.
Employer Identification Number: 136085918

2020
Helen & Milton Kimmelman Foundation
745 Fifth Ave., Suite 2204
New York 10151-0001

Established in 1982 in NY.
Donor(s): Milton Kimmelman.†
Financial data (yr. ended 11/30/87): Assets, $10,496,050 (M); gifts received, $977,082; expenditures, $4,206,947, including $4,157,068 for 96 grants (high: $1,500,000; low: $50).
Purpose and activities: Giving primarily for Jewish welfare funds and other Jewish organizations, and the visual and performing arts, including museums; support also for medical research and education, and the environment.
Types of support: General purposes, matching funds, program-related investments, building funds.
Application information: Contributes only to pre-selected organizations. Applications not accepted.
Trustee: Helen Kimmelman.
Employer Identification Number: 133110688

2021
The Calvin Klein Foundation
c/o Nathan Berkman & Co.
29 Broadway, Suite 2800
New York 10006

Established in 1981 in NY.
Financial data (yr. ended 6/30/87): Assets, $318 (M); gifts received, $143,500; expenditures, $147,251, including $147,050 for 61 grants (high: $11,000; low: $275).
Purpose and activities: Support for Jewish organizations, health agencies, cultural institutions, and general charities.
Limitations: Giving primarily in NY.
Application information:
Deadline(s): None
Trustees: James Coe, Andrew Rosen.
Employer Identification Number: 133094765

2022
David L. Klein, Jr. Memorial Foundation, Inc.
c/o L.J. Podell
2181 Ralph Ave.
Brooklyn 11234

Incorporated in 1959 in NY.
Donor(s): David L. Klein,† Miriam Klein, Endo Laboratories, Inc.
Financial data (yr. ended 2/28/87): Assets, $2,355,843 (M); gifts received, $50,250; expenditures, $156,695, including $125,181 for 114 grants (high: $39,500; low: $10).
Purpose and activities: Emphasis on hospitals, medical research, Jewish welfare funds, temple support, higher education, and cultural activities.
Limitations: Giving primarily in NY. No grants to individuals.
Application information: Contributes only to pre-selected organizations. Applications not accepted.
Officer and Trustees: Miriam Klein, Pres.; Saretta Barnet, Marjorie Traub.
Employer Identification Number: 136085432

2023
Klock Company Trust
(also known as Jay E. and Lucia DeL. Klock Kingston Foundation)
c/o Key Trust Co.
260 Fair St.
Kingston 12401 (914) 339-6750

Established in 1966 in NY.
Financial data (yr. ended 12/31/87): Assets, $3,112,143 (M); expenditures, $228,938, including $199,500 for 28 grants (high: $28,000; low: $1,000).
Purpose and activities: Grants for hospitals and health services, youth organizations, social services, religious support, cultural programs, and education.
Limitations: Giving limited to Kingston and Ulster counties, NY.
Application information:
Initial approach: Letter
Deadline(s): Before end of quarters: Mar., June, Sept., and Dec.
Write: Earle H. Foster
Trustees: Harry Dubois Frey, Key Trust Co.
Employer Identification Number: 146038479

2024
Louis & Rose Klosk Fund
c/o Chemical Bank
30 Rockefeller Plaza, 60th Fl.
New York 10112 (212) 621-2148

Trust established in 1970 in NY.
Donor(s): Louis Klosk.†
Financial data (yr. ended 12/31/87): Assets, $3,108,659 (M); expenditures, $125,438, including $94,500 for 34 grants (high: $12,500; low: $500).
Purpose and activities: Giving for Jewish welfare funds, hospitals, care for the aged, arts, and higher education.
Limitations: Giving primarily in NY.
Application information:
Deadline(s): None
Write: Barbara Strohmeier, V.P.; Chemical Bank
Trustees: Barry Cooper, Nathan Cooper, Chemical Bank.
Employer Identification Number: 136328994

2025
The Seymour H. Knox Foundation, Inc.
3750 Marine Midland Center
Buffalo 14203 (716) 854-6811

Incorporated in 1945 in NY.
Donor(s): Seymour H. Knox, Marjorie K.C. Klopp,† Dorothy K.G. Rogers.†
Financial data (yr. ended 12/31/87): Assets, $14,691,260 (M); expenditures, $918,335, including $756,174 for 57 grants (high: $300,000; low: $100).
Purpose and activities: Giving for the arts, higher and secondary education, hospitals, civic organizations, and community funds.
Types of support: General purposes.
Limitations: Giving primarily in the Buffalo, NY, area. No grants to individuals.
Application information: Contributes only to pre-selected oraganizations. Applications not accepted.
Initial approach: Letter
Deadline(s): None
Board meeting date(s): May and Dec.
Write: Seymour H. Knox, Pres.
Officers: Seymour H. Knox, Pres.; Northrup R. Knox, V.P. and Treas.; Hazard K. Campbell, V.P.; Seymour H. Knox III, V.P.; Samuel D. Magavern, Secy.
Directors: Frederick S. Pierce, Henry Z. Urban.
Employer Identification Number: 160839066

2026
The Kohlberg Foundation
c/o Kohlberg & Co.
116 Radio Circle
Mount Kisco 10549 (914) 241-8598

Established in 1962 in New York.

Donor(s): Jerome Kohlberg.
Financial data (yr. ended 11/30/87): Assets, $9,814,764 (M); gifts received, $2,202,235; expenditures, $437,984, including $385,815 for 74 grants (high: $25,000; low: $100).
Purpose and activities: Emphasis on higher education and culture.
Types of support: Continuing support.
Application information:
Write: Morton I. Cohen
Trustees: Karen Davis, Jerome Kohlberg, Jr., Nancy S. Kohlberg, Pam Vinal.
Employer Identification Number: 136116079

2027
Kosciuszko Foundation, Inc.
15 East 65th St.
New York 10021-6595 (212) 734-2130

Incorporated in 1925 in NY.
Financial data (yr. ended 6/30/88): Assets, $10,927,061 (M); gifts received, $644,599; expenditures, $1,064,536, including $36,075 for 6 grants (high: $13,495; low: $90) and $438,757 for 127 grants to individuals.
Purpose and activities: A private operating foundation which promotes Polish culture in the U.S. and Poland, and maintains a library of Polish publications. Scholarship grants for Polish scholars desiring to study in the U.S., and for American scholars desiring to study in Poland, or for graduate and postgraduate studies in the United States. The foundation also organizes summer courses at Polish universities for American students.
Types of support: Student aid, fellowships, exchange programs, publications.
Limitations: Giving primarily in Poland and the U.S.
Publications: Newsletter, informational brochure, application guidelines.
Application information: Application form required.
Initial approach: Letter
Deadline(s): Nov. 15 for foreign exchange students, and Mar. 15 for summer session
Board meeting date(s): Apr. and Nov.
Write: Joseph E. Gore, Pres. or Irena Budesa-Gagic, Controller
Officer: Joseph E. Gore, Pres. and Exec. Dir.
Number of staff: 10 full-time professional; 2 part-time support.
Employer Identification Number: 131628179

2028
Koussevitzky Music Foundation, Inc.
200 Park Ave.
New York 10166 (212) 351-3092

Established in 1942 in NY.
Donor(s): Olga Koussevitzky,† Serge Koussevitzky.†
Financial data (yr. ended 3/31/88): Assets, $1,410,494 (M); expenditures, $48,906, including $9,000 for 2 grants and $10,000 for 1 grant to an individual.
Purpose and activities: The foundation has suspended giving pending development of a new program.
Types of support: Grants to individuals.
Application information:
Deadline(s): Nov. 30
Write: Ellis J. Freedman, Esq., Secy.
Officers: Jacob Druckman, Pres.; Ellis J. Freedman, Secy.; John Grozier, Treas.
Directors: Leonard Bernstein, Elliott Carter, Mario Davidovsky, Andrew Imbrie, Fred Lerdahl, Gunther Schuller, Michael Tilson Thomas.
Employer Identification Number: 046128361

2029
E. A. Kraft Charitable Trust
c/o Chemical Bank
30 Rockefeller Plaza, 60th Fl.
New York 10112 (212) 621-2143

Established in 1978.
Financial data (yr. ended 7/31/87): Assets, $37,153 (M); expenditures, $138,408, including $136,000 for 31 grants (high: $10,000; low: $1,000).
Purpose and activities: Giving for secondary and higher education, hospitals and health, social services, cultural programs, and Episcopal religious organizations.
Limitations: Giving primarily in New York, NY.
Application information:
Deadline(s): None
Write: Mrs. Barbara Strohmeier
Trustees: Alfred Ferguson, Logan Fulrath, Jr., Chemical Bank.
Employer Identification Number: 136761770

2030
Henry R. Kravis Foundation, Inc.
c/o Kohlberg Kravis Roberts & Co.
Nine West 57th St.
New York 10019

Established in 1985 in NY.
Donor(s): Henry R. Kravis.
Financial data (yr. ended 11/30/87): Assets, $4,040,458 (M); gifts received, $4,000,000; expenditures, $1,033,088, including $1,025,000 for 4 grants (high: $750,000; low: $50,000).
Purpose and activities: Support primarily for the arts and culture, including a museum, and for Jewish welfare.
Limitations: No grants to individuals.
Application information: Contributes only to pre-selected organizations. Applications not accepted.
Officers and Directors:* Henry R. Kravis,* Chair. and Pres.; Thomas Hudson, Secy.; Richard I. Beattie, Jerome Kohlberg, Jr.
Employer Identification Number: 133341521

2031
Samuel H. Kress Foundation
174 East 80th St.
New York 10021 (212) 861-4993

Incorporated in 1929 in NY.
Donor(s): Samuel H. Kress,† Claude W. Kress,† Rush H. Kress.†
Financial data (yr. ended 8/31/87): Assets, $63,967,746 (M); expenditures, $2,515,773, including $1,365,202 for 120 grants (high: $130,000; low: $100; average: $5,000-$12,500) and $291,129 for grants to individuals.
Purpose and activities: Giving through six main programs: 1) fellowships for pre-doctoral research in art history; 2) advanced training and research in conservation of works of art; 3) development of scholarly resources in the fields of art history and conservation; 4) conservation and restoration of monuments in western Europe; 5) archaeological fieldwork emphasizing art history; 6) occasional related projects.
Types of support: Professorships, internships, fellowships, research, publications, conferences and seminars.
Limitations: No support for art history programs below the pre-doctoral level, or the purchase of works of art. No grants for living artists, or for operating budgets, continuing support, annual campaigns, endowments, deficit financing, capital funds, or films; no loans.
Publications: Annual report (including application guidelines).
Application information: Application forms required for fellowships in art history and art conservation.
Initial approach: Proposal
Copies of proposal: 1
Deadline(s): Nov. 30 for research fellowships in art history; Jan. 31 for fellowships in art conservation
Board meeting date(s): Usually in Oct. and May
Final notification: 3 months
Write: Dr. Marilyn Perry, Pres.
Officers and Trustees: Franklin D. Murphy, Chair.; W. Clarke Wescoe, Vice-Chair. and Treas.; Marilyn Perry, Pres.; John C. Fontaine, V.P.; William Bader, Secy.; Lyman Field, Immaculada de Habsburgo.
Number of staff: 2 full-time professional; 1 part-time professional; 3 full-time support.
Employer Identification Number: 131624176
Recent arts and culture grants:
Allentown Art Museum, Allentown, PA, $50,000. Toward renovation of existing space for improved conservation and storage facilities for textiles and works on paper. 1987.
American Academy in Rome, NYC, NY, $120,000. Toward Kress Fellowships in Italian Art History and Classical Art and Archaeology. 1987.
American Academy in Rome, NYC, NY, $20,000. Toward excavation of Roman Forum. 1987.
Archaeological Institute of America, Boston, MA, $125,000. Toward Kress Lectureship in Ancient Art. 1987.
Boston University, Boston, MA, $12,500. For Kress University Fellowship in art history. 1987.
Brown University, Providence, RI, $12,500. For Kress University Fellowship in art history. 1987.
Bryn Mawr College, Bryn Mawr, PA, $12,500. For Kress University Fellowship in art history. 1987.
Columbia University, NYC, NY, $12,500. For Kress University Fellowship in art history. 1987.
Cornell University, Ithaca, NY, $12,500. For Kress University Fellowship in art history. 1987.

Harvard University, Cambridge, MA, $51,000. Toward Kress Fellowship in History of Art at Villa I Tatti, Florence, Italy. 1987.
Indiana University, Fort Wayne, IN, $12,500. For Kress University Fellowship in art history. 1987.
Johns Hopkins University, Baltimore, MD, $12,500. For Kress University Fellowship in art history. 1987.
Johns Hopkins University, Baltimore, MD, $12,500. For Kress University Fellowship in art history. 1987.
National Gallery of Art, Center for Advanced Study in Visual Arts, DC, $402,000. Toward Kress Fellowships in History of Art. 1987.
New York University, NYC, NY, $12,500. For Kress University Fellowship in art history. 1987.
Princeton University, Princeton, NJ, $12,500. For Kress University Fellowship in art history. 1987.
Stanford University, Stanford, CA, $12,500. For Kress University Fellowship in art history. 1987.
University of California, Berkeley, CA, $12,500. For Kress University Fellowship in art history. 1987.
University of California, Santa Barbara, CA, $12,500. For Kress University Fellowship in art history. 1987.
University of Chicago, Chicago, IL, $12,500. For Kress University Fellowship in art history. 1987.
University of Illinois, Chicago, IL, $12,500. For Kress University Fellowship in art history. 1987.
University of Iowa, Iowa City, IA, $12,500. For Kress University Fellowship in art history. 1987.
University of Kansas, Lawrence, KS, $12,500. For Kress University Fellowship in art history. 1987.
University of London, Warburg Institute, London, England, $50,000. Toward computerization of scholarly publications program. 1987.
University of Minnesota, Minneapolis, MN, $12,500. For Kress University Fellowship in art history. 1987.
University of Missouri, Columbia, MO, $12,500. For Kress University Fellowship in art history. 1987.
University of North Carolina, Chapel Hill, NC, $12,500. For Kress University Fellowship in art history. 1987.
University of Oregon, Portland, OR, $12,500. For Kress University Fellowship in art history. 1987.
University of Pennsylvania, Philadelphia, PA, $12,500. For Kress University Fellowship in art history. 1987.
University of Washington, Seattle, WA, $12,500. For Kress University Fellowship in art history. 1987.
University of Wisconsin, Madison, WI, $12,500. For Kress University Fellowship in art history. 1987.
World Monuments Fund, NYC, NY, $1,000,000. To establish Kress Foundation European Preservation Program. 1987.
Yale University, New Haven, CT, $12,500. For Kress University Fellowship in art history. 1987.

2032
The Mathilde and Arthur B. Krim Foundation, Inc.
c/o Orion Pictures
711 Fifth Ave.
New York 10022 (212) 758-5100

Donor(s): Arthur B. Krim.
Financial data (yr. ended 12/31/86): Assets, $140,172 (M); gifts received, $269,063; expenditures, $241,168, including $238,076 for 81 grants (high: $94,500; low: $30; average: $3,000).
Purpose and activities: Emphasis on higher education, medical research, cultural programs, health agencies, public policy, social services, civil rights, Jewish organizations, and an institute of sociology.
Types of support: Continuing support, research.
Limitations: Giving primarily in NY.
Publications: 990-PF.
Application information: Applications not accepted.
Write: Arthur B. Krim, Chair.
Director: Arthur B. Krim, Chair.
Number of staff: None.
Employer Identification Number: 136219851

2033
The H. Frederick Krimendahl II Foundation
c/o Goldman, Sachs & Co., Tax Dept.
85 Broad St., 30th Fl.
New York 10004-2106

Established in 1968 in NY.
Donor(s): H. Frederick Krimendahl II.
Financial data (yr. ended 5/31/88): Assets, $2,908,129 (M); gifts received, $274,000; expenditures, $79,325, including $68,928 for 67 grants (high: $5,000; low: $50).
Purpose and activities: Support primarily for youth; support also for education, arts, and culture.
Limitations: No grants to individuals.
Application information: Contributes only to pre-selected organizations. Applications not accepted.
Trustees: Constance M. Krimendahl, H. Frederick Krimendahl II, Nancy C. Krimendahl, James S. Marcus, Elizabeth K. Wolf.
Employer Identification Number: 237000391

2034
Charles and Bertha Kriser Foundation, Inc.
211 East 43rd St.
New York 10017

Established in NY.
Donor(s): Sidney P. Kriser, Richard Feldstein, Judy Feldstein, R.C. Mahon & Co., and others.
Financial data (yr. ended 5/31/86): Assets, $1,881,881 (M); gifts received, $160,000; expenditures, $202,014, including $197,413 for 79 grants (high: $50,000; low: $23).
Purpose and activities: Emphasis on Jewish welfare organizations; support also for health and hospitals, cultural programs, and higher education.
Limitations: Giving primarily in NY.
Officers: David Kriser, Pres.; Sidney Kriser, Secy.
Employer Identification Number: 136188243

2035
The Albert Kunstadter Family Foundation
1035 Fifth Ave.
New York 10028 (212) 249-1733

Incorporated in 1952 in IL.
Donor(s): Members of the Kunstadter family.
Financial data (yr. ended 12/31/88): Assets, $2,636,738 (M); expenditures, $192,737 for 67 grants (high: $10,000; low: $1,000; average: $2,000-$5,000).
Purpose and activities: Local, national, and, where possible, international giving, including support for education and the arts.
Types of support: Special projects, general purposes, operating budgets.
Limitations: Giving primarily in East Coast states between Boston, MA, and Washington, DC. No support for religious purposes. No grants to individuals, or for deficit financing, building funds, land acquisition, scholarships and fellowships, or matching gifts; no loans.
Publications: Annual report (including application guidelines).
Application information:
Initial approach: Letter
Copies of proposal: 1
Deadline(s): Submit short proposal preferably before Nov.
Board meeting date(s): June and as required
Final notification: 3 weeks for negative responses, 1 to 3 months for positive ones
Write: John W. Kunstadter, Pres., or Geraldine S. Kunstadter, Chair.
Officers and Directors: Geraldine S. Kunstadter, Chair.; John W. Kunstadter, Pres. and Treas.; Christopher Kunstadter, V.P.; Peter Kunstadter, V.P.; Lisa Kunstadter, Secy.; Elizabeth Kunstadter, Sally Lennington Kunstadter.
Number of staff: None.
Employer Identification Number: 366047975

2036
L and L Foundation
781 Fifth Ave.
New York 10022

Incorporated in 1963 in NY.
Donor(s): Lawrence E. Brinn.
Financial data (yr. ended 12/31/86): Assets, $5,006,595 (M); gifts received, $2,000; expenditures, $241,179, including $190,450 for 32 grants (high: $50,000; low: $100).
Purpose and activities: Emphasis on hospitals, higher education, cultural programs, including the performing arts, and youth and child welfare agencies.
Limitations: Giving primarily in NY. No grants to individuals.
Application information: Contributes only to pre-selected organizations. Applications not accepted.
Write: Lawrence E. Brinn, Pres.

Officers and Directors: Lawrence E. Brinn, Pres. and Treas.; Mildred F. Cunningham, V.P.; Peter F. De Gaetano, Secy.
Employer Identification Number: 136155758

2037
Eugene M. Lang Foundation
100 East 42nd St., 3rd Fl.
New York 10017 (212) 687-4741

Established in 1968 in NY.
Donor(s): Eugene M. Lang.
Financial data (yr. ended 12/31/88): Assets, $22,695,000 (M); expenditures, $1,928,000, including $1,749,749 for 85 grants (high: $1,257,000; low: $25; average: $100-$20,000).
Purpose and activities: Support for higher education, cultural programs, and hospitals.
Types of support: Operating budgets, continuing support, annual campaigns, seed money, emergency funds, scholarship funds, professorships, internships, fellowships, special projects, conferences and seminars, land acquisition.
Limitations: Giving primarily in NY and neighboring area, including PA. No grants to individuals, or for building funds, equipment and materials, capital or endowment funds, deficit financing, publications, or matching gifts; no loans.
Application information:
Initial approach: Letter
Deadline(s): None
Board meeting date(s): Apr. and Nov.
Write: Eugene M. Lang, Trustee
Trustees: David A. Lang, Eugene M. Lang, Stephen Lang, Theresa Lang.
Number of staff: 1 part-time professional; 1 full-time support.
Employer Identification Number: 136153412

2038
Larsen Fund, Inc.
Time & Life Bldg.
New York 10020
Additional address: 2960 Post Rd., Suite 100, Southport, CT 06490; Tel.: (203) 255-5318

Incorporated in 1941 in NY.
Donor(s): Roy E. Larsen.†
Financial data (yr. ended 12/31/87): Assets, $6,345,691 (M); expenditures, $460,323, including $359,995 for 58 grants (high: $25,000; low: $500).
Purpose and activities: Grants largely for higher education, conservation, the arts, research, and social services.
Types of support: General purposes, fellowships, professorships, research, annual campaigns, building funds, capital campaigns, conferences and seminars, consulting services, endowment funds, internships, land acquisition, lectureships, scholarship funds, seed money, special projects.
Limitations: Giving primarily in the New York, NY, area, Minneapolis, MN, area, and CT. No grants to individuals.
Publications: Annual report (including application guidelines).
Application information:
Initial approach: Letter
Copies of proposal: 1
Deadline(s): Submit proposal at least 60 days prior to meeting dates
Board meeting date(s): Beginning of May and Dec.
Write: Marcelle Coudrai
Officers and Directors:* Robert R. Larsen,* Pres. and Treas.; Christopher Larsen,* V.P.; Ann Larsen Simonson,* V.P.; Jonathan Z. Larsen,* Secy.; Marcelle Coudrai.
Number of staff: 2 full-time support.
Employer Identification Number: 136104430

2039
Lasdon Foundation, Inc.
Ten Rockefeller Plaza, Suite 1111
New York 10020-1903 (212) 977-8420

Incorporated in 1946 in DE.
Donor(s): W.S. Lasdon,† Stanley S. Lasdon, J.S. Lasdon,† M.S. Lasdon.†
Financial data (yr. ended 11/30/88): Assets, $3,064,163 (M); expenditures, $251,613, including $162,625 for 70 grants (high: $30,000; low: $100).
Purpose and activities: To further research in the medical sciences through grants to universities and medical institutions; support also for the performing arts and general civic projects.
Types of support: Research, matching funds, continuing support, annual campaigns.
Limitations: No grants to individuals, or for building or endowment funds, operating budgets, or program support.
Application information:
Initial approach: Letter
Copies of proposal: 1
Deadline(s): Submit proposal preferably in Mar. or Sept.; no set deadline
Board meeting date(s): Annually
Final notification: Application for grants not necessarily acknowledged
Write: Stanley S. Lasdon, Pres.
Officers and Directors: Stanley S. Lasdon, Pres. and Treas.; Gene S. Lasdon, V.P.; Mildred D. Lasdon, V.P.
Number of staff: 1 full-time support.
Employer Identification Number: 131739997

2040
William and Mildred Lasdon Foundation
Ten Rockefeller Plaza, Suite 1111
New York 10020-1903

Established in 1947 in DE.
Donor(s): Jacob S. Lasdon, William S. Lasdon.
Financial data (yr. ended 12/31/87): Assets, $1,818,443 (M); gifts received, $1,065,000; expenditures, $58,190, including $53,008 for 73 grants (high: $5,000; low: $75).
Purpose and activities: Giving primarily for hospitals, museums, and other arts organizations.
Limitations: Giving primarily in NY.
Officers: Mildred D. Lasdon, Pres.; Nanette L. Laitman, Secy.-Treas.
Employer Identification Number: 237380362

2041
Albert and Mary Lasker Foundation, Inc.
865 First Ave., Apt. 15E
New York 10017 (212) 421-9010

Incorporated in 1942 in NY.
Donor(s): Albert D. Lasker,† Mary W. Lasker.
Financial data (yr. ended 12/31/87): Assets, $3,567,409 (M); gifts received, $41,250; expenditures, $721,832, including $290,082 for grants (high: $24,999), $8,934 for 1 grant to an individual and $127,683 for foundation-administered programs.
Purpose and activities: Primarily concerned with medical research; annual Lasker awards given to honor and encourage outstanding medical research; support also for a beautification program, health programs, and the arts.
Application information:
Deadline(s): None
Write: Mary W. Lasker, Pres.
Officers and Directors: Mary W. Lasker, Pres.; Alice Fordyce, Exec. V.P.; Catherine G. Blair, V.P.; William McC. Blair, V.P.; James W. Fordyce, Secy.-Treas.; Christopher Brody, Anne B. Fordyce, Dr. Jordan Gutterman, David Morse, Edwin C. Whitehead.
Employer Identification Number: 131680062

2042
Abe and Frances Lastfogel Foundation
c/o Wallin, Simon, Black and Co.
1350 Ave. of the Americas
New York 10019 (212) 586-5100

Established in 1972 in CA.
Donor(s): Abe Lastfogel,† Frances Lastfogel.†
Financial data (yr. ended 12/31/86): Assets, $3,669,197 (M); gifts received, $359,630; expenditures, $346,617, including $345,885 for 168 grants (high: $50,000; low: $80; average: $500-$3,000).
Purpose and activities: Grants for Jewish welfare funds, education, cultural programs, health and social service agencies, including those affiliated with the motion picture industry.
Types of support: Annual campaigns, endowment funds, program-related investments, special projects.
Limitations: Giving primarily in the Los Angeles, CA, area and NY.
Publications: 990-PF.
Application information:
Write: Lawrence Lewis, V.P.
Officers and Directors:* Walter Zifkin,* Pres.; Lawrence Lewis,* V.P.; Lee Stevens,* V.P.; Roger Davis, Secy.-Treas.
Employer Identification Number: 237146829

2043
The Lauder Foundation, Inc.
767 Fifth Ave., 37th Floor
New York 10153 (212) 572-4285

Incorporated in 1962 in NY.
Donor(s): Estee Lauder, Joseph H. Lauder,† Leonard A. Lauder, Ronald S. Lauder.
Financial data (yr. ended 11/30/86): Assets, $9,523,240 (M); gifts received, $1,500; expenditures, $1,311,805, including

$1,295,501 for 101 grants (high: $200,000; average: $1,000-$50,000).
Purpose and activities: Emphasis on museums, education, Jewish organizations, social service agencies, cultural programs, and conservation; some support for public affairs organizations and hospitals.
Limitations: Giving primarily in the New York, NY, metropolitan area.
Application information:
Deadline(s): None
Board meeting date(s): As needed
Final notification: 4 to 8 weeks
Write: Margaret Gunderman
Officers and Directors: Estee Lauder, Pres.; Leonard A. Lauder, Secy.-Treas.
Number of staff: None.
Employer Identification Number: 136153743

2044
Lawrence Foundation
c/o Lawrence Aviation Industries, Inc.
Sheep Pasture Rd.
Port Jefferson Station 11776 (516) 473-1800

Established in 1943 in MA and NY.
Donor(s): Lawrence Aviation Industries, Inc.
Financial data (yr. ended 12/31/86): Assets, $2,242,696 (M); expenditures, $217,257, including $196,178 for 171 grants (high: $10,000; low: $12).
Purpose and activities: Giving primarily for higher education, hospitals and health associations; support also for social services and cultural affairs.
Limitations: Giving primarily in New York, with emphasis on Long Island.
Application information:
Deadline(s): None
Write: Gerald Cohen, Trustee
Trustee: Gerald Cohen.
Employer Identification Number: 116035412

2045
John S. and Florence G. Lawrence Foundation, Inc.
Eight Freer St., Suite 160
Lynbrook 11563 (516) 887-9485

Established in 1955 in NY.
Donor(s): John S. Lawrence.
Financial data (yr. ended 4/30/88): Assets, $1,761,894 (M); expenditures, $86,327, including $71,612 for 91 grants (high: $24,200; low: $50).
Purpose and activities: Giving primarily for Jewish welfare organizations and religious activities; support also for education, hospitals, and the arts.
Types of support: Operating budgets, continuing support, annual campaigns, emergency funds, fellowships, general purposes, research, scholarship funds.
Limitations: No grants to individuals, or for seed money, deficit financing, capital funds, endowment funds, matching gifts, non-grant support, research, demonstration projects, program support, publications, conferences or seminars; no loans.
Application information:
Initial approach: Letter
Deadline(s): None
Board meeting date(s): Mar.
Write: John S. Lawrence, Pres.
Officers and Directors: John S. Lawrence, Pres. and Treas.; Florence G. Lawrence, V.P. and Secy.; James G. Lawrence, V.P.; Betsy P. Schiff, V.P.; George J. Hutt, David M. Levitan.
Number of staff: 1 part-time support.
Employer Identification Number: 136099026

2046
Samuel J. & Ethel Lefrak Foundation, Inc.
97-77 Queens Blvd.
Rego Park 11374

Established in 1963.
Donor(s): Samuel J. Lefrak, L.S.S. Leasing Corp.
Financial data (yr. ended 12/31/86): Assets, $261,013 (L); gifts received, $23,000; expenditures, $167,291.
Purpose and activities: Giving primarily for education, hospitals and health agencies, and cultural institutions; some support for Jewish giving and general charitable giving.
Limitations: Giving primarily in New York, NY.
Officer: Samuel J. Lefrak, Pres.
Employer Identification Number: 116043788

2047
Robert Lehman Foundation, Inc.
c/o Kelly, Drye & Warren
101 Park Ave.
New York 10178 (212) 808-7946

Incorporated in 1943 in NY.
Donor(s): Robert Lehman.†
Financial data (yr. ended 9/30/87): Assets, $42,873,586 (M); expenditures, $2,218,803, including $1,911,870 for 16 grants (high: $696,988; low: $4,960).
Purpose and activities: Support for the maintenance, conservation, and preservation of the Robert Lehman collection at The Metropolitan Museum of Art; some support also for higher education and cultural programs, with emphasis on visual arts and related teaching activities and publications.
Limitations: Giving primarily in the northeastern U.S., with emphasis on New York, NY.
Application information:
Deadline(s): None
Board meeting date(s): As required
Write: Paul C. Guth, Exec. Secy.
Officers and Directors: Philip H. Isles, Pres.; Edwin L. Weisl, V.P.; Paul C. Guth, Exec. Secy.; Robert A. Bernhard, Treas.; James M. Hester, Michael M. Thomas.
Number of staff: None.
Employer Identification Number: 136094018

2048
Lemberg Foundation, Inc.
60 East 42nd St., Rm. 1814
New York 10165 (212) 682-9595

Incorporated in 1945 in NY.
Donor(s): Samuel Lemberg.†
Financial data (yr. ended 12/31/86): Assets, $6,783,868 (M); gifts received, $79,264; expenditures, $344,951, including $309,068 for 110 grants (high: $35,000; low: $15).
Purpose and activities: Support for Jewish welfare funds, higher education, temple support, and the performing arts.
Types of support: Building funds, endowment funds, special projects, research, scholarship funds, fellowships.
Limitations: No grants for matching gifts.
Application information:
Initial approach: Letter, proposal, or telephone
Copies of proposal: 1
Board meeting date(s): As required
Write: John Usdan, Treas.
Officers: Suzanne Usdan, Pres.; Adam Usdan, Secy.; John Usdan, Treas.
Number of staff: 2 part-time support.
Employer Identification Number: 136082064

2049
Edgar M. Leventritt Foundation, Inc.
Jay Cox Rd.
Cold Spring 10516

Established in 1939 in NY.
Financial data (yr. ended 12/31/87): Assets, $1,497,975 (M); expenditures, $82,448, including $66,500 for 11 grants (high: $27,000; low: $100).
Purpose and activities: Support for higher education and cultural programs, including music.
Limitations: No grants to individuals, no loans or scholarships.
Officers: Edgar R. Berner, Pres.; T. Roland Berner, V.P. and Treas.; Thomas R. Berner, V.P.; Olga Formissano, Secy.
Employer Identification Number: 136111037

2050
Lever Brothers Company Contributions Program
390 Park Ave.
New York 10022 (212) 906-4685

Financial data (yr. ended 12/31/88): Total giving, $149,915, including $85,200 for 27 grants (high: $5,500; low: $100; average: $500-$2,500) and $64,715 for 465 employee matching gifts.
Purpose and activities: Support for a wide range of programs, including culture and the arts, business education, child welfare, civic affairs, civil rights, community development, community funds, conservation, crime and law enforcement, ecology, the disadvantaged, drug abuse, education, employment training, engineering, family services, the handicapped, health, higher education, historic preservation, the homeless, hospitals, hunger, law and justice, libraries, literacy, minorities, museums, music, Native Americans, the performing arts, public affairs, rehabilitation, science and technology, and youth. Provides product donations.
Types of support: Employee matching gifts, general purposes, operating budgets, employee-related scholarships, in-kind gifts.
Limitations: Giving primarily in Baltimore, MD; Commerce, CA; Hammond, IN; St. Louis, MO;

Cartersville, GA; Edgewater and Englewood, NJ; and New York City, NY.
Publications: Application guidelines.
Application information:
Initial approach: Proposal
Copies of proposal: 1
Deadline(s): None
Board meeting date(s): Feb.
Write: Shirley Loxley, Community Affairs Mgr.
Number of staff: 1

2051
Lever Brothers Company Foundation, Inc.
390 Park Ave.
New York 10022 (212) 906-4685

Incorporated in 1952 in NY.
Donor(s): Lever Brothers Co.
Financial data (yr. ended 12/31/88): Assets, $829,591 (M); expenditures, $253,301, including $202,718 for 143 grants (high: $18,500; low: $100; average: $1,000) and $50,097 for 417 employee matching gifts.
Purpose and activities: Grants largely for health and human services, higher education, civil rights, hospitals, community development, civic affairs, and cultural programs.
Types of support: Operating budgets.
Limitations: Giving primarily in areas of company operations in NY, CA, GA, IN, MD, and MO. No support for religious or international organizations. No grants to individuals, or for building funds (except for hospitals) or endowment funds; no loans.
Publications: Application guidelines.
Application information:
Initial approach: Letter or proposal
Copies of proposal: 1
Deadline(s): Dec. 31
Board meeting date(s): Feb.
Final notification: 1 month after meeting
Write: Shirley Loxley, Community Affairs Mgr., Unilever United States, Inc.
Officers: Leonard Gugick,* Pres.; R.L. Marquis, Secy.
Directors:* C.L. Roberts, W.M. Volpi.
Number of staff: 1 part-time professional; 1 part-time support.
Employer Identification Number: 136122117

2052
Levien Foundation
745 Fifth Ave., Suite 605
New York 10151-0016

Established in 1960 in NY.
Financial data (yr. ended 12/31/87): Assets, $1,127,075 (M); expenditures, $47,092.
Purpose and activities: Support primarily for Jewish giving and health agencies and hospitals; grants also for cultural institutions.
Types of support: Research, general purposes.
Limitations: Giving primarily in NY.
Officer: Francis Levien, Mgr.
Employer Identification Number: 136077798

2053
Mortimer Levitt Foundation, Inc.
c/o E. Rubenstein
215 East 68th St.
New York 10021-5718
Application address: 18 East 50th St., New York, NY 10022

Established in 1966 in NY.
Donor(s): Mortimer Levitt, The Custom Shops.
Financial data (yr. ended 2/28/87): Assets, $1,166,551 (M); gifts received, $144,868; expenditures, $45,561, including $45,478 for 64 grants (high: $5,000; low: $50).
Purpose and activities: Support for the arts, including museums, and youth.
Limitations: Giving primarily in New York, NY.
Application information:
Initial approach: Letter
Deadline(s): None
Write: Mortimer Levitt, Pres.
Officers: Mortimer Levitt, Pres.; A. Levitt, V.P. and Secy.; E. Rubenstein, Treas.
Employer Identification Number: 136204678

2054
The Jerome Levy Foundation
c/o Warshaw, Burstein, Cohen, Schlesinger & Kuh
555 Fifth Ave.
New York 10017
Application address: P.O. Box 26, Chappaqua, NY 10514

Trust established in 1955 in NY.
Donor(s): Leon Levy, S. Jay Levy.
Financial data (yr. ended 10/31/87): Assets, $616,763 (M); gifts received, $26,500; expenditures, $587,677, including $565,050 for 30 grants (high: $250,000; low: $50).
Purpose and activities: Grants largely for Jewish welfare funds, the fine arts, and higher education; support also for organizations interested in freedom of expression.
Application information: Contributes only to pre-selected organizations. Applications not accepted.
Write: S. Jay Levy, Trustee
Trustees: Leon Levy, S. Jay Levy.
Employer Identification Number: 136159573

2055
Bertha & Isaac Liberman Foundation
c/o Richard Mark
Peat Marwick & Co., 345 Park Ave.
New York 10154
Application address: 45 East 89th St., New York, NY 10028

Established in 1947 in NY.
Donor(s): Isaac Liberman.†
Financial data (yr. ended 6/30/87): Assets, $3,871,834 (M); gifts received, $1,196,291; expenditures, $105,351, including $99,600 for 9 grants (high: $40,100; low: $1,000).
Purpose and activities: Support for a Young Men's Hebrew Association, higher education, and a Jewish welfare organization.
Types of support: General purposes.
Limitations: No grants to individuals.
Application information:
Deadline(s): None
Write: Jeffrey Klein, Pres.
Officers: Jeffrey Klein, Pres.; Seymour Klein, V.P. and Secy.; Bertha Liberman, Treas.
Employer Identification Number: 136119056

2056
Lindau Foundation, Inc.
Box 329, R.D. 2
Pine City 14871

Established in 1973 in NY.
Financial data (yr. ended 4/30/88): Assets, $1,045,947 (M); expenditures, $101,034, including $93,250 for 29 grants (high: $25,000; low: $500).
Purpose and activities: Emphasis on community funds, cultural programs, hospitals, and education.
Types of support: General purposes.
Limitations: Giving primarily in Elmira, NY.
Application information: Contributes primarily to pre-selected organizations. Applications not accepted.
Officers: Whitney S. Powers, Jr., Pres.; Patricia L. Powers, V.P.; Bela C. Tifft, Secy.
Employer Identification Number: 161020706

2057
Jacques and Yulla Lipchitz Foundation, Inc.
Six East 43rd St.
New York 10017

Established in 1962.
Donor(s): Yulla Lipchitz.
Financial data (yr. ended 2/28/87): Assets, $3,244,425 (M); expenditures, $123.
Purpose and activities: Gifts of works of art by Jacques Lipchitz to various museums.
Application information:
Initial approach: Letter
Write: Hanno D. Mott, V.P.
Officers: Yulla Lipchitz, Pres.; Hanno D. Mott, V.P.
Employer Identification Number: 136151503

2058
Howard and Jean Lipman Foundation, Inc.
522 Fifth Ave.
New York 10036

Established in 1959 in NY.
Donor(s): Howard W. Lipman, Jean Lipman.
Financial data (yr. ended 6/30/88): Assets, $1,098,639 (L); expenditures, $63,613, including $60,750 for 12 grants (high: $25,000; low: $250; average: $5,062).
Purpose and activities: Giving primarily for art museums; support also for hospitals.
Types of support: Endowment funds.
Publications: 990-PF.
Application information: Contributes only to pre-selected organizations. Applications not accepted.
Officers: Howard W. Lipman, Pres.; Peter W. Lipman, V.P.; Charles H. Leavitt, Secy.; Jean Lipman, Treas.
Employer Identification Number: 136066963

2059
The Kenneth & Evelyn Lipper Foundation
112 East 70th St.
New York 10021
Application address: c/o Evelyn Lipper, 375 Park Ave., New York, NY 10152; Tel.: (212) 486-8181

Established about 1982 in NY.
Donor(s): Gruss Petroleum Corp., Evmar Oil Corp., and others.
Financial data (yr. ended 8/31/87): Assets, $834,049 (M); expenditures, $164,767, including $137,275 for 47 grants (high: $20,000; low: $100).
Purpose and activities: Giving primarily for Jewish welfare, education, hospitals and a home for the aged, international affairs, and cultural programs.
Limitations: Giving primarily in NY.
Application information:
Deadline(s): None
Trustees: Evelyn Lipper, Kenneth Lipper.
Employer Identification Number: 133188873

2060
The Lucius N. Littauer Foundation, Inc.
60 East 42nd St., Suite 2910
New York 10165 (212) 697-2677

Incorporated in 1929 in NY.
Donor(s): Lucius N. Littauer.†
Financial data (yr. ended 12/31/87): Assets, $18,150,066 (M); expenditures, $1,398,470, including $1,197,950 for 137 grants (high: $150,000; low: $500).
Purpose and activities: Grants primarily for the social sciences and the humanities; support for higher education with emphasis on Jewish and Middle Eastern studies, and for refugee aid, including resettlement and rehabilitation; other interests include history and biography, language and literature, philosophy, economics, political science, and religion.
Types of support: Research, publications, conferences and seminars, endowment funds, matching funds, fellowships, lectureships, professorships, scholarship funds, special projects.
Limitations: No grants to individuals.
Application information:
Initial approach: Proposal
Copies of proposal: 1
Deadline(s): None
Board meeting date(s): Semiannually and as required
Final notification: 3 months
Write: William Lee Frost, Pres.
Officers and Directors: Harry Starr, Chair.; William Lee Frost, Pres. and Treas.; Issai Hosiosky, V.P. and Secy.; Charles Berlin, Berthold Bilski, George Harris, Henry A. Lowett, Peter J. Solomon.
Number of staff: 1 full-time professional; 1 part-time professional.
Employer Identification Number: 131688027

2061
Frances and John L. Loeb Foundation
c/o Peat Marwick Main Co.
345 Park Ave.
New York 10154 (212) 909-5000

Incorporated in 1937 in NY.
Donor(s): John L. Loeb, Frances L. Loeb.
Financial data (yr. ended 10/31/87): Assets, $4,140,226 (M); gifts received, $1,504,020; expenditures, $399,729, including $386,602 for 166 grants (high: $50,000; low: $100; average: $100-$10,000).
Purpose and activities: Giving for higher education, hospitals and health services, and cultural programs, including museums, and the performing arts; some support also for social services and international activities.
Application information: Contributes only to pre-selected organizations. Applications not accepted.
Officers and Trustees: John L. Loeb, Pres. and Treas.; Frances L. Loeb, V.P.; John L. Loeb, Jr., Secy.; Judith L. Chiara, Arthur L. Loeb.
Number of staff: None.
Employer Identification Number: 136085598

2062
Loews Foundation
One Park Ave., 15th Fl.
New York 10016 (212) 545-2642

Trust established in 1957 in NY.
Donor(s): Loews Corp., and subsidiaries.
Financial data (yr. ended 12/31/87): Assets, $376,476 (M); gifts received, $1,275,000; expenditures, $904,489, including $892,243 for 36 grants (high: $500,000; low: $250; average: $1,000-$25,000) and $12,210 for 90 employee matching gifts.
Purpose and activities: Grants primarily for Jewish welfare funds, higher education, including employee matching gifts and employee-related scholarships through the National Merit Scholarship Corp., and cultural organizations.
Types of support: Employee matching gifts, employee-related scholarships.
Limitations: No grants to individuals.
Application information: Applications for employee-related scholarship program available from foundation.
Deadline(s): None
Board meeting date(s): As required
Write: Daria Mychajluk
Trustees: Preston R. Tisch, Roy Posner, C.G. Sposato, Jr., Laurence A. Tisch.
Employer Identification Number: 136082817

2063
Lucille Lortel Foundation, Inc.
c/o Hecht & Co.
1500 Broadway
New York 10036

Established in 1980 in NY.
Donor(s): Lucille Lortel.
Financial data (yr. ended 6/30/88): Assets, $503,686 (M); expenditures, $173,380, including $159,875 for 40 grants (high: $100,000; low: $75).
Purpose and activities: Support for cultural organizations, including theaters, and libraries.
Limitations: Giving primarily in New York, NY.
Application information: Contributes only to pre-selected organizations. Applications not accepted.
Officers: Lucille Lortel, Pres.; Michael Hecht, Secy.-Treas.
Employer Identification Number: 133036521

2064
The Henry Luce Foundation, Inc.
111 West 50th St., Rm. 3710
New York 10020 (212) 489-7700

Incorporated in 1936 in NY.
Donor(s): Henry R. Luce.†
Financial data (yr. ended 12/31/88): Assets, $350,227,791 (M); gifts received, $580,621; expenditures, $15,426,000, including $13,321,266 for 186 grants (high: $1,000,000; low: $3,000; average: $25,000-$300,000) and $293,203 for 15 grants to individuals.
Purpose and activities: Grants for specific projects in the broad areas of Asian affairs, higher education and scholarship, theology, the arts, and public affairs. The Luce Scholars Program gives a select group of young Americans, not Asian specialists, a year's work/study experience in the East and Southeast Asia. The Henry R. Luce Professorship Program provides five- or eight-year support for a limited number of integrative academic programs in the humanities and social sciences at private colleges and universities. Funding in the arts focuses on research and scholarship in American art; direct support for specific projects at major museums throughout the country; dissertation support to selected university departments of art history. The Luce Fund for Southeast Asian Studies offers support to an invited group of ten American universities on a competitive basis to improve the quality of Southeast Asian Studies. The United States-China Cooperative Research Program is a competitive grant program to encourage thematic research projects jointly directed by American and Chinese Scholars.
Types of support: Seed money, special projects, research, professorships, internships, exchange programs.
Limitations: Giving for international activities limited to East and Southeast Asia. No support for journalism or media projects. No grants to individuals (except for the Luce Scholars Program), or for endowment or domestic building funds, general operating support, scholarships, or fellowships, annual fund drives; no loans.
Publications: Annual report, informational brochure.
Application information: Nominees for scholars programs accepted from institutions only; individual applications cannot be considered; Luce Fund for Southeast Asian Studies by invitation only; American Art proposals by invitation only.
Initial approach: Letter
Copies of proposal: 1
Deadline(s): Apr. 1, Henry R. Luce Professorship; June 15, American Art; 1st Monday in Dec., Luce Scholar nominations; Oct. 3, Luce Fund for

Southeast Asian Studies; Jan. 15, U.S.-China Cooperative Research; none, program grants
Board meeting date(s): June, Sept., and Dec.
Final notification: 1 month to 1 year; program grants awarded in late fall and end of year
Write: Robert E. Armstrong, Exec. Dir.
Officers and Directors: Henry Luce III, Pres.; Robert E. Armstrong, V.P. and Exec. Dir.; John C. Evans, V.P. and Secy.-Treas.; Mrs. Maurice T. Moore, V.P.; Margaret Boles Fitzgerald, James I. McCord, Thomas L. Pulling, David V. Ragone, Charles C. Tillinghast, Jr.
Number of staff: 6 full-time professional; 4 full-time support.
Employer Identification Number: 136001282
Recent arts and culture grants:
Archives of American Art of the Smithsonian Institution, DC, $150,000. To provide further support for Archives' expanded regional collection activities. 12/9/87.
Boston University, Department of Art History, Boston, MA, $75,000. To provide further support for dissertation fellowships in American art. 12/9/87.
City University of New York, Graduate School and University Center, Department of Art History, NYC, NY, $120,000. To provide further support for dissertation fellowships in American art. 12/9/87.
Columbia University, Department of Art History, NYC, NY, $120,000. To provide further support for dissertation fellowships in American art. 12/9/87.
Harvard University, Fine Arts Library, Cambridge, MA, $50,000. To support photographic exchange between American and Chinese art museums. 12/9/87.
Harvard University, John King Fairbank Center for East Asian Research, Cambridge, MA, $25,000. To support completion of two research projects by Professor John K. Fairbank: Cambridge History of China and Robert Hart's China Journal. 6/9/88.
Honolulu Academy of Arts, Honolulu, HI, $38,000. To support research and planning for exhibition and catalogue, Ke Ola 'O Ka 'Aina/The Life of the Land. 12/9/87.
Metropolitan Museum of Art, NYC, NY, $1,000,000. To augment earlier award for Henry R. Luce Center for Study of American Art by providing for computerization of facility and for development of educational materials and programs. 12/9/87.
Municipal Art Society, NYC, NY, $100,000. To support program agenda for 1988 and 1989. 12/9/87.
National Gallery of Art, DC, $175,000. For preparation and publication of catalogue, Eighteenth and Nineteenth Century American Paintings. 3/31/88.
New York Landmarks Conservancy, NYC, NY, $75,000. For Conservancy's Religious Properties Program. 6/09/88.
Stanford University, Department of Art History, Palo Alto, CA, $75,000. To provide further support for dissertation fellowships in American art. 12/9/87.
University of Delaware, Department of Art History, Newark, DE, $120,000. To provide further support for dissertation fellowships in American art. 12/9/87.
University of Michigan, Department of the History of Art, Ann Arbor, MI, $75,000. To provide further support for dissertation fellowships in American art. 12/9/87.
University of San Francisco, Institute for Chinese-Western Cultural History, San Francisco, CA, $180,000. For activities of Institute for Chinese-Western Cultural History. 6/09/88.
Yale University, Department of Art History, New Haven, CT, $120,000. To provide further support for dissertation fellowships in American art. 12/9/87.

2065
MacAndrews and Forbes Foundation
36 East 63rd St.
New York 10021

Established in 1982 in NY.
Donor(s): MacAndrews & Forbes Co., MacAndrews & Forbes Group, Technicolor, Inc., Wilbur Chocolate Co.
Financial data (yr. ended 12/31/87): Assets, $81,938 (M); gifts received, $1,707,394; expenditures, $1,881,813, including $1,881,537 for 53 grants (high: $559,594; low: $75; average: $500-$50,000).
Purpose and activities: Support for jewish giving, health services, culture, and higher education.
Limitations: Giving primarily in New York, NY.
Application information:
Initial approach: Letter
Deadline(s): None
Write: Richard E. Halperin, Pres.
Officers: Richard E. Halperin,* Pres.; Fred L. Tepperman,* V.P. and Treas.; Frederick W. McNabb, Jr., Secy.
Directors:* Ronald O. Perelman, Bruce Slovin.
Employer Identification Number: 133116648

2066
James A. Macdonald Foundation
One North Broadway
White Plains 10601 (914) 428-9305

Incorporated in 1966 in NY.
Donor(s): Flora Macdonald Bonney.†
Financial data (yr. ended 12/31/87): Assets, $4,638,952 (M); expenditures, $349,302, including $305,387 for 265 grants (high: $25,000; low: $100; average: $200-$600) and $48,000 for 2 loans.
Purpose and activities: Emphasis on Protestant church support, secondary education, community funds, hospitals, youth agencies, and historic preservation.
Types of support: Operating budgets, continuing support, annual campaigns, seed money, emergency funds, building funds, equipment, land acquisition, endowment funds, scholarship funds, special projects, research, fellowships, renovation projects.
Limitations: Giving primarily in NY. No grants to individuals or for matching gifts; no loans.
Application information:
Initial approach: Letter
Copies of proposal: 1
Deadline(s): None
Board meeting date(s): Irregularly, but at least quarterly
Write: Walter J. Handelman, Secy.
Officers: Blanche B. Handelman,* Pres.; Walter J. Handelman,* Secy.; Alan L. Model, Treas.
Directors:* Alice H. Model.
Number of staff: None.
Employer Identification Number: 136199690

2067
The Macmillan Foundation
866 Third Ave.
New York 10022

Incorporated in 1967 in DE.
Donor(s): Macmillan, Inc.
Financial data (yr. ended 12/31/86): Assets, $2,880,799 (M); expenditures, $146,512, including $114,466 for grants.
Purpose and activities: Emphasis on cultural organizations, including the performing arts and libraries, and higher education.
Types of support: General purposes, operating budgets, annual campaigns, endowment funds.
Limitations: Giving primarily in NY, particularly in the New York City metropolitan area. No grants to individuals, or for building funds, scholarships, fellowships, or matching gifts; no loans.
Application information:
Initial approach: Proposal
Copies of proposal: 1
Deadline(s): None
Board meeting date(s): As required
Final notification: 2 months
Write: Philip E. Hoversten, V.P.
Officers: Edward P. Evans,* Chair. and Pres.; Philip E. Hoversten, V.P., Finance; William F. Reilly, V.P.; Beverly C. Chell, Secy.; Richard Marangelo, Treas.
Directors:* William R. Reilly.
Number of staff: None.
Employer Identification Number: 136260248

2068
Josiah Macy, Jr. Foundation
44 East 64th St.
New York 10021 (212) 486-2424

Incorporated in 1930 in NY.
Donor(s): Kate Macy Ladd.†
Financial data (yr. ended 6/30/88): Assets, $87,836,555 (M); expenditures, $4,602,007, including $2,928,411 for 41 grants (high: $275,000; low: $1,000; average: $20,000-$200,000), $68,110 for 37 employee matching gifts and $50,000 for 1 foundation-administered program.
Purpose and activities: Major interest in medicine and health. Major grant programs are Minorities in Medicine, Medical Education, with emphasis on improving its effectiveness, and training of physicians and other health care professionals; support also for Macy Conferences, usually on issues relevant to current program areas.
Types of support: Special projects.
Limitations: No grants to individuals, or for travel, capital or endowment funds, operating budgets, annual fund appeals, seed money, emergency funds, deficit financing, research, publications, conferences not run by the

foundation, scholarships, or fellowships; no loans.
Publications: Annual report, informational brochure (including application guidelines).
Application information: The Pathobiology Program has been discontinued.
Initial approach: Letter
Copies of proposal: 1
Deadline(s): None
Board meeting date(s): Jan., May, and Sept.
Final notification: Within 1 month
Write: Thomas H. Meikle, Jr., M.D., Pres.
Officers: Clarence F. Michalis,* Chair.; Thomas H. Meikle, Jr.,* Pres.; Maxine E. Bleich, V.P.; Rina Forlini, Secy.-Treas.
Directors:* Lawrence K. Altman, Harold Amos, Louis Auchincloss, Alexander G. Bearn, E. Virgil Conway, Charles B. Finch, S. Parker Gilbert, Patricia A. Graham, Bernard W. Harleston, Lawrence S. Huntington, David L. Luke III, Mary Patterson McPherson, Walter N. Rothschild, Jr.
Number of staff: 3 full-time professional; 5 full-time support.
Employer Identification Number: 135596895
Recent arts and culture grants:
New York Hall of Science, Biology Department, Corona, NY, $300,000. To support development of biology exhibition, What Is A Germ. 9/16/87.

2069
The Russell Maguire Foundation, Inc.
c/o Berman and Hecht
Ten East 40th St., Rm. 710
New York 10016
Additional address: 74 Harbor Dr., Greenwich, CT 06830

Incorporated in 1941 in NY.
Donor(s): Russell Maguire,† and others.
Financial data (yr. ended 12/31/87): Assets, $2,948,001 (M); expenditures, $252,953, including $152,545 for 64 grants (high: $21,500; low: $40).
Purpose and activities: Emphasis on arts and cultural programs; support also for a community fund, education, health associations, and social service agencies.
Limitations: Giving primarily in NY and CT.
Application information:
Write: Elizabeth Gale, Dir.
Directors: F. Richards Ford III, Natasha B. Ford, Elizabeth S. Gale, Suzanne S. Maguire.
Employer Identification Number: 136162698

2070
A. L. Mailman Family Foundation, Inc.
707 Westchester Ave.
White Plains 10604 (914) 681-4448

Foundation established in 1976 in FL as The Dr. Marilyn M. Segal Foundation, Inc.
Donor(s): Abraham L. Mailman,† The Mailman Foundation, Inc.
Financial data (yr. ended 12/31/87): Assets, $12,803,902 (M); gifts received, $32,212; expenditures, $853,311, including $687,816 for 25 grants (high: $50,000; low: $5,000).
Purpose and activities: Support primarily for programs committed to the preservation and strengthening of the family, with a special interest in children and youth who are disadvantaged by socio-economic status, race, and emotional or physical disabilities; giving also for educational efforts to stimulate moral and intellectual growth and the development of social responsibility; and for research in and refinement of developmental, individualized education.
Types of support: Seed money, matching funds, special projects, research, publications, technical assistance.
Limitations: No grants to individuals, or for operating budgets, capital or endowment funds, continuing support, annual campaigns, emergency funds, or deficit financing.
Publications: Annual report.
Application information:
Initial approach: Letter
Copies of proposal: 1
Deadline(s): Submit proposal preferably in Sept. and Feb.; deadline Mar. 1 and Oct. 1
Board meeting date(s): Jan. and June
Final notification: 5 months
Write: Luba H. Lynch, Secy.
Officers: Marilyn M. Segal, Chair.; Richard D. Segal,* Pres.; Luba H. Lynch, Secy.; Kurt Lichten,* Treas.
Trustees:* Betty S. Bardige, Vito G. DiCristina, Jonathan R. Gordon, Jay B. Langner, Patricia S. Lieberman, Wendy S. Masi.
Number of staff: 1 full-time professional; 1 full-time support; 1 part-time support.
Employer Identification Number: 510203866
Recent arts and culture grants:
Childrens Museum of Manhattan, NYC, NY, $10,000. For High School Internship Program. Interns become directly involved with research, design, construction and preparation of museum exhibits, help with clerical responsibilities and learn to work with groups of children. 1987.

2071
The Mailman Foundation, Inc.
460 Park Ave.
New York 10022 (212) 751-7171

Incorporated in 1943 in DE.
Donor(s): Joseph L. Mailman, Abraham L. Mailman.†
Financial data (yr. ended 12/31/87): Assets, $4,122,028 (M); expenditures, $499,169, including $498,771 for 83 grants (high: $100,000; low: $30).
Purpose and activities: Support for Jewish welfare funds, hospitals, higher education, temple support, and the arts.
Publications: Annual report.
Application information: Contributes only to pre-selected organizations. Applications not accepted.
Write: Vito G. DiCristina, Secy.-Treas.
Officers and Trustees: Joseph L. Mailman, Pres.; Phyllis Mailman, V.P.; Vito G. DiCristina, Secy.-Treas.; Joseph S. Mailman, Joshua L. Mailman, Joan M. Wolfe.
Employer Identification Number: 136161556

2072
The Mandeville Foundation, Inc.
230 Park Ave.
New York 10169 (212) 697-4785

Incorporated in 1963 in CT.
Donor(s): Ernest W. Mandeville.
Financial data (yr. ended 12/31/87): Assets, $6,177,767 (M); expenditures, $843,657, including $598,135 for 63 grants (high: $118,960; low: $200; average: $1,000-$15,000).
Purpose and activities: Giving primarily for higher and secondary education, cultural programs, and social service agencies.
Limitations: Giving primarily in NY and CT.
Application information:
Deadline(s): None
Final notification: 90 days
Write: Hubert T. Mandeville, Pres.
Officers: Hubert T. Mandeville, Pres.; P. Kempton Mandeville, V.P.
Directors: Maurice C. Greenbaum, Meredith H. Hollis, Deborah S. Mandeville.
Number of staff: 2
Employer Identification Number: 066043343

2073
Meyer & Min Manischewitz Foundation, Inc.
c/o Robert A. Mann
785 Fifth Ave.
New York 10022-1051

Established in 1965 in NY.
Financial data (yr. ended 12/31/87): Assets, $1,509,409 (M); expenditures, $61,166, including $57,675 for 69 grants (high: $6,000; low: $100).
Purpose and activities: Support primarily for arts and culture, social services, and Jewish organizations.
Limitations: Giving primarily in NY and CA. No grants to individuals.
Application information: Contributes only to pre-selected organizations. Applications not accepted.
Officers and Directors: Robert A. Mann, Pres.; Gerald Barrett, Secy.; Alan Bralower.
Employer Identification Number: 136185013

2074
Manufacturers Hanover Foundation
270 Park Ave.
New York 10017 (212) 286-7124

Trust established in 1956 in NY.
Donor(s): Manufacturers Hanover Trust Co.
Financial data (yr. ended 12/31/87): Assets, $15,165,933 (M); expenditures, $1,167,101, including $611,500 for 11 grants (high: $341,500; low: $10,000; average: $10,000-$50,000) and $484,507 for 1,648 employee matching gifts.
Purpose and activities: Interests include a community fund, higher and secondary education, hospitals, cultural programs, youth agencies, public policy and community development organizations, and health agencies.
Types of support: Employee matching gifts, annual campaigns, building funds, endowment funds, general purposes, continuing support.

Limitations: Giving primarily in areas in which the company operates, primarily the New York, NY, metropolitan area. No support for private foundations. No grants to individuals, or for scholarships, fellowships, or special projects; no loans.
Publications: Annual report.
Application information:
Initial approach: Letter
Copies of proposal: 1
Deadline(s): Submit proposal preferably between Sept. and Dec.; deadline Mar. 31
Board meeting date(s): May
Final notification: June 1
Write: Matthew Trachtenberg, Agent
Advisory Committee: John F. McGillicuddy, Chair.
Trustee: Manufacturers Hanover Trust Co.
Employer Identification Number: 136143284

2075
Marble Fund, Inc.
200 Park Ave., Rm. 4406
New York 10166-0001 (212) 687-0466

Established in 1952 in NY.
Donor(s): M. William Levy, Marion H. Levy, Caryn L. Magid.
Financial data (yr. ended 12/31/87): Assets, $469,720 (M); gifts received, $199,486; expenditures, $136,860, including $134,261 for 131 grants (high: $25,000; low: $25).
Purpose and activities: Giving for education, health and medical research, community and rural development, the performing arts, and the environment and wildlife conservation.
Types of support: Annual campaigns, building funds, capital campaigns, general purposes, research, seed money, technical assistance.
Limitations: Giving primarily in NY.
Application information:
Initial approach: Letter
Deadline(s): None
Write: Marion H. Levy, Pres.
Officers: Marion H. Levy, Pres.; William G. Levy, V.P.; Caryn L. Magid, V.P.; M. William Levy, Secy.-Treas.
Number of staff: 2 part-time support.
Employer Identification Number: 136084387

2076
James S. Marcus Foundation
c/o Goldman, Sachs & Co.
85 Broad St., Tax Dept.
New York 10004

Established in 1969.
Donor(s): James S. Marcus.
Financial data (yr. ended 5/31/87): Assets, $1,518,345 (M); expenditures, $79,129, including $74,697 for 71 grants (high: $2,000; low: $100).
Purpose and activities: Giving for the arts and cultural programs, particularly opera; some support for health agencies, social services, and higher education.
Limitations: Giving primarily in NY. No grants to individuals.
Application information: Presently not receiving applications; contributes only to pre-selected organizations.
Trustees: H. Frederick Krimendahl II, Ellen F. Marcus, James S. Marcus.
Employer Identification Number: 237044611

2077
Joseph Martinson Memorial Fund
c/o Phillips, Nizer, Benjamin, Krim & Ballon
40 West 57th St.
New York 10019

Trust established in 1950 in NY.
Donor(s): Joseph B. Martinson.†
Financial data (yr. ended 12/31/87): Assets, $1,600,000 (M); expenditures, $120,000, including $100,000 for 75 grants.
Purpose and activities: Support largely for the performing arts and museums.
Limitations: Giving primarily in NY, VT, AZ, and CT. No grants to individuals.
Application information:
Write: Paul Martinson, Trustee
Trustees: Paul Martinson, Howard Graff, Frances Sirota, Citibank, N.A.
Employer Identification Number: 136161532

2078
The Richard Mather Fund
c/o Key Trust Co.
201 South Warren St.
Syracuse 13202 (315) 470-5222
Additional address: c/o W.L. Broad, Box 4967, Syracuse, NY 13221

Trust established in 1955 in NY.
Donor(s): Flora Mather Hosmer,† R.C. Hosmer, Jr.,† Hosmer Descendants Trust.
Financial data (yr. ended 12/31/87): Assets, $2,206,000 (M); gifts received, $16,900; expenditures, $157,000, including $127,000 for 16 grants (high: $40,000; low: $100; average: $1,000-$5,000).
Purpose and activities: Emphasis on cultural organizations.
Types of support: Capital campaigns, continuing support, endowment funds, general purposes, matching funds, publications, special projects.
Limitations: Giving primarily in central NY, with emphasis on Syracuse. No grants to individuals; no loans.
Publications: Informational brochure (including application guidelines).
Application information: Funds substantially committed.
Initial approach: Letter; mass mail solicitations not considered
Copies of proposal: 1
Board meeting date(s): As required
Write: John S. Hancock, Trustee
Trustees: William L. Broad, John S. Hancock, S. Sterling McMillan III, Elizabeth H. Schaefer.
Number of staff: None.
Employer Identification Number: 156018423

2079
Mathis-Pfohl Foundation
5-46 46th Ave.
Long Island City 11101 (718) 784-4800

Incorporated in 1947 in IA.
Donor(s): Members of the Pfohl family and associated companies.
Financial data (yr. ended 11/30/86): Assets, $2,747,716 (M); gifts received, $28,000; expenditures, $113,969, including $106,525 for 82 grants (high: $25,000; low: $100).
Purpose and activities: Grants for higher and secondary education, hospitals and health organizations, religious institutions, social service and youth agencies, and cultural programs.
Application information:
Initial approach: Letter
Deadline(s): None
Board meeting date(s): As required
Write: Ann Pfohl Kirby, V.P.
Officers: James M. Pfohl, Pres.; Ann Pfohl Kirby, V.P. and Secy.; Lynn P. Quigley, V.P. and Treas.
Employer Identification Number: 116013764

2080
Hale Matthews Foundation
100 Park Ave., 33rd Fl.
New York 10017

Established in 1963.
Donor(s): Hale Matthews.†
Financial data (yr. ended 12/31/87): Assets, $1,687,411 (M); expenditures, $129,389, including $115,000 for 12 grants (high: $25,000; low: $1,000; average: $7,500).
Purpose and activities: Giving for the theatre and the performing arts, and medical and general charitable purposes.
Types of support: Matching funds, fellowships, general purposes.
Limitations: Giving primarily in NY.
Application information: Applications not accepted.
Officers and Trustees: William N. Ashbey, Pres.; Frances G. Scaife, V.P.; Helen Brann, Secy.; Richard G. Hewitt, Treas.
Employer Identification Number: 136157267

2081
Edelman Division Matz Foundation
253 Broadway
New York 10007

Trust established in 1970 in NY as one of two successor trusts to the Matz Foundation.
Donor(s): Israel Matz.†
Financial data (yr. ended 6/30/86): Assets, $2,200,376 (M); expenditures, $195,718, including $168,325 for 33 grants (high: $75,075; low: $500).
Purpose and activities: Emphasis on Jewish welfare funds and cultural institutions, higher and other education, and health services.
Limitations: Giving primarily in NY.
Trustees: Ethel M. Edelman.
Employer Identification Number: 237082997

2082
Israel Matz Foundation
14 East Fourth St., Rm. 403
New York 10012

Trust established in 1925 in NY.
Donor(s): Israel Matz.†
Financial data (yr. ended 12/31/87): Assets, $1,578,685 (M); expenditures, $157,670.
Purpose and activities: To extend financial grants-in-aid to indigent Hebrew scholars, writers, and public workers and their dependents, primarily in Israel; also to publish Hebrew classics and to advance Hebrew literature and culture.
Types of support: Grants to individuals, publications.
Limitations: Giving primarily in Israel and in New York City.
Application information:
Initial approach: Letter
Deadline(s): 6 months before needed
Write: Dr. Milton Arfa, Chair.
Officers and Trustees: Milton Arfa, Chair.; Rivka Friedman, Exec. Secy.; Zvi Almog, Sidney D. Braun, Abraham S. Halkin, Hayim Leaf, Shlomo Sharan.
Employer Identification Number: 136121533

2083
Helen Mayer Charitable Trust
c/o Norstar Trust Co.
One East Ave.
Rochester 14638

Established in 1959 in NY.
Donor(s): Helen Shumway Mayer.
Financial data (yr. ended 11/30/87): Assets, $839,689 (M); gifts received, $315,011; expenditures, $260,959, including $258,625 for 27 grants (high: $25,000; low: $350).
Purpose and activities: Grants for religious support, historic preservation, and culture.
Application information: Contributes only to pre-selected organizations. Applications not accepted.
Trustees: Helen Shumway Mayer, Norstar Trust Co.
Employer Identification Number: 166022958

2084
The Louis B. Mayer Foundation
One Battery Park Plaza, 29th Fl.
New York 10004 (212) 908-2713

Trust established in 1947 in CA.
Donor(s): Louis B. Mayer.†
Financial data (yr. ended 12/31/87): Assets, $6,398,575 (M); expenditures, $1,465,198, including $1,306,000 for 11 grants (high: $1,000,000; low: $7,000; average: $20,000-$50,000).
Purpose and activities: Support for basic innovation, research, and development in areas of education, arts, letters, and medicine.
Types of support: Building funds, continuing support, endowment funds, equipment, internships, operating budgets, professorships, renovation projects, research, seed money, special projects.
Limitations: No grants to individuals; no loans.
Application information:
Initial approach: Letter, proposal, or telephone
Copies of proposal: 1
Deadline(s): Submit proposal between Mar. 1 and Dec. 30
Board meeting date(s): Quarterly
Write: Kathy Foer
Officers and Trustees: Irene Mayer Selznick, Pres; Thomas J. McGrath, V.P.; Lewis H. Lapham, Secy.; Carol Farkas, Treas.; Jeffrey Selznick.
Number of staff: None.
Employer Identification Number: 952232340

2085
William and Helen Mazer Foundation, Inc.
c/o Cohen and Randall
1100 Franklin Ave.
Garden City 11530 (516) 877-2720

Incorporated in 1979 in NY.
Donor(s): Abraham Mazer Family Fund, Inc., William Mazer.
Financial data (yr. ended 9/30/87): Assets, $1,067,524 (M); expenditures, $151,379, including $147,789 for 96 grants (high: $47,000; low: $10).
Purpose and activities: Emphasis on higher education, including medical education, and hospitals; support also for the performing arts, Jewish welfare organizations, and a peace fund.
Application information:
Initial approach: Letter
Deadline(s): None
Write: William Mazer, Pres.
Officers and Directors: William Mazer, Pres. and Treas.; Helen Mazer, V.P. and Secy.; Norman H. Cohen.
Employer Identification Number: 133029517

2086
James J. McCann Charitable Trust and McCann Foundation, Inc.
(also known as McCann Foundation)
35 Market St.
Poughkeepsie 12601 (914) 452-3085

McCann Foundation, Inc. established in NY in 1967; trust established in 1969 in NY; foundations function as single unit and financial data is combined.
Donor(s): James J. McCann.†
Financial data (yr. ended 12/31/87): Assets, $23,512,105 (M); expenditures, $1,591,982, including $1,305,431 for grants.
Purpose and activities: Giving primarily for secondary and higher education (including scholarship funds), recreation, civic projects, social services, cultural programs, church support and religious associations, and hospitals.
Types of support: Continuing support, annual campaigns, seed money, building funds, equipment, land acquisition, scholarship funds, fellowships, publications, conferences and seminars.
Limitations: Giving limited to Poughkeepsie and Dutchess County, NY. No grants to individuals, or for operating budgets, emergency or endowment funds, deficit financing, or matching gifts; no loans.
Publications: Annual report.
Application information:
Initial approach: Letter or proposal
Copies of proposal: 1
Deadline(s): Submit proposal preferably in Feb. or Aug.; no deadline
Board meeting date(s): Jan. and July
Final notification: 60 days
Write: John J. Gartland, Jr., Pres.
Officers and Trustees:* John J. Gartland, Jr.,* Pres.; William L. Gardner, Jr.,* V.P.; Richard V. Corbally, Secy.
Number of staff: 1 part-time professional; 1 full-time support.
Employer Identification Number: 146050628

2087
The Michael W. McCarthy Foundation
World Financial Ctr., South Tower
New York 10080

Trust established in 1958 in NY.
Donor(s): Michael W. McCarthy, Margaret E. McCarthy.
Financial data (yr. ended 12/31/87): Assets, $2,269,802 (M); expenditures, $166,520, including $143,491 for 17 grants (high: $98,366; low: $225).
Purpose and activities: Support largely for higher education and for Roman Catholic church support and religious associations.
Application information: Contributes only to pre-selected organizations. Applications not accepted.
Trustee: Michael W. McCarthy.
Employer Identification Number: 136150919

2088
Frederick McDonald Trust
c/o Norstar Trust Company
69 State St.
Albany 12201 (518) 447-4189

Established in 1950.
Donor(s): Frederick McDonald.
Financial data (yr. ended 12/31/88): Assets, $1,000,860 (M); expenditures, $131,878, including $129,500 for 33 grants (high: $20,000; low: $1,000; average: $2,000-$4,000).
Purpose and activities: Giving primarily for hospitals and health agencies; support also for youth agencies and a community fund.
Types of support: Annual campaigns, equipment, operating budgets.
Limitations: Giving limited to Albany, NY. No grants to individuals.
Application information: Application form required.
Deadline(s): Oct. 1
Write: R.F. Galvin, Sr. Trust Officer
Trustee: Norstar Trust Company.
Number of staff: None.
Employer Identification Number: 146014233

2089
Dextra Baldwin McGonagle Foundation, Inc.
445 Park Ave.
New York 10022 (212) 758-8970
Additional address: 40 Crossing at Blind Brook, Purchase, NY 10577-2210

Incorporated in 1967 in NY.
Donor(s): Mrs. Dextra Baldwin McGonagle.†
Financial data (yr. ended 12/31/88): Assets, $6,937,921 (M); expenditures, $361,741, including $289,600 for 80 grants (high: $51,500; low: $25; average: $2,000).
Purpose and activities: Support for hospitals and higher education; grants also for social service agencies, religious organizations, and cultural programs.
Types of support: Annual campaigns, seed money, building funds, equipment, research, endowment funds.
Limitations: Giving primarily in NY and CA. No grants to individuals, or for matching gifts.
Application information: Applications not accepted.
Board meeting date(s): As required
Write: David B. Spanier, Pres.
Officers and Directors: Maury L. Spanier, Chair.; David B. Spanier, Pres.; Helen G. Spanier, V.P. and Secy.-Treas.
Number of staff: 3 part-time support.
Employer Identification Number: 136219236

2090
The Donald C. McGraw Foundation, Inc.

46 Summit Ave.
Bronxville 10708 (914) 779-1682

Incorporated in 1963 in NY.
Donor(s): Donald C. McGraw.†
Financial data (yr. ended 1/31/88): Assets, $4,828,818 (L); gifts received, $145,369; expenditures, $312,039, including $308,000 for 33 grants (high: $50,000; low: $1,000).
Purpose and activities: Grants largely for hospitals and medical research, education, church support, cultural programs, and social service agencies.
Limitations: Giving primarily in NY and NJ.
Application information:
Initial approach: Letter
Deadline(s): None
Write: John L. Cady, V.P.
Officers and Directors: Donald C. McGraw, Jr., Pres.; John L. Cady, V.P. and Secy.; John L. McGraw, V.P. and Treas.
Employer Identification Number: 136165603

2091
The McGraw-Hill Foundation, Inc.

1221 Ave. of the Americas
New York 10020 (212) 512-6113

Incorporated in 1978 in NY.
Donor(s): McGraw-Hill, Inc.
Financial data (yr. ended 12/31/88): Assets, $63,505 (M); gifts received, $1,880,000; expenditures, $1,844,355, including $974,912 for 139 grants (high: $145,000; low: $100; average: $1,000-$5,000) and $867,837 for 3,773 employee matching gifts.
Purpose and activities: Program emphasis is on education; significant support also given in the areas of health and welfare, arts and cultural organizations, and civic activities.
Types of support: General purposes, operating budgets, continuing support, annual campaigns, seed money, emergency funds, special projects, research, scholarship funds, employee-related scholarships, exchange programs, fellowships, matching funds, employee matching gifts.
Limitations: Giving limited to areas of company operations, or to national organizations. No support for religious or political organizations or United Way member agencies. No grants to individuals, or for capital, building, or endowment funds, conferences, travel, courtesy advertising, films, or publications; no loans.
Publications: Application guidelines.
Application information:
Initial approach: Proposal
Copies of proposal: 1
Deadline(s): None
Board meeting date(s): Quarterly
Final notification: 4-6 weeks
Write: Susan A. Wallman, Admin.
Officers: Mary A. Cooper,* Pres.; Frank D. Penglase, V.P. and Treas.; Susan A. Wallman, Admin. and Secy.
Directors:* Kay Knight Clarke, Frank J. Kaufman, Robert N. Landes, Donald S. Rubin, Ralph R. Schulz, Thomas J. Sullivan.
Number of staff: 2 full-time professional; 1 full-time support; 1 part-time support.
Employer Identification Number: 132955464

2092
McGraw-Hill, Inc. Corporate Giving Program

1221 Ave. of the Americas
New York 10020 (212) 512-6113

Financial data (yr. ended 12/31/88): Total giving, $10,015,860, including $2,245,860 for grants and $7,770,000 for in-kind gifts.
Purpose and activities: Support for the arts and culture, dance, education, including educational associations and educational research, fine arts, libraries, literacy, museums, performing arts, theater, and volunteerism.
Types of support: Continuing support, in-kind gifts.
Application information: Applications not accepted.
Write: Susan A. Wallman, Admin.
Number of staff: 2 full-time professional; 1 full-time support; 1 part-time support.

2093
The Andrew W. Mellon Foundation

140 East 62nd St.
New York 10021 (212) 838-8400

Trust established in 1940 in DE as Avalon Foundation; incorporated in 1954 in NY; merged with Old Dominion Foundation and renamed The Andrew W. Mellon Foundation in 1969.
Donor(s): Ailsa Mellon Bruce,† Paul Mellon.
Financial data (yr. ended 12/31/88): Assets, $1,558,000,000 (M); expenditures, $59,794,884 for 208 grants (high: $3,250,000; low: $5,000; average: $25,000-$800,000).
Purpose and activities: Grants on selective basis in higher education, cultural affairs, including historic preservation, the humanities, museums, performing arts, population, and in certain environmental and public affairs areas. Graduate fellowship program in the humanities administered by the Woodrow Wilson National Fellowship Foundation, which makes all awards. The foundation is reviewing its areas of programmatic activity. Though no substantial change in the general designation of those areas is expected, there may well be shifts of focus and purpose within the individual areas.
Types of support: Continuing support, endowment funds, research, internships, fellowships, matching funds, special projects.
Limitations: No support for primarily local organizations. No grants to individuals (including scholarships and fellowships); no loans.
Publications: Annual report (including application guidelines).
Application information:
Initial approach: Descriptive letter or proposal
Copies of proposal: 1
Deadline(s): None
Board meeting date(s): Mar., June, Oct., and Dec.
Final notification: After board meetings
Write: Neil L. Rudenstine, Exec. V.P.
Officers: William G. Bowen,* Pres.; Neil L. Rudenstine, Exec. V.P.; James M. Morris, Secy.; Kenneth J. Herr, Treas.
Trustees:* William O. Baker, Chair.; William G. Bowen, Charles E. Exley, Jr., Hanna Holborn Gray, Timothy Mellon, Arjay Miller, Frank H.T. Rhodes, Charles A. Ryskamp, John R. Stevenson, John C. Whitehead.
Number of staff: 9 full-time professional; 14 full-time support.
Employer Identification Number: 131879954
Recent arts and culture grants:
American Academy in Rome, NYC, NY, $250,000. To support postdoctoral fellowships in School of Classical Studies. 10/7/87.
American Council of Learned Societies, NYC, NY, $1,500,000. For matching endowment in support of IREX. 1988.
American Council of Learned Societies, NYC, NY, $1,000,000. Toward editorial costs of American National Biography. 1988.
American Council of Learned Societies, NYC, NY, $400,000. To support IREX-sponsored collaborative programs between American and East European scholars in humanities and social sciences. 1988.
American Dance Festival, NYC, NY, $95,000. To develop and extend its artistic activity. 12/17/87.
Carnegie-Mellon University, Mellon Institute, Pittsburgh, PA, $855,000. To support Research Center on Materials of the Artist and Conservator. 1988.
Colorado Dance Festival, Boulder, CO, $45,000. To develop and extend its artistic activity. 12/17/87.
Columbia University, Avery Library, NYC, NY, $100,000. To create on videodisc computerized catalogue of architectural drawings. 1988.
Columbia University, Research Center for Arts and Culture, NYC, NY, $165,000. For Artist Training and Career Project. 1988.
Council for Basic Education, DC, $180,000. For fellowship program in humanities for secondary school teachers. 1988.

Dance USA, DC, $75,000. For series of archive-management and preservation workshops. 1988.
Detroit Institute of Arts, Detroit, MI, $400,000. For matching endowment in support of research and publication of substantial scholary quality. 10/7/87.
Eugene ONeill Memorial Theater Center, Waterford, CT, $75,000. To develop and extend its artistic activity. 12/17/87.
Foundation of the American Institute for Conservation of Historic and Artistic Works, DC, $25,000. Toward costs of publishing papers from Gilding Conservation Symposium. 1988.
Frick Collection, NYC, NY, $25,000. To improve bibliographic services in its Arts Reference Library. 1988.
Great Lakes Theater Festival, Cleveland, OH, $95,000. To develop and extend its artistic activity. 12/17/87.
Harvard University, Cambridge, MA, $1,650,000. For program of Mellon Faculty Fellowships in Humanities. 10/7/87.
Historical Society of Pennsylvania, Philadelphia, PA, $175,000. For matching grant to promote access to and use of its collections. 10/7/87.
Huntington Library, Art Gallery and Botanical Garden, San Marino, CA, $150,000. For matching grant in form of endowment to promote access to and use of its collections. 10/7/87.
Jacobs Pillow Dance Festival, Lee, MA, $95,000. To develop and extend its artistic activity. 12/17/87.
K Q E D, San Francisco, CA, $30,000. Toward costs of American Landscape project. 1988.
La Jolla Playhouse, La Jolla, CA, $95,000. To develop and extend its artistic activity. 12/17/87.
Library of Congress, DC, $50,000. Toward costs of study to reassess Library's mission, strategies, and management practices. 1988.
Library of Congress, DC, $27,000. For international symposium on preservation of serial literature, and for film on preservation binding. 1988.
Massachusetts Institute of Technology, Cambridge, MA, $350,000. Toward curriculum development for new Humanities, Arts, and Social-Sciences distribution requirements for undergraduates. 12/17/87.
Metropolitan Museum of Art, NYC, NY, $250,000. Toward production costs of The Genius of Place, one-hour film about Frederick Law Olmsted to be presented on public television. 10/7/87.
Missouri Botanical Garden, Saint Louis, MO, $950,000. For program of botanical research and for Latin American Plant Sciences Network. 1988.
Municipal Art Society, NYC, NY, $35,000. For conservation intern training program. 1988.
Music-Theater Performing Group, NYC, NY, $75,000. To develop amd extend its artistic activity. 12/17/87.
National Arts Stabilization Fund, NYC, NY, $2,500,000. For program to strengthen financial resources of arts institutions. 1988.
National Faculty of Humanities, Arts and Sciences, Atlanta, GA, $200,000. To expand activities of its Northwest Region program. 1988.
National Humanities Center, Research Triangle Park, NC, $900,000. For its fellowship program. 1988.
National Humanities Center, Research Triangle Park, NC, $675,000. For use as bridging general support funds. 1988.
New York Historical Society, NYC, NY, $50,000. For self-study of institutional needs and priorities. 1988.
Northeast Document Conservation Center, Andover, MA, $125,000. Toward costs of field-service program. 10/7/87.
Palace of Arts and Science Foundation, San Francisco, CA, $350,000. For Exploratorium's publication program. 1988.
Partners for Livable Places, DC, $225,000. Toward extending Economics of Amenity program to include libraries, museums, and academic institutions. 10/7/87.
Peabody Museum of Salem, Salem, MA, $200,000. For matching endowment for research and publication of substantial scholary quality. 10/7/87.
River Arts Repertory, Woodstock, NY, $45,000. To develop and extend its artistic activity. 12/17/87.
School of American Ballet, NYC, NY, $500,000. For permanent endowment for School's Teachers' Fund. 10/7/87.
Smithsonian Institution, DC, $700,000. To support Cooperative Smithsonian Institution-University Programs in Structure and Evolution of Terrestrial Ecosystems. 1988.
Smithsonian Institution, Center for Asian Art, DC, $300,000. For matching endowment for research and publication of substantial scholary quality. 10/7/87.
Smithsonian Institution, Cooper-Hewitt Museum, DC, $200,000. For matching endowment for research and publication of substantial scholary quality. 10/7/87.
Studio Museum in Harlem, NYC, NY, $35,000. To support curatorial services for its James VanDerZee collection. 1988.
University of California, Berkeley, CA, $500,000. For preservation microfilming of embrittled humanities collections in the library. 1988.
University of California, Berkeley, CA, $350,000. For use by Bay Area Writing Project in support of National Writing Project. 1988.
University of California, Riverside, CA, $25,000. For planning costs of English National Union Catalogue to 1800. 1988.
University of Denver, Denver, CO, $11,425. For conference at Rocky Mountain Regional Conservation Center. 1988.
University of Iowa, Iowa City, IA, $140,000. For book-conservation apprenticeships and training workshops for experienced book conservators. 1988.
University of Michigan, Ann Arbor, MI, $950,000. For editorial costs of The Middle English Dictionary. 1988.
W G B H Educational Foundation, Boston, MA, $100,000. Toward support of NOVA public television series in association with Worldwatch Institute and based upon Worldwatch's State of the World publications. 12/17/87.
Williamstown Theater Festival, Williamstown, MA, $95,000. To develop and extend its artistic activity. 12/17/87.
Woodrow Wilson National Fellowship Foundation, Princeton, NJ, $4,500,000. For program of Mellon Fellowships in the Humanities. 1988.
Yale University, New Haven, CT, $1,500,000. For matching endowment for program of Directed Studies in Humanities. 1988.
Yale University, New Haven, CT, $500,000. For preservation-microfilming of embrittled humanities collections in library. 1988.

2094
The Memton Fund, Inc.

60 East 42nd St., Suite 1651
New York 10165 (212) 972-0398

Incorporated in 1936 in NY.
Donor(s): Albert G. Milbank,† Charles M. Cauldwell.†
Financial data (yr. ended 12/31/86): Assets, $5,330,805 (M); expenditures, $311,954, including $232,000 for 91 grants (high: $15,000; low: $1,000; average: $1,000-$5,000).
Purpose and activities: Emphasis on higher education, cultural organizations, community funds, health services, and youth and child welfare agencies.
Types of support: General purposes, operating budgets, continuing support, annual campaigns, seed money, emergency funds, deficit financing, endowment funds, scholarship funds, capital campaigns.
Limitations: No grants to individuals, or for building funds, equipment, land acquisition, renovation projects, matching gifts, special projects, research, publications, or conferences; no loans.
Application information:
Initial approach: Telephone
Copies of proposal: 1
Deadline(s): Feb.
Board meeting date(s): Mar. and Oct.
Write: Lillian Daniels, Secy.
Officers and Directors: David L. Milbank, Pres.; Samuel L. Milbank, V.P.; Lillian I. Daniels, Secy.-Treas.; Elenita M. Drumwright, Marjorie M. Farrar, Francis H. Musselman, Samuel S. Polk, Daphne M. White.
Number of staff: 1 full-time professional; 2 part-time professional.
Employer Identification Number: 136096608

2095
The Robert and Joyce Menschel Foundation

c/o Goldman, Sachs & Co.
85 Broad St.
New York 10004

Established in 1958 in NY.
Donor(s): Robert B. Menschel.
Financial data (yr. ended 10/31/88): Assets, $3,805,417 (M); expenditures, $135,063, including $123,910 for 128 grants (high: $15,000; low: $20).
Purpose and activities: Giving for social welfare, the arts, hospitals, and higher education.
Application information: All grants initiated by the foundation. Applications not accepted.

Officers: Robert B. Menschel, Pres. and Treas.; Joyce F. Menschel, V.P. and Secy.
Number of staff: None.
Employer Identification Number: 136098443

2096
The Sue and Eugene Mercy, Jr. Foundation
c/o Goldman, Sachs & Co., Tax Dept.
85 Broad St.
New York 10004

Established in 1967 in NY.
Donor(s): Eugene Mercy, Jr.
Financial data (yr. ended 12/31/87): Assets, $2,994,362 (M); gifts received, $840,000; expenditures, $672,124, including $660,335 for 139 grants (high: $350,000; low: $50).
Purpose and activities: Emphasis on Jewish giving, including welfare funds, secondary education, and hospitals; support also for higher education and culture, particularly music.
Limitations: Giving primarily in New York City, NY.
Officers and Directors: Eugene Mercy, Jr., Pres. and Treas.; Sue Mercy, V.P.; Robert E. Mnuchin, Secy.
Employer Identification Number: 136217050

2097
Merlin Foundation
c/o Schulte, Roth & Zabel
900 Third Ave.
New York 10022 (212) 758-0404

Established in 1978 in NY.
Donor(s): Audrey Sheldon Poon.†
Financial data (yr. ended 9/30/87): Assets, $1,444,823 (M); gifts received, $752,708; expenditures, $100,725, including $82,780 for 15 grants.
Purpose and activities: Emphasis on higher education in music and the arts, and cultural programs; some support also for welfare funds.
Application information:
Initial approach: Letter
Deadline(s): None
Write: William D. Zabel, Pres.
Officers: William D. Zabel, Pres. and Treas.; Roger S. Altman, V.P.; Thomas H. Baer, V.P.; John J. McLaughlin, Secy.
Employer Identification Number: 237418853

2098
The Ingram Merrill Foundation
104 East 40th St., Suite 302
New York 10016
Application address: P.O. Box 202, Village Station, New York, NY 10014

Trust established in 1956 in NY.
Donor(s): James I. Merrill.
Financial data (yr. ended 12/31/87): Assets, $132,214 (M); gifts received, $10,000; expenditures, $213,010, including $189,300 for 22 grants to individuals (high: $15,000; low: $3,000).
Purpose and activities: Concerned primarily with the advancement of the cultural and fine arts through aid to individual writers, poets, and artists.
Types of support: Grants to individuals.
Limitations: No grants for the performing arts.
Application information: Application form required.
Board meeting date(s): May
Write: Milton Maurer, Trustee
Selection Committee: Harry Ford, Chair.; Patrick Marla, Secy.; John Hollander, David M. Kalstone, Joseph D. McClatchy, Jr.
Trustees: Huyler C. Held, Robert A. Magowan, Jr., Milton Maurer.
Employer Identification Number: 136042498

2099
Merrill Lynch & Company Foundation, Inc.
World Headquarters, South Tower
World Financial Center
New York 10080-6106 (212) 236-4319

Incorporated in 1950 in DE.
Donor(s): Merrill Lynch, Pierce, Fenner & Smith, Inc.
Financial data (yr. ended 12/31/87): Assets, $12,300,000 (M); gifts received, $2,000,000; expenditures, $1,338,002, including $1,268,500 for 75 grants (high: $200,000; low: $1,500; average: $15,000).
Purpose and activities: Emphasis on education, especially higher education; support also for the arts, cultural programs, health, civic affairs, and community services.
Types of support: General purposes, operating budgets, special projects, research, capital campaigns, continuing support, endowment funds, publications, renovation projects, scholarship funds.
Limitations: No support for religious purposes or social, fraternal, or athletic organizations. No grants to individuals, or for deficit financing, matching gifts, or conferences; no loans.
Publications: Annual report, corporate giving report, 990-PF, application guidelines.
Application information:
Initial approach: Proposal or letter
Copies of proposal: 1
Deadline(s): None
Board meeting date(s): Mar., June, Sept., and Dec.
Final notification: 3 months
Write: Westina L. Matthews, Secy.
Officers: John A. Fitzgerald,* Pres.; William A. Schreyer,* V.P.; Daniel P. Tully,* V.P.; Westina L. Matthews, Secy.; Thomas Lombardi, Treas.
Trustees:* Matthew W. McKenna.
Number of staff: None.
Employer Identification Number: 136139556

2100
Merrill Lynch & Company, Inc. Corporate Contributions Program
World Financial Center
World Headquarters
New York 10080-6106 (212) 236-4319

Financial data (yr. ended 12/31/88): Total giving, $6,594,052, including $5,217,261 for 1,797 grants (high: $250,000; low: $25) and $1,376,791 for 5,421 employee matching gifts.
Purpose and activities: Merrill Lynch and subsidiaries support health, culture and the arts, civic and community affairs, and community development. In addition to direct cash grants, the company underwrites cultural events, and awards grants on behalf of employee volunteers through the Employee Community Involvement Program. In 1986, the company joined the Corporate Special Projects Fund, a collaborative philanthropic effort of six corporations, which supports programs to improve the quality of life in New York City. Programs reflect combined foundation and corporate giving.
Types of support: Employee matching gifts, scholarship funds.
Limitations: Giving primarily in the main headquarters area of NY, NJ, and CT, and operating locations. No support for fraternal, social, athletic, political, or religious organizations. No grants to individuals, or for operating support of government agencies, or to reduce an operating deficit or liquidate a debt.
Publications: Corporate giving report (including application guidelines).
Application information: Include organization description, amount requested and proposed use of funds, project timetable, evaluation method, board list, most recently audited financial statement and current financial statement, operating budget, and IRS 501(c)(3) status letter.
Initial approach: Proposal letter
Copies of proposal: 1
Deadline(s): None
Final notification: Within 60 days
Write: Westina Matthews, Mgr., Corp. Contribs.
Administrators: John A. Fitzgerald, Pres., Merill Lynch and Co. Fdn., Inc.; Westina Matthews, Mgr., Corp. Contribs.
Number of staff: 8

2101
Joyce Mertz-Gilmore Foundation
218 East 18th St.
New York 10003 (212) 475-1137

Incorporated in 1959 in NY.
Donor(s): Joyce Mertz Gilmore.†
Financial data (yr. ended 12/31/87): Assets, $32,767,510 (M); gifts received, $2,439,746; expenditures, $3,683,521, including $3,061,541 for 238 grants (high: $350,000; low: $1,000; average: $5,000-$25,000).
Purpose and activities: Current concerns include human rights and democratic values, the protection and enhancement of the environment, alternative defense and common security issues, and New York City cultural, social, and civic concerns.
Types of support: Operating budgets, general purposes, special projects.
Limitations: No grants to individuals, or for capital or endowment funds, conferences, scholarships, fellowships, or matching gifts; no loans.
Publications: Annual report, program policy statement, application guidelines, grants list, financial statement, informational brochure (including application guidelines).
Application information: Submit proposal upon request of foundation only. Application form required.
Initial approach: Letter

Copies of proposal: 1
Deadline(s): Jan. 31 and July 31
Board meeting date(s): Apr. and Nov. for grant decisions
Final notification: Within 2 weeks of meeting
Write: Larry E. Condon, Pres.

Officers and Directors: LuEsther T. Mertz, Chair.; Larry E. Condon, Pres.; Elizabeth Burke Gilmore, Secy.; Charles Bloomstein, Treas.; Harlan Cleveland, C. Virgil Martin, Richard J. Mertz, Franklin W. Wallin.
Number of staff: 2 full-time professional; 2 full-time support; 1 part-time support.
Employer Identification Number: 132872722
Recent arts and culture grants:
Acting Company, NYC, NY, $5,000. For general support. 1987.
Alliance of Resident Theaters, NYC, NY, $5,000. For general support. 1987.
Alvin Ailey American Dance Theater, NYC, NY, $5,000. For general support. 1987.
American Place Theater, NYC, NY, $5,000. For general support. 1987.
Asolo Theater Festival Association, Sarasota, FL, $100,000. For general support. 1987.
Boys Choir of Harlem, NYC, NY, $5,000. For general support. 1987.
Bronx Museum of the Arts, Bronx, NY, $5,000. For general support. 1987.
Brooklyn Museum, Brooklyn, NY, $5,000. For general support. 1987.
Chamber Music Society of Lincoln Center, NYC, NY, $5,000. For general support. 1987.
City Center Theater, NYC, NY, $5,000. For general support. 1987.
Dance Notation Bureau, NYC, NY, $5,000. For general support. 1987.
Dance Theater Workshop, NYC, NY, $5,000. For general support. 1987.
Elisa Monte Dance Company, NYC, NY, $10,000. For general support. 1987.
Executive Service Corps, National, NYC, NY, $5,000. For Arts Consulting Program. 1987.
Feld Ballet, NYC, NY, $5,000. For general support. 1987.
Hudson Guild, NYC, NY, $5,000. For general support. 1987.
International Arts Relations (INTAR), NYC, NY, $5,000. For general support. 1987.
John and Mable Ringling Museum of Art Foundation, Sarasota, FL, $10,000. For general support. 1987.
Joyce Theater Foundation, NYC, NY, $150,000. For general support. 1987.
Kitchen, The, NYC, NY, $5,000. For general support. 1987.
Lambs Theater Company, NYC, NY, $5,000. For general support. 1987.
Lincoln Center for the Performing Arts, Lincoln Center Institute for the Arts in Education, NYC, NY, $7,500. For general support. 1987.
Lincoln Center Theater, NYC, NY, $10,000. For general support. 1987.
Mabou Mines Development Foundation, NYC, NY, $5,000. For general support. 1987.
Manhattan Theater Club, NYC, NY, $5,000. For general support. 1987.
Municipal Art Society, NYC, NY, $20,000. To evaluate development plans for Columbus Circle and to preserve Hudson waterfront on Upper West Side. 1987.
Museum of the City of New York, NYC, NY, $5,000. For general support. 1987.
Music-Theater Performing Group, NYC, NY, $5,000. For general support. 1987.
Musica Sacra, NYC, NY, $5,000. For general support. 1987.
National Public Radio, DC, $10,000. To support acquisition of international reports from free-lance reporters. 1987.
New York Botanical Garden, Bronx, NY, $5,000. To provide training in natural resource management to Bronx Park employees. 1987.
New York Botanical Garden, Bronx, NY, $5,000. For general support. 1987.
New York Botanical Garden, Institute for Economic Botany, Bronx, NY, $20,000. For research throughout world to identify species of plants that are underutilized as food or fuel sources. 1987.
New York City Opera, NYC, NY, $5,000. For general support. 1987.
New York Foundation for the Arts, NYC, NY, $5,000. For documentary film on Solidarity period in Poland. 1987.
New York Landmarks Conservancy, NYC, NY, $25,000. For rehabilitation projects which preserve housing for local residents and families. 1987.
New York Public Library, Performing Arts Research Center, NYC, NY, $5,000. For general support. 1987.
New York Shakespeare Festival, NYC, NY, $10,000. For general support. 1987.
New York Studio School of Drawing, Painting and Sculpture, NYC, NY, $7,500. For scholarship fund. 1987.
Obor, Clinton, CT, $15,000. For project to promote indigenous editorial leadership in Thailand and Pakistan by providing seed money and expertise to organizations wishing to publish wide range of books. 1987.
Rosalind Newman and Dancers, NYC, NY, $5,000. For general support. 1987.
Studio Museum in Harlem, NYC, NY, $5,000. For general support. 1987.
Theater Off Park, NYC, NY, $5,000. For general support. 1987.
Town Hall Foundation, NYC, NY, $5,000. For general support. 1987.
W N E T Channel 13, NYC, NY, $20,000. For general support. 1987.
W N E T Channel 13, NYC, NY, $5,000. For general support. 1987.

2102
Metropolitan Life Foundation

One Madison Ave.
New York 10010-3690 (212) 578-6272

Incorporated in 1976 in NY.
Donor(s): Metropolitan Life Insurance Co.
Financial data (yr. ended 12/31/88): Assets, $97,378,807 (M); expenditures, $8,208,109, including $7,169,456 for 840 grants (high: $750,000; low: $100; average: $1,000-$25,000), $166,666 for 2 grants to individuals, $510,715 for 608 employee matching gifts and $3,215,993 for loans.
Purpose and activities: To make donations for education, health, including medical research and substance abuse programs, civic purposes, and United Way chapters; grants also for cultural programs, including public broadcasting; also makes program-related investments.
Types of support: Operating budgets, continuing support, employee matching gifts, research, program-related investments, general purposes, publications, special projects, capital campaigns, equipment, matching funds, scholarship funds, employee-related scholarships, seed money.
Limitations: No support for private foundations, religious, fraternal, athletic, political, social, or veterans' organizations; organizations already receiving support through United Way campaigns; local chapters of national organizations; disease-specific organizations; labor groups; organizations with international programs; organizations primarily engaged in patient care or direct treatment, drug treatment centers and community health clinics; hospital capital fund campaigns; or elementary or secondary schools. No grants to individuals (except for 2 medical research awards), or for endowment funds, courtesy advertising, or festival participation.
Publications: Corporate giving report, application guidelines, program policy statement.
Application information: Application form required for special programs where requests for proposals are issued.
Initial approach: Letter
Copies of proposal: 1
Deadline(s): Varies for competitive awards programs; none for grants
Board meeting date(s): About 6 times a year
Final notification: 4 to 6 weeks
Write: Sibyl C. Jacobson, Pres.

Officers: John J. Creedon,* Chair.; Sibyl C. Jacobson,* Pres.; Paul S. Entmacher, M.D.,* V.P.; William J. Howard, Counsel and Secy.; Arthur G. Typermass,* Treas.
Directors:* Richard W. Keough, Donald A. Odell.
Number of staff: None.
Employer Identification Number: 132878224
Recent arts and culture grants:
Affiliate Artists, NYC, NY, $22,000. 1987.
American Ballet Theater, NYC, NY, $10,000. 1987.
American Council for the Arts, NYC, NY, $18,000. 1987.
American Dance Festival, NYC, NY, $8,500. For Metropolitan Life Foundation Young Choreographers Award. 1987.
American Museum of Natural History, NYC, NY, $12,500. 1987.
American Symphony Orchestra League, DC, $6,000. For book which describes successful projects for volunteer symphony associations. 1987.
American Theater Wing, NYC, NY, $10,000. For distribution of Working in the Theater videocassettes to university theater departments, drama schools and arts institutions. 1987.
Arts and Business Council, NYC, NY, $25,000. 1987.
Association of Science Technology Centers, DC, $5,000. For Vision Exhibit. 1987.
Ballet Hispanico of New York, NYC, NY, $10,000. 1987.
Brooklyn Academy of Music, Brooklyn, NY, $5,000. 1987.

Business Committee for the Arts, NYC, NY, $5,000. 1987.
Carnegie Hall Restoration Campaign, NYC, NY, $30,000. 1987.
Dramatists Guild, NYC, NY, $7,000. For Young Playwright's Festival. 1987.
International Arts Relations (INTAR), NYC, NY, $10,000. For Minority Visual Arts. 1987.
Joffrey Ballet, NYC, NY, $10,000. For revival of L'Apres-midi d'un Faune. 1987.
John F. Kennedy Center for the Performing Arts, DC, $15,000. 1987.
Lincoln Center for the Performing Arts, NYC, NY, $45,000. 1987.
Lyric Opera of Chicago, Chicago, IL, $7,000. 1987.
Metropolitan Museum of Art, NYC, NY, $70,000. 1987.
Metropolitan Museum of Art, NYC, NY, $60,000. For building fund. 1987.
Metropolitan Museum of Art, NYC, NY, $10,000. 1987.
Montclair Art Museum, Montclair, NJ, $5,000. For Minority Visual Arts. 1987.
Museum of African American Art, Los Angeles, CA, $7,000. For Minority Visual Arts program, for special catalog of black art to introduce artists to black children. 1987.
Museum of Contemporary Hispanic Art, NYC, NY, $20,000. For Minority Visual Arts. 1987.
Museum of Modern Art, NYC, NY, $15,000. For Anniversary Campaign. 1987.
Museum of Science and Industry, Chicago, IL, $5,000. 1987.
National Center of Afro-American Artists, Roxbury, MA, $20,000. For Minority Visual Arts. 1987.
National Corporate Fund for Dance, NYC, NY, $10,000. 1987.
National Corporate Theater Fund, NYC, NY, $6,000. 1987.
National Foundation for Advancement in the Arts, Miami, FL, $5,000. 1987.
New York Botanical Garden, Bronx, NY, $5,000. 1987.
New York City Ballet, NYC, NY, $5,000. 1987.
New York City Opera, NYC, NY, $10,000. 1987.
New York Foundation for the Arts, NYC, NY, $6,000. 1987.
New York Shakespeare Festival, NYC, NY, $5,000. 1987.
Pennsylvania Academy of the Fine Arts, Philadelphia, PA, $5,000. For Minority Visual Arts. 1987.
Pittsburgh Center for the Arts, Pittsburgh, PA, $5,000. 1987.
Pittsburgh Symphony Society, Pittsburgh, PA, $5,000. 1987.
Portland Art Museum of the Oregon Art Institute, Portland, OR, $5,000. For Minority Visual Arts. 1987.
Rutgers, The State University of New Jersey Foundation, Zimmerli Art Museum, New Brunswick, NJ, $15,000. For Minority Visual Arts. 1987.
Saint Louis Conservatory and Schools for the Arts (CASA), Saint Louis, MO, $7,000. 1987.
San Antonio Museum Association, San Antonio, TX, $8,000. For Minority Visual Arts program, for exhibition of works by Mexican-American artists. 1987.
Tampa Bay Performing Arts Center, Tampa, FL, $10,000. 1987.
Triton Museum of Art, Santa Clara, CA, $5,000. For Minority Visual Arts program, for exhibition by emerging local Asian-American artists. 1987.
Very Special Arts, Madison, WI, $15,000. For Itzhak Perlman Award and to supply curriculum materials for schools. 1987.
W N E T Channel 13, NYC, NY, $5,000. 1987.

2103
Metropolitan Life Insurance Company Corporate Giving Program

One Madison Ave.
New York 10010-3690 (212) 578-221

Financial data (yr. ended 12/31/88): $2,082,616 for grants (high: $1,500,000; low: $1,000).
Purpose and activities: Support for health care, health research and illness prevention, health and safety, higher, precollege, and minority education, public policy and research, art centers and councils, botanic gardens, zoos, dance, museums, music, libraries and art education, community improvement, employment training, equal opportunity, law and justice, family and youth, public broadcasting, and the United Way.
Types of support: Operating budgets, continuing support, employee matching gifts, research, general purposes, special projects, publications.
Limitations: No support for private foundations, religious, fraternal, athletic, polictical, social, or veterans' organizations, organizations already receiving support through United Way campaigns, local chapters of national organizations, disease-specific organizations, labor groups, organizations with international programs, organizations primarily engaged in patient care or direct treatment, drug treatment centers and community health clinics, or elementary or secondary schools. No grants to individuals, or for endowment funds, courtesy advertising, festival participation, or hospital capital fund campaigns.
Publications: Corporate giving report.
Application information: Include brief description of the organization, including, purpose of grant, history, and governing board; audited financial statement; 501(c)(3) letter; 990 IRS form.
Initial approach: Letter
Write: Sibyl Jacobson, Pres., Metropolitan Life Foundation

2104
Mex-Am Cultural Foundation, Inc.

c/o Grant, Herrmann, Schwartz & Klinger
One Wall St.
New York 10005 (212) 943-8126

Established in 1986 in NY.
Donor(s): The Wolfgang Schoenborn Trust.
Financial data (yr. ended 9/30/87): Assets, $2,334,656 (M); gifts received, $2,330,844; expenditures, $124,050, including $100,000 for 4 grants (high: $35,000; low: $20,000).
Purpose and activities: Support primarily for cultural organizations that promote programs related to Mexican arts and its culture.
Limitations: Giving primarily in New York, NY.
Application information:
Initial approach: Letter
Deadline(s): None
Write: Andrew M. Klinger, Trustee
Trustees: William J. Brown, Eduardo Fernandez Hernandez, Andrew M. Klinger, Evelyn Rather, Milton Schwartz.
Employer Identification Number: 133328723

2105
Barbara and Clifford Michel Foundation, Inc.

80 Pine St.
New York 10005 (212) 701-3200
Additional Tel.: (212) 344-3090

Incorporated in 1951 in NY.
Donor(s): Barbara R. Michel,† Clifford W. Michel.†
Financial data (yr. ended 12/31/87): Assets, $596,888 (M); gifts received, $120,000; expenditures, $123,621, including $114,500 for 14 grants (high: $35,000; low: $1,000).
Purpose and activities: Support for higher and secondary education, hospitals, cultural programs, and projects concerned with law and justice.
Types of support: Operating budgets, continuing support, annual campaigns, building funds, equipment, endowment funds, capital campaigns.
Limitations: No grants to individuals, or for seed money, emergency funds, deficit financing, land acquisition, demonstration projects, publications, conferences, research, scholarships, or fellowships; no loans.
Publications: 990-PF.
Application information:
Deadline(s): None
Board meeting date(s): June and Dec.
Final notification: 2 to 3 weeks
Write: Clifford L. Michel, Pres.
Officers: Clifford L. Michel, Pres.; Clifford F. Michel, V.P.; Denise Riccardelli, Secy.; Lynn R. Falcone, Treas.
Number of staff: None.
Employer Identification Number: 136082879

2106
Milbank Memorial Fund

One East 75th St.
New York 10021 (212) 570-4804

Incorporated in 1905 in NY.
Donor(s): Elizabeth Milbank Anderson.†
Financial data (yr. ended 12/31/87): Assets, $31,427,463 (M); expenditures, $1,199,263, including $755,559 for 36 grants (high: $78,007; low: $1,300) and $427,169 for foundation-administered programs.
Purpose and activities: A private operating foundation currently supporting projects which promote improvement in occupational health, with initial emphasis upon the health and welfare of migrant workers. In addition to grantmaking, the foundation has published the Milbank Quarterly, a scholarly journal in the health field since 1923.
Types of support: Research, special projects.
Limitations: No grants to individuals, or for annual campaigns, building or endowment funds, deficit financing, operating budgets,

general purposes, or matching gifts; no new scholarships or fellowships; no loans.
Publications: Annual report (including application guidelines), grants list.
Application information:
Initial approach: Letter, proposal, or telephone
Copies of proposal: 1
Deadline(s): Apr. 1, Sept. 1, and Nov. 1
Board meeting date(s): Mar., May, Oct., and Dec.
Final notification: 4 weeks after meetings
Officers: Robert H. Ebert,* Pres.; David P. Willis, V.P.; Audrey Irwin, Secy.; Sara C. Romano, Treas.
Directors:* Francis H. Musselman, Chair.; Samuel L. Milbank, Vice-Chair.; Leroy E. Burney, M.D., Rashi Fein, Ellen V. Futter, Peter M. Gottsegen, Rosemary A. Stevens, Alan T. Wenzell.
Number of staff: 3 full-time professional; 3 full-time support; 1 part-time support.
Employer Identification Number: 135562282
Recent arts and culture grants:
Hudson River Film and Video Company, Garrison, NY, $20,000. For documentary for National Public Television on present and future of American agriculture. 3/88.

2107
Kathryn & Gilbert Miller Fund, Inc.
c/o Peat, Marwick, Mitchell & Co.
345 Park Ave.
New York 10154

Incorporated in 1952 in NY.
Donor(s): Kathryn B. Miller.†
Financial data (yr. ended 3/31/87): Assets, $3,888,514 (M); expenditures, $1,463,548, including $1,438,533 for 40 grants (high: $300,000; low: $500).
Purpose and activities: Grants primarily for cultural programs, hospitals and medical research, and higher and secondary education.
Officers and Directors: Charles Looker, Pres.; Philip J. Hirsch, V.P. and Treas.; Jerold Zieselman, Secy.
Employer Identification Number: 136121254

2108
Mitsubishi International Corporate Contributions Program
520 Madison Ave.
New York 10022 (212) 605-2000

Purpose and activities: Company gives support generally in five broad categories: organizations concerned primarily with United States-Japan relations, educational organizations, cultural organizations, charitable organizations, and regional organizations oriented toward the Japanese-American and Japanese business community.
Limitations: Giving primarily in headquarters city and major operating locations.
Application information:
Copies of proposal: 1
Write: Martha Gellens, Mgr., Public Affairs

2109
The Mnuchin Foundation
c/o Goldman, Sachs & Co.
85 Broad St., Tax Dept., 30th Fl.
New York 10004

Established in 1980 in NY.
Donor(s): Robert E. Mnuchin.
Financial data (yr. ended 4/30/87): Assets, $2,108,836 (M); gifts received, $1,241,941; expenditures, $233,359, including $232,470 for 55 grants (high: $75,000; low: $25).
Purpose and activities: Emphasis on Jewish welfare, health, the arts, dance, and education.
Limitations: Giving primarily in NY.
Application information:
Deadline(s): None
Trustees: Eugene Mercy, Jr., Adrian Mnuchin, Robert E. Mnuchin.
Employer Identification Number: 133050751

2110
The Dom Mocquereau Foundation, Inc.
c/o Davis Polk & Wardwell
499 Park Ave.
New York 10022 (212) 759-3076

Incorporated about 1926 in NY.
Donor(s): Justine B. Ward.†
Financial data (yr. ended 9/30/87): Assets, $1,139,557 (M); expenditures, $270,426, including $155,500 for 7 grants (high: $50,000; low: $6,000) and $30,128 for 3 grants to individuals.
Purpose and activities: Support only for teaching of Gregorian chant by gifts to charitable organizations in the U.S., France, Switzerland, Holland, Italy, and Portugal, and by direct payment of salary of teachers of Gregorian chant.
Types of support: Grants to individuals, professorships.
Limitations: No grants for scholarships; no loans.
Application information:
Initial approach: Letter
Deadline(s): None
Write: James F. Dolan, Pres.
Officers: James F. Dolan,* Pres.; Theodore Marier, Exec. V.P.; Bernard F. Curry,* 2nd V.P. and Treas.; Maureen S. Bateman,* Secy.
Trustees:* Jean Lallemand, Thomas Mastroianni, Martin F. Shea.
Employer Identification Number: 237118643

2111
Leo Model Foundation, Inc.
c/o Schneidman & Assoc.
405 Park Ave.
New York 10022

Established in 1970 in NY.
Donor(s): Model Charitable Lead Trust, Jane and Leo Model Foundation.
Financial data (yr. ended 12/31/87): Assets, $6,457,595 (M); gifts received, $1,312,077; expenditures, $865,699, including $817,520 for 117 grants (high: $175,000; low: $500).
Purpose and activities: Support for museums and the arts, secondary and higher education, and public interest organizations.
Application information: Contributes only to pre-selected organizations. Applications not accepted.
Officers: Allen Model, Pres.; Peter H. Model, V.P.; John A. Nevins, Secy.-Treas.
Employer Identification Number: 237084119

2112
The Ambrose Monell Foundation
c/o Fulton, Duncombe & Rowe
30 Rockefeller Plaza, Rm. 3217
New York 10112 (212) 586-0700

Incorporated in 1952 in NY.
Donor(s): Maude Monell Vetlesen.†
Financial data (yr. ended 12/31/86): Assets, $94,441,256 (M); expenditures, $3,962,709, including $3,688,500 for 104 grants (high: $250,000; low: $1,000; average: $5,000-$100,000).
Purpose and activities: For the "improvement of the physical, mental, and moral condition of humanity throughout the world"; giving largely for hospitals and health services, medical and chemical research, museums, performing arts, and other cultural activities, and higher and secondary education; support also for social services, research in political science, mental health, aid to the handicapped, and geophysical research.
Types of support: General purposes, research, building funds, endowment funds, operating budgets.
Limitations: No grants to individuals.
Application information:
Initial approach: Proposal
Copies of proposal: 1
Deadline(s): None
Board meeting date(s): Dec.
Write: Harmon Duncombe, Pres.
Officers and Directors: Harmon Duncombe, Pres. and Treas.; George Rowe, Jr., V.P. and Secy.; Eugene P. Grisanti, Henry G. Walter, Jr.
Number of staff: None.
Employer Identification Number: 131982683

2113
MONY Financial Services Foundation
1740 Broadway, MD 4-6
New York 10019

Established in 1987 in NY; direct corporate giving since the early 1940's.
Donor(s): The Mutual Life Insurance Co. of New York.
Financial data (yr. ended 12/31/87): Assets, $478,723 (M); gifts received, $1,478,802; expenditures, $1,092,684, including $380,145 for 84 grants (high: $25,000; low: $25) and $353,966 for employee matching gifts.
Purpose and activities: The foundation has identified "The Changing American Family" as its principal focus for funding. As always, change creates new needs and problems. The MONY Financial Services address the changes of society in transition by directing resources to organizations and programs that demonstrate an ability to effectively combat the social problems arising from these changes. MONY will consider grants that address such areas as, but not limited to: affordable and accessible child care alternatives for single parents;

improved educational and training opportunities for women and minorities; and increased community-based services that allow the elderly to remain at home and prevent institutionalization with emphasis on innovative and well-managed programs that will enhance the quality of life of the individuals and families who comprise our diverse communities. Types of support include employee volunteer programs, employee matching gifts, challenge matches, and in-kind donations.
Types of support: Employee matching gifts, special projects, employee-related scholarships, matching funds.
Limitations: Giving primarily in communities where MONY maintains offices. No support for private foundations, fully participating members of the United Way, or religious, fraternal, athletic, social, or veterans' organizations. No grants for capital fund drives, endowments, or deficit financing.
Publications: Application guidelines.
Application information:
Initial approach: Letter of inquiry
Copies of proposal: 1
Deadline(s): May 1
Board meeting date(s): Sept. 15
Final notification: Oct. 1
Write: Lynn Stekas, Pres.
Officers: Lynn Stekas, Pres.; Thomas G. Napurano, C.F.O.; Robert F. Colby, Secy.; Frederick P. Winters, Treas.
Directors: James A. Attwood, Gray Castle, Lawrence Clark, Gordon E. Perry, Albert J. Schiff, Floyd L. Smith.
Employer Identification Number: 133398852

2114
Edward S. Moore Foundation, Inc.
c/o Walter, Conston, Alexander and Green
90 Park Ave.
New York 10016 (212) 210-9400
Application address: 55 Old Field Point Rd., Greenwich, CT 06830; Tel.: (203) 629-4591

Foundation established in 1957 in NY.
Donor(s): Edward S. Moore, Jr.,† Evelyn N. Moore,† Carolyn N. Moore, and others.
Financial data (yr. ended 12/31/87): Assets, $21,732,100 (M); expenditures, $947,674, including $762,250 for 80 grants (high: $30,000; low: $1,000; average: $2,500-$25,000).
Purpose and activities: Support for youth agencies, hospitals, education, and cultural programs, including museums; and churches.
Types of support: Operating budgets, continuing support, annual campaigns, seed money, emergency funds, building funds, equipment, land acquisition, endowment funds, matching funds, internships, scholarship funds, special projects, research.
Limitations: Giving primarily in NY and CT. No grants to individuals, or for deficit financing, publications, or conferences; no loans.
Publications: Annual report, 990-PF.
Application information:
Initial approach: Letter
Deadline(s): None
Board meeting date(s): Jan., Apr., July, and Oct.
Final notification: 3 to 6 months
Write: John W. Cross III, Pres.
Officers and Directors: John W. Cross III, Pres.; Marion Moore Gilbert, V.P.; Donald Vail, Secy.; Alexander Jackson, Treas.
Number of staff: 1 full-time professional.
Employer Identification Number: 136127365

2115
Morgan Guaranty Trust Company of New York Charitable Trust
23 Wall St.
New York 10015 (212) 483-2058

Trust established in 1961 in NY.
Donor(s): Morgan Guaranty Trust Co. of New York.
Financial data (yr. ended 12/31/88): Assets, $6,112,365 (M); expenditures, $7,411,618, including $5,847,450 for 384 grants (high: $150,000; low: $2,000; average: $2,000-$25,000) and $1,564,168 for 7,782 employee matching gifts.
Purpose and activities: Emphasis is on helping to find solutions to social problems and needs through support of competent agencies in fields of health, social services, culture, education, the environment, and international affairs. Special attention to job training, youth programs, international relief, housing, economic development, and advocacy and citizen involvement programs in New York City. Matches employee gifts to educational programs, cultural institutions, hospitals and health care agencies, human services and local development organizations, and international organizations.
Types of support: Employee matching gifts, operating budgets, annual campaigns, seed money, building funds, equipment, land acquisition, special projects, matching funds, technical assistance, general purposes, capital campaigns, endowment funds, renovation projects.
Limitations: Giving primarily in the New York City, NY, area, except for selected institutions of higher education, and international affairs. No support for organizations working with specific disabilities or diseases. No grants to individuals, or for scholarships, fellowships, or conferences; no loans.
Publications: Corporate giving report, application guidelines, program policy statement, grants list.
Application information: Application form required.
Initial approach: Proposal
Copies of proposal: 1
Deadline(s): Sept. 15
Board meeting date(s): Monthly
Final notification: 3 months
Write: Roberta Ruocco, V.P., Morgan Guaranty Trust Co. of New York
Advisory Committee: Lewis T. Preston, John F. Ruffle, Dennis Weatherstone.
Trustee: Morgan Guaranty Trust Co. of New York.
Number of staff: 6 full-time professional; 5 full-time support.
Employer Identification Number: 136037931
Recent arts and culture grants:
Alliance for the Arts, NYC, NY, $5,000. 1987.
Alliance of Resident Theaters, NYC, NY, $10,000. 1987.
American Composers Orchestra, NYC, NY, $5,000. 1987.
American Museum in Britain, Friends of the, NYC, NY, $12,000. 1987.
Arts and Business Council, NYC, NY, $5,500. 1987.
Asia Society, NYC, NY, $18,750. 1987.
Brazilian Cultural Foundation, NYC, NY, $6,000. 1987.
Brooklyn Academy of Music, Brooklyn, NY, $32,500. For support of last of four installments of gift and first of two installments for Next Wave Festival. 1987.
Brooklyn Botanic Garden, Brooklyn, NY, $7,000. For operating purposes. 1987.
Brooklyn Botanic Garden Fund, Brooklyn, NY, $15,000. For capital support. 1987.
Brooklyn Childrens Museum, Brooklyn, NY, $5,000. 1987.
Brooklyn Museum, Brooklyn, NY, $7,500. For last of two installments of gift. 1987.
Brooklyn Philharmonic Symphony Orchestra, Brooklyn, NY, $5,000. For programs to increase exposure to the arts. 1987.
Carnegie Hall Foundation, NYC, NY, $25,000. For last of four installments of gift. 1987.
Carnegie Hall Foundation, NYC, NY, $7,500. Toward arts in education in New York City. 1987.
Carnegie Hall Society, NYC, NY, $5,310. For support as part of Foundation's program of matching gifts to cultural institutions. 1987.
Childrens Art Carnival, NYC, NY, $7,500. For last of two installments toward arts in education in New York City. 1987.
Chinese Cultural Center, NYC, NY, $5,000. For support as part of Foundation's program of matching gifts to cultural institutions. 1987.
Cincinnati Institute of Fine Arts, Cincinnati, OH, $5,500. For support as part of Foundation's program of matching gifts to cultural institutions. 1987.
Circle Repertory Theater Company, NYC, NY, $5,000. 1987.
Columbia University, Teachers College, NYC, NY, $37,500. For first of two installments for the Writing Project. 1987.
Cooper Union for the Advancement of Science and Art, NYC, NY, $50,000. For capital support. 1987.
Creative Time, NYC, NY, $5,000. For programs to increase exposure to arts. 1987.
Cultural Council Foundation, NYC, NY, $5,000. 1987.
Dance Theater Workshop, NYC, NY, $40,000. For support which includes last of two installments of gift for New York Dance and Performance Awards and first of two installments of gift. 1987.
Dog Museum of America, NYC, NY, $5,200. For support as part of Foundation's program of matching gifts to cultural institutions. 1987.
Drawing Center, NYC, NY, $6,000. For last of two installments of gift. 1987.
Educational Broadcasting Corporation, NYC, NY, $18,120. For support as part of Foundation's program of matching gifts to cultural institutions. 1987.
Elder Craftsmen, NYC, NY, $5,000. 1987.
Ensemble Studio Theater, NYC, NY, $25,000. For support which includes last of two installments of gift. 1987.
Film Forum, NYC, NY, $7,500. For last of two installments of gift. 1987.

Film/Video Arts, NYC, NY, $6,000. For first of two installments of gift. 1987.
Foundation for Independent Video and Film, NYC, NY, $6,000. 1987.
Harvard University, Cambridge, MA, $12,500. For first of two installments for Busch-Reisinger Museum. 1987.
House Foundation for the Arts, NYC, NY, $5,000. 1987.
Houston Grand Opera Association, Houston, TX, $10,000. For support as part of Foundation's program of matching gifts to cultural institutions. 1987.
Independent Committee on Arts Policy, NYC, NY, $7,500. 1987.
Institute for Art and Urban Resources, Long Island City, NY, $10,000. For last of two installments of gift. 1987.
Japan Society, NYC, NY, $25,000. 1987.
John F. Kennedy Center for the Performing Arts, DC, $5,000. For last of two installments of gift. 1987.
Joyce Theater Foundation, NYC, NY, $20,000. For first of two installments of gift. 1987.
Juilliard School, NYC, NY, $6,050. For support as part of Foundation's program of matching gifts to educational institutions. 1987.
Kitchen Center for Video, Music and Dance, NYC, NY, $8,500. 1987.
La Mama Experimental Theater Club, NYC, NY, $5,000. 1987.
Learning Through an Expanded Arts Program (LEAP), NYC, NY, $8,000. Toward arts in education in New York City. 1987.
Lincoln Center for the Performing Arts, NYC, NY, $50,000. 1987.
Lincoln Center for the Performing Arts, Lincoln Center Institute, NYC, NY, $10,000. For last of two installments toward arts in education in New York City. 1987.
Lower Manhattan Cultural Council, NYC, NY, $6,000. 1987.
Lucinda Childs Dance Company, NYC, NY, $5,000. 1987.
Manhattan Theater Club, NYC, NY, $10,000. For last of two installments of gift. 1987.
Media Center for Children, NYC, NY, $5,000. For last of two installments toward arts in education in New York City. 1987.
Meet the Composer, NYC, NY, $10,000. For last of two installments of gift. 1987.
Metropolitan Museum of Art, NYC, NY, $15,295. For support as part of Foundation's program of matching gifts to cultural institutions. 1987.
Metropolitan Museum of Art, NYC, NY, $12,500. 1987.
Metropolitan Opera Association, NYC, NY, $11,900. For support as part of Foundation's program of matching gifts to cultural institutions. 1987.
Metropolitan Opera Guild, NYC, NY, $7,500. Toward arts in education in New York City. 1987.
Museum of Modern Art, NYC, NY, $42,500. For support which includes last of two installments of gift for Project Series and first of two installments of gift. 1987.
Museum of Modern Art, NYC, NY, $25,000. For third of four installments of gift. 1987.
Music-Theater Performing Group, NYC, NY, $7,500. For last of two installments of gift. 1987.
Musica Sacra, NYC, NY, $5,000. For first of two installments of gift. 1987.
National Dance Institute, NYC, NY, $7,500. Toward arts in education in New York City. 1987.
New York Botanical Garden, Bronx, NY, $25,000. For capital support. 1987.
New York Botanical Garden, Bronx, NY, $10,000. For operating purposes. 1987.
New York City Ballet, NYC, NY, $25,000. For last of two installments of gift. 1987.
New York City Ballet, NYC, NY, $5,745. For support as part of Foundation's program of matching gifts to cultural institutions. 1987.
New York City Mission Society, Cadet Corps, NYC, NY, $7,000. 1987.
New York City Opera, NYC, NY, $20,000. For last of two installments of gift. 1987.
New York Dance Center, NYC, NY, $25,000. For first of two installments of gift. 1987.
New York Foundation for the Arts, NYC, NY, $10,000. 1987.
New York School for Circus Arts, NYC, NY, $5,000. For programs to increase exposure to arts. 1987.
New York Zoological Society, Bronx, NY, $5,000. For operating purposes. 1987.
Original Ballets Foundation, NYC, NY, $12,500. For new Ballet School toward arts in education in New York City. 1987.
Paul Taylor Dance Foundation, NYC, NY, $15,000. 1987.
Performance Space 122, NYC, NY, $5,000. 1987.
Philadelphia College of Art, Philadelphia, PA, $7,650. For support as part of Foundation's program of matching gifts to educational institutions. 1987.
Pick Up Performance Company, NYC, NY, $6,000. For first of two installments of gift. 1987.
Pierpont Morgan Library, NYC, NY, $12,500. 1987.
Playwrights Horizons, NYC, NY, $6,500. For last of two installments of gift. 1987.
Poets and Writers, NYC, NY, $7,000. 1987.
Pratt Institute, Brooklyn, NY, $25,000. For capital support. 1987.
Saint Augustine School of the Arts, Bronx, NY, $5,000. Toward arts in education in New York City. 1987.
Saint Lukes Performing Arts Ensemble, NYC, NY, $7,500. 1987.
Second Stage Theater, NYC, NY, $6,000. For first of two installments of gift. 1987.
Spanish Theater Repertory Company, NYC, NY, $5,000. For last of two installments of gift. 1987.
Studio in a School Association, NYC, NY, $15,000. Toward arts in education in New York City. 1987.
Studio Museum in Harlem, NYC, NY, $10,000. For last of two installments of gift. 1987.
Symphony Space, NYC, NY, $7,500. For last of two installments toward arts in education in New York City. 1987.
Teachers and Writers Collaborative, NYC, NY, $7,500. For last of two installments. 1987.
Theater Development Fund, NYC, NY, $5,000. For first of two installments of gift. 1987.
Theater for the New City Foundation, NYC, NY, $6,500. 1987.
Trisha Brown Dance Company, NYC, NY, $5,000. 1987.
United States, Government of, Department of the Treasury, DC, $25,000. For preservation of the Treasury Building. 1987.
Vivian Beaumont Theater, NYC, NY, $25,000. Toward Sarafina production. 1987.
Waverly Consort, NYC, NY, $5,000. For first of two installments of gift. 1987.
Whitney Museum of American Art, NYC, NY, $7,500. For last of two installments of gift. 1987.
WPA Theater, NYC, NY, $6,000. For first of two installments of gift. 1987.

2116
Morgan Guaranty Trust Company of New York Corporate Giving Program

23 Wall Street
New York 10015 (212) 483-2058

Financial data (yr. ended 12/31/88): $2,642,251 for grants.
Purpose and activities: Morgan's philanthropy concentrates on six areas: education, health, social services, cultural activities, international activities, and the environment. Within these major areas of concern, Morgan focuses its efforts on helping people help themselves. Morgan matches contributions by its employees, retirees, directors, members of the Directors Advisory Council, and the spouse of any eligible person from amounts of $10 up to a total of $6,000 each calendar year; gifts of cash, securities, and real estate are matched dollar-for-dollar in six categories of giving: education, health care, human services, culture, international affairs, and the environment. Types of support include in-kind donations, supplying effective expertise for specific programs through the firm's strong volunteer network, and paying for top-flight summer interns from relevant graduate programs to work for non-profit organizations. Funds also come from the firm's offices and subsidiaries worldwide. Programs reflect combined foundation and corporate giving.
Types of support: Capital campaigns, employee matching gifts, matching funds, general purposes, operating budgets, special projects, in-kind gifts.
Limitations: Giving primarily in New York, NY, except in the fields of higher education and international affairs; those few grants made outside NY are likely to be to national organizations. No support for religious organizations unless their programs are secular in nature, for work with specific diseases and disabilities, programs dealing with chemical dependency, or for scholarly research. No grants to individuals, or for scholarships and fellowships.
Publications: Corporate giving report, informational brochure.
Application information: Submit two copies of grant application, and one copy of proposal and supporting materials; proposal should include organization's history, goals, and constituencies served, annual report if available, lists of directors and staff, recent financial audit, budget for current year and next year, list of major donors, 501(c)(3). Application form required.
Initial approach: Request application from bank; for a specific project request,

provide a project description including purpose, budget, duration, directors' names/qualifications, and evaluation methods; for capital support, give program description, amount, finish date
Deadline(s): Grants are made on a calendar-year basis; for proposal to be considered in the same year in which it is submitted, it must be received by Sept. 15
Final notification: 3 months; proposals will not be considered until all requested information has been received; Morgan will discontinue consideration of any proposal that remains incomplete 2 months after acknowledgement of its receipt
Write: Roberta A. Ruocco, V.P., Community Relations and Public Affairs Dept.

Community Relations and Public Affairs Dept.: R. Barkley Calkins, Jeanne Erwin Linnes, Robert F. Longley, Laura D. Roosevelt, Roberta A. Ruocco, Hildy J. Simmons, James T. Wallis.

2117
Morgan Stanley Foundation
1251 Ave. of the Americas, 31st Fl.
New York 10020 (212) 703-6610

Trust established in 1961 in NY.
Donor(s): Morgan Stanley & Co., Inc.
Financial data (yr. ended 12/31/88): Assets, $6,800,000 (M); gifts received, $2,000,000; expenditures, $1,171,397, including $970,500 for grants (average: $3,500-$10,000) and $200,897 for employee matching gifts.
Purpose and activities: Giving primarily for programs in social welfare; grants also for business schools, cultural programs, and hospitals.
Types of support: Operating budgets, continuing support, employee matching gifts, general purposes.
Limitations: Giving primarily in the New York, NY, metropolitan area. No grants to individuals, or for emergency, endowment or building funds; deficit financing, equipment, land acquisition, scholarships, fellowships, special projects, research, publications, or conferences; no loans.
Publications: Program policy statement.
Application information:
Initial approach: Letter
Copies of proposal: 1
Deadline(s): None
Board meeting date(s): Quarterly and as required
Final notification: 3-6 months
Write: Patricia Schaefer
Trustees: John Barr, Anson Beard, Jr., Kenneth DeRegt, Edward Dunn, John Wilson.
Staff: Patricia Schaefer.
Number of staff: 1 part-time professional; 1 part-time support.
Employer Identification Number: 136155650

2118
The William T. Morris Foundation, Inc.
230 Park Ave., Suite 622
New York 10169 (212) 986-8036

Trust established in 1937; incorporated in 1941 in DE.
Donor(s): William T. Morris.†
Financial data (yr. ended 6/30/87): Assets, $37,484,353 (M); expenditures, $1,452,708, including $1,036,900 for 71 grants (high: $50,000; low: $3,000; average: $5,000-$20,000).
Purpose and activities: Giving primarily to religious, charitable, scientific, and/or educational institutions.
Limitations: Giving primarily in the northeastern states, especially NY and CT.
Application information:
Initial approach: Letter and proposal
Copies of proposal: 1
Deadline(s): None
Board meeting date(s): As required
Final notification: 6 to 8 weeks
Write: E.A. Antonelli, Pres.
Officers and Directors: E.A. Antonelli, Pres.; W.F. Wheeler, Jr., V.P.; P.W. Krehbiel, Secy.; A.C. Laske, Jr., Treas.; Arthur C. Laske.
Number of staff: 3 full-time professional.
Employer Identification Number: 131600908

2119
Enid & Lester S. Morse, Jr. Foundation, Inc.
60 East 42nd St.
New York 10165-0015

Established in 1967 in NY.
Financial data (yr. ended 3/31/87): Assets, $37,136 (M); gifts received, $110,000; expenditures, $260,743, including $260,695 for 90 grants (high: $100,000; low: $25).
Purpose and activities: Giving primarily for the arts, including the performing arts, and higher education.
Officers: Lester S. Morse, Jr., Pres.; Enid Morse, V.P.; Richard Morse, Treas.
Director: Lawrence A. Wien.
Employer Identification Number: 136220174

2120
Mosbacher Foundation, Inc.
515 Madison Ave.
New York 10022

Incorporated in 1948 in NY.
Donor(s): Emil Mosbacher, Gertrude Mosbacher, Emil Mosbacher, Jr., Barbara Mosbacher, Robert Mosbacher.
Financial data (yr. ended 12/31/87): Assets, $2,977 (M); gifts received, $280,000; expenditures, $455,481, including $453,264 for 169 grants (high: $50,000; low: $45).
Purpose and activities: Grants primarily for higher education, cultural programs, including museums, and international studies.
Application information: Contributes only to pre-selected organizations. Applications not accepted.
Officers: Robert Mosbacher, Pres.; Barbara Mosbacher, Secy.-Treas.
Employer Identification Number: 136155392

2121
Henry and Lucy Moses Fund, Inc.
c/o Moses and Singer
1271 Ave. of the Americas
New York 10020 (212) 246-3700

Incorporated in 1942 in NY.
Donor(s): Henry L. Moses,† Lucy G. Moses.
Financial data (yr. ended 12/31/87): Assets, $7,457,471 (M); gifts received, $2,107,376; expenditures, $4,339,890, including $4,270,102 for 183 grants (high: $1,000,000; low: $500).
Purpose and activities: Support for hospitals and medical schools, Jewish and other welfare funds, higher education, youth, minority, and social service agencies, the aged, the handicapped, cultural programs, and environmental concerns, including Central Park in New York City.
Types of support: Building funds, endowment funds, research, scholarship funds, fellowships, general purposes, matching funds, professorships, continuing support, annual campaigns, capital campaigns, operating budgets.
Limitations: Giving primarily in the New York, NY, metropolitan area. No grants to individuals; no loans.
Application information: Support currently limited to previous grant recipients. Applications not accepted.
Board meeting date(s): Usually in Feb., May, Aug., and Oct.
Write: Henry Schneider, Treas.
Officers and Directors: Lucy G. Moses, Pres.; Alfred W. Bressler, V.P.; Arthur M. Fishberg, M.D., V.P.; Felix A. Fischman, V.P.; Lillian E. Rachlin, Secy.; Henry Schneider, Treas.
Number of staff: None.
Employer Identification Number: 136092967

2122
J. Malcolm Mossman Charitable Trust
c/o Chemical Bank
30 Rockefeller Plaza
New York 10112 (212) 621-2148

Established in 1971.
Financial data (yr. ended 12/31/87): Assets, $470,395 (M); expenditures, $205,262, including $199,050 for 93 grants (high: $10,000; low: $500).
Purpose and activities: Giving primarily for social service and youth agencies, higher and secondary education, cultural programs, health, and church support, with some emphasis on Roman Catholic organizations.
Limitations: Giving primarily in NY. No grants to individuals.
Application information:
Initial approach: Letter
Deadline(s): None
Write: Barbara Strohmeier
Trustees: Irving Goodstein, Chemical Bank.
Employer Identification Number: 136354042

2123
Musicians Foundation, Inc.
200 West 55th St., No. 41
New York 10019-5218 (212) 247-5332

Established in 1914 in NY.
Donor(s): Noel Murphy,† and others.
Financial data (yr. ended 4/30/88): Assets, $1,202,231 (M); expenditures, $127,558, including $83,908 for 36 grants to individuals (high: $6,685; low: $200).
Purpose and activities: Financial assistance to professional musicians in critical need.
Types of support: Grants to individuals.
Publications: Informational brochure, application guidelines.
Application information:
Deadline(s): None
Write: Brent Williams, Exec. Dir.
Officer: Brent Williams, Exec. Dir.
Number of staff: None.
Employer Identification Number: 131790739

2124
The Napier Foundation
c/o Chemical Bank
30 Rockefeller Plaza, 60th Fl.
New York 10112 (212) 621-2148
Application address: Michael Cunsolini, Napier Co., Napier Park, Meriden, CT 06450

Donor(s): Napier Co.
Financial data (yr. ended 7/31/87): Assets, $2,451,813 (M); expenditures, $133,035, including $118,984 for 71 grants (high: $11,400; low: $100).
Purpose and activities: Emphasis on higher and secondary education, youth and social agencies, hospitals, and cultural programs.
Limitations: Giving primarily in the Meriden, CT, area.
Application information:
Deadline(s): None
Write: Barbara Strohmeier, V.P., Chemical Bank
Trustees: John E. Benison, Eugene E. Bertolli, Michael G. Consolini, Eleanor S. Cooney, Ronald J. Meoni, Robert M. Meyers, Howard C. Schaefer, John A. Shulga, Carter H. White, Chemical Bank.
Employer Identification Number: 136029883

2125
The Nash Family Foundation, Inc.
c/o Spicer & Oppenheim
Seven World Trade Center
New York 10048

Established in 1964 in NY.
Donor(s): Jack Nash, Leo Levy, Helen Nash.
Financial data (yr. ended 6/30/88): Assets, $2,757,996 (M); expenditures, $49,487, including $41,387 for 42 grants (high: $15,000; low: $10).
Purpose and activities: Emphasis on Jewish giving, education, the arts, and museums.
Limitations: Giving primarily in New York, NY.
Application information: Contributes only to pre-selected organizations. Applications not accepted.
Officers and Directors: Jack Nash, Pres.; Arthur Aeder, V.P.; Ludwig Braumann, V.P.; Helen Nash, Treas.; Joshua Nash, Pamela Rohr.
Employer Identification Number: 136168559

2126
Nathanson-Abrams Family Foundation
c/o Roberta Abrams
1230 Ave. of the Americas, Suite 2010
New York 10020

Established in 1980.
Financial data (yr. ended 2/28/87): Assets, $1,102,930 (M); expenditures, $120,385, including $112,795 for grants.
Purpose and activities: Support for museums, universities, and public charities.
Types of support: Annual campaigns, building funds, capital campaigns, conferences and seminars, operating budgets.
Officer: Roberta Abrams, Treas.
Employer Identification Number: 133030314

2127
National Broadcasting Company, Inc. Corporate Giving Program
30 Rockefeller Plaza
New York 10112 (212) 664-4458

Financial data (yr. ended 12/31/88): Total giving, $1,150,000, including $1,000,000 for 241 grants (high: $60,000; low: $250) and $150,000 for 10 grants to individuals.
Purpose and activities: Supports non-profit performing arts groups and broadcasting-related organizations.
Types of support: Operating budgets, special projects, employee-related scholarships.
Limitations: Giving primarily in New York, NY; Chicago, IL; Los Angeles, CA; Cleveland, OH; Miami, FL; Washington, D.C.; Denver, CO; and Seattle, WA. No support for religious groups. No grants to individuals (including NBC employees), or for capital campaigns or endowments.
Publications: Newsletter, application guidelines.
Application information: Proposal including description and history of project and organization, budget, purpose statement indicating project's benefits, explanation of why NBC was considered to be a contributor, annual report or audited financial statement, and 501(c)(3) status letter. Application form required.
Initial approach: Letter
Copies of proposal: 1
Deadline(s): Aug. 1
Write: Andrew Brenner, Admin.
Number of staff: 1 full-time professional.

2128
National Fuel Gas Corporate Giving Program
30 Rockefeller Plaza
New York 10112 (212) 541-7533

Financial data (yr. ended 9/30/88): Total giving, $241,000, including $146,000 for grants, $80,000 for 145 grants to individuals and $15,000 for 5 in-kind gifts.
Purpose and activities: Supports fine arts institutes and general education, including private colleges and employee-related scholarships. Support also for community development, crime and law enforcement, hospital building funds, theater, and women's programs; includes in-kind donations.
Types of support: Annual campaigns, building funds, capital campaigns, conferences and seminars, employee-related scholarships, scholarship funds, student aid, in-kind gifts.
Limitations: Giving primarily in headquarters city and major operating locations in 22 counties in western NY state and northwestern PA.
Publications: Newsletter.
Application information:
Write: Bernard J. Kennedy, Pres. and C.E.O.
Number of staff: 2 part-time professional; 2 part-time support.

2129
Alice & Fred Netter Foundation, Inc.
c/o K. Fred Netter
411 Theodore Fremd Ave.
Rye 10580-1410

Established in 1965 in NY.
Donor(s): K. Fred Netter.
Financial data (yr. ended 12/31/87): Assets, $1,168,911 (M); gifts received, $69,641; expenditures, $52,988, including $43,015 for 97 grants (high: $6,000; low: $25; average: $50-$1,000).
Purpose and activities: Support for music, education, including education for minorities, Jewish welfare, medical research, sociology, and general charitable giving.
Types of support: Annual campaigns, building funds, capital campaigns, research.
Limitations: Giving primarily in NY.
Application information: Contributes only to pre-selected organizations. Applications not accepted.
Officers and Trustees: K. Fred Netter, Pres. and Treas.; Alfred E. Netter, V.P.; Ronald A. Netter, V.P.; Kenneth J. Bialkin, Secy.; Alice Netter.
Number of staff: None.
Employer Identification Number: 136176542

2130
Roy R. and Marie S. Neuberger Foundation, Inc.
522 Fifth Ave.
New York 10036 (212) 790-9676

Incorporated in 1954 in NY.
Donor(s): Roy R. Neuberger, Marie S. Neuberger.
Financial data (yr. ended 12/31/86): Assets, $8,130,506 (M); expenditures, $478,122, including $469,930 for 178 grants (high: $200,000; low: $25; average: $2,513).
Purpose and activities: Grants primarily for cultural programs, including the fine arts, and higher education.
Limitations: No grants to individuals.
Application information:
Initial approach: Letter
Board meeting date(s): Apr.
Write: Roy R. Neuberger, Pres.

Officers and Directors: Roy R. Neuberger, Pres. and Treas.; Ann N. Aceves, V.P.; James A. Neuberger, V.P.; Marie S. Neuberger, V.P.; Roy S. Neuberger, V.P.; Charles H. Levitt, Secy.; Mary Piatoff.
Number of staff: None.
Employer Identification Number: 136066102

2131
The New York Community Trust

415 Madison Ave.
New York 10017 (212) 758-0100

Community foundation established in 1923 in NY by resolution and declaration of trust.
Financial data (yr. ended 12/31/88): Assets, $634,966,791 (M); gifts received, $46,310,165; expenditures, $48,310,165, including $42,708,287 for 6,300 grants (high: $2,125,000; low: $100; average: $5,000-$35,000), $107,988 for 221 employee matching gifts, $774,540 for foundation-administered programs and $200,000 for loans.
Purpose and activities: A composite of many charitable funds. The grant program of each fund is handled separately, designed to meet objectives suggested by founder. Priority given to applications for special support for projects having particular significance for the New York City area. Loan guarantee program improves access to commercial lending.
Types of support: Seed money, matching funds, consulting services, technical assistance, special projects, research, publications, conferences and seminars, loans.
Limitations: Giving primarily in the metropolitan New York, NY, area. No support for religious purposes, or for transportation, or manpower development by non-advised grant program. No grants to individuals, or for deficit financing, emergency funds, building campaigns, endowment funds, or general operating support.
Publications: Informational brochure, annual report, application guidelines, newsletter, occasional report.
Application information:
Initial approach: Proposal with cover letter
Copies of proposal: 1
Deadline(s): None
Board meeting date(s): Feb., Apr., June, July, Oct., and Dec.
Final notification: 10 to 12 weeks
Write: Herbert B. West, Dir.
Officers: Herbert B. West,* Pres.; Lorie A. Slutsky, Exec. V.P.; Karen Metcalf, V.P., Finance and Admin.; Joyce M. Bove, V.P., Program; Sidney S. Whelan, Jr., V.P., Donor Relations; Kieran J. Lawlor, Controller.
Distribution Committee:* William Parsons, Chair.; Barbara S. Preiskel, Vice-Chair.; Frank H. Detweiler, Consulting Member; Arthur G. Altschul, Aida Alvarez, William M. Evarts, Jr., Barry H. Garfinkel, Judah Gribetz, Robert M. Kaufman, Bernard J. Pisani, M.D., Mrs. Laurance S. Rockefeller.
Trustees: The Bank of New York, Bankers Trust Co., Barclays Bank of New York, N.A., Brown Brothers Harriman Trust Co., The Chase Manhattan Bank, N.A., Chemical Bank, Citibank, N.A., Fiduciary Trust Co. International, Manufacturers Hanover Trust Co., Marine Midland Bank, N.A., Morgan Guaranty Trust Co. of New York, Republic National Bank of New York, Rockefeller Trust Co., IBJ Schroder Bank & Trust Co., J. & W. Seligman Trust Co., United States Trust Company.
Number of staff: 25 full-time professional; 2 part-time professional; 15 full-time support; 1 part-time support.
Employer Identification Number: 133062214
Recent arts and culture grants:
American Council for the Arts, NYC, NY, $10,000. For Arts Research Seminar Program. 3/10/88.
Appalshop, Whitesburg, KY, $12,000. For support of Headwaters, television documentary on community issues in Kentucky coalfields. 2/10/88.
Arts Connection, NYC, NY, $15,000. For research study to evaluate impact of arts study on educational achievement and personnel. 2/9/88.
Bronx Council on the Arts, Bronx, NY, $71,000. To provide theater program for visually impaired and sighted elderly at senior centers in Bronx. 2/8/88.
Concert Artists Guild, NYC, NY, $24,000. To broaden organization's financial base. 12/7/87.
Connecticut Players Foundation, New Haven, CT, $5,000. Toward work of Long Wharf Theater. 12/28/87.
Cypress Hills Local Development Corporation, Cypress Hills, NY, $15,000. To support efforts to implement historic district designation in Cypress Hills. 12/7/87.
Drawing Center, NYC, NY, $35,000. To strengthen membership of unique arts center. 8/1/88.
Educational Video Center, NYC, NY, $20,000. Toward renewal funding for alternative school video/writing project. 4/11/88.
Elder Craftsmen, NYC, NY, $17,000. To cover costs of agency's volunteer services program. 12/7/87.
Elders Share The Arts, Bronx, NY, $15,000. To train staff in new programs sites in NYC to use agency's approach and evaluate program. 10/8/87.
Electronic Arts Intermix, NYC, NY, $5,000. For Catalogue Project. 10/30/87.
Film Society of Lincoln Center, NYC, NY, $20,000. To underwrite demographic study of readership for film comment. 10/30/87.
Henry Street Settlement, NYC, NY, $15,000. To develop model curriculum for study of local culture and history. 12/7/87.
Hospital Audiences, NYC, NY, $69,000. To provide arts programs and workshops to blind and visually-impaired persons. 8/1/88.
Hospital Audiences, NYC, NY, $20,000. For second-year support of Hospital Audience's Haiomnibus Program. 8/1/88.
Independent Committee on Arts Policy, NYC, NY, $10,000. For preparation of national policy document aimed at 1988 Presidential candidates. 4/10/88.
Jewish Museum, NYC, NY, $10,000. To support Tribute to Radio Station - W E V D. 8/8/88.
Juilliard School, NYC, NY, $11,500. For renewal of Anna Schoen-Rene Fund Student Loan Program. 7/31/88.
Learning Through an Expanded Arts Program (LEAP), NYC, NY, $15,000. To expand arts-in-education program in public schools in the Bronx. 12/7/87.
Light Opera of Manhattan, NYC, NY, $10,000. For publicity to advertise new theater location. 2/24/88.
Metropolitan Opera Association, NYC, NY, $25,000. For 1987-88 support of young artists development program and in-school residency program. 12/7/87.
Metropolitan Opera Association, NYC, NY, $11,500. To provide loans to enable young vocalists to continue their advanced musical education. 7/31/88.
Metropolitan Opera Guild, NYC, NY, $20,000. To support training program for public school teachers. 10/13/87.
Mind Builders Creative Arts Company, Bronx, NY, $15,000. To update and computerize organization's management systems. 6/8/88.
Music-Theater Performing Group, NYC, NY, $25,000. To assist in building audience base. 12/7/87.
New Museum of Contemporary Art, NYC, NY, $7,500. For five-year program plan. 6/20/88.
New York School for Circus Arts, NYC, NY, $10,000. To help children at Saint Luke's Hospital cope with their hospitalization. 3/1/88.
Orpheus Chamber Ensemble, NYC, NY, $26,000. For marketing and development campaign. 2/4/88.
Pentacle, NYC, NY, $7,500. For marketing project-training program for experimental and minority choreographers and dance companies. 5/5/88.
Philharmonic-Symphony Society of New York, NYC, NY, $25,000. To provide additional support for Symphony Orchestra Library Information Project. 10/15/87.
Poets and Writers, NYC, NY, $20,000. For marketing campaign to new audiences. 2/4/88.
Queens County Art and Cultural Center, Flushing, NY, $35,000. To implement neighborhood-intensive marketing strategy. 10/15/87.
Saint Lukes Ensemble, NYC, NY, $17,000. For Children's Free Opera and Dance concerts in Brooklyn, Bronx and Staten Island. 4/11/88.
Save the Theaters, NYC, NY, $25,000. For organizational development funds to increase base of individual support. 2/4/88.
South Street Seaport Museum, NYC, NY, $25,000. To continue support for campaign to increase museum's membership. 6/6/88.
Studio in a School Association, NYC, NY, $23,000. To support visual arts programs for public elementary schools in Bronx. 10/13/87.
Symphony Space, NYC, NY, $30,000. To support fundraising and publicity campaign. 10/13/87.
Theater Communications Group, NYC, NY, $40,000. To strengthen major organization serving American nonprofit theater. 4/11/88.
Theater for the Forgotten, Long Island City, NY, $15,000. For salary and fringe benefits of program director of changing scenes program. 12/7/87.
Theater for the New City Foundation, NYC, NY, $20,000. To increase individual contributions. 8/1/88.

Town Hall Foundation, NYC, NY, $25,000. To help re-establish Town Hall as leading arts organization. 4/11/88.
Whitney Museum of American Art, NYC, NY, $15,000. To be used for two full-time instructors for artreach program. 8/1/88.

2132
New York Life Foundation
51 Madison Ave.
New York 10010 (212) 576-7341

Established in 1979 in NY.
Donor(s): New York Life Insurance Co.
Financial data (yr. ended 12/31/87): Assets, $22,165,054 (M); expenditures, $2,212,314, including $2,062,976 for 648 grants (high: $360,000; low: $25; average: $500-$10,000) and $99,188 for employee matching gifts.
Purpose and activities: Grants to national and local organizations. Priority areas are AIDS and literacy; support also for higher education, including insurance education, in both direct grants and employee matching gifts; community funds; community development and urban affairs; hospitals; cultural programs; and youth and social service agencies.
Types of support: General purposes, scholarship funds, operating budgets, building funds, special projects, employee matching gifts.
Limitations: No support for public educational institutions; fraternal, social, professional, veterans', or athletic organizations; religious or sectarian organizations or activities whose services are limited to members of any one religious group; grant-making foundations; preschool, primary, or secondary educational institutions; or United Way-member organizations already receiving foundation support. No grants to individuals, or for seminars, conferences, trips, memorials, endowments, capital campaigns, research-related programs, or matching gifts; no loans.
Publications: Application guidelines.
Application information:
Initial approach: Letter
Copies of proposal: 1
Deadline(s): None
Board meeting date(s): No formal schedule
Final notification: Varies
Write: Carol J. Reuter, Exec. Dir.
Officers: Donald K. Ross,* Chair.; Edmund R. Harnedy,* Secy.; William E. Keiter,* Treas.; Carol J. Reuter, Exec. Dir.
Directors:* George A.W. Bundschuh, John T. DeBardeleben, Harry G. Hohn, Malcolm MacKay, Walter Shur.
Number of staff: 3 full-time professional; 1 full-time support.
Employer Identification Number: 132989476

2133
New York Stock Exchange Foundation, Inc.
11 Wall St.
New York 10005 (212) 656-2060

Incorporated in 1983 in NY.
Donor(s): New York Stock Exchange.
Financial data (yr. ended 12/31/87): Assets, $6,102,536 (M); gifts received, $2,200,000; expenditures, $1,273,842, including $261,546 for 36 grants (high: $70,000; low: $500) and $54,109 for employee matching gifts.
Purpose and activities: Support for higher education, community development, social services, and arts and cultural institutions.
Types of support: Employee matching gifts.
Limitations: Giving primarily in New York, NY.
Application information:
Initial approach: Letter
Write: James E. Buck, Secy.
Officers: Richard R. Shinn,* Chair.; James E. Buck, Secy.; John P. Johnson, Treas.
Directors:* John Brademas, James C. Bradford, Jr., John A. Georges, William A. Schreyer, Donald Stone, W. Clarke Wescoe.
Employer Identification Number: 133203195

2134
New York Telephone Company Giving Program
1095 Ave. of the Americas, Room 2506
New York 10036 (212) 395-2295

Purpose and activities: New York Telephone evaluates each applicant organization on its merits. Specifically, the company reviews the quality of the program, its service to the public, the size and type of constituency it serves, the organization's management, and its accountability, finances and fundraising practices. Because the company considers it important that an applicant receive widespread support from the community in which it functions, the applicant organization's community impact and interest are also assessed. To assure that its contributions are used where they have the greatest value, New York Telephone gives only where a genuine need for funding is demonstrated, and only to programs that do not duplicate the work of public agencies. The contributions program covers three general areas: health and welfare, education, and culture and civic affairs. The grants are disbursed in the following categories: General Operating Expense-for day-to-day expenses of the organization; Capital Grants-for construction, remodeling or restoration of physical facilities; Leadership Grants-for noteworthy projects of certain non-profit organizations; Special Grants-for a specific project by an organization are in some cases sponsored 100 percent by the company.
Types of support: Capital campaigns, employee matching gifts, operating budgets, special projects, equipment, conferences and seminars, matching funds, research, seed money.
Limitations: Giving primarily in NY. No support for discriminatory organizations, political groups, national health organizations, elementary or secondary education, or religious groups for denominational purposes. No grants to individuals, or for goodwill or special occasion advertising, or operating expenses of United Way recipients.
Application information: Include description of organization and its growth areas, statement of objectives and long-range plans, lists of board members and corporate officers, budget and audited financial statement, 501 (c)(3).
Initial approach: Letter, phone or full application
Deadline(s): Applications accepted throughout the year
Board meeting date(s): Charitable Contributions Committee meets as needed
Final notification: Minimum of 12 weeks to process applications
Write: Barbara Wright, Staff Dir., Contribs.

2135
The New York Times Company Foundation, Inc.
229 West 43rd St.
New York 10036 (212) 556-1091

Incorporated in 1955 in NY.
Donor(s): The New York Times Co.
Financial data (yr. ended 12/31/87): Assets, $1,883,112 (M); gifts received, $5,100,000; expenditures, $4,898,542, including $4,670,860 for 594 grants (high: $220,000; low: $500; average: $1,000-$10,000) and $523,730 for 486 employee matching gifts.
Purpose and activities: Grants primarily for higher and secondary education, including support for minority education and a matching gifts program; support also for urban affairs, cultural programs, journalism, and environmental concerns.
Types of support: Annual campaigns, conferences and seminars, continuing support, emergency funds, employee matching gifts, endowment funds, exchange programs, fellowships, general purposes, internships, operating budgets, publications, research, scholarship funds, seed money, employee-related scholarships.
Limitations: Giving primarily in the New York, NY, metropolitan area and in localities served by affiliates of the company. No support for sectarian religious institutions or for health-related purposes; grants for urban affairs seldom made on the neighborhood level. No grants to individuals, or for capital and building funds; no loans.
Publications: Annual report (including application guidelines).
Application information:
Initial approach: Letter
Copies of proposal: 1
Deadline(s): Submit proposal in the early part of the year; no set deadline
Board meeting date(s): Mar. and Sept.
Final notification: Varies
Write: Fred M. Hechinger, Pres.
Officers: Fred M. Hechinger,* Pres.; Walter E. Mattson,* Exec. V.P.; David L. Gorham, Sr. V.P.; Solomon B. Watson IV, V.P.; Laura Corwin, Secy.
Directors:* Arthur Ochs Sulzberger, Chair.; John F. Akers, William R. Cross, Jr., Richard L. Gelb, Louis V. Gerstner, Jr., Marian S. Heiskell, Ruth S. Holmberg, George B. Munroe, Charles H. Price II, George L. Shinn, Donald M. Stewart, Iphigene Ochs Sulzberger, Judith P. Sulzberger, M.D., Cyrus R. Vance, Esq., Theodore R. Wagner.
Number of staff: 1 full-time professional.
Employer Identification Number: 136066955
Recent arts and culture grants:
Alvin Ailey American Dance Theater, NYC, NY, $10,000. 1987.
Amas Repertory Theater, NYC, NY, $5,000. 1987.

American Academy of Dramatic Arts, NYC, NY, $5,000. For minority scholarships. 1987.
American Ballet Theater, NYC, NY, $5,000. 1987.
American Council for the Arts, NYC, NY, $7,000. 1987.
American Craft Council, NYC, NY, $10,000. 1987.
American Dance Festival, NYC, NY, $10,000. 1987.
American Museum of Natural History, NYC, NY, $15,000. 1987.
American Music Center, NYC, NY, $5,000. 1987.
American Symphony Orchestra League, NYC, NY, $10,000. For New York concert. 1987.
American Trust for the British Library, Cambridge, MA, $25,000. 1987.
Arts Connection, NYC, NY, $15,000. For dance program in New York City public schools. 1987.
Asia Society, NYC, NY, $5,000. 1987.
Big Apple Circus, NYC, NY, $5,000. 1987.
Brooklyn Academy of Music, Brooklyn, NY, $20,000. Toward 125th anniversary. 1987.
Brooklyn Botanic Garden, Brooklyn, NY, $5,000. 1987.
Brooklyn Museum, Brooklyn, NY, $10,000. 1987.
Business Committee for the Arts, NYC, NY, $5,000. 1987.
Carnegie Hall Society, NYC, NY, $35,000. For plaque for Sydney Gruson. 1987.
Circle in the Square, NYC, NY, $5,000. 1987.
Circle Repertory Theater Company, NYC, NY, $7,000. 1987.
Clurman Theater, NYC, NY, $5,000. 1987.
Columbia University, Teachers College, NYC, NY, $5,000. For teaching of writing project. 1987.
Cultural Assistance Center, NYC, NY, $10,000. 1987.
Cultural Council Foundation, NYC, NY, $10,000. 1987.
Cunningham Dance Foundation, NYC, NY, $5,000. 1987.
Dance Magazine Foundation, NYC, NY, $5,000. 1987.
Dance Notation Bureau, NYC, NY, $5,000. 1987.
Dance Theater of Harlem, NYC, NY, $5,000. 1987.
Dance Theater Workshop, NYC, NY, $5,000. 1987.
Ensemble Studio Theater, NYC, NY, $5,000. 1987.
Eugene ONeill Memorial Theater Center, Waterford, CT, $20,000. For variety of educational programs in theater arts. 1987.
First New York International Festival of the Arts, NYC, NY, $250,000. 1987.
Florida Studio Theater, Sarasota, FL, $5,000. 1987.
Florida West Coast Music, Sarasota, FL, $5,000. 1987.
Folger Shakespeare Library, DC, $5,000. For Guild Book Worker's 80th Anniversary Exhibit. 1987.
Forest History Society, Santa Cruz, CA, $10,000. 1987.
Forty-Second Street E.T.C., NYC, NY, $5,000. Toward 42nd Street Festival. 1987.
Intar Hispanic American Theater, NYC, NY, $5,000. 1987.
International Center of Photography, NYC, NY, $5,000. 1987.
Japan Society, NYC, NY, $5,000. 1987.
Jewish Museum, NYC, NY, $5,000. 1987.
Joyce Theater, NYC, NY, $5,000. 1987.
LaFourche Heritage Society, Thibodaux, LA, $5,000. 1987.
Lincoln Center for the Performing Arts, NYC, NY, $100,000. 1987.
Little Orchestra Society, NYC, NY, $5,000. 1987.
Manhattan Theater Club, NYC, NY, $5,000. 1987.
Marie Selby Botanical Gardens, Sarasota, FL, $10,000. 1987.
Memphis Orchestral Society, Memphis, TN, $10,000. 1987.
Metropolitan Museum of Art, NYC, NY, $170,000. 1987.
Middlebury College, Middlebury, VT, $5,000. For training of teachers at Breadloaf School of English. 1987.
Municipal Art Society, NYC, NY, $5,000. 1987.
Museum of Broadcasting, NYC, NY, $10,000. 1987.
Museum of Modern Art, NYC, NY, $15,000. 1987.
Museum of the City of New York, NYC, NY, $5,000. 1987.
National Dance Institute, NYC, NY, $10,000. To support dance programs in public schools. 1987.
National Public Radio, DC, $10,000. For educational projects. 1987.
Negro Ensemble Company, NYC, NY, $5,000. 1987.
New York Botanical Garden, Bronx, NY, $25,000. 1987.
New York City Ballet, NYC, NY, $20,000. 1987.
New York City Opera, NYC, NY, $20,000. 1987.
New York Historical Society, NYC, NY, $10,000. For 1987 Summer History Institute. 1987.
New York Landmarks Preservation Foundation, NYC, NY, $5,000. 1987.
New York Philharmonic, NYC, NY, $15,000. 1987.
New York Shakespeare Festival, NYC, NY, $15,000. For Shakespeare-Broadway and high schools. 1987.
New York Shakespeare Festival, NYC, NY, $10,000. 1987.
New York State Broadcasters Association, Albany, NY, $5,000. 1987.
New York Youth Symphony, NYC, NY, $6,000. 1987.
New York Zoological Society, Bronx, NY, $25,450. 1987.
New York Zoological Society, Bronx, NY, $10,000. For Wildlife Conservation International Program. 1987.
Paper Bag Players, NYC, NY, $7,000. 1987.
Parsons School of Design, NYC, NY, $5,000. For graduate program in architecture and design criticism. 1987.
Paul Taylor Dance Foundation, NYC, NY, $10,000. 1987.
PEN American Center, NYC, NY, $5,000. 1987.
Philharmonia Virtuosi Corporation, Dobbs Ferry, NY, $10,000. 1987.
Pierpont Morgan Library, NYC, NY, $10,000. 1987.
Playwrights Horizons, NYC, NY, $10,000. 1987.
Poets and Writers, NYC, NY, $7,500. 1987.
Putnam Museum, Moline, IL, $10,000. 1987.
Ringling Museum of Art Foundation, Sarasota, FL, $5,000. 1987.
Roundabout Theater Company, NYC, NY, $10,000. 1987.
Saint Johns River Community College, Palatka, FL, $10,000. Toward Florida School of the Arts. 1987.
Santa Rosa Symphony Association, Santa Rosa, CA, $10,000. 1987.
Sarasota Opera Association, Sarasota, FL, $12,000. 1987.
School of American Ballet, NYC, NY, $5,000. 1987.
Second Stage Theater, NYC, NY, $5,000. 1987.
Skowhegan School of Painting and Sculpture, Skowhegan, ME, $10,000. For scholarships. 1987.
Solomon R. Guggenheim Museum, NYC, NY, $12,000. 1987.
South Street Seaport Museum, NYC, NY, $5,000. 1987.
Thalian Hall, Wilmington, NC, $20,000. 1987.
Theater, The, Sarasota, FL, $20,000. 1987.
Town Hall Foundation, NYC, NY, $6,000. 1987.
University of Kentucky, Lexington, KY, $5,000. For fine arts series. Grant shared with Southeast Community College. 1987.
University of North Alabama, Florence, AL, $8,000. Toward Video Encyclopedia of the 20th Century. 1987.
University of Southern Maine, Portland, ME, $25,000. To create library for historic collection. 1987.
Vivian Beaumont Theater, NYC, NY, $20,000. 1987.
W N E T Channel 13, NYC, NY, $25,000. 1987.
W N Y C Foundation, NYC, NY, $10,000. For Frick Museum concerts. 1987.
Whitney Museum of American Art, NYC, NY, $10,000. 1987.
YM-YWHA, 92nd Street, NYC, NY, $15,000. For general operations including support for poetry center. 1987.
YM-YWHAs of Greater New York, Associated, NYC, NY, $5,000. For second annual Jewish Book Fair. 1987.
Young Concert Artists, NYC, NY, $5,000. 1987.

2136
The New-Land Foundation, Inc.

200 Park Ave., Suite 3014
New York 10166 (212) 867-5500

Incorporated in 1941 in NY.
Donor(s): Muriel M. Buttinger.†
Financial data (yr. ended 12/31/88): Assets, $15,822,407 (M); gifts received, $161,036; expenditures, $1,787,803, including $1,575,343 for 139 grants.
Purpose and activities: Grants for civil rights, mental health, environmental preservation, public interest, arms control and disarmament, cultural programs, minority and medical education, and social service and youth agencies.
Types of support: General purposes, annual campaigns, seed money, research, conferences

and seminars, continuing support, internships, matching funds, operating budgets, special projects.
Limitations: No grants to individuals; no loans.
Publications: Application guidelines.
Application information:
Initial approach: Proposal
Copies of proposal: 1
Deadline(s): Feb. 1 and Aug. 1
Board meeting date(s): Spring and fall
Final notification: For positive responses only
Write: Robert Wolf, Pres.
Officers and Directors: Robert Wolf, Pres.; Constance Harvey, V.P.; Hal Harvey, V.P.; Renee G. Schwartz, Secy.-Treas.; Joan Harvey, Anna Frank Loeb, Albert Solnit.
Number of staff: None.
Employer Identification Number: 136086562

2137
Samuel I. Newhouse Foundation, Inc.
c/o Paul Scherer
360 Madison Ave.
New York 10017

Incorporated in 1945 in NY.
Donor(s): Samuel I. Newhouse,† Mitzi E. Newhouse.†
Financial data (yr. ended 10/31/87): Assets, $60,262,791 (M); gifts received, $1,000; expenditures, $3,828,191, including $3,729,324 for 408 grants (high: $250,000; low: $100; average: $500-$1,000).
Purpose and activities: Establishment of Newhouse Communications Center at Syracuse University for education and research in mass communications; giving for community funds, hospitals, Jewish welfare funds, higher and secondary education, music and the arts, and youth agencies; support also for journalism associations.
Application information: Applications not accepted.
Officers and Directors: Donald E. Newhouse, V.P.; Samuel I. Newhouse, Jr., V.P.; Norman N. Newhouse, Secy.; Theodore Newhouse, Treas.; Richard E. Diamond.
Number of staff: None.
Employer Identification Number: 116006296

2138
Jerome A. and Estelle R. Newman Assistance Fund, Inc.
707 Westchester Ave., Suite 405
White Plains 10604-3102 (914) 993-0777

Incorporated in 1954 in NY.
Donor(s): Howard A. Newman, Jerome A. Newman.†
Financial data (yr. ended 6/30/87): Assets, $8,359,550 (M); expenditures, $987,456, including $957,085 for 26 grants (high: $415,000; low: $250; average: $250-$15,000).
Purpose and activities: Support for higher education, hospitals, aid to the handicapped, Jewish welfare funds, and the performing arts.
Limitations: Giving primarily in NY. No grants to individuals or loans to individuals.
Application information:
Initial approach: Letter
Deadline(s): None
Board meeting date(s): Sept.
Final notification: Varies
Officers: Howard A. Newman,* Chair.; William C. Newman,* Pres.; Patricia Nanon,* V.P.; Elizabeth L. Newman,* V.P.; Robert H. Haines,* Secy.; Michael Greenberg, Treas.
Directors:* Andrew H. Levy, William C. Scott.
Number of staff: None.
Employer Identification Number: 136096241

2139
Henry Nias Foundation, Inc.
639 Seney Ave.
Mamaroneck 10543 (914) 698-5036

Incorporated in 1955 in NY.
Donor(s): Henry Nias.†
Financial data (yr. ended 11/30/86): Assets, $10,619,000 (M); expenditures, $583,313, including $514,000 for 53 grants (high: $25,000; low: $2,500; average: $5,000-$15,000).
Purpose and activities: Emphasis on hospitals, aid to the handicapped, medical school student loan funds, education, cultural programs, youth, the aged, and Jewish welfare funds.
Limitations: Giving limited to the New York City, NY, metropolitan area.
Application information: Applications by invitation only.
Deadline(s): Aug. 31
Board meeting date(s): Sept. and Oct.
Final notification: Grants paid in Nov.
Write: Henry L. Fleischman, Pres.
Officers and Directors: Henry L. Fleischman, Pres. and Treas.; Albert J. Rosenberg, V.P. and Secy.; Stanley Edelman, M.D., V.P.; Richard J. Edelman, Charles D. Fleischman, William F. Rosenberg.
Number of staff: None.
Employer Identification Number: 136075785

2140
Edward John Noble Foundation, Inc.
32 East 57th St.
New York 10022 (212) 759-4212
Business office address: P.O. Box 162, Washington Depot, CT 06794

Trust established in 1940 in CT; incorporated in 1982.
Donor(s): Edward John Noble.†
Financial data (yr. ended 12/31/88): Assets, $86,179,103 (M); expenditures, $3,389,550, including $2,410,929 for 65 grants (high: $295,000; low: $250; average: $5,000-$50,000).
Purpose and activities: Grants to major cultural organizations in New York City, especially for their educational programs. Selected projects concerned with conservation and ecology primarily related to activities on an island off the coast of GA. Supports private college and university environmental studies programs in the Northeast and programs to improve educational opportunity for gifted and talented disadvantaged children in New York City. Programs in health education efforts related to family planning and the problems of overpopulation.
Types of support: Continuing support, scholarship funds, matching funds, general purposes, endowment funds, special projects.
Limitations: Giving primarily in the metropolitan New York, NY, area for arts organizations and their educational programs; St. Catherine's Island, GA, and the eastern states for conservation projects and population control; and the Northeast for private colleges and universities. No support for television, films, or performances. No grants to individuals, or for publications, building funds, or equipment; no loans.
Publications: Biennial report (including application guidelines).
Application information:
Initial approach: Letter or proposal
Copies of proposal: 1
Deadline(s): 6 weeks before board meeting dates
Board meeting date(s): June and Dec.
Final notification: 3 months
Write: June Noble Larkin, Chair.
Officers: June Noble Larkin,* Chair. and Pres.; Nancy K. Breslin,* Secy.; Frank Y. Larkin,* Treas.; John F. Joline III, Exec. Dir.
Directors:* Mimi Coleman, Robert G. Goelet, Howard Phipps, Jr., Frank P. Piskor, E.J. Noble Smith, Jeremy T. Smith, Carroll L. Wainwright, Jr., Alan N. Weeden.
Number of staff: 3 full-time professional; 2 full-time support.
Employer Identification Number: 061055586
Recent arts and culture grants:
Affiliate Artists, NYC, NY, $25,000. To match National Endowment for the Arts grant. 12/7/87.
American Museum of Natural History, NYC, NY, $185,691. For Archaeological Research Project on St. Catherine's Island. 12/7/87.
Brooklyn Philharmonic Symphony Orchestra, Brooklyn, NY, $15,000. For music instruction in Brooklyn schools. 6/13/88.
Bryant Park Restoration Corporation, NYC, NY, $10,000. For Music and Dance Half-Price Tickets Booth. 12/7/87.
Lincoln Center for the Performing Arts, NYC, NY, $35,000. For Great Performers Kronos Quartet concert series in 1988-1989. 6/13/88.
Museum of Broadcasting, NYC, NY, $250,000. For Scholars' Room. 6/13/88.
Museum of Modern Art, NYC, NY, $56,250. Toward important acquisition. 12/7/87.
National Soaring Museum, Elmira, NY, $10,000. For education program. 6/13/88.
New York Botanical Garden, Institute of Economic Botany, Bronx, NY, $28,050. For ethnobotanical research on tropical rain forest resources. 6/13/88.
New York Zoological Society, Bronx, NY, $295,000. For St. Catherine's Island Survival Center for Endangered Species. 12/7/87.
Philharmonic-Symphony Society of New York, NYC, NY, $10,000. For Annual Fund. 12/7/87.
Third Street Music School Settlement, NYC, NY, $50,000. To support expanded development staff. 6/13/88.
Young Concert Artists, NYC, NY, $75,000. For endowment of residency program. 6/13/88.
Youth Symphony Orchestra of New York, NYC, NY, $5,000. For general support. 6/13/88.

2141
Normandie Foundation, Inc.
c/o Norman-Weil Office
147 East 48th St.
New York 10022 (212) 759-7185

Incorporated in 1966 in NY.
Donor(s): Andrew E. Norman, The Aaron E. Norman Fund, Inc.
Financial data (yr. ended 12/31/86): Assets, $1,837,505 (M); expenditures, $77,209, including $62,700 for grants.
Purpose and activities: Grants primarily for cultural programs, with emphasis on a school for circus arts, and for civil liberties, and minority and civil rights organizations.
Types of support: General purposes.
Limitations: No grants to individuals, or for building or endowment funds, scholarships, fellowships, or matching gifts; generally no loans.
Application information:
Initial approach: Letter
Copies of proposal: 1
Deadline(s): None
Board meeting date(s): June and Dec.
Final notification: 6 months
Write: Andrew E. Norman, Pres.
Officers: Andrew E. Norman, Pres. and Treas.; Nancy N. LaSalle, V.P. and Secy.; Helen D. Norman, V.P.
Number of staff: None.
Employer Identification Number: 136213564

2142
Norstar Bank of Upstate NY Foundation
c/o Norstar Bank of Upstate New York, Trust Dept.
69 State St.
Albany 12201 (518) 447-4162

Trust established in 1962 in NY.
Donor(s): Norstar Bank of Upstate New York.
Financial data (yr. ended 9/30/88): Assets, $5,439,735 (M); gifts received, $4,101,155; expenditures, $580,760, including $575,025 for 135 grants (high: $125,000; low: $25).
Purpose and activities: Emphasis on community funds, higher education, hospitals and health associations, and youth agencies; support also for civic affairs and the arts.
Types of support: Building funds, equipment, land acquisition, research, capital campaigns.
Limitations: Giving primarily in the Albany, Utica, and Newburgh, NY, areas. No grants to individuals, or for endowment funds, scholarships, fellowships, or matching gifts; no loans.
Application information: Application form required.
Initial approach: Proposal
Copies of proposal: 2
Deadline(s): None
Board meeting date(s): Distribution committee meets 3 or 4 times a year as required
Final notification: Shortly after meeting
Write: Robert F. MacFarland, Chair.
Trustee: Norstar Bank of Upstate New York.
Number of staff: None.
Employer Identification Number: 146105570

2143
North American Reassurance Corporate Giving Program
237 Park Ave.
New York 10017 (212) 907-8000

Financial data (yr. ended 12/31/88): $49,000 for grants (high: $5,000; low: $500; average: $500-$1,000).
Purpose and activities: Supports civic programs, cultural institutes, education, medical research, minority programs, urban affairs, and welfare programs.
Application information:
Initial approach: Letter
Write: Michel Sales, Pres. and C.E.O.

2144
Northern New York Community Foundation, Inc.
(Formerly Watertown Foundation, Inc.)
P.O. Box 6106
Watertown 13601 (315) 782-7110

Community foundation incorporated in 1929 in NY.
Financial data (yr. ended 12/31/88): Assets, $3,109,621 (M); gifts received, $141,014; expenditures, $739,666, including $395,023 for 46 grants (high: $80,000; low: $333) and $200,834 for 199 grants to individuals.
Purpose and activities: To promote charitable, educational, cultural, recreational, and health programs through grants to community organizations and agencies and a student scholarship program.
Types of support: Annual campaigns, seed money, building funds, equipment, land acquisition, matching funds, student aid, special projects, research, publications, conferences and seminars, renovation projects, capital campaigns.
Limitations: Giving limited to Jefferson County, NY. No grants for endowment funds or deficit financing.
Publications: Annual report.
Application information:
Initial approach: Letter or telephone
Copies of proposal: 1
Deadline(s): Feb. 1, May 1, Aug. 1, and Nov. 1
Board meeting date(s): Mar., June, Sept., and Dec.
Final notification: 1 to 2 months
Write: James W. Higgins, Exec. Dir.
Officers: Robert G. Horr, Jr.,* Pres.; Everett G. Foster,* V.P.; Anderson Wise,* Secy.-Treas.; James W. Higgins, Exec. Dir.; Lee T. Hirschey.
Directors:* Norman R. Ahlheim, Frances P. Carter, Floyd J. Chandler, John Doldo, Jr., Richard O. Flechtner, Barbara D. Hanrahan, P. Owen Willaman.
Number of staff: 1 full-time professional; 1 part-time professional; 2 full-time support.
Employer Identification Number: 156020989

2145
NYNEX Corporate Giving Program
1113 Westchester Ave., 1st Fl.
White Plains
New York 10604-3510

Financial data (yr. ended 12/31/87): $13,724,700 for grants (high: $100,000; low: $100).
Purpose and activities: Support for economic, continuing, and general education, community affairs, literary, and arts, including music and theater, job development, public broadcasting, United Way agencies, for children, youth, and minorities. Considers projects concerned with urban problems and rural issues, and elementary and secondary education programs. Types of support offered include employee volunteer programs and company in-house services, and short term projects. Maintains an employee gift-matching program for education.
Types of support: Employee-related scholarships, special projects, technical assistance, matching funds, in-kind gifts.
Limitations: Giving primarily in operating locations in NY and MA. No grants to individuals or for religious, political, or discriminatory organizations, United Way recipients, advertising, or dinner programs.
Application information: Include annual budget, audited financial statements from the previous two years, 501(c)(3), 990-PF, lists of board members and contributors as well as list of contributions amount. Application form required.
Initial approach: By letter
Board meeting date(s): Committee meets quarterly
Write: Barbara W. Bates, Dir., Corp. Contribs.
Number of staff: 4 full-time professional; 1 part-time professional.

2146
NYNEX Foundation
1113 Westchester Ave., 1st Fl.
White Plains 10604-3510 (914) 644-7226

Established in 1985 in NY.
Donor(s): NYNEX Corp.
Financial data (yr. ended 12/31/87): Assets, $25,174,622 (M); gifts received, $3,000,000; expenditures, $1,494,278, including $1,441,750 for 47 grants (high: $150,000; low: $1,500; average: $10,000-$50,000).
Purpose and activities: Giving in three areas: educational organizations of all levels, economic and community development, including support for cultural institutions, and innovative solutions to the problems of the less advantaged, such as the elderly and unemployed.
Types of support: Special projects.
Limitations: Giving primarily in areas of company operations concentrated in New England and NY. No support for organizations which duplicate work of federal, state, or local public agencies, or religious organizations. No grants to individuals, or for advertising, or operating expenses of organizations supported by the United Way.

Publications: Annual report (including application guidelines), informational brochure (including application guidelines).
Application information:
Initial approach: Proposal with letter
Deadline(s): None
Board meeting date(s): Contributions Committee meets 4 times a year
Final notification: 4 to 6 months
Write: Barbara W. Bates, Prog. Dir.
Officers: W.G. Burns,* Pres.; R.F. Burke,* V.P. and Secy.; Grace J. Fippinger, V.P. and Treas.; D.K. Emmons, Exec. Dir.; M. Goldstein, Comptroller.
Directors:* Delbert C. Staley.
Number of staff: 5 part-time professional; 2 part-time support.
Employer Identification Number: 133319048

2147
O.C.F. Foundation, Inc.
122 East 42nd St.
New York 10168

Incorporated in 1940 in NY.
Donor(s): International Minerals and Metals Corp.
Financial data (yr. ended 12/31/87): Assets, $1,600,155 (M); expenditures, $159,662, including $137,945 for 39 grants (high: $35,000; low: $60).
Purpose and activities: Support for Jewish welfare funds and cultural activities; some support for social services.
Limitations: Giving primarily in NY.
Application information: Contributes only to pre-selected organizations. Applications not accepted.
Officers: H. Fred Baerwald, Pres.; Anne Halpern, V.P.; Philip J. Maron, Secy.; Gregor Leinsdorf, Treas.
Employer Identification Number: 136007727

2148
A. Lindsay and Olive B. O'Connor Foundation
P.O. Box D
Hobart 13788 (607) 538-9248

Trust established in 1965 in NY.
Donor(s): Olive B. O'Connor.†
Financial data (yr. ended 12/31/87): Assets, $33,971,080 (M); expenditures, $2,684,464, including $2,371,754 for 122 grants (high: $275,000; low: $132; average: $1,000-$20,000).
Purpose and activities: Emphasis on "quality of life," including hospitals, libraries, community centers, higher education, nursing and other vocational education, youth agencies, religious organizations, and historic restoration; support also for town, village, and environmental improvement.
Types of support: General purposes, continuing support, annual campaigns, seed money, emergency funds, building funds, equipment, land acquisition, endowment funds, special projects, research, publications, conferences and seminars, scholarship funds, matching funds, loans, technical assistance, program-related investments, renovation projects.
Limitations: Giving primarily in Delaware County, NY, and contiguous rural counties in upstate NY. No grants to individuals, or for operating budgets or deficit financing.
Publications: Program policy statement.
Application information: Application form required.
Initial approach: Letter
Copies of proposal: 1
Deadline(s): Apr. 1
Board meeting date(s): May or June and Sept. or Oct.; committee meets monthly to consider grants under $5,000
Final notification: 1 week to 10 days after semiannual meeting
Write: Donald F. Bishop, II, Exec. Dir.
Officer: Donald F. Bishop II, Exec. Dir.
Advisory Committee: Olive B. Price, Chair.; Robert L. Bishop II, Vice-Chair.; Robert L. Bishop, Exec. Secy.; Donald F. Bishop, Charlotte Bishop Hill, William J. Murphy, Eugene E. Peckham.
Trustee: Chase Lincoln First Bank, N.A.
Number of staff: 2
Employer Identification Number: 166063485

2149
Sylvan and Ann Oestreicher Foundation, Inc.
645 Madison Ave.
New York 10022 (212) 759-8500

Incorporated in 1948 in NY.
Donor(s): Sylvan Oestreicher.†
Financial data (yr. ended 4/30/88): Assets, $3,091,374 (M); expenditures, $147,307, including $135,639 for 134 grants (high: $21,000; low: $75).
Purpose and activities: Grants primarily for religious welfare funds, hospitals, and higher education; support also for the handicapped, youth agencies, religious associations, and cultural programs.
Application information:
Deadline(s): None
Write: Robert F. Welch, Secy.
Officers and Directors: Ann Oestreicher, Pres.; Merwin Lewis, V.P.; Robert F. Welch, Secy.
Employer Identification Number: 136085974

2150
Ralph E. Ogden Foundation, Inc.
Pleasant Hill Rd.
Mountainville 10953

Incorporated in 1947 in DE.
Donor(s): Ralph E. Ogden,† H. Peter Stern, Margaret H. Ogden.†
Financial data (yr. ended 12/31/87): Assets, $17,406,503 (M); expenditures, $977,806, including $892,675 for 24 grants (high: $757,675; low: $1,000).
Purpose and activities: Support primarily for the arts, especially a local art center.
Limitations: Giving primarily in Mountainville, NY, and New York City.
Application information: Contributes only to pre-selected organizations. Applications not accepted.
Officers and Trustees: H. Peter Stern, Pres.; Leslie A. Jacobson, V.P.; Spencer L. Koslan, Secy.; Eugene L. Cohan, Treas.; Frederick Lubcher, David Sachs, Beatrice Stern, Elisabeth Ellen Stern, John Peter Stern.
Employer Identification Number: 141455902

2151
F. W. Olin Foundation, Inc.
780 Third Ave.
New York 10017 (212) 832-0508
Minnesota address: William B. Horn, V.P., 2700 Foshay Tower, Minneapolis, MN 55402; Tel.: (612) 341-2581

Incorporated in 1938 in NY.
Donor(s): Franklin W. Olin.†
Financial data (yr. ended 12/31/87): Assets, $218,670,318 (M); expenditures, $15,130,443, including $13,801,300 for 12 grants (high: $3,467,000; low: $31,300; average: $3,000,000-$6,000,000).
Purpose and activities: Primarily for constructing and equipping new academic buildings and libraries at private four-year, accredited, degree-granting colleges and universities, with a preference for funding undergraduate buildings. Awards limited to institutions with enrollment of more than 500 full-time students.
Types of support: Building funds, equipment.
Limitations: No support for colleges and universities with enrollments of less than 500 full-time undergraduate students. No grants to individuals, or for operating budgets, research, scholarships, fellowships, matching gifts, special projects, general support, or non-academic buildings and facilities funds; no loans.
Publications: Program policy statement (including application guidelines).
Application information: Submit original application to New York office and 1 copy to Minneapolis office; geographic location is given negative weight for proposals in areas of previous foundation support, especially during the last 2 years.
Initial approach: Letter (no more than 5 pages)
Copies of proposal: 2
Deadline(s): Submit applications preferably from Jan. 1 to Oct. 31
Board meeting date(s): As required
Final notification: Mar. of following year for positive response
Write: Lawrence W. Milas, Pres.
Officers and Directors:* Lawrence W. Milas, Pres.; William B. Horn, V.P.; William B. Norden, Secy. and Counsel; William J. Schmidt, Treas.; Carlton T. Helming.
Number of staff: 4 full-time professional; 2 part-time professional; 2 full-time support.
Employer Identification Number: 131820176
Recent arts and culture grants:
Bard College, Annandale-on-Hudson, NY, $3,393,000. For Humanities Center building construction. 1987.
Bates College, Lewiston, ME, $31,300. For Arts Center building construction. 1987.

2152
John M. Olin Foundation, Inc.
100 Park Ave., Suite 2701
New York 10017 (212) 661-2670

Incorporated in 1953 in DE.
Donor(s): John M. Olin.†
Financial data (yr. ended 12/31/88): Assets, $73,292,834 (M); expenditures, $15,570,118, including $14,383,741 for 200 grants (high: $942,000; low: $1,500; average: $10,000-$200,000).
Purpose and activities: Support for public policy research, strategic and international studies, studies of American political institutions, and law and the legal system, with emphasis on the application of fundamental American principles of freedom and justice.
Types of support: Seed money, research, special projects, publications, conferences and seminars, general purposes, professorships, fellowships, continuing support, internships, lectureships.
Limitations: No support for programs without significant import for national affairs. No grants to individuals, or for annual campaigns, operating budgets, or building or endowment funds; no loans.
Publications: Annual report, program policy statement, application guidelines.
Application information:
Initial approach: Proposal
Copies of proposal: 1
Deadline(s): None
Board meeting date(s): 4 times a year
Final notification: Usually within 90 days
Write: James Piereson, Exec. Dir.
Officers and Trustees: William E. Simon, Pres.; George J. Gillespie III, Secy.-Treas.; James Piereson, Exec. Dir.; Richard M. Furlaud, Charles F. Knight, Walter F. O'Connell, Eugene F. Williams, Jr.
Number of staff: 5 full-time professional; 2 full-time support.
Employer Identification Number: 376031033
Recent arts and culture grants:
ETV Endowment of South Carolina, Columbia, SC, $75,000. For broadcast and distribution of documentary film Angola by South Carolina Educational Television. 1987.
ETV Endowment of South Carolina, Columbia, SC, $50,000. For television series American Interests 1986-87. 1987.
ETV Endowment of South Carolina, Columbia, SC, $50,000. For television series American Interests 1987-88. 1987.
Greater Washington Educational Television Association, DC, $25,000. For film documentary on Chautauqua-Soviet town meeting in Riga called, Washington on the Baltic. 1987.
National Endowment for the Humanities, DC, $12,000. For 1987 Jefferson Lecture. 1987.
Radio Free Europe, Radio Liberty Fund, DC, $60,000. For John M. Olin Senior Fellow and summer internship program. 1987.
Southern Educational Communications Association, Columbia, SC, $150,000. For William F. Buckley, Jr.'s television series, Firing Line. 1987.

2153
The Omnicom Foundation, Inc.
c/o The Omnicom Group, Inc.
909 Third Ave.
New York 10022

Established in 1987 in NY.
Donor(s): Omnicom Group, Inc., DDB Needham Worldwide.
Financial data (yr. ended 12/31/87): Assets, $2,250 (M); gifts received, $14,500; expenditures, $12,250, including $12,250 for 8 grants (high: $5,000; low: $500).
Purpose and activities: First year of operation: 1987; supports arts, communication, and education.
Types of support: Annual campaigns, general purposes.
Limitations: Giving primarily in New York City.
Officers: Dennis Hewitt,* Pres.; Barry J. Wagner,* Secy.; Frank J. Holzmann, Treas.
Directors:* G. Gary de Paolo, Lloyd Highbloom, Thomas J. Watson.
Employer Identification Number: 133450486

2154
Orion Capital Corporate Giving Program
30 Rockefeller Plaza Suite 2820
New York 10112 (212) 541-4646

Financial data (yr. ended 12/31/88): $2,450 for 4 grants (high: $1,000; low: $100).
Purpose and activities: Supports cultural institutes, general education and private colleges, and public policy programs.
Types of support: Annual campaigns.
Limitations: Giving primarily in headquarters city, and major operating locations in NY, CT, and CA.
Application information:
Initial approach: Letter
Write: Alan R. Gruber, Chair. and C.E.O.

2155
Edward B. Osborn Charitable Trust
c/o United States Trust Co. of New York
45 Wall St.
New York 10005

Trust established in 1961 in NY.
Donor(s): Edward B. Osborn.
Financial data (yr. ended 10/31/86): Assets, $3,841,709 (M); expenditures, $158,206, including $132,068 for 13 grants (high: $15,000; low: $500).
Purpose and activities: Giving for hospitals and medical research, with some support for cultural programs, secondary schools, parks, and youth agencies.
Limitations: Giving primarily in NY and FL.
Officer and Trustees: James W. Anderson, V.P.; Mrs. Edward B. Osborn, U.S. Trust Co. of New York.
Employer Identification Number: 136071296

2156
Osceola Foundation, Inc.
51 East 42nd St., Suite 1601
New York 10017

Incorporated in 1963 in NY.
Donor(s): Katherine Sperry Beinecke Trust.
Financial data (yr. ended 12/31/86): Assets, $4,295,789 (M); gifts received, $1,595,473; expenditures, $685,780, including $562,861 for 65 grants (high: $185,794; low: $10) and $18,715 for 4 grants to individuals.
Purpose and activities: Giving primarily for higher education, including some scholarships, and historic preservation, including a rare book library; some support for performing arts organizations.
Types of support: Student aid.
Application information:
Initial approach: Letter
Deadline(s): Prior to end of year; scholarship applications should be made well in advance of tuition due dates
Write: Walter Beinecke, Jr., Pres.
Officers and Directors: Walter Beinecke, Jr., Pres. and Treas.; Perry Ashley, Secy.; Deborah Kinsella Beale, Walter Beinecke III, Barbara Collar, Ann Oliver.
Employer Identification Number: 136094234

2157
OSG Foundation
1114 Ave. of the Americas, 12th Fl.
New York 10036

Donor(s): Overseas Shipholding Group, Inc.
Financial data (yr. ended 12/31/87): Assets, $812,511 (M); gifts received, $348,400; expenditures, $654,269, including $652,781 for 112 grants (high: $150,000; low: $50).
Purpose and activities: Giving for Jewish welfare funds, hospitals, education, and the arts.
Application information: Applications not accepted.
Officers and Directors: Raphael Recanati, Pres.; Michael A. Recanati, V.P. and Secy.-Treas.; Morton P. Hyman, V.P.; Morris Feder.
Employer Identification Number: 133099337

2158
The Overbrook Foundation
521 Fifth Ave., Rm. 1821
New York 10175 (212) 661-8710

Incorporated in 1948 in NY.
Donor(s): Frank Altschul,† Helen G. Altschul,† Arthur G. Altschul, Margaret A. Lang.
Financial data (yr. ended 12/31/87): Assets, $48,069,237 (M); gifts received, $253,800; expenditures, $2,078,998, including $1,523,300 for 183 grants (high: $176,000; low: $100; average: $1,000-$10,000).
Purpose and activities: Grants for arts and cultural programs, child welfare, civil rights, community funds, conservation, elementary, secondary, and higher education, hospitals, international affairs, medical research, museums, and social services.
Types of support: General purposes.
Limitations: Giving primarily in NY and CT. No grants to individuals.
Application information:

Initial approach: Letter
Deadline(s): None
Board meeting date(s): Usually in Apr. and Nov.
Final notification: Within 6 weeks
Write: M. Sheila McGoldrick
Officers and Directors: Arthur G. Altschul, Pres. and Treas.; Edith A. Graham, V.P.; Margaret A. Lang, V.P.; Diana L. Altschul, Secy.; Stephen F. Altschul, Robert C. Graham, Jr., Frances L. Labaree, Bethuel M. Webster.
Number of staff: 2 part-time professional; 4 part-time support.
Employer Identification Number: 136088860

2159
William S. Paley Foundation, Inc.
51 West 52nd St., Rm. 3490
New York 10019 (212) 765-3333

Incorporated in 1936 in NY.
Donor(s): William S. Paley.
Financial data (yr. ended 12/31/87): Assets, $16,411,499 (M); expenditures, $741,879, including $103,541 for 2 grants (high: $83,541; low: $20,000).
Purpose and activities: Emphasis on a museum of broadcasting, education, cultural programs, and health services.
Types of support: General purposes, fellowships.
Limitations: Giving primarily in NY. No grants to individuals.
Application information:
Initial approach: Proposal
Deadline(s): None
Board meeting date(s): 3rd Wednesday in Oct.
Write: John S. Minary, Secy.
Officers and Directors:* William S. Paley,* Pres.; John S. Minary,* Secy.; Sidney W. Harl,* Treas.; George J. Gillespie III, Kate C. Paley, William C. Paley, Walter N. Thayer.
Employer Identification Number: 136085929

2160
Paramount Communications Foundation, Inc.
(Formerly Gulf + Western Foundation, Inc.)
15 Columbus Circle
New York 10023 (212) 373-8517

Incorporated in 1954 in NY.
Donor(s): Paramount Communications, Inc.
Financial data (yr. ended 10/31/87): Assets, $37,891 (M); gifts received, $3,162,293; expenditures, $2,896,644, including $2,587,877 for 292 grants (high: $205,245; low: $10; average: $1,000-$5,000) and $308,767 for 730 employee matching gifts.
Purpose and activities: Administers philanthropic giving of operating units on behalf of the corporation. Purposes relate to employee needs or interests and/or business interests of the corporation. Administers an employee matching gifts program.
Types of support: Operating budgets, continuing support, employee matching gifts, internships, employee-related scholarships.
Limitations: Giving primarily in areas of company operations, and to national organizations. No grants to individuals, or for annual campaigns, seed money, emergency funds, deficit financing, equipment, land acquisition, renovation, endowment funds, research, demonstration projects, publications, or conferences; no loans.
Application information:
Initial approach: Letter
Copies of proposal: 1
Deadline(s): None
Board meeting date(s): 4 times a year
Final notification: 6 weeks to 6 months
Write: Gloria S. White, Exec. Dir.
Officers: Samuel J. Silberman,* Chair.; Edward T. Weaver,* Pres.; Elsa M. Rivlin, Secy.; Raymond M. Nowak, Treas.; Gloria S. White, Exec. Dir.
Trustees:* Donald Oresman.
Number of staff: 2 full-time professional; 2 full-time support.
Employer Identification Number: 136089816

2161
The Park Foundation
100 East 42nd St., Suite 1850
New York 10017

Incorporated in 1949 in DC.
Donor(s): John P. Kennedy, Jr. Foundation.
Financial data (yr. ended 12/31/87): Assets, $11,412 (M); gifts received, $160,000; expenditures, $157,537, including $157,382 for 55 grants (high: $23,305; low: $1,000).
Purpose and activities: Assistance to "the indigent, sick, and infirm"; emphasis on higher and secondary education and child welfare; support also for rehabilitation of the handicapped, Roman Catholic welfare agencies, and cultural programs.
Types of support: General purposes.
Limitations: Giving primarily in NY, MA, and DC.
Application information:
Deadline(s): None
Write: Richard S. Waite, Asst. Treas.
Officers: Jean K. Smith,* V.P.; Joseph E. Hakim, Treas.
Trustees:* Stephen E. Smith.
Employer Identification Number: 136163065

2162
Josephine Bay Paul and C. Michael Paul Foundation, Inc.
c/o Martin L. Schneider Associates
12 Monroe Pl.
Brooklyn 11201-2630 (718) 875-5100

Incorporated in 1962 in NY.
Donor(s): Josephine Bay Paul.†
Financial data (yr. ended 1/31/88): Assets, $2,821,533 (M); expenditures, $449,921, including $220,060 for 41 grants (high: $65,000; low: $1,000).
Purpose and activities: Grants for professional chamber music ensembles, selected festivals or presenters, and conservatories to promote chamber music and career development opportunities for performers.
Types of support: Continuing support, operating budgets, general purposes, matching funds, seed money, special projects, technical assistance.
Publications: Program policy statement, 990-PF.
Application information:
Initial approach: Letter
Copies of proposal: 1
Deadline(s): Preferably Jan. and Aug.
Board meeting date(s): Apr. and Oct.
Write: Frederick Bay, Pres. and Exec. Dir.
Officers and Directors: Synnova B. Hayes, Chair.; Frederick Bay, Pres. and Exec. Dir.; Daniel A. Demarest, Secy.; Hans Ege, Treas.
Number of staff: 1 part-time professional; 1 part-time support.
Employer Identification Number: 131991717

2163
Henry and Rose Pearlman Foundation, Inc.
c/o Ralph Levitt
36 West 44th St.
New York 10036 (212) 944-0235

Incorporated in 1953 in NY.
Donor(s): Henry Pearlman,† Rose Pearlman, Eastern Cold Storage Insulation Co., Inc.
Financial data (yr. ended 11/30/86): Assets, $20,359,861 (M); gifts received, $871,000; expenditures, $26,753, including $26,199 for 15 grants (high: $5,000; low: $15).
Purpose and activities: A private operating foundation; grants locally for museums, arts organizations, and social agencies.
Limitations: Giving primarily in NY.
Application information:
Deadline(s): None
Write: Rose Pearlman, Pres.
Officers and Directors: Rose Pearlman, Pres.; Alex W. Pearlman, V.P.; Marge Scheuer, Secy.; Dorothy Edelman, Treas.
Employer Identification Number: 136159092

2164
PepsiCo Foundation, Inc.
700 Anderson Hill Rd.
Purchase 10577 (914) 253-3153

Incorporated in 1962 in NY.
Donor(s): PepsiCo, Inc., Frito-Lay, Inc.
Financial data (yr. ended 12/31/87): Assets, $15,053,941 (M); gifts received, $20,341,635; expenditures, $5,641,086, including $5,639,251 for 1,956 grants (high: $484,383; low: $20).
Purpose and activities: Support for education and other non-profit organizations where employees are involved as volunteers.
Types of support: Employee matching gifts.
Limitations: Giving primarily in areas of company operations in NY; and to national and regional organizations. No grants to individuals.
Publications: Informational brochure, program policy statement, application guidelines.
Application information:
Initial approach: Proposal
Deadline(s): None
Board meeting date(s): At least annually
Final notification: Within 3 months
Write: Jacqueline R. Millan, V.P., Contribs.
Officers: Donald M. Kendall,* Chair.; Joseph F. McCann,* Pres.; Jacqueline R. Millan, V.P., Contribs.; Douglas Cram, Secy.; Claudia Morf, Treas.

Directors:* D. Wayne Calloway, Robert G. Dettmer, Roger A. Enrico, Michael H. Jordan, Harvey C. Russell.
Number of staff: 2 full-time professional; 2 full-time support.
Employer Identification Number: 136163174

2165
The Pfizer Foundation, Inc.
235 East 42nd St.
New York 10017 (212) 573-3351

Incorporated in 1953 in NY.
Donor(s): Pfizer Inc.
Financial data (yr. ended 12/31/88): Assets, $3,449,654 (M); expenditures, $1,144,279, including $1,131,500 for 156 grants (high: $100,000; low: $1,000; average: $1,000-$5,000).
Purpose and activities: Grants primarily for higher education, health, civic and community welfare, culture, and international affairs.
Types of support: Operating budgets, continuing support, annual campaigns, seed money, emergency funds, building funds, equipment, matching funds, professorships, internships, scholarship funds, fellowships, special projects, research, publications, conferences and seminars, capital campaigns.
Limitations: Giving primarily in areas of company operations, with emphasis on local New York City or national organizations. No support for religious organizations for religious purposes, veterans', fraternal or labor organizations, non tax-exempt foundations, or anti-business organizations. No grants to individuals, or for deficit financing, employee matching gifts, goodwill advertising, or land acquisition; no loans.
Publications: Annual report (including application guidelines).
Application information:
Initial approach: Proposal
Copies of proposal: 1
Deadline(s): None
Board meeting date(s): As required
Final notification: 3 months
Write: Wyndham Anderson, Exec. V.P.
Officers and Directors: Robert A. Wilson, Pres.; Wyndham Anderson, Exec. V.P.; James R. Gardner, V.P.; Terence J. Gallagher, Secy.; Kevin S. Keating, Treas.
Number of staff: None.
Employer Identification Number: 136083839

2166
The Carl and Lily Pforzheimer Foundation, Inc.
70 Pine St., Rm. 3030
New York 10270 (212) 422-5484

Incorporated in 1942 in NY.
Donor(s): Members of the Pforzheimer family and others.
Financial data (yr. ended 12/31/87): Assets, $26,351,311 (M); expenditures, $885,880, including $454,062 for 18 grants (high: $80,000; low: $2,000).
Purpose and activities: Collaborates with established libraries and educational institutions in connection with the Carl H. Pforzheimer Library in the general field of American and English literature; giving primarily for higher and secondary education; support also for cultural programs and a national municipal organization.
Types of support: Seed money, professorships, internships, scholarship funds.
Limitations: No grants to individuals, or for building or endowment funds, research programs, or matching gifts; no loans.
Application information:
Initial approach: Letter or proposal
Copies of proposal: 1
Deadline(s): None
Board meeting date(s): Apr., June, Oct., and Dec.
Final notification: Immediately following board meeting
Write: Carl H. Pforzheimer, Jr., Pres.
Officers: Carl H. Pforzheimer, Jr.,* Pres.; Carl H. Pforzheimer III,* V.P. and Treas.; Martin F. Richman, Secy.
Directors:* Nancy Aronson, Richard W. Couper, George Frelinghuysen, Jill L. Leinbach, Carol K. Pforzheimer.
Number of staff: 4 full-time professional; 2 full-time support.
Employer Identification Number: 135624374
Recent arts and culture grants:
Caramoor Center for Music and the Arts, Katonah, NY, $15,000. For unrestricted support. 1987.
Metropolitan Opera Guild, NYC, NY, $10,000. For unrestricted support. 1987.
New York Council for the Humanities, NYC, NY, $5,000. For unrestricted support. 1987.
W N E T Channel 13, NYC, NY, $80,000. For Intellectuals in Exile. 1987.

2167
Philip Morris Companies Corporate Contributions Program
120 Park Ave.
New York 10017 (212) 880-3489
*Philip Morris:*1930 Maple St.,Box 1498, Louisville, KY 40201, Box 26603, Richmond, VA 23261; 3321 Hwy.29S,Box 1098, Concord, NC 28025, Mission Viejo Realty Grp.;24800 Chrisanta Dr.,Mission Viejo,CA 92691;8822 S. Ridgeline Blvd.,Highlands Ranch, CO 80126

Financial data (yr. ended 12/31/88): Total giving, $19,700,000, including $16,465,000 for grants (high: $500,000; low: $500; average: $5,000-$25,000), $1,235,000 for grants to individuals and $2,000,000 for employee matching gifts.
Purpose and activities: Philip Morris Companies corporate headquarters and the subsidiaries (except for General Foods and Kraft, which have their own foundations) follow the same guidelines for giving. Philip Morris commits itself to assisting organizations that enrich the quality of life in areas of company operations, stimulating the growth of new knowledge, creating a social atmosphere conducive to equal opportunities for all, and strengthening public confidence in the business sector. Support is for higher education, health and welfare, culture and humanities, and conservation and the environment; also for the United Way, employee matching gifts, and scholarships for employees' dependents.
Types of support: Employee matching gifts, general purposes, operating budgets, special projects, continuing support, emergency funds, endowment funds, matching funds, professorships, scholarship funds, research, employee-related scholarships.
Limitations: Giving primarily in areas of company operations in NY, VA, KY, NC, WI, CA, and CO; some support for national programs which affect the general welfare and for local programs which address national concerns. No support for religious or fraternal organizations, United Way recipients, public television or radio, elementary and secondary schools, or youth organizations. No grants to individuals, or for capital or building fund drives.
Publications: Informational brochure.
Application information: Local requests to the nearest operating company for local managers to assess and recommend to headquarters office as seen fit. Other requests to headquarters. Proposals should include description of organization, list of board members, list of donors, description of project, the population to be served, audited financial statement and IRS 501 (c)(3) status letter.
Deadline(s): Applications are preferred in first quarter of the year, or 3 months before board meetings
Board meeting date(s): Mar., June, and Oct.
Write: Anne T. Dowling, Mgr., Corp. Contribs. & Support
Number of staff: 5 full-time professional; 6 full-time support.

2168
Tatiana Piankova Foundation
781 Fifth Ave.
New York 10022

Established about 1983 in NY.
Donor(s): Susan Polachek.
Financial data (yr. ended 7/31/87): Assets, $2,494,425 (M); expenditures, $90,290, including $78,420 for 22 grants (high: $10,000; low: $200).
Purpose and activities: Giving primarily for the arts, cultural institutions, and social service organizations.
Application information:
Deadline(s): None
Write: Lawrence E. Brinn, Pres.
Officers and Directors: Lawrence E. Brinn, Pres.; Mildred F. Cunningham, V.P. and Secy.; Peter F. De Gaetano.
Employer Identification Number: 133142090

2169
Pine Level Foundation, Inc.
c/o Ernst & Whinney
787 Seventh Ave.
New York 10019

Incorporated in 1968 in CT as a successor to the Stetson Foundation, a trust established in 1936 in CT.
Donor(s): Iola Wise Stetson.
Financial data (yr. ended 12/31/87): Assets, $1,108,172 (M); expenditures, $94,083, including $74,264 for 72 grants (high: $6,000; low: $250).

Purpose and activities: Giving for cultural programs, conservation, education, and health agencies.
Limitations: Giving primarily in CT and NY.
Application information:
Initial approach: Letter
Deadline(s): None
Write: Iola Haverstick, Pres.
Officers and Directors: Iola Haverstick, Pres.; Elizabeth Kratovil, V.P.; S. Alexander Haverstick, Secy.
Employer Identification Number: 237008912

2170
Pinewood Foundation
100 Park Ave.
New York 10017

Incorporated in 1956 in NY as Celeste and Armand Bartos Foundation.
Donor(s): Celeste G. Bartos, D.S. and R.H. Gottesman Foundation.
Financial data (yr. ended 10/31/88): Assets, $10,096,334 (M); expenditures, $1,561,432, including $1,428,450 for 58 grants (high: $200,300; low: $38).
Purpose and activities: Giving for higher education and cultural programs, with emphasis on the arts.
Limitations: Giving primarily in New York, NY.
Application information: Contributes only to pre-selected organizations. Applications not accepted.
Officers: Celeste G. Bartos,* Pres.; Armand P. Bartos,* V.P.; Edgar Wachenheim III, V.P.; Peter C. Siegfried, Secy.; Benjamin Glowatz, Treas.
Directors:* Adam Bartos.
Employer Identification Number: 136101581

2171
The Pisces Foundation
210 South St.
New York 10002 (212) 619-6255

Incorporated in 1951 in NY.
Donor(s): Dorothy Schiff, New York Post Corp.
Financial data (yr. ended 12/31/86): Assets, $6,900,295 (M); gifts received, $121,563; expenditures, $307,072, including $224,660 for 90 grants.
Purpose and activities: Emphasis on education, hospitals, public television, and juvenile crime prevention.
Limitations: Giving primarily in NY. No grants to individuals, or for endowment or capital funds, or matching gifts; no loans.
Application information:
Initial approach: Letter
Deadline(s): None
Board meeting date(s): Monthly except Aug.
Write: Adele Hall Sweet, Exec. V.P.
Officers: Dorothy Schiff, Pres.; Adele Hall Sweet, Exec. V.P.; Sarah-Ann Kramarsky, Secy.; Mortimer W. Hall, Treas.
Number of staff: 1 full-time support.
Employer Identification Number: 136018311

2172
Henry B. Plant Memorial Fund, Inc.
c/o United States Trust Co. of New York
45 Wall St.
New York 10005

Incorporated in 1947 in NY.
Donor(s): Amy P. Statter.
Financial data (yr. ended 12/31/87): Assets, $4,857,591 (M); expenditures, $250,892, including $210,000 for 83 grants (high: $30,000; low: $500).
Purpose and activities: Emphasis on hospitals, population control, cultural programs, the environment, and health agencies.
Limitations: Giving primarily in NY.
Application information:
Initial approach: Letter
Deadline(s): None
Officers and Directors: Mrs. J. Phillip Lee, Pres.; Phyllis S. Oxman, V.P.
Employer Identification Number: 136077327

2173
The Pollock-Krasner Foundation, Inc.
725 Park Ave.
New York 10021 (212) 517-5400
Application address: P.O. Box 4957, New York, NY 10185; FAX No.: (212) 288-2836

Established in 1984 in DE.
Donor(s): Lee Krasner.†
Financial data (yr. ended 6/30/88): Assets, $24,101,514 (M); expenditures, $1,588,728, including $833,175 for 94 grants to individuals (high: $25,000; low: $1,000).
Purpose and activities: Giving exclusively to needy and worthy individual working artists (painters, sculptors, and graphic and mixed-media artists) who have embarked on professional careers; grants may be used for professional or personal requirements.
Types of support: Grants to individuals.
Limitations: No support for organizations or institutions; no individual grants to students, photographers, commercial or performance artists, or craftsmen. No grants for no tuition payments.
Publications: Informational brochure (including application guidelines), annual report, application guidelines.
Application information: Application form required.
Initial approach: Letter
Deadline(s): None
Board meeting date(s): Regularly throughout the year
Final notification: As soon as possible
Write: Charles C. Bergman, Exec. V.P.
Officers and Directors:* Gerald Dickler,* Chair.; Eugene Victor Thaw,* Pres.; Charles C. Bergman, Exec. V.P.
Number of staff: 6 full-time professional; 1 part-time professional; 2 full-time support.
Employer Identification Number: 133255693

2174
Mrs. Cheever Porter Foundation
c/o Adams & Becker
Seven High St.
Huntington 11743
Application address: c/o Kelley, Drye & Warren, 101 Park Ave., New York, NY 10178

Established in 1962 in NY.
Financial data (yr. ended 6/30/87): Assets, $2,555,404 (M); expenditures, $261,297, including $236,500 for 24 grants (high: $50,000; low: $1,000).
Purpose and activities: Giving primarily for higher education, the arts, and animal welfare.
Application information:
Initial approach: Letter
Deadline(s): None
Write: Alton E. Peters, Dir.
Directors: Alton E. Peters, Edgar Scott, Jr., Clifford E. Starkins.
Employer Identification Number: 136093181

2175
The Pratt-Northam Foundation
c/o Hunt & Hunt
5564 Woodlawn Ave.
Lowville 13367
Application address: P.O. Box 104, Lowville, NY 13367

Incorporated in 1962 in NY.
Donor(s): Hazel Northam.†
Financial data (yr. ended 12/31/87): Assets, $1,897,869 (M); expenditures, $219,797, including $174,945 for 42 grants (high: $35,000; low: $1,125).
Purpose and activities: Grants and workerships provided for educational, cultural or charitable objectives.
Limitations: Giving limited to the Black River Valley region of NY.
Application information: Application form required.
Deadline(s): None
Write: Donald Exford
Directors: John A. Beach, Richard C. Cummings, Lee Hirschey, Lyle W. Hornbeck, Donald M. Hunt, Livingston Lansing, Edward Sieber.
Number of staff: None.
Employer Identification Number: 166088207

2176
The Louis and Harold Price Foundation, Inc.
654 Madison Ave., Suite 2005
New York 10021 (212) 753-0240
Additional tel.: (212) 752-9335

Incorporated in 1951 in NY.
Donor(s): Louis Price,† Harold Price.
Financial data (yr. ended 12/31/87): Assets, $25,702,604 (M); expenditures, $1,844,021, including $1,639,335 for 282 grants (high: $1,113,000; low: $25; average: $100-$5,000).
Purpose and activities: Support for a business institute, Jewish welfare funds, hospitals, community funds, and higher education, including scholarship funds; grants also for youth agencies, camps for children, temple support, medical research, the arts, and services for the blind and other handicapped.
Types of support: Endowment funds, operating budgets, scholarship funds, special projects, continuing support, research, annual campaigns.
Limitations: Giving primarily in metropolitan New York, NY, and Los Angeles, CA. No grants to individuals, or for building funds.

Publications: 990-PF.
Application information:
Initial approach: Letter or proposal
Copies of proposal: 1
Deadline(s): None
Board meeting date(s): Feb., May, and as required
Final notification: 1 to 3 months
Write: Harold Price, Pres.
Officers and Trustees: Harold Price, Pres.; Pauline Price, V.P. and Secy.; Gloria Appel, David Gerstein, Rosemary L. Guidone, Milton Slotkin, Linda Vitti.
Number of staff: 1 full-time professional.
Employer Identification Number: 136121358

2177
The Prospect Hill Foundation, Inc.
420 Lexington Ave., Suite 3020
New York 10170 (212) 370-1144

Incorporated in 1960 in NY; absorbed The Frederick W. Beinecke Fund in 1983.
Donor(s): William S. Beinecke.
Financial data (yr. ended 12/31/88): Assets, $34,145,781 (M); expenditures, $1,653,795 for 156 grants (high: $420,000; low: $2,500; average: $5,000-$25,000).
Purpose and activities: The Prospect Hill Foundation has a broad range of philanthropic interests. Prospective applicants are requested to obtain guidelines prior to submitting an inquiry.
Types of support: Matching funds, operating budgets, publications, general purposes.
Limitations: Giving primarily in the northeastern U.S., including NY, NJ, and RI; support for youth and social agencies primarily in the NY area. No support for religious activities. No grants to individuals, or for research.
Publications: Grants list, informational brochure (including application guidelines).
Application information:
Initial approach: Letter
Deadline(s): None
Board meeting date(s): 4 times annually
Final notification: 4 weeks
Write: Constance Eiseman, Exec. Dir.
Officers: William S. Beinecke,* Pres.; Elizabeth G. Beinecke,* V.P.; John B. Beinecke,* V.P.; Constance Eiseman, Secy. and Exec. Dir.; Michael A. Yesko, Treas.
Directors:* Frederick W. Beinecke, Frances Beinecke Elston, Sarah Beinecke Richardson.
Number of staff: 1 full-time professional; 1 full-time support; 6 part-time support.
Employer Identification Number: 136075567
Recent arts and culture grants:
American Craft Council, NYC, NY, $24,955. To computerize artists registry and catalogue book collection. 1987.
Cunningham Dance Foundation, NYC, NY, $10,000. For general support. 1987.
Historic Hudson Valley, Tarrytown, NY, $10,000. To restore greenhouse and gardens of Montgomery Place, Federal mansion in Dutchess County. 1987.
Lincoln Center Theater, NYC, NY, $20,000. For general support. 1987.
Metropolitan Museum of Art, NYC, NY, $10,000. For general support. 1987.
New York Botanical Garden, Bronx, NY, $20,000. For general support. 1987.
New York City Ballet, NYC, NY, $53,000. For 1987 repertory fund and final payment of grant to match National Endowment for the Arts challenge grant. 1987.
New York Philharmonic, NYC, NY, $32,000. For general support. 1987.
Sagamore Institute, Racquette Lake, NY, $5,000. For restoration of secondary buildings for use as living museum. 1987.
Trinity Repertory Company, Providence, RI, $15,000. For endowment campaign. 1987.
Wave Hill, Bronx, NY, $7,500. For new map and guide to Wave Hill woods, and for improved trail signage. 1987.

2178
Prudential-Bache Foundation
100 Gold St.
New York 10292 (212) 214-7507

Incorporated in 1965 in NY.
Donor(s): Bache Halsey Stuart Shields, Inc.
Financial data (yr. ended 1/31/88): Assets, $22,020 (M); gifts received, $435,000; expenditures, $435,580, including $435,535 for 150 grants (high: $25,000; low: $100).
Purpose and activities: Emphasis on social services, higher education, hospitals, cultural programs, and Jewish and Roman Catholic welfare funds.
Application information:
Deadline(s): None
Write: Bruno G. Bissetta, Treas.
Officers: H. Virgil Sherrill, Pres.; Charles Christofilis, V.P. and Secy.; Bruno G. Bissetta, Treas.
Directors:* George McGough, Leland Paton.
Employer Identification Number: 136193023

2179
The Pumpkin Foundation
c/o Joseph H. Reich & Co.
900 Third Ave.
New York 10022 (212) 753-5150

Donor(s): Joseph H. Reich.
Financial data (yr. ended 6/30/88): Assets, $1,263,827 (M); gifts received, $0; expenditures, $17,916, including $13,835 for 26 grants (high: $3,400; low: $40).
Purpose and activities: Support primarly for education, the arts and museums.
Application information:
Write: Joseph H. Reich
Trustees: Carol F. Reich, Janet H. Reich, Joseph H. Reich.
Employer Identification Number: 136279814

2180
Quantum Chemical Corporation Contributions Committee
99 Park Avenue
New York 10016-1502 (212) 551-0438

Financial data (yr. ended 12/31/87): Total giving, $1,130,000, including $924,700 for grants and $205,300 for 904 employee matching gifts.
Purpose and activities: Supports education, the arts and sciences, cultural programs, health care and hospitals, youth, welfare, and United Way.
Types of support: General purposes, employee matching gifts, annual campaigns, building funds, capital campaigns, conferences and seminars, continuing support, endowment funds, equipment, fellowships, grants to individuals, research, scholarship funds, employee-related scholarships, special projects, scholarship funds, student loans.
Limitations: Giving primarily in operating areas.
Publications: Informational brochure.
Application information: Proposal indicating proof of tax-exempt status.
Initial approach: Send letter of intention along with organizational fact sheet
Copies of proposal: 1
Deadline(s): Summer or early fall
Write: Arden Melick, Dir. Corp. Communications
Administrators: Susan Jablonski, Corp. Comm. Assoc.; Carlotta Wilsen, Comm. Relations Admin.
Number of staff: 4

2181
The R. and D. Fund, Inc.
1700 Broadway, Rm. 1702
New York 10019

Incorporated in 1952 in NY.
Donor(s): Members of the Straus family.
Financial data (yr. ended 12/31/87): Assets, $72,721 (M); gifts received, $141,213; expenditures, $154,358, including $152,211 for 75 grants (high: $35,700; low: $10).
Purpose and activities: Grants only to charities of personal interest to the donors, with emphasis on fine arts and cultural programs, international affairs, higher education, and hospitals.
Application information: Contributes only to pre-selected organizations. Applications not accepted.
Officers: Ralph I. Straus, Pres.; Donald B. Straus, V.P.; Tricia McKenna, Secy.-Treas.
Employer Identification Number: 136118829

2182
The Harold K. Raisler Foundation, Inc.
599 Lexington Ave.
New York 10022 (212) 319-2660

Incorporated in 1957 in NY.
Financial data (yr. ended 12/31/87): Assets, $1,675,000 (M); expenditures, $70,500, including $61,900 for grants.
Purpose and activities: Grants for higher education, hospitals, cultural programs, temple support, and Jewish welfare funds.
Limitations: No grants to individuals.
Application information:
Initial approach: Letter
Copies of proposal: 2
Board meeting date(s): May
Write: Harold K. Raisler, Pres.
Officer and Directors: Harold K. Raisler, Pres. and Treas.; Robert K. Raisler, V.P. and Secy.
Employer Identification Number: 136094406

2183
The Robert K. Raisler Foundation, Inc.
599 Lexington Ave.
New York 10022 (212) 319-2660

Incorporated in 1958 in NY.
Financial data (yr. ended 12/31/87): Assets, $1,619,700 (M); expenditures, $89,000, including $80,000 for grants.
Purpose and activities: Emphasis on higher education, Jewish welfare funds, cultural programs, temple support, and health agencies.
Officers and Directors: Robert K. Raisler, Pres. and Treas.; Harold K. Raisler, V.P. and Secy.
Employer Identification Number: 136094433

2184
Walter Reade Foundation, Inc.
c/o Simpson, Thacher, and Bartlett
One Battery Park Plaza
New York 10004 (212) 908-2713

Donor(s): Walter Reade Organization, Inc.
Financial data (yr. ended 12/31/87): Assets, $1,996,308 (M); expenditures, $44,881, including $36,100 for 3 grants (high: $35,000; low: $500).
Purpose and activities: Grants primarily for a theatre institute; support also for education and a political science institute.
Limitations: No grants to individuals.
Application information: Contributes only to pre-selected organizations. Applications not accepted.
Write: Stephen P. Duggan, Treas.
Officers: Gertrude B. Reade, Pres.; Dolly Reade Borgia, V.P.; Steven P. Duggan, Treas.
Employer Identification Number: 216014506

2185
Reader's Digest Association Giving Program
Pleasantville 10570 (914) 241-5370

Financial data (yr. ended 12/21/87): $1,093,972 for grants.
Purpose and activities: Support for a variety of cultural, social service, and civic programs in areas where Reader's Digest employees live.
Types of support: Continuing support, program-related investments, general purposes.
Limitations: Giving primarily in communities where employees live.
Publications: Informational brochure.
Application information:
Initial approach: Letter of inquiry
Deadline(s): None
Write: J. Edward Hall, V.P.
Administrators: J. Edward Hall, V.P.
Number of staff: 2 part-time professional; 2 part-time support.

2186
Reader's Digest Foundation
c/o Readers Digest Association, Inc.
Pleasantville 10570 (914) 241-5370

Incorporated in 1938 in NY.
Donor(s): The Reader's Digest Association, Inc., DeWitt Wallace,† Lila Acheson Wallace.†
Financial data (yr. ended 12/31/87): Assets, $19,329,307 (M); gifts received, $1,100,000; expenditures, $2,642,709, including $1,163,600 for 91 grants (high: $125,000; low: $8,500; average: $10,000-$60,000) and $807,116 for 662 employee matching gifts.
Purpose and activities: Particular interest in journalism education and in programs that offer pre-college youth a variety of character-building experiences, including programs that assist young people in acquiring those basic skills critical to building a solid educational base.
Types of support: Employee matching gifts, general purposes, scholarship funds, program-related investments, continuing support, employee-related scholarships.
Limitations: No support for religious organizations or endeavors; legislative or lobbying efforts; veterans', political, or fraternal organizations; charitable dinners or fundraising events; private foundations; cultural organizations; environmental groups; television, film or video productions; local chapters of national organizations; or medical research or health-related activities. No grants to individuals, or for capital, building or endowment funds, operating budgets, annual campaigns, seed money, emergency funds, deficit financing, special projects, publications, workshops, or conferences and seminars; no loans.
Publications: Annual report (including application guidelines).
Application information:
Initial approach: Letter
Copies of proposal: 1
Deadline(s): Feb., June, and Oct.
Final notification: 90 days
Write: J. Edward Hall, Pres.
Officers: George V. Grune,* Chair.; J. Edward Hall,* Pres.; Richard F. McLoughlin,* V.P.; Mary Graniero, Secy.; Ross Jones, Treas.
Directors:* Kenneth O. Gilmore, Barbara J. Morgan, John A. Pope, Jr., Francis G. Ronnenberg.
Number of staff: 2 part-time professional; 1 full-time support; 1 part-time support.
Employer Identification Number: 136120380

2187
The Reed Foundation, Inc.
30 Rockefeller Plaza, Suite 4528
New York 10112-0119 (212) 977-5294

Incorporated in 1949 in NY.
Donor(s): Samuel Rubin.†
Financial data (yr. ended 12/31/88): Assets, $11,179,990 (M); expenditures, $1,133,850, including $1,002,533 for 101 grants (high: $90,000; low: $265; average: $1,000-$10,000).
Purpose and activities: Emphasis on education, cultural affairs, and human rights; provides support for "projects of newly-formed organizations or innovative or timely programs of existing institutions for which other funding may be difficult to obtain."
Types of support: Endowment funds, research, conferences and seminars, scholarship funds, fellowships, exchange programs, matching funds, general purposes, building funds, capital campaigns, continuing support, operating budgets, program-related investments, publications, renovation projects, seed money, special projects.
Limitations: Giving primarily in the New York, NY, metropolitan area; some giving in New York State, CT, DC, IL, and VT. No grants to individuals.
Publications: Program policy statement.
Application information:
Initial approach: Letter
Copies of proposal: 1
Deadline(s): None
Board meeting date(s): Bimonthly
Final notification: Immediately following board meetings
Write: J. Sinclair Armstrong, Secy.
Officers and Directors: Reed Rubin, Pres.; J. Sinclair Armstrong, Secy.; Jane Gregory Rubin, Treas.
Number of staff: 1 part-time professional; 1 part-time support.
Employer Identification Number: 131990017

2188
Kurt P. Reimann Foundation, Inc.
c/o Benjamin Nadel & Co.
437 Fifth Ave.
New York 10016 (212) 683-0071

Established in 1971.
Donor(s): Auguste Reimann,† Kurt P. Reimann, Mrs. Kurt P. Reimann.
Financial data (yr. ended 11/30/86): Assets, $9,480,978 (M); expenditures, $223,957, including $217,111 for 12 grants (high: $48,189; low: $1,500).
Purpose and activities: Grants mainly for cultural programs, with emphasis on music and the performing arts; support also for a college.
Application information:
Deadline(s): None
Write: Reimer Koch-Weser, Pres.
Officers: Reimer Koch-Weser, Pres.; Anna Ellsam, V.P.; Benjamin Nadel, Treas.
Employer Identification Number: 221712688

2189
Revlon Foundation, Inc.
767 Fifth Ave.
New York 10153

Incorporated in 1955 in NY.
Donor(s): Revlon, Inc., and its subsidiaries.
Financial data (yr. ended 12/31/87): Assets, $147,409 (M); gifts received, $2,415,000; expenditures, $2,306,102, including $2,267,508 for 44 grants (high: $661,000; low: $500) and $38,508 for 147 employee matching gifts.
Purpose and activities: Emphasis on women's interest groups, minorities, and health care which are national in scope or where company has subsidiaries, and cultural organizations which focus on main areas of interest listed above; support also for higher education, conservation, and community funds.
Types of support: Employee matching gifts.
Limitations: No grants to individuals; employee matching gifts awarded to educational institutions only.
Application information: Applications not accepted.
Write: Roger Shelley, Pres.

Officers: Richard E. Halperin,* Pres.; Nancy T. Gardiner, Exec. V.P.; Wade H. Nichols III, V.P. and Secy.; John Bulzacchelli, V.P. and Treas.
Directors:* Howard Gritts, Ronald O. Perelman.
Employer Identification Number: 136126130

2190
Rich Foundation, Inc.
1145 Niagara St.
P.O. Box 245
Buffalo 14213

Established in 1961.
Financial data (yr. ended 12/31/87): Assets, $642,811 (M); gifts received, $180,000; expenditures, $189,261, including $177,192 for 161 grants (high: $10,000; low: $25).
Purpose and activities: Emphasis on community funds, the arts, hospitals, church support, youth programs, and education, especially higher education.
Limitations: Giving primarily in NY.
Officer: David A. Rich, Exec. Dir.
Employer Identification Number: 166026199

2191
Anne S. Richardson Charitable Trust
c/o Chemical Bank
30 Rockefeller Plaza
New York 10112 (212) 621-2143

Trust established in 1965 in CT.
Donor(s): Anne S. Richardson.†
Financial data (yr. ended 7/31/88): Assets, $8,000,301 (M); expenditures, $486,113, including $396,400 for 25 grants (high: $10,000; low: $700).
Purpose and activities: Interests include conservation, education, and cultural programs.
Limitations: Giving primarily in CT and NY. No grants to individuals, or for endowment funds, scholarships, or fellowships; no loans.
Application information:
Initial approach: Letter or proposal
Copies of proposal: 2
Deadline(s): Submit proposal preferably in Jan., Mar., June, or Oct.; no set deadline
Board meeting date(s): Feb., Apr., July, and Nov.
Write: Patricia Kelly
Trustees: Chemical Bank.
Employer Identification Number: 136192516

2192
Smith Richardson Foundation, Inc.
210 East 86th St., 6th Fl.
New York 10028 (212) 861-8181
Application address for Early Intervention/Education and Indigenous Self-Help projects: Peter L. Richardson, V.P., 266 Post Road East, Westport, CT 06880

Incorporated in 1935 in NC.
Donor(s): H.S. Richardson, Sr.,† Grace Jones Richardson.†
Financial data (yr. ended 12/31/87): Assets, $217,989,584 (M); expenditures, $13,552,209, including $11,380,387 for 82 grants (high: $1,149,336; low: $38,800).
Purpose and activities: The grants-in-aid program has two main thrusts: 1) a public affairs program, aimed at supporting and promoting a vigorous economy and free society, mainly through support of public policy research projects and educational programs focusing on business and the economy; 2) to aid in developing the qualities of leadership that will make society fully responsive to the great demands being placed upon it in today's world, through support of the Center for Creative Leadership in Greensboro, NC. Two new grants programs were established in 1986: Early Intervention/Education projects for at-risk children, and Indigenous Self-Help/Mutual Aid projects which would include community oriented efforts that focus on child development and family support issues in economically disadvantaged areas.
Types of support: Research, publications, conferences and seminars, seed money, matching funds, special projects.
Limitations: No support for programs in the arts, historic restoration, or regional or community programs concerning employment, recreation, or regional or community health and welfare. No grants to individuals, or for deficit financing, building or endowment funds, scholarships, fellowships, operating budgets, or research in the physical sciences; no loans.
Publications: Annual report (including application guidelines).
Application information: Most projects funded are initiated by the foundation.
Initial approach: Proposal
Copies of proposal: 1
Deadline(s): None
Board meeting date(s): Usually in Mar., June, Sept., and Dec.
Final notification: 30 to 60 days
Write: A. Devon Gaffney, Dir. of Research
Officers: H. Smith Richardson, Jr.,* Chair.; R. Randolph Richardson,* Pres.; Charles W. Cheek,* V.P. and Secy.; R. Larry Coble, Treas.
Trustees:* Robert H. Mulreany, Heather S. Richardson, Peter L. Richardson, Stuart S. Richardson.
Number of staff: 5 full-time professional; 2 full-time support.
Employer Identification Number: 560611550
Recent arts and culture grants:
Arts Center, Carrboro, NC, $75,000. For general support. 1987.
ETV Endowment of South Carolina, Spartanburg, SC, $75,000. To provide partial underwriting of PBS American Interests series. 1987.

2193
The Frederick W. Richmond Foundation, Inc.
245 East 58th St., Suite 10A
New York 10022 (212) 752-1668

Incorporated in 1962 in NY.
Donor(s): Frederick W. Richmond.
Financial data (yr. ended 4/30/87): Assets, $3,206,747 (M); expenditures, $268,237, including $224,450 for 49 grants (high: $25,000; low: $250; average: $2,000).
Purpose and activities: Major interest in pilot projects in education and the arts.
Types of support: Special projects, seed money, fellowships.
Limitations: No grants to individuals.
Publications: 990-PF, program policy statement.
Application information:
Initial approach: Letter
Copies of proposal: 1
Deadline(s): None
Board meeting date(s): Biannually
Final notification: 3 months
Write: Timothy E. Wyman, Pres.
Officers: Timothy E. Wyman,* Pres.; William J. Butler,* Secy.; Gerald K. Warner, Treas.; Pauline Nunen, Exec. Dir.
Directors:* Barbara Bode, Helen Fioratti, Steven N. Kaufmann, Frederick W. Richmond.
Number of staff: 1 full-time professional; 1 part-time professional; 1 part-time support.
Employer Identification Number: 136124582

2194
The Ridgefield Foundation
c/o Oppenheim, Appel, Dixon & Co.
101 Park Ave.
New York 10178 (212) 692-9570

Incorporated in 1956 in NY.
Donor(s): Henry J. Leir, Erna D. Leir, Continental Ore Corp., International Ore and Fertilizer Corp.
Financial data (yr. ended 2/28/87): Assets, $4,578,793 (M); gifts received, $1,270,015; expenditures, $228,526, including $176,950 for 56 grants (high: $25,000; low: $125; average: $100-$500).
Purpose and activities: Support for education in the U.S. and Israel, Jewish welfare funds, social service agencies, and cultural programs; most support is for past donees or for organizations recommended by board members.
Limitations: No grants to individuals, or for scholarships, fellowships, or matching gifts; no loans.
Application information: Unsolicited applicants are usually not funded; most support is for past donees or organizations recommended by board members.
Initial approach: Letter
Copies of proposal: 2
Deadline(s): Submit proposal preferably in Sept.
Board meeting date(s): Oct.
Write: Marguerite M. Riposanu, Secy.
Officers: Henry J. Leir,* Pres.; Louis J. Lipton,* V.P.; Marguerite M. Riposanu, Secy.; Samuel Sitkoff,* Treas.
Directors:* Arthur S. Hoffman, Erna D. Leir, Jean Mayer, Jerome Shelby.
Number of staff: 1 part-time professional.
Employer Identification Number: 136093563

2195
The Gerald & May Ellen Ritter Memorial Fund
c/o Proskauer Rose Goetz & Mendelsohn
300 Park Ave.
New York 10022 (212) 909-7708

Fund established in 1980 in NY.
Donor(s): May Ellen Ritter,† Gerald Ritter.†

Financial data (yr. ended 4/30/87): Assets, $1,877,215 (M); expenditures, $692,344, including $673,000 for 34 grants (high: $175,000; low: $1,000; average: $500-$50,000).
Purpose and activities: Support for higher education, cultural organizations, including music and other performing arts, social service and youth agencies, temple support, and Jewish welfare funds.
Types of support: Building funds, equipment, land acquisition, endowment funds, matching funds, scholarship funds, fellowships, research, loans, publications, conferences and seminars, continuing support, operating budgets, annual campaigns, seed money, emergency funds, deficit financing, special projects.
Limitations: Giving primarily in New York, NY. No grants to individuals.
Application information:
Initial approach: Letter or proposal
Deadline(s): None
Board meeting date(s): Quarterly
Final notification: Varies
Write: Gerald Silbert, Pres.
Officers: Gerald Silbert,* Chair. and Pres.; Lawrence Lachman,* Sr. V.P.; Ramie J. Silbert,* V.P.; Terry F. Silbert,* V.P.; Rita Rothman, Secy.; Herbert T. Weinstein,* Treas.
Number of staff: None.
Employer Identification Number: 133037300

2196
Rochester Gas and Electric Corporate Giving Program
89 East Avenue
Rochester 14649 (716) 546-2700

Financial data (yr. ended 12/31/88): $487,000 for grants.
Purpose and activities: Support for health and welfare (75 percent), education (19 percent), civic affairs (3 percent), and the arts and culture (3 percent).
Limitations: Giving primarily in the franchise area: nine counties centering around Rochester, NY.
Application information: Applications not accepted.
Write: David C. Heiligman, V.P.

2197
Rockefeller Brothers Fund
1290 Ave. of the Americas
New York 10104 (212) 373-4200

Incorporated in 1940 in NY.
Donor(s): John D. Rockefeller, Jr.,† Mrs. Martha Baird Rockefeller,† Mrs. Abby Rockefeller Mauze,† David Rockefeller, John D. Rockefeller, 3rd,† Laurance S. Rockefeller, Nelson A. Rockefeller,† Winthrop Rockefeller.†
Financial data (yr. ended 12/31/87): Assets, $219,435,159 (M); gifts received, $192,500; expenditures, $11,005,923, including $7,631,438 for 136 grants (high: $400,000; low: $5,000; average: $10,000-$75,000).
Purpose and activities: "Support of efforts in the U.S. and abroad that contribute ideas, develop leaders, and encourage institutions in the transition to global interdependence and that counter world trends of resource depletion, militarization, protectionism, and isolation which now threaten to move humankind everywhere further away from cooperation, trade and economic growth, arms restraint, and conservation." There are four major giving categories: 1) One World, with two major components: sustainable resource use and world security, including issues related to arms control, international relations, development, trade, and finance; 2) New York City; 3) Nonprofit Sector; and 4) Special Concerns. Two new concerns include focusing effective action on public health and related issues involved with the AIDS crisis in New York City, and dealing with the current crisis in South Africa.
Types of support: General purposes, seed money, special projects, conferences and seminars, internships, exchange programs, matching funds, consulting services, continuing support, research, technical assistance, endowment funds.
Limitations: No support for churches, hospitals, or community centers. No grants to individuals (including research, graduate study, or the writing of books), or for endowment or building funds; no loans.
Publications: Annual report (including application guidelines).
Application information:
Initial approach: Letter
Copies of proposal: 1
Deadline(s): None
Board meeting date(s): June and Nov.
Final notification: 3 months
Write: Benjamin R. Shute, Jr., Secy.
Officers: Colin G. Campbell, Pres.; Russell A. Phillips, Jr., Exec. V.P.; Benjamin R. Shute, Jr., Secy.; David G. Fernald, Treas.
Trustees:* David Rockefeller, Jr., Chair.; Abby M. O'Neill, Vice-Chair.; Laura R. Chasin, Peggy Dulany, James H. Evans, Peter C. Goldmark, Jr., Neva R. Goodwin, Hugh B. Price, George Putnam, Laurance Rockefeller, Rodman C. Rockefeller, Sharon P. Rockefeller, Steven C. Rockefeller, S. Frederick Starr, Russell E. Train.
Number of staff: 6 full-time professional; 1 part-time professional; 13 full-time support; 1 part-time support.
Employer Identification Number: 131760106
Recent arts and culture grants:
Columbia University, NYC, NY, $300,000. For final contribution to general support of university's Center for United States-China Arts Exchange to be used as funds functioning as endowment. 11/14/87.
Columbia University, NYC, NY, $75,000. For final conference of 3-year project of research and exchange in general arts education organized by university's Center for United States-China Arts exchange with Project Zero. 11/14/87.
National Trust for Historic Preservation, DC, $35,000. For expenses associated with Pocantico planning project. 1/27/87.
Studio Museum in Harlem, NYC, NY, $30,000. For development of business and architectural plans for expanded museum shop. 10/6/87.

2198
Rockefeller Family Fund, Inc.
1290 Ave. of the Americas, Rm. 3450
New York 10104 (212) 373-4252

Incorporated in 1967 in NY.
Donor(s): Members of the Rockefeller family.
Financial data (yr. ended 12/31/87): Assets, $27,738,390 (M); gifts received, $474,748; expenditures, $2,681,753, including $1,937,500 for 85 grants (high: $55,000; low: $2,002).
Purpose and activities: Grants primarily for advocacy activities to promote arms control, the environment, the women's movement, and public-interest activities centered on institutional responsiveness. Through 1988, giving also to nonpartisan organizations that help citizens comprehend and exercise the right to vote through the Citizen Education and Participation Program. Starting in 1988, the Fund will also support advocacy activities in education, primarily at preschool and primary levels.
Types of support: Operating budgets, continuing support, seed money, special projects.
Limitations: No support for international programs. No grants to individuals, or for building funds, renovation projects, deficit financing, research, endowment funds, matching gifts, scholarships, or fellowships; no loans.
Publications: Annual report (including application guidelines), newsletter.
Application information:
Initial approach: Letter or proposal
Copies of proposal: 1
Deadline(s): None
Board meeting date(s): June and Dec.; executive committee usually meets every 8 weeks
Final notification: 1 to 3 months
Write: Donald K. Ross, Dir.
Officers: Richard M. Chasin,* Pres.; Nancy Anderson,* V.P.; Anne Bartley,* V.P.; Clare Buden,* V.P.; Diana N. Rockefeller,* V.P.; Wendy Rockefeller,* V.P.; Donald K. Ross, Dir. and Secy.; David G. Fernald, Treas.
Trustees:* Hope Aldrich, Dana Chasin, Laura Chasin, Alida Rockefeller Dayton, Bruce Mazlish, Alida R. Messinger, Catharine O'Neill, Mary Louise Pierson, Richard G. Rockefeller, Steven C. Rockefeller, Abby R. Simpson.
Number of staff: 2 full-time professional; 1 full-time support; 1 part-time support.
Employer Identification Number: 136257658
Recent arts and culture grants:
Rails to Trails Conservancy, DC, $45,000. For membership campaign to create national constituency for preserving rail corridors as trails for recreation and wildlife preserves. 3/88.

2199
The Rockefeller Foundation
1133 Ave. of the Americas
New York 10036 (212) 869-8500

Incorporated in 1913 in NY.
Donor(s): John D. Rockefeller, Sr.†
Financial data (yr. ended 12/31/88): Assets, $1,828,914,091 (M); expenditures,

$77,372,147, including $50,630,076 for 870 grants (high: $1,150,000; low: $1,000; average: $10,000-$150,000), $5,014,827 for 309 grants to individuals, $23,291 for 62 employee matching gifts, $5,180,480 for 5 foundation-administered programs and $5,000,000 for 1 loan.

Purpose and activities: "To promote the well-being of mankind throughout the world." Concentrates its activities on science-based, international development in agriculture, health, and population sciences; arts and humanities; and equal opportunity. A "Special Interests and Explorations" category permits the foundation to maintain flexibility in grantmaking. Programs are carried out through the awarding of grants and fellowships, and the dissemination of information through publications and close association with the media. In addition, the foundation operates a Study and Conference Center in Bellagio, Italy, which is available for international conferences and brief residencies.

Types of support: Matching funds, fellowships, research, publications, conferences and seminars, special projects, grants to individuals, program-related investments.

Limitations: No support for appraising or subsidizing cures or inventions; the establishment of local hospitals, churches, schools, libraries, or welfare agencies or their building or operating funds; financing altruistic movements involving private profit; or propaganda or attempts to influence legislation. No grants for personal aid to individuals, or for capital or endowment funds, general support, or scholarships; no loans.

Publications: Annual report, program policy statement, occasional report, informational brochure, application guidelines.

Application information: Informational brochures available for fellowship programs.

Initial approach: Letter
Copies of proposal: 1
Deadline(s): Specified in individual brochures
Board meeting date(s): Usually in Apr., June, Sept., and Dec.
Write: Lynda Mullen, Secy.

Officers: Peter C. Goldmark,* Pres.; Kenneth Prewitt, Sr. V.P.; Hugh B. Price, V.P.; Nan S. Robinson, V.P. for Administration; Frank Karel, V.P. for Communications; Lynda Mullen, Secy.; Jack R. Meyer, Treas.

Trustees:* John R. Evans, Chair.; John Brademas, Harold Brown, Frances FitzGerald, W. David Hopper, Alice Stone Ilchman, Richard H. Jenrette, Tom Johnson, Arthur Levitt, Jr., Robert C. Maynard, Eleanor Holmes Norton, Harry Woolf.

Number of staff: 59 full-time professional; 54 full-time support; 4 part-time support.

Employer Identification Number: 131659629

Recent arts and culture grants:

African Council on Communication Education, Nairobi, Kenya, $41,300. For workshop on use of theater as method of communicating information about reproductive health to young people in rural areas of sub-Saharan Africa. 1988.

African Theatre Exchange (ATEX), England, $20,000. Toward expenses relating to African symposium workshop in Mauritius. 1988.

American Association of Museums, DC, $30,000. Toward Museum Data Collection Program. 1988.

American Council for the Arts, NYC, NY, $18,500. Toward publication and dissemination of book entitled Aspects of International Cultural Exchange: Looking to the Year 2000. 1988.

American Council of Learned Societies, NYC, NY, $300,000. To support basic scholarly research toward production of American National Biography. 1988.

American Council of Learned Societies, NYC, NY, $30,000. For use by International Research and Exchanges Board to continue scholarly projects associated with archival exchange between U.S. and Soviet Union. 1988.

American Dance Festival, NYC, NY, $76,000. Toward continuation of International Choreographers Workshop. 1988.

American Music Center, NYC, NY, $20,000. For coordination of American Music Week activities in U.S.. 1988.

American Music Theater Festival, Philadelphia, PA, $65,000. Toward commissioning and workshop expenses for Latin Connection project. 1988.

American Place Theater, NYC, NY, $25,000. Toward further development and production of original theater pieces that illuminate American history and culture. 1988.

American Repertory Theater, Cambridge, MA, $50,000. Toward expenses of two theatrical workshop/residencies to facilitate collaboration with international artists. 1988.

Appalshop, Whitesburg, KY, $25,000. For residency of playwright John O'Neal. 1988.

Appalshop, Whitesburg, KY, $17,500. To support American Festival of regional and ethnic work. 1988.

Arts and Business Council, NYC, NY, $25,000. Toward costs of Sybil Simon Multicultural Arts Administration Internship Program. 1988.

Association of College, University and Community Arts Administrators, DC, $100,000. For establishment of national task force on presenting and touring of contemporary artists. 1988.

Association of Hispanic Arts, NYC, NY, $30,000. For further development of publication, AHA! Hispanic News. 1988.

Available Potential Enterprises, Northampton, MA, $5,000. For playwright-in-residence to be named by theater. 1988.

Baltimore Theater Project, Baltimore, MD, $44,360. Toward residency and touring project involving Argentina's Teatro del Sur. 1988.

Biennale of Sydney, Sydney, Australia, $20,000. For participation of American entries in 1988 Biennale; 18 visual artists were presented. 1988.

Boston Dance Umbrella, Boston, MA, $25,000. Toward humanities conferences and contextual activities surrounding presentation of Tour de Fuerza and Africa Oye. 1988.

Bronx Museum of the Arts, Bronx, NY, $80,000. Toward exhibition, Latin American Spirit in the United States: 1920-1970. 1988.

Brooklyn Academy of Music, Brooklyn, NY, $200,000. To continue support of Next Wave Festival. 1988.

Brooklyn Academy of Music, Brooklyn, NY, $50,000. For planning and development of Pacific Rim Festival. 1988.

Brooklyn Institute of Arts and Sciences, Brooklyn, NY, $25,000. For use by Brooklyn Museum toward three-day conference and educational programs related to Hispanic Art in the United States exhibition. 1988.

Budapest New York Theater Arts Foundation, NYC, NY, $5,000. Toward participation of Squat Theater in Milan Oltre Festival. 1988.

California Afro-American Museum Foundation, Los Angeles, CA, $50,000. Toward exhibition entitled Introspectives: Contemporary Art by Americans and Brazilians of African Descent. 1988.

California Institute of the Arts, Valencia, CA, $5,000. Toward performance costs of Hungers, interdiscplinary theater piece, at Ars Electronica festival in Linz, Austria. 1988.

Capital Repertory Company, Albany, NY, $25,000. For residency of playwright Lynn Alvarez. 1988.

Cast Theater, Hollywood, CA, $5,000. For playwright-in-residence to be named by theater. 1988.

Center for Contemporary Arts of Santa Fe, Santa Fe, NM, $25,000. Toward organization and touring expenses of Ceremony of Memory. 1988.

Center for Puppetry Arts, Atlanta, GA, $15,000. For expenses of international participants in its Puppetry of the Americas festival and accompanying conference. 1988.

Center Theater Group of Los Angeles, Los Angeles, CA, $8,000. For use by Mark Taper Forum's Improvisational Theatre Project toward theatrical performances at Munich's Theatre of the World ASSITEJ Festival and at Vienna Festival. 1988.

Childrens Theater Company and School, Minneapolis, MN, $25,000. For residency of playwright Constance Congdon. 1988.

Chocolate Bayou Theater Company, Houston, TX, $5,000. For playwright-in-residence to be named by theater. 1988.

Civil Rights Project, Boston, MA, $200,000. Toward production, with accompanying educational materials, of sequel to Eyes on the Prize, public television series that documented early years of civil rights movement, and establishment of archive based on two series. 1988.

Civil Rights Project, Boston, MA, $100,000. To help production, with accompanying educational materials, of sequel to Eyes on the Prize, public television series that documented early years of civil rights movement, and establishment of archive based on two series; as part of American Public Schools awards. 1988.

Civil Rights Project, Boston, MA, $100,000. To help production, with accompanying educational materials, of sequel to Eyes on the Prize, public television series that documented early years of civil rights movement, and establishment of archive based on two series. 1988.

Civil Rights Project, Boston, MA, $47,300. Toward reprinting and distributing educational materials to accompany its public television series, Eyes on the Prize. 1988.

Civil Rights Project, Boston, MA, $47,300. Toward reprinting and distributing educational materials to accompany public television series, Eyes on the Prize. 1988.
Collective for Living Cinema, NYC, NY, $10,000. Toward conference, publication, and touring package based on Misrepresentations: A Corrective Film Series. 1988.
Colonus, Brooklyn, NY, $10,000. Toward artistic and production expenses of part IV of The Warrior Ant. 1988.
Community Programs in the Arts and Sciences (COMPAS), Saint Paul, MN, $90,000. For program to improve writing instruction in Saint Paul secondary schools. 1988.
Contemporary Arts Center, New Orleans, LA, $24,000. To assist American regional artists, especially minority and interdisciplinary artists, to develop collaborative projects and reach new audiences. 1988.
Council of American Overseas Research Centers, DC, $25,000. Toward further development of programs on behalf of American scholars working abroad. 1988.
Dance Exchange, DC, $5,000. Toward participation of Liz Lerman/Exchange and Dancers of the Third Age in London Dance Umbrella's 10th anniversary festival. 1988.
Dance Theater Workshop, NYC, NY, $225,000. To support Suitcase Fund, program of reciprocal touring by artists and companies from United States and abroad. 1988.
Dance Theater Workshop, NYC, NY, $25,000. For grant-in-aid to support Suitcase Fund, program of reciprocal touring by artists and companies from United States and abroad. 1988.
Diverse Works, Houston, TX, $18,000. To assist American regional artists, especially minority and interdisciplinary artists, to develop collaborative projects and reach new audiences. 1988.
Educational Testing Service, Princeton, NJ, $215,000. To continue collaborating with Harvard University's Project Zero on development of new approaches to instruction and testing in arts and humanities. 1988.
Eighty Langton Street, San Francisco, CA, $24,000. To assist American regional artists, especially minority and interdisciplinary artists, to develop collaborative projects and reach new audiences. 1988.
Eureka Theater Company, San Francisco, CA, $5,000. For playwright-in-residence to be named by theater. 1988.
European Cooperation Fund, Oxford, England, $150,000. Toward establishing program of support for publishing and translating Central European writing. 1988.
Foundation for Independent Video and Film, NYC, NY, $30,000. To continue research for directory of resources for independent film and video production in Africa, Asia, and Latin America, and to publish Latin American resource guide. 1988.
Friends of Puerto Rico, NYC, NY, $10,000. For use by Museum of Contemporary Hispanic Art toward exhibition costs and accompanying educational materials for exhibition, Homage to Jose Campeche. 1988.
Great Lakes Theater Festival, Cleveland, OH, $40,000. Toward artistic expenses and costs relating to production of Blood Wedding and four-month festival Festival Fantastico. 1988.
Hallwalls, Buffalo, NY, $18,000. To assist American regional artists, especially minority and interdisciplinary artists, to develop collaborative projects and reach new audiences. 1988.
Harvard University, Cambridge, MA, $235,000. To continue collaborating with Educational Testing Service on development of new approaches to instruction and testing in arts and humanities. 1988.
Illusion Theater and School, Minneapolis, MN, $5,000. For playwright-in-residence to be named by theater. 1988.
Independent Broadcasting Associates, Littleton, MA, $39,000. Toward adaptation for classroom use of 10-part series of half-hour radio broadcasts on Indian culture and society. 1988.
Independent Committee on Arts Policy, NYC, NY, $22,000. Toward 1988 activities and preparation of national arts policy briefing paper. 1988.
Indiana University, Bloomington, IN, $10,800. For use by African studies program toward African ethnomusicology curriculum program. 1988.
Institute of Contemporary Art, Boston, MA, $25,000. For curatorial research on Latin American art and development of series of small exhibitions. 1988.
Institute of International Education, NYC, NY, $50,000. For development of comprehensive information clearinghouse on international arts exchange. 1988.
Institute of International Education, NYC, NY, $25,000. Toward further development of its international exchange activities, as part of arts awards. 1988.
Institute of International Education, NYC, NY, $23,750. Toward publication and dissemination of book entitled Aspects of International Cultural Exchange: Looking to the Year 2000. 1988.
Intermedia Arts Minnesota, Minneapolis, MN, $16,000. To assist American regional artists, especially minority and interdisciplinary artists, to develop collaborative projects and reach new audiences. 1988.
International African Institute, London, England, $60,000. Toward development of training programs in documentation and educational activities, and toward development of exchange and networks among museums. 1988.
International Arts Relations (INTAR), NYC, NY, $25,000. For residency of playwright Jose Rivera. 1988.
International Arts Relations (INTAR), NYC, NY, $17,500. Toward David Avalos exhibition. 1988.
International Centre of Theatre Research, Paris, France, $200,000. To make available to international television audiences English-language version of Indian epic, The Mahabharata, as adapted by Peter Brook and International Centre of Theatre Research. 1988.
International Congress on Women in Music, La Crescenta, CA, $5,000. Toward participating in 1988 International Congress on Women in Music in Bremen and Heidelberg, Germany. 1988.
International House of Philadelphia, Philadelphia, PA, $30,000. For dissemination of film series entitled Latin American Visions. 1988.
Jacobs Pillow Dance Festival, Lee, MA, $60,000. Toward international and intercultural dance projects. 1988.
Johns Hopkins University, Baltimore, MD, $220,400. Toward program of resident fellowships in history of art and anthropology. 1988.
Jose Limon Dance Foundation, NYC, NY, $25,000. Toward revival and presentation of Missa Brevis at Festival del Centro Historico de la Ciudad de Mexico. 1988.
Jose Limon Dance Foundation, NYC, NY, $20,000. Toward participation in Festival Internacional Cervantino and Festival Cultural Sinalda in Mexico. 1988.
K T C A Twin Cities Public Television, Minneapolis, MN, $150,000. To support performing arts television series, Alive From Off Center. 1988.
La Mama Experimental Theater Club, NYC, NY, $200,000. To take aggressive role in producing and presenting next generation of important Third World artists. 1988.
La Mama Experimental Theater Club, NYC, NY, $25,000. For intercultural theater production. 1988.
Los Angeles Contemporary Exhibitions (LACE), Los Angeles, CA, $24,000. To assist American regional artists, especially minority and interdisciplinary artists, to develop collaborative projects and reach new audiences. 1988.
Los Angeles Educational Partnership, Los Angeles, CA, $150,000. To foster professional renewal of teachers through interdisciplinary activity in arts and humanities. 1988.
Mabou Mines Development Foundation, NYC, NY, $25,000. For residency of playwright Eric Overmyer. 1988.
Makerere University, Kampala, Uganda, $10,000. Toward purchase and installation of sculpture, The War Victim, by Francis Naggenda. 1988.
Mary Luft and Company, Miami, FL, $40,000. Toward 1988 New Music America Festival, to be held in Miami. 1988.
Mary Luft and Company, Miami, FL, $7,500. Toward coordinating American participation in two festivals celebrating modern music: 1988: Ano Internacional de la Musica Argentina Congresso y Festival in September 1988 and New York Days in Rotterdam in December 1988. 1988.
Mary McLeod Bethune Memorial Museum and Archives, DC, $50,000. Toward further costs of its development efforts. 1988.
Meet the Composer, NYC, NY, $350,000. For continuation of composers-in-residence program. 1988.
Meet the Composer, NYC, NY, $150,000. To bridge distance between jazz and rest of serious music community by initiating national fellowship program for jazz composers; fellowships include commission and residency with performing arts group. 1988.

Mexican Museum, San Francisco, CA, $5,000. For participation of humanities scholars in symposium, From the Inside Out: Mexican Folk Art in a Contemporary Context. 1988.
Milwaukee Repertory Theater, Milwaukee, WI, $5,000. Toward presentation of The Tale of Lear, at Toga International Arts Festival, in Japan. 1988.
Missouri Botanical Garden, Saint Louis, MO, $300,000. To initiate formation of Latin American plant sciences network to expand graduate training opportunities, stimulate research in new disciplines, and promote intraregional collaboration. 1988.
Movement Theater International, Philadelphia, PA, $18,000. For participation by African artists in its 1988 Festival. 1988.
Museum of Fine Arts of Houston, Houston, TX, $40,000. Toward development of exhibition of outstanding artists of Argentina and Uruguay from late 19th century to present. 1988.
Music-Theater Performing Group, NYC, NY, $25,000. Toward development of inter-cultural music-theatre works. 1988.
Music-Theater Performing Group, NYC, NY, $7,500. To participate in Festival de Otono, Madrid, and Festival de Ville, Paris. 1988.
National Jazz Service Organization, DC, $30,000. For program activities. 1988.
National Museums of Kenya, Institute of Primate Research, Kenya, $30,250. To study in baboons contraceptive vaccine developed by National Institute of Immunology in New Delhi, India. 1988.
National Museums of Kenya, Institute of Primate Research, Kenya, $25,110. To enable Mohamed Isahakia to study development and application of antisperm monoclonal antibodies. 1988.
National Public Radio, DC, $200,000. Toward general support. 1988.
National Public Radio, DC, $30,300. Toward six one-month residencies for ethnic-minority journalists. 1988.
Negro Ensemble Company, NYC, NY, $25,000. Toward initiating pilot phase of theater collaborative as well as institutional evaluation and planning project. 1988.
New Radio and Performing Arts, Brooklyn, NY, $35,000. Toward radio series featuring work by minority and international artists. 1988.
New York Foundation for the Arts, NYC, NY, $25,000. Toward second national conference on systems of support for individual artists. 1988.
New York Shakespeare Festival, NYC, NY, $175,000. For Festival Latino. 1988.
Nexus, Atlanta, GA, $18,000. To assist American regional artists, especially minority and interdisciplinary artists, to develop collaborative projects and reach new audiences. 1988.
Oberlin College, Oberlin, OH, $25,000. Toward planning for Jazz Masterwork Editions. 1988.
Opera America, DC, $200,000. To continue its program, Opera for the Eighties and Beyond. 1988.
Original Ballets Foundation, NYC, NY, $60,000. To expand services of New Ballet School and to undertake thorough evaluation of its past and present activity. 1988.
Original Ballets Foundation, NYC, NY, $15,000. For Feld Ballet's participation in five Italian festivals. 1988.
Orpheus Chamber Ensemble, NYC, NY, $10,000. To participate in Bath International Festival of Music and Arts. 1988.
Painted Bride Art Center, Philadelphia, PA, $24,000. To assist American regional artists, especially minority and interdisciplinary artists, to develop collaborative projects and reach new audiences. 1988.
Pan Asian Repertory Theater, NYC, NY, $7,500. For participation in 1988 Edinburgh Festival Fringe. 1988.
Performing Arts Journal, NYC, NY, $35,000. Toward series of publications that focus on interculturalism. 1988.
Philadelphia Alliance for Teaching Humanities in the Schools, Philadelphia, PA, $170,000. For administration of CHART (Collaborative for Humanities and Arts Teaching) network. CHART enables teachers to expand their knowledge and then reform classes. 1988.
Philadelphia Alliance for Teaching Humanities in the Schools, Philadelphia, PA, $58,300. Toward CHART administration's evaluation project. 1988.
Philadelphia Alliance for Teaching Humanities in the Schools, Philadelphia, PA, $25,000. Toward CHART's technical assistance meetings. 1988.
Philadelphia Museum of Art, Philadelphia, PA, $50,000. Toward exhibition, Jasper Johns: Work Since 1974, presented in U.S. pavilion at 43rd Venice Biennale. 1988.
Pick Up Performance Company, NYC, NY, $35,000. Toward development, production, and touring of large-scale choreographic work by David Gordon entitled Made in U.S.A. 1988.
Pittsburgh Public School District, Pittsburgh, PA, $150,000. Toward Arts PROPEL Dissemination Project. 1988.
Players Project, NYC, NY, $10,000. Toward participation in Cervantino Festival in Mexico City and Guanajuato. 1988.
Playwrights Horizons, NYC, NY, $25,000. For residency of playwright Craig Lucas. 1988.
Playwrights Unlimited, Mill Valley, CA, $5,000. For playwright-in-residence to be named by theater. 1988.
Puerto Rican Traveling Theater Company, NYC, NY, $5,000. For playwright-in-residence to be named by theater. 1988.
Randolph Street Gallery, Chicago, IL, $18,000. To assist American regional artists, especially minority and interdisciplinary artists, to develop collaborative projects and reach new audiences. 1988.
Readers International, Columbia, LA, $30,000. Toward library marketing campaign for translations of contemporary world literature. 1988.
Real Art Ways, Hartford, CT, $16,000. To assist American regional artists, especially minority and interdisciplinary artists, to develop collaborative projects and reach new audiences. 1988.
Research Foundation of the State University of New York, Buffalo, NY, $25,000. For use by SUNY-Buffalo toward First International Women's Playwrights Conference. 1988.
Rice University, Center for Cultural Studies, Houston, TX, $225,000. Toward program of resident fellowships. 1988.
River Arts Repertory Company, NYC, NY, $25,000. For residency of playwright Richard Nelson. 1988.
Roadside Attractions, Detroit, MI, $5,000. For playwright-in-residence to be named by theater. 1988.
Saint Louis Art Museum, Saint Louis, MO, $150,000. To mount exhibition devoted to art and social context of Caribbean festival tradition. 1988.
Salzburg Seminar in American Studies, Cambridge, MA, $60,000. Toward August 1988 international session on Gender and the Humanities. 1988.
Smithsonian Institution, DC, $150,000. To conduct experiments in exhibitions presenting non-Western cultures and American cultural minorities. 1988.
Smithsonian Institution, DC, $25,000. For use by National Museum of African Art in further planning for exhibition on nomadic architecture. 1988.
Smithsonian Institution, DC, $15,000. Toward symposium entitled Afro-Americans and the Evolution of a Living Constitution. 1988.
Social and Public Arts Resource Center, Venice, CA, $15,000. For educational activities to accompany exhibition of contemporary mural art entitled World Wall. 1988.
South Carolina Committee for the Humanities, Columbia, SC, $150,000. Toward rural education project in arts and humanities, as part of CHART awards. 1988.
Spanish Theater Repertory Company, NYC, NY, $100,000. Toward Repertorio Espanol's Latin American Director's Project. 1988.
Spoleto Festival USA, Charleston, SC, $50,000. For production and presentation of The Warrior Ant. 1988.
Stephen Petronio Dance Company, NYC, NY, $5,000. For participation in Holland Festival and Festival International Montpellier-Danse. 1988.
Studio Museum in Harlem, NYC, NY, $45,000. Toward planning for The Decade Show, major exhibition and survey of art of 1980's. 1988.
Studio Museum in Harlem, NYC, NY, $25,000. To continue research for exhibition of contemporary African art. 1988.
Sundance Institute for Film and Television, Salt Lake City, UT, $60,000. To increase production opportunities for American minority filmmakers and distribution within U.S. of works by Latin American filmmakers. 1988.
Syracuse University, Syracuse, NY, $5,000. Toward preparing U.S. entries at Second Biannual International Video Festival in Medellin, Colombia. 1988.
Theater for a New Audience, NYC, NY, $10,000. Toward educational components of its Shakespeare Celebration. 1988.
Theater for the New City Foundation, NYC, NY, $25,000. For residency of playwright Harry Kondoleon. 1988.
Trisha Brown Dance Company, NYC, NY, $5,000. Toward participating in 1988 National Theatre Dance Festival in Taipei, Taiwan. 1988.

University of California, Los Angeles, CA, $50,000. For use by Wight Art Gallery toward planning costs of exhibition, Defining Chicano Art. 1988.
University of Hawaii, Center for Pacific Island Studies, Manoa, HI, $83,400. Toward program of resident fellowships, as part of fellowships in the humanities awards. 1988.
University of Maryland Foundation, College Park, MD, $82,700. Toward program of resident fellowships in Department of Spanish and Portuguese and Research Center for Arts and Humanities. 1988.
University of New Mexico, Southwest Hispanic Research Institute, Albuquerque, NM, $224,000. Toward program of resident fellowships, as part of fellowships in the humanities awards. 1988.
University of Pennsylvania, Center for the Study of Black Literature and Culture, Philadelphia, PA, $219,100. Toward program of resident fellowships. 1988.
Urban Bush Women, NYC, NY, $25,000. Toward expenses for training of company members and research and development of new works. 1988.
Urban Bush Women, NYC, NY, $9,000. Toward presenting Heat at Festival International Montpellier-Danse and at London Dance Umbrella's Tenth Annual Festival. 1988.
Vanderbilt University, Center for Latin American and Iberian Studies, Nashville, TN, $25,000. Toward costs of completing Cambridge History of Latin American Literature. 1988.
Victory Gardens Theater, Chicago, IL, $5,000. For playwright-in-residence to be named by theater. 1988.
W G B H Educational Foundation, Boston, MA, $250,000. To enhance public knowledge of Latin America through prime-time public television series on its contemporary history entitled The Other Americas. 1988.
W G B H Educational Foundation, Boston, MA, $25,000. Toward New Television, series of experimental works by video artists. 1988.
W H Y Y-TV, Philadelphia, PA, $65,000. Toward 1988 INPUT (International Public Television) conference. 1988.
W N E T Channel 13, NYC, NY, $87,500. Toward continuation of Channel Crossings, its television series of dramas and documentaries produced abroad. 1988.
W N E T Channel 13, NYC, NY, $25,000. Toward New Television, series of experimental works by video artists. 1988.
W N Y C Foundation, NYC, NY, $65,000. For continuation of Window on World Television, series of foreign television programming presented to U.S. viewers. 1988.
Washington Project for the Arts (WPA), DC, $20,000. Toward research and development of exhibition, The Blues Aesthetic: Black Culture and Modernism, which examines influence of Afro-American culture on 20th century modernism. 1988.
World Music Productions, DC, $35,000. Toward nationally distributed public radio series on contemporary African music. 1988.
Yale University, New Haven, CT, $50,000. Toward artistic expenses relating to production of The Warrior Ant. 1988.

2200
Richard & Dorothy Rodgers Foundation
c/o Dorothy Rodgers
598 Madison Ave.
New York 10022

Established in 1952 in NY.
Donor(s): Richard Rodgers,† Dorothy Rodgers.
Financial data (yr. ended 12/31/87): Assets, $2,195,671 (M); gifts received, $454,000; expenditures, $432,422, including $423,775 for 127 grants (high: $71,000; low: $50).
Purpose and activities: Support for hospitals, culture, Jewish, and general giving.
Limitations: Giving primarily in New York, NY.
Application information: Contributes only to pre-selected organizations. Applications not accepted.
Officers: Dorothy Rodgers, Pres. and Treas.; Lawrence B. Bottenweiser, Secy.
Employer Identification Number: 136062852

2201
The Felix and Elizabeth Rohatyn Foundation, Inc.
(Formerly Felix G. Rohatyn Foundation)
c/o Lazard Freres & Co.
One Rockefeller Plaza
New York 10020

Established in 1968.
Donor(s): Felix G. Rohatyn.
Financial data (yr. ended 12/31/86): Assets, $3,461,203 (M); gifts received, $1,010,000; expenditures, $535,576, including $530,820 for 81 grants (high: $250,000; low: $100).
Purpose and activities: Emphasis on education, particularly higher education, the performing arts, community development, international affairs organizations, and public policy groups.
Types of support: General purposes, equipment.
Limitations: Giving primarily in the New York, NY, area. No grants to individuals.
Application information:
Initial approach: Letter
Deadline(s): None
Write: Felix G. Rohatyn, Pres.
Officers: Felix G. Rohatyn, Pres.; Elizabeth Rohatyn, V.P.; Melvin L. Heineman, Secy.-Treas.
Number of staff: None.
Employer Identification Number: 237015644

2202
Romill Foundation
1045 Sixth Ave.
New York 10018
Additional address: c/o Wilmington Trust Company, 10th and Market Sts., Wilmington, DE 19890

Trust established in 1960 in SC.
Donor(s): Roger Milliken.
Financial data (yr. ended 12/31/87): Assets, $2,801,883 (M); gifts received, $363,493; expenditures, $1,036,269, including $1,031,039 for 28 grants (high: $456,039; low: $1,000; average: $2,500-$65,000).
Purpose and activities: Grants primarily for educational associations and higher education; some support for public interest and cultural organizations.
Types of support: General purposes.
Limitations: Giving primarily in Spartanburg County, SC.
Application information:
Initial approach: Letter
Deadline(s): None
Board meeting date(s): As required
Write: Lawrence Heagney, Treas.
Officer: Lawrence Heagney, Treas.
Trustees: Gerrish H. Milliken, Justine V.R. Milliken, Minot K. Milliken.
Number of staff: None.
Employer Identification Number: 136102069

2203
Billy Rose Foundation, Inc.
One Dag Hammarskjold Plaza, 47th Fl.
New York 10163 (212) 349-4141

Incorporated in 1958 in NY.
Donor(s): Billy Rose.†
Financial data (yr. ended 12/31/87): Assets, $9,251,113 (M); expenditures, $1,358,821, including $1,294,865 for 78 grants (high: $325,000; low: $2,000; average: $2,500-$25,000).
Purpose and activities: Support for museums, particularly a museum in Israel, the performing and fine arts, higher education, and medical research.
Types of support: Research, special projects.
Limitations: Giving primarily in New York, NY. No grants to individuals.
Application information:
Initial approach: Letter
Deadline(s): None
Board meeting date(s): Usually in June
Final notification: Varies
Write: Terri C. Mangino, Exec. Dir.
Officers and Directors: Arthur Cantor,* Chair.; Morris Shilensky,* Pres.; James R. Cherry,* V.P. and Secy.-Treas.; Charles Wohlstetter, V.P.; Terri C. Mangino, Exec. Dir.
Number of staff: 1 full-time professional.
Employer Identification Number: 136165466

2204
Frederick P. & Sandra P. Rose Foundation
380 Madison Ave.
New York 10017

Established in 1982 in DE.
Donor(s): Frederick P. Rose.
Financial data (yr. ended 11/30/86): Assets, $569,726 (M); gifts received, $165,000; expenditures, $276,209, including $275,000 for 5 grants (high: $160,000; low: $5,000).
Purpose and activities: Giving primarily for higher education; support also for cultural organizations.
Application information: Contributes only to pre-selected organizations. Applications not accepted.
Officers and Directors: Frederick P. Rose, Pres.; Sandra P. Rose, V.P.; Jonathan F.P. Rose, Secy.-Treas.; Deborah Rose, Elihu Rose.
Employer Identification Number: 133136740

2205
Joseph Rosen Foundation, Inc.
P.O. Box 334, Lenox Hill Station
New York 10021 (212) 249-1550

Incorporated in 1948 in NY.
Financial data (yr. ended 6/30/87): Assets, $9,012,532 (M); gifts received, $434,050; expenditures, $364,718, including $342,169 for 235 grants (high: $24,000; low: $50).
Purpose and activities: Grants largely for Jewish welfare funds, and temple support, child welfare, higher education, health services, and cultural organizations, especially the performing arts.
Application information: Contributes only to pre-selected organizations. Applications not accepted.
Officers and Directors: Abraham A. Rosen, Pres.; Jonathan P. Rosen, V.P. and Secy.; Miriam Rosen, Treas.
Employer Identification Number: 136158412

2206
The Rosenstiel Foundation
c/o Lewis Helphand & Co.
1185 Ave. of the Americas
New York 10036-2602

Incorporated in 1950 in OH.
Donor(s): Lewis S. Rosenstiel.†
Financial data (yr. ended 12/31/86): Assets, $10,795,446 (M); expenditures, $702,823, including $577,175 for 105 grants (high: $103,525; low: $500).
Purpose and activities: Grants largely for Polish cultural programs, the performing arts, health organizations, hospitals, and higher education.
Limitations: Giving primarily in NY and FL.
Application information: Contributes only to pre-selected organizations. Applications not accepted.
Officers: Blanka A. Rosenstiel, Pres.; Elizabeth R. Kabler, V.P.; Maurice C. Greenbaum, Secy.
Employer Identification Number: 066034536

2207
The Ida and William Rosenthal Foundation, Inc.
90 Park Ave.
New York 10016 (212) 953-1415

Incorporated in 1953 in NY.
Donor(s): Ida Rosenthal,† William Rosenthal.†
Financial data (yr. ended 8/31/87): Assets, $4,554,910 (M); expenditures, $278,447, including $203,917 for 43 grants (high: $25,000; low: $250).
Purpose and activities: Grants primarily for scholarships at selected secondary, undergraduate, and graduate institutions; support also for community and minority organizations in the NY metropolitan area and Hudson County, NJ; support for theatre, dance and museum projects in NY.
Types of support: Continuing support, seed money, endowment funds, scholarship funds, capital campaigns.
Limitations: Giving primarily in NY and NJ; some support also in GA, FL, and WV. No grants to individuals, or for matching gifts; no loans.
Application information:
Initial approach: Letter
Copies of proposal: 1
Deadline(s): None
Board meeting date(s): As required
Write: Catherine C. Brawer, V.P.
Officers and Directors: Beatrice Coleman, Pres.; Robert H. Stroup, V.P. and Secy.; David C. Masket, V.P. and Treas.; Catherine Coleman Brawer, V.P.; Robert A. Brawer, V.P.; Elizabeth Coleman, V.P.
Number of staff: 1 part-time professional; 1 part-time support.
Employer Identification Number: 136141274

2208
The William Rosenwald Family Fund, Inc.
122 East 42nd St., 24th Fl.
New York 10168 (212) 697-2420

Incorporated in 1938 in CT.
Donor(s): William Rosenwald, and family.
Financial data (yr. ended 12/31/86): Assets, $15,737,424 (M); gifts received, $226,656; expenditures, $652,868, including $580,800 for 40 grants (high: $260,000; low: $100).
Purpose and activities: Emphasis on Jewish welfare funds; some support for higher education, including medical education, cultural activities, and hospitals.
Limitations: Giving primarily in NY.
Application information:
Initial approach: Proposal
Deadline(s): None
Write: David P. Steinmann, Secy.
Officers: William Rosenwald,* Pres. and Treas.; Nina Rosenwald,* V.P.; Alice R. Sigelman,* V.P.; Elizabeth R. Varet,* V.P.; David P. Steinmann, Secy.
Directors:* Hulbert S. Aldrich, Bernard E. Brandes, Samuel Hoffman, Henry Z. Steinway, Frank D. Williams.
Employer Identification Number: 131635289

2209
Arthur Ross Foundation, Inc.
20 East 74th St., 4-C
New York 10021 (212) 737-7311

Incorporated in 1955 in NY.
Donor(s): Arthur Ross.
Financial data (yr. ended 12/31/88): Assets, $6,097,468 (M); gifts received, $89,750; expenditures, $1,068,838, including $925,771 for 70 grants (high: $87,971; low: $50).
Purpose and activities: Support for higher education and cultural institutions, especially museums and parks.
Limitations: Giving primarily in NY.
Publications: Annual report.
Application information: Contributes only to pre-selected organizations. Applications not accepted.
Write: Arthur Ross, Pres.
Officers and Directors: Arthur Ross, Pres. and Treas.; Clifford A. Ross, Exec. V.P.; Janet C. Ross, V.P.; George J. Gillespie III, Secy.; Tom Bernstein, John H. Dobkin, William T. Golden, Leo Gottlieb, Ralph M. Sussman, Paul E. Taylor, Jr., Edgar Wachenheim III.
Employer Identification Number: 136121436

2210
Stanley & Elsie Roth Foundation, Inc.
c/o Stanley Roth, Jr.
10 East 70th St., Apt. 14C
New York 10021-4947

Incorporated in 1974 in NJ.
Donor(s): Stanley Roth, Sr.†
Financial data (yr. ended 12/31/87): Assets, $1,449,515 (M); expenditures, $261,224, including $238,000 for 32 grants (high: $100,000; low: $872).
Purpose and activities: Giving largely for universities, museums, care for the aged, and hospitals.
Limitations: No grants to individuals.
Publications: 990-PF.
Application information:
Initial approach: Letter
Deadline(s): Sept. 30
Board meeting date(s): May 5 and Nov. 11
Final notification: Dec. 31
Write: Richard S. Borisoff, V.P.
Officers and Directors: Stanley Roth, Jr., Pres.; Richard S. Borisoff, V.P.; Robert Roth, V.P.; Joseph S. Iseman, Secy.-Treas.
Number of staff: None.
Employer Identification Number: 237400784

2211
Robert and Maurine Rothschild Fund, Inc.
c/o Perelsom Johnson & Runes
560 Lexington Avenue
New York 10022

Incorporated in 1948 in NY.
Donor(s): Herbert M. Rothschild,† Nannette F. Rothschild, and others.
Financial data (yr. ended 12/31/87): Assets, $1,478,551 (M); expenditures, $130,356, including $101,550 for 68 grants (high: $52,000; low: $25).
Purpose and activities: Emphasis on the arts, including museums, and community development and higher education.
Application information:
Initial approach: Letter
Deadline(s): None
Write: The Directors
Directors: Katherine Jackson, Maurine Rothschild, Peter Rothschild, Robert F. Rothschild.
Employer Identification Number: 136059064

2212
Robert E. & Judith O. Rubin Foundation
c/o Goldman, Sachs & Co. - Tax Dept.
85 Broad St., 30th Fl.
New York 10004

Established in 1980 in NY.
Donor(s): Robert E. Rubin.
Financial data (yr. ended 8/31/87): Assets, $1,207,154 (M); gifts received, $747,184; expenditures, $565,608, including $562,975 for 47 grants (high: $250,000; low: $100).

Purpose and activities: Giving primarily for higher education, hospitals, and Jewish welfare; support also for cultural programs.
Application information: Applications not accepted.
Trustees: Judith O. Rubin, Robert E. Rubin, Roy J. Zuckerberg.
Employer Identification Number: 133050749

2213
Samuel Rubin Foundation, Inc.

777 United Nations Plaza
New York 10017 (212) 697-8945

Established in 1958 in NY.
Donor(s): Samuel Rubin Foundation, Inc.
Financial data (yr. ended 6/30/87): Assets, $12,185,466 (M); expenditures, $1,034,334, including $854,541 for 117 grants (high: $235,000; low: $800; average: $2,000-$15,000).
Purpose and activities: Grants for the pursuit of peace and justice; for an equitable reallocation of the world's resources; and to promote social, economic, political, civil, and cultural rights.
Types of support: General purposes, seed money.
Limitations: No grants to individuals, or for endowments or building funds.
Publications: Program policy statement, 990-PF.
Application information:
Initial approach: Proposal
Deadline(s): None
Board meeting date(s): Quarterly
Final notification: 2 weeks following board meetings
Write: Cora Weiss, Pres.
Officers and Directors: Cora Weiss, Pres.; Judy Weiss, V.P.; Charles L. Mandelstam, Secy.; Peter Weiss, Treas.; Ralph Shikes, Daniel Weiss, Tamara Weiss.
Number of staff: 1 full-time professional; 1 part-time professional; 1 full-time support.
Employer Identification Number: 136164671
Recent arts and culture grants:
PTV Production, NYC, NY, $5,000. 1987.

2214
Helena Rubinstein Foundation, Inc.

405 Lexington Ave.
New York 10174 (212) 986-0806

Incorporated in 1953 in NY.
Donor(s): Helena Rubinstein Gourielli.†
Financial data (yr. ended 5/31/88): Assets, $38,258,900 (M); expenditures, $4,897,091, including $4,530,283 for 245 grants (high: $300,000).
Purpose and activities: Focus on projects that benefit women and children. Funding primarily for education, community services, health care and medical research, and the arts.
Types of support: Operating budgets, seed money, professorships, internships, scholarship funds, fellowships, research, publications, continuing support, general purposes.
Limitations: Giving primarily in New York City, NY. No grants to individuals, or for emergency funds, or film or video projects; no loans.
Publications: Annual report (including application guidelines), application guidelines.
Application information:
Initial approach: Letter
Copies of proposal: 1
Deadline(s): None
Board meeting date(s): Nov. and May
Final notification: 1 to 3 months
Write: Diane Moss, Exec. Dir.
Officers and Directors: Roy V. Titus, Chair.; Mrs. Roy V. Titus, Vice-Chair.; Oscar Kolin, Pres.; Diane Moss, V.P. and Exec. Dir.; Robert S. Friedman, Secy.-Treas.; Gertrude G. Michelson, Martin E. Segal.
Number of staff: 4 full-time professional; 1 full-time support; 1 part-time support.
Employer Identification Number: 136102666
Recent arts and culture grants:
Acting Company, NYC, NY, $25,000. For general support. 11/13/87.
Acting Company, NYC, NY, $9,000. For general support. 6/8/88.
Alvin Ailey American Dance Theater, NYC, NY, $30,000. For general support of Repertory Ensemble. 5/24/88.
Alvin Ailey American Dance Theater, NYC, NY, $30,000. To underwrite creation of new works for Thirtieth Anniversary Season. 5/27/88.
America-Israel Cultural Foundation, NYC, NY, $100,000. For scholarship endowment fund to be established in honor of Leonard Bernstein's 70th birthday. 11/25/87.
America-Israel Cultural Foundation, NYC, NY, $35,000. For Helena Rubinstein Foundation Scholarships to students in arts in Israel. 6/8/88.
American Composers Orchestra, NYC, NY, $5,000. To commission American women composers to create music and perform at Carnegie Hall. 6/8/88.
American Friends of the Israel Museum, NYC, NY, $10,000. Toward educational activities for children at Ruth Youth Wing of Museum. 11/25/87.
American Museum of Natural History, Department of Education, NYC, NY, $7,500. For community programming. 6/8/88.
American Public Radio, Saint Paul, MN, $45,000. For general support. 11/25/87.
Arts Connection, NYC, NY, $7,000. For tutoring and counseling component of Young Talent Program. 6/8/88.
Asia Society, Performing Arts Department, NYC, NY, $5,000. For school program. 5/24/88.
Bargemusic, Brooklyn, NY, $5,000. For program support for women performers. 5/24/88.
Bezalel Academy of Arts and Design, Friends of, NYC, NY, $25,000. For scholarships to students at Bezalel Academy of Arts and Design in Israel. 5/24/88.
Brooklyn Academy of Music, Brooklyn, NY, $15,000. For general support of Performing Arts Program for Young People. 6/8/88.
Brooklyn Childrens Museum, Brooklyn, NY, $7,500. For expansion of Early Childhood Program. 5/24/88.
Brooklyn Museum, Brooklyn, NY, $20,000. For Helena Rubinstein Foundation scholarships for students enrolled in Young Artists Museum Classes and for general support. 6/8/88.
Brooklyn Philharmonic Symphony Orchestra, Brooklyn, NY, $5,000. For in-School Performance and Instruction Program and Free Schooltime Concerts. 11/25/87.
Carnegie Hall Corporation, NYC, NY, $10,000. For classical music concerts for special education students. 11/25/87.
Chamber Music Society of Lincoln Center, NYC, NY, $10,000. For Together With Chamber Music series and Student Ticket Subsidy program. 5/24/88.
Childrens Art Carnival, NYC, NY, $15,000. For general support of educational arts programs for minority youth. 11/25/87.
Childrens Museum of Manhattan, NYC, NY, $20,000. For program support. 11/25/87.
Cooper-Hewitt Museum, The Smithsonians National Museum of Design, NYC, NY, $10,000. For partial-tuition scholarships for candidates in Master of Arts Program in Decorative Arts. 6/8/88.
Doing Art Together, NYC, NY, $5,000. For general support of P.S. 86-Lehman College collaborative art outreach program of child/parent/teacher workshops. 5/24/88.
Drawing Center, NYC, NY, $5,000. For internships. 11/25/87.
East End Arts and Humanities Council, Riverhead, NY, $5,000. For support of Dance Subscription Series. 5/24/88.
Friars Foundation, NYC, NY, $10,000. For grant awards to arts and charitable organizations. 5/24/88.
Guild Hall of East Hampton, East Hampton, NY, $5,000. For support of exhibition. 11/25/87.
Harbor Festival Foundation, NYC, NY, $10,000. For general support. 11/25/87.
Institute of International Education, NYC, NY, $10,000. For Arts International Program. 5/24/88.
Jewish Museum, NYC, NY, $25,000. For education department programs for school children. 11/25/87.
Joffrey Ballet, Foundation for the, NYC, NY, $7,500. For general support. 6/8/88.
Juilliard School, NYC, NY, $60,000. For scholarships for graduate music students. 6/24/88.
Kibbutz Neve-Eitan, Israel, $325,000. Toward renovation and reconstruction of Cultural Center and repair of parking area and access roads. 11/25/87.
Lincoln Center for the Performing Arts, NYC, NY, $15,000. For general support. 5/24/88.
Lincoln Center Institute, NYC, NY, $5,000. For general support. 5/24/88.
Lincoln Center Theater, NYC, NY, $25,000. For general support. 5/24/88.
Lincoln Center Theater, NYC, NY, $10,000. Toward documentary film about Sarafina!. 5/24/88.
Manhattan School of Music, NYC, NY, $15,000. For scholarships for women. 6/8/88.
Martha Graham Center of Contemporary Dance, NYC, NY, $5,000. For scholarships for women dancers in Martha Graham School's Trainee Program. 6/8/88.
Museum of Broadcasting, NYC, NY, $10,000. For seed funding for three Saturday morning radio workshops for children. 5/24/88.

Museum of Modern Art, NYC, NY, $100,000. For installation of improved lighting in Roy and Niuta Titus Theater 1. 5/24/88.
Museum of Modern Art, NYC, NY, $50,000. For general support. 6/8/88.
Museum of Modern Art, NYC, NY, $10,000. For general support. 10/5/87.
Museum of the City of New York, NYC, NY, $8,500. For education department programs for school children. 11/25/87.
National Museum of American Jewish History, Philadelphia, PA, $6,000. For family programming. 11/25/87.
New Ballet School, Associate School of the Feld Ballet, NYC, NY, $15,000. For general support. 5/24/88.
New School for Social Research, NYC, NY, $150,000. Toward transition fund to support merger of Mannes College of Music with New School for Social Research. 5/24/88.
New York City Ballet, New York State Theater, NYC, NY, $25,000. For general support. 5/24/88.
New York City School Volunteer Program, NYC, NY, $20,000. For salary support of Cultural Resources Project Coordinator. 11/25/87.
New York Dance Center, NYC, NY, $35,000. For expenses incurred through efforts to find tenant/partner for 890 Broadway. 5/24/88.
New York Public Library, Schomburg Center for Research in Black Culture, NYC, NY, $5,000. For general support. 5/27/88.
New York Shakespeare Festival, NYC, NY, $75,000. For support of Free Shakespeare in the Park. 6/8/88.
New York University, Tisch School of the Arts, NYC, NY, $24,000. For scholarships to students in Institute of Film and Television. 5/24/88.
New York Zoological Society, Bronx, NY, $15,000. For teaching fellowships at Bronx Zoo. 11/25/87.
New York Zoological Society, Bronx Zoo, Bronx, NY, $15,000. For Helena Rubinstein Teaching Fellowships at Bronx Zoo. 6/8/88.
Parsons School of Design, NYC, NY, $40,000. For scholarships to candidates in M.F.A. in Painting program. 6/8/88.
Public Art Fund, NYC, NY, $7,500. For MTA Gets You There Subway Poster Project. 5/24/88.
Queens Museum, Flushing, NY, $7,500. To New York City Panorama in a Box project, educational program for public school children. 11/25/87.
Repertorio Espanol, NYC, NY, $5,000. For study guide to Spanish-language performances for junior high and high school students. 5/24/88.
School of American Ballet, NYC, NY, $15,000. For scholarships for young women. 5/24/88.
Solomon R. Guggenheim Museum, NYC, NY, $10,000. For production costs of WORKS AND PROCESS, a Performing Arts Series. 11/25/87.
State University College at Buffalo, Western New York Institute for the Arts in Education, Buffalo, NY, $5,000. For general support. 11/25/87.
Staten Island Childrens Museum, Staten Island, NY, $7,000. For exhibition support. 5/24/88.
Statue of Liberty-Ellis Island Foundation, NYC, NY, $10,000. For construction of Student Orientation Center in Ellis Island Immigration Museum. 5/24/88.
Studio in a School Association, NYC, NY, $5,000. For visual arts instruction program in P.S. 6 in Bronx. 11/25/87.
Symphony Space, NYC, NY, $7,500. For Curriculum Arts Project. 11/25/87.
TADA, NYC, NY, $10,000. To assist with lease commitment for office, rehearsal, and performance space at Stage Arts Theater on West 28th Street. 12/15/87.
Tanglewood Music Center, Symphony Hall, Tanglewood, MA, $20,000. For Helena Rubinstein Fellowship for woman conductor; and for endowment to support annual scholarships for women in Conducting Seminar at Tanglewood. 5/24/88.
Teachers and Writers Collaborative, NYC, NY, $8,500. For writing and arts workshops in New York City public schools and for publications. 11/25/87.
Tel Aviv Museum, American Friends of the, NYC, NY, $50,000. For Helena Rubinstein Youth Workshops of Tel Aviv Museum, to be located in Art Education Center. 6/8/88.
Tel Aviv Museum, American Friends of the, NYC, NY, $50,000. For book, periodical, microfilm and equipment purchases for Helena Rubinstein Art Library of Tel Aviv Museum. 6/8/88.
Tel Aviv Museum, American Friends of the, NYC, NY, $20,000. For maintenance of Helena Rubinstein Pavilion. 6/8/88.
Twyla Tharp Dance Foundation, NYC, NY, $5,000. For preservation of video archive. 11/25/87.
Victor DAmico Institute of Art, Amagansett, NY, $5,000. For general support. 6/8/88.
W N E T Channel 13, NYC, NY, $200,000. To underwrite children's educational programming. 11/25/87.
W N Y C Foundation, NYC, NY, $10,000. For Kids America, a children's radio program. 11/25/87.
W N Y C Foundation, NYC, NY, $5,000. For program support. 5/24/88.
Whitney Museum of American Art, NYC, NY, $1,000,000. For Museum Studies Component of Independent Study Program for endowment fund, income to be designated for stipends for Helena Rubinstein Fellows; balance for Fellow's stipends each year. 6/8/88.
Whitney Museum of American Art, NYC, NY, $40,000. For Free Admission Program for College Students. 5/31/88.
Whitney Museum of American Art, NYC, NY, $5,000. For general support. 11/4/87.
YM-YWHA, 92nd Street, NYC, NY, $20,000. For New York Chamber Symphony. 11/25/87.
Young Concert Artists, NYC, NY, $27,000. For program support. 6/8/88.

2215
Rudin Foundation, Inc.
345 Park Ave.
New York 10154 (212) 644-8500

Incorporated in 1960 in NY.
Financial data (yr. ended 12/31/86): Assets, $961,039 (M); gifts received, $372,700; expenditures, $424,565, including $420,903 for 141 grants (high: $175,000; low: $100; average: $500-$2,000).
Purpose and activities: Grants for higher education, community development, and cultural organizations.
Limitations: Giving primarily in New York, NY.
Application information:
Initial approach: Letter
Deadline(s): None
Write: Susan H. Rapaport, Admin.
Officers and Directors: Jack Rudin, Pres.; Lewis Rudin, V.P.; Morton Witzling, Secy.; Milton N. Hoffman, Treas.; May Rudin, Lewis Steinman, Adelaide Rudin Zisson.
Employer Identification Number: 136113064

2216
Samuel and May Rudin Foundation, Inc.
345 Park Ave.
New York 10154 (212) 644-8500

Incorporated in 1976 in NY.
Donor(s): Samuel Rudin.†
Financial data (yr. ended 6/30/88): Assets, $3,396,588 (M); gifts received, $9,129,987; expenditures, $10,747,296, including $10,499,840 for 263 grants (high: $1,000,000; low: $250; average: $10,000-$50,000).
Purpose and activities: Support primarily for higher education, social service and religious welfare agencies, hospitals and health associations, and museums, performing arts groups, and other cultural programs.
Limitations: Giving primarily in New York City, NY.
Application information:
Initial approach: Letter
Deadline(s): None
Write: Susan H. Rapaport, Admin.
Officers and Directors: Jack Rudin, Pres.; Lewis Rudin, Exec V.P. and Secy.-Treas.; Beth Rudin DeWoody, V.P.; Eric Rudin, V.P.; Madeleine Rudin Johnson, Katherine Rudin, William Rudin.
Employer Identification Number: 132906946

2217
The Nina M. Ryan Foundation, Inc.
Jaycox Rd.
Cold Spring 10516

Incorporated in 1947 in NY.
Financial data (yr. ended 12/31/87): Assets, $2,265,315 (M); expenditures, $84,391, including $68,655 for 58 grants (high: $10,000; low: $25).
Purpose and activities: Grants primarily for cultural programs, with emphasis on music and music education, and for higher education; support also for community funds.
Limitations: No grants for No grants, scholarships or loans.
Application information: Applications not accepted.
Officers: Winifred B. Parker, Pres.; R.F. Bell, V.P.; Richard O. Berner, V.P.; T. Roland Berner, V.P. and Treas.; Olga Formissano, Secy.
Employer Identification Number: 136111038

2218
Sacharuna Foundation
c/o Palisades Management Corp.
515 Madison Ave., Rm. 4100
New York 10022

Established in 1985 in NY.
Donor(s): Lavinia Currier, Jack Robinson.
Financial data (yr. ended 12/31/87): Assets, $9,414,440 (M); gifts received, $10,000; expenditures, $505,414, including $460,500 for 19 grants (high: $100,000; low: $1,000).
Purpose and activities: Giving primarily for conservation, environmental, and wildlife organizations. Some support for historic preservation and cultural programs.
Application information: Contributes only to pre-selected organizations. Applications not accepted.
Trustee: Lavinia Currier.
Employer Identification Number: 133264132

2219
Saks Fifth Avenue Corporate Giving Program
12 East 49th St.
New York 10017 (212) 940-4195

Purpose and activities: Supports humanities and culture, civic affairs, and health and social services.
Types of support: General purposes, special projects.
Limitations: Giving primarily in major operating areas.
Application information: Include organization description, amount requested, audited financial statement and 501(c)(3).
Initial approach: Brief letter to director of Corporate Contributions Committee or local manager of nearest branch store
Deadline(s): None
Write: Paul Leblang, Dir., Corp. Contribs. Comm.

2220
The Salomon Foundation, Inc.
One New York Plaza
New York 10004 (212) 747-2400

Established in 1985 in NY.
Donor(s): Salomon, Inc.
Financial data (yr. ended 12/31/87): Assets, $8,322,770 (M); gifts received, $10,000; expenditures, $2,050,516, including $1,279,100 for 272 grants (high: $125,000; low: $500) and $715,929 for employee matching gifts.
Purpose and activities: Support for higher, elementary and secondary education; arts and culture; community activities; libraries; and medical research and health. The foundation also sponsors an employee matching gifts program for education.
Types of support: Employee matching gifts.
Limitations: Giving primarily in New York City, NY, area and other geographic locations where branch offices are situated, notably Los Angeles and San Francisco, CA; Dallas, TX; Chicago, IL; Atlanta, GA; and Boston, MA. No grants to individuals.
Application information:
Initial approach: Letter
Copies of proposal: 1
Deadline(s): None
Write: Jane Heffner, Secy.
Officers: John H. Gutfreund,* Pres.; Jane E. Heffner, Secy.; Donald M. Feuerstein, Treas.
Directors:* Warren E. Buffet, Gedale B. Horowitz, William F. May, William J. Voute.
Employer Identification Number: 133388259

2221
Richard & Edna Salomon Foundation, Inc.
45 Rockefeller Plaza
New York 10111 (212) 903-1216

Established in 1964 in NY.
Donor(s): Richard B. Salomon.
Financial data (yr. ended 12/31/87): Assets, $2,894,655 (M); expenditures, $584,140, including $578,250 for 47 grants (high: $201,000; low: $250).
Purpose and activities: Giving for the arts, education, and social services.
Types of support: General purposes.
Limitations: No grants to individuals.
Application information:
Initial approach: Letter
Deadline(s): None
Write: R.M. Schleicher, V.P.
Officers: Richard B. Salomon,* Pres.; Raymond M. Schleicher,* V.P. and Treas.; Merwin Lewis, Secy.
Directors:* Edna Salomon, Richard E. Salomon.
Employer Identification Number: 136163521

2222
Saltzman Foundation, Inc.
350 Fifth Ave.
New York 10118-0001

Established in 1950 in NY.
Financial data (yr. ended 3/31/88): Assets, $1,160,367 (M); gifts received, $25,000; expenditures, $55,908, including $52,100 for 19 grants (high: $30,000; low: $50).
Purpose and activities: Support primarily for higher education, museums, health, hospitals, libraries, and child development.
Limitations: Giving primarily in NY.
Application information:
Write: Arnold A. Saltzman, Pres.
Officers and Directors: Arnold A. Saltzman, Pres. and Treas.; Joan Saltzman, Secy.; Roth Tuishoff.
Employer Identification Number: 136142471

2223
The Fan Fox and Leslie R. Samuels Foundation, Inc.
30 Rockefeller Plaza, Suite 1933
New York 10112 (212) 315-2940

Incorporated in 1959 in UT; reincorporated in 1981 in NY.
Donor(s): Leslie R. Samuels,† Fan Fox Samuels.†
Financial data (yr. ended 7/31/88): Assets, $88,302,175 (M); gifts received, $21,385,000; expenditures, $5,394,173, including $4,334,193 for 136 grants (high: $300,000; low: $300; average: $5,000-$300,000).
Purpose and activities: Grants largely for the performing arts, health care, social services, and education, especially programs for the young and the elderly.
Types of support: Continuing support, seed money, building funds, equipment, research, matching funds, special projects.
Limitations: Giving primarily in the New York, NY, metropolitan area. No grants to individuals, or for scholarships or fellowships; no loans.
Publications: Annual report (including application guidelines).
Application information:
Initial approach: Letter
Copies of proposal: 1
Deadline(s): None
Board meeting date(s): Oct., Jan., Apr., July, and as necessary
Final notification: 4 months
Write: Marvin A. Kaufman, Pres.
Officers and Directors: Morton J. Bernstein, Chair.; Marvin A. Kaufman, Pres.; Joseph C. Mitchell, V.P. and Treas.; Carlos D. Moseley, V.P.; Muriel Nasser, Secy.
Number of staff: 3 full-time professional; 1 full-time support.
Employer Identification Number: 133124818

2224
Sasco Foundation
145 East 74th St., Suite 1C
New York 10021

Trust established in 1951 in NY.
Donor(s): Leila E. Riegel,† Katherine R. Emory.
Financial data (yr. ended 12/31/87): Assets, $4,057,765 (M); expenditures, $150,247, including $118,500 for 79 grants (high: $5,000; low: $500; average: $500-$2,000).
Purpose and activities: Grants for hospitals, higher and secondary education, youth agencies, cultural programs, and conservation.
Limitations: Giving primarily in NY, CT, and ME. No grants to individuals.
Application information:
Initial approach: Proposal
Deadline(s): Nov. 30
Write: Ann Brownell Sloane, Admin.
Trustees: Manufacturers Hanover Trust Co.
Employer Identification Number: 136046567

2225
Denise & Andrew Saul Foundation
c/o Eisner & Lubin
250 Park Ave.
New York 10177

Established in 1984 in NY.
Donor(s): Andrew M. Saul.
Financial data (yr. ended 9/30/87): Assets, $1,095,165 (M); expenditures, $839,974, including $836,627 for 14 grants (high: $250,000; low: $866; average: $10,000-$100,000).
Purpose and activities: Giving primarily for cultural programs; support also for education and hospitals.

Application information: Contributes only to pre-selected organizations. Applications not accepted.
Officers and Trustees: Andrew M. Saul, Pres. and Treas.; Denise M. Saul, V.P. and Secy.; Lynn T. Fischer, Sidney J. Silberman.
Number of staff: None.
Employer Identification Number: 133254182

2226
The Scherman Foundation, Inc.
315 West 57th St., Suite 2D
New York 10019 (212) 489-7143

Incorporated in 1941 in NY.
Donor(s): The Scherman family.
Financial data (yr. ended 12/31/88): Assets, $52,609,550 (M); expenditures, $3,242,004, including $2,679,800 for 130 grants (high: $125,000; low: $5,000; average: $10,000-$25,000).
Purpose and activities: Grants largely for conservation, disarmament and peace, family planning, human rights and liberties, the arts, and social welfare.
Types of support: Operating budgets, continuing support, seed money, emergency funds, matching funds, program-related investments, special projects, general purposes, technical assistance.
Limitations: Giving primarily in New York, NY, for arts and social welfare. No support for colleges, universities, or other higher educational institutions. No grants to individuals, or for building or endowment funds, scholarships, or fellowships.
Publications: Annual report (including application guidelines), application guidelines.
Application information:
Initial approach: Letter
Copies of proposal: 1
Deadline(s): None
Board meeting date(s): Quarterly
Final notification: 3 months
Write: David F. Freeman, Exec. Dir.
Officers: Axel G. Rosin,* Pres.; Katharine S. Rosin,* Secy.; David F. Freeman, Treas. and Exec. Dir.
Directors:* Helen Edey, M.D., Archibald R. Murray, Susanna Sahatdjian, Anthony M. Schulte, Karen R. Sollins, Marcia Thompson.
Number of staff: 1 full-time professional; 1 part-time professional; 1 full-time support.
Employer Identification Number: 136098464
Recent arts and culture grants:
Acting Company, Group I Acting Company, NYC, NY, $30,000. For general support. 1987.
American Museum of Natural History, NYC, NY, $25,000. For general support. 1987.
Black Spectrum Theater Company, Jamaica, NY, $15,000. For general support. 1987.
Bloomingdale House of Music, NYC, NY, $20,000. For general support. 1987.
Bronx Museum of the Arts, Bronx, NY, $7,500. For general support. 1987.
Brooklyn Museum, Brooklyn Institute of Arts and Sciences, Brooklyn, NY, $20,000. For general support. 1987.
Chamber Music Society of Lincoln Center, NYC, NY, $5,000. For general support. 1987.
Circle Repertory Theater Company, NYC, NY, $10,000. For general support. 1987.
Dance Theater of Harlem, NYC, NY, $20,000. For general support. 1987.
Dance Theater Workshop, NYC, NY, $25,000. For general support. 1987.
Elder Craftsmen, NYC, NY, $15,000. For general support. 1987.
Equity Library Theater, NYC, NY, $10,000. For general support. 1987.
Harlem School of the Arts, NYC, NY, $25,000. For general support. 1987.
Laura Dean Dancers and Musicians, NYC, NY, $10,000. For general support. 1987.
Learning Through an Expanded Arts Program (LEAP), NYC, NY, $15,000. For general support. 1987.
Music-Theater Performing Group, NYC, NY, $10,000. For general support. 1987.
National Theater of the Deaf, Chester, CT, $10,000. For general support. 1987.
New York Botanical Garden, NYC, NY, $25,000. For general support. 1987.
New York Zoological Society, NYC, NY, $25,000. For general support. 1987.
New York Zoological Society, NYC, NY, $5,000. For Buddhist Perception of Nature Project. 1987.
Pierpont Morgan Library, NYC, NY, $15,000. For general support. 1987.
Poets and Writers, NYC, NY, $10,000. For general support. 1987.
Printmaking Workshop, NYC, NY, $10,000. For general support. 1987.
Public Interest Radio, NYC, NY, $20,000. For general support. 1987.
Saint Lukes Chamber Ensemble, NYC, NY, $10,000. For performing arts ensemble. 1987.
School of American Ballet, NYC, NY, $20,000. For general support. 1987.
Skowhegan School of Painting and Sculpture, NYC, NY, $10,000. For general support. 1987.
Spanish Theater Repertory Company, Repertorio Espanol, NYC, NY, $15,000. For general support. 1987.
Studio Museum in Harlem, NYC, NY, $15,000. For general support. 1987.
Teachers and Writers Collaborative, NYC, NY, $5,000. For general support. 1987.
Volunteer Lawyers for the Arts, NYC, NY, $10,000. For general support. 1987.
W B A I-FM, NYC, NY, $10,000. For general support. Grant made through Pacifica Foundation. 1987.
W G B H Educational Foundation, Boston, MA, $50,000. For WGBH Humanities Challenge. 1987.
W N E T Channel 13, NYC, NY, $10,000. For general support. 1987.
W N Y C Foundation, NYC, NY, $10,000. For general support. 1987.
West End Symphony, NYC, NY, $15,000. For Music Outreach Program. 1987.
YM-YWHA, 92nd Street, NYC, NY, $25,000. For performing arts program. 1987.
Young Audiences, New York Committee, NYC, NY, $15,000. For general support. 1987.
Young Concert Artists, NYC, NY, $10,000. For general support. 1987.

2227
S. H. and Helen R. Scheuer Family Foundation, Inc.
104 East 40th St.
New York 10016-1801 (212) 573-8350

Incorporated in 1943 in NY.
Donor(s): Members of the Scheuer family.
Financial data (yr. ended 11/30/87): Assets, $28,427,774 (M); gifts received, $5,851,691; expenditures, $8,068,556, including $7,594,823 for 249 grants (high: $1,000,000; low: $100).
Purpose and activities: Emphasis on local Jewish welfare funds, higher education, and cultural programs.
Limitations: Giving primarily in New York, NY.
Application information: Applications not accepted.
Board meeting date(s): As necessary
Write: Wilbur Daniels, Exec. Dir.
Officers: Amy Scheuer Cohen, Pres.; Richard J. Scheuer, V.P.; Harvey Brecher, Secy.; Harold Cohen, Treas.
Number of staff: 1 full-time professional.
Employer Identification Number: 136062661

2228
Sarah I. Schieffelin Residuary Trust
c/o The Bank of New York
48 Wall St.
New York 10015

Established in 1976.
Donor(s): Sarah I. Schieffelin.†
Financial data (yr. ended 3/31/86): Assets, $5,357,551 (M); expenditures, $303,866, including $265,538 for 30 grants (high: $26,579; low: $1,000).
Purpose and activities: Giving for conservation, wildlife preservation, cultural programs, health, social services, and church support. Giving generally limited to continuing support for specified recipients.
Limitations: Giving primarily in NY.
Application information: Contributes only to pre-selected organizations. Applications not accepted.
Trustees: Thomas Fenlon, The Bank of New York.
Employer Identification Number: 136724459

2229
The Schiff Foundation
485 Madison Ave., 20th Fl.
New York 10022 (212) 751-3180

Incorporated in 1946 in NY.
Donor(s): John M. Schiff,† Edith B. Schiff,† David T. Schiff, Peter G. Schiff.
Financial data (yr. ended 12/31/88): Assets, $9,270,000 (M); expenditures, $1,036,000, including $1,030,000 for 120 grants (high: $400,000; low: $25; average: $500-$25,000).
Purpose and activities: Giving for special medical programs, certain youth and social service agencies, museums, and education; funds substantially committed to organizations of interest to the donors.
Types of support: Annual campaigns, capital campaigns, general purposes, professorships, research, special projects.

Limitations: Giving primarily in NY. No grants to individuals.
Application information: No new commitments at this time.
Initial approach: Proposal
Copies of proposal: 1
Deadline(s): Submit proposal preferably between May and Oct.
Write: David T. Schiff, Pres.
Officers and Directors:* David T. Schiff,* Pres.; Peter G. Schiff,* V.P.; Sandra Frey Davies, Secy.; Humberto Lopez, Treas.
Employer Identification Number: 136088221

2230
The Schimmel Foundation
885 Third Ave.
New York 10022 (212) 777-3080

Incorporated 1n 1960 in NY.
Donor(s): Norbert Schimmel.
Financial data (yr. ended 12/31/87): Assets, $1,056,458 (M); expenditures, $174,070, including $161,300 for 38 grants (high: $51,375; low: $25).
Purpose and activities: Giving primarily to art museums, including donations of works of art; support also for Jewish organizations.
Limitations: No support for private foundations. No grants to individuals.
Application information:
Initial approach: Letter
Deadline(s): None
Write: Norbert Schimmel, Mgr.
Directors: Norbert Schimmel, Mgr.; Alan Bloom, Leon Pomerance, Jules Schimmel.
Employer Identification Number: 136145185

2231
Schlumberger Foundation, Inc.
277 Park Ave.
New York 10172 (212) 350-9455

Schlumberger Foundation established as a trust in 1954 in TX; terminated in 1982 and assets transferred to Schlumberger Horizons, Inc., a DE foundation; in 1982 name changed from Schlumberger Horizons, Inc. to Schlumberger Foundation, Inc.
Donor(s): Schlumberger, Ltd.
Financial data (yr. ended 12/31/86): Assets, $11,534,602 (M); expenditures, $1,485,635, including $1,432,022 for 98 grants (high: $200,000; low: $1,000; average: $2,000-$20,000).
Purpose and activities: Grants limited to selected colleges and universities for scholarships, fellowships, and endowed professorships in engineering and other natural sciences; small number of grants awarded in the educational, medical, and humanitarian areas.
Types of support: Scholarship funds, fellowships, professorships, general purposes, research, special projects.
Limitations: Giving limited to the North American continent. No grants to individuals, or for building funds or operating budgets.
Application information:
Initial approach: Letter
Deadline(s): None
Board meeting date(s): Feb. or Mar.
Final notification: Within 3 weeks
Write: Arthur W. Alexander, Exec. Secy.
Officers and Directors: Arthur W. Alexander, Exec. Secy.; George H. Jewell, Arthur Lindenauer, Roy Shourd.
Trustee Bank: Texas Commerce Bank.
Number of staff: 2
Employer Identification Number: 237033142

2232
David Schwartz Foundation, Inc.
720 Fifth Ave.
New York 10019 (212) 682-6640

Incorporated in 1945 in NY.
Donor(s): Jonathan Logan, Inc., David Schwartz, and others.
Financial data (yr. ended 5/31/87): Assets, $18,791,449 (M); expenditures, $1,672,051, including $1,458,896 for 90 grants (high: $231,500; low: $10).
Purpose and activities: Emphasis on higher education, cultural programs, and social welfare; support also for hospitals, health agencies, and Jewish organizations.
Types of support: General purposes.
Limitations: Giving primarily in NY, with emphasis on New York City. No grants to individuals.
Application information: Funds currently committed. Applications not accepted.
Board meeting date(s): At least once a year, usually in May or June
Write: Richard J. Schwartz, Pres.
Officers and Directors: Richard J. Schwartz, Pres.; Lois R. Zenkel, V.P.; Stephen D. Gardner, Irene Schwartz, Bruce Zenkel.
Number of staff: None.
Employer Identification Number: 226075974

2233
Arnold and Marie Schwartz Fund for Education and Health Research
465 Park Ave.
New York 10022

Incorporated in 1971 in DE.
Donor(s): Arnold Schwartz Charitable Trust.
Financial data (yr. ended 3/31/88): Assets, $5,561,943 (M); expenditures, $513,722, including $422,090 for 69 grants (high: $103,810; low: $20; average: $500-$10,000).
Purpose and activities: Grants largely for higher education, hospitals, medical research, music, and religious organizations.
Limitations: Giving primarily in the New York City, NY, area.
Application information:
Deadline(s): None
Officers: Marie D. Schwartz, Pres.; Ruth Kerstein,* Secy.
Directors:* Sylvia Kassel.
Employer Identification Number: 237115019

2234
Scovill Foundation, Inc.
499 Park Ave.
New York 10022 (212) 750-0200

Incorporated in 1961 in CT.
Donor(s): Scovill Manufacturing Co.
Financial data (yr. ended 12/31/86): Assets, $1,034,611 (M); expenditures, $259,015, including $255,620 for 122 grants (high: $38,000; low: $25).
Purpose and activities: Emphasis on community funds, hospitals, youth agencies, cultural organizations, and educational institutions.
Types of support: Operating budgets, continuing support, seed money, building funds, employee matching gifts.
Limitations: Giving primarily in areas of company operations. No grants to individuals.
Application information:
Initial approach: Proposal
Copies of proposal: 1
Deadline(s): None
Board meeting date(s): Mar.
Final notification: 3 months
Write: Laura B. Resnikoff, Trustee
Trustees: John W. Moore, Jr., Laura B. Resnikoff.
Employer Identification Number: 066022942

2235
The Evelyn Sharp Foundation
1370 Ave. of the Americas
New York 10019 (212) 603-1333

Incorporated in 1952 in NY.
Donor(s): Evelyn Sharp, and others.
Financial data (yr. ended 6/30/87): Assets, $4,576,174 (M); expenditures, $235,159, including $224,500 for 23 grants (high: $61,000; low: $2,000).
Purpose and activities: Emphasis on the performing arts and museums, education, population control, and medical research and hospitals.
Limitations: Giving primarily in NY.
Application information:
Initial approach: Letter
Deadline(s): None
Write: Mrs. Evelyn Sharp, Pres.
Officers and Trustees: Evelyn Sharp, Pres.; Mrs. Philip Bastedo, V.P.; Mary Cronson, V.P.; Emerson Foote, V.P.; Albert Francke III, V.P.; Jeremiah Milbank, Jr., V.P.; Peter J. Sharp, V.P.
Employer Identification Number: 136119532

2236
Emma A. Sheafer Charitable Trust
c/o Morgan Guaranty Trust Co. of New York
Nine West 57th St.
New York 10019 (212) 483-2248
Application address: c/o Morgan Guaranty Trust Co. of NY, 23 Wall St., New York, NY 10005

Trust established in 1975 in NY.
Donor(s): Emma A. Sheafer.†
Financial data (yr. ended 12/31/87): Assets, $2,768,034 (M); expenditures, $150,526, including $103,016 for 10 grants (high: $15,000; low: $1,150).
Purpose and activities: Giving limited to performing arts groups.
Types of support: General purposes, continuing support, seed money, deficit financing, building funds, equipment, land acquisition, endowment funds.

Limitations: Giving limited to NY, with emphasis on New York City. No grants to individuals, or for research, scholarships, fellowships, or matching gifts; no loans.
Application information:
Initial approach: Letter
Copies of proposal: 1
Deadline(s): Mid-Apr. and mid-Oct.
Board meeting date(s): June and Dec.
Final notification: 2 months
Write: Robert F. Longley, Sr. V.P., Morgan Guaranty Trust Co. of New York
Trustees: John C. Russell, Morgan Guaranty Trust Co. of New York.
Number of staff: None.
Employer Identification Number: 510186114

2237
Eric P. Sheinberg Foundation
c/o Goldman, Sachs & Co.
85 Broad St., Tax Dept., 30th Fl.
New York 10004

Donor(s): Eric P. Sheinberg.
Financial data (yr. ended 6/30/87): Assets, $2,706,315 (M); gifts received, $791,985; expenditures, $91,610, including $89,180 for 61 grants (high: $20,000; low: $25).
Purpose and activities: Support for health and welfare organizations, arts and cultural programs, and higher education.
Types of support: General purposes.
Limitations: Giving primarily in New York, NY. No grants to individuals.
Application information: Applications not accepted.
Trustees: Eric P. Sheinberg, Michael Steinhardt.
Employer Identification Number: 137004291

2238
Ralph C. Sheldon Foundation, Inc.
710 Hotel Jamestown Bldg.
Jamestown 14701 (716) 664-9850

Incorporated in 1948 in NY.
Donor(s): Julia S. Livengood, Isabell M. Sheldon.
Financial data (yr. ended 5/31/87): Assets, $4,372,536 (M); gifts received, $1,149,192; expenditures, $1,194,838, including $797,593 for 37 grants (high: $194,100; low: $800; average: $35,000).
Purpose and activities: Giving primarily for youth and social service agencies and cultural programs.
Types of support: General purposes, building funds, equipment, annual campaigns, capital campaigns, emergency funds.
Limitations: Giving primarily in southern Chautauqua County, NY. No support for religious organizations. No grants to individuals.
Application information: Application form required.
Copies of proposal: 1
Deadline(s): None
Final notification: Immediately after determination
Write: Paul B. Sullivan, Exec. Dir.
Officers and Directors: Elizabeth Y. Sheldon, Pres.; Walter L. Miller, V.P.; Robert G. Wright, V.P.; Paul B. Sullivan, Secy. and Exec. Dir.; Miles L. Lasser, Treas.; Barclay O. Wellman.
Number of staff: 1 part-time professional; 1 full-time support; 1 part-time support.
Employer Identification Number: 166030502

2239
Shendell Foundation
122 East 42nd St., Suite 2500
New York 10168-0002

Established in 1962 in NY.
Donor(s): Isaac Shendell.
Financial data (yr. ended 10/31/87): Assets, $751,589 (M); gifts received, $564,494; expenditures, $339,498, including $335,000 for 8 grants (high: $100,000; low: $25,000).
Purpose and activities: Giving primarily for music and for higher education, including medical education.
Application information:
Initial approach: Proposal
Deadline(s): None
Write: Gordon S. Oppenheimer, Trustee
Trustees: Gordon S. Oppenheimer, Andrew Segal, Charles Segal.
Employer Identification Number: 136097659

2240
C. D. Shiah Charitable Foundation
75 Rockefeller Plaza, Suite 1501
New York 10019 (212) 484-8780

Established in 1981 in NY.
Financial data (yr. ended 6/30/87): Assets, $1,467,401 (M); expenditures, $109,250, including $104,500 for 7 grants (high: $50,000; low: $1,500).
Purpose and activities: Emphasis on Chinese-American programs, secondary and higher education, and performing arts.
Limitations: No grants to individuals.
Application information:
Initial approach: Proposal
Write: Oded Aboodi, Trustee
Trustee: Oded Aboodi.
Employer Identification Number: 133076929

2241
The Shubert Foundation, Inc.
234 West 44th St.
New York 10036 (212) 944-3777

Incorporated in 1945 in DE.
Donor(s): Lee Shubert,† J.J. Shubert.†
Financial data (yr. ended 5/31/88): Assets, $106,371,000 (M); gifts received, $234,000; expenditures, $3,238,000, including $2,565,000 for 175 grants (high: $100,000; low: $1,000; average: $10,000-$20,000) and $202,000 for 1 foundation-administered program.
Purpose and activities: To build and perpetuate the live performing arts, particularly the professional theater, in the U.S. Support both of theatrical institutions and of those other elements of the performing arts and related institutions necessary to maintain and support the theater. The foundation also operates a theatrical archive. Grants almost always made exclusively for general operating funds.
Types of support: Operating budgets.
Limitations: No grants to individuals, or for capital or endowment funds, research, conduit organizations, audience development, direct subsidies to reduce admission prices, productions for specialized audiences, scholarships, fellowships, or matching gifts; no loans.
Publications: Annual report (including application guidelines).
Application information: Application form required.
Initial approach: Letter or telephone
Copies of proposal: 2
Deadline(s): Submit proposal preferably in Oct. or Nov.; deadline Dec. 1
Board meeting date(s): Monthly
Final notification: May
Write: Lynn L. Seidler, Exec. Dir.
Officers and Directors:* Gerald Schoenfeld,* Chair.; Bernard B. Jacobs,* Pres.; John W. Kluge,* V.P.; Michael I. Sovern,* V.P.; Irving M. Wall,* Secy.; Lee J. Seidler,* Treas.; Lynn L. Seidler, Exec. Dir.
Number of staff: 2 full-time professional; 1 full-time support.
Employer Identification Number: 136106961
Recent arts and culture grants:
A Contemporary Theater, Seattle, WA, $10,000. 1987.
Acting Company, NYC, NY, $30,000. 1987.
Actors Equity Association, NYC, NY, $25,000. Toward non-traditional casting project. 1987.
Actors Fund, NYC, NY, $25,000. 1987.
Actors Studio, NYC, NY, $7,500. 1987.
Actors Theater of Louisville, Louisville, KY, $75,000. 1987.
Actors Theater of Saint Paul, Saint Paul, MN, $10,000. 1987.
Alaska Repertory Theater, Anchorage, AK, $10,000. 1987.
Alley Theater, Houston, TX, $10,000. 1987.
Alliance for the Arts, NYC, NY, $30,000. For Kerttu Shubert Culture Award. 1987.
Alliance of Resident Theaters, NYC, NY, $20,000. 1987.
Alliance Theater Company, Atlanta, GA, $12,500. 1987.
Alvin Ailey American Dance Theater, NYC, NY, $30,000. 1987.
Amas Repertory Theater, NYC, NY, $7,500. 1987.
American Academy of Dramatic Arts, NYC, NY, $7,500. 1987.
American Ballet Theater, NYC, NY, $60,000. 1987.
American Conservatory Theater, San Francisco, CA, $25,000. 1987.
American Dance Festival, NYC, NY, $5,000. 1987.
American Jewish Theater, NYC, NY, $5,000. 1987.
American Museum of the Moving Image, Astoria, NY, $5,000. 1987.
American Music Theater Festival, Philadelphia, PA, $25,000. Toward Music Theater Production Partnership. 1987.
American Music Theater Festival, Philadelphia, PA, $10,000. 1987.
American Place Theater, NYC, NY, $10,000. 1987.
American Repertory Theater, Cambridge, MA, $35,000. 1987.
Arena Stage, DC, $40,000. 1987.

Arts/Boston, Boston, MA, $7,500. 1987.
Ballet Hispanico of New York, NYC, NY, $5,000. 1987.
Berkeley Repertory Theater, Berkeley, CA, $10,000. 1987.
Big Apple Circus, NYC, NY, $5,000. 1987.
Boarshead Theater, Lansing, MI, $5,000. 1987.
Brooklyn Academy of Music, Brooklyn, NY, $30,000. 1987.
California Institute of the Arts, Valencia, CA, $7,500. 1987.
Capital Repertory Company, Albany, NY, $5,000. 1987.
Carnegie Hall, NYC, NY, $15,000. 1987.
Carnegie-Mellon University, Department of Drama, Pittsburgh, PA, $15,000. 1987.
Center Stage, Baltimore, MD, $15,000. 1987.
Chicago Theater Foundation, Chicago, IL, $7,500. 1987.
Childrens Art Carnival, NYC, NY, $5,000. 1987.
Circle in the Square, NYC, NY, $65,000. 1987.
Circle Repertory Theater Company, NYC, NY, $45,000. 1987.
City Center Theater, NYC, NY, $10,000. 1987.
Cleveland Play House, Cleveland, OH, $7,500. 1987.
Columbia University, NYC, NY, $100,000. Toward Presidential Scholars Program. 1987.
Columbia University, NYC, NY, $7,500. Toward School of Law VLA Clinical Program. 1987.
Columbia University, NYC, NY, $7,500. Toward Entertainment Law Program. 1987.
Columbia University, Oscar Hammerstein II Center for Theater Studies, NYC, NY, $50,000. 1987.
Corcoran Gallery of Art, DC, $10,000. 1987.
CSC Repertory, NYC, NY, $5,000. 1987.
Cultural Alliance of Greater Washington, DC, $7,500. 1987.
Cultural Council Foundation, NYC, NY, $10,000. 1987.
Cunningham Dance Foundation, NYC, NY, $10,000. 1987.
Dallas Theater Center, Dallas, TX, $15,000. 1987.
Dance Theater of Harlem, NYC, NY, $25,000. 1987.
Dance Theater Workshop, NYC, NY, $12,500. 1987.
Denver Center Theater Company, Denver, CO, $15,000. 1987.
Drama League, NYC, NY, $5,000. 1987.
Dramatists Guild, NYC, NY, $15,000. Toward Young Playwrights Festival. 1987.
East West Players, Los Angeles, CA, $5,000. 1987.
El Teatro Campesino, San Juan Bautista, CA, $7,500. 1987.
Empty Space Theater, Seattle, WA, $10,000. 1987.
Ensemble Studio Theater, NYC, NY, $40,000. 1987.
Equity Library Theater, NYC, NY, $7,500. 1987.
Eugene ONeill Memorial Theater Center, Waterford, CT, $50,000. 1987.
Eureka Theater Company, San Francisco, CA, $7,500. 1987.
Executive Mansion Preservation Society, NYC, NY, $5,000. 1987.
Feld Ballet, NYC, NY, $25,000. 1987.
Folger Theater Group, DC, $7,500. 1987.
Fords Theater Society, DC, $20,000. 1987.
Forty Second Street Theater Row, NYC, NY, $20,000. 1987.
Foundation for the Extension and Development of the American Professional Theater, NYC, NY, $15,000. 1987.
Fund for the Borough of Brooklyn, Brooklyn, NY, $7,500. Toward Celebrate Brooklyn. 1987.
GeVa Theater, Rochester, NY, $10,000. 1987.
Goodman Theater, Chicago, IL, $30,000. 1987.
Goodspeed Opera House, East Haddam, CT, $25,000. 1987.
Guthrie Theater, Minneapolis, MN, $20,000. 1987.
Harlem School of the Arts, NYC, NY, $10,000. 1987.
Harold Clurman Theater, NYC, NY, $10,000. 1987.
Hartford Stage Company, Hartford, CT, $12,500. 1987.
Hartman Regional Theater, Stamford, CT, $7,500. 1987.
Houston Ballet, Houston, TX, $10,000. 1987.
Hubbard Street Dance Company, Chicago, IL, $5,000. 1987.
Hudson Guild Theater, NYC, NY, $5,000. 1987.
Indiana Repertory Theater, Indianapolis, IN, $7,500. 1987.
International Arts Relations (INTAR), NYC, NY, $7,500. 1987.
International Center of Photography, NYC, NY, $10,000. 1987.
Joffrey Ballet, NYC, NY, $35,000. 1987.
Joyce Theater, NYC, NY, $25,000. For theater exchange. 1987.
Joyce Theater, NYC, NY, $10,000. For dance project. 1987.
Juilliard School, NYC, NY, $12,500. For Theater Center. 1987.
Kitchen, The, NYC, NY, $5,000. 1987.
La Jolla Playhouse, La Jolla, CA, $7,500. 1987.
La Mama Experimental Theater Club, NYC, NY, $7,500. 1987.
Lambs Theater Company, NYC, NY, $10,000. 1987.
Lar Lubovitch Dance Company, NYC, NY, $5,000. 1987.
Laura Dean Dancers and Musicians, NYC, NY, $5,000. 1987.
Lincoln Center for the Performing Arts, NYC, NY, $20,000. Toward Mostly Mozart Festival. 1987.
Lincoln Center for the Performing Arts, NYC, NY, $10,000. Toward Great Performers Series. 1987.
Lincoln Center Theater, NYC, NY, $25,000. 1987.
Long Wharf Theater, New Haven, CT, $50,000. Toward New Play Program. 1987.
Long Wharf Theater, New Haven, CT, $35,000. 1987.
Los Angeles Theater Center, Los Angeles, CA, $40,000. 1987.
Lucinda Childs Dance Company, NYC, NY, $5,000. 1987.
Mabou Mines, NYC, NY, $7,500. 1987.
Magic Theater, San Francisco, CA, $10,000. 1987.
Manhattan Theater Club, NYC, NY, $90,000. 1987.
Margaret Jenkins Dance Company, San Francisco, CA, $5,000. 1987.
Mark Taper Forum, Los Angeles, CA, $90,000. 1987.
Martha Graham Dance Company, NYC, NY, $7,500. 1987.
McCarter Theater Company, Princeton, NJ, $10,000. 1987.
Meet the Composer, NYC, NY, $5,000. 1987.
Metropolitan Opera Association, NYC, NY, $20,000. 1987.
Milwaukee Repertory Theater, Milwaukee, WI, $12,500. 1987.
Museum of the City of New York, NYC, NY, $20,000. 1987.
Music-Theater Performing Group, Lenox Arts Center, NYC, NY, $10,000. 1987.
Musical Theater Works, NYC, NY, $5,000. 1987.
National Dance Institute, NYC, NY, $10,000. 1987.
National Institute for Music Theater, DC, $7,500. 1987.
National Theater of the Deaf, Chester, CT, $12,500. 1987.
Negro Ensemble Company, NYC, NY, $75,000. 1987.
New Dramatists, NYC, NY, $15,000. 1987.
New Federal Theater, NYC, NY, $10,000. 1987.
New York City Ballet, NYC, NY, $60,000. 1987.
New York City Opera, NYC, NY, $25,000. 1987.
New York Foundation for the Arts, NYC, NY, $5,000. Toward Early Stages Program. 1987.
New York Public Library, NYC, NY, $20,000. For Performing Arts Research Center. 1987.
New York Shakespeare Festival, NYC, NY, $250,000. 1987.
New York University, Tisch School of the Arts, NYC, NY, $50,000. 1987.
Nikolais/Louis Foundation for Dance, NYC, NY, $5,000. 1987.
ODC, San Francisco, CA, $5,000. 1987.
Old Globe Theater, San Diego, CA, $15,000. 1987.
Oregon Shakespearean Festival, Ashland, OR, $5,000. 1987.
Pacific Northwest Ballet, Seattle, WA, $5,000. 1987.
Pan Asian Repertory Theater, NYC, NY, $5,000. 1987.
Paul Taylor Dance Company, NYC, NY, $17,500. 1987.
Peoples Light and Theater Company, Malvern, PA, $7,500. 1987.
Perseverance Theater, Douglas, AK, $5,000. 1987.
Pilobolus, Washington, CT, $5,000. 1987.
Pittsburgh Public Theater, Pittsburgh, PA, $10,000. 1987.
Playwrights Center, Minneapolis, MN, $7,500. 1987.
Playwrights Horizons, NYC, NY, $35,000. 1987.
Portland Stage Company, Portland, ME, $5,000. 1987.
Puerto Rican Traveling Theater Company, NYC, NY, $10,000. 1987.
Repertory Theater of Saint Louis, Saint Louis, MO, $10,000. 1987.
Richmond Ballet, Richmond, VA, $5,000. 1987.
Roundabout Theater Company, NYC, NY, $10,000. 1987.
Salt Lake Acting Company, Salt Lake City, UT, $5,000. 1987.

San Francisco Ballet, San Francisco, CA, $20,000. 1987.
School of American Ballet, NYC, NY, $7,500. 1987.
Seattle Repertory, Seattle, WA, $25,000. 1987.
Second Stage Theater, NYC, NY, $12,500. 1987.
South Coast Repertory, Costa Mesa, CA, $20,000. 1987.
Spanish Theater Repertory Company, NYC, NY, $5,000. 1987.
Spoleto Festival USA, Charleston, SC, $5,000. 1987.
Steppenwolf Theater, Chicago, IL, $10,000. 1987.
Studio Arena Theater, Buffalo, NY, $7,500. 1987.
Symphony Space, NYC, NY, $7,500. 1987.
Syracuse Stage, Syracuse, NY, $10,000. 1987.
Theater Communications Group, NYC, NY, $7,500. 1987.
Theater Development Fund, NYC, NY, $20,000. 1987.
Theater for the New City, NYC, NY, $7,500. 1987.
Town Hall, NYC, NY, $7,500. 1987.
Trinity Square Repertory Company, Providence, RI, $15,000. 1987.
Trisha Brown Dance Company, NYC, NY, $5,000. 1987.
Twyla Tharp Dance Foundation, NYC, NY, $15,000. 1987.
Victory Gardens Theater, Chicago, IL, $10,000. 1987.
Volunteer Lawyers for the Arts, NYC, NY, $10,000. 1987.
Washington Opera, DC, $10,000. 1987.
Whole Theater Company, Montclair, NJ, $10,000. 1987.
Williamstown Theater Festival, Williamstown, MA, $7,500. 1987.
Wisdom Bridge Theater, Chicago, IL, $10,000. 1987.
Womens Project, NYC, NY, $5,000. 1987.
WPA Theater, NYC, NY, $12,500. 1987.
Yale University, Yale School of Drama/Yale Repertory Theater, New Haven, CT, $60,000. 1987.
York Theater Company, NYC, NY, $5,000. 1987.

2242
Simon Foundation, Inc.
c/o Charles Simon
One New York Plaza
New York 10004 (212) 747-6013

Incorporated in 1954 in NY.
Donor(s): Charles Simon.
Financial data (yr. ended 12/31/87): Assets, $489,112 (M); expenditures, $252,671, including $240,645 for 72 grants (high: $25,000; low: $50).
Purpose and activities: Emphasis on cultural programs and museums, higher education, hospitals, and youth agencies.
Types of support: General purposes, scholarship funds.
Limitations: Giving primarily in NY.
Application information: Contributes only to pre-selected organizations. Applications not accepted.
Officers and Directors: Charles Simon, Pres. and Treas.; George DeSipio, V.P. and Secy.; Daniel M. Kelly.
Employer Identification Number: 136088838

2243
Sidney, Milton and Leoma Simon Foundation
23 Crestview Dr.
Pleasantville 10570

Established in 1964.
Donor(s): Milton Simon.†
Financial data (yr. ended 5/31/87): Assets, $9,791,307 (M); expenditures, $579,010, including $402,500 for 57 grants (high: $12,500; low: $2,500).
Purpose and activities: Grants primarily for the handicapped, performing arts, medical research, Jewish welfare funds, and hospitals.
Types of support: Research.
Application information:
Initial approach: Letter or proposal
Deadline(s): None
Write: Joseph C. Warner, Trustee
Trustees: Joseph C. Warner, Meryll Warner, Alan Wechsler.
Employer Identification Number: 136175218

2244
Skirball Foundation
c/o Bergreen & Bergreen
660 Madison Ave.
New York 10021 (212) 832-8500

Established in 1950 in OH.
Donor(s): Members of the Skirball family, Skirball Investment Co.
Financial data (yr. ended 12/31/87): Assets, $28,830,944 (M); gifts received, $24,752,376; expenditures, $2,187,176, including $2,106,360 for 31 grants (high: $1,000,000; low: $100; average: $500-$10,000).
Purpose and activities: Giving primarily for Jewish welfare and temple support; support also for education, the arts, and medicine.
Limitations: Giving primarily in CA. No grants to individuals.
Application information:
Write: Morris H. Bergreen, Pres.
Officers and Trustees: Morris H. Bergreen, Pres.; Martin Blackman, Secy.; Robert D. Goldfarb, V.P.; A. Skirball-Kenis, V.P.; George H. Heyman, Jr., Treas.; Robert M. Tanenbaum.
Employer Identification Number: 346517957

2245
The Slade Foundation, Inc.
c/o Bear Stearns Companies, Inc.
245 Park Ave.
New York 10167

Incorporated in 1952 in NY.
Donor(s): John H. Slade.
Financial data (yr. ended 7/31/88): Assets, $541,173 (M); gifts received, $255,000; expenditures, $158,612, including $156,443 for 16 grants (high: $150,000; low: $20).
Purpose and activities: Giving for Jewish welfare funds and organizations, and for cultural programs and social services; support also for organizations in Israel.
Limitations: Giving primarily in New York, NY and Israel.
Application information: Contributes only to pre-selected organizations. Applications not accepted.
Officers and Directors:* John H. Slade,* Pres.; Milton B. Evlau,* V.P.; George Maxwell, Secy.-Treas.
Employer Identification Number: 136065039

2246
C. F. Roe Slade Foundation
c/o J.T. Jackson
P.O. Box 1944
New York 10116-1944

Established in 1969 in NY.
Donor(s): Marie-Antoinette Slade.†
Financial data (yr. ended 6/30/86): Assets, $598,754 (M); gifts received, $62,000; expenditures, $116,227, including $108,392 for 10 grants (high: $30,000; low: $5,000).
Purpose and activities: Support for education, culture, health services, and conservation.
Application information: Contributes only to pre-selected organizations. Applications not accepted.
Trustees: Kathleen McLaughlin Jeffords, Jean T.J. Scully, Leonard T. Scully, Donald Vail.
Employer Identification Number: 136205873

2247
Alan B. Slifka Foundation, Inc.
11 Hanover Sq.
New York 10005

Established in 1963 in NY.
Donor(s): Alan B. Slifka.
Financial data (yr. ended 11/30/87): Assets, $1,900,706 (M); gifts received, $484,000; expenditures, $448,641, including $440,709 for 302 grants (high: $50,000; low: $5).
Purpose and activities: Support primarily for Jewish welfare organizations and cultural activities; some support also for education and child welfare.
Limitations: Giving primarily in NY.
Officer: Alan B. Slifka, Pres.
Employer Identification Number: 136192257

2248
Joseph & Sylvia Slifka Foundation
477 Madison Ave.
New York 10022

Established in 1944.
Financial data (yr. ended 10/31/87): Assets, $1,992,931 (M); gifts received, $2,880; expenditures, $116,582, including $102,516 for 63 grants (high: $25,000; low: $100).
Purpose and activities: Support primarily for Jewish welfare, hospitals, higher education, culture, and the arts.
Application information:
Initial approach: Letter
Deadline(s): None
Write: Joseph Slifka, Pres.
Officer: Joseph Slifka, Pres.
Employer Identification Number: 136106433

2249
Alfred P. Sloan Foundation
630 Fifth Ave., 25th Fl.
New York 10111-0242 (212) 582-0450

Incorporated in 1934 in DE.
Donor(s): Alfred P. Sloan, Jr.,† Irene Jackson Sloan,† New Castle Corp.
Financial data (yr. ended 12/31/88): Assets, $541,886,057 (M); expenditures, $28,526,382, including $21,740,386 for grants (high: $2,395,000; low: $3,000; average: $10,000-$300,000) and $3,200,000 for grants to individuals.
Purpose and activities: Interests in science and technology, education, economics and management, and related problems of society; Sloan fellowships for basic research in the sciences are administered entirely through institutions.
Types of support: General purposes, seed money, research, fellowships, conferences and seminars, special projects.
Limitations: No support for the creative or performing arts, humanities (except through the New Liberal Arts Program), medical research, religion, or primary or secondary education. No grants to individuals directly, or for endowment or building funds, or equipment not related directly to foundation-supported projects; no loans.
Publications: Annual report, informational brochure, program policy statement, application guidelines.
Application information: Nomination forms available for fellowship candidates; direct applications not accepted.
Initial approach: Letter
Copies of proposal: 1
Deadline(s): Sept. 15 for fellowship program; no deadline for others
Board meeting date(s): Throughout the year (grants of $30,000 or less); 5 times a year (grants over $30,000)
Final notification: Early in year for research fellowships; within 3 months for others
Write: Ralph E. Gomory, Pres.
Officers: Ralph E. Gomory,* Pres.; Stewart F. Campbell, Financial V.P. and Secy.; Arthur L. Singer, Jr., V.P.
Trustees:* Howard W. Johnson, Chair.; Lucy Wilson Benson, Stephen L. Brown, Lloyd C. Elam, S. Parker Gilbert, Marvin L. Goldberger, Ralph E. Gomory, Howard H. Kehrl, Donald N. Langengerg, Cathleen Synge Morawetz, Frank Press, Lewis T. Preston, James D. Robinson III, Harold T. Shapiro, Roger B. Smith.
Number of staff: 8 full-time professional; 9 full-time support.
Employer Identification Number: 131623877
Recent arts and culture grants:
Rutgers, The State University of New Jersey Foundation, New Brunswick, NJ, $200,000. For partial support of Edison Papers. 4/21/88.
Smithsonian Institution, DC, $311,000. For continued support of videohistory program, Science in National Life. 10/8/87.
Smithsonian Institution, DC, $300,000. For third year funding of Smithsonian's Videohistory Program. 10/12/88.
W G B H Educational Foundation, Boston, MA, $50,000. For documentary film entitled, The Hidden City. 10/12/88.

2250
John Sloan Memorial Foundation, Inc.
220 East 42nd St., 16th Fl.
New York 10017 (212) 682-3060

Established in 1979 in NY.
Financial data (yr. ended 12/31/87): Assets, $1,368,288 (M); expenditures, $297,468, including $288,000 for 11 grants (high: $60,000; low: $2,500).
Purpose and activities: Giving limited to organizations and activities concerning American Art, preferably for the period from 1880 to 1950.
Application information:
Initial approach: Letter
Deadline(s): None
Write: Harry B. Clark, Treas.
Officers: Helen F. Sloan, Pres.; Donald E. McNicol, V.P.; Harry B. Clark, Treas.
Employer Identification Number: 132988798

2251
The Smith Barney Foundation
1345 Ave. of the Americas
New York 10105

Incorporated in 1965 in NY.
Donor(s): Smith Barney, Harris Upham & Co., Inc.
Financial data (yr. ended 12/31/87): Assets, $296,407 (M); gifts received, $27,065; expenditures, $370,921, including $370,750 for grants.
Purpose and activities: Grants primarily for community funds, higher education, including business education, youth agencies, urban affairs, and the arts.
Application information: Contributes only to preselected organizations. Applications not accepted.
Officers and Directors:* Henry U. Harris, Jr.,* Chair.; John A. Orb,* Pres.; Jeffrey H. Kahn,* V.P.; J. Perry Ruddick,* Treas.
Employer Identification Number: 136187938

2252
George D. Smith Fund, Inc.
c/o Lawrence W. Milas, V.P.
805 Third Ave., 20th Fl.
New York 10022

Incorporated in 1956 in DE.
Donor(s): George D. Smith, Sr.†
Financial data (yr. ended 12/31/86): Assets, $19,757,878 (M); expenditures, $865,378, including $845,100 for 9 grants (high: $175,000; low: $100; average: $50,000-$175,000).
Purpose and activities: Primarily supports basic research in molecular and cellular physiology and in cardiovascular diagnostic methods at two university medical centers; support also for higher education and public television.
Types of support: Research.
Limitations: Giving primarily in CA and UT.
Application information: Applications not accepted.
Officers and Trustees:* George D. Smith, Jr.,* Pres. and Secy.-Treas.; H.D. Burgess, V.P.; Lawrence W. Milas, V.P.; C.M. Smith,* V.P.
Employer Identification Number: 136138728

2253
The John Ben Snow Foundation, Inc.
P.O. Box 376
Pulaski 13142 (315) 298-6401
New Jersey office: 202 Mountain Ave., Westfield, NJ 07090

Incorporated in 1948 in NY.
Donor(s): John Ben Snow.†
Financial data (yr. ended 3/31/88): Assets, $3,835,196 (M); expenditures, $212,185, including $152,800 for 20 grants (high: $20,000; low: $200; average: $5,000-$10,000).
Purpose and activities: Giving for higher and secondary educational institutions, youth agencies, hospitals, and community betterment projects.
Types of support: Building funds, matching funds, scholarship funds, special projects, fellowships, equipment.
Limitations: Giving limited to central NY, with focus on Oswego County. No grants to individuals, or for operating budgets, endowment funds, or contingency financing.
Publications: Annual report (including application guidelines).
Application information: Application form required.
Initial approach: Letter
Copies of proposal: 1
Deadline(s): Submit proposal between Sept. and Apr.; deadline Mar. 15
Board meeting date(s): June
Write: Vernon F. Snow, Pres.
Officers: Vernon F. Snow, Pres.; Allen R. Malcolm, Exec. V.P. and Secy.-Treas.; William P. Ellwood, Bruce Malcolm, Rollan Melton, Royle Melton, David H. Snow.
Number of staff: 2 part-time support.
Employer Identification Number: 136112704
Recent arts and culture grants:
Joffrey Ballet, NYC, NY, $7,300. For support for junior company to perform in Central New York. 1987.
Pulaski Historical Society, Pulaski, NY, $9,700. For renovation of building to increase preservation and display facilities. 1987.
Syracuse University Press, Syracuse, NY, $13,000. For John Ben Snow annual literary prize. 1987.

2254
John Ben Snow Memorial Trust
P.O. Box 378
Pulaski 13142 (315) 298-6401

Trust established in 1974 in NY.
Donor(s): John Ben Snow.†
Financial data (yr. ended 12/31/88): Assets, $16,279,023 (M); expenditures, $1,210,672, including $961,380 for 38 grants (high: $75,000; low: $2,000; average: $5,000-$25,000).
Purpose and activities: Giving primarily for education, especially scholarship funds and for research; cultural institutions, especially libraries; medical and health organizations; and environmental groups; and community development.
Types of support: Seed money, equipment, research, publications, scholarship funds, fellowships, matching funds, renovation projects.

Limitations: Giving primarily in central NY, and New York City. No support for government agencies or unspecified projects. No grants to individuals or for operating budgets or endowment funds; no loans.
Publications: Annual report (including application guidelines).
Application information: Application form required.
Initial approach: Letter
Copies of proposal: 1
Deadline(s): Submit proposal preferably from July through Mar.; deadline Mar. 15
Final notification: 3 months
Write: Vernon F. Snow, Trustee
Trustees: Allen R. Malcolm, Rollan D. Melton, Vernon F. Snow, Irving Trust Co.
Number of staff: 2 part-time support.
Employer Identification Number: 136633814
Recent arts and culture grants:
Akwesasne Cultural Center, Hogansburg, NY, $30,000. For completion of library grounds. 1987.
Brookgreen Gardens, Murrells Inlet, SC, $10,000. For long range land development plans. 1987.
Folger Shakespeare Library, DC, $25,000. For Bicentennial programs and public events. 1987.
International Folk Art Foundation, Santa Fe, NM, $5,000. For establishment of permnanent Hispanic heritage wing. 1987.
International Museum of Photography at George Eastman House, Rochester, NY, $15,000. For building renovation and expansion of George Eastman House. 1987.
Lincoln Center Institute for the Arts in Education, NYC, NY, $20,000. For aesthetic education for teachers. 1987.
New York Historical Association, Cooperstown, NY, $25,000. For fellowships for students in museum studies. 1987.
New York Public Library, NYC, NY, $40,000. For exhibition of Bicentennial documents and books. 1987.
Oregon State University, Center for the Humanities, Corvallis, OR, $33,000. For Bicentennial Education Symposium. 1987.
Preservation/Revitalization of Pulaski, Pulaski, NY, $50,000. For development of historic downtown and river walkway. 1987.
YMCA, Frost Valley, Oliveria, NY, $25,000. For restoration of spillway at Straus House Conference Center. 1987.

2255
Sokoloff Foundation, Inc.
200 East 78th St.
New York 10021 (212) 744-5337

Financial data (yr. ended 12/31/87): Assets, $1,564,983 (M); expenditures, $90,787, including $73,925 for 45 grants (high: $20,000; low: $50).
Purpose and activities: Giving for Jewish welfare funds, social services, and the arts.
Application information:
Deadline(s): None
Write: Stephen Sokoloff, Pres.
Officers: Stephen Sokoloff, Pres.; H. Sol Tunick, Secy.
Employer Identification Number: 136155196

2256
The Soling Family Foundation
c/o Solico Penthouse
205 East 42nd St.
New York 10017

Established in 1985 in NY.
Donor(s): Chester Soling.
Financial data (yr. ended 5/31/88): Assets, $2,147,048 (M); expenditures, $351,661, including $277,035 for grants (high: $191,335).
Purpose and activities: Support primarily for a child care organization; giving also for museums, theatres and higher education.
Limitations: Giving primarily in MA and NY. No grants to individuals.
Application information: Contributes only to pre-selected organizations. Applications not accepted.
Officers: Chester Soling, Pres.; Carole Soling, Secy.; Caytha Jentis.
Employer Identification Number: 133288798

2257
The Abraham & Beverly Sommer Foundation
c/o Estate of Abraham Sommer
810 Seventh Ave.
New York 10019-5818

Established in 1977 in NY.
Donor(s): Beverly Sommer.
Financial data (yr. ended 12/31/87): Assets, $728,258 (M); gifts received, $250,000; expenditures, $162,562, including $161,945 for 21 grants (high: $50,200; low: $20).
Purpose and activities: Support primarily for Jewish giving; support also for higher education, environmental preservation, and culture, including support for an opera company.
Limitations: Giving primarily in NY. No grants to individuals.
Application information: Contributes only to pre-selected organizations. Applications not accepted.
Officers: Beverly Sommer, Pres.; Amy Sommer, V.P.; Robert S. Puder, Secy.-Treas.
Employer Identification Number: 132960992

2258
Sony Corporation of America Foundation, Inc.
Nine West 57th St.
New York 10019 (212) 418-9404

Established in 1972 in NY.
Donor(s): Sony Corp. of America.
Financial data (yr. ended 12/31/86): Assets, $1,763,503 (M); gifts received, $342,500; expenditures, $498,603, including $476,286 for grants and $22,317 for employee matching gifts.
Purpose and activities: Grants largely for hospitals, higher education, including scholarships for children of company employees, community funds, the performing arts, and Japanese and other cultural programs.
Types of support: General purposes, operating budgets, continuing support, annual campaigns, seed money, emergency funds, deficit financing, building funds, equipment, land acquisition, endowment funds, employee matching gifts, internships, employee-related scholarships.
Limitations: No grants to individuals (except for scholarships for children of company employees), or for special projects, research, publications, or conferences; no loans.
Application information:
Initial approach: Letter
Copies of proposal: 1
Deadline(s): None
Board meeting date(s): Quarterly
Final notification: 1 week
Write: Kenneth L. Nees, V.P.
Officers and Directors: Akio Morita, Chair.; Kenji Tamiya, Pres.; Kenneth L. Nees, V.P. and Secy.; Robert D. Dillon, Jr., V.P.; Norio Ohga, V.P.; Harvey L. Schein, V.P.
Number of staff: None.
Employer Identification Number: 237181637

2259
Nate B. and Frances Spingold Foundation, Inc.
55 East 59th St.
New York 10022-1104 (212) 418-8440

Incorporated in 1955 in NY.
Donor(s): Frances Spingold,† Nathan Breither Spingold.†
Financial data (yr. ended 11/30/86): Assets, $10,242,507 (M); gifts received, $10,000; expenditures, $2,410,730, including $920,152 for 74 grants (high: $67,967; low: $90; average: $1,000-$37,000).
Purpose and activities: To improve the human condition through health and human services, with emphasis on meeting pediatric, geriatric and gerontological needs; expand opportunities for research and higher education, particularly in the medical sciences; and foster the development of the visual, performing and communication arts by providing opportunities for talented young artists, and by making arts available to more people.
Types of support: Conferences and seminars, fellowships, internships, matching funds, professorships, research, scholarship funds, special projects.
Limitations: Giving primarily in the New York, NY, metropolitan area and in Israel. No support for international activities. No grants to individuals, or for building or endowment funds, annual campaigns, or general operating purposes; no loans.
Publications: Annual report (including application guidelines).
Application information:
Initial approach: Proposal
Copies of proposal: 1
Deadline(s): None
Board meeting date(s): Monthly
Final notification: 90 days
Write: James R. Halperin, Exec. V.P.
Officers and Directors: H. Peter Tepperman, Pres.; James R. Halperin, Exec. V.P.; Melvyn C. Levitan, V.P.
Number of staff: None.
Employer Identification Number: 136107659

2260
The Bernard & Anne Spitzer Foundation, Inc.
800 Fifth Ave.
New York 10021-7299

Donor(s): Bernard Spitzer.
Financial data (yr. ended 12/31/87): Assets, $575,760 (M); gifts received, $400,000; expenditures, $333,788, including $332,850 for grants (high: $325,000).
Purpose and activities: Support primarily for culture and Jewish welfare substantial grant to a college.
Limitations: Giving primarily in NY.
Officers: Bernard Spitzer, Pres.; Anne Spitzer.
Employer Identification Number: 133098005

2261
The Seth Sprague Educational and Charitable Foundation
c/o U.S. Trust Co. of New York
45 Wall St.
New York 10005 (212) 806-4500

Trust established in 1939 in NY.
Donor(s): Seth Sprague.†
Financial data (yr. ended 12/31/88): Assets, $32,628,000 (M); expenditures, $2,077,000, including $1,620,000 for 424 grants.
Purpose and activities: Emphasis on health and human services, education, culture and the arts, and civic affairs and community development.
Types of support: Operating budgets, seed money, general purposes, matching funds, special projects.
Limitations: Giving primarily in NY and MA. No grants to individuals; no loans.
Publications: Application guidelines.
Application information:
Initial approach: Proposal or letter
Copies of proposal: 1
Deadline(s): Apr. 15 and Oct. 1
Board meeting date(s): Mar., June, Sept., and Nov. (grants awarded at June and Nov. meetings)
Final notification: No notice unless grant is made
Write: Maureen Augusciak, Sr. V.P., or Anne L. Smith Ganey, Asst. V.P., U.S. Trust Co. of New York
Trustees: Walter G. Dunnington, Jr., Arline Ripley Greenleaf, Jacqueline DeN. Simpkins, U.S. Trust Co. of New York.
Number of staff: None.
Employer Identification Number: 136071886

2262
The Spunk Fund, Inc.
675 Third Ave., Suite 1510
New York 10017 (212) 972-8330

Incorporated in 1981 in NY.
Donor(s): Marianne Gerschel.
Financial data (yr. ended 6/30/88): Assets, $10,103,293 (M); gifts received, $5,603; expenditures, $1,045,132, including $681,269 for 52 grants (high: $49,523; low: $1,000).
Purpose and activities: Support primarily for medical research, education, and cultural programs.
Types of support: General purposes, research.
Limitations: Giving primarily in NY.
Publications: Informational brochure (including application guidelines).
Application information:
Deadline(s): Apr. 1; applications accepted from Sept. through Mar.
Final notification: June
Write: Marianne Gerschel, Pres.
Officers: Marianne Gerschel, Pres. and Treas.; Joseph Erdman, Secy.; Judith K. Dimon, Exec. Dir.
Number of staff: 3 full-time professional; 1 full-time support.
Employer Identification Number: 133116094

2263
The Starr Foundation
70 Pine St.
New York 10270 (212) 770-6882

Incorporated in 1955 in NY.
Donor(s): Cornelius V. Starr,† and others.
Financial data (yr. ended 12/31/87): Assets, $425,604,761 (M); gifts received, $4,000; expenditures, $26,271,295, including $25,142,354 for 278 grants (high: $1,500,000; low: $1,000) and $700,036 for 316 grants to individuals.
Purpose and activities: Grants largely for education with emphasis on higher education, including scholarships under specific programs; support also for culture, health, welfare, and social sciences.
Types of support: Continuing support, building funds, endowment funds, professorships, student aid, scholarship funds, fellowships, research, general purposes.
Limitations: No grants to individuals (except through foundation's scholarship programs), or for matching gifts; no loans.
Publications: 990-PF.
Application information:
Initial approach: Letter
Copies of proposal: 1
Deadline(s): None
Board meeting date(s): Feb. and Sept.
Final notification: Varies
Write: Mr. Ta Chun Hsu, Pres.
Officers: Ta Chun Hsu,* Pres.; Marion I. Breen,* V.P.; Ida E. Galler, Secy.; Frank R. Tengi, Treas.
Directors:* Maurice R. Greenberg, Chair.; Houghton Freeman, Edwin A.G. Manton, John J. Roberts, Ernest E. Stempel.
Number of staff: 1 full-time professional; 3 full-time support.
Employer Identification Number: 136151545
Recent arts and culture grants:
American Club (AERA), Jakarta Pusat, Indonesia, $5,000. For An American Festival in Solo in Indonesia. 9/26/88.
Asia Society, NYC, NY, $15,000. For renewed support for 1987. 11/19/87.
Associated Japan-America Societies of the United States, NYC, NY, $10,000. For 1987-88 budget. 8/3/87.
Brooklyn Botanic Garden, Brooklyn, NY, $250,000. To meet challenge grant to fund design and display of bonsai collection in C.V. Starr Bonsai House. 7/8/87.
Carnegie Hall, NYC, NY, $100,000. Toward audience development through expanded programming. 8/15/88.
Church of Jesus Christ of Latter Day Saints, Mormon Tabernacle Choir, Salt Lake City, UT, $15,000. Toward support of concert program. 2/24/88.
Hun School of Princeton, Princeton, NJ, $45,000. For Fine Arts Center-75th Anniversary Campaign. 9/26/88.
Japan Society, NYC, NY, $11,000. For renewed support for 1988. 7/5/88.
Lincoln Center for the Performing Arts, NYC, NY, $125,000. Toward support of Consolidated Corporate Fund for 1988. 2/24/88.
Maryland Institute College of Art, Baltimore, MD, $60,000. For support of international programs. 11/19/87.
McCarter Theater Company, Princeton, NJ, $10,000. For renewed support for 1988. 7/5/88.
Metropolitan Museum of Art, NYC, NY, $5,000. Toward renewed support for 1988. 6/20/88.
New York Landmarks Conservancy, NYC, NY, $6,000. For renewed support for 1988. 2/24/88.
New York Shakespeare Festival, NYC, NY, $25,000. For renewed support of free summer performances in 1988. 4/18/88.
Opera Orchestra of New York, NYC, NY, $25,000. Toward support of Young Artists Program. 12/17/87.
Philharmonic-Symphony Society of New York, NYC, NY, $25,000. For support of Free Park Concerts program. 4/18/88.
Professional Childrens School, NYC, NY, $10,000. For Scholarship Endowment Fund. 7/5/88.
Prospect Park Alliance, Brooklyn, NY, $50,000. For project to restore Prospect Park's historic Carousel. 8/12/88.
San Antonio Festival, San Antonio, TX, $20,000. For renewed support. 9/26/88.
Thai-American Friendship Committee, DC, $25,000. To support U.S. Geodesic Dome Pavilion in Bangkok. 4/18/88.
Utah Symphony Society, Utah Symphony Orchestra, Salt Lake City, UT, $15,000. Toward support of annual fund campaign. 2/24/88.

2264
Janet Upjohn Stearns Charitable Trust
c/o Morgan Guaranty Trust Company of New York
Nine West 57th St.
New York 10019

Established in 1961 in NY.
Financial data (yr. ended 12/31/87): Assets, $1,311,214 (M); expenditures, $109,122, including $89,500 for 9 grants (high: $5,000; low: $1,000).
Purpose and activities: Funds for secondary education, culture, and social services.
Trustees: James Dolan, Davis, Polk & Wardwell, Morgan Guaranty Trust Co. of New York.
Advisory Committee: Janet T. Beck, G.E. Eisenhardt, Janet W. Ley, Robin Munn.
Employer Identification Number: 136035045

2265
Philip H. & Lois R. Steckler Foundation, Inc.
c/o Philip H. Steckler, Jr.
522 Fifth Ave.
New York 10036

Established in 1969 in NY.
Donor(s): Philip H. Steckler, Jr.
Financial data (yr. ended 7/31/87): Assets, $1,719,006 (M); gifts received, $368,667; expenditures, $209,597, including $182,616 for 164 grants (high: $50,000; low: $10).
Purpose and activities: Giving primarily for hospitals and health services; some support for education, churches, youth services, and cultural activities.
Limitations: Giving primarily in New York, NY.
Application information: Contributes only to pre-selected organizations. Applications not accepted.
Officers and Directors: Philip H. Steckler, Jr., Pres. and Treas.; Philip H. Steckler, V.P.; Lois R. Steckler, Secy.; Donald R. Kurtz, Charles H. Levitt, Philip H. Steckler III, Philip A. Straus.
Employer Identification Number: 132621420

2266
The Steele-Reese Foundation
c/o Messrs. Davidson, Dawson & Clark
330 Madison Ave.
New York 10017 (212) 557-7700
Application addresses: John R. Bryden, 760 Malabu Dr., Lexington, KY 40502; Christine Brady, P.O. Box 23, Carmen, ID 83462
Scholarship application address: Lydia Schofield, Scholarship Dir. for Idaho, Box 922, Salmon, ID 83467

Trust established in 1955 in NY.
Donor(s): Eleanor Steele Reese,† Emmet P. Reese.†
Financial data (yr. ended 8/31/88): Assets, $23,179,853 (M); expenditures, $1,152,768, including $945,750 for 29 grants (high: $100,000; low: $2,000) and $75,000 for 71 grants to individuals.
Purpose and activities: Principally to aid organized charities in southern Appalachia and ID and adjacent states. Support for education, including scholarships, health, welfare, conservation, and the humanities, with a strong preference for rural projects; student aid paid through institutions.
Types of support: General purposes, operating budgets, equipment, endowment funds, matching funds, professorships, scholarship funds, student aid.
Limitations: Giving primarily in southern Appalachia, particularly KY, and in the Northwest, with emphasis on ID; scholarship program limited to students from Lemhi and Custer counties, ID. No grants for continuing support, annual campaigns, seed money, emergency or building funds, deficit financing, research, or land acquisition; no loans; grants to individuals confined to scholarships and paid through institutions.
Publications: Annual report (including application guidelines).
Application information: High school seniors can apply for scholarships through their schools.
Initial approach: Letter
Copies of proposal: 3
Deadline(s): None; payments are generally made in Feb. and Aug.
Board meeting date(s): Monthly
Final notification: 3 to 6 months
Write: William T. Buice, III, in NY for general matters; Dr. John R. Bryden for southern applicants; and Mrs. Christine Brady for northwestern applicants
Trustees: William T. Buice III, Robert T.H. Davidson, Morgan Guaranty Trust Co. of New York.
Number of staff: 3 part-time support.
Employer Identification Number: 136034763
Recent arts and culture grants:
Childrens Museum of Oak Ridge, Oak Ridge, TN, $50,000. For endowment fund and for Appalachian Arts project. 1987.
Kentucky Educational Television Foundation, Lexington, KY, $50,000. Toward two-to-one matching grant for endowment. 1987.
Oregon High Desert Museum, Bend, OR, $40,000. For educational functions of museum. 1987.
Panida Theater Committee, Sandpoint, ID, $10,000. For final payment toward fire and safety equipment in restoration. 1987.
Pilchuck School, Seattle, WA, $25,000. Toward endowment of school devoted to out of glasswork. 1987.
Teachers and Writers Collaborative, NYC, NY, $6,000. For writer-in-residence demonstration program in Salmon, Idaho with local schools and adult community groups. 1987.

2267
The Miriam & Harold Steinberg Foundation, Inc.
527 West 34th St.
New York 10001

Established in 1960 in NY.
Donor(s): Harold Steinberg, Grammercy Holding Corp., Harmir Realty Co.
Financial data (yr. ended 6/30/87): Assets, $2,282,176 (M); expenditures, $831,527, including $818,565 for 37 grants (high: $488,450; low: $100; average: $100-$10,000).
Purpose and activities: Support primarily for Jewish welfare and cultural programs.
Application information: Contributes only to pre-selected organizations. Applications not accepted.
Officers: Harold Steinberg, Pres. and Treas.; Morris Steinberg, Secy.
Employer Identification Number: 136126000

2268
Jerome L. Stern Family Foundation, Inc.
(Formerly Jerome L. and Jane Stern Foundation, Inc.)
342 Madison Ave., Rm. 1912
New York 10173 (212) 972-8165

Incorporated in 1944 in NY.
Donor(s): Members of the Stern family.
Financial data (yr. ended 2/28/87): Assets, $3,011,188 (M); gifts received, $9,768; expenditures, $217,657, including $190,370 for 70 grants (high: $52,100; low: $10).
Purpose and activities: Emphasis on Jewish religious education, temple support, and Jewish welfare funds; some support also for museums.
Limitations: Giving primarily in NY.
Application information: Applications not accepted.
Officers and Directors: Jerome L. Stern, Chair., V.P., and Secy.; Jane M. Stern, Pres.; Geoffrey S. Stern, V.P.; Henriette J. Stern, Treas.; Ronald A. Stern.
Employer Identification Number: 136127063

2269
The Stevens Kingsley Foundation, Inc.
125 Broad St.
New York 10004-2425

Established in 1960 in NY.
Financial data (yr. ended 12/31/87): Assets, $1,068,564 (M); expenditures, $76,148, including $63,820 for 14 grants (high: $16,000; low: $400).
Purpose and activities: Support primarily for libraries, community development, historic preservation, and education.
Types of support: Building funds, equipment, seed money, renovation projects.
Limitations: Giving primarily in Rome, NY.
Officers and Directors: Donald R. Osborn, Pres.; Henry Christensen III, Secy.; Joseph F. Lord, Treas.; George B. Grow, William Curtis Pierce, George B. Waters.
Employer Identification Number: 136150722

2270
The Philip A. and Lynn Straus Foundation, Inc.
1037 Constable Dr. South
Mamaroneck 10543

Incorporated about 1957 in NY.
Donor(s): Philip A. Straus.
Financial data (yr. ended 3/31/87): Assets, $11,813,053 (M); gifts received, $1,948,354; expenditures, $538,489, including $495,490 for 100 grants (high: $62,000; low: $50).
Purpose and activities: Giving for higher education, Jewish welfare funds, international cooperation, child welfare, civil rights organizations, and cultural programs.
Limitations: Giving primarily in NY.
Application information: Contributes only to pre-selected organizations. Applications not accepted.
Write: Philip A. Straus, Pres.
Officers and Trustees: Philip A. Straus, Pres.; Lynn G. Straus, V.P. and Treas.; John W. Herz, Secy.
Employer Identification Number: 136161223

2271
Alan & Katherine Stroock Fund
c/o Stroock & Stroock & Lavan
Seven Hanover Square
New York 10004-2594 (212) 806-6068

Established in 1958 in NY.
Donor(s): Alan M. Stroock,† Katherine W. Stroock.
Financial data (yr. ended 12/31/87): Assets, $49,484 (M); gifts received, $313,249;

expenditures, $359,925, including $357,470 for 30 grants (high: $200,000; low: $25).
Purpose and activities: Support primarily for higher education, cultural programs, and Jewish concerns.
Limitations: No grants to individuals.
Application information: Contributes only to pre-selected organizations. Applications not accepted.
Officers and Directors: Ronald J. Stein, Pres.; Henry A. Loeb, V.P.; Judith Jahnke, Secy.; Morton L. Deitch, Treas.; Barbara Lamar.
Employer Identification Number: 136086102

2272
William Matheus Sullivan Musical Foundation, Inc.
c/o Hugh Ross
410 East 57th St.
New York 10022 (212) 755-8158

Incorporated in 1956 in NY.
Donor(s): William Matheus Sullivan,† Arcie Lubetkin.†
Financial data (yr. ended 12/31/87): Assets, $2,822,350 (M); gifts received, $3,000; expenditures, $146,835, including $75,000 for 11 grants (high: $55,000; low: $500) and $5,800 for 24 grants to individuals.
Purpose and activities: To advance the careers of gifted young singers who have completed their formal music training, either directly or by finding engagements for them via assistance given to orchestras, operatic societies, or other musical groups; grants based on financial need of applicant.
Types of support: Grants to individuals, continuing support, special projects.
Limitations: No support for general fields of music education and vocal or instrument training. No grants for building or endowment funds, or for operating budgets.
Publications: Application guidelines.
Application information: Requests for New York auditions should be accompanied by resume and copy of contract for at least one engagement with full orchestra after Nov.; West Coast auditions may be reestablished soon. Application form required.
Initial approach: Letter or proposal, detailing educational and musical experience
Copies of proposal: 1
Deadline(s): Oct. 1st for the following fall
Board meeting date(s): 5 or 6 times a year as required
Write: Hugh Ross, Exec. Dir.
Officers and Trustees: Spencer Byard, Pres.; Hugh Ross, V.P. and Exec. Dir.; Jose T. Moscoso, Secy.; Peter J. Merrill, Treas.; Rose Bampton, George L. Boveroux, Jr., Bruce Donnell, Edward O. Downes, Barbara B. Last, Gail M.L. Lavielle, David Lloyd, Lee Schaenen.
Number of staff: 1 full-time professional.
Employer Identification Number: 136069096

2273
The Sulzberger Foundation, Inc.
229 West 43rd St.
New York 10036 (212) 556-1750

Incorporated in 1956 in NY.
Donor(s): Arthur Hays Sulzberger,† Iphigene Ochs Sulzberger.
Financial data (yr. ended 12/31/86): Assets, $11,470,177 (M); gifts received, $1,500,000; expenditures, $615,691, including $563,118 for 143 grants (high: $56,500; low: $100).
Purpose and activities: Grants largely for education, cultural programs, hospitals, community funds, and welfare funds.
Types of support: Annual campaigns, building funds, capital campaigns, conferences and seminars, consulting services, continuing support, emergency funds, endowment funds, equipment, exchange programs, fellowships, general purposes, internships, lectureships, operating budgets, professorships, program-related investments, renovation projects, scholarship funds, seed money, special projects, technical assistance.
Limitations: Giving primarily in NY and Chattanooga, TN. No grants to individuals, or for matching gifts; no loans.
Publications: 990-PF.
Application information:
Initial approach: Telephone
Deadline(s): None
Board meeting date(s): Jan. and as required
Write: Marian S. Heiskell, Pres.
Officers and Directors: Marian S. Heiskell, Pres.; Arthur Ochs Sulzberger, V.P. and Secy.-Treas.; Ruth S. Holmberg, V.P.; Judith P. Sulzberger, V.P.; Iphigene Ochs Sulzberger.
Number of staff: 3 part-time support.
Employer Identification Number: 136083166

2274
Surdna Foundation, Inc.
250 Park Ave., Rm. 528
New York 10177 (212) 697-0630

Incorporated in 1917 in NY.
Donor(s): John E. Andrus.†
Financial data (yr. ended 6/30/88): Assets, $302,275,638 (M); gifts received, $1,583,784; expenditures, $16,205,138, including $14,465,586 for 120 grants (high: $5,150,000; low: $6,500).
Purpose and activities: Support primarily for social concerns, including youth and child welfare; higher and medical education, health care delivery, medical research, and cultural affairs. The necessary objective of all grants is to bring the benefits of the programs supported to significantly broad groups of the population.
Types of support: Seed money, emergency funds, equipment, matching funds, internships, scholarship funds, fellowships, special projects, research, endowment funds, renovation projects, technical assistance.
Limitations: Giving limited to the northeastern states, with emphasis on NY. No grants to individuals, or for annual campaigns, building funds, land acquisition, or conferences and seminars; no loans.
Publications: Annual report (including application guidelines).
Application information:
Initial approach: Letter and preliminary outline
Copies of proposal: 1
Deadline(s): July 1, Oct. 1, Jan. 1, and Apr. 1
Board meeting date(s): Sept., Nov., Feb., and May
Final notification: 2 weeks
Write: Edward Skloot, Exec. Dir.
Officers: Edward F. McGee,* Pres.; John Lynagh,* V.P. and Secy.; Russell R. Roetger,* V.P.; Donald R. Spaidal,* Treas.; Edward Skloot, Exec. Dir.; Lindsley Homrighausen, Admin. for Grants.
Directors:* John E. Andrus III, Chair.; Peter B. Benedict, Lawrence S.C. Griffith, Julia A. Moon, Samuel S. Thorpe III.
Number of staff: 1 full-time professional; 1 full-time support.
Employer Identification Number: 136108163
Recent arts and culture grants:
American Antiquarian Society, Worcester, MA, $100,000. 1987.
Arts Resources in Collaboration, NYC, NY, $15,000. 1987.
Bargemusic, Brooklyn, NY, $20,000. 1987.
Brooklyn Institute of Arts and Sciences, Brooklyn, NY, $34,000. 1987.
Chamber Music Society of Lincoln Center, NYC, NY, $25,000. 1987.
Early Music Foundation, NYC, NY, $20,000. 1987.
Hudson River Museum of Westchester, Yonkers, NY, $50,000. 1987.
Joyce Theater Foundation, NYC, NY, $20,000. 1987.
Juilliard School, NYC, NY, $100,000. 1987.
Jupiter Symphony of New York, NYC, NY, $30,000. 1987.
La Mama Experimental Theater Club, NYC, NY, $25,000. 1987.
Marlboro School of Music, Marlboro, VT, $25,000. 1987.
Metropolitan Opera Association, NYC, NY, $50,000. 1987.
Minnesota Opera Company, Saint Paul, MN, $30,000. 1987.
Municipal Art Society, NYC, NY, $40,000. 1987.
National Theater of the Deaf, NYC, NY, $22,000. 1987.
New England Conservatory of Music, Boston, MA, $75,000. 1987.
New York City Hispanic-American Dance Company, NYC, NY, $35,000. 1987.
New York Shakespeare Festival, NYC, NY, $30,000. 1987.
Original Ballets Foundation, NYC, NY, $25,000. 1987.
Paul Taylor Dance Foundation, NYC, NY, $40,000. 1987.
Performing Arts Repertory Theater Foundation, NYC, NY, $20,000. 1987.
Philharmonia Virtuosi, Dobbs Ferry, NY, $25,000. 1987.
Philharmonic-Symphony Society of New York, NYC, NY, $50,000. 1987.
Playwrights Horizons, NYC, NY, $60,000. 1987.
Rhode Island School of Design, Providence, RI, $100,000. 1987.
Saint Lukes Chamber Ensemble, NYC, NY, $50,000. 1987.
Skowhegan School of Painting and Sculpture, Skowhegan, ME, $25,000. 1987.
Storm King Art Center, Mountainville, NY, $35,000. 1987.
Symphony Space, NYC, NY, $17,500. 1987.
Vivian Beaumont Theater, NYC, NY, $50,000. 1987.

Westminster Choir College, Princeton, NJ, $50,000. 1987.
Young Audiences, NYC, NY, $50,000. 1987.
Young Concert Artists, NYC, NY, $50,000. 1987.

2275
Texaco Philanthropic Foundation Inc.
2000 Westchester Ave.
White Plains 10650 (914) 253-4150

Incorporated in 1979 in DE.
Donor(s): Texaco, Inc.
Financial data (yr. ended 12/31/88): Assets, $14,163,644 (M); expenditures, $6,710,926, including $5,659,255 for 586 grants (high: $850,500; low: $300; average: $1,000-$10,000) and $998,265 for 2,451 employee matching gifts.
Purpose and activities: To enhance the quality of life by providing support for cultural programs, higher education, social welfare, public and civic organizations, hospitals and health agencies, and environmental protection.
Types of support: Employee matching gifts, fellowships, research, employee-related scholarships, special projects, scholarship funds.
Limitations: Giving primarily in areas of company operations to local organizations; support also for national organizations that serve a large segment of the population. No support for religious organizations, private foundations , fraternal, social, or veterans' organizations, social functions, commemorative journals, or meetings, or political activities. No grants to individuals, or for general operating support, capital funds (except for selected private non-profit hospitals) or endowments; no loans.
Publications: Annual report (including application guidelines).
Application information:
Initial approach: Proposal
Copies of proposal: 1
Deadline(s): None
Board meeting date(s): Quarterly
Final notification: 2 months
Write: Maria Mike-Mayer, Secy.
Officers: William C. Weitzel, Jr.,* Pres.; Maria Mike-Mayer, Secy.; David C. Crikelair, Treas.
Directors:* Lorene L. Rogers, Chair.; John D. Ambler, William S. Barrack, Jr., Paul B. Hicks, Jr., George Parker, Jr.
Number of staff: 5
Employer Identification Number: 133007516
Recent arts and culture grants:
Academy of Natural Sciences of Philadelphia, Philadelphia, PA, $5,000. 1987.
Affiliate Artists, NYC, NY, $15,500. 1987.
American Museum of Natural History, NYC, NY, $5,000. 1987.
Audubon Park and Zoological Garden, New Orleans, LA, $10,000. 1987.
Bakersfield Symphony, Bakersfield, CA, $10,000. 1987.
Baton Rouge Symphony, Baton Rouge, LA, $5,000. 1987.
Business Arts Fund, Houston, TX, $10,000. 1987.
Business Committee for the Arts, NYC, NY, $5,000. 1987.
Cherokee National Historical Society, Tahlequah, OK, $7,500. 1987.
Classical America, NYC, NY, $5,000. 1987.
Corcoran Gallery of Art, DC, $5,000. 1987.
Council for the Arts in Westchester, White Plains, NY, $20,000. 1987.
Denver Museum of Natural History, Denver, CO, $5,500. 1987.
Denver Zoological Foundation, Denver, CO, $15,000. 1987.
Dutchess Arts Fund, Poughkeepsie, NY, $5,000. 1987.
Five Civilized Tribes Museum, Muskogee, OK, $5,000. 1987.
Grand Opera House, Wilmington, DE, $22,500. 1987.
Houston Ballet, Houston, TX, $25,000. 1987.
Houston Lyric Theater Foundation, Wortham Theater Center, Houston, TX, $50,000. 1987.
Houston Lyric Theater Foundation, Wortham Theater Center, Houston, TX, $20,000. 1987.
Houston Symphony Society, Houston, TX, $25,000. 1987.
Houston Symphony Society, Houston, TX, $5,000. 1987.
Hudson River Museum of Westchester, Yonkers, NY, $5,000. 1987.
Huntington Library, Art Gallery and Botanical Garden, San Marino, CA, $5,000. 1987.
Iowa Historical Museum Foundation, Des Moines, IA, $10,000. 1987.
James Dick Foundation for the Performing Arts, Festival Institute at Round Top, Round Top, TX, $5,000. 1987.
John F. Kennedy Center for the Performing Arts, DC, $20,000. 1987.
Lincoln Center for the Performing Arts, NYC, NY, $25,000. 1987.
Los Angeles County Museum of Natural History Foundation, Los Angeles, CA, $5,000. 1987.
Los Angeles Music Center, Los Angeles, CA, $10,000. 1987.
Los Angeles Philharmonic, Los Angeles, CA, $50,000. 1987.
Lyric Opera of Chicago, Chicago, IL, $45,000. 1987.
Metropolitan Museum of Art, NYC, NY, $5,000. 1987.
Metropolitan Opera Association, NYC, NY, $820,500. 1987.
Mid-Hudson Civic Center, Poughkeepsie, NY, $5,000. 1987.
Midland-Odessa Symphony and Chorale, Midland, TX, $5,000. 1987.
National Symphony Orchestra, DC, $10,000. 1987.
New Orleans City Ballet, New Orleans, LA, $12,500. 1987.
New Orleans Museum of Art, New Orleans, LA, $9,500. 1987.
New Orleans Opera Association, New Orleans, LA, $10,000. 1987.
New Orleans Philharmonic Symphony Society, New Orleans, LA, $14,000. 1987.
Port Arthur Historical Society, Port Arthur, TX, $10,000. 1987.
Texas Opera Theater, Houston, TX, $5,000. 1987.
Thomas Gilcrease Institute of American History and Art, Tulsa, OK, $20,000. 1987.
Tulsa Ballet Theater, Tulsa, OK, $7,500. 1987.
Tulsa Opera, Tulsa, OK, $18,000. 1987.
Tulsa Philharmonic Orchestra, Tulsa, OK, $15,000. 1987.
Ventura County Symphony Association, Ventura, CA, $10,000. 1987.
W H I L - Stereo FM 91, Mobile, AL, $10,400. 1987.
Washington Opera, DC, $5,000. 1987.
Wichita Symphony, Wichita, KS, $6,500. 1987.

2276
Texaco, Inc. Foundation
c/o Texaco, Inc.
2000 Westchester Ave.
White Plains 10650 (914) 253-4150

Incorporated in 1969 in OK; renamed as Texaco, Inc. Foundation in 1984 following Getty Oil Co.'s merger with Texaco, Inc.
Donor(s): Texaco, Inc.
Financial data (yr. ended 12/31/88): Assets, $727,761 (M); expenditures, $525,355, including $525,300 for 7 grants (high: $400,000; low: $8,800; average: $10,000-$50,000).
Purpose and activities: To enhance the quality of life by providing support for cultural programs, higher education, social welfare, public affairs and civic organizations, hospitals and health agencies, and environmental protection.
Types of support: Research, special projects.
Limitations: No support for religious organizations or private foundations. No grants to individuals, or for capital funds or endowments.
Application information:
Initial approach: Proposal or letter
Copies of proposal: 1
Deadline(s): None
Board meeting date(s): As required
Final notification: 2 months
Write: Maria Mike-Mayer, Secy.
Officers: William C. Weitzel, Jr.,* Pres.; Maria Mike-Mayer, Secy.; David C. Crikelair, Treas.
Directors:* Lorene L. Rogers, Chair.; William S. Barrack, Jr., Paul B. Hicks, Jr., George Parker, Jr.
Employer Identification Number: 237063751

2277
Eugene V. & Clare E. Thaw Charitable Trust
726 Park Ave.
New York 10021

Established in 1981 in NY.
Donor(s): Eugene V. Thaw.
Financial data (yr. ended 5/31/88): Assets, $3,577,294 (M); gifts received, $664,649; expenditures, $374,559, including $353,369 for 20 grants (high: $83,000; low: $1,000).
Purpose and activities: A private operating foundation; giving for arts and culture; limited support for social services.
Application information: Contributes only to pre-selected organizations. Applications not accepted.
Trustees: Clare E. Thaw, Eugene V. Thaw.
Employer Identification Number: 133081491

2278
J. Walter Thompson Company Fund, Inc.
466 Lexington Ave.
New York 10017 (212) 210-7000

Incorporated in 1953 in NY.
Donor(s): J. Walter Thompson Co.
Financial data (yr. ended 11/30/88): Assets, $899,182 (M); expenditures, $195,600, including $126,600 for 10 grants (high: $40,000; low: $1,000; average: $1,500-$5,000) and $65,134 for 137 employee matching gifts.
Purpose and activities: Giving to arts, community funds, and educational organizations, including an employee matching gift program for education. Grants generally restricted to organizations which have received longstanding support from the fund.
Types of support: Employee matching gifts, employee-related scholarships, scholarship funds.
Limitations: No grants to individuals.
Application information:
Initial approach: Letter
Copies of proposal: 1
Board meeting date(s): Mar.-Apr.
Write: Nancy Fitzpatrick, Secy.
Officers and Directors:* Edward A. Haymes,* Chair.; Burt Manning,* Pres.; Susan Mirsky,* V.P.; Nancy Fitzpatrick,* Secy.; Donna Matteo, Treas.
Number of staff: None.
Employer Identification Number: 136020644

2279
The Thorne Foundation
435 East 52nd St.
New York 10022

Incorporated in 1930 in NY.
Donor(s): Landon K. Thorne,† Julia L. Thorne.†
Financial data (yr. ended 12/31/87): Assets, $2,442,494 (M); expenditures, $202,179, including $167,655 for 30 grants (high: $25,000; low: $100).
Purpose and activities: Emphasis on higher education, museums, and cultural programs.
Limitations: Giving primarily in NY.
Application information:
Initial approach: Proposal
Write: Miriam A. Thorne, Pres.
Officers: Miriam A. Thorne, Pres.; David H. Thorne, V.P.; John B. Jessup, Secy.-Treas.
Employer Identification Number: 136109955

2280
The Oakleigh L. Thorne Foundation
1633 Broadway, 30th Fl.
New York 10019

Incorporated in 1959 in NY.
Donor(s): Commerce Clearing House, Inc.
Financial data (yr. ended 12/31/87): Assets, $212,576 (M); gifts received, $300,000; expenditures, $342,357, including $341,700 for 112 grants (high: $80,000; low: $200).
Purpose and activities: Emphasis on community funds, hospitals, health agencies, higher and secondary education, youth agencies, conservation programs, and cultural programs.
Types of support: General purposes, operating budgets, continuing support, annual campaigns, seed money, emergency funds, deficit financing, building funds, equipment, land acquisition, endowment funds, special projects, research, publications, capital campaigns, renovation projects.
Limitations: No grants to individuals, or for scholarships, fellowships, or matching gifts; no loans.
Application information:
Initial approach: Letter
Copies of proposal: 1
Deadline(s): None
Board meeting date(s): Quarterly
Final notification: 6 months
Write: Oakleigh B. Thorne, Pres.
Officers and Directors: Oakleigh B. Thorne, Pres. and Treas.; Ellen L. Klingener, V.P.; Horace C. Stephenson, V.P.
Number of staff: None.
Employer Identification Number: 510243758

2281
Louis Comfort Tiffany Foundation
P.O. Box 480
Canal Street Station
New York 10013 (212) 431-9880

Association established in 1918 in NY.
Donor(s): Louis Comfort Tiffany.†
Financial data (yr. ended 12/31/87): Assets, $4,210,046 (M); expenditures, $391,765, including $300,000 for 20 grants to individuals.
Purpose and activities: To encourage talented and advanced artists of the fine arts (painting, sculpture, and the graphic arts) and the industrial crafts (ceramics, textile design, glass design, metal work) by awarding a limited number of grants biannually.
Types of support: Grants to individuals.
Limitations: No grants for general support, or capital or endowment funds.
Application information: Awards are by nomination only. Applications not accepted.
Write: Angela Westwater, Pres.
Officers and Trustees: Angela Westwater, Pres.; Gerard E. Jones, Secy.; Robert Meltzer, Treas.; William Bailey, Robert Blackburn, Thomas S. Buechner, Amanda Burden, Stephen Greene, Lewis Iselin, Bill N. Lacy, Roy Lichtenstein, David Pease, Martin Puryear, David A. Ross, Paul J. Smith, Diane Waldman.
Number of staff: None.
Employer Identification Number: 131689389

2282
Time Inc. Foundation
Time & Life Bldg., Rm. 4173
Rockefeller Center
New York 10020 (212) 841-8030

Established in 1983 in NY.
Donor(s): Time-Warner, Inc.
Financial data (yr. ended 12/31/87): Assets, $445,564 (M); gifts received, $423,409; expenditures, $273,319, including $273,200 for 21 grants (high: $54,000; low: $600).
Purpose and activities: Giving mainly for cultural programs, urban affairs, and youth agencies.
Types of support: Operating budgets.
Application information: Contributes only to preselected organizations. Applications not accepted.
Officers: Donald M. Wilson, Pres.; Emelda M. Cathcart, V.P.; William M. Guttman, Secy.; Kevin D. Senie, Treas.
Directors: Reginald K. Brach, Jr., Glenn A. Britt, Ray Cave, Michael J. Fuchs, Gerald M. Levin, Kelso F. Sutton.
Employer Identification Number: 133131902

2283
The Tinker Foundation, Inc.
55 East 59th St.
New York 10022 (212) 421-6858

Trust established in 1959 in NY; incorporated in 1975 in NY.
Donor(s): Edward Larocque Tinker.†
Financial data (yr. ended 12/31/88): Assets, $48,721,972 (M); expenditures, $3,020,997, including $1,893,300 for 56 grants and $92,500 for 10 grants to individuals.
Purpose and activities: To promote better understanding among the peoples of the U.S., Latin America, Portugal, and Spain. Grants in aid of projects in the social sciences, international relations, marine sciences, natural resource development and some assistance for projects focused on Antarctica. Support also offered for conferences, meetings, seminars, and public affairs programs, and occasionally for programs furthering the education of the Spanish- and Portuguese-speaking peoples in the U.S.
Types of support: Special projects, research, conferences and seminars, exchange programs, matching funds, lectureships, seed money.
Limitations: Giving limited to projects related to Latin America, Spain, and Portugal. No support for projects concerned with health or medical issues. No grants to individuals, or for building or endowment funds, annual campaigns, or operating budgets.
Publications: Annual report (including application guidelines), grants list.
Application information: The foundation has terminated its Postdoctoral Fellowship Program. Final installments of fellowships will be paid out in 1988.
Initial approach: Letter
Copies of proposal: 1
Deadline(s): Institutional grants: Mar. 1 for summer meeting and Oct. 1 for winter meeting; Field Research Grants: Oct. 1
Board meeting date(s): Institutional grants: June and Dec.; Field Research Grants: Dec.
Final notification: Institutional and Field Research grants: 2 weeks after board meetings
Write: Martha T. Muse, Chair.
Officers and Directors: Martha T. Muse, Chair., Pres., and C.E.O.; Grayson Kirk, V.P.; Raymond L. Brittenham, Secy.; Gordon T. Wallis, Treas.; John N. Irwin II, Charles McC. Mathias, W. Clarke Wescoe.
Number of staff: 5 full-time professional; 3 full-time support.
Employer Identification Number: 510175449

Recent arts and culture grants:
Missouri Botanical Garden, Saint Louis, MO, $50,000. To establish Tinker Latin American Postgraduate Fellowship in Tropical Botany. 1987.
Woodrow Wilson International Center for Scholars, DC, $30,000. To Latin American Program to support continuation of annual Editors' Conference in addition to outreach activities, including dialogues and discussion groups for policymakers and scholars from Washington area. 1987.
Woodrow Wilson International Center for Scholars, DC, $15,000. Toward conference on Portugal to be organized by West European Program. 1987.

2284
Tisch Foundation, Inc.
667 Madison Ave.
New York 10021-8087 (212) 841-1547

Incorporated in 1957 in FL.
Donor(s): Hotel Americana, Tisch Hotels, Inc., members of the Tisch family, and closely held corporations.
Financial data (yr. ended 12/31/87): Assets, $76,022,587 (M); expenditures, $2,635,208, including $2,452,120 for 118 grants (high: $1,003,400; low: $100).
Purpose and activities: Emphasis on higher education, including institutions in Israel, and research related programs; support also for Jewish organizations and welfare funds, museums, and secondary education.
Types of support: Continuing support, building funds, equipment, research.
Limitations: No grants to individuals, or for endowment funds, scholarships, fellowships, or matching gifts; no loans.
Application information: Contributes only to pre-selected organizations. Applications not accepted.
Board meeting date(s): Mar., June, Sept., Dec., and as required
Write: Laurence A. Tisch, Sr. V.P.
Officers and Directors: Preston R. Tisch, Pres.; Laurence A. Tisch, Sr. V.P.; E. Jack Beatus, Secy.-Treas.; Joan H. Tisch, Wilma S. Tisch.
Number of staff: None.
Employer Identification Number: 591002844

2285
Rose & John Tishman Fund, Inc.
175 East 79th St.
New York 10021-0432

Established in 1957 in NY.
Donor(s): Rose Tishman.
Financial data (yr. ended 12/31/87): Assets, $872,455 (M); gifts received, $225,000; expenditures, $119,572, including $57,770 for 82 grants (high: $20,000; low: $20) and $54,500 for 1 grant to an individual.
Purpose and activities: Support for Jewish organizations and general charitable giving.
Types of support: Grants to individuals.
Application information:
Initial approach: Letter
Deadline(s): None
Write: Rose F. Tishman, V.P.
Officers: John Tishman, Pres.; Daniel R. Tishman, V.P. and Treas.; Katherine Blacklock, V.P.; Rose Tishman, V.P.; Kathleen Kotown, Secy.
Employer Identification Number: 136151766

2286
William S. & Frances B. Todman Foundation
c/o Reid & Priest
40 West 57th St.
New York 10019

Established in 1980 in NY.
Donor(s): Frances B. Todman.
Financial data (yr. ended 11/30/87): Assets, $3,777 (M); gifts received, $207,860; expenditures, $207,500, including $207,500 for 11 grants (high: $150,000; low: $1,000).
Purpose and activities: Support primarily for medical research, Jewish giving, and the arts.
Limitations: Giving primarily in NY and FL. No grants to individuals.
Application information: Contributes only to pre-selected organizations. Applications not accepted.
Trustees: Lisa Todman Plough, Frances B. Todman, William S. Todman, Jr.
Employer Identification Number: 133064427

2287
Mildred Faulkner Truman Foundation
c/o Chase Lincoln First Bank, N.A.
P.O. Box 1412
Rochester 14603
Application address: 212 Front St., P.O. Box 236, Owego, NY 13827; Tel.: (607) 687-1350

Established in 1985 in NY.
Donor(s): Mildred Faulkner Truman.†
Financial data (yr. ended 8/31/87): Assets, $3,934,671 (M); expenditures, $263,988, including $222,904 for 36 grants (high: $25,000; low: $400).
Purpose and activities: Giving for youth and child welfare, education, social services, and cultural programs.
Limitations: Giving primarily in Tioga County, NY.
Application information:
Deadline(s): None
Write: Irene C. Graven, Acting Exec. Dir.
Officers: Harold Newcomb, Chair.; Edwin B. Bartow, Vice-Chair.; Robert Williams, Secy.; Dorothy Goodrich, Treas.
Trustees: John J. Donnelly, James V. Guido, Fred R. McFadden, John C. Murphy, Carl Saddlemire.
Corporate Trustee: Chase Lincoln First Bank, N.A.
Employer Identification Number: 166293320

2288
The Trust for Mutual Understanding
30 Rockefeller Plaza, Rm. 5600
New York 10112

Established in 1984 in NY.
Financial data (yr. ended 4/30/87): Assets, $17,554,094 (M); expenditures, $573,270, including $410,506 for 9 grants (high: $80,000; low: $16,000).
Purpose and activities: Support for an academy of the sciences, an opera company, theater and other cultural programs.
Application information: Contributes only to pre-selected organizations. Applications not accepted.
Trustees: Richard Lanier, Elizabeth J. McCormack, Donal C. O'Brien, Jr.
Employer Identification Number: 133212724

2289
Michael Tuch Foundation, Inc.
122 East 42nd St., No. 1616
New York 10168 (212) 986-9082

Incorporated in 1946 in NY.
Donor(s): Michael Tuch.†
Financial data (yr. ended 12/31/87): Assets, $4,817,501 (M); gifts received, $59,132; expenditures, $298,402, including $243,233 for 93 grants (high: $7,000; low: $250; average: $1,000).
Purpose and activities: Emphasis on higher education, cultural programs, including the performing arts, Jewish welfare funds, and child welfare.
Types of support: Endowment funds, scholarship funds, fellowships.
Limitations: Giving primarily in New York, NY. No support for religion or health. No grants to individuals, or for study, or new general support.
Application information:
Write: Eugene Tuck, Pres.
Officers: Eugene Tuck, Pres. and Exec. Dir.; Elizabeth Tuck, 1st V.P.; Martha Rozett, 2nd V.P.; Jacques J. Stone, Secy.-Treas.
Trustee: Jonathon S. Tuck.
Employer Identification Number: 136002848

2290
Unilever United States Corporate Giving Program
390 Park Avenue
New York 10022 (212) 888-1260

Purpose and activities: Supports elementary, secondary, economic and general education, public and private colleges; scholarships; legal services; hospitals, programs for international groups, minorities, job development, youth service, environmental issues, political and civic affairs. Community funding includes United Way. Employee gift matching for education and cultural projects. Provides non-financial assistance through in-kind donations, use of company facilities, and employee volunteer programs. Funding decisions are favorably influenced by employee involvement. Company considers national programs.
Types of support: Employee matching gifts, in-kind gifts.
Limitations: Giving primarily in headquarter city and national operating areas.
Application information:
Initial approach: Letter and proposal
Board meeting date(s): Decisions made in Feb.
Write: Shirley Loxley, Comm. Affairs Mgr.

2291
United States Trust Company of New York Foundation
c/o U.S. Trust Co. of New York
45 Wall St.
New York 10005 (212) 806-4420

Trust established in 1955 in NY.
Donor(s): U.S. Trust Co. of New York.
Financial data (yr. ended 12/31/87): Assets, $48,028 (L); gifts received, $400,177; expenditures, $374,872, including $282,532 for 80 grants (high: $50,000; low: $25; average: $3,000-$5,000) and $92,160 for 281 employee matching gifts.
Purpose and activities: Support for cultural, health, educational, and civic and urban affairs organizations that assist in building or maintaining an improved quality of life. Preference given to innovative, broad-based, privately supported, and efficient organizations in which company employees are active.
Types of support: Operating budgets, annual campaigns, seed money, building funds, equipment, land acquisition, endowment funds, matching funds, employee matching gifts, special projects, research, capital campaigns, general purposes, publications.
Limitations: Giving primarily in the New York metropolitan area and other primary market areas of the company. No support for religious or political organizations or member agencies of the United Way. No grants to individuals, or for emergency funds, deficit financing, scholarships, or fellowships; no loans.
Publications: Informational brochure (including application guidelines).
Application information:
Initial approach: Letter or proposal
Copies of proposal: 1
Deadline(s): Apr. 1
Board meeting date(s): Mar., May, Sept., and Nov.
Final notification: 2 to 3 months
Write: Carol A. Strickland, V.P.
Corporate Contributions Committee: Carol A. Strickland, V.P. and Corp. Secy.
Number of staff: 2 part-time professional; 2 part-time support.
Employer Identification Number: 136072081

2292
United States-Japan Foundation
145 East 32nd St., 12th Fl.
New York 10016 (212) 481-8753
Tokyo, Japan, office address: Nihon Shobo Kaikan, 9th Fl., 2-9-16 Toranomon, Minato-ku, Tokyo; Tel.: 03-591-4002

Foundation incorporated in 1980 in NY.
Donor(s): The Japan Shipbuilding Industry Foundation.
Financial data (yr. ended 12/31/87): Assets, $81,523,855 (M); expenditures, $4,599,030, including $3,307,699 for 45 grants (high: $284,313; low: $3,012; average: $10,000-$25,000).
Purpose and activities: To strengthen cooperation and understanding between the people of the U.S. and Japan through grants in: 1) Exchange of persons and ideas, involving American and Japanese leaders drawn from local communities, the professions, state and local governments, and other groups; 2) Education, with emphasis on pre-college education; and 3) Nongovernmental dialogue in such fields as energy, technology, international finance, and defense.
Types of support: Exchange programs, special projects, publications, internships, fellowships, matching funds, conferences and seminars, research, seed money.
Limitations: No support for projects in the arts involving performances, exhibitions, or productions, or for sports exchanges, student exchanges, scholarly research, or scholarly conferences. No grants to individuals, or for building or endowment funds; no loans.
Publications: Annual report, newsletter.
Application information:
Initial approach: Letter
Deadline(s): None
Board meeting date(s): May and Nov.
Final notification: 6 months to 1 year
Write: Ronald Aqua, Prog. Dir.
Officers: Stephen W. Bosworth, Pres.; Maximilian Kempner, Secy.; Stephen W. Montanye, Controller.
Trustees:* William D. Eberle, Chair.; Kiichi Saeki, Vice-Chair.; Thomas A. Bartlett, Robin Chandler Duke, Orville L. Freeman, Tadao Ishikawa, Hiroyuki Itami, Jonathan Mason, Robert S. McNamara, Isao Nakauchi, Richard W. Petree, Shizuo Saito, Robert W. Sarnoff, Yohei Sasakawa, Ryuzo Sejima, Ayako Sono, Phillips Talbot, Joseph D. Tydings, Yoshio Terasawa, Henry G. Walter, Jr., John S. Wadsworth, Jr.
Number of staff: 6 full-time professional; 4 full-time support.
Employer Identification Number: 133054425
Recent arts and culture grants:
National Public Radio, DC, $103,000. For full-time reporting capability from Tokyo that will enhance and increase National Public Radio's coverage of news and issues from Japan and the Far East. 1987.
Nebraskans for Public Television, Lincoln, NE, $75,000. For production of two half-hour public television programs entitled Japan: Toward the 21st Century, and development of interactive videodiscs and accompanying print materials. 1987.
W N E T Channel 13, NYC, NY, $150,258. For second year of Japan Project at WNET. 1987.

2293
Uris Brothers Foundation, Inc.
300 Park Ave.
New York 10022 (212) 407-9512

Incorporated in 1956 in NY.
Donor(s): Percy Uris,† Harold D. Uris,† and related business interests.
Financial data (yr. ended 10/31/88): Assets, $21,695,694 (M); expenditures, $1,570,216, including $1,492,400 for 73 grants (high: $500,000; low: $500) and $250,000 for loans.
Purpose and activities: Grants for the arts, cultural programs, education and youth, social service agencies, and housing for the homeless.
Types of support: Building funds, special projects, capital campaigns, technical assistance, general purposes, loans, program-related investments, renovation projects.
Limitations: Giving primarily in New York, NY. No grants to individuals, or for endowment funds.
Application information:
Initial approach: Letter or brief proposal
Copies of proposal: 1
Deadline(s): None
Board meeting date(s): Quarterly
Write: Ms. Alice Paul, Exec. Dir.
Officers: Susan Halpern,* Pres.; Jane Bayard,* V.P.; Linda Sanger,* V.P.; Alice Paul,* Secy. and Exec. Dir.; Benjamin Gessula, Treas.
Directors:* Ruth Uris, Chair.; Robert H. Abrams, Robert L. Bachner.
Number of staff: 1 part-time professional.
Employer Identification Number: 136115748

2294
Utica Foundation, Inc.
233 Genesee St.
Utica 13501 (315) 738-4977

Community foundation incorporated in 1952 in NY.
Financial data (yr. ended 12/31/87): Assets, $2,894,528 (L); gifts received, $1,162,728; expenditures, $125,653, including $99,737 for 36 grants (high: $10,000; low: $350).
Purpose and activities: Support for social and health services, scholarship programs of institutions for aid to local students, and cultural programs.
Types of support: General purposes, seed money, building funds, equipment, conferences and seminars, professorships, matching funds, scholarship funds, capital campaigns.
Limitations: Giving limited to Utica, Oneida, and Herkimer counties, NY. No support for religious purposes. No grants to individuals, or for endowment funds, deficit financing, or operating budgets; no loans.
Publications: Annual report, application guidelines.
Application information: Application form required.
Initial approach: Letter
Copies of proposal: 7
Board meeting date(s): 3 to 4 times a year, in May and as required
Final notification: 2 to 3 months
Write: Addison M. White, Pres.
Officers and Directors: Addison M. White, Pres.; Mrs. Thomas G. Hineline, V.P.; Arthur H. Turner, V.P.; William L. Schrauth, Secy.; James S. Kernan, Jr., Treas.; Rev. P. Arthur Brindisi, Vincent R. Corrou, Jr., Irving Cramer, M.D., Victor T. Ehre, John L. Knower, Harold J. Moore, Burrel Samuels, Msgr. Charles Sewall, Dwight E. Vicks, Jr., William B. Westcott, Jr.
Trustee Banks: Marine Midland Bank, N.A., Norstar Bank of Upstate New York.
Number of staff: 1 part-time support.
Employer Identification Number: 156016932
Recent arts and culture grants:
Central New York Community Arts Council, Utica, NY, $5,000. Toward purchase of computer equipment. 1987.
Childrens Museum of History, Natural History and Science, Utica, NY, $5,000. Toward installment of new side entrance door and platform for railroad exhibit. 1987.
Utica Zoological Society, Utica, NY, $6,000. For first installment of grant toward cost of Walkway-Overlook. 1987.

2295
Utica National Group Foundation, Inc.
P.O. Box 530
Utica 13503 (315) 735-3321

Established in 1987 in NY.
Donor(s): Utica Mutual Insurance Co.
Financial data (yr. ended 12/31/88): Assets, $790,152 (M); expenditures, $4,174, including $3,000 for 1 grant.
Purpose and activities: Grants for an arts fund.
Limitations: Giving primarily in the greater Utica, NY, area.
Application information: Application form required.
Deadline(s): First 15 days of each calendar quarter
Write: John R. Zapisek, Treas.
Officers: W. Craig Heston,* Pres.; Wallace H. Watkins, V.P.; John P. Sullivan, Secy.; John R. Zapisek, Treas.
Directors:* Robert M. Best, Edward W. Duffy, John G. Haehl, Herbert P. Ladds, Jr., David R. Newcomb, Randall H. Pakula, Robert L. Tarnow, Donald B. Thrush.
Employer Identification Number: 161313450

2296
van Ameringen Foundation, Inc.
509 Madison Ave.
New York 10022 (212) 758-6221

Incorporated in 1950 in NY.
Donor(s): Arnold Louis van Ameringen.†
Financial data (yr. ended 12/31/88): Assets, $26,580,353 (M); expenditures, $1,738,704, including $1,492,257 for 42 grants (high: $108,996).
Purpose and activities: Grants chiefly to promote mental health and social welfare through preventive measures, treatment, and rehabilitation; some general local giving.
Types of support: Operating budgets, continuing support, seed money, matching funds, special projects, research, publications.
Limitations: Giving primarily in the urban Northeast from Boston, MA, to Washington, DC, including NY and PA. No support for international activities and institutions in other countries, or for mental retardation, the physically handicapped, drug abuse, or alcoholism. No grants to individuals, or for annual campaigns, deficit financing, or emergency, capital, endowment funds, scholarships, or fellowships; no loans.
Publications: Annual report, informational brochure (including application guidelines).
Application information:
Initial approach: Proposal
Copies of proposal: 1
Deadline(s): 2 months before board meetings
Board meeting date(s): Mar., June, and Nov.
Final notification: Within 60 days
Write: Patricia Kind, Pres.
Officers and Directors: Patricia Kind, Pres., Treas., and C.E.O.; Lily vA. Auchincloss, V.P.; Harmon Duncombe, Secy.; Mrs. Arnold Louis van Ameringen, Honorary Chair.; Henry P. van Ameringen, Henry G. Walter, Jr.
Number of staff: 1 full-time professional; 1 full-time support.
Employer Identification Number: 136125699
Recent arts and culture grants:
Educational Broadcasting Corporation, NYC, NY, $50,000. For production of documentary entitled Who Lives, Who Dies. 11/19/87.
Museum of Modern Art, NYC, NY, $30,000. For support of Annual Fund. 11/19/87.
New York School for Circus Arts, NYC, NY, $10,000. Toward Clown Care Unit at St. Lukes Roosevelt Hospital Center. 11/19/87.

2297
H. van Ameringen Foundation
509 Madison Ave.
New York 10022

Established in 1950.
Donor(s): Henry van Ameringen, Mrs. Arnold Louis van Ameringen.
Financial data (yr. ended 12/31/87): Assets, $320,362 (M); gifts received, $325,000; expenditures, $130,857, including $130,250 for 26 grants (high: $25,000; low: $500).
Purpose and activities: Giving for cultural programs, conservation, mental health, education, and social services.
Limitations: Giving primarily in NY.
Application information: Applications not accepted.
Trustee: Henry van Ameringen.
Employer Identification Number: 136215329

2298
G. Unger Vetlesen Foundation
c/o Fulton, Duncombe, and Rowe
30 Rockefeller Plaza
New York 10112 (212) 586-0700

Incorporated in 1955 in NY.
Donor(s): George Unger Vetlesen.†
Financial data (yr. ended 12/31/87): Assets, $32,794,108 (M); expenditures, $1,452,381, including $1,294,825 for 29 grants (high: $250,000; low: $5,000; average: $5,000-$50,000).
Purpose and activities: Established a biennial international science award for discoveries in the earth sciences; grants for biological, geophysical, and environmental research, including scholarships, and cultural organizations, including those emphasizing Norwegian-American relations and maritime interests. Support also for public policy research, and libraries.
Types of support: General purposes, special projects.
Limitations: No grants to individuals.
Application information:
Initial approach: Proposal
Copies of proposal: 1
Deadline(s): Nov. 1
Board meeting date(s): Dec.
Final notification: Positive determination, by Dec. 31; negative determination, no response
Write: George Rowe, Jr., Pres.
Officers and Directors: George Rowe, Jr., Pres.; Harmon Duncombe, V.P. and Treas.; Joseph T.C. Hart, Secy.; Eugene P. Grisanti, Henry G. Walter, Jr.
Number of staff: None.
Employer Identification Number: 131982695

2299
Viacom International Corporate Contributions Program
1211 Ave. of the Americas
New York 10036 (212) 575-5175

Purpose and activities: Supports cultural institutions and children's programs.
Application information:
Write: Elizabeth A. Martin, Mgr., Corp. Communications

2300
The Vidda Foundation
c/o Carter, Carter, & Rupp
10 East 40th St., Suite 2103
New York 10016 (212) 696-4052

Established in 1979 in NY.
Donor(s): Ursula Corning.
Financial data (yr. ended 5/31/88): Assets, $980,544 (M); gifts received, $600,025; expenditures, $1,066,998, including $998,323 for 27 grants (high: $243,000; low: $750).
Purpose and activities: Giving primarily to educational projects, cultural programs, including an educational film-making company, church music funds, conservation, hospitals, and social services.
Types of support: General purposes, building funds, special projects, endowment funds, research, operating budgets.
Limitations: Giving primarily in NY. No grants to individuals.
Application information:
Initial approach: Letter or proposal
Copies of proposal: 3
Deadline(s): Submit proposal preferably in Oct. and Apr.
Board meeting date(s): Nov. and May
Final notification: 2 months
Write: Gerald E. Rupp, Mgr.
Trustees: Gerald E. Rupp, Mgr.; Ann Fraser Brewer, Ursula Corning, Thomas T. Fraser, Christophe Velay.
Number of staff: 2 part-time professional; 1 part-time support.
Employer Identification Number: 132981105

2301
Doris Warner Vidor Foundation, Inc.
317 East 64th St.
New York 10021

Established in 1972.
Financial data (yr. ended 11/30/86): Assets, $1,817,247 (M); expenditures, $203,774, including $192,280 for 77 grants (high: $30,000; low: $50).
Purpose and activities: Emphasis on cultural programs; support also for higher and secondary education, health, and hospitals.
Limitations: Giving primarily in the greater New York City, NY, metropolitan area.
Application information: Applications not accepted.
Officers: Warner Leroy, Pres.; Quentin Vidor, V.P.; Lewis Brian Vidor, Secy.; Linda Janklow, Treas.
Employer Identification Number: 237252504

2302
Vinmont Foundation, Inc.
888 East 19th St.
Brooklyn 11230 (718) 377-0178

Incorporated in 1947 in NY.
Donor(s): Lily H. Weinberg,† Robert C. Weinberg.†
Financial data (yr. ended 12/31/87): Assets, $1,421,497 (M); gifts received, $50,000; expenditures, $127,835, including $111,300 for 86 grants (high: $6,000; low: $250).
Purpose and activities: Giving primarily for black and Native American development nationally; and for social service agencies, urban planning, and restoration in metropolitan New York City.
Types of support: Operating budgets, continuing support, annual campaigns, seed money, emergency funds.
Limitations: Giving primarily in the New York, NY, metropolitan area; national support for minorities. No grants to individuals, or for capital or endowment funds, research, special projects, publications, conferences, scholarships, fellowships, or matching gifts; no loans.
Publications: Program policy statement.
Application information: Rarely funds unsolicited proposals.
Initial approach: Letter or proposal
Copies of proposal: 1
Deadline(s): None
Board meeting date(s): Feb., Apr., Sept., and Nov.
Final notification: 6 months
Write: William R. Nye, Treas.
Officers: Myron S. Isaacs, Pres.; Ethel E. Wortis, Secy.; William R. Nye, Treas.
Director: L. Franklyn Lowenstein.
Number of staff: None.
Employer Identification Number: 131577203

2303
The Laura B. Vogler Foundation, Inc.
P.O. Box 94
Bayside 11361 (718) 423-3000

Incorporated in 1959 in NY.
Donor(s): Laura B. Vogler,† John J. Vogler.†
Financial data (yr. ended 10/31/88): Assets, $3,254,901 (M); expenditures, $189,886, including $135,500 for 61 grants (high: $5,000; low: $1,000; average: $2,000-$5,000).
Purpose and activities: Giving for education, youth assistance, community services, and health care.
Types of support: Seed money, emergency funds, special projects, research, scholarship funds.
Limitations: Giving limited to the New York, NY, metropolitan area, including Long Island. No grants to individuals, or for building or endowment funds, annual fundraising campaigns, or matching gifts; no loans.
Publications: Annual report (including application guidelines).
Application information: Application form required.
Initial approach: Letter
Copies of proposal: 1
Deadline(s): 30 days prior to board meeting
Board meeting date(s): Jan., Apr., July, and Oct.
Final notification: 2 to 3 months
Write: D. Donald D'Amato, Pres.
Officers and Trustees: D. Donald D'Amato, Pres. and C.E.O.; Lawrence L. D'Amato, Secy.-Treas.; Max L. Kupferberg, I. Jerry Lasurdo, Stanley C. Pearson, Robert T. Waldbauer, Karen M. Yost.
Number of staff: 2 part-time professional.
Employer Identification Number: 116022241
Recent arts and culture grants:
New York Hall of Science, Corona, NY, $5,000. To expand volunteer program. 1987.

2304
DeWitt Wallace-Reader's Digest Fund, Inc.
(Formerly DeWitt Wallace Fund, Inc.)
1270 Ave. of the Americas, Suite 2118
New York 10020 (212) 397-6630

Incorporated in 1965 in NY.
Donor(s): DeWitt Wallace.†
Financial data (yr. ended 12/31/87): Assets, $454,943,758 (M); expenditures, $6,230,474, including $6,124,400 for 130 grants (high: $1,000,000; low: $5,000; average: $15,000-$80,000).
Purpose and activities: Support primarily for independent schools and activities fostering qualities of leadership and character in young people, including endowed scholarship programs at independent secondary schools, and educational projects; some support also for conservation programs, zoology, and cultural programs.
Types of support: Operating budgets, continuing support, internships, scholarship funds, exchange programs, special projects.
Limitations: Giving primarily in New York City and the northeast; some support for national programs. No support for public television, film, or media projects; colleges and universities; local chapters of national organizations; religious, fraternal, or veterans' organizations; government and public policy organizations; or private foundations. No grants to individuals, or for annual campaigns, endowments, emergency or capital funds, deficit financing, or scholarly research; no loans.
Publications: Biennial report (including application guidelines).
Application information: Funds largely committed; most projects initiated by the Fund; proposals considered for funding from only one Wallace Fund per year.
Initial approach: Brief letter (no more than 3 pages)
Copies of proposal: 1
Deadline(s): None
Board meeting date(s): 3 times per year
Final notification: 8 to 10 weeks
Write: M. Christine DeVita, Treas.
Officers: George V. Grune,* Chair. and Pres.; Donald C. Platten,* Secy.; M. Christine DeVita, Treas., Exec. Dir., and General Counsel.
Directors:* Richard F. McLoughlin, Kenneth O. Gilmore, William G. Bowen, Laurance S. Rockefeller.
Number of staff: 7
Employer Identification Number: 136183757
Recent arts and culture grants:
Alternate ROOTS (Regional Organization of Theaters South), Atlanta, GA, $7,500. For 1987 performance festival. 1987.
Alvin Ailey American Dance Theater, NYC, NY, $25,000. For new works. Grant made through Dance Theater Foundation. 1987.
American Associates of the Royal Academy Trust, NYC, NY, $12,500. For exchanges of US-UK art exhibits. 1987.
American Dance Festival, Durham, NC, $5,000. For Young Choreographers and Composers in Residence Program. 1987.
American Federation of Musicians, NYC, NY, $10,000. For general support of 1987 Congress of Strings. 1987.
American Museum of Natural History, NYC, NY, $50,000. For renovation of Theodore Roosevelt Hall. 1987.
Arena Stage, DC, $25,000. For play development program. Grant made through Washington Drama Society. 1987.
Artpark, Lewiston, NY, $10,000. For Artists-in-Residence Program. Grant made through Natural Heritage Trust. 1987.
Berkshire Theater Festival, Stockbridge, MA, $5,000. For operating support. 1987.
Boston Symphony Orchestra, Boston, MA, $25,000. To endow annual Reader's Digest Fellowship for composer at Tanglewood Music Center. 1987.
Bronx Arts Ensemble, Bronx, NY, $5,000. For operating support. 1987.
Center Theater Group of Los Angeles, Los Angeles, CA, $25,000. For year-long residency by Spalding Gray and other new work. 1987.
Childrens Museum, Boston, MA, $50,000. For Early Adolescent Initiative. 1987.
Colorado Dance Festival, Boulder, CO, $7,500. For Phase II of Jazz Tap Project. 1987.
Columbia University, Teachers College, NYC, NY, $75,000. To support Writing Project's expansion into teaching reading. 1987.
Dance Theater Workshop, NYC, NY, $7,500. To support production of performances by emerging choreographers. 1987.
Dance USA, DC, $5,000. To support needs assessment for national commissioning program. 1987.
Ensemble Studio Theater, NYC, NY, $15,000. Toward support for annual Marathon of new one-act plays. 1987.
Eugene ONeill Memorial Theater Center, Waterford, CT, $10,000. For National Opera/Music Theater Conference. 1987.
Exploratorium, San Francisco, CA, $20,000. For Explainers program, in which high school students act as museum guides. 1987.
Feld Ballet, NYC, NY, $15,000. For support of New Ballet School which provides free dance training for public school children in New York City. Grant made through Original Ballet Foundation. 1987.
Glimmerglass Opera Theater, Cooperstown, NY, $20,000. For program development and planning. 1987.
Group I Acting Company, NYC, NY, $7,500. For support of new production of Eric Overmyer's On the Verge. 1987.
Haleakala, The Kitchen, NYC, NY, $7,500. For 1987/88 Theater Series. 1987.
Harlem School of the Arts, NYC, NY, $10,000. For operating support. 1987.

House Foundation for the Arts, NYC, NY, $10,000. To support creation of new work by Meredith Monk. 1987.
Joffrey Ballet, Foundation for the, NYC, NY, $50,000. For new ballets. 1987.
Joyce Theater Foundation, NYC, NY, $7,500. For Sampler Series. 1987.
Long Wharf Theater, New Haven, CT, $10,000. For operating support. Grant made through Connecticut Players Foundation. 1987.
Manhattan Theater Club, NYC, NY, $15,000. For second stage play development program. 1987.
Metropolitan Museum of Art, NYC, NY, $120,000. To support videotape presentation of Lila Acheson Wallace Wing. 1987.
Millay Colony for the Arts, Austerlitz, NY, $10,000. For Reader's Digest Endowed Fellowships. 1987.
National Dance Institute, NYC, NY, $15,000. For operating support for in-school program of dance training for public school children. 1987.
New Business Ventures for Not-for-Profit Organizations, NYC, NY, $10,000. For operating support. 1987.
New York Botanical Garden, Bronx, NY, $100,000. For continued work on Hemlock Forest study. 1987.
New York Shakespeare Festival, NYC, NY, $50,000. To support new work. 1987.
New York Zoological Society, Bronx, NY, $15,000. To support work training program for Bronx Zoo's summer employees. 1987.
New York Zoological Society, NYC, NY, $1,000,000. For renovation of Central Park Zoo. 1987.
North Carolina School of the Arts Foundation, Winston-Salem, NC, $12,500. For Reader's Digest Endowed Scholarship Fund. 1987.
Old Globe Theater, San Diego, CA, $10,000. For Play Discovery Festival. 1987.
Opera Orchestra of New York, NYC, NY, $5,000. To support Young Artists Program. 1987.
Paul Taylor Dance Company, NYC, NY, $25,000. To support new work by Paul Taylor. 1987.
Philharmonic-Symphony Society of New York, Music Assistance Fund, NYC, NY, $16,000. To support Reader's Digest Endowed Fellowship for minority musician. 1987.
Pierpont Morgan Library, NYC, NY, $15,000. For operating support. 1987.
Preservation League of New York State, Albany, NY, $5,000. For Architectural Heritage Year 1986 and general support. 1987.
Saint Lukes Performing Arts Ensemble, NYC, NY, $7,500. For operating support. 1987.
Society of Illustrators, NYC, NY, $10,000. For annual scholarship competition for art students. 1987.
Spanish Theater Repertory Company, NYC, NY, $15,000. For Playwright-in-Residence program. 1987.
Sundance Institute for Film and Television, Salt Lake City, UT, $10,000. To support dance/film laboratory. 1987.
University of Manitoba, Manitoba, Canada, $50,000. For Endowed Scholarship Fund for Canadian women who wish to pursue graduate studies in fine art in U. S.. 1987.
Visual Communicators Education Fund, NYC, NY, $7,500. For scholarships for graphic arts and advertising design students. 1987.
Vivian Beaumont Theater, NYC, NY, $100,000. To support production of new works at Lincoln Center Theater. 1987.
Westchester Conservatory of Music, White Plains, NY, $20,000. For Reader's Digest Endowed Scholarship Fund, now designated for minority and disadvantaged students. 1987.
YM-YWHA, 92nd Street, NYC, NY, $55,000. To support pilot literature project for high school students. 1987.

2305
Lila Wallace-Reader's Digest Fund, Inc.

(Formerly L.A.W. Fund, Inc.)
1270 Ave. of the Americas, Suite 2118
New York 10020 (212) 397-6630

Incorporated in 1956 in NY.
Donor(s): Lila Acheson Wallace.†
Financial data (yr. ended 12/31/87): Assets, $338,892,056 (M); expenditures, $2,137,800, including $2,106,000 for 57 grants (high: $250,000; low: $5,000; average: $20,000-$60,000).
Purpose and activities: Support for the visual and performing arts, museums, conservation and beautification of the environment, and restoration of historic structures and gardens of particular historic interest; limited support for the areas of arts in education, and youth services.
Types of support: Operating budgets, continuing support, special projects, general purposes.
Limitations: Giving primarily in New York City and the northeast; some support for national programs. No support for public television, film, or media projects; colleges and universities; local chapters of national organizations; religious, fraternal, or veterans' organizations; government and public policy organizations; or private foundations. No grants to individuals, or for annual campaigns, building or endowment funds, capital purposes, or scholarly research.
Publications: Biennial report (including application guidelines).
Application information: Funds largely committed; most new projects initiated by the fund; proposals considered for funding from only 1 Wallace Fund per year.
Initial approach: Letter (no more than 3 pages)
Copies of proposal: 1
Deadline(s): None
Board meeting date(s): 3 times a year
Final notification: 8 to 12 weeks
Write: M. Christine DeVita, Treas.
Officers: George V. Grune,* Chair. and Pres.; Donald C. Platten,* Secy.; M. Christine DeVita, Treas., Exec. Dir., and General Counsel.
Directors:* William G. Bowen, Kenneth O. Gilmore, Richard F. Loughlin, Laurance S. Rockefeller.
Number of staff: 11
Employer Identification Number: 136086859
Recent arts and culture grants:
American Repertory Theater, Cambridge, MA, $50,000. For new works initiative. 1987.
American Trust for the British Library, Cambridge, MA, $10,000. For general support. 1987.
Appalshop, Whitesburg, KY, $5,000. To support Roadside Theater's plays-in-progress. 1987.
Ballet Theater Foundation, American Ballet Theater, NYC, NY, $50,000. For commissioned ballet by Clark Tippet and other new work. 1987.
Berkeley Repertory Theater, Berkeley, CA, $25,000. For new work by Amlin Gray and the Parallel Season. 1987.
Brooklyn Academy of Music, Brooklyn, NY, $50,000. For new opera/music theater initiative. 1987.
Brooklyn Botanic Garden Corporation, Brooklyn, NY, $10,000. For Children's Garden Program. 1987.
Bucket Dance Theater, Rochester, NY, $15,000. For new work by Garth Fagan. 1987.
Chicago Theater Group, Goodman Theater, Chicago, IL, $25,000. For new work. 1987.
Creative Time, NYC, NY, $5,000. For free dance performances in Central Park. 1987.
Dance Theater of Harlem, NYC, NY, $50,000. For development of new full-length production by Arthur Mitchell and Billy Wilson. 1987.
Dance Works, NYC, NY, $5,000. For The Space at Pentacle. 1987.
Dancing in the Streets, Brooklyn, NY, $5,000. To support Grand Central Dances. 1987.
Danspace Project, NYC, NY, $5,000. For performers' fees for 1987 season. 1987.
Dean Dance and Music Foundation, NYC, NY, $15,000. For development of new work by Laura Dean. 1987.
Drawing Center, NYC, NY, $25,000. To support viewing program and Selections shows. 1987.
Field Papers, NYC, NY, $5,000. For new work by Dana Reitz. 1987.
Foundation of the Dramatists Guild, NYC, NY, $10,000. To support free playwrighting in public high schools. 1987.
Institute for Art and Urban Resources, Long Island City, NY, $25,000. To support National Studio Program. 1987.
Institute of Contemporary Art, Boston, MA, $50,000. For education programs. 1987.
John F. Kennedy Center for the Performing Arts, DC, $125,000. To support Center's 1987-88 and 1988-89 ballet seasons. 1987.
Lubovitch Dance Foundation, NYC, NY, $5,000. For new work by Lar Lubovitch. 1987.
Lucinda Childs Dance Foundation, NYC, NY, $15,000. For new works by Ms. Childs. 1987.
Marlboro School of Music, Philadelphia, PA, $7,500. For Marlboro Music, training and performance program for young musicians. 1987.
Meet the Composer, NYC, NY, $250,000. To support music commissioning program. 1987.
Meet the Composer, NYC, NY, $100,000. To support Orchestra Residencies Program. 1987.
Music-Theater Performing Group, Lenox Arts Center, NYC, NY, $30,000. For production support for Vienna: Lusthaus and other works

by Martha Clarke and to help replace destroyed sets and costumes. 1987.
National Gallery of Art, DC, $50,000. For Patrons' Permanent Fund for acquisition of new works. 1987.
New York City Hispanic-American Dance Company, NYC, NY, $10,000. For Reader's Digest Scholarships for low-income students at Ballet Hispanico's School. 1987.
New York Historical Society, NYC, NY, $10,000. For operating expenses. 1987.
Pacific Northwest Ballet Association, Seattle, WA, $25,000. For new works by Ian Horvath and Kent Stowell. 1987.
Pennsylvania Ballet Association, Philadelphia, PA, $25,000. For new ballets. 1987.
Pick Up Performance Company, NYC, NY, $15,000. For new works by David Gordon. 1987.
Second Stage Theater, NYC, NY, $15,000. For Coastal Disturbances by Tina Howe and other works. 1987.
Smithsonian Institution, DC, $50,000. For gardens and mural in public concourse of new Quadrangle building. 1987.
Spoleto Festival USA, Charleston, SC, $105,000. For chamber music series by young professional musicians. 1987.
Studio Museum in Harlem, NYC, NY, $25,000. To expand in-school arts in education program. 1987.
Symphony Space, NYC, NY, $30,000. To support Selected Shorts programs. 1987.
Symphony Space, NYC, NY, $15,000. For Wall to Wall concerts, 12-hour free music marathons. 1987.
Theater and Arts Foundation of San Diego County, La Jolla Playhouse, La Jolla, CA, $50,000. For two new productions on second stage. 1987.
Theaterworks/USA, NYC, NY, $15,000. For operating support for children's theater. 1987.
Trinity Repertory Company, Providence, RI, $25,000. For new work. 1987.
Trisha Brown Dance Company, NYC, NY, $15,000. For new work by Trisha Brown. 1987.
Twyla Tharp Dance Foundation, NYC, NY, $25,000. For new work by Twyla Tharp. 1987.
Volunteer Lawyers for the Arts, NYC, NY, $10,000. For operating support for legal services program for artists. 1987.
Young Concert Artists, NYC, NY, $5,000. For operating support. 1987.

2306
Miriam G. and Ira D. Wallach Foundation

100 Park Ave.
New York 10017

Incorporated in 1956 in NY.
Financial data (yr. ended 10/31/86): Assets, $12,561,300 (M); gifts received, $301,963; expenditures, $1,209,766, including $1,154,073 for 91 grants (high: $285,000; low: $100; average: $500-$25,000).
Purpose and activities: Support primarily for higher education, and international relations, including peace; some support for social services, Jewish organizations, and cultural programs.
Limitations: Giving primarily in NY.
Officers: Ira D. Wallach,* Pres.; Edgar Wachenheim III,* V.P.; James G. Wallach,* V.P.; Kenneth L. Wallach,* V.P.; Miriam G. Wallach,* V.P.; Peter C. Siegfried, Secy.; Benjamin Glowatz, Treas.
Directors:* Sue W. Wachenheim, Kate B. Wallach, Mary K. Wallach, Susan S. Wallach.
Employer Identification Number: 136101702

2307
Warner Communications Foundation, Inc.

c/o Warner Communications, Inc.
75 Rockefeller Plaza
New York 10019 (212) 484-8022

Established in 1959.
Donor(s): Warner Communications, Inc.
Financial data (yr. ended 9/30/87): Assets, $174,802 (M); expenditures, $735,000, including $735,000 for 8 grants (high: $250,000; low: $10,000).
Purpose and activities: Support for hospitals, museums, cultural programs and historic preservation, and education. Due to changes within the company, no new grants currently being awarded; foundation continues to make payments on earlier commitments.
Limitations: Giving primarily in NY.
Application information: Applications currently not accepted.
Write: Mary E. McCarthy, Dir. of Corp. Contribs.
Officers and Directors:* Deane F. Johnson,* Chair.; Warren A. Christie, V.P.; Eli T. Bruno, Secy.; David R. Haas,* Treas.
Administrator: Mary E. McCarthy, Dir. of Corp. Contribs.
Employer Identification Number: 136085361

2308
Frank Weeden Foundation

11 Broadway
New York 10004 (212) 344-8470

Established about 1963 in CA.
Donor(s): Frank Weeden,† Alan N. Weeden, Donald E. Weeden, John D. Weeden, Mabel H. Weeden, William F. Weeden, M.D.
Financial data (yr. ended 6/30/88): Assets, $20,138,362 (M); expenditures, $719,931, including $576,966 for 36 grants (high: $152,000; low: $1,000; average: $10,000-$20,000).
Purpose and activities: Giving primarily to environmental organizations working to insure species diversity, and organizations working to keep population within the limits of the world's resources to sustain them; giving also for youth, the arts, and education.
Types of support: General purposes, land acquisition.
Limitations: No grants to individuals.
Publications: Annual report.
Application information:
Initial approach: Letter
Copies of proposal: 1
Deadline(s): None
Board meeting date(s): Mar., June, Sept., and Dec.
Write: Alan N. Weeden, Pres.
Officers and Directors: Alan N. Weeden, Pres.; William F. Weeden, V.P.; John D. Weeden, Secy.-Treas.; Donald E. Weeden.
Number of staff: 1 part-time support.
Employer Identification Number: 946109313

2309
The Louis A. Wehle Foundation

445 St. Paul St.
Rochester 14605

Established in 1952 in NY.
Donor(s): Genesee Brewing Co., Inc.
Financial data (yr. ended 4/30/87): Assets, $735,640 (M); gifts received, $75,000; expenditures, $120,286, including $115,150 for 22 grants (high: $53,000; low: $100).
Purpose and activities: Grants primarily for social services, culture, and education.
Types of support: General purposes, building funds, annual campaigns, capital campaigns, continuing support, equipment, operating budgets.
Limitations: Giving primarily in the greater Rochester, NY, area.
Application information:
Initial approach: Proposal
Copies of proposal: 1
Deadline(s): None
Board meeting date(s): As required
Final notification: Following board meeting
Write: John L. Wehle, Jr., Trustee
Trustees: John L. Wehle, Sr., John L. Wehle, Jr., Marjorie S. Wehle, Robert G. Wehle.
Employer Identification Number: 166027209

2310
Theodore & Renee Weiler Foundation, Inc.

16 North Chatsworth Ave.
Larchmont 10538

Established in 1965 in NY.
Donor(s): Theodore R. Weiler.
Financial data (yr. ended 12/31/87): Assets, $1,766,202 (M); expenditures, $77,411, including $67,179 for 61 grants (high: $10,000; low: $50).
Purpose and activities: Grants for Jewish giving, culture, education, and health and social services.
Limitations: Giving primarily in New York City, NY, and Palm Beach, FL.
Application information: Contributes only to pre-selected organizations. Applications not accepted.
Trustees: Theodore R. Weiler, Pres.; Alan Safir, V.P.; Rhoda Weiler, Secy.; Richard Kandel, Treas.
Employer Identification Number: 136181441

2311
Sanford I. Weill Charitable Foundation, Inc.

65 East 55th St.
New York 10022 (212) 891-8878

Donor(s): Sanford I. Weill.
Financial data (yr. ended 12/31/87): Assets, $1,048,295 (M); gifts received, $2,625;

expenditures, $35,327, including $34,375 for 16 grants (high: $10,000; low: $275).
Purpose and activities: Support for culture, social services, and the aged.
Limitations: Giving primarily in NY.
Application information: Application form required.
Deadline(s): None
Write: Sanford I. Weill, Pres.
Officers: Sanford I. Weill, Pres.; Kenneth J. Bialkin, Mgr.; Joan H. Weill, Mgr.
Employer Identification Number: 136223609

2312
Kurt Weill Foundation for Music, Inc.
Seven East 20th St.
New York 10003 (212) 505-5240

Established in 1962.
Donor(s): Lotte Lenya.†
Financial data (yr. ended 12/31/86): Assets, $1,652,794 (M); gifts received, $25; expenditures, $349,002, including $19,000 for 8 grants (high: $5,000; low: $1,000), $47,000 for 2 grants to individuals and $140,013 for 3 foundation-administered programs.
Purpose and activities: A private operating foundation; programs include maintenance of archives and research center and production consultation. Awards grants to organizations and individuals for projects "intended to promote greater understanding of the artistic legacies of Kurt Weill or Lotte Lenya."
Types of support: Research, publications, fellowships, grants to individuals, special projects.
Publications: Informational brochure (including application guidelines), newsletter.
Application information: Application form required.
Initial approach: Letter, proposal
Copies of proposal: 1
Deadline(s): Nov. 15
Final notification: Feb. 1
Write: David Farneth, Dir.
Officers and Trustees: Kim Kowalke, Pres.; Henry Marx, V.P.; Lys Symonette, V.P.; Milton Coleman, Treas.; Harold Prince, Julius Rudel, Guy Stern.
Number of staff: 4 full-time professional; 2 full-time support; 1 part-time support.
Employer Identification Number: 136139518

2313
Harold M. & Anna M. Weinberg Family Foundation, Inc.
25 Robert Pitt Dr.
Monsey 10952

Established in 1956 in NY.
Donor(s): Edward Weinberg, James Weinberg.
Financial data (yr. ended 12/31/87): Assets, $85,246 (M); gifts received, $68,000; expenditures, $120,625, including $119,355 for 91 grants (high: $72,500; low: $10).
Purpose and activities: Support primarily for Jewish welfare; some support for cultural programs and health.
Application information: Contributes only to pre-selected charitable organizations. Applications not accepted.
Officers: James Weinberg, Pres.; Edward Weinberg, Treas.
Employer Identification Number: 136160074

2314
Wellington Foundation, Inc.
14 Wall St., Suite 1702
New York 10005

Incorporated in 1955 in NY.
Donor(s): Herbert G. Wellington,† Herbert G. Wellington, Jr., Elizabeth D. Wellington.†
Financial data (yr. ended 12/31/86): Assets, $1,947,172 (M); expenditures, $362,485, including $356,500 for 23 grants (high: $100,000; low: $1,000).
Purpose and activities: To support recognized medical, educational, and cultural programs.
Application information: Contributes only to pre-selected organizations. Applications not accepted.
Officers and Directors: Herbert G. Wellington, Jr., Pres. and Treas.; Patricia B. Wellington, V.P.; Thomas D. Wellington, Secy.
Employer Identification Number: 136110175

2315
The Margaret L. Wendt Foundation
1325 Liberty Bldg.
Buffalo 14202 (716) 855-2146

Trust established in 1956 in NY.
Donor(s): Margaret L. Wendt.†
Financial data (yr. ended 1/31/87): Assets, $41,280,939 (M); expenditures, $1,474,839, including $970,031 for 71 grants (high: $80,000; low: $200; average: $5,000-$15,000).
Purpose and activities: Emphasis on education, the arts, and social services; support also for churches and religious organizations, health associations, public interest organizations, and youth agencies.
Limitations: Giving primarily in Buffalo and western NY. No grants to individuals, or for scholarships.
Application information:
Initial approach: Letter
Copies of proposal: 4
Deadline(s): 1 month prior to board meeting
Board meeting date(s): Quarterly; no fixed dates
Final notification: Usually 4 to 6 months
Write: Robert J. Kresse, Secy.
Officers and Trustees: Ralph W. Loew, Chair.; Robert J. Kresse, Secy.; Thomas D. Lunt.
Number of staff: 1 part-time support.
Employer Identification Number: 166030037

2316
Nina W. Werblow Charitable Trust
c/o Ehrenkranz, Ehrenkranz and Schultz
375 Park Ave.
New York 10152 (212) 751-5959

Trust established in NY.
Donor(s): Nina W. Werblow.†
Financial data (yr. ended 2/28/87): Assets, $4,910,725 (M); expenditures, $227,669, including $160,207 for 47 grants (high: $21,707; low: $500).
Purpose and activities: Giving for hospitals, Jewish welfare organizations, higher education, social service agencies, and cultural programs.
Limitations: Giving primarily in New York City, NY.
Application information:
Initial approach: Letter
Deadline(s): Sept. 30
Write: Roger A. Goldman, Trustee
Trustees: Lillian Ahrens Carver, Joel S. Ehrenkranz, Roger A. Goldman.
Employer Identification Number: 136742999

2317
The Western New York Foundation
Main Seneca Bldg., Suite 1402
237 Main St.
Buffalo 14203 (716) 847-6440

Incorporated in 1951 in NY as The Wildroot Foundation; present name adopted in 1958.
Donor(s): Welles V. Moot.†
Financial data (yr. ended 7/31/88): Assets, $4,082,009 (M); expenditures, $267,233, including $195,282 for 18 grants (high: $50,000; low: $320; average: $10-$15,000).
Purpose and activities: Grants to nonprofit institutions, with emphasis on capital needs, seed funds for new projects, or expanding services. Support primarily for the performing arts, youth agencies, the natural sciences, and social service agencies.
Types of support: Seed money, building funds, equipment, land acquisition, endowment funds, special projects, publications, conferences and seminars, matching funds, loans, capital campaigns, renovation projects, technical assistance.
Limitations: Giving limited to the 8th Judicial District of NY (Erie, Niagara, Genesee, Wyoming, Allegany, Cattaraugus, and Chautauqua counties). No support for hospitals or religious organizations. No grants to individuals, or for scholarships, fellowships, or generally for operating budgets or deficit financing.
Publications: Annual report.
Application information: Application form required.
Initial approach: Letter (not more than 1 and 1/2 pages) and a copy of IRS exemption letter
Copies of proposal: 2
Deadline(s): None
Board meeting date(s): 3 or 4 times a year
Final notification: 6 to 8 weeks
Write: Welles V. Moot, Jr., Pres.
Officers and Trustees: Welles V. Moot, Jr., Pres.; Cecily M. Johnson, V.P.; Robert S. Scheu, V.P.; John R. Moot, Secy.; Richard Moot, Treas.; John N. Walsh III.
Number of staff: 1 full-time professional.
Employer Identification Number: 160845962

2318
The Whitehead Foundation
c/o Goldman, Sachs & Co.
85 Broad St., 30th Fl.
New York 10004

Established in 1982 in NY.
Donor(s): John C. Whitehead Foundation.
Financial data (yr. ended 6/30/87): Assets, $19,298,805 (M); gifts received, $732,500; expenditures, $376,762, including $316,625 for 49 grants (high: $50,000; low: $500).
Purpose and activities: Giving for higher education, church support, the arts, and civic organizations.
Limitations: Giving primarily in NY and NJ.
Trustees: Arthur G. Altschul, John L. Weinberg, Jaan W. Whitehead, John C. Whitehead.
Employer Identification Number: 133119344

2319
Mrs. Giles Whiting Foundation
30 Rockefeller Plaza
New York 10112 (212) 698-2500

Incorporated in 1963 in NY.
Donor(s): Mrs. Giles Whiting.†
Financial data (yr. ended 11/30/87): Assets, $18,719,916 (M); expenditures, $1,423,557, including $936,700 for 9 grants (high: $300,000; low: $1,700; average: $25,000-$150,000) and $163,000 for 10 grants to individuals.
Purpose and activities: Grants only to seven graduate schools conducting programs of Whiting Fellowships in the Humanities. Support also for emerging writers through Whiting Writers' Awards.
Types of support: Fellowships, grants to individuals.
Limitations: No grants to individuals (except for Whiting Writers' Award program for which applications are not invited), or for general support, capital funds, matching gifts, research, special projects, publications, or conferences; no loans.
Publications: Multi-year report.
Application information: Funds fully committed. Applications not accepted.
Board meeting date(s): May and Nov.
Write: Robert H.M. Ferguson, Secy.
Officers: Robert M. Pennoyer,* Pres.; Mary St. John Douglas,* V.P.; Harry W. Havemeyer,* V.P.; Robert H.M. Ferguson, Secy.-Treas.
Trustees:* Robert L. Belknap.
Number of staff: 1 full-time professional; 2 part-time professional.
Employer Identification Number: 136154484

2320
Lawrence A. Wien Foundation, Inc.
c/o Wien, Malkin & Bettex
60 East 42nd St.
New York 10165

Incorporated in 1953 in NY.
Donor(s): Lawrence A. Wien, Mae L. Wien, and others.
Financial data (yr. ended 6/30/87): Assets, $5,052,133 (M); expenditures, $1,529,988, including $1,516,020 for 275 grants (low: $100).
Purpose and activities: Grants primarily for higher education, Jewish religious and social organizations and welfare funds, cultural programs, and social services; support also for hospitals and health services.
Limitations: Giving primarily in New York, NY.
Application information:
Write: Lawrence A. Wien, Pres.
Officers and Directors: Lawrence A. Wien, Pres. and Treas.; Peter L. Malkin, Secy.; Isabel W. Malkin, Enid W. Morse, Lester S. Morse, Jr.
Employer Identification Number: 136095927

2321
The Wikstrom Foundation
c/o Norstar Trust Co.
P.O. Box 43
Syracuse 13202 (315)4247-707

Established in 1960 in NY.
Donor(s): A.S. Wikstrom.†
Financial data (yr. ended 12/31/86): Assets, $1,896,822 (M); gifts received, $21,001; expenditures, $158,637, including $132,323 for grants (high: $50,000; average: $1,000-$20,000).
Purpose and activities: Grants primarily for cultural programs and higher education; support also for programs for the elderly, and for Roman Catholic organizations, including church support.
Types of support: Operating budgets, annual campaigns, building funds, equipment, endowment funds, matching funds, capital campaigns, conferences and seminars, continuing support, general purposes, publications, renovation projects, research, seed money, special projects.
Limitations: Giving limited to NY and FL. No grants to individuals; no loans.
Application information:
Initial approach: Letter
Deadline(s): None
Write: Roderick Brace, Trust Officer, Norstar Trust Co.
Trustee: Norstar Trust Co.
Number of staff: None.
Employer Identification Number: 146014286

2322
John Wiley & Sons Corporate Contributions Program
605 Third Ave.
New York 10158 (212) 850-6000

Financial data (yr. ended 4/30/88): $188,300 for employee matching gifts.
Purpose and activities: Support for AIDS, animal welfare, the arts, including dance, film, music, theater, fine and performing arts, hunger, the homeless, international affairs, literacy, and education, including education for minorities.
Types of support: Annual campaigns, capital campaigns, employee matching gifts, fellowships, lectureships, publications, scholarship funds.
Limitations: Giving primarily in New York City, NY.
Application information: Applications not accepted.
Write: Deborah E. Wiley, Vice-Chair.
Number of staff: 2 part-time support.

2323
Elaine P. and Richard U. Wilson Foundation
c/o Chase Lincoln First Bank, N.A.
P.O. Box 1412
Rochester 14603

Established in 1963 in NY.
Donor(s): Katherine M. Wilson.†
Financial data (yr. ended 12/31/86): Assets, $5,320,336 (M); expenditures, $429,333, including $412,750 for 16 grants (high: $250,000; low: $3,000).
Purpose and activities: Emphasis on higher and secondary education, Protestant church support, cultural programs, and museums.
Limitations: Giving primarily in NY.
Application information: Contributes only to pre-selected organizations. Applications not accepted.
Trustee: Chase Lincoln First Bank, N.A.
Employer Identification Number: 166042023

2324
Marie C. and Joseph C. Wilson Foundation
160 Allens Creek Rd.
Rochester 14618 (716) 461-4699

Trust established in 1963 in NY.
Donor(s): Katherine M. Wilson,† Joseph C. Wilson.†
Financial data (yr. ended 12/31/87): Assets, $9,274,197 (M); expenditures, $688,953, including $339,392 for 36 grants (high: $50,000; low: $100; average: $1,000-$25,000) and $32,487 for 1 foundation-administered program.
Purpose and activities: Giving primarily for social services, health and medical research, education, housing, and youth agencies; some support for the arts.
Types of support: Operating budgets, continuing support, annual campaigns, seed money, emergency funds, building funds, endowment funds, matching funds, internships, scholarship funds, fellowships, special projects, research, conferences and seminars.
Limitations: Giving primarily in Rochester, NY. No support for political organizations. No grants to individuals.
Publications: Annual report (including application guidelines).
Application information:
Initial approach: 1-page letter; submit full proposal only at request of foundation
Copies of proposal: 12
Deadline(s): 6 weeks before board meetings
Board meeting date(s): Feb., May, and Sept.; grants considered in Feb. and Sept. only
Final notification: 3 months
Write: Ruth H. Fleischmann, Exec. Dir.
Officer: Ruth H. Fleischmann, Exec. Dir.
Board of Managers: Janet C. Wilson, Pres.; Joan W. Dalbey, Marie O. Dalbey, Katherine Dalbey Ensign, Deidre Wilson Garton, Judith W. Martin, Katherine W. Roby, Deirdre Hart Wilson, J. Richard Wilson, Marie C. Wilson.
Trustee: Chase Lincoln First Bank, N.A.
Number of staff: 1 part-time professional; 1 part-time support.
Employer Identification Number: 166042022

2325
Robert Wilson Foundation
50 West 34th St., No. 23A14
New York 10001 (212) 586-7620

Trust established in 1964 in NY.
Donor(s): Robert W. Wilson, Marillyn B. Wilson.
Financial data (yr. ended 12/31/87): Assets, $212,842 (L); expenditures, $318,053, including $299,045 for 70 grants (high: $30,000; low: $100; average: $500-$25,000).
Purpose and activities: Emphasis on music, especially opera, social services, historic preservation, population control, the arts, and conservation.
Types of support: Building funds, equipment, land acquisition, matching funds, loans.
Limitations: Giving primarily in New York City, NY. No grants to individuals, or for endowment funds, research, scholarships, or fellowships.
Publications: Annual report.
Application information:
Initial approach: Telephone or proposal
Copies of proposal: 1
Deadline(s): Submit proposal preferably in Jan. or Feb.; no set deadline
Board meeting date(s): As required
Write: Robert W. Wilson, Trustee
Trustees: Marillyn B. Wilson, Robert W. Wilson.
Number of staff: None.
Employer Identification Number: 116037280

2326
The Winfield Foundation
c/o D. Troxell
342 Madison Ave., No. 1818
New York 10173 (212) 245-7580

Incorporated in 1941 in NY.
Donor(s): Frasier W. McCann,† Helena M. Charlton.†
Financial data (yr. ended 12/31/88): Assets, $1,410,188 (M); gifts received, $100,000; expenditures, $147,010, including $117,250 for 25 grants (high: $53,750; low: $500; average: $1,000-$5,000).
Purpose and activities: Emphasis on historic preservation, music, and hospitals.
Limitations: Giving primarily in NY. No grants to individuals, or for research-related programs, scholarships, fellowships, or matching gifts; no loans.
Application information:
Initial approach: Letter
Copies of proposal: 1
Board meeting date(s): Semiannually
Write: Franklin W. McCann, Pres.
Officers and Directors: Franklin W. McCann,* Pres.; Jonathan W. McCann,* V.P.; D. Chase Troxell, V.P. and Secy.; Helen Hooke, Secy.; Gordon S. Gavan.
Employer Identification Number: 136158017

2327
The Norman and Rosita Winston Foundation, Inc.
c/o Summit Rovins and Feldesman
445 Park Ave.
New York 10022 (212) 702-2200

Incorporated in 1954 in NY.
Donor(s): Norman K. Winston,† The N.K. Winston Foundation, Inc.
Financial data (yr. ended 12/31/87): Assets, $41,859,032 (M); gifts received, $500,268; expenditures, $2,447,001, including $2,002,500 for 85 grants (high: $150,000; low: $1,000; average: $5,000-$50,000).
Purpose and activities: Emphasis on higher education, including medical and theological education, hospitals, and cultural programs.
Types of support: General purposes.
Limitations: Giving primarily in NY. No grants to individuals.
Application information:
Initial approach: Proposal
Copies of proposal: 1
Deadline(s): None
Board meeting date(s): 2 to 4 times a year
Final notification: By the end of Dec.
Write: Joel M. Rudell, Secy.
Officers: Julian S. Perlman,* Pres.; Arthur Levitt, Jr.,* V.P. and Treas.; Joel M. Rudell, Secy.
Trustee: Simon H. Rifkind.
Number of staff: None.
Employer Identification Number: 136161672

2328
Robert Winthrop Charitable Trust
c/o Wood Struchers & Winthrop
P.O. Box 18
New York 10005

Financial data (yr. ended 11/30/87): Assets, $1,169,133 (M); gifts received, $277,161; expenditures, $257,003, including $239,965 for 88 grants (high: $30,000; low: $200).
Purpose and activities: Support primarily for wildlife preservation; support also for higher education, historic preservation, medical research and for museums.
Application information: Contributes only to pre-selected organizations. Applications not accepted.
Trustees: Cornelia Bonnie, Robert Winthrop.
Employer Identification Number: 237441147

2329
Woodner Foundation
660 Madison Ave.
New York 10021 (212) 644-0630

Established in 1960 in NY.
Donor(s): Ian Woodner.
Financial data (yr. ended 12/31/86): Assets, $34 (M); gifts received, $339,700; expenditures, $415,666, including $415,484 for 34 grants (high: $288,165; low: $100).
Purpose and activities: Emphasis on cultural programs, including museums, and a university.
Application information:
Initial approach: Letter
Deadline(s): None
Write: Ian Woodner, Pres.
Officers: Ian Woodner, Pres.; Paula Vial, V.P. and Secy.
Employer Identification Number: 136162669

2330
Wrightson-Ramsing Foundation, Inc.
c/o Trident Oil Corp.
375 Park Ave., Suite 3408
New York 10152 (212) 758-2835

Incorporated in 1952 in NY.
Donor(s): Martha Wrightson Ramsing.
Financial data (yr. ended 12/31/86): Assets, $1,636,071 (M); gifts received, $34,000; expenditures, $121,616, including $109,205 for grants (high: $50,000).
Purpose and activities: Grants primarily for cultural programs and museums, higher education, and welfare.
Application information:
Initial approach: Letter
Deadline(s): None
Write: Thor H. Ramsing, Pres.
Officers and Directors: Thor H. Ramsing, Pres. and Treas.; Martha Wrightson Ramsing, V.P.; Anthony A. Bliss, Byron L. Ramsing, Martha R. Zoubek.
Employer Identification Number: 131967462

2331
Wunsch Foundation, Inc.
841 63rd St.
Brooklyn 11220 (718) 238-2525

Incorporated in 1943 in NY.
Donor(s): Joseph W. Wunsch, Eric M. Wunsch, Samuel Wunsch, WEA Enterprises Co., Inc.
Financial data (yr. ended 12/31/87): Assets, $4,124,184 (M); gifts received, $30,000; expenditures, $242,291, including $228,250 for 14 grants (high: $71,250; low: $100).
Purpose and activities: Giving primarily for higher education, fine arts, museums, and Israel.
Limitations: No grants to individuals.
Application information:
Initial approach: Letter
Deadline(s): None
Write: Eric M. Wunsch, Pres.
Officers and Directors: Eric M. Wunsch, Pres.; Ethel Wunsch, Secy.
Employer Identification Number: 116006013

2332
Harold L. Wyman Foundation, Inc.
33 Puritan Dr.
Port Chester 10573

Established in 1965 in New York.
Financial data (yr. ended 9/30/87): Assets, $1,753,010 (M); expenditures, $67,988, including $56,150 for 30 grants (high: $7,000; low: $500).
Purpose and activities: Support for cultural activities, health associations, social services, and youth organizations.
Limitations: Giving primarily in NY.
Application information: Contributes only to pre-selected charitable organizations. Applications not accepted.

Initial approach: Letter
Write: Walter G. Korntheuer, Secy.
Officers: Otto Korntheuer,* Pres.; Walter C. Korntheuer, Secy.-Treas.
Trustees:* George C. Barron.
Employer Identification Number: 136201289

2333
William & Vina B. Yerdon Foundation
c/o First American Bank of New York
50 State St.
Albany 12207

Established in 1975 in NY.
Financial data (yr. ended 4/30/87): Assets, $1,231,011 (M); expenditures, $69,319, including $59,000 for 12 grants (high: $15,000; low: $1,000).
Purpose and activities: Support for community development, civic affairs, social services and cultural organizations.
Trustee: First American Bank of New York.
Employer Identification Number: 237366678

2334
Arthur Young & Company New York Combined Appeal Plan Trust
Arthur Young & Company
277 Park Ave.
New York 10172-0001 (212) 407-2600

Donor(s): Arthur Young and Co.
Financial data (yr. ended 7/31/87): Assets, $41,602 (M); gifts received, $68,492; expenditures, $67,255, including $67,200 for 17 grants (high: $45,400; low: $300).
Purpose and activities: Support for culture and the arts, the disabled, welfare programs, community and social services.
Limitations: Giving primarily in New York, NY. No grants to individuals.
Application information: Contributes only to preselected organizations. Applications not accepted.
Write: John Howell
Combined Appeal Committee: John Howell, Chair.; Mark Besca, Annette Ehrhart, George Kunath, Thomas McConville, Rosemarie Meschi, David Nugent, Mary O'Donnell, Janice Robertson, Phyllis Schlesinger.
Employer Identification Number: 237323557

2335
The Young & Rubicam Foundation
c/o R. John Cooper, Pres.
285 Madison Ave.
New York 10017 (212) 210-3000

Incorporated in 1955 in NY.
Donor(s): Young & Rubicam, Inc.
Financial data (yr. ended 12/31/86): Assets, $36,425 (M); gifts received, $558,102; expenditures, $575,425, including $463,719 for 106 grants (high: $83,300; low: $100) and $111,643 for 348 employee matching gifts.
Purpose and activities: Grants primarily for a matching gifts program; foundation directors initiate contributions for selected community funds, cultural programs, including the performing arts, community development, and youth agencies.
Types of support: Employee matching gifts.
Limitations: No grants to individuals, or for capital or endowment funds, scholarships, fellowships, operating budgets, continuing support, annual campaigns, seed money, emergency funds, deficit financing, special projects, research, publications, or conferences; no loans.
Application information: Applications not accepted.
Board meeting date(s): June and Nov.
Officers and Directors: R. John Cooper, Pres.; Joan Hafey, V.P.; Mark Stroock, V.P.; Robert Tallman, Jr., Secy.; Dennis E. Hewitt, Treas.
Number of staff: 5 part-time support.
Employer Identification Number: 136156199

2336
Youths' Friends Association, Inc.
c/o Seidman & Seidman
15 Columbus Circle
New York 10023
Application address: P.O. Box 5387, Hilton Head, SC 29938; Tel.: (803) 671-5060

Incorporated in 1950 in NY.
Donor(s): Johan J. Smit,† Mrs. Johan J. Smit.†
Financial data (yr. ended 12/31/87): Assets, $5,400,000 (M); expenditures, $252,000, including $172,500 for 85 grants (high: $15,000; low: $1,000).
Purpose and activities: Grants largely for character-building, with emphasis on higher and secondary education, health agencies, hospitals, youth agencies, child welfare, and music; some support also for churches and religious associations.
Limitations: No grants to individuals.
Application information:
Initial approach: Letter
Copies of proposal: 1
Deadline(s): None
Board meeting date(s): Semiannually
Write: Walter J. Graver, Secy.-Treas.
Officers and Directors: Herman J. Meinert, Pres.; Sheila Smit, V.P.; Walter Graver, Secy.-Treas.; Marion Meinert, Stephen C. Smit.
Employer Identification Number: 136097828

2337
Charles Zarkin Memorial Foundation, Inc.
c/o Wachtell, Lipton, Rosen & Katz
299 Park Ave.
New York 10171

Incorporated in 1969 in NY.
Donor(s): Fay Zarkin.†
Financial data (yr. ended 12/31/87): Assets, $3,778,819 (M); expenditures, $202,908, including $143,000 for 12 grants (high: $60,000; low: $3,000).
Purpose and activities: Emphasis on Jewish welfare funds, youth agencies, hospitals, higher education, and cultural programs.
Limitations: Giving primarily in New York, NY. No grants to individuals.
Application information: Contributes only to pre-selected organizations. Applications not accepted.
Board meeting date(s): Dec.
Officers: Martin Lipton,* Pres. and Treas.; Leonard Rosen,* V.P.; Estelle Oleck,* V.P.; Constance Monte, Secy.
Trustees:* Robert B. McKay, Lester Pollack.
Number of staff: None.
Employer Identification Number: 237149277

2338
The Zilkha Foundation, Inc.
30 Rockefeller Plaza
New York 10112-0153 (212) 765-8661

Incorporated in 1948 in NY.
Donor(s): Selim K. Zilkha, Ezra K. Zilkha, Zilkha & Sons, Inc.
Financial data (yr. ended 8/31/88): Assets, $161,781 (M); gifts received, $365,104; expenditures, $337,732, including $324,991 for 79 grants (high: $63,640; low: $55).
Purpose and activities: A small family foundation of which a large part of funds are designated for specific charities; grants primarily for higher education, Jewish welfare and educational funds, the performing arts, and intercultural organizations; support also for a hospital.
Limitations: No grants to individuals.
Application information: Grants awarded largely at the initiative of the officers.
Initial approach: Letter
Deadline(s): Aug. 31
Board meeting date(s): Dec.
Write: Ezra K. Zilkha, Pres.
Officers: Ezra K. Zilkha, Pres. and Treas.; Cecile E. Zilkha, V.P. and Secy.
Number of staff: None.
Employer Identification Number: 136090739

2339
Arthur Zimtbaum Foundation, Inc.
c/o Elihu H. Modlin
EAB Plaza
Uniondale 11506 (516) 294-2660

Incorporated in 1955 in NY.
Donor(s): Arthur Zimtbaum,† Rose B. LeVantine.
Financial data (yr. ended 12/31/87): Assets, $1,211,634 (M); expenditures, $169,638, including $139,000 for 19 grants (high: $20,000; low: $500).
Purpose and activities: Giving for medical research, cultural programs, and higher education.
Limitations: Giving primarily in NY.
Application information:
Initial approach: Written proposal
Deadline(s): None
Write: Rose B. LeVantine, Pres.
Officers: Rose B. LeVantine, Pres.; Elihu H. Modlin, V.P. and Secy.; Herbert Merin, Treas.
Directors: William J. Burke, Paulette L. LeVantine, Andrew Merin, Charles Modlin.
Employer Identification Number: 116016391

NORTH CAROLINA

2340
ABC Foundation
c/o Cone Mills Corp.
1201 Maple St.
Greensboro 27405

Trust established in 1944 in NC.
Donor(s): Cone Mills Corp.
Financial data (yr. ended 10/31/87): Assets, $4,035,019 (M); expenditures, $480,650, including $338,844 for 81 grants (high: $40,000; low: $300) and $60,633 for 49 grants to individuals.
Purpose and activities: Grants for higher education, community funds, culture, and child welfare.
Limitations: Giving limited to areas of company operations in NC. No grants to individuals.
Application information:
Initial approach: Letter
Copies of proposal: 1
Board meeting date(s): Annually and as required
Write: Lacy G. Baynes, Trustee
Trustees: Lacy G. Baynes, W.O. Leonard, Dewey L. Trogdon, North Carolina National Bank.
Employer Identification Number: 566040774

2341
Akers Foundation, Inc.
P.O. Box 2726
Gastonia 28053

Incorporated in 1955 in NC.
Financial data (yr. ended 12/31/87): Assets, $1,462,873 (M); expenditures, $129,287, including $109,530 for 55 grants (high: $12,500; low: $80).
Purpose and activities: Giving primarily for Protestant church support, education, and social services; support also for cultural programs.
Limitations: Giving primarily in NC.
Application information:
Deadline(s): None
Write: John M. Akers, Pres.
Officers: John M. Akers, Pres. and Treas.; C. Scott Akers, V.P.; Charles W. Akers, Secy.
Employer Identification Number: 566044428

2342
Mary Reynolds Babcock Foundation, Inc.
102 Reynolda Village
Winston-Salem 27106-5123 (919) 748-9222

Incorporated in 1953 in NC.
Donor(s): Mary Reynolds Babcock,† Charles H. Babcock.†
Financial data (yr. ended 8/31/88): Assets, $46,088,914 (M); expenditures, $3,270,054, including $2,911,510 for 140 grants (high: $115,000; low: $650).
Purpose and activities: Supports active participation by citizens in the protection of the environment, the development of public policy, the well-being of children and adolescents, education, grassroots organizing, opportunity for women, rural issues, and the arts.
Types of support: Operating budgets, seed money, emergency funds, special projects, program-related investments, employee matching gifts, loans, matching funds.
Limitations: Giving primarily in NC and the southeastern U.S., and to national organizations. No support for medical and health programs, research, film or video production, international activities, local or community programs (except where the program is a model for the region or nation), or for tax-supported educational institutions outside NC. No grants to individuals, or for endowment funds, building funds, renovation projects, scholarships, or fellowships; no student loans.
Publications: Annual report (including application guidelines), program policy statement.
Application information: Application form required.
Initial approach: Proposal
Copies of proposal: 1
Deadline(s): Submit proposal between Dec. and Feb. or June and Aug.; deadlines Mar. 1 and Sept. 1
Board meeting date(s): May and Nov.
Final notification: 1st week of months following board meetings
Write: William L. Bondurant, Exec. Dir.
Officers: L. Richardson Preyer,* Pres.; Barbara B. Millhouse,* V.P.; Kenneth F. Mountcastle, Jr.,* Secy.; Zachary T. Smith,* Treas.; William L. Bondurant, Exec. Dir.
Directors:* Betsy M. Babcock, Bruce M. Babcock, Reynolds Lassiter, Katharine B. Mountcastle, Katharine R. Mountcastle, Laura Mountcastle, William R. Rogers, Isabel Stewart, Paul N. Ylvisaker.
Number of staff: 3 full-time professional; 2 full-time support.
Employer Identification Number: 560690140
Recent arts and culture grants:
Bard College, Annandale-on-Hudson, NY, $20,000. To assist in publication of educational catalog to accompany first comprehensive exhibition of Black Mountain artists. 1987.
Middlebury College, Breadloaf School of English, Middlebury, VT, $90,000. To support tuition of fifteen North Carolina writing teachers. 1987.
Public Interest Video Network, New Voices Radio Reports, DC, $15,000. To produce radio reports on key issues and increase their listening audience. 1987.
Reynolda House, Winston-Salem, NC, $75,000. For Twentieth Anniversary goals. 1987.
Southeastern Center for Contemporary Art, Winston-Salem, NC, $50,000. Toward salaries for curator of national exhibitions and director of development. 1987.
Western North Carolina Public Radio, Asheville, NC, $22,900. For enhancement of public radio programming in western North Carolina. 1987.

2343
Bank of Granite Foundation
P.O. Box 128
Granite Falls 28630-1402

Financial data (yr. ended 12/31/87): Assets, $63,803 (M); gifts received, $35,000; expenditures, $33,597, including $33,550 for 23 grants (high: $5,000; low: $300).
Purpose and activities: Support for education, with emphasis on higher education, social services, the arts, including music, civic affairs, including the homeless, and public policy.
Limitations: Giving primarily in NC.
Application information: Contributions to preselected charitable organizations. Applications not accepted.
Trustees: Walter Carpenter, Jr., John A. Forlines, Jr., Joe A. Jones.
Employer Identification Number: 566075867

2344
BarclaysAmerican/Foundation, Inc.
201 South Tryon St.
P.O. Box 31488
Charlotte 28231 (704) 339-5000

Incorporated in 1959 in NC.
Donor(s): BarclaysAmerican Corp., and subsidiaries.
Financial data (yr. ended 12/31/87): Assets, $1,247,394 (M); gifts received, $51,767; expenditures, $375,382, including $355,917 for 299 grants (high: $50,000; low: $100; average: $5,000) and $19,465 for 151 employee matching gifts.
Purpose and activities: Grants largely for education and community funds; support also for youth agencies, the arts, and medical institutions.
Types of support: Operating budgets, continuing support, annual campaigns, building funds, employee matching gifts.
Limitations: Giving limited to areas of company operations. No grants to individuals, or for endowment funds, scholarships, fellowships, or research; no loans.
Application information:
Initial approach: Letter
Copies of proposal: 2
Deadline(s): None
Board meeting date(s): Apr. and Dec.
Final notification: 6 months
Write: Robert V. Knight, Jr., Secy.-Treas.
Officers and Directors: Edward F. Hill, Pres. and Chair.; Harry L. Dalton, V.P.; Robert V. Knight, Jr., Secy.-Treas.; Douglas W. Booth.
Employer Identification Number: 566060973

2345
The Belk Foundation
c/o I.N. Howard, Trustee
2801 West Tyvola Rd.
Charlotte 28217-4500

Trust established in 1928 in NC.
Donor(s): The Belk Mercantile Corps.
Financial data (yr. ended 5/31/88): Assets, $18,434,408 (M); gifts received, $587,794; expenditures, $817,621, including $710,200 for 40 grants (high: $100,000; low: $500).

Purpose and activities: Grants largely for community funds and higher education; support also for youth agencies and cultural programs.
Limitations: Giving primarily in NC and SC.
Application information:
Deadline(s): None
Trustees: I.N. Howard, First Union National Bank.
Advisors: Thomas M. Belk, Chair.; Claudia Belk, Irwin Belk, John M. Belk, Katherine Belk, B. Frank Matthews, Leroy Robinson.
Employer Identification Number: 566046450

2346
The Mary Duke Biddle Foundation
1044 West Forest Hills Blvd.
Durham 27707 (919) 493-5591

Trust established in 1956 in NY.
Donor(s): Mary Duke Biddle.†
Financial data (yr. ended 12/31/87): Assets, $13,510,671 (M); expenditures, $775,427, including $577,159 for 96 grants (high: $7,500; low: $500; average: $2,000-$5,000).
Purpose and activities: Support for higher and secondary education, specified churches, cultural programs, particularly music, projects in the arts, and aid to the community and to the handicapped; half of the income is committed to Duke University.
Types of support: Seed money, research, conferences and seminars, scholarship funds, fellowships, professorships, general purposes, matching funds, special projects.
Limitations: Giving limited to New York, NY, and NC. No support for public education. No grants to individuals, or for building or endowment funds or operating budgets; no loans.
Publications: Annual report.
Application information:
Initial approach: Letter
Copies of proposal: 1
Deadline(s): None
Board meeting date(s): Mar., June, Sept., and Dec.
Final notification: Approximately 90 days for negative responses
Write: James H. Semans, Chair., or Douglas C. Zinn, Asst. to the Chair.
Officers and Trustees: James H. Semans, M.D., Chair.; Mary D.B.T. Semans, Vice-Chair.; T.S. Kenan III, Secy.-Treas.; Archie K. Davis, Mary T. Jones.
Number of staff: 2 part-time professional; 2 part-time support.
Employer Identification Number: 136068883
Recent arts and culture grants:
American Composers Orchestra, NYC, NY, $5,000. 1987.
American Council for the Arts, NYC, NY, $5,000. 1987.
American Dance Festival, NYC, NY, $10,000. For performance of North Carolina Dance Theater. 1987.
Concert Artists Guild, NYC, NY, $5,000. 1987.
Duke University, Durham, NC, $192,700. For arts and humanities. 1987.
Duke University, Durham, NC, $162,479. For music. 1987.
Durham Arts Council, Durham, NC, $18,500. For development of Emergency Artists Program, providing modest grants to young artists at critical stage in their development. 1987.
Mint Museum of Art, Charlotte, NC, $5,000. 1987.
North Carolina Arts Celebration, Chapel Hill, NC, $5,000. 1987.
North Carolina School of the Arts, Winston-Salem, NC, $5,000. 1987.
North Carolina Shakespeare Festival, High Point, NC, $5,000. 1987.
North Carolina Symphony, Raleigh, NC, $12,000. 1987.
Penland School of Crafts, Penland, NC, $5,000. 1987.
Winston-Salem Arts Council, Winston-Salem, NC, $5,000. Toward producing and distributing brochure, nationwide, about program for emerging artists. 1987.

2347
Blue Bell Foundation
c/o Wrangler Co.
335 Church Court
Greensboro 27401 (919) 373-3580

Trust established in 1944 in NC.
Donor(s): Blue Bell, Inc.
Financial data (yr. ended 9/30/87): Assets, $3,784,532 (M); expenditures, $222,583, including $187,751 for 95 grants (high: $18,420; low: $10) and $21,773 for 140 employee matching gifts.
Purpose and activities: Grants for higher and secondary education, including matching gifts, community funds, hospitals, and cultural programs.
Types of support: Employee matching gifts.
Limitations: Giving primarily in areas where corporation has plants.
Application information:
Initial approach: Letter
Deadline(s): None
Write: Mickey Conklin
Advisory Committee: D.P. Laws, H.V. Moore, T.L. Wentherford.
Trustee: Wachovia Bank & Trust Co., N.A.
Employer Identification Number: 566041057

2348
The Blumenthal Foundation
P.O. Box 34689
Charlotte 28234 (704) 377-6555

Trust established in 1953 in NC.
Donor(s): I.D. Blumenthal,† Herman Blumenthal, Radiator Specialty Co.
Financial data (yr. ended 4/30/88): Assets, $19,067,751 (M); gifts received, $63,927; expenditures, $975,287, including $922,904 for 178 grants (high: $300,500; low: $8; average: $100-$23,000).
Purpose and activities: Giving for higher education, Jewish welfare organizations, and programs in the arts and humanities; also supports Wildacres, a conference center in North Carolina, which invites groups in a variety of disciplines to use its facilities.
Types of support: Building funds, equipment, operating budgets, emergency funds, research, general purposes, publications, matching funds, annual campaigns, conferences and seminars, seed money, special projects.
Limitations: Giving primarily in NC, with emphasis on Charlotte. No grants to individuals, or for scholarships or fellowships; no loans.
Application information:
Initial approach: Letter or proposal
Copies of proposal: 1
Deadline(s): 15 days before board meetings
Board meeting date(s): Mar., June, Sept., and Dec.
Final notification: 1 to 3 months
Write: Herman Blumenthal, Trustee
Trustees: Samuel Blumenthal, Herman Blumenthal, Chair.; Alan Blumenthal, Anita Blumenthal, Philip Blumenthal.
Number of staff: 3
Employer Identification Number: 560793667

2349
Kathleen Price and Joseph M. Bryan Family Foundation
One North Pointe, Suite 170
3101 North Elm St.
Greensboro 27408 (919) 288-5455

Incorporated in 1955 in NC.
Donor(s): Kathleen Price Bryan,† Joseph M. Bryan, Sr., Kathleen Bryan Edwards, Nancy Bryan Faircloth, Joseph M. Bryan, Jr.
Financial data (yr. ended 12/31/88): Assets, $30,186,241 (M); gifts received, $7,672; expenditures, $1,930,613, including $1,604,305 for 64 grants (high: $250,000; low: $1,000; average: $5,000-$100,000).
Purpose and activities: Grants principally in the fields of education, arts and culture, human services, public interest, and youth.
Types of support: Continuing support, seed money, equipment, general purposes, operating budgets, scholarship funds, technical assistance, special projects, endowment funds, building funds, renovation projects.
Limitations: Giving primarily in NC and the Southeast. No grants to individuals, or to private foundations; or, generally, for annual fund drives, research, or loans.
Publications: Program policy statement, application guidelines, grants list.
Application information: Telephone or personal interviews with Exec. Dir. are encouraged prior to deadlines; site visits are made when possible. Application form required.
Initial approach: Letter
Copies of proposal: 1
Deadline(s): Mar. 1 and Sept. 1
Board meeting date(s): May and Nov.
Final notification: 2 weeks after board meetings
Write: Robert K. Hampton, Exec. Dir.
Officers and Trustees: Kathleen Bryan Edwards, Pres.; Joseph M. Bryan, Jr., V.P. and Treas.; Nancy Bryan Faircloth, V.P.; Robert K. Hampton, Secy. and Exec. Dir.
Number of staff: 1 full-time professional; 1 full-time support.
Employer Identification Number: 566046952

2350
Burlington Industries Corporate Giving Program

3330 West Friendly Ave.
Greensboro 27410 (919) 379-2000

Financial data (yr. ended 9/30/88): $136,273 for 58 grants (high: $50,000; low: $50; average: $1,000-$5,000).
Purpose and activities: Support for community and urban programs, culture, education, united campaigns, health care, and public broadcasting. Types of support include loaned staff, gifts of used or surplus equipment or furniture and the donation of products manufactured by the company.
Types of support: In-kind gifts, consulting services, equipment.
Limitations: Giving primarily in headquarters city, major U.S. operating areas and operating locations in foreign countries. No grants to individuals, or for general operating budgets or endowments.
Publications: Informational brochure (including application guidelines).
Application information: Include description of project, proposed budget, financial statement and 501(c)(3) status letter.
Initial approach: Letter of inquiry or by telephone
Copies of proposal: 1
Board meeting date(s): Decisions made in Mar., June, Sept., and Dec. by Donations Committee
Write: Park R. Davidson, Asst. V.P., Finance

2351
Burlington Industries Foundation

P.O. Box 21207
3330 West Friendly Ave.
Greensboro 27420 (919) 379-2515

Trust established in 1943 in NC.
Donor(s): Burlington Industries, Inc., and subsidiary companies.
Financial data (yr. ended 9/30/88): Assets, $7,300,533 (M); expenditures, $1,401,532, including $962,508 for 177 grants (high: $100,000; low: $100; average: $500-$5,000), $24,250 for 50 grants to individuals and $414,774 for 962 employee matching gifts.
Purpose and activities: To support educational, charitable, cultural, and similar causes. Grants to colleges and universities generally in the geographical area of plants, where the company recruits annually for employees. Grants to various community and civic causes based upon recommendation of the company's local management; includes support for youth agencies, hospitals, and some health associations. Grants to individuals are only to help employees cope with hardship caused by disasters.
Types of support: Matching funds, annual campaigns, building funds, professorships, scholarship funds, fellowships, employee matching gifts.
Limitations: Giving primarily in areas of company operations in NC, SC, and VA. Generally no grants for sectarian or denominational religious organizations, national organizations, private secondary schools, or historic preservation projects. No grants to individuals (except for company employees and their families in distress), or for conferences, seminars, workshops, outdoor dramas, films, documentaries, endowment funds, or medical research operating expenses; no loans.
Publications: Program policy statement, application guidelines.
Application information:
Initial approach: Telephone, letter, or proposal
Copies of proposal: 1
Deadline(s): None
Board meeting date(s): Quarterly
Write: Park R. Davidson, Exec. Dir.
Officer and Trustees: Park R. Davidson, Exec. Dir.; J.C. Cowan, Jr., Donald R. Hughes, J. Kenneth Lesley, Charles A. McLendon, Jr.
Number of staff: None.
Employer Identification Number: 566043142

2352
Burroughs Wellcome Contributions Program

Burroughs Wellcome Co.
3030 Cornwallis Rd.
Research Triangle Pk. 27709 (919) 248-4177

Financial data (yr. ended 8/31/88): Total giving, $2,942,702, including $2,310,563 for 1,000 grants (high: $500,000; low: $10; average: $10-$500,000), $104,912 for employee matching gifts and $527,227 for 75 in-kind gifts.
Purpose and activities: Supports biomedical research, AIDS information and research, medical education, arts and cultural programs, elementary, secondary, and higher education, civic organizations, health and human service organizations through employee matching gifts to United Way, and scholarships to children of company employees through the National Merit Scholarship Corporation; other forms of support include employee matching gifts to schools, foundations, hospitals, and public radio and television stations, in-kind donations of employee talent and surplus materials; international health care projects receive product donations.
Types of support: In-kind gifts, annual campaigns, building funds, conferences and seminars, employee matching gifts, fellowships, lectureships, matching funds, publications, special projects.
Limitations: Giving primarily in Research Triangle Park and Greenville, NC, for health and human services, and civic and cultural programs; some support for national organizations. No support for political or religious groups. No grants to individuals.
Publications: Corporate giving report (including application guidelines).
Application information: Letters requesting contributions for NC charities should be addressed to Arline Erwin; requests for charities outside NC should be addressed to Joan Guilkey; biomedical research requests may be referred to the Burroughs Wellcome Fund.
Initial approach: Letter, including IRS exemption number
Copies of proposal: 1
Deadline(s): None
Board meeting date(s): As needed
Write: Joan Guilkey, Contribs./Donations Mgr.
Contributions Committee: Thomas E. Kennedy, Chair. and V.P., Corp. Affairs; John E. Kelsey, Ph.D., Dir., Technical and Admin. Operations; Peter Reckert, V.P., Marketing; Joan Guilkey, Contribs. Mgr.
Number of staff: 1 full-time professional; 3 full-time support.

2353
The Cannon Foundation, Inc.

P.O. Box 548
Concord 28026-0548 (704) 786-8216

Incorporated in 1943 in NC.
Donor(s): Charles A. Cannon,† Cannon Mills Co.
Financial data (yr. ended 9/30/88): Assets, $87,220,799 (M); expenditures, $4,704,019, including $4,110,629 for 59 grants (high: $600,000; low: $1,000; average: $2,500-$100,000).
Purpose and activities: Support for hospitals, higher and secondary education, and cultural programs; grants also for Protestant church support, and social service and youth agencies.
Types of support: Annual campaigns, building funds, equipment, matching funds, renovation projects.
Limitations: Giving primarily in NC, especially in the Cabarrus County area. No grants to individuals, or for operating budgets, seed money, emergency funds, deficit financing, land acquisition, endowment funds, demonstration projects, research, publications, conferences, seminars, scholarships, or fellowships; no loans.
Publications: Application guidelines.
Application information: Application form required.
Initial approach: Letter
Copies of proposal: 1
Deadline(s): Submit proposal in Jan., Apr., July, and Oct.; deadline Jan. 15, Apr. 15, July 15, and Oct. 15
Board meeting date(s): Mar., June, Sept., and Dec.
Final notification: Within 2 weeks of board action
Write: Dan L. Gray, Exec. Dir.
Officers and Directors: Mariam C. Hayes, Pres.; W.C. Cannon, V.P.; T.C. Haywood, Secy.-Treas.; Dan L. Gray, Exec. Dir.; G.A. Batte, Jr., W.S. Fisher, Elizabeth L. Quick, T.L. Ross.
Number of staff: 1 full-time professional; 2 full-time support.
Employer Identification Number: 566042532

2354
Connemara Fund

P.O. Box 20124
Greensboro 27420

Established in 1968 in NC.
Donor(s): Mary R. Jackson.†
Financial data (yr. ended 6/30/88): Assets, $5,332,715 (M); expenditures, $248,210, including $225,600 for 52 grants (high: $25,000; low: $900; average: $3,000).

Purpose and activities: Grants primarily for church support and religious welfare associations; support also for child welfare, social services, and cultural programs.
Types of support: Continuing support, general purposes.
Limitations: Giving primarily in the New England area. No grants to individuals.
Application information:
Initial approach: Proposal or letter
Copies of proposal: 1
Board meeting date(s): As required
Final notification: 2 months
Write: Herrick Jackson, Trustee
Trustees: Herrick Jackson, Robert W. Jackson, Alison Jackson Van Dyk.
Number of staff: 1 part-time support.
Employer Identification Number: 566096063

2355
The Josephus Daniels Charitable Foundation
215 South McDowell St.
Raleigh 27601 (919) 829-4694

Established in 1964 in NC.
Donor(s): The News and Observer Publishing Co.
Financial data (yr. ended 12/31/87): Assets, $2,577,096 (M); gifts received, $437,595; expenditures, $542,345, including $513,584 for 219 grants (high: $105,000; low: $50).
Purpose and activities: Support for education, including higher education, and community development; support also for the arts and programs that benefit the disadvantaged.
Types of support: Annual campaigns, building funds, capital campaigns, continuing support, emergency funds, endowment funds, equipment, publications, renovation projects, scholarship funds, seed money, special projects.
Limitations: Giving primarily in NC and SC. No support for religious or political organizations. No grants to individuals, or for conferences or seminars.
Publications: Informational brochure (including application guidelines).
Application information:
Initial approach: Letter
Deadline(s): None
Board meeting date(s): Monthly
Write: Witt Clarke, Secy.-Treas.
Officers: Frank A. Daniels, Jr., Pres.; Melvin L. Finch, V.P.; Witt Clarke, Secy.-Treas.
Employer Identification Number: 566065260

2356
The Dickson Foundation, Inc.
2000 First Union Plaza
Charlotte 28282 (704) 372-5404

Incorporated in 1944 in NC.
Donor(s): American and Efird Mills, Inc.
Financial data (yr. ended 12/31/87): Assets, $16,571,705 (M); expenditures, $784,917, including $709,917 for 231 grants (high: $30,000; low: $100).
Purpose and activities: Support for secondary and higher education, including scholarship funds, community funds, youth agencies, and hospitals.
Types of support: Scholarship funds, general purposes.
Limitations: Giving primarily in NC. No grants to individuals, or for building or endowment funds.
Application information:
Initial approach: Letter
Deadline(s): None
Board meeting date(s): Annually and as required
Officers and Directors: R. Stuart Dickson, Chair.; Alan T. Dickson, Pres.; Rush S. Dickson III, V.P.; Thomas W. Dickson, V.P.; Colleen S. Colbert, Secy.-Treas.
Employer Identification Number: 566022339

2357
Duke Power Company Foundation
422 South Church St.
Charlotte 28242 (704) 373-3224
Scholarship address: Scholastic Excellence Awards Program, Duke Power Co. Fdn., P.O. Box 33189, Charlotte, NC 28242

Established in 1984 in NC.
Donor(s): Duke Power Co.
Financial data (yr. ended 12/31/88): Assets, $2,143,673 (M); gifts received, $573,120; expenditures, $5,022,843, including $4,967,474 for 1,768 grants (high: $100,000; low: $50; average: $500-$10,000) and $43,650 for 89 grants to individuals.
Purpose and activities: Supports those organizations, institutions, and programs that are able to demonstrate a broad base of support among the business and civic community. Support is directed to: health and human services, education, civic programs, the homeless, environment, engineering, and culture and art. Awards competitive scholarships to students whose parents live in company areas and to employees' or retirees' children.
Types of support: Employee-related scholarships, student aid, capital campaigns, employee matching gifts, general purposes, matching funds.
Limitations: Giving primarily in the company's headquarters and service areas in NC and SC. No support for single sectarian or denominational religious, veterans', or fraternal organizations; organizations where the foundation would be the only donor; hospitals supported by the Duke Endowment; or to organizations primarily supported by tax dollars (education excepted).
Application information: Application form required for scholarships only; students must be nominated by school official.
Initial approach: Proposal
Copies of proposal: 1
Deadline(s): Scholarships: Oct. 15; all others anytime
Write: Robert C. Allen, V.P.
Officers: William S. Lee,* Chair.; Douglas W. Booth,* Pres.; Robert C. Allen, V.P. and Exec. Dir.; John P. O'Keefe, Secy.; David L. Hauser, Treas.
Trustees:* Steve C. Griffith, Jr., William H. Grigg, Warren H. Owen.
Employer Identification Number: 581586283

2358
Durham Corporation Giving Program
2610 Wycliff Road
Raleigh 27607 (919) 881-2219
Mailing address: P.O. Box 27807, Raleigh, NC 27611

Financial data (yr. ended 12/31/88): Total giving, $171,808, including $162,903 for grants and $8,905 for 53 employee matching gifts.
Purpose and activities: Support for United Way, private higher education, health and welfare, community development, and arts and culture. Types of support include loaned staff and use of company printing facilities.
Types of support: Employee matching gifts, capital campaigns, building funds, in-kind gifts.
Limitations: No grants to individuals, or for endowments.
Application information:
Initial approach: Letter
Final notification: 4 weeks
Write: Floyd E. Slapper, V.P. and Secy.

2359
Percy B. Ferebee Endowment
c/o Wachovia Bank & Trust Co., N.A.
P.O. Box 3099
Winston-Salem 27150 (919) 748-5269

Established in 1973 in NC.
Donor(s): Percy Ferebee.†
Financial data (yr. ended 12/31/86): Assets, $1,888,856 (M); expenditures, $118,129, including $46,462 for 7 grants (high: $17,500; low: $2,000; average: $5,000) and $51,686 for 105 grants to individuals.
Purpose and activities: Emphasis on scholarships to individuals, and educational, cultural, and civic development.
Types of support: Student aid, annual campaigns, seed money, emergency funds, building funds, equipment, land acquisition.
Limitations: Giving primarily in Cherokee, Clay, Graham, Jackson, Macon, and Swain counties, NC, and the Cherokee Indian Reservation. No grants to individuals (except for scholarships), or for operating budgets.
Publications: Informational brochure (including application guidelines).
Application information: Application form required.
Initial approach: Proposal
Copies of proposal: 1
Deadline(s): Submit proposal preferably in Sept.; deadline for scholarships, Feb. 15; for grants, Oct. 1
Board meeting date(s): May and Nov.
Final notification: 10 days
Write: E. Ray Cope, V.P., Wachovia Bank & Trust Co., N.A.
Awards Advisory Committee: John Parris, Chair.; Mrs. Frela Owl Beck, Ty W. Burnette, James Conley, Maggie Alice Sandlin Crisp, J. Smith Howell, John Waldroup, Bill Walker.
Trustee: Wachovia Bank & Trust Co., N.A.
Number of staff: None.
Employer Identification Number: 566118992

2360
The Doak Finch Foundation
c/o NCNB National Bank Trust Group
One NCNB Plaza T09-1
Charlotte 28255
Application address: 10 Welloskie Dr., Thomasville, NC 27360

Trust established in 1961 in NC.
Donor(s): Doak Finch.
Financial data (yr. ended 10/31/88): Assets, $2,728,604 (M); expenditures, $205,496, including $174,800 for 21 grants (high: $50,000; low: $1,000; average: $3,000-$5,000).
Purpose and activities: Giving to schools, social service agencies, and cultural organizations.
Limitations: Giving limited to the Thomasville, NC, area.
Application information:
Initial approach: Letter or proposal
Copies of proposal: 1
Deadline(s): Feb.
Board meeting date(s): No established dates
Write: Manager of Institutional Services
Trustee: NCNB National Bank.
Directors: J.C. Dorety, Helen Finch, Richard J. Finch, Jane F. Turner, David R. Williams.
Employer Identification Number: 566042823

2361
The First Union Foundation
First Union Plaza, 0143
Charlotte 28288 (704) 374-6649
Addresses of contributions coordinators: First Union Natl. Bank, Marketing Div. T-2, Box 1329, Greenville, SC 29602; First Union Corp., GA, P.O. Box 56566, Atlanta, GA 30343; First Union Natl. Bank, P.O. Box 2080, Jacksonville, FL 32231

Established in 1987 in NC.
Donor(s): First Union Corp.
Financial data (yr. ended 12/31/87): Assets, $4,975,785 (M); expenditures, $1,337,691, including $1,312,169 for 670 grants (high: $38,200; low: $25).
Purpose and activities: Support for higher education, special programs for public elementary and secondary schools, and other educational programs, arts funds or councils, public broadcasting, visual and performing arts, historic preservation and libraries, and community improvement, leadership development, and environmental protection. Special consideration for children and youth and the disadvantaged to help them become productive and self-sufficient. Types of support include capital grants, made only when there is a community-wide fundraising campaign that includes the entire business community. A grant is made for one year only and does not imply that a grant will be made the following year unless a multi-year pledge is made.
Types of support: Building funds, capital campaigns, endowment funds, operating budgets, renovation projects, special projects.
Limitations: Giving primarily in FL, GA, NC, and SC. No support for religious, veterans', or fraternal organizations, retirement homes, pre-college level schools except through employee matching gifts or for a special project for a public school, or organizations supported through the United Way, except for approved capital campaigns.
Application information:
Initial approach: Proposal to the nearest First Union Bank
Deadline(s): Sept. 1 for consideration in next year's budget
Board meeting date(s): Mar., June, Sept., and Dec.
Write: Ann D. Thomas, V.P., Corp. Contribs.
Directors: Ann D. Thomas, Dir., Corp. Contribs.; B.D. Allen, Marion A. Cowell, Jr., Ben T. Craig, Edward E. Crutchfield, Jr., John R. Georgius, J. Robert Lee, Walter K. Nussbaum, B.J. Walker.
Trustee: First Union National Bank of North Carolina.
Employer Identification Number: 566288589

2362
Foundation For The Carolinas
301 South Brevard St.
Charlotte 28202 (704) 376-9541

Community foundation incorporated in 1958 in NC.
Financial data (yr. ended 12/31/88): Assets, $35,769,162 (M); gifts received, $6,167,004; expenditures, $5,606,762, including $5,052,204 for 1,739 grants (high: $500,000; low: $100; average: $1,000-$20,000).
Purpose and activities: Support primarily for education, human services, religion, the arts, health and medical research, youth programs, the aged, the environment, historic preservation, and public interest and civic programs.
Types of support: Seed money, matching funds, scholarship funds.
Limitations: Giving primarily to organizations serving the citizens of NC and SC, with emphasis on the Central Piedmont region. No grants to individuals, or for deficit financing, capital campaigns, operating budgets, publications, conferences, or endowment funds.
Publications: Annual report (including application guidelines), newsletter, program policy statement.
Application information: Application form required.
Initial approach: Letter
Copies of proposal: 15
Deadline(s): Feb. 1, June 1, and Oct. 1
Board meeting date(s): Quarterly, with annual meeting in Mar.; distribution committee meets monthly
Final notification: 2 months
Write: William L. Spencer, Pres.
Officers: F. Kenneth Iverson,* Chair.; Larry J. Dagenhart,* 1st Vice-Chair.; Monroe T. Gilmour,* Vice-Chair.; William L. Spencer, Pres.; Barbara T. Hautau, V.P.; Robin L. Hinson,* Secy.; Graeme M. Keith,* Treas.
Directors:* John V. Andrews, and 39 additional directors.
Number of staff: 4 full-time professional; 2 part-time professional; 4 full-time support; 1 part-time support.
Employer Identification Number: 566047886

2363
Community Foundation of Gaston County, Inc.
(Formerly Garrison Community Foundation of Gaston County, Inc.)
P.O. Box 123
Gastonia 28053 (704) 864-0927

Community foundation incorporated in 1978 in NC.
Financial data (yr. ended 12/31/88): Assets, $3,470,902 (M); gifts received, $923,540; expenditures, $441,666, including $425,531 for grants and $9,000 for grants to individuals.
Purpose and activities: Support for the arts, education, health services, museums and youth organizations; support also for medical grants to children 18 or under.
Types of support: Seed money, building funds, equipment, endowment funds, scholarship funds, special projects, renovation projects, general purposes.
Limitations: Giving limited to NC, particularly Gaston County. No grants for exchange programs, fellowships, program-related investments, annual campaigns, deficit financing, continuing support, technical assistance, professorships, or internships; no loans.
Publications: Annual report, occasional report, informational brochure.
Application information: Application form is required for Children's Medical Aid Fund only.
Initial approach: Letter
Copies of proposal: 1
Deadline(s): Feb. 15 and Aug. 15
Board meeting date(s): Feb. and Sept.
Write: Rebecca B. Carter, Exec. Dir.
Officers: W. Duke Kimbrell, Pres.; Rebecca B. Carter, Exec. Dir.
Employer Identification Number: 589830716

2364
Karl and Anna Ginter Foundation
c/o NCNB National Bank Trust Group
One NCNB Plaza T09-1
Charlotte 28255

Established in 1968 in NC.
Donor(s): Karl Ginter.
Financial data (yr. ended 12/31/88): Assets, $1,615,804 (M); expenditures, $104,439, including $94,500 for 16 grants (high: $20,000; low: $1,000; average: $5,000-$6,000).
Purpose and activities: Emphasis on higher education; grants also for cultural programs.
Limitations: Giving primarily in Mecklenburg County, NC.
Application information: Funds are mostly committed.
Initial approach: Proposal or letter
Copies of proposal: 1
Deadline(s): Sept. 30
Board meeting date(s): Nov.
Final notification: Dec. 31
Write: Mgr., Institutional Services
Directors: Stamford R. Brookshire, Joseph W. Grier, Jr., Thomas R. Payne.
Trustee: NCNB National Bank.
Employer Identification Number: 566094355

2365
Glaxo Corporate Giving Program
Five Moore Dr.
Research Triangle Park 27709 (919) 248-2588

Purpose and activities: Glaxo believes "in being a conscientious corporate citizen as well as a contributing and active member of the communities within which we work." While the foundation emphasizes projects having a statewide effect, the corporate giving program concentrates on three counties in NC: Durham, Wake, and Orange. Support for health, welfare, education, culture and the arts, and civic and community services. Programs reflect foundation and corporate giving.
Types of support: Program-related investments, seed money, special projects.
Limitations: Giving primarily in Durham, Wake, and Orange Counties, NC.
Application information: Include funds, in hand or pledged, and from whom; line-item budget for the project, and list of board members.
Initial approach: Proposal
Copies of proposal: 1
Board meeting date(s): Monthly
Write: Kathryn H. Wallace, Contribs. Admin.
Number of staff: 1 full-time professional; 1 full-time support.

2366
The Foundation of Greater Greensboro, Inc.
First Citizens Bank, Suite 307
P.O. Box 207
Greensboro 27402 (919) 379-9100

Community foundation established in 1983.
Financial data (yr. ended 6/30/88): Assets, $2,802,426 (M); gifts received, $454,808; expenditures, $308,373, including $202,015 for grants.
Purpose and activities: Grants primarily for cultural affairs and the arts, civic affairs and community development, education, health and social services.
Types of support: Emergency funds, equipment, general purposes, renovation projects, seed money, special projects.
Limitations: Giving limited to the Greater Greensboro, NC, area.
Publications: Annual report, application guidelines, program policy statement, newsletter.
Application information: Application form required.
Initial approach: Proposal (3 pages or less)
Copies of proposal: 1
Deadline(s): 30 days prior to monthly meeting
Write: Paul W. Stephanz, Exec. Dir.
Officers and Directors: Cynthia E. Doyle, Pres.; Carolyn W. Fee, Treas.; and 26 additional directors.
Number of staff: 1 full-time professional; 1 full-time support.
Employer Identification Number: 561380249

2367
The John W. and Anna H. Hanes Foundation
c/o Wachovia Bank & Trust Co., N.A.
P.O. Box 3099, MC 31022
Winston-Salem 27150 (919) 770-5274

Trust established in 1947 in NC.
Financial data (yr. ended 12/31/88): Assets, $12,321,005 (M); expenditures, $632,929, including $554,399 for 41 grants (high: $57,000; low: $2,000; average: $1,000-$25,000).
Purpose and activities: Support for cultural programs, historic preservation, conservation, health and education, child welfare, social services, and community programs.
Types of support: Annual campaigns, seed money, emergency funds, building funds, equipment, land acquisition, endowment funds, matching funds, special projects, research, publications.
Limitations: Giving limited to NC, particularly Forsyth County. No grants to individuals, or for operating expenses.
Publications: Program policy statement, application guidelines.
Application information: Application form required.
Initial approach: Telephone or letter
Copies of proposal: 1
Deadline(s): 15th day of month preceding board meeting
Board meeting date(s): Jan., Apr., July, and Oct.
Final notification: 10 days
Write: Joyce T. Adger, V.P., Wachovia Bank & Trust Co., N.A.
Trustees: Frank Borden Hanes, Sr., Frank Borden Hanes, Jr., Gordon Hanes, R. Philip Hanes, Jr., Wachovia Bank & Trust Co., N.A.
Number of staff: None.
Employer Identification Number: 566037589

2368
James G. Hanes Memorial Fund/Foundation
c/o Wachovia Bank & Trust Co., N.A.
P.O. Box 3099, MC 31022
Winston-Salem 27150 (919) 770-5274

Trusts established in 1957 and 1972 in NC.
Financial data (yr. ended 10/31/88): Assets, $9,511,107 (M); gifts received, $437,112; expenditures, $11,602,307, including $1,033,830 for 39 grants (high: $380,000; low: $1,000; average: $1,000-$25,000).
Purpose and activities: Support for health and education projects, cultural programs, conservation, and community programs.
Types of support: Annual campaigns, seed money, emergency funds, building funds, equipment, land acquisition, matching funds, special projects, research, publications, endowment funds.
Limitations: Giving primarily in NC and the Southeast. No grants to individuals, or for general operational or maintenance purposes.
Publications: Informational brochure (including application guidelines).
Application information: Application form required.
Initial approach: Proposal
Copies of proposal: 1
Deadline(s): Mar. 15, June 15, Sept. 15, and Dec. 15
Board meeting date(s): Jan., Apr., July, and Oct.
Final notification: 10 days
Write: Joyce T. Adger, V.P., Wachovia Bank & Trust Co., N.A.
Distribution Committee: Eldridge C. Hanes, Chair.; Edward K. Crawford, James G. Hanes III, Douglas R. Lewis, Drewry Hanes Nostitz, Frank F. Willingham.
Trustee: Wachovia Bank & Trust Co., N.A.
Number of staff: None.
Employer Identification Number: 566036987

2369
Alex Hemby Foundation
4419 Sharon Rd.
Charlotte 28211

Established in 1950 in NC.
Donor(s): Hemby Investment Co.
Financial data (yr. ended 12/31/87): Assets, $5,364,136 (M); expenditures, $353,411, including $306,700 for 37 grants (high: $75,000; low: $50).
Purpose and activities: Giving for higher and other education, health associations and hospitals, and cultural programs.
Application information:
Initial approach: Letter
Deadline(s): None
Write: T.E. Hemby, Jr., Trustee
Trustees: Mrs. B.W. Leahy, Mrs. Hilda W. Hemby, T.E. Hemby, Jr.
Employer Identification Number: 566046767

2370
Hillsdale Fund, Inc.
P.O. Box 20124
Greensboro 27420 (919) 274-5471

Incorporated in 1963 in NC.
Donor(s): The L. Richardson family.
Financial data (yr. ended 12/31/87): Assets, $15,286,583 (M); expenditures, $826,292, including $654,314 for 50 grants (high: $235,000; low: $1,400).
Purpose and activities: Interests include the general fields of education, conservation, the arts and humanities.
Limitations: Giving primarily in NC and the southeastern states. No grants to individuals, or for operating budgets.
Application information: Submit 13 copies of brochures and printed material.
Initial approach: Proposal
Copies of proposal: 1
Deadline(s): Approximately one month prior to biannual board meetings
Board meeting date(s): Usually in Apr. and Nov.
Write: Sion A. Boney, Admin. V.P.
Officers and Trustees: Lunsford Richardson, Jr., Pres.; Sion A. Boney, Admin. V.P. and Secy.-Treas.; Sion A. Boney III, J. Peter Gallagher, Margaret W. Gallagher, Laurinda V. Lowenstein, Louise Boney McCoy, Beatrix P. Richardson, Beatrix W. Richardson, Eudora L. Richardson, Molly R. Smith, Richard G. Smith III, Margaret R. White.
Number of staff: 1 part-time support.

Employer Identification Number: 566057433

2371
Integon Foundation
500 West Fifth St.
Winston-Salem 27152 (919) 770-2000

Established in 1967 in NC.
Financial data (yr. ended 12/31/87): Expenditures, $109,000 for 35 grants (high: $5,000; low: $500; average: $1,000-$5,000) and $16,000 for employee matching gifts.
Purpose and activities: The Integon Foundation reflects management's view that a strong community, supported by a broad range of quality educational, social, and cultural services is essential for business progress. Support for community development, arts and culture, and the United Way; support also for business education and leadership development, human services, including drug abuse programs; in-kind donations through loaned staff, gifts of used or surplus equipment or furniture, use of facilities for meetings or seminars, and access to printing facilities.
Types of support: Employee matching gifts, capital campaigns, special projects, consulting services, building funds, lectureships, in-kind gifts.
Limitations: Giving primarily in Winston-Salem; some giving in Piedmont and Triad in the state of NC; no support for national organizations. No support for churches or religious denominations, political parties, political candidates, or organizations involved in lobbying. No grants to individuals, or for operating fund drives.
Publications: Application guidelines.
Application information: Include project description, amount requested, financial statements for past two years, 501(c)(3), and list of board.
Initial approach: Letter or telephone call
Copies of proposal: 1
Deadline(s): Requests should be received during the month prior to the Board meeting
Board meeting date(s): Nov., Feb., May, and Aug.
Write: Turner Coley
Number of staff: 1 part-time professional; 1 part-time support.
Employer Identification Number: 566085755

2372
Jefferson-Pilot Foundation
c/o Jerry King, Jefferson Pilot Broadcasting Co.
One Julian Price Place
Charlotte 28208

Financial data (yr. ended 11/30/87): Assets, $90,064 (M); expenditures, $81,698, including $79,650 for 24 grants (high: $20,000; low: $500).
Purpose and activities: Emphasis on educational funding, public television and radio, and communications.
Managers: Gerald King, W. Roger Soles.
Trustee: NCNB National Bank of NC.
Employer Identification Number: 566040780

2373
May Gordon Latham Kellenberger Historical Foundation
c/o NCNB National Bank Trust Group
One NCNB Plaza T09-1
Charlotte 28255
Additional address: P.O. Box 908, New Bern, NC 28560

Established in 1979.
Donor(s): May Gordon Latham Kellenberger.
Financial data (yr. ended 11/30/86): Assets, $5,077,921 (M); gifts received, $39,277; expenditures, $226,686, including $175,870 for 23 grants (high: $40,000; low: $600).
Purpose and activities: "To aid and support projects related to Tryon Palace and Historical New Bern," with emphasis on building, restoration, and preservation.
Types of support: Building funds, special projects, publications, renovation projects, research.
Limitations: Giving limited to New Bern, NC.
Application information:
Initial approach: Letter or proposal
Copies of proposal: 1
Deadline(s): June 1 and Dec. 1
Write: Mgr., Institutional Services
Trustee: NCNB National Bank.
Directors: Robert D. Douglas, Jr., Chair.; Gertrude S. Carraway, Vice-Chair.; George A. Ives, Jr., Secy.-Treas.; Ella Bengel, Patric Dorsey, Sidney R. French, Mrs. H. Dail Holderness, W.S. Price, Jr., John C. Thomas, E. Newsom Williams.
Employer Identification Number: 581360279

2374
Kenan Family Foundation
P.O. Box 2729
Chapel Hill 27515-2729

Established in 1984 in NC.
Donor(s): Frank H. Kenan.
Financial data (yr. ended 12/31/87): Assets, $1,487,617 (M); gifts received, $500,000; expenditures, $22,225, including $13,000 for 2 grants (high: $11,000; low: $2,000).
Purpose and activities: Support for education, economics and humanities.
Application information: Contributes only to pre-selected organizations. Applications not accepted.
Officers and Directors: Frank H. Kenan, Pres.; Thomas S. Kenan III, V.P. and Treas.; Braxton Schell, Secy.; Owen Gwyn, Jr., Annice Hawkins Kenan, Elizabeth Price Kenan, Owen G. Kenan.
Employer Identification Number: 581587972

2375
Effie Allen Little Foundation
P.O. Box 340
Wadesboro 28170 (704) 694-3114

Established in 1954 in NC.
Donor(s): Charles L. Little, Sr.
Financial data (yr. ended 12/31/88): Assets, $1,383,304 (M); expenditures, $85,613, including $46,403 for 22 grants (high: $15,000; low: $100; average: $100-$5,000).
Purpose and activities: Giving primarily for higher and other education; support also for social service and youth organizations.
Types of support: Annual campaigns, scholarship funds, continuing support, operating budgets, special projects.
Limitations: Giving primarily in Anson County, NC.
Publications: 990-PF.
Application information: Applications not accepted.
Deadline(s): None
Board meeting date(s): As needed
Write: Dora Anne Little, Pres.
Officers and Directors: Charles L. Little, Sr., Chair.; Dora Anne Little, Pres.; Henry W. Little III, Secy.-Treas.; Mrs. Charles L. Little, Mrs. Hal W. Little.
Number of staff: None.
Employer Identification Number: 566048449

2376
Martha and Spencer Love Foundation
c/o NCNB National Bank
One NCNB Plaza T09-1
Charlotte 28255

Trust established in 1947 in NC.
Donor(s): J. Spencer Love,† Martha E. Love Ayers.
Financial data (yr. ended 12/31/87): Assets, $1,937,066 (M); gifts received, $100; expenditures, $185,000, including $162,500 for 5 grants (high: $140,000; low: $2,500; average: $5,000).
Purpose and activities: Emphasis on higher education, the arts, Protestant church support, and social welfare programs.
Limitations: Giving primarily in NC.
Application information:
Initial approach: Proposal or letter
Copies of proposal: 1
Board meeting date(s): As required
Write: Manager, Institutional Services
Trustee: NCNB National Bank.
Directors: Howard Holderness, Charles E. Love, Cornelia S. Love, Julian Love, Martin E. Love, Lela Love Popov, E.R. Zane.
Employer Identification Number: 566040789

2377
Marsh Foundation, Inc.
P.O. Box 35329
Charlotte 28235

Donor(s): Marsh Realty Co.
Financial data (yr. ended 12/31/87): Assets, $880,913 (M); gifts received, $9,800; expenditures, $6,492, including $315 for 1 grant.
Purpose and activities: Support for arts and science.
Officers: Lex Marsh, Pres. and Treas.; John S. Johnston, V.P. and Secy.; G. Alex Marsh III, V.P.
Employer Identification Number: 566056515

2378
NCNB Corporate Charities
One NCNB Plaza
Charlotte 28255 (704) 374-8571

Purpose and activities: Supports United Way, higher education, community development, arts and cultural activities and social and human services. Types of support include volunteer recruitment, employee volunteer programs and in-kind donations, including loaned staff, gifts of used or surplus equipment or furniture, contributions of the company's primary goods or services and use of its facilities for seminars or meetings. Employee matching gifts for post-secondary education only.
Types of support: In-kind gifts, building funds, employee matching gifts, scholarship funds, employee-related scholarships, capital campaigns, special projects, equipment.
Limitations: Giving primarily in NCNB's service area in the southeastern U.S.: FL, SC, NC, and the areas of Baltimore, MD, Atlanta, GA, and Prince William County, VA. No support for religious organizations or athletic events. No grants to individuals.
Publications: Annual report.
Application information:
Initial approach: Full written proposal
Copies of proposal: 1
Deadline(s): Budgets prepared in summer of preceding year
Final notification: If rejected, will send notice
Write: Molly V. Philips, Dir., Public Policy
Number of staff: 4 full-time professional; 2 full-time support.

2379
Neisler Foundation, Inc.
P.O. Box 99
Kings Mountain 28086

Established in 1952 in NC.
Financial data (yr. ended 12/31/87): Assets, $1,379,645 (M); expenditures, $87,802, including $58,875 for 41 grants (high: $21,000; low: $100).
Purpose and activities: Support primarily for education, community funds, local fire departments, historical societies, libraries and religious giving.
Trustee: First Union National Bank of North Carolina.
Employer Identification Number: 566042484

2380
Peoples Bank Foundation
c/o Peoples Bank & Trust Co.
Box 872
Rocky Mount 27802 (919) 977-4001

Established in 1954 in NC.
Financial data (yr. ended 12/31/87): Assets, $895 (M); gifts received, $118,930; expenditures, $134,391, including $130,206 for 241 grants (high: $11,000; low: $25).
Purpose and activities: Grants primarily for higher education; support also for youth, social services, culture, and community funds.
Application information: Application form required.
Deadline(s): None
Write: Robert R. Mauldin
Trustee: Peoples Bank & Trust Co.
Employer Identification Number: 566050776

2381
Pepsi-Cola of Charlotte Foundation, Inc.
P.O. Box 241167
Charlotte 28224

Established in 1987 in NC.
Donor(s): Pepsi-Cola Bottling Co. of Charlotte, Inc.
Financial data (yr. ended 12/31/87): Assets, $273,468 (M); gifts received, $300,000; expenditures, $26,532, including $26,500 for 4 grants (high: $25,000; low: $200).
Purpose and activities: Support for housing, family services, youth, and music.
Limitations: Giving limited to the Charlotte, NC, area. No grants to individuals.
Application information:
Initial approach: Proposal
Deadline(s): None
Write: Dale Halton, Pres.
Officers: Dale Halton, Pres.; Darrell Holland, Secy.; Phil Halton, V.P. and Treas.
Employer Identification Number: 561591985

2382
Proctor Foundation
c/o Wachovia Bank & Trust Co.
P.O. Box 3099
Winston-Salem 27150 (919) 770-5269

Established in 1974 in NC.
Donor(s): Lucille S. Proctor.†
Financial data (yr. ended 12/31/86): Assets, $1,302,661 (M); expenditures, $110,561, including $93,921 for 27 grants (high: $25,000; low: $200; average: $500-$3,000).
Purpose and activities: Emphasis on higher education and youth; some support also for the handicapped and cultural organizations.
Types of support: Continuing support, annual campaigns, seed money, emergency funds, general purposes, building funds, equipment, land acquisition, renovation projects, matching funds.
Limitations: Giving primarily in Rowan County, NC. No grants to individuals, or for deficit financing or endowments; no loans.
Application information:
Initial approach: Letter
Deadline(s): None
Board meeting date(s): Jan. and Sept.
Final notification: 10 days after board meetings
Write: Martha B. Carlisle
Officers and Directors: Lucille P. Norvell, Pres.; Patricia P. Rendleman, V.P.; James L. Woodson, Secy.; Richard J. Rendleman, Treas.; Henrietta S. Anthony, Edwin O. Norvell.
Employer Identification Number: 237398904

2383
Kate B. Reynolds Charitable Trust
BB & T Building
Eight West Third St., Suite M3
Winston-Salem 27101 (919) 723-1456

Trust established in 1947 in NC.
Donor(s): Kate B. Reynolds.†
Financial data (yr. ended 8/31/88): Assets, $132,963,287 (M); expenditures, $5,090,612, including $4,660,374 for 97 grants (high: $200,000; low: $2,210; average: $10,000-$100,000).
Purpose and activities: Seventy-five percent of net income to be distributed for the health care of those in need statewide; twenty-five percent for the benefit of poor and needy residents of Winston-Salem and Forsyth County.
Types of support: Operating budgets, continuing support, annual campaigns, seed money, emergency funds, matching funds, building funds, capital campaigns, equipment, general purposes, renovation projects, research, special projects.
Limitations: Giving limited to NC; social welfare grants limited to Winston-Salem and Forsyth County; health care giving, state-wide. No grants to individuals, or for endowment funds; grants on a highly selective basis for construction of facilities or purchase of equipment.
Publications: Annual report (including application guidelines), program policy statement, informational brochure, application guidelines.
Application information: Applicant should contact the executive secretary prior to submitting a written application. Application form required.
Initial approach: Proposal
Copies of proposal: 1
Deadline(s): Jan. 15, May. 15, and Aug. 15 for Poor and Needy Trust; Apr. 1 and Oct. 1 for Health Care Trust
Board meeting date(s): Advisory committee for Poor and Needy Trust meets in Feb., June, and Sept.; for Health Care grants in May and Nov.
Final notification: 1 week after committee meeting
Write: W. Vance Frye, Exec. Secy.
Trustee: Wachovia Bank & Trust Co., N.A.
Number of staff: 1 full-time professional; 1 full-time support.
Employer Identification Number: 566036515
Recent arts and culture grants:
Experiment in Self-Reliance, Winston-Salem, NC, $5,000. For operating expenses for Love Community Choir. 1987.

2384
Z. Smith Reynolds Foundation, Inc.
101 Reynolda Village
Winston-Salem 27106-5199 (919) 725-7541

Incorporated in 1936 in NC.
Donor(s): Nancy S. Reynolds,† Mary Reynolds Babcock,† Richard J. Reynolds, Jr.,† William N. Reynolds.†
Financial data (yr. ended 12/31/88): Assets, $192,067,565 (M); gifts received, $7,880,991; expenditures, $8,199,016, including $7,593,579 for 206 grants (low: $300; average:

$15,000-$35,000) and $15,000 for 3 grants to individuals.
Purpose and activities: Giving primarily for education, the arts, health care, youth, community and economic development, social services, public policy, environment, improvement of the criminal justice system, and minority and women's issues.
Types of support: Operating budgets, continuing support, annual campaigns, seed money, building funds, equipment, land acquisition, matching funds, special projects, publications, conferences and seminars, general purposes.
Limitations: Giving limited to NC. No grants to individuals (except for Nancy Susan Reynolds Awards for community leadership), or for research or program-related investments; no loans.
Publications: Annual report (including application guidelines).
Application information: Application form required.
Initial approach: Letter, telephone, or proposal
Copies of proposal: 1
Deadline(s): Feb. 1 and Aug. 1
Board meeting date(s): 2nd Friday in May and Nov.
Final notification: 4 months after deadline
Write: Thomas W. Lambeth, Exec. Dir.
Officers: Zachary T. Smith,* Pres.; Smith W. Bagley,* V.P.; Thomas W. Lambeth, Secy. and Exec. Dir.; Joseph G. Gordon,* Treas.
Trustees:* Josephine D. Clement, Daniel G. Clodfelter, Hubert Humphrey, Katharine B. Mountcastle, Mary Mountcastle, Stephen L. Neal, Jane S. Patterson, Sherwood H. Smith, Jr.
Number of staff: 3 full-time professional; 2 full-time support.
Employer Identification Number: 586038145
Recent arts and culture grants:
African-American Dance Ensemble, Durham, NC, $25,000. For organizational development project. 1987.
Asheville Alumnae Delta House, Asheville, NC, $15,000. For youth cultural arts and tutorial project, as part of minority awards. 1987.
Beaufort Historical Association, Beaufort, NC, $20,000. For development program for Old Town Beaufort Historical Restoration. 1987.
Black Artists Guild, Kinston, NC, $15,000. For educational and artistic programs for youth in black community. 1987.
C.S. Brown School Auditorium Restoration Association, Winton, NC, $25,000. For operational support of cultural arts center and museum, as part of minority awards. 1987.
Charlotte Hawkins Brown Historical Society, Sedalia, NC, $50,000. For operational support and preservation of North Carolina African-American history. 1987.
Crossroads of Wilmington, Wilmington, NC, $20,000. For academic, social and cultural enrichment programs for low-income minority children. 1987.
Eastern Music Festival, Greensboro, NC, $10,000. To upgrade Festival's programs and activities. 1987.
Greenville Museum of Art, Greenville, NC, $5,000. For Collection Preservation Treatment Project. 1987.
Highlands Studio for the Arts, Highlands, NC, $10,000. For children-and-the-arts continuing education program. 1987.
Hyde County Grassroots Arts Council, Swan Quarter, NC, $10,000. To support music as performing art to benefit students and public. 1987.
National Humanities Center, Research Triangle Park, NC, $25,000. For operational support of Center. 1987.
North Carolina Agency for Public Telecommunications, Raleigh, NC, $35,000. For production of North Carolina Community Colleges' Literacy series. 1987.
North Carolina Humanities Committee, Greensboro, NC, $5,000. For statewide conference on literacy. 1987.
Randolph Arts Guild, Asheboro, NC, $10,000. To establish arts facility in downtown Asheboro. 1987.
Reynolda House, Winston-Salem, NC, $217,500. For operational support of American Museum of Art and for renovation of Reynolda House. 1987.
Rutherford County Arts Council, Forest City, NC, $20,000. For Folkroots program, cultural heritage project. 1987.
Saint Johns Museum of Art, Wilmington, NC, $5,000. For installation, preventive conservation and storage of permanent art collection. 1987.
University of North Carolina, Chapel Hill, NC, $35,000. For Program in Humanities and Human Values. 1987.
University of North Carolina, Center for Public Television, Chapel Hill, NC, $10,000. For production of documentary on Black Mountain College. 1987.
Watermark Association of Artisans, Northeastern Education and Development Foundation, Elizabeth City, NC, $35,000. For expansion of facilities for its crafts marketing cooperative for low-income women. 1987.

2385
Grace Jones Richardson Trust
P.O. Box 20124
Greensboro 27420

Trust established in 1962 in CT.
Donor(s): Grace Jones Richardson.†
Financial data (yr. ended 12/31/87): Assets, $22,388,438 (M); expenditures, $313,525, including $230,000 for 174 grants (high: $10,000).
Purpose and activities: Emphasis on community funds, social services, religious giving, health services, conservation, higher education, and cultural programs.
Limitations: No grants to individuals.
Application information: Applications not accepted.
Board meeting date(s): As required
Trustees: Peter L. Richardson, Robert R. Richardson, Stuart S. Richardson.
Number of staff: 1 part-time support.
Employer Identification Number: 066023003

2386
The Florence Rogers Charitable Trust
P.O. Box 36006
Fayetteville 28303 (919) 484-2033

Trust established in 1961 in NC.
Donor(s): Florence L. Rogers.†
Financial data (yr. ended 3/31/88): Assets, $3,863,337 (M); expenditures, $245,025, including $143,097 for 29 grants (high: $30,000; low: $200; average: $2,000-$5,000), $25,080 for 3 employee matching gifts and $10,200 for 4 foundation-administered programs.
Purpose and activities: Support for art programs, education, recreation, child welfare, and the general quality of life in the area. Preference is given to seed money for new ideas.
Types of support: Conferences and seminars, emergency funds, matching funds, operating budgets, publications, renovation projects, research, seed money, special projects.
Limitations: Giving primarily in Fayetteville, Cumberland County, and southeastern NC. No grants to individuals, or for building or endowment funds, scholarships, or fellowships; no loans.
Publications: Informational brochure (including application guidelines).
Application information:
Initial approach: Letter or telephone
Copies of proposal: 1
Board meeting date(s): Monthly
Final notification: 3 months
Write: JoAnn Barnette Stancil, Admin.
Officer: JoAnn Barnette Stancil, Admin.
Trustees: Nolan P. Clark, John C. Tally.
Number of staff: 1 full-time professional; 1 part-time professional; 2 part-time support.
Employer Identification Number: 566074515

2387
The RosaMary Foundation
c/o Wachovia Bank & Trust Co, N.A.
P.O. Box 3099
Winston-Salem 27150
Application address: P.O. Box 51299, New Orleans, LA 70151

Trust established in 1939 in LA.
Donor(s): Members of the A.B. Freeman family.
Financial data (yr. ended 12/31/87): Assets, $23,218,884 (M); expenditures, $1,266,488, including $1,017,437 for 34 grants (high: $170,000; low: $250).
Purpose and activities: Emphasis on a community fund, higher and secondary education, including church-related schools, civic affairs, and cultural programs.
Types of support: Annual campaigns, building funds, capital campaigns, continuing support, endowment funds, research, seed money, special projects.
Limitations: Giving primarily in the greater New Orleans, LA, area. No grants to individuals.
Application information:
Initial approach: Proposal in letter form
Copies of proposal: 1
Deadline(s): None
Board meeting date(s): Approximately 2 times a year beginning in spring

Write: Louis M. Freeman, Chair.
Trustees: Louis M. Freeman, Chair.; Adelaide W. Benjamin, Richard W. Freeman, Jr., Charles Keller, Jr., Rosa F. Keller, Mary Elizabeth Wisdom.
Number of staff: None.
Employer Identification Number: 726024696

2388
Sigmund Sternberger Foundation, Inc.
P.O. Box 3111
Greensboro 27402 (919) 373-1500

Incorporated in 1957 in NC.
Donor(s): Sigmund Sternberger,† Rosa Sternberger Williams.†
Financial data (yr. ended 3/31/87): Assets, $9,223,412 (M); gifts received, $499,000; expenditures, $489,229, including $404,950 for 38 grants (high: $75,000; low: $500) and $16,450 for 18 grants to individuals.
Purpose and activities: Support for higher education, including scholarship funds, and individual scholarships for children of members of the Revolution Masonic Lodge and to residents of Guilford County pursuing undergraduate studies in NC; grants also for the arts and human service agencies. Emphasis on special one-time projects, seed money and emergency needs.
Types of support: Seed money, emergency funds, special projects, scholarship funds, student aid, capital campaigns, operating budgets.
Limitations: Giving primarily in Guilford County, NC. No loans.
Publications: Application guidelines.
Application information: Application form required.
Initial approach: Letter
Copies of proposal: 1
Deadline(s): None
Board meeting date(s): Usually in Mar., June, Dec., and as required
Final notification: 3 months
Write: Robert O. Klepfer, Jr., Exec. Dir.
Officers: Mrs. A.J. Tannenbaum,* Pres.; Sidney J. Stern, Jr.,* Secy.-Treas.; Robert O. Klepfer, Jr., Exec. Dir.
Directors:* Howard E. Carr, Charles M. Reid, Jeanne Tannenbaum, Sigmund I. Tannenbaum, M.D., Rabbi Arnold S. Task.
Number of staff: 1 part-time professional.
Employer Identification Number: 566045483

2389
Greater Triangle Community Foundation
Headquarters Park
2222 Chapel Hill Nelson Hwy.
Durham 27713 (919) 544-4006

Incorporated in 1983 in NC.
Financial data (yr. ended 6/30/88): Assets, $4,119,635 (M); gifts received, $2,580,500; expenditures, $950,000, including $252,931 for grants.
Purpose and activities: Support primarily for education, the arts, health, conservation and social sciences.
Types of support: Scholarship funds, seed money, special projects.
Limitations: Giving primarily in the Durham, Orange, and Wake County, NC, area. No grants for annual campaigns, continuing support, employee matching gifts, operating budgets, program-related investments; no loans.
Publications: Annual report, newsletter, application guidelines.
Application information: Application form required.
Initial approach: Letter
Copies of proposal: 13
Deadline(s): Feb. 15
Board meeting date(s): Apr.
Final notification: May 1
Write: Shannon St. John, Exec. Dir.
Executive Director: Shannon St. John.
Number of staff: 2 full-time professional; 1 full-time support.
Employer Identification Number: 561380796

2390
Valdese Manufacturing Company Foundation, Inc.
P.O. Drawer 10
Valdese 28690-0010

Financial data (yr. ended 12/31/87): Assets, $4,376 (M); expenditures, $3,514, including $3,500 for 3 grants (high: $2,500; low: $500).
Purpose and activities: Support for arts and culture, and social services.
Application information: Contributes only to preselected organizations. Applications not accepted.
Officers: William Galloway, Pres. and Treas.; Edward Pascal, V.P. and Secy.
Employer Identification Number: 566061867

2391
Volvo GM Heavy Truck Corporate Giving Program
P.O. Box 26115
Greensboro 27402-6115 (919) 279-2000

Financial data (yr. ended 12/31/88): $100,000 for 73 grants (high: $2,500; low: $250; average: $250-$2,500).
Purpose and activities: Support for community development, ecology, education, including building funds, libraries, health, hospitals, hospices, and fine and performing arts.
Types of support: Annual campaigns, building funds, emergency funds, general purposes.
Limitations: Giving primarily in NC, OH, UT, and VA.
Application information: Applications not accepted.
Write: Thage Berggren, Pres.
Number of staff: 1 part-time support.

2392
The Wachovia Foundation Inc.
c/o Wachovia Bank & Trust Co., N.A.
P.O. Box 3099
Winston-Salem 27150

Incorporated in 1982 in NC.
Donor(s): Wachovia Bank & Trust Co., N.A.
Financial data (yr. ended 12/31/88): Assets, $5,096,247 (M); gifts received, $2,495,733; expenditures, $1,091,949, including $913,144 for 142 grants (high: $50,000; low: $275) and $177,032 for 960 employee matching gifts.
Purpose and activities: Emphasis on higher education and community projects, including community funds.
Types of support: Building funds, capital campaigns, special projects, endowment funds, research, operating budgets, annual campaigns, renovation projects, grants to individuals.
Limitations: Giving primarily in NC. No grants to individuals.
Application information:
Initial approach: Contact local bank office
Deadline(s): None
Board meeting date(s): Monthly
Write: John F. McNair III, Pres. and C.E.O., Wachovia Bank & Trust Co., N.A.
Officers: John G. Medlin, Jr., Pres.; John F. McNair III, V.P. and Treas.; J. Scott Cramer, V.P.; Hans W. Wanders, V.P.; James G. Vanderberry, Secy.
Number of staff: 2 part-time support.
Employer Identification Number: 581485946

2393
The Winston-Salem Foundation
229 First Union National Bank Bldg.
Winston-Salem 27101 (919) 725-2382

Community foundation established in 1919 in NC by declaration of trust.
Financial data (yr. ended 12/31/88): Assets, $49,157,236 (M); gifts received, $7,079,087; expenditures, $4,410,698, including $3,837,062 for grants (high: $100,000; low: $100; average: $15,000), $99,880 for grants to individuals and $335,707 for loans to individuals.
Purpose and activities: Student aid primarily to bona fide residents of Forsyth County, NC; support also for non-profit organizations of all types, especially educational, social service and health programs, the arts, and civic affairs.
Types of support: Seed money, emergency funds, student aid, special projects, matching funds, general purposes, student loans, fellowships, research, continuing support.
Limitations: Giving primarily in the greater Forsyth County, NC, area; some support for northwest NC. No grants for annual campaigns, land acquisition, publications, or conferences.
Publications: Annual report, application guidelines, newsletter, grants list.
Application information: Application form required for student aid or student loans and includes $20 application fee.
Initial approach: Telephone
Copies of proposal: 1
Deadline(s): Jan. 1, Apr. 1, July 1, and Oct. 1
Board meeting date(s): Jan., Mar., June, Sept., and Nov. (applications not considered at Jan. meeting)
Final notification: 1 month
Write: Henry M. Carter, Jr., Exec. Dir.
Officer: Henry M. Carter, Jr., Exec. Dir.
Foundation Committee: John F. McNair III, Chair.; F. Hudnall Christopher, Jr., Vice-Chair.; Herbert Brenner, Victor I. Flow, Jr., Mrs. Roberta W. Irwin, Barbara K. Phillips, C. Edward Pleasants, Jr., A. Tab Williams III.

Trustees: Branch Banking & Trust Co., First Citizens Bank & Trust Co., First Union National Bank, NCNB National Bank, Southern National Bank, Wachovia Bank & Trust Co., N.A.
Number of staff: 4 full-time professional; 3 full-time support.
Employer Identification Number: 566037615
Recent arts and culture grants:
Arts Council, Winston-Salem, NC, $27,500. To support spin-off of Urban Arts, division of Arts Council, into independent arts programming agency. 9/13/88.
Carolina Consort, Winston-Salem, NC, $5,000. To support baroque orchestra's first subscription concert series in Spring 1989. 6/14/88.
Fiddle and Bow Society, Winston-Salem, NC, $7,000. To help initiate international music series and to continue supporting Opening Acts of local musicians. 6/14/88.
Love Community Choir, Winston-Salem, NC, $6,000. To continue support for community choir for underserved youth. 6/14/88.
Piedmont Chamber Singers, Winston-Salem, NC, $6,000. To hire part-time marketing consultant for choir. 6/14/88.
Urban Arts, Winston-Salem, NC, $10,000. To ensure availability of technical assistance to area small and medium-sized arts organizations. 6/14/88.
Winston-Salem Symphony, winston-Salem, NC, $25,000. To help support addition of assistant conductor and director of development to community's symphony orchestra staff. 3/15/88.
Winston-Salem Theater Alliance, Winston-Salem, NC, $5,000. To help provide semi-professional theater company with home theater and means to develop broadened audience base. 6/14/88.

2394
Margaret C. Woodson Foundation, Inc.
P.O. Box 829
Salisbury 28145 (704) 633-5000

Incorporated in 1954 in NC.
Donor(s): Margaret C. Woodson.†
Financial data (yr. ended 12/31/86): Assets, $6,655,998 (M); gifts received, $311,689; expenditures, $369,093, including $345,520 for 25 grants (high: $58,000; low: $250).
Purpose and activities: Giving for higher education, cultural programs, child welfare, and hospitals.
Limitations: Giving primarily in Davie and Rowan counties, NC. No grants for research.
Application information:
Deadline(s): Jan. 31
Write: James L. Woodson, Pres.
Officers: James L. Woodson,* Pres.; Esther C. Shay,* V.P.; Roy C. Hoffner, Secy.; Charles Cunningham,* Treas.
Directors:* Paul L. Bernhardt, Beulah Hillard, Mary Holt W. Woodson, Paul B. Woodson.
Employer Identification Number: 566064938

NORTH DAKOTA

2395
Fargo-Moorhead Area Foundation
315 North Eighth St.
Fargo 58102 (701) 234-0756
Additional address: P.O. Box 1609, Fargo, ND 58107

Community foundation established in 1960 in ND.
Financial data (yr. ended 12/31/86): Assets, $2,977,718 (M); gifts received, $55,231; expenditures, $514,429, including $422,463 for 56 grants (high: $42,706; low: $138; average: $1,000-$10,000).
Purpose and activities: Grants for educational, scientific, medical, surgical, hygenic, musical, and artistic purposes; support also for the preservation of art and historical records and relics, public health, housing, and civic improvements; giving for the care of children, the aged, sick, helpless, poor and incompetent, as well as for the improvement of moral, mental, social, and physical well-being.
Types of support: Continuing support, annual campaigns, seed money, emergency funds, building funds, equipment, matching funds, scholarship funds, renovation projects, capital campaigns, conferences and seminars, consulting services, exchange programs, general purposes, operating budgets, publications, special projects, technical assistance.
Limitations: Giving primarily in the city of Fargo and Cass County, ND, and the city of Moorhead and Clay County, MN. No grants to individuals, or for deficit financing, land acquisition, or medical research; no loans.
Publications: Program policy statement, application guidelines, informational brochure, annual report.
Application information: Application form required.
Initial approach: Letter or telephone
Copies of proposal: 8
Deadline(s): Submit proposal preferably in Jan. or Mar.; deadline Apr. 1
Board meeting date(s): Quarterly
Final notification: May 30
Write: Susan M. Hunke, Exec. Dir.
Officers: Marcia Kierscht,* Chair.; Roger L. Sullivan, Secy.
Distribution Committee:* Esther Allen, Richard B. Crockett, Edward Ellenson, Robert Feder, Norman M. Jones, Edward R. Stern, James M. Swedback.
Trustee Banks: American Bank and Trust Co., Dakota First Trust Co., First Interstate Bank and Trust, First Trust Co. of North Dakota, Norwest Capital Bank ND, N.A.
Number of staff: 1 full-time professional; 1 part-time support.
Employer Identification Number: 456010377

2396
Tom & Frances Leach Foundation, Inc.
P.O. Box 1136
Bismarck 58502 (701) 255-0479

Established in 1955 in ND.
Donor(s): Tom Leach,† Frances Leach.†
Financial data (yr. ended 12/31/87): Assets, $5,072,654 (M); expenditures, $458,632, including $274,498 for 44 grants (high: $50,000; low: $500; average: $1,000-$5,000).
Purpose and activities: Giving to higher education, social service and youth agencies, hospitals and health services, and cultural programs.
Types of support: Scholarship funds, capital campaigns, continuing support, endowment funds, general purposes, operating budgets, special projects.
Limitations: Giving primarily in ND, particularly in Bismarck and Mandan, and in Tulsa, OK.
Publications: Annual report.
Application information: Application form required.
Initial approach: Letter
Copies of proposal: 1
Deadline(s): Oct. 1
Board meeting date(s): Nov.
Final notification: Dec.
Write: Clement C. Weber, Exec. Dir.
Officers: Ernest R. Fleck,* Pres.; James P. Wachter,* V.P.; Russell R. Mather,* Secy.-Treas.; Clement C. Weber, Exec. Dir.
Directors:* Frank J. Bavendick, Julia B. Blakely, Robert P. Hendrickson, Gilbert N. Olson, Paul D. Schliesman.
Number of staff: 1 full-time professional; 1 full-time support.
Employer Identification Number: 456012703

2397
MDU Resources Foundation
400 North Fourth St.
Bismarck 58501 (701) 222-7828

Established in 1983 in ND.
Donor(s): MDU Resources Group, Inc., Williston Basin Interstate Pipeline Co., Knife River, Coal Mining Co.
Financial data (yr. ended 12/31/87): Assets, $245,271 (M); expenditures, $254,586, including $253,965 for 149 grants (high: $30,000; low: $50).
Purpose and activities: Grants for education, community development, hospitals and health services, and cultural programs.
Types of support: General purposes, scholarship funds, building funds.
Limitations: Giving primarily in areas of company operations of MDU Resources Group and its divisions and subsidiaries in ND, MT, and SD.
Application information: Application form required.
Deadline(s): None
Write: Robert E. Wood, Pres.
Officers and Directors: Robert E. Wood, Pres.; Alvin J. Wittmaier, V.P.; H.J. Mellen, Jr., Secy.-Treas.; Douglas C. Kane, Joseph R. Maichel.
Employer Identification Number: 450378937

2398
Myra Foundation
P.O. Box 1536
Grand Forks 58206-1536 (701) 775-9420

Incorporated in 1941 in ND.
Donor(s): John E. Myra.†
Financial data (yr. ended 12/31/87): Assets, $2,489,194 (M); expenditures, $263,987, including $169,986 for 23 grants (high: $44,500; low: $500; average: $7,390).
Purpose and activities: Emphasis on civic projects, health, cultural organizations, higher and secondary education, social services, the aged, and youth development.
Limitations: Giving limited to Grand Forks County, ND. No grants to individuals, or for endowment funds, research, or matching gifts; no loans.
Publications: Informational brochure (including application guidelines).
Application information: Application form required.
Initial approach: Letter
Copies of proposal: 1
Deadline(s): None
Board meeting date(s): Quarterly
Write: Edward C. Gillig, Pres.
Officers: Edward C. Gillig, Pres.; Hilda Johnson, V.P.; Robert F. Hansen, Secy.-Treas.
Employer Identification Number: 450215088

2399
North Dakota Community Foundation
1002 East Central Ave.
Bismarck 58501 (701) 222-8349

Established in 1977 in ND.
Financial data (yr. ended 12/31/88): Assets, $2,413,869 (M); gifts received, $231,709; expenditures, $227,352, including $105,535 for 136 grants (high: $4,500; low: $100; average: $1,000).
Purpose and activities: Unrestricted funds largely for aid to the elderly and disadvantaged; support also for health services, including mental health, youth agencies, parks and recreation, and arts and cultural programs.
Types of support: Operating budgets, continuing support, annual campaigns, seed money, building funds, equipment, matching funds, scholarship funds, special projects, research, publications, conferences and seminars, student aid.
Limitations: Giving primarily in ND. No support for lobbying or sectarian purposes; low priority given to national or out-of-state organizations, hospitals, organizations with substantial and professional fundraising programs, or organizations that raise money through gambling activities. No grants to individuals (except for scholarships), or for emergency or endowment funds, deficit financing, or land acquisition; no loans.
Publications: Annual report, newsletter.
Application information: Application by foundation invitation only for unrestricted grants. Application form required.
Initial approach: Letter
Copies of proposal: 1
Board meeting date(s): Annually in 2nd quarter of year
Write: Richard H. Timmins, Pres.
Officers and Directors: Vernon E. Wagner, Chair.; Mark Butz, Vice-Chair.; Richard H. Timmins, Pres.; Donald L. Schmid, Secy.-Treas.; Jan Berg, Keith Bjerke, Francis Forster, David Gipp, Sarah Andrews Herman, Ray Hoffman, Jo Jacobson, Karnes Johnson, Theodore F. Kessel, Sr., J. Gerald Niles, John Pierson.
Number of staff: 2 full-time professional; 1 full-time support.
Employer Identification Number: 450336015

2400
Earl C. Reineke Foundation
P.O. Box 1880
Fargo 58107

Established in 1960 in ND.
Financial data (yr. ended 12/31/87): Assets, $116,457 (M); gifts received, $0; expenditures, $206,983, including $201,538 for 2 grants (high: $192,690; low: $8,848).
Purpose and activities: Support primarily for the restoration of an historic theatre; supoort also for a public radio station.
Types of support: Equipment, renovation projects.
Limitations: Giving primarily in Fargo, ND.
Application information:
Initial approach: Letter
Deadline(s): None
Write: John M. Riley, Trustee
Trustees: John G. Early, Thomas G. Early, John M. Riley.
Employer Identification Number: 456013651

2401
Alex Stern Family Foundation
Bill Stern Bldg., Suite 202
609-1/2 First Ave., North
Fargo 58102 (701) 237-0170

Established in 1964 in ND.
Donor(s): William Stern,† Sam Stern,† Edward A. Stern.†
Financial data (yr. ended 12/31/88): Assets, $6,872,036 (M); expenditures, $422,096, including $338,593 for 63 grants (high: $30,000; low: $90; average: $5,375).
Purpose and activities: Emphasis on cultural programs, social service agencies, and youth agencies; grants also for community organizations, temple support, and human interest and human services organizations.
Types of support: Special projects, continuing support, annual campaigns, emergency funds, building funds, equipment, research, conferences and seminars, professorships, matching funds, lectureships, operating budgets, publications, scholarship funds.
Limitations: Giving limited to the Fargo, ND, and Moorhead, MN, areas. No grants to individuals, or for endowment funds; no loans.
Publications: Application guidelines.
Application information: Application form required.
Initial approach: Letter, telephone, or proposal
Copies of proposal: 3
Deadline(s): Submit application preferably between Apr. and Dec.; no set deadline
Final notification: Within a few months
Write: A.M. Eriksmoen, Exec. Dir.
Officer and Trustees: A.M. Eriksmoen, Exec. Dir.; W.R. Amundson, J.L. McCormick.
Number of staff: 1 full-time professional; 1 part-time professional.
Employer Identification Number: 456013981
Recent arts and culture grants:
Cass County Historical Society, West Fargo, ND, $5,000. Toward construction costs for agricultural display building. 1987.
Fargo Public Schools, Creative Arts Studio, Fargo, ND, $10,000. For funding access for handicapped and disabled at Clara Barton School. 1987.
Fargo Theater, Fargo, ND, $5,000. Toward purchase and remodeling of theater building. 1987.
Fargo-Moorhead Civic Opera Company, West Fargo, ND, $5,000. Toward production expenses. 1987.
Fargo-Moorhead Orchestral Association, Fargo, ND, $5,500. Toward musical educational programs provided to area schools. 1987.
Prairie Public Television, Fargo, ND, $10,000. For second installment of grant for programing expenses. 1987.

OHIO

2402
Acme Cleveland Foundation
30195 Chagrin Blvd., Suite 300
Pepper Pike 44124 (216) 292-2100

Incorporated in 1969 in OH.
Donor(s): Acme-Cleveland Corp.
Financial data (yr. ended 12/31/87): Assets, $134,948 (M); expenditures, $41,624, including $36,460 for grants and $5,155 for employee matching gifts.
Purpose and activities: Emphasis on community funds, higher education, health agencies and hospitals, youth activities, and cultural organizations.
Types of support: Operating budgets, continuing support, general purposes, annual campaigns, building funds, endowment funds, special projects, employee matching gifts.
Limitations: Giving limited to areas of company operations, especially Cleveland, OH, and Detroit, MI. No grants to individuals, or for research programs, scholarships, or fellowships; no loans.
Application information:
Initial approach: Proposal
Copies of proposal: 1
Deadline(s): Submit proposal preferably between Dec. 1 and Feb. 15
Board meeting date(s): Contribution committee meets at the end of Feb.
Write: Mel A. Vogel
Officers: W. Paul Cooper,* Pres.; D.M. Flammang, Secy.-Treas.

Directors:* Theodore M. Alfred, B. Charles Ames, W. David Dance, Stephen M. Dubrul, Jr., John D. Dwyer, Martin J. Koldyke, Karl H. Rudolph, Robert M. Taylor.
Employer Identification Number: 346527528

2403
Akron Community Foundation
One Cascade Plaza
Akron 44308 (216) 376-8522

Community foundation incorporated in 1955 in OH.
Financial data (yr. ended 3/31/88): Assets, $8,204,727 (M); gifts received, $451,611; expenditures, $860,529, including $757,333 for 112 grants (high: $158,000; low: $100; average: $1,000-$10,000).
Purpose and activities: To promote charitable, benevolent, educational, recreational, health, esthetic, cultural, and public welfare activities; to support a program of research leading to the improvement of the health, education, and general well-being of all citizens of the Akron area; to give toward the support of experimental and demonstration programs, through established or new agencies; to test the validity of research findings in various fields of community planning directed toward the efficient and adequate coordination of public and private services organized to meet human needs.
Types of support: Operating budgets, building funds, matching funds, research, special projects.
Limitations: Giving primarily in Summit County, OH. No grants to individuals, or for endowment funds, scholarships, or fellowships; no loans.
Publications: Annual report, application guidelines, newsletter.
Application information: No more than 1 grant to an organization in a 12-month period.
Initial approach: Proposal, letter, or telephone
Copies of proposal: 1
Deadline(s): Mar. 15, July 15, and Dec. 1
Board meeting date(s): Generally May, Sept., and Jan.
Final notification: 2 to 3 months
Write: John L. Feudner, Jr., Exec. Dir.
Officers: Tom H. Barrett,* Pres.; George T. Parry,* V.P.; Allan Johnson, Secy.; Ernest J. Novack, Jr.,* Treas.; John L. Feudner, Jr., Exec. Dir.
Trustees:* Bruce S. Bailey, Randolph Baxter, Ann Amer Brennan, Robert W. Briggs, Michael J. Connor, Howard L. Flood, Karl S. Hay, Judith Isroff, David A. Lieberth, Tom Merryweather, Bruce Rothmann, Melvin D. Sacks, Sandra Smith, Gale R. Urda, Charles F. Zodrow.
Trustee Banks: Bank One of Akron, First National Bank of Ohio, National City Bank, Society National Bank.
Number of staff: 1 part-time professional; 1 full-time support.
Employer Identification Number: 237029875
Recent arts and culture grants:
Akron Childrens Theater Productions, Akron, OH, $5,000. To assist with purchase of sound system. 1988.
Akron Civic Theater, Community Hall Foundation, Akron, OH, $40,000. To assist in meeting challenge grant. 1988.
Akron Symphony Orchestra, Akron, OH, $13,000. To support 1987-88 in-school concerts. 1988.
Akron Symphony Orchestra, Akron, OH, $12,000. For in-school concerts ('86-'87). 1988.
Akron Symphony Orchestra, Akron, OH, $10,000. To underwrite 1988 Subscription Concert. 1988.
Childrens Concert Society of Akron, Akron, OH, $5,000. For 1987-88 season. 1988.
Cuyahoga Valley Youth Ballet, Cuyahoga Falls, OH, $6,360. For portable dance floor and shoes. 1988.
ETC All American Youth Show Choir, Stow, OH, $5,000. To purchase cargo van. 1988.
Kent State University, Kent, OH, $20,000. To purchase permanent facility for WKSU-FM. 1988.
Musical Arts Association, Blossom Music Center, Cleveland, OH, $20,000. To sponsor 1987 concert. 1988.
Tuesday Musical Club, Akron, OH, $15,000. To assist with performance at E.J. Thomas Hall. 1988.
Weathervane Community Playhouse, Akron, OH, $25,000. To assist with capital project. 1988.

2404
The William H. Albers Foundation, Inc.
P.O. Box 38360
Cincinnati 45238-0360

Incorporated in 1982 in OH.
Financial data (yr. ended 4/30/88): Assets, $1,444,397 (M); expenditures, $114,858, including $95,000 for 30 grants (high: $10,000; low: $200).
Purpose and activities: Emphasis on secondary and higher education, cultural programs, youth agencies, and hospitals.
Types of support: General purposes, building funds, operating budgets.
Limitations: Giving primarily in Cincinnati, OH.
Application information:
Write: Irene A. Dornheggen, Pres.
Officer and Trustees: Irene A. Dornheggen, Pres.; Ann M. Kallaher, James L. Leonard, Luke J. Leonard.
Employer Identification Number: 316023881

2405
Eleanora C. U. Alms Trust
c/o Fifth Third Bank, Dept. 00850 Trust Div.
38 Fountain Sq. Plaza
Cincinnati 45263 (513) 579-6034

Trust established in 1939 in OH.
Donor(s): Eleanora C.U. Alms.†
Financial data (yr. ended 9/30/87): Assets, $2,539,865 (M); expenditures, $125,009, including $109,120 for 11 grants (high: $25,000; low: $5,000; average: $10,000).
Purpose and activities: Support for charitable, educational, and artistic activities.
Types of support: Building funds.
Limitations: Giving limited to the greater Cincinnati, OH, area. No support for political or religious purposes, or to other foundations. No grants to individuals, or for operating budgets; no loans.
Publications: Application guidelines.
Application information:
Initial approach: Letter
Copies of proposal: 1
Deadline(s): Early Feb., May, Aug., or Nov.
Board meeting date(s): Mar., June, Sept., and Dec.
Write: Carolyn F. McCoy, Mgr.
Trustee: Fifth Third Bank.
Employer Identification Number: 316019723
Recent arts and culture grants:
Cincinnati Art Museum, Cincinnati, OH, $25,000. For gallery renovation. 1987.
Cincinnati Ballet Company, Cincinnati, OH, $5,000. For Nutcracker production costs. 1987.
Cincinnati Childrens Theater, Cincinnati, OH, $7,500. For sets and costumes for Bicentennial production. 1987.
Cincinnati Historical Society, Cincinnati, OH, $10,000. For film on history of city government. 1987.
Fine Arts Fund, Cincinnati, OH, $5,500. For annual campaign. 1987.
Friends of the William Howard Taft Birthplace, Cincinnati, OH, $10,000. For restoration costs for exhibits for Charles P. Taft room. 1987.
Music Hall, Cincinnati, OH, $100,000. For capital campaign. 1987.

2406
Amcast Industrial Foundation
3931 South Dixie Ave.
Kettering 45439 (513) 298-5251
Mailing address: P.O. Box 98, Dayton, OH 45401

Incorporated in 1952 in OH.
Donor(s): Amcast Industrial Corp. (formerly Dayton Malleable, Inc.).
Financial data (yr. ended 8/31/88): Assets, $547,984 (M); gifts received, $178,279; expenditures, $172,136, including $167,583 for 79 grants (high: $21,371; low: $25) and $4,553 for 28 employee matching gifts.
Purpose and activities: Grants mainly for community funds, arts and cultural programs, social services, health, and higher education; includes matching gifts for education.
Types of support: Continuing support, annual campaigns, emergency funds, building funds, employee matching gifts, special projects, research, employee-related scholarships.
Limitations: Giving primarily in areas of company operations. No grants to individuals (except employee-related scholarships), or for operating budgets, seed money, deficit financing, equipment, land acquisition, endowment funds, scholarships, fellowships, publications, or conferences; no loans.
Publications: Financial statement, informational brochure.
Application information: Letters to the foundation are routed to the different divisions which then make grant recommendations to the foundations. Applicants may write to the division in their area directly.
Board meeting date(s): Nov. and Aug.
Write: Thomas G. Amato, Secy.

Officers and Trustees: Leo W. Ladehoff, Pres.; Thomas G. Amato, Secy.
Number of staff: None.
Employer Identification Number: 316016458

2407
The American Financial Corporation Foundation

One East Fourth St.
Cincinnati 45202 (513) 579-2121

Established in 1971 in OH.
Donor(s): American Financial Corp.
Financial data (yr. ended 12/31/87): Assets, $117,066 (M); gifts received, $2,150,000; expenditures, $2,158,815, including $2,156,435 for 111 grants (high: $250,000; low: $15; average: $500-$20,000).
Purpose and activities: Foundation is primarily a conduit for corporate contributions to local charities. Giving primarily for organizations promoting social change, economic study, and social welfare, including hospitals, and public interest organizations; grants also for education and the arts.
Types of support: Building funds, endowment funds, operating budgets, special projects.
Limitations: Giving primarily in the Cincinnati, OH, area. No grants to individuals.
Application information:
Initial approach: Letter
Copies of proposal: 1
Board meeting date(s): As required
Final notification: 60 days
Write: Sandra W. Heimann, Secy.
Officers: Carl H. Lindner,* Pres.; Robert D. Lindner,* V.P.; Sandra W. Heimann, Secy.; Sherwood W. McIntire, Treas.
Trustees:* Ronald F. Walker.
Number of staff: None.
Employer Identification Number: 237153009

2408
The American Foundation Corporation

720 National City Bank Bldg.
Cleveland 44114 (216) 241-6664

Incorporated in 1974 as successor to trust established in 1944 in OH.
Donor(s): Corning, Murfey and Norweb families and others.
Financial data (yr. ended 12/31/87): Assets, $16,946,361 (M); gifts received, $22,675; expenditures, $1,064,220, including $1,064,220 for 186 grants (high: $197,124; low: $8; average: $200-$36,000).
Purpose and activities: Emphasis on an arboretum, the arts, higher and secondary education, child welfare, and community funds.
Types of support: Annual campaigns, general purposes, continuing support.
Limitations: Giving primarily in the Cleveland, OH, area, and CA. No grants to individuals, or for capital or endowment funds, special projects, research, scholarships, fellowships, or matching gifts; no loans.
Application information: Funds presently committed. Applications not accepted.
Board meeting date(s): As necessary
Write: Maria G. Muth, Treas.
Officers: Malvin E. Bank, Secy.; Maria G. Muth, Treas.
Trustees: Henry H. Corning, Nathan E. Corning, T. Dixon Long, Spencer L. Murfey, Jr., William W. Murfey.
Number of staff: None.
Employer Identification Number: 237348126

2409
American Greetings Corporate Giving Program

10500 American Rd.
Cleveland 44144-2388 (216) 252-7300

Purpose and activities: Supports arts and culture, health and welfare, education, and civic affairs.
Types of support: Capital campaigns, matching funds, operating budgets.
Limitations: Giving primarily in corporate headquarters and major operating areas.
Publications: Corporate report.
Application information: Include budget and proof of 501(c)(3) status.
Initial approach: Letter
Deadline(s): None
Final notification: 6 weeks. All requests will be answered
Write: Harvey Levin, V.P.

2410
American Society of Ephesus, Inc.

(also known as George B. Quatman Foundation)
327 North Elizabeth St.
Lima 45801 (419) 225-2261

Incorporated in 1958.
Financial data (yr. ended 12/31/86): Assets, $1,500,173 (M); expenditures, $115,000, including $100,000 for 15 grants (high: $80,000; low: $75).
Purpose and activities: Formed primarily for the purpose of the restoration and preservation of the Christian shrines contained in the ruins of the ancient city of Ephesus that lies on the western coast of Turkey facing the Aegean Sea. Once the annual budget for this program is completed, it normally consumes all available income. Should any monies be remaining, consideration is primarily given to a donation to a Christian shrine that would have the common focal point and usage by the public in general.
Types of support: Renovation projects.
Limitations: Giving primarily in Ephesus, Turkey; some local giving in the Lima, OH, area. No grants for research, scholarships, or church maintenance or reconstruction.
Publications: 990-PF, occasional report, informational brochure.
Application information:
Write: Joseph B. Quatman, V.P.
Officers: George W. Quatman, Jr.,* Pres.; Joseph B. Quatman,* V.P.; Anne Lehmann, Secy.-Treas.
Trustees:* Anthony J. Bowers, John D. Quatman, Joseph E. Quatman, Jr.
Number of staff: 1 part-time professional; 1 part-time support.
Employer Identification Number: 346560998

2411
Anderson Foundation

P.O. Box 119
Maumee 43537 (419) 891-6481

Trust established in 1949 in OH.
Donor(s): Partners in The Andersons.
Financial data (yr. ended 12/31/87): Assets, $4,737,945 (M); gifts received, $104,100; expenditures, $612,217, including $542,042 for 162 grants (high: $136,854; low: $50) and $35,024 for 121 employee matching gifts.
Purpose and activities: Grants for higher and secondary education, social service and youth agencies, community funds, civic and community efforts, cultural programs, religious organizations, and educational and research associations.
Types of support: Capital campaigns, conferences and seminars, employee matching gifts, employee-related scholarships, annual campaigns, building funds, emergency funds, general purposes, matching funds, publications, research, scholarship funds, seed money, special projects.
Limitations: Giving primarily in the greater Toledo, OH, area, including Maumee, Columbus, and Findlay. Grants also to organizations located within 50 miles of The Andersons plants in the following cities: Delphi, Frankfort, and Dunkirk, IN; Champaign, IL; and Albion, Potterville, Webberville, and White Pigeon, MI. No grants to individuals, or for endowment funds or travel.
Publications: Application guidelines.
Application information:
Initial approach: Letter or telephone
Copies of proposal: 1
Deadline(s): 1st week of months of board meetings
Board meeting date(s): Bimonthly beginning in Feb.
Final notification: Generally 2 months; depends on completeness of proposal
Write: Tammy Smahaj, Secy. to the Chair.
Trustees: Thomas H. Anderson, Chair.; Andrew T. Anderson, Christopher J. Anderson, Michael J. Anderson, Robert G. Bristow, Beverly J. McBride, Ruth M. Miller.
Number of staff: 1 full-time professional.
Employer Identification Number: 346528868

2412
William P. Anderson Foundation

c/o Central Trust Co.
Fifth and Main Sts.
Cincinnati 45202 (513) 651-8439

Incorporated in 1941 in OH.
Financial data (yr. ended 10/31/87): Assets, $3,565,190 (M); expenditures, $201,187, including $135,500 for 38 grants (high: $10,000; low: $500) and $31,287 for 4 grants to individuals.
Purpose and activities: Emphasis on hospitals, community funds, educational institutions, child welfare and youth agencies, including problems of juvenile delinquency, health agencies, conservation, and the arts.
Types of support: Annual campaigns, building funds, capital campaigns.
Limitations: Giving primarily in Cincinnati, OH, and Boston, MA. No grants to individuals.

Application information: The foundation no longer awards scholarships to individual students; existing commitments will be paid out.
Initial approach: Letter
Deadline(s): None
Board meeting date(s): Oct. and Nov.
Write: Paul D. Myers, Secy.
Officers and Trustees: William G. Anderson, Pres. and Treas.; Vachael Anderson Coombe, V.P.; Harry W. Whittaker, V.P.; Paul D. Myers, Secy.; Grenville Anderson, William P. Anderson V, Eva Jane Coombe, Michael A. Coombe, Margot A. Pattison, C. Lawson Reed, Dorothy W. Reed, Katharine W. Taft.
Employer Identification Number: 316034059

2413
The Andersons Giving Program
P.O. Box 119
Maumee 43537 (419) 893-5050

Financial data (yr. ended 12/31/87): $187,400 for grants (high: $180,000).
Purpose and activities: Supports education, scientific research, the United Way, youth service and religious/non-sectarian organizations. Also available is employee gift matching for education, hospitals, cultural projects and public broadcasting.
Types of support: Employee matching gifts.
Limitations: Giving primarily in headquarters city and major operating locations.
Application information: Applications not accepted.
Write: Beverly Lane, Contribs. Secy.

2414
The Andrews Foundation
1127 Euclid Ave., Suite 210
Cleveland 44115 (216) 621-3215

Incorporated in 1951 in OH.
Donor(s): Mrs. Matthew Andrews.†
Financial data (yr. ended 12/31/88): Assets, $4,931,996 (M); expenditures, $341,508, including $301,900 for 67 grants (high: $100,000; low: $500).
Purpose and activities: Giving for higher and secondary education, the performing arts, a child development center, and associations concerned with alcoholism and the handicapped.
Types of support: Annual campaigns, building funds, capital campaigns, endowment funds, general purposes.
Limitations: Giving limited to northeastern OH. No grants to individuals.
Application information:
Initial approach: Letter
Copies of proposal: 1
Deadline(s): None
Board meeting date(s): Usually in Nov.
Write: Richard S. Tomer, Pres.
Officers and Trustees: Richard S. Tomer, Pres. and Treas.; Barbara J. Baxter, V.P.; James H. Dempsey, Jr., Secy.; Laura S. Baxter.
Number of staff: None.
Employer Identification Number: 346515110

2415
The Mildred Andrews Fund
1220 Huntington Bldg.
Cleveland 44115

Trust established in 1972 in OH.
Donor(s): Peter Putnam, and others.
Financial data (yr. ended 12/31/87): Assets, $32,045,394 (M); gifts received, $18,506,069; expenditures, $1,008,304, including $363,934 for 33 grants (high: $100,112; low: $50).
Purpose and activities: A private operating foundation; giving for the arts and higher education.
Limitations: Giving primarily in the Cleveland, OH, area.
Application information:
Write: Peter Putnam, Trustee
Trustee: Peter Putnam.
Employer Identification Number: 237158695

2416
The Evenor Armington Fund
c/o Huntington Trust Co., N.A.
P.O. Box 1558
Columbus 43260
Application address: The Huntington National Bank, Trust Dept., 41 South High St., Columbus, OH 43216; Tel.: (614) 463-3707

Established in 1954 in OH.
Donor(s): Everett Armington, and members of the Armington family.
Financial data (yr. ended 6/30/88): Assets, $4,789,988 (M); expenditures, $48,392, including $18,000 for 3 grants (high: $8,000; low: $4,000).
Purpose and activities: Grants primarily for special projects, usually short-term, in education, child welfare, medical research, health, the arts, the environment, and public policy organizations, including human rights, peace and justice, and the struggle against poverty.
Types of support: Operating budgets, continuing support, annual campaigns, emergency funds, research, publications, special projects.
Limitations: No grants for deficit financing, or for general purposes.
Application information: Most grants are initiated by the advisors. Applications not accepted.
Deadline(s): Nov. 15
Board meeting date(s): Summer
Advisors: Catherine Armington, David E. Armington, Paul S. Armington, Peter Armington, Rosemary Armington.
Trustee: Huntington National Bank.
Number of staff: None.
Employer Identification Number: 346525508

2417
The Ashtabula Foundation, Inc.
c/o Society Bank of Eastern Ohio, N.A.
4717 Main Ave.
Ashtabula 44004 (216) 992-6818

Community foundation incorporated in 1922 in OH.
Financial data (yr. ended 12/31/87): Assets, $7,688,391 (M); gifts received, $68,732; expenditures, $411,516, including $307,112 for 33 grants (high: $64,801; low: $125).
Purpose and activities: To administer charitable trusts; support for health, welfare, and cultural programs, with emphasis on a community fund and church support.
Limitations: Giving limited to the Ashtabula, OH, area.
Publications: Application guidelines.
Application information: Application guidelines for scholarship funds available. Application form required.
Initial approach: Proposal
Copies of proposal: 4
Deadline(s): Feb. 1, May 1, Aug. 1, and Nov. 1
Board meeting date(s): Mar., June, Sept., and Dec.
Officers and Trustees: Frank Koski, Pres.; Wilbur Anderson, V.P.; Tom Anderson, Secy.-Treas.; Douglas Hedberg, Eleanor Jammal, Maynard Walker, Glen Warner, John Zaback, William C. Zweier.
Trustee Bank: Society Bank of Eastern Ohio, N.A.
Employer Identification Number: 346538130

2418
Edward M. Barr Charitable Trust
c/o Mahoning National Bank, Trust Dept.
23 Federal Plaza, P.O. Box 479
Youngstown 44501 (216) 742-7000

Established in 1973 in Ohio.
Financial data (yr. ended 12/31/87): Assets, $1,377,361 (M); expenditures, $82,778, including $72,000 for 5 grants (high: $50,000; low: $5,500).
Purpose and activities: Giving primarily for social services, especially the Salvation Army; support also for cultural programs, and denominational giving.
Types of support: Building funds, capital campaigns, equipment, renovation projects.
Limitations: Giving primarily in Youngstown, OH.
Application information:
Initial approach: Letter
Deadline(s): None
Write: Patrick A. Sebastiano, Sr. V.P. and Sr. Trust Officer, Mahoning National Bank of Youngstown
Trustee: Mahoning National Bank of Youngstown.
Members: John C. Litty, Jr., Gregory L. Ridler, Patrick A. Sebastiano.
Employer Identification Number: 346687006

2419
Battelle Memorial Institute Giving Program
Office of Community Affairs
505 King Ave.
Columbus 43201 (614) 424-6424

Purpose and activities: Supports civic affairs, culture, education, health and human services.
Types of support: Annual campaigns, capital campaigns, conferences and seminars.
Limitations: Giving primarily in Columbus, OH, and the Tri-Cities in WA.

Application information:
Initial approach: Initial contact by phone or a preliminary letter
Copies of proposal: 1
Deadline(s): None
Write: John S. Christie, V.P., Corp. Dev.

2420
Elsie and Harry Baumker Charitable Foundation, Inc.
2828 Barrington Dr.
Toledo 43606

Incorporated in 1982 in OH.
Donor(s): Elsie Baumker.†
Financial data (yr. ended 12/31/87): Assets, $1,404,445 (M); expenditures, $79,799, including $77,400 for 21 grants (high: $7,500; low: $500).
Purpose and activities: Giving primarily for health services and social service and youth agencies; support also for higher education and cultural programs.
Limitations: Giving primarily in OH, with emphasis on Toledo.
Application information:
Deadline(s): None
Final notification: 3 months
Trustees: Gladys M. Preis, Mgr.; Howard L. Ness, Nancy Preis.
Employer Identification Number: 341300465

2421
The Leon A. Beeghly Fund
c/o Bank One, Youngstown N.A.
Six Federal Plaza West
Youngstown 44503 (216) 743-3151
Mailing address: 808 Stambaugh Bldg., Youngstown, OH 44503

Trust established in 1940 in OH.
Donor(s): Leon A. Beeghly,† Mabel L. Beeghly.†
Financial data (yr. ended 12/31/88): Assets, $3,732,886 (M); expenditures, $852,783, including $808,182 for 72 grants (high: $92,000; low: $200; average: $5,000-$10,000).
Purpose and activities: Emphasis on Protestant church support and religious associations, higher education, cultural programs, community development, hospitals, community funds, and aid to the handicapped; support also for family services and programs that benefit women, youth, and the disadvantaged and the aged.
Types of support: General purposes, building funds, equipment, endowment funds, professorships, scholarship funds, capital campaigns, annual campaigns, continuing support, emergency funds, operating budgets, renovation projects, special projects.
Limitations: Giving primarily in the Youngstown, OH, metropolitan area; limited giving in western PA. No grants to individuals, or for research, special projects, publications, or conferences; no loans.
Publications: Program policy statement, application guidelines.
Application information:
Initial approach: Proposal
Copies of proposal: 1
Deadline(s): None
Board meeting date(s): Quarterly
Final notification: 1 to 6 months
Write: James L. Beeghly, Exec. Secy.
Appointing Committee: James L. Beeghly, Exec. Secy.; John D. Beeghly, R.T. Beeghly.
Trustee: Bank One, Youngstown, N.A.
Number of staff: 1 part-time support.
Employer Identification Number: 346514043

2422
The Belden Brick Company Charitable Trust
700 Tuscarawas St., W.
P.O. Box 20910
Canton 44701-0910 (216) 456-0031

Donor(s): Belden Brick Co.
Financial data (yr. ended 12/31/87): Assets, $331,365 (M); gifts received, $30,000; expenditures, $21,533, including $21,252 for 25 grants (high: $6,225; low: $25).
Purpose and activities: Support for health, recreation, welfare agencies, education, and cultural organizations.
Types of support: Operating budgets, building funds.
Limitations: Giving primarily in Canton and Massillon, OH.
Application information:
Initial approach: Letter
Final notification: 2 months
Write: William H. Belden, Sr.
Trustees: Paul B. Belden, Jr., William H. Belden, Sr., Paul W. Hartburg, Jr.
Number of staff: 3 part-time professional.
Employer Identification Number: 346565519

2423
The Benua Foundation, Inc.
17 South High St., Rm. 730
Columbus 43215

Incorporated in 1952 in DE.
Donor(s): A.R. Benua, Ebco Manufacturing Co.
Financial data (yr. ended 12/31/87): Assets, $8,476,000 (M); expenditures, $360,694, including $346,050 for 115 grants (high: $25,000; low: $200).
Purpose and activities: Giving for conservation, higher education, youth and health agencies, and cultural programs.
Limitations: Giving primarily in OH.
Trustees: John M. Bowsher, Eleanor L. Craig, MacLee Henny.
Employer Identification Number: 316026443

2424
Loren M. Berry Foundation
3055 Kettering Blvd., Suite 418
Dayton 45439 (513) 293-0398

Incorporated in 1960 in OH.
Donor(s): Loren M. Berry.†
Financial data (yr. ended 12/31/87): Assets, $7,000,000 (M); expenditures, $376,660, including $374,660 for 80 grants (high: $25,000; low: $100).
Purpose and activities: Emphasis on higher education, hospitals, youth agencies, medical research, cultural programs, church support, and patriotic organizations.
Limitations: Giving primarily in OH. No grants to individuals, or for operating budgets.
Application information:
Initial approach: Letter
Deadline(s): None
Board meeting date(s): Mar., June, Sept., and Dec.
Write: William T. Lincoln, Treas.
Officers and Trustees: John W. Berry, Sr., Pres.; William T. Lincoln, Treas.; Charles Berry, David Berry, George Berry, John W. Berry, Jr., Martha B. Fraim, William Fraim, Elizabeth Gray, Leland Henry, James O. Payne.
Employer Identification Number: 316026144

2425
The William Bingham Foundation
1250 Leader Bldg.
Cleveland 44114 (216) 781-3275

Incorporated in 1955 in OH.
Donor(s): Elizabeth B. Blossom.†
Financial data (yr. ended 12/31/87): Assets, $22,584,000 (M); expenditures, $1,076,000, including $768,905 for 34 grants (high: $150,000; low: $1,000; average: $1,000-$25,000).
Purpose and activities: Support for the arts, education, including higher education, conservation, health, and welfare.
Types of support: General purposes, special projects, seed money, building funds, equipment, endowment funds, research, publications, conferences and seminars, scholarship funds, matching funds, program-related investments, operating budgets, capital campaigns, land acquisition, professorships, renovation projects.
Limitations: Giving primarily in the eastern U.S., with some emphasis on the Cleveland, OH, area. No grants to individuals; no loans.
Publications: Annual report (including application guidelines), application guidelines.
Application information: Full proposals accepted only on request of foundation in response to applicant's initial letter.
Initial approach: Letter of 2 pages or less
Copies of proposal: 1
Deadline(s): Submit letter preferably in Feb. or July; deadline for solicited proposal, 2 months prior to board meeting dates
Board meeting date(s): Usually May and Oct.
Final notification: 3 to 6 months
Write: Laura C. Hitchcox, Dir.
Officers: Mary E. Gale,* Pres.; Thomas F. Allen, Secy.; C. Bingham Blossom,* Treas.; Laura C. Hitchcox, Dir.
Trustees:* Dudley S. Blossom, Laurel Blossom, Benjamin Gale, Thomas H. Gale, Elizabeth B. Heffernan.
Number of staff: 1 full-time professional.
Employer Identification Number: 346513791
Recent arts and culture grants:
Academy of the Arts, Easton, MD, $5,000. For support of Gifted and Talented Program for high school art students. 5/16/87.
Fairmount Center for Creative and Performing Arts, Novelty, OH, $10,000. For window replacement. 11/14/87.
Film Arts Foundation, San Francisco, CA, $10,000. For completion of film entitled, Movement From the Soul: The Dance Innovations of Isadora Duncan. 5/16/87.

National Public Radio, DC, $25,000. To support News and Information Fund for coverage of education. 5/16/87.
University of Massachusetts, Amherst, MA, $30,000. For microfilming of The Papers of Elizabeth Cady Stanton and Susan B. Anthony. 11/14/87.
Volunteer Lawyers for the Arts, NYC, NY, $5,000. For general support. 11/14/87.
YMCA of Greater New York, Center for the Arts, NYC, NY, $5,000. For support of Writers Community series of The Writer's Voice. 11/14/87.
Young Audiences of Maryland, Baltimore Chapter, Baltimore, MD, $10,000. For matching grant to endowment fund. 5/16/87.

2426
Blade Foundation
c/o The Toledo Blade, Personnel Office
541 Superior St.
Toledo 43604 (419) 245-6290

Established in 1969 in OH.
Donor(s): Blade Communications, Inc.
Financial data (yr. ended 9/30/87): Assets, $467,291 (M); gifts received, $300,000; expenditures, $141,401, including $137,025 for 42 grants (high: $37,000; low: $100) and $4,000 for 9 grants to individuals.
Purpose and activities: Support for cultural and educational institutions and social service organizations; scholarships limited to children or legal dependents of full-time employees of the Toledo Blade with at least 3 years employment; officers' and directors' children are not eligible.
Types of support: Student aid.
Limitations: Giving primarily in OH.
Application information:
Deadline(s): Mar. 1 for scholarships
Officers and Trustees: William Block, Jr., Pres.; Allan Block, V.P.; John R. Block, V.P.; William Block, Jr., V.P.; Newell Kest, V.P.; Harold O. Davis, Secy.; John W. Harms, Treas.
Employer Identification Number: 346559843

2427
BP America Corporate Giving Program
200 Public Square 35-A
Cleveland 44114-2375 (216) 586-8621

Financial data (yr. ended 12/31/87): Total giving, $10,319,559, including $8,120,612 for grants (high: $930,000; low: $50), $1,048,947 for 4,778 employee matching gifts and $1,150,000 for loans.
Purpose and activities: Supports education, health and human services, civic and community affairs, urban development, and culture and the arts. Types of support include employee matching gifts for higher education, hospitals and culture, in-kind donations; and program-related investments for the social investments program.
Types of support: Capital campaigns, building funds, employee matching gifts, equipment, fellowships, general purposes, matching funds, operating budgets, research, scholarship funds, special projects.
Limitations: No support for religious, political, or fraternal organizations. No grants to individuals.
Publications: Corporate giving report (including application guidelines).
Application information: Include list of officers and directors, most recently audited financial statement, complete budget, funding sources for previous 12 months, 501(c)(3) and most recent Form 990-Income Tax Return of Organization Exempt from Income Tax.
Initial approach: Phone or letter
Copies of proposal: 1
Deadline(s): Applications accepted throughout the year
Write: Lance C. Buhl, Mgr., Corp. Contribs.
Number of staff: 7 full-time professional; 5 full-time support.

2428
Louise Brown Foundation
2000 Huntington Bldg.
Cleveland 44115 (216) 696-4700

Established in 1971 in OH.
Donor(s): Louise I. Brown.
Financial data (yr. ended 11/30/87): Assets, $0 (M); expenditures, $201,288, including $199,055 for 46 grants (high: $40,000; low: $100).
Purpose and activities: Support for cultural organizations, and higher and other education.
Limitations: Giving primarily in Cleveland, OH.
Application information:
Write: Richard T. Watson, Trustee
Trustees: Louise I. Brown, Willard W. Brown, Richard T. Watson.
Employer Identification Number: 237194549

2429
Kenneth Calhoun Charitable Trust
c/o Society National Bank
800 Superior Ave.
Cleveland 44101
Application address: c/o Society National Bank, 157 South Main St., Akron, OH 44308

Established in 1982 in OH.
Donor(s): Kenneth Calhoun.†
Financial data (yr. ended 7/31/87): Assets, $3,865,556 (M); expenditures, $210,198, including $181,418 for 44 grants (high: $50,000; low: $75; average: $500-$10,000).
Purpose and activities: Giving for hospitals, cultural programs, education, youth agencies, and social services.
Limitations: Giving limited to the greater Akron, OH, area with an emphasis on Summit County.
Application information:
Initial approach: Letter
Copies of proposal: 1
Deadline(s): June 30
Write: Karen Krino, Sr. Trust Officer, Society National Bank
Trustee: Society National Bank.
Employer Identification Number: 341370330

2430
M. E. & F. J. Callahan Foundation
29500 Solon Rd.
Solon 44139-3474

Established in 1975 in OH.
Financial data (yr. ended 12/31/87): Assets, $271,994 (M); gifts received, $150,000; expenditures, $134,137, including $133,925 for 37 grants (high: $28,280; low: $35).
Purpose and activities: Giving to performing arts, especially music.
Limitations: No grants to individuals.
Application information: Contributes only to pre-selected organizations. Applications not accepted.
Officers: F.J. Callahan, Pres.; Mary E. Callahan, V.P.; John F. Fant, Jr., Secy.
Employer Identification Number: 510164320

2431
The Camden Foundation
c/o Fifth Third Bank
Dept. 00861
Cincinnati 45263 (513) 579-4327

Established in 1952 in OH.
Financial data (yr. ended 12/31/88): Assets, $1,160,585 (M); expenditures, $55,501, including $49,300 for 12 grants (high: $18,000; low: $1,000).
Purpose and activities: Giving primarily for museums, the arts, education, and general charitable projects.
Application information: Application form required.
Initial approach: Letter or telephone
Deadline(s): None
Write: Eileen McCaulay
Trustee: Fifth Third Bank.
Employer Identification Number: 316024141

2432
The Robert Campeau Family Foundation (U.S.)
(Formerly Federated Department Stores Foundation)
Seven West Seventh St.
Cincinnati 45202 (513) 579-7166

Originally incorporated in 1952 in OH and later dissolved; reestablished in 1980 in OH.
Donor(s): Federated Department Stores, Inc.
Financial data (yr. ended 1/31/88): Assets, $22,117,952 (M); expenditures, $7,288,443, including $6,392,237 for 721 grants (high: $300,000; low: $500; average: $1,000-$15,000) and $788,849 for employee matching gifts.
Purpose and activities: Emphasis on higher education and cultural, civic, and health and welfare programs; matching employee gifts to educational and cultural organizations and contributions of $1,000 or more to local organizations at the request of the divisions of the company; support also for civic and urban affairs, hospitals, social services, especially population control and community funds, and public policy organizations.
Types of support: Employee matching gifts, general purposes, building funds, matching funds, special projects.

Limitations: Giving primarily in communities of company operations; Miami, FL, Atlanta, GA, Boston and Somerville, MA, Brooklyn and New York, NY, Cincinnati and Columbus, OH, Memphis, TN, Seattle, WA, and Paramus, NJ. No support for religious organizations for religious purposes. No grants to individuals.
Publications: Annual report.
Application information: Local organizations should apply directly to local division of Federated Dept. Stores.
Initial approach: Proposal
Copies of proposal: 1
Deadline(s): None
Final notification: 6 to 8 weeks
Write: Patricia Ikeda, Exec. Dir.
Officers: Ilse Campeau,* Chair. and Pres.; Robert Campeau,* Vice-Chair.; Ronald W. Tysoe,* Sr. V.P.; Roland Villemaire, V.P. and Treas.; Thomas G. Cody, Secy.
Trustees:* His Eminence G. Emmett Cardinal Carter, Russell S. Davis, J. Roy Weir, James M. Zimmerman.
Number of staff: 1 part-time professional; 3 part-time support.
Employer Identification Number: 310996760

2433
The Don M. Casto Foundation
209 East State St.
Columbus 43215

Incorporated in 1962 in OH.
Donor(s): Members of the Casto family and family-related businesses.
Financial data (yr. ended 5/31/87): Assets, $1,165,852 (M); gifts received, $50,000; expenditures, $128,620, including $121,600 for 34 grants (high: $20,000; low: $25).
Purpose and activities: Giving primarily for cultural programs, community funds, hospitals, and higher and secondary education.
Limitations: Giving primarily in OH.
Application information: Generally does not accept unsolicited applications.
Trustees: Frank S. Benson, Jr., Frank S. Benson III, Don M. Casto III.
Employer Identification Number: 316049506

2434
Cayuga Foundation
c/o Trustcorp Bank, Ohio
Three Seagate
Toledo 43603 (419) 259-8288

Established in 1960 in OH.
Financial data (yr. ended 12/31/87): Assets, $1,496,050 (M); expenditures, $90,655, including $64,400 for 26 grants (high: $10,000; low: $200).
Purpose and activities: Grants primarily for health and education, especially higher education; support also for cultural programs and denominational giving.
Types of support: General purposes, scholarship funds, building funds.
Limitations: Giving primarily in Toledo, OH, and NY.
Application information:
Initial approach: Proposal
Write: Gerald Miller
Corporate Trustee: The Toledo Trust Co.
Advisors: Donald J. Keue, Elizabeth K. McIntosh, Elizabeth M. Pfenzinger.
Employer Identification Number: 346504822

2435
Charities Foundation
One Sea Gate
Toledo 43666 (419) 247-1888

Trust established in 1937 in OH.
Donor(s): Owens-Illinois, Inc., William E. Levis,† Harold Boeschenstein,† and others.
Financial data (yr. ended 12/31/87): Assets, $5,088,024 (M); expenditures, $1,274,171, including $1,256,009 for 103 grants (high: $381,600; low: $125; average: $750-$20,000).
Purpose and activities: Contributions from the foundation are initiated internally, with emphasis on higher and other education, community funds, cultural programs, conservation, youth and social service agencies, and civic and public affairs organizations.
Types of support: General purposes.
Limitations: Giving primarily in OH, with emphasis on Toledo. No grants to individuals, or for scholarships.
Publications: Annual report, 990-PF.
Application information: All funds presently committed. Applications not accepted.
Write: Grayce A. Neimy, Secy.
Officer: Luis C. Isaza, Mgr.
Trustees: Jerome A. Bohland, Henry A. Page, Jr., Carter Smith.
Number of staff: 1 part-time support.
Employer Identification Number: 346554560

2436
Cincinnati Bell Foundation, Inc.
201 East Fourth St.
Cincinnati 45202 (513) 397-1250

Established in 1984 in OH.
Donor(s): Cincinnati Bell, Inc.
Financial data (yr. ended 12/31/87): Assets, $1,324,087 (M); gifts received, $500,000; expenditures, $567,597, including $530,505 for grants and $17,000 for 197 employee matching gifts.
Purpose and activities: Supports the arts, education including higher education, health, hospitals, welfare, youth, media and communications, with priority to programs that are broadly supported by other organizations.
Types of support: Annual campaigns, capital campaigns, employee matching gifts.
Limitations: Giving primarily in the greater Cincinnati, OH area, and in Northern KY, and any other city in which company has a significant corporate presence.
Publications: Informational brochure (including application guidelines).
Application information:
Initial approach: Letter
Copies of proposal: 1
Deadline(s): None
Write: C.W. Wright, Exec. Dir.
Officers: Dwight H. Hibbard, Pres.; Betty S. Kromer, Secy.-Treas.; C.W. Wright, Exec. Dir.
Trustees: Scott Aiken, John T. LaMacchia, Dennis J. Sullivan, Jr.
Number of staff: 1
Employer Identification Number: 311125542

2437
The Greater Cincinnati Foundation
802 Carew Tower
441 Vine St.
Cincinnati 45202-2817 (513) 241-2880

Community foundation established in 1963 in OH by bank resolution and declaration of trust.
Financial data (yr. ended 12/31/88): Assets, $68,435,500 (M); gifts received, $8,478,692; expenditures, $5,923,094, including $5,554,094 for grants (high: $300,000; low: $500).
Purpose and activities: Grants for a broad range of both new and existing activities in general categories of arts and culture and humanities, civic affairs, education, health, and social services, including youth agencies.
Types of support: Seed money, capital campaigns, building funds, equipment, program-related investments, special projects, matching funds, loans, technical assistance, renovation projects.
Limitations: Giving limited to the greater Cincinnati, OH, area. No support for sectarian religious purposes. No grants to individuals, or for operating budgets, annual campaigns, deficit financing, endowment funds, scholarships, fellowships, internships, exchange programs, or scholarly research.
Publications: Annual report (including application guidelines), newsletter, application guidelines.
Application information: Application form required.
Initial approach: Letter or telephone, followed by interview with foundation staff
Copies of proposal: 22
Deadline(s): 90 days prior to board meetings
Board meeting date(s): Mar., June, Sept., and Dec.
Final notification: Immediately following board meetings
Write: Patricia A. Massey, Program Officer
Officers: William O. Coleman, Dir.; William T. Bahlman, Jr., Assoc. Dir.; Herbert R. Brown, Assoc. Dir.; Charles W. Goering, Assoc. Dir.; Daniel LeBlond, Assoc. Dir.; Walter L. Lingle, Jr., Assoc. Dir.; Nelson Schwab, Jr., Assoc. Dir.; Robert Westheimer, Assoc. Dir.
Governing Board: Robert G. Stachler, Chair.; Kay Pettengill, Vice-Chair.; William D. Atteberry, Cynthia Booth, Richard B. Budde, M.D., William A. Friedlander, Louise A. Head, Charles S. Mechem, Jr., John L. Strubbe.
Trustee Banks: AmeriTrust Co., Banc One Ohio Corp., The Central Trust Co. of Northern Ohio, N.A., Fifth Third Bank, Huntington National Bank, The Lebanon-Citizens National Bank, The Northside Bank & Trust Co., Peoples Liberty Bank of Northern Kentucky, Provident Bank, Society Bank, N.A., Star Bank.
Number of staff: 2 full-time professional; 3 full-time support.
Employer Identification Number: 310669700
Recent arts and culture grants:
Art Academy of Cincinnati, Cincinnati, OH, $32,670. 1987.

Art Academy of Cincinnati, Cincinnati, OH, $30,000. 1987.
CCA Artists Fire Fund Project, Cincinnati, OH, $8,250. 1987.
Cincinnati Art Museum, Cincinnati, OH, $24,025. 1987.
Cincinnati Artists Group Effort, Cincinnati, OH, $5,000. 1987.
Cincinnati Ballet Company, Cincinnati, OH, $35,000. 1987.
Cincinnati Fire Museum, Cincinnati, OH, $10,000. For Jacob E. Davis Volunteer Leadership Award. 1987.
Cincinnati Historical Society, Cincinnati, OH, $36,281. 1987.
Cincinnati Historical Society, Cincinnati, OH, $10,000. 1987.
Cincinnati Institute of Fine Arts, Cincinnati, OH, $20,000. For Fine Arts Fund, a funding vehicle for various arts and performing arts agencies. 1987.
Cincinnati Nature Center, Milford, OH, $18,590. 1987.
Cincinnati Nature Center, Milford, OH, $5,000. 1987.
Cincinnati Opera Association, Cincinnati, OH, $21,200. 1987.
Cincinnati Opera Association, Cincinnati, OH, $15,145. To renovate 100-year old Beck Building to store stage sets. 1987.
Cincinnati Playhouse in the Park, Cincinnati, OH, $13,650. 1987.
Cincinnati Symphony Orchestra, Cincinnati, OH, $27,125. 1987.
Fine Arts Fund, Cincinnati, OH, $92,835. 1987.
Friends of the William Howard Taft Birthplace, Cincinnati, OH, $30,000. 1987.
Historic Southwest Ohio, Cincinnati, OH, $10,000. 1987.
Historic Southwest Ohio, Cincinnati, OH, $5,403. 1987.
Metropolitan Opera Association, NYC, NY, $6,000. 1987.
Music Hall Association of Cincinnati, Cincinnati, OH, $50,000. 1987.
National Trust for Historic Preservation, Cincinnati, OH, $10,000. 1987.
Northern Kentucky Arts Council, Covington, KY, $5,000. To increase communication with artists, audiences and funders about programs in area. 1987.
Peaslee Neighborhood Center, Steel Drum Band, Cincinnati, OH, $10,000. For steel-drum instruments for music instruction and to increase self-esteem and teamwork among children. 1987.
School for Creative Performing Arts, Friends of the, Cincinnati, OH, $32,112. 1987.
Taft Museum, Cincinnati, OH, $5,000. To design and construct handicapped/wheelchair entrance. 1987.
W C E T-Greater Cincinnati Television Educational Foundation, Cincinnati, OH, $10,000. 1987.
W C E T-Greater Cincinnati Television Educational Foundation, Cincinnati, OH, $7,458. 1987.
Zoological and Botanical Society of Cincinnati, Cincinnati, OH, $25,881. 1987.

2438
The Cleveland Electric Illuminating Company Giving Program

P.O. Box 5000
Cleveland 44101 (216) 447-3100

Financial data (yr. ended 12/31/88): $151,964 for grants.
Purpose and activities: Supports civic and community affairs, environmental concerns, the arts, including museums and music, education, health, youth, and United Way.
Types of support: Annual campaigns, building funds, capital campaigns.
Limitations: Giving primarily in Northeastern OH, mostly in Cleveland. No grants to individuals, or for endowments or scholarships.
Application information:
Initial approach: Summary of proposal, one-two pages
Copies of proposal: 1
Deadline(s): None
Board meeting date(s): Committee meetings monthly
Final notification: All requests will be answered
Contributions Committee: Jacquita Hauserman, Chair.; Tanzie D. Adams, Secy.; Gary Greben.

2439
The Cleveland Electric Illuminating Foundation

P.O. Box 5000
Cleveland 44101 (216) 622-9800
Application address: 55 Public Square, Cleveland, OH 44113; Tel.: (216) 479-6512

Incorporated in 1961 in OH.
Donor(s): The Cleveland Electric Illuminating Co.
Financial data (yr. ended 12/31/87): Assets, $13,947,008 (M); expenditures, $1,285,894, including $1,073,505 for 121 grants (high: $120,000; low: $40; average: $100-$10,000) and $156,000 for employee matching gifts.
Purpose and activities: Emphasis on qualifying nonprofit organizations in health, welfare, civic, cultural, or educational endeavors; support also for community funds.
Types of support: Annual campaigns, building funds, equipment, operating budgets, employee matching gifts, continuing support.
Limitations: Giving limited to northeastern OH, with emphasis on Cleveland. No support for political organizations. Generally, no grants to individuals, or for endowment funds, deficit financing, research, scholarships, or fellowships; no loans.
Publications: Informational brochure, annual report.
Application information:
Initial approach: Cover letter with proposal
Copies of proposal: 1
Deadline(s): None
Board meeting date(s): Contributions Committee usually meets monthly
Final notification: 7 weeks
Write: Gary J. Greben, Chair., Contribs. Comm.
Officers: Robert M. Ginn,* Chair.; Robert J. Farling,* Pres.; John S. Levicki, V.P.; Carl E. Chancellor, Secy.; Terrence R. Moran, Treas.
Trustees:* Richard A. Miller, William E. Conway, Roy H. Holdt, Sister Mary Martha Reinhard, S.N.D., Karl H. Rudolph, Craig R. Smith, Herbert E. Strawbridge, Allan J. Tomlinson, Jr., Harold L. Williams.
Number of staff: 2 part-time professional; 1 part-time support.
Employer Identification Number: 346514181

2440
The Cleveland Foundation

1400 Hanna Bldg.
Cleveland 44115 (216) 861-3810

Community foundation established in 1914 in OH by bank resolution and declaration of trust.
Financial data (yr. ended 12/31/88): Assets, $498,766,658 (M); gifts received, $11,092,644; expenditures, $26,521,084, including $22,238,337 for 710 grants (high: $800,000; average: $1,000-$800,000) and $1,875,000 for loans.
Purpose and activities: The pioneer community foundation which has served as a model for most community foundations in the U.S.; grants are made to private tax-exempt and governmental agencies and programs serving the greater Cleveland area in the fields of civic and cultural affairs, education and economic development, and health and social services. Current priorities are in economic development, neighborhood development, downtown revitalization, lakefront enhancement, programs dealing with the young, the aged and special constituencies, health care for the medically indigent and for underserved populations, and the professional performing and visual arts. Grants mainly as seed money for innovative projects or to developing institutions or services addressing unmet needs in the community. Very limited support for capital purposes for highly selective construction or equipment projects which serve the program priorities listed above.
Types of support: Seed money, special projects, matching funds, consulting services, technical assistance, program-related investments, renovation projects.
Limitations: Giving limited to the greater Cleveland area, with primary emphasis on Cleveland, Cuyahoga, Lake, and Geauga Counties, OH, unless specified by donor. No support for sectarian or religious activities, community services such as fire and police protection, and library and welfare services. No grants to individuals, or for endowment funds, operating costs, debt reduction, fundraising campaigns, publications, films and audiovisual materials (unless they are an integral part of a program already being supported), memberships, travel for bands, sports teams, classes and similar groups; capital support for planning, construction, renovation, or purchase of buildings, equipment and materials, land acquisition, or renovation of public space unless there is strong evidence that the program is of priority to the foundation.
Publications: Annual report (including application guidelines), newsletter, occasional report, application guidelines, informational brochure.
Application information:

Initial approach: Letter, proposal, or telephone
Copies of proposal: 2
Deadline(s): Mar. 31, June 30, Sept. 15, and Dec. 31
Board meeting date(s): Distribution committee meets in Mar., June, Sept., and Dec.
Final notification: 1 month
Write: Steven A. Minter, Dir.
Officers: Steven A. Minter, Dir.; Michael J. Hoffmann, Secy.; Philip T. Tobin, Admin. Officer and Treas.
Distribution Committee: Richard W. Pogue, Chair.; John J. Dwyer, Vice-Chair.; Elmo A. Bean, James M. Delaney, Henry J. Goodman, Jerry V. Jarrett, Adrienne L. Jones, E. Bradley Jones, Lindsay J. Morgenthaler, Harvey G. Oppmann, Alfred M. Rankin, Jr.
Trustees: AmeriTrust Co., Bank One, Cleveland, N.A., Huntington National Bank, National City Bank, Society National Bank.
Number of staff: 15 full-time professional; 5 part-time professional; 17 full-time support.
Employer Identification Number: 340714588
Recent arts and culture grants:
Accord Associates, Cleveland, OH, $15,000. For debut Concert Series. 9/88.
Art Studio, Cleveland, OH, $50,000. To support new position of administrative director. Grant shared with Highland View Hospital. 12/88.
ARTS E.T.C., Cleveland, OH, $25,000. For start-up and first year operating costs listed in core budget. 9/88.
Case Western Reserve University, Weatherhead School of Management, Cleveland, OH, $60,000. For new arts management program. 12/87.
Cleveland Ballet, Cleveland, OH, $200,000. For Leadership Gift for Capitalization Campaign. 9/88.
Cleveland Ballet, Cleveland, OH, $100,000. For artistic support to add four apprentice dancers and expand employment for all dancers from 36 to 38 weeks. 6/88.
Cleveland Center for Contemporary Art, Cleveland, OH, $30,000. For operation of Galleria space and special exhibition and lecture series. 9/88.
Cleveland Education Fund, Cleveland, OH, $66,768. Toward Andover-Bread Loaf Writing workshop for Cleveland teachers. 12/88.
Cleveland Historic Warehouse District Development Corporation, Cleveland, OH, $45,000. For general operating support and specific public projects. 12/88.
Cleveland Institute of Music, Cleveland, OH, $37,750. For concerts and master classes involving distinguished guest artists with Contemporary Music Ensemble. 6/88.
Cleveland Modern Dance Association, DANCECLEVELAND, Cleveland, OH, $40,000. For artistic fees for Paul Taylor Dance Company residency. 6/88.
Cleveland Museum of Natural History, Cleveland, OH, $2,600,000. For principal distribution from Isaac T. and Gertrude P. Kahn Funds. 12/88.
Cleveland Museum of Natural History, Cleveland, OH, $200,000. Toward construction of new wing and its programs. 6/88.
Cleveland Museum of Natural History, Cleveland, OH, $44,736. For development of specimen loan program. 3/88.
Cleveland Opera, Cleveland, OH, $125,000. For production of The Pearl Fishers by Georges Bizet. 6/88.
Cleveland Play House, Cleveland, OH, $150,000. To expand size and professional qualifications of artistic staff. 6/88.
Cleveland Public Radio, Cleveland, OH, $81,550. To purchase remote/portable sound equipment and develop cultural programming. 6/88.
Cleveland Public Radio, Cleveland, OH, $20,000. To continue cultural arts programming in 1989. 12/88.
Cleveland Public Theater, Cleveland, OH, $35,000. For core personnel and guest artists. 12/88.
Cleveland State University, Cleveland, OH, $15,800. For Sacred Landmarks Research Group Exhibition. 12/88.
Cuyahoga Community College, Cleveland, OH, $20,000. For special marketing of 10th annual Tri-C Jazzfest. 12/88.
Darius Milhaud Society, Cleveland, OH, $5,000. For production costs of Milhaud opera, Medee, for 1989 festival, Medea in the Arts and Real World. 12/88.
East Cleveland Community Theater and Arts Center, East Cleveland, OH, $20,000. For administrative director. 6/88.
Eleanor B. Rainey Memorial Institute, Cleveland, OH, $9,000. To repair building's lighting, paint interior walls, and replace plumbing. 3/88.
Findlay Area Arts Council, Findlay, OH, $19,700. For production costs of three annual Gilbert and Sullivan performances. 6/88.
Findlay Area Youtheater, Findlay, OH, $10,000. To establish and develop Kids Summer Stock (KSS) program. 9/88.
Findlay College, Findlay, OH, $5,000. For space and utilization study to be used in developing building plans for Mazza Gallery. 6/88.
Great Lakes Theater Festival, Cleveland, OH, $150,000. For 1988 production of Lorca's Blood Wedding. 3/88.
Hancock Historical Museum Association, Findlay, OH, $35,000. To establish education program model. 12/87.
Harriet Tubman Museum and Cultural Association, Cleveland, OH, $15,000. For start-up and first-year operating costs. 9/88.
Karamu House, Cleveland, OH, $300,000. For deficit elimination. 9/88.
Kenneth C. Beck Center for the Cultural Arts, Lakewood, OH, $100,000. For support of marketing director and operations manager and related office expenses. 12/87.
Koch School of Music, Lakewood, OH, $15,000. For renovation and/or purchase of new home in city of Lakewood. 12/87.
Lyric Opera of Cleveland, Cleveland, OH, $15,000. For 1988 Cleveland premiere of Cavalli's La Calisto. 3/88.
Making the Dream Come True, Cleveland, OH, $15,000. For orchestra costs for Martin Luther King concert by Cleveland Orchestra. 12/88.
Musical Arts Association, Cleveland, OH, $70,000. Toward performance of American, new and unusual music, and continuation of Great Composers of Our Time series. 3/88.
Musical Arts Association, Cleveland, OH, $69,300. Toward performance of American, new and unusual music, and continuation of Great Composers of Our Time series. 3/88.
Musical Arts Association, Cleveland, OH, $50,000. For Sustaining Fund of Cleveland Orchestra. 12/87.
Musical Arts Association, Cleveland, OH, $50,000. For Sustaining Fund of Cleveland Orchestra. 12/88.
Musical Arts Association, Cleveland, OH, $5,000. Toward Cleveland Orchestra presenting Martin Luther King, Jr. concert at Cory United Methodist Church. 12/87.
New Organization for the Visual Arts (NOVA), Cleveland, OH, $6,020. To promote and expand use of Northeast Ohio Artists Slide Registry. 6/88.
Northeastern Ohio Areawide Coordinating Agency, Cleveland, OH, $7,250. For directory on historic preservation activities in region. 6/88.
Ohio Chamber Ballet, Akron, OH, $50,000. For creation of new ballet by Heinz Poll. 3/88.
Playhouse Square Foundation, Cleveland, OH, $100,000. For pre-production costs of Gospel at Colonus. 12/87.
Robert Page Singers and Orchestra, Cleveland, OH, $30,000. Toward addition of marketing staff. 12/87.
Rock and Roll Hall of Fame and Museum, Cleveland, OH, $600,000. Toward construction of museum in Cleveland. 6/88.
Rockefeller Park Cultural Arts Association, Cleveland, OH, $7,500. For Rockefeller Park Gardenfest '88. 6/88.
SPACES, Cleveland, OH, $9,555. For exhibition, seminars, and publications associated with completion of collaborative streetscape project in Warehouse District. 12/87.
Temple Museum of Jewish Religious Art, Cleveland, OH, $10,000. Toward Mounting of The Loom and the Cloth: Exhibition of Fabrics of Jewish Life. 12/87.
Tom Evert Dance Company, Euclid, OH, $20,000. For engagement of general manager. 9/88.
Western Reserve Fine Arts Association, Madison, OH, $15,000. To engage full-time director. 3/88.

2441
The George W. Codrington Charitable Foundation

1100 National City Bank Bldg.
Cleveland 44114 (216) 566-5500

Trust established in 1955 in OH.
Donor(s): George W. Codrington.†
Financial data (yr. ended 12/31/87): Assets, $7,907,383 (M); expenditures, $475,323, including $417,000 for 76 grants.
Purpose and activities: Giving primarily for higher education and hospitals; support also for community funds, museums, youth and health agencies, and music.
Limitations: Giving limited to Cuyahoga County, OH, and surrounding area. No grants

to individuals or for endowment funds; no loans.
Publications: Annual report (including application guidelines).
Application information:
Initial approach: Full proposal
Copies of proposal: 5
Deadline(s): Submit proposal preferably the month before board meetings
Board meeting date(s): Mar., June, Sept., and Dec.
Write: Earl P. Schneider, Chair., Supervisory Board
Officer: Raymond T. Sawyer, Secy.
Supervisory Board: Earl P. Schneider, Chair.; W. Paul Cooper, Vice-Chair.; John J. Dwyer, William E. McDonald, Curtis E. Moll.
Trustee: AmeriTrust Co.
Number of staff: None.
Employer Identification Number: 346507457

2442
The Columbus Foundation
1234 East Broad St.
Columbus 43205 (614) 251-4000

Community foundation established in 1943 in OH by resolution and declaration of trust.
Financial data (yr. ended 12/31/88): Assets, $135,000,000 (M); gifts received, $15,082,000; expenditures, $11,235,000, including $10,271,000 for 1,700 grants (high: $200,000; low: $100; average: $5,000-$25,000).
Purpose and activities: A public charitable foundation for receiving funds for distribution to charitable organizations mainly in the central OH region. Grants made to strengthen existing agencies or to initiate new programs in the following categories: arts and humanities, civic affairs, conservation and environmental protection, education, health, mental health and retardation, and social service agencies.
Types of support: Seed money, matching funds, capital campaigns, land acquisition, publications, renovation projects, special projects, technical assistance, continuing support.
Limitations: Giving limited to central OH from unrestricted funds. No support for religious purposes, or for projects normally the responsibility of a public agency. No grants to individuals, or generally for budget deficits, conferences, scholarly research, or endowment funds.
Publications: Annual report, application guidelines, newsletter.
Application information: Grant requests to the Columbus Youth Foundation must be submitted by the 1st Fridays in Feb. and Oct. for consideration at meetings held in Apr. and Dec.; requests to the Ingram-White Castle Foundation must be submitted by the 1st Fridays in Feb. and Sept. for consideration in Apr. and Nov. Application form required.
Initial approach: Meeting with staff
Copies of proposal: 4
Deadline(s): 1st Friday in Dec., Mar., May, and Aug.
Board meeting date(s): Feb., May, July, and Oct.
Final notification: After quarterly meeting
Write: James I. Luck, Pres.
Officers: James I. Luck, Pres.; Tullia Brown Hamilton, V.P.; Dorothy M. Reynolds, V.P.
Governing Committee: Shirle N. Westwater, Chair.; John W. Kessler, Vice-Chair.; Eldon W. Ward, Vice-Chair.; Robert S. Crane, Jr., Thekla R. Shackelford, Leslie H. Wexner, John Walton Wolfe.
Trustee Banks and Trustee Committee: BancOhio National Bank, Bank One Trust Co., N.A., Huntington Trust Co.
Number of staff: 8 full-time professional; 9 full-time support.
Employer Identification Number: 316044264
Recent arts and culture grants:
Alliance for Dance and Movement Arts, Ohio Dance, Cleveland, OH, $5,000. To support Ohio Dance Festival. 2/19/88.
Ballet Metropolitan, Columbus, OH, $60,000. For matching grant. 7/15/88.
Center of Science and Industry, Columbus, OH, $65,000. To support Super Summer Science Show for 1989 entitled Robots and Beyond: The Age of Intelligent Machines. 2/19/88.
Center of Science and Industry, Columbus, OH, $55,000. To support CIVIC, computer consortium for nonprofit organizations. 2/19/88.
Columbus Museum of Art, Columbus, OH, $15,000. To support development of facility plan. 5/20/88.
Columbus Symphony Orchestra, Columbus, OH, $150,000. For challenge grant. 7/15/88.
Columbus, City of, Department of Recreation and Parks, Columbus, OH, $10,000. To acquire sculpture by Jack Greaves for island park. 4/15/88.
Jefferson Academy of Music, Columbus, OH, $5,000. To support String Ensemble Residency program and children's concert series. 7/15/88.
Ohio State University Research Foundation, Columbus, OH, $5,000. To stage production of The Green Table for University Dance Company. 5/15/87.
Opera/Columbus, Columbus, OH, $50,000. To underwrite production of Salome. 7/15/88.
Players Theater of Columbus, Columbus, OH, $50,000. For matching grant of increased and new contributions from board members and donors. 7/15/88.
Players Theater of Columbus Foundation, Columbus, OH, $5,000. To help meet challenge grant. 5/15/87.
Saint Stephens Community House, Columbus, OH, $10,000. To support expansion of youth fine arts program in dance. 5/20/88.
Tiffin Theater, Tiffin, OH, $18,000. To purchase tickets for performances at theater and distribute through Commission on Aging to frail and indigent elderly in Seneca County. 4/15/88.

2443
The Corbett Foundation
800 Broadway, Suite 1007
Cincinnati 45202-1333 (513) 241-3320

Incorporated in 1958 in OH.
Donor(s): J. Ralph Corbett, Patricia A. Corbett.
Financial data (yr. ended 4/30/88): Assets, $6,727,921 (M); gifts received, $190,000; expenditures, $1,106,466, including $810,813 for 13 grants (high: $500,000; low: $1,000).
Purpose and activities: Support primarily for culture and the arts, including music, education, and community projects.
Limitations: Giving primarily in OH, with emphasis on Cincinnati. No grants to individuals.
Application information:
Initial approach: Proposal
Deadline(s): None
Final notification: Within 2 months
Write: Jean S. Reis, V.P.
Officers and Trustees: Patricia A. Corbett, Pres. and Treas.; Jean S. Reis, V.P. and Secy.; William J. Baechtold, J. Ralph Corbett, Thomas R. Corbett, Alan J. Lehn, Jack M. Watson, Perry B. Wydman.
Employer Identification Number: 316050360

2444
James M. Cox, Jr. Foundation, Inc.
Fourth and Ludlow Sts.
Dayton 45402
Application address: c/o Cox Enterprises, Inc., P.O. Box 105720, Atlanta, GA 30348

Established in 1969 in GA.
Financial data (yr. ended 12/31/87): Assets, $6,445,644 (M); expenditures, $270,840, including $265,000 for 5 grants (high: $100,000; low: $15,000).
Purpose and activities: Support primarily for environmental conservancy and mental health; some support for museums and education.
Types of support: General purposes.
Application information:
Write: Carl R. Gross, Treas.
Officers and Trustees:* James Cox Kennedy,* Pres.; Barbara Cox Anthony,* V.P.; Chester E. Finn, Secy.; Carl R. Gross,* Treas.
Employer Identification Number: 237256190

2445
Dana Corporation Foundation
P.O. Box 1000
Toledo 43697 (419) 535-4500

Incorporated in 1956 in OH.
Donor(s): Dana Corp.
Financial data (yr. ended 12/31/87): Assets, $8,535,794 (M); gifts received, $2,000,000; expenditures, $1,736,297, including $1,529,526 for 232 grants (high: $161,342; low: $100; average: $500-$20,000) and $179,589 for employee matching gifts.
Purpose and activities: Emphasis on community funds, higher education including an employee matching gifts program, social services, health services, civic affairs, youth agencies, and cultural programs.
Types of support: Employee matching gifts, annual campaigns, building funds, continuing support, emergency funds, equipment, land acquisition, operating budgets, seed money, capital campaigns.
Limitations: Giving primarily in areas of company operations. No grants to individuals, or for scholarships or fellowships; no loans.
Application information:
Initial approach: Proposal
Copies of proposal: 1

Deadline(s): None
Board meeting date(s): Apr., Aug., and Dec. or May, Sept., and Jan.
Final notification: 60 to 90 days
Write: Pauline Marzollini, Asst. Secy.
Officers and Directors: C.H. Hirsch, Pres.; T.J. Fairhurst, V.P.; R.M. Leonardi, Secy.; R.A. Habel, Treas.; B.N. Cole, Robert A. Cowie, J.R. Gregory, R.J. Lipford, N.L. Revenaugh.
Number of staff: 1 part-time professional.
Employer Identification Number: 346544909

2446
Dayco Charitable Foundation, Inc.
1301 East 9th St., Suite 3600
Cleveland 44114-1824

Established in 1972.
Donor(s): Dayco Corp.
Financial data (yr. ended 12/31/87): Assets, $19,616 (M); gifts received, $200,000; expenditures, $216,797, including $216,694 for 37 grants (high: $100,000; low: $50).
Purpose and activities: Giving for community funds, social services, civic affairs, Jewish welfare, the arts, higher education, and hospitals.
Limitations: Giving primarily in OH.
Officers: N.G. Crnkovich, Pres.; D.S. Gutridge, V.P.; P.J. Neroni, V.P.; P.W. Phillips, V.P.; D. Daly, Secy.; S. Paul, Treas.
Employer Identification Number: 237223605

2447
The Dayton Foundation
1895 Kettering Tower
Dayton 45423 (513) 222-0410

Community foundation established in 1921 in OH by resolution and declaration of trust.
Financial data (yr. ended 12/31/86): Assets, $17,859,979 (M); gifts received, $9,926,827; expenditures, $1,436,792, including $1,158,466 for 397 grants (high: $30,000; low: $350; average: $4,000-$5,000) and $42,900 for 104 grants to individuals.
Purpose and activities: To assist public charitable, benevolent and educational purposes which benefit local citizens and respond to a wide variety of community needs, including cultural programs, community development, health and social services, and youth; "to help launch new projects which represent a unique and unduplicated opportunity for the community," and to generate matching funds.
Types of support: Seed money, building funds, equipment, matching funds, technical assistance, special projects, capital campaigns, conferences and seminars, consulting services, emergency funds, endowment funds, renovation projects.
Limitations: Giving limited to the greater Dayton, OH, area. No grants to individuals (except for awards to teachers and municipal employees), or for continuing support, annual campaigns, deficit financing, endowment funds, or research.
Publications: Annual report (including application guidelines), newsletter.
Application information:
Initial approach: Proposal, telephone, or letter
Copies of proposal: 1
Deadline(s): Submit proposal preferably 4 weeks before board meeting
Board meeting date(s): Bimonthly beginning in Jan.
Final notification: 4 to 6 weeks
Write: Frederick Bartenstein III, Dir.
Officer: Frederick Bartenstein III, Dir.
Distribution Committee: Frederick C. Smith, Chair.; John E. Moore, Vice-Chair.; Richard F. Glennon, Anne S. Greene, Jesse Philips.
Trustees and Bank Trustees: Avery Allen, Michael J. Alley, William A. Harrell, Donald Kasle, Jerry L. Kirby, Frederick Schantz, Trace B. Swisher, Bank One, Dayton, The Central Trust Co. of Northern Ohio, N.A., Citizens Federal Savings and Loan, Fifth Third Bank, The First National Bank, Huntington National Bank, Society Bank, N.A.
Number of staff: 2 full-time professional; 3 part-time professional; 3 full-time support; 2 part-time support.
Employer Identification Number: 316027287
Recent arts and culture grants:
Dayton Ballet Association, Dayton, OH, $5,000. To help underwrite production costs of The Night Before Christmas. 1987.
Dayton Black Cultural Festival, Dayton, OH, $5,000. Toward start-up fund for 1988 festival. 1987.
Dayton Museum of Natural History, Dayton, OH, $25,000. Toward capital campaign which will finance Indian Village Interpretive Center, new planetarium, and expansion and renovation of museum. 1987.
Friends of Aullwood, Dayton, OH, $10,000. For support, as response to Marie Aull's challenge, which will result in operating endowment for Aullwood Audubon Center and Farm. 1987.
Human Race, Dayton, OH, $24,000. To help establish resident repertory theater which will perform at Biltmore Hotel's Muse Space and at Victory Theater. 1987.
Montgomery County Historical Society, Dayton, OH, $5,000. Toward cost of dismantling historic Cooper Building's limestone facade at Second and Main Streets. 1987.

2448
The Dayton Power & Light Company Foundation
Courthouse Plaza, S.W.
P.O. Box 1247
Dayton 45402 (513) 259-7225

Established in 1984 in OH.
Donor(s): Dayton Power & Light Co.
Financial data (yr. ended 12/31/87): Assets, $10,401,981 (M); gifts received, $5,000,000; expenditures, $577,017, including $551,252 for 114 grants (high: $175,000; low: $100; average: $25-$250,000).
Purpose and activities: Support for civic affairs, community development, engineering, health and welfare, arts and culture, and education; includes in-kind giving.
Types of support: Capital campaigns, operating budgets, employee-related scholarships, scholarship funds, in-kind gifts.
Limitations: Giving primarily in southwest OH.
Application information:
Copies of proposal: 1
Deadline(s): None
Board meeting date(s): Apr. and Dec.
Write: Kathleen G. Regan
Officers and Trustees: Stephen F. Kozair, Pres.; Judy W. Lansaw, Secy.; Thomas M. Jenkins, Treas.
Number of staff: 1 full-time professional; 1 part-time support.
Employer Identification Number: 311138883

2449
George H. Deuble Foundation
c/o AmeriTrust Co.
Box 5937
Cleveland 44101
Mailing address: c/o DCC Corp., P.O. Box 2288, North Canton, OH 44720; Tel.: (216) 494-0494

Trust established in 1947 in OH.
Donor(s): George H. Deuble.†
Financial data (yr. ended 12/31/88): Assets, $12,500,000 (M); expenditures, $603,887, including $603,887 for 81 grants (high: $50,000; low: $20).
Purpose and activities: Grants for youth agencies, higher education, hospitals, cultural programs, and a community fund.
Types of support: Continuing support, annual campaigns, emergency funds, building funds, equipment, endowment funds, matching funds, scholarship funds, loans, conferences and seminars.
Limitations: Giving primarily in the Stark County, OH, area. No grants to individuals, or for operating budgets, seed money, deficit financing, general endowments, land acquisition, research, or publications.
Application information:
Initial approach: Letter
Deadline(s): None
Board meeting date(s): Monthly
Final notification: 1 month
Write: Andrew H. Deuble, Trustee
Officer and Trustees: Walter C. Deuble, Pres.; Andrew H. Deuble, Stephen G. Deuble, Charles A. Morgan, AmeriTrust Co.
Number of staff: None.
Employer Identification Number: 346500426

2450
The Eagle-Picher Foundation
580 Walnut St.
P.O. Box 779
Cincinnati 45201 (513) 721-7010

Incorporated in 1953 in MI; merged with The Union Steel Foundation in 1969.
Donor(s): Eagle-Picher Industries, Inc.
Financial data (yr. ended 10/31/88): Assets, $42,535 (M); gifts received, $54,540; expenditures, $218,951, including $218,435 for 92 grants (high: $19,000; low: $100).
Purpose and activities: Grants largely for community funds, cultural programs, youth agencies, hospitals, social services, and higher education.
Limitations: Giving primarily in areas of company operations. No grants to individuals,

or for endowment funds or matching gifts; no loans.
Application information:
Initial approach: Letter
Copies of proposal: 1
Deadline(s): None
Board meeting date(s): As required
Write: J.R. Nall, Pres.
Officers and Directors: J. Rodman Nall, Pres.; David N. Hall, V.P. and Treas.; Corinne M. Faris, Secy.; James A. Ralston.
Employer Identification Number: 316029997

2451
The Eaton Charitable Fund
Eaton Center
Cleveland 44114 (216) 523-4822

Trust established in 1953 in OH.
Donor(s): Eaton Corp.
Financial data (yr. ended 12/31/87): Assets, $11,924,133 (M); gifts received, $3,525,332; expenditures, $3,525,332, including $2,108,917 for grants (high: $376,221; low: $200; average: $1,000-$10,000) and $590,238 for 1,793 employee matching gifts.
Purpose and activities: High priority to local organizations which serve the needs of company's employees and offer them opportunity to provide leadership, voluntary service, and personal financial support, including vigorous support for United Way concept. General operating support and capital grants to health, human services, medical research, civic and cultural organizations, and independent college funds. Support for educational institutions preferably for engineering, scientific, technological, and business-related projects; capital campaigns limited to educational institutions with programs of direct interest to Eaton. Capital grants to health care facilities limited to geographic areas where there is a shortage of beds, facilities which serve needs of employees, and have reduced their ratio of beds to general public and shortened average stay, and projects that will increase productivity and lower cost of health care.
Types of support: Operating budgets, building funds, employee matching gifts, annual campaigns, special projects, in-kind gifts.
Limitations: Giving primarily in areas of company operations. No support for religious denominations, fraternal organizations, and organizations which could be members of a United Fund or federated community fund but who choose not to participate. No grants to individuals, or for endowment funds, or fundraising events outside of specific company interests; no loans.
Publications: Corporate giving report, annual report, application guidelines.
Application information: Contribution requests should be made through a local Eaton manager wherever possible.
Initial approach: Letter or proposal
Copies of proposal: 1
Deadline(s): None
Board meeting date(s): Quarterly
Final notification: 60 to 90 days
Write: Frederick B. Unger, Dir., Community Affairs
Officer: Frederick B. Unger, Dir. of Community Affairs.
Corporate Contributions Committee: Marshall Wright, Chair.; William E. Butler, John D. Evans, Floyd M. Wilkerson.
Trustee: Society National Bank of Cleveland.
Number of staff: 2 part-time professional; 1 part-time support.
Employer Identification Number: 346501856

2452
The Cyrus Eaton Foundation
3552 Fairmount Blvd.
Shaker Heights 44118 (216) 371-4656

Established in 1955 in DE.
Financial data (yr. ended 12/31/85): Assets, $1,596,349 (M); expenditures, $73,322, including $56,500 for 24 grants (high: $9,000; low: $500).
Purpose and activities: Giving primarily for cultural programs, public affairs, social services, and hospitals.
Limitations: Giving primarily in OH, with emphasis on Cleveland, and in CA, DC, FL, and IL.
Application information:
Initial approach: Letter
Deadline(s): None
Write: Alice J. Gulick, V.P.
Officers and Trustees:* Hester Butterfield,* Pres.; Barring Coughlin,* V.P. and Secy.; Alice J. Gulick,* V.P.; Henry W. Gulick, Treas.
Employer Identification Number: 237440277

2453
Electric Power Equipment Company Foundation
60 East Spring St.
Columbus 43215-2583 (614) 224-5215

Financial data (yr. ended 9/30/86): Assets, $636,676 (M); expenditures, $50,475, including $48,950 for 120 grants (high: $9,000; low: $25; average: $100-$500).
Purpose and activities: Support for health, social services, youth, arts and culture, education, and religious giving.
Application information: Contributes only to preselected organizations. Applications not accepted.
Officers: J.H. McAtee, Chair.; L.F. Wehrle, Vice-Chair.; T.A. Feibel, Secy.; W.B. Langley, Treas.
Employer Identification Number: 316035112

2454
The Thomas J. Emery Memorial
c/o Frost and Jacobs
2500 Central Trust Center
Cincinnati 45202 (513) 621-3124

Incorporated in 1925 in OH.
Donor(s): Mary Muhlenberg Emery.†
Financial data (yr. ended 12/31/87): Assets, $15,155,291 (M); expenditures, $976,611, including $857,686 for 49 grants (high: $106,850; low: $1,000).
Purpose and activities: Emphasis on higher and secondary education, a community fund, cultural activities, social service and youth agencies, and hospitals.
Limitations: Giving primarily in Cincinnati, OH.
Application information:
Initial approach: Letter
Deadline(s): None
Board meeting date(s): 4 times a year
Final notification: 30 days to 3 months
Write: Henry W. Hobson, Jr., Pres.
Officers and Trustees: Henry W. Hobson, Jr., Pres.; Charles M. Barrett, M.D., V.P.; Frank T. Hamilton, Secy.; Walter L. Lingle, Jr., Treas.; Charles M. Barrett, M.D., Lee A. Carter.
Number of staff: 2 part-time support.
Employer Identification Number: 310536711

2455
Walter and Marian English Foundation
c/o Walter English Co.
1227 Bryden Rd.
Columbus 43205 (614) 253-7458
Application address: Station E, Box 6869, Columbus, OH 43205

Established about 1978 in Ohio.
Donor(s): Walter English.
Financial data (yr. ended 12/31/87): Assets, $1,448,318 (M); gifts received, $100,000; expenditures, $57,891, including $50,050 for 26 grants (high: $12,500; low: $100).
Purpose and activities: Giving primarily for civic affairs, cultural programs, education, health, and social services.
Limitations: Giving limited to Franklin County, OH. No grants to individuals.
Application information:
Initial approach: Letter
Deadline(s): May 1 and Sept. 1
Write: Ellen E. Wiseman, Mgr.
Trustees: Marian English, Walter English.
Manager: Ellen E. Wiseman.
Employer Identification Number: 310921799

2456
John F. and Doris E. Ernsthausen Charitable Foundation
c/o Society National Bank, Trust Tax
P.O. Box 6179
Cleveland 44101
Application address: Citizens Bank Bldg., Norwalk, OH 44857

Trust established in 1956 in OH.
Donor(s): John F. Ernsthausen, Doris E. Ernsthausen.
Financial data (yr. ended 6/30/87): Assets, $7,620,890 (M); expenditures, $29,533.
Purpose and activities: Giving for Methodist church support, care of the aged, higher and secondary education, a community fund, and cultural programs.
Limitations: Giving primarily in OH.
Application information:
Deadline(s): None
Write: Cornelius J. Ruffing, Mgr.
Managers: Paul L. Carpenter, Loyal L. Chaney, John F. Ernsthausen, Earle H. Lowe, Cornelius J. Ruffing.
Trustee: Society National Bank.
Employer Identification Number: 346501908

2457
Ferro Foundation
1000 Lakeside Ave.
Cleveland 44114-1183 (216) 641-8580

Incorporated in 1959 in OH.
Donor(s): Ferro Corp.
Financial data (yr. ended 4/30/88): Assets, $366,686 (M); gifts received, $250,000; expenditures, $201,371, including $201,200 for 45 grants (high: $67,500; low: $500).
Purpose and activities: Emphasis on a community fund, higher education, cultural programs, and hospitals.
Types of support: Operating budgets, building funds.
Limitations: Giving primarily in OH.
Application information:
Write: A. Posnick, Pres.
Officers and Trustees:* Adolph Posnick,* Pres.; A.C. Bersticker,* V.P.; J.V. Goodger, Secy.-Treas.; H.R. Ortino,* Treas.
Employer Identification Number: 346554832

2458
The Fifth Third Foundation
c/o The Fifth Third Bank
Dept. 00850, Fifth Third Ctr.
Cincinnati 45263 (513) 579-6034

Trust established in 1948 in OH.
Donor(s): Fifth Third Bancorporation.
Financial data (yr. ended 12/31/87): Assets, $6,402,765 (M); gifts received, $200,000; expenditures, $493,861, including $465,086 for grants (high: $180,000; low: $100).
Purpose and activities: Emphasis on higher education, hospitals, health agencies, youth, social services, cultural programs, and community development.
Types of support: Continuing support, annual campaigns, seed money, building funds, equipment, special projects, publications, capital campaigns, renovation projects, scholarship funds.
Limitations: Giving primarily in the Cincinnati, OH, area. No grants to individuals, or for endowment funds, or fellowships; no loans.
Publications: Application guidelines.
Application information:
Initial approach: Proposal
Copies of proposal: 1
Deadline(s): Submit proposal from Jan. through Dec.; no set deadline
Board meeting date(s): Monthly
Write: Carolyn F. McCoy, Foundation Officer
Trustee: Fifth Third Bancorporation.
Number of staff: 1
Employer Identification Number: 316024135

2459
Roger S. Firestone Foundation
c/o Bank One, Akron
50 South Main St.
Akron 44308

Established in 1983 in Ohio.
Financial data (yr. ended 12/31/87): Assets, $6,472,384 (M); expenditures, $160,921, including $73,500 for 10 grants (high: $25,000; low: $1,000).
Purpose and activities: Emphasis on art institutions, cultural programs, and education, particularly higher education; support also for social service agencies.
Types of support: General purposes.
Limitations: Giving primarily in AZ, DC, and NY.
Application information:
Initial approach: Proposal
Deadline(s): None
Write: C.J. Goldthorpe
Trustees: John D. Firestone, Herbert T. McDevitt, Gay F. Wray.
Employer Identification Number: 341388255

2460
Elizabeth Firestone-Graham Foundation
c/o Bank One Akron, N.A.
50 South Main St.
Akron 44308

Established in 1983 in Ohio.
Financial data (yr. ended 11/30/86): Assets, $1,872,292 (M); gifts received, $300,581; expenditures, $418,521, including $393,000 for 10 grants (high: $106,000; low: $5,000).
Purpose and activities: Giving primarily for higher education and the arts.
Application information:
Initial approach: Proposal
Deadline(s): Submit proposal between July 1 and Sept. 30
Write: C.J. Goldthorpe
Officer and Trustees: Ray A. Graham III, Pres.; Barbara F. Graham.
Employer Identification Number: 341388252

2461
Harvey Firestone, Jr. Foundation
c/o Bank One, Akron
50 South Main St.
Akron 44308

Established in 1983 in Ohio.
Financial data (yr. ended 12/31/87): Assets, $7,652,182 (M); expenditures, $150,432, including $47,500 for 29 grants (high: $5,000; low: $250).
Purpose and activities: Emphasis on hospitals and education; support also for cultural programs, social services, and denominational giving.
Types of support: General purposes.
Limitations: Giving primarily in the eastern U.S.
Application information:
Initial approach: Proposal
Deadline(s): Submit application from July 1 through Sept. 30
Write: C.J. Goldthorpe
Trustees: Anne F. Ball, Martha F. Ford, Elizabeth F. Willis.
Employer Identification Number: 341388254

2462
Firman Fund
1010 Hanna Bldg.
Cleveland 44115-2078 (216) 363-6480

Incorporated in 1951 in OH.
Donor(s): Pamela H. Firman.
Financial data (yr. ended 12/31/87): Assets, $5,945,685 (M); expenditures, $340,757, including $303,526 for 102 grants (high: $26,000; low: $50; average: $100-$50,000).
Purpose and activities: Grants largely for hospitals, higher and secondary education, cultural programs, youth agencies, and community funds.
Types of support: Annual campaigns, general purposes, building funds.
Limitations: Giving primarily in OH. No grants to individuals, or for research; no loans.
Application information:
Initial approach: Proposal or letter
Copies of proposal: 1
Deadline(s): 6 weeks prior to meetings
Board meeting date(s): Apr. and Nov.
Write: Pamela H. Firman, Pres. or Carol L. Colangelo, Secy.
Officers: Pamela H. Firman,* Pres.; Cynthia F. Webster,* V.P.; Carol L. Colangelo, Secy.; M.G. Mikolaj, Treas.
Trustees:* Royal Firman III.
Employer Identification Number: 346513655

2463
The Fleischmann Foundation
4001 Carew Tower
Cincinnati 45202

Incorporated in 1931 in OH.
Donor(s): Julius Fleischmann.†
Financial data (yr. ended 12/31/87): Assets, $3,232,815 (M); gifts received, $75,950; expenditures, $171,418, including $158,721 for 37 grants (high: $83,950; low: $50).
Purpose and activities: Emphasis on the humanities, including support for museums, especially for a museum of natural history, and the arts.
Limitations: Giving primarily in OH.
Application information:
Deadline(s): None
Write: Charles Fleischmann III, Pres.
Officers: Charles Fleischmann III, Pres. and Treas.; Eric B. Yeiser, V.P.; Burd Blair S. Fleischmann, Secy.
Trustees: Burd S. Schlessinger, Leonard A. Weakly.
Employer Identification Number: 316025516

2464
Albert W. and Edith V. Flowers Charitable Trust
c/o Society Bank of Eastern Ohio, N.A.
126 Central Plaza North
Canton 44702 (216) 489-5422
Application address: c/o Society Bank of Eastern Ohio, N.A., P.O. Box 500, Canton, OH 44701

Trust established in 1968 in OH.
Donor(s): Albert W. Flowers,† Edith V. Flowers.†
Financial data (yr. ended 12/31/86): Assets, $1,507,051 (M); expenditures, $98,180, including $87,877 for grants.
Purpose and activities: Emphasis on Protestant church support, a home for the aged, youth agencies, higher and secondary education, and cultural programs.

Limitations: Giving primarily in Stark County, OH.
Application information:
Initial approach: Letter
Deadline(s): Nov. 15
Write: Stephen C. Donatini
Trustees: F.E. McCullough, Albert C. Printz, Ronald B. Tynan, Society Bank of Eastern Ohio, N.A.
Employer Identification Number: 346608643

2465
The S. N. Ford and Ada Ford Fund
P.O. Box 849
Mansfield 44901 (419) 526-3493
Application address: Distribution Committee, 35 North Park St., Mansfield, OH 44901

Trust established in 1947 in OH.
Donor(s): Ada Ford, M.D.†
Financial data (yr. ended 12/31/87): Assets, $5,858,014 (M); expenditures, $479,610, including $55,500 for 11 grants (high: $10,000; low: $1,000) and $336,877 for 462 grants to individuals.
Purpose and activities: Assistance to the aged and the sick, and scholarships for the youth of Richland County.
Types of support: Building funds, student aid, grants to individuals.
Limitations: Giving primarily in Richland County, OH. No grants for endowment funds, or for operating budgets, special projects, general support, research, or matching gifts; no loans.
Publications: Annual report.
Application information: Application form required.
Initial approach: Telephone
Deadline(s): None
Board meeting date(s): Monthly
Final notification: 2 months
Write: Ralph H. LeMunyon, Pres.
Distribution Committee: Ralph H. LeMunyon, Pres.; Burton Preston, V.P.; Catherine A. Dorsey, Secy. and Investigator; David L. Upham, Secy.; Stephen B. Bogner, Walter J. Kinkel.
Trustee: First Buckeye Bank.
Employer Identification Number: 340842282
Recent arts and culture grants:
Mansfield Symphony Society, Mansfield, OH, $10,000. 1987.

2466
Forest City Enterprises Charitable Foundation, Inc.
10800 Brookpark Rd.
Cleveland 44130

Trust established in 1976 in OH.
Donor(s): Forest City Enterprises, Inc.
Financial data (yr. ended 1/31/87): Assets, $13,639 (M); gifts received, $400,000; expenditures, $412,422, including $412,277 for 248 grants (high: $20,000; low: $20).
Purpose and activities: Support for Jewish welfare funds, a community fund, and several other fields, including crime and law enforcement, leadership development, drug abuse programs, the homeless, and hunger. Additional support for education, including adult and elementary education, and cultural programs.
Types of support: Annual campaigns, employee-related scholarships.
Application information:
Copies of proposal: 1
Deadline(s): None
Write: Nathan Shafran, Trustee
Officers and Trustees: Max Ratner, Pres.; Sam Miller, V.P.; Helen F. Morgan, Secy.; Albert Ratner, Charles Ratner, Nathan Shafran, J. Maurice Struchen.
Number of staff: 3
Employer Identification Number: 341218895

2467
The Harry K. & Emma R. Fox Charitable Foundation
900 Bond Court Bldg.
Cleveland 44114 (216) 621-8400

Trust established in 1959 in OH.
Donor(s): Emma R. Fox.†
Financial data (yr. ended 12/31/86): Assets, $4,000,000 (M); expenditures, $250,000, including $235,000 for 62 grants (high: $16,500; low: $700; average: $1,000-$10,000).
Purpose and activities: Giving to hospitals, education, cultural programs, youth agencies, and human services.
Limitations: Giving primarily in northeastern OH. No grants to individuals, or for endowment funds or matching gifts; no loans.
Publications: Application guidelines.
Application information:
Initial approach: Full proposal
Copies of proposal: 4
Deadline(s): May 15 and Nov. 15
Board meeting date(s): June and Dec.
Final notification: 6 months
Write: Harold E. Friedman, Secy.
Officer: Harold E. Friedman, Secy.
Trustees: Marjorie S. Schweid, Chair.; George Rosenfeld, Vice-Chair.; National City Bank.
Number of staff: 1 part-time professional.
Employer Identification Number: 346511198

2468
Frisch's Restaurants, Inc. Giving Program
2800 Gilbert Ave.
Cincinnati 45206 (513) 961-2660

Purpose and activities: Supports arts and culture, education, and civic affairs through various programs, Arts Event Sponsorship, Product Donations, Civic and Educational Sponsorships, and Arts/Civic Fund Drives.
Types of support: Annual campaigns, continuing support, equipment, general purposes, in-kind gifts.
Limitations: Giving primarily in company marketing areas in FL, IN, KS, KY, OH, OK, TX.
Application information: Include complete budget, IRS letter and list of contributors and board members.
Initial approach: Letter
Copies of proposal: 1
Deadline(s): Applications accepted throughout the year
Board meeting date(s): Monthly
Final notification: 4 weeks
Write: Louis J. Ullman, Sr. V.P., Finance

2469
The William O. and Gertrude Lewis Frohring Foundation, Inc.
3200 National City Center
Cleveland 44114 (216) 621-0200

Trust established in 1958 in OH; incorporated in 1963.
Donor(s): William O. Frohring,† Gertrude L. Frohring.†
Financial data (yr. ended 12/31/87): Assets, $3,318,030 (M); expenditures, $281,141, including $248,250 for 47 grants (high: $50,000; low: $450; average: $3,864).
Purpose and activities: Giving mainly to health, education, and the arts.
Types of support: Operating budgets, continuing support, annual campaigns, seed money, emergency funds, building funds, equipment, land acquisition.
Limitations: Giving primarily in Geauga, Lake, and Cuyahoga counties, OH. No grants to individuals, or for deficit financing, endowment funds, matching gifts, scholarships, or fellowships; no loans.
Application information:
Initial approach: Letter
Copies of proposal: 1
Deadline(s): Submit proposal preferably in Mar. and Aug.; deadline 1 week before board meetings
Board meeting date(s): May and Oct.
Final notification: 3 weeks after board meetings
Write: William W. Falsgraf, Asst. Secy.
Officers and Trustees: Glenn H. Frohring, Chair.; Lloyd W. Frohring, Treas.; William W. Falsgraf, Elaine A. Szilagyi.
Employer Identification Number: 346516526

2470
The GAR Foundation
50 South Main St.
P.O. Box 1500
Akron 44309 (216) 376-5300

Trust established in 1967 in OH.
Donor(s): Ruth C. Roush,† Galen Roush.†
Financial data (yr. ended 12/31/87): Assets, $109,465,263 (M); expenditures, $6,326,616, including $5,927,051 for 160 grants (high: $500,000; low: $1,000; average: $10,000-$75,000).
Purpose and activities: Grants to higher and secondary educational institutions for programs promoting the private enterprise economic system, and for the arts, hospitals, and civic and social service agencies, including youth activities.
Types of support: Equipment, general purposes, endowment funds, matching funds, research, scholarship funds.
Limitations: Giving primarily in northeastern OH, with emphasis on Akron. No support for medical research. No grants to individuals, or for fundraising campaigns, or general operating expenses of the donee not directly related to its exempt purpose.
Publications: Application guidelines.
Application information: Application form required.
Initial approach: Proposal
Copies of proposal: 1

Deadline(s): 1st of month prior to board meeting date
Board meeting date(s): Feb., May, Aug., and Nov.
Final notification: Jan. 1, Apr. 1, July 1 and Oct. 1
Write: Lisle M. Buckingham, Trustee
Distribution Committee: Lisle M. Buckingham,* Joseph Clapp, John L. Tormey, S.R. Werner, Charles F. Zodrow.
Trustees:* National City Bank, Akron.
Number of staff: 1 full-time professional; 4 part-time professional.
Employer Identification Number: 346577710

2471
GenCorp Foundation, Inc.
175 Ghent Rd.
Fairlawn 44313-3300 (216) 869-4440

Incorporated in 1961 in OH as successor to The General Tire Foundation, a trust established in 1950 in OH.
Donor(s): GenCorp, Inc.
Financial data (yr. ended 11/30/88): Assets, $28,700,882 (M); expenditures, $1,371,759, including $936,101 for 187 grants (high: $50,000; low: $300) and $166,038 for employee matching gifts.
Purpose and activities: Emphasis on higher education, community funds, and youth agencies; support also for social services and cultural programs.
Types of support: Employee matching gifts, annual campaigns, employee-related scholarships, general purposes, continuing support.
Limitations: Giving primarily in areas of company operations, including AZ, AR, CA, IN, MS, NH, NY, OH, PA, and TN. No grants to individuals, or for endowment funds, or research; no loans.
Application information:
Initial approach: Letter
Copies of proposal: 1
Deadline(s): None
Board meeting date(s): As required
Final notification: 2 months
Write: Joseph M. Leyden, Pres.
Officer and Trustee: Joseph M. Leyden, Pres. and Secy.
Number of staff: None.
Employer Identification Number: 346514223

2472
Gerlach Foundation, Inc.
37 West Broad St., 5th Fl.
Columbus 43215

Incorporated in 1953 in OH.
Donor(s): Pauline Gerlach,† John J. Gerlach, John B. Gerlach.
Financial data (yr. ended 11/30/86): Assets, $5,938,411 (M); expenditures, $240,179, including $109,860 for 35 grants (high: $41,000; low: $50).
Purpose and activities: Emphasis on higher education and social services; support also for cultural programs.
Types of support: General purposes.
Limitations: Giving primarily in OH. No grants to individuals.
Application information: Contributes only to pre-selected organizations. Applications not accepted.
Write: John J. Gerlach, Pres.
Officers: John J. Gerlach, Pres.; Gretchen Gerlach, V.P.; John B. Gerlach, Secy.-Treas.
Employer Identification Number: 316023912

2473
Gould Inc. Foundation
35129 Curtis Blvd.
Eastlake 44094 (216) 953-5000

Incorporated in 1951 in OH.
Donor(s): Gould, Inc.
Financial data (yr. ended 12/31/87): Assets, $3,033,037 (M); expenditures, $386,442, including $186,854 for 30 grants (high: $33,000; low: $150; average: $2,000-$5,000), $78,921 for 50 grants to individuals and $90,633 for 530 employee matching gifts.
Purpose and activities: To strengthen the socio-economic environment in areas of corporate operations and of selected educational and scientific institutions; grants largely for community funds, higher education, scholarships for children of employees, hospitals, cultural activities, and youth agencies; support also for national organizations recognized as beneficial to the broader national community.
Types of support: Employee-related scholarships, annual campaigns, building funds, equipment, endowment funds, research, employee matching gifts.
Limitations: Giving primarily in areas of corporate operations. No support for groups that discriminate against minorities; disease-related organizations, other than special projects undertaken within Gould Inc.; or religious and fraternal groups which do not benefit entire commmunities. No grants to individuals (except company-employee scholarships); no loans.
Application information: Write to principal manager of local Gould facility.
Initial approach: Letter or proposal
Copies of proposal: 1
Deadline(s): Jan. 31 for scholarships; no set deadline for general grants
Board meeting date(s): Jan. and as required
Write: Joseph Huss, V.P., Human Resources, Gould, Inc.
Officers: C.D. Ferguson, Pres.; Jerry W. Gaskin, V.P.; M.C. Veysey, V.P. and Secy.
Number of staff: 2 part-time professional.
Employer Identification Number: 346525555

2474
The Gradison & Company Foundation
580 Building
Cincinnati 45202 (513) 579-5000

Financial data (yr. ended 12/31/87): Assets, $96,371 (M); gifts received, $67,000; expenditures, $92,493, including $92,308 for 83 grants (high: $17,500; low: $25).
Purpose and activities: Support for United Appeal, culture, youth, higher education, schools for the handicapped, civic affairs, health, and social services.
Application information: Contributes only to preselected charitable organizations. Applications not accepted.
Write: David L. Amrine, Treas. and Cont.
Trustees: David W. Ellis, Robert B. Shott, Donald E. Weston.
Employer Identification Number: 311018948

2475
Walter L. and Nell R. Gross Charitable Trust
105 East Fourth St., Rm. 710
Cincinnati 45202 (513) 721-5086

Established in 1955 in OH.
Donor(s): Members of the Gross family.
Financial data (yr. ended 12/31/87): Assets, $2,767,177 (M); expenditures, $59,044, including $46,018 for 20 grants (high: $9,950; low: $150).
Purpose and activities: Support for higher and secondary education, youth agencies, cultural programs, hospitals and health agencies, and Protestant church support.
Limitations: Giving primarily in OH.
Application information: Applications not accepted.
Write: Walter L. Gross, Jr., or Thomas R. Gross, Trustees
Advisory Board: Walter L. Gross, Jr., Thomas R. Gross, Patricia G. Linnemann.
Employer Identification Number: 316033247

2476
The George Gund Foundation
One Erieview Plaza
Cleveland 44114-1773 (216) 241-3114

Incorporated in 1952 in OH.
Donor(s): George Gund.†
Financial data (yr. ended 12/31/87): Assets, $237,474,933 (M); expenditures, $8,842,891, including $7,621,885 for 310 grants (high: $250,000; low: $750; average: $25,000-$35,000).
Purpose and activities: Priority to education projects, with emphasis on new concepts and methods of teaching and learning, and on increasing educational opportunities for the disadvantaged; programs advancing economic revitalization and job creation; projects promoting neighborhood development; projects for improving human services, employment opportunities, housing for minority and low-income groups, and meeting the special needs of women; support also for ecology, civic affairs, and the arts.
Types of support: Operating budgets, continuing support, seed money, emergency funds, land acquisition, matching funds, internships, scholarship funds, special projects, publications, conferences and seminars, program-related investments, exchange programs, renovation projects, research.
Limitations: Giving primarily in northeastern OH. Generally no grants to individuals, or for building or endowment funds, equipment, or renovation projects.
Publications: Annual report (including application guidelines).
Application information:
Initial approach: Proposal

Copies of proposal: 1
Deadline(s): Jan. 15, Apr. 15, July 15, and Oct. 15
Board meeting date(s): Mar., June, Oct., and Dec.
Final notification: 8 weeks
Write: David Bergholz, Exec. Dir.

Officers and Trustees: Frederick K. Cox, Pres. and Treas.; Geoffrey Gund, V.P.; William G. Caples, Secy.; David Bergholz, Exec. Dir.; Kathleen L. Barber, Ann L. Gund, George Gund III, Llura A. Gund.

Number of staff: 3 full-time professional; 3 full-time support.

Employer Identification Number: 346519769

Recent arts and culture grants:

Accord Associates, Cleveland, OH, $10,000. For continued support for Debut Series which involves public performances and school appearances by professional black classical musicians. 10/22/87.
American Documentary, NYC, NY, $25,000. To assist in underwriting thirteen-part series highlighting films of independent filmmakers and focuses on important social issues. 6/22/88.
Arts Midwest, Minneapolis, MN, $35,000. For support of performing arts touring program and minority arts administration fellowship program. 3/10/88.
Association of Ohio Dance Companies, Cleveland, OH, $5,000. For project, New Choreography from Folk Dances and Oral Traditions. 3/10/88.
Broadway School of Music and the Arts, Cleveland, OH, $15,000. For challenge grant to assist in meeting School's operating requirements. 10/22/87.
Cleveland Artists Foundation, Cleveland, OH, $30,000. To expand exhibition program of Northeast Ohio Art Museum. 10/22/87.
Cleveland Center for Contemporary Art, Cleveland, OH, $50,000. For start-up operating and program support for satellite exhibition facility located in Cleveland's new Galleria complex. 10/22/87.
Cleveland Center for Contemporary Art, Cleveland, OH, $5,000. To produce catalog of John Pearson's art to accompany exhibition of his work. 3/10/88.
Cleveland Childrens Museum, Cleveland, OH, $25,000. For educational outreach program to accompany Museum's new exhibit entitled Water, Water Everywhere. 10/22/87.
Cleveland Museum of Art, Cleveland, OH, $38,000. To assist with establishment of archives. 6/22/88.
Cleveland Museum of Natural History, Cleveland, OH, $200,000. Toward construction and endowment of new wing. 6/22/88.
Cleveland Music School Settlement, Cleveland, OH, $22,100. For Live with the Arts program. 3/10/88.
Cleveland Music School Settlement, Cleveland, OH, $6,950. For expenses of Teens-in-Training On the Road Summer Program. 10/22/87.
Cleveland Opera, Cleveland, OH, $30,000. For continued development of local performing arts group. 10/22/87.
Cleveland Play House, Cleveland, OH, $25,000. To assist in underwriting new Artistic Director's salary during six-month transition period. 12/10/87.
Cleveland Public Radio, Cleveland, OH, $5,864. For production and airing of programs dealing with local and regional public education issues. 12/10/87.
Cuyahoga Community College, Cleveland, OH, $5,000. To assist in underwriting Showtime at High Noon Series during 1987/88 season. 12/10/87.
East Cleveland Community Theater and Arts Center, East Cleveland, OH, $12,500. For emergency operating support to meet budget shortfall caused by changes in National Endowment for the Arts' funding strategy. 10/22/87.
Eleanor B. Rainey Memorial Institute, Cleveland, OH, $6,390. For coordinated summer arts program for residents of Cleveland's Near East Side neighborhoods. 10/22/87.
Fairmount Theater of the Deaf, Cleveland, OH, $15,000. To support efforts to revitalize and strengthen operations. 3/10/88.
Film Arts Foundation, San Francisco, CA, $15,000. Toward documentary film entitled Turning the Tide, describing ways in which key national figures have changed their minds regarding our nation's defense strategies. 12/10/87.
Great Lakes Historical Society, Vermilion, OH, $85,000. For supplemental assistance for program planning and predesign services related to proposed development of Great Lakes Maritime Educational Center. 12/10/87.
Great Lakes Historical Society, Vermilion, OH, $60,000. For additional planning and feasibility studies related to development of Great Lakes Museum. 6/22/88.
Great Lakes Shakespeare Festival, Cleveland, OH, $25,000. For special project entitled Festival Fantastico which highlights Spanish arts. 6/22/88.
Lyric Opera of Cleveland, Cleveland, OH, $17,500. For continued operating support. 3/10/88.
Musical Arts Association, Cleveland, OH, $50,000. For one-time challenge grant to enable Association to generate additional operating support. 12/10/87.
National Archives Trust Fund Board, DC, $20,000. To support collection and microfilming of papers of Margaret Sanger, coordinated by Consortium for Women's History, and to distribute material to Ohio libraries. 3/10/88.
National Public Radio, DC, $60,000. To expand Midwest office. 3/10/88.
New Day Press, Cleveland, OH, $11,410. To reprint series of books for young children on black history prior to Reconstruction Period. 6/22/88.
New Organization for the Visual Arts (NOVA), Cleveland, OH, $10,000. For start-up support for new Artists Information Center. 10/22/87.
Nordonia Hills City School District, Northfield, OH, $35,000. To assist with statewide expansion of program entitled Power of the Pen. 3/10/88.
Ohio Chamber Ballet, Akron, OH, $45,000. To assist in meeting challenge grant from National Endowment for the Arts to enable Ballet to expand its services to more Ohio cities. 3/10/88.
Old Brooklyn Community Development Corporation, Cleveland, OH, $90,000. To renovate Broadvue Theatre into facility to be leased by Great Lakes Theatre Festival. 10/22/87.
Playhouse Square Foundation, Cleveland, OH, $250,000. For operating assistance over interim period until more permanent sources of support are developed, plus assistance toward creation of Musical Incubator. 12/10/87.
Rockefeller Park Cultural Arts Association, Cleveland, OH, $5,000. To support Rockefeller Park Cultural Arts Festival. 6/22/88.
SPACES, Cleveland, OH, $5,000. For support of Hidden City Revealed project which will be undertaken in collaboration with Committee for Public Art in Warehouse District. 10/22/87.
Strongsville Historical Society, Strongsville, OH, $20,000. To assist with expenses of moving historic Lathrop House and Bradley Home. 6/22/88.
Tom Evert Dance Company, Euclid, OH, $6,000. To assist with personnel expenses during 1987/88 season. 12/10/87.
Western Reserve Historical Society, Cleveland, OH, $7,500. For Connecticut/Ohio Western Reserve Film Project. 6/22/88.
Western Reserve Historical Society, Cleveland, OH, $7,240. For expenses of reprinting book entitled Cleveland Architecture 1876-1976. 6/22/88.

2477
The Hamilton Community Foundation, Inc.

319 North Third St.
Hamilton 45011 (513) 863-1389

Community foundation incorporated in 1951 in OH.

Financial data (yr. ended 12/31/88): Assets, $9,198,587 (M); gifts received, $863,131; expenditures, $971,100, including $915,471 for 200 grants (high: $25,000; low: $10; average: $1,000-$20,000) and $6,665 for foundation-administered programs.

Purpose and activities: Grants for local institutions, with emphasis on youth and child welfare agencies and scholarships. Grants also for health agencies and cultural programs.

Types of support: Seed money, emergency funds, scholarship funds, conferences and seminars.

Limitations: Giving limited to Butler County, OH. No grants to individuals, or for operating budgets, continuing support, annual campaigns, deficit financing, capital or endowment funds, matching gifts, program support, research, demonstration projects, or publications; no loans.

Publications: Annual report, application guidelines.

Application information:
Initial approach: Proposal
Copies of proposal: 10
Deadline(s): Submit proposal 30 days prior to 1st Monday of months in which board meets

Board meeting date(s): Feb., Apr., June, Oct., and Dec.
Final notification: 2 months
Write: Cynthia V. Parrish, Exec. Dir.

Officers: Anne B. Carr, Pres.; Cynthia V. Parrish, Exec. Dir.
Trustees: David Belew, Don W. Fitton, Jr., Richard J. Fitton, William Hartford, Lamont Jacobs, William Keck, Joseph L. Marcum, Lee H. Parrish, Joel H. Schmidt, John A. Whalen.
Trustee Banks: Second National Bank, First National Bank and Trust Co.
Number of staff: 1 part-time professional; 1 part-time support.
Employer Identification Number: 316038277

2478
The Hankins Foundation
3835-4 Lander Rd.
Chagrin Falls 44022

Trust established in 1952 in OH.
Donor(s): Edward R. Hankins,† Ann H. Long,† Jane H. Lockwood,† Ruth L. Hankins.
Financial data (yr. ended 12/31/87): Assets, $2,607,401 (M); expenditures, $210,457, including $171,388 for 82 grants (high: $27,500; low: $250).
Purpose and activities: Emphasis on higher education, community funds, health agencies and hospitals, youth and social service agencies, and cultural programs.
Limitations: Giving primarily in OH. No grants to individuals; no loans.
Application information:
Initial approach: Proposal
Copies of proposal: 1
Deadline(s): None
Board meeting date(s): As required
Write: Miss Ruth L. Hankins, Trustee

Trustees: Ruth L. Hankins, Richard R. Hollington, Jr., Edward G. Lockwood, Gordon G. Long, Janet L. Tarwater.
Employer Identification Number: 346565426

2479
Grace and John T. Harrington Foundation
c/o Bank One Youngstown, N.A.
P.O. Box 359
Youngstown 44501 (216) 742-6871

Established in 1954 in OH.
Financial data (yr. ended 12/31/87): Assets, $1,414,997 (M); expenditures, $118,317, including $104,667 for 11 grants (high: $41,667; low: $2,000; average: $2,000-$10,000).
Purpose and activities: Giving primarily for arts and culture, education, and social services.
Types of support: General purposes.
Publications: 990-PF.
Application information:
Deadline(s): None

Trustees: John T. Thornton, Peter Thornton, William W. Thornton, Bank One, Youngstown, N.A.
Employer Identification Number: 346514087

2480
Haskell Fund
1010 Hanna Bldg.
Cleveland 44115 (216) 696-5528

Incorporated in 1955 in OH.
Donor(s): Melville H. Haskell,† Coburn Haskell, Melville H. Haskell, Jr., Mark Haskell.
Financial data (yr. ended 12/31/88): Assets, $1,989,065 (M); expenditures, $138,524, including $120,700 for 51 grants (high: $14,000; low: $250; average: $1,000-$5,000).
Purpose and activities: Giving locally for community services and nationally for higher and secondary education, hospitals, and health agencies.
Types of support: Annual campaigns, building funds, continuing support, endowment funds, general purposes, operating budgets, scholarship funds, special projects.
Limitations: Giving primarily in the Cleveland, OH, area for community service grants; other grants awarded nationally. No grants to individuals.
Publications: Annual report.
Application information:
Initial approach: Proposal
Copies of proposal: 1
Board meeting date(s): Within the first 2 weeks of June
Write: Donald C. Cook, Treas.

Officers: Coburn Haskell,* Pres.; Schuyler A. Haskell,* V.P.; Betty J. Tuite, Secy.; Donald C. Cook, Treas.
Trustees:* Mary H. Haywood, Melville H. Haskell, Jr.
Employer Identification Number: 346513797

2481
The Hershey Foundation
Two Bratenahl Place
Bratenahl 44108
Application address: 11530 Madison Rd., Huntsberg, OH 44046

Established in 1986 in OH.
Donor(s): Jo Hershey Selden.
Financial data (yr. ended 6/30/88): Assets, $1,262,194 (M); gifts received, $700,000; expenditures, $68,427, including $66,900 for 6 grants (high: $51,000; low: $400).
Purpose and activities: Support primarily for a Montessori School; support also for a theatre and for the musical arts.
Types of support: Building funds, general purposes.
Limitations: Giving primarily in OH.
Application information: Application form required.
Copies of proposal: 2
Write: Jo Hershey Selden, Pres.

Officers: Jo Hershey Selden, Pres.; Carole H. Walters, V.P.; Debra S. Guren, Secy.; Georgia A. Froelich, Loren Hershey.
Employer Identification Number: 341525626

2482
The Higbee Foundation
100 Public Square
Cleveland 44113 (216) 579-3402

Trust established in 1975 in OH as successor to Higbee McKelvey Charitable Foundation.
Donor(s): The Higbee Co.
Financial data (yr. ended 1/31/88): Assets, $4,904 (M); gifts received, $265,231; expenditures, $292,586, including $292,460 for 173 grants (high: $120,000; low: $25).
Purpose and activities: Emphasis on community funds; support also for higher education, hospitals, and cultural organizations.
Limitations: Giving primarily in OH. No grants to individuals.
Publications: 990-PF, application guidelines.
Application information:
Initial approach: Proposal, letter, or telephone
Copies of proposal: 1
Deadline(s): Submit proposal by Jan. 1
Board meeting date(s): Jan.

Trustees: Robert R. Broadbent, R.B. Campbell.
Number of staff: None.
Employer Identification Number: 510173783

2483
Hoover Company Corporate Giving Program
101 East Maple St.
North Canton 44720 (216) 499-9200

Purpose and activities: Support for United Way, youth, hospitals, higher education, health associations, and culture.
Limitations: Giving primarily in areas where company has manufacturing facilities, mainly Stark County, OH, area. No grants to individuals.
Application information:
Initial approach: Letter

2484
Letha E. House Foundation
698 East Washington St., Suite 1-B
Medina 44256 (216) 723-6404

Established in 1967 in OH.
Financial data (yr. ended 6/30/87): Assets, $1,339,637 (M); expenditures, $155,664, including $139,050 for 8 grants.
Purpose and activities: Support primarily for historical restoration projects.
Types of support: Renovation projects, operating budgets.
Limitations: Giving primarily in the Medina County, OH, area.
Application information:
Initial approach: Letter
Deadline(s): None
Write: Charles Clark Griesinger, Trustee

Trustees: Charles Clark Griesinger, Paul M. Jones, Old Phoenix National Bank of Medina.
Employer Identification Number: 237025122

2485
The Huffy Foundation, Inc.
P.O. Box 1204
Dayton 45401 (513) 866-6251

Incorporated in OH in 1959 as Huffman Foundation; name changed in 1978.
Donor(s): Huffy Corp.
Financial data (yr. ended 6/30/88): Assets, $478,574 (M); gifts received, $336,000; expenditures, $209,646, including $197,253 for 78 grants (high: $45,000; low: $100; average: $1,000) and $9,600 for 32 employee matching gifts.
Purpose and activities: Support for higher education, cultural programs, youth agencies, community funds, civic affairs, and health.
Types of support: Operating budgets, continuing support, annual campaigns, seed money, emergency funds, matching funds, scholarship funds, special projects, publications, employee matching gifts, conferences and seminars, building funds, capital campaigns, consulting services, general purposes.
Limitations: Giving primarily in areas of company operations in OH, CO, CA, and WI. Generally no operational grant support for agencies covered by the United Way. No grants to individuals, or for deficit financing, endowment funds, research, or fellowships; no loans.
Publications: Informational brochure (including application guidelines).
Application information:
Initial approach: Letter or proposal
Copies of proposal: 1
Deadline(s): None
Board meeting date(s): Apr., Aug., and Dec.
Final notification: Approximately 2 weeks after board meetings
Write: R.R. Wieland, Secy.
Officers: Harry A. Shaw,* Pres.; R.R. Wieland, Secy.
Trustees:* F.C. Smith, Chair.; S.J. Northrop.
Number of staff: None.
Employer Identification Number: 316023716

2486
Gilbert W. & Louise Ireland Humphrey Foundation
1010 Hanna Bldg.
Cleveland 44115 (216) 363-6486

Incorporated in 1951 in OH.
Donor(s): Gilbert W. Humphrey,† Louise Ireland Humphrey.
Financial data (yr. ended 12/31/88): Assets, $1,463,273 (M); expenditures, $181,248, including $171,500 for 21 grants (high: $46,000; low: $500; average: $1,000-$5,000).
Purpose and activities: Emphasis on educational institutions, music, cultural programs, a community fund, hospitals, and social service agencies.
Limitations: Giving primarily in OH. No grants to individuals.
Publications: 990-PF.
Application information: Funds committed to the same charities each year; foundation rarely considers new appeals.
Initial approach: Letter
Copies of proposal: 1
Deadline(s): Submit proposal preferably in 1st quarter of year; deadline Sept. 1
Board meeting date(s): 1st Tuesday of Nov.
Write: Louise Ireland Humphrey, Pres.
Officers and Trustees:* Louise Ireland Humphrey,* Pres.; Margaret H. Bindhardt,* V.P.; M.G. Mikolaj,* Secy.; George M. Humphrey II, Treas.
Employer Identification Number: 346525832

2487
George M. and Pamela S. Humphrey Fund
1010 Hanna Bldg.
Cleveland 44115 (216) 363-6487

Incorporated in 1951 in OH.
Donor(s): George M. Humphrey,† Pamela S. Humphrey.†
Financial data (yr. ended 12/31/86): Assets, $6,645,060 (M); expenditures, $980,755, including $420,000 for 41 grants (high: $75,000; low: $500; average: $5,000).
Purpose and activities: Support for hospitals, higher and secondary education, and community funds; support also for cultural programs and health agencies.
Types of support: Operating budgets, continuing support, annual campaigns, emergency funds, building funds, equipment, endowment funds, matching funds, professorships, internships, research, technical assistance.
Limitations: Giving primarily in OH. No grants to individuals; no loans.
Publications: Annual report.
Application information:
Initial approach: Letter or proposal
Copies of proposal: 1
Deadline(s): Submit proposal preferably in Feb. or Oct.; deadline Oct. 15
Board meeting date(s): Apr. and Nov.
Final notification: 1 month
Write: Carol H. Butler, Pres.
Officers: Carol H. Butler,* Pres.; John G. Butler,* V.P.; H.N. Putnam, Secy.-Treas.
Trustees:* Pamela B. Rutter.
Employer Identification Number: 346513798

2488
Hunter Foundation
1010 Hanna Blvd.
Cleveland 44115 (216) 363-6483

Established in 1956 in OH.
Financial data (yr. ended 12/31/87): Assets, $1,242,252 (M); expenditures, $113,795, including $102,500 for 23 grants (high: $15,000; low: $1,000).
Purpose and activities: Giving for hospitals and medical purposes, social services, higher education, and an environmental museum.
Limitations: Giving primarily in AZ and KY. No grants to individuals.
Application information:
Initial approach: Proposal
Deadline(s): Aug. 31
Board meeting date(s): 1st 2 weeks in Sept.
Write: J.A. Horning, Treas.
Officers: Barbara Hunter,* Pres.; J. Rukin Jelks, Jr., V.P.; R.S. St. John, Secy.; J.A. Horning, Treas.
Trustees:* Carolyn G. Jelks.
Employer Identification Number: 346513679

2489
Huntington Bancshares Corporate Giving Program
41 S. High St.
Columbus 43287 (614) 476-8300

Purpose and activities: Supports economic development, arts and culture, education, job development, minority programs, health associations, and youth services.
Types of support: Employee matching gifts, general purposes, annual campaigns, capital campaigns, endowment funds, fellowships, scholarship funds.
Application information:
Copies of proposal: 1
Deadline(s): By year end
Write: Dorothy R. Brownley, V.P., Dir. of Corp. Relations
Number of staff: 2 full-time professional.

2490
John F. and Loretta A. Hynes Foundation
c/o Mahoning National Bank of Youngstown
Box 479
Youngstown 44501 (216) 742-7000

Established in 1957 in OH.
Financial data (yr. ended 12/31/87): Assets, $1,291,380 (M); expenditures, $96,465, including $85,500 for 13 grants (high: $12,500; low: $1,000).
Purpose and activities: Giving primarily for arts organizations, hospitals, education, and youth programs.
Types of support: Equipment, capital campaigns, special projects, renovation projects.
Limitations: Giving primarily in the Youngstown, OH, area. No grants to individuals.
Application information:
Initial approach: Proposal
Deadline(s): None
Write: Patrick A. Sebastiano, Sr. V.P. and Trust Officer, Mahoning National Bank of Youngstown
Officers: John M. Newman, Chair.; W.W. Bresnahan, Vice-Chair.
Members: William J. Mullen, Arthur G. Young.
Trustee Bank: Mahoning National Bank of Youngstown.
Employer Identification Number: 346516440

2491
Iddings Foundation
Kettering Tower, Suite 1620
Dayton 45423 (513) 224-1773

Trust established in 1973 in OH.
Donor(s): Roscoe C. Iddings,† Andrew S. Iddings.†
Financial data (yr. ended 12/31/88): Assets, $7,631,469 (M); expenditures, $519,497,

including $454,806 for 68 grants (high: $30,000; low: $500; average: $5-$10,000).
Purpose and activities: Grants for pre-college and higher education, health care, mental health, care of the aged and handicapped, youth agencies, cultural programs, the environment, community welfare, and population control.
Types of support: Operating budgets, continuing support, annual campaigns, seed money, emergency funds, building funds, equipment, land acquisition, scholarship funds, special projects, publications, consulting services, capital campaigns, conferences and seminars, general purposes, matching funds, renovation projects.
Limitations: Giving limited to OH, with emphasis on the Dayton metropolitan area. No grants to individuals, or for endowment funds or deficit financing; no loans.
Publications: Informational brochure (including application guidelines), multi-year report.
Application information:
Initial approach: Letter or telephone
Copies of proposal: 8
Deadline(s): Mar. 1, June 1, Sept. 1, or Nov. 1
Board meeting date(s): Apr., July, Oct., and Dec.
Final notification: 1 week following meeting of distribution committee
Write: Maribeth A. Eiken, Admin.
Trustee: Bank One, Dayton, N.A.
Number of staff: 1 part-time professional.
Employer Identification Number: 316135058

2492
The Louise H. and David S. Ingalls Foundation, Inc.
301 Tower East
20600 Chagrin Blvd.
Shaker Heights 44122 (216) 921-6000

Incorporated in 1953 in OH.
Donor(s): Louise H. Ingalls,† Edith Ingalls Vignos, Louise Ingalls Brown, David S. Ingalls,† David S. Ingalls, Jr., Jane I. Davison, Anne I. Lawrence.
Financial data (yr. ended 12/31/87): Assets, $10,460,053 (M); expenditures, $589,483, including $563,000 for 23 grants (high: $99,000; low: $2,000).
Purpose and activities: "The improvement of the physical, educational, mental, and moral condition of humanity throughout the world"; grants largely for higher and secondary education; support also for community funds, health, and cultural programs. Support mainly to organizations known to the trustees.
Types of support: Special projects, building funds, capital campaigns, research, endowment funds, equipment.
Limitations: Giving primarily in Cleveland, OH.
Application information:
Initial approach: Proposal
Copies of proposal: 5
Deadline(s): None
Board meeting date(s): As required
Write: David S. Ingalls, Jr., Pres.
Officers: David S. Ingalls, Jr.,* Pres. and Treas.; Louise Ingalls Brown,* V.P.; Edith Ingalls Vignos,* V.P.; James H. Dempsey, Jr., Secy.
Trustees:* Jane I. Davison, Anne I. Lawrence.
Number of staff: 2 part-time support.
Employer Identification Number: 346516550

2493
The Ireland Foundation
1010 Hanna Bldg.
Cleveland 44115 (216) 363-6486

Incorporated in 1951 in OH.
Donor(s): Margaret Allen Ireland,† R. Livingston Ireland,† Kate Ireland, and members of the Ireland family.
Financial data (yr. ended 12/31/88): Assets, $7,326,496 (M); expenditures, $462,396, including $390,000 for 73 grants (high: $100,000; low: $100; average: $1,000-$5,000).
Purpose and activities: Grants largely for educational and charitable programs, with emphasis on nursing, higher and secondary education, and hospitals; grants also for music.
Types of support: General purposes.
Limitations: Giving primarily in Cleveland, OH. No grants to individuals.
Application information: Funds committed to the same charities each year; foundation rarely considers new appeals. Applications not accepted.
Initial approach: Letter and brief proposal
Board meeting date(s): 1st Tuesday of Nov.
Officers: Louise Ireland Humphrey,* Pres. and Treas.; Kate Ireland,* V.P.; M.G. Mikolaj, Secy.
Trustees:* R.L. Ireland III.
Employer Identification Number: 346525817

2494
Irwin J. Jaeger Foundation
c/o Barbara S. Bromberg
1700 Central Trust Tower
Cincinnati 45202

Donor(s): Irwin J. Jaeger.
Financial data (yr. ended 11/30/87): Assets, $1,017,742 (M); gifts received, $795,275; expenditures, $70,288, including $70,065 for 15 grants (high: $45,250; low: $100).
Purpose and activities: Giving primarily to Jewish organizations.
Types of support: Continuing support, equipment, operating budgets.
Officer: Irwin J. Jaeger, Pres. and Treas.
Trustees: Patricia Jaeger, Richard Jaeger.
Employer Identification Number: 237154491

2495
Isaac & Esther Jarson - Stanley & Mickey Kaplan Foundation
(Formerly Isaac N. and Esther M. Jarson Charitable Trust)
105 East Fourth St., Suite 710
Cincinnati 45202 (513) 721-5086

Trust established in 1955 in OH.
Financial data (yr. ended 12/31/87): Assets, $3,087,372 (M); expenditures, $125,549, including $110,850 for 53 grants (high: $30,000; low: $50).
Purpose and activities: Giving for civic affairs, education, and cultural programs.
Limitations: Giving primarily in Cincinnati, OH.
Application information:
Write: Stanley M. Kaplan or Myran J. Kaplan, Mgrs.
Managers: Myran J. Kaplan, Stanley M. Kaplan.
Employer Identification Number: 316033453

2496
The Martha Holden Jennings Foundation
710 Halle Bldg.
1228 Euclid Ave.
Cleveland 44115 (216) 589-5700
Business office: 20620 North Park Blvd., No. 215, Shaker Heights, OH 44118; Tel.: (216) 932-7337

Incorporated in 1959 in OH.
Donor(s): Martha Holden Jennings.†
Financial data (yr. ended 12/31/87): Assets, $44,444,622 (M); gifts received, $22,037; expenditures, $2,361,105, including $1,251,600 for 117 grants (high: $100,000; low: $750; average: $1,000-$30,000) and $432,844 for 16 foundation-administered programs.
Purpose and activities: Giving to foster development of the capabilities of young people through improving the quality of teaching in secular elementary and secondary schools; program includes awards in recognition of outstanding teaching; special educational programs for teachers in the fields of the humanities, the arts, and the sciences; awards to deserving students in furtherance of their recognized abilities; curriculum development projects; school evaluation studies; and educational television programs.
Types of support: Continuing support, seed money, matching funds, professorships, scholarship funds, special projects, conferences and seminars.
Limitations: Giving limited to OH. No grants to individuals (except awards by nomination), or for operating budgets, annual campaigns, travel, emergency funds, deficit financing, capital or endowment funds, research, or publications; no loans.
Publications: Annual report, newsletter, program policy statement, application guidelines.
Application information: Application form required for Grants to Teachers Program.
Initial approach: 1-page project summary, cover letter, budget, and proposal
Copies of proposal: 10
Deadline(s): 20th of each month preceding month in which application is to be considered
Board meeting date(s): Advisory and Distribution Committee meets monthly, except Aug. and Dec.
Final notification: 6 to 8 weeks
Write: Joan M. Johnson, Prog. Dir.
Officers and Trustees: Arthur S. Holden, Jr., Chair.; George B. Chapman, Jr., Pres.; William F. Hauserman, V.P.; Frank W. Milbourn, V.P.; John H. Gherlein, Secy.; Allen H. Ford, Treas.; Robert M. Ginn, Claire D. Holden.
Number of staff: 1 full-time professional; 1 part-time professional; 3 part-time support.

Employer Identification Number: 340934478
Recent arts and culture grants:
Chautauqua Institution, Chautauqua, NY, $15,000. For scholarship support in 1987. 1987.
Childrens Concert Society of Akron, Akron, OH, $5,000. For in-school concerts. 1987.
Cincinnati Opera Association, Cincinnati, OH, $10,000. For Education Outreach Program. 1987.
Cleveland Ballet, Cleveland, OH, $33,000. For educational mini-performances. 1987.
Cleveland Health Education Museum, Cleveland, OH, $20,000. For Family Discovery Center. 1987.
Cleveland Institute of Art, Cleveland, OH, $7,200. For Cuyahoga County Regional Scholastic Art Awards Competition. 1987.
Cleveland Institute of Music, Cleveland, OH, $15,000. For Preparatory Department Scholarships. 1987.
Cleveland Institute of Music, Cleveland, OH, $15,000. For support for Encore School for Strings. 1987.
Cleveland Modern Dance Association, Cleveland, OH, $11,425. For dance scholarships. 1987.
Cleveland Museum of Natural History, Cleveland, OH, $11,250. For archaeological field experience. 1987.
Cleveland Music School Settlement, Cleveland, OH, $8,000. For Summer Music Program. 1987.
Cleveland Music School Settlement, Cleveland, OH, $6,000. For benefit concert at Severance Hall. 1987.
Cleveland Play House, Cleveland, OH, $30,000. For Educational Outreach/Student Matinee Programs. 1987.
Cleveland Public Radio, Cleveland, OH, $7,000. For Kids America. 1987.
Cleveland School of the Arts, Friends of the, Cleveland, OH, $33,000. For tutoring support for students. 1987.
Columbus Symphony Orchestra, Columbus, OH, $15,000. For Young People's Concerts and Docent Program. 1987.
Dayton Opera Association, Dayton, OH, $5,000. For Student Audience Performances. 1987.
Fairmount Theater of the Deaf, Cleveland, OH, $30,000. For education and outreach program. 1987.
Fairport Childrens Theater, Fairport Harbor, OH, $12,000. For theater for children, by children. 1987.
Findlay City Schools, Findlay, OH, $6,500. For Perceptual Skills in Drawing Workshop. 1987.
Great Lakes Shakespeare Festival, Cleveland, OH, $25,000. For Theater Festival Education Program. 1987.
Lakewood Little Theater Fine Arts Foundation, Lakewood, OH, $40,000. For Beck Center Educational Programs. 1987.
Lima Area Arts Council, Lima, OH, $6,000. For Arts Educational Partnership. 1987.
Lyric Opera of Cleveland, Cleveland, OH, $7,500. For Education Outreach Program. 1987.
Musical Arts Association, Cleveland, OH, $50,000. For Cleveland Orchestra Youth Orchestra. 1987.
Muskingum College, New Concord, OH, $10,000. For Appalachian Children's Theater Series. 1987.
New Cleveland Opera Company, Cleveland, OH, $18,000. For Cleveland Opera on Tour Educational Programming. 1987.
Nordonia Hills City School District, Northfield, OH, $5,000. For Interscholastic Writing Tournaments. 1987.
Northern Ohio Childrens Performing Music Foundation, Cleveland, OH, $5,500. For Singing Angels Concert. 1987.
Oberlin College, Conservatory of Music, Oberlin, OH, $5,000. For summer youth symphony orchestra. 1987.
Ohio Wesleyan University, Delaware, OH, $7,150. For summer seminar in writing instruction. 1987.
Opera Association of Central Ohio, Columbus, OH, $15,000. For Columbus Symphony Orchestra In-School Education Program. 1987.
Playhouse Square Foundation, Cleveland, OH, $10,000. For Children's Theater Series. 1987.
Toledo Opera Association, Toledo, OH, $10,200. For Opera-On-Wheels Component of Outreach Programs. 1987.
University Circle, Cleveland, OH, $20,000. For Cultural Education Project. 1987.
Youngstown Area Arts Council, Youngstown, OH, $5,850. For Arts Holiday Student Program. 1987.

2497
The Juilfs Foundation
8485 Broadwell Rd.
Cincinnati 45244

Established in 1962 in OH.
Financial data (yr. ended 12/31/86): Assets, $2,073,639 (M); expenditures, $70,362, including $67,663 for 38 grants (high: $25,000; low: $100).
Purpose and activities: Emphasis on higher education, hospitals, the arts, youth agencies and a community fund.
Limitations: Giving primarily in OH.
Trustees: George C. Juilfs, Howard W. Juilfs, Faye Kuluris.
Employer Identification Number: 316027571

2498
The Robert E., Harry A., and M. Sylvia Kangesser Foundation
1801 East Ninth St., No. 1220
Cleveland 44114 (216) 621-5747

Incorporated in 1947 in OH.
Donor(s): Robert E. Kangesser,† Harry A. Kangesser,† M. Sylvia Kangesser.†
Financial data (yr. ended 12/31/88): Assets, $3,500,000 (M); expenditures, $340,000, including $320,000 for 23 grants (high: $150,000; low: $200).
Purpose and activities: Support largely for Jewish educational organizations; support also for non-denominational health services and medical services, and civic affairs.
Types of support: General purposes, building funds, annual campaigns, continuing support, operating budgets, capital campaigns.
Limitations: Giving primarily in the greater Cleveland, OH, area.
Application information:
Initial approach: Proposal
Deadline(s): Aug. 31
Board meeting date(s): Usually in Sept. or Oct.
Write: David G. Kangesser, Pres.
Officers and Trustees: David G. Kangesser, Pres.; Helen Kangesser, V.P.; Hedy Kangesser, Treas.
Employer Identification Number: 346529478

2499
The Kettering Family Foundation
1440 Kettering Tower
Dayton 45423 (513) 228-1021

Incorporated in 1955 in IL; reincorporated in 1966 in OH.
Donor(s): E.W. Kettering,† V.W. Kettering, J.K. Lombard, S.K. Williamson, P.D. Williamson, M.D., Richard D. Lombard, B. Weiffenbach,† Charles F. Kettering III.
Financial data (yr. ended 12/31/88): Assets, $345,173 (M); gifts received, $1,000; expenditures, $305,996, including $226,300 for 17 grants (high: $50,000; low: $300; average: $5,000-$25,000).
Purpose and activities: Support largely for higher and secondary education, cultural programs, conservation, and specialized medical research.
Types of support: Operating budgets, annual campaigns, seed money, emergency funds, deficit financing, building funds, equipment, land acquisition, endowment funds, special projects, research, publications, conferences and seminars, capital campaigns, continuing support, general purposes, matching funds.
Limitations: No support for foreign or religious organizations. No grants to individuals, or for scholarships or fellowships; no loans.
Publications: Annual report.
Application information:
Initial approach: Letter stating amount requested
Copies of proposal: 1
Deadline(s): Mar. 1 and Sept. 1
Board meeting date(s): Mid-May and mid-Nov.
Final notification: 1 month after board meetings
Write: Jack L. Fischer, Secy.
Officers: Charles F. Kettering III,* Pres.; Susan K. Beck,* V.P.; Debra L. Williamson,* V.P.; Jane K. Lombard,* Secy.-Treas.; Jack L. Fischer, Secy.; Jonathan G. Verity, Treas.
Trustees:* Matthew B. Beck, Kyle W. Cox, Mark A. Cox, Douglas J. Cushnie, Karen W. Cushnie, Linda K. Danneberg, William H. Danneberg, Lisa S. Kettering, Virginia W. Kettering, Richard J. Lombard, Douglas E. Williamson, Leslie G. Williamson, P.D. Williamson, M.D., Susan K. Williamson.
Number of staff: None.
Employer Identification Number: 310727384
Recent arts and culture grants:
Art Students League of Denver, Denver, CO, $5,000. For studio equipment acquisition. 1987.
Citizen Exchange Council, NYC, NY, $10,000. For continued operating support. 1987.

Community School of Performing Arts, Los Angeles, CA, $10,000. For scholarship. 1987.
Denver Botanic Gardens, Denver, CO, $15,000. For endowment. 1987.
Southwest Public Communications Foundation, Fort Worth, TX, $5,000. For project on Mind's Eye: Black Visionary Art in America. 1987.

2500
The Kettering Fund

1440 Kettering Tower
Dayton 45423 (513) 228-1021

Established in 1958 in OH.
Donor(s): Charles F. Kettering.†
Financial data (yr. ended 6/30/88): Assets, $72,734,550 (M); expenditures, $1,280,932, including $1,138,500 for 22 grants (high: $300,000; low: $1,000; average: $5,000-$25,000).
Purpose and activities: Grants for scientific, medical, social, and educational studies and research; support also for cultural programs.
Limitations: Giving primarily in OH. No grants to individuals, no fellowships or scholarships; no loans.
Application information:
Initial approach: Brief outline of proposal in letter form
Copies of proposal: 1
Deadline(s): Apr. 1 and Oct. 1
Board meeting date(s): Usually in mid-May and mid-Nov.
Final notification: 10 days to 2 weeks after meeting date
Write: Jack L. Fischer
Distribution Committee: Jean S. Kettering, Virginia W. Kettering,* Jane K. Lombard, Susan K. Williamson.
Trustees:* Bank One, Dayton.
Number of staff: None.
Employer Identification Number: 316027115
Recent arts and culture grants:
Arts Center Foundation, Dayton, OH, $1,000,000. For general support. 1987.
Asia Society, NYC, NY, $200,000. For National Center for Education about Asia. 1987.
Aullwood Audubon Center and Forum, Dayton, OH, $25,000. For general support. 1987.
Dayton Art Institute, Dayton, OH, $56,000. For facility redesign and improvement. 1987.
Dayton Museum of Natural History, Dayton, OH, $500,000. For renovation and expansion of current museum. 1987.
Dayton Performing Arts Fund, Dayton, OH, $165,000. For general support. 1987.
Montgomery County Historical Society, Dayton, OH, $5,000. For continued general support. 1987.
W C E T-Greater Cincinnati Television Educational Foundation, Cincinnati, OH, $10,000. For production of series directed at first grade science curriculum. 1987.
W P T D/W P T O, Channels 16/14, Dayton, OH, $5,000. For continued annual support. 1987.

2501
The Klein Foundation

1771 East 30th St.
Cleveland 44114-4469 (216) 623-0370

Established in 1979 in OH.
Donor(s): East Texas Periodicals.
Financial data (yr. ended 9/30/87): Assets, $27,831 (M); gifts received, $115,000; expenditures, $112,724, including $112,724 for 61 grants (high: $30,250; low: $50).
Purpose and activities: Support primarily for the arts and for museums; support also for higher education, churches, and for environment conservation.
Limitations: Giving primarily in Cleveland, OH.
Application information:
Deadline(s): None
Officers: G. Robert Klein, Chair.; George R. Klein, Pres.; Marilyn E. Brown, Secy.
Employer Identification Number: 341288590

2502
Knight Foundation

One Cascade Plaza
Akron 44308 (216) 253-9301

Incorporated in 1950 in OH.
Donor(s): John S. Knight,† James L. Knight, and their families and associates.
Financial data (yr. ended 12/31/88): Assets, $482,371,219 (M); expenditures, $22,470,400, including $18,488,458 for 317 grants (high: $2,000,000; low: $1,000; average: $5,000-$100,000) and $1,000,000 for 1 loan.
Purpose and activities: Grants primarily for education, cultural, health, and social service programs initiated by organizations in cities where Knight-Ridder properties are located; giving on a national scale for print journalism.
Types of support: Special projects, building funds, capital campaigns, endowment funds, fellowships, general purposes, matching funds, scholarship funds, seed money.
Limitations: Giving limited to areas where Knight-Ridder newspapers are published: CA, CO, FL, GA, IN, KS, KY, MI, MN, MS, NC, ND, OH, PA, SC, and SD for Cities Program; Journalism and Arts and Culture programs are national in scope. No support for organizations with grantmaking activities other than community foundations. No grants to individuals, or for annual fundraising campaigns or dinners; genral operating support; operating deficits; trips or uniforms for bands; films, videos, or television programs; honoraria; scholarly research leading to a book; group travel; memorials; or medical research.
Publications: Annual report (including application guidelines), application guidelines, informational brochure (including application guidelines).
Application information: Considers only 1 request from an organization during a 12-month period; all proposals must have endorsment of president of organization or institution requesting grant.
Initial approach: Letter
Copies of proposal: 2
Deadline(s): Jan. 1, Apr. 1, July 1, and Oct. 1
Board meeting date(s): Mar., June, Sept., and Dec.
Final notification: 2 weeks after meeting dates
Write: Creed C. Black, Pres.
Officers and Trustees: James L. Knight, Chair.; Lee Hills, Vice-Chair.; Creed C. Black, Pres.; James D. Spaniolo, V.P. and Secy.; David J. Catrow, Treas.; W. Gerald Austen, James K. Batten, Alvah H. Chapman, Jr., Charles E. Clark, C.C. Gibson, Gordon E. Heffern, Rolfe Neill, Beverly Knight Olson, Henry King Stanford, Barbara Knight Toomey.
Number of staff: 4 full-time professional; 3 full-time support; 1 part-time support.
Employer Identification Number: 346519827
Recent arts and culture grants:
Academy of Natural Sciences of Philadelphia, Philadelphia, PA, $150,000. For new earth sciences exhibit. 1987.
Akron Art Museum, Akron, OH, $500,000. To furnish major leadership gift to expand permanent endowment fund. 1987.
American Federation of Arts, NYC, NY, $50,000. For general support. 1987.
American Music Theater Festival, Philadelphia, PA, $35,000. For international symposium on contemporary music theater. 1987.
Art in the Stations, Detroit, MI, $20,000. To match grant from Skillman Foundation to acquire a major work of art for Fort/Cass Station of Detroit People Mover. 1987.
Arts Center of Catawba Valley, Hickory, NC, $10,000. For challenge grant to establish endowment. 1987.
Broward Performing Arts Foundation, Fort Lauderdale, FL, $75,000. To build performing arts center. 1987.
Center for the Fine Arts Association, Miami, FL, $500,000. For Endowment Fund, the income of which will be used exclusively for exhibitions. 1987.
Colorado Dance Festival, Boulder, CO, $5,000. For general support for season. 1987.
Colorado Music Festival, Boulder, CO, $10,000. For general support of 1988 summer concert season. 1987.
Columbus Discovery Commemorative Fund, Miami, FL, $300,000. Toward challenge grant for benefit of endowments of Greater Miami Opera and Historical Association of Southern Florida and for capital needs of Museum of Science and Space Transit Planetarium. 1987.
Columbus Museum, Columbus, GA, $30,000. To install opening exhibitions in this newly refurbished museum and to increase endowment. 1987.
Columbus Philharmonic Guild, Columbus, GA, $8,000. For general support. 1987.
Community Hall Foundation, Akron, OH, $50,000. To add to permanent endowment of Akron Civic Theater. 1987.
Como Conservatory Restoration Fund, Saint Paul, MN, $20,000. To help restore and renovate Como Park Conservatory. 1987.
Edison Institute, Dearborn, MI, $75,000. For major new permanent exhibit, The Automobile in American Life, at Henry Ford Museum and Greenfield Village. 1987.
Episcopal Hospital, Philadelphia, PA, $12,500. To restore and protect stained glass windows in Chapel of Episcopal Hospital. 1987.
Fairchild Tropical Garden, Miami, FL, $35,000. For general support. 1987.

Film Society of Miami, Miami, FL, $10,000. For general support. 1987.
Florida Trust for Historic Preservation, Tallahassee, FL, $25,000. To endow Education Fund of Bonnet House. 1987.
Friends of Logan Square Foundation, Philadelphia, PA, $90,000. For rehabilitation of Swann Memorial Fountain, the centerpiece of Logan Square. 1987.
Greater Akron Musical Association, Akron, OH, $400,000. To challenge Akron community to donate to endowment of Akron Symphony Orchestra. 1987.
Greater Akron Musical Association, Akron, OH, $30,000. For general support. 1987.
Historical Society of Pennsylvania, Philadelphia, PA, $100,000. For permanent exhibition, Inheriting America. 1987.
Ida Cason Callaway Foundation, Pine Mountain, GA, $12,500. Toward construction of Day Butterfly Center. 1987.
John Bartram Association, Philadelphia, PA, $9,000. To match challenge grant from J.N. Pew Jr. Charitable Trust to restore buildings and gardens in oldest surviving botanical garden in North America. 1987.
Kent State University Foundation, Kent, OH, $10,000. For capital campaign for WKSU-FM, public broadcasting radio station. 1987.
Leon County Schools, Tallahassee, FL, $9,000. For North Florida Writing Project, a teacher training center. 1987.
Living Arts and Science Center, Lexington, KY, $15,000. For elevator and housing to make this museum and teaching center accessible to handicapped children. 1987.
Long Beach Grand Opera, Long Beach, CA, $25,000. To help provide staff development position. 1987.
Long Beach Museum of Art Foundation, Long Beach, CA, $25,000. For annual operating support. 1987.
Long Beach Symphony Association, Long Beach, CA, $5,000. For continued support of Kinderkonzerts. 1987.
Miami City Ballet, Miami, FL, $25,000. For general support and to provide matching funds for endowment. 1987.
Miami Youth Museum, Miami, FL, $5,000. For traveling exhibit, Through The Looking Glass: Drawings by Elizabeth Layton. 1987.
Michigan Opera Theater, Detroit, MI, $10,000. For general support. 1987.
Minnesota Public Radio, Saint Paul, MN, $50,000. To underwrite broadcasts of Saint Paul Chamber Orchestra. 1987.
Museum of Science, Miami, FL, $45,000. For general support. 1987.
Musical Arts Association, Cleveland, OH, $20,000. For Sustaining Fund of Blossom Music Center. Grant shared with Cleveland Orchestra. 1987.
New World Symphony, Miami, FL, $50,000. For inaugural season. 1987.
Northwest Indiana Public Broadcasting, Highland, IN, $20,000. To finish studio and erect tower for new public television station. 1987.
Northwest Indiana Symphony Society, Whiting, IN, $10,000. For symphony chorus. 1987.
Ohio Chamber Ballet, Akron, OH, $25,000. For general support. 1987.
Ohio Historical Society, Columbus, OH, $10,000. To match National Endowment for the Humanities grant to build permanent endowment. 1987.
Opera Company of Philadelphia, Philadelphia, PA, $15,000. For general support. 1987.
Opera Guild of Greater Miami, Miami, FL, $40,000. For general support. 1987.
Painted Bride Art Center, Philadelphia, PA, $10,000. For building renovations which will create fully equipped exhibition gallery. 1987.
Pasadena Symphony Association, Pasadena, CA, $5,000. For general support. 1987.
Pennsylvania Academy of the Fine Arts, Philadelphia, PA, $20,000. For general support. 1987.
Pennsylvania Ballet Association, Philadelphia, PA, $20,000. For general support. 1987.
Pennsylvania Opera Theater, Philadelphia, PA, $15,000. For education program, In Every Way The Arts. 1987.
Philadelphia Company, Philadelphia, PA, $10,000. For production of Citizen Tom Paine during Bicentennial Celebration of U.S. Constitution. 1987.
Philadelphia Museum of Art, Philadelphia, PA, $30,000. For general support. 1987.
Philadelphia Orchestra Association, Philadelphia, PA, $25,000. For general support. 1987.
Philharmonic Orchestra of Florida, Fort Lauderdale, FL, $25,000. For general support to match challenge grant from State of Florida. 1987.
Saint Bernard Church Memorial Trust Fund, Akron, OH, $25,000. For restoration and preservation for this historic building. 1987.
Saint Louis County Heritage and Arts Center, Duluth, MN, $10,000. For management computerization project. 1987.
San Jose Childrens Discovery Museum, San Jose, CA, $150,000. For building fund of this new museum. 1987.
Save Orchestra Hall, Detroit, MI, $100,000. To complete restoration of this new home for Detroit Symphony Orchestra. 1987.
Smithsonian Institution, DC, $10,000. To encourage thoughtful historical study of nation's space program. 1987.
Springer Opera House Arts Association, Columbia, GA, $50,000. For endowment fund to assure continued maintenance of this performing arts facility. 1987.
Summit County Historical Society of Akron, Akron, OH, $5,000. To computerize administrative records. 1987.
Tallahassee Symphony Orchestra, Tallahassee, FL, $5,490. For guest conductors. 1987.
W.O. Smith Nashville Community Music School, Nashville, TN, $10,000. To support program of music instruction for low income children. 1987.
Weathervane Community Playhouse, Akron, OH, $30,000. For endowment funds. 1987.
Western Reserve Historical Society, Cleveland, OH, $25,000. To restore 1845 Jonathan Herrick House in Hale Farm and Village. 1987.
Wichita Symphony Society, Wichita, KS, $25,000. For three concert tour in Southwest Kansas. 1987.
Winthrop College, Rock Hill, SC, $25,000. For Carolina Young Writers' Conference. 1987.
Yes 150 Foundation, Troy, MI, $20,000. To publish The Buildings of Michigan, a project of Michigan Sesquicentennial Commission. 1987.
Zoological Society of Florida, Miami, FL, $50,000. To rebuild Sulawesi Villge, children's petting zoo at Miami Metrozoo. 1987.
Zoological Society of Middle Tennessee, Nashville, TN, $10,000. For planning and developing seed money to build zoo for largest city in U.S. without zoological park. 1987.

2503
The Kroger Company Giving Program

1014 Vine St.
Cincinnati 45201 (513) 762-4443

Purpose and activities: Support for social services, arts and humanities, health, the homeless, drug abuse and nutrition. Also support for benefits and other fundraisers.
Limitations: Giving primarily in major operating locations.
Application information: Include: organization description; amount requested; purpose for which funds are sought; recently audited financial statement; 501(c)(3).
Initial approach: Brief letter or proposal
Write: Paul A. Bernish, V.P. and Secy.

2504
Kulas Foundation

1662 Hanna Bldg.
Cleveland 44115 (216) 861-3139

Incorporated in 1937 in OH.
Donor(s): Fynette H. Kulas,† E.J. Kulas.†
Financial data (yr. ended 12/31/87): Assets, $17,066,860 (M); gifts received, $228,335; expenditures, $1,191,559, including $1,006,576 for 72 grants (high: $105,000; low: $125; average: $2,000-$30,000).
Purpose and activities: Grants largely to music institutions and for higher education; some support also for local performing arts and social services.
Types of support: Building funds, continuing support, equipment, professorships, renovation projects, special projects.
Limitations: Giving limited to the greater Cleveland, OH, area. No grants to individuals, or for endowment funds.
Application information: Application form required.
Initial approach: Letter
Copies of proposal: 5
Deadline(s): Submit proposal preferably six weeks before a meeting; no set deadline
Board meeting date(s): Feb., May, Aug., and Nov.
Final notification: After board meetings
Write: Allen C. Holmes, Pres.
Officers: Allen C. Holmes,* Pres.; Richard W. Pogue,* V.P.; Sarah E. Werder, Secy.
Trustees:* Herbert E. Strawbridge.
Number of staff: 1 full-time support.
Employer Identification Number: 340770687

2505
The Laub Foundation
19583 Coffinberry Blvd.
Fairview Park 44126 (216) 331-4028
Application address: Five Ocean Ave., South Harwich, MA 02661

Incorporated in 1958 in OH.
Donor(s): Herbert J. Laub,† Elsie K. Laub.†
Financial data (yr. ended 10/31/87): Assets, $2,601,518 (M); expenditures, $175,146, including $137,825 for 36 grants (high: $6,000; low: $600).
Purpose and activities: Grants primarily for scholarship programs of colleges and private schools, cultural programs, and youth agencies.
Types of support: Scholarship funds, operating budgets, continuing support, annual campaigns, seed money, emergency funds, building funds, equipment, matching funds, fellowships, publications, conferences and seminars.
Limitations: Giving primarily in Cuyahoga County, OH, and adjacent counties. No grants to individuals, or for deficit financing or endowment funds; no loans.
Publications: Annual report.
Application information: Final distribution of grants made at Aug. meeting.
Initial approach: Letter followed by proposal
Copies of proposal: 2
Deadline(s): None
Board meeting date(s): Feb., May, Aug., and Nov.
Final notification: After Aug. meeting
Write: Malcolm D. Campbell, Jr., Pres.
Officers and Trustees: Malcolm D. Campbell, Jr., Pres. and Treas.; Amie Campbell, V.P.; Robert B. Nelson, Secy.; Laurence A. Bartell, Katherine C. Berry, Thomas C. Westropp.
Number of staff: 1 part-time professional.
Employer Identification Number: 346526087

2506
Fred A. Lennon Foundation
29500 Solon Rd.
Solon 44139 (216) 248-4600

Established in 1965 in OH.
Financial data (yr. ended 11/30/87): Assets, $8,951,087 (M); gifts received, $800,000; expenditures, $1,710,596, including $1,689,310 for 158 grants (high: $401,800; low: $100; average: $100-$100,000).
Purpose and activities: Giving for higher education and Roman Catholic church support; grants also for public policy, hospitals, cultural programs, social services, and community funds.
Limitations: Giving primarily in OH.
Application information:
Initial approach: Proposal
Deadline(s): None
Write: John F. Fant, Jr., Asst. Secy.
Officers: Fred A. Lennon, Pres.; A.P. Lennon, V.P.; F.J. Callahan, Secy.
Employer Identification Number: 346572287

2507
The Lincoln Electric Foundation
c/o Society National Bank
22801 St. Clair Ave.
Cleveland 441019 (216) 481-8100

Trust established in 1952 in OH.
Donor(s): Lincoln Electric Co.
Financial data (yr. ended 12/31/87): Assets, $909,860 (M); gifts received, $450,000; expenditures, $459,788, including $455,550 for 40 grants (high: $96,000; low: $500; average: $500-$20,000).
Purpose and activities: Emphasis on higher education and a community fund; grants also for hospitals and medical services, social service agencies, cultural programs, and civic institutions.
Limitations: Giving primarily in OH, with emphasis on Cleveland.
Application information:
Initial approach: Letter
Deadline(s): Sept. 20
Board meeting date(s): Nov.
Write: Ellis F. Smolik, Secy.-Treas.
Officer and Trustee: Ellis F. Smolik, Secy.-Treas.; Society National Bank.
Number of staff: 1
Employer Identification Number: 346518355

2508
The Community Foundation of Greater Lorain County
1865 North Ridge Rd., E., Suite A
Lorain 44055 (216) 277-0142
Additional tel.: (216) 323-4445

Community foundation incorporated in 1980 in OH.
Financial data (yr. ended 12/31/88): Assets, $10,471,058 (M); gifts received, $700,529; expenditures, $680,224, including $331,381 for 35 grants (high: $64,224; low: $100) and $27,900 for grants to individuals.
Purpose and activities: Giving for social services, education, health, civic affairs, and cultural programs.
Types of support: Student aid, special projects, general purposes, matching funds, technical assistance, scholarship funds, seed money.
Limitations: Giving limited to Lorain County, OH, and its immediate vicinity. No grants to individuals (except for scholarships), or for annual campaigns, deficit financing, or capital campaigns.
Publications: Annual report, informational brochure (including application guidelines), application guidelines, newsletter.
Application information:
Initial approach: Proposal
Copies of proposal: 1
Deadline(s): Feb. 15 and Aug. 15 for general grants; May 1 for scholarships
Board meeting date(s): Apr. and Oct. for general grants; June for scholarships
Write: Carol G. Simonetti, Exec. Dir.
Officers and Trustees: Scribner L. Fauver, Pres.; John S. Corogin, V.P.; Gerda Klein, Secy.; Billy S. Rowland, Treas.; Robert S. Cook, Frank Jacinto, Larry D. Jones, Sr., James W. McGlamery, Robert C. Singleton, Donald W. Stevenson, Elizabeth W. Thomas, John A. Vanek, Andrew J. Warhola, Rickie Weiss, J. Milton Yinger, Molly Young.
Number of staff: 3 full-time professional; 2 full-time support.
Employer Identification Number: 341322781

2509
The Lubrizol Foundation
29400 Lakeland Blvd.
Wickliffe 44092 (216) 943-4200

Incorporated in 1952 in OH.
Donor(s): The Lubrizol Corp.
Financial data (yr. ended 12/31/87): Assets, $2,202,169 (M); gifts received, $805,875; expenditures, $907,025, including $709,520 for grants and $187,665 for employee matching gifts.
Purpose and activities: Emphasis on higher education, social services, civic and cultural programs, youth agencies, and hospitals.
Types of support: Operating budgets, continuing support, annual campaigns, emergency funds, building funds, equipment, matching funds, professorships, internships, scholarship funds, fellowships, research, employee matching gifts, capital campaigns, general purposes.
Limitations: Giving primarily in OH, with emphasis on Cleveland. No grants to individuals, or for seed money, deficit financing, endowment funds, demonstration projects, publications, or conferences; no loans.
Publications: Annual report.
Application information:
Initial approach: Proposal
Copies of proposal: 1
Deadline(s): None
Board meeting date(s): As required, usually 3 or 4 times a year
Final notification: 2 weeks after meeting
Write: Douglas W. Richardson, Pres.
Officers and Trustees: L.E. Coleman, Chair. and C.E.O.; Douglas W. Richardson, Pres. and C.O.O.; Lucy M. Miller, Secy.-Treas.; W.T. Beargie, J.C. Davis, David K. Ford, K.H. Hopping, J.F. Klemens, W.M. LeSuer, F. Alex Nason, M.J. O'Connor.
Number of staff: 1 full-time support; 1 part-time support.
Employer Identification Number: 346500595

2510
The John C. Markey Charitable Fund
P.O. Box 191
Bryan 43506

Established in 1966 in OH.
Donor(s): John C. Markey.†
Financial data (yr. ended 6/30/87): Assets, $3,321,404 (M); expenditures, $285,765, including $206,520 for 78 grants (high: $91,500; low: $100).
Purpose and activities: Grants for a local chapter of the YWCA, higher and other education, Protestant church support, hospitals, and libraries and other cultural organizations.
Application information:
Write: John R. Markey, Pres.
Officers and Trustees: John R. Markey, Pres. and Treas.; Catherine M. Anderson, V.P.; Arthur S. Newcomer, Secy.; L.W. Lisle.
Employer Identification Number: 346572724

2511
Roy & Eva Markus Foundation, Inc.
c/o Board of Education, Rm. 152
1380 East Sixth St.
Cleveland 44114

Trust established in 1954 in OH; incorporated in 1967.
Donor(s): Roy C. Markus,† Eva Markus, Eli C. Markus,† Seymour H. Levy,† Robert C. Coplan.
Financial data (yr. ended 7/31/87): Assets, $1,583,946 (M); gifts received, $100,000; expenditures, $241,887, including $212,900 for 34 grants (high: $70,000; low: $100).
Purpose and activities: Giving largely for higher education, mainly through local scholarship funds; support also for health, cultural programs, and Jewish welfare funds.
Types of support: Scholarship funds, research.
Limitations: Giving primarily in OH and CA. No grants to individuals.
Publications: Annual report.
Application information: Funds committed for the foreseeable future.
Officers and Trustees:* Eva Markus,* Pres.; Robert C. Coplan,* Exec. V.P. and Secy.; Mark A. Levy,* V.P.; Shirley H. Levy,* V.P.; E.M. Glickman, Treas.
Employer Identification Number: 341018827

2512
David Meade Massie Trust
65 East Second St.
P.O. Box 41
Chillicothe 45601 (614) 772-5070

Financial data (yr. ended 12/31/87): Assets, $3,461,472 (M); expenditures, $246,827, including $206,766 for 2 grants (high: $201,848; low: $4,918).
Purpose and activities: Emphasis on community development, especially volunteer fire departments, and on youth, health, and social service agencies; support also for education and cultural programs.
Limitations: Giving limited to Chillicothe and Ross County, OH.
Publications: Program policy statement, application guidelines.
Application information: Application form required.
Deadline(s): Mar. 1, June 1, Sept. 1, and Dec. 1
Board meeting date(s): Mar. 15, June 15, Sept. 15, and Dec. 15
Write: Marilyn Carnes
Trustees: Louis A. Ginther, Joseph G. Kear, Joseph P. Sulzer.
Employer Identification Number: 316022292

2513
Elizabeth Ring Mather and William Gwinn Mather Fund
650 Citizens Bldg.
850 Euclid Ave.
Cleveland 44114 (216) 861-5341

Incorporated in 1954 in OH.
Donor(s): Elizabeth Ring Mather.†
Financial data (yr. ended 12/31/86): Assets, $6,156,099 (M); gifts received, $491,255; expenditures, $628,399, including $549,179 for 44 grants (high: $367,057; low: $100; average: $200-$20,000).
Purpose and activities: Giving generally for specific civic purposes, including the arts, hospitals and health agencies, higher and secondary education, conservation, and social welfare.
Types of support: Annual campaigns, building funds, equipment, general purposes, publications, endowment funds.
Limitations: Giving primarily in OH, with emphasis on the greater Cleveland area. No grants to individuals, or for scholarships, fellowships, or matching gifts; no loans.
Application information:
Initial approach: Letter
Deadline(s): None
Board meeting date(s): June and Dec.
Write: James D. Ireland, Pres.
Officers and Trustees: James D. Ireland, Pres. and Treas.; Theodore R. Colborn, Secy.; Cornelia I. Hallinan, Cornelia W. Ireland, George R. Ireland, James D. Ireland III, Lucy E. Ireland, R. Henry Norweb, Jr.
Number of staff: 1 part-time professional.
Employer Identification Number: 346519863

2514
The S. Livingston Mather Charitable Trust
803 Tower East
20600 Chagrin Blvd.
Shaker Heights 44122 (216) 942-6484

Trust established in 1953 in OH.
Donor(s): S. Livingston Mather.†
Financial data (yr. ended 12/31/88): Assets, $3,061,000 (M); expenditures, $157,000 for 55 grants (high: $27,500; low: $150; average: $1,000-$10,000).
Purpose and activities: Support for education, child welfare, youth programs, mental health, social services, cultural programs, and environment and natural resources. Support for both general operations and specific projects.
Types of support: Operating budgets, continuing support, seed money, emergency funds, building funds, equipment, special projects, annual campaigns, renovation projects, scholarship funds, capital campaigns.
Limitations: Giving primarily in northeast OH. No support for science and medical research programs, or in areas "appropriately supported by the government and/or the United Way". No grants to individuals, or for deficit financing or mass mailing solicitation; no loans.
Publications: Biennial report (including application guidelines).
Application information: Mass mail solicitations not considered.
Initial approach: Letter or telephone
Copies of proposal: 1
Deadline(s): None
Board meeting date(s): Quarterly, and as required
Final notification: 2 months
Write: S. Sterling McMillan, Secy.
Distribution Committee: S. Sterling McMillan,* Secy.; Elizabeth M. McMillan, Madeleine M. Offutt.
Trustees:* AmeriTrust Co.
Number of staff: 1 part-time support.
Employer Identification Number: 346505619

2515
John A. McAlonan Trust
c/o National City Bank
P.O. Box 2130
Akron 44309-2130 (216) 375-8332

Trust established in 1958 in OH.
Donor(s): John A. McAlonan.†
Financial data (yr. ended 12/31/86): Assets, $3,796,340 (M); expenditures, $208,915, including $183,545 for 28 grants (high: $10,000; low: $1,000).
Purpose and activities: Giving for cultural programs and facilities, youth agencies, hospitals, the handicapped, and education.
Limitations: Giving limited to the Akron, OH, area. No grants to individuals.
Application information:
Initial approach: Letter or proposal
Copies of proposal: 6
Board meeting date(s): May and Nov.
Write: Mary H. Hembree, Trust Officer, National City Bank
Trustee: National City Bank.
Employer Identification Number: 346513095

2516
McDonald & Company Securities Foundation
(Formerly McDonald & Company Foundation)
2100 Society Bldg.
Cleveland 44114 (216) 443-2300

Donor(s): McDonald & Co. Securities, Inc.
Financial data (yr. ended 3/25/88): Assets, $619,650 (M); gifts received, $48,400; expenditures, $95,103, including $91,095 for 104 grants (high: $18,000; low: $100).
Purpose and activities: Support for health associations, culture and the arts, elementary education programs, and community and social services; support for higher education only through the Ohio Foundation for Independent Colleges.
Types of support: General purposes.
Limitations: Giving primarily in northeastern OH; primarily Cleveland. No support for secondary schools.
Application information:
Deadline(s): None
Write: Gordon A. Price
Officers: Thomas M. O'Donnell, Chair. and Pres.; Willard E. Carmel,* V.P.; E. Robert Hawken, Jr., Secy.; Gordon A. Price, Treas.
Trustees:* Dean G. Lauritzen, Edward L. Tabol.
Number of staff: None.
Employer Identification Number: 341386528

2517
Lois Sisler McFawn Trust No. 2
c/o AmeriTrust Co.
P.O. Box 5937
Cleveland 44101 (216) 687-5632

Trust established in 1956 in OH.
Donor(s): Lois Sisler McFawn.
Financial data (yr. ended 12/31/88): Assets, $9,055,088 (M); expenditures, $345,187, including $286,400 for 39 grants (high: $30,000; low: $1,000).

Purpose and activities: Emphasis on education, hospitals, minority group programs, cultural activities, and youth agencies.
Types of support: General purposes, building funds, equipment, research, internships.
Limitations: Giving primarily in the Akron, OH, area. No grants to individuals, or for matching gifts, continuing support, seed money, emergency funds, deficit financing, land acquisition, publications, or conferences; no loans.
Publications: Application guidelines.
Application information:
Initial approach: Proposal
Copies of proposal: 1
Deadline(s): None
Board meeting date(s): Usually in June and Dec.
Write: Donald F. Barney, Trust Officer
Distribution Committee: Michael Connor, H. Flood, J. Guinter, Fredrick Myers, John Ong.
Trustee: AmeriTrust Co.
Number of staff: None.
Employer Identification Number: 346508111

2518
The Mead Corporate Giving Program
Courthouse Plaza Northeast
Dayton 45463 (513) 222-6323

Purpose and activities: Supports civic and community affairs, the environment, libraries, performing arts, dance, theater, wildlife, youth, federated campaigns, education, health, hospitals, science, United Way, and welfare. Also provides employee matching gifts for education.
Limitations: Giving primarily in areas of company operations; no support for national organizations. No grants to individuals.
Publications: Informational brochure.
Application information: Include description of the project, budget, a financial report, 501(c)(3) status report and list of board and donors.
Initial approach: Not formalized
Copies of proposal: 1
Deadline(s): None
Write: Ronald F. Budzik, Exec. Dir.
Number of staff: None.

2519
The Mead Corporation Foundation
Courthouse Plaza Northeast
Dayton 45463 (513) 222-6323

Trust established in 1957 in OH.
Donor(s): The Mead Corp.
Financial data (yr. ended 12/31/87): Assets, $22,318,490 (M); gifts received, $6,000,000; expenditures, $2,252,944, including $1,807,995 for 619 grants (high: $150,000; low: $25; average: $200-$30,000) and $200,468 for 308 employee matching gifts.
Purpose and activities: Emphasis on community funds, higher education, critical human services needs, and arts.
Types of support: Annual campaigns, building funds, conferences and seminars, continuing support, emergency funds, employee matching gifts, equipment, fellowships, matching funds, operating budgets, research, scholarship funds, seed money, special projects, employee-related scholarships.
Limitations: Giving primarily in areas of company operations. No support for national, fraternal, labor, or veterans' organizations, political organizations, or religious organizations for religious purposes. Grants rarely to tax-supported institutions except for public colleges and universities. No grants to individuals, or for endowment funds, advertising, dinners, or tickets; no loans; normally no operating support for organizations already receiving substantial support through United Way.
Publications: Application guidelines, informational brochure, program policy statement.
Application information: Applicants for grants in Mead operating communities should contact or apply to the local Mead unit manager. Application form required.
Initial approach: Proposal
Deadline(s): None
Board meeting date(s): Feb., Apr., July, Oct., and Dec.
Final notification: 2 months
Write: Ronald F. Budzik, Exec. Dir.
Officers: Ronald F. Budzik, Exec. Dir.; K.A. Strawn, Admin. Officer and Secy.; William D. Bloebaum, Jr., Treas.
Trustee: First National Bank of Cincinnati.
Distribution Committee: James Van Vleck, Chair.; Charles W. Joiner, Steven C. Mason, Charles Mazza, John C. McCurrach, Frederick J. Robbins.
Number of staff: 1 full-time support; 3 part-time support.
Employer Identification Number: 316040645

2520
Nelson Mead Fund
c/o Rend & Co.
2060 Kettering Tower
Dayton 45423

Established in 1965 in OH.
Financial data (yr. ended 11/30/87): Assets, $692,844 (M); gifts received, $151,134; expenditures, $226,163, including $222,266 for 75 grants (high: $22,300; low: $25).
Purpose and activities: Support primarily for conservation and wildlife preservation; giving also for Christian religious organizations, civic and cultural groups, and educational institutions.
Application information: Contributes only to pre-selected organizations. Applications not accepted.
Trustees: Nelson S. Mead, Ruth C. Mead.
Employer Identification Number: 316064591

2521
Merrell Dow Pharmaceuticals Corporate Giving Program
10123 Alliance Road
Cincinnati 45242 (513) 948-9111

Purpose and activities: Support for higher and other education, fine arts, and community development.
Limitations: Giving primarily in greater Cincinnati, OH and greater Indianapolis, IN, areas. No support for organizations receiving support from the United Way.
Application information:
Initial approach: Direct request to K.A. Lohr
Copies of proposal: 1
Write: Kenneth A. Lohr, Dir., Comm. Relations
Administrator: Kenneth A. Lohr, Dir. Community Relations.
Number of staff: 1 part-time professional; 1 part-time support.

2522
Mill-Rose Foundation, Inc.
7995 Tyler Blvd.
Mentor 44060

Donor(s): Mill-Rose Co.
Financial data (yr. ended 6/30/88): Assets, $17,689 (M); gifts received, $45,750; expenditures, $53,612, including $53,568 for 39 grants (high: $9,983; low: $30).
Purpose and activities: Support for youth, education, social services, health services, religion, the arts, and community funds.
Limitations: Giving primarily in OH.
Application information:
Initial approach: Letter
Write: Victor Miller, Trustee
Trustees: Nina C. Alban, Carolyn Miller, Eric W. Miller, Lawrence W. Miller, Mildred Miller, Paul M. Miller, Richard M. Miller, Victor Miller.
Employer Identification Number: 341345012

2523
Lewis N. Miller Charitable Trust
Elyria Savings and Trust National Bank
105 Court St.
Elyria 44035

Established in 1985 in OH.
Financial data (yr. ended 12/31/86): Assets, $2,008,882 (M); expenditures, $130,997, including $119,897 for 9 grants.
Purpose and activities: Support for animal welfare, higher education, social services, cultural programs, health associations, and a church.
Trustee: Elyria Savings and Trust National Bank.
Employer Identification Number: 346834475

2524
Clement O. Miniger Memorial Foundation
Hillcrest Hotel, Rm. 229
Madison Ave. at 16th St.
Toledo 43612
Mailing address: P.O. Box 333, Toledo, OH 43691

Incorporated in 1952 in OH.
Donor(s): George M. Jones, Jr., Eleanor Miniger Jones.
Financial data (yr. ended 12/31/87): Assets, $5,317,562 (M); expenditures, $186,358, including $166,700 for 27 grants (high: $38,000; low: $1,000).
Purpose and activities: Giving for higher education, youth agencies, social services, and cultural programs.
Limitations: Giving primarily in OH.
Application information: Applications not accepted.

Officers and Trustees: George M. Jones, Jr., Pres.; Ford R. Weber, V.P.; John C. Eberly, Exec. Secy. and Treas.; Richard Day, Thomas DeVilbiss, George M. Jones III, John A. Morse.
Employer Identification Number: 346523024

2525
The Minster Machine Company Foundation
West Fifth St.
Minster 45865-1027

Financial data (yr. ended 11/30/87): Assets, $531,001 (M); expenditures, $45,661, including $43,925 for 29 grants (high: $20,000; low: $100).
Purpose and activities: Support for social services, health, civic affairs, community funds, single-disease associations, culture, and youth.
Officers: John F. Herkenhoff, Pres.; Howard H. Fark, V.P.; Harold J. Winch, V.P.; Robert J. Sudhoff, Secy.-Treas.
Employer Identification Number: 346559271

2526
The Harry C. Moores Foundation
c/o Francis E. Caldwell
3010 Hayden Rd.
Columbus 43218 (614) 846-0389

Trust established in 1961 in OH.
Donor(s): Harry C. Moores.†
Financial data (yr. ended 9/30/87): Assets, $17,012,429 (M); expenditures, $760,029, including $729,500 for 72 grants (high: $50,000; low: $1,000; average: $1,000-$20,000).
Purpose and activities: Local grants largely for rehabilitation of the handicapped, Protestant church support, hospitals, higher education, social service agencies concerned with the aged, child welfare, and the retarded, and cultural programs.
Types of support: Seed money, scholarship funds, general purposes, capital campaigns, annual campaigns.
Limitations: Giving primarily in the Columbus, OH, area. No grants to individuals, or for endowment funds, or matching gifts; no loans.
Application information:
Initial approach: Proposal in letter form
Copies of proposal: 1
Deadline(s): Submit proposal between Oct. and July; deadline Aug. 1
Board meeting date(s): Apr. or May and Aug. or Sept.
Final notification: By Oct. 15 (if affirmative)
Write: David L. Fenner, Secy.
Officers and Trustees: John J. Gerlach, Chair.; David L. Fenner, Secy.; Francis E. Caldwell, Treas.; William C. Jones, William H. Leighner.
Number of staff: None.
Employer Identification Number: 316035344

2527
The Murch Foundation
830 Hanna Bldg.
Cleveland 44115

Incorporated in 1956 in OH.
Donor(s): Maynard H. Murch.†
Financial data (yr. ended 12/31/87): Assets, $8,162,060 (M); expenditures, $490,452, including $475,000 for 82 grants (high: $45,000; low: $1,000).
Purpose and activities: Emphasis on museums and cultural programs, higher and secondary education, hospitals and health agencies, and community recreation.
Types of support: Annual campaigns, capital campaigns, endowment funds, general purposes, renovation projects, scholarship funds.
Limitations: Giving primarily in OH. No grants to individuals.
Application information: Contributes only to pre-selected organizations. Applications not accepted.
Officers and Trustees: Maynard H. Murch IV, Pres. and Treas.; James H. Dempsey, Jr., V.P. and Secy.; Creighton B. Murch, V.P.; Robert B. Murch, V.P.
Employer Identification Number: 346520188

2528
John P. Murphy Foundation
100 Public Square, 10th Fl.
Cleveland 44113 (216) 579-3650

Incorporated in 1960 in OH.
Donor(s): John P. Murphy.†
Financial data (yr. ended 9/30/88): Assets, $29,183,173 (M); expenditures, $1,603,853, including $1,329,415 for 74 grants (high: $150,000; low: $1,000; average: $5,000-$50,000).
Purpose and activities: Giving for higher and secondary (restricted) education; support also for the arts, community and civic affairs, social service and youth agencies, and hospitals.
Types of support: Operating budgets, building funds, equipment, general purposes, capital campaigns, continuing support, annual campaigns, exchange programs, matching funds, publications, renovation projects, research, special projects.
Limitations: Giving primarily in the greater Cleveland, OH, area. No grants to individuals, or for endowment funds; no loans.
Publications: Annual report, informational brochure.
Application information:
Initial approach: Letter
Copies of proposal: 1
Deadline(s): None; all applications on hand considered at bimonthly meetings
Board meeting date(s): Bimonthly
Final notification: Within 2 weeks of meeting
Write: Herbert E. Strawbridge, Pres. and Secy.
Officers and Trustees: Herbert E. Strawbridge, Pres. and Secy.; Claude M. Blair, V.P.; Robert G. Wright, V.P.; Paul L. Volk, Treas.
Number of staff: 1 part-time support.
Employer Identification Number: 346528308

2529
Louis S. and Mary Myers Foundation
1293 South Main St.
Akron 44301

Established in 1956 in OH.
Financial data (yr. ended 12/31/87): Assets, $1,014,670 (M); gifts received, $167,070; expenditures, $134,616, including $132,675 for 20 grants (high: $52,000; low: $250).
Purpose and activities: Giving primarily to Jewish and Jewish welfare organizations; support also for the arts.
Application information:
Write: Pat Hill
Officer: Louis S. Myers, Pres.
Trustees: Mary Myers, Stephen E. Myers.
Employer Identification Number: 346555862

2530
National City Bank Giving Program
1900 E. Ninth St.
Cleveland 44114 (216) 575-2000

Financial data (yr. ended 12/31/86): $1,057,971 for 246 grants.
Purpose and activities: Supports arts and culture, health and welfare, education and civic affairs; also provides technical assistance, employee volunteer support, and low-interest-rate loans to revitalize housing, neighborhoods, and businesses.
Types of support: Technical assistance, loans, in-kind gifts.
Limitations: Giving primarily in areas of company operations in Cuyahoga, Geauga, Lake, Lorain, Medina, and Summit counties, OH; some support for national or regional organizations.
Application information:
Initial approach: Letter of inquiry describing project
Deadline(s): Best time to apply is before Nov. 10
Board meeting date(s): Bi-monthly
Final notification: 12 weeks
Write: Dennis T. Brennan, Asst. V.P., Public Affairs

2531
National City Corporate Giving Program
National City Center
1900 East Ninth St.
Cleveland 44114 (216) 575-2000

Financial data (yr. ended 12/31/88): Total giving, $4,214,749, including $4,121,217 for 500 grants (high: $10,000; low: $1,000; average: $1,000-$5,000), $67,877 for 450 employee matching gifts and $25,655 for 15 in-kind gifts.
Purpose and activities: Supports alcohol/drug treatment, civic affairs, urban affairs and development, arts and culture, education, health care, housing, hunger, handicapped, minority programs, youth and women's issues, public broadcasting and the United Way.
Types of support: Annual campaigns, building funds, employee matching gifts, research, employee-related scholarships, capital campaigns.
Limitations: Giving primarily in headquarters city and operating locations in Cleveland, Akron, Dayton, Toledo, Columbus, Columbiana, Norwalk, and Sandusky, OH; Louisville, Lexington, Ashland, Bowling Green, and Owensboro, KY; and New Albany, and Salem, IN.

Publications: Informational brochure (including application guidelines), program policy statement.
Application information:
Initial approach: Written proposal
Copies of proposal: 1
Deadline(s): 10th Jan., Mar., May., Jul., Sept., and Nov.
Board meeting date(s): Approx. 25th of above months
Write: Allen C. Waddle, Sr. V.P., Public Affairs Dept.

2532
Nationwide Foundation
One Nationwide Plaza
Columbus 43216 (614) 249-4310

Incorporated in 1959 in OH.
Donor(s): Nationwide Mutual Insurance Co., and affiliates.
Financial data (yr. ended 12/31/87): Assets, $16,306,700 (M); expenditures, $2,198,194, including $1,956,722 for 139 grants (high: $1,056,996; low: $500; average: $1,000-$8,000) and $211,478 for 1,118 employee matching gifts.
Purpose and activities: Giving primarily for human services agencies; support also for cultural programs, community funds, and higher education, including employee matching gifts.
Types of support: Operating budgets, continuing support, annual campaigns, seed money, emergency funds, special projects, research, scholarship funds, employee matching gifts, capital campaigns.
Limitations: Giving primarily in OH, particularly Columbus, and other communities where the company maintains offices. No support for public elementary and secondary schools, or fraternal or veterans' organizations. No grants to individuals, or for building funds; no loans.
Publications: Informational brochure (including application guidelines).
Application information:
Initial approach: Letter
Copies of proposal: 1
Deadline(s): Sept. 1
Board meeting date(s): Feb., May, Aug., and Nov.
Final notification: Feb.
Write: J. Richard Bull, V.P.
Officers: Paul A. Donald,* Pres.; Peter F. Frenzer, Exec. V.P., Investments; D.R. McFerson, Sr. V.P., Finance; Gordon E. McCutchan, Sr. V.P. and General Counsel; Gerald W. Woodard, V.P. and Treas.; J. Richard Bull, V.P. and Chair., Contrib. Comm.; W.E. Fitzpatrick, Secy.
Trustees:* John E. Fisher, Chair.; Charles L. Fuellgraf, Jr., James M. Lewis, John L. Marakas, Frank B. Sollars, Carl H. Stitzlein.
Number of staff: 1 part-time professional; 1 part-time support.
Employer Identification Number: 316022301

2533
The NCR Foundation
1700 South Patterson Blvd.
Dayton 45479 (513) 445-2577

Incorporated in 1953 in OH.
Donor(s): NCR Corp.
Financial data (yr. ended 12/31/87): Assets, $9,739,840 (M); gifts received, $5,000,000; expenditures, $3,392,996, including $2,630,765 for grants and $708,631 for employee matching gifts.
Purpose and activities: Emphasis on higher education, particularly computer science, an employee matching gift program, and community funds; some support for cultural programs and urban affairs.
Types of support: Operating budgets, annual campaigns, seed money, emergency funds, building funds, equipment, research, scholarship funds, employee-related scholarships, employee matching gifts, continuing support.
Limitations: Giving primarily in areas of company operations, with emphasis on Dayton, OH. No grants to individuals; no loans.
Application information:
Initial approach: Letter or proposal
Copies of proposal: 1
Deadline(s): None
Board meeting date(s): Mar., June, Sept., and Dec.
Final notification: 3 to 6 months
Write: R.F. Beach, V.P.
Officers: W.S. Anderson,* Pres.; R.F. Beach, V.P.; C.P. Russ III, Secy.; M.S. Combs, Treas.
Trustees:* Charles A. Anderson, G.A. Costanzo, Harry Holiday, Jr., Cathleen Synge Morawetz.
Number of staff: 2
Employer Identification Number: 316030860

2534
The L. and L. Nippert Charitable Foundation
c/o The Central Trust Co. of Northern Ohio, N.A.
P.O. Box 1198
Cincinnati 45201 (513) 651-8421

Established in 1981.
Donor(s): Louis Nippert, Louise D. Nippert.
Financial data (yr. ended 12/31/86): Assets, $3,940,895 (M); expenditures, $139,873, including $115,750 for 31 grants (high: $25,000; low: $500; average: $2,000-$8,000).
Purpose and activities: Broad and unrestricted giving, with some focus on education, conservation, and music.
Types of support: Annual campaigns, building funds, capital campaigns, endowment funds, equipment, land acquisition, operating budgets, publications, renovation projects, scholarship funds, seed money, special projects.
Limitations: Giving primarily in OH.
Publications: Application guidelines.
Application information:
Initial approach: Proposal
Copies of proposal: 4
Deadline(s): First of Mar., July, and Nov.
Board meeting date(s): Apr., Aug., and Dec.
Final notification: 1 month after meetings
Write: Betty C. Scheid, Trust Officer
Trustees: Louis Nippert, Louise D. Nippert, The Central Trust Co. of Northern Ohio, N.A.
Number of staff: 1
Employer Identification Number: 316219757

2535
The Nord Family Foundation
(Formerly Nordson Foundation)
385 Midway Plaza, Suite 312
Elyria 44035 (216) 324-2822
Additional tel.: (216) 233-8401

Trust established in 1952 in OH.
Donor(s): Walter G. Nord,† Mrs. Walter G. Nord,† Nordson Corp., Evan W. Nord.
Financial data (yr. ended 10/31/88): Assets, $51,642,645 (M); gifts received, $2,602,035; expenditures, $2,057,871, including $1,709,230 for 89 grants (high: $152,000; low: $100; average: $3,000-$5,000), $40,000 for 2 foundation-administered programs and $15,128 for loans.
Purpose and activities: Emphasis on projects to assist the disadvantaged and minorities, including giving for secondary and higher education, social services, health, cultural affairs, and civic activities. New initiatives in 1988 were creation of Public Service Institute, Child Care Resource Center, and a day care center for low to moderate income families.
Types of support: Operating budgets, continuing support, seed money, emergency funds, equipment, matching funds, consulting services, technical assistance, loans, special projects, publications, employee matching gifts, general purposes, program-related investments.
Limitations: Giving primarily in the Lorain and Cuyahoga county areas, OH. No grants to individuals, or for deficit financing, research, scholarships, fellowships, or conferences.
Publications: Annual report (including application guidelines).
Application information:
Initial approach: Proposal, letter, or telephone
Copies of proposal: 1
Deadline(s): Submit proposal at least 1 month before meetings
Board meeting date(s): Jan., June, and Oct.
Final notification: 1 to 3 months
Write: Jeptha J. Carrell, Exec. Dir.
Officers and Trustees:* Evan W. Nord,* Pres.; Eric T. Nord,* V.P.; William D. Ginn,* Secy.; Jeptha J. Carrell, Exec. Dir.
Number of staff: 5 full-time professional; 2 part-time professional; 1 full-time support.
Employer Identification Number: 346539234
Recent arts and culture grants:
Allen Memorial Art Museum, Oberlin, OH, $30,000. For public education program. 1987.
Lorain County Arts Council, Elyria, OH, $5,000. For research/script for dramatization for public television of Toni Morrison's book, The Bluest Eye. 1987.
W V I Z TV Channel 25, Cleveland, OH, $11,000. For local acquisition, McNeil/Lehrer News Hour. 1987.

2536
Charles G. O'Bleness Foundation No. 2
c/o The Huntington National Bank, Trust Department
41 South High St.
Columbus 43215

Established in 1962 in OH.
Financial data (yr. ended 12/31/87): Assets, $1,026,427 (M); expenditures, $103,120, including $91,071 for 7 grants (high: $37,471; low: $3,600).
Purpose and activities: Giving primarily for an arts center, secondary education, and hospitals.
Limitations: Giving primarily in Athens County, OH.
Application information:
Deadline(s): Oct. 15
Trustee: Huntington National Bank.
Advisors: John Clark, John M. Jones.
Employer Identification Number: 316022855

2537
Oerlikon Motch Corporation Foundation
1250 East 222nd St.
Euclid 44117-1190 (216) 486-3600

Financial data (yr. ended 12/31/86): Assets, $309,777 (M); expenditures, $27,103, including $25,700 for 24 grants (high: $10,000; low: $200).
Purpose and activities: Support for higher education, culture and the arts, welfare, and community and social services.
Application information:
Write: Dianne S. Wrona, Secy.
Officers and Directors: R.J. Mayer, Pres.; R. Siewert, V.P.; D.S. Wrona, Secy.; G.D. Babbitt, L. Reiss.
Employer Identification Number: 346555823

2538
Ohio Bell Foundation
45 Erieview Plaza, Rm. 870
Cleveland 44114 (216) 822-2423

Established in 1987 in OH.
Donor(s): Ohio Bell.
Financial data (yr. ended 12/31/88): Assets, $17,797,000 (M); gifts received, $10,000,000; expenditures, $2,314,488, including $2,001,634 for 389 grants (high: $475,000; low: $100; average: $100-$475,000), $281,071 for 2,134 employee matching gifts and $16,910 for 10 in-kind gifts.
Purpose and activities: Support for civic affairs, community development, art and culture, education, and health.
Types of support: Continuing support, employee matching gifts, general purposes, special projects.
Limitations: Giving limited to OH, except for employee matching gifts for education. No support for religious organizations for religious purposes, lobbying, direct patient care, or sports or athletic events. No grants to individuals, or for special event advertising.
Publications: Annual report (including application guidelines).
Application information:
Initial approach: Proposal
Copies of proposal: 1
Deadline(s): None
Board meeting date(s): Periodic
Write: William W. Boag, Jr., Exec. Dir.
Officers: Donald W. Morrison,* Secy.; Robert E. Cogan, Treas.; William W. Boag, Jr., Exec. Dir.
Trustees: Douglas E. Fairbanks, Robert J. Hudzik, Leo R. Reichard.
Number of staff: 1 full-time professional; 2 full-time support.
Employer Identification Number: 341536258

2539
Ohio Savings Charitable Foundation
1600 Ohio Savings Plaza
Cleveland 44114

Financial data (yr. ended 11/30/88): Assets, $377,095 (M); expenditures, $12,898, including $11,170 for 32 grants (high: $2,100; low: $25).
Purpose and activities: Support for Jewish giving, Christian charities, social services, health services, youth, arts, education, and minorities.
Limitations: Giving primarily in Cleveland, OH.
Trustees: Robert Goldberg, Chair.; David Goldberg.
Employer Identification Number: 237055858

2540
The Ohio Valley Foundation
c/o The Fifth Third Bank
Dept. 00850
Cincinnati 45263 (513) 579-6034

Incorporated in 1946 in OH.
Donor(s): John J. Rowe.†
Financial data (yr. ended 12/31/87): Assets, $2,522,579 (M); expenditures, $122,663, including $112,500 for 12 grants (high: $25,000; low: $2,000; average: $10,000).
Purpose and activities: Giving primarily for education, youth agencies, and cultural programs.
Types of support: Building funds, capital campaigns.
Limitations: Giving primarily in the greater Cincinnati, OH, area. No grants to individuals, or for endowment funds or operating budgets.
Application information:
Initial approach: Proposal
Copies of proposal: 1
Deadline(s): Nov. 15
Board meeting date(s): Dec.
Final notification: Immediately after Dec. meeting
Write: Carolyn F. McCoy, Fdn. Officer
Trustees: Clement Buenger, Donald Meihaus, William S. Rowe, N. Beverly Tucker, John W. Warrington.
Number of staff: None.
Employer Identification Number: 316008508

2541
Owens-Corning Foundation, Inc.
P.O. Box 1688
Toledo 43603-1688 (419) 248-8000
Application address: Employee Services & Community Relations/Owens Corning Fiberglass/One Levis Square, Toledo, OH 43659

Financial data (yr. ended 12/31/88): Assets, $363,233 (M); expenditures, $18,535, including $15,000 for 1 grant.
Purpose and activities: Support for education, including religious schools, science and technology, community development and funds, civic affairs, civil rights, the homeless and housing, museums, performing arts, and drug rehabilitation.
Types of support: Annual campaigns, employee matching gifts, equipment, operating budgets, renovation projects, scholarship funds.
Limitations: Giving primarily in major corporate manufacturing locations.
Application information:
Initial approach: Letter
Deadline(s): None
Board meeting date(s): 3rd Tuesday of each month
Write: Emerson J. Ross, Mgr.
Officers: Bradford C. Oelman,* Pres.; Rodney A. Nowland, V.P. and Secy.; Emerson J. Ross, Treas.
Directors:* John E. Gates, Robert D. Heddens, Lewis W. Saxby.
Trustee: Ohio Citizens Bank.
Number of staff: 1 part-time professional; 1 part-time support.
Employer Identification Number: 341270856

2542
The Payne Fund
1770 Huntington Bldg.
Cleveland 44115 (216) 696-1621

Incorporated in 1929 in OH.
Donor(s): Frances P. Bolton.†
Financial data (yr. ended 12/31/87): Assets, $2,528,000 (M); gifts received, $296,400; expenditures, $479,300, including $409,833 for 17 grants (high: $60,000; low: $1,500).
Purpose and activities: To initiate, assist, or conduct research and experiments in education and other activities in behalf of the welfare of mankind; support also for higher education, and cultural programs.
Application information: Contributes only to pre-selected organizations. Applications not accepted.
Officers and Directors: Charles P. Bolton,* Pres.; Kenyon C. Bolton III,* V.P.; Philip P. Bolton,* V.P.; Thomas C. Bolton,* V.P.; William B. Bolton,* Secy.-Treas.; John B. Bolton, Barbara Bolton Gratry, Mary Bolton Hooper, Frederick B. Taylor.
Employer Identification Number: 135563006

2543
Penn Central Corporate Giving Program
One East Fourth St.
Cincinnati 45202 (513) 579-6600

Financial data (yr. ended 12/31/88): Total giving, $341,302, including $290,970 for 34 grants (high: $100,000; low: $25; average: $25-$100,000) and $50,332 for 141 employee matching gifts.
Purpose and activities: Supports education, health, hospitals, welfare, culture, arts, civic and social activities.
Types of support: Employee matching gifts, general purposes.

Limitations: Giving primarily in headquarters city and major operating areas.
Application information: Include complete budget, IRS letter, board list, contributors' list, and audited statement.
Initial approach: Query letter describing project
Deadline(s): None
Final notification: 6-8 weeks
Write: David H. Street, Sr. V.P. of Finance

2544
The Perkins Charitable Foundation
401 Euclid Ave., Rm. 480
Cleveland 44114

Trust established in 1950 in OH.
Donor(s): Members of the Perkins family.
Financial data (yr. ended 12/31/87): Assets, $6,939,523 (M); expenditures, $383,222, including $341,250 for 36 grants (high: $50,000; low: $200).
Purpose and activities: Giving for higher and secondary education, museums, hospitals, community funds, and conservation.
Limitations: Giving primarily in OH. No grants to individuals.
Trustees: Jacob B. Perkins, Leigh H. Perkins, Ralph Perkins, Jr., Sallie P. Sullivan.
Employer Identification Number: 346549753

2545
Peterloon Foundation
1900 Carew Tower
Cincinnati 45202

Established in 1958.
Donor(s): John J. Emery.†
Financial data (yr. ended 11/30/87): Assets, $2,681,913 (M); expenditures, $279,003, including $72,200 for 21 grants (high: $10,000; low: $500).
Purpose and activities: Giving for arts and cultural programs, education, and social agencies.
Limitations: Giving primarily in OH.
Officers: Lela Emery Steele, Pres. and Treas.; Melissa Emery Lanier, V.P.; Henry H. Chatfield, Secy.
Trustees: Ethan Emery, Irene E. Goodale, Paul George Sittenfeld.
Employer Identification Number: 316037801

2546
The Thomas F. Peterson Foundation
3200 National City Center
Cleveland 44114 (216) 621-0200

Established in 1953.
Financial data (yr. ended 10/31/86): Assets, $1,547,523 (M); gifts received, $20,000; expenditures, $72,475, including $48,300 for 16 grants (high: $20,000; low: $100).
Purpose and activities: Giving for higher education, cultural programs, and youth agencies.
Types of support: General purposes, scholarship funds.
Limitations: Giving primarily in OH. No grants to individuals.
Application information:
Deadline(s): None
Write: James E. Chapman, Secy.
Officers and Trustees:* Ethel B. Peterson,* Pres.; Barbara P. Ruhlman,* V.P.; James E. Chapman, Secy.; John D. Drinko,* Treas.
Employer Identification Number: 346524958

2547
Jesse Philips Foundation
4801 Springfield St.
Dayton 45401
Scholarship application address: c/o Ruth Richardson, Dayton Board of Education, Dayton Public Schools, 348 West First St., Dayton, OH 45402

Incorporated in 1960 in OH.
Donor(s): Jesse Philips, Philips Industries, Inc., and subsidiaries.
Financial data (yr. ended 2/28/87): Assets, $14,408,990 (M); gifts received, $2,245,563; expenditures, $2,101,256, including $2,053,151 for 620 grants (high: $333,500; low: $20).
Purpose and activities: Giving for Jewish welfare funds, hospitals, higher education, cultural programs, social services, and community development. Scholarships or study loans limited to high school students in Montgomery County, OH, or to Jesse Philips Scholars and paid through institutions.
Types of support: Scholarship funds.
Limitations: Giving primarily in Dayton, OH.
Application information: Application forms required for scholarship program.
Deadline(s): May I for scholarships
Write: Jesse Philips, Pres.
Officers and Trustees: Jesse Philips, Pres.; Caryl Philips, V.P.; Milton Roisman, V.P.; E.L. Ryan, Jr., Secy.; Thomas C. Haas, Treas.
Employer Identification Number: 316023380

2548
Place Fund
6000 Parkland Blvd.
Mayfield Heights 44124

Established in 1986 in OH.
Donor(s): Peter B. Lewis.
Financial data (yr. ended 12/31/87): Assets, $279,035 (M); gifts received, $308,000; expenditures, $780,406, including $766,072 for 3 grants (high: $752,071; low: $5,000).
Purpose and activities: Support for a Jewish community organization; giving also to a theater festival.
Types of support: Land acquisition.
Limitations: Giving primarily in Cleveland, OH.
Officers and Trustees: Peter B. Lewis, Pres.; Adam J. Lewis, V.P.; John D. Garson, Secy.-Treas.
Employer Identification Number: 341532635

2549
PMI Food Equipment Group Giving Program
Corp. Communications Dept.
World Headquarters
Troy 45374 (513) 332-3150

Purpose and activities: Supports arts and humanities, civic and public affairs, higher education, community service organizations, youth services, and engineering; priority given to organizations that have proven their effectiveness in producing positive results. Consideration also for "start-up" organizations addressing developing community needs.
Types of support: Employee matching gifts, exchange programs, employee-related scholarships, scholarship funds.
Limitations: Giving primarily in OH. No support for organizations limiting services to members of any one religious group or for organizations already funded by United Way or other federated programs. No grants to individuals, or for organizations with a limited constituency, travel, tuition, registration fees, membership dues, purchase of tickets for fund raising, goodwill advertisements; no loans.
Publications: Informational brochure.
Application information: Include general program information, brief history of purpose and achievements, proposal, budget, audited financial statement, 501(c)(3) status letter, list of board and officers and statement of fund raising expenses as a percentage of overall organization, administrative and program costs.
Initial approach: Written proposal
Copies of proposal: 1
Deadline(s): None
Final notification: All requests will be answered within 60 days
Write: Sandy Borror, Coord., Corp. Contribs.
Number of staff: 1 full-time professional.

2550
The William B. Pollock II and Kathryn Challiss Pollock Foundation
c/o Bank One Youngstown, N.A.
Six Federal Plaza West
Youngstown 44503

Trust established in 1952 in OH.
Donor(s): William B. Pollock II, Kathryn Challiss Pollock.
Financial data (yr. ended 12/31/87): Assets, $2,075,337 (M); expenditures, $148,605, including $123,810 for 43 grants (high: $17,500; low: $50; average: $100-$2,000).
Purpose and activities: Support for hospitals, community funds, Protestant church support, cultural activities, education, youth and health agencies, and population control.
Types of support: Operating budgets, continuing support, annual campaigns, seed money, emergency funds, deficit financing, building funds, equipment, land acquisition, endowment funds, research, special projects, publications, conferences and seminars.
Limitations: Giving limited to the Youngstown, OH, area. No grants to individuals, or for matching gifts, or scholarships and fellowships; no loans.
Publications: 990-PF.
Trustees: Franklin S. Bennett, Jr., Bank One, Youngstown, N.A.
Number of staff: None.
Employer Identification Number: 346514079

2551
William Powell Company Foundation
2535 Spring Grove Ave.
Cincinnati 45214 (513) 852-2000
Application address: P.O. Box 14534, Cincinnati, OH 45250

Financial data (yr. ended 11/30/88): Assets, $298,270 (M); expenditures, $14,157, including $13,650 for 10 grants (high: $7,500; low: $50).
Purpose and activities: Support for United Appeal, fine arts, higher education, and zoological society.
Limitations: Giving primarily in Cincinnati, OH. No grants to individuals.
Application information:
Initial approach: Letter
Deadline(s): None
Write: Mr. V. Anderson Coombe, Trustee
Trustee: V. Anderson Coombe.
Employer Identification Number: 316043487

2552
The Procter & Gamble Fund
P.O. Box 599
Cincinnati 45201 (513) 983-3913

Incorporated in 1952 in OH.
Donor(s): The Procter & Gamble Cos.
Financial data (yr. ended 6/30/88): Assets, $34,729,192 (M); expenditures, $14,043,267, including $13,975,164 for 1,054 grants (high: $1,799,950; low: $50).
Purpose and activities: Grants nationally for private higher education and economic and public policy research organizations; support also for community funds, hospitals, youth agencies, urban affairs, and aid to the handicapped; generally limited to areas of domestic company operations.
Types of support: Annual campaigns, building funds, continuing support, emergency funds, equipment, land acquisition, matching funds, employee-related scholarships, employee matching gifts.
Limitations: Giving primarily in areas in the U.S. and where the company and its subsidiaries have large concentrations of employees; national giving for higher education and economic and public affairs. No grants to individuals.
Publications: Informational brochure.
Application information: Grant requests from colleges and universities are discouraged, as most grants are initiated by the trustees within specified programs.
Initial approach: Proposal
Copies of proposal: 1
Deadline(s): None
Board meeting date(s): Jan., Apr., July, and Oct.
Final notification: 1 month
Write: R.R. Fitzpatrick, V.P.
Officers: G.S. Gendell,* Pres.; R.R. Fitzpatrick,* V.P.; P.F. Wieting,* V.P.; B.J. Nolan, V.P. and Secy.; Edwin H. Eaton, Treas.
Trustees:* S.J. Fitch, J.W. Nethercott.
Number of staff: 5 full-time professional; 2 full-time support.
Employer Identification Number: 316019594
Recent arts and culture grants:
Albany Area Arts Council, Albany, NY, $10,000. 1987.
American Museum of Natural History, NYC, NY, $6,000. 1987.
Art Academy of Cincinnati, Cincinnati, OH, $6,100. 1987.
Cape Girardeau Civic Center, Cape Girardeau, MO, $5,000. 1987.
Cincinnati Institute of Fine Arts, Cincinnati, OH, $365,000. 1987.
Colonial Williamsburg Foundation, Williamsburg, VA, $5,000. 1987.
Fords Theater Society, DC, $12,500. 1987.
Fund for the Arts, Lexington, KY, $5,000. 1987.
Greater Cincinnati Television Educational Foundation, Cincinnati, OH, $12,000. 1987.
Historic Southwest Ohio, Cincinnati, OH, $5,000. 1987.
John F. Kennedy Center for the Performing Arts, DC, $30,000. 1987.
Lincoln Center for the Performing Arts, NYC, NY, $7,000. 1987.
Memphis Arts Council, Memphis, TN, $16,500. 1987.
Metropolitan Opera Association, NYC, NY, $6,000. 1987.
National Railroad Museum, Green Bay, WI, $7,500. 1987.
National Symphony Orchestra Association of Washington, D.C., DC, $5,000. 1987.
Paramount Civic Center, Wilkes-Barre, PA, $25,000. 1987.
Philharmonic Society of Northeastern Pennsylvania, Avoca, PA, $7,500. 1987.
University of Cincinnati, W G U C Radio, Cincinnati, OH, $7,500. 1987.
University of Iowa, Natural History Museum-Iowa Hall, Iowa City, IA, $5,000. 1987.
Zoological Society of Cincinnati, Cincinnati, OH, $6,000. 1987.

2553
Progressive Corporate Giving Program
6000 Parkland Blvd.
Mayfield Heights 44143 (216) 464-8000
Mailing address: P.O. Box 5070, Cleveland, OH 44101

Financial data (yr. ended 12/31/88): Total giving, $810,000, including $799,000 for 50 grants (high: $75,000; low: $250) and $11,000 for 25 employee matching gifts.
Purpose and activities: Supports the arts and culture, civic affairs, education, environment, health, minority programs, and social sciences; emphasis is on innovative and creative projects that are difficult to fund through traditional sources and address an important or new community need.
Types of support: Employee matching gifts, matching funds, employee-related scholarships, seed money, special projects.
Limitations: Giving primarily in Austin, TX; Cleveland, OH; Colorado Springs, CO; Richmond, VA; Sacramento, CA; and Tampa, FL. No support for religious organizations for religious purposes. No grants to individuals.
Publications: Application guidelines.
Application information: Include project description, organization history, time frame for project, names of project administrators, complete budget, list of board members and contributors, 501(c)(3), and an audited financial statement.
Initial approach: Initial contact by letter with complete proposal
Copies of proposal: 1
Deadline(s): None
Board meeting date(s): Quarterly
Final notification: 8 weeks
Write: Jennifer S. Frutchy, Contribs. Mgr.
Number of staff: 1 full-time professional; 1 part-time support.

2554
Reeves Foundation
232-4 West Third St.
P.O. Box 441
Dover 44622 (216) 364-4660

Trust established in 1966 in OH.
Donor(s): Margaret J. Reeves,† Helen F. Reeves,† Samuel J. Reeves.†
Financial data (yr. ended 12/31/88): Assets, $12,351,322 (M); expenditures, $889,666, including $736,288 for 18 grants (high: $200,000; low: $2,101).
Purpose and activities: Emphasis on historical societies and health agencies; grants also for cultural activities, youth agencies, higher education, and church support. Priority given to capital improvement projects.
Types of support: Operating budgets, continuing support, building funds, equipment, matching funds, research, scholarship funds, special projects.
Limitations: Giving primarily in OH, with emphasis on the Dover area. No grants to individuals, or for annual campaigns, seed money, emergency funds, deficit financing, land acquisition, renovation projects, endowment funds, fellowships, special projects, publications, or conferences; no loans.
Application information:
Initial approach: Proposal
Copies of proposal: 2
Deadline(s): 15th of months prior to those when board meets
Board meeting date(s): Bimonthly starting in Feb.
Final notification: 2 to 7 weeks
Write: Don A. Ulrich, Exec. Dir.
Officers: Margaret H. Reeves,* Pres.; Thomas R. Scheffer,* V.P.; W.E. Lieser, Treas.; Don A. Ulrich,* Exec. Dir.
Trustees:* Jeffry Wagner.
Number of staff: 1 full-time professional; 1 full-time support.
Employer Identification Number: 346575477

2555
The Reinberger Foundation
27600 Chagrin Blvd.
Cleveland 44122 (216) 292-2790

Established in 1968 in OH.
Donor(s): Clarence T. Reinberger,† Louise F. Reinberger.†
Financial data (yr. ended 12/31/88): Assets, $42,176,251 (M); expenditures, $2,334,602, including $1,810,530 for 53 grants (high: $200,000; low: $500; average: $20,000-$50,000).

Purpose and activities: Support for the arts, social welfare, Protestant churches, higher education, and medical research.
Types of support: Operating budgets, continuing support, annual campaigns, building funds, equipment, endowment funds, matching funds, scholarship funds, research, publications, special projects, deficit financing, capital campaigns.
Limitations: Giving primarily in the Cleveland and Columbus, OH, areas. No grants to individuals, or for seed money, emergency funds, land acquisition, demonstration projects, or conferences; no loans.
Publications: 990-PF.
Application information:
Initial approach: Proposal
Copies of proposal: 1
Deadline(s): None
Board meeting date(s): Mar., June, Sept., and Dec.
Final notification: 6 months
Write: Robert N. Reinberger, Co-Dir.
Managers: Robert N. Reinberger, Co-Dir.; William C. Reinberger, Co-Dir.; Richard H. Oman, Secy.; AmeriTrust Co.
Number of staff: 2 full-time professional.
Employer Identification Number: 346574879

2556
Reliance Electric Company Charitable, Scientific and Educational Trust
29325 Chagrin Blvd.
Pepper Pike 44122 (216) 266-1913

Trust established in 1952 in OH.
Donor(s): Reliance Electric Co.
Financial data (yr. ended 10/31/88): Assets, $185,000 (M); gifts received, $650,000; expenditures, $710,000, including $515,000 for 60 grants (high: $20,000; low: $500; average: $500-$5,000) and $180,000 for employee matching gifts.
Purpose and activities: Emphasis on community funds, higher education, hospitals, cultural programs, and social services; also funds an employee matching gifts program.
Types of support: Employee matching gifts.
Limitations: Giving primarily in OH within proximity of major company facilities. No support for national health organizations. No grants to individuals.
Application information:
Initial approach: Proposal
Copies of proposal: 1
Deadline(s): May., Oct., and Dec.
Board meeting date(s): Quarterly
Write: Byron O. Lutman, Secy.
Officer: Byron O. Lutman, Secy.
Trustee: AmeriTrust Co.
Number of staff: None.
Employer Identification Number: 346505329

2557
The Reynolds and Reynolds Company Foundation
P.O. Box 2608
Dayton 45401 (513) 449-4490

Established in 1986 in OH.
Financial data (yr. ended 9/30/87): Assets, $11,728 (M); gifts received, $375,096; expenditures, $377,168, including $377,076 for grants.
Purpose and activities: "The foundation focuses attention on a program of giving to promote a healthy environment for neighbors, employees and their families, and the business community." Support for health, education, arts, and community activities; organizations not falling precisely into these categories may also be considered for grants. Programs will be judged on their impact in the local community and how they fit into the total contributions program. Support is given to traditional, established organizations and to organizations which propose worthy, innovative programs. At times, when the foundation sees a need for a specific program for which it has not received an application, it may solicit a grant that addresses the perceived need. The United Way is also strongly supported.
Limitations: Giving primarily in areas of company operations, with emphasis on Dayton, OH. No support for sectarian organizations with an exclusively religious purpose, fraternal or veterans' organizations, primary or secondary schools (except for occasional special projects), or tax-supported universities and colleges (except for occasional special projects. No grants to individuals, or for courtesy advertising; organizations receiving funds from the United Way generally not considered.
Publications: Application guidelines.
Application information: Outside of Dayton area, write to local facility manager.
Initial approach: Proposal
Final notification: 3 months
Trustee: Robert C. Nevin.
Employer Identification Number: 311168299

2558
Robbins & Myers Foundation
1400 Kettering Tower
Dayton 45423 (513) 222-2610

Incorporated in 1966 in OH.
Donor(s): Robbins & Myers, Inc.
Financial data (yr. ended 8/31/88): Assets, $20,000 (M); gifts received, $60,000; expenditures, $40,867, including $39,000 for grants (high: $20,625; low: $100).
Purpose and activities: Giving primarily for community funds, education, cultural programs, and youth activities.
Types of support: Annual campaigns, employee-related scholarships.
Limitations: Giving primarily in areas of company operations. No grants to individuals.
Application information:
Initial approach: Letter
Deadline(s): None
Write: Daniel W. Duval, Pres.
Officers and Managers: Daniel W. Duval, Pres.; H.E. Becker, Secy.; George M. Walker, Treas.
Employer Identification Number: 316064597

2559
The Samuel Rosenthal Foundation
Halle Bldg., Suite 810
1228 Euclid Ave.
Cleveland 44115-8125 (216) 523-8125

Trust established in 1959 in OH.
Donor(s): Work Wear Corp., Inc., and subsidiaries.
Financial data (yr. ended 3/31/89): Assets, $9,600,000 (M); expenditures, $641,900, including $601,530 for 39 grants (high: $413,500; low: $50).
Purpose and activities: Grants for general, secular, vocational, Hebrew, and Jewish education; support also for the arts, health and welfare funds, and the aged.
Types of support: General purposes.
Limitations: Giving primarily in Cleveland, OH. No grants to individuals.
Publications: Application guidelines.
Application information:
Initial approach: Proposal
Copies of proposal: 1
Deadline(s): None
Board meeting date(s): 4 times a year
Final notification: After meeting
Write: Charlotte R. Kramer, Trustee
Trustees: Cynthia R. Boardman, Jane R. Horvitz, Charlotte R. Kramer, Mark R. Kramer, Leighton A. Rosenthal.
Number of staff: 2 part-time support.
Employer Identification Number: 346558832

2560
The Rubbermaid Foundation
1147 Akron Rd.
Wooster 44691-0800 (216) 264-6464

Established in 1986 in OH.
Donor(s): Rubbermaid, Inc.
Financial data (yr. ended 12/31/87): Assets, $2,883,355 (M); expenditures, $282,924, including $272,499 for 33 grants (high: $75,000; low: $150).
Purpose and activities: Support for the arts, higher and secondary education, economics, and health.
Types of support: Annual campaigns.
Limitations: No grants to individuals.
Application information:
Initial approach: Letter
Deadline(s): None
Write: Richard Gates, Pres.
Officers and Trustees: Richard D. Gates, Pres.; Joseph G. Meehan, V.P.; James A. Morgan, Secy.; Stanley C. Gault, Walter W. Williams.
Employer Identification Number: 341533729

2561
Fran and Warren Rupp Foundation
40 Sturges Ave.
Mansfield 44902-1912 (419) 522-2345

Established in 1977.
Donor(s): Fran Rupp, Warren Rupp.
Financial data (yr. ended 12/31/87): Assets, $1,723,916 (M); expenditures, $85,889, including $61,127 for 14 grants (high: $12,000; low: $500).

Purpose and activities: Emphasis on the arts and social service agencies.
Types of support: General purposes.
Limitations: Giving primarily in OH. No grants to individuals.
Application information:
Initial approach: Letter
Deadline(s): None
Write: Donald Smith, Secy.
Officers and Trustees: Warren Rupp, Pres.; Fran Rupp, V.P.; Donald Smith, Secy.-Treas.
Employer Identification Number: 341230690

2562
Josephine S. Russell Charitable Trust
c/o The Central Trust Co. of Northern Ohio, N.A.
P.O. Box 1198
Cincinnati 45201 (513) 651-8377

Trust established in 1976 in OH.
Donor(s): Josephine Schell Russell.†
Financial data (yr. ended 6/30/87): Assets, $5,236,997 (M); expenditures, $275,380, including $248,800 for 23 grants (high: $20,000; low: $1,000; average: $5,000-$10,000).
Purpose and activities: Emphasis on education and aid to the handicapped; support also for social service agencies, cultural programs, health, and scientific and literary purposes.
Types of support: Seed money, equipment, land acquisition, special projects, publications, building funds, capital campaigns, renovation projects.
Limitations: Giving limited to the greater Cincinnati, OH, area. No grants to individuals, or for endowment funds, operating budgets, continuing support, annual campaigns, deficit financing, scholarships, or conferences; no loans.
Publications: Informational brochure (including application guidelines).
Application information:
Initial approach: Letter, telephone, or proposal
Copies of proposal: 8
Deadline(s): 1 month prior to board meetings
Board meeting date(s): Alternate months beginning with Jan.
Final notification: 3 months
Write: Mrs. Nancy C. Gurney, Exec. Asst.
Trustee: The Central Trust Co. of Northern Ohio, N.A.
Number of staff: 1 part-time professional.
Employer Identification Number: 316195446

2563
Sandusky Foundry and Machine Company Foundation
615 West Market St.
P.O. Box 5012
Sandusky 44870-1281

Donor(s): Sandusky Foundry and Machine Co.
Financial data (yr. ended 12/31/87): Assets, $142,692 (M); gifts received, $50,000; expenditures, $32,504, including $32,250 for 14 grants (high: $10,000; low: $150).
Purpose and activities: Support for education, youth, United Way, culture, and social services.
Application information: Contributes only to preselected organizations. Applications not accepted.
Trustees: Carlos G. Alafita, Edward A. McPhillamy, Charles W. Rainger, Dean K. Rogers, Daniel A. Scott.
Employer Identification Number: 346596951

2564
The Schey Foundation
2167 Savannah Pkwy.
Westlake 44145

Established in 1985 in OH.
Donor(s): Ralph E. Schey, Walter A. Rajki.
Financial data (yr. ended 6/30/87): Assets, $2,316,086 (M); gifts received, $400,000; expenditures, $96,221, including $93,545 for 21 grants (high: $58,500; low: $20).
Purpose and activities: Giving primarily to a school of business building fund, a business education foundation, and an opera association.
Types of support: Building funds.
Limitations: Giving primarily in OH.
Application information: Contributes only to pre-selected organizations. Applications not accepted.
Officer and Trustees: Ralph E. Schey, Pres.; David E. Cook, Lucille L. Schey.
Employer Identification Number: 341502219

2565
Jacob G. Schmidlapp Trust No. 2
c/o Fifth Third Bank
Dept. 00850, Trust Div.
Cincinnati 45263 (513) 579-6034

Trust established in 1916 in OH.
Donor(s): Jacob G. Schmidlapp.†
Financial data (yr. ended 12/31/87): Assets, $2,120,000 (M); expenditures, $125,760, including $102,600 for 7 grants (high: $25,000; low: $2,500; average: $5,000).
Purpose and activities: Grants for education, with emphasis on capital programs for higher educational institutions and cultural programs, primarily in the greater Cincinnati area.
Types of support: Equipment, building funds, capital campaigns, land acquisition, seed money, renovation projects.
Limitations: Giving primarily in the greater Cincinnati, OH, area; support also in KY and IN. No support for religious or political purposes. No grants to individuals, or for endowment funds, operating budgets, scholarships, or fellowships; no loans.
Publications: Annual report (including application guidelines), application guidelines.
Application information:
Initial approach: Letter or telephone
Copies of proposal: 1
Deadline(s): First day of months preceding board meetings
Board meeting date(s): Mar., June, Sept., and Dec.
Final notification: Middle of months in which board meets
Write: Carolyn F. McCoy, Fdn. Officer, Fifth Third Bank
Trustee: Fifth Third Bank.
Number of staff: 1
Employer Identification Number: 316020109

2566
The Sears Family Foundation
907 Park Bldg.
Cleveland 44114 (216) 241-6434

Trust established in 1949 in OH.
Donor(s): Anna L. Sears,† Lester M. Sears,† Ruth P. Sears,† Mary Ann Swetland.†
Financial data (yr. ended 12/31/88): Assets, $2,017,098 (M); gifts received, $29,655; expenditures, $181,073, including $167,300 for 52 grants (high: $50,000; low: $250; average: $500-$1,000).
Purpose and activities: Giving for health, education, welfare, and environmental projects.
Types of support: General purposes, operating budgets, continuing support, annual campaigns, seed money, emergency funds, deficit financing, building funds, equipment, land acquisition, matching funds, research, capital campaigns.
Limitations: Giving limited to the Cleveland, OH, area. No grants to individuals, or for scholarships or fellowships; no loans.
Publications: 990-PF.
Application information:
Initial approach: Letter
Copies of proposal: 1
Deadline(s): Submit proposal preferably before Dec.
Board meeting date(s): As needed
Final notification: 60 days
Write: David W. Swetland, Trustee
Officer and Trustees: Polly M. Swetland, Secy.; Ruth Swetland Eppig, David Sears Swetland, David W. Swetland.
Number of staff: 2 part-time support.
Employer Identification Number: 346522143

2567
Second Foundation
1525 National City Bank Bldg.
Cleveland 44114 (216) 696-4200

Established in 1984 in OH.
Donor(s): 1525 Foundation.
Financial data (yr. ended 12/31/88): Assets, $24,022,658 (M); expenditures, $1,608,469, including $1,535,080 for 12 grants (high: $1,079,476; low: $500; average: $5,000-$100,000).
Purpose and activities: Support primarily for culture and education.
Types of support: Continuing support, endowment funds, general purposes, matching funds, research, equipment, professorships.
Limitations: Giving primarily in OH, especially the Cleveland area.
Publications: 990-PF.
Application information:
Initial approach: Proposal
Deadline(s): None
Board meeting date(s): As required; at least monthly
Final notification: Within 1 month of receipt
Write: Bernadette Walsh, Asst. Secy.
Officers and Directors: Hubert H. Schneider, Pres.; Thelma G. Smith, V.P.; Phillip A. Ranney, Secy.-Treas.
Number of staff: 2
Employer Identification Number: 341436198

2568
The Della Selsor Trust
P.O. Box 1488
Springfield 45501

Established in 1966 in OH.
Donor(s): Della Selsor.†
Financial data (yr. ended 12/31/87): Assets, $2,000,000 (M); expenditures, $80,000, including $65,000 for 33 grants (high: $10,000; low: $200).
Purpose and activities: Grants to youth and cultural organizations, and hospitals; support also for a church.
Types of support: Annual campaigns, building funds, capital campaigns.
Limitations: Giving primarily in Clark and Madison counties, OH.
Application information:
Initial approach: Letter or telephone call
Deadline(s): None
Write: Trustees
Trustees: Glenn W. Collier, Oscar T. Martin.
Employer Identification Number: 510163338

2569
The Louise Taft Semple Foundation
1800 First National Bank Center
Cincinnati 45202 (513) 381-2838

Incorporated in 1941 in OH.
Donor(s): Louise Taft Semple.†
Financial data (yr. ended 12/31/87): Assets, $10,979,817 (M); expenditures, $1,279,815, including $1,072,533 for 36 grants (high: $500,000; low: $1,500; average: $5,000-$30,000).
Purpose and activities: Support for the fine arts, social services and a community fund, higher and secondary education, hospitals, and health organizations.
Types of support: Building funds, endowment funds, scholarship funds, fellowships, professorships, matching funds.
Limitations: Giving primarily in Cincinnati, OH. No grants to individuals, or for general purposes or research; no loans.
Application information:
Initial approach: Letter
Deadline(s): None
Board meeting date(s): Apr., July, Oct., and Dec.
Final notification: 3 months
Write: Dudley S. Taft, Pres.
Officers: Dudley S. Taft,* Pres.; James R. Bridgeland, Jr.,* Secy.; Norma Gentzler, Treas.
Trustees:* Mrs. John T. Lawrence, Jr., Walter L. Lingle, Jr., Nellie Taft, Robert Taft, Jr., Mrs. Robert A. Taft II.
Number of staff: None.
Employer Identification Number: 310653526

2570
The Richard H. and Ann Shafer Foundation
Eight East Long St., Rm. 400
Columbus 43215 (614) 224-8111

Donor(s): Richard A. Shafer,† Ohio Road Paving Co.
Financial data (yr. ended 12/31/87): Assets, $1,926,234 (M); gifts received, $5,000; expenditures, $97,277, including $92,600 for 27 grants (high: $30,000; low: $100).
Purpose and activities: Emphasis on hospitals and health agencies, higher education, cultural programs, and social service agencies.
Limitations: Giving limited to OH.
Application information:
Initial approach: Proposal
Deadline(s): Dec. 15
Write: Fannie L. Shafer, Mgr.
Trustees: Fannie L. Shafer, Mgr.; Homer W. Lee, John Reese.
Employer Identification Number: 316029095

2571
Sheller-Globe Foundation
c/o Ohio Citizens Bank
P.O. Box 1688
Toledo 43603 (419) 255-8840
Application address: Sheller Globe Corp., 1505 Jefferson Sve., Toledo, Ohio 43697; Tel.: (419) 255-8840

Trust established in 1956 in OH.
Donor(s): Sheller-Globe Corp.
Financial data (yr. ended 12/31/87): Assets, $305,921 (M); gifts received, $100,000; expenditures, $149,718, including $145,601 for 18 grants (high: $30,000; low: $1,000).
Purpose and activities: Primarily local giving, with emphasis on community funds, youth agencies, hospitals, the arts, and higher education.
Limitations: Giving primarily in OH. No grants to individuals.
Application information:
Initial approach: Letter
Copies of proposal: 1
Board meeting date(s): As required
Write: William H. Patterson, Mgr.
Advisory Committee: Chester Devenow, Alfred Grava, Lawrence King, William H. Patterson, Ralph Hill.
Trustee: Ohio Citizens Trust Co.
Employer Identification Number: 346518486

2572
The Sherman-Standard Register Foundation
626 Albany St.
Dayton 45408

Incorporated in 1955 in OH.
Donor(s): Standard Register Co.
Financial data (yr. ended 11/30/88): Assets, $616,647 (M); gifts received, $200,000; expenditures, $190,528, including $190,033 for 66 grants (high: $47,000; low: $120).
Purpose and activities: Giving for community funds, higher education, youth agencies, health, civic affairs, and culture.
Limitations: Giving primarily in OH.
Application information: Applications not accepted.
Officers: William P. Sherman, Pres.; J.L. Sherman, V.P.; Otto F. Stock, Secy.; Craig J. Brown, Treas.
Employer Identification Number: 316026027

2573
The Sherwick Fund
c/o The Cleveland Foundation
1400 Hanna Bldg.
Cleveland 44115 (216) 861-3810

Incorporated in 1953 in OH.
Donor(s): John Sherwin, Frances Wick Sherwin.
Financial data (yr. ended 12/31/87): Assets, $9,660,556 (M); expenditures, $583,212, including $512,933 for grants.
Purpose and activities: A supporting fund of The Cleveland Foundation; emphasis on youth agencies, health, education, social services, cultural programs, and community funds.
Types of support: Seed money.
Limitations: Giving limited to the greater Cleveland, OH, area and Lake County. No grants to individuals, or for endowment funds, general operating budgets, or deficit financing; no loans.
Publications: Annual report, application guidelines, program policy statement.
Application information:
Initial approach: Full proposal or letter of inquiry
Copies of proposal: 2
Deadline(s): Apr. 1 and Oct. 1
Board meeting date(s): Usually in June and Dec.
Final notification: 1 month after board meets
Write: Mary Louise Hahn, Secy.-Treas.
Officers: John Sherwin,* Chair.; John Sherwin, Jr.,* Pres.; Homer C. Wadsworth,* V.P.; Mary Louise Hahn, Secy.-Treas.
Trustees:* John J. Dwyer, Harvey G. Oppmann.
Number of staff: 1 full-time professional; 1 part-time support.
Employer Identification Number: 346526395

2574
The Sherwin-Williams Foundation
101 Prospect Ave., N.W., 12th Fl.
Cleveland 44115 (216) 566-2511

Incorporated in 1964 in OH.
Donor(s): The Sherwin-Williams Co.
Financial data (yr. ended 12/31/87): Assets, $1,986,170 (L); gifts received, $2,368,500; expenditures, $466,846, including $411,750 for 138 grants (high: $30,000; low: $250; average: $1,000-$3,000) and $54,846 for 305 employee matching gifts.
Purpose and activities: Supports health and human services agencies, higher education, civic affairs, and cultural programs.
Types of support: Operating budgets, building funds, equipment, employee matching gifts.
Limitations: Giving primarily in areas of company headquarters and plants; most grants are in Cleveland, OH. No support for sectarian, labor, veterans' or fraternal organizations, or for organizations assisted by taxes; no operating support for organizations assisted by United Way. No grants to individuals, or for endowment funds, annual campaigns, seed money, emergency funds, deficit financing, land acquisition, special projects, research, scholarships, fellowships, publications, advertising, or conferences; no loans.
Application information:
Initial approach: Letter

Copies of proposal: 1
Deadline(s): Submit proposal preferably in Jan., Apr., July, or Oct.
Board meeting date(s): Mar., June, Sept., and Dec.
Final notification: 1 month
Write: Barbara Gadosik, Dir., Corp. Contribs.
Trustees: John G. Breen, Chair.; Thomas A. Commes, T. Kroeger, Thomas R. Miklich.
Number of staff: 1 full-time professional; 1 part-time support.
Employer Identification Number: 346555476

2575
The Simmons Charitable Trust
c/o Miners & Mechanics Savings & Trust Co.
124 North Fourth St.
Steubenville 43952

Established in 1977 in OH.
Financial data (yr. ended 5/31/88): Assets, $1,846,855 (M); expenditures, $81,961, including $68,725 for 29 grants (high: $10,000; low: $225) and $7,329 for 1 grant to an individual.
Purpose and activities: Grants for health and social services agencies, youth organizations, education, and religious giving; awards music scholarships to students of Steubenville High School.
Types of support: Student aid.
Limitations: Giving primarily in Jefferson County, OH, with emphasis on Steubenville.
Application information:
Initial approach: Letter
Trustee: Miners and Mechanics Savings & Trust.
Employer Identification Number: 346743541

2576
The Slemp Foundation
c/o Star Bank, N.A., Cincinnati
P.O. Box 1118
Cincinnati 45201 (513) 632-4585

Trust established in 1943 in VA.
Donor(s): C. Bascom Slemp.†
Financial data (yr. ended 6/30/87): Assets, $7,618,752 (M); gifts received, $1,300; expenditures, $449,037, including $177,750 for 26 grants (high: $54,000; low: $50) and $205,600 for 257 grants to individuals.
Purpose and activities: Giving for the maintenance of three named institutions; charitable and educational purposes and for the improvement of health of residents of Lee and Wise counties, VA, or their descendants, wherever located; also giving for scholarships, a museum, libraries, and hospitals.
Types of support: Student aid, building funds, emergency funds, endowment funds, equipment, lectureships, renovation projects, scholarship funds, seed money.
Limitations: Giving limited to Lee and Wise counties, VA.
Publications: 990-PF.
Application information: Application forms provided for scholarship applicants.
Initial approach: Letter
Copies of proposal: 1
Deadline(s): Oct. 1 for scholarships
Board meeting date(s): Apr., July, and Nov.
Trustees: Campbell S. Edmonds, Mary Virginia Edmonds, John A. Reid, Nancy E. Smith.
Employer Identification Number: 316025080

2577
The Eleanor Armstrong Smith Charitable Fund
1100 National City Bank Bldg.
Cleveland 44114 (216) 566-5500

Established in 1974 in OH.
Financial data (yr. ended 12/31/87): Assets, $3,226,938 (M); expenditures, $207,976, including $184,562 for 15 grants (high: $75,000; low: $610).
Purpose and activities: Support primarily for the environment, health care, and the arts, including a musical arts association.
Types of support: General purposes.
Limitations: Giving primarily in the Cleveland, OH, area. No grants to individuals; no loans.
Application information:
Initial approach: Letter
Write: Andrew L. Fabens, III
Trustee: Eleanor A. Smith.
Employer Identification Number: 237374137

2578
The Smith Family Foundation
19701 North Park Blvd.
Shaker Heights 44122

Incorporated in 1986 in OH.
Financial data (yr. ended 10/31/87): Assets, $278,180 (M); gifts received, $400,000; expenditures, $135,148, including $134,292 for 59 grants (high: $35,000; low: $50).
Purpose and activities: Support primarily for higher education, community funds and the performing arts.
Types of support: General purposes.
Application information: Contributes only to pre-selected organizations. Applications not accepted.
Trustees: Gretchen P. Smith, Ward Smith.
Employer Identification Number: 346874008

2579
The Kelvin and Eleanor Smith Foundation
1100 National City Bank Bldg.
Cleveland 44114
Application address: 29425 Chagrin Blvd., Suite 303, Pepper Pike, OH 44122

Incorporated in 1955 in OH.
Donor(s): Kelvin Smith.†
Financial data (yr. ended 10/31/88): Assets, $29,857,125 (M); gifts received, $651,727; expenditures, $1,225,997, including $952,833 for 41 grants (high: $133,333; low: $1,500).
Purpose and activities: Giving for education, cultural affairs, hospitals, and conservation.
Types of support: Operating budgets, continuing support, annual campaigns, seed money, building funds, equipment.
Limitations: Giving primarily in the greater Cleveland, OH, area. No grants to individuals, or for endowment funds, scholarships, fellowships, or matching gifts; no loans.
Publications: Application guidelines.
Application information:
Initial approach: Letter
Copies of proposal: 2
Deadline(s): None
Board meeting date(s): May and Oct.
Final notification: 2 to 3 months
Write: Douglas W. Richardson, Pres.
Officers and Trustees: John L. Dampeer, Pres. and Treas.; Lucia S. Nash, V.P.; Cara S. Stirn, V.P.; Ellen Mavec, Secy.; Douglas W. Richardson, Ralph S. Tyler, Jr.
Number of staff: None.
Employer Identification Number: 346555349

2580
The South Waite Foundation
AmeriTrust Co.
900 Euclid Ave.
Cleveland 44101

Incorporated in 1953 in OH.
Donor(s): Francis M. Sherwin,† Margaret H. Sherwin.
Financial data (yr. ended 12/31/87): Assets, $1,869,046 (M); expenditures, $142,216, including $125,738 for 26 grants (high: $12,400; low: $500).
Purpose and activities: Grants usually to those local organizations that the foundation is familiar with; emphasis on community funds, the arts, secondary education, health and medical research, and youth organizations.
Limitations: Giving limited to the Cleveland, OH, area. No grants to individuals, or for scholarships.
Application information:
Deadline(s): Oct.
Officers and Trustees: Brian Sherwin, Pres.; Margaret H. Sherwin, V.P.; Donald W. Gruetner, Secy.-Treas.; Sherman Dye.
Employer Identification Number: 346526411

2581
The Standard Products Foundation
2130 West 110th St.
Cleveland 44102 (216) 281-8300

Incorporated in 1953 in OH.
Donor(s): Standard Products Co.
Financial data (yr. ended 6/30/87): Assets, $8,342,060 (M); expenditures, $338,224, including $331,544 for 111 grants (high: $50,000; low: $100).
Purpose and activities: Emphasis on community funds, higher education, hospitals, cultural programs, and social service and youth agencies.
Limitations: Giving primarily in Cleveland, OH.
Application information:
Initial approach: Letter
Deadline(s): None
Write: Robert C. Jacob, V.P.
Officers and Trustees: James S. Reid, Jr., Pres.; Robert C. Jacob, V.P.; James E. Chapman, Secy.; Joseph A. Robinson, Treas.; E.B. Brandon, John T. Frieg.
Employer Identification Number: 346525047

2582
Star Bank, N.A., Cincinnati Foundation
(Formerly The First National Bank of Cincinnati Foundation)
c/o The First National Bank of Cincinnati
425 Walnut St.
Cincinnati 45202 (513) 632-4524

Trust established in 1967 in OH.
Financial data (yr. ended 12/31/87): Assets, $1,155,860 (M); gifts received, $220,000; expenditures, $503,350, including $500,804 for 49 grants (high: $87,500; low: $200).
Purpose and activities: Grants for community funds, hospitals, cultural programs, and higher education.
Types of support: General purposes, building funds, equipment, land acquisition, operating budgets.
Limitations: Giving limited to the greater Cincinnati, OH, area. No grants to individuals, or for endowment funds, research, scholarships, fellowships, or matching gifts; no loans.
Application information:
Initial approach: Letter
Deadline(s): None
Board meeting date(s): Monthly
Write: David L. Dowen
Officers and Trustees: Oliver W. Waddell, Chair.; Samuel M. Cassidy, Pres.; Herman J. Guckenberger, Jr., Secy.; James R. Bridgeland, Jr., J.P. Hayden, Jr., Mark T. Johnson, Thomas J. Klinedinst, William N. Liggett, Philip M. Meyers, Jr., Thomas E. Petry, William W. Wommack.
Number of staff: None.
Employer Identification Number: 316079013

2583
The Stocker Foundation
3535 East Erie Ave.
Lorain 44054 (216) 288-4581
Additional address: P.O. Box 2118, Lorain, OH 44054

Incorporated in 1979 in OH.
Donor(s): Beth K. Stocker.
Financial data (yr. ended 9/30/87): Assets, $8,043,366 (M); gifts received, $175,000; expenditures, $500,838, including $440,343 for 68 grants (high: $25,000; low: $300; average: $2,000-$10,000).
Purpose and activities: Emphasis on short-term youth development programs, social service agencies offering solutions to specific problems, education (including higher education), aid to the handicapped, and cultural programs.
Types of support: Operating budgets, continuing support, seed money, emergency funds, building funds, equipment, endowment funds, matching funds, scholarship funds, publications, renovation projects, research, special projects.
Limitations: Giving primarily in Lorain County, OH, and southern AZ. No support for religious organizations for religious purposes, governmental services, or public school services required by law. No grants to individuals, or for annual campaigns or deficit financing; no loans.
Publications: Application guidelines, informational brochure (including application guidelines).
Application information:
Initial approach: Telephone, letter, or proposal
Copies of proposal: 5
Deadline(s): Feb. 1, May 15, and Oct. 1
Board meeting date(s): Mid-winter, summer, and fall
Final notification: 1 month after board meetings
Write: Sara Jane Norton, Dir.
Officers and Trustees: Beth K. Stocker, Pres.; Sara Jane Norton, Secy.-Treas. and Dir.; Mary Ann Dobras, Anne Woodling, Nancy Elizabeth Woodling.
Corporate Trustee: Ameritrust Co.
Number of staff: 1 part-time professional; 1 part-time support.
Employer Identification Number: 341293603

2584
The Stouffer Corporation Fund
29800 Bainbridge Rd.
Solon 44139 (216) 248-3600

Incorporated in 1952 in OH.
Donor(s): The Stouffer Corp.
Financial data (yr. ended 6/30/88): Assets, $1,629,020 (M); gifts received, $500,000; expenditures, $407,808, including $402,550 for 277 grants (high: $77,500; low: $100; average: $250-$1,000).
Purpose and activities: Grants primarily for community funds, higher education, cultural programs, and health.
Types of support: Operating budgets, continuing support, annual campaigns, seed money, emergency funds, building funds, equipment, endowment funds, scholarship funds, special projects, capital campaigns, renovation projects.
Limitations: Giving primarily in OH. No grants to individuals, or for matching gifts, research, publications, or conferences; no loans.
Application information:
Initial approach: Letter
Copies of proposal: 1
Deadline(s): Submit proposal preferably in Aug. through Oct.
Board meeting date(s): Sept., Nov., Feb., and May
Write: Robert W. Loehr, Secy.
Officers: Thomas Stauffer, Pres.; Powell Woods, V.P.; Robert W. Loehr, Secy.-Treas.
Trustees: Richard Atkinson, James M. Biggar, Ed Frantz, William Hulett, David Jennings, Anthony Martino, Wayne Partin, John Quagliata.
Number of staff: None.
Employer Identification Number: 346525245

2585
The Frank M. Tait Foundation
Courthouse Plaza, S.W., 10th Fl.
Dayton 45402 (513) 222-2401

Incorporated in 1955 in OH.
Donor(s): Frank M. Tait,† Mrs. Frank M. Tait.†
Financial data (yr. ended 12/31/88): Assets, $4,446,734 (M); expenditures, $268,085, including $215,785 for 40 grants (high: $22,130; low: $50; average: $1,000-$5,000).
Purpose and activities: Support for youth agencies and cultural programs.
Types of support: Annual campaigns, seed money, building funds, equipment, special projects, capital campaigns, matching funds.
Limitations: Giving limited to Montgomery County, OH. No grants to individuals, or for endowment funds, operating budgets, continuing support, emergency funds, deficit financing, research, publications, conferences, scholarships, or fellowships; no loans.
Publications: Annual report (including application guidelines).
Application information:
Initial approach: Letter
Copies of proposal: 1
Deadline(s): Mar. 15, June 15, Sept. 15, and Dec. 15
Board meeting date(s): Apr., July, Oct., and Jan.
Final notification: 2 months
Write: Susan T. Rankin, Exec. Dir.
Officers: Richard F. Beach,* Pres.; Frederick W. Schantz, V.P.; Susan T. Rankin, Secy.-Treas. and Exec. Dir.
Trustees:* Irvin G. Bieser, Peter H. Forster, Alexander J. Williams.
Number of staff: 1 part-time professional.
Employer Identification Number: 316037499

2586
Nelson Talbott Foundation
911 East Ohio Bldg.
Cleveland 44114

Established in 1947 in OH.
Donor(s): Nelson S. Talbott.
Financial data (yr. ended 9/30/87): Assets, $1,487,951 (M); gifts received, $10,283; expenditures, $65,882, including $40,947 for 69 grants.
Purpose and activities: Support primarily for cultural institutions, wilderness societies, environmental concerns, and social services.
Limitations: Giving primarily in Cleveland, OH.
Trustees: Malvin Banks, Josephine L. Talbott, Nelson S. Talbott.
Employer Identification Number: 316039441

2587
Tamarkin Foundation
P.O. Box 1588
Youngstown 44501-1588 (216) 792-3811

Established in 1968.
Donor(s): Tamarkin Co., Project Four, Inc., S&H Co., members of the Tamarkin family.
Financial data (yr. ended 12/31/86): Assets, $483,016 (M); gifts received, $292,980; expenditures, $159,169, including $158,950 for 31 grants (high: $115,300; low: $50).
Purpose and activities: Primarily giving for Jewish welfare agencies and temple support; also support for hospitals and cultural institutions.
Types of support: Operating budgets, special projects, building funds.
Limitations: Giving primarily in OH.
Application information:
Deadline(s): None

Write: Bertram Tamarkin, Pres., or Nathan H. Monus, Secy.
Officers and Trustees: Bertram Tamarkin, Pres.; Jerry P. Tamarkin, V.P.; Nathan H. Monus, Secy.; Jack P. Tamarkin, Treas.; Arthur N.K. Friedman, Michael I. Monus.
Employer Identification Number: 341023645

2588
The Timken Company Charitable Trust
1835 Dueber Ave., S.W.
Canton 44706 (216) 438-4005

Trust established in 1947 in OH.
Donor(s): The Timken Co.
Financial data (yr. ended 12/31/87): Assets, $1,004,902 (M); expenditures, $226,182, including $214,675 for 30 grants (high: $33,250; low: $350; average: $1,000-$15,000).
Purpose and activities: Support primarily for higher education and community funds; some support for cultural programs.
Types of support: Operating budgets.
Limitations: Giving primarily in OH. No grants to individuals.
Application information:
Deadline(s): None
Final notification: Varies
Write: Ward J. Timken, Advisor
Advisor: Ward J. Timken.
Trustee: The Central Trust Co. of Northern Ohio, N.A.
Number of staff: 3 full-time professional; 3 full-time support.
Employer Identification Number: 346534265

2589
Timken Foundation of Canton
236 Third St., S.W.
Canton 44702 (216) 455-5281

Incorporated in 1934 in OH.
Donor(s): Members of the Timken family.
Financial data (yr. ended 9/30/88): Assets, $121,190,000 (M); expenditures, $5,861,000, including $5,687,000 for 43 grants (high: $1,007,000; low: $2,000).
Purpose and activities: To promote broad civic betterment by capital fund grants; grants largely for colleges, schools, hospitals, cultural centers, conservation and recreation, and other charitable institutions.
Types of support: Building funds, equipment, capital campaigns.
Limitations: Giving primarily in areas of Timken Company domestic operations. No grants to individuals, or for operating budgets.
Application information:
Deadline(s): None
Board meeting date(s): As required
Final notification: As soon as possible
Write: Don D. Dickes, Secy.
Officers and Trustees: Ward J. Timken, Pres.; W.R. Timken, V.P.; W.R. Timken, Jr., V.P.; Joseph F. Toot, Jr., V.P.; Don D. Dickes, Secy.-Treas.
Number of staff: 1 full-time professional; 1 part-time support.
Employer Identification Number: 346520254

2590
Toledo Community Foundation, Inc.
1540 National Bank Bldg.
Toledo 43604-1108 (419) 241-5049

Community foundation established in 1924 in OH by trust agreement; reactivated in 1973.
Financial data (yr. ended 12/31/87): Assets, $13,224,736 (M); gifts received, $795,204; expenditures, $1,569,197, including $1,381,632 for 355 grants (high: $38,667; low: $250; average: $15,000-$20,000).
Purpose and activities: Support for projects which promise to affect a broad segment of the citizens of northwestern OH or which tend to help those living in an area not being adequately served by local community resources. Areas of interest include social services and youth programs, arts and culture, hospitals and health asociations, education, conservation, religion, government and urban affairs, and united funds.
Types of support: Seed money, matching funds, conferences and seminars, equipment, renovation projects, special projects.
Limitations: Giving primarily in northwestern OH, with emphasis on the greater Toledo area. No grants to individuals, or for annual campaigns, operating budgets, or endowment funds.
Publications: Annual report, informational brochure, application guidelines.
Application information: Application form required.
Copies of proposal: 1
Deadline(s): Submit proposal preferably in months when board meets; deadlines Mar. 1, June 1, Sept. 1, and Dec. 1
Board meeting date(s): Jan., Apr., July, and Oct.
Final notification: 2 months
Write: Miriam M. Bixler, Dir.
Officers and Trustees: Lawrence T. Foster, Pres.; Steven Timonere, V.P.; Thomas H. Anderson, Secy.; Robert J. Kirk, Treas.; Robert V. Franklin, Caroline Jobst, Marvin S. Kobacker, Duane Stranahan, Jr., H. Lawrence Thompson, Jr.
Number of staff: 3 full-time professional; 1 full-time support.
Employer Identification Number: 237284004

2591
The Toledo Trust Foundation
c/o Toledo Trust Co.
Three Seagate
Toledo 43603 (419) 259-8217

Trust established in 1953 in OH.
Donor(s): The Toledo Trust Co.
Financial data (yr. ended 12/31/86): Assets, $374,036 (M); gifts received, $500,000; expenditures, $464,883, including $460,976 for 46 grants (high: $111,000; low: $25; average: $1,000-$10,000) and $2,557 for 11 employee matching gifts.
Purpose and activities: Support for community funds and higher and secondary education; grants also for cultural activities and youth agencies.
Types of support: Operating budgets, continuing support, annual campaigns, emergency funds, building funds, equipment, land acquisition, consulting services, technical assistance, program-related investments, employee matching gifts, matching funds.
Limitations: Giving primarily in OH. No grants to individuals, or for start-up funds, deficit financing, or matching gifts; no loans.
Application information:
Initial approach: Letter
Deadline(s): None
Board meeting date(s): Monthly
Final notification: 2 months
Write: James E. Lupe, V.P., Toledo Trust Co.
Trustees: Edwin M. Bergsmark, Robert Foster, George W. Haigh, The Toledo Trust Co.
Number of staff: None.
Employer Identification Number: 346504808

2592
Tremco Foundation
10701 Shaker Blvd.
Cleveland 44104

Trust established in 1950 in OH.
Donor(s): Tremco Manufacturing Co.
Financial data (yr. ended 12/31/86): Assets, $1,397,933 (M); gifts received, $200,000; expenditures, $234,011, including $225,355 for 150 grants (high: $50,600; low: $20; average: $300) and $4,885 for 43 employee matching gifts.
Purpose and activities: Emphasis on community funds, higher education, and cultural programs.
Types of support: Building funds, capital campaigns, continuing support, employee matching gifts, fellowships, general purposes, employee-related scholarships, scholarship funds.
Limitations: Giving primarily in Cleveland, OH. No grants to individuals, or for annual campaigns, conferences and seminars, consulting services, deficit financing, endowment funds, equipment, exchange programs, internships, land acquisition, matching funds, operating budgets, professorships, publications, renovation projects, research, seed money, special projects, or technical assistance; no loans.
Trustees: Leigh Carter, Gordon D. Harnett, Mark A. Steinbock.
Employer Identification Number: 346527566

2593
The Treu-Mart Fund
c/o The Cleveland Foundation
1400 Hanna Bldg.
Cleveland 44115 (216) 861-3810
Additional address: c/o R. Michael Cole, The Jewish Community Federation of Cleveland, 1750 Euclid Ave., Cleveland, OH 44115; Tel.: (216) 566-9200

Established in 1980 in OH.
Donor(s): Elizabeth M. Treuhaft, William C. Treuhaft.†
Financial data (yr. ended 12/31/87): Assets, $1,802,539 (M); gifts received, $1,000; expenditures, $103,531, including $93,800 for grants (high: $20,000; low: $1,000).
Purpose and activities: Supporting organization of The Cleveland Foundation and The Jewish Community Federation of

Cleveland; organization grants primarily for projects benefitting residents of the greater Cleveland area, especially those incorporating demonstration or research elements. Support largely for community development, cultural programs, health planning, and social service activities, including Jewish welfare agencies.
Types of support: Research, special projects.
Limitations: Giving primarily in Cleveland, OH. No grants to individuals, or for operating budgets or annual campaigns.
Publications: Annual report, program policy statement, application guidelines.
Application information:
Initial approach: Proposal
Copies of proposal: 2
Deadline(s): Feb. 1 and Sept. 1
Board meeting date(s): Usually in Mar. and Oct.
Final notification: 3 months
Write: Mary Louise Hahn, Treas.
Officers: Elizabeth M. Treuhaft,* Chair.; Arthur W. Treuhaft,* Pres.; Homer C. Wadsworth,* V.P.; Henry L. Zucker,* V.P.; Howard R. Berger, Secy.; Mary Louise Hahn, Treas.
Trustees:* Frances M. King, Albert B. Ratner, Lloyd S. Schwenger.
Number of staff: 1 full-time professional; 1 full-time support.
Employer Identification Number: 341323364

2594
The Treuhaft Foundation
10701 Shaker Blvd.
Cleveland 44104 (216) 229-0166

Trust established in 1955 in OH.
Donor(s): Mrs. William C. Treuhaft, William C. Treuhaft.†
Financial data (yr. ended 12/31/87): Assets, $12,595,919 (M); expenditures, $1,188,963, including $1,101,049 for 78 grants (high: $240,000; low: $125; average: $200-$50,000).
Purpose and activities: Support for higher education, Jewish welfare funds, music and cultural programs, and health and welfare programs.
Types of support: Operating budgets, annual campaigns, seed money, emergency funds, building funds, endowment funds, professorships, special projects, research, publications, conferences and seminars.
Limitations: Giving primarily in the Cleveland, OH, area. No grants to individuals, or for capital grants, deficit financing, or hardware or software equipment; general support only to specific organizations of interest to the Treuhaft family; no loans.
Application information:
Initial approach: Letter
Deadline(s): None
Board meeting date(s): As required
Final notification: After board meeting
Write: Mrs. William C. Treuhaft, Chair.
Trustees: Mrs. William C. Treuhaft, Chair.; Irwin M. Feldman, Arthur W. Treuhaft.
Number of staff: None.
Employer Identification Number: 341206010

2595
Trinova Corporate Giving Program
1705 Indian Wood Circle
Maumee 43537 (419) 891-2200
Application addresses: organizations in northwest OH, write to the Maumee OH, address. Others write to the nearest subsidiary or plant

Purpose and activities: Trinova has a highly decentralized giving program. Contributions of $5,000 or more are paid through Trinova Philanthropic Foundation. Contributions less than $5,000 are paid through the direct giving program. Areas of interest include the arts, business, higher education, educational research, health, and youth.
Types of support: Annual campaigns, building funds, continuing support, employee matching gifts, general purposes.
Limitations: Giving limited to northwest OH for headquarters; operating companies handle requests in their areas.
Application information: At this time, guidelines and support area programs are in the process of being evaluated. Requests should be addressed to the nearest plant or subsidiary.
Initial approach: Letter; write to nearest operating company of Trinova, Vickers, or Aeroquip
Copies of proposal: 1
Deadline(s): None
Final notification: As soon as proposal is received
Write: Richard G. Rump, Mgr., Financial Communications

2596
Trinova Corporation Philanthropic Foundation
(Formerly Libbey-Owens-Ford Philanthropic Foundation)
1705 Indian Wood Circle
Maumee 43537

Donor(s): Trinova Corp.**Financial data** (yr. ended 12/31/87): Assets, $707,959 (M); gifts received, $155,170; expenditures, $7,118.
Purpose and activities: To promote a healthy and vibrant society by supporting those health, educational, cultural, and social organizations that work to advance the public welfare in the interests of the company, its employees, customers, shareowners, and the general public. Contributions are distributed in the greater Toledo area and company plant communities; some support is given to national organizations.
Limitations: Giving primarily in the greater Toledo, OH, area. No grants to individuals or for endowments; no loans.
Application information:
Initial approach: Proposal
Deadline(s): None
The Toledo Trust Co.
Employer Identification Number: 346504806

2597
TRW Corporate Giving Program
1900 Richmond Rd.
Cleveland 44124 (216) 291-7164

Financial data (yr. ended 12/31/88): $1,000,000 for grants.
Purpose and activities: Support for community and civic affairs, arts and culture, environmental concerns, equal rights, health, legal services, education, science, United Way, welfare, women's issues and youth programs in their areas. Types of support include volunteer recruitment and use of company facilities and donations of the company's primary goods or services. Each division gives up to $5,000 per year.
Types of support: Annual campaigns, general purposes, research, scholarship funds, in-kind gifts.
Application information: Include project description, project budget, a financial report, 501(c)(3), and board donors lists.
Write: Donna Cummings, Mgr. Contribs.

2598
TRW Foundation
1900 Richmond Rd.
Cleveland 44124 (216) 291-7164

Incorporated in 1953 in OH as the Thompson Products Foundation; became the Thompson Ramo Wooldridge Foundation in 1958, and adopted its present name in 1965.
Donor(s): TRW, Inc.
Financial data (yr. ended 12/31/88): Assets, $18,000,000 (M); gifts received, $14,000,000; expenditures, $7,117,708, including $5,610,212 for 367 grants (high: $375,000; low: $500; average: $2,500-$50,000), $7,000 for 5 grants to individuals and $1,448,643 for 3,470 employee matching gifts.
Purpose and activities: Grants largely for higher education, particularly for engineering, technical, science, and/or business administration programs, and community funds; limited support for hospitals, welfare agencies, youth agencies, and civic and cultural organizations.
Types of support: Employee matching gifts, scholarship funds, professorships, fellowships, research, operating budgets, equipment, general purposes, matching funds, special projects.
Limitations: Giving primarily in TRW plant communities, with some emphasis on Cleveland, OH. No support for religious purposes, fraternal or labor organizations, or private elementary or secondary schools. No grants to individuals, or for endowment funds.
Publications: Annual report, program policy statement, application guidelines, grants list.
Application information: The employee-related scholarship program was discontinued in 1986; past obligations continue to be paid.
Initial approach: Proposal
Copies of proposal: 1
Deadline(s): Submit proposals preferably in Aug. or Sept.; deadline Sept. 1 for organizations already receiving support from the foundation
Board meeting date(s): Dec.
Final notification: 60 to 90 days
Write: Donna L. Cummings, Mgr.

Officers: Howard V. Knicely, Pres.; Edward N. Button,* V.P.; Alan F. Senger, V.P.; James M. Roosevelt, Secy.; Robert G. Gornall, Treas.; Edward J. Toth, Cont.
Trustees:* Martin A. Coyle, Joseph T. Gorman.
Number of staff: 2 full-time professional; 2 full-time support.
Employer Identification Number: 346556217
Recent arts and culture grants:
Business Committee for the Arts, NYC, NY, $5,000. For operating support. 1987.
California Museum Foundation, Los Angeles, CA, $10,000. For aerospace wing support. 1987.
Cleveland Ballet, Cleveland, OH, $32,000. For operating support. Grant shared with San Jose Ballet. 1987.
Cleveland Institute of Art, Cleveland, OH, $25,000. For multiyear pledge for capital campaign. 1987.
Cleveland Opera, Cleveland, OH, $25,000. For operating support. 1987.
Cleveland Play House, Cleveland, OH, $45,000. For multiyear pledge for capital campaign. 1987.
Fords Theater, DC, $5,000. For operating support. 1987.
Great Lakes Theater Festival, Cleveland, OH, $45,000. For operating support. 1987.
Henry Ford Museum and Greenfield Village, Dearborn, MI, $5,000. For special exhibit support. 1987.
Japan Society, NYC, NY, $10,000. For special project support. 1987.
John F. Kennedy Center for the Performing Arts, DC, $10,000. For operating support. 1987.
Lawrence Hall of Science, Berkeley, CA, $5,000. For special project support for education program. 1987.
Los Angeles Music Center, Los Angeles, CA, $45,000. For operating support. 1987.
Musical Arts Association, Cleveland, OH, $25,000. For operating support. 1987.
Orange County Performing Arts Center, Costa Mesa, CA, $35,000. For multiyear pledge for capital campaign. 1987.
Orchestra Hall, Detroit, MI, $5,000. For capital campaign. 1987.
Playhouse Square Foundation, Cleveland, OH, $60,000. For multiyear pledge for capital campaign. 1987.
University Circle, Cleveland, OH, $7,500. For operating support. 1987.
Western Reserve Historical Society, Cleveland, OH, $10,000. For operating support. 1987.
Wolf Trap Foundation for the Performing Arts, Vienna, VA, $7,500. For operating support for capital campaign. 1987.

2599
Marcia Brady Tucker Foundation, Inc.
106 Colonial Center Bldg.
Cincinnati 45227 (513) 561-3164

Incorporated in 1941 in NY.
Donor(s): Marcia Brady Tucker.†
Financial data (yr. ended 12/31/86): Assets, $7,569,804 (M); gifts received, $94,699; expenditures, $508,805, including $447,201 for 54 grants (high: $60,000).
Purpose and activities: Support mainly for education, conservation, and medical, religious or cultural institutions.
Types of support: Matching funds, capital campaigns, emergency funds, equipment, scholarship funds, seed money.
Limitations: No grants to individuals.
Application information: Grants made only on the initiative of the foundation. Applications not accepted.
Write: Luther Tucker, Pres.
Officers and Directors: Luther Tucker, Pres.; Marcia T. Boogaard, Secy.; Carll Tucker III, Treas.; Elizabeth Sanders, Naomi Stoehr, Gay Tucker, Luther Tucker, Jr., Nicholas Tucker, Toinette Tucker.
Number of staff: 1 part-time support.
Employer Identification Number: 136161561

2600
Van Dorn Foundation
2700 East 79th St.
Cleveland 44104 (216) 361-5234

Established in 1985 in OH.
Donor(s): Van Dorn Co.
Financial data (yr. ended 12/31/88): Assets, $17,754 (M); gifts received, $200,000; expenditures, $322,112, including $272,377 for 188 grants (high: $5,000; low: $25) and $49,735 for 46 employee matching gifts.
Purpose and activities: Interests include higher and secondary education, cultural organizations, health, and community funds.
Types of support: Annual campaigns, capital campaigns, employee matching gifts.
Limitations: Giving primarily in the greater Cleveland, OH, area.
Application information:
Initial approach: Letter, outlining usage of monies requested
Copies of proposal: 1
Deadline(s): None
Board meeting date(s): Quarterly
Final notification: By end of calendar year
Write: Herman R. Ceccardi, Treas.
Officers and Trustees: Lawrence C. Jones, Chair.; Robert N. Jones, Pres.; Campbell W. Elliott, V.P., Public Affairs; Dennis A. Buss, V.P.; Wolfgang Liebertz, V.P.; Richard A. Plociak, V.P.; George M. Smart, V.P.; Samuel H. Smith, Jr., V.P.; John L. Dampeer, Secy.; Herman R. Ceccardi, Treas.; James R. Heckman, Cont.
Employer Identification Number: 341464280

2601
The Van Wert County Foundation
101-1/2 East Main St.
Van Wert 45891 (419) 238-1743

Incorporated in 1925 in OH.
Donor(s): Charles F. Wassenberg,† Gaylord Saltzgaber,† John D. Ault,† Kernan Wright,† Richard L. Klein,† Hazel Gleason,† Constance Eirich.†
Financial data (yr. ended 12/31/87): Assets, $5,469,958 (M); gifts received, $130,110; expenditures, $309,323, including $193,828 for grants (high: $33,000; low: $190; average: $500) and $60,498 for 102 grants to individuals.
Purpose and activities: Emphasis on scholarships in art, music, agriculture, and home economics; support also for elementary and secondary education, youth agencies, an art center, recreational facilities, and programs dealing with alcoholism and drug abuse.
Types of support: General purposes, equipment, student aid.
Limitations: Giving limited to Van Wert County, OH. No grants for endowment funds, or for matching gifts; no loans.
Publications: 990-PF, application guidelines.
Application information: Application forms and guidelines issued for scholarship program.
Initial approach: Letter or proposal
Copies of proposal: 1
Deadline(s): Submit proposal in May or Nov.; deadlines May 25 and Nov. 25
Board meeting date(s): June and Dec.
Final notification: 1 week
Write: Robert W. Games, Exec. Secy.
Officer: Robert W. Games, Exec. Secy.
Trustees: D.L. Brumback, Jr., William S. Derry, A.C. Diller, Kenneth Koch, G.E. Leslie, Watson Ley, Paul W. Purmont, Jr., Charles Ross, C. Allan Runser, Donald C. Sutton, Roger Thompson, Sumner Walters, Larry Wendel, G. Dale Wilson, Michael R. Zedaker.
Number of staff: 1 part-time professional; 1 part-time support.
Employer Identification Number: 340907558

2602
Walter E. and Caroline H. Watson Foundation
P.O. Box 450
Youngstown 44501 (216) 744-9000

Trust established in 1964 in OH.
Donor(s): Walter E. Watson.†
Financial data (yr. ended 12/31/87): Assets, $3,954,765 (M); expenditures, $251,409, including $249,732 for 64 grants (high: $46,974; low: $250; average: $1,000-$5,000).
Purpose and activities: To support public institutions of learning in OH and public and charitable institutions in the Mahoning Valley, OH; emphasis on hospitals, youth agencies, community development, and cultural programs.
Types of support: Annual campaigns, equipment, general purposes, renovation projects, special projects.
Limitations: Giving primarily in OH. No grants to individuals, or for endowment funds or operating budgets.
Application information:
Board meeting date(s): Semiannually
Trustee: The Dollar Savings and Trust Co.
Employer Identification Number: 346547726

2603
The Raymond John Wean Foundation
c/o Second National Bank of Warren, Trust Dept.
108 Main St.
Warren 44481 (216) 394-5600

Trust established in 1949 in OH.
Donor(s): Raymond J. Wean.†
Financial data (yr. ended 12/31/86): Assets, $31,291,968 (M); gifts received, $6,597,590;

expenditures, $1,083,775, including $933,834 for 608 grants (high: $75,000; low: $50; average: $100-$20,000).
Purpose and activities: Grants for higher and secondary education, hospitals, health agencies, youth agencies, Protestant church support, cultural programs, and social services.
Types of support: Continuing support.
Limitations: Giving primarily in OH, Palm Beach, FL, and PA, especially Pittsburgh.
Application information: Contributes only to pre-selected organizations. Applications not accepted.
Board meeting date(s): As required
Write: Raymond J. Wean, Jr., Chair.
Administrators: Raymond J. Wean, Jr., Chair.; Raymond J. Wean III, Vice-Chair.; Clara G. Petrosky, Secy.; Gordon B. Wean.
Trustee: Second National Bank of Warren.
Number of staff: None.
Employer Identification Number: 346505038

2604
Maxwell C. Weaver Foundation
c/o First National Bank of Cincinnati
P.O. Box 1118
Cincinnati 45201 (513) 632-4579

Established in 1985 in OH.
Financial data (yr. ended 12/31/87): Assets, $1,030,208 (M); expenditures, $93,609, including $83,341 for 14 grants (high: $23,850; low: $1,000).
Purpose and activities: Support primarily for arts and health programs for youth; support also for secondary education.
Application information:
Deadline(s): None
Write: Terry Crilley
Trustee: First National Bank of Cincinnati.
Employer Identification Number: 316275346

2605
The S. K. Wellman Foundation
1800 Huntington Bldg.
Cleveland 44115
Application address: 548 Leader Bldg., Cleveland, OH 44114; Tel.: (216) 696-4640

Incorporated in 1951 in OH.
Donor(s): S.K. Wellman.†
Financial data (yr. ended 12/31/86): Assets, $5,619,887 (M); expenditures, $369,228, including $328,000 for 63 grants (high: $25,000; low: $500).
Purpose and activities: Grants for education, cultural activities, health agencies, and social services.
Limitations: Giving primarily in OH. No grants to individuals.
Publications: Application guidelines.
Application information:
Initial approach: Letter
Deadline(s): Dec. 31
Write: R. Dugald Pearson, Exec. Secy.
Officers: John M. Wilson, Jr.,* Pres.; R. Dugald Pearson, Exec. Secy.
Trustees:* Franklin B. Floyd, Suzanne O'Gara, Mrs. John M. Wilson, Jr.
Employer Identification Number: 346520032

2606
White Consolidated Industries Foundation, Inc.
c/o White Consolidated Industries, Inc.
11770 Berea Rd.
Cleveland 44111 (216) 252-8385

Established in 1951 in OH.
Donor(s): White Consolidated Industries, Inc., The Tappan, Co.
Financial data (yr. ended 12/31/87): Assets, $1,329,020 (M); expenditures, $480,000, including $437,000 for grants (high: $56,000; low: $100) and $18,000 for 150 employee matching gifts.
Purpose and activities: Emphasis on community funds, higher education, hospitals, and cultural organizations.
Types of support: General purposes, building funds, equipment, research, continuing support, operating budgets, employee matching gifts.
Limitations: Giving primarily in Cleveland and Columbus, OH.
Application information: Application form required.
Initial approach: Proposal
Copies of proposal: 1
Deadline(s): None
Board meeting date(s): As required
Write: Daniel R. Elliott, Jr., Chair.
Officers and Trustees: Daniel R. Elliott, Jr., Chair.; Donald C. Blasius, V.P.; Lawrence W. Kenney, V.P. and Treas.; W.G. Bleakley, V.P.
Employer Identification Number: 046032840

2607
The E. F. Wildermuth Foundation
4770 Indianola Ave., Suite 140
Columbus 43214 (614) 846-5838

Established in 1962.
Financial data (yr. ended 12/31/86): Assets, $2,972,329 (M); expenditures, $191,898, including $122,016 for 25 grants (high: $40,000; low: $500).
Purpose and activities: Grants primarily for higher education, particularly optometric schools and research; support also for the arts and a church.
Limitations: Giving primarily in OH.
Application information:
Deadline(s): Aug. 15
Write: Homer W. Lee, Treas.
Trustees: H. Wald Ewalt, Pres.; Faurest Borton, V.P.; David R. Patterson, V.P.; Bettie A. Kalb, Secy.; Homer W. Lee, Treas.; Karl Borton, J. Patrick Campbell, Genevieve Connable, W. Daniel Driscoll, David T. Patterson, Phillip N. Phillipson.
Employer Identification Number: 316050202

2608
Williamson Company Foundation
3500 Madison Rd.
Cincinnati 45209-1185

Financial data (yr. ended 12/31/87): Expenditures, $50,444 for 51 grants (high: $17,917; low: $50).
Purpose and activities: Support for United Way, public health and welfare, culture, and education.
Trustee: W.D. Wilder.
Employer Identification Number: 316031985

2609
The Marguerite M. Wilson Foundation
29525 Chagrin Blvd., No. 305
Pepper Pike 44122 (216) 292-5730

Established in 1953 in Ohio.
Financial data (yr. ended 12/31/87): Assets, $1,516,574 (M); expenditures, $88,586, including $82,000 for 6 grants (high: $30,000; low: $1,000).
Purpose and activities: Emphasis on hospitals, private schools, cultural organizations, and social services.
Limitations: Giving primarily in OH. No grants to individuals.
Application information:
Deadline(s): None
Final notification: Response only to those applications which the trustees wish to pursue
Officers and Trustees: Pauline W. Horner, Pres. and Treas.; James H. Dempsey, Jr., Secy.; Holly Munger Book, Douglas M. Horner, James M. Horner, Jr., Myron W. Munger, Robert L. Munger, Jr.
Employer Identification Number: 346521259

2610
Wodecroft Foundation
2100 DuBois Tower
Cincinnati 45202 (513) 621-6747

Trust established in 1958 in OH.
Donor(s): Roger Drackett.
Financial data (yr. ended 12/31/86): Assets, $5,402,995 (M); expenditures, $159,840, including $154,000 for 39 grants (high: $15,000; low: $500).
Purpose and activities: Emphasis on cultural programs, hospitals, and conservation.
Limitations: Giving primarily in OH. No grants to individuals.
Application information:
Initial approach: Letter
Board meeting date(s): As required
Write: H. Truxtun Emerson, Jr., Secy.
Officers and Trustees: Richard W. Barrett, Chair.; H. Truxtun Emerson, Jr., Secy.; Jeanne H. Drackett.
Employer Identification Number: 316047601

2611
Wolfe Associates Inc.
34 South Third St.
Columbus 43216 (614) 461-5220

Incorporated in 1973 in OH.
Donor(s): The Dispatch Printing Co., The Ohio Co., WBNS TV, Inc., RadiOhio, Inc., Video Indiana, Inc.
Financial data (yr. ended 6/30/88): Assets, $5,765,431 (M); gifts received, $1,840,333; expenditures, $669,416, including $620,858 for 59 grants (high: $232,500; low: $500;

average: $1,000-$10,000) and $38,750 for 26 employee matching gifts.
Purpose and activities: Giving for a community fund, higher and secondary education, hospitals and medical research, cultural activities, and youth and social service agencies.
Types of support: Operating budgets, continuing support, annual campaigns, emergency funds, building funds, equipment, matching funds, professorships, employee matching gifts, scholarship funds.
Limitations: Giving primarily in central OH. No grants to individuals, or for research, demonstration projects, publications, or conferences.
Publications: Program policy statement, application guidelines.
Application information:
Initial approach: Letter
Deadline(s): None
Board meeting date(s): Mar., June, Sept., and Dec.
Final notification: After board meeting
Write: A. Kenneth Pierce, Jr., V.P.
Officers: John W. Wolfe, Pres.; A. Kenneth Pierce, Jr., V.P. and Secy.-Treas.; Nancy Wolfe Lane, V.P.; William C. Wolfe, Jr., V.P.
Number of staff: None.
Employer Identification Number: 237303111

2612
The Wuliger Foundation, Inc.
Bond Court Bldg.
1300 East Ninth St.
Cleveland 44114 (216) 522-1310

Incorporated in 1956 in OH.
Donor(s): Ernest M. Wuliger, Allan M. Unger, Ohio-Sealy Mattress Manufacturing Co.
Financial data (yr. ended 12/31/87): Assets, $2,558,019 (M); gifts received, $1,538,250; expenditures, $1,187,586, including $1,169,630 for 117 grants (high: $327,500; low: $20; average: $500-$30,000).
Purpose and activities: Giving for Jewish welfare funds; support also for higher education, hospitals, and the arts.
Limitations: Giving primarily in OH. No grants to individuals.
Application information:
Initial approach: Proposal
Deadline(s): None
Board meeting date(s): As necessary
Final notification: Within 2 weeks if possible
Write: Ernest M. Wuliger, Pres.
Officers: Ernest M. Wuliger, Pres. and Treas.; Maurice Saltzman, V.P.; Timothy F. Wuliger, Secy.
Number of staff: None.
Employer Identification Number: 346527281

2613
XTEK Foundation
11451 Reading Rd.
Cincinnati 45241 (513) 733-7800

Incorporated in 1962 in OH.
Donor(s): XTEK, Inc.
Financial data (yr. ended 12/31/87): Assets, $353,253 (M); gifts received, $9,150; expenditures, $88,091, including $88,091 for 37 grants (high: $40,000; low: $100).
Purpose and activities: Emphasis on a community fund, cultural programs, and higher education; support also for health and youth agencies.
Limitations: Giving primarily in the Greater Cincinnati, OH, area.
Application information:
Deadline(s): None
Write: James D. Kiggen, Pres.
Officers: James D. Kiggen, Pres.; Robert C. Wood, Secy.
Employer Identification Number: 316029606

2614
The Leo Yassenoff Foundation
37 North High St., Suite 304
Columbus 43215 (614) 221-4315

Incorporated in 1947 in DE.
Donor(s): Leo Yassenoff.†
Financial data (yr. ended 12/31/87): Assets, $10,176,234 (M); expenditures, $1,374,375, including $1,263,719 for 109 grants (high: $300,000; low: $200; average: $1,000-$20,000).
Purpose and activities: Support primarily for social services, education, health and hospitals, youth agencies, religion, civic affairs, and arts and cultural programs.
Types of support: Seed money, emergency funds, building funds, equipment, land acquisition, matching funds, technical assistance, special projects, research, publications, scholarship funds, capital campaigns, renovation projects, general purposes.
Limitations: Giving limited to Franklin County, OH. No support for religious purposes, except to donor-designated recipients. No grants to individuals, or for operating support, annual campaigns, endowments, deficit financing, or debt reduction; no loans.
Publications: Annual report, application guidelines.
Application information:
Initial approach: Telephone, letter, or proposal
Copies of proposal: 1
Deadline(s): 1st business day of every other month beginning in Jan.
Board meeting date(s): Every other month beginning in Jan.
Final notification: 2 months
Write: Cynthia A. Cecil Lazarus, Exec. Dir.
Officers and Trustees:* Melvin L. Schottenstein,* Chair.; Frederick E. Dauterman, Jr.,* Vice-Chair.; Mary J. Hoover,* Secy.-Treas.; Cynthia A. Cecil Lazarus, Exec. Dir.
Number of staff: 1 full-time professional; 1 part-time professional; 1 full-time support; 1 part-time support.
Employer Identification Number: 310829426

2615
The Youngstown Foundation
c/o The Dollar Savings & Trust Company
P.O. Box 450
Youngstown 44501 (216) 744-9000

Community foundation established in 1918 in OH by bank resolution.
Financial data (yr. ended 12/31/87): Assets, $24,147,938 (M); gifts received, $985,959; expenditures, $2,276,279, including $2,091,161 for 144 grants (high: $298,900; low: $200; average: $1,000-$20,000) and $4,500 for 9 loans to individuals.
Purpose and activities: To support local charitable and educational agencies for the betterment of the community; grants for capital purposes, with emphasis on aid to crippled children, community funds, youth agencies, music and cultural programs, and hospitals.
Types of support: Building funds, equipment, annual campaigns, student loans, general purposes, renovation projects, special projects.
Limitations: Giving limited to the Youngstown, OH, area. No grants to individuals (except for limited student loans), or for endowment funds, operating budgets, seed money, emergency funds, deficit financing, continuing support, land acquisition, demonstration projects, publications, conferences, research, scholarships, fellowships, or matching gifts.
Publications: 990-PF, informational brochure.
Application information:
Initial approach: Proposal
Copies of proposal: 1
Deadline(s): None
Board meeting date(s): Jan., Mar., May, July, Sept., Nov., and Dec.
Write: Herbert H. Pridham, Secy.
Officer: Herbert H. Pridham, Secy.; Aileen Gottschling.
Distribution Committee: D.W. McGowan, Chair.; William M. Cafaro, Vice-Chair.; C. Gilbert James, William R. Powell, Bernard J. Yozwiak.
Trustee: The Dollar Savings and Trust Co.
Number of staff: None.
Employer Identification Number: 346515788

OKLAHOMA

2616
Mary K. Ashbrook Foundation for El Reno, Oklahoma
P.O. Box 627
El Reno 73036 (405) 262-4684

Established in 1978 in OK.
Donor(s): Mary K. Ashbrook.†
Financial data (yr. ended 6/30/87): Assets, $1,553,392 (M); expenditures, $166,213, including $142,538 for 15 grants (high: $55,000; low: $500).
Purpose and activities: Grants for education, cultural programs, civic affairs, community development, and welfare; support also for a hospital.
Types of support: Continuing support, seed money, emergency funds, building funds, equipment, land acquisition, matching funds, scholarship funds, special projects.

Limitations: Giving limited to El Reno, OK. No grants to individuals, or for deficit financing, endowment funds, research, fellowships, demonstration projects, publications, or conferences; no loans.
Publications: Application guidelines.
Application information: Application form required.
Initial approach: Letter or telephone
Deadline(s): Submit proposal by first of each month
Board meeting date(s): Monthly
Final notification: 1 month
Write: Virginia Sue Douglas, Trustee
Trustees: Betty Dittmer, Virginia Sue Douglas, Alleen Poole.
Number of staff: None.
Employer Identification Number: 731049531

2617
Hu & Eva Maud Bartlett Foundation
P.O. Box 1368
Sapulpa 74067

Established in 1950 in OK.
Financial data (yr. ended 12/31/87): Assets, $1,020,915 (M); expenditures, $74,251, including $53,710 for 4 grants (high: $50,710; low: $750).
Purpose and activities: Support primarily for a medical center; giving also for historical preservation and general charitable purposes.
Limitations: Giving primarily in Sapulpa, OK.
Application information:
Initial approach: Letter
Deadline(s): None
Trustees: Barbara Benedict, Charley Sherwood, Sherry Sherwood.
Employer Identification Number: 736092249

2618
Grace & Franklin Bernsen Foundation
2600 Fourth National Bank Bldg.
Tulsa 74119

Established in 1985 in OK.
Donor(s): Grace Bernsen,† Franklin Bernsen.†
Financial data (yr. ended 9/30/88): Assets, $19,564,729 (M); expenditures, $1,118,131, including $736,750 for 34 grants (high: $100,000; low: $1,000).
Purpose and activities: Support primarily for Christian religious organizations, the arts, medical sciences and youth organizations.
Types of support: General purposes.
Limitations: Giving primarily in in the Tulsa, OK, area.
Trustees: Howard M. Maher, Paul R. Peterson, Donald E. Pray, John D. Strong.
Number of staff: 3 full-time professional.
Employer Identification Number: 237009414

2619
Max and Tookah Campbell Foundation
P.O. Box 701051
Tulsa 74170

Trust established in 1964 in OK.
Donor(s): Max W. Campbell.†
Financial data (yr. ended 12/31/87): Assets, $5,423,241 (M); expenditures, $489,175, including $261,226 for 67 grants (high: $25,000; low: $50).
Purpose and activities: Emphasis on Protestant church support and higher education; grants also for hospitals and health agencies, cultural programs, and youth agencies.
Limitations: Giving primarily in OK.
Application information: Contributes only to pre-selected organizations. Applications not accepted.
Trustees: Pauline Holderman, Joan Lepley Hunt, Robert G. Hunt.
Employer Identification Number: 736111626

2620
H. A. and Mary K. Chapman Charitable Trust
One Warren Place, Suite 1816
6100 South Yale
Tulsa 74136 (918) 496-7882

Trust established in 1976 in OK.
Donor(s): H.A. Chapman.†
Financial data (yr. ended 12/31/88): Assets, $36,004,235 (M); expenditures, $2,016,038, including $1,615,500 for 36 grants (high: $467,000; low: $1,000; average: $44,875).
Purpose and activities: Grants largely for education, particularly higher education, and a hospital, social services and cultural programs.
Limitations: Giving primarily in Tulsa, OK.
Application information: Application form required.
Deadline(s): None
Board meeting date(s): Quarterly and as needed
Write: Donne Pitman, Trustee
Trustees: Ralph L. Abercrombie, Donne W. Pitman.
Number of staff: None.
Employer Identification Number: 736177739

2621
The Cuesta Foundation, Inc.
One Williams Center, Suite 4400
Tulsa 74172

Incorporated in 1962 in OK.
Donor(s): Charles W. Oliphant, Allene O. Mayo, Allen G. Oliphant, Jr., Gertrude O. Sundgren, Eric B. Oliphant, Nancy B. Deane.
Financial data (yr. ended 4/30/87): Assets, $1,936,152 (M); gifts received, $1,000; expenditures, $168,274, including $153,750 for 63 grants (high: $25,000; low: $500; average: $2,000).
Purpose and activities: Emphasis on higher education; support also for the performing arts, social agencies, and a population control organization.
Types of support: Building funds, continuing support, endowment funds.
Limitations: Giving primarily in OK. No grants to individuals.
Publications: Financial statement, informational brochure.
Application information:
Initial approach: Letter or proposal
Copies of proposal: 1
Deadline(s): Sept. 1
Write: Donald P. Carpenter, Treas.
Officers and Directors: Charles W. Oliphant, Chair.; Eric B. Oliphant, Pres.; Richard E. Wright III, Secy.; Donald P. Carpenter, Treas.; Allene O. Mayo, Arline B. Oliphant, Gertrude O. Oliphant.
Employer Identification Number: 736091550

2622
First Interstate Bank of Oklahoma Foundation
P.O. Box 25189
Oklahoma City 73125-0189 (405) 272-4000

Established in 1987 in OK.
Donor(s): First Interstate Bank of Oklahoma.
Financial data (yr. ended 12/31/87): Assets, $0 (M); expenditures, $0.
Purpose and activities: Support for health and welfare, education, and civic and cultural programs. Major supporter of United Way and Allied Arts; no grants were made in 1987, first year of operation.
Types of support: Capital campaigns, equipment, operating budgets.
Limitations: Giving limited to OK. No support for partisan political organizations, sectarian organizations, or foundations which are themselves grant-making bodies. No grants to individuals, or for trips or tours, advertising, or endowments.
Application information: Letter or telephone call for guidelines and application form. Application form required.
Board meeting date(s): Foundation board meets monthly
Write: Sheila Mayberry, Admin. Asst.
Officers: Richard G. Hastings III,* Chair.; Sheila Mayberry, Secy.
Directors:* Lynn Groves, Ann Herring, Jay Jones, Veda Ware.
Employer Identification Number: 736237244

2623
The Glass-Glen Burnie Foundation
116 East Delaware
Nowata 74048

Established in 1986 in OK.
Donor(s): Julian W. Glass, Jr.
Financial data (yr. ended 12/31/87): Assets, $1,012,021 (M); gifts received, $130,032; expenditures, $60,426, including $25,000 for 1 grant.
Purpose and activities: A private operating foundation in the process of establishing a museum; support for historic preservation and general charitable purposes.
Limitations: No grants to individuals.
Publications: Annual report.
Application information: Contributes only to pre-selected organizations. Applications not accepted.
Director: R. Lee Taylor, Exec. Dir.
Trustees: David D. Denham, Julian W. Glass, Jr., Patrick C. Hayes, Irene S. Wischer.
Number of staff: 1 part-time support.
Employer Identification Number: 731267576

2624
Herbert and Roseline Gussman Foundation
3200 First National Tower
Tulsa 74103

Established in 1951 in OK.
Donor(s): Herbert Gussman, Roseline Gussman, Barbara Gussman, Ellen Jane Adelson.
Financial data (yr. ended 12/31/87): Assets, $2,250,599 (M); expenditures, $446,973, including $437,257 for 58 grants (high: $210,100; low: $10).
Purpose and activities: Emphasis on Jewish giving, cultural programs, health services, and educational institutions.
Limitations: Giving primarily in OK.
Application information: Applications not accepted.
Trustees: Herbert Gussman, Roseline Gussman.
Employer Identification Number: 736090063

2625
Harris Foundation, Inc.
6403 Northwest Grand Blvd.
Oklahoma City 73116 (405) 848-3371

Incorporated in 1938 in OK.
Donor(s): Vernon V. Harris.†
Financial data (yr. ended 12/31/87): Assets, $1,323,596 (M); expenditures, $373,594, including $352,470 for 58 grants (high: $45,000; low: $150).
Purpose and activities: Support for higher education, youth and health agencies, Protestant church support, social services, and cultural programs.
Types of support: Building funds, equipment, fellowships, operating budgets, renovation projects.
Limitations: Giving primarily in OK, with emphasis on Oklahoma City.
Publications: Financial statement.
Application information:
Deadline(s): None
Write: Margaret Harris Long, Pres.
Officers and Directors: Margaret Harris Long, Pres.; Pat J. Patterson, Secy.; Judith Harris Garrett, Jane C. Harris, William J. Harris, William V. Harris, Robert F. Long.
Employer Identification Number: 736093072

2626
The Helmerich Foundation
1579 East 21st St.
Tulsa 74114 (918) 742-5531

Established in 1965 in OK.
Donor(s): W.H. Helmerich.†
Financial data (yr. ended 9/30/88): Assets, $13,876,453 (M); gifts received, $1,143,381; expenditures, $1,094,481, including $1,000,000 for 5 grants (high: $250,000; low: $50,000).
Purpose and activities: Giving of large capital gifts, with emphasis on Protestant church support and religious organizations, and on cultural programs, youth and health agencies, and a community development project.
Types of support: Building funds, equipment, capital campaigns, operating budgets.
Limitations: Giving limited to the Tulsa, OK, area. No grants to individuals, or for general support, continuing support, annual campaigns, seed money, emergency funds, deficit financing, land acquisition, endowment funds, matching gifts, scholarships, fellowships, program support, research, demonstration projects, publications, or conferences; no loans.
Publications: Application guidelines, program policy statement.
Application information:
Initial approach: Letter
Copies of proposal: 1
Deadline(s): None
Board meeting date(s): As required
Final notification: 4 weeks
Write: W.H. Helmerich III, Trustee
Trustee: W.H. Helmerich III.
Number of staff: None.
Employer Identification Number: 736105607

2627
Historical Preservation, Inc.
429 Northwest 16th St.
Oklahoma City 73103 (405) 272-4363

Established in 1971 in OK.
Donor(s): Carolyn Skelly Burford, Mrs. Hugh M. Johnson.†
Financial data (yr. ended 12/31/88): Assets, $1,788,354 (L); expenditures, $109,489, including $6,525 for 4 grants (high: $5,000; low: $25; average: $25-$5,000).
Purpose and activities: Giving is primarily concerned with the preservation, restoration and maintenance of historic sites, located within and around the Heritage Hills Historical Preservation District; the perpetuation of the historical and cultural heritage of the area; and assisting in the development of projects for zoning and land use to eliminate blighting influences and foster planning, development, beautification, and improvement within the parameters of historical preservation.
Types of support: Equipment, building funds, renovation projects, special projects, publications.
Limitations: Giving limited to the Heritage Hills Historical Preservation District in Oklahoma City, OK, and surrounding urban areas. No grants to individuals.
Application information:
Write: G.P. Johnson Hightower, Treas.
Officers: Chuck Wiggin, Pres.; Bill Carey, 1st V.P.; John Hefner, 2nd V.P.; John Yoeckel, Community Liaison Representative; Gary Bloom, Secy.; G.P. Johnson Hightower, Treas.
Employer Identification Number: 237023817

2628
Willard Johnston Foundation, Inc.
6100 North Western
Oklahoma City 73118-1098 (405) 840-5585

Established in 1951 in OK.
Financial data (yr. ended 12/31/87): Assets, $1,170,060 (M); expenditures, $90,079, including $59,745 for grants.
Purpose and activities: Support for higher education, health and social services, and the arts.
Types of support: General purposes, scholarship funds.
Limitations: Giving primarily in Oklahoma City, Ok.
Application information:
Initial approach: Letter
Deadline(s): None
Write: George J. Records, Mgr.
Manager: George J. Records.
Employer Identification Number: 736093829

2629
The Kerr Foundation, Inc.
6301 North Western, Suite 130
Oklahoma City 73118 (405) 842-1510

Incorporated in 1963 in OK, and reincorporated in 1985.
Donor(s): Grayce B. Kerr Flynn.†
Financial data (yr. ended 12/31/87): Assets, $19,905,058 (M); expenditures, $1,567,017, including $1,038,170 for 44 grants (high: $150,000; low: $150; average: $10,000-$50,000) and $150,000 for loans.
Purpose and activities: Giving primarily for education, cultural activities, and health. Generally all grants are challenge grants.
Types of support: Matching funds.
Limitations: Giving primarily in TX, AR, KS, CO, MO, NM, and OK. No grants to individuals, or generally for continuing support.
Publications: Application guidelines.
Application information: Application form required.
Initial approach: Letter
Copies of proposal: 4
Deadline(s): None
Board meeting date(s): Quarterly
Write: Anne Holzberlein, Admin. Asst.
Officers and Trustees: Robert S. Kerr, Jr., Pres. and Chair.; Lou C. Kerr, V.P. and Secy.; Gerald R. Marshall, Treas.; Royce Hammons, Sharon Kerr, Steven Kerr, Elmer B. Staats.
Number of staff: 2 part-time professional; 1 full-time support.
Employer Identification Number: 731256122

2630
The Robert S. and Grayce B. Kerr Foundation, Inc.
6301 North Western, Suite 220
Oklahoma City 73118 (405) 848-0975

Chartered in 1986 in OK.
Donor(s): Grayce B. Kerr Flynn.†
Financial data (yr. ended 1/31/87): Assets, $18,957,125 (M); gifts received, $9,845; expenditures, $1,253,758, including $979,313 for 31 grants (high: $200,000; low: $500).
Purpose and activities: Grants primarily for education, including higher education, the performing and visual arts, environmental conservation, and human services.
Types of support: Emergency funds, equipment, fellowships, general purposes, matching funds, operating budgets, renovation projects, scholarship funds, seed money, special projects, technical assistance, building funds, conferences and seminars, internships.
Limitations: Giving limited to OK. No support for sectarian religious activities. No grants to individuals, or for endowments, annual

campaigns, memberships, or medical or scientific research.
Publications: Informational brochure.
Application information: Application form required.
Initial approach: Letter
Copies of proposal: 7
Deadline(s): Mar. 1 and Oct. 1
Board meeting date(s): June and Dec.
Final notification: 1 week after board meeting
Write: Anne Hodges Morgan, Pres.
Officers and Trustees: Joffa Kerr, Chair.; Anne Hodges Morgan, Pres.; N. Martin Stringer, Secy.; William G. Kerr, Treas.
Number of staff: 1 full-time professional; 1 full-time support.
Employer Identification Number: 731256123

2631
Kirkpatrick Foundation, Inc.
1300 North Broadway Dr.
Oklahoma City 73103 (405) 235-5621

Incorporated in 1955 in OK.
Donor(s): Eleanor B. Kirkpatrick, John E. Kirkpatrick, Kirkpatrick Oil Co., Joan E. Kirkpatrick, Kathryn T. Blake.†
Financial data (yr. ended 12/31/88): Assets, $18,546,000 (M); expenditures, $1,065,451, including $906,817 for 129 grants (high: $571,432; low: $100; average: $100-$25,000) and $2,394 for 1 in-kind gift.
Purpose and activities: Support for community programs, education, cultural programs, including fine and performing arts groups and historic preservation, and social service projects.
Types of support: Operating budgets, continuing support, annual campaigns, emergency funds, endowment funds, seed money, special projects.
Limitations: Giving primarily in Oklahoma City, OK. No support for hospitals, religious organizations, or mental health agencies. No grants to individuals; no loans.
Publications: Informational brochure.
Application information: Application form required.
Copies of proposal: 1
Deadline(s): 2 weeks before board meets
Board meeting date(s): Mar., June, Sept., and Dec.
Write: Marilyn B. Myers, Dir.
Officers and Directors: John E. Kirkpatrick, Chair.; Joan E. Kirkpatrick, Pres.; Christian K. Keesee, V.P.; Eleanor J. Maurer, Secy.; Eleanor B. Kirkpatrick, Treas.; Jack Abernathy, John L. Belt, Douglas Cummings, Dan Hogan, Marilyn B. Myers, Charles E. Nelson, Morrison G. Tucker.
Number of staff: 2 part-time professional; 1 full-time support; 1 part-time support.
Employer Identification Number: 730701736

2632
J. A. LaFortune Foundation
1801 Fourth National Bank Bldg.
Tulsa 74119

Established in 1945 in OK.
Financial data (yr. ended 12/31/87): Assets, $463,123 (M); expenditures, $123,857, including $120,000 for 10 grants (high: $50,000; low: $500).
Purpose and activities: Giving primarily for higher education, community development and cultural programs.
Limitations: No grants to individuals; no loans.
Application information: Generally contributes to pre-selected organizations.
Initial approach: Letter
Deadline(s): None
Write: Corinne Childs, Treas.
Officers and Trustees: Gertrude L. LaFortune, Pres.; Robert J. LaFortune, Secy.; Corinne Childs, Treas.; J.A. LaFortune, Jr., Mary Ann L. Wilcox.
Employer Identification Number: 736092073

2633
The J. E. and L. E. Mabee Foundation, Inc.
3000 Mid-Continent Tower
Tulsa 74103 (918) 584-4286

Incorporated in 1948 in DE.
Donor(s): J.E. Mabee,† L.E. Mabee.†
Financial data (yr. ended 8/31/88): Assets, $455,194,780 (M); expenditures, $14,232,342, including $13,047,900 for 78 grants (high: $1,500,000; low: $2,000; average: $100,000-$500,000).
Purpose and activities: To aid Christian religious organizations, charitable organizations, vocational and technical schools, and institutions of higher learning; and to support hospitals and other agencies and institutions engaged in the discovery, treatment, and care of diseases.
Types of support: Building funds, equipment, matching funds, capital campaigns, land acquisition, renovation projects, continuing support.
Limitations: Giving limited to OK, TX, KS, AR, MO, and NM. No support for secondary or elementary education, or tax-supported institutions. No grants to individuals, or for research, endowment funds, scholarships, fellowships, or operating expenses; no loans.
Publications: Program policy statement, application guidelines.
Application information:
Initial approach: Proposal
Copies of proposal: 1
Deadline(s): Mar. 1, June 1, Sept. 1, and Dec. 1
Board meeting date(s): Jan., Apr., July, and Oct.
Final notification: After board meetings
Write: Guy R. Mabee, Chair.
Officers and Trustees: Guy R. Mabee, Chair.; John H. Conway, Jr., Vice-Chair. and Secy.-Treas.; John W. Cox, Vice-Chair.; Joe Mabee, Vice-Chair.; Donald P. Moyers, Vice-Chair.
Number of staff: 5 part-time professional; 6 full-time support.
Employer Identification Number: 736090162
Recent arts and culture grants:
Galveston Historical Foundation, Galveston, TX, $100,000. For building renovation. 1987.
Lamesa Dawson County Museum Association, Lamesa, TX, $100,000. For museum renovation. 1987.
Oklahoma Veterans Memorial, Oklahoma City, OK, $25,000. For new museum. 1987.
Resource Center of the Ninety-Nines, Oklahoma City, OK, $100,000. For museum renovation. 1987.
San Antonio Art Institute, San Antonio, TX, $750,000. For new multi-purpose building. 1987.

2634
McCasland Foundation
P.O. Box 400
McCasland Bldg.
Duncan 73534 (405) 252-5580

Trust established in 1952 in OK.
Donor(s): Members of the McCasland family, Mack Oil Co., Jath Oil Co., and others.
Financial data (yr. ended 12/31/87): Assets, $21,707,012 (M); gifts received, $367,500; expenditures, $1,071,674, including $939,272 for 120 grants (high: $135,000; low: $100; average: $1,000-$40,000).
Purpose and activities: Emphasis on higher education, hospitals, community welfare, and cultural programs.
Types of support: Scholarship funds, general purposes, building funds.
Limitations: Giving primarily in OK and the Southwest, including TX and KS.
Application information:
Initial approach: Letter
Deadline(s): None
Board meeting date(s): Variable; usually quarterly
Final notification: After board meetings
Write: W.H. Phelps, Trustee
Trustees: Mary Frances Maurer, T.H. McCasland, Jr., W.H. Phelps.
Number of staff: None.
Employer Identification Number: 736096032

2635
The McMahon Foundation
714-716 C Ave.
P.O. Box 2156
Lawton 73502 (405) 355-4622

Incorporated in 1940 in OK.
Donor(s): Eugene D. McMahon,† Louise D. McMahon.†
Financial data (yr. ended 3/31/87): Assets, $27,016,087 (M); expenditures, $1,147,520, including $797,764 for 25 grants (high: $243,000; low: $400; average: $1,000-$55,000).
Purpose and activities: Support for education, social welfare and youth agencies, the arts, and community development projects.
Types of support: Annual campaigns, building funds, capital campaigns, emergency funds, equipment, general purposes, land acquisition, matching funds, renovation projects, scholarship funds.
Limitations: Giving primarily in Lawton and Comanche County, OK.
Application information:
Initial approach: Letter
Copies of proposal: 1
Deadline(s): 1 week prior to board meeting
Board meeting date(s): Monthly
Final notification: 2-3 days after board meeting
Write: James F. Wood, Dir.

Officers: Gale Sadler,* Secy.-Treas.; James F. Wood, Dir.
Trustees:* Charles S. Graybill, M.D., Chair.; Manville Redman, Vice-Chair.; Kenneth Bridges, Ronald E. Cagle, M.D., Orban E. Sanders, Frank C. Sneed.
Number of staff: 1 full-time professional; 1 full-time support.
Employer Identification Number: 730664314

2636
The Samuel Roberts Noble Foundation, Inc.

P.O. Box 2180
Ardmore 73402 (405) 223-5810

Trust established in 1945 in OK; incorporated in 1952.
Donor(s): Lloyd Noble.†
Financial data (yr. ended 10/31/88): Assets, $318,315,572 (M); gifts received, $1,000; expenditures, $17,940,028, including $7,623,285 for 138 grants (high: $407,400; low: $1,000; average: $5,000-$150,000), $57,500 for 52 grants to individuals, $65,945 for 32 employee matching gifts and $8,406,905 for foundation-administered programs.
Purpose and activities: Supports its own three operating programs: 1) basic biomedical research pertaining to cancer and degenerative diseases; 2) plant research, with the objective of genetic engineering of plants; and 3) agricultural research, consultation, and demonstration, along with wildlife management, for the benefit of rural and urban people. Primarily, grants are for higher education, for health research pertaining to cancer and degenerative diseases, and for health delivery systems. Matching gift program for Noble Co. employees.
Types of support: Research, employee-related scholarships, seed money, building funds, equipment, endowment funds, matching funds, employee matching gifts.
Limitations: Giving primarily in the Southwest, with emphasis on OK. No grants to individuals (except through the scholarship program for children of employees of Noble organizations); no loans.
Publications: Annual report.
Application information: Application form required.
Initial approach: Letter
Copies of proposal: 1
Deadline(s): 6 weeks prior to board meeting dates
Board meeting date(s): Usually in Jan., Apr., July, and Oct.
Final notification: 2 weeks after board meetings
Write: John F. Snodgrass, Pres.
Officers: John F. Snodgrass,* Pres.; Larry Pulliam, V.P. and Treas.; M.K. Patterson, Jr., V.P.; Jackie N. Skidmore, Secy.
Trustees:* Ann Noble Brown, David R. Brown, Michael A. Cawley, Vivian N. Dubose, William R. Goddard, John R. March, Edward E. Noble, Mary Jane Noble, Sam Noble, Joseph L. Parker.
Number of staff: 63 full-time professional; 57 full-time support; 10 part-time support.
Employer Identification Number: 730606209
Recent arts and culture grants:
Ballet Oklahoma, Oklahoma City, OK, $6,000. For Apprentice Program. 1987.
Cimarron Circuit Opera Company, Norman, OK, $31,500. To purchase portable sound and stage equipment to enhance performance quality while on tour. 1987.
McCurtain County Historical Society, Idabel, OK, $125,000. For Barnes-Stevenson House purchase. 1987.
McCurtain County Historical Society, Idabel, OK, $49,697. For Barnes-Stevenson House renovations and repairs. 1987.
National Cowboy Hall of Fame and Western Heritage Center, Oklahoma City, OK, $500,000. For operating and endowment fund drive. 1987.
Oklahoma Heritage Association, Oklahoma City, OK, $20,000. For Trackmaker series research and publication. 1987.
Oklahoma Symphony Orchestra, Oklahoma City, OK, $5,000. For general operating support. 1987.
Philbrook Art Center, Tulsa, OK, $400,000. Toward Museum School construction. 1987.
Robert W. Woodruff Arts Center, Atlanta, GA, $10,000. For annual support campaign. 1987.
Westminster Schools, Atlanta, GA, $200,000. Toward construction of Broyles Art and Student Activities Center. 1987.

2637
The Vivian Bilby Noble Foundation, Inc.

P.O. Box 817
Ardmore 73402 (405) 223-5810

Trust established in 1936 in OK; incorporated in 1959.
Donor(s): Lloyd Noble.†
Financial data (yr. ended 12/31/88): Assets, $2,445,797 (M); expenditures, $126,956, including $121,440 for 19 grants (high: $17,000; low: $1,000; average: $5,000-$10,000).
Purpose and activities: Emphasis on education, church support, and youth agencies; some support also for cultural programs and community social service organizations.
Types of support: Operating budgets, continuing support, annual campaigns, building funds, equipment, land acquisition, endowment funds, capital campaigns, general purposes, renovation projects, special projects.
Limitations: Giving primarily in the southwestern U.S. No grants to individuals, or for seed money, emergency funds, deficit financing, matching gifts, scholarships, fellowships, research, publications, or conferences; no loans.
Publications: Application guidelines.
Application information: Application form required.
Initial approach: Letter
Copies of proposal: 1
Deadline(s): Submit proposal preferably in June through Aug.; deadline Aug. 31
Board meeting date(s): Oct. and as needed
Final notification: 2 months
Write: Larry Pulliam, Asst. Secy.
Officers and Trustees: Edward E. Noble, Pres.; Sam Noble, V.P.; Ann Noble Brown, Secy.-Treas.
Number of staff: 2
Employer Identification Number: 736090116

2638
Oklahoma City Community Foundation, Inc.

115 Park Ave.
Oklahoma City 73103 (405) 235-5603
Additional address: P.O. Box 1146, Oklahoma City, OK 73101

Community foundation incorporated in 1968 in OK.
Financial data (yr. ended 6/30/88): Assets, $34,342,591 (M); gifts received, $3,838,758; expenditures, $1,598,289, including $1,358,826 for 284 grants (high: $335,289; low: $25; average: $3,000-$10,000).
Purpose and activities: Giving to charitable, educational, health, and cultural organizations.
Types of support: Scholarship funds, fellowships, matching funds, operating budgets, continuing support, annual campaigns, seed money, emergency funds, building funds, equipment, research, special projects.
Limitations: Giving primarily in greater Oklahoma City, OK. No grants to individuals, or for endowment funds or deficit financing; no loans.
Publications: Annual report, newsletter.
Application information:
Initial approach: Telephone
Copies of proposal: 1
Deadline(s): June 30 and Dec. 31
Board meeting date(s): Jan., Apr., July, and Oct.
Write: Nancy B. Anthony, Exec. Dir.
Officers: Dan Hogan III,* Pres.; Gerald R. Marshall,* V.P.; John L. Belt, Secy.; Eleanor J. Maurer, Treas.; Nancy B. Anthony, Exec. Dir.
Trustees:* Ray Anthony, Richard Harrison, John Kirkpatick, Clayton Rich, Nancy Soule, James Tolbert, Morrison G. Tucker.
Trustee Banks: Bank Oklahoma, First Interstate Bank and Trust, Liberty National Bank & Trust Co. of Oklahoma City, Trust Co. of Oklahoma.
Number of staff: 1 full-time professional; 2 part-time support.
Employer Identification Number: 237024262
Recent arts and culture grants:
Canterbury Choral Society, Oklahoma City, OK, $12,000. For Oklahoma City Centennial Grant. 1987.
Dance Conspiracy, Oklahoma City, OK, $12,000. For Oklahoma City Centennial Grant. 1987.
Lyric Theater of Oklahoma, Oklahoma City, OK, $11,000. 1987.
Metropolitan Library, Oklahoma City, OK, $12,000. For Oklahoma City Centennial Grant. Grant shared with American Institute of Architects. 1987.
Oklahoma City Arts Council, Oklahoma City, OK, $12,000. For Oklahoma City Centennial Grant. 1987.
Oklahoma Zoological Trust, Oklahoma City, OK, $7,000. For Oklahoma City Grant to purchase saltwater aquariums for education program. 1987.
William Fremont Harn Gardens, Oklahoma City, OK, $15,291. 1987.
William Fremont Harn Gardens, Oklahoma City, OK, $12,000. For Oklahoma City Centennial Grant. 1987.

2639
Oklahoma Gas and Electric Company Giving Program
P.O. Box 321
Oklahoma City 73101 (405) 272-3195

Financial data (yr. ended 12/31/88): $181,333 for grants.
Purpose and activities: Considers civic affairs, health associations, hospital building funds, education, the arts including fine arts and museums, and general charitable giving.
Application information:
Write: James G. Harlow, Jr., Chair., Pres., and C.E.O.

2640
Phillips Petroleum Foundation, Inc.
Phillips Bldg., 16th Fl.
Bartlesville 74004 (918) 661-6248

Incorporated in 1973 in OK.
Donor(s): Phillips Petroleum Co.
Financial data (yr. ended 12/31/87): Assets, $0 (M); gifts received, $5,074,389; expenditures, $5,074,389, including $3,627,120 for 660 grants (high: $594,118; low: $20; average: $1,000-$25,000) and $1,446,793 for 687 employee matching gifts.
Purpose and activities: Support for education, civic and youth organizations, cultural programs, and social service and health agencies.
Types of support: Employee matching gifts, operating budgets, annual campaigns, seed money, building funds, equipment, land acquisition, renovation projects, research, conferences and seminars, scholarship funds, fellowships, professorships, internships, exchange programs, matching funds, continuing support, general purposes, capital campaigns.
Limitations: Giving primarily in areas of company operations, particularly OK, TX, CO, and other states in the South and Southwest. Generally no grants to religious organizations or specialized health agencies. No grants to individuals, or for trips or fundraising dinners; no loans.
Publications: Application guidelines.
Application information:
Initial approach: Proposal, letter, or telephone
Copies of proposal: 1
Deadline(s): None
Board meeting date(s): Mar. and as required
Final notification: 8 to 12 weeks
Write: John C. West, Exec. Mgr.
Officers: R.W. Peters, Jr.,* Pres.; R.H. Schultz,* V.P.; J.B. Whitworth,* V.P.; G.C. Meese, Secy.; Betsy L. Swan, Treas.; John C. West, Exec. Mgr.
Directors:* D.J. Billam, D.L. Cone, L.M. Francis, J.W. Middleton, Stanley R. Mueller, J.W. O'Toole, J.G. Wilson.
Number of staff: 1 part-time professional; 1 part-time support.
Employer Identification Number: 237326611

2641
Public Service Company of Oklahoma Corporate Giving Program
212 East 6th
P.O. Box 201
Tulsa 74119 (918) 599-2000

Financial data (yr. ended 12/31/88): Total giving, $450,000, including $440,000 for 250 grants (high: $130,000; low: $100) and $10,000 for 5 in-kind gifts.
Purpose and activities: Company has general widespread giving program; interests include the elderly, alcoholism, culture, child welfare, energy, ecology, historic preservation, libraries, leadership development, and education, including vocational education; small gifts are the norm except for the United Way and capital campaigns.
Types of support: Annual campaigns, building funds, capital campaigns, conferences and seminars, continuing support, deficit financing, emergency funds, employee matching gifts, endowment funds, equipment, general purposes, internships, lectureships, matching funds, operating budgets, professorships, publications, research, employee-related scholarships, special projects, in-kind gifts.
Limitations: Giving primarily in service area in OK.
Publications: Application guidelines.
Application information: Detailed financial information needed for capital campaign requests.
Initial approach: Letter
Copies of proposal: 1
Deadline(s): None, but 60-90 days lead time is desirable
Board meeting date(s): Monthly
Final notification: Usually 60 days
Write: William R. Stratton, V.P. and C.F.O.
Number of staff: 5

2642
Robert Glenn Rapp Foundation
2301 N.W. 39th Expressway, Suite 300
Oklahoma City 73112 (405) 525-8331

Trust established about 1953 in OK.
Donor(s): Florence B. Clark.†
Financial data (yr. ended 12/31/86): Assets, $2,471,698 (M); expenditures, $535,000, including $535,000 for 2 grants (high: $500,000; low: $35,000).
Purpose and activities: Emphasis on higher education; support also for medical research, hospitals, secondary education, and cultural programs.
Limitations: Giving primarily in OK, with emphasis on Oklahoma City. No grants to individuals.
Application information: Grantmaking has been temporarily suspended.
Initial approach: Letter
Deadline(s): Oct. 1
Board meeting date(s): Annually, usually in the latter part of the year
Write: Trustees
Trustees: Stanley B. Catlett, James H. Milligan, Lois Darlene Milligan.
Number of staff: None.
Employer Identification Number: 730616840

2643
Scrivner Corporate Giving Program
5701 North Shartel
Box 26030
Oklahoma City 73126 (405) 841-5500

Financial data (yr. ended 12/31/88): Total giving, $75,000, including $60,000 for grants, $5,000 for 2 employee matching gifts and $10,000 for in-kind gifts.
Purpose and activities: Support for culture and the arts, and adult, business, secondary, and higher education, literacy, family and child welfare, community development, crime and law enforcement, health associations, homeless, medical research, social services, and youth programs; includes in-kind giving.
Types of support: In-kind gifts, annual campaigns, building funds, capital campaigns, continuing support, employee matching gifts, endowment funds, equipment, program-related investments, scholarship funds.
Limitations: Giving primarily in communities where company does business, especially in central OK.
Application information:
Initial approach: Letter
Copies of proposal: 1
Write: Mike Brake, Dir. of Corp. Communications
Administrator: Mike Brake, Dir. Corp. Communications.
Number of staff: 1

2644
Shin'en Kan, Inc.
P.O. Box 1111
Bartlesville 74005

Established in 1980 in OK.
Financial data (yr. ended 12/31/87): Assets, $5,883,230 (M); expenditures, $2,186,855, including $2,154,434 for 4 grants (high: $2,048,434; low: $1,000).
Purpose and activities: Support primarily for the development and construction of a museum devoted to Japanese art and the furtherance of the understanding and appreciation of the architecture of Bruce Goff.
Types of support: Building funds, general purposes.
Application information: Contributes only to pre-selected organizations. Applications not accepted.
Write: Joe D. Price, Pres.
Officers: Joe D. Price,* Pres.; Etsuko Y. Price,* V.P.; W.E. Yount, Secy.-Treas.
Directors:* Ralph E. Lerner.
Employer Identification Number: 731106645

2645
Harold C. & Joan S. Stuart Foundation
Box 1349
Tulsa 74101 (918) 743-7814

Established in 1969 in OK.
Financial data (yr. ended 12/31/87): Assets, $1,029,973 (M); expenditures, $47,881, including $42,324 for 53 grants (high: $20,000; low: $50; average: $100-$500).
Purpose and activities: Giving primarily for social services and youth, including a

community fund; support also for cultural programs and health associations.
Types of support: General purposes.
Limitations: Giving primarily in the Tulsa, OK, area.
Application information:
Write: Harold C. Stuart, Trustee
Trustees: Harold C. Stuart, Joan S. Stuart.
Employer Identification Number: 237052178

2646
C. W. Titus Foundation
1801 Philtower Bldg.
Tulsa 74103 (918) 582-8095

Established in 1968 in OK.
Financial data (yr. ended 12/31/86): Assets, $6,810,580 (M); expenditures, $216,114, including $167,871 for 38 grants (high: $50,000; low: $1,000).
Purpose and activities: Giving for hospitals and health services, cultural programs, the handicapped, and social service agencies.
Limitations: Giving primarily in OK and MO.
Application information:
Deadline(s): None
Trustees: Rosemary T. Reynolds, Timothy T. Reynolds.
Employer Identification Number: 237016981

2647
Vose Foundation
(Formerly First National Foundation, Inc.)
120 Park Ave.
P.O. Box 25189
Oklahoma City 73125 (405) 235-0330

Incorporated in 1954 in OK.
Donor(s): First National Bank and Trust Co.
Financial data (yr. ended 12/31/87): Assets, $512,480 (M); expenditures, $255,672, including $250,000 for 1 grant.
Purpose and activities: Emphasis on community funds, higher education, cultural programs, youth agencies, and hospitals.
Types of support: Annual campaigns, seed money, building funds, equipment, consulting services, technical assistance, scholarship funds.
Limitations: Giving primarily in Oklahoma City, OK. No grants to individuals, or for matching gifts; no loans.
Publications: Application guidelines.
Application information:
Initial approach: Letter
Deadline(s): None
Write: Rainey Williams, Pres.
Number of staff: 2
Employer Identification Number: 736099287

2648
The Herman and Mary Wegener Foundation, Inc.
1711 First National Bldg.
Oklahoma City 73102 (405) 235-7200

Incorporated in 1954 in OK.
Donor(s): Herman H. Wegener.†
Financial data (yr. ended 12/31/87): Assets, $2,257,045 (M); expenditures, $337,654, including $279,700 for 33 grants (high: $20,000; low: $200).
Purpose and activities: Emphasis on hospitals and education; grants also for cultural programs, youth agencies, and social agencies.
Types of support: Building funds, operating budgets, special projects.
Limitations: Giving primarily in Oklahoma City, OK. No grants to individuals, or for endowment funds.
Application information:
Initial approach: Letter
Deadline(s): Nov. 1
Board meeting date(s): Quarterly
Officers and Trustees: Willis B. Sherin, Pres.; Lee Holmes, V.P.; May Fry, Secy.; Clenard Wegener, Treas.; Wanda B. Burnett, Rosemary Fields, Kenneth Wegener, Raymond Lee Wegener, Willis B. Wegener.
Employer Identification Number: 736095407

2649
The Williams Companies Foundation, Inc.
P.O. Box 2400
Tulsa 74102 (918) 588-2106

Incorporated in 1974 in OK.
Donor(s): The Williams Companies, Inc.
Financial data (yr. ended 12/31/88): Assets, $8,652,000 (M); expenditures, $1,097,000, including $1,073,942 for 179 grants (high: $297,253; low: $50; average: $1,000-$30,000).
Purpose and activities: Support primarily for higher education, health and human services, cultural programs, and civic projects; employee matching gifts for United Way campaign.
Types of support: General purposes, building funds, equipment, seed money, emergency funds, matching funds.
Limitations: Giving primarily in locations where the Williams Companies has a strong business presence, with emphasis on Tulsa, OK. Generally, no support for national organizations. No grants to individuals, or for scholarships or fellowships; no loans.
Application information:
Initial approach: Proposal
Copies of proposal: 1
Deadline(s): None
Board meeting date(s): Varies
Final notification: Approximately 1 month
Write: Hannah D. Robson, Mgr.
Officers: Joseph H. Williams,* Chair.; Vernon T. Jones, Pres.; Keith E. Bailey,* V.P.; David M. Higbee, Secy.-Treas.; Hannah D. Robson, Mgr.
Directors:* John C. Bumgarner, Jr., J. Furman Lewis.
Number of staff: 1 part-time professional; 1 part-time support.
Employer Identification Number: 237413843

2650
The R. A. Young Foundation
6401 North Pennsylvania Ave., Suite 209
Oklahoma City 73116 (405) 840-4444

Incorporated in 1953 in OK.
Donor(s): Raymond A. Young.
Financial data (yr. ended 11/30/86): Assets, $3,553,127 (M); expenditures, $157,692, including $150,000 for 31 grants (high: $50,000; low: $25).
Purpose and activities: Giving for Protestant church support and religious service associations, higher education, and arts and culture.
Limitations: Giving primarily in OK.
Application information:
Initial approach: Letter
Deadline(s): None
Write: Raymond A. Young, Pres.
Officers and Trustees: Raymond A. Young, Pres.; Carolyn Young Hodnett, V.P.; Verna N. Young, Secy.-Treas.
Employer Identification Number: 736092654

2651
John Steele Zink Foundation
1259 East 26th St.
Tulsa 74114 (918) 749-8249

Established in 1972.
Donor(s): John Steele Zink,† Jacqueline A. Zink.
Financial data (yr. ended 10/31/88): Assets, $34,977,166 (M); expenditures, $1,066,308, including $998,973 for 54 grants (high: $414,000; low: $150).
Purpose and activities: Support for higher education and cultural programs.
Limitations: Giving primarily in Tulsa, OK.
Application information:
Initial approach: Letter or telephone
Deadline(s): None
Write: Jacqueline A. Zink, Trustee
Trustees: Horace Balling, Swannie Zink Tarbel, Jacqueline A. Zink, John Smith Zink.
Employer Identification Number: 237246964

OREGON

2652
The Autzen Foundation
P.O. Box 3709
Portland 97208 (503) 226-6051

Incorporated in 1951 in OR.
Donor(s): Thomas J. Autzen.†
Financial data (yr. ended 12/31/88): Assets, $7,413,084 (M); expenditures, $486,667, including $465,900 for grants (high: $15,000; low: $100; average: $200-$10,000).
Purpose and activities: Support for higher education, conservation, arts, the performing arts, and youth agencies.
Types of support: Continuing support, seed money, building funds, matching funds, special projects.
Limitations: Giving primarily in OR. No grants to individuals, or for scholarships or fellowships; no loans.
Application information: Include copy of IRS exemption letter, general budget, project budget, and list of board of directors.
Initial approach: Letter
Copies of proposal: 1
Deadline(s): Mar. 30 and Oct. 31
Board meeting date(s): May and Dec.

Final notification: 3 to 4 months
Write: Vivienne B. Snow, Admin.
Officers and Directors: Thomas E. Autzen, Pres.; Duane Autzen, V.P.; Henry C. Houser, Secy.
Number of staff: 1 part-time professional.
Employer Identification Number: 936021333

2653
Bend Foundation
416 Northeast Greenwood
Bend 97701 (503) 382-1662
Additional address: 510 Baker Bldg., Minneapolis, MN 55402

Trust established in 1947 in IL.
Donor(s): Brooks-Scanlon, Inc., Brooks Resources Corp.
Financial data (yr. ended 12/31/87): Assets, $2,236,336 (M); gifts received, $2,000; expenditures, $200,068, including $129,905 for 16 grants (high: $25,000; low: $500) and $26,000 for 2 grants to individuals.
Purpose and activities: Grants for higher education, cultural programs, and a community fund.
Types of support: Continuing support, annual campaigns, seed money, building funds, equipment, land acquisition, matching funds, student aid.
Limitations: Giving limited to central OR, with preference for the city of Bend and Deschutes County. No grants for operating budgets, deficit financing, endowment funds, special projects, research, publications, or conferences; no loans.
Application information:
Initial approach: Letter or proposal
Copies of proposal: 1
Deadline(s): Submit proposal preferably in Dec.
Board meeting date(s): Feb. or Mar.
Final notification: A few months
Write: Michael P. Hollern, Trustee
Trustees: Conley Brooks, Conley Brooks, Jr., Michael P. Hollern, William L. Smith.
Number of staff: None.
Employer Identification Number: 416019901

2654
The Carpenter Foundation
711 East Main St., Suite 18
P.O. Box 816
Medford 97501 (503) 772-5851

Incorporated in 1957 in OR.
Donor(s): Helen Bundy Carpenter,† Alfred S.V. Carpenter,† Harlow Carpenter.
Financial data (yr. ended 6/30/88): Assets, $8,658,629 (M); expenditures, $533,219, including $388,774 for 57 grants (high: $22,500; low: $1,000; average: $2,000-$10,000).
Purpose and activities: Grants for higher and secondary education, including scholarship funds, human services, art and architecture, and the performing arts.
Types of support: Operating budgets, seed money, equipment, matching funds, technical assistance, scholarship funds, research.
Limitations: Giving primarily in Jackson and Josephine counties, OR. No grants to individuals, or for deficit financing, endowment funds, or demonstration projects.
Publications: Application guidelines, annual report.
Application information:
Initial approach: Proposal or letter
Copies of proposal: 1
Deadline(s): Submit proposal 4 weeks before board meeting
Board meeting date(s): Usually in Mar., June, Sept., and Dec.
Final notification: 1 to 2 weeks
Write: Dunbar Carpenter, Treas.
Officers and Trustees: Emily C. Mostue, Jane H. Carpenter, Pres.; Dunbar Carpenter, Treas.; Karen C. Allan, Robertson Collins, Mrs. Robert Ogle.
Associate Trustees: Jerilyn Holt, Sheila Kimball, Bill Moffat, William Thorndike, Jr.
Number of staff: 1 part-time support.
Employer Identification Number: 930491360

2655
Clark Foundation
255 Southwest Harrison St., GA 2
Portland 97201 (503) 223-5290

Established in 1968 in OR.
Donor(s): Maurie D. Clark.
Financial data (yr. ended 12/31/86): Assets, $53,226 (M); gifts received, $296,500; expenditures, $352,462, including $318,900 for 143 grants (high: $18,000; low: $500).
Purpose and activities: Emphasis on building funds for higher education and for churches and religious associations; grants also for cultural programs, youth agencies, secondary education, the environment, and medical care.
Types of support: Building funds.
Limitations: Giving primarily in the Portland, OR, area. No grants to individuals, or for endowment funds, research, or matching gifts; no loans.
Application information:
Initial approach: Letter
Copies of proposal: 1
Deadline(s): None
Board meeting date(s): Bimonthly
Write: Jean Ameele
Officers: Maurie D. Clark, Pres. and Treas.; David A. Kekel, V.P.; Patrick E. Becker, Secy.
Employer Identification Number: 237423789

2656
The Collins Foundation
909 Terminal Sales Bldg.
Portland 97205 (503) 227-7171

Incorporated in 1947 in OR.
Donor(s): Members of the Collins family.
Financial data (yr. ended 12/31/88): Assets, $41,252,107 (M); expenditures, $3,055,958, including $2,771,626 for 154 grants (high: $320,166; low: $750; average: $3,000-$25,000).
Purpose and activities: Emphasis on higher education, youth, hospices, and health agencies, social welfare, and the arts and cultural programs.
Types of support: Building funds, equipment, research, matching funds, program-related investments, special projects.
Limitations: Giving limited to OR, with emphasis on Portland. No grants to individuals, or for deficit financing, legislative lobbying, endowment funds, general purposes, delayed projects, scholarships, fellowships, operating budgets, or annual campaigns.
Publications: Annual report (including application guidelines), informational brochure.
Application information:
Initial approach: Letter
Copies of proposal: 1
Deadline(s): None
Board meeting date(s): Approximately 6 times a year
Final notification: 4 to 8 weeks
Write: William C. Pine, Exec. V.P.
Officers: Maribeth W. Collins,* Pres.; William C. Pine, Exec. V.P.; Grace Collins Goudy,* V.P.; Thomas B. Stoel, Secy.; Eugene E. Sharp, Treas.
Trustees:* Ralph Bolliger.
Number of staff: 1 part-time professional; 1 part-time support.
Employer Identification Number: 936021893
Recent arts and culture grants:
Arts Celebration, Portland, OR, $5,000. For jazz concert, Artquake. 1987.
Chamber Music Northwest, Portland, OR, $6,000. For Catlin Gabel series. 1987.
Contemporary Crafts Association, Portland, OR, $10,000. For 1987-88 program. 1987.
Neskowin Coast Foundation, Neskowin, OR, $5,000. For Music Festival 1987. 1987.
Oregon Educational and Public Broadcasting Service Foundation, Portland, OR, $200,000. For construction of new broadcast center. 1987.
Oregon Educational and Public Broadcasting Service Foundation, Portland, OR, $30,000. To underwrite The Collectors. 1987.
Oregon Military Museum and Research Foundation, Lake Oswego, OR, $10,000. For construction of additional space. 1987.
Oregon Museum of Science and Industry, Portland, OR, $25,000. For Early Childhood Education Project. 1987.
Oregon Shakespearean Festival, Ashland, OR, $50,000. To match NEA grant. 1987.
Oregon Symphony Society, Portland, OR, $50,000. For 1987-88 season. 1987.
Peter Britt Gardens Music and Arts Festival Association, Medford, OR, $25,000. For Agnes Flanagan Guest Artist endowment. 1987.
Portland Art Association, Portland, OR, $45,000. For renovation and reinstallation of Winslow B. Ayer Wing galleries. 1987.
Portland Art Association, Portland, OR, $5,000. For Pacific Northwest College of Art faculty exchange enrichment. 1987.
Portland Childrens Museum, Friends of the, Portland, OR, $5,000. For Customs House exhibit. 1987.
Portland Civic Theater, Portland, OR, $25,000. For equipment. 1987.
Portland Opera Association, Portland, OR, $50,000. For Cash Stabilization Fund. 1987.
Portland Youth Philharmonic Association, Portland, OR, $6,000. For musical education. 1987.
Rogue Valley Opera Association, Ashland, OR, $5,000. For 1987 productions. 1987.
Saint Francis of Assisi Episcopal Church, Wilsonville, OR, $15,000. For organ. 1987.

Storefront Actors Theater, Portland, OR, $7,500. For marketing program. 1987.
Tigard Area Historical and Preservation Association, Portland, OR, $15,000. For LaVerne Sharp Memorial Parlor. 1987.
Troutdale Historical Society, Troutdale, OR, $5,000. For historic barn museum. 1987.
Umatilla County Historical Society, Pendleton, OR, $5,000. For restoration of Union Pacific railroad depot. 1987.
West Coast Chamber Orchestra, Portland, OR, $6,000. For 1987 season. 1987.
Young Audiences of Oregon, Portland, OR, $10,000. For multicultural performances. 1987.

2657
Henry Failing Fund
P.O. Box 2971
Portland 97208

Established in 1947 in OR.
Financial data (yr. ended 12/31/87): Assets, $2,155,342 (M); gifts received, $0; expenditures, $137,825, including $127,550 for 8 grants (high: $15,944; low: $15,943).
Purpose and activities: Support primarily for education and hospitals; giving also for an art association.
Limitations: Giving primarily in Portland, OR.
Trustee: First Interstate Bank of Oregon.
Employer Identification Number: 936021362

2658
First Interstate Bank of Oregon, N.A. Charitable Foundation
P.O. Box 3131
Portland 97208
Application address: 1300 Southwest Fifth Ave., Portland, OR 97201

Incorporated in 1983 in OR.
Donor(s): First Interstate Bank of Oregon, N.A.
Financial data (yr. ended 12/31/87): Assets, $217,440 (M); gifts received, $830,000; expenditures, $840,842, including $839,437 for 204 grants (high: $310,300; low: $25; average: $100-$5,000).
Purpose and activities: Support for community funds, education, with emphasis on higher education, cultural programs, and child and animal welfare.
Limitations: Giving limited to OR. No support for political or religious organizations. No grants to individuals, or for seminars or conferences.
Application information: Submit information on specific project budget material, and copy of 501(c)(3).
Initial approach: Letter or proposal
Deadline(s): None
Board meeting date(s): As necessary
Final notification: 2 to 4 months
Write: Harleen Katke, Trustee
Trustees: Robert Ames, David S. Belles, Floyd Bennett, Robert J. Derby, Harleen Katke, Robert G. Murray.
Agent: First Interstate Bank of Oregon, N.A.
Number of staff: None.
Employer Identification Number: 930836170

2659
Fohs Foundation
P.O. Box 1001
Roseburg 97470 (503) 673-0141

Trust established in 1937 in NY.
Donor(s): F. Julius Fohs,† Mrs. Cora B. Fohs.†
Financial data (yr. ended 12/31/86): Assets, $6,194,295 (M); expenditures, $364,173, including $292,000 for 9 grants (high: $200,000; low: $1,000).
Purpose and activities: To promote science, art, education, health, healthful recreation and good citizenship of children and adults; research in general, charitable, humanitarian, sociological and educational problems; support for Ella Fohs children's and senior citizens' camps in CT; grants for Jewish-sponsored educational institutions, particularly in Israel.
Application information:
Initial approach: Letter
Copies of proposal: 1
Deadline(s): None
Board meeting date(s): Apr. or May
Write: Charlotte Richards, Secy.-Treas.
Officer: Charlotte Richards, Secy.-Treas.
Trustees: Frances F. Sohn, Chair.; Fuller Holloway, Vice-Chair.
Number of staff: 1 part-time support.
Employer Identification Number: 746003165

2660
Lorene Sails Higgins Charitable Trust
c/o The Bank of California
P.O. Box 3121
Portland 97208 (503) 225-2924

Trust established in 1968 in OR.
Donor(s): Lorene Sails Higgins.
Financial data (yr. ended 12/31/86): Assets, $3,759,493 (M); expenditures, $417,188, including $349,220 for 29 grants (high: $54,500; low: $1,000).
Purpose and activities: Emphasis on cultural programs, the performing arts, higher education, and religious institutions with emphasis on Christian Science projects.
Types of support: Building funds, equipment, matching funds.
Limitations: Giving primarily in the Portland, OR, metropolitan area. No grants to individuals, or for endowment funds, general support, scholarships, or fellowships; no loans.
Publications: Program policy statement, application guidelines.
Application information: Contributes only to pre-selected organizations. Applications not accepted.
Write: Marc Grignon, Trust Officer, The Bank of California
Trustees: The Bank of California, N.A., Wood, Tatum, Mosser, Brooke, & Holder.
Number of staff: None.
Employer Identification Number: 936050051

2661
Hyster Company Corporate Giving Program
P.O. Box 2902
Portland 97208 (503) 721-6000

Purpose and activities: Supports local organizations, the arts and general education; in-kind services including printing, meeting space, donated material, and company products and services; technical assistance including advertising, planning, account/fiscal management, legal, marketing, general management, and design programs.
Types of support: Building funds, matching funds, scholarship funds, in-kind gifts.
Limitations: Giving primarily in headquarters city and major operating offices.
Application information: Include project budget, board and contributions list, audited statement and 501(c)(3) status.
Initial approach: Proposal and letter
Deadline(s): Aug. and Sept.
Final notification: 4-6 weeks
Write: David Earnest, Public Relations Mgr.

2662
The Jackson Foundation
c/o U.S. National Bank of Oregon
P.O. Box 3168
Portland 97208 (503) 275-5718

Trust established in 1960 in OR; Philip Ludwell Jackson Charitable and Residual Trusts were merged into The Jackson Foundation in 1981.
Donor(s): Maria C. Jackson.†
Financial data (yr. ended 6/30/87): Assets, $8,836,487 (M); expenditures, $602,000, including $508,998 for 123 grants (high: $66,570; low: $500; average: $1,000-$5,000).
Purpose and activities: Support largely to aid needy persons through social service agencies; grants for higher and secondary education, cultural programs, hospitals, community and civic organizations, and youth agencies.
Types of support: Seed money, emergency funds, building funds, equipment, special projects, technical assistance, renovation projects, consulting services.
Limitations: Giving limited to OR. No support for churches or temples. No grants to individuals, or for endowment funds, matching gifts, scholarships, fellowships, or building or equipment funds for religious organizations; no loans to individuals.
Application information: Application form required.
Initial approach: Request for application form
Copies of proposal: 4
Deadline(s): Aug. 25, Nov. 25, and Mar. 25
Board meeting date(s): Sept., Dec., Apr., and as required
Final notification: 3 or 4 weeks
Write: Frank E. Staich, Asst. V.P., U.S. National Bank of Oregon
Trustees: Milo Ormseth, Gordon M. Tretheway, United States National Bank of Oregon.
Number of staff: 3
Employer Identification Number: 936020752

2663
The Jeld-Wen Foundation
(Formerly Jeld-Wen, Wenco Foundation)
3303 Lakeport Blvd.
P.O. Box 1329
Klamath Falls 97601 (503) 882-3451

Established in 1969.
Donor(s): Jeld-Wen Fiber Products, Inc. of Iowa, Jeld-Wen Co. of Arizona, Wenco, Inc. of North Carolina, Wenco, Inc. of Ohio, and other Jeld-Wen, Wenco companies.
Financial data (yr. ended 12/31/87): Assets, $7,979,926 (M); gifts received, $1,490,047; expenditures, $715,705, including $530,301 for 116 grants (high: $100,000; low: $348).
Purpose and activities: The foundation prioritizes requests on the basis of demonstrated impact toward making our communities better places to live. An assessment is also made as to how many company employees will use the services. Projects that improve the existing service or provide new ones, usually involving capital or seed money, and annual support for existing organizations through the United Way are major categories for giving.
Types of support: General purposes, seed money, building funds, equipment, land acquisition, special projects, scholarship funds, matching funds.
Limitations: Giving primarily in areas of company operations; in AZ, FL, IA, KY, NC, OH, OR, SD, and WA projects should serve communities in which company plants exist; projects in adjacent communities may be accepted if sufficient members of employees reside in the area and would benefit. No support for activities that are specifically religious or that duplicate services provided by other government or private agencies. No grants to individuals; no loans.
Publications: Program policy statement, application guidelines.
Application information: Application form required.
Initial approach: Proposal or letter; prefer not to receive telephone calls
Copies of proposal: 1
Deadline(s): Submit proposal preferably in Mar.; no set deadline
Board meeting date(s): Mar., June, Sept., and Dec.
Final notification: 2 weeks after meetings
Write: R.C. Wendt, Secy.
Officer and Trustees: R.C. Wendt, Secy.; W.B. Early, T.H. Schnormeier, Richard L. Wendt, L.V. Wetter.
Number of staff: None.
Employer Identification Number: 936054272

2664
The S. S. Johnson Foundation
P.O. Box 356
Redmond 97756 (503) 548-8104

Incorporated in 1948 in CA.
Donor(s): Samuel S. Johnson, Elizabeth Hill Johnson.
Financial data (yr. ended 5/31/88): Assets, $3,063,331 (M); expenditures, $185,437, including $149,777 for 127 grants (high: $10,000; low: $10; average: $500-$1,000), $7,725 for 14 grants to individuals and $7,400 for 7 loans to individuals.
Purpose and activities: Support for educational, scientific, cultural, religious, health, and welfare organizations, primarily for limited emergency operational funds and limited non-recurring emergency grants or loans to students through educational institutions.
Types of support: Operating budgets, seed money, emergency funds, matching funds, scholarship funds, student aid, conferences and seminars, student loans, equipment, special projects.
Limitations: Giving primarily in the Pacific Northwest, primarily OR and northern CA. No support for foreign organizations. No grants for continuing support, annual campaigns, deficit financing, capital support, research, or endowments.
Publications: 990-PF.
Application information: Application form required for scholarships. Application form required.
Initial approach: Letter
Copies of proposal: 1
Deadline(s): None
Board meeting date(s): July and Jan.
Final notification: 2 to 3 weeks
Write: Elizabeth Hill Johnson, Pres.
Officers: Elizabeth Hill Johnson,* Pres. and Treas.; Shirley K. Comini, Secy.
Directors:* Robert W. Hill, Elizabeth K. Johnson, Patricia Johnson Nelson, Ralf H. Stinson, M.D.
Number of staff: 1 part-time support.
Employer Identification Number: 946062478

2665
Louisiana-Pacific Foundation
111 Southwest Fifth Ave.
Portland 97204 (503) 221-0800

Established in 1973 in OR.
Donor(s): Louisiana-Pacific Corp.
Financial data (yr. ended 12/31/88): Assets, $24,329 (L); gifts received, $765,000; expenditures, $751,973, including $751,907 for 134 grants (high: $160,000; low: $225; average: $1,000-$5,000).
Purpose and activities: Giving for higher education, including employee-related scholarships, and community funds; some support for health, youth agencies, and the arts.
Types of support: Annual campaigns, capital campaigns, continuing support, general purposes, employee-related scholarships.
Limitations: Giving primarily in areas of plant locations.
Application information: Application form required for scholarships.
Initial approach: Letter
Copies of proposal: 1
Board meeting date(s): Quarterly
Write: Robert E. Erickson, Trustee
Officers: Harry A. Merlo,* Chair. and Pres.; Larry C. Campbell,* V.P.; Donald R. Holman, Secy.; John C. Hart, Treas.
Trustees:* Gary R. Maffei, Robert E. Erickson.
Number of staff: None.
Employer Identification Number: 237268660

2666
Maybelle Clark Macdonald Fund
405 Northwest 18th Ave.
Portland 97209
Application address: 5270-7 Southwest Landing Square Dr., Portland, OR 97201

Established about 1970.
Donor(s): Maybelle Clark Macdonald.
Financial data (yr. ended 6/30/88): Assets, $287,550 (M); gifts received, $102,212; expenditures, $108,671, including $105,481 for 43 grants (high: $20,000; low: $25).
Purpose and activities: Giving largely for local cultural programs and Roman Catholic church support.
Limitations: Giving primarily in OR.
Application information:
Initial approach: Letter
Deadline(s): None
Write: Maybelle Clark Macdonald, Pres.
Officers: Maybelle Clark Macdonald, Pres.; Fred C. Macdonald, Secy.; Daniel A. Callahan, Treas.
Employer Identification Number: 237108002

2667
Mentor Graphics Foundation
8500 Southwest Creekside Place
Beaverton 97005-7191 (503) 626-7000

Established in 1985 in OR.
Donor(s): Mentor Graphics.
Financial data (yr. ended 12/31/87): Assets, $274,038 (M); gifts received, $180,000; expenditures, $103,719, including $103,018 for 75 grants (high: $12,500; low: $10).
Purpose and activities: Support for community funds, culture, youth, social services, and higher educatiion.
Limitations: Giving primarily in areas where Mentor Graphics has major operations.
Application information:
Initial approach: Letter
Deadline(s): 3 weeks prior to bimonthly meeting
Write: Marti Brown, Admin.
Officers and Directors: Frank S. Delia, V.P. and Secy.; John C. Carveth, V.P. and Treas.; Berkeley T. Merchant, V.P.; Richard J. Anderson, Frank J. Costa, Brian Kiernan.
Employer Identification Number: 930870309

2668
Fred Meyer Charitable Trust
1515 Southwest Fifth Ave., Suite 500
Portland 97201 (503) 228-5512

Trust established by will in 1978; obtained IRS status in OR in 1982.
Donor(s): Fred G. Meyer.†
Financial data (yr. ended 3/31/89): Assets, $256,120,715 (M); expenditures, $12,088,931, including $11,113,904 for 174 grants (high: $750,000; low: $500; average: $20,000-$200,000).
Purpose and activities: The trust provides two types of funding: 1) general purpose grants, primarily in OR for education, the arts and humanities, health, and social welfare; and 2) special program grants, primarily in AK, ID, MT, OR, and WA, in the areas of Aging and Independence, and Support for Children at Risk. Under general purpose, the Trust operates the Small Grants Program, which provides awards of $500 to $8,000 for small projects in OR.
Types of support: Seed money, building funds, equipment, matching funds, technical

assistance, program-related investments, special projects, research, general purposes, operating budgets, renovation projects.
Limitations: Giving primarily in OR, except for special programs which also include WA, ID, MT and AK. No support for sectarian or religious organizations for religious purposes. No grants to individuals, or for operating budgets, endowment funds, annual campaigns, deficit financing, scholarships, or fellowships or indirect or overhead costs, except as specifically and essentially related to the grant project; occasional program-related loans only.
Publications: Annual report, informational brochure (including application guidelines), program policy statement.
Application information: Special guidelines for aging program, Children at Risk program, and Small Grants Program. Application form required.
Initial approach: Proposal
Copies of proposal: 1
Deadline(s): 1989: July 1 for aging program; Apr. 1 and Oct. 1 for Children at Risk program; Jan. 15, Apr. 15, July 15, and Oct. 15 for Small Grants Program; no set deadline for other grants
Board meeting date(s): Monthly
Final notification: 3 to 5 months for proposals that pass first screening; 1 to 2 months for those that don't
Write: Charles S. Rooks, Exec. Dir.
Officers: Charles S. Rooks, Secy. and Exec. Dir.; Wayne G. Pierson, Treas.
Trustees: Travis Cross, Pauline Lawrence, Warne Nunn, G. Gerald Pratt, Oran B. Robertson.
Number of staff: 5 full-time professional; 5 full-time support.
Employer Identification Number: 930806316
Recent arts and culture grants:
Constitution Project, Portland, OR, $238,000. To produce public television program, Road from Runnymede, which chronicles origin of U.S. Constitution, and to distribute film and related curriculum materials to schools. 11/4/88.
Eugene Ballet, Eugene, OR, $86,000. To purchase portable truss and provide fee support for rural communities. 5/6/88.
High Desert Museum, Bend, OR, $16,000. For feasibility study regarding renovation and operation of Malheur Field Station as educational extension of High Desert Museum. 3/4/88.
Imaginarium, Anchorage, AK, $150,000. For Science Explorer Program, project which will hire at-risk youth to assist young children with hands-on exhibits in Imaginarium, science museum for children. 8/5/88.
K C T S/9 Public Television, Seattle, WA, $13,000. For production of public television documentary on elder abuse, The Golden Years. 3/4/88.
Lelooska Foundation, Ariel, WA, $48,000. For repair of traditional masks and costumes used in public presentations of sacred songs, dances, and myths of Kwakiutl and other Pacific Northwest native groups. 1/6/88.
Metolius, City of, Metolius, OR, $11,200. To restore historic railroad station as community center. 5/6/88.
Oregon Art Institute, Portland, OR, $1,000,000. To renovate galleries. 4/8/88.
Oregon Historical Society, Portland, OR, $250,000. To renovate portion of Sovereign Hotel that will be used for offices of Society Press and to develop Society Bookstore. 11/4/88.
Oregon Historical Society, Portland, OR, $30,000. For oral history project relating to Fred G. Meyer and his involvement in development of business in Northwest. 1/6/88.
Oregon Maritime Center and Museum, Portland, OR, $80,000. For employment of director and public relations efforts. 9/1/88.
Pacific Ballet Theater, Portland, OR, $100,000. For general support of remainder of Portland Ballet Theater's 1987-88 season. 2/5/88.
Planned Parenthood of Columbia-Willamette, Portland, OR, $48,000. To continue Teens and Company, program in which teenage actors utilize dramatic vignettes to demonstrate how to handle difficult situations and convey accurate information about sex-related topics. 12/2/88.
Umatilla County Historical Society, Pendleton, OR, $50,000. To construct brick tower on grounds of Umatilla County Courthouse to house restored 1888 Seth Thomas Tower Clock. 9/1/88.
Umatilla County Saturday Academy, Pendleton, OR, $20,000. To bring professionals in music and arts to classrooms in eastern Oregon. 9/30/88.
Wildlife Safari, Winston, OR, $75,000. For development of North American Exhibit area. 12/4/87.

2669
Northwest Natural Gas Company Contributions Program
220 N.W. Second Ave.
Portland 97209 (503) 226-4211

Financial data (yr. ended 12/31/88): Total giving, $285,000, including $278,337 for 735 grants (average: $100-$5,000) and $6,663 for 31 in-kind gifts.
Purpose and activities: Supports education, including public and private colleges, civic affairs and community development, arts and culture, welfare, and health programs.
Types of support: General purposes, annual campaigns, capital campaigns, employee-related scholarships.
Limitations: Giving primarily in company service area: Willamette Valley of OR, north and central coast, southwest WA. No support for programs already funded under the United Way umbrella. No grants for dinner benefits.
Publications: Application guidelines.
Application information: Application form required.
Initial approach: Letter to chairman of Contributions Committee asking for application and guidelines
Copies of proposal: 1
Board meeting date(s): Quarterly
Write: C.J. Rue, Chair., Contribs. Comm.
Administrator: C.J. Rue, Chair., Contribs. Comm.
Number of staff: 2 part-time professional.

2670
The Oregon Community Foundation
1110 Yeon Bldg.
522 Southwest Fifth Ave.
Portland 97204 (503) 227-6846

Community foundation established in 1973 in OR.
Financial data (yr. ended 6/30/88): Assets, $40,220,276 (M); gifts received, $3,798,447; expenditures, $6,190,787, including $5,769,012 for grants (high: $737,992; average: $3,500-$10,000).
Purpose and activities: To "meet educational, cultural, medical, social and civic needs in all areas and at all levels of society throughout the state."
Types of support: Operating budgets, seed money, building funds, equipment, land acquisition, technical assistance, scholarship funds, special projects, matching funds, renovation projects.
Limitations: Giving limited to OR. No support for films, or for religious organizations for religious purposes. No grants to individuals, or for emergency funding, endowments, annual campaigns, deficit financing, research, publications, or conferences, unless so designated by a donor; no loans.
Publications: Annual report, newsletter, program policy statement, application guidelines.
Application information: Application form required.
Initial approach: 1-page letter
Copies of proposal: 12
Deadline(s): Submit application preferably in Mar. or Aug.; deadlines Apr. 1 and Sept. 1
Board meeting date(s): Jan., June, Sept., and Nov.
Final notification: 3 months
Write: Gregory A. Chaille, Exec. Dir.
Officers: Donald C. Frisbee,* Pres.; Robert W. Chandler,* V.P.; Sally McCracken,* V.P.; William Swindells, Jr.,* V.P.; Gwyneth Gamble Booth,* Secy.; Kenneth Lewis,* Treas.; Gregory A. Chaille, Exec. Dir.
Directors:* Edwin M. Baker, John D. Gray, Richard F. Hensley, Alice Koehler, Louis B. Perry, Walter C. Reynolds, M.D., Jess Rogerson.
Participating Banks: The Bank of California, N.A., First Interstate Bank of Oregon, The Oregon Bank, United States National Bank of Oregon.
Number of staff: 4 full-time professional; 1 part-time professional; 2 full-time support.
Employer Identification Number: 237315673
Recent arts and culture grants:
Centro Cultural of Washington County, Hillsboro, OR, $10,000. 1988.
Chamber Music Northwest, Portland, OR, $7,000. 1988.
Columbia River Maritime Museum, Astoria, OR, $5,000. 1988.
Eugene Ballet, Eugene, OR, $8,000. 1988.
Eugene Symphony, Eugene, OR, $5,300. 1988.
Forest History Society, Durham, NC, $5,000. 1988.
High Desert Museum, Bend, OR, $23,000. 1988.
Historic Preservation League of Oregon, Portland, OR, $10,000. 1988.
Mission Mill Museum, Salem, OR, $12,500. 1988.

National Society of Colonial Dames, Portland, OR, $10,000. 1988.
New Rose Theater, Portland, OR, $5,500. 1988.
Oregon Art Institute, Portland, OR, $351,961. 1988.
Oregon Historical Society, Portland, OR, $14,722. 1988.
Oregon Institute for Literary Arts, Portland, OR, $52,881. 1988.
Oregon Museum of Science and Industry, Portland, OR, $7,844. 1988.
Oregon Public Broadcasting Foundation, Portland, OR, $236,675. 1988.
Oregon School of Design, Portland, OR, $15,000. 1988.
Oregon Shakespearean Festival, Ashland, OR, $19,250. 1988.
Oregon Symphony Association, Portland, OR, $222,042. 1988.
Peter Britt Gardens Music and Arts Festival Association, Medford, OR, $5,000. 1988.
Portland Center for the Performing Arts, Portland, OR, $667,289. 1988.
Portland Opera Association, Portland, OR, $192,333. 1988.
Portland Repertory Theater, Portland, OR, $5,000. 1988.
Portland Youth Philharmonic, Portland, OR, $11,929. 1988.
Umatilla County Historical Society, Pendleton, OR, $5,000. 1988.
University of Oregon, Department of Architecture, Eugene, OR, $8,500. 1988.
University of Oregon, Museum of Art, Eugene, OR, $5,000. 1988.

2671
PacifiCorp Foundation
111 Southwest Columbia St., Suite 840
Portland 97201-5813 (503) 464-6000

Established in 1988 in OR.
Purpose and activities: Support primarily for health and welfare, civic and community affairs, culture and the arts, and education.
Limitations: Giving primarily in major operating areas in the west. No grants to individuals, or for operating support for religious organizations, or endowments.
Application information:
Initial approach: Brief letter
Deadline(s): None
Write: Ernest Bloch II, Exec. Dir.
Employer Identification Number: 943089826

2672
Pioneer Trust Bank, N.A. Foundation
P.O. Box 2305
Salem 97308-2305

Financial data (yr. ended 12/31/87): Assets, $312,109 (M); expenditures, $16,484, including $16,050 for 35 grants (high: $1,000; low: $25; average: $100-$5,000).
Purpose and activities: Supprt for health, social services and youth, arts and culture, conservation, religious giving, and the United Way.
Limitations: Giving primarily in Salem, OR, and its surrounding areas.
Application information:
Initial approach: Letter
Deadline(s): Oct. 31
Trustee: Pioneer Trust Bank, N.A.
Employer Identification Number: 930881673

2673
Security Pacific Bank Oregon Corporate Contributions
P.O. Box 3066
Portland 97208

Financial data (yr. ended 12/31/88): $64,415 for 62 grants (high: $10,940; low: $175).
Purpose and activities: Support for health and welfare, including federated funds and national health organizations, hospital and health programs, and social services; education; culture; and civic affairs; SPBO also participates in the Security Pacific Foundation Employee Matching Gift Program. Support is primarily made through unrestricted operating grants and capital grants for major building projects.
Types of support: Capital campaigns, building funds, operating budgets.
Limitations: Giving primarily in areas of company operations throughout OR. No support for military, fraternal, professional organizations or service clubs, churches or religious groups, marathons, political organizations or programs, advocacy organizations, or organizations receiving in excess of 50 percent of their funding from government agencies. No grants to individuals, or for research or study projects, or advertising in charitable journals.
Application information: Proposal including 501(c)(3), list of board members, current year's operating budget (if requesting capital funds, detailed statement of total project cost), statement of current financial position, most recent audited financial statement, list of current donors.
Initial approach: Proposal
Write: Ed Dewald, Chair., Social Policy Committee

2674
Tektronix Foundation
P.O. Box 500
Beaverton 97077 (503) 627-7084

Incorporated in 1952 in OR.
Donor(s): Tektronix, Inc.
Financial data (yr. ended 12/31/87): Assets, $2,580,887 (M); gifts received, $2,757,032; expenditures, $2,323,246, including $1,726,659 for 159 grants (high: $163,318; low: $25), $42,450 for 34 grants to individuals and $245,221 for employee matching gifts.
Purpose and activities: Giving for education, especially physical sciences and employee matching gifts, community funds and other social service programs, health agencies, and some limited arts grants; support also for scholarship programs for children of company employees.
Types of support: Operating budgets, continuing support, annual campaigns, seed money, building funds, equipment, land acquisition, employee matching gifts, fellowships, employee-related scholarships, renovation projects.
Limitations: Giving primarily in OR. No grants to individuals (except for employee-related scholarships), or for emergency or endowment funds, demonstration projects, matching or challenge gifts, deficit financing, research, publications, or conferences; no loans.
Application information:
Initial approach: Proposal
Copies of proposal: 1
Deadline(s): 1 month before board meeting
Board meeting date(s): Feb., May, Aug., and Nov.
Final notification: Following board meeting, for grant recipients only
Write: Dianna Smiley, Admin.
Officers and Trustees: Jean Vollum, Chair.; Charles H. Frost, Vice-Chair.; William B. Webber, Secy.; Larry N. Choruby, Treas.; Tom Long, Steve Vollum, William D. Walker.
Number of staff: 1 part-time professional; 1 part-time support.
Employer Identification Number: 936021540

2675
The Herbert A. Templeton Foundation
1717 S.W. Park Ave.
Portland 97201 (503) 223-0036

Incorporated in 1955 in OR.
Donor(s): Herbert A. Templeton,† Members of the Templeton family.
Financial data (yr. ended 12/31/88): Assets, $4,058,534 (M); expenditures, $355,786, including $306,135 for 137 grants (high: $15,000; low: $100; average: $500-$5,000).
Purpose and activities: Grants to educational, youth, cultural, and social service organizations operating in OR or having programs significantly affecting OR residents; present emphasis on program and direct services.
Types of support: Operating budgets, continuing support, seed money, emergency funds, scholarship funds, special projects, general purposes.
Limitations: Giving limited to OR. No support for medical services, scientific research or technology, the aged, or parochial education. No grants to individuals, or for program-related investments, fellowships, building or endowment funds, or matching gifts; no loans.
Publications: Program policy statement (including application guidelines).
Application information:
Initial approach: Letter or proposal
Copies of proposal: 1
Deadline(s): Submit proposal preferably from July through Sept.; deadline Sept. 30
Board meeting date(s): Jan., Apr., July, Oct., and Nov.; most grant requests processed at meetings in Oct. or Nov.
Final notification: Nov. or Dec.
Write: Mrs. Ruth B. Richmond, V.P.
Officers and Trustees: Jane T. Bryson, Pres.; Ruth B. Richmond, V.P.; Terrence R. Pancoast, Secy.-Treas.; James E. Bryson, John R. Olsen, Hall Templeton, William B. Webber.
Number of staff: 1 part-time support.
Employer Identification Number: 930505586

2676
Rose E. Tucker Charitable Trust
900 Southwest Fifth Ave., 24th Fl.
Portland 97204 (503) 224-3380

Trust established about 1976 in OR.
Donor(s): Rose E. Tucker,† Max and Rose Tucker Foundation.
Financial data (yr. ended 6/30/88): Assets, $13,350,953 (M); expenditures, $717,830, including $587,605 for 157 grants (high: $25,000; low: $500; average: $2,500-$12,000).
Purpose and activities: Priority given to programs in fields of education, health and welfare, community development, social services, arts and culture, and care and education of underprivileged and handicapped.
Types of support: Building funds, scholarship funds, general purposes, operating budgets, equipment, special projects, capital campaigns, land acquisition.
Limitations: Giving primarily in OR, with emphasis on the Portland metropolitan area. No support for religion, or private foundations. No grants to individuals, or for fellowships, operating budgets, or debt reduction; no loans.
Publications: Application guidelines, annual report (including application guidelines), grants list.
Application information:
Initial approach: Proposal
Copies of proposal: 1
Deadline(s): None
Board meeting date(s): Approximately every 2 months
Final notification: Within 10 days of board meetings
Write: Thomas B. Stoel or Milo Ormseth, Trustees
Trustees: Milo Ormseth, Thomas B. Stoel, United States National Bank of Oregon.
Number of staff: 1 part-time support.
Employer Identification Number: 936119091
Recent arts and culture grants:
High Desert Museum, Bend, OR, $15,000. For capital campaign. 1987.
Japanese Garden Society of Oregon, Portland, OR, $5,000. For facilities. 1987.
Oregon Art Institute, Portland, OR, $5,000. For statewide program. 1987.
Oregon Coast Aquarium, South Beach, OR, $12,500. For capital campaign. 1987.
Oregon Public Broadcasting, Portland, OR, $5,000. For history series. 1987.
Oregon Shakespearean Festival, Ashland, OR, $7,500. For shop expansion project. 1987.
Portland Civic Theater, Portland, OR, $5,000. For current projects. 1987.
Storefront Theater, Portland, OR, $5,000. For Marketing Program. 1987.

2677
William S. Walton Charitable Trust
c/o United States National Bank of Oregon
P.O. Box 3168
Portland 97208

Trust established in 1958 in OR.
Donor(s): William S. Walton.†
Financial data (yr. ended 5/31/87): Assets, $728,892 (M); expenditures, $152,833, including $135,000 for 15 grants (high: $25,000; low: $2,000; average: $2,500-$15,000).
Purpose and activities: Giving primarily for youth agencies, higher education, cultural programs, and Protestant welfare funds. Support for capital improvements only, including building funds, equipment and materials and renovation projects.
Types of support: Building funds, equipment, renovation projects.
Limitations: Giving limited to the Salem, OR, area. No grants to individuals, or for endowment funds, general operating support, scholarships, fellowships, or matching gifts; no loans.
Application information:
Initial approach: Full proposal
Copies of proposal: 1
Deadline(s): Submit proposal preferably from June through Aug.; deadline Sept. 15
Board meeting date(s): Oct.
Final notification: October 30
Write: Floyd K. Bowers, Trustee
Trustees: Floyd K. Bowers, United States National Bank of Oregon.
Number of staff: 2 part-time professional.
Employer Identification Number: 930432836

2678
Wessinger Foundation
1133 West Burnside
Portland 97209 (503) 222-4351

Established in 1979.
Financial data (yr. ended 9/30/88): Assets, $4,060,016 (M); expenditures, $257,594, including $199,750 for 25 grants (high: $50,000; low: $250).
Purpose and activities: Giving for higher education, cultural programs, youth agencies, social services, and historic preservation organizations.
Limitations: Giving limited to the Pacific Northwest, with emphasis on the Tri-County area.
Application information:
Initial approach: Letter
Deadline(s): None
Officers and Directors: W.W. Wessinger, Pres.; Fred G. Wessinger, V.P.; Thomas B. Steol, Secy.; Donald Frisbee, John C. Hampton.
Employer Identification Number: 930754224

2679
Wheeler Foundation
1211 S.W. Fifth Ave., Suite 2906
Portland 97204-1911 (503) 228-0261

Established in 1965 in OR.
Donor(s): Coleman H. Wheeler,† Cornelia T. Wheeler.
Financial data (yr. ended 12/31/88): Assets, $4,286,526 (M); gifts received, $20,000; expenditures, $263,290, including $240,125 for 95 grants (high: $15,000; low: $250; average: $1,000).
Purpose and activities: Emphasis on higher and secondary education, medical services and research, cultural programs, and youth agencies.
Types of support: General purposes.
Limitations: Giving primarily in OR. No grants to individuals, or for endowment funds.
Application information:
Initial approach: Letter along with copy of IRS determination letter
Copies of proposal: 1
Deadline(s): None
Board meeting date(s): Mar., June, Sept., and Dec.
Write: Samuel C. Wheeler, Pres.
Officers and Directors: Samuel C. Wheeler, Pres.; John C. Wheeler, V.P.; David A. Kekel, Secy.-Treas.; Lil M. Hendrickson.
Number of staff: 1 part-time professional.
Employer Identification Number: 930553801

2680
The Woodard Family Foundation
P.O. Box 97
Cottage Grove 97424

Incorporated in 1952 in OR.
Financial data (yr. ended 6/30/87): Assets, $2,344,425 (M); expenditures, $99,850, including $79,506 for 39 grants (high: $20,700; low: $25).
Purpose and activities: Support for education, community development, social services, and culture.
Limitations: Giving primarily in OR.
Officers: Carlton Woodard, Pres.; Dutee Woodard, V.P.; Kim Woodard, Secy.-Treas.
Employer Identification Number: 936026550

PENNSYLVANIA

2681
Action Industries Charitable Foundation
460 Nixon Rd.
Cheswick 15024 (412) 782-4800

Established in 1976 in PA.
Donor(s): Action Industries, Inc.
Financial data (yr. ended 12/31/87): Assets, $565,376 (M); expenditures, $87,433, including $86,733 for 15 grants (high: $63,750; low: $50).
Purpose and activities: Support for culture, community funds, Jewish giving, and education, including higher education.
Limitations: Giving primarily in Pittsburgh, PA.
Application information:
Initial approach: Letter
Deadline(s): None
Write: Amos Comay, Trustee
Trustees: Steven H. Berez, Sholom D. Comay, David Shapira.
Employer Identification Number: 251299973

2682
Air Products and Chemicals, Inc. Corporate Giving Program
Public Affairs Dept.
Allentown 18195 (215) 481-8079

Financial data (yr. ended 9/30/88): Total giving, $1,553,500, including $768,500 for grants (high: $160,000; low: $500; average: $1,000-$5,000), $460,000 for 1,700 employee matching gifts and $325,000 for in-kind gifts.
Purpose and activities: Supports education, health, welfare, chemistry, community development, drug abuse issues, civic improvement, culture and the arts.
Types of support: Capital campaigns, employee matching gifts, operating budgets, matching funds, special projects.
Limitations: Giving primarily in headquarters city and major operating areas.
Publications: Informational brochure.
Application information: Include budget, 501(c)(3), and list of contributors and board.
Initial approach: Letter and proposal
Copies of proposal: 1
Deadline(s): None
Board meeting date(s): Monthly
Final notification: Within 3 months
Write: Pamela S. Handwerk, Mgr., Corp. Philanthropy
Number of staff: 1 full-time professional.

2683
The Air Products Foundation
Route 222
Trexlertown 18087 (215) 481-8079
Additional address: c/o Manager, Corporate Philanthropy, Air Products and Chemicals, Inc., Allentown, PA 18195

Incorporated in 1979 in PA.
Donor(s): Air Products and Chemicals, Inc.
Financial data (yr. ended 9/30/88): Assets, $2,636,241 (M); gifts received, $3,000,000; expenditures, $966,583, including $963,071 for 245 grants (high: $250,000; low: $42).
Purpose and activities: Support for the areas of higher education, health, welfare, community investment, culture and art.
Types of support: Operating budgets, continuing support, annual campaigns, seed money, emergency funds, building funds, equipment, special projects, capital campaigns, renovation projects.
Limitations: Giving primarily in areas of company operations throughout the U.S. No support for sectarian religious purposes, political or veterans' organizations, labor groups, national capital campaigns of health organizations, hospital operating expenses, elementary or secondary schools, or organizations receiving support from the United Way. No grants to individuals; no loans.
Publications: Informational brochure (including application guidelines).
Application information:
Initial approach: Proposal
Copies of proposal: 1
Deadline(s): None
Board meeting date(s): Monthly
Final notification: 3 months
Write: Pamela Handwerk, Contribs. Officer
Officers: Leon C. Holt, Jr.,* Chair.; C.P. Powell, V.P.; Richard A. Gray, Jr., Secy.; Ronald D. Barclay, Treas.
Trustees:* Dexter F. Baker, P.L. Thibaut Brian, Jack B. St. Clair, R.M. Davis, R.F. Dee, Walter F. Light.
Number of staff: 1 full-time professional; 1 part-time support.
Employer Identification Number: 232130928

2684
Alco Standard Foundation
P.O. Box 834
Valley Forge 19482-0834 (215) 296-8000

Established in 1974 in PA.
Donor(s): Alco Standard Corp.
Financial data (yr. ended 12/31/87): Assets, $628,752 (M); gifts received, $500,000; expenditures, $236,242, including $151,375 for 145 grants (high: $15,980; low: $25) and $83,379 for 515 employee matching gifts.
Purpose and activities: Emphasis on community funds, education, including an employee matching gift program, hospitals, health, youth, and cultural programs.
Types of support: Employee matching gifts, matching funds.
Limitations: Giving primarily in areas of company operations.
Officers and Directors:* Tinkham Veale III,* Chair.; Ray B. Mundt,* Pres.; William F. Drake, Jr.,* V.P.; O. Gordon Brewer, Jr., Treas.
Employer Identification Number: 237378726

2685
Alcoa Foundation
1501 Alcoa Bldg.
Pittsburgh 15219-1850 (412) 553-2348

Trust established in 1952 in PA; incorporated in 1964.
Donor(s): Aluminum Co. of America.
Financial data (yr. ended 12/31/88): Assets, $215,624,666 (M); expenditures, $12,755,197, including $9,107,326 for 1,381 grants (average: $5,000-$25,000), $448,000 for grants to individuals, $1,204,338 for 1,870 employee matching gifts and $250,000 for loans.
Purpose and activities: Grants chiefly for education, especially higher education, arts and cultural programs, health and welfare organizations, hospitals, civic and community development, and youth organizations.
Types of support: Annual campaigns, building funds, conferences and seminars, continuing support, emergency funds, employee matching gifts, equipment, fellowships, matching funds, operating budgets, research, scholarship funds, seed money, employee-related scholarships, capital campaigns, general purposes, renovation projects, special projects.
Limitations: Giving primarily in areas of company operations. No support for sectarian or religious organizations, political purposes, or elementary or secondary schools. No grants to individuals (except for employee-related scholarships), or for endowment funds; no loans.
Publications: Annual report, informational brochure (including application guidelines).
Application information:
Initial approach: Proposal
Copies of proposal: 1
Deadline(s): None
Board meeting date(s): Monthly
Final notification: 1 to 4 months
Write: Earl L. Gadbery, Pres.
Officers: Earl L. Gadbery,* Pres.; Kathleen R. Burgan, Secy.-Treas.
Directors:* Ernest J. Edwards, Richard L. Fischer, F. Worth Hobbs, Vincent R. Scorsone, Robert F. Slagle, Donald R. Whitlow.
Corporate Trustee: Mellon Bank, N.A.
Number of staff: 4 full-time professional; 3 full-time support.
Employer Identification Number: 251128857

2686
Allegheny Foundation
P.O. Box 268
Pittsburgh 15230 (412) 392-2900

Incorporated in 1953 in PA.
Donor(s): Richard M. Scaife.
Financial data (yr. ended 12/31/88): Assets, $20,852,456 (M); expenditures, $1,531,118, including $1,198,500 for 20 grants (high: $600,000; low: $5,000).
Purpose and activities: Emphasis on organizations concerned with historic preservation and higher education.
Types of support: General purposes, equipment, publications, seed money, operating budgets.
Limitations: Giving primarily in western PA, with emphasis on Pittsburgh. No grants to individuals, or for endowment funds, scholarships, or fellowships; no loans.
Publications: Annual report.
Application information:
Initial approach: Letter
Copies of proposal: 1
Deadline(s): None
Board meeting date(s): Dec.
Final notification: Dec.
Write: Joanne B. Beyer, Pres.
Officers: Richard M. Scaife,* Chair.; Joanne B. Beyer,* Pres.
Trustees:* Margaret R. Battle, Peter B. Bell, Ralph H. Goettler, Doris O'Donnell, Nathan J. Stark, George Weymouth, Arthur P. Ziegler, Jr.
Number of staff: 1 full-time professional; 2 part-time support.
Employer Identification Number: 256012303

2687
Allegheny International Foundation
Two Oliver Plaza
P.O. Box 456
Pittsburgh 15230 (412) 562-4153

Incorporated in 1953 in IL as Chemetron Foundation.
Donor(s): Chemetron Corp., Allegheny International, Inc.
Financial data (yr. ended 12/31/87): Assets, $29,664 (M); expenditures, $4,062, including $3,907 for 4 grants (high: $3,357; low: $100).
Purpose and activities: Support largely for higher education, community funds, hospitals, cultural programs, and youth agencies.
Types of support: Matching funds.
Limitations: No support for religious or fraternal organizations. No grants to individuals.
Application information:
Initial approach: Letter

Deadline(s): None
Write: S.H. Iapalucci, Pres.
Officers: S.H. Iapalucci,* Pres.; J.T. Dougherty, V.P. and Secy.
Directors:* R.J. Weiland.
Employer Identification Number: 366058055

2688
Allegheny Ludlum Corporate Giving Program
1000 Six PPG Pl.
Pittsburgh 15222 (412) 394-2836

Financial data (yr. ended 12/31/88): $92,214 for 42 grants (high: $25,000; low: $100; average: $250-$2,000).
Purpose and activities: Support for civic affairs, community development, cultural programs, social services, Jewish welfare, urban affairs, youth, women, and general charitable giving.
Limitations: Giving primarily in operating locations in CT, IN, NY, OK and PA. No grants to individuals.
Application information:
Initial approach: By mail
Copies of proposal: 1
Deadline(s): None
Write: Jon D. Walton, Chair., Contribs. Comm.
Number of staff: None.

2689
Allegheny Ludlum Foundation
1000 Six PPG Place
Pittsburgh 15222-5479 (412) 394-2836

Established in 1981 in PA.
Donor(s): Allegheny Ludlum Corp.
Financial data (yr. ended 12/31/88): Assets, $1,748,044 (M); gifts received, $500,000; expenditures, $630,348, including $623,107 for 99 grants (high: $211,000; low: $250; average: $500-$5,000).
Purpose and activities: Support primarily for community funds, hospitals, and youth agencies; some support for education.
Types of support: Annual campaigns, building funds, capital campaigns, continuing support, emergency funds, publications, employee-related scholarships, scholarship funds.
Limitations: Giving primarily in PA, IN, CT, NY, and OK. No grants to individuals.
Application information:
Initial approach: Letter
Copies of proposal: 1
Deadline(s): None
Write: Jon D. Walton, Chair. Contribs. Comm.
Trustees: J.L. Murdy, R.P. Simmons, Jon D. Walton, Pittsburgh National Bank.
Number of staff: None.
Employer Identification Number: 256228755

2690
AMPCO-Pittsburgh Foundation, Inc.
600 Giant St., Suite 4600
Pittsburgh 15219 (412) 456-4418

Established in 1957 in PA.
Donor(s): AMPCO-Pittsburgh Corp.
Financial data (yr. ended 12/31/87): Assets, $2,465,071 (M); gifts received, $1,053,289; expenditures, $110,162, including $74,890 for 95 grants (high: $5,000; low: $20) and $25,500 for 31 grants to individuals.
Purpose and activities: Grants primarily for youth, culture, and education; college scholarships awarded to children of full-time company employees.
Types of support: Student aid.
Application information: Application form required for scholarships.
Deadline(s): May 15 for scholarships
Final notification: Late July for scholarships
Write: Rose Hoover, Asst. Secy.
Officers and Trustees: Louis Berkman,* Chair.; Marshall L. Berkman,* Pres.; Robert A. Paul,* V.P. and Treas.; E.H. Moores, Secy.
Employer Identification Number: 396043867

2691
The Annenberg Fund, Inc.
Two Radnor Corp. Center, No. 101
Radnor 19087 (215) 964-8613

Incorporated in 1951 in DE.
Donor(s): Walter H. Annenberg.
Financial data (yr. ended 12/31/87): Assets, $32,350,200 (M); expenditures, $8,159,146, including $8,031,520 for 291 grants (high: $1,500,000; low: $100; average: $100-$100,000).
Purpose and activities: Emphasis on higher education, health and medical research, including medical education, cultural programs, and community services.
Types of support: Research, building funds, general purposes.
Limitations: Giving primarily in PA, CA, and NY. No grants to individuals.
Application information: Applications not accepted.
Board meeting date(s): Irregularly
Write: Alice C. Cory, Secy.
Officers and Directors: Walter H. Annenberg, Pres.; Leonore Annenberg, V.P.; William J. Henrich, Jr., V.P.; Alice C. Cory, Secy.-Treas; Wallis Annenberg.
Number of staff: 5
Employer Identification Number: 236286756

2692
Arronson Foundation
2400 One Reading Center
Philadelphia 19107

Established in 1957 in DE.
Donor(s): Gertrude Arronson.†
Financial data (yr. ended 10/31/87): Assets, $6,673,210 (M); expenditures, $594,709, including $560,143 for 45 grants (high: $185,000; low: $250).
Purpose and activities: Emphasis on Jewish giving, education, particularly higher education; support also for cultural programs and hospitals.
Officers: Harold E. Kohn, Pres.; Edith Kohn, V.P.; Joseph C. Kohn, V.P.; Stuart H. Savett, V.P.; Bayard M. Graf, Secy.-Treas.
Employer Identification Number: 236259604

2693
Babcock Charitable Trust
2220 Palmer St.
Pittsburgh 15218 (412) 351-3515

Established in 1957 in PA.
Donor(s): Fred C. Babcock.
Financial data (yr. ended 12/31/87): Assets, $1,516,994 (M); gifts received, $1,224,000; expenditures, $20,767, including $20,356 for 49 grants (high: $1,900; low: $25).
Purpose and activities: Support primarily for secondary and higher education, community funds, youth organizations and cultural programs.
Application information:
Initial approach: Letter
Deadline(s): None
Write: Fred C. Babcock, Trustee
Trustees: Fred C. Babcock, Jean B. Harbeck, Carl P. Stillitano.
Employer Identification Number: 256035161

2694
Barra Foundation, Inc.
8200 Flourtown Ave., Suite 12
Wyndmoor 19118 (215) 233-5115

Incorporated in 1963 in DE.
Donor(s): Robert L. McNeil, Jr.
Financial data (yr. ended 12/31/87): Assets, $23,084,749 (M); expenditures, $1,833,759, including $1,501,453 for 187 grants (high: $300,000; low: $250; average: $500-$10,000).
Purpose and activities: Giving for the advancement and diffusion of knowledge and its effective application to human needs in certain fields, particularly in Eighteenth Century American art and material culture. Projects must be pilot studies or enterprises requiring foresight, not supported by other agencies or individuals; publication or studies required.
Types of support: Matching funds, publications, special projects.
Limitations: Giving primarily in the Philadelphia, PA, area. No grants to individuals, or for annual or capital campaigns, building or endowment funds, operating budgets, deficit drives, scholarships, fellowships, or ongoing programs; no loans.
Publications: Program policy statement.
Application information: Application form required.
Initial approach: Letter
Copies of proposal: 3
Deadline(s): None
Board meeting date(s): Dec. and as appropriate
Final notification: 3 to 6 months
Write: Robert L. McNeil, Jr., Pres.
Officers and Directors: Robert L. McNeil, Jr., Pres. and Treas.; William T. Tredennick, V.P.; George M. Brodhead, Secy.; Herman R. Hutchinson, E. Marshall Nuckols, Jr.
Number of staff: 1 part-time support.
Employer Identification Number: 236277885

2695
Bayer-Mobay Foundation
Mobay Rd.
Pittsburgh 15205-9741 (412) 394-5542

Established in 1985 in PA.
Donor(s): Mobay Corp.
Financial data (yr. ended 12/31/87): Assets, $7,099,946 (M); gifts received, $295,000; expenditures, $490,347, including $457,620 for 67 grants (high: $115,000; low: $125).
Purpose and activities: Support for a community fund, higher education, culture and civic affairs.
Application information: Application form required.
Deadline(s): None
Write: W.C. Ostern, Pres.
Officers: W.C. Ostern, Pres.; E.L. Reichard, V.P.; R.W. Brown, V.P. and Secy.-Treas.
Employer Identification Number: 251508079

2696
Helen D. Groome Beatty Trust
c/o Mellon Bank (East), N.A.
P.O. Box 7899
Philadelphia 19101-7899 (215) 585-3208

Trust established in 1951 in PA.
Donor(s): Helen D. Groome Beatty.†
Financial data (yr. ended 9/30/87): Assets, $5,275,840 (M); expenditures, $317,162, including $274,197 for 94 grants (high: $11,575; low: $1,000).
Purpose and activities: To provide capital support for charitable and educational institutions, with emphasis on higher education, hospitals, and cultural programs.
Types of support: Building funds, renovation projects.
Limitations: Giving primarily in the Philadelphia, PA, metropolitan area. No grants to individuals, or for endowment funds, or operating budgets.
Publications: Application guidelines.
Application information:
Initial approach: Proposal, telephone, or letter
Copies of proposal: 1
Deadline(s): Apr. 15 or Oct. 15
Board meeting date(s): May 15 and Nov. 15
Write: Patricia M. Kling, Trust Officer, Mellon Bank (East), N.A.
Trustee: Mellon Bank, N.A.
Employer Identification Number: 236224798

2697
Bell Telephone Company of Pennsylvania Giving Program
One Pkwy., 9th FL-A
Philadelphia 19102 (215) 466-2257

Financial data (yr. ended 12/31/88): Total giving, $2,487,548, including $2,352,947 for grants (average: $1,000-$400,000) and $134,601 for 740 employee matching gifts.
Purpose and activities: Supports education, health, welfare, civic affairs, culture and the arts.
Types of support: General purposes, capital campaigns, special projects, employee matching gifts.
Limitations: Giving primarily in operating territory, Harrisburg and Pittsburgh, PA. No support for political, fraternal, religious, and veterans' organizations. No grants to individuals.
Application information:
Initial approach: Letter and proposal, along with IRS form indicating nonprofit, 501(C)(3) status
Copies of proposal: 1
Deadline(s): Third quarter
Board meeting date(s): Jan. of each year
Final notification: 2 weeks
Write: Charles D. Fulton, Corp. Contribs. Mgr.
Number of staff: 7

2698
Claude Worthington Benedum Foundation
1400 Benedum-Trees Bldg.
Pittsburgh 15222 (412) 288-0360

Incorporated in 1944 in PA.
Donor(s): Michael Late Benedum,† Sarah N. Benedum.†
Financial data (yr. ended 12/31/88): Assets, $146,790,484 (M); expenditures, $7,920,551, including $7,056,551 for 79 grants (high: $1,000,000; low: $3,000; average: $10,000-$125,000).
Purpose and activities: Grants are made in areas of education, health and human services, community and economic development, and the arts. Funds are provided for projects that address regional problems and needs, that establish demonstration projects with strong potential for replication in WV, or that make outstanding contributions to the area. Local initiatives and voluntary support are encouraged by the foundation.
Types of support: Matching funds, consulting services, building funds, operating budgets, technical assistance, special projects, program-related investments, seed money.
Limitations: Giving limited to WV and to the greater Pittsburgh, PA, area. No support for national health and welfare campaigns, medical research, or religious activities. No grants to individuals.
Publications: Biennial report (including application guidelines).
Application information:
Initial approach: Letter or telephone
Copies of proposal: 1
Board meeting date(s): Mar., June, Sept., and Dec.
Final notification: Up to 6 months
Write: Paul R. Jenkins, Pres.
Officers: Henry A. Bergstrom,* Chair.; Paul R. Jenkins,* Pres.; David L. Wagner, V.P. and Treas.; Elizabeth Pusateri, Secy.
Trustees:* Paul G. Benedum, Jr., Harry C. Hamm, Jennings Randolph, Hulett C. Smith, George A. Stinson.
Number of staff: 5 full-time professional; 1 part-time professional; 3 full-time support.
Employer Identification Number: 251086799

2699
Beneficia Foundation
One Pitcairn Place
Jenkintown 19046-3593 (215) 887-6700

Incorporated in 1953 in PA.
Donor(s): Members of the Theodore Pitcairn Family.
Financial data (yr. ended 4/30/87): Assets, $11,338,289 (M); expenditures, $652,364, including $535,500 for 50 grants (high: $214,300; low: $500).
Purpose and activities: Emphasis on conservation, music, the arts, education, and church support.
Limitations: Giving primarily in PA. No grants to individuals.
Application information:
Deadline(s): Mar. 31
Write: Feodor U. Pitcairn, Exec. Secy.
Officers and Directors: Laren Pitcairn, Pres.; Miriam P. Mitchell, V.P.; Feodor U. Pitcairn, Exec. Secy.; Mark J. Pennink, Treas.; Diene P. Cooper, Douglas J. Cooper, J. Daniel Mitchell, John D. Mitchell, Mark J. Pennink, Kirstin O. Pitcairn, Mary Eleanor Pitcairn.
Number of staff: None.
Employer Identification Number: 246015630

2700
Bergstrom Foundation
1800 Benedum Trees Bldg.
Pittsburgh 15222 (412) 471-1751

Established in 1960 in PA.
Donor(s): Henry A. Bergstrom, Margaret A. Bergstrom.
Financial data (yr. ended 12/31/86): Assets, $1,395,355 (M); expenditures, $77,554, including $61,400 for 25 grants (high: $25,000; low: $100).
Purpose and activities: Giving primarily for education, particularly higher education, and cultural programs.
Types of support: General purposes.
Limitations: Giving primarily in the Pittsburgh, PA, area. No grants to individuals.
Application information:
Deadline(s): None
Write: Henry A. Bergstrom, Pres.
Officer and Trustees: Henry A. Bergstrom, Pres.; Henry A. Bergstrom, Jr.
Employer Identification Number: 251112093

2701
Allen H. & Selma W. Berkman Charitable Trust
One Oxford Centre, 40th Fl.
Pittsburgh 15219 (412) 392-2020
Application address: 5000 Fifth Ave., Pittsburgh, PA 15232

Established in 1972 in PA.
Donor(s): Allen H. Berkman, Selma W. Berkman.
Financial data (yr. ended 10/31/88): Assets, $1,732,295 (M); gifts received, $103,710; expenditures, $154,821, including $149,000 for 37 grants (high: $50,000; low: $250; average: $1,500).
Purpose and activities: Giving primarily for higher and other educational institutions, and

social services, including programs for the aged, child development, and the handicapped; support also for health and hospitals; the performing arts, historic preservation, and other cultural programs; and community and urban development.
Types of support: Special projects, annual campaigns, building funds, capital campaigns, continuing support, emergency funds, endowment funds, fellowships, general purposes, operating budgets, scholarship funds, technical assistance, research, program-related investments.
Limitations: Giving primarily in the Pittsburgh, PA, area.
Publications: Annual report, 990-PF.
Application information:
Initial approach: Letter
Copies of proposal: 1
Deadline(s): Sept. 1
Write: Allen H. Berkman, Trustee
Trustees: Barbara B. Ackerman, Allen H. Berkman, Richard L. Berkman, Selma W. Berkman, Susan B. Rahm.
Number of staff: None.
Employer Identification Number: 256144060

2702
Bethlehem Area Foundation
430 East Broad St.
Bethlehem 18018 (215) 867-7588

Community foundation established in 1967 in PA.
Financial data (yr. ended 6/30/88): Assets, $2,728,804 (M); gifts received, $81,156; expenditures, $180,069, including $146,508 for 31 grants (high: $10,000; low: $1,000; average: $2,000-$6,000).
Purpose and activities: Giving primarily for health, education and training, social services, and welfare; support also for cultural programs and civic needs.
Types of support: Seed money, emergency funds, building funds, equipment, land acquisition, matching funds, special projects, capital campaigns, renovation projects, publications.
Limitations: Giving limited to the Bethlehem, PA, area. No support for sectarian religious purposes. No grants to individuals, or for operating budgets, continuing support, annual campaigns, deficit financing, endowments, scholarships, or research; no loans.
Publications: Annual report (including application guidelines), grants list, application guidelines, program policy statement.
Application information: Capital funding: must submit invoice copies when requesting release of funds. Program: brief progress report in June; program evaluation by Oct.
Initial approach: Letter
Copies of proposal: 5
Deadline(s): Submit proposal from June 1 to Aug. 1
Board meeting date(s): Oct.
Final notification: Oct.
Write: Eleanor A. Boylston, Exec. Dir.
Officers: Msgr. John McPeak,* Chair.; Joseph F. Leeson, Jr.,* Vice-Chair.; Eleanor A. Boylston, Secy. and Exec. Dir.
Board of Governors:* Curtis H. Barnette, Martha Cusimano, John R. Mendenhall, Jose Perna, Cidney B. Spillman, Nancy W. Swan, Edwin F. Van Billiard.
Trustee Banks: First Valley Bank, Lehigh Valley Bank, Meridian Bank.
Number of staff: 1 part-time professional.
Employer Identification Number: 231686634

2703
Bethlehem Steel Corporate Giving Program
Martin Tower
8th & Eaton Aves., Rm. 435
Bethlehem 18016 (215) 694-2424

Financial data (yr. ended 12/31/88): Total giving, $1,000,000, including $970,000 for grants (high: $50,000; low: $1,000; average: $1,000-$5,000) and $30,000 for in-kind gifts.
Purpose and activities: Supports education, health, human services, economic education, public policy, arts, culture and civic affairs.
Types of support: Capital campaigns, general purposes, continuing support.
Limitations: Giving primarily in major operating locations.
Application information: Present moratorium on new requests. Applications not accepted.
Write: James F. Kostecky, Dir., Corp. Support
Number of staff: 3 full-time professional; 1 part-time professional.

2704
Binswanger Foundation
c/o The Binswanger Co.
1845 Walnut St.
Philadelphia 19103 (215) 448-6000

Donor(s): Binswanger Corp.
Financial data (yr. ended 12/31/87): Assets, $959,903 (M); gifts received, $146,975; expenditures, $235,691, including $223,310 for grants (high: $83,000).
Purpose and activities: Support for Jewish giving, United Way, civic affairs, culture, including the fine and performing arts and music, and higher education.
Limitations: No grants to individuals.
Application information:
Initial approach: Letter
Deadline(s): None
Write: Frank G. Binswanger, Sr.
Officers: Frank G. Binswanger, Sr., Chair.; Frank G. Binswanger, Jr., Vice-Chair.; Samuel Levy, Secy.; John K. Binswanger, Treas.
Employer Identification Number: 236296506

2705
H. M. Bitner Charitable Trust
One Mellon Bank Ctr.
Pittsburgh 15258 (412) 234-4695

Established in PA in 1955.
Donor(s): H.M. Bitner, Evelyn H. Bitner.
Financial data (yr. ended 12/31/86): Assets, $1,499,000 (M); expenditures, $97,690, including $75,250 for 39 grants (high: $5,000; low: $500; average: $1,000).
Purpose and activities: Giving for higher and other education, cultural programs, including performing arts, hospitals, medical research, and social service agencies.
Types of support: General purposes, operating budgets.
Application information: Application guidelines available from the foundation upon request.
Write: Eileen Wilhem, Asst. V.P., Mellon Bank, N.A.
Trustees: Jessie N. Bitner, John Howard Bitner, Linnea McQuiston, Evelyn Bitner Pearson, Mellon Bank, N.A.
Employer Identification Number: 256018931

2706
The Buhl Foundation
Four Gateway Center, Rm. 1522
Pittsburgh 15222 (412) 566-2711

Trust established in 1927 in PA.
Donor(s): Henry Buhl, Jr.†
Financial data (yr. ended 6/30/88): Assets, $34,583,787 (M); expenditures, $1,332,503, including $985,023 for 41 grants (high: $115,000; low: $2,500; average: $5,000-$50,000).
Purpose and activities: Emphasis on "developmental or innovative" grants to regional institutions, with special interest in education at all levels and in regional concerns, particularly those related to problems of children and youth.
Types of support: Seed money, special projects, research, continuing support.
Limitations: Giving primarily in southwestern PA, particularly the Pittsburgh area. No support for religious activities or nationally funded organizations. No grants to individuals, or for building or endowment funds, operating budgets, scholarships, fellowships, equipment, land acquisition, annual campaigns, emergency funds, deficit financing, renovation projects, publications, conferences or seminars (unless grant-related); no loans.
Publications: Annual report, informational brochure (including application guidelines).
Application information: Submit final proposal upon invitation only.
Initial approach: Letter
Copies of proposal: 1
Deadline(s): None
Board meeting date(s): Monthly
Final notification: Approximately 3 months normally
Write: Dr. Doreen E. Boyce, Exec. Dir.
Officers and Managers:* John G. Frazer, Jr.,* Pres.; Francis B. Nimick, Jr.,* V.P.; William H. Rea,* V.P.; Katherine E. Schumacher, Secy.; John M. Arthur,* Treas.; Doreen E. Boyce, Exec. Dir.
Number of staff: 2 full-time professional; 2 full-time support.
Employer Identification Number: 250378910
Recent arts and culture grants:
Carnegie, The, Buhl Science Center, Pittsburgh, PA, $1,000,000. For new Science Center Planetarium. 4/20/88.
Fort Ligonier Association, Ligonier, PA, $10,000. Toward funds required to match National Endowment for Humanities award to endow education and curatorial programs. 2/5/88.
International Poetry Forum, Pittsburgh, PA, $30,000. To support initiation of publication program, The Spoken Page. 9/25/87.

2707
Alpin J. and Alpin W. Cameron Memorial Fund
c/o First Pennsylvania Bank, N.A.
Fifteenth and Chestnut Sts.
Philadelphia 19101

Trust established in 1957 in PA.
Financial data (yr. ended 9/30/87): Assets, $2,477,269 (M); gifts received, $3,405; expenditures, $120,434, including $103,250 for 58 grants (high: $7,500; low: $500).
Purpose and activities: Emphasis on higher education, cultural programs, and hospitals.
Limitations: Giving primarily in the Philadelphia, PA, area.
Application information:
Write: Gregory D'Angelo, Trust Admin., First Pennsylvania Bank, N.A.
Trustee: First Pennsylvania Bank, N.A.
Employer Identification Number: 236213225

2708
Charles Talbot Campbell Foundation
c/o The Union National Bank of Pittsburgh
P.O. Box 837
Pittsburgh 15230

Trust established in 1975 in PA.
Donor(s): Charles Talbot Campbell.†
Financial data (yr. ended 12/31/88): Assets, $4,225,000 (M); expenditures, $288,000, including $280,000 for 13 grants (high: $75,000; low: $5,000; average: $20,000).
Purpose and activities: Emphasis on hospitals and ophthalmological research, agencies for the handicapped, and music.
Limitations: Giving primarily in PA. No support for community funds, including United Way. No grants to individuals; no loans.
Application information:
Copies of proposal: 1
Write: William M. Schmidt, V.P.
Trustee: Union National Bank of Pittsburgh.
Employer Identification Number: 251287221

2709
E. Rhodes & Leona B. Carpenter Foundation
c/o Joseph A. O'Connor, Jr., Morgan, Lewis & Bockius
2000 One Logan Square
Philadelphia 19103

Established in 1975 in VA.
Donor(s): E. Rhodes Carpenter.†
Financial data (yr. ended 12/31/86): Assets, $15,948,611 (M); gifts received, $4,086,105; expenditures, $320,111, including $200,000 for 1 grant.
Purpose and activities: Main areas of interest include the arts, education, human health, and scientific research.
Limitations: Giving primarily in areas east of the Mississippi River. No support for local church congregations or parishes. No grants to individuals.
Application information:
Initial approach: Letter
Deadline(s): None
Officers: Ann Day, Pres.; Paul Day, Jr., V.P. and Secy.-Treas.
Director: M.H. Reinhart.
Employer Identification Number: 510155772

2710
Carpenter Technology Corporation Foundation
101 West Bern St.
P.O. Box 662
Reading 19601 (215) 371-2214

Incorporated in 1953 in NJ; re-incorporated in 1981 in DE as the Carpenter Technology Corporation Foundation.
Donor(s): Carpenter Technology Corp.
Financial data (yr. ended 9/30/88): Assets, $564,322 (M); gifts received, $300,000; expenditures, $250,344, including $219,562 for 91 grants (high: $83,000; low: $100) and $30,471 for 220 employee matching gifts.
Purpose and activities: Support for community funds, health and welfare, culture and the arts, civic and public affairs, and higher education, including giving toward scholarship funds. Company also has an employee matching gifts program toward colleges and universities.
Types of support: Employee matching gifts, scholarship funds, building funds, general purposes, fellowships, research, special projects, employee-related scholarships.
Limitations: Giving primarily in areas of company operations, especially the Reading, PA, area. No grants to individuals.
Publications: Program policy statement, application guidelines.
Application information: Application form required for scholarships.
Initial approach: Letter
Deadline(s): Dec. of preceding academic year for scholarships
Board meeting date(s): Semiannually
Write: W.J. Pendleton, V.P.
Officers: Paul R. Roedel,* Pres.; W.J. Pendleton, V.P.; Daniel K. Rothermel, Secy.; John A. Schuler, Treas.
Directors:* H.O. Beaver, Jr., Chair.; T. Beaver, Jr., W.E.C. Dearden, C.R. Garr, A.E. Humphrey, J.L. Jones, Frederick C. Langenberg, A.J. Lena, H.R. Sharbaugh, S. James Spitz, Jr., H.W. Walker II.
Employer Identification Number: 232191214

2711
Louis N. Cassett Foundation
Three Mellon Bank Center, 32nd Fl.
Philadelphia 19102-2468 (215) 963-3391

Trust established in 1946 in PA.
Donor(s): Louis N. Cassett.†
Financial data (yr. ended 12/31/86): Assets, $5,500,000 (M); expenditures, $450,000, including $450,000 for 132 grants (high: $40,000; low: $100; average: $3,000).
Purpose and activities: Support for higher education, hospitals, medical research, and health agencies, including aid to the handicapped; some support also for cultural programs.
Types of support: Annual campaigns, building funds.
Limitations: Giving primarily in the northeastern U.S. No grants to individuals or for endowment funds.
Application information:
Initial approach: Proposal
Copies of proposal: 1
Deadline(s): Submit proposal in 2nd half of year
Board meeting date(s): As required
Write: Joseph Oberndorf, Trustee
Trustees: Albert J. Elias, Carol Gerstley Katz, Joseph Oberndorf.
Number of staff: None.
Employer Identification Number: 236274038

2712
CIGNA Corporate Giving Program
One Logan Sq.
Philadelphia 19103 (215) 523-5255
Application address in CT: James N. Mason, Jr., Dir., Civic Affairs, CIGNA Corp., W-A, 900 Cottage Grove Ave., Bloomfield, CT 06002

Financial data (yr. ended 12/31/88): $6,980,000 for loans.
Purpose and activities: CIGNA sometimes complements Foundation programs with direct contributions to community relations projects, including support for civic and cultural events, in-kind donations of materials and services, and memberships in civic organizations. The Community Investment Program is a joint effort of CIGNA investment and public affairs professionals that makes targeted below-market rate investments to community development projects which are socially productive, but which do not meet conventional lending criteria for risk and yield; investments are made in the areas of community economic development, housing, and culture and the arts, with an emphasis on those projects which produce affordable housing or create jobs in economically depressed areas, particularly in Hartford and Philadelphia. CIGNA recognizes the efforts of employee volunteers who work in educational and social service organizations through the Grants-for-Givers program, Volunteer of the Month Award, and the Annual Community Service Award.
Types of support: In-kind gifts.
Limitations: Giving primarily in the greater Philadelphia, PA, area, and the greater Hartford, CT, area. No support for sectarian religious activities, or research and treatment of specific diseases, political organizations or campaigns, lobbying groups, or organizations primarily funded by United Way. No grants to individuals, or for capital campaigns, endowment drives, improvements or expansions, or hospital campaigns.
Application information: Letter including description of organization, project and goals, budget, list of board members, 501(c)(3) and most recent 990 form.
Copies of proposal: 1
Deadline(s): None
Write: Jeffrey P. Lindtner, Exec. Dir., CIGNA Fdn.

2713
CIGNA Foundation
One Logan Sq.
Philadelphia 19103 (215) 523-5255
Organizations in the greater Hartford area, write to: James N. Mason, Dir., Civic Affairs, CIGNA Corp., W-A, 900 Cottage Grove Ave., Bloomfield, CT 06002

Incorporated in 1962 in PA; merged with Connecticut General Contributions and Civic Affairs Department in 1982.
Donor(s): CIGNA Corp.
Financial data (yr. ended 12/31/87): Assets, $1,369,316 (M); gifts received, $7,599,963; expenditures, $8,114,288, including $6,940,322 for 413 grants (high: $935,424; low: $100; average: $2,000-$100,000) and $1,059,867 for employee matching gifts.
Purpose and activities: Support for a broad range of programs in education, health and human services, civic affairs, and the arts, with priority placed on public secondary education, higher education for minority students, programs which favorably influence CIGNA's business environment, community economic development, and culture and the arts. Special emphasis on increasing literacy, career education, and minority higher education, programs which contribute to an improved understanding of societal issues significant to business and economic development in Philadelphia, PA and Hartford, CT.
Types of support: Employee matching gifts, general purposes, annual campaigns, seed money, emergency funds, fellowships, matching funds, operating budgets, scholarship funds, employee-related scholarships, special projects.
Limitations: Giving primarily in Hartford, CT, and Philadelphia, PA; and to selected national organizations. No support for religious organizations for religious purposes, political organizations or campaigns, or disease-specific research or treatment organizations. No grants to individuals, or endowment drives, capital campaigns, organizations receiving major support through the United Way or other CIGNA-supported federated funding agencies, or hospital capital improvements and expansions.
Publications: Annual report (including application guidelines).
Application information: In the Greater Hartford area, direct requests to Bloomfield, CT office; other requests go to Philadelphia, PA office.
Initial approach: Letter of one or two pages
Deadline(s): None
Board meeting date(s): Biennially
Final notification: 6 weeks
Write: Jeffrey P. Lindtner, Exec. Dir.
Officers: Barry F. Wiksten, Pres.; Jeffrey P. Lindtner, Exec. Dir.; Thomas J. Wagner, Secy.
Directors: James W. Walker, Jr., Chair.; Thomas H. Dooley, Caleb L. Fowler, Donald M. Levinson, G. Robert O'Brien, James G. Stewart, George R. Trumbull.
Number of staff: 6
Employer Identification Number: 236261726

2714
Claneil Foundation, Inc.
One Plymouth Meeting, Suite 511
Plymouth Meeting 19462 (215) 828-6331

Incorporated in 1968 in DE.
Donor(s): Henry S. McNeil.
Financial data (yr. ended 12/31/87): Assets, $5,861,863 (M); expenditures, $383,816, including $337,038 for grants.
Purpose and activities: Support largely for arts education, higher and secondary education, cultural programs, health and social services, and family planning.
Limitations: Giving primarily in PA.
Application information:
Initial approach: Proposal
Deadline(s): None
Write: Dr. Henry A. Jordan, Exec. Dir.
Officers and Directors: Lois F. McNeil, Pres.; Barbara M. Jordan, V.P.; Warrin C. Meyers, V.P.; George M. Brodhead, Secy.; Langhorne B. Smith, Treas.; Henry A. Jordan, Exec. Dir.
Employer Identification Number: 236445450

2715
The Anne L. and George H. Clapp Charitable and Educational Trust
c/o Mellon Bank, N.A.
One Mellon Bank Ctr.
Pittsburgh 15230 (412) 234-5598

Donor(s): George H. Clapp.†
Financial data (yr. ended 9/30/88): Assets, $9,221,105 (M); expenditures, $547,476, including $453,500 for 37 grants (high: $30,500; low: $3,000).
Purpose and activities: Giving primarily for education, hospitals, health and social services, cultural programs, a community fund, and youth agencies.
Limitations: Giving primarily in the Pittsburgh, PA, area.
Application information:
Initial approach: Letter; application form provided after initial contact
Deadline(s): None
Write: William B. Outy, V.P., Mellon Bank, N.A.
Trustees: William E. Collins, Katherine Clapp Galbraith, Mellon Bank, N.A.
Employer Identification Number: 256018976

2716
Ethel D. Colket Foundation
1632 Chestnut St.
Philadelphia 19103

Established in 1964 in PA.
Financial data (yr. ended 8/31/87): Assets, $1,620,634 (M); gifts received, $0; expenditures, $47,666, including $35,000 for 14 grants (high: $8,000; low: $500).
Purpose and activities: Support primarily for hospitals; giving also for opera, ballet, and other musical activities; contributions to churches and other religious, scientific, literary or educational activities.
Limitations: Giving primarily in the Delaware Valley, PA, area.
Application information:
Initial approach: Letter
Deadline(s): None
Trustee: Provident National Bank.
Employer Identification Number: 236292917

2717
Colonial Penn Group Corporate Giving Program
Colonial Penn Plaza
5 Penn Center Plaza
Philadelphia 19181 (215) 988-8000

Financial data (yr. ended 12/31/86): $400,000 for grants (high: $190,000; low: $250; average: $1,000-$1,500).
Purpose and activities: Support for 1) Health-emphasis on research programs designed to improve the health care of the elderly; also considers support for programs that work toward the reduction of health care costs through either preventive medicine or other types of programs; 2) Education-emphasis on higher education, with particular emphasis upon those institutions located in primary operating areas. Also focus attention and contributions upon gerontological programs within higher education. Additional support through employee matching gifts to education; 3) Welfare-support for organizations that aid underprivileged citizens in the community and that help to promote general social improvement; particular attention to those requests that do not duplicate, overlap or neutralize the efforts of the community-wide endeavors to which Colonial Penn has already contributed; in addition, support to new community organizations which do not qualify for participation in community-federated drives; 4) Human Rights-striving for the elimination of discrimination based on stereotypes, contributions in this area are made to organizations that address themselves to the inequities and discriminations against the elderly, blacks, women and others; 5) Civic-support for nonprofit organizations and causes that work together to help solve the more pressing needs of communities; 6) Cultural-in order to help provide a wholesome environment in which to live, work, and conduct business, corporate giving in this area is focused on community organizations and institutions, outside of the area of higher education as such, in the visual and performing arts, the humanities, and the physical and natural sciences. It is Colonial Penn's policy that exceptions to the guidelines as outlined above should not be made unless extreme exigencies accompany the requests.
Types of support: Matching funds, general purposes.
Limitations: Giving primarily in major operating areas.
Application information: The administration of Colonial Penn Group's corporate giving program is the responsibility of the Corporate Contributions Committee, which consists of six persons, is appointed by the Chair., and is chaired by the Sr. V.P. of Corporate Affairs.
Initial approach: Proposal
Write: Nina Kenney, V.P. and Chair., Contribs. Comm.

2718
Consolidated Natural Gas Company Foundation
c/o CNG Tower
625 Liberty Ave.
Pittsburgh 15222-3199 (412) 227-1185

Established about 1984 in PA.
Donor(s): Consolidated Natural Gas Co.
Financial data (yr. ended 12/31/87): Assets, $4,787,622 (M); gifts received, $5,300,000; expenditures, $3,502,627, including $3,256,324 for 757 grants and $189,243 for employee matching gifts.
Purpose and activities: Support for human services, community funds and development, education, and culture and the arts.
Types of support: Employee matching gifts, operating budgets, matching funds, annual campaigns, building funds, capital campaigns, conferences and seminars, continuing support, equipment, general purposes, matching funds, operating budgets, renovation projects, special projects.
Limitations: Giving primarily in PA, OH, WV, NY, LA, OK, and areas where the company has business interests. No support for fraternal, political, or labor organizations, or organizations for strictly sectarian purposes. No grants to individuals, or for operating funds of United Way-supported organizations, fundraising activities, or courtesy advertising.
Publications: Multi-year report, informational brochure (including application guidelines).
Application information:
Initial approach: Letter
Deadline(s): Sept. 1 for support renewal requests
Board meeting date(s): varies
Write: Ray N. Ivey, V.P.
Officers and Directors: D.E. Weatherwax, Pres.; Ray N. Ivey, V.P. and Exec. Dir.; S.M. Banda, Secy. and Mgr.; R.J. Bean, Jr., R.T. Fetters, D.P. Hunt, R. Gifford, L.J. Timms, Jr., R.E. Wright.
Trustee: Mellon Bank, N.A.
Employer Identification Number: 136077762

2719
Copernicus Society of America
1950 Pennsylvania Ave.
P.O. Box 385
Fort Washington 19034 (215) 628-3632

Established in 1972 in PA.
Donor(s): Edward J. Piszek, Sr.
Financial data (yr. ended 6/30/87): Assets, $6,045,225 (M); gifts received, $5,000; expenditures, $466,150, including $361,151 for 16 grants.
Purpose and activities: Grants largely for cultural programs and historic preservation.
Types of support: Continuing support, endowment funds, publications, conferences and seminars.
Limitations: No grants to individuals, or for special projects, operating budgets, annual campaigns, seed money, emergency funds, deficit financing, building funds, equipment and materials, land acquisition, matching gifts, scholarships, fellowships, or research; no loans.
Publications: Program policy statement, application guidelines.
Application information:
Initial approach: Proposal
Copies of proposal: 1
Deadline(s): None
Board meeting date(s): Monthly
Final notification: 5 to 6 weeks
Write: P. Erik Nelson, Exec. Dir.
Officers: Edward J. Piszek, Sr.,* Chair. and Pres.; Helen P. Nelson,* V.P. and Secy.; Francis Keenan, V.P.; Edward J. Piszek, Jr.,* V.P.; George Piszek,* V.P.; William P. Piszek,* V.P.; Anne P. Reitenbaugh,* V.P.; Olga P. Piszek,* Treas.; P. Erik Nelson, Exec. Dir.
Directors:* James Draper, Bernard J. McLafferty, Harold B. Montgomery.
Number of staff: 1 full-time professional; 3 part-time support.
Employer Identification Number: 237184731

2720
Copperweld Foundation
Four Gateway Center, 22nd Fl.
Pittsburgh 15222-1211 (412) 263-3200

Established in 1941 in PA.
Financial data (yr. ended 6/30/88): Assets, $1,101,459 (M); expenditures, $61,900, including $58,950 for 44 grants (high: $10,000; low: $100).
Purpose and activities: Support primarily for health, welfare, civic affairs, culture, environment, family planning, minority education, and educational organizations.
Types of support: General purposes.
Limitations: Giving primarily in Pittsburgh, PA.
Publications: Application guidelines.
Application information:
Initial approach: Proposal
Copies of proposal: 1
Deadline(s): None
Board meeting date(s): June 15 and Dec. 15
Write: Douglas E. Young
Trustees: James R. Murray, John D. Turner, Douglas E. Young.
Employer Identification Number: 256035603

2721
Corestates Foundation
c/o PNB, Public Responsibility Dept.
Fifth & Market Sts.
Philadelphia 19106 (215) 973-4181

Financial data (yr. ended 12/31/87): Assets, $222,847 (M); gifts received, $16,500; expenditures, $11,822, including $11,492 for 4 grants (high: $5,000; low: $800).
Purpose and activities: Support for education, and civic and cultural affairs; main emphasis is on neighborhood economic development.
Types of support: Capital campaigns.
Limitations: Giving primarily in Philadelphia, PA, and Bucks, Chester, Delaware, and Montgomery counties.
Application information:
Initial approach: Letter
Directors: Thomas H. Bamford, Joseph Bond, G. Morris Dorrance, Bronal Z. Harris, Thomas J. Patterson, Jr.
Employer Identification Number: 222625990

2722
Earle M. Craig and Margaret Peters Craig Trust
One Mellon Bank Ctr.
Pittsburgh 15258 (412) 234-5248

Trust established in 1953 in PA.
Donor(s): Earle M. Craig,† Margaret Peters Craig.†
Financial data (yr. ended 12/31/86): Assets, $2,667,720 (M); expenditures, $934,550, including $925,000 for grants (average: $1,000-$20,000).
Purpose and activities: Giving largely for higher education, private secondary schools, hospitals, Protestant churches and religious organizations, the arts, public policy research, and social agencies.
Types of support: Operating budgets, continuing support, annual campaigns, seed money, emergency funds, building funds, equipment, land acquisition, endowment funds, research, publications, conferences and seminars.
Limitations: Giving primarily in PA; support also in TX, NY, and New England, including ME. No grants to individuals, or for deficit financing, matching gifts, scholarships, fellowships, or demonstration projects; no loans.
Application information: Family directs distribution of funds. Applications not accepted.
Board meeting date(s): As required
Write: Edward S. McKenna, Asst. V.P., Mellon Bank, N.A.
Trustee: Mellon Bank, N.A.
Number of staff: None.
Employer Identification Number: 256018660

2723
Crown American Corporate Giving Program
131 Market St.
Johnstown 15907 (814) 536-4441

Financial data (yr. ended 1/31/89): $80,000 for 302 grants (high: $10,000; low: $10).
Purpose and activities: Supports higher, secondary, business, elementary, and adult education, arts, catholic giving, community development, fine arts, historic preservation, libraries, literacy, museums, recreation, and youth.
Types of support: Capital campaigns, consulting services, general purposes, matching funds, scholarship funds, special projects.
Limitations: Giving primarily in Johnstown, PA and other areas where Crown America Corp. has properties in PA, NY, NJ, KY, TN, WV, VA, NC, GA, MD, and IN.
Application information:
Initial approach: Must be written request
Deadline(s): None
Write: Donna Gambol, V.P., Communications

2724
Cyclops Foundation
650 Washington Rd.
Pittsburgh 15228 (412) 343-4000

Trust established in 1953 in PA.
Donor(s): Cyclops Corp.

Financial data (yr. ended 12/31/87): Assets, $13,900 (M); gifts received, $300,000; expenditures, $384,062, including $365,003 for 79 grants (high: $75,000; low: $200) and $18,774 for employee matching gifts.
Purpose and activities: Grants primarily for community funds, higher education, hospitals, and cultural organizations located in communities where the company is a significant employer.
Types of support: Annual campaigns, seed money, building funds, equipment, land acquisition, employee matching gifts, capital campaigns, scholarship funds.
Limitations: Giving primarily in areas of company operations in PA and OH. No grants to individuals, or for endowment funds, research, fellowships, challenge grants, special projects, deficit financing, operating budgets, continuing support, emergency funds, publications, or conferences; no loans.
Publications: Application guidelines.
Application information:
Initial approach: Letter
Copies of proposal: 1
Deadline(s): None
Final notification: 1 to 2 months
Write: Susan J. Rutter, Mgr.-Cash & Banking
Trustees: William H. Knoell, James F. Will.
Number of staff: None.
Employer Identification Number: 256067354

2725
Dauphin Deposit Trust Foundation
Box 2961
Harrisburg 17105 (717) 255-2045

Donor(s): Dauphin Deposit Bank & Trust Co.
Financial data (yr. ended 12/31/87): Assets, $64,382 (M); gifts received, $57,500; expenditures, $59,980, including $59,950 for 28 grants (high: $27,000; low: $250).
Purpose and activities: Support for social services, youth, the United Way, and historic preservation.
Limitations: Giving primarily in PA.
Application information:
Initial approach: Proposal
Deadline(s): None
Write: Larry A. Hartman, V.P. and Trust Officer, Dauphin Deposit Trust Co.
Employer Identification Number: 236419900

2726
Debemac Foundation
c/o Drinker Biddle & Reath
1345 Chestnut St.
Philadelphia 19107-3426

Established in 1958 in PA.
Donor(s): Lewis H. Van Dusen, Jr., Maria P.W. Van Dusen, Marian A. Boyer.
Financial data (yr. ended 9/30/87): Assets, $260,762 (M); gifts received, $191,497; expenditures, $868,918, including $864,045 for 27 grants (high: $425,000; low: $20).
Purpose and activities: Support primarily for a science museum and planetarium and a hospital.
Application information: Contributes only to pre-selected organizations. Applications not accepted.
Officers: John E. Littleton, Pres.; John N. Childs, Jr., V.P.; Henry S. Robinson, Secy.; Robert J. Harbison, Treas.
Trustees: John C. Garner, Daniel R. Ross, Lewis H. Van Dusen, Jr.
Employer Identification Number: 236222789

2727
DeFrees Family Foundation, Inc.
419 Third Ave.
P.O. Box 708
Warren 16365 (814) 723-8150

Established in 1978 in PA.
Donor(s): Joseph H. DeFrees,† members of the DeFrees family.
Financial data (yr. ended 12/31/88): Assets, $3,440,247 (M); expenditures, $166,322, including $158,000 for 12 grants (high: $100,000; low: $1,000).
Purpose and activities: Giving primarily for education, particularly higher education.
Types of support: Special projects, research, publications, scholarship funds.
Limitations: Giving primarily in the Warren, PA, area. No support for relief projects. No grants to individuals; no loans.
Publications: Application guidelines.
Application information:
Initial approach: Proposal
Deadline(s): Mar. 1, July 1, and Oct. 1
Board meeting date(s): Apr., Aug., and Nov.
Write: Harold A. Johnson, Pres.
Officers and Directors: Harold A. Johnson, Pres. and Treas.; Barbara B. DeFrees, V.P.; Charles W.S. DeFrees, Secy.
Employer Identification Number: 251320042
Recent arts and culture grants:
Chautauqua Institution, Chautauqua, NY, $25,000. For endowment for lectureship. 1987.
Roger Tory Peterson Institute for the Study of Natural History, Jamestown, NY, $5,000. For facilities for study of natural history. 1987.
Thomas Struthers Trust, Warren, PA, $5,000. For improvements to theater. 1987.
Thomas Struthers Trust, Warren, PA, $5,000. for summer playhouse. 1987.

2728
Dietrich American Foundation
1811 Chestnut St., Suite 304
Philadelphia 19103 (215) 988-0050

Established in 1963 in DE.
Financial data (yr. ended 12/31/88): Assets, $14,465,883 (M); expenditures, $880,234, including $760,750 for 7 grants (high: $375,000; low: $250).
Purpose and activities: Support primarily for historic preservation, museums and the arts.
Types of support: Operating budgets.
Application information:
Initial approach: Letter
Deadline(s): None
Board meeting date(s): Jan.
Write: H. Richard Dietrich, Jr., Pres.
Officers: H. Richard Dietrich, Jr., Pres.; Lowell S. Thomas, Jr., Secy.; Frederic C. Barth, Treas.
Number of staff: 2 part-time professional.
Employer Identification Number: 516017453

2729
The Dietrich Foundation, Inc.
1811 Chestnut St., Suite 304
Philadelphia 19103 (215) 988-0050

Incorporated in 1953 in DE.
Donor(s): Members of the Dietrich family, Dietrich American Foundation.
Financial data (yr. ended 12/31/88): Assets, $4,692,719 (M); gifts received, $375,000; expenditures, $674,762, including $561,743 for 17 grants (high: $230,000; low: $1,500; average: $15,000).
Purpose and activities: Grants primarily for museums, conservation, music, and visual, performing, and community arts.
Types of support: Continuing support, operating budgets, special projects, publications.
Limitations: Giving primarily in PA. No grants to individuals.
Application information:
Initial approach: Letter
Copies of proposal: 1
Board meeting date(s): Usually in Jan.
Write: Daniel W. Dietrich II, Pres.
Officers and Directors: Daniel W. Dietrich II, Pres. and Treas.; Joseph G.J. Connolly, Secy.
Number of staff: 2
Employer Identification Number: 236255134

2730
William B. Dietrich Foundation
(Formerly The Dietrich Foundation, Incorporated)
1811 Chestnut St., Suite 304
Philadelphia 19103 (215) 988-0050

Incorporated in 1936 in DE.
Donor(s): Daniel W. Dietrich Foundation, Inc., Henry D. Dietrich,† Dietrich American Foundation.
Financial data (yr. ended 12/31/88): Assets, $6,021,025 (M); gifts received, $375,000; expenditures, $260,869, including $191,435 for 12 grants (high: $75,000; low: $100; average: $15,000).
Purpose and activities: Grants largely for conservation, higher and secondary education, museums, local historic restoration programs, and community funds.
Types of support: Research, operating budgets, special projects, building funds, capital campaigns, matching funds.
Limitations: Giving primarily in PA. No grants to individuals.
Application information:
Initial approach: Letter
Copies of proposal: 1
Board meeting date(s): Jan., Apr., July, and Oct.
Write: William B. Dietrich, Pres.
Officers and Directors: William B. Dietrich, Pres. and Treas.; Frank G. Cooper, Secy.
Number of staff: 2
Employer Identification Number: 231515616

2731
Dolfinger-McMahon Foundation
One Franklin Plaza, 15th Fl.
Philadelphia 19102 (215) 854-6318

Trust established in 1957 in PA, and originally comprised of four separate trusts: T/W of Henry Dolfinger as modified by will of Mary McMahon; 1935 D/T of Henry Dolfinger as modified by will of Caroline D. McMahon; Residuary T/W of Caroline D. McMahon; Dolfinger-McMahon Trust for Greater Philadelphia; In 1986 the 1935 D/T of H. Dolfinger was merged with the residuary T/W of C. McMahon.
Donor(s): Caroline D. McMahon,† Mary M. McMahon.†
Financial data (yr. ended 9/30/88): Assets, $9,764,133 (M); expenditures, $601,732, including $457,393 for 88 grants (high: $17,000; low: $1,000).
Purpose and activities: Emphasis on experimental, demonstration, or "seed money" projects in race relations, aid to the handicapped, higher and secondary education, social and urban programs, church programs, and health agencies. Beginning in 1981, the foundation has given increased consideration to true emergency situations. Grants limited to $20,000 in any one year to a single project or program.
Types of support: Operating budgets, seed money, emergency funds, matching funds, special projects, publications, conferences and seminars, deficit financing, scholarship funds, loans.
Limitations: Giving limited to the greater Philadelphia, PA, area. No support for medical or scientific research or for special interest advocacy through legislative lobbying or solicitation of government agencies. No grants to individuals; no support for medical or scientific research or for special interest advocacy through legislative lobbying or solicitation of government agencies, or for endowment funds, physical facilities, renovations or building repairs, building funds, scholarships, or fellowships.
Publications: Annual report (including application guidelines), application guidelines.
Application information:
Initial approach: Proposal
Copies of proposal: 2
Deadline(s): Submit proposal preferably in Mar. or Sept.; must actually be received on or before Apr. 1 or Oct. 1
Board meeting date(s): Apr., Oct., and as required
Final notification: 1 week to 10 days following semiannual meeting
Write: Joyce E. Robbins, Exec. Secy.
Officer: Joyce E. Robbins, Exec. Secy.
Trustees: Maurice Heckscher, Roland Morris.
Number of staff: None.
Recent arts and culture grants:
Academy of Natural Sciences of Philadelphia, Philadelphia, PA, $6,300. For Membership Development Project. 1987.
Bucks County Historical Society, Doylestown, PA, $7,500. To establish full-time Development Office. 1987.
Foundation for Todays Art/Nexus, Philadelphia, PA, $10,000. For salary support of Director. 1987.
Moore College of Art, Young People's Art Workshop, Philadelphia, PA, $7,500. To provide scholarships to poorer children to attend program, thus complementing their school education, developing their creative skills and exposing them to the arts. 1987.
Painted Bride Art Center, Philadelphia, PA, $5,390. For new series in Latin and Hispanic arts. 1987.
Pennsylvania Ballet Association, Philadelphia, PA, $5,000. For Exchange Program in connection with presentation of A Midsummers Night's Dream at Academy of Music. 1987.
Philadelphia Company, Philadelphia, PA, $10,000. For developing new scripts to be implemented during 1985/86 season. 1987.
Suburban Music School, Media, PA, $5,000. To hire part-time fundraiser as part of efforts to establish permanent development office for first year of this office. 1987.
Zoological Society of Philadelphia, Philadelphia, PA, $18,300. For stipend to develop and implement long-range audio/visual program at zoo, creating educational videos to be used at zoo and on public television. 1987.

2732
The Eberly Foundation
P.O. Box 2023
Uniontown 15401-0526 (412) 437-7557

Established in 1963 in PA.
Financial data (yr. ended 12/31/88): Assets, $3,358,826 (M); expenditures, $111,050, including $66,204 for 6 grants (high: $50,000; low: $1,575).
Purpose and activities: Support primarily for community development, elementary education, health organizations, the performing arts and historic preservation.
Types of support: Building funds, special projects.
Limitations: Giving primarily in PA, WV and OK.
Application information:
Initial approach: Letter
Deadline(s): None
Write: Robert E. Eberly, Pres.
Officer: Robert E. Eberly, Pres. and Treas.; Patricia Hillman Miller, Secy.
Trustees:* Carolyn E. Blaney, Ruth Ann Carter, Jill Drost, Robert E. Eberly, Jr., Margaret E. George, Jacob D. Moore.
Employer Identification Number: 237070246

2733
Edgewater Corporation Charitable Trust
c/o Joseph Rosati, Edgewater Corp.
300 College Ave.
Oakmont 15139 (412) 826-7340

Financial data (yr. ended 12/31/87): Assets, $294,810 (M); expenditures, $23,938, including $21,140 for 8 grants (high: $15,250; low: $40).
Purpose and activities: Gives to United Way, social services, and culture.
Limitations: Giving primarily in PA.
Application information:
Initial approach: Letter
Deadline(s): None
Trustee: Pittsburgh National Bank.
Employer Identification Number: 256022200

2734
The Erie Community Foundation
502 G. Daniel Baldwin Bldg.
P.O. Box 1818
Erie 16507 (814) 454-0843

Community foundation established as Erie Endowment Foundation in 1935 in PA; renamed in 1970.
Financial data (yr. ended 12/31/88): Assets, $13,599,043 (M); gifts received, $3,004,134; expenditures, $1,082,337, including $910,225 for 117 grants (high: $67,000; low: $285; average: $1,000-$25,000).
Purpose and activities: Giving for social service and youth agencies, education, the visual and performing arts, hospitals, health agencies, and religious organizations.
Types of support: Seed money, emergency funds, building funds, equipment, matching funds, research, annual campaigns, capital campaigns, conferences and seminars, annual campaigns, capital campaigns, conferences and seminars.
Limitations: Giving primarily in Erie County, PA. No grants to individuals (except for scholarships from restricted funds), or for operating budgets, continuing support, annual campaigns, deficit financing, land acquisition, endowment funds, special projects, publications, or conferences; no loans.
Publications: Annual report.
Application information: Application form required.
Initial approach: Letter or telephone
Copies of proposal: 6
Deadline(s): Submit proposal preferably in Feb., May, Aug., or Nov.; deadlines 1st of the month of board meetings
Board meeting date(s): Mar., June, Sept., and Dec.
Final notification: 3 to 4 weeks
Write: Edward C. Doll, Chair.
Officers and Trustees: Edward C. Doll, Chair.; Charles H. Bracken, Pres.; William F. Grant, V.P.; Ray L. McGarvey, Secy.-Treas.; David W. Doupe, M.D., Albert F. Duval, John R. Falcone, Ann V. Greene, F. William Hirt, Ernest L. Lake.
Trustee Banks: The First National Bank of Pennsylvania, Marine Bank, Mellon Bank, N.A., PennBank Erie.
Number of staff: 3 part-time support.
Employer Identification Number: 256032032
Recent arts and culture grants:
Arts Council of Erie, Erie, PA, $35,000. For annual fund drive. 1987.
Erie Art Museum, Erie, PA, $5,000. For Annex Development Project. 1987.
Erie Bayfront Ballet, Erie, PA, $18,500. For expansion project. 1987.
Erie Civic Ballet, Erie, PA, $5,000. For Nutcracker performance. 1987.
W Q L N-TV, Public Broadcasting of Northwest Pennsylvania, Erie, PA, $15,000. For TV and Radio Broadcasting operations. 1987.

2735
Leon Falk Family Trust
3315 Grant Bldg.
Pittsburgh 15219

Trust established in 1952 in PA.
Financial data (yr. ended 12/31/86): Assets, $325,000 (M); gifts received, $140,000; expenditures, $140,000, including $140,000 for 15 grants (high: $55,000; low: $1,000).
Purpose and activities: Emphasis on the performing arts, Jewish welfare funds, and a community fund.
Types of support: Special projects, annual campaigns, operating budgets, building funds.
Limitations: Giving primarily in Pittsburgh, PA.
Application information:
Write: Louis A. Devin, Jr., Secy.
Officer: Louis A. Devin, Jr., Secy.
Trustees: Sholom D. Comay, Leon Falk, Jr., Loti G. Falk, Marjorie L. Falk, Sigo Falk.
Employer Identification Number: 256065756

2736
Farber Foundation
1401 Walnut St.
Philadelphia 19102

Financial data (yr. ended 12/31/88): Assets, $1,942,996 (M); gifts received, $175,000; expenditures, $94,354, including $93,995 for 56 grants (high: $30,000; low: $50; average: $50-$30,000).
Purpose and activities: Giving primarily for Jewish organizations, higher education and a broad range of general charitable programs.
Application information: Contributes only to pre-selected organizations. Applications not accepted.
Officers: Jack Farber, Pres.; Stephen V. Dubin, V.P. and Secy.; James G. Baxter, V.P. and Treas.
Employer Identification Number: 236254221

2737
Samuel S. Fels Fund
2214 Land Title Bldg.
100 South Broad St.
Philadelphia 19110 (215) 567-2808

Incorporated in 1935 in PA.
Donor(s): Samuel S. Fels.†
Financial data (yr. ended 12/31/87): Assets, $26,307,086 (M); expenditures, $1,953,641, including $1,429,432 for 142 grants (high: $275,000; low: $500; average: $3,000-$20,000) and $25,000 for loans.
Purpose and activities: Grants for continuing support of major projects instituted by the fund itself, principally the Fels Research Institute, Temple University Medical School and the Fels Center of Government, University of Pennsylvania. Additional grants for short-term assistance to projects and organizations that help to demonstrate and evaluate ways to prevent, lessen, or resolve contemporary social problems, or that seek to provide permanent improvements in the provision of services for the improvement of daily life; to increase the stability of arts organizations and enrich the cultural life of the city of Philadelphia; limited aid to locally based university presses.
Types of support: Seed money, emergency funds, matching funds, technical assistance, special projects, research, conferences and seminars, continuing support, general purposes, internships, professorships, publications.
Limitations: Giving limited to the city of Philadelphia, PA. No support for national organizations. No grants to individuals, or for endowment or building funds, travel, scholarships, or fellowships.
Publications: Annual report, application guidelines.
Application information: Applicant must request guidelines before submitting proposals. Application form required.
Copies of proposal: 1
Board meeting date(s): Monthly except Aug.
Write: Kathryn Smith Pyle, Exec. Dir.
Officers: Nochem S. Winnet,* Pres.; Iso Briselli,* V.P.; Kathryn Smith Pyle, Secy. and Exec. Dir.; David C. Melnicoff, Treas.
Member-Directors:* Brother Daniel Burke, F.S.C., Raymond K. Denworth, Jr., Sandra Featherman, Wilbur E. Hobbs, David H. Wice.
Number of staff: 1 full-time professional; 1 part-time professional; 1 part-time support.
Employer Identification Number: 231365325
Recent arts and culture grants:
American Music Theater Festival, Philadelphia, PA, $8,500. For general support. 1987.
Balch Institute for Ethnic Studies, Philadelphia, PA, $5,000. For Blacks in Philadelphia exhibit. 1987.
Concerto Soloists, Philadelphia, PA, $12,535. For Young Artists competition. 1987.
Curtis Institute of Music, Philadelphia, PA, $5,000. For general support. 1987.
Junior League of Philadelphia, Philadelphia, PA, $5,000. For Fairmount Waterworks restoration. 1987.
Opera Company of Philadelphia, Philadelphia, PA, $10,000. For general support. 1987.
Pennsylvania Academy of the Fine Arts, Philadelphia, PA, $5,000. For Gallery completion. 1987.
Philadelphia Chamber Orchestra, Philadelphia, PA, $5,000. For general support. 1987.
Philadelphia Orchestra Association, Philadelphia, PA, $100,000. For Oboe Chair endowment. 1987.
Statue of Liberty-Ellis Island Foundation, NYC, NY, $10,000. For Statue of Liberty restoration. 1987.
Temple University, Philadelphia, PA, $9,754. For University Press book subsidies: The Leaders of Philadelphia's Black Community, 1787-1848; Philadelphia's Black Elite. 1987.
University of Pennsylvania, University Museum, Philadelphia, PA, $5,232. 1987.

2738
J. B. Finley Charitable Trust
c/o Pittsburgh National Bank
Pittsburgh 15265 (412) 762-2586

Trust established in 1919 in PA.
Donor(s): J.B. Finley.†
Financial data (yr. ended 9/30/88): Assets, $2,758,427 (M); gifts received, $0; expenditures, $170,815, including $153,640 for 38 grants (high: $20,000; low: $1,000; average: $100-$10,000).
Purpose and activities: Emphasis on Protestant church support and religious organizations, higher and secondary education, and cultural programs; support also for a community fund and a hospital.
Types of support: Building funds, general purposes, equipment, matching funds, seed money, special projects.
Limitations: Giving primarily in PA.
Publications: Informational brochure, application guidelines.
Application information: Application form required.
Initial approach: Letter
Copies of proposal: 1
Deadline(s): Apr. 15 and Oct. 15
Board meeting date(s): End of May and Nov.
Final notification: Mid June and Dec.
Write: Secy., Charitable Trust Comm.
Trustee: Pittsburgh National Bank.
Employer Identification Number: 256024443

2739
Foster Charitable Trust
P.O. Box 67
Pittsburgh 15230 (412) 928-8900

Trust established in 1962 in PA.
Donor(s): Foster Industries, Inc.
Financial data (yr. ended 12/31/87): Assets, $2,998,343 (M); expenditures, $370,524, including $365,934 for 49 grants (high: $200,000; low: $334).
Purpose and activities: Grants primarily to Jewish welfare funds, hospitals, higher education and the arts.
Limitations: No grants to individuals, or for endowment funds, or operating budgets.
Application information:
Initial approach: Letter
Copies of proposal: 1
Deadline(s): None
Board meeting date(s): As required
Write: Bernard S. Mars, Trustee
Trustees: J.R. Foster, Jay L. Foster, H. Roy Gordon, Bernard S. Mars, Milton Porter.
Number of staff: None.
Employer Identification Number: 256064791

2740
Henry C. Frick Educational Commission
Centre City Tower
650 Smithfield St.
Pittsburgh 15222 (412) 232-3335

Trust established in 1909 in PA.
Donor(s): Henry C. Frick.†
Financial data (yr. ended 12/31/86): Assets, $4,070,026 (M); expenditures, $180,474, including $98,906 for 26 grants (high: $8,000; low: $83; average: $1,000-$30,000).
Purpose and activities: To improve or enhance the quality of public elementary and secondary education. Invites and gives preference to proposals that provide for or encourage interaction among the various community elements that make up and contribute to public education.
Types of support: Seed money, matching funds, special projects, research, publications, conferences and seminars.

Limitations: Giving limited to the city of Pittsburgh, and Allegheny, Fayette, Greene, Washington, and Westmoreland counties in southwestern PA. No grants to individuals, or for annual campaigns, deficit financing, capital or endowment funds, scholarships, or fellowships; no loans.
Publications: Program policy statement, application guidelines, informational brochure, grants list.
Application information:
Initial approach: Letter or telephone
Copies of proposal: 1
Deadline(s): Oct. and Feb.
Board meeting date(s): Mar., June, and Dec.
Final notification: 2 weeks after board meetings
Write: Jane C. Burger, Exec. Dir.
Officers: Albert C. Van Dusen,* Pres.; Sandra J. McLaughlin,* V.P.; Joseph C. Swaim, Jr.,* Secy.-Treas.; Jane C. Burger, Exec. Dir.
Trustees:* Doreen E. Boyce, Henry Clay Frick II, David Henderson, George D. Lockhart, Rev. Donald S. Nesti.
Number of staff: 1 part-time professional; 2 part-time support.
Employer Identification Number: 250965374
Recent arts and culture grants:
Pittsburgh History and Landmarks Foundation, Pittsburgh, PA, $5,000. Toward development of pilot implementation of docent outreach program for Pittsburgh and Allegheny County Schools. 12/87.

2741
The Helen Clay Frick Foundation
P.O. Box 86190
Pittsburgh 15221 (412) 371-0600

Trust established in 1947 in PA.
Donor(s): Miss Helen C. Frick.†
Financial data (yr. ended 12/31/87): Assets, $78,959,892 (M); gifts received, $4,015,457; expenditures, $3,605,720, including $1,737,748 for 35 grants (high: $1,256,000; low: $1,000; average: $1,000-$25,000).
Purpose and activities: Grants to an art reference library in New York City, a nature sanctuary in Westchester County, NY, a historical society in Westmoreland County, PA; support also for cultural organizations, groups concerned with conservation and horticulture, and educational institutions.
Types of support: Annual campaigns, publications, operating budgets, general purposes, continuing support, capital campaigns.
Limitations: Giving primarily in Pittsburgh, PA, and NY. No grants to individuals.
Application information: Most funds are currently committed. Applications not accepted.
Initial approach: Letter
Copies of proposal: 1
Deadline(s): 6 weeks in advance of meeting
Board meeting date(s): Jan., May, Sept., and Nov.
Final notification: 3 weeks after meeting
Write: DeCourcy E. McIntosh, Exec. Dir.
Officers: DeCourcy E. McIntosh, Secy. and Exec. Dir.; Walter F. Cooley, Jr.,* Treas.
Trustees:* Henry Clay Frick II,* Chair.; I. Townsend Burden III,* Vice-Chair.; Peter P. Blanchard III, Mrs. Edward N. Dane, Henry Clay Frick III, Thomas J. Hilliard, J. Fife Symington III, Edward R. Weidlein, Jr., C. Holmes Wolfe, Jr., Mellon Bank, N.A.
Number of staff: 3 full-time professional; 1 full-time support.
Employer Identification Number: 256018983

2742
Edwin B. Garriques Trust
c/o Duane Morris & Heckscher
1500 One Franklin Plaza
Philadelphia 19102 (215) 854-6379

Established in 1922 in PA.
Financial data (yr. ended 12/31/88): Assets, $2,013,000 (M); expenditures, $110,000 for 4 grants (high: $60,000; low: $15,000).
Purpose and activities: Grants to accredited schools of music for scholarship assistance.
Types of support: Scholarship funds.
Limitations: Giving primarily in the Philadelphia, PA, area. No grants to individuals.
Application information:
Initial approach: Letter
Deadline(s): None
Write: Seymour Wagner, Secy.
Officers: Robert Montgomery Scott, Chair.; Seymour Wagner, Secy.
Trustee: Fidelity Bank, N.A.
Employer Identification Number: 236220616

2743
Elsie Lee Garthwaite Memorial Foundation
c/o Quinlan and Co., Ltd.
510 Walnut St., 11th Fl.
Philadelphia 19106
Application address: 1100 Barberry Rd., Bryn Mawr, PA 19010

Donor(s): Albert A. Garthwaite, Jr.
Financial data (yr. ended 12/31/87): Assets, $1,179,881 (M); gifts received, $74,417; expenditures, $10,166.
Purpose and activities: Support primarily for health associations and educational and cultural institutions.
Application information:
Deadline(s): None
Write: Albert A. Garthwaite, Jr., Pres.
Officers: Albert A. Garthwaite, Jr., Pres.; John B. Webb, V.P.; Patricia J. Turney, Secy.; C. Robert Turney, Treas.
Trustees: John Acuff, and 8 other trustees.
Employer Identification Number: 236290877

2744
The Albert M. Greenfield Foundation
2207 Oakwyn Rd.
Lafayette Hill 19444
Application address: One Beekman Pl., Apt. 2A, New York, NY 10022

Incorporated in 1953 in PA.
Donor(s): Albert M. Greenfield,† Etelka J. Greenfield.†
Financial data (yr. ended 8/31/87): Assets, $5,521,035 (M); expenditures, $218,650, including $187,850 for 19 grants (high: $50,000; low: $1,000).
Purpose and activities: Emphasis on the arts, music, and higher education.
Limitations: Giving primarily in the Philadelphia, PA, area. No grants for endowment funds; no loans.
Application information:
Initial approach: Letter
Copies of proposal: 1
Deadline(s): None
Board meeting date(s): As required
Write: Elizabeth M. Petrie, Chair.
Officers and Trustees: Elizabeth M. Petrie, Chair.; Gordon K. Greenfield, Pres.; Elizabeth G. Zeidman, Secy.; Gustave G. Amsterdam, Bruce H. Greenfield.
Employer Identification Number: 236050816

2745
Evelyn A. J. Hall Charitable Trust
Two Radnor Corp. Center, No. 101
Radnor 19087 (215) 964-8613

Trust established in 1952 in NY.
Donor(s): Evelyn A. Hall.
Financial data (yr. ended 12/31/87): Assets, $10,551,147 (M); expenditures, $1,158,847, including $1,085,450 for 86 grants (high: $254,250; low: $100; average: $100-$25,000).
Purpose and activities: Giving for museums, hospitals, medical research, higher education, conservation, preservation, social services, and youth agencies.
Types of support: General purposes.
Limitations: Giving primarily in New York, NY, and FL. No grants to individuals.
Application information: Applications not accepted.
Write: Alice C. Cory
Trustee: Walter H. Annenberg.
Number of staff: 5
Employer Identification Number: 236286760

2746
Hamilton Bank Foundation
(Formerly The National Central Foundation)
c/o Hamilton Bank
P.O. Box 3959
Lancaster 17604 (717) 291-3512

Incorporated in 1965 in PA.
Donor(s): Hamilton Bank.
Financial data (yr. ended 12/31/87): Assets, $60,067 (M); gifts received, $358,588; expenditures, $441,723, including $441,629 for 283 grants (high: $25,000; low: $25).
Purpose and activities: Emphasis on community funds and higher education, including employee matching gifts; support also for hospitals, youth agencies, and arts organizations.
Types of support: Employee matching gifts.
Limitations: Giving limited to seven counties of south central PA.
Application information:
Write: Eloise C. Aurand, Dir., Pub. Rel.
Employer Identification Number: 236444555

2747
The Greater Harrisburg Foundation
127 Pine St.
Harrisburg 17101 (717) 236-5040

Established in 1920 in PA; assets first acquired in 1940; grants first made in the mid-1940's.
Financial data (yr. ended 12/31/87): Assets, $2,215,250 (M); gifts received, $889,279; expenditures, $367,000, including $261,709 for 175 grants (high: $50,000; low: $10; average: $2,000).
Purpose and activities: Giving for education, health, human services, community development, and arts and humanities; priority assigned to funding new projects and awarding seed money to organizations which may not be eligible for support elsewhere.
Types of support: Seed money, special projects.
Limitations: Giving primarily in PA, with emphasis on Dauphin, Cumberland, Franklin, and Perry counties. No grants to individuals, or for operating or capital expenses.
Publications: Annual report (including application guidelines), informational brochure, application guidelines.
Application information:
Initial approach: Proposal
Copies of proposal: 1
Deadline(s): Apr. 15 for spring round; Sept. 1 for fall round
Board meeting date(s): June and Nov. for grantmaking; Feb. for policy review
Final notification: 2 weeks following meeting date
Write: Diane L. Swartzkopf, Pres.
Distribution Committee: John M. Aichele, William H. Alexander, Tita Eberly, George C. Eppinger, Lois Lehrman Grass, Gerald H. Hempt, Jacqueline M. Little, John M. Schrantz, Conrad M. Siegel, Elsie W. Swenson, Nathan H. Waters, Jr., Esq.
Staff: Diane L. Swartzkopf, Pres.
Distribution Committee Banks: Citizens National Bank, Citizens National Bank of Greencastle, Farmers Trust Co., The First National Bank, First National Bank and Trust Co., GHF, Inc., Juniata Valley Bank, CCNB Bank, Commonwealth National Bank, Dauphin Deposit Bank & Trust Co., Farmers and Merchants Trust Co., First Bank and Trust Co., Fulton Bank, Hamilton Bank, Pennsylvania National Bank and Trust Co., Valley Bank and Trust Co.
Number of staff: 1 full-time professional; 2 part-time professional; 1 full-time support.
Employer Identification Number: 236294219

2748
Harsco Corporation Fund
c/o Harsco Corporation
P.O. Box 8888
Camp Hill 17011-8888 (717) 763-7064

Trust established in 1956 in PA.
Donor(s): Harsco Corp.
Financial data (yr. ended 12/31/87): Assets, $7,758,975 (M); gifts received, $100,000; expenditures, $410,647, including $395,562 for 119 grants (high: $111,000; low: $50).
Purpose and activities: Grants largely to community funds and health agencies in areas of corporation operations; educational and performing arts grants primarily for matching gifts. Requests for contributions originate with local operating management and are approved or disapproved at the fund's central office. Scholarship program for children of employees administered through National Merit Scholarship Corp.
Types of support: General purposes, operating budgets, continuing support, employee-related scholarships, employee matching gifts.
Limitations: Giving primarily in areas of company operations. No grants to individuals, or for special projects, building or endowment funds, or research programs; no loans.
Publications: Program policy statement.
Application information: Application form required for employee-related scholarships.
Initial approach: Letter
Deadline(s): Jan. 12 for scholarships; no set deadline for grants
Board meeting date(s): Apr. and as required
Write: Richard Y. Eby, Secy. (Grants); Demaris K. Hetrick, Admin. Public Relations (Scholarship Prog.)
Officers: Jeffrey J. Burdge,* Pres.; W.W. Gambill,* V.P.; Richard Y. Eby, Secy.; George F. Rezich, Treas.
Trustees:* Robert F. Nation.
Employer Identification Number: 236278376

2749
Lita Annenberg Hazen Charitable Trust
100 Matsonford Rd.
Two Radnor Corp. Ctr., No. 101
Radnor 19087 (215) 894-8613

Trust established in 1952 in NY.
Donor(s): Lita Hazen.
Financial data (yr. ended 12/31/87): Assets, $8,078,499 (M); expenditures, $474,566, including $425,430 for 28 grants (high: $250,000; low: $200).
Purpose and activities: Grants largely for medical research, hospitals, education, and cultural programs; some support for social services, especially Jewish welfare agencies.
Types of support: Annual campaigns, general purposes, scholarship funds.
Limitations: Giving primarily in New York, NY. No grants to individuals.
Application information: Contributes only to pre-selected organizations. Applications not accepted.
Write: A.C. Cory
Trustee: Walter H. Annenberg.
Number of staff: 5
Employer Identification Number: 236286759

2750
H. J. Heinz Company Foundation
P.O. Box 57
Pittsburgh 15230 (412) 456-5772

Trust established in 1951 in PA.
Donor(s): H.J. Heinz Co.
Financial data (yr. ended 4/30/87): Assets, $8,336,715 (M); gifts received, $6,700,000; expenditures, $4,699,352, including $3,830,783 for grants and $840,333 for 2,037 employee matching gifts.
Purpose and activities: Support mainly for community funds; grants also for higher education, including employee matching gifts, hospitals, youth and social agencies, cultural programs, and research in nutrition.
Types of support: Annual campaigns, building funds, continuing support, employee matching gifts, operating budgets, seed money, technical assistance, emergency funds, equipment, internships, scholarship funds, fellowships, special projects, research, publications, conferences and seminars, professorships, endowment funds, capital campaigns.
Limitations: Giving primarily in areas of company operations. No grants to individuals, or for deficit financing, or land acquisition; no loans.
Publications: Program policy statement, application guidelines.
Application information:
Initial approach: Letter
Copies of proposal: 1
Deadline(s): None
Board meeting date(s): As necessary
Final notification: Varies
Write: Elizabeth Atkinson, Admin.
Officers and Trustees: Anthony F.J. O'Reilly, Chair.; Karyll A. Davis, Secy.; R. Derek Finlay, S.D. Wiley, Mellon Bank, N.A.
Number of staff: 1 full-time professional; 1 full-time support.
Employer Identification Number: 256018924

2751
Howard Heinz Endowment
30 CNG Tower
625 Liberty Ave.
Pittsburgh 15222-3199 (412) 391-5122

Trust established in 1941 in PA.
Donor(s): Howard Heinz,† Elizabeth Rust Heinz.†
Financial data (yr. ended 12/31/87): Assets, $387,569,090 (M); expenditures, $14,256,160, including $12,907,174 for 158 grants (high: $1,852,442; low: $2,500; average: $20,000-$250,000).
Purpose and activities: After gifts to certain agencies with which Mr. Heinz was associated during his life, the Endowment supports music and the arts, education, health, social services, and urban and international affairs, usually with one-time, non-renewable grants for new programs, seed money, and capital projects.
Types of support: Seed money, building funds, annual campaigns, emergency funds, general purposes, equipment, endowment funds, research, scholarship funds, matching funds, program-related investments, operating budgets, renovation projects, capital campaigns.
Limitations: Giving limited to PA, with emphasis on Pittsburgh and the Allegheny County area; educational grants limited to Pittsburgh and Allegheny County. No grants to individuals; no loans.
Publications: Annual report (including application guidelines).
Application information: Application form required.
Initial approach: Letter, proposal, or telephone
Copies of proposal: 1
Deadline(s): 90 days before meeting date

Board meeting date(s): June and Dec.
Final notification: 3 to 4 months
Write: Alfred W. Wishart, Jr., Exec. Dir.
Officers: Jack E. Kime, Assoc. Dir., Chief Financial and Admin. Officer; Alfred W. Wishart, Jr., Exec. Dir.; Dixon R. Brown, Dir. of Finance.
Trustees: Henry John Heinz III, Chair.; Drue Heinz, Joseph W. Oliver, William H. Rea, William W. Scranton, Mellon Bank, N.A.
Number of staff: 7 full-time professional; 2 part-time professional; 9 full-time support.
Employer Identification Number: 251064784
Recent arts and culture grants:
Carnegie Museum of Art, Pittsburgh, PA, $105,000. Toward 1988 Special Exhibitions Program. 12/14/87.
Carnegie, The, Pittsburgh, PA, $11,000,000. Toward $117.5 million capital campaign, Second Century Fund. 12/14/87.
Carnegie, The, Three Rivers Arts Festival, Pittsburgh, PA, $90,000. Toward artistic programming for site-specific sculpture program in Point State Park, and performing arts series at Fulton Theater during 1988 festival. 12/14/87.
Civic Light Opera Association of Greater Pittsburgh, Pittsburgh, PA, $50,000. For general operating support for 1987-88. 12/14/87.
Fort Ligonier Memorial Foundation, Ligonier, PA, $30,000. Toward capital campaign. 12/14/87.
Hawthornden Literary Institute, Pittsburgh, PA, $180,000. For operating support for 1988. 12/14/87.
Pittsburgh Ballet Theater, Pittsburgh, PA, $75,000. For general operating support for 1987-88. 12/14/87.
Pittsburgh Dance Council, Pittsburgh, PA, $30,000. For general operating support for 1987-88. 12/14/87.
Pittsburgh Filmmakers, Pittsburgh, PA, $48,000. To continue Filmmakers at Fulton Theater Project for 1987-88 season. 11/15/87.
Pittsburgh History and Landmarks Foundation, Pittsburgh, PA, $50,000. Toward publication of book of photographs by Clyde Hare. 12/14/87.
Pittsburgh Opera, Pittsburgh, PA, $75,000. For general operating support for 1987-88 season. 12/14/87.
Pittsburgh Public Theater, Pittsburgh, PA, $75,000. For general operating support for 1987-88. 12/14/87.
Pittsburgh Symphony Society, Pittsburgh, PA, $90,000. Toward 1987-88 Sustaining Fund Campaign. 12/14/87.
Pittsburgh Trust for Cultural Resources, Pittsburgh, PA, $960,816. For 1988 operating support. 12/14/87.
Pittsburgh Trust for Cultural Resources, Pittsburgh, PA, $285,000. Toward first year of three-year Facade Restoration Program. 12/14/87.
Pittsburgh Trust for Cultural Resources, Pittsburgh, PA, $15,000. For study of financial health of arts organizations in Pittsburgh. 12/14/87.
Program to Encourage Minority Arts in Pittsburgh, Pittsburgh, PA, $50,000. For special grants program to fund minority projects in 1988-89. 12/14/87.
Renaissance and Baroque Society of Pittsburgh, Pittsburgh, PA, $20,000. For special programming in celebration of 20th anniversary season. 12/14/87.

2752
Vira I. Heinz Endowment
The CNG Tower
625 Liberty Ave., 30th Fl.
Pittsburgh 15222-3199 (412) 391-5122

Trust established in 1983 in PA.
Donor(s): Vira I. Heinz.†
Financial data (yr. ended 12/31/87): Assets, $186,486,059 (M); expenditures, $4,703,633, including $4,063,001 for 88 grants (high: $1,000,000; low: $500).
Purpose and activities: Support for education, human services, arts and humanities, health and nutrition, religion and values, and economic development.
Types of support: Capital campaigns, general purposes, renovation projects, seed money, special projects, technical assistance, building funds.
Limitations: Giving limited to Pittsburgh and western PA, although in certain cases support may be considered on a national or international basis. No grants for general endowments.
Publications: Annual report, informational brochure.
Application information: Application form required.
Initial approach: Letter, proposal, or telephone
Deadline(s): 90 days prior to board meeting
Board meeting date(s): Mar. and Oct.
Final notification: 3 to 4 months
Write: Alfred W. Wishart, Jr., Exec. Dir.
Administrator: Alfred W. Wishart, Jr., Exec. Dir.
Trustees: James M. Walton, Chair.; William H. Rea, Helen P. Rush, John T. Ryan, S. Donald Wiley, Mellon Bank, N.A.
Number of staff: 8 full-time professional; 1 part-time professional; 8 full-time support.
Employer Identification Number: 256235878
Recent arts and culture grants:
Carnegie Museum of Art, Pittsburgh, PA, $30,000. For general operating support for 1987-88. 10/30/87.
Carnegie-Mellon University, Art Gallery, Pittsburgh, PA, $20,000. Toward exhibition of work by Barry Le Va. 10/30/87.
Civic Light Opera Association of Greater Pittsburgh, Pittsburgh, PA, $25,000. For general operating support for 1987-88. 10/30/87.
Pittsburgh Ballet Theater, Pittsburgh, PA, $25,000. For general operating support for 1987-88. 10/30/87.
Pittsburgh Dance Council, Pittsburgh, PA, $10,000. For general operating support for 1987-88. 10/30/87.
Pittsburgh Opera, Pittsburgh, PA, $25,000. For general operating support for 1987-88. 10/30/87.
Pittsburgh Public Theater, Pittsburgh, PA, $25,000. For general operating support for 1987-88. 10/30/87.
Pittsburgh Symphony Society, Pittsburgh, PA, $25,000. For general operating support for 1987-88. 10/30/87.
Pittsburgh Symphony Society, Pittsburgh, PA, $5,000. Toward celebration for Performing Arts in Pittsburgh as tribute to H.J. Heinz II. 10/30/87.
Tuesday Musical Club, Pittsburgh, PA, $10,000. To commission musical work for 100th anniversary celebration in 1989. 10/30/87.

2753
H. J. & Drue Heinz Foundation
USX Tower, Suite 4440
600 Grant St.
Pittsburgh 15219 (412) 456-5731

Established in 1954 in PA.
Financial data (yr. ended 12/31/88): Assets, $2,201,413 (M); gifts received, $1,196,450; expenditures, $1,460,844, including $1,422,612 for 29 grants (high: $300,000; low: $500).
Purpose and activities: Emphasis on culture, conservation, and higher education.
Types of support: Special projects.
Limitations: Giving primarily in PA, NY, and Washington, DC.
Application information: Contributes only to pre-selected organizations. Applications not accepted.
Officer and Trustee: Dixon R. Brown, Secy.
Number of staff: 1 full-time professional.
Employer Identification Number: 256018930

2754
The Hillman Foundation, Inc.
2000 Grant Bldg.
Pittsburgh 15219 (412) 338-3466

Incorporated in 1951 in DE.
Donor(s): John Hartwell Hillman, Jr.,† J.H. Hillman & Sons Co., Hillman Land Co., and family-owned corporations.
Financial data (yr. ended 12/31/88): Assets, $42,614,328 (M); expenditures, $2,608,194, including $2,242,875 for 59 grants (high: $326,475; low: $4,000; average: $4,000-$200,000).
Purpose and activities: Program areas include cultural advancement and the arts, education, health and medicine, civic and community affairs, social services, youth, and religion.
Types of support: Continuing support, seed money, endowment funds, matching funds, professorships, special projects, building funds, equipment, land acquisition, capital campaigns, renovation projects.
Limitations: Giving primarily in Pittsburgh and southwestern PA. No grants to individuals, or for operating budgets, annual campaigns, deficit financing, travel, or conferences; no loans.
Publications: Annual report (including application guidelines).
Application information:
Initial approach: Letter
Copies of proposal: 1
Deadline(s): None
Board meeting date(s): Apr., June, Oct., and Dec., and at annual meeting in May
Final notification: 3 to 4 months

Write: Ronald W. Wertz, Exec. Dir.
Officers: Henry L. Hillman,* Pres.; C.G. Grefenstette,* V.P.; Ronald W. Wertz, Exec. Dir. and Secy.; David H. Ross, Treas.
Directors:* H. Vaughan Blaxter III, Douglas G. Sisterson, Lawrence M. Wagner.
Number of staff: 3 full-time professional; 1 full-time support.
Employer Identification Number: 256011462
Recent arts and culture grants:
Bidwell Education, Music and Recreation Center, Pittsburgh, PA, $35,000. Toward renovation of second floor of Center to accommodate music program, administrative offices and restrooms. 4/12/88.
Carnegie, The, Pittsburgh, PA, $5,000,000. Toward Second Century Fund capital campaign in support of capital projects, endowment, program development and ongoing operations. 6/21/88.
Carnegie, The, Museum of Natural History, Pittsburgh, PA, $75,725. To purchase 26 mineral specimens that will be exhibited in Systematic and Masterpiece Sections of Hillman Hall of Minerals and Gems. 2/23/88.
Carnegie, The, Museum of Natural History, Pittsburgh, PA, $8,000. To establish Carnegie Mineralogical Award which recognizes contributions that promote and improve preservation, conservation, and educational use of minerals and mineral collecting. 2/8/88.
Pittsburgh Ballet Theater, Pittsburgh, PA, $20,000. Toward implementing recommendations made by Academy for Educational Development (AED) management study. 4/12/88.
Pittsburgh Childrens Museum, Pittsburgh, PA, $50,000. Toward winter quarterly program, Magic of the Season, renovation of facility and general program support. 12/1/87.
Pittsburgh Opera Theater, Pittsburgh, PA, $5,000. Toward series of three chamber operas to be presented at Carnegie Music Hall. 9/26/88.
Soldiers and Sailors Memorial Hall of Allegheny County, Pittsburgh, PA, $7,200. Toward cost of cleaning and restoring five major paintings. 6/21/88.

2755
The Henry L. Hillman Foundation
2000 Grant Bldg.
Pittsburgh 15219 (412) 338-3466

Established in 1964 in PA.
Donor(s): Henry L. Hillman.
Financial data (yr. ended 12/31/88): Assets, $13,627,080 (M); expenditures, $648,951, including $604,750 for 44 grants (high: $203,000; low: $500; average: $1,000-$5,000).
Purpose and activities: Support for the arts and cultural programs, youth, conservation, civic affairs, community development, church support, secondary education, social services, and hospitals.
Types of support: Operating budgets, continuing support, annual campaigns, seed money, emergency funds, building funds, equipment, matching funds, special projects, renovation projects, capital campaigns.
Limitations: Giving primarily in Pittsburgh and southwestern PA. No grants to individuals, or for deficit financing, land acquisition, endowment funds, research, publications, or conferences; no loans.
Application information:
Initial approach: Letter
Copies of proposal: 1
Deadline(s): None
Board meeting date(s): Mar. and Dec.
Final notification: 3 to 4 months
Write: Ronald W. Wertz, Exec. Dir.
Officers: Henry L. Hillman,* Pres.; Ronald W. Wertz,* Exec. Dir. and Secy.; David H. Ross, Treas.
Directors:* H. Vaughan Blaxter III.
Number of staff: 1 part-time professional.
Employer Identification Number: 256065959

2756
The Margaret Mellon Hitchcock Foundation
c/o Mellon Bank, N.A.
P.O. Box 185
Pittsburgh 15258 (412) 234-5892

Trust established in 1961 in PA.
Donor(s): Margaret Mellon Hitchcock.
Financial data (yr. ended 12/31/86): Assets, $1,900,424 (M); expenditures, $168,238, including $151,000 for 25 grants (high: $50,000; low: $1,000).
Purpose and activities: Grants largely for hospitals, music, aid to the handicapped, and secondary education.
Limitations: Giving primarily in the New York, NY, area. No grants to individuals, or for building or endowment funds, operating budgets, or special projects.
Application information: Application form required.
Board meeting date(s): Oct. or Nov.
Write: Leonard B. Richards III, V.P., Mellon Bank, N.A.
Officer: A.A. Vestal, Secy.
Trustees: Margaret Mellon Hitchcock, Thomas Hitchcock III, Alexander M. Laughlin, Mellon Bank, N.A.
Employer Identification Number: 256018992

2757
The Holstrom Family Foundation
P.O. Box 1310
Doylestown 18901

Established in 1984 in NY.
Donor(s): Carleton Holstrom, Bear Stearns & Co.
Financial data (yr. ended 11/30/88): Assets, $597,189 (M); expenditures, $116,900, including $109,875 for 33 grants (high: $25,000; low: $100).
Purpose and activities: First year of operation, 1985; initial grants awarded for cultural programs, education, Jewish welfare, hospitals, and social services.
Limitations: Giving primarily in New York City, NY, and in NJ.
Application information: Contributes only to pre-selected organizations. Applications not accepted.
Officers: Carleton Holstrom, Pres.; Christina L. Holstrom, V.P.; Mary Beth Kineke, V.P.; Marcia O. Holstrom, Secy.; Cynthia J. Cawthorne, Treas.
Employer Identification Number: 222611162

2758
Janet A. Hooker Charitable Trust
100 Matsonford Rd.
Two Radnor Corp. Ctr., No. 101
Radnor 19087 (215) 964-8613

Trust established in 1952 in NY.
Donor(s): Janet A. Neff Hooker.
Financial data (yr. ended 12/31/87): Assets, $8,306,169 (M); expenditures, $646,752, including $595,000 for 40 grants (high: $74,000; low: $1,000).
Purpose and activities: Support largely for arts and culture, historic preservation, conservation, medical research and health services, and social service agencies; giving also for animal welfare, religion, and education.
Types of support: Annual campaigns, general purposes.
Limitations: Giving primarily in NY, FL, and DC. No grants to individuals.
Application information: Applications not accepted.
Write: A.C. Cory
Trustee: Walter H. Annenberg.
Number of staff: 5 full-time professional.
Employer Identification Number: 236286762

2759
Elizabeth S. Hooper Foundation
223 Lancaster Ave., Suite 200
Devon 19333

Established in 1967.
Donor(s): Interstate Marine Transport Co., Interstate Towing Co., Interstate Ocean Transport Co., and members of the Hooper family.
Financial data (yr. ended 6/30/87): Assets, $1,273,577 (M); gifts received, $325,000; expenditures, $478,008, including $470,300 for 142 grants (high: $50,000; low: $100).
Purpose and activities: Giving largely for higher and secondary education; grants also for cultural programs, public policy organizations, health, and Protestant church support.
Types of support: Building funds, special projects, general purposes, emergency funds, research, scholarship funds, operating budgets.
Officers and Directors: Adrian S. Hooper, Pres.; Thomas Hooper, V.P.; Bruce H. Hooper, Secy.; Ralph W. Hooper, Treas.; John P. Lally.
Employer Identification Number: 236434997

2760
John M. Hopwood Charitable Trust
c/o Pittsburgh National Bank
Trust Dept. - 965
Pittsburgh 15265

Trust established about 1948 in PA.
Donor(s): John M. Hopwood.†
Financial data (yr. ended 12/31/86): Assets, $9,061,998 (M); gifts received, $38,115;

expenditures, $604,436, including $555,550 for 75 grants (high: $65,000; low: $1,000).
Purpose and activities: Giving for hospitals, higher education, youth and social service agencies, cultural programs, community funds, and church support.
Limitations: Giving primarily in PA and FL.
Application information:
Initial approach: Letter
Deadline(s): None
Write: James R. Smith, V.P., Pittsburgh National Bank
Trustees: William T. Hopwood, Pittsburgh National Bank.
Employer Identification Number: 256022634

2761
The Hoyt Foundation
c/o First National Bank Bldg.
P.O. Box 1488
New Castle 16103 (412) 652-5511

Incorporated in 1962 in PA.
Donor(s): May Emma Hoyt,† Alex Crawford Hoyt.
Financial data (yr. ended 10/31/88): Assets, $8,390,487 (M); expenditures, $522,145, including $287,050 for 36 grants (high: $65,000; low: $200) and $147,859 for 208 grants to individuals.
Purpose and activities: Emphasis on higher education, including scholarships, and a hospital; some support also for cultural programs.
Types of support: Student aid, annual campaigns, building funds, capital campaigns, continuing support, seed money.
Limitations: Giving limited to residents of, or organizations located in Lawrence County, PA.
Application information: Application form required.
Initial approach: Proposal
Deadline(s): July 15 and Dec. 15 for scholarships
Board meeting date(s): Monthly
Write: Dorothy A. Patton
Officers and Directors: Thomas V. Mansell, Pres. and Secy.; A. Wayne Cole, Thomas J. O'Shane, Paul H. Reed, John W. Sant.
Number of staff: 1 part-time support.
Employer Identification Number: 256064468

2762
Milton G. Hulme Charitable Foundation
720 Frick Bldg.
Pittsburgh 15219 (412) 281-2007

Established in 1960 in PA.
Donor(s): Glover & MacGregor, Inc.
Financial data (yr. ended 12/31/86): Assets, $3,107,113 (M); expenditures, $126,082, including $123,100 for 49 grants (high: $20,000; low: $250).
Purpose and activities: Giving primarily for hospitals, higher education, and music; some support for youth agencies.
Limitations: Giving primarily in PA. No grants to individuals.
Application information:
Initial approach: Letter, proposal, or telephone
Copies of proposal: 1
Deadline(s): Submit proposal preferably in early Dec.; deadline Dec. 15
Board meeting date(s): Dec.
Final notification: 2 weeks after application deadline
Write: Helen C. Hulme, Trustee
Trustees: Nathalie H. Curry, Helen C. Hulme, Jocelyn H. MacConnell, Helen H. Shoup.
Number of staff: 2 part-time support.
Employer Identification Number: 256062896

2763
The Hunt Foundation
c/o Mellon Bank, N.A.
P.O. Box 185
Pittsburgh 15230 (412) 281-8734
Additional address: Mellon Bank, One Mellon Bank Ctr., Rm. 3845, Pittsburgh, PA 15258

Trust established in 1951 in PA.
Donor(s): Roy A. Hunt,† and members of the Hunt family.
Financial data (yr. ended 12/31/86): Assets, $10,887,627 (M); expenditures, $588,205, including $477,135 for 215 grants (high: $5,000; low: $500; average: $1,000).
Purpose and activities: Grants generally initiated by the trustees, with emphasis on higher education; smaller grants for secondary education, and cultural and conservation programs.
Types of support: Annual campaigns, building funds, capital campaigns, endowment funds, general purposes.
Limitations: Giving primarily in the Pittsburgh, PA, and Boston, MA, areas. No grants to individuals.
Application information:
Initial approach: Letter
Copies of proposal: 1
Deadline(s): May 1 and Oct. 1
Board meeting date(s): June and Nov.
Final notification: July and Dec.
Write: L.B. Richards
Trustees: Alfred M. Hunt, Andrew McQ. Hunt, Christopher M. Hunt, Daniel K. Hunt, Helen M. Hunt, John B. Hunt, Marion McM. Hunt, Richard McM. Hunt, Roy A. Hunt III, Susan M. Hunt, Torrence M. Hunt, Torrence M. Hunt, Jr., William E. Hunt, Rachel Hunt Knowles, Mellon Bank, N.A.
Number of staff: 2 part-time professional; 2 part-time support.
Employer Identification Number: 256018925

2764
The Roy A. Hunt Foundation
600 Grant St., 56th Fl.
Pittsburgh 15219 (412) 281-8734

Established in 1966 in PA.
Donor(s): Roy A. Hunt.†
Financial data (yr. ended 5/31/87): Assets, $19,918,353 (M); expenditures, $3,341,415, including $3,167,375 for 23 grants (high: $2,515,625; low: $7,500; average: $7,500-$50,000).
Purpose and activities: Grants initiated by the trustees, primarily to support the Hunt Institute for Botanical Documentation at Carnegie-Mellon University; smaller grants for higher and secondary education, Protestant church support, and cultural programs.
Types of support: Annual campaigns, building funds, endowment funds, general purposes.
Limitations: Giving primarily in the Pittsburgh, PA, area. No grants to individuals.
Application information: Applications not accepted.
Deadline(s): May 1 and Oct. 1 for solicited proposals only
Board meeting date(s): June and Nov.
Final notification: July and Dec.
Write: Torrence M. Hunt, Jr., Admin. Trustee
Officer: K. Sidney Neuman, Secy.
Trustees: Susan Hunt Hollingsworth, Andrew McQ. Hunt, Christopher M. Hunt, Daniel K. Hunt, Helen McM. Hunt, John B. Hunt, Marion McM. Hunt, Richard McM. Hunt, Roy A. Hunt III, Torrence M. Hunt, Torrence M. Hunt, Jr., Rachel Hunt Knowles.
Number of staff: 2 part-time professional; 2 part-time support.
Employer Identification Number: 256105162
Recent arts and culture grants:
Carnegie-Mellon University, Hunt Institute for Botanical Documentation, Pittsburgh, PA, $220,000. For education. 1987.
Carnegie, The, Pittsburgh, PA, $25,000. For fine arts. 5/88.

2765
Hunt Manufacturing Company Foundation
230 South Broad St.
Philadelphia 19102 (215) 732-7700

Established in 1955 in NJ.
Donor(s): Hunt Manufacturing Co.
Financial data (yr. ended 11/28/88): Assets, $8,745 (M); gifts received, $484,540; expenditures, $481,806, including $456,219 for 104 grants (high: $54,500; low: $150; average: $1,000-$5,000), $24,602 for 16 grants to individuals and $985 for 13 employee matching gifts.
Purpose and activities: Grants largely for cultural programs, inner-city revitalization, public policy research, civic groups, and higher education, including scholarships for the children of company employees; some support also for youth and health agencies, and for community funds.
Types of support: Operating budgets, continuing support, annual campaigns, seed money, building funds, equipment, scholarship funds, employee-related scholarships, employee matching gifts, special projects, technical assistance.
Limitations: Giving primarily in Philadelphia, PA, Fresno, CA, Florence, KY, Statesville, NC, and Florence, AL. No grants to individuals (except for employee-related scholarships), or for endowment funds or matching gifts; no loans.
Publications: Application guidelines, 990-PF.
Application information:
Initial approach: Proposal
Copies of proposal: 1
Deadline(s): 1 month prior to board meeting dates
Board meeting date(s): Jan., Apr., July, and Oct.
Final notification: 3 months

Write: William E. Parshall, Secy.
Officers: Ronald Naples,* Pres.; William E. Parshall, Secy.; Rudolph M. Peins, Jr.,* Treas.
Trustees:* John Carney, Dave Kalberer, Rudolph Peins, Phyllis Perry, Scott Venella.
Number of staff: 1 full-time professional; 1 full-time support.
Employer Identification Number: 226062897

2766
Incom International Charitable Trust, Inc.
661 Anderson Dr.
P.O. Box 3823
Pittsburgh 15230

Financial data (yr. ended 12/31/87): Assets, $5,271 (M); expenditures, $87,521, including $87,100 for 83 grants (high: $14,000; low: $100).
Purpose and activities: Support for higher education, hospitals and health associations, community and social services, rehabilitation centers, youth, and the arts.
Types of support: General purposes, operating budgets, capital campaigns.
Application information:
Deadline(s): None
Trustees: Richard H. Allen, Paul L. Soske, Mellon Bank, N.A.
Employer Identification Number: 251337101

2767
Independence Foundation
2500 Philadelphia National Bank Bldg.
Philadelphia 19107-3493 (215) 563-8105

Established in 1932 as International Cancer Research Foundation; incorporated as Donner Foundation in 1945 in DE; divided in 1961 into Independence Foundation and a newly formed William H. Donner Foundation.
Donor(s): William H. Donner.†
Financial data (yr. ended 12/31/88): Assets, $69,006,000 (M); expenditures, $3,441,476, including $2,997,271 for grants.
Purpose and activities: Giving largely for independent secondary education, especially in the form of student loan funds; support for a limited number of educational and cultural organizations; support also for student aid in nursing education.
Types of support: Endowment funds, professorships, general purposes, scholarship funds, fellowships.
Limitations: No grants to individuals, or for building and development funds, travel, research, publications, operating budgets, college scholarships, graduate fellowships, or matching gifts.
Publications: Program policy statement, application guidelines, annual report.
Application information:
Initial approach: Letter
Copies of proposal: 5
Deadline(s): 3 weeks before meetings
Board meeting date(s): Mar., June, Sept., and Dec.
Final notification: 3 to 6 weeks
Write: Robert A. Maes, Pres.
Officers and Directors: Robert A. Maes, Pres.; Alexander F. Barbieri, Secy.; Viola MacInnes, Treas.; Frederick H. Donner, Robert M. Scott.
Number of staff: 3 full-time professional.
Employer Identification Number: 231352110
Recent arts and culture grants:
Library Company of Philadelphia, Philadelphia, PA, $6,000. For general support. 1987.
W H Y Y-TV, Philadelphia, PA, $5,000. For general support. 1987.

2768
The J.D.B. Fund
404 Swedesford Rd.
P.O. Box 157
Gwynedd 19436 (215) 699-2233

Trust established in 1966 in PA.
Donor(s): John Drew Betz.
Financial data (yr. ended 12/31/87): Assets, $7,675,891 (M); expenditures, $1,820,201, including $1,767,611 for 43 grants (high: $725,000; low: $1,000).
Purpose and activities: All grants originate with the trustees. Grants to health associations, hospitals, conservation organizations, societies or agencies devoted to historic preservation, and civic affairs.
Types of support: Building funds, equipment, land acquisition, matching funds.
Limitations: Giving primarily in Philadelphia, PA, and the surrounding area. No support for arts and sciences or medical research. No grants to individuals, or for endowment funds; no loans for general support of established universities, charities, foundations, or hospitals; scholarships and fellowships; demonstration projects, publications, or conferences.
Application information: Contributes only to pre-selected organizations. Applications not accepted.
Board meeting date(s): Monthly
Write: Paul J. Corr, Mgr.
Manager: Paul J. Corr.
Trustees: Claire S. Betz, John Drew Betz.
Number of staff: 2
Employer Identification Number: 236418867

2769
Henry Janssen Foundation, Inc.
2650 Westview Dr.
Wyomissing 19610

Incorporated in 1931 in DE.
Donor(s): Members of the Janssen family.
Financial data (yr. ended 12/31/86): Assets, $9,524,236 (M); expenditures, $460,104, including $389,500 for 36 grants (high: $50,000; low: $500).
Purpose and activities: Emphasis on hospitals, health, cultural programs, Protestant church support, higher education, and community funds.
Limitations: Giving primarily in PA, particularly Reading and Berks County.
Application information: Contributes only to pre-selected organizations. Applications not accepted.
Write: Helene L. Master, V.P.
Officers and Trustees: Elsa L. Bowman, Pres.; Helene L. Master, V.P.; John W. Bowman, Secy.; El Roy P. Master, Treas.; F. Eugene Stapleton.
Employer Identification Number: 231476340

2770
Donald P. Jones Foundation
P.O. Box 58910
Philadelphia 19102-3910

Established in 1953 in PA.
Financial data (yr. ended 12/31/87): Assets, $1,008,251 (M); expenditures, $51,605, including $10,082 for 27 grants (high: $3,510; low: $25) and $27,344 for 41 in-kind gifts.
Purpose and activities: Support primarily for health, youth, the arts, education, and labor.
Limitations: Giving primarily in PA.
Application information:
Deadline(s): None
Write: Donald P. Jones, Trustee
Trustees: Arthur W. Jones, Donald P. Jones, Ethel G. Jones.
Employer Identification Number: 236259820

2771
K. M. & G. Foundation
Six PPG Place
Pittsburgh 15222 (412) 456-3963

Financial data (yr. ended 12/31/87): Assets, $82,660 (M); gifts received, $132,000; expenditures, $73,739, including $73,585 for 60 grants (high: $17,000; low: $25).
Purpose and activities: Support for social services, youth, arts and culture, higher and other education, business and economics, health and hospitals, community development, international affairs, civic affairs, and the United Way; includes scholarship funds.
Types of support: General purposes, employee-related scholarships.
Limitations: Giving primarily in Pittsburgh, PA.
Application information:
Initial approach: Letter
Deadline(s): None
Write: Kelley Murray, Asst. to Chair.
Officers: William H. Genge, Chair.; Edward L. Graf, Secy.
Employer Identification Number: 256076887

2772
Samuel and Rebecca Kardon Foundation
c/o Landsburg Platt & Co.
117 South 17th St.
Philadelphia 19103 (215) 561-6633

Trust established in 1952 in PA.
Donor(s): Emanuel S. Kardon, American Bag & Paper Corp.
Financial data (yr. ended 12/31/87): Assets, $6,461,106 (M); gifts received, $13,200; expenditures, $406,603, including $359,725 for 48 grants (high: $250,000; low: $100; average: $500-$2,000).
Purpose and activities: Emphasis on Jewish welfare funds, music and higher and secondary education; support also for hospitals, and social service agencies.

Limitations: Giving primarily in PA.
Application information:
Initial approach: Letter
Deadline(s): None
Write: Emanuel S. Kardon, Pres.
Officer and Trustee: Emanuel S. Kardon, Pres.
Employer Identification Number: 236278123

2773
The Katz Foundation
Papercraft Park
Pittsburgh 15238 (412) 362-8000

Trust established in 1960 in PA.
Donor(s): Members of the Katz family.
Financial data (yr. ended 12/31/86): Assets, $1,236,649 (M); gifts received, $32,375; expenditures, $312,890, including $282,673 for 65 grants (high: $184,511; low: $35).
Purpose and activities: Giving primarily for Jewish welfare funds, youth, and cultural programs.
Limitations: Giving primarily in PA. No grants to individuals, or for operating budgets.
Application information: Contributes only to pre-selected organizations. Applications not accepted.
Copies of proposal: 2
Write: William Katz, Trustee
Trustees: Hyman I. Katz, Joseph M. Katz, Mrs. Joseph M. Katz, Marshall P. Katz, William Katz.
Employer Identification Number: 256062917

2774
Earl Knudsen Charitable Foundation
P.O. Box 1791
Pittsburgh 15230

Established about 1975.
Donor(s): Earl Knudsen.†
Financial data (yr. ended 12/31/88): Assets, $3,300,000 (M); expenditures, $176,800, including $154,750 for 30 grants (high: $40,000; low: $250; average: $5,000).
Purpose and activities: Emphasis on higher education, hospitals, youth agencies, Protestant church support, and cultural programs.
Types of support: General purposes.
Limitations: Giving primarily in PA. No grants to individuals, or for endowment funds, scholarships, fellowships, or matching gifts; no loans.
Application information:
Initial approach: Proposal
Copies of proposal: 1
Deadline(s): None
Board meeting date(s): Quarterly and as required
Write: William M. Schmidt, Secy.
Trustees: Roy Thomas Clark, Edwin F. Rodenbaugh, Union National Bank of Pittsburgh.
Employer Identification Number: 256062530

2775
John Crain Kunkel Foundation
1400 Market St., Suite 203
Camp Hill 17011 (717) 763-1784

Established in 1965 in PA.
Financial data (yr. ended 12/31/86): Assets, $7,610,028 (M); expenditures, $355,270, including $266,150 for 11 grants (high: $60,000; low: $6,000).
Purpose and activities: Emphasis on a hospital, higher and secondary education, cultural programs, and social agencies.
Limitations: Giving primarily in PA.
Application information:
Initial approach: Letter
Deadline(s): None
Write: Hasbrouck S. Wright, Exec. Trustee
Trustees: Hasbrouck S. Wright, Exec. Trustee; W.M. Kunkel, K.R. Stark.
Employer Identification Number: 237026914

2776
The Lancaster County Foundation
29 East King St., Rm. 14
Lancaster 17602 (717) 397-1629

Community foundation established in 1924 in PA.
Donor(s): Martin M. Harnish.†
Financial data (yr. ended 4/30/88): Assets, $6,974,370 (M); expenditures, $361,801, including $356,108 for 45 grants (high: $27,000; low: $1,500; average: $3,000-$10,000) and $1,100 for 3 grants to individuals.
Purpose and activities: Giving for welfare, social services, especially aid to the handicapped, health services, youth agencies, education, and cultural programs.
Types of support: Building funds, equipment, renovation projects, special projects, seed money, student aid, matching funds.
Limitations: Giving limited to Lancaster County, PA. No support for governmental agencies. No grants to individuals (except for a limited number of scholarships from donor-designated funds), or for operating budgets, continuing support, annual campaigns, deficit financing, land acquisition, endowment funds, fellowships, or conferences and seminars; no loans.
Publications: Annual report, application guidelines.
Application information: Application form required.
Copies of proposal: 2
Deadline(s): Oct. 15
Board meeting date(s): Varies
Final notification: Jan. 31
Write: Nancy L. Neff, Exec. Secy.
Trustees: David H. Acox, Jr., Chair.; Robert Luttrell, Vice-Chair.; and 12 trustee banks.
Distribution Committee: Donald B. Hostetter, Chair.; R. Wesley Shope, Vice-Chair.; Nancy L. Neff, Exec. Secy.; John R. Baldwin, John I. Hartman, Jr., S. Dale High, C. Edwin Ireland, Dawn K. Johnston, Bruce P. Ryder.
Number of staff: 1 part-time support.
Employer Identification Number: 236419120

2777
The R. K. Laros Foundation
3529 Magnolia Dr.
Easton 18042

Trust established in 1952 in PA.
Donor(s): Russell K. Laros.†
Financial data (yr. ended 12/31/86): Assets, $2,338,492 (M); expenditures, $102,400, including $86,803 for 11 grants (high: $15,000; low: $2,000).
Purpose and activities: Emphasis on higher education, community programs, historic preservation, and a hospital.
Types of support: General purposes.
Limitations: Giving limited to the Lehigh Valley area of eastern PA. No grants to individuals, or for endowment funds or operating budgets.
Application information:
Initial approach: Proposal
Copies of proposal: 6
Deadline(s): None
Board meeting date(s): Annually between May and Sept.
Write: Robert A. Spillman, Secy.
Officers: R.K. Laros, Jr., M.D., Pres.; Herman E. Collier, Jr., M.D., V.P.; Talbot Shelton, V.P.; Robert A. Spillman, Secy.; James G. Whilden, M.D., Treas.
Employer Identification Number: 236207353

2778
Laurel Foundation
Three Gateway Ctr., 6 North
Pittsburgh 15222 (412) 765-2400

Incorporated in 1951 in PA.
Donor(s): Cordelia S. May.
Financial data (yr. ended 12/31/87): Assets, $15,633,262 (M); expenditures, $978,590, including $756,000 for 45 grants (high: $50,000; low: $500).
Purpose and activities: Grants largely to organizations operating in the fields of higher and secondary education, conservation, health, cultural programs, and population planning, with concentration on projects originating in the Pittsburgh area; support also for immigration reform.
Types of support: General purposes, building funds, special projects, conferences and seminars, equipment, land acquisition, operating budgets, publications, lectureships.
Limitations: Giving primarily in western PA. No grants to individuals.
Publications: Annual report, application guidelines.
Application information:
Initial approach: Letter
Copies of proposal: 1
Deadline(s): Submit proposal preferably between Jan. and Apr. or July and Oct.; deadlines are May 1 and Nov. 1
Board meeting date(s): June and Dec.
Write: Gregory D. Curtis, Pres.
Officers: Gregory D. Curtis, Pres. and Secy.; Roger F. Meyer, V.P. and Treas.; Mrs. John F. Kraft, Jr.,* V.P.
Trustees:* Cordelia S. May, Chair.; Curtis S. Scaife, Robert E. Willison.
Number of staff: 2 part-time professional; 2 part-time support.
Employer Identification Number: 256008073

2779
The Lebovitz Fund
3050 Tremont St.
Allentown 18104 (215) 820-5053

Established in 1944 in PA.

Financial data (yr. ended 7/31/87): Assets, $1,426,796 (M); gifts received, $11,104; expenditures, $118,260, including $97,958 for 78 grants (high: $59,000; low: $20).
Purpose and activities: Support for conservation, culture and Jewish giving.
Limitations: Giving primarily in MI.
Application information:
Initial approach: Letter
Write: Herbert C. Lebovitz, Treas.
Officers: Clara H. Lebovitz, Pres.; Beth Ann Segal, Secy.; Herbert C. Lebovitz, Treas.
Director: Jonathan Javitch, James Lebovitz.
Employer Identification Number: 236270079

2780
Lockhart Iron and Steel Company Charitable Trust
c/o Union National Bank of Pittsburgh
Fourth Ave. & Wood St.
Pittsburgh 15278-2241

Financial data (yr. ended 12/31/87): Assets, $41,977 (M); expenditures, $9,866, including $9,400 for 15 grants (high: $2,000; low: $200).
Purpose and activities: Support for social services, youth, religion, and the arts.
Limitations: Giving primarily in Pittsburgh, PA.
Trustee: Union National Bank of Pittsburgh.
Employer Identification Number: 256020647

2781
The Ludwick Institute
c/o Ballard, Spahr, Andrews & Ingersoll
30 South 17th St., 20th Fl.
Philadelphia 19103 (215) 636-4964

Financial data (yr. ended 4/30/88): Assets, $2,125,000 (M); expenditures, $111,794, including $101,975 for 13 grants (high: $32,000; low: $1,000).
Purpose and activities: Support for education, particularly of disadvantaged youths, and for the study of the natural sciences; grants also for culture, with emphasis on museums.
Limitations: Giving limited to Philadelphia, PA.
Application information:
Initial approach: Proposal
Deadline(s): Apr.
Board meeting date(s): May and Oct.
Write: Hugh A.A. Sargent, Pres.
Officers: Hugh A.A. Sargent, Pres.; F.W. Elliott Farr, V.P.; L. Wilbur Zimmerman, V.P.; Victor J. Lang, Jr., Secy.; William M. Davison IV, Treas.; and 9 managers.
Employer Identification Number: 236256408

2782
The Lukens Foundation
50 South First Ave.
Coatesville 19320 (215) 383-2504

Trust established in 1966 in PA.
Donor(s): Lukens, Inc.
Financial data (yr. ended 12/31/87): Assets, $918,939 (L); expenditures, $177,388, including $163,968 for grants (high: $22,500; low: $100) and $8,154 for employee matching gifts.
Purpose and activities: Emphasis on community funds; conservation; cultural programs, including museums and performing arts; health and welfare efforts; human service projects; and education, including an employee matching gift program supporting institutions of secondary and higher education.
Types of support: Continuing support, annual campaigns, emergency funds, building funds, equipment, matching funds, employee matching gifts.
Limitations: Giving primarily in areas of domestic company operations. No grants to individuals, or for endowment funds or research; no loans.
Publications: Informational brochure.
Application information: Application form required.
Initial approach: Letter
Copies of proposal: 1
Deadline(s): Submit proposal preferably in Oct.; deadline Dec. 1
Board meeting date(s): Jan., Feb., Mar., and Apr.
Final notification: 4 months
Write: W. Evelyn Walker, Secy.
Officer: W. Evelyn Walker, Secy. and Admin.
Trustees: W.R. Wilson, Chair.; John R. Bartholdson, John van Roden, Robert Schaal.
Employer Identification Number: 236424112

2783
Samuel P. Mandell Foundation
Two Mellon Bank Center, Suite 1104
Philadelphia 19102 (215) 569-3600

Trust established in 1955 in PA.
Donor(s): Samuel P. Mandell.†
Financial data (yr. ended 12/31/87): Assets, $9,234,321 (M); expenditures, $900,192, including $709,157 for 194 grants (high: $200,000; low: $18).
Purpose and activities: Emphasis on Jewish welfare funds, hospitals and health services, higher education, cultural programs, and community affairs.
Limitations: Giving primarily in PA. No support for private operating foundations. No grants to individuals.
Application information:
Initial approach: Letter
Deadline(s): None
Write: John L. Ricketts, Exec. Secy.
Officer: John L. Ricketts, Exec. Secy.
Trustees: Judith Delfiner, Gerald Mandell, M.D., Morton Mandell, M.D., Ronald Mandell, Seymour Mandell.
Number of staff: 2 part-time support.
Employer Identification Number: 236274709

2784
The Martin Foundation
c/o MME, Inc., Huntington Plaza
3993 Huntington Pike
Huntington Valley 19006-1927

Established in 1981 in PA.
Donor(s): Alfred S. Martin.
Financial data (yr. ended 3/31/88): Assets, $1,613,359 (M); expenditures, $91,775, including $72,200 for 27 grants (high: $10,000; low: $500).
Purpose and activities: Grants for culture, higher and secondary education, youth programs, and community funds.
Application information:
Initial approach: Letter
Deadline(s): None
Write: Jovina Armento
Officer and Trustees: Alfred S. Martin, Mgr.; William W. Allen III, George J. Hartnett, Mary M. Martin, W. James Quigley.
Employer Identification Number: 232182719

2785
James H. Matthews & Company Educational and Charitable Trust
P.O. Box 4999
Pittsburgh 15206-3011 (412) 363-2500

Financial data (yr. ended 9/30/88): Assets, $473,055 (M); gifts received, $117,000; expenditures, $56,445, including $55,620 for 33 grants (high: $2,500; low: $500).
Purpose and activities: Supports community funds, social services, culture and the arts, and medical research.
Limitations: Giving primarily in Pittsburgh, PA.
Trustees: William M. Hauber, Thomas N. Kennedy, J.L. Parker, Robert Reed.
Employer Identification Number: 256028582

2786
J. S. McCormick Company Charitable Trust
25th St. & A.V.R.R.
Pittsburgh 15222

Donor(s): The J.S. McCormick Co.
Financial data (yr. ended 12/31/88): Assets, $2,899 (M); gifts received, $10,000; expenditures, $10,460, including $10,460 for 67 grants (high: $200; low: $50).
Purpose and activities: Support for social services, youth, health services, culture and the arts, and education.
Limitations: Giving primarily in Pittsburgh, PA.
Application information: Contributes only to preselected organizations. Applications not accepted.
Trustees: Robert G. Lind, Thomas F. Nelson, Eileen A. O'Malley, Curtin E. Schafer, Jr.
Employer Identification Number: 256032057

2787
McCune Foundation
1104 Commonwealth Bldg.
316 Fourth Ave.
Pittsburgh 15222 (412) 644-8779

Established in 1979 in PA.
Donor(s): Charles L. McCune.†
Financial data (yr. ended 9/30/88): Assets, $218,621,330 (M); expenditures, $11,135,842, including $10,158,285 for grants (high: $1,000,000; low: $50,000; average: $150,000-$350,000).
Purpose and activities: Giving primarily for independent higher education, health, and social services; support includes challenge grants. Preference is given to the organizations supported by the donor.

Types of support: Equipment, endowment funds, building funds, matching funds, capital campaigns, renovation projects, scholarship funds, seed money, special projects.
Limitations: Giving primarily in southwestern PA, with emphasis on the Pittsburgh area. No grants to individuals, or for general operating purposes; no loans.
Publications: Annual report (including application guidelines), grants list, financial statement.
Application information: Applicants are encouraged to wait 3 years after receiving a grant before reapplying.
Initial approach: Letter
Copies of proposal: 1
Deadline(s): Nov. 1 and Mar. 15
Board meeting date(s): Jan. and June
Final notification: 4 months
Write: Earland I. Carlson, Exec. Dir.
Distribution Committee: Richard D. Edwards, John R. McCune, Robert F. Patton.
Trustee: Union National Bank of Pittsburgh.
Number of staff: 2 full-time professional; 2 full-time support.
Employer Identification Number: 256210269
Recent arts and culture grants:
Carnegie, The, Pittsburgh, PA, $1,000,000. Toward construction of new Buhl Science Center. 1987.
Fort Ligonier Association, Ligonier, PA, $35,000. For endowment to staff Education and Collections Deapartments, as part of capital campaign awards. 1987.
Fund for the Bicentennical Celebration of Common Pleas Court, Pittsburgh, PA, $10,000. Toward restoration of courtroom in Allegheny County Courthouse. 1987.

2788
Katherine Mabis McKenna Foundation, Inc.
c/o Mellon Bank, N.A.
P.O. Box 185
Pittsburgh 15230
Application address: P.O. Box 186, LaTrobe, PA 15650; Tel.: (412) 537-6901

Incorporated in 1969 in PA.
Donor(s): Katherine M. McKenna.
Financial data (yr. ended 12/31/87): Assets, $9,384,496 (M); gifts received, $38,789; expenditures, $691,576, including $520,870 for 63 grants (high: $50,000; low: $400; average: $1,000-$10,000).
Purpose and activities: Giving for higher education, medical organizations, civic affairs, and cultural programs.
Types of support: General purposes, operating budgets, annual campaigns, seed money, building funds, equipment, endowment funds, special projects, scholarship funds, capital campaigns, internships, land acquisition.
Limitations: Giving primarily in western PA. No grants to individuals, or for matching gifts; no loans.
Application information:
Initial approach: Letter
Copies of proposal: 1
Deadline(s): Submit proposal preferably in Jan. through July; deadline Nov. 1
Board meeting date(s): Mar., June, Sept., and Dec.
Final notification: 3 to 6 months
Write: T. William Boxx, Secy.
Officer: T. William Boxx, Secy.-Treas.
Director: Linda McKenna Boxx.
Trustee: Mellon Bank, N.A.
Number of staff: 2
Employer Identification Number: 237042752

2789
John McShain Charities, Inc.
540 North Seventeenth St.
Philadelphia 19130 (215) 564-2322

Incorporated in 1949 in PA.
Donor(s): John McShain, John McShain, Inc., and others.
Financial data (yr. ended 3/31/87): Assets, $47,775,889 (M); expenditures, $2,805,542, including $2,355,619 for 198 grants (high: $300,000; low: $10; average: $100-$50,000).
Purpose and activities: Support for higher and secondary education, Roman Catholic church support, and social welfare and cultural programs.
Limitations: Giving primarily in Philadelphia, PA. No grants to individuals.
Application information:
Initial approach: Letter
Deadline(s): None
Board meeting date(s): Mar.
Final notification: 3 months
Write: John McShain, Fdn. Dir.
Officers and Directors: John McShain, Fdn. Dir.; William L. Shinners, V.P.; Mary Tompkins, Secy.-Treas.
Number of staff: None.
Employer Identification Number: 236276091

2790
Mellon Bank (East) Foundation
3 Mellon Bank Plaza
Philadelphia 19102 (215) 553-3032
Application address: P.O. Box 7236, Philadelphia, PA 19101

Trust established in 1955 in PA.
Donor(s): Girard Trust Bank.
Financial data (yr. ended 12/31/87): Assets, $2,239,245 (M); gifts received, $510,000; expenditures, $316,707, including $313,550 for 233 grants (high: $200,000; low: $100).
Purpose and activities: Emphasis on senior citizens, youth, cultural programs, community funds, civic affairs, and conservation.
Types of support: General purposes, operating budgets.
Limitations: Giving primarily in PA.
Trustee: Mellon Bank, N.A.
Employer Identification Number: 236227144

2791
Mellon Bank Corporate Giving Program
One Mellon Bank Center, Rm. 368
Pittsburgh 15258 (412) 234-5000

Purpose and activities: Through cash donations and in-kind contributions, Mellon encourages grass root efforts designed to promote job creation, support small businesses, create central business districts, provide affordable neighborhood housing, offer needed health and human services, and enrich the overall quality of life. Direct grants are made to organizations in the following categories: neighborhood and economic development, education, health and human services, and arts and culture. Technical assistance and loans are given for housing and small business. The Mellon Bank Community Development Corporation makes low-interest loans for housing and economic development in low- and moderate-income areas. Mellon also considers in-kind contributions of notions, meeting and exhibit space, furnishings, and employee volunteers; focus is on fundraising, marketing, and promotional efforts designed to broaden the resource base of a nonprofit organization, complement volunteer commitment, and afford visibility to the group and Mellon; to this end support is given for technical assistance, brochures, and special events. Programs reflect combined foundation and corporate giving.
Types of support: Employee matching gifts, operating budgets, capital campaigns, general purposes, building funds, seed money, in-kind gifts.
Limitations: Giving primarily in PA, MD, and DE where Mellon Bank Corporation operates offices; no support for national organizations or those which operate outside the U.S. No support for fraternal organizations, political parties, religious organizations, individual United Way agencies which receive funds from the United Way, or specialized health campaigns. No grants to individuals (loans or assistance), or for scholarships, fellowships or travel grants.
Application information: Include organization and project description and budget, 501(c)(3), audited financial statement and contributors and board lists.
Initial approach: Letter; grantseekers should submit requests directly to the Mellon Bank in their area
Board meeting date(s): Monthly
Final notification: 6 weeks
Write: Sylvia Clark, V.P.

2792
Mellon Bank Foundation
One Mellon Bank Ctr., Rm. 572
Pittsburgh 15258-0001 (412) 234-6266

Established in 1974 in PA.
Donor(s): Mellon Bank, N.A.
Financial data (yr. ended 12/31/87): Assets, $2,260,020 (M); gifts received, $1,202,500; expenditures, $1,290,245, including $1,275,954 for 83 grants (high: $125,000; low: $500; average: $1,500-$10,000).
Purpose and activities: Giving primarily to serve the overall vitality of local communities, with emphasis on economic development, including business development, employment and retraining initiatives, health and welfare, higher education, and cultural programs.
Types of support: Operating budgets, continuing support, annual campaigns, building funds, matching funds, technical assistance, special projects, capital campaigns, general purposes, seed money.
Limitations: Giving primarily in southwestern PA. No support for fraternal or religious

organizations, specialized health campaigns or other highly specialized projects with little or no positive impact on local communities, or United Way agencies (unless authorized to solicit corporations). No grants to individuals, or for emergency funds, deficit financing, equipment, land acquisition, scholarships, fellowships, research, publications, or conferences; no loans.
Publications: Corporate giving report (including application guidelines), informational brochure.
Application information:
Initial approach: Proposal
Copies of proposal: 1
Deadline(s): None
Board meeting date(s): Monthly
Final notification: 2 months
Write: Sylvia Clark, V.P.
Officers: Sandra J. McLaughlin,* Chair. and Pres.; Sylvia Clark, V.P. and Secy.; Steven G. Elliott, Treas.
Trustees:* Joseph F. DiMario, George T. Farrell, Richard A. Gaugh, Martin G. McGuinn, W. Keith Smith.
Number of staff: None.
Employer Identification Number: 237423500

2793
Matthew T. Mellon Foundation
c/o Mellon Bank, N.A.
One Mellon Bank Ctr.
Pittsburgh 15258 (412) 234-5892

Established in 1946 in PA.
Financial data (yr. ended 12/31/87): Assets, $1,154,703 (M); gifts received, $500,000; expenditures, $194,290, including $189,000 for 4 grants (high: $84,000; low: $5,000).
Purpose and activities: Support primarily for a medical institute; support also for a Scottish-Irish trust and the arts.
Types of support: Building funds.
Application information:
Deadline(s): None
Write: Leonard B. Richards
Trustees: George D. Lockhart, James R. Mellon, A.A. Vestal, James M. Walton, Mellon Bank, N.A.
Employer Identification Number: 251286841

2794
Richard King Mellon Foundation
525 William Penn Place
Pittsburgh 15219 (412) 392-2800

Trust established in 1947 in PA; incorporated in 1971 in PA.
Donor(s): Richard K. Mellon.†
Financial data (yr. ended 12/31/88): Assets, $728,518,000 (M); expenditures, $33,842,575, including $29,111,565 for 127 grants (high: $8,000,000; low: $3,000).
Purpose and activities: Local grant programs emphasize conservation, higher education, cultural and civic affairs, social services, medical research and health care; support also for conservation of natural areas and wildlife preservation elsewhere in the U.S.
Types of support: Seed money, building funds, equipment, land acquisition, research, matching funds, general purposes, continuing support, operating budgets, renovation projects.
Limitations: Giving primarily in Pittsburgh and western PA, except for nationwide conservation programs. No grants to individuals, or for fellowships or scholarships except through National Merit Scholarship Corporation.
Publications: Annual report (including application guidelines), informational brochure.
Application information:
Initial approach: Proposal
Copies of proposal: 1
Deadline(s): Apr. 1 and Oct. 1; submit proposal between Jan. and Mar. or July and Sept.
Board meeting date(s): June and Dec.
Final notification: 1 to 6 months
Write: George H. Taber, V.P.
Officers: Seward Prosser Mellon,* Pres.; George H. Taber,* V.P. and Dir.; Robert B. Burr, Jr., Secy.; Andrew W. Mathieson,* Treas.
Trustees:* Richard P. Mellon, Chair.; Arthur M. Scully, Jr., Mason Walsh, Jr.
Number of staff: 8 part-time professional; 1 full-time support; 10 part-time support.
Employer Identification Number: 251127705
Recent arts and culture grants:
Carnegie Institute, Pittsburgh, PA, $8,000,000. Toward capital campaign. 1987.
Pacific Tropical Botanical Garden, Lawai, HI, $950,000. For land acquisition. 1987.
Pittsburgh Ballet Theater, Pittsburgh, PA, $75,000. For operating support. 1987.
Pittsburgh Childrens Museum, Pittsburgh, PA, $213,000. To adapt main floor into major exhibition and performance area. 1987.
Pittsburgh Public Theater Corporation, Pittsburgh, PA, $85,000. For operating support. 1987.

2795
Meridian Foundation
c/o Meridian Bancorp, Inc.
1700 Arch Street, Mezzanine
Philadelphia 19103 (215) 854-3114

Trust established in 1956 in PA as the American Bank Foundation.
Donor(s): Meridian Bancorp, Inc.
Financial data (yr. ended 12/31/87): Assets, $34,850 (M); gifts received, $419,717; expenditures, $429,327, including $429,056 for 95 grants (high: $45,750; low: $100).
Purpose and activities: Support for community funds, higher education, health and welfare, arts and culture, and civic affairs. Maximum grant for capital campaigns is 5 percent of goal; special emphasis on economic and community development.
Types of support: Annual campaigns, building funds, capital campaigns.
Limitations: Giving primarily in southeastern PA: Berks, Bucks, Chester, Dauphin, Delaware, Lancaster, Lebanon, Lehigh, Montgomery, Philadelphia, and Schuykill counties. No grants to individuals, or for endowment funds, scholarships, or fellowships; no loans.
Publications: Application guidelines.
Application information: Requests for multi-year support, capital campaigns, or grants over $5,000 handled by foundation directly. Smaller, single-year gifts are decided on by the local foundation committee for each subsidiary.
Initial approach: Proposal
Copies of proposal: 1
Deadline(s): 1 month prior to board meetings
Board meeting date(s): Feb., May, Aug., and Nov.
Write: Nora Mead Brownell, Dir., Corp. Communications and Community Relations
Officer: Nora Mead Brownell, Dir., Corp. Communications and Community Relations.
Trustee: Meridian Bancorp, Inc.
Number of staff: None.
Employer Identification Number: 231976387

2796
Mine Safety Appliances Company Charitable Trust
c/o Mine Safety Appliances Co.
P.O. Box 426
Pittsburgh 15230

Trust established in 1951 in PA.
Donor(s): Mine Safety Appliances Co.
Financial data (yr. ended 12/31/87): Assets, $5,307,036 (M); expenditures, $568,797, including $510,542 for 106 grants (high: $110,000; low: $100; average: $300-$30,000).
Purpose and activities: Emphasis on community funds, higher education, hospitals, and health care; some support for the performing arts.
Types of support: General purposes.
Limitations: Giving primarily in PA. No grants to individuals, or for matching gifts; no loans.
Application information:
Initial approach: Letter
Copies of proposal: 1
Deadline(s): None
Board meeting date(s): Quarterly
Final notification: varies
Write: James E. Herald, Secy.
Officer: James E. Herald, Secy.
Trustee: Pittsburgh National Bank.
Number of staff: None.
Employer Identification Number: 256023104

2797
The Motter Foundation
3900 East Market St.
York 17402

Financial data (yr. ended 2/28/88): Assets, $552,313 (M); gifts received, $24,000; expenditures, $47,066, including $46,500 for 49 grants (high: $9,000; low: $250).
Purpose and activities: Support for health associations, youth organizations, Jewish giving, higher education, cultural groups, and services for the handicapped.
Officers: John C. Motter, Pres.; Frank Motter, Secy.
Trustees: Ed Motter, Fred Motter.
Employer Identification Number: 236280401

2798
Mudge Foundation
c/o Pittsburgh National Bank
Trust Div.
Pittsburgh 15265 (412) 355-3866

Established in 1955 in PA.
Financial data (yr. ended 12/31/86): Assets, $1,585,649 (M); expenditures, $77,947, including $69,100 for 7 grants (high: $40,000; low: $500).
Purpose and activities: Grants for natural resources and science projects, including medical research; support also for museums of natural history.
Types of support: General purposes, research.
Limitations: Giving primarily in TX, ME, and PA.
Application information:
Initial approach: Letter
Deadline(s): None
Write: H. Flood
Trustee: Pittsburgh National Bank.
Employer Identification Number: 256023150

2799
Florence R. C. Murray Charitable Trust
c/o The Philadelphia National Bank
P.O. Box 7618, F.C. 1-6-17
Philadelphia 19101-7618 (215) 973-2792

Established in 1980 in PA.
Donor(s): Florence R.C. Murray.†
Financial data (yr. ended 7/31/88): Assets, $3,421,062 (M); expenditures, $526,508, including $479,380 for 27 grants (high: $50,000; low: $2,666).
Purpose and activities: Emphasis on youth programs; support also for cultural, recreational, educational, and welfare organizations, and for hospitals and programs on race relations.
Types of support: Endowment funds, general purposes, matching funds, operating budgets, research, scholarship funds, special projects.
Limitations: Giving primarily in the five-county Philadelphia, PA, area. No grants to individuals, or for construction, multi-year grants, or deficit financing; no loans.
Application information:
Initial approach: Letter or proposal
Copies of proposal: 1
Deadline(s): Mar. 1 and Sept. 1
Board meeting date(s): Usually spring and autumn
Final notification: One month
Write: Bruce M. Brown, V.P., The Philadelphia National Bank
Trustees: William E. Lingelbach, Jr., William F. McDonald, Sr., Philadelphia National Bank.
Number of staff: 2 part-time professional; 1 part-time support.
Employer Identification Number: 236721607

2800
Gustav Oberlaender Foundation, Inc.
P.O. Box 896
Reading 19603

Incorporated in 1934 in DE.
Donor(s): Gustav Oberlander.†
Financial data (yr. ended 12/31/87): Assets, $1,758,562 (M); expenditures, $132,784, including $112,800 for grants.
Purpose and activities: Emphasis on cultural programs, hospitals, community funds, social services, higher education, and youth agencies.
Limitations: Giving primarily in PA.
Application information:
Initial approach: Letter or full proposal
Deadline(s): None
Write: Harold O. Leinbach, Pres.
Officers and Trustees: Harold O. Leinbach, Pres.; Richard O. Leinbach, V.P.; John M. Ennis, Secy.-Treas.; Paula Leinbach, Henry B. Sellers, Greta Smith, Jean L. Ziemer.
Employer Identification Number: 236282493

2801
Parklands Foundation
1500 One Franklin Plaza
Philadelphia 19102 (215) 854-6373

Established in 1977.
Donor(s): Charles H. Woodward.
Financial data (yr. ended 2/28/87): Assets, $94,961 (M); expenditures, $100,223, including $100,000 for 1 grant.
Purpose and activities: Giving limited to municipal entities for the development, improvement, and maintenance of parks and recreation areas.
Limitations: Giving primarily in Philadelphia, PA, Charlestown, SC, and ME.
Application information:
Deadline(s): None
Write: Martin A. Heckscher, Pres.
Officers and Directors: Martin A. Heckscher, Pres.; Sheldon M. Bonavitz, Secy.-Treas.; Donald Auten.
Employer Identification Number: 232026438

2802
The William Penn Foundation
1630 Locust St.
Philadelphia 19103-6305 (215) 732-5114

Incorporated in 1945 in DE.
Donor(s): Otto Haas,† Phoebe W. Haas,† Otto Haas & Phoebe W. Haas Charitable Trusts.
Financial data (yr. ended 12/31/88): Assets, $466,688,422 (M); gifts received, $9,577,431; expenditures, $25,191,754, including $23,195,743 for 392 grants (high: $1,000,000; low: $1,330) and $99,006 for 238 employee matching gifts.
Purpose and activities: At the beginning of 1987 the foundation adopted a new set of grant-making categories: (1) environment; (2) culture; and (3) human development, including programs for children, adolescents, elderly; and (4) community fabric (institutions, services, and intergroup relations). Also sponsors a matching gift program for board members, former board members, and employees of the foundation.
Types of support: Seed money, equipment, matching funds, special projects, emergency funds, land acquisition, renovation projects, technical assistance.
Limitations: Giving limited to the Philadelphia, PA, area, and Camden County, NJ. No support for sectarian religious activities, recreational programs, or programs focusing on a particular disease or treatment for addiction. No grants to individuals, or for operating budgets, continuing support, annual campaigns, deficit financing, hospital building funds, endowment funds, scholarships, fellowships, research, publications, travel, films, or conferences; no loans.
Publications: Annual report, application guidelines.
Application information:
Initial approach: Proposal
Copies of proposal: 1
Deadline(s): None
Board meeting date(s): Jan., Mar., Apr., June, July, Sept., Oct., and Dec.
Final notification: 2 to 3 months
Write: Bernard C. Watson, Ph.D., Pres. and C.E.O.
Officers: Bernard C. Watson,* Pres. and C.E.O.; Fran M. Coopersmith, V.P. for Finance and Treas.; Harry E. Cerino, V.P. for Progs.; Roland H. Johnson, Secy. and Sr. Prog. Officer.
Directors:* John C. Haas, Chair.; William D. Haas, Vice-Chair.; Frederick W. Anton III, Ernesta D. Ballard, Mary C. Carroll, Nelson A. Diaz, Richard G. Gilmore, Carole F. Haas, Chara C. Haas, David W. Haas, Frederick R. Haas, Janet F. Haas, John O. Haas, Philip C. Herr II, Robert Montgomery Scott, Paul M. Washington.
Number of staff: 10 full-time professional; 1 part-time professional; 10 full-time support.
Employer Identification Number: 231503488
Recent arts and culture grants:
Academy of Natural Sciences of Philadelphia, Philadelphia, PA, $250,000. For new education and library facilities. 8/88.
American Music Theater Festival, Philadelphia, PA, $190,000. To commission, develop, and produce new works. 2/88.
Archdiocese of Philadelphia, Philadelphia, PA, $13,281. For cultural, educational, and health care enrichment of summer day camps. 5/88.
Asociacion de Musicos Latino Americanos, Philadelphia, PA, $50,000. For general support. 2/88.
Black Peoples Unity Movement Day Care Program, Camden, NJ, $6,514. For cultural, educational, and health care enrichment of summer day camps. 5/88.
Boys and Girls Clubs of Metropolitan Philadelphia, Philadelphia, PA, $108,853. For cultural, educational, and health care enrichment of summer day camps. 5/88.
Bushfire Theater of Performing Arts, Philadelphia, PA, $280,000. For challenge grant for artistic and administrative staff and capital improvements. 8/88.
Camden County Council on Economic Opportunity, Camden, NJ, $29,732. For cultural, educational, and health care enrichment of summer day camps. 5/88.
Central Philadelphia Development Corporation, Philadelphia, PA, $120,000. For background research to develop programs to preserve historic structures in Center City. 8/88.
Chester County Historical Society, West Chester, PA, $41,420. To support Community/Museum Education Project. 12/88.
Church of the Advocate, Philadelphia, PA, $19,000. Toward its historic restoration project. 10/88.

Civil Rights Project, Boston, MA, $250,000. For Eyes on the Prize: Part II, eight-part television documentary on Civil Rights Movement from the '60s to the early '80s. 8/88.
Crime Prevention Association, Philadelphia, PA, $25,523. For cultural, educational, and health care enrichment of summer day camps. 5/88.
Dance Conduit, Philadelphia, PA, $15,000. For reconstruction and performance of Doris Humphrey's Dawn in New York. 6/88.
Diversified Community Services, Philadelphia, PA, $6,290. For cultural, educational, and health care enrichment of summer day camps. 5/88.
Fabric Workshop, Philadelphia, PA, $40,000. For new equipment to expand artistic opportunities. 8/88.
Franklin Institute, Philadelphia, PA, $1,000,000. Toward construction and equipping of Futures Center. 4/88.
Fredric R. Mann Music Center, Philadelphia, PA, $225,000. To upgrade acoustical and amplification systems. 1/88.
Friends Neighborhood Guild, Philadelphia, PA, $9,265. For cultural, educational, and health care enrichment of summer day camps. 5/88.
Friends of Logan Square Foundation, Philadelphia, PA, $100,000. For restoration of Swann Memorial Fountain. 6/88.
Friends of the Delaware Canal, Point Pleasant, PA, $25,000. Toward activities to restore this 60-mile linear park. 11/88.
Hartranft Community Corporation, Philadelphia, PA, $9,000. For cultural, educational, and health care enrichment of summer day camps. 5/88.
Kardon Institute of Music for the Handicapped, Philadelphia, PA, $50,000. Toward establishment of program for hearing impaired. 1/88.
Lutheran Social Mission Society of Philadelphia, Philadelphia, PA, $22,313. For cultural, educational, and health care enrichment of summer day camps. 5/88.
Melanie Stewart and Company Dance, Philadelphia, PA, $12,000. To support home concert series. 3/88.
Movement Theater International, Philadelphia, PA, $100,000. For renovations to Tabernacle Church to create performing arts theater. 8/88.
Museum of American Jewish History, Philadelphia, PA, $120,000. For conservation and collections care activities. 4/88.
Neighborhood Center, Camden, NJ, $33,800. For cultural, educational, and health care enrichment of summer day camps. 5/88.
New Freedom Theater, Philadelphia, PA, $651,040. For activities to enhance artistic productions. 8/88.
OPEN, Philadelphia, PA, $9,653. For cultural, educational, and health care enrichment of summer day camps. 5/88.
Opera Company of Philadelphia, Philadelphia, PA, $300,000. For performance of Handel's Messiah in conjuction with School District of Philadelphia. 8/88.
Opera North, Philadelphia, PA, $137,500. For artistic director's salary and production costs. 2/88.
Pennsbury Society, Morrisville, PA, $10,000. To research and develop permanent exhibit on reconstruction of Pennsbury Manor. 6/88.
Philadelphia Art Alliance, Philadelphia, PA, $50,000. For restoration of its historic building. 8/88.
Philadelphia Art Alliance, Philadelphia, PA, $15,000. For information on artists project to be conducted by Columbia University Research Center for Arts and Culture. 2/88.
Philadelphia College of Textiles and Science, Philadelphia, PA, $85,000. For cataloguing and documentation of textile collection. 2/88.
Philadelphia Company, Philadelphia, PA, $100,000. For Stages program to develop new works. 4/88.
Philadelphia Dance Alliance, Philadelphia, PA, $20,000. For long-range planning. 5/88.
Philadelphia Dance Company, Philadelphia, PA, $75,000. For dancers' rehearsals fees for development of new works. 1/88.
Philadelphia Festival Theater for New Plays, Philadelphia, PA, $40,000. For production costs of Magda and Calas. 1/88.
Philadelphia Historic Preservation Corporation, Philadelphia, PA, $50,000. For preservation of historic buildings and districts. 12/88.
Philadelphia Museum of Art, Philadelphia, PA, $1,100,720. To support local artists and promote Philadelphia as major regional art center, in collaborative program with Pennsylvania Academy of Fine Arts and Institute of Contemporary Art. 1/88.
Philadelphia Singers, Philadelphia, PA, $33,750. To support Choirs in Concerts, choral music education program for high school music and graduate choral conducting students. 12/88.
Philadelphia Society for the Preservation of Landmarks, Philadelphia, PA, $70,000. For collections management and documentation project for four historic houses. 4/88.
Please Touch Museum, Philadelphia, PA, $78,540. To strengthen Museum's Division of Interpretation. 8/88.
Rutgers, The State University of New Jersey Foundation, New Brunswick, NJ, $28,732. For museum education enrichment program for children and youth. 8/88.
Taller Puertorriqueno, Philadelphia, PA, $60,200. To develop and expand artistic programs. 4/88.
Taller Puertorriqueno, Philadelphia, PA, $6,773. For cultural, educational, and health care enrichment of summer day camps. 5/88.
Terry Beck Troupe, Philadelphia, PA, $15,000. For artists' salaries. 3/88.
United Communities Southeast Philadelphia, Philadelphia, PA, $12,566. For cultural, educational, and health care enrichment of summer day camps. 5/88.
University of Pennsylvania, Philadelphia, PA, $225,000. To support children's program, Kids Corner on WXPN-FM. 12/88.
University of Pennsylvania, Annenberg Center for Communication, Philadelphia, PA, $8,000. For Back-to-School Children's Festival at Penn's Landing. 7/88.
University of Pennsylvania, School of Arts and Sciences, Philadelphia, PA, $396,300. Toward establishing Center for the Study of Black Literature and Culture. 1/88.
Urban Coalition of Philadelphia Foundation, Philadelphia, PA, $10,000. To provide admissions for low-income children and families to Africamericas Festival. 4/88.
West Chester Community Center, West Chester, PA, $12,305. For cultural, educational, and health care enrichment of summer day camps. 5/88.
Woodrock, Philadelphia, PA, $8,140. For cultural, educational, and health care enrichment of summer day camps. 5/88.
Wyck Association, Philadelphia, PA, $71,398. For collections management and documentation project for three historic houses in Germantown: Wyck, Cliveden, and Loudoun. 4/88.
Yellow Springs Institute for Contemporary Studies and the Arts, Chester Springs, PA, $50,000. For multicultural program expansion. 4/88.
YMCA of Brandywine, Coatesville, PA, $14,941. For cultural, educational, and health care enrichment of summer day camps. 5/88.
YMCA, Philadelphia Metro, Philadelphia, PA, $55,240. For cultural, educational, and health care enrichment of summer day camps. 5/88.
Young Audiences of Eastern Pennsylvania, Philadelphia, PA, $37,520. To expand programming in Philadelphia public schools. 4/88.
YWCA of Camden County, Camden, NJ, $24,539. For cultural, educational, and health care enrichment of summer day camps. 5/88.
YWCA of Philadelphia, Philadelphia, PA, $23,139. For cultural, educational, and health care enrichment of summer day camps. 5/88.

2803
Pennsylvania Power & Light Company Giving Program

Two North Ninth Street
Allentown 18101 (215) 770-5151

Financial data (yr. ended 12/31/88): Total giving, $903,090, including $726,648 for grants, $47,880 for grants to individuals and $128,562 for 680 employee matching gifts.
Purpose and activities: "The company has a charitable contributions committee composed of our Chief Executive Officer, three Executive/Senior Vice Presidents, one Division Vice President, and a Secretary. Due to the nature of our business, our contributions are directed to organizations within, or principally benefiting, our service area. Solicitations for funds directed to national, regional, or metropolitan areas outside our service territory are, with few exceptions, declined." The company is organized into 6 divisions and specific funds are allocated for recipients in each division. Funds are also allocated to recipients of a systemwide nature. Supports education, the arts, civic and community affairs, health, United Way, and youth.
Types of support: Equipment, building funds, scholarship funds, special projects, employee matching gifts, employee-related scholarships.
Limitations: Giving primarily in service area, approximately 1,000 square miles in central eastern PA.
Application information:

Initial approach: Letter
Board meeting date(s): At least twice annually, once to review policies, and in Sept. to approve budget for coming year
Write: Robert K. Campbell, Pres. and C.E.O.
Number of staff: None.

2804
Pennwalt Foundation
Pennwalt Bldg.
Three Benjamin Franklin Pkwy.
Philadelphia 19102 (215) 587-7653

Trust established in 1957 in PA.
Donor(s): Pennwalt Corp.
Financial data (yr. ended 12/31/87): Assets, $331,063 (M); gifts received, $1,238,400; qualifying distributions, $1,212,652, including $935,310 for 467 grants (high: $60,629; low: $25), $906,000 for 92 grants to individuals and $186,439 for 581 employee matching gifts.
Purpose and activities: Grants primarily for community funds; higher education, including employee-related scholarships and matching gifts; and cultural programs, including museums and public broadcasting; support also for civic affairs, and health and medicine.
Types of support: Operating budgets, general purposes, continuing support, annual campaigns, seed money, emergency funds, deficit financing, building funds, equipment, land acquisition, matching funds, employee matching gifts, employee-related scholarships, renovation projects.
Limitations: Giving primarily in areas of company operations, with some emphasis on the Philadelphia, PA, area. No support for public education; veterans', fraternal, or labor organizations; or sectarian religious organizations. No grants to individuals (except for employee-related scholarships), or for endowment funds, special projects, research, publications, conferences, courtesy advertising, or entertainment promotions; no loans.
Application information:
Initial approach: Proposal
Copies of proposal: 1
Deadline(s): None
Board meeting date(s): Mar., June, Sept., and Dec.
Final notification: 1 to 3 months
Write: George L. Hagar, Exec. Secy.
Trustees: Anthony P. Fortino, Seymour S. Preston III, George Reath, Jr.
Number of staff: 1 part-time professional; 1 full-time support.
Employer Identification Number: 236256818

2805
The Pew Charitable Trusts
Three Pkwy., Suite 501
Philadelphia 19102-1305 (215) 568-3330

Pew Memorial Trust, J.N. Pew, Jr. Charitable Trust, J. Howard Pew Freedom Trust, Mabel Pew Myrin Trust, Medical Trust, Knollbrook Trust, and Mary Anderson Trust, created in 1948, 1956, 1957, 1957, 1975, 1965, and 1957 respectively.
Donor(s): Mary Ethel Pew,† Mabel Pew Myrin,† J. Howard Pew,† Joseph N. Pew, Jr.†
Financial data (yr. ended 12/31/88): Assets, $2,519,746,836 (M); expenditures, $140,390,855, including $135,906,632 for grants (high: $3,000,000; low: $2,500).
Purpose and activities: Giving primarily in culture, education, health and human services, conservation and the environment, public policy and religion. In culture, support is given in the Philadelphia area to foster cultural activities of the highest quality, promote an environment that encourages artistic and institutional advancement, and increase awareness and appreciation of Philadelphia's diverse cultural resources. Nationally, support is given to advance specific cultural areas or disciplines, address critical cultural needs, and support the dissemination of creative solutions to problems shared by broad national constituencies. In education, support is given to maintain academic excellence, strengthen the liberal arts and sciences, support institutional diversity, make higher education more accessible to disadvantaged populations, and encourage better understanding of major issues affecting the quality of education. In health and human services, support is given to programs that encourage community development in the Philadelphia area, promote greater self-sufficiency and meaningful, productive lifestyles among groups at risk, strengthen institutions in the health professions, advance the biomedical sciences, improve health care delivery systems, encourage the elderly and the physically and mentally handicapped to live to their fullest potential, build the capacities of individuals and communities, strengthen indigenous policies and programs in developing countries that promote improved health status and sustained economic and social development. In conservation and the environment, support is given to advance the field of conservation through research and training, strengthen the field's infrastructure, and encourage collaboration among the various disciplines involved with resource management and development. In public policy, support is given to improve understanding of the free enterprise system and American civic values and responsibilities, and to encourage research and debate on the implications of contemporary policy concerns on U.S. security, international relations, and the economy. In religion, support is given to promote the development and application of Judeo-Christian values and encourage better understanding of how those values shape our lives and civic responsibilities. Support is also given to improve theological education, encourage interdenominational and interfaith understanding, and strengthen ministry and the work of congregations in their communities.
Types of support: Seed money, matching funds, continuing support, renovation projects, building funds, equipment, research, operating budgets, special projects, capital campaigns, general purposes, internships, technical assistance.
Limitations: No grants to individuals, or for endowment funds, deficit financing, scholarships, or fellowships except those identified or initiated by the trusts.
Publications: Annual report (including application guidelines), grants list, occasional report, informational brochure (including application guidelines).
Application information: Contact foundation for specific guidelines and limitations in each program area.
Initial approach: Letter, telephone, or proposal
Copies of proposal: 1
Deadline(s): Music-Jan. 1; museums/visual arts-Apr. 1; theater-June 1; dance-Sept. 1; all others-none
Board meeting date(s): Feb., Apr., June, Sept., and Dec.
Final notification: Approximately 3 weeks after board meetings
Write: Rebecca W. Rimel, Exec. Dir.
Officers: Thomas W. Langfitt, M.D.,* Pres.; Rebecca W. Rimel, Exec. Dir.
Directors:* Susan W. Catherwood, Robert G. Dunlop, Howard O. Guess, Robert E. McDonald, J. Howard Pew II, J.N. Pew III, John G. Pew, Jr., Joseph N. Pew IV, M.D., R. Anderson Pew, Richard C. Sorlien, Ethel Benson Wister.
Trustee: The Glenmede Trust Co.
Number of staff: 22 full-time professional; 33 full-time support; 5 part-time support.
Recent arts and culture grants:
Academy of Natural Sciences of Philadelphia, Philadelphia, PA, $1,050,000. For general operations, and construction of new multipurpose building. 6/88.
Academy of Natural Sciences of Philadelphia, Philadelphia, PA, $30,000. To complete second edition of Groundwater Contamination in the United States. 4/88.
Aid to Artisans, Farmington, CT, $35,000. To evaluate feasibility of craft development program in Ghana. 12/87.
American Ballet Competition, Philadelphia, PA, $25,000. For NextMove Festival. 12/87.
American Ballet Competition, Philadelphia, PA, $10,000. To support commissioning of Philadelphia Section of David Gordon's new dance United States as part of NextMove Festival. 12/87.
American Dance Festival, NYC, NY, $40,000. To support residencies of Philadelphia-based choreographers and dancers at annual American Dance Festival. 12/87.
American Folklore Society, Columbus, OH, $250,000. For Philadelphia Folklore Project, as part of 1989 AFS Centennial celebration. 12/87.
American Music Center, NYC, NY, $10,000. To support score-copying program for Philadelphia composers and ensembles. 4/88.
American Music Theater Festival, Philadelphia, PA, $225,000. For general operations. 4/88.
American Poetry Center, Philadelphia, PA, $18,000. To support 1988 Poetry Week activities. 9/87.
Association of College, University and Community Arts Administrators, Madison, WI, $100,000. To support national task force to examine role of presenting and touring performing arts in United States. 2/88.
Basically Bach Festival of Philadelphia, Philadelphia, PA, $10,000. To support artistic fees for 1988 festival. 4/88.
Brandywine Workshop, Philadelphia, PA, $32,500. To support traveling exhibition of Afro-American abstract artists; exhibition of computer-generated images and related

workshops/ and lecture series by Native American artists. 6/88.

Bucks County Community College, Newton, PA, $17,000. For support of planning phase of Philadelphia Photography Sesquicentennial Project. 4/88.

Bushfire Theater of Performing Arts, Philadelphia, PA, $7,000. To support 52nd Street Writers Workshop, program for local playwrights. 9/87.

Center Theater Group of Los Angeles, Los Angeles, CA, $100,000. For production fund to co-produce and/or present works developed by Philadelphia theaters. 9/87.

CHOICE: Concern for Health Options-Information, Care and Education, Philadelphia, PA, $100,000. To support Project Connect, interactive theater and counseling program for preteens. 2/88.

Choral Arts Society of Philadelphia, Philadelphia, PA, $10,000. To support subscription series of choral/symphonic works. 4/88.

Chorus America, Philadelphia, PA, $50,000. To help foster greater recognition of significant American choral works through support of performance costs. 4/88.

Church Memorial Park, Chester, Canada, $42,000. To support capital expenditures and operations. 2/88.

Clay Studio, Philadelphia, PA, $36,900. To support lecture series, and American Clay Artists Exhibition. 6/88.

Colonial Williamsburg Foundation, Williamsburg, VA, $600,000. To support restoration and interpretation of Williamsburg Courthouse. 9/87.

Colorado Dance Festival, Boulder, CO, $5,000. To support residency of Philadelphia-based artist Steve Krieckhaus at 1988 Colorado Dance Festival. 4/88.

Concerto Soloists, Philadelphia, PA, $50,000. For matching grant to support European tour in April 1989. 4/88.

Council for Basic Education, DC, $71,000. For Independent Study Fellowships in Humanities for Philadelphia teachers. 9/87.

Dance Theater Workshop, NYC, NY, $270,000. Toward National Performance Network. 9/87.

Dance Umbrella, Cambridge, MA, $18,000. To present performances by Philadelphia-based artist LaVaughn Robinson at 1988 Jazz Tap Festival and Hellmutt Gottschild and Karen Bamonte. 2/88.

Danceteller, Philadelphia, PA, $10,000. Toward artistic salaries and expenses. 12/87.

District One Community Education Center, Philadelphia, PA, $30,000. For Independent Performing Artists Project. 12/87.

District One Community Education Center, Philadelphia, PA, $20,000. For partial matching support for capital improvements in two performing spaces. 12/87.

Earmark, Philadelphia, PA, $76,000. For production and distribution of radio series At The Bride. 12/87.

Educational Broadcasting Corporation, NYC, NY, $500,000. For development and production of television programs on Philadelphia Orchestra and Pennsylvania Ballet to be featured on Great Performances. 12/87.

Fabric Workshop, Philadelphia, PA, $77,000. To support artistic and educational programming, and capital improvements. 6/88.

Franklin Institute, Philadelphia, PA, $4,500,000. For partially matching grant for development and construction of The Future Center. 12/87.

Friends of Logan Square Foundation, Philadelphia, PA, $350,000. For restoration of Swann Memorial Fountain. 12/87.

Greater Philadelphia Cultural Alliance, Philadelphia, PA, $50,000. For general operations. 12/87.

Group Motion Multi-Media Dance Theater, Philadelphia, PA, $25,000. To support Visiting Artists Workshop and Performance Series, and Twentieth Anniversary Festival. 4/88.

Headlands Arts Center, Sausalito, CA, $33,000. To support residencies of eight Philadelphia-based artists. 6/88.

Highlands Historical Society, Fort Washington, PA, $58,000. To support historic structures report for Highlands property in Fort Washington, Pennsylvania. 2/88.

John F. Kennedy Center for the Performing Arts, DC, $112,000. To support Pennsylvania/Milwaukee Ballet, and Philadelphia Singers and Concerto Soloists Chamber Orchestra of Philadelphia as part of Center's 1988-89 season. 4/88.

Mann Music Center, Philadelphia, PA, $200,000. For performances by American Ballet Theater. 12/87.

Mann Music Center, Philadelphia, PA, $50,000. For performances by Ballet National de Espana., 12/87.

Mary Luft and Company, New Music America/Miami Festival, Miami, FL, $25,000. To support residency of Relache, and commissioning and performance of new collaborative work by artist Peter Rose as part of 1988 festival. 4/88.

Meet the Composer, NYC, NY, $450,000. For Composers/Choreographers Collaboration Project to encourage commissioning of original musical and choreography works for American dance companies. 12/87.

Melanie Stewart and Company Dance, Philadelphia, PA, $30,000. For artistic and administrative salaries. 12/87.

Modern Language Association of America, NYC, NY, $238,700. To establish two national programs to support foreign language instruction and to complete Wing Short-Title Catalog Revision Project. 2/88.

Movement Theater International, Philadelphia, PA, $50,000. For artists' fees and direct production costs associated with 1988 Movement Theater Festival. 12/87.

Movement Theater International, Philadelphia, PA, $15,000. For staff expansion and training. 12/87.

Movement Theater International, Philadelphia, PA, $10,000. For presentation of Philadelphia-based artists as part of festival's core performance program. 12/87.

Mozart on the Square, Philadelphia, PA, $14,000. To support artistic fees. 4/88.

Museum of American Jewish History, Philadelphia, PA, $75,000. To support temporary exhibitions, supplementary programs, and collections management activities. 6/88.

Museum of Modern Art, NYC, NY, $485,000. For Museum Education Consortium, in support of second phase of national collaborative project to research and develop interactive videodisc technology for use in museums. 6/88.

National Association of Artists Organizations, DC, $35,000. For feasibility study concerning national visual arts touring network. 6/88.

National Captioning Institute, Falls Church, VA, $85,000. For challenge grant for support of public affairs television closed-captioned programming. 12/87.

National Gallery of Art, DC, $265,000. For exhibition of still life paintings by Raphaelle Peale, co-organized with Pennsylvania Academy of the Fine Arts. 6/88.

National Public Radio, DC, $1,185,000. For History Reporting Unit and coverage of Delaware Valley for Performance Today. 12/87.

New Arts Program, Kutztown, PA, $29,000. To continue and expand Philadelphia artists' consultation and residency program. 6/88.

New Arts Program, Kutztown, PA, $9,000. To expand artist consultation/residency program to Philadelphia. 9/87.

New York City Ballet, NYC, NY, $50,000. For creation and production of new ballet choreographed by Philadelphia artist Robert Weiss to be featured in New York City Ballet's American Music Festival. 12/87.

New York Foundation for the Arts, NYC, NY, $60,000. To support conference in Philadelphia to examine role and needs of artists in Philadelphia cultural community. 2/88.

New York Historical Society, NYC, NY, $200,000. For comprehensive cataloging program. 12/87.

New York Zoological Society, Wildlife Conservation International, Bronx, NY, $280,000. For conservation training for indigenous scientists and wildlife managers as part of research projects in Africa, Asia, and Latin America. 12/87.

Opera Company of Philadelphia, Philadelphia, PA, $600,000. For partially challenge grant to support opera productions; Pavarotti Voice Competition; a special Messiah concert; and Jessye Norman concert. 4/88.

Our Lady of the Lake University of San Antonio, San Antonio, TX, $250,000. Toward renovation of Fine Arts Building as new Humanities Center. 9/87.

Pennsbury Society, Morrisville, PA, $57,000. To support maintenance and repairs at Pennsbury Manor. 4/88.

Pennsylvania Academy of the Fine Arts, Philadelphia, PA, $350,000. To support three exhibitions, and purchase of conservation equipment. 6/88.

Pennsylvania Ballet Association, Philadelphia, PA, $750,000. Toward renovation and equipping of new rehearsal facility. 12/87.

Pennsylvania Ballet Association, Philadelphia, PA, $300,000. For support of general operations. 12/87.

Pennsylvania Historical and Museum Commission, Friends of the, Harrisburg, PA, $120,000. To support restoration, conservation, and interpretation of Gideon

Gilpin House and adjacent out buildings at Brandywine Battlefield Park, Chadds Ford, Pennsylvania. 2/88.
Pennsylvania Opera Theater, Philadelphia, PA, $110,000. For general operations. 4/88.
Pentacle, NYC, NY, $36,000. To include ten Philadelphia-based dance companies in year-long marketing and technical assistance program. 12/87.
Peoples Light and Theater Company, Malvern, PA, $135,000. To support operations. 9/87.
Peoples Light and Theater Company, Malvern, PA, $75,000. For matching grant toward renovation and expansion of existing farmhouse as artists' residence. 9/87.
Philadelphia Alliance for Teaching Humanities in the Schools, Philadelphia, PA, $1,125,000. For programs designed to strengthen language, arts, literature, and history education in School District of Philadelphia. 9/87.
Philadelphia Area Repertory Theater, Philadelphia, PA, $15,000. Toward partial matching grant for artistic salaries. 9/87.
Philadelphia Art Alliance, Philadelphia, PA, $20,000. To support capital improvement program. 6/88.
Philadelphia Chamber Music Society, Philadelphia, PA, $5,000. To introduce work of Philadelphia-based composers to leading national chamber ensembles in order to encourage commissioning of new works. 4/88.
Philadelphia Company, Philadelphia, PA, $50,000. To support general operations. 9/87.
Philadelphia Company, Philadelphia, PA, $22,000. For full-time project director for STAGES. Grant made as part of Trust's program, Artistic Development Initiative, to encourage artistic development of nonprofit theater in Philadelphia area, and to increase local and national recognition of Philadelphia area theater community. 9/87.
Philadelphia Dance Company, Philadelphia, PA, $60,000. To develop and present new works by black choreographers. 12/87.
Philadelphia Drama Guild, Philadelphia, PA, $250,000. For grant, partially challenge, to support operations. 9/87.
Philadelphia Drama Guild, Philadelphia, PA, $115,000. Toward Playwrights of Philadelphia Festival. Grant made as part of Trust's program, Artistic Development Initiative, to encourage artistic development of nonprofit theater in Philadelphia area, and to increase local and national recognition of Philadelphia area theater community. 9/87.
Philadelphia Festival Theater for New Plays, Philadelphia, PA, $60,000. For grant, partially matching, to support operations. 9/87.
Philadelphia Historic Preservation Corporation, Philadelphia, PA, $165,000. To support Philadelphia Architectural Salvage Program. 2/88.
Philadelphia Museum of Art, Philadelphia, PA, $780,000. To support special exhibitions; research and planning for future exhibitions; and programs of Division of Education. 6/88.
Philadelphia Orchestra Association, Philadelphia, PA, $350,000. For general operations. 6/88.
Philadelphia Singers, Philadelphia, PA, $100,000. To support general operations; new position of Executive Director; and commissioning of new choral work. 4/88.
Philadelphia Society for the Preservation of Landmarks, Philadelphia, PA, $60,000. To develop long-range, systematic plan for continuing care and maintenance of society's four historic properties; and to support restoration and repairs of Grumbelthorpe. 4/88.
Philadelphia Theater Caravan, Philadelphia, PA, $110,000. For artistic salaries and costs associated with New Productions Fund. 9/87.
Philadelphia Volunteer Lawyers for the Arts, Philadelphia, PA, $55,000. For collaborative project with Business Volunteers for the Arts and Community Accountants, to provide technical services to Philadelphia cultural community concerning real estate issues. 6/88.
Philadelphia Volunteer Lawyers for the Arts, Philadelphia, PA, $16,000. To support operations. 9/87.
Philadelphia Volunteer Lawyers for the Arts, Philadelphia, PA, $9,000. For conference and part-time coordinator to address real estate needs of Philadelphia cultural community. 9/87.
Pierpont Morgan Library, NYC, NY, $150,000. To catalogue selected major research collections of library. 12/87.
Please Touch Museum, Philadelphia, PA, $46,500. To support increased staff salaries. 6/88.
Preservation Coalition of Greater Philadelphia, Philadelphia, PA, $55,000. To continue and expand Historic Neighborhoods Preserved program. 2/88.
Preservation Fund of Pennsylvania, Lancaster, PA, $250,000. For emergency fund to help preserve or protect threatened historic structures in Philadelphia. 12/87.
Print Club, Philadelphia, PA, $39,000. To support artists' residencies. 6/88.
Prints in Progress, Philadelphia, PA, $40,000. To support ongoing workshop activities. 6/88.
Relache, Philadelphia, PA, $70,000. To support artists' fees, and production and promotional costs. 4/88.
Riverside Symphony, NYC, NY, $14,000. To support commissioning, performance, and recording of major orchestral work by Philadelphia-based composer Maurice Wright. 4/88.
Rosenbach Museum and Library, Philadelphia, PA, $85,000. To support long-range capital planning. 6/88.
Samuel S. Fleisher Art Memorial, Philadelphia, PA, $192,000. To support gallery and studio renovations, and collaborative international project as part of 1992 Columbus Quinticentennary. 6/88.
Schuylkill Valley Nature Center, Philadelphia, PA, $96,000. For Management Intern Program. 12/87.
Schuylkill Valley Nature Center, Philadelphia, PA, $44,000. For regional cooperative planning program. 12/87.
Settlement Music School of Philadelphia, Philadelphia, PA, $100,000. For parking lot lighting improvements and expansion at school's branches. 6/88.
Smithsonian Institution, National Zoological Park/Conservation and Research Center, DC, $200,000. For grant, partially matching, to support Wildlife Management and Training Program. 9/87.
South Street Dance Company, Philadelphia, PA, $10,000. For body/language/88 project to showcase work by artists working in mixed disciplines. 12/87.
Spoleto Festival USA, Charleston, SC, $25,000. For co-production and presentation of American Music Theater Festival production of The Warrior Ant during 1988 festival. 2/88.
Strings for Schools, Malvern, PA, $6,000. To support teaching concerts in schools to expand children's music appreciation. 4/88.
Susan Hess Modern Dance, Philadelphia, PA, $26,000. For Solos project. 12/87.
Susan Hess Modern Dance, Philadelphia, PA, $21,000. To support Three Choreographers Working project. 12/87.
Taller Puertorriqueno, Philadelphia, PA, $16,000. To support exhibitions and visiting artists programs, and residency and training of two Philadelphia-based artists at Mission Cultural Center in San Francisco. 6/88.
Temple University, Tyler School of Art, Philadelphia, PA, $35,000. To support artists' lecture series. 6/88.
Theater Project, Baltimore, MD, $40,000. To commission new work from and provide developmental residency for Philadelphia-based performing arts company. 12/87.
University of Pennsylvania, Annenberg Center for Communication Arts and Sciences, Philadelphia, PA, $210,000. Toward capital improvements and renovations in Prince and Zellerbach Theaters. 9/87.
University of Pennsylvania, Annenberg Center for Communication Arts and Sciences, Philadelphia, PA, $40,000. For Dance Celebration. 9/87.
University of Pennsylvania, Annenberg Center for Communication Arts and Sciences, Philadelphia, PA, $25,000. Toward Annenberg Center Theater Series. 9/87.
University of Pennsylvania, Annenberg Center for the Communication Arts and Sciences, Philadelphia, PA, $40,000. To support commissioning of new dance work by Paul Taylor to premiere in 1988-89 season of Dance Celebration. 4/88.
University of Pennsylvania, Morris Arboretum, Philadelphia, PA, $400,000. For grant, partially challenge, to complete construction of landscaped parking area. 9/87.
University of the Arts, Philadelphia, PA, $29,000. To support master classes, public seminar, and concerts to be held in conjunction with 1988 Mellon Jazz Festival. 4/88.
W H Y Y-TV, Philadelphia, PA, $223,000. For Arts reporting on radio, and production of television program with Philadelphia Museum of Art. 6/88.
Walnut Street Theater Corporation, Philadelphia, PA, $100,000. For grant, partially challenge, to support operations. 9/87.
Walnut Street Theater Corporation, Philadelphia, PA, $15,000. For associate artistic director's salary. Grant made as part of Trust's program, Artistic Development

Initiative, to encourage artistic development of nonprofit theater in Philadelphia area, and to increase local and national recognition of Philadelphia area theater community. 9/87.

We the People 200, 1988 Africamericas Festival, Philadelphia, PA, $11,000. To support Sacred Black Music Concert and Jazz Concert as part of festival. 4/88.

Wilma Theater, Philadelphia, PA, $80,000. For grant, partially matching, to support operations. 9/87.

Wilma Theater, Philadelphia, PA, $74,000. For exceptional artistic costs associated with two plays of 1987-88 season. Grant made as part of Trust's program, Artistic Development Initiative, to encourage artistic development of nonprofit theater in Philadelphia area, and to increase local and national recognition of Philadelphia area theater community. 9/87.

Young Audiences of Eastern Pennsylvania, Philadelphia, PA, $10,000. For performances and workshops as part of intergenerational programs. 12/87.

Zero Moving Dance Company, Philadelphia, PA, $50,000. For artistic development. 12/87.

Zero Moving Dance Company, Philadelphia, PA, $40,000. Toward one-week season at Joyce Theatre in New York City. 12/87.

2806
Philadelphia Electric Company Giving Program

2301 Market St.
P.O. Box 8699
Philadelphia 19101 (215) 841-4000

Financial data (yr. ended 12/31/88): $2,000,000 for grants.
Purpose and activities: Supports health and welfare, civic affairs, education, and arts and culture.
Types of support: Capital campaigns, general purposes, operating budgets, scholarship funds.
Limitations: Giving primarily in headquarters city and major operating locations. No grants to individuals.
Application information: Include organization and project description and budget, board list and 501(c)(3).
Initial approach: Letter
Board meeting date(s): Monthly
Final notification: 6-8 weeks
Write: John H. Austin Jr., Pres. and C.O.O.

2807
The Philadelphia Foundation

Two Mellon Bank Ctr., Suite 2017
Philadelphia 19102 (215) 563-6417

Community foundation established in 1918 in PA by bank resolution.
Donor(s): 129 different funds.
Financial data (yr. ended 4/30/87): Assets, $60,865,000 (M); gifts received, $4,446,597; expenditures, $4,569,280, including $4,174,650 for 389 grants (high: $123,252; low: $276; average: $500-$15,000).
Purpose and activities: For the purpose of promoting charitable, educational, and civic activities; most of the funds have specific purposes or named beneficiary institutions, with emphasis on health and welfare, including hospitals and community activities; grants also for education and cultural programs.
Types of support: Operating budgets, continuing support, seed money, emergency funds, matching funds, special projects, consulting services, technical assistance.
Limitations: Giving limited to Philadelphia and to Bucks, Chester, Delaware, and Montgomery counties in southeastern PA, except for designated funds. No support for national organizations, government agencies, large budget agencies, private schools, religious organizations, or umbrella-funding organizations. No grants to individuals, or for annual or capital campaigns, building funds, land acquisition, endowment funds, scholarships, fellowships, research, publications, tours or trips, conferences, or deficit financing; no loans.
Publications: Annual report, application guidelines, program policy statement, informational brochure.
Application information: Application form required.
Initial approach: Proposal, including cover sheet and statistical form
Copies of proposal: 1
Deadline(s): Submit proposal preferably during May and June or Nov. and Dec.; proposals not accepted Aug.-0ct. and Feb.-Apr.; deadlines July 31 and Jan. 15
Board meeting date(s): Apr. and Nov.
Final notification: 3 to 4 months
Write: John E. Ruthrauff, Dir.
Officer: John E. Ruthrauff, Dir.
Managers: Don Jose Stovall, Chair.; Ernesta Drinker Ballard, David Brenner, Carmen Febo-San Miguel, M.D., Peter Hearn, Walter R. Livingston, Jr., Mary MacGregor Mather, Leon C. Sunstein, Jr., Peter Vaughn.
Trustees: Continental Bank, Fidelity Bank, N.A., First Pennsylvania Bank, N.A., Mellon Bank, N.A., Meridian Bank, Philadelphia National Bank, Provident National Bank.
Number of staff: 6 full-time professional; 3 full-time support.
Employer Identification Number: 231581832
Recent arts and culture grants:

Afro American Historical and Cultural Museum, Philadelphia, PA, $14,840. 1987.

American Poetry Center, Philadelphia, PA, $6,000. 1987.

Asociacion de Musicos Latino Americanos, Philadelphia, PA, $5,032. 1987.

Big Small Theater, Philadelphia, PA, $6,000. 1987.

Brandywine Graphic Workshop, Philadelphia, PA, $6,000. 1987.

Bushfire Theater of Performing Arts, Philadelphia, PA, $6,000. 1987.

Chester East Side Ministries, Philadelphia, PA, $8,000. For support, as part of Foundation's support to cultural organizations and activities. 1987.

Danceteller, Philadelphia, PA, $5,000. 1987.

Genealogical Society of Pennsylvania, Philadelphia, PA, $5,000. 1987.

New Freedom Theater, Philadelphia, PA, $10,405. 1987.

Pan-African Studies Community Education Program, Philadelphia, PA, $8,000. 1987.

Penjerdel Regional Foundation, Philadelphia, PA, $5,000. 1987.

Pennsylvania Academy of the Fine Arts, Philadelphia, PA, $5,500. 1987.

Pennsylvania Ballet Association, Philadelphia, PA, $5,500. 1987.

Pennsylvania Opera Theater, Philadelphia, PA, $6,500. 1987.

Peoples Light and Theater Company, Malvern, PA, $10,000. 1987.

Philadelphia Dance Company, Philadelphia, PA, $10,190. 1987.

Philadelphia Orchestra Association, Philadelphia, PA, $5,208. To support Special School Concert for area youngsters from public schools. 1987.

Philadelphia Theater Caravan, Philadelphia, PA, $10,000. 1987.

Relache, Philadelphia, PA, $15,000. 1987.

Society Hill Playhouse, Philadelphia, PA, $7,500. 1987.

Taller Puertorriqueno, Philadelphia, PA, $22,000. 1987.

Theater Center of Philadelphia, Philadelphia, PA, $10,000. 1987.

University of Pennsylvania, Annenberg Center, Philadelphia, PA, $37,880. For outreach and ticket subsidy fund. 1987.

University of Pennsylvania, Annenberg Center, Philadelphia, PA, $25,252. For professional theater programming. 1987.

University of Pennsylvania, Annenberg Center, Philadelphia, PA, $21,067. For outreach, community service and education. 1987.

W H Y Y-TV, Philadelphia, PA, $9,585. 1987.

Zoological Society of Philadelphia, Philadelphia, PA, $5,500. 1987.

2808
Philadelphia National Bank Corporate Giving Program

Fifth & Market Sts.
Philadelphia 19106 (215) 973-4181

Purpose and activities: Support for education and civic and cultural affairs; main focus is neighborhood economic development; grants are for local organizations only and range from $500 - $10,000. Most larger grants are for capital campaigns. In addition, there is an employee matching gift program for degree granting institutions.
Types of support: Capital campaigns, employee matching gifts.
Limitations: Giving limited to Philadelphia, PA, and Philadelphia, Bucks, Chester, Delaware, and Montgomery counties.
Application information: Application form required.
Initial approach: Proposal
Deadline(s): None
Write: John Whealin, Asst. V.P. or Bronal Harris, Public Responsibility Officer

2809
The Pittsburgh Foundation

30 CNG Tower
625 Liberty Ave., 30th Fl.
Pittsburgh 15222-3199 (412) 391-5122

Community foundation established in 1945 in PA by bank resolution and declaration of trust.
Financial data (yr. ended 12/31/87): Assets, $108,690,270 (M); gifts received, $4,331,215;

expenditures, $5,256,531, including $4,608,585 for 274 grants (high: $100,000; low: $500; average: $5,000-$50,000).
Purpose and activities: Organized for the permanent administration of funds placed in trust for public charitable and educational purposes; funds used for programs to support special projects of regularly established agencies, capital and equipment needs, research of a nontechnical nature, and demonstration projects. Grants primarily for human services, health, education, urban affairs, and the arts. Unless specified by the donor, grants are generally nonrecurring.
Types of support: Special projects, seed money, building funds, equipment, research, renovation projects, technical assistance.
Limitations: Giving limited to Pittsburgh and Allegheny County, PA. No support for churches, private schools, or hospitals. No grants to individuals, or for annual campaigns, endowment funds, travel, operating budgets, scholarships, fellowships, or research of a highly technical or specialized nature; no loans to individuals.
Publications: Annual report, application guidelines, newsletter.
Application information: Application form required.
Initial approach: Letter or proposal
Copies of proposal: 1
Deadline(s): 60 days prior to board meeting
Board meeting date(s): Mar., June, Sept., and Dec.
Final notification: 4 to 6 weeks
Write: Alfred W. Wishart, Jr., Exec. Dir.
Officers: Alfred W. Wishart, Jr., Exec. Dir.; Jack E. Kime, Assoc. Dir. and Chief Financial and Admin. Officer; Dana M. Phillips, Planning and Evaluation Officer.
Distribution Committee: Sholom D. Comay, Chair.; William J. Copeland, Vice-Chair.; Dorothy R. Williams, Treas.; Byrd R. Brown, Jeanne C. Caliguiri, Douglas D. Danforth, Robert Dickey III, Arthur J. Edmunds, Benjamin R. Fisher, Jr., Sherin H. Knowles, Phyllis Moorman Goode, John L. Propst, Frieda G. Shapira.
Trustee Banks: First Seneca Bank, Equibank, Mellon Bank, N.A., Pittsburgh National Bank, Union National Bank of Pittsburgh.
Number of staff: 8 full-time professional; 1 part-time professional; 12 full-time support.
Employer Identification Number: 250965466
Recent arts and culture grants:
Carnegie-Mellon University, Art Gallery, Pittsburgh, PA, $5,000. For Perspectives from Pennsylvania, exhibition of work of 18 Pennsylvania painters. 12/9/87.
Carnegie, The, Pittsburgh, PA, $5,000. To support Jazz Symposium and concert for students, April 1988. 12/9/87.
Institute for Urban Design, Pittsburgh, PA, $5,000. Toward publication of book entitled Smokestack City, USA: Redesigning 19th Century Cities for 21st Century Success. 9/23/87.
Laurel Highlands Regional Theater, Pittsburgh, PA, $5,000. Toward purchase of church to use as theater. 12/9/87.
Manchester Craftsmens Guild, Pittsburgh, PA, $10,000. For operating support. 12/9/87.
Mattress Factory, Pittsburgh, PA, $10,000. For operating support. 12/9/87.
Performing Arts for Children, Pittsburgh, PA, $5,000. For operating support. 12/9/87.
Phipps Friends, Pittsburgh, PA, $20,000. To carry out marketing and user study of Phipps Conservatory. 12/9/87.
Pittsburgh Ballet Theater, Pittsburgh, PA, $40,000. For production of The Great Gatsby. 9/23/87.
Pittsburgh Center for the Arts, Pittsburgh, PA, $10,000. To mount national search for new executive director, and for 1987-88 operating support. 9/23/87.
Pittsburgh Public Theater, Pittsburgh, PA, $7,500. For development consultancy for 1987-88 operating year. 12/9/87.
Pittsburgh Trust for Cultural Resources, Pittsburgh, PA, $10,000. For study of financial health of arts organizations in Pittsburgh. 12/9/87.
Three Rivers Arts Festival, Pittsburgh, PA, $20,000. For site specific sculpture program at 1988 Festival. 12/9/87.
University of Pittsburgh, Three Rivers Shakespeare Festival, Pittsburgh, PA, $5,000. Toward Rotating Repertory Conversion Phase I, Planning Study. 12/9/87.

2810
Pittsburgh National Bank Foundation
(Formerly Pittsburgh National Foundation)
c/o Pittsburgh National Bldg., 14th Fl.
Fifth Ave. and Wood St.
Pittsburgh 15222 (412) 762-3137

Established in 1970 in PA.
Donor(s): Pittsburgh National Bank.
Financial data (yr. ended 12/31/87): Assets, $5,059,288 (M); gifts received, $1,218,895; expenditures, $1,343,839, including $1,282,089 for 226 grants (high: $386,881; low: $25; average: $1,000-$35,000) and $46,117 for 187 employee matching gifts.
Purpose and activities: Giving for community funds, education, hospitals and health, cultural programs, youth agencies, public policy, community development, and social services.
Types of support: Operating budgets, continuing support, annual campaigns, seed money, emergency funds, deficit financing, general purposes, building funds, equipment, land acquisition, matching funds, employee matching gifts.
Limitations: Giving limited to southwestern PA. No support for religious purposes. No grants to individuals, or for endowment; no loans.
Application information:
Initial approach: Letter
Copies of proposal: 1
Deadline(s): None
Board meeting date(s): Monthly
Final notification: Approximately 6 weeks
Write: D. Paul Beard, Secy.
Trustee: Pittsburgh National Bank.
Officer: D. Paul Beard, Secy.
Number of staff: 2 part-time professional; 2 part-time support.
Employer Identification Number: 251202255

2811
PMA Foundation
925 Chestnut St.
Philadelphia 19107

Established in 1981 in PA.
Donor(s): PMA Industries, Inc.
Financial data (yr. ended 12/31/87): Assets, $59,826 (M); gifts received, $150,000; expenditures, $117,878, including $117,731 for 86 grants (high: $25,000; low: $25).
Purpose and activities: Grants primarily for higher education through an employee matching gifts program, culture, and community funds.
Types of support: Employee matching gifts.
Limitations: Giving primarily in PA.
Trustees: Frederick W. Anton III, David L. Johnson, Douglas M. Moe.
Employer Identification Number: 232159233

2812
PPG Industries Foundation
One PPG Place
Pittsburgh 15272 (412) 434-2970

Incorporated in 1951 in PA.
Donor(s): PPG Industries, Inc.
Financial data (yr. ended 12/31/87): Assets, $13,516,930 (M); expenditures, $4,822,463, including $3,890,854 for 1,082 grants (high: $363,000; low: $1,000; average: $5,000-$20,000) and $564,449 for 3,426 employee matching gifts.
Purpose and activities: Giving primarily for social services, including community funds and youth organizations, higher education, health and safety organizations, cultural programs, and civic and community affairs.
Types of support: Annual campaigns, capital campaigns, operating budgets, emergency funds, research, scholarship funds, employee-related scholarships, employee matching gifts, continuing support, special projects.
Limitations: Giving primarily in areas of company operations, with emphasis on the Pittsburgh, PA, region. No support for religious groups for religious purposes. No grants to individuals, or for endowment funds, advertising, benefits, grants (other than matching gifts) of less than $100, or operating support of United Way member agencies; no loans.
Publications: Annual report (including application guidelines).
Application information: Grant decisions made by the Screening Committee and the Board of Directors.
Initial approach: Letter
Copies of proposal: 1
Deadline(s): Sept. 1
Board meeting date(s): Usually in June and Dec.
Final notification: Following board meetings
Write: Roslyn Rosenblatt, Exec. Dir.
Officers and Directors:* Vincent Sarni,* Chair.; Frank V. Breeze,* Vice-Chair.; E.J. Slack,* Pres.; Robert H. Mitchel,* V.P.; Guy Zoghby,* V.P.; Edward Mazeski, Jr., Secy.; Lawrence M. Call, Treas.; Roslyn Rosenblatt,* Exec. Dir.
Number of staff: 1 full-time professional; 1 full-time support; 1 part-time support.

Employer Identification Number: 256037790
Recent arts and culture grants:
Alabama Space Science Exhibit Commission, Huntsville, AL, $5,000. 1987.
Carnegie Institute, Pittsburgh, PA, $15,000. For Three Rivers Arts Festival. 1987.
Friends of the New Zoo, Pittsburgh, PA, $10,000. For King Environmental Center. 1987.
Museum of Flight, Seattle, WA, $5,000. 1987.
Pittsburgh Ballet Theater, Pittsburgh, PA, $10,000. For capital support. 1987.
Pittsburgh Opera, Pittsburgh, PA, $10,000. 1987.
Pittsburgh Symphony Society, Pittsburgh, PA, $18,000. 1987.
River City Brass Band, Pittsburgh, PA, $15,000. 1987.
Statue of Liberty-Ellis Island Foundation, NYC, NY, $25,000. 1987.
United Jewish Federation of Greater Pittsburgh, Pittsburgh, PA, $5,000. For Pittsburgh Holocaust Center. 1987.
W Q E D Metropolitan Pittsburgh Public Broadcasting, Pittsburgh, PA, $50,000. 1987.

2813
PQ Corporation Foundation
Valley Forge Executive Mall, Bldg. 11
Valley Forge 19482 (215) 293-7200

Financial data (yr. ended 6/30/87): Assets, $28,845 (M); expenditures, $22,960, including $22,925 for grants.
Purpose and activities: Support for culture and community affairs.
Limitations: Giving primarily in PA.
Officers: Dale J. Shimer, Pres.; Ernest G. Posner, Secy.; Michael R. Imbriani, Treas.
Directors: James D. McDonald, John M. Reed.
Employer Identification Number: 232302993

2814
The Presser Foundation
Presser Place
Bryn Mawr 19010 (215) 525-4797

Founded in 1916; incorporated in 1939 in PA.
Donor(s): Theodore Presser.†
Financial data (yr. ended 6/30/87): Assets, $24,000,000 (M); expenditures, $1,100,000, including $600,000 for grants.
Purpose and activities: To provide scholarship aid grants to accredited colleges and universities for worthy undergraduate students of music; to increase music education in institutions of learning and to popularize the teaching of music as a profession; to administer emergency aid through small grants to worthy music teachers in need.
Types of support: Grants to individuals, scholarship funds, building funds, conferences and seminars, equipment, fellowships, matching funds, renovation projects, seed money, special projects.
Application information: Application forms available for financial aid to needy music teachers and for scholarships.
Deadline(s): None
Write: Henderson Supplee III, Pres.
Officers and Trustees: Henderson Supplee III, Pres.; Boyd T. Barnard, Robert Capanna, William M. Davison IV, Morris Duane, Raymond S. Green, Edwin E. Heidakka, Thomas M. Hyndman, Jr., Bruce Montgomery, Charles F. Nagel, Edith A. Reinhardt, Felix C. Robb, Michael Stairs, James D. Winsor III, Philip W. Young.
Number of staff: 1 full-time professional.
Employer Identification Number: 232164013

2815
Provident Mutual Life Insurance Company of Philadelphia Giving Program
1600 Market Street
P.O. Box 7378
Philadelphia 19101 (215) 636-5000

Financial data (yr. ended 12/31/88): Total giving, $575,000, including $517,000 for grants, $43,000 for employee matching gifts and $15,000 for in-kind gifts.
Purpose and activities: Supports arts and culture, health and welfare, education and civic affairs.
Types of support: Matching funds, employee matching gifts.
Limitations: Giving primarily in headquarters city.
Application information: Proposal including project description and budget.
Initial approach: Letter and proposal
Deadline(s): Sept. and Oct.
Final notification: 4-6 weeks
Write: Keith Bratz, Asst. Dir., Communications

2816
Provident National Bank Giving Program
Public Affairs Dept.
Broad and Chestnut Sts.
Philadelphia 19110 (215) 585-7659

Financial data (yr. ended 12/31/88): Total giving, $1,300,000, including $1,275,000 for 200 grants and $25,000 for employee matching gifts.
Purpose and activities: Supports arts and culture, health and welfare, employment and community development, and education and civic affairs.
Types of support: Annual campaigns, building funds, capital campaigns, continuing support, employee matching gifts, general purposes, operating budgets, special projects.
Limitations: Giving primarily in headquarters city and major operating locations in Philadelphia, Bucks, Montgomery, Delaware, and Chester counties, PA.
Publications: Corporate giving report.
Application information: Proposal including project budget and description, lists of board members and major contributors, audited financial statement, annual report, 501(c)(3).
Initial approach: Letter and proposal
Copies of proposal: 1
Deadline(s): Sept.-Oct.
Board meeting date(s): Jan. and May
Final notification: Within 12 weeks
Write: Sara S. Moran, Public Affairs Officer
Number of staff: 1

2817
The Provincial Foundation
2023 Pine St.
Philadelphia 19103 (215) 735-3862

Established in 1958 in PA.
Financial data (yr. ended 1/31/88): Assets, $1,127,626 (M); expenditures, $84,202, including $56,545 for 120 grants (high: $5,000; low: $100; average: $438).
Purpose and activities: Grants for culture, health and social services, Jewish organizations, and higher education.
Limitations: Giving primarily in Philadelphia, PA. No grants to individuals.
Publications: Annual report (including application guidelines).
Application information:
Initial approach: Letter
Copies of proposal: 1
Board meeting date(s): Jan., Apr., July, and Sept.
Officers: Arthur Klein, Pres.; Esther Klein, V.P.; Michael Temin, Secy.
Number of staff: 1 part-time professional.
Employer Identification Number: 231422090

2818
The Quaker Chemical Foundation
Elm and Lee Sts.
Conshohocken 19428 (215) 828-4250

Trust established in 1959 in PA.
Donor(s): Quaker Chemical Corp.
Financial data (yr. ended 6/30/88): Assets, $456,180 (M); gifts received, $538,000; expenditures, $424,391, including $240,860 for 152 grants (high: $25,000; low: $20; average: $2,500), $104,911 for 35 grants to individuals and $78,620 for 398 employee matching gifts.
Purpose and activities: Grants largely for higher education, including scholarships and matching gifts, and for local community funds, hospitals, and cultural programs.
Types of support: Scholarship funds, employee matching gifts, employee-related scholarships, matching funds.
Limitations: Giving primarily in CA, MI, and PA. No grants to individuals (except company-employee scholarships), or for building or endowment funds; no loans.
Publications: Application guidelines.
Application information:
Initial approach: Proposal
Copies of proposal: 1
Deadline(s): Apr. 30
Board meeting date(s): Quarterly
Final notification: July
Write: Karl H. Spaeth, Chair.
Trustees: Karl H. Spaeth, Chair.; Edwin J. Delattre, Linda P. Huhn-Sarge, Alan G. Keyser, J. Everett Wick, Jane Williams.
Number of staff: None.
Employer Identification Number: 236245803

2819
Reedman FCS Foundation
c/o Reedman Corp.
U.S. Route One
Langhorne 19047-9801 (215) 757-4961

Financial data (yr. ended 12/31/87): Assets, $241,267 (M); gifts received, $93,261; expenditures, $7,704, including $7,552 for 51 grants (high: $2,000; low: $10).
Purpose and activities: Support primarily for health, including hospitals, medical research, and various single-disease health associations and foundations; some support for civic affairs and culture.
Limitations: No grants to individuals.
Application information:
Initial approach: Letter or proposal; include proof of organization's tax-exempt status and spell out requested amount
Write: John E. Keating, Mgr.
Officer: Ralph Reedman, Jr., Pres.
Directors: Herbert Reedman, Sr., Stanley Reedman, Sr., Thomas Reedman, Sr.
Employer Identification Number: 222463892

2820
Herbert M. Rehmeyer Trust
c/o The York Bank & Trust Co.
21 East Market St.
York 17401
Application address: 35 South Duke St., York, PA 17401; Tel.: (717) 843-7841

Established in 1981.
Financial data (yr. ended 4/30/88): Assets, $1,251,097 (M); expenditures, $138,063, including $118,650 for 37 grants (high: $10,000; low: $400).
Purpose and activities: Grants largely for arts and cultural programs, including historical societies; support also for youth and social service agencies, higher education, and hospitals and health agencies.
Limitations: Giving primarily in York County, PA.
Application information: Application form required.
Deadline(s): Oct. 1
Write: Henry Leader, Trustee
Trustees: Henry Leader, Lester Naylor, The York Bank & Trust Co.
Employer Identification Number: 236708035

2821
Reliance Insurance Companies Foundation
Four Penn Center Plaza
Philadelphia 19103

Trust established in 1967 in PA.
Donor(s): Reliance Insurance Company.
Financial data (yr. ended 12/31/87): Assets, $18,492 (M); gifts received, $30,000; expenditures, $26,023, including $10,951 for 6 grants and $15,059 for 96 employee matching gifts.
Purpose and activities: Support for community funds and development, cultural programs, higher education, including an employee matching gift program.
Types of support: Employee matching gifts, general purposes.
Limitations: Giving primarily in PA.
Application information:
Deadline(s): None
Trustees: Saul P. Steinberg, Robert M. Steinberg.
Employer Identification Number: 236420936

2822
Rider-Pool Foundation
c/o Provident National Bank
1632 Chestnut St.
Philadelphia 19103 (215) 585-5679
Additional address: P.O. Box 7648, Philadelphia, PA 19101

Established in 1957 in PA.
Donor(s): Dorothy Rider-Pool.
Financial data (yr. ended 12/31/87): Assets, $4,956,000 (M); expenditures, $200,000, including $200,000 for grants (high: $50,000; low: $5,000; average: $15,000).
Purpose and activities: Giving for the prevention of cruelty to children or animals; some support for cultural programs.
Types of support: General purposes, building funds, emergency funds, endowment funds, fellowships, renovation projects, research, special projects.
Limitations: Giving primarily in Allentown, PA.
Application information:
Initial approach: Letter or proposal
Deadline(s): None
Write: John R. McNeil III, V.P., Provident National Bank
Trustees: Edward L. Donnely, Leon C. Holt, Provident National Bank.
Employer Identification Number: 236207356

2823
Rittenhouse Foundation
225 South 15th St.
Philadelphia 19102 (215) 735-3863

Incorporated in 1952 in PA.
Donor(s): Philip Klein.†
Financial data (yr. ended 12/31/87): Assets, $1,815,000 (M); expenditures, $168,406, including $114,675 for 137 grants (high: $14,000; low: $100).
Purpose and activities: To assist charitable and educational institutions, with emphasis on higher education, music and the arts, and youth agencies.
Types of support: Continuing support, seed money, equipment, publications, scholarship funds.
Limitations: Giving primarily in the Philadelphia, PA, area. No grants to individuals, or for endowment funds or operating budgets; no loans.
Publications: Annual report (including application guidelines).
Application information:
Initial approach: Letter
Copies of proposal: 1
Deadline(s): None
Board meeting date(s): Jan., Apr., July, and Sept.
Final notification: 30 days
Write: Arthur Klein, Pres.
Officers and Directors:* Arthur Klein,* Pres. and Treas.; Esther Klein,* Exec. V.P.; Michael Temin, Secy.
Number of staff: 1 part-time professional; 2 part-time support.
Employer Identification Number: 236005622

2824
Donald & Sylvia Robinson Family Foundation
6507 Wilkins Ave.
Pittsburgh 15217 (412) 661-1200

Financial data (yr. ended 10/31/87): Assets, $1,688,669 (M); expenditures, $85,987, including $79,948 for 53 grants (high: $25,000; low: $100).
Purpose and activities: Support for Jewish welfare funds and the performing arts.
Types of support: Annual campaigns, emergency funds.
Application information:
Write: Donald Robinson, Trustee
Trustees: Donald Robinson, Sylvia Robinson.
Number of staff: None.
Employer Identification Number: 237062017

2825
Milton and Shirley Rock Foundation
229 South 18th St.
Philadelphia 19103 (215) 875-2828

Established in 1985 in PA.
Financial data (yr. ended 8/31/87): Assets, $2,145,641 (M); expenditures, $126,252, including $120,920 for 10 grants (high: $52,500; low: $920).
Purpose and activities: Support for cultural programs and a university.
Limitations: Giving primarily in Philadelphia, PA.
Application information: Contributes only to pre-selected organizations. Applications not accepted.
Officers and Directors: Milton L. Rock, Pres.; Robert H. Rock, V.P.; Susan Rock Herzog, V.P.
Number of staff: None.
Employer Identification Number: 222670382

2826
The Rockwell Foundation
3212 USX Tower
600 Grant St.
Pittsburgh 15219 (412) 765-3990

Trust established in 1956 in PA.
Donor(s): Willard F. Rockwell,† and family.
Financial data (yr. ended 12/31/88): Assets, $8,965,580 (M); expenditures, $442,726, including $425,950 for 140 grants (high: $30,000; low: $50).
Purpose and activities: Giving for higher and secondary education; support also for the fine and performing arts, child welfare and family services, conservation, hospitals and health agencies, historic preservation, and religion.
Types of support: Annual campaigns, building funds, capital campaigns, continuing support, endowment funds, equipment, general purposes, operating budgets, scholarship funds, seed money.

Limitations: Giving primarily in PA. No grants to individuals, or for fellowships; no loans.
Application information:
Initial approach: Letter or telephone
Copies of proposal: 1
Board meeting date(s): As required
Write: H. Campbell Stuckeman, Secy.
Officer and Trustees: H. Campbell Stuckeman, Secy.; George Peter Rockwell, Russell A. Rockwell, Willard F. Rockwell, Jr.
Number of staff: None.
Employer Identification Number: 256035975

2827
Rockwell International Corporation Trust

600 Grant St.
Pittsburgh 15219 (412) 565-7436

Trust established in 1959 in PA.
Donor(s): Rockwell International Corp.
Financial data (yr. ended 9/30/88): Assets, $33,415,497 (M); gifts received, $20,000,000; expenditures, $10,300,555, including $9,602,606 for 1,289 grants (high: $500,000; low: $25; average: $1,000-$50,000) and $598,902 for 628 employee matching gifts.
Purpose and activities: Giving for higher education, primarily engineering education; and organizations which provide services in communities where donor has facilities; support also for cultural programs, health, and human services.
Types of support: Operating budgets, building funds, employee matching gifts, scholarship funds, fellowships, professorships.
Limitations: Giving primarily in areas of corporate operations, except for selected national organizations and universities which are sources of recruits. No grants to individuals, or for hospital building campaigns or general endowments; no loans.
Publications: Informational brochure.
Application information:
Initial approach: Proposal
Copies of proposal: 1
Deadline(s): None
Board meeting date(s): Monthly
Final notification: 60 to 90 days
Write: J.J. Christin, Secy., Trust Comm., or W.R. Fitz, Asst. Secy.
Trust Committee: J.J. Christin, Secy.
Trustee: Pittsburgh National Bank.
Number of staff: 4
Employer Identification Number: 251072431
Recent arts and culture grants:
Air Force Armament Museum, Fort Walton, FL, $10,000. 1987.
Air Force Museum Foundation, Wright-Patterson A.F.B., OH, $100,000. 1987.
Alabama Space and Rocket Center, Huntsville, AL, $33,000. 1987.
Association of Science Technology Centers, DC, $5,000. 1987.
Bel Canto Chorus, Milwaukee, WI, $5,000. 1987.
Bidwell Cultural and Training Center, Manchester Craftsmens Guild, Pittsburgh, PA, $6,500. 1987.
British American Arts Association, Bethesda, MD, $25,000. 1987.
British American Arts Association, Imperial War Museum, Bethesda, MD, $25,000. 1987.
Buhl Science Center, Pittsburgh, PA, $5,000. 1987.
Business Committee for the Arts, NYC, NY, $5,000. 1987.
California Chamber Symphony Society, Los Angeles, CA, $5,000. 1987.
California Museum of Science and Industry, Los Angeles, CA, $5,000. 1987.
Carnegie Institute, Pittsburgh, PA, $25,000. 1987.
Cedar Rapids Art Association, Cedar Rapids, IA, $15,000. 1987.
Childrens Museum at La Habra, La Habra, CA, $5,000. 1987.
Civic Light Opera Association of Greater Pittsburgh, Pittsburgh, PA, $7,000. 1987.
Dallas Opera, Dallas, TX, $7,500. 1987.
Florentine Opera Company, Milwaukee, WI, $10,000. 1987.
Huntington Library, Art Gallery and Botanical Garden, San Marino, CA, $10,000. 1987.
Huntington Library, Art Gallery and Botanical Garden, San Marino, CA, $5,000. 1987.
Jacksonville Jazz Festival, WJCT, Jacksonville, FL, $5,000. 1987.
John F. Kennedy Center for the Performing Arts, DC, $8,000. 1987.
Lincoln Center for the Performing Arts, NYC, NY, $11,000. 1987.
Los Angeles County Museum of Art, Los Angeles, CA, $5,000. 1987.
Los Angeles County Museum of Natural History, Los Angeles, CA, $5,000. 1987.
Los Angeles County Museum of Natural History, Los Angeles, CA, $5,000. 1987.
Metropolitan Museum of Art, NYC, NY, $6,000. 1987.
Mid-Columbia Symphony Society, Richland, WA, $11,000. 1987.
Milwaukee Art Museum, Milwaukee, WI, $10,000. 1987.
Milwaukee Ballet Company, Milwaukee, WI, $5,000. 1987.
Milwaukee Festival of Parades, Milwaukee, WI, $12,000. 1987.
Milwaukee Repertory Theater, Milwaukee, WI, $10,000. 1987.
Milwaukee Symphony Orchestra, Milwaukee, WI, $30,000. 1987.
Milwaukee Zoo, Milwaukee, WI, $20,000. 1987.
Milwaukee Zoo, Milwaukee, WI, $10,000. 1987.
Museum of Flight, Seattle, WA, $40,000. 1987.
Museum of Science and Industry, Chicago, IL, $100,000. 1987.
Music Center of Los Angeles County, Los Angeles, CA, $60,000. 1987.
Orange County Business Committee for the Arts, Costa Mesa, CA, $5,000. 1987.
Orange County Performing Arts Center, Costa Mesa, CA, $25,000. 1987.
Pittsburgh Ballet Theater, Pittsburgh, PA, $17,500. 1987.
Pittsburgh Opera, Pittsburgh, PA, $15,000. 1987.
Pittsburgh Opera, Pittsburgh, PA, $5,000. 1987.
Pittsburgh Public Theater, Pittsburgh, PA, $15,000. 1987.
Pittsburgh Symphony, Pittsburgh, PA, $24,000. 1987.
Pittsburgh Symphony Association, Pittsburgh, PA, $5,000. 1987.
Pittsburgh Symphony Society, Pittsburgh, PA, $20,000. 1987.
Pittsburgh Trust for Cultural Resources, Pittsburgh, PA, $5,000. 1987.
Ronald Reagan Presidential Foundation, DC, $50,000. 1987.
Science Station, Cedar Rapids, IA, $17,000. 1987.
South Carolina Museum, Charles H. Townes Center, Columbia, SC, $10,000. 1987.
South Coast Repertory Theater, Costa Mesa, CA, $5,000. 1987.
Statue of Liberty-Ellis Island Foundation, NYC, NY, $175,000. 1987.
Submarine Force Library and Museum Association, Groton, CT, $5,000. 1987.
Thomas Gilcrease Museum Association, Tulsa, OK, $5,000. 1987.
United Performing Arts Center, Milwaukee, WI, $80,000. 1987.
United States Navy Memorial Foundation, Arlington, VA, $25,000. 1987.
W Q E D Metropolitan Pittsburgh Public Broadcasting, Pittsburgh, PA, $8,000. 1987.
Woodruff Arts Center, Atlanta Arts Alliance, Atlanta, GA, $5,000. 1987.

2828
Alexis Rosenberg Foundation

c/o Fidelity Bank, N.A.
Broad & Walnut Sts.
Philadelphia 19109

Established in 1983 in PA.
Donor(s): Alexis Rosenberg.†
Financial data (yr. ended 6/30/87): Assets, $1,855,873 (M); expenditures, $106,333, including $92,625 for 18 grants (high: $15,000; low: $1,000).
Purpose and activities: Giving only to organizations to aid "Youth of America," including grants for higher education, hospitals and rehabilitation, and cultural programs.
Limitations: Giving primarily in PA. No grants to individuals.
Application information:
Initial approach: Proposal
Deadline(s): None
Officers and Directors: Robert Greenfield, Pres.; Charles Kahn, Secy.-Treas.; Edward Daley.
Trustee Bank: Fidelity Bank, N.A.
Employer Identification Number: 232222722

2829
Lawrence Saunders Fund

c/o Fidelity Bank, N.A.
Broad & Walnut Sts.
Philadelphia 19109

Established in 1970 in PA.
Financial data (yr. ended 12/31/87): Assets, $1,114,576 (M); expenditures, $64,013, including $53,329 for 60 grants (high: $7,500; low: $100).
Purpose and activities: Support primarily for educational institutions, social service and youth organizations, and cultural programs, including libraries.
Application information:
Initial approach: Letter

Deadline(s): None
Trustees: Kenneth N. Gemmill, Fidelity Bank, N.A.
Employer Identification Number: 236488524

2830
Sarah Scaife Foundation, Inc.
P.O. Box 268
Pittsburgh 15230 (412) 392-2900

Trust established in 1941; incorporated in 1959 in PA; present name adopted in 1974.
Donor(s): Sarah Mellon Scaife.†
Financial data (yr. ended 12/31/87): Assets, $169,870,980 (M); expenditures, $9,788,585, including $8,295,500 for 92 grants (high: $1,000,000; low: $3,000; average: $25,000-$100,000).
Purpose and activities: Grants primarily directed toward public policy programs that address major international and domestic issues; also supports local cultural, health and recreational projects.
Types of support: Operating budgets, continuing support, seed money, equipment, matching funds, fellowships, research, special projects, publications, conferences and seminars, general purposes.
Limitations: Giving limited to PA for culture, health and recreation; giving nationally for public policy programs. No support for national organizations for general fundraising campaigns. No grants to individuals, or for deficit financing or scholarships; no loans.
Publications: Annual report (including application guidelines).
Application information:
Initial approach: Letter or proposal
Copies of proposal: 1
Deadline(s): None
Board meeting date(s): Feb., May, Sept., and Nov.
Final notification: 2 to 4 weeks
Write: Richard M. Larry, Pres.
Officers: Richard Mellon Scaife, Chair.; Richard M. Larry,* Pres.; Donald C. Sipp, V.P., Investments; Barbara L. Slaney, V.P.; R. Daniel McMichael, Secy.; Gerald Walsh, Treas.
Trustees:* Anthony J.A. Bryan, Peter Denby, Edwin J. Feulner, Jr., Allan H. Meltzer, James M. Walton.
Number of staff: 5
Employer Identification Number: 251113452
Recent arts and culture grants:
Brandywine Conservancy, Chadds Ford, PA, $2,000,000. For Third Decade Fund Campaign. 1987.
Vanderbilt University, Nashville, TN, $50,000. For Television News Archive. 1987.

2831
Sharon Steel Foundation
P.O. Box 190
Farrell 16120 (412) 981-1375

Trust established in 1953 in PA.
Donor(s): Sharon Steel Corp.
Financial data (yr. ended 12/31/87): Assets, $3,390,406 (M); expenditures, $433,116, including $423,750 for 58 grants (high: $100,000; low: $100).
Purpose and activities: Support for higher education, music, community funds, hospitals, medical research, civic affairs, and youth activities.
Officers and Trustees: Victor Posner, Chair.; Steven Posner, Mgr.; Jack Coppersmith.
Employer Identification Number: 256063133

2832
Esther Simon Charitable Trust
Two Radner Corp. Center, No. 101
Radnor 19087 (215) 964-8613

Trust established in 1952 in NY.
Donor(s): Mrs. Esther Simon.
Financial data (yr. ended 12/31/87): Assets, $8,753,000 (M); expenditures, $648,848, including $592,667 for 50 grants (high: $100,000; low: $1,000; average: $1,000-$15,000).
Purpose and activities: Grants to charitable, cultural, and educational institutions, including hospitals and social service organizations.
Types of support: Annual campaigns, general purposes.
Limitations: Giving primarily in New York, NY. No grants to individuals.
Application information: Applications not accepted.
Trustee: Walter H. Annenberg.
Number of staff: 5
Employer Identification Number: 236286763

2833
W. W. Smith Charitable Trust
101 Bryn Mawr Ave., Suite 200
Bryn Mawr 19010 (215) 525-9667

Trust established in 1977 in PA.
Donor(s): William Wikoff Smith.†
Financial data (yr. ended 6/30/88): Assets, $89,669,913 (M); expenditures, $3,463,749, including $2,734,116 for 130 grants (high: $243,543; low: $5,000; average: $5,000-$40,000).
Purpose and activities: Support for financial aid programs for qualified needy undergraduate students at accredited universities and colleges, hospital programs for the medical care of the poor and needy, basic scientific medical research programs dealing with cancer, AIDS, and heart disease, and programs of organizations providing shelter, food, and clothing for children and the aged.
Types of support: Scholarship funds, research, operating budgets, seed money, emergency funds, building funds, equipment, land acquisition, special projects, publications, matching funds, general purposes, continuing support, renovation projects.
Limitations: Giving primarily in the Delaware Valley, including Philadelphia and its neighboring counties; grants to colleges and hospitals (for indigent care) by invitation only. No grants to individuals, or for deficit financing or existing endowment funds; no loans; no grants over 3 years.
Publications: Biennial report (including application guidelines).
Application information: Free medical care and college financial aid programs by invitation only; applications for medical research grants must be submitted in quadruplicate; application forms required for medical research only.
Initial approach: Proposal or letter
Copies of proposal: 1
Deadline(s): For free medical care, Feb. 1; for social service programs, Feb. 1 and Aug. 1; for college scholarships, May; for cancer and AIDS research, June 15; and for heart research, Sept. 15
Board meeting date(s): For medical care, Mar.; social services, Mar. and Sept.; scholarships, June; cancer and AIDS research, Sept.; heart research, Dec.
Final notification: 1 month after trustees meet
Write: Bruce M. Brown, Trust Admin.
Trustees: Mary L. Smith, Philadelphia National Bank.
Number of staff: 5 part-time professional; 1 part-time support.
Employer Identification Number: 236648841
Recent arts and culture grants:
Moore College of Art, Philadelphia, PA, $15,000. For student financial aid program. 1987.
Philadelphia College of Art, Philadelphia, PA, $35,000. For student financial aid program. 1987.
Philadelphia College of Art, Philadelphia, PA, $5,000. For scholarship program. 1987.

2834
Ethel Sergeant Clark Smith Memorial Fund
101 Bryn Mawr Ave., Suite 200
Bryn Mawr 19010 (215) 525-9667
Application address: Find Code 1-6-17, Personal Trust Div., Philadelphia National Bank, P.O. Box 7618, Philadelphia, PA 19101-7618; Tel: (215) 973-2792

Trust established in 1977 in PA.
Donor(s): Ethel Sergeant Clark Smith.†
Financial data (yr. ended 5/31/88): Assets, $9,567,767 (M); expenditures, $680,109, including $587,285 for 23 grants (high: $150,000; low: $1,000; average: $5,000-$25,000).
Purpose and activities: Giving for hospitals, social service organizations, libraries, colleges, arts and culture, museums, historical buildings, recreation, music and drama facilities, and programs for women, the handicapped, and exceptional persons.
Types of support: Building funds, continuing support, emergency funds, equipment, general purposes, land acquisition, operating budgets, research, special projects, exchange programs, matching funds, renovation projects, scholarship funds, seed money.
Limitations: Giving limited to Delaware County, PA or organizations benefitting county residents. No support for secondary schools, one-disease organizations, salaries, or consultants. No grants to individuals, or for funds on a long-term basis, deficit financing, scholarships, or fellowships; no gifts longer than 3 years; no loans.
Publications: Biennial report (including application guidelines).
Application information: Personal visits prior to proposal submission discouraged.
Initial approach: Letter or proposal
Copies of proposal: 1

Deadline(s): Mar. 1 and Sept. 1
Board meeting date(s): May and Nov.
Final notification: 1 month
Write: Bruce M. Brown, V.P. for Charitable Trusts, Philadelphia National Bank
Trustee: Philadelphia National Bank.
Number of staff: 3 part-time professional; 2 part-time support.
Employer Identification Number: 236648857

2835
The Snider Foundation
1804 Rittenhouse Square
Philadelphia 19103

Established in 1977 in PA.
Financial data (yr. ended 4/30/87): Assets, $1,290,062 (M); gifts received, $1,166,433; expenditures, $294,165, including $293,845 for 62 grants (high: $100,000; low: $100).
Purpose and activities: Support primarily for the arts; support also for museums, higher education, and Jewish welfare.
Limitations: Giving primarily in Philadelphia, PA.
Application information: Contributes only to pre-selected organizations. Applications not accepted.
Officers: Edward M. Snider, Pres.; Sanford Lipstein, Secy.-Treas.
Trustees: Fred A. Snabel.
Employer Identification Number: 232047668

2836
W. P. Snyder Charitable Fund
3720 One Oliver Plaza
Pittsburgh 15222 (412) 471-1331

Trust established in 1950 in PA.
Donor(s): W.P. Snyder, Jr.,† W.P. Snyder III, The Shenango Furnace Co.
Financial data (yr. ended 12/31/86): Assets, $8,845,363 (M); expenditures, $488,606, including $452,700 for 37 grants (high: $150,000; low: $500).
Purpose and activities: Emphasis on community funds, higher and secondary education, and hospitals; support also for cultural programs, including historic preservation, and social agencies.
Types of support: General purposes.
Limitations: Giving primarily in PA.
Application information:
Deadline(s): None
Write: John K. Foster, Trustee
Trustees: John K. Foster, G. Whitney Snyder, W.P. Snyder III.
Employer Identification Number: 256034967

2837
Sordoni Foundation, Inc.
45 Owen St.
Forty Fort 18704 (717) 283-1211

Incorporated in 1946 in PA.
Donor(s): Andrew J. Sordoni, Sr.,† Andrew J. Sordoni, Jr.,† Andrew J. Sordoni III, Mrs. Andrew J. Sordoni, Sr.,† Mrs. Andrew J. Sordoni, Jr.,† Mrs. Andrew J. Sordoni III, and others.
Financial data (yr. ended 7/31/87): Assets, $5,851,179 (M); gifts received, $1,000; expenditures, $228,667, including $196,370 for 34 grants (high: $35,000; low: $100) and $4,500 for 7 grants to individuals.
Purpose and activities: Giving for higher education; support also for cultural programs, health care, and medical research.
Types of support: Building funds, equipment, capital campaigns, continuing support, seed money, special projects.
Limitations: Giving primarily in northeastern PA. No grants to individuals, or for scholarships.
Application information: The foundation has discontinued the scholarships to individuals program. No new grants will be awarded.
Initial approach: Letter
Deadline(s): None
Board meeting date(s): As required
Write: Benjamin Badman, Jr., Exec. V.P.
Officers and Directors: Andrew J. Sordoni III, Pres.; Benjamin Badman, Jr., Exec. V.P. and Secy.-Treas.; Helen Mary Sekera, V.P.; Jule Ayers, Margaret B. English, Thomas H. Kiley, Roy E. Morgan.
Employer Identification Number: 246017505

2838
Spang & Company Charitable Trust
c/o Union National Bank of Pittsburgh
P.O. Box 751
Butler 16003-0751 (412) 287-8781

Established in 1972.
Donor(s): Spang & Co., Magnetics, Inc.
Financial data (yr. ended 12/31/87): Assets, $861,773 (M); gifts received, $17,900; expenditures, $105,207, including $97,710 for 58 grants (high: $24,000; low: $50).
Purpose and activities: Giving to hospitals and community funds, community development, cultural organizations, particularly a public library, and youth and social service agencies.
Limitations: Giving primarily in the Butler, PA, area.
Application information:
Initial approach: Proposal
Deadline(s): 90 days before end of calendar quarter
Write: C.R. Dorsch
Trustee: Frank E. Rath, Jr., Union National Bank of Pittsburgh.
Employer Identification Number: 256020192

2839
Alexander C. & Tillie S. Speyer Foundation
1202 Renedum Trees Bldg.
Pittsburgh 15222 (412) 281-7225

Established in 1962 in PA.
Donor(s): Members of the Speyer family.
Financial data (yr. ended 12/31/87): Assets, $2,609,235 (M); gifts received, $57,088; expenditures, $95,816, including $57,088 for 47 grants (high: $10,500; low: $10).
Purpose and activities: Giving primarily for education, culture, and Jewish organizations.
Application information:
Deadline(s): None
Write: A.C. Speyer, Jr., Mgr.
Trustees: A.C. Speyer, Jr., Darthea Speyer.
Employer Identification Number: 256051650

2840
SPS Foundation
c/o SPS Technologies
Jenkintown 19046 (215) 572-3000

Trust established in 1953 in PA.
Donor(s): SPS Technologies, Inc.
Financial data (yr. ended 12/31/87): Assets, $544,179 (M); gifts received, $210,000; expenditures, $202,066, including $198,875 for 210 grants (high: $53,000; low: $25; average: $100-$500).
Purpose and activities: Giving for community funds, higher education, hospitals, youth activities, and the arts.
Types of support: Operating budgets, continuing support, annual campaigns, emergency funds, building funds, equipment, employee matching gifts, special projects, research.
Limitations: Giving primarily in PA, Cleveland, OH, and Santa Ana, CA. No grants to individuals, or for seed money, land acquisition, matching funds, scholarships, fellowships, demonstration projects, publications, or conferences and seminars; no loans.
Application information:
Deadline(s): None
Final notification: 1 month
Write: Rockwell M. Groves, Chair., Gifts Comm.
Manager: Rockwell M. Groves, Chair., Gifts Comm.
Trustees: H. Thomas Hallowell, Joseph Rhein, John R. Selby, Jr.
Number of staff: None.
Employer Identification Number: 236294553

2841
James Hale Steinman Foundation
P.O. Box 128
Lancaster 17603
Scholarship application address: Eight West King St., Lancaster, PA 17603

Trust established in 1952 in PA.
Donor(s): James Hale Steinman,† Louise Steinman von Hess,† Lancaster Newspapers, Inc., and others.
Financial data (yr. ended 12/31/87): Assets, $6,112,179 (M); expenditures, $405,267, including $333,690 for 38 grants (high: $236,641; low: $250) and $40,000 for 24 grants to individuals.
Purpose and activities: Giving for historic preservation, education (including scholarships to newspaper carriers and children of employees of Steiman Enterprises), social services, and a community fund.
Types of support: Employee-related scholarships, annual campaigns, capital campaigns.
Limitations: Giving primarily in Lancaster, PA.
Application information: Application form available for employee-related scholarships. Application form required.

Deadline(s): For scholarships, Feb. 28 of senior year of high school
Board meeting date(s): Dec.
Write: M. Steven Weaver, Secy., Scholarship Committee
Officers and Trustees: Caroline S. Nunan, Chair.; Beverly R. Steinman, Vice-Chair.; Jack S. Gerhart, Secy.; Willis W. Shenk, Treas.; John M. Buckwalter, Caroline N. Hill, Hale S. Krasne.
Number of staff: None.
Employer Identification Number: 236266377

2842
John Frederick Steinman Foundation
Eight West King St.
Lancaster 17603

Trust established in 1952 in PA.
Donor(s): John Frederick Steinman,† Shirley W. Steinman,† Lancaster Newspapers, Inc., and others.
Financial data (yr. ended 12/31/87): Assets, $9,148,617 (M); gifts received, $300,000; expenditures, $1,176,716, including $1,102,855 for 82 grants (high: $541,105; low: $500) and $30,000 for 14 grants to individuals.
Purpose and activities: Giving for higher and secondary education, community funds, social services, youth, hospitals, and the handicapped; also funds a fellowship program limited to graduate study in mental health or a related field.
Types of support: Fellowships, annual campaigns, capital campaigns.
Limitations: Giving primarily in PA, with emphasis on the Lancaster area.
Application information: Application for fellowship program available upon request.
Deadline(s): Feb. 1 for fellowships
Write: Jack S. Gerhart, Secy.; for fellowships, Jay H. Wenrich, Fellowship Prog. Secy.
Officers and Trustees: Pamela M. Thye, Chair.; Jack S. Gerhart, Secy.; Willis W. Shenk, Treas.; John M. Buckwalter, Henry Pildner, Jr., Samuel C. Williams, Jr.
Employer Identification Number: 236266378

2843
Stockton Rush Bartol Foundation
230 South Broad St., Suite 1300
Philadelphia 19102 (215) 875-5402

Established in 1984 in PA.
Donor(s): George E. Bartol III.
Financial data (yr. ended 11/30/87): Assets, $3,518,612 (M); expenditures, $181,751, including $157,195 for 40 grants (high: $15,000; low: $500; average: $1,000-$5,000).
Purpose and activities: Support for the arts and cultural organizations.
Types of support: General purposes, special projects, building funds, continuing support, operating budgets, publications, renovation projects, seed money, research.
Limitations: Giving limited to Bucks, Chester, Delaware, Montgomery, and Philadelphia counties, PA. No support for religious or social organizations. No grants to individuals.
Publications: Annual report (including application guidelines), grants list, application guidelines.
Application information: Applicants must reapply annually. Application form required.
Initial approach: Letter requesting application
Deadline(s): May 1 and Nov. 1
Board meeting date(s): June and Dec.
Write: Mary Kuhn, Exec. Dir.
Officers: Mildred Blair Bartol MacInnes, Chair.; Cynthia W. Drayton, Pres.; William Parshall, Secy.-Treas.
Trustees: Mary Farr Bartol, Katherine Selma Bartol Lunt, Victoria Grier Bartol Vallely, Mary Rush Bartol Wolzon.
Number of staff: 1 part-time professional.
Employer Identification Number: 232318470

2844
Strauss Foundation
c/o Fidelity Bank
135 South Broad St.
Philadelphia 19109

Trust established in 1951 in PA.
Donor(s): Maurice L. Strauss.
Financial data (yr. ended 12/31/87): Assets, $38,202,216 (M); expenditures, $1,331,656, including $942,870 for 364 grants (high: $41,500; low: $100) and $315,000 for 1 foundation-administered program.
Purpose and activities: Emphasis on Jewish welfare funds in the U.S. and Israel, child welfare and youth agencies, education, hospitals, and cultural programs.
Limitations: Giving primarily in PA and for organizations in Israel. No grants to individuals.
Application information: Unsolicited applications are not encouraged.
Initial approach: Letter
Deadline(s): None
Trustees: Henry A. Gladstone, Scott R. Isdaner, Sandra S. Krause, Benjamin Strauss, Robert Perry Strauss.
Corporate Trustee: Fidelity Bank, N.A.
Employer Identification Number: 236219939

2845
Margaret Dorrance Strawbridge Foundation of Pennsylvania I, Inc.
Five Penn Center Plaza
Philadelphia 19103

Established in 1985 in PA.
Donor(s): Margaret Dorrance Strawbridge Foundation.
Financial data (yr. ended 12/31/87): Assets, $3,603,238 (M); gifts received, $155,497; expenditures, $239,165, including $208,250 for 13 grants (high: $50,000; low: $1,000).
Purpose and activities: Grants for hospitals and medical research, and culture; some support for education.
Limitations: No grants to individuals, or for endowment funds.
Application information:
Initial approach: Proposal
Deadline(s): None
Board meeting date(s): Quarterly
Write: George Strawbridge, Sr., V.P.
Officers: George Strawbridge, Jr., Pres.; George Strawbridge, Sr., V.P. and Secy.-Treas.
Employer Identification Number: 232373081

2846
The Stroud Foundation
c/o Mellon Bank (East)
P.O. Box 7236
Philadelphia 19101
Application address: Landhope R.D. 2, West Grove, PA 19390

Trust established in 1961 in PA.
Donor(s): Joan M. Stroud.
Financial data (yr. ended 12/31/86): Assets, $1,306,222 (M); gifts received, $1,024,677; expenditures, $249,700, including $239,500 for 54 grants (high: $69,500; low: $100).
Purpose and activities: Grants largely for higher and secondary education and a natural science museum; some support also for cultural programs and environment.
Types of support: General purposes, continuing support, annual campaigns, seed money, emergency funds, building funds, equipment, land acquisition, endowment funds, research, scholarship funds.
Limitations: No grants to individuals, or for matching gifts; no loans.
Application information:
Initial approach: Letter
Copies of proposal: 1
Deadline(s): None
Board meeting date(s): Quarterly
Write: W.B. Dixon Stroud, Mgr.
Managers: Joan S. Blaine, T. Sam Means, Joan M. Stroud, Morris W. Stroud, W.B. Dixon Stroud, Truman Welling.
Number of staff: None.
Employer Identification Number: 236255701

2847
Sun Company Corporate Giving Program
100 Matsonford Rd.
Radnor 19087 (215) 293-6000

Financial data (yr. ended 12/31/87): $6,700,000 for grants (high: $1,000,000; low: $25; average: $5,000-$10,000).
Purpose and activities: Supports education, health, human services and federated drives, civic affairs, including citizenship, economic development, employment, public information, policy research, arts, historic preservation, music, literacy, humanities, women, and youth.
Types of support: Employee matching gifts, equipment, building funds, capital campaigns, general purposes, research, scholarship funds.
Limitations: Giving primarily in areas where Sun has major facilities.
Publications: Informational brochure (including application guidelines).
Application information: Include project description and budget, financial report, IRS 501(c)(3) status proof and board list.
Initial approach: Letter
Write: Robert L. Simons, Dir., Corp. Contribs.
Number of staff: 2

2848
Superior-Pacific Fund
Seven Wynnewood Rd.
Wynnewood 19096
Scholarship application address: Superior Tube Co. Scholarship Comm., P.O. Box 616, Devault, PA 19432; Tel.: (215) 647-2701

Trust established in 1952 in PA.
Donor(s): Superior Tube Co., Pacific Tube Co.
Financial data (yr. ended 12/31/86): Assets, $6,522,722 (M); gifts received, $50,006; expenditures, $352,046, including $319,975 for 87 grants (high: $75,000; low: $25) and $11,500 for 16 grants to individuals.
Purpose and activities: Grants primarily for higher and secondary education, including scholarships for children of company employees, community funds, hospitals, health agencies, and music.
Types of support: Employee-related scholarships.
Application information: Application form required.
Deadline(s): Jan. 10
Officers and Directors: Paul E. Kelly, Pres.; Richard H. Gabel, Paul E. Kelly, Jr., William G. Warden III.
Employer Identification Number: 236298237

2849
Susquehanna-Pfaltzgraff Foundation
P.O. Box 2026
York 17405
Application address: 140 East Market St., York, PA 17401; Tel.: (717) 848-5500

Established in 1966 in PA.
Financial data (yr. ended 12/31/87): Assets, $320,236 (M); gifts received, $175,000; expenditures, $155,295, including $154,284 for 35 grants (high: $29,000; low: $100).
Purpose and activities: Primarily giving to youth and social service organizations, and cultural programs.
Application information:
Initial approach: Letter
Write: John L. Finlayson
Officers and Directors:* Louis J. Appell, Jr.,* Pres. and Treas.; George N. Appell,* V.P.; Helen P. Appell,* V.P.; William H. Simpson, Secy.
Employer Identification Number: 236420008

2850
Tasty Baking Foundation
2801 Hunting Park Ave.
Philadelphia 19129 (215) 221-8500

Established in 1955 in PA.
Donor(s): Tasty Baking Co.
Financial data (yr. ended 12/31/87): Assets, $216,448 (M); gifts received, $100,000; expenditures, $117,066, including $116,875 for 61 grants (high: $7,500; low: $200).
Purpose and activities: Giving for arts, education, health, the disadvantaged, general welfare, and low-income housing.
Types of support: General purposes.
Limitations: Giving limited to the Greater Philadelphia, PA, area.
Application information: Application form required.
Initial approach: Letter
Copies of proposal: 1
Deadline(s): 2 weeks prior to monthly meeting of trustees
Write: K. Grim
Officers and Trustees: Philip J. Baur, Jr., Chair.; John M. Pettine, Secy.-Treas.; Elizabeth H. Gemmill, Nelson G. Harris.
Number of staff: 1
Employer Identification Number: 236271018

2851
Teleflex Foundation
155 South Limerick Rd
Limerick 19468-1699 (215) 948-5100

Established in 1980 in PA.
Donor(s): Teleflex, Inc.
Financial data (yr. ended 12/31/88): Assets, $430,000 (M); gifts received, $300,000; expenditures, $190,000, including $190,000 for 106 grants (high: $12,500; low: $100; average: $1,000-$5,000).
Purpose and activities: Support for higher and elementary education, hospitals and medical research, health, science and technology, community and social services, public affairs, culture, environmental issues, and urban affairs and welfare.
Types of support: General purposes, employee matching gifts, seed money.
Limitations: Giving primarily in areas of plant locations in CA, DE, MA, ME, MI, NJ, NY, OH, PA, and TX.
Application information:
Initial approach: Written request
Copies of proposal: 1
Deadline(s): None
Board meeting date(s): Fall/Spring
Final notification: Within 60 days
Write: Robert Bertschy, Dir.
Officers: Lennox K. Black, Pres.; Bonnie Groff, Secy.; Robert Bertschy, Treas.
Directors: M.C. Chisholm, Diane Fukuda, William Haussmann, John H. Remer, Palmer Retzlaff.
Number of staff: 1 part-time professional; 1 part-time support.
Employer Identification Number: 232104782

2852
Harry C. Trexler Trust
1227 Hamilton St.
Allentown 18102 (215) 434-9645

Trust established in 1934 in PA.
Donor(s): Harry C. Trexler,† Mary M. Trexler.†
Financial data (yr. ended 3/31/88): Assets, $42,155,803 (M); gifts received, $4,920; expenditures, $1,655,848, including $1,576,047 for 52 grants (high: $525,349; low: $500; average: $7,000-$40,000).
Purpose and activities: The will provides that one-fourth of the income shall be added to the corpus, one-fourth paid to the City of Allentown for park purposes, and the remainder distributed to such charitable organizations and objects as shall be "of the most benefit to humanity," but limited to Allentown and Lehigh County, particularly for hospitals, churches, institutions for the care of the crippled and orphans, youth agencies, social services, cultural programs, and support of ministerial students at two named PA institutions.
Types of support: Building funds, matching funds, general purposes, operating budgets, continuing support, land acquisition, capital campaigns, renovation projects.
Limitations: Giving limited to Allentown and Lehigh County, PA. No grants to individuals, or for endowment funds, research, scholarships, or fellowships; no loans.
Publications: Annual report, application guidelines.
Application information:
Initial approach: Letter
Copies of proposal: 5
Deadline(s): Jan. 31 for consideration at annual fund distribution
Board meeting date(s): Monthly; however, grant distribution takes place annually after Mar. 31
Final notification: June 1
Write: Thomas H. Christman, Secy. to the Trustees
Trustees: Kathryn Stephanoff, Chair.; Dexter F. Baker, Philip I. Berman, Carl J.W. Hessinger, Richard K. White, M.D.
Staff: Thomas H. Christman, Secy. to the Trustees.
Number of staff: 1 full-time professional; 1 full-time support.
Employer Identification Number: 231162215

2853
Union Pacific Corporate Giving Program
Martin Tower
Eighth and Eaton Aves.
Bethlehem 18018 (215) 861-3215

Financial data (yr. ended 12/31/88): Total giving, $1,909,500, including $1,065,500 for grants (high: $130,000; low: $500; average: $5,000-$10,000), $187,000 for 284 grants to individuals and $657,000 for employee matching gifts.
Purpose and activities: Union Pacific Foundation administers the wide-ranging philanthropic activities of Union Pacific Corporation and its operating companies - Union Pacific Railroad Company, Union Pacific Resources Company and Union Pacific Realty Company. Union Pacific Foundation grants are made primarily to private institutions of higher education, health, social welfare, and arts, located in communities served by the Union Pacific companies, which are principally in the West; the foundation has more implicit guidelines than the direct giving program which considers programs not filling the foundation's specifications. In addition to direct grants, the non-foundation giving program consists of scholarship aid to the children of employees and employee matching gifts programs.
Types of support: Building funds, capital campaigns, employee matching gifts, equipment, matching funds, renovation projects, employee-related scholarships, special projects.
Limitations: Giving primarily in locations where Union Pacific maintains operations.
Application information: Include project report and budget, lists of board members, major donors, financial report and 501 (c)(3) status letter. Application form required.
Initial approach: Letter/proposal; company considers unsolicited requests for funding
Copies of proposal: 1
Deadline(s): August 15th

Board meeting date(s): End of Jan.
Final notification: Formal notification to accepted applicants
Write: C.N. Olsen, Pres., Union Pacific Foundation

2854
Union Pacific Foundation
Martin Tower
Eighth and Eaton Aves.
Bethlehem 18018 (215) 861-3215

Incorporated in 1955 in UT.
Donor(s): Union Pacific Corp.
Financial data (yr. ended 12/31/88): Assets, $7,662,105 (M); gifts received, $13,000,000; expenditures, $6,856,618, including $6,845,500 for 795 grants (high: $200,000; low: $500; average: $1,000-$10,000).
Purpose and activities: Grants primarily to non-tax-supported institutions of higher education, health (including hospitals and hospices), social services, and fine and performing arts groups and other cultural programs. The foundation does not sponsor an employee matching gifts program.
Types of support: Operating budgets, continuing support, annual campaigns, building funds, equipment, matching funds, scholarship funds, renovation projects, capital campaigns, general purposes, special projects.
Limitations: Giving primarily in areas of company operations, particularly in the midwestern and western U.S. in AR, CA, CO, ID, IL, KS, LA, MO, NE, NV, OK, OR, TX, UT, WA, and WY. No support for tax-supported institutions or affiliates (other than United Ways); specialized national health and welfare organizations; political, religious, or labor groups; social clubs, fraternal or veterans' organizations; support for United Way-affiliated organizations restricted to capital projects. No grants to individuals, or for sponsorship of dinners, benefits, seminars, or other special events.
Publications: Application guidelines, informational brochure.
Application information: Application form required.
Initial approach: Letter
Copies of proposal: 1
Deadline(s): Aug. 15
Board meeting date(s): Late Jan. for consideration for the following year
Final notification: Feb. through May
Write: Charles N. Olsen, Pres.
Officers: Charles N. Olsen,* Pres. and Secy.; L.W. Matthews III, V.P., Finance; John R. Mendenhall, V.P., Taxes; G.M. Stuart, Treas.
Trustees:* Drew Lewis, Chair.; and 23 additional trustees.
Number of staff: 1 full-time professional; 1 full-time support.
Employer Identification Number: 136406825

2855
USX Foundation, Inc.
(Formerly United States Steel Foundation, Inc.)
600 Grant St., Rm. 2640
Pittsburgh 15219-4776 (412) 433-5237

Incorporated in 1953 in DE.
Donor(s): USX Corp., and certain subsidiaries.
Financial data (yr. ended 11/30/88): Assets, $14,279,028 (M); gifts received, $5,000,000; expenditures, $6,282,780, including $5,853,000 for 217 grants (high: $1,500,000; low: $150; average: $1,000-$25,000) and $90,870 for 136 employee matching gifts.
Purpose and activities: Support to higher education, primarily the private sector, including college and university development grants, special purpose grants, project assistance, matching gifts, manpower development grants, and support to educational associations; scientific and research grants, including capital, operating, project, and research support; civic and cultural grants for capital and operating needs; medicine and health grants for research, capital, and operating purposes; and national and community social services support, including the United Way and other voluntary agencies.
Types of support: General purposes, operating budgets, continuing support, annual campaigns, seed money, emergency funds, building funds, equipment, land acquisition, endowment funds, special projects, research, employee matching gifts, capital campaigns, renovation projects.
Limitations: Giving primarily in areas of company operations; support also to activities of a national nature. No support for religious organizations for religious purposes. No grants to individuals, or for conferences, seminars, travel, scholarships, fellowships, publications, or films; no loans.
Publications: Annual report (including application guidelines), application guidelines.
Application information:
Initial approach: 1- or 2-page proposal letter
Copies of proposal: 1
Deadline(s): Public, cultural, and scientific affairs, Jan. 15; aid to education, Apr. 15; medical, health, and national and community social services, July 15
Board meeting date(s): Following board meetings
Write: William A. Gregory, Jr., Mgr.
Officers: Peter B. Mulloney,* Pres.; William E. Lewellen, V.P. and Treas.; Gary A. Glynn, V.P., Investments; Robert M. Hernandez, V.P. and Compt.; Richard M. Hays, Secy.; William A. Gregory, Jr., Mgr.; Dominic B. King, General Counsel; John T. Mills, Tax Counsel.
Trustees:* David M. Roderick, Chair.; W. Bruce Thomas, Vice-Chair.; Neil A. Armstrong, Charles A. Corry, John H. Filer, David C. Garrett, Jr., James A.D. Geier, Thomas C. Graham, David C. Jones, Paul E. Lego, John F. McGillicuddy, John M. Richman, Mark Shepherd, Jr., William E. Swales, T.A. Wilson.
Number of staff: 2 full-time professional; 2 full-time support.
Employer Identification Number: 136093185

2856
Vicary Foundation, Inc.
5050 West 38th St.
Erie 16506-1307 (814) 833-5120

Established in 1958 in PA.
Financial data (yr. ended 12/31/87): Assets, $1,007,702 (M); expenditures, $67,622, including $53,200 for 26 grants (high: $5,000; low: $250).
Purpose and activities: Support primarily for community organizations and for social services; support also for education and the arts.
Limitations: Giving primarily in Erie, PA.
Application information:
Deadline(s): None
Write: Charles A. Curtze, Trustee
Officer and Trustees: Charles C. Vicary, Secy.-Treas.; Charles A. Curtze, Louise V. Curtze, James W. Vicary, Mary W. Vicary.
Employer Identification Number: 256035971

2857
The Warwick Foundation
108 West Court St.
Doylestown 18901 (215) 348-3199

Established in 1961 in PA.
Donor(s): Helen H. Gemmill, Kenneth Gemmill.
Financial data (yr. ended 12/31/87): Assets, $3,266,018 (M); expenditures, $150,520, including $133,480 for 49 grants (high: $7,200; low: $200).
Purpose and activities: Giving primarily for the United Way and higher education in the form of scholarship money to colleges and universities; support also for cultural and civic affairs.
Types of support: Scholarship funds, operating budgets.
Limitations: Giving primarily in the Bucks County and Philadelphia, PA, areas. No grants to individuals.
Application information:
Initial approach: Letter
Deadline(s): None
Final notification: No response to application unless affirmative
Write: Grace M. Huber, Secy.
Officer: Grace M. Huber, Secy. and Mgr.
Trustees: Elizabeth Gemmill, Helen H. Gemmill, John Gemmill, Kenneth W. Gemmill, William Gemmill, Catharine Lowen.
Number of staff: None.
Employer Identification Number: 236230662

2858
Robert S. Waters Charitable Trust
c/o Mellon Bank, N.A.
One Mellon Bank Ctr.
Pittsburgh 15258 (412) 234-5784

Trust established in 1952 in PA.
Donor(s): Robert S. Waters.†
Financial data (yr. ended 12/31/86): Assets, $3,422,529 (M); gifts received, $111,804; expenditures, $179,705, including $141,800 for 36 grants (high: $23,000; low: $500).
Purpose and activities: Emphasis on cultural programs, conservation, secondary education, social services, and historic preservation.
Limitations: Giving primarily in PA. No grants to individuals, or scholarships, or fellowships; no loans.
Application information: Application form required.
Initial approach: Letter
Copies of proposal: 2
Deadline(s): None
Board meeting date(s): Sept.

Write: Barbara K. Robinson, V.P., Mellon Bank, N.A.
Trustees: John P. Davis, Jr., Mellon Bank, N.A.
Employer Identification Number: 256018986

2859
Robert and Mary Weisbrod Foundation
Trust Dept.
c/o Union National Bank of Pittsburgh
Pittsburgh 15278-2241

Established in 1968 in PA.
Donor(s): Mary E. Weisbrod.†
Financial data (yr. ended 12/31/87): Assets, $6,928,736 (M); expenditures, $413,336, including $352,000 for 23 grants (high: $100,000; low: $1,000).
Purpose and activities: Emphasis on hospitals, social service agencies, and music organizations.
Limitations: Giving primarily in the Pittsburgh, PA, area.
Application information:
Initial approach: Proposal
Deadline(s): None
Write: The Distribution Committee
Distribution Committee: Donald L. McCaskey, Francis B. Nimick, William R. Watkins.
Trustee: Union National Bank of Pittsburgh.
Employer Identification Number: 256105924

2860
Franklin H. & Ruth L. Wells Foundation
4718 Old Gettysburg Rd., Suite 405
Mechanicsburg 17055 (717) 763-1157

Established in 1983 in PA.
Donor(s): Ruth L. Wells Annuity Trust, Frank Wells Marital Trust.
Financial data (yr. ended 5/31/88): Assets, $4,323,993 (M); gifts received, $592,868; expenditures, $449,409, including $398,076 for 37 grants (high: $100,000; low: $1,000; average: $2,000-$15,000).
Purpose and activities: Support for social service agencies, cultural programs, and education.
Types of support: Building funds, capital campaigns, emergency funds, equipment, land acquisition, renovation projects, seed money, special projects.
Limitations: Giving primarily in Dauphin, Cumberland, and Perry counties, PA. No support for religious activities. No grants for operating expenses, endowments, or debts.
Application information:
Initial approach: Letter
Deadline(s): None
Write: Miles J. Gibbons, Exec. Dir
Committee: Miles J. Gibbons, Exec. Dir.; Clifford S. Charles, Gladys R. Charles, Ellen R. Cramer.
Trustee: Dauphin Deposit Bank & Trust Co.
Number of staff: 1 part-time professional; 1 part-time support.
Employer Identification Number: 222541749

2861
Westinghouse Foundation
c/o Westinghouse Electric Corp.
11 Stanwix St.
Pittsburgh 15222 (412) 642-3017

Established in 1987 in PA as a result of the merger of Westinghouse Educational Foundation, Westinghouse International Educational Foundation and Westinghouse Electric Fund.
Donor(s): Westinghouse Electric Corp.
Financial data (yr. ended 12/31/88): Assets, $8,373,427 (M); gifts received, $8,150,000; qualifying distributions, $10,667,879, including $10,667,769 for 638 grants (high: $1,986,313; low: $1,000), $195,000 for 65 grants to individuals and $1,064,579 for 8,069 employee matching gifts.
Purpose and activities: Grants primarily for United Way organizations where the company has a major presence. Support also for youth, the disadvantaged, minority education, educational associations, social service agencies, hospitals, and selected cultural grants in plant cities; expanded emphasis on civic and economic development; support also for grants to targeted colleges and universities for science and engineering.
Types of support: Employee matching gifts, special projects.
Limitations: No support for religious organizations or specialized health campaigns. No grants to individuals, or for operating budgets, annual campaigns, seed money, land acquisition, equipment, renovation projects, deficit financing, conferences, research, emergency or endowment funds, scholarships, or fellowships; no loans.
Publications: Annual report (including application guidelines), application guidelines.
Application information:
Initial approach: Telephone or proposal
Copies of proposal: 1
Deadline(s): None
Board meeting date(s): Jan., Apr., July, and Sept.
Final notification: 2 months
Write: C.M. Springer, Pres. or C.L. Kubelick, Mgr., University & Education Programs
Officer: C.M. Springer, Pres.; C.L. Kubelick, Secy.
Trustees: R.F. Pugliese, Chair.; G.M. Clark, G.C. Dorman, D.C. Korb, R.A. Linder, E.P. Massaro, H.F. Murray, W.A. Powe, M.C. Sardi, J.B. Yasinsky.
Number of staff: 3 full-time professional; 3 full-time support.
Employer Identification Number: 251357168
Recent arts and culture grants:
American-Australian Bicentennial Foundation, DC, $5,000. For education and cultural program. 1987.
British American Arts Association, Bethesda, MD, $17,000. For redevelopment program. 1987.
Carnegie Institute, Pittsburgh, PA, $35,000. For conservancy programs in Museums of Art and Natural History. 1987.
Carnegie Institute, Pittsburgh, PA, $9,769. For matching support. 1987.
Civic Light Opera Association of Greater Pittsburgh, Pittsburgh, PA, $6,500. For program for disabled, elderly, and economically disadvantaged. 1987.
Common Pleas Court Bicentennial, Pittsburgh, PA, $25,000. For restoration of 100-year-old courtroom. 1987.
Community Arts Council of Western North Carolina, Asheville, NC, $6,000. For renovation program. 1987.
Generations Together, Pittsburgh, PA, $25,000. For artist resource program and senior mentors for high school students. 1987.
Grand Rapids Art Museum, Grand Rapids, MI, $5,000. For Profiles, minority artists program. 1987.
Japan Society, NYC, NY, $25,000. For publication support for capital campaign. 1987.
K F A E, Richland, WA, $8,217. For matching support. 1987.
Maryland Center for Public Broadcasting, Owings Mill, MD, $17,085. For matching support. 1987.
Museum of Modern Art, NYC, NY, $5,000. For advancement of understanding of visual arts program. 1987.
National Council for Families and Television, Princeton, NJ, $25,000. For project support. 1987.
New York City Opera, NYC, NY, $10,000. For new Malcom X opera. 1987.
Pittsburgh Ballet Theater, Pittsburgh, PA, $50,000. For scholarships for economically disadvantaged students, commission of new work, and for program support. 1987.
Pittsburgh Dance Council, Pittsburgh, PA, $12,000. For public school students program, minority attendance program, and for support for transition to Benedum Center. 1987.
Pittsburgh Opera, Pittsburgh, PA, $10,000. For general program support. 1987.
Pittsburgh Opera Theater, Pittsburgh, PA, $5,400. For Saturday performances for minority audiences. 1987.
Pittsburgh Public Theater, Pittsburgh, PA, $15,000. For outreach program for economically disadvantaged. 1987.
Pittsburgh Symphony Society, Pittsburgh, PA, $60,000. For annual sustaining fund campaign and Far East tour. 1987.
Pittsburgh Symphony Society, Pittsburgh, PA, $27,912. For matching support. 1987.
Pittsburgh Youth Symphony Orchestra Association, Pittsburgh, PA, $5,000. To represent U.S. at Aberdeen International Youth Festival, Scotland. 1987.
Pittsburgh Zoo, Pittsburgh, PA, $61,166. For equipment and program support. 1987.
River City Brass Band, Pittsburgh, PA, $15,000. For program support. 1987.
W D U Q-FM, Pittsburgh, PA, $5,975. For matching support. 1987.
W E T A-FM, DC, $6,884. For matching support. 1987.
W Q E D Metropolitan Pittsburgh Public Broadcasting, Pittsburgh, PA, $80,000. For capital campaign and equipment. 1987.
W Q E D Metropolitan Pittsburgh Public Broadcasting, Pittsburgh, PA, $52,937. For matching support. 1987.
W Q E D-FM, Pittsburgh, PA, $14,471. For matching support. 1987.

2862
Whalley Charitable Trust
1205 Graham Ave.
Windber 15963
Application address: c/o G. Lesko, 1210 Graham Ave., Windber, PA 15963

Trust established in 1961 in PA.
Donor(s): John J. Whalley, John Whalley, Jr., Mary Whalley.
Financial data (yr. ended 12/31/86): Assets, $2,506,185 (M); expenditures, $133,449, including $113,988 for 60 grants (high: $20,000; low: $15).
Purpose and activities: Support for health, civic affairs, education, religious organizations, and cultural programs.
Limitations: Giving primarily in PA.
Trustees: David Klementik, G. Lesko.
Employer Identification Number: 237128436

2863
The Whitaker Foundation
4718 Old Gettysburg Rd., Suite 405
Mechanicsburg 17055-4325 (717) 763-1391

Trust established in 1975 in NY.
Donor(s): U.A. Whitaker,† Helen F. Whitaker.†
Financial data (yr. ended 12/31/87): Assets, $292,018,330 (M); gifts received, $2,487,016; expenditures, $14,051,283, including $13,077,479 for 185 grants (high: $2,500,000; low: $270; average: $40,000-$60,000).
Purpose and activities: Support for projects which integrate engineering with biomedical research; grants also to local community service agencies, educational institutions, and cultural organizations.
Types of support: Seed money, building funds, equipment, land acquisition, research, special projects, renovation projects, capital campaigns.
Limitations: Giving primarily in the U.S. and Canada for Biomedical Engineering Research Program; and in the Harrisburg, PA, area for community service, educational, and cultural organizations. No support for sectarian religious purposes. No grants to individuals, or for operating budgets of established programs, deficit financing, annual campaigns, emergency funds, publications, conferences, seminars, or endowment funds; no loans.
Publications: Program policy statement, informational brochure (including application guidelines).
Application information: Application procedures are outlined in program policy statements for medical research grants and regional program.
Initial approach: Letter or telephone for regional program; preliminary application for medical research program
Copies of proposal: 1
Deadline(s): Jan. 2, May 1, and Sept. 1 for regional program proposals, and Feb. 15, June 15, and Oct. 15 for Biomedical Engineering Research Program
Board meeting date(s): Feb., June, and Oct. for governing committee
Final notification: 5 months
Write: Miles J. Gibbons, Jr., Exec. Dir.
Officer: Miles J. Gibbons, Jr., Exec. Dir.
Committee Members: C.J. Fredricksen, Chair.; Robert K. Campbell, Allan W. Cowley, M.D., Eckley B. Coxe IV, G. Burtt Holmes, Ruth W. Holmes, Portia W. Shumaker.
Trustee: Chemical Bank.
Number of staff: 2 full-time professional; 1 part-time professional; 2 full-time support.
Employer Identification Number: 222096948
Recent arts and culture grants:
Allied Arts Fund, Harrisburg, PA, $9,000. To support administrative expenses for 1987-88. 10/1/87.
Central Pennsylvania Youth Ballet, Carlisle, PA, $7,000. For Apple Computer System. 2/1/88.
Dauphin County Historical Society, Harrisburg, PA, $45,000. Toward restoration of John Harris Mansion. 6/22/87.
Friends of Fort Hunter, Harrisburg, PA, $30,000. To restore Centennial Barn. 6/22/87.
Hershey Museum of American Life, Hershey, PA, $10,825. For enlargement of lecture-meeting room. 10/1/87.
New York University, NYC, NY, $149,605. For research project, Kinematic and Kinetic Upper Extremity Requirements of String Instrumentalists. 2/1/88.
Pennsylvania Arts Coalition, Pittsburgh, PA, $10,000. For Commonwealth of Pennsylvania Governor's Awards for Excellence in the Arts, Humanities and Sciences. 2/1/88.
State Museum of Pennslvania, Friends of the, Harrisburg, PA, $5,000. For two projectors and related equipment. 10/1/87.
W I T F-TV/FM South Central Educational Broadcasting Council, Harrisburg, PA, $12,000. For School Learning Channel. 6/22/87.

2864
The Helen F. Whitaker Fund
4718 Old Gettysburg Rd., Suite 405
Mechanicsburg 17055 (717) 763-1600

Established in 1983 in NY.
Financial data (yr. ended 7/31/88): Assets, $11,349,253 (M); gifts received, $6,416,729; expenditures, $802,380, including $776,932 for 4 grants (high: $218,932; low: $70,000).
Purpose and activities: Support primarily for educational institutions and charitable organizations supporting the development of the professional careers of young musicians and arts administrators, or the development of the business and professional careers of women.
Types of support: General purposes, seed money.
Application information:
Initial approach: Letter
Copies of proposal: 3
Deadline(s): None
Board meeting date(s): As needed
Write: Miles J. Gibbons, Jr.
Trustee: Chemical Bank.
Number of staff: 2
Employer Identification Number: 222459399

2865
Willary Foundation
c/o Northeastern Bank of Pennsylvania
P.O. Box 937
Scranton 18501-0937

Established in 1968 in PA.
Financial data (yr. ended 12/31/87): Assets, $1,003,774 (M); expenditures, $14,820, including $9,518 for 16 grants (high: $5,000; low: $26).
Purpose and activities: Support primarily for music.
Limitations: Giving primarily in Northeastern PA. No grants to individuals; no loans.
Trustees: Mary L. Scranton, William W. Scranton, Northeastern Bank of Pennsylvania.
Employer Identification Number: 237014785

2866
The C. K. Williams Foundation
P.O. Box 7236
Philadelphia 19101-7236

Established in 1963 in PA.
Financial data (yr. ended 12/31/87): Assets, $3,196,823 (M); gifts received, $78,917; expenditures, $73,095, including $63,000 for 10 grants (high: $35,000; low: $1,000).
Purpose and activities: Support primarily for museums and public television.
Types of support: General purposes.
Application information: Contributes only to pre-selected organizations. Applications not accepted.
Board meeting date(s): N
Officers and Directors: Joan W. Rhame, Pres. and Secy.; Charles K. Williams, Josephine C. Williams.
Employer Identification Number: 236292772

2867
Williamsport Foundation
102 West Fourth St.
Williamsport 17701 (717) 326-2611

Community foundation established in 1916 in PA by bank resolution.
Financial data (yr. ended 12/31/85): Assets, $16,881,759 (M); gifts received, $120,340; expenditures, $2,093,610, including $1,841,971 for 79 grants (high: $239,223; average: $1,000-$30,000).
Purpose and activities: Support for civic affairs, including recreation, cultural programs, youth agencies, higher education, and hospitals.
Types of support: Building funds, emergency funds, equipment, general purposes, matching funds, program-related investments, research, seed money, special projects, loans.
Limitations: Giving limited to organizations located in the greater Williamsport, PA, area. No grants to individuals, or for endowment funds or operating budgets.
Publications: Annual report.
Application information:
Initial approach: Letter
Copies of proposal: 5
Deadline(s): None
Board meeting date(s): At least 4 times a year
Final notification: 2 months
Write: Harold D. Hershberger, Jr., Secy.

Administrative Committee: John E. Person, Jr., Chair.; Harold D. Hershberger, Jr., Secy.; Ralph R. Cranmer, William C. Nichols, Mary Elizabeth Stockwell.
Trustees: Commonwealth Bank & Trust Co., Northern Central Bank, Williamsport National Bank.
Number of staff: None.
Employer Identification Number: 246013117

2868
Wolf Foundation
P.O. Box 1267
York 17405 (218) 846-0250

Established in 1969 in PA.
Financial data (yr. ended 12/31/87): Assets, $406,241 (M); gifts received, $222,735; expenditures, $168,071, including $166,742 for 51 grants (high: $30,000; low: $50).
Purpose and activities: Support for health organizations, and youth; some support for religion and arts.
Types of support: General purposes.
Application information:
Initial approach: Letter
Deadline(s): None
Officers: William B. Zimmerman, Chair.; Thomas W. Wolf, Pres.; George Hodged, Secy.-Treas.
Employer Identification Number: 237028494

2869
Wyomissing Foundation, Inc.
1015 Penn Ave.
Wyomissing 19610 (215) 376-7496

Incorporated in 1929 in DE.
Donor(s): Ferdinand Thun,† and family.
Financial data (yr. ended 12/31/88): Assets, $12,572,440 (M); expenditures, $607,636, including $469,300 for 55 grants (high: $58,000; low: $750; average: $1,000-$20,000).
Purpose and activities: Giving primarily for hospitals, higher education, civic affairs, youth and social service agencies, and a community fund; support also for conservation and music.
Types of support: Operating budgets, continuing support, annual campaigns, seed money, emergency funds, building funds, equipment, matching funds, capital campaigns.
Limitations: Giving primarily in Berks County, PA, and contiguous counties; limited support also in the mid-Atlantic area. No grants to individuals, or for endowment funds, deficit financing, land acquisition, publications, conferences, scholarships, or fellowships; no loans.
Publications: Program policy statement, application guidelines, annual report, financial statement.
Application information:
Initial approach: Proposal not exceeding 2 pages (excluding supporting materials)
Copies of proposal: 1
Deadline(s): Submit proposal preferably in Feb., May, Aug., or Oct.; deadline 25th of month preceding board meeting
Board meeting date(s): Mar., June, Sept., and Nov.
Final notification: 3 months
Write: Lawrence A. Walsky, Secy.
Officers: Marlin Miller, Jr.,* Pres.; Mrs. Herbert Karasin,* V.P.; Lawrence A. Walsky, Secy.; Alfred Hemmerich,* Treas.
Trustees:* Anna M. Cherney, Victoria F. Guthrie, Mrs. Herbert Karasin, Sidney D. Kline, Jr., Paul R. Roedel, Peter Thun.
Number of staff: 1 part-time professional; 1 part-time support.
Employer Identification Number: 231980570

2870
Yarway Foundation
Norristown and Narcissa Rds.
Blue Bell 19422 (215) 825-2100

Trust established in 1959 in PA.
Donor(s): Yarway Corp.
Financial data (yr. ended 12/31/87): Assets, $89,486 (M); expenditures, $38,096, including $16,500 for 6 grants (high: $5,000; low: $500) and $21,000 for 6 grants to individuals.
Purpose and activities: Grants primarily for higher education, including the D. Robert Yarnell-Bernard G. Waring Scholarship Award Program for children of company employees; support also for cultural, civic, health and welfare agencies.
Types of support: Employee-related scholarships.
Limitations: Giving primarily in PA.
Application information: Application form required.
Initial approach: Letter
Deadline(s): Nov. 15
Write: Lillian Houlihan, Personnel Dept.
Trustees: H. Hayes Baker, Joseph F. Barclay, Jr., David W. Dupert.
Employer Identification Number: 236265621

PUERTO RICO

2871
Puerto Rico Community Foundation
Banco Popular Center, Suite 900
Hato Rey 00918 (809) 751-3885

Incorporated in 1984 in PR.
Financial data (yr. ended 12/31/87): Assets, $4,741,195 (M); gifts received, $2,625,089; expenditures, $1,526,688, including $969,136 for 72 grants.
Purpose and activities: Foundation "seeks to contribute to the achievement of a healthier economy and enhance quality of life in Puerto Rico"; giving in areas such as economic development, education, community development, science and technological innovation, health, the arts, criminal justice, and civic affairs.
Limitations: Giving primarily in PR. No support for religious organizations or commonly accepted community services. No grants to individuals, or for operating expenses of established agencies, publications, annual campaigns, endowments, deficit financing, or scholarships; generally no grants for equipment, building, or renovation funds.
Publications: Annual report, newsletter, informational brochure (including application guidelines).
Application information:
Initial approach: Letter
Deadline(s): June 1, Sept. 1, Nov. 1, and Feb. 15
Board meeting date(s): July, Oct., Dec., and Apr.
Final notification: Within 2 weeks of board meetings
Write: Ethel Rios de Betancourt, Pres.
Officer: Ethel Rios de Betancourt, Pres.
Directors: Manuel H. Dubon, Chair.; Amalia Betanzos, and 18 additional directors.
Number of staff: 4 full-time professional; 4 full-time support.
Employer Identification Number: 660413230

RHODE ISLAND

2872
Armbrust Foundation
735 Allens Ave.
Providence 02905

Trust established about 1951 in RI.
Donor(s): Armbrust Chain Co.
Financial data (yr. ended 12/31/87): Assets, $1,414,988 (M); gifts received, $25,000; expenditures, $94,820, including $91,001 for 47 grants (high: $13,000; low: $100).
Purpose and activities: Emphasis on a community fund, Protestant church support, and hospitals and health services; support also for education, and cultural and environmental programs.
Limitations: Giving primarily in RI.
Application information: Contributes only to preselected organizations. Applications not accepted.
Trustees: Adelaide P. Armbrust, Howard W. Armbrust.
Employer Identification Number: 056088332

2873
Attleboro Pawtucket Savings Bank Charitable Foundation
c/o Pawtucket Saving Bank
286 Main St., P.O. Box 188
Pawtucket 02862 (401) 724-5000

Donor(s): Attleboro Pawtucket Savings Bank.
Financial data (yr. ended 11/30/87): Assets, $40,059 (M); gifts received, $60,000; expenditures, $44,800, including $44,700 for 45 grants (high: $35,000; low: $25).
Purpose and activities: Support for social services, health services, youth, the arts, music, civic affairs, and employment.
Limitations: Giving primarily in Blackstone Valley, Kent County, and Greater Attleboro, RI, areas.

Application information:
Initial approach: Letter
Deadline(s): None
Write: William E. Corrigan Jr., Trustee
Trustees: Paul E. Benson, William E. Corrigan, Jr., Linda M. Mallory.
Employer Identification Number: 050419220

2874
Chace Fund, Inc.
731 Hospital Trust Bldg.
Providence 02903

Established in 1947 in RI.
Financial data (yr. ended 12/31/87): Assets, $599,771 (M); gifts received, $179,360; expenditures, $148,264, including $132,611 for 25 grants (high: $5,000; low: $150).
Purpose and activities: Support primarily for community organizations; support also for education, social services, hospitals and the arts.
Types of support: General purposes.
Limitations: Giving primarily in NY, RI, and MA.
Application information:
Initial approach: Letter
Deadline(s): None
Write: Malcolm G. Chace, III
Officers: Malcolm G. Chace III, Pres.; Arnold B. Chace, Jr., V.P.; Robert A. Casale, Secy.-Treas.
Employer Identification Number: 056008849

2875
Mary Dexter Chafee Fund
c/o The Rhode Island Hospital Trust National Bank
One Hospital Trust Plaza
Providence 02903 (401) 278-8700

Established in 1933 in RI.
Financial data (yr. ended 6/30/87): Assets, $1,393,904 (M); expenditures, $119,010, including $94,500 for 20 grants (high: $20,000; low: $500).
Purpose and activities: Giving primarily for social services, education, cultural organizations, conservation, and historic preservation.
Limitations: Giving primarily in RI. No grants to individuals.
Application information:
Initial approach: Proposal; must include copy of latest annual report
Deadline(s): None
Officers: Dorothy C. Scott, Pres.; Richard S. Chafee, Secy.; William G. Chafee, Treas.
Agent: The Rhode Island Hospital Trust National Bank.
Employer Identification Number: 056006295

2876
The Champlin Foundations
P.O. Box 637
Providence 02901-0637 (401) 421-3719

Trusts established in 1932, 1947, and 1975 in DE.
Donor(s): George S. Champlin,† Florence C. Hamilton,† Hope C. Neaves.
Financial data (yr. ended 12/31/88): Assets, $209,907,639 (M); gifts received, $2,939,158; expenditures, $12,768,000, including $11,297,639 for 158 grants (high: $2,350,000; low: $600; average: $15-$50,000).
Purpose and activities: Support for conservation, education, health, historic preservation, libraries, scientific and cultural activities, youth, the elderly, and social services.
Types of support: Building funds, equipment, land acquisition, renovation projects, scholarship funds, capital campaigns.
Limitations: Giving primarily in RI. No grants to individuals, or for general support, program or operating budgets, matching gifts, special projects, research, publications, conferences, or continuing support; no loans.
Publications: Program policy statement, application guidelines, annual report, grants list.
Application information:
Initial approach: 1-page letter
Copies of proposal: 1
Deadline(s): Submit proposal preferably between Apr. 1 and Aug. 31; deadline Aug. 31
Board meeting date(s): Nov.
Final notification: After Nov. meeting; 1 month for rejections
Write: David A. King, Exec. Dir.
Distribution Committee: David A. King, Exec. Dir.; Francis C. Carter, John Gorham, Louis R. Hampton, Robert W. Kenyon, Norma B. LaFreniere, John W. Linnell, Mario F. Veltri.
Trustee: Bank of Delaware.
Number of staff: 3 part-time professional; 1 part-time support.
Employer Identification Number: 516010168
Recent arts and culture grants:
Beneficent Congregational Church, Providence, RI, $50,000. For major repairs. 1987.
Blackstone Valley Historical Society, Cumberland, RI, $5,095. 1987.
Bristol Historical and Preservation Society, Bristol, RI, $25,000. 1987.
Gilbert Stuart Memorial, Saunderstown, RI, $10,000. 1987.
Providence Preservation Society, Providence, RI, $15,000. 1987.
Rhode Island Historical Society, Providence, RI, $23,125. For equipment necessary to update computer connection with other research libraries. 1987.
Rhode Island Philharmonic Orchestra, Providence, RI, $12,500. 1987.
Roger Williams Park Museum of Natural History, Providence, RI, $100,000. Toward cost of restoration. 1987.
Scituate Preservation Society, Scituate, RI, $10,000. 1987.
Touro National Heritage Trust, NYC, NY, $15,000. For preservation project in Newport, RI. 1987.

2877
Citizens Charitable Foundation
c/o Citizens Trust Co.
870 Westminster St.
Providence 02903 (401) 456-7285

Established in 1967 in RI.
Donor(s): Citizens Savings Bank, F.S.B., Citizens Trust Co.
Financial data (yr. ended 12/31/86): Assets, $904,741 (M); gifts received, $275,000; expenditures, $282,890, including $275,387 for 67 grants (high: $134,000; low: $500; average: $3,000).
Purpose and activities: Giving primarily for community funds, higher education, hospitals, arts and culture, and youth and civic agencies.
Types of support: Building funds, equipment, land acquisition, special projects, technical assistance, employee-related scholarships.
Limitations: Giving primarily in RI. No support for United Way member agencies except for capital funds. No grants to individuals, or for endowment funds, general support, research programs, or matching gifts; no loans.
Publications: Annual report (including application guidelines).
Application information:
Initial approach: Letter
Copies of proposal: 6
Deadline(s): Submit proposal preferably in June; no set deadline
Board meeting date(s): Mar., June, Sept., and Dec.
Final notification: 3 to 6 months
Write: D. Faye Sanders, Chair.
Trustees: D. Faye Sanders, Chair.; Jonathan A. Barnes, Flordeliza G. Inonog, James H. Sweet.
Number of staff: None.
Employer Identification Number: 056022653

2878
The Cranston Foundation
c/o Leo G. Hutchings, Trustee
1381 Cranston St.
Cranston 02920 (401) 943-4800

Trust established in 1960 in RI.
Donor(s): Cranston Print Works Co.
Financial data (yr. ended 6/30/87): Assets, $826,466 (M); gifts received, $414,492; expenditures, $261,918, including $184,300 for 138 grants (high: $15,000; low: $50), $61,819 for 35 grants to individuals and $13,375 for employee matching gifts.
Purpose and activities: Grants largely for higher education, including a scholarship program for children of Cranston Corporation employees. Support also for community funds, hospitals, and cultural programs.
Types of support: Employee-related scholarships, operating budgets, scholarship funds, employee matching gifts.
Limitations: Giving primarily in RI and MA.
Application information:
Initial approach: Proposal
Deadline(s): Apr. 15
Board meeting date(s): At least quarterly
Trustees: Leo G. Hutchings, Frederic L. Rockefeller, Richard Schein, George W. Shuster.
Employer Identification Number: 056015348

2879
Norman & Rosalie Fain Fund Trust
505 Central Ave.
Pawtucket 02861 (401) 725-8028

Established in 1964 in RI.
Financial data (yr. ended 12/31/87): Assets, $1,184,594 (M); expenditures, $102,212,

including $96,595 for 26 grants (high: $25,000; low: $100).
Purpose and activities: Support primarily for Planned Parenthood; support also for Jewish welfare and the arts.
Limitations: Giving primarily in RI.
Application information:
Initial approach: Letter
Deadline(s): None
Write: Norman M. Fain
Trustees: Norman M. Fain, Rosalie B. Fain.
Employer Identification Number: 056022655

2880
Fleet Charitable Trust
c/o Fleet National Bank
111 Westminster St.
Providence 02903 (401) 278-6979

Trust established in 1955 in RI.
Donor(s): Fleet National Bank.
Financial data (yr. ended 12/31/87): Assets, $25,894,600 (M); gifts received, $521,917; expenditures, $1,241,521, including $1,081,217 for 84 grants (high: $363,000; low: $200), $14,000 for 14 grants to individuals and $55,152 for employee matching gifts.
Purpose and activities: Giving primarily for capital purposes of major charities, including United Way, health, higher education, including an employee matching gift program, hospitals, arts, and museums. Support also for work/study scholarships paid to colleges on behalf of RI high school seniors from minority groups.
Types of support: Annual campaigns, emergency funds, building funds, equipment, employee matching gifts, capital campaigns, matching funds.
Limitations: Giving limited to RI-based organizations. No grants for endowment or operating funds; no loans.
Publications: Application guidelines, program policy statement.
Application information: Scholarship candidates must be nominated by highschool guidance counselor and submit a letter stating needs.
Initial approach: Proposal
Copies of proposal: 1
Deadline(s): None
Board meeting date(s): Quarterly
Final notification: 2 months after board meeting
Write: Ms. Nancy L. Langrall, Asst. V.P., Fleet National Bank
Trustee: Fleet National Bank.
Number of staff: None.
Employer Identification Number: 056007619

2881
The Edward E. Ford Foundation
297 Wickenden St.
Providence 02903 (401) 751-2966

Trust established in 1957 in NY.
Donor(s): Edward E. Ford.†
Financial data (yr. ended 9/30/88): Assets, $44,540,248 (M); expenditures, $2,283,314, including $1,899,380 for 60 grants (high: $35,000; low: $10,000).
Purpose and activities: Primary interest in independent secondary education. Independent secondary schools must hold full and active membership in National Association of Independent Schools to be eligible for consideration.
Types of support: Annual campaigns, seed money, building funds, equipment, land acquisition, endowment funds, matching funds, scholarship funds, special projects, research, publications, renovation projects.
Limitations: Giving limited to the U.S. and its protectorates. No support for elementary or college-level schools, or to organizations that have been applicants within the last three years. No grants to individuals, or for emergency funds or deficit financing.
Publications: Annual report (including application guidelines).
Application information: Application form required.
Initial approach: Letter or telephone
Copies of proposal: 12
Deadline(s): Submit proposal during months prior to stated deadlines: Feb. 1, Apr. 1, and Sept. 15
Board meeting date(s): Apr., June, and Nov.
Final notification: 6 weeks for formal reply; informal reply sooner
Write: Philip V. Havens, Exec. Dir.
Officer: Philip V. Havens, Exec. Dir.
Advisory Board: William C. Fowle, Chair.; H. Ward Reighley, Vice-Chair.; Gillian Attfield, Gillian R. Brooks, Frank H. Detweiler, Lawrence L. Hlavacek, Julia F. Menard, Lyman W. Menard.
Trustee: Manufacturers Hanover Trust Co.
Number of staff: 1 full-time professional; 1 full-time support.
Employer Identification Number: 136047243
Recent arts and culture grants:
Montgomery Bell Academy, Grades 7-12, Nashville, TN, $30,000. To establish endowment to support fine arts professional development fund. 11/17/87.
Providence Country Day School, Grades 5-12, East Providence, RI, $35,000. Toward renovation of Lund Science and Fine Arts Building. 11/17/87.

2882
Haffenreffer Family Fund
c/o Fleet National Bank
100 Westminster St.
Providence 02903 (401) 274-4564

Trust established in 1943 in RI.
Donor(s): Members of the Haffenreffer family.
Financial data (yr. ended 12/31/87): Assets, $4,508,085 (M); expenditures, $256,247, including $205,150 for 81 grants (high: $40,000; low: $100).
Purpose and activities: Assistance to charitable and educational institutions in which members of the family are actively interested; with emphasis on higher and secondary education, community funds, church support, cultural programs, and hospitals.
Limitations: Giving primarily in RI and southeastern New England.
Application information:
Initial approach: Letter
Deadline(s): None
Write: Stanley C. Bodell, Jr.
Trustees: Patricia H. Blackall, Norman H. Fain, Carl W. Haffenreffer, David H. Haffenreffer, Rudolph F. Haffenreffer III, Rudolf F. Haffenreffer IV, William H. Heisler III, Andrew M. Hunt.
Employer Identification Number: 056012787

2883
Horace A. Kimball and S. Ella Kimball Foundation
c/o Rhode Island Hospital Trust National Bank
One Hospital Trust Plaza
Providence 02903
Additional address: R.F.D. Woodville, Hope Valley, RI 02832

Incorporated in 1956 in DE.
Donor(s): H. Earle Kimball.†
Financial data (yr. ended 9/30/87): Assets, $3,670,012 (M); expenditures, $216,402, including $184,800 for 19 grants (high: $25,000; low: $500).
Purpose and activities: Emphasis on health services, secondary education, community funds, youth agencies, programs for the elderly, and cultural programs; support also for volunteer fire and ambulance corps.
Limitations: Giving primarily in RI. No grants to individuals.
Publications: 990-PF.
Application information: Application form required.
Copies of proposal: 3
Deadline(s): None
Board meeting date(s): Varies
Write: Thomas F. Black, III, Pres.
Officers and Trustees: Thomas F. Black III, Pres.; T. Dexter Clarke, Secy.-Treas.; Norman D. Baker, Jr.
Number of staff: 1 part-time support.
Employer Identification Number: 056006130

2884
Little Family Foundation
c/o The Rhode Island Hospital Trust National Bank
P.O. Box 1597
Providence 02901-1597 (401) 278-8752

Trust established in 1946 in RI.
Donor(s): Royal Little.
Financial data (yr. ended 12/31/88): Assets, $12,746,724 (M); expenditures, $1,238,918, including $1,100,000 for 150 grants (high: $250,000; low: $1,000; average: $5,000).
Purpose and activities: Support for scholarship funds at designated business schools; Rhode Island Junior Achievement for programs in secondary schools; and various charities in New England, including youth agencies, cultural programs, and hospitals.
Types of support: Operating budgets, continuing support, annual campaigns, emergency funds, building funds, equipment, endowment funds, matching funds, scholarship funds.
Limitations: No grants to individuals, or for seed money, deficit financing, or land acquisition; no loans.
Publications: Application guidelines.

Application information: For scholarships, application is by letter to designated business school; deadline Sept. 1.
Initial approach: Letter
Copies of proposal: 1
Board meeting date(s): Quarterly
Write: Shawn P. Buckless, Trust Off., The Rhode Island Hospital Trust National Bank
Trustees: Augusta Willoughby Little Bishop, E. Janice Leeming, Arthur D. Little, Cameron R. Little, The Rhode Island Hospital Trust National Bank.
Employer Identification Number: 056016740

2885
Nortek Foundation
50 Kennedy Plaza
Providence 02903-2360

Established in 1974 in CA.
Donor(s): Nortek, Inc.
Financial data (yr. ended 12/31/87): Assets, $1,615,841 (M); gifts received, $86,097; expenditures, $95,495, including $59,065 for 56 grants (high: $7,500; low: $20).
Purpose and activities: Support primarily for higher education, arts and culture, health associations, and various civic organizations.
Limitations: Giving primarily in Providence, RI. No grants to individuals.
Application information: Contributes to preselected organizations. Applications not accepted.
Officers and Directors: Ralph R. Papitto, Chair.; Richard L. Bready, Vice-Chair.; John R. Potter, Secy.; Richard J. Harris, Treas.
Employer Identification Number: 237376137

2886
Old Stone Bank Charitable Foundation
180 South Main St.
Providence 02903 (401) 278-2213

Established in 1969 in RI.
Donor(s): Old Stone Bank.
Financial data (yr. ended 12/31/87): Assets, $620,501 (M); gifts received, $300,000; expenditures, $329,409, including $316,384 for 34 grants (high: $166,000; low: $550) and $12,891 for 64 employee matching gifts.
Purpose and activities: Giving primarily for community funds, education, cultural activities, social services, health, and civic improvement.
Types of support: Seed money, building funds, land acquisition, program-related investments, employee matching gifts, special projects, capital campaigns, matching funds.
Limitations: Giving limited to RI. No support for member agencies of United Way or other united appeals, or religious or political organizations. No grants to individuals, or for endowment funds, scholarships, fellowships, publications, conferences, or general operating support; no loans.
Publications: Annual report (including application guidelines), financial statement, grants list, program policy statement, informational brochure.
Application information:
Initial approach: Letter or telephone
Copies of proposal: 1
Deadline(s): 1st day of month when board meets
Board meeting date(s): Bimonthly beginning in Jan.
Final notification: 4 to 6 weeks
Write: Kay H. Low, Coord.
Distribution Committee: Ernest Corner, Chair.; Kay H. Low, Coord.; Theodore W. Barnes, Bernard V. Buonanno, Ernest Corner, Thomas P. Dimeo, Winfield W. Major, Thomas F. Schutte, Richmond Viall, Jr., Robert A. Riesman.
Number of staff: 1 part-time professional.
Employer Identification Number: 237029175

2887
Providence Journal Charitable Foundation
75 Fountain St.
Providence 02902 (401) 277-7206

Trust established in 1956 in RI.
Donor(s): Providence Journal Co.
Financial data (yr. ended 12/31/87): Assets, $2,834,839 (M); gifts received, $43,032; expenditures, $526,233, including $525,236 for 66 grants (high: $146,000; low: $1,000).
Purpose and activities: Emphasis on higher education and a community fund; support also for youth agencies, cultural programs, and hospitals.
Limitations: Giving primarily in RI. No grants to individuals.
Application information:
Initial approach: Letter or proposal
Copies of proposal: 1
Deadline(s): None
Board meeting date(s): Monthly
Write: Harry Dyson, Trustee
Trustees: Benjamin L. Cook, Jr., Harry Dyson, Stephen Hamblett, Paul C. Nicholson, Jr., John C.A. Watkins.
Employer Identification Number: 056015372

2888
The Rhode Island Community Foundation
957 North Main St.
Providence 02904 (401) 274-4564

Community foundation incorporated in 1916 in RI (includes The Rhode Island Community Foundation).
Financial data (yr. ended 12/31/88): Assets, $65,000,000 (M); gifts received, $3,591,989; expenditures, $3,283,118, including $3,260,741 for 776 grants and $27,000 for 6 grants to individuals.
Purpose and activities: To promote educational and charitable activities which will tend to improve the living conditions and well-being of the inhabitants of RI; grants for capital and operating purposes principally to agencies working in the fields of education, health care, the arts and cultural affairs, youth, the aged, social services, urban affairs, historic preservation, and the environment. Some restricted grants for scholarships and medical research.
Types of support: Fellowships, operating budgets, seed money, emergency funds, building funds, equipment, land acquisition, matching funds, consulting services, technical assistance, special projects, scholarship funds, research, publications, conferences and seminars, renovation projects, capital campaigns, general purposes.
Limitations: Giving limited to RI. No support for sectarian purposes, or medical research (except as specified by donors). No grants to individuals, or for endowment funds, annual campaigns, or deficit financing; no loans.
Publications: Annual report, program policy statement, application guidelines, newsletter, informational brochure.
Application information: Priority given to first 25 applications received prior to each board meeting.
Initial approach: Telephone, meeting, or letter
Copies of proposal: 5
Deadline(s): None
Board meeting date(s): Jan., Mar., May, July, Sept., and Nov.
Final notification: 3 months
Write: Douglas M. Jansson, Exec. Dir.
Officer: Douglas M. Jansson, Secy. and Exec. Dir.
Distribution Committee and Board of Directors: Robert H.I. Goddard, Chair.; Melvin Alperin, Patricia H. Blackall, Paul J. Choquette, William H. Heisler, B. Jae Clanton, Edward Maggiacomo.
Trustees: The Rhode Island Hospital Trust National Bank, Fleet National Bank, Citizens Bank, Old Stone Trust Co.
Number of staff: 2 full-time professional; 2 part-time professional; 1 full-time support; 2 part-time support.
Employer Identification Number: 050208270

2889
Rhode Island Hospital Trust Corporate Giving Program
One Hospital Trust Plaza
Providence 02903 (401) 278-7683

Financial data (yr. ended 12/31/87): Total giving, $1,057,579, including $661,987 for grants and $395,592 for in-kind gifts.
Purpose and activities: Support for United Way, education, employment, and training, higher education, health and human services, culture and the arts, civic and community affairs, foreign contributions, memberships, benefits, and program ads; also provides in-kind donations of personnel time, products, and facilities.
Types of support: In-kind gifts.
Limitations: Giving limited to RI.
Application information:
Initial approach: Letter
Write: Susan Baxter, Asst. V.P., Corp. Communications

2890
The Textron Charitable Trust
P.O. Box 878
Providence 02903 (401) 421-2800
Scholarship application addresses: Arthur Susman, National Merit Scholarship Corp., One American Plaza, Evanston, IL 60201; Philip Benson, College Scholarship Service, Box 176, Princeton, NJ 08541

Trust established in 1953 in VT.
Donor(s): Textron, Inc.
Financial data (yr. ended 12/31/87): Assets, $13,897,836 (M); gifts received, $1,655,730; expenditures, $2,952,964, including $1,986,429 for 443 grants (high: $115,000; low: $100; average: $500-$50,000) and $916,305 for 882 employee matching gifts.
Purpose and activities: Giving primarily for community funds, higher education, including scholarship programs, hospital and health agencies; support also for youth clubs, urban programs, minorities, and cultural programs.
Types of support: Building funds, equipment, matching funds, employee matching gifts, technical assistance, employee-related scholarships, capital campaigns, general purposes, special projects.
Limitations: Giving primarily in areas of company operations nationwide. No grants to individuals, or for endowment funds, land acquisition, deficit financing, research, demonstration projects, or publications; no loans.
Publications: Application guidelines.
Application information:
Initial approach: Proposal
Copies of proposal: 1
Deadline(s): None
Board meeting date(s): Quarterly
Final notification: 8 weeks
Write: Delores A. Francis, Mgr., Contribs. Program
Contributions Committee: Raymond W. Caine, Jr., Chair.
Trustee: The Rhode Island Hospital Trust National Bank.
Number of staff: 1 full-time professional; 1 full-time support.
Employer Identification Number: 256115832

SOUTH CAROLINA

2891
The Arkwright Foundation
P.O. Box 1086
Spartanburg 29304 (803) 585-9213

Incorporated in 1945 in SC.
Donor(s): Members of the M.L. Cates and W.S. Montgomery fami.
Financial data (yr. ended 12/31/87): Assets, $4,999,443 (M); expenditures, $409,433, including $307,943 for 84 grants (high: $31,000; low: $15).
Purpose and activities: Grants largely for a community fund, higher and secondary education, youth agencies, cultural programs, and Protestant church support.
Limitations: Giving primarily in SC.
Application information:
Initial approach: Letter, personal visit, or telephone
Deadline(s): None
Write: Joe W. Smith, Secy.-Treas.
Officers and Trustees: MacFarlane L. Cates, Sr., Chair.; Walter S. Montgomery, Vice-Chair.; Joe W. Smith, Secy.-Treas.; MacFarlane L. Cates, Jr., J.C. Kirkland, W.S. Montgomery, Jr.
Employer Identification Number: 576000066

2892
The Bailey Foundation
P.O. Box 1276
Clinton 29325 (803) 833-6830

Trust established in 1951 in SC.
Donor(s): M.S. Bailey & Son, Bankers, Clinton Investment Co.
Financial data (yr. ended 8/31/88): Assets, $3,878,200 (M); gifts received, $69,884; expenditures, $325,192, including $220,600 for 17 grants (high: $67,000; low: $100), $17,000 for 10 grants to individuals, $21,050 for 14 employee matching gifts and $43,000 for 27 loans to individuals.
Purpose and activities: Support primarily for higher education, including a student loan and scholarship program for children of employees of M.S. Bailey & Son, Bankers; support also for churches, community services, social services, libraries, museums, and child development.
Types of support: Employee-related scholarships, student loans, employee matching gifts, building funds, capital campaigns, endowment funds, matching funds, renovation projects.
Limitations: Giving primarily in Laurens County, SC, and in NC. No support for political organizations. No grants to individuals (except scholarships for children of company employees), or for operating expenses.
Application information: Applications for students available from personnel officers at Clinton Mills and Bailey Bank. Application form required.
Deadline(s): Apr. 15 of applicant's senior year in high school
Board meeting date(s): Quarterly
Write: H. William Carter, Jr., Admin.
Trustee: M.S. Bailey & Son, Bankers.
Advisory Committee: Emily F. Bailey, George H. Cornelson, C. Bailey Dixon, Robert M. Vance, James Von Hollen, Mercer V. Wise.
Grants Advisory Committee: Clarice W. Johnson, W.E. Little, James MacDonald, Joseph O. Nixon, Donny Ross, Donny Wilder.
Number of staff: 1
Employer Identification Number: 576018387

2893
Lucy Hampton Bostick Charitable Trust
c/o H. Simmons Tate, Jr.
P.O. Box 11889
Columbia 29211

Established in 1968 in SC.
Financial data (yr. ended 7/31/88): Assets, $1,296,563 (M); expenditures, $99,284, including $79,800 for 7 grants (high: $25,000; low: $300).
Purpose and activities: Grants for cultural organizations and education.
Types of support: General purposes.
Limitations: Giving primarily in SC.
Application information: Contributes only to pre-selected organizations. Applications not accepted.
Trustees: A. Mason Gibbs, N. Simmons Tate, Jr., George R.P. Walker.
Employer Identification Number: 576042059

2894
Builder Marts America Foundation, Inc.
P.O. Box 47
Greenville 29602-0047

Financial data (yr. ended 6/30/87): Assets, $165,602 (M); gifts received, $100,000; expenditures, $61,081, including $60,850 for 13 grants (high: $30,000; low: $100).
Purpose and activities: Support for education, culture and community and social sevices.
Types of support: General purposes.
Limitations: Giving primarily in Greenville, SC.
Application information: Contributes only to pre-selected organizations. Applications not accepted.
Trustees: A.F. Burgess, Clarence B. Bauknight, Macon G. Patton.
Employer Identification Number: 570658040

2895
Citizens and Southern National Bank of South Carolina Corporate Giving Program
1801 Main St.
Columbia 29222 (803) 765-8011

Financial data (yr. ended 12/31/87): $415,875 for grants.
Purpose and activities: Supports education, general health care, United Way, youth service, international groups and fine arts institutes.
Types of support: General purposes, matching funds, annual campaigns, building funds, capital campaigns, endowment funds.
Limitations: Giving primarily in SC. No grants to individuals, or for operating budgets, scholarships (except employee-related), fellowships, research, special projects, publications or conferences. No loans are available.
Publications: Application guidelines.
Application information: Include description of organization, amount requested, recently audited financial statement, 501(c)(3), purpose.
Initial approach: Letter or proposal
Copies of proposal: 1
Deadline(s): Applications accepted throughout the year
Board meeting date(s): Mar., June, Sept., and Dec.
Final notification: 3 months after submission of complete application
Write: Betty Davenport, Fdn. Secy.
Number of staff: 1

2896
Gregg-Graniteville Foundation, Inc.
P.O. Box 418
Graniteville 29829 (803) 663-7552

Incorporated in 1949 in SC.
Financial data (yr. ended 12/31/88): Assets, $12,102,240 (M); expenditures, $688,250,

including $546,046 for 39 grants (high: $341,149; low: $100; average: $5,000), $49,540 for 39 grants to individuals and $341,149 for 1 foundation-administered program.
Purpose and activities: Emphasis on education, recreation, religion, health, youth agencies, and community funds; scholarships only for children of Graniteville Co. employees and residents of Graniteville, Vaucluse, and Warrenville, SC.
Types of support: Continuing support, annual campaigns, seed money, emergency funds, building funds, endowment funds, matching funds, employee-related scholarships, research, special projects, capital campaigns, equipment.
Limitations: Giving primarily in Aiken County, SC, and Richmond County, GA. No grants to individuals (except for scholarships for children of company employees and residents of specified areas), or for operating budgets, deficit financing, land acquisition, publications, or conferences; no loans.
Publications: Annual report.
Application information: Application form required.
Initial approach: Letter
Copies of proposal: 1
Deadline(s): None
Board meeting date(s): Bimonthy or as required
Final notification: 1 month
Write: Joan F. Phibbs, Secy.
Officers: Robert P. Timmerman,* Pres.; John W. Cunningham,* V.P.; Jerry R. Johnson,* V.P.; Joan F. Phibbs, Secy.-Treas.
Directors:* Robert M. Bell, Carl W. Littlejohn, Jr., William C. Lott, James A. Randall, Clyde F. Strom.
Number of staff: 1 full-time professional.
Employer Identification Number: 570314400
Recent arts and culture grants:
Aiken County Arts Council, Aiken, SC, $5,000. 1987.

2897
Hartz Foundation
10 Valencia Circle
Myrtle Beach 29572

Incorporated in 1956 in MN.
Financial data (yr. ended 7/31/88): Assets, $4,427,080 (M); expenditures, $262,185, including $227,029 for 99 grants (high: $25,000; low: $75).
Purpose and activities: Giving for Protestant church support, higher and secondary education, hospitals, community development, and public broadcasting.
Limitations: Giving primarily in MN. No grants to individuals, or for building or endowment funds; no loans.
Application information:
Initial approach: Proposal
Copies of proposal: 1
Deadline(s): None
Board meeting date(s): Sept.
Write: Onealee Hartz, Secy.
Officers: Gene Beito, Pres.; Dwight Tanquist, V.P.; Onealee Hartz, Secy.-Treas.
Director: Orin Green.
Employer Identification Number: 416041638

2898
The Liberty Corporation Foundation
P.O. Box 789
Greenville 29602 (803) 292-4367

Established in 1965 in SC.
Donor(s): Liberty Corp.
Financial data (yr. ended 8/31/88): Assets, $198,094 (M); gifts received, $185,000; expenditures, $323,296, including $268,866 for 37 grants (high: $84,850; low: $1,500) and $53,975 for employee matching gifts.
Purpose and activities: Support primarily for higher education, including an employee matching gifts program, and for a community fund; some grants also to youth agencies and cultural institutions.
Types of support: Employee matching gifts.
Limitations: No grants to individuals.
Application information:
Initial approach: Proposal
Deadline(s): None
Write: Mary Anne Bunton, V.P.
Officers: W. Hayne Hipp,* Pres.; Mary Anne Bunton, V.P.; R.G. Hilliard,* V.P.; R.T. Coleman, Secy.; Barry L. Edwards, Treas.
Directors:* F.M. Hipp, Chair.; Macon G. Patton.
Employer Identification Number: 570468195

2899
Everett N. McDonnell Foundation
c/o Wallace Evans, Managing Agent
16 Starboard Tack
Salem 29676

Incorporated in 1946 in IL.
Donor(s): Everett N. McDonnell.†
Financial data (yr. ended 10/31/88): Assets, $2,795,453 (M); expenditures, $120,532, including $100,900 for grants (high: $20,000).
Purpose and activities: Giving for hospitals, health agencies, church support, and higher education.
Limitations: Giving primarily in IL and GA.
Application information: Applications not accepted.
Officers and Directors:* Florence L. McDonnell,* Pres. and Treas.; Gwyneth O. Moran, V.P.; John D. Marshall,* Secy.
Employer Identification Number: 366109359

2900
Post and Courier Foundation
134 Columbus St.
Charleston 29403-4800

Incorporated in 1951 in SC.
Donor(s): Evening Post Publishing Co.
Financial data (yr. ended 12/31/87): Assets, $1,098,910 (M); gifts received, $376,702; expenditures, $336,061, including $311,363 for 79 grants (high: $50,000; low: $60) and $19,726 for 16 grants to individuals.
Purpose and activities: Emphasis on higher education, including scholarships for news carriers; also support for community development, conservation, crime and law enforcement and health associations; scholarships for outstanding newspaper carriers in Charleston.
Types of support: Employee-related scholarships, building funds, capital campaigns, continuing support, matching funds, program-related investments, special projects.
Limitations: Giving primarily in Charleston, SC.
Application information:
Initial approach: Proposal
Deadline(s): None
Write: J.F. Smoak, Fdn. Mgr.
Officers: Peter Manigault, Pres.; Ivan V. Anderson, Jr., Exec. V.P.; Joseph F. Smoak, V.P. and Treas.; Arthur M. Wilcox, Secy.
Employer Identification Number: 576020356

2901
The Self Foundation
P.O. Drawer 1017
Greenwood 29648 (803) 229-2571

Incorporated in 1942 in SC.
Donor(s): James C. Self.†
Financial data (yr. ended 12/31/88): Assets, $22,455,914 (M); expenditures, $1,287,054, including $994,720 for 24 grants (high: $300,000; low: $1,000; average: $10,000).
Purpose and activities: Primary interest in health care and higher education; support also for cultural programs, and activities for youth and the elderly; grants mainly for capital or special purposes.
Types of support: Seed money, emergency funds, building funds, equipment, matching funds, technical assistance, special projects, renovation projects.
Limitations: Giving limited to SC, with emphasis on Greenwood. No grants to individuals, or for endowment funds, land acquisition, operating budgets, continuing support, annual campaigns, deficit financing, publications, conferences, scholarships, fellowships, or research-related programs; no loans.
Publications: Annual report (including application guidelines).
Application information: Application form required.
Initial approach: Proposal
Copies of proposal: 1
Deadline(s): Submit proposal preferably in the 2 months prior to board meetings; deadlines, 1st day of month in which board meets
Board meeting date(s): 3rd week in Mar., June, Sept., and Dec.
Final notification: 10 days after board meeting
Write: Frank J. Wideman, Jr., Exec. V.P.
Officers: James C. Self,* Pres.; Frank J. Wideman, Jr., Exec. V.P.; James C. Self, Jr.,* V.P.; W.M. Self,* Secy.; Kenneth E. Young, Treas.
Trustees:* Virginia S. Brennan, Emmett I. Davis, Lynn W. Hodge, William B. Patrick, Jr., Sally E. Self, M.D., Paul E. Welder.
Number of staff: 1 full-time professional.
Employer Identification Number: 570400594
Recent arts and culture grants:
Greenwood Performing Arts, Greenwood, SC, $7,500. For one-for-one challenge grant. 1987.

South Carolina Historical Society, Charleston, SC, $25,000. For challenge grant to assist with cost of new climate control, fire and burglar alarm systems in fireproof building. 1987.

2902
John I. Smith Charities, Inc.

c/o NCNB South Carolina, Trust Dept.
P.O. Box 608
Greenville 29602 (803) 271-5934

Established in 1985 in SC.
Donor(s): John Q. Smith.†
Financial data (yr. ended 7/31/87): Assets, $7,071,348 (M); gifts received, $2,122,577; expenditures, $801,952, including $653,000 for 23 grants (high: $200,000; low: $2,000).
Purpose and activities: Support for educational and religious institutions, and community organizations.
Types of support: Capital campaigns, emergency funds, endowment funds, general purposes, scholarship funds.
Limitations: Giving primarily in SC.
Application information:
Initial approach: Letter
Board meeting date(s): Quarterly
Write: Wilbur Y. Bridgers, Pres.
Officers and Director: Wilbur Y. Bridgers, Pres. and Secy.; W. Thomas Smith, V.P. and Treas.; Jefferson V. Smith III.
Trustee: NCNB South Carolina.
Number of staff: None.
Employer Identification Number: 570806327

2903
South Carolina National Charitable & Educational Foundation

1426 Main St.
Columbia 29226

Established in 1961.
Donor(s): South Carolina National Bank.
Financial data (yr. ended 12/31/87): Assets, $972,706 (M); gifts received, $811,666; expenditures, $898,920, including $884,775 for grants.
Purpose and activities: Giving for higher education, youth agencies, cultural programs, and a community fund.
Types of support: Building funds, employee matching gifts, general purposes, matching funds, renovation projects, scholarship funds, special projects.
Limitations: Giving limited to SC, except for matching gifts. No grants to individuals.
Publications: Program policy statement.
Application information:
Initial approach: Letter or proposal
Deadline(s): None
Write: James B. Murphy, Jr., Secy.
Officers and Trustees: John A. Warren, Chair.; James B. Murphy, Jr., Secy.; Rufus C. Barkley, Jr., W. Hayne Hipp, James G. Lindley, Robert S. McCoy, Jr.
Employer Identification Number: 576019497

2904
The Spartanburg County Foundation

805 Montgomery Bldg.
Spartanburg 29301 (803) 582-0138

Community foundation incorporated in 1943 in SC.
Financial data (yr. ended 12/31/88): Assets, $14,594,779 (M); gifts received, $1,249,539; expenditures, $867,167, including $658,037 for 141 grants (high: $30,000; low: $400; average: $5,000-$10,000).
Purpose and activities: To provide "for the mental, moral, intellectual and physical improvement, assistance and relief of the inhabitants of Spartanburg County." Support for local projects in education, arts, humanities, recreation, health, and welfare.
Types of support: Continuing support, seed money, emergency funds, building funds, equipment, matching funds, conferences and seminars, consulting services, scholarship funds, renovation projects, lectureships.
Limitations: Giving limited to Spartanburg County, SC. No grants to individuals, or for operating budgets, annual campaigns, deficit financing, land acquisition, or endowment funds; no loans.
Publications: Annual report (including application guidelines), informational brochure.
Application information:
Initial approach: Telephone
Copies of proposal: 1
Deadline(s): Submit proposal preferably in 1st 6 months of year, and at least 40 days before board meetings. Grants are considered in Mar., June, Sept., and Dec.
Board meeting date(s): Monthly
Final notification: 1 month following board meeting
Write: James S. Barrett, Exec. Dir.
Officers: John E. Keith, Secy.; W. Marshall Chapman, Treas.; James S. Barrett, Exec. Dir.
Trustees:* Harry R. Phillips, Jr., Chair.; Richard H. Pennell, Vice-Chair.; Elaine Freeman, John E. Keith, John T. Wardlaw, Kurt Zimmerli.
Number of staff: 1 full-time professional; 1 part-time professional; 1 full-time support; 1 part-time support.
Employer Identification Number: 570351398

2905
Spring Industries Corporate Giving Program

Executive Office Bldg.
P.O. Box 70
Fort Mill 29715 (803) 547-2901

Purpose and activities: Supports community and civic service programs, federated campaigns, culture and arts, health, hospitals, education and youth service. Provides company in-house services and donations of the company's primary goods or services; dominant focus on operating communities.
Limitations: Giving primarily in AL, GA, NC, and SC.
Application information: Include description of the project, budget, a financial report, 501(c)(3) status letter and major donor list.
Write: Robert L. Thompson Jr., V.P., Public Affairs

2906
Springs Foundation, Inc.

104 East Springs St.
Lancaster 29720 (803) 286-2196
Additional address: P.O. Drawer 460, Lancaster, SC 29720

Incorporated in 1942 in DE.
Donor(s): Elliott W. Springs,† Anne Springs Close, Frances Ley Springs.†
Financial data (yr. ended 12/31/88): Assets, $20,507,785 (M); gifts received, $3,680; expenditures, $1,566,588, including $1,148,244 for 41 grants (high: $750,000; low: $500; average: $5,000-$50,000) and $136,314 for loans.
Purpose and activities: Support largely for recreation, and education, including public schools and student loans; support for community services, churches, hospitals, and medical scholarships.
Types of support: Building funds, equipment, endowment funds, publications, professorships, matching funds, general purposes, special projects, student aid, student loans.
Limitations: Giving primarily in Lancaster County and/or the townships of Fort Mill and Chester, SC. No grants to individuals (except through the Springs Medical Scholarship Program).
Publications: Annual report (including application guidelines).
Application information: Application form required for student loans.
Initial approach: Telephone or brief letter
Copies of proposal: 1
Deadline(s): None
Board meeting date(s): Apr., Sept., and Dec.
Final notification: 3 months
Write: Charles A. Bundy, Pres.
Officers and Directors: Anne Springs Close, Chair.; Charles A. Bundy, Pres.; R.C. Hubbard, V.P. and Secy.; Crandall C. Bowles, V.P. and Treas.; James Bradley, Derick S. Close, Elliott Springs Close, H.W. Close, Jr., Katherine A. Close, Leroy Springs Close, Frances Close Hart, Pat Close Hastings, J.W. Medford.
Number of staff: 1 full-time professional; 2 full-time support.
Employer Identification Number: 570426344
Recent arts and culture grants:
Lancaster County Council of the Arts, Lancaster, SC, $16,500. For operating support and for Lancaster appearance of Charlotte Symphony Orchestra. 1987.
South Carolina Department of Parks, Recreation and Tourism, Columbia, SC, $5,000. For appearance of Columbia Symphony Orchestra during weekend opening of new amphitheater at Andrew Jackson State Park. 1987.

2907
F. W. Symmes Foundation

c/o South Carolina National Bank
P.O. Box 969
Greenville 29602 (803) 239-6843

Trust established in 1954 in SC.
Donor(s): F.W. Symmes.†
Financial data (yr. ended 3/31/88): Assets, $7,828,321 (M); expenditures, $532,491,

including $464,875 for 9 grants (high: $100,000; low: $1,000; average: $36,000).
Purpose and activities: Emphasis on church support, child welfare, hospitals, youth agencies, music, and recreation.
Limitations: Giving primarily in SC. No grants to individuals.
Publications: Application guidelines, informational brochure.
Application information:
Initial approach: Letter or telephone
Copies of proposal: 5
Deadline(s): 4 weeks before board meetings
Board meeting date(s): Semiannually
Final notification: 2 weeks following meeting
Write: Victoria G. Dotson, Trust Off., South Carolina National Bank
Trustees: William H. Orders, Wilson C. Wearn, F. McKinnon Wilkinson, South Carolina National Bank.
Number of staff: None.
Employer Identification Number: 576017472

2908
Trident Community Foundation
11 Broad St.
Charleston 29401-3001 (803) 723-3635
Additional tel.: (803) 723-2124

Incorporated in l974 in SC.
Financial data (yr. ended 6/30/88): Assets, $2,682,540 (M); gifts received, $1,376,616; expenditures, $286,259, including $116,030 for grants (high: $15,000; low: $100; average: $1,500-$5,000), $10,500 for grants to individuals, $33,000 for 2 foundation-administered programs and $13,475 for loans.
Purpose and activities: Giving for the arts and humanities, education, environment, and health and social services.
Types of support: Emergency funds, program-related investments, publications, renovation projects, scholarship funds, seed money, special projects, technical assistance, student aid, operating budgets.
Limitations: Giving primarily in Berkeley, Charleston, and Dorchester counties, SC. No grants for scholarships, annual campaigns, endowments, equipment, deficit financing, or generally for building funds; no loans.
Publications: Annual report (including application guidelines), newsletter.
Application information: Application form required.
Initial approach: Letter
Copies of proposal: 5
Board meeting date(s): 3rd Tuesday of every other month
Final notification: Within 3 months of each proposal deadline
Write: Ruth Heffron, Exec. Dir.
Officers and Directors: Henry Smythe, Jr., Pres.; George Bullwinkel, Jr., V.P.; Louise Maybank, Secy.; Conrad Zimmerman, Jr., Treas.; Ruth H. Heffron, Exec. Dir.; Richard Hendry, Dir. of Program Dev.; Ann Stein.
Number of staff: 2 full-time professional; 2 part-time professional; 2 part-time support.
Employer Identification Number: 237390313

TENNESSEE

2909
Arthur F. Adams Foundation, Inc.
4487 Talltrees Dr.
Memphis 38117

Financial data (yr. ended 12/31/87): Assets, $130,370 (M); expenditures, $133,634, including $132,000 for 3 grants (high: $80,000; low: $2,000).
Purpose and activities: Support primarily for a hospital and an opera company.
Limitations: Giving primarily in Miami, FL.
Application information:
Deadline(s): None
Write: Henry W. Clark, Pres.
Officers: Henry W. Clark, Pres.; William Warren, Exec. V.P.; H. Willis Day, V.P.; Richard Chadman, Secy.-Treas.
Employer Identification Number: 596151030

2910
Aladdin Industries Foundation, Inc.
703 Murfreesboro Rd.
Nashville 37210-4521 (615) 748-3360

Incorporated in 1964 in TN.
Donor(s): Aladdin Industries.
Financial data (yr. ended 12/31/88): Assets, $1,290,580 (M); expenditures, $48,254, including $41,000 for 13 grants (high: $10,000; low: $500).
Purpose and activities: Support primarily for youth; with funding also for the aged, music, business, education, and drug abuse.
Types of support: General purposes, employee-related scholarships, seed money.
Limitations: Giving primarily in TN.
Application information:
Initial approach: Letter
Deadline(s): Current calender year
Board meeting date(s): Quarterly
Write: L.B. Jenkins, Secy.-Treas.
Officer and Directors: L.B. Jenkins, Secy.-Treas.; V.S. Johnson III, F.R. Meyer.
Employer Identification Number: 620701769

2911
Dantzler Bond Ansley Foundation
c/o Third National Bank, Trust Dept.
P.O. Box 305110
Nashville 37230-5110 (615) 748-5207

Incorporated in 1980 in TN.
Donor(s): Mildred B. Ansley.†
Financial data (yr. ended 4/30/87): Assets, $5,452,980 (M); expenditures, $377,168, including $349,100 for 28 grants (high: $50,000; low: $2,000).
Purpose and activities: Support primarily for health and medical research, higher and secondary education, and cultural programs.
Types of support: Annual campaigns, capital campaigns.
Limitations: Giving primarily in middle TN and Nashville, TN.
Application information:
Copies of proposal: 3
Deadline(s): May 31
Write: Kim Williams, Trust Officer
Trustees: Frank Drowota, Thomas F. Frist, Fred Russell.
Employer Identification Number: 592111990

2912
BBC Foundation
450 Machellan Bldg.
722 Chestnut St.
Chattanooga 37402
Application address: 428 McCallie Ave., Chattanooga, TN 37402; Tel.: (615) 756-5880

Financial data (yr. ended 12/31/86): Assets, $1,566,652 (M); expenditures, $71,889, including $62,200 for 19 grants (high: $10,000; low: $1,000).
Purpose and activities: Support primarily for schools, cultural programs, and health services.
Types of support: General purposes.
Application information:
Deadline(s): None
Write: Carl J. Arnold, Secy.-Treas.
Officers and Trustees: H. Clay Evans Johnson, Chair.; Betty J. Farmer, Vice-Chair.; Barbara J. Prickett, Vice-Chair.; Carl J. Arnold, Secy.-Treas.
Employer Identification Number: 581577719

2913
Belz Foundation
P.O. Box 171199
Memphis 38187-1199

Incorporated in 1952 in TN.
Donor(s): Jack A. Belz, Philip Belz, and others.
Financial data (yr. ended 12/31/86): Assets, $5,182,801 (M); gifts received, $1,170,874; expenditures, $394,574, including $391,130 for 352 grants (high: $223,955; low: $5).
Purpose and activities: Emphasis on Jewish welfare funds, temple support, education, and cultural organizations.
Limitations: Giving primarily in Memphis, TN. No grants to individuals.
Managers: Jack A. Belz, Martin S. Belz, Philip Belz, Raymond Shainberg, Jack Weil, Jimmie D. Williams.
Employer Identification Number: 626046715

2914
Benwood Foundation, Inc.
1600 American National Bank Bldg.
Chattanooga 37402 (615) 267-4311

Incorporated in 1944 in DE; in 1945 in TN.
Donor(s): George Thomas Hunter.†
Financial data (yr. ended 12/31/87): Assets, $58,776,779 (M); expenditures, $8,689,336, including $8,346,713 for 100 grants (high: $5,000,000; low: $250; average: $1,000-$100,000).
Purpose and activities: Support for higher and secondary education, welfare agencies, health agencies and hospitals, cultural programs, including the performing arts, beautification, and Christian religious organizations.
Types of support: Research, annual campaigns, seed money, emergency funds,

deficit financing, building funds, equipment, land acquisition, conferences and seminars, endowment funds, professorships, scholarship funds, matching funds, general purposes, continuing support, renovation projects.
Limitations: Giving primarily in the Chattanooga, TN, area. No grants to individuals, or for building or operating funds of churches; no loans.
Publications: Application guidelines.
Application information: Application form required.
Initial approach: Letter
Copies of proposal: 6
Deadline(s): End of each month preceding board meetings
Board meeting date(s): Jan., Apr., July, and Oct.
Final notification: 3 days after board meeting
Write: William A. Walter, Exec. Dir.
Officers and Trustees: Walter R. Randolph, Jr., Chair.; Sebert Brewer, Jr., Pres.; Scott L. Probasco, Jr., V.P.; E.Y. Chapin III, Secy.-Treas.; William A. Walter, Exec. Dir.
Number of staff: 1 full-time professional; 2 full-time support.
Employer Identification Number: 620476283

2915
Bernal Foundation
c/o Werthan Industries
P.O. Box 1310
Nashville 37202 (615) 259-9331

Established in 1953 in TN.
Donor(s): Albert Werthan, Members of the Werthan Family.
Financial data (yr. ended 12/31/87): Assets, $673,800 (M); gifts received, $102,147; expenditures, $189,093, including $177,593 for 224 grants (high: $20,000; low: $50).
Purpose and activities: Support primarily for higher and other education, Jewish temples, and Jewish welfare funds; giving also for a community fund.
Limitations: Giving primarily in TN.
Application information:
Initial approach: Letter
Deadline(s): None
Board meeting date(s): June
Write: Albert Werthan, Chair.
Officers: Albert Werthan, Chair.; Bernard Werthan, Jr., Secy.; Morris Werthan II, Treas.
Employer Identification Number: 626037906

2916
T. W. Briggs Welcome Wagon Foundation, Inc.
2670 Union Ave. Extension, Suite 1122
Memphis 38112-4402 (901) 323-0213

Established in 1957.
Financial data (yr. ended 9/30/87): Assets, $4,779,786 (M); gifts received, $75,329; expenditures, $272,359, including $214,185 for 31 grants (high: $67,000; low: $25).
Purpose and activities: Giving for higher education, social services, museums, a community fund, and youth agencies.
Limitations: Giving primarily in TN.
Application information:
Deadline(s): None
Officers and Directors: Hubert A. McBride, Chair.; S. Herbert Rhea, Pres. and Treas.; William T. Morris, V.P.; Eleanor Prest, Secy.; Margaret Hyde, Harry J. Phillips, Sr., Spence Wilson.
Employer Identification Number: 626039986

2917
George Newton Bullard Foundation
c/o Kraft Brothers, Esstman, Patton, and Harrell
404 James Robertson Pkwy.
Nashville 37219

Established in 1967 in TN.
Donor(s): Ella Hayes Trust.
Financial data (yr. ended 12/31/86): Assets, $10,786,584 (M); gifts received, $917,098; expenditures, $511,948, including $440,850 for 183 grants (high: $24,002; low: $100).
Purpose and activities: Emphasis on social agencies; support for churches and religious associations, higher and secondary education, and cultural programs.
Limitations: Giving primarily in TN.
Trustees: George N. Bullard, Jr., Elizabeth B. Stadler.
Employer Identification Number: 626077171

2918
The Robert H. and Monica M. Cole Foundation
c/o First American Trust Co., Trust Dept.
505 South Gay St.
Knoxville 37902

Established in 1976.
Financial data (yr. ended 9/30/87): Assets, $2,320,905 (M); expenditures, $152,939, including $142,682 for 31 grants (high: $50,000; low: $500; average: $1,000-$5,000).
Purpose and activities: Grants for medical research on Parkinson's disease, and for cultural programs and civic affairs.
Types of support: Operating budgets, research.
Limitations: Giving limited to eastern TN, including Knoxville, and southeast KY.
Application information:
Write: Mark A. Goodson, Trust Officer, First American Trust Co.
Trustees: Monica M. Cole, William W. Davis, J. Robert Page, First American Trust Co.
Employer Identification Number: 626137973

2919
Brownlee Currey Foundation
c/o Commerce Union Bank, Trust Dept.
One Commerce Place
Nashville 37219 (615) 749-3336

Established in 1967.
Financial data (yr. ended 12/31/86): Assets, $2,238,035 (M); expenditures, $155,414, including $150,200 for 25 grants (high: $100,000; low: $100).
Purpose and activities: Giving primarily for cultural programs, education, health, and a community fund.
Types of support: Annual campaigns, research.
Application information:
Initial approach: Letter
Deadline(s): None
Write: M. Kirk Scobey, Sr. V.P. and Trust Officer, Commerce Union Bank
Officers: Margaret C. Henley, Pres.; Brownlee O. Currey, Jr., V.P.
Trustee: Commerce Union Bank.
Employer Identification Number: 626077710

2920
East Tennessee Foundation
709 Market St.
P.O. Box 590
Knoxville 37901 (615) 524-1223

Incorporated in 1958 in TN.
Financial data (yr. ended 12/31/87): Assets, $4,800,000 (M); gifts received, $3,700,000; expenditures, $330,000, including $215,000 for 62 grants (high: $25,000; low: $1,000; average: $5,000) and $5,000 for 2 grants to individuals.
Purpose and activities: Support for the arts, education, community development and youth services.
Types of support: Conferences and seminars, consulting services, equipment, matching funds, operating budgets, publications, renovation projects, research, technical assistance, fellowships, special projects.
Limitations: Giving limited to Knoxville, TN and its 16 surrounding counties.
Publications: Annual report (including application guidelines), newsletter, informational brochure.
Application information: Application form provided for application to the arts fund and the youth endowment.
Initial approach: Letter or phone
Write: Katharine Pearson, Exec. Dir.
Officers: Natalie L. Haslam, Chair.; John R. Cooper, Pres.; Katherine Pearson, Exec. Dir.
Number of staff: 3 full-time professional.
Employer Identification Number: 620807696

2921
First Tennessee Bank Corporate Giving Program
165 Madison Ave.
P.O. Box 84
Memphis 38103 (901) 523-4382

Financial data (yr. ended 12/31/86): Total giving, $927,480, including $912,480 for grants (high: $174,000; low: $50; average: $5,000-$50,000) and $15,000 for in-kind gifts.
Purpose and activities: Supports higher education, and corporate initiated projects for elementary and secondary schools, health, welfare, culture and the arts. National health agencies supported only through local chapters and limited to a maximum of $100 annually. In addition to contributions, First Tennessee is also interested in supporting community organizations through sponsorships and marketing promotions. The objective of these projects is to involve the First Tennessee target audience. And as part of its commitment to the community, First Tennessee participates in the Volunteer Center's Corporate Neighbor program. The purpose of the First Tennessee Volunteer-bank is to help communities by providing organizations and events with individuals who are willing to commit time and

resources, as well as help employees expand their horizons, skills and capabilities through volunteer experience. From time to time, First Tennessee has equipment and furniture which is still usable but has been retired from service in the Bank and is available for donation.
Types of support: In-kind gifts, technical assistance, operating budgets, annual campaigns, seed money, special projects.
Limitations: Giving primarily in headquarters city and major operating locations. No support for charities sponsored by a single civic organization, agencies supported by the United Way, or united arts funds, religious, veteran, social, athletic, or fraternal organizations, or charities which redistribute funds to other charities, except for united fund-type organizations. No grants to individuals, or for deficit financing, endowments, or multi-year commitments of 4 years or more.
Publications: Application guidelines.
Application information: Narrative/letter, complete budget, 501(c)(3), application form, board and contributors lists, audited statement and annual report.
Initial approach: Letter of inquiry with description of project
Copies of proposal: 1
Deadline(s): Applications accepted throughout the year
Final notification: 4 weeks
Write: Rebecca Theobald, Community Investment Rep.
Number of staff: 2 part-time professional.

2922
Genesco Corporate Giving Program
Genesco Park Admin. Bldg.
Nashville 37202 (615) 367-8281

Financial data (yr. ended 01/31/88): Total giving, $83,805, including $78,805 for 39 grants (high: $35,000; low: $100) and $5,000 for in-kind gifts.
Purpose and activities: Supports federated campaigns, culture and the arts, education, including business and minority education, employment, foreign policy, health, literacy, and community services including alcohol/drug treatment programs. Types of support include volunteer recruitment and donations of the company's primary goods or services.
Types of support: Annual campaigns, capital campaigns, internships, in-kind gifts.
Limitations: Giving primarily in Nashville, TN and Allentown, PA. No grants for advertising or dinners.
Application information: Include description of project, annual report, financial statement, 501(c)(3) status report, list of board members and donors and a proposal budget.
Initial approach: Letter of inquiry
Copies of proposal: 1
Deadline(s): First of each month
Board meeting date(s): First week of each month
Final notification: Will send rejection notice
Write: John Pennington, Dir. Pub. Rel.
Number of staff: 1 part-time professional.

2923
Hamico, Inc.
1715 West 38th St.
Chattanooga 37409

Incorporated in 1956 in TN.
Donor(s): Chattem, Inc.
Financial data (yr. ended 12/31/88): Assets, $2,814,339 (M); gifts received, $57,406; expenditures, $77,721, including $76,090 for 27 grants (high: $10,000; low: $150).
Purpose and activities: Emphasis on higher, secondary, and elementary education, and on cultural and health programs.
Types of support: Continuing support, endowment funds.
Limitations: Giving primarily in Chattanooga, TN.
Application information: Contributes only to pre-selected organizations. Applications not accepted.
Officers and Trustees: Alex Guerry, Pres.; James E. Abshire, Jr., V.P.; Durwood C. Harvey, Secy.-Treas.; Ray W. Evans, Alexander Guerry III, James M. Holbert, Vernon L. Staggs.
Number of staff: None.
Employer Identification Number: 626040782

2924
The HCA Foundation
c/o Hospital Corp. of America
One Park Plaza, P.O. Box 550
Nashville 37202-0550 (615) 320-2165

Established in 1982 in TN.
Donor(s): Hospital Corp. of America.
Financial data (yr. ended 12/31/88): Assets, $22,199,295 (M); expenditures, $2,877,714, including $2,128,943 for 237 grants (high: $363,000; low: $500; average: $1,000-$20,000) and $267,969 for 382 employee matching gifts.
Purpose and activities: Giving primarily for health management and policy exploration; support also for education, especially higher education, the arts and cultural programs, social services, civic and community affairs, and the United Way.
Types of support: Matching funds, general purposes, land acquisition, special projects, building funds, professorships, publications, conferences and seminars, renovation projects, capital campaigns, equipment, continuing support, employee matching gifts, operating budgets, research, employee-related scholarships.
Limitations: Giving primarily in Nashville, TN, and to groups that are national in scope. No support for social, religious, fraternal, labor, athletic, or veterans' groups (except for specific programs of broad public benefit), political entities, schools below the college level, private foundations, or individual United Way agencies. No grants to individuals, or for endowment funds, dinners, tables, or tickets to fund-raising events, promotional materials including goodwill advertising, publications, trips, or tours.
Publications: Biennial report (including application guidelines), informational brochure, application guidelines.
Application information: Information brochures available for HCA Teacher Awards Program, HCA Volunteer Service Awards, HCA Achievement Awards for Non-Profit Management, and employee-related scholarship program.
Initial approach: Telephone or letter
Copies of proposal: 1
Deadline(s): None
Board meeting date(s): Jan., Apr., July, and Oct.
Final notification: Within 4 months
Write: Ida F. Cooney, Exec. Dir.
Officers: Donald S. MacNaughton,* Chair. and Pres.; Ida F. Cooney, V.P. and Exec. Dir.; Peter F. Bird, Secy.-Treas. and Sr. Prog. Officer.
Directors:* Robert C. Crosby, Thomas F. First, Jr., Charles J. Kane, R. Clayton McWhorter, Roger E. Mick, Irving S. Shapiro.
Number of staff: 4 full-time professional; 1 full-time support.
Employer Identification Number: 621134070

2925
Hazel Montague Hutcheson Foundation
c/o American National Bank & Trust Co.
736 Market St.
Chattanooga 37402 (615) 757-3203

Established in 1962 in TN.
Donor(s): Hazel G.M. Montague.†
Financial data (yr. ended 6/30/88): Assets, $2,565,332 (M); expenditures, $142,184, including $131,979 for 39 grants (high: $10,200; low: $500; average: $1,000-$3,000).
Purpose and activities: Support for private secondary schools, Protestant church support, health agencies, and cultural programs.
Types of support: Annual campaigns.
Limitations: Giving primarily in TN and FL. No grants for scholarships; no loans.
Application information: Applications not accepted.
Board meeting date(s): Varies
Write: Peter T. Cooper
Trustees: Betty R. Hutcheson, Theodore M. Hutcheson, W. Frank Hutcheson, Hazel Hutcheson Meadow.
Number of staff: None.
Employer Identification Number: 626045925

2926
J. R. Hyde Foundation, Inc.
3030 Poplar Ave.
Memphis 38111 (901) 325-4245

Incorporated in 1961 in TN.
Donor(s): J.R. Hyde.†
Financial data (yr. ended 8/31/88): Assets, $14,688,291 (M); gifts received, $750,000; expenditures, $835,523, including $765,179 for 91 grants (high: $50,000; low: $600) and $17,500 for 7 grants to individuals.
Purpose and activities: Grants for higher education, including scholarships for the children of Malone & Hyde employees, secondary education, cultural programs, community funds, and social service and youth agencies and Protestant church support.
Types of support: Scholarship funds, employee-related scholarships.
Limitations: Giving primarily in the mid-South. No grants to individuals (except for company-employee scholarships), or for general support,

capital or endowment funds, research programs, or matching grants; no loans.
Application information:
Deadline(s): None
Board meeting date(s): Sept. and as required
Write: Ms. Margaret R. Hyde, Pres.
Officers: Margaret R. Hyde, Pres.; Joe R. Hyde III, V.P.; Jane Hyde Scott, Secy.-Treas.
Trustee: First Tennessee Bank.
Employer Identification Number: 620677725

2927
Interstate Packaging Foundation Charitable Trust
P.O. Box AG
White Bluff 37187-0922 (615) 256-2088

Financial data (yr. ended 4/30/88): Assets, $45,368 (M); gifts received, $10,332; expenditures, $14,475, including $13,845 for 34 grants (high: $5,100; low: $50).
Purpose and activities: Support for Jewish giving, health, including, single-disease associations, culture, youth and youth volunteerism, higher education, civic affairs, and social services.
Application information:
Initial approach: Proposal
Deadline(s): None
Write: Jerald Doochin
Trustees: Michael Doochin, Jerald Doochin.
Employer Identification Number: 621031459

2928
Leu Foundation, Inc.
2409 Abbot Martin Rd.
Nashville 37315

Established in 1976 in NE.
Donor(s): Frank Leu, Marjorie Skala.
Financial data (yr. ended 12/31/86): Assets, $1,454,276 (M); gifts received, $44,000; expenditures, $82,172, including $27,000 for grants (high: $10,000) and $28,500 for grants to individuals.
Purpose and activities: Support primarily for higher education, including student aid; support also for religion and culture.
Types of support: Student aid.
Limitations: Giving for scholarships primarily in North Platte, NE.
Application information: Completion of application form required for scholarship.
Deadline(s): None
Write: Frank Leu, Pres.
Officers and Trustees: Frank Leu, Pres. and Mgr.; Dennis Barkley, Treas.; Cynthia Leu, Edna Nelson, Marjorie Skala.
Employer Identification Number: 470576937

2929
Lyndhurst Foundation
Suite 701, Tallan Bldg.
100 West Martin Luther King Blvd.
Chattanooga 37402-2561 (615) 756-0767

Incorporated in 1938 in DE.
Donor(s): Cartter Lupton,† Central Shares Corp.
Financial data (yr. ended 12/31/88): Assets, $108,980,679 (M); expenditures, $12,536,499, including $10,872,890 for 60 grants (high: $5,000,000; low: $600; average: $4,000-$75,000) and $650,000 for 35 grants to individuals.
Purpose and activities: Support primarily for revitalization in Chattanooga, including grants for education, the arts, city involvement and economic development; support also for educational reform, primarily focused on the quality of teaching in elementary and secondary schools (including awards for teachers); limited support for cultural programs. Lyndhurst Prizes, awarded to individuals whose work embodies values the foundation considers important, are given solely at the initiative of the foundation.
Types of support: General purposes, seed money, matching funds, operating budgets, program-related investments, special projects, grants to individuals.
Limitations: Giving limited to the southeastern U.S., especially Chattanooga, TN. No grants to individuals, or for scholarships, fellowships, building or endowment funds, equipment, deficit financing, medical or university-based research, publications, or conferences; no general support for hospitals, colleges, universities, or religious organizations; no loans.
Publications: Annual report, application guidelines.
Application information: Applications or nominations not accepted for Lyndhurst Prizes; application form required for Lyndhurst Teachers' Awards.
Initial approach: Letter
Copies of proposal: 1
Deadline(s): Feb. 15 for Lyndhurst Teachers' Awards; Jan. 25, Mar. 25, June 25, Aug. 25, and Oct. 25 for other grants
Board meeting date(s): Jan., Mar., May, Aug., Oct., and Dec.
Final notification: 3 months
Write: Jack E. Murrah, Exec. Dir.
Officers: Jack E. Murrah, Exec. Dir.; Allen McCallie, Secy.; Charles B. Chitty, Treas.
Trustees:* John T. Lupton,* Chair.; Robert Coles, Mai Bell Hurley, Deaderick C. Montague.
Number of staff: 5 full-time professional; 4 full-time support.
Employer Identification Number: 626044177
Recent arts and culture grants:
Allied Arts of Greater Chattanooga, Chattanooga, TN, $30,000. For series of seminars on impact of urban design on city's image and on its economy. 1987.
Appalshop, Whitesburg, KY, $100,000. For general support. 1987.
Arts and Education Council, Chattanooga, TN, $6,600. To host meeting of distinguished authors and critics for purpose of creating Fellowship of Southern Writers, organization designed both to recognize and to stimulate high achievement in southern writing. 1987.
Association of Visual Artists, Chattanooga, TN, $25,000. For first-year operating costs for organization dedicated to promotion of visual art and artists who create it in Chattanooga area. 1987.
Belmont College, Graduate School of Business, Nashville, TN, $52,750. To collect and organize papers and documents related to administration of Governor Lamar Alexander and to make this information accessible to researchers. 1987.
Center City Corporation, Chattanooga, TN, $500,000. For construction costs of Miller Plaza in downtown Chattanooga. 1987.
Center City Corporation, Chattanooga, TN, $60,000. For operating costs of Miller Plaza which entails leasing retail space, planning programs for stage, and overseeing use of pavilion. 1987.
Chattanooga Ballet, Chattanooga, TN, $30,000. For general support. 1987.
Chattanooga Nature Center, Chattanooga, TN, $50,000. To enable teachers of natural sciences to participate in training programs at Yellowstone National Park, barrier islands of Georgia, and in Mount Saint Helen's region in summers. 1987.
Chattanooga Nature Center, Chattanooga, TN, $15,000. For consultant services to Nature Center and Reflection Riding to investigate potential of cooperative capital campaign. 1987.
Chattanooga Regional History Museum, Chattanooga, TN, $75,000. To design and build exhibits highlighting five major periods of Chattanooga's history. 1987.
Chattanooga Regional History Museum, Chattanooga, TN, $34,800. For second phase of two-year planning program which supported research and exhibit development for Chattanooga's museum of local history. 1987.
Chattanooga Symphony and Opera Association, Chattanooga, TN, $143,500. For core orchestra which has created 24 full-time positions. 1987.
Chattanooga Symphony and Opera Association, Chattanooga, TN, $5,000. To conduct pre-concert lectures to help audience better understand and appreciate historical and cultural context of music being performed. 1987.
Chattanooga, City of, Chattanooga, TN, $320,000. For renovation and expansion of Tivoli Theater and creation of adjacent Tivoli Center, new cultural complex in downtown Chattanooga. 1987.
Chattanooga, City of, Human Services Department, Chattanooga, TN, $30,000. For second-year support for program initiated by Chattanooga Head Start, using Wolf Trap training in both public and private day care centers. Through this program, both local artists and early childhood educators are trained in effective ways to use arts with preschoolers. 1987.
Childrens Literature for Children, Atlanta, GA, $5,000. For organization that is dedicated to teaching children to read books. The model, which originated at The Westminster Schools, is being applied at two of Atlanta's inner-city schools. 1987.
Duke University, Durham, NC, $5,000. For Duke University and the University of North Carolina at Chapel Hill to conduct semester-long seminar to bring together faculty from both universities to discuss planning Center for Documentary Studies. 1987.
Friends of the Festival, Chattanooga, TN, $75,000. To conduct comprehensive evaluation of Riverbend Festival to determine its strengths, weaknesses and options for future. 1987.
Friends of the Festival, Chattanooga, TN, $20,000. For general support for Riverbend

Festival, week-long series of events in sports, arts and music. 1987.
Little Theater, Chattanooga, TN, $44,000. For marketing outreach project. 1987.
New York Center for Visual History, NYC, NY, $5,000. For production of Voices and Visions, thirteen-part series on American poetry which is targeted toward high school students throughout nation. 1987.
South Carolina Arts Commission, Columbia, SC, $5,000. For project Carolina Connections: A Festival for Writers and Readers, which will bring together writers and readers at festival, conference and book fair. 1987.
Southeastern Center for Contemporary Art, Winston-Salem, NC, $50,000. For development of The Next Generation, exhibit which identifies, celebrates and promotes understanding of works of emerging black artists. 1987.
University of Tennessee, School of Architecture, Knoxville, TN, $36,000. For continued support of urban design consultant for Chattanooga. 1987.

2930
R. J. Maclellan Charitable Trust
Provident Bldg.
Chattanooga 37402 (615) 755-1291

Trust established in 1954 in TN.
Donor(s): Robert J. Maclellan.†
Financial data (yr. ended 12/31/87): Assets, $39,002,645 (M); expenditures, $2,931,666, including $2,861,453 for 66 grants (high: $1,294,230; low: $932; average: $5,000-$50,000).
Purpose and activities: Giving for higher and theological education, social service and youth agencies, Protestant religious associations, and cultural programs.
Types of support: Continuing support, annual campaigns, seed money, building funds, equipment, matching funds, scholarship funds, operating budgets.
Limitations: Giving primarily in the Chattanooga, TN, area. No grants to individuals, or for emergency funds, deficit financing, land acquisition, renovations, endowment funds, special projects, research, publications, or conferences; no loans.
Application information:
Initial approach: Letter
Copies of proposal: 1
Deadline(s): 3 weeks before board meetings
Board meeting date(s): 10 times annually
Final notification: 1 week after meeting
Write: Hugh O. Maclellan, Sr., Chair.
Trustees: Hugh O. Maclellan, Sr., Chair.; Dudley Porter, Jr., American National Bank & Trust Co. of Chattanooga.
Number of staff: 1 full-time professional; 1 full-time support.
Employer Identification Number: 626037023

2931
Magic Chef Foundation, Inc.
740 King Edward Ave., S.E.
Cleveland 37311

Established in 1984 in TN.
Donor(s): Magic Chef Industries.
Financial data (yr. ended 6/30/87): Assets, $2,148,483 (M); gifts received, $600,000; expenditures, $406,621, including $402,900 for 19 grants (high: $100,000; low: $1,000).
Purpose and activities: Giving primarily for higher education, social services, with an emphasis of child welfare and youth organizations, and the arts.
Limitations: Giving primarily in TN. No grants to individuals.
Application information: Contributes only to preselected organizations. Applications not accepted.
Officers and Directors:* S.B. Rymer, Jr.,* Pres.; D.J. Krumm,* V.P.; Donald C. Byers, Secy.; Jerry Schiller,* Treas.
Employer Identification Number: 626047469

2932
Massengill-DeFriece Foundation, Inc.
Holston Plaza, Suite 208
516 Holston Ave.
Bristol 37620 (615) 764-3833

Incorporated in 1949 in TN.
Donor(s): Frank W. DeFriece,† Pauline M. DeFriece,† Frank W. DeFriece, Jr.
Financial data (yr. ended 12/31/86): Assets, $3,561,174 (M); expenditures, $190,540, including $160,000 for 13 grants (high: $60,000; low: $500; average: $12,000).
Purpose and activities: Support for private higher education, museums, health, youth, and religion.
Types of support: Continuing support, annual campaigns, emergency funds, equipment, matching funds, capital campaigns, endowment funds, operating budgets, professorships, special projects.
Limitations: Giving primarily in the Bristol, TN, and Bristol, VA, areas. No grants to individuals, or for special projects, research, publications, or conferences; no loans.
Application information:
Initial approach: Letter
Copies of proposal: 1
Board meeting date(s): Usually quarterly
Final notification: 2 to 4 months
Write: Frank W. DeFriece, Jr., V.P.
Officers and Directors: Albert S. Kelly, Jr., Pres.; Frank W. DeFriece, Jr., V.P.; Josephine D. Wilson, V.P.; John C. Paty, Jr., Secy.-Treas.; Mark W. DeFriece, Paul E. DeFriece, C. Richard Hagerstrom, Jr.
Number of staff: 1 part-time support.
Employer Identification Number: 626044873

2933
Jack C. Massey Foundation
310 25th Ave. N., Suite 109
Nashville 37203

Trust established in 1966 in TN.
Donor(s): Jack C. Massey.
Financial data (yr. ended 12/31/86): Assets, $6,063,882 (M); expenditures, $961,737, including $877,481 for 191 grants (high: $200,000; low: $50).
Purpose and activities: Emphasis on higher and secondary education and medical research; grants also for cultural programs.
Types of support: Research.
Limitations: Giving primarily in TN.
Application information: Contributes only to pre-selected organizations. Applications not accepted.
Write: Jack C. Massey, Trustee
Officers: Omega C. Sattler, Secy.; Clarence Edmonds,* Treas.
Trustees:* Barbara M. Clark, Jack C. Massey, J. Brad Reed.
Employer Identification Number: 626065672

2934
The Memphis-Plough Community Foundation
c/o Community Foundation of Greater Memphis
1755 Lynnfield Rd., Suite 285
Memphis 38119 (901) 761-3806

Community foundation incorporated in 1969 in TN.
Financial data (yr. ended 4/30/88): Assets, $18,995,502 (M); gifts received, $3,323,271; expenditures, $3,181,733, including $2,851,607 for 328 grants (high: $150,000; low: $50; average: $100-$200,000).
Purpose and activities: Support for education, social services, religion, health, the arts, and science.
Types of support: Seed money, program-related investments.
Limitations: Giving limited to Memphis and Shelby County, western TN, northern MS, and the surrounding vicinity. No grants to individuals, or for operating budgets, continuing support, capital or building funds, annual campaigns, emergency funds, deficit financing, endowment funds, matching gifts, scholarships, fellowships, or research; no loans.
Publications: Annual report (including application guidelines), newsletter, informational brochure, program policy statement (including application guidelines), application guidelines.
Application information: Application form required.
Initial approach: Letter or telephone
Copies of proposal: 10
Deadline(s): May 15 and Nov. 15 (unrestricted)
Board meeting date(s): Unrestricted fund grant requests reviewed in June and Dec.; donor grant recommendations reviewed in Mar., June, Sept., and Dec.
Final notification: 1 month after deadline
Write: Lisa Bell, Prog. Officer
Officers and Governors:* James D. Witherington,* Chair.; Mrs. Harry J. Phillips,* Vice-Chair.; John K. Fockler,* Pres.; Donn Southern, Secy.; Willis H. Willey III,* Treas.; Lisa Bell, Prog. and Communications Officer; and 23 additional governors.
Agency Banks: Commerce Union Bank, Commercial and Industrial Bank, First American Bank, First Tennessee Bank, National Bank of Commerce, Union Planters National Bank.
Number of staff: 5 full-time professional; 2 full-time support; 2 part-time support.
Employer Identification Number: 237047899

2935
The Justin and Valere Potter Foundation
c/o Sovran Bank/Central South
One Commerce Place
Nashville 37219 (615) 749-3336

Trust established in 1951 in TN.
$17,559,527 (M); expenditures, $1,614,629, including $1,477,300 for 33 grants (high: $250,000; low: $5,000; average: $10,000-$75,000).
Purpose and activities: Giving primarily for higher education, including scholarship funds and medical education; support also for cultural programs, social services, and medical research.
Types of support: Scholarship funds, operating budgets, special projects, research.
Limitations: Giving primarily in Nashville, TN.
Application information:
Initial approach: Letter
Deadline(s): None
Board meeting date(s): As needed
Write: M. Kirk Scobey, Sr. V.P. & Trust Officer, Sovran Bank/Central South
Distribution Committee: Justin P. Wilson, Chair.; Albert L. Menefee, Jr., David K. Wilson.
Trustee: Sovran Bank/Central South.
Number of staff: None.
Employer Identification Number: 626033081

2936
Provident Life and Accident Insurance Corporate Giving Program
Fountain Square
Chattanooga 37402 (615) 755-8996

Purpose and activities: Support for education, public broadcasting, medical research, and health care, programs to help minorities, culture and the arts, and civic and community concerns.
Types of support: Employee matching gifts, capital campaigns, endowment funds, general purposes, special projects, scholarship funds.
Limitations: Giving primarily in headquarters city, headquarters state and major operating locations. No grants to individuals, or for operating funds for colleges and universities.
Application information:
Initial approach: Letter of inquiry
Deadline(s): Early fall preferred for receiving applications but will be accepted throughout the year
Board meeting date(s): Meets approximately every 3 months
Write: Jim Steele, Treas., Provident Life and Accident Insurance Co., and Secy., Contrib. Comm.

2937
The William B. Stokely, Jr. Foundation
620 Campbell Station Rd.
Station West, Suite Y
Knoxville 37922 (615) 966-4878

Incorporated in 1951 in IN.
Donor(s): William B. Stokely, Jr.†
Financial data (yr. ended 12/31/87): Assets, $7,500,000 (M); expenditures, $443,704, including $402,738 for grants.
Purpose and activities: Emphasis on higher education; some support also for hospitals, health agencies, and cultural programs.
Limitations: Giving primarily in the east TN area. No grants to individuals.
Application information:
Initial approach: Letter or proposal
Copies of proposal: 1
Deadline(s): Submit proposal preferably in the fall
Board meeting date(s): Feb., May, Aug., and Nov.
Write: William B. Stokely III, Pres.
Officers: William B. Stokely III,* Pres.; Kay H. Stokely,* Exec. V.P.; Andrea A. White-Randall, V.P.
Directors:* Mrs. Horace Burnett, William B. Stokely IV.
Number of staff: 1 full-time professional.
Employer Identification Number: 356016402

2938
Werthan Foundation
P.O. Box 1310
Nashville 37202 (615) 259-9331

Trust established in 1945 in TN.
Donor(s): Werthan Bag Corp., Bernard Werthan, Albert Werthan, Werthan Industries, Inc.
Financial data (yr. ended 11/30/86): Assets, $5,734,523 (M); gifts received, $180,801; expenditures, $464,419, including $391,505 for 72 grants (high: $90,000; low: $100; average: $5,000).
Purpose and activities: Emphasis on Jewish welfare funds, higher education, and a community fund; support also for cultural programs.
Limitations: Giving primarily in TN.
Application information:
Initial approach: Letter
Deadline(s): None
Board meeting date(s): June
Write: Albert Werthan, Chair.
Officers and Trustees: Albert Werthan, Chair.; Bernard Werthan, Jr., Secy.; Herbert M. Shayne, Treas.; Morris Werthan II, Werthan Industries, Inc.
Number of staff: None.
Employer Identification Number: 626036283

2939
Woods-Greer Foundation
c/o American National Bank and Trust Co., Trust Dept.
736 Market St., P.O. Box 1638
Chattanooga 37401 (615) 757-3203

Established in 1976.
Donor(s): C. Cecil Woods.†
Financial data (yr. ended 5/31/88): Assets, $1,702,269 (M); expenditures, $100,636, including $85,000 for 15 grants (high: $25,000; low: $500; average: $1,000-$5,000).
Purpose and activities: Giving mainly for higher education, Christian religious organizations, and the arts.
Types of support: Operating budgets, continuing support, annual campaigns, building funds, equipment, publications, scholarship funds, matching funds.
Limitations: Giving primarily in the southeastern U.S. No grants to individuals; no loans.
Application information: Applications not accepted.
Initial approach: Proposal
Copies of proposal: 1
Deadline(s): Submit proposal preferably in Apr. or May; no set deadline
Board meeting date(s): July
Write: Peter T. Cooper, Secy.-Treas.
Officers: The Very Rev. C. Cecil Woods, Jr., Chair.; Marie Cartinhour Woods, Vice-Chair.; Peter T. Cooper, Secy.-Treas.
Trustees: William G. Brown, Ellen Woods Polansky, Kathleen Woods Van Devender, Margaret C. Woods-Denkler, Carolyn Taylor Woods.
Number of staff: None.
Employer Identification Number: 626126272

TEXAS

2940
Abell-Hanger Foundation
303 West Wall, Rm. 615
Midland 79701 (915) 684-6655
Mailing address: P.O. Box 430, Midland, TX 79702

Incorporated in 1954 in TX.
Donor(s): George T. Abell,† Gladys H. Abell.†
Financial data (yr. ended 6/30/88): Assets, $46,714,490 (M); expenditures, $3,923,482, including $3,228,498 for 91 grants (high: $600,000; low: $350; average: $20,000-$35,000).
Purpose and activities: Support primarily for higher education, youth activities, cultural programs, health services, the handicapped, and social welfare agencies.
Types of support: General purposes, operating budgets, continuing support, annual campaigns, seed money, building funds, endowment funds, matching funds, scholarship funds, research, equipment, capital campaigns, special projects.
Limitations: Giving limited to TX, preferably within the Permian Basin. No grants to individuals, or for individual scholarships or fellowships; no loans.
Publications: 990-PF, annual report (including application guidelines).
Application information: Application form required.
Initial approach: Request and complete application forms
Copies of proposal: 1
Deadline(s): Sept. 30, Jan. 31, and May 31
Board meeting date(s): Oct. 15, Feb. 15, and June 15
Final notification: 1 month

Write: David L. Smith, Mgr.
Officers: John P. Butler,* Pres.; James I. Trott,* V.P.; Lester Van Pelt, Jr., Secy.-Treas.; David L. Smith, Mgr.
Trustees:* Robert L. Leibrock, John F. Younger.
Number of staff: 1 full-time professional; 2 part-time professional; 1 full-time support; 1 part-time support.
Employer Identification Number: 756020781
Recent arts and culture grants:
Ballet Midland, Midland, TX, $15,000. For general operating support. 1987.
Midland Arts Assembly, Midland, TX, $8,000. For general operating support. 1987.
Midland Independent School District, Midland, TX, $65,000. For high school band programs and alternative school. 1987.
Midland Symphony and Chorale Association, Midland, TX, $35,000. For general operating support. 1987.
Petroleum Museum, Midland, TX, $200,000. For general operating support. 1987.
Texas Association of Museums, Austin, TX, $5,500. For annual conference. 1987.

2941
The J. S. Abercrombie Foundation
5005 Riverway, Suite 500
Houston 77056 (713) 627-2500

Trust established in 1950 in TX.
Donor(s): J.S. Abercrombie.†
Financial data (yr. ended 12/31/86): Assets, $9,608,935 (M); expenditures, $1,796,335, including $1,700,508 for 36 grants (high: $150,000; low: $500; average: $10,000-$100,000).
Purpose and activities: Giving primarily for medical and higher education and health; support also for social welfare and cultural programs.
Types of support: Operating budgets, building funds, research, special projects.
Limitations: Giving primarily in TX. No grants to individuals.
Application information:
Initial approach: Proposal
Copies of proposal: 1
Deadline(s): Submit proposal preferably in Apr. or Oct.; deadlines May 15 and Nov. 15
Board meeting date(s): June and Dec.
Final notification: 4 to 6 weeks after meetings for positive responses
Write: Thomas M. Weaver, Mgr.
Officers: Josephine E. Abercrombie,* Pres.; Seth A. McMeans, Secy.; John B. Howenstine,* Treas.
Trustees:* Edwina Gregg, George A. Robinson, Jamie A. Robinson.
Number of staff: None.
Employer Identification Number: 746048281

2942
Community Foundation of Abilene
402 Cypress, Suite 708
P.O. Box 1001
Abilene 79604 (915) 676-3883

Incorporated in 1985 in TX.
Financial data (yr. ended 6/30/88): Assets, $3,296,135 (M); gifts received, $2,510,988; expenditures, $1,066,025, including $925,812 for 60 grants (high: $300,000; low: $25; average: $2,000-$8,000) and $38,990 for foundation-administered programs.
Purpose and activities: Support for social services, health organizations, education, and civic affairs.
Types of support: Annual campaigns, building funds, conferences and seminars, consulting services, emergency funds, equipment, land acquisition, matching funds, operating budgets, program-related investments, publications, renovation projects, research, scholarship funds, fellowships, seed money, technical assistance.
Limitations: Giving primarily in the Abilene, TX, area. No grants for continuing support, deficit financing, employee matching gifts, endowment funds, or program-related investments; no loans.
Application information:
Initial approach: Letter
Write: Nancy E. Dark, Exec. Dir.
Officer: Nancy E. Dark, Exec. Dir.
Trustees: Joe Canon, Chair.; Tucker S. Bridwell, Vice-Chair.; Lawrence E. Gill, Secy.; G. Philip Morehead, Treas.; Dr. Jesse C. Fletcher, and 10 additional trustees.
Number of staff: 1 full-time professional; 1 full-time support.
Employer Identification Number: 752045832

2943
The Allbritton Foundation
5615 Kirby Dr., Suite 310
Houston 77005

Established in 1958 in TX.
Donor(s): Joe L. Allbritton, Perpetual Corp., and others.
Financial data (yr. ended 11/30/86): Assets, $2,976 (M); gifts received, $816,000; expenditures, $814,645, including $813,000 for 10 grants (high: $500,000; low: $500).
Purpose and activities: Grants mainly for Christian religious organizations, education, and cultural programs.
Types of support: Building funds, capital campaigns, continuing support, endowment funds, fellowships, general purposes, professorships, scholarship funds.
Publications: Annual report.
Officers: Joe L. Allbritton,* Pres.; Barbara B. Allbritton,* V.P.; Virginia L. White, Secy.-Treas.
Trustees:* Lawrence I. Hebert, Stephen A. Massey, Thomas W. Wren.
Number of staff: 1 part-time support.
Employer Identification Number: 746051876

2944
Amarillo Area Foundation, Inc.
700 First National Place
801 South Fillmore
Amarillo 79101 (806) 376-4521

Community foundation established as a trust in 1957 in TX.
Financial data (yr. ended 12/31/88): Assets, $18,266,372 (M); gifts received, $1,538,578; expenditures, $2,368,319, including $2,076,639 for 63 grants (high: $744,500; low: $74; average: $10,000-$20,000).
Purpose and activities: Support for community development, including education, arts and cultural programs, and health organizations, especially a medical center.
Types of support: Seed money, emergency funds, building funds, equipment, land acquisition, matching funds, consulting services, technical assistance, scholarship funds, special projects, research, student aid.
Limitations: Giving primarily in 26 most northern counties of TX Panhandle. No grants to individuals (except for limited scholarships from designated funds), or for operating budgets, annual campaigns, deficit financing, endowment funds, publications, or conferences; no loans.
Publications: Annual report, application guidelines.
Application information: Application form required.
Initial approach: Letter or telephone
Copies of proposal: 1
Deadline(s): Semi-monthly
Board meeting date(s): Quarterly; executive committee meets semi-monthly
Write: Jim Allison, Exec. Dir.
Officers and Directors: John Stiff,* Pres.; Betty Cooper,* 1st V.P.; Tom Patterson,* 2nd V.P.; Dr. John Bridwell,* Secy.; Don Patterson, Treas.; and 21 other directors.
Number of staff: 3 full-time professional.
Employer Identification Number: 750978220
Recent arts and culture grants:
Amarillo Art Center, Amarillo, TX, $78,740. 1987.
Carson County Square House Museum, Panhandle, TX, $10,119. 1987.
Don Harrington Discovery Center, Amarillo, TX, $276,473. 1987.

2945
American Airlines Contributions Committee
Box 619616, M.D. 3D24
Dallas 75261-9616 (817) 355-3545

Purpose and activities: Support for the arts and culture, including fine arts, performing arts, and theater and hospitals; also, in-kind support.
Types of support: Annual campaigns, conferences and seminars, employee matching gifts, special projects, in-kind gifts.
Limitations: Giving primarily in cities in the U.S. that are served by American Airlines.
Application information:
Initial approach: Need request in writing
Copies of proposal: 1
Write: Barbara Schreffler, Admin.
Number of staff: 1 full-time professional.

2946
American Petrofina Foundation
8350 North Central Expy.
Dallas 75206 (214) 750-2400
Application address: P.O. Box 2159, Dallas, TX 75221

Incorporated in 1974 in TX.
Donor(s): American Petrofina, Inc.
Financial data (yr. ended 6/30/88): Assets, $2,500,000 (M); expenditures, $267,712, including $242,000 for 91 grants.

Purpose and activities: Giving to non-profit organizations; interests include health, community funds, cultural programs, education, and civic affairs.
Types of support: Continuing support, annual campaigns, seed money, emergency funds, building funds, equipment, research, scholarship funds, employee matching gifts, matching funds.
Limitations: Giving primarily in TX. No grants to individuals.
Application information: Proposal should include information on background and purpose of organization.
Initial approach: Proposal
Copies of proposal: 1
Deadline(s): None
Board meeting date(s): Approximately once per calendar quarter
Final notification: Affirmative only
Write: M. Leon Oliver, V.P.
Officers and Directors: Ronald W. Haddock, Pres.; Brendan O'Connor, V.P. and Treas.; M. Leon Oliver, V.P.; Kenneth W. Perry, V.P.; William W. Phelps, V.P.; Glenn E. Selvidge, V.P.
Employer Identification Number: 237391423

2947
Josephine Anderson Charitable Trust
P.O. Box 8
Amarillo 79105 (806) 376-7873

Trust established in TX.
Donor(s): Josephine Anderson.†
Financial data (yr. ended 2/29/88): Assets, $4,692,537 (M); expenditures, $378,984, including $193,300 for 41 grants (high: $20,000; low: $300).
Purpose and activities: Emphasis on health associations, social services and youth agencies, cultural programs, churches, and education.
Limitations: Giving primarily in Amarillo, TX. No grants to individuals.
Application information:
Deadline(s): None
Write: L.A. White or Imadell Carter
Officers and Trustees: L.A. White, Managing Trustee; Imadell Carter, Secy.
Employer Identification Number: 751469596

2948
The Dene Anton Foundation
(Formerly The Judge Roy and Dene Hofheinz Trust)
c/o NCNB Texas, Trust Dept.
P.O. Box 2518
Houston 77001 (713) 652-6526

Established in 1984 in TX.
Donor(s): Roy M. Hofheinz Charitable Foundation.
Financial data (yr. ended 9/30/88): Assets, $1,603,748 (M); expenditures, $885,955, including $869,820 for 28 grants (high: $237,750; low: $100).
Purpose and activities: Support primarily for music organizations, medical research, and general charitable giving.
Types of support: Operating budgets, program-related investments.
Limitations: Giving primarily in CA. No grants to individuals.
Application information:
Initial approach: Letter
Deadline(s): None
Write: Mrs. Dene Hofheinz Anton, Trustee
Trustees: Dene Hofheinz Anton, NCNB Texas.
Employer Identification Number: 760093912

2949
The Armstrong Foundation
(Formerly The Texas Educational Association)
P.O. Box 470338
Fort Worth 76147-0338 (817) 737-7251
Application address: P.O. Drawer 2299, Matchez, MS 39120

Incorporated in 1949 in TX.
Donor(s): George W. Armstrong, Sr.†
Financial data (yr. ended 12/31/87): Assets, $9,155,664 (M); expenditures, $595,500, including $434,258 for 94 grants (high: $45,000; low: $100).
Purpose and activities: To support educational undertakings "through financial assistance to schools, colleges, universities and other educational mediums advocating the perpetuation of constitutional government." Grants only for educational programs on American ideals and traditional values; support also for youth agencies, cultural programs and religious activities.
Types of support: Conferences and seminars, internships, publications, research, general purposes.
Limitations: Giving primarily in TX. No grants to individuals, or for capital or endowment funds, or operating budgets; no loans.
Publications: Application guidelines.
Application information:
Initial approach: Proposal
Copies of proposal: 1
Deadline(s): None
Board meeting date(s): Mar., June, Sept., and Dec.
Final notification: 2 months
Write: Thomas K. Armstrong, Pres.
Officers: Thomas K. Armstrong, Pres.; John H. James, V.P. and Treas.; Thomas K. Armstrong, Jr., V.P.; J. Hatcher James III, V.P.; Laura J. Harrison, Secy.
Number of staff: 3 part-time professional; 1 full-time support; 1 part-time support.
Employer Identification Number: 756003209

2950
Joe & Wilhelmina Barnhart Foundation
5620 Greenbriar
Houston 77005

Established in 1967 in TX.
Donor(s): Joseph M. Barnhart, Robert J. Barnhart, Wilhelmina B. Traylor.
Financial data (yr. ended 12/31/87): Assets, $1,001,152 (M); gifts received, $100,000; expenditures, $59,000, including $45,020 for 19 grants (high: $30,000; low: $25).
Purpose and activities: Support for an elementary school; giving also to community arts and cultural institutions, a college and a children's hospital.
Limitations: Giving primarily in Beeville and Houston, TX.
Application information: Contributes only to pre-selected organizations. Applications not accepted.
Trustees: Walter S. Baker, Jr., Joseph M. Barnhart, Robert J. Barnhart, Robert Leslie, Bland McReynolds, Margaret Price, Wilhelmina B. Traylor.
Employer Identification Number: 746088946

2951
Bass Foundation
309 Main St.
Fort Worth 76102 (817) 336-0494

Established in 1945 in TX.
Donor(s): Perry R. Bass, Lee Bass, Edward Bass, Sid Richardson Carbon and Gasoline Co., Perry R. Bass, Inc.
Financial data (yr. ended 12/31/88): Assets, $300).
Purpose and activities: Giving primarily for the arts and cultural institutions; some support for conservation.
Types of support: General purposes.
Publications: 990-PF.
Application information: Applications not accepted.
Write: Valleau Wilkie, Jr.
Officers and Directors: Perry R. Bass, Pres.; Nancy Lee Bass, V.P.; Shaye Arnold, Secy.-Treas.
Number of staff: 1 part-time professional.
Employer Identification Number: 756033983

2952
The Bass Foundation
4224 Thanksgiving Tower
Dallas 75201 (214) 754-7190

Trust established in 1945 in TX; in 1983, foundation split up into Bass Foundation and Harry Bass Foundation.
Donor(s): Harry W. Bass, Sr., Mrs. Harry W. Bass, Sr.
Financial data (yr. ended 12/31/86): Assets, $2,465,542 (M); expenditures, $112,067, including $112,000 for 19 grants (high: $50,000; low: $100; average: $200-$10,000).
Purpose and activities: Support for cultural programs, education, and hospitals.
Types of support: Building funds, general purposes.
Limitations: Giving primarily in the Dallas, TX, metropolitan area, and the Salt Lake City, UT, area.
Application information:
Initial approach: Proposal
Deadline(s): None
Board meeting date(s): As required
Write: Richard D. Bass
Trustees: Richard D. Bass, Thurman R. Taylor, Harry M. Wittingdon.
Number of staff: None.
Employer Identification Number: 756013540

2953
Sarah Campbell Blaffer Foundation
913 River Oaks Bank & Trust Bldg.
2001 Kirby Dr.
Houston 77019 (713) 528-5279

Incorporated in 1964 in TX.
Donor(s): Sarah C. Blaffer.†
Financial data (yr. ended 12/31/87): Assets, $30,763,150 (M); gifts received, $1,885,951; expenditures, $724,486, including $90,000 for 6 grants (high: $25,000; low: $5,000) and $205,489 for foundation-administered programs.
Purpose and activities: A private operating foundation that awards grants for cultural programs, church support, and secondary and higher education; also operates a program of art exhibits.
Limitations: Giving primarily in TX. No grants to individuals, or for endowment funds, scholarships, or fellowships; no loans.
Application information:
Initial approach: Letter
Copies of proposal: 1
Deadline(s): Submit proposal from Jan. through Aug.; deadline Sept. 30
Board meeting date(s): Mar. and Oct.
Write: Edward Joseph Hudson, Jr., Secy.
Officers and Trustees: Charles W. Hall, Pres.; Jane Blaffer Owen, V.P. and Treas.; Cecil Blaffer von Furstenberg, V.P.; Edward Joseph Hudson, Jr., Secy.; Gilbert M. Denman, Jr.
Employer Identification Number: 746065234

2954
J. B. & Margaret Blaugrund Foundation
918 First City National Bank
El Paso 79901

Established in 1958 in TX.
Financial data (yr. ended 7/31/87): Assets, $1,243,170 (M); expenditures, $53,993, including $48,250 for grants (high: $5,000; low: $250).
Purpose and activities: Giving primarily for the United Jewish Appeal and other Jewish welfare organizations; support also for cultural programs, social service and youth agencies, and health associations and hospitals.
Limitations: No support for individuals.
Application information: Contributes only to pre-selected organizations. Applications not accepted.
Write: Ann B. Marks, Pres.
Officers: Ann B. Marks, Pres.; Maurice J. Blauguard, V.P.; J. Alan Marks, Secy.-Treas.
Number of staff: None.
Employer Identification Number: 746040400

2955
The Mr. & Mrs. Joe W. Bratcher, Jr. Foundation
c/o H. David Hughes
1300 One Republic Plaza, 333 Guadalupe St.
Austin 78701

Established in 1985 in TX.
Donor(s): Joe W. Bratcher, Jr., Mrs. Joe W. Bratcher, Jr.
Financial data (yr. ended 12/31/87): Assets, $1,151,793 (M); gifts received, $50,000; expenditures, $78,231, including $72,750 for 7 grants (high: $25,000; low: $750).
Purpose and activities: Giving primarily for a capital raising fund for a hospital; support also for the performing arts and animal welfare.
Limitations: No grants to individuals.
Application information:
Initial approach: Letter
Deadline(s): Sept. 30
Write: Joe W. Bratcher, Jr., Pres.
Officers: Joe W. Bratcher, Jr., Pres.; Rhobie K. Bratcher, Secy.
Director: Joe W. Bratcher III.
Employer Identification Number: 742387803

2956
B. C. & Addie Brookshire Kleberg County Charitable Foundation
c/o Texas Commerce Bank-Corpus Christi, Trust Dept.
P.O. Drawer 749
Corpus Christi 78403 (512) 883-3621

Established in 1958.
Financial data (yr. ended 6/30/88): Assets, $1,143,409 (M); expenditures, $82,813, including $71,894 for 17 grants (high: $12,500; low: $500).
Purpose and activities: Giving for youth recreation agencies, community centers, education, and cultural programs.
Types of support: Building funds, equipment, renovation projects, scholarship funds, special projects.
Limitations: Giving primarily in Kleberg County, TX.
Application information:
Deadline(s): None
Write: Carly M. Ivy
Trustee: Texas Commerce Bank-Corpus Christi.
Employer Identification Number: 746108397

2957
The Brown Foundation, Inc.
2118 Welch Ave.
P.O. Box 130646
Houston 77219 (713) 523-6867

Incorporated in 1951 in TX.
Donor(s): Herman Brown,† Margarett Root Brown,† George R. Brown,† Alice Pratt Brown.†
Financial data (yr. ended 6/30/88): Assets, $357,596,290 (M); gifts received, $3,820; expenditures, $19,563,915, including $16,740,135 for 178 grants (high: $2,621,057; low: $800) and $43,365 for 27 employee matching gifts.
Purpose and activities: Support principally for the arts and education.
Types of support: Operating budgets, continuing support, annual campaigns, seed money, building funds, equipment, land acquisition, endowment funds, matching funds, professorships, fellowships, special projects, research, publications, capital campaigns, renovation projects.
Limitations: Giving primarily in TX, with emphasis on Houston. No grants to individuals; no loans.
Publications: Application guidelines.
Application information:
Initial approach: Proposal
Copies of proposal: 1
Deadline(s): None
Board meeting date(s): Feb., June, and Oct.
Final notification: 3 months
Write: Katherine B. Dobelman, Exec. Dir.
Officers: Maconda Brown O'Connor,* Chair.; Isabel Brown Wilson,* Pres.; C.M. Hudspeth,* V.P.; M.S. Stude,* V.P.; Nancy Brown Wellin,* V.P.; Louisa Stude Sarofim,* Secy.; Katherine B. Dobelman, Treas. and Exec. Dir.
Trustees:* Nancy O'Connor Abendshein, Walter Negley, Thomas I. O'Connor, James R. Paden.
Number of staff: 1 full-time professional; 6 full-time support.
Employer Identification Number: 746036466
Recent arts and culture grants:
Alley Theater, Houston, TX, $100,000. To establish New Plays Production Fund. 1988.
American Associates of the Royal Academy Trust, NYC, NY, $50,000. For exhibitions in U.S.. 1988.
Archives of American Art of the Smithsonian Institution, NYC, NY, $150,000. For purchase of Pach Collection. 1988.
Archives of American Art of the Smithsonian Institution, NYC, NY, $70,000. For general operating fund. 1988.
Arkansas Arts Center Foundation, Little Rock, AR, $10,000. For general operations. 1988.
Armand Bayou Nature Center, Houston, TX, $10,000. Toward general operating fund. 1988.
Asia Society/Houston, Houston, TX, $5,000. For education series. 1988.
Childrens Museum of Houston, Houston, TX, $25,000. For Kidtechnics exhibit. 1988.
Cleveland Institute of Art, Cleveland, OH, $250,000. For scholarship and faculty endowment. 1988.
Contemporary Art in San Antonio, San Antonio, TX, $10,000. For Blue Star Art Space Exhibition schedule. 1988.
Contemporary Arts Association of Houston, Houston, TX, $100,000. For establishment of operating endowment. 1988.
Contemporary Arts Association of Houston, Houston, TX, $75,000. For exhibtion fund. 1988.
Contemporary Arts Association of Houston, Houston, TX, $20,000. Toward 87-88 annual program fund campaign. 1988.
Corpus Christi Aquarium Association, Corpus Christi, TX, $600,000. For capital fund and construction drive. 1988.
Diverse Works, Houston, TX, $25,000. Toward general operations. 1988.
Farrell Dyde Dance Theater, Houston, TX, $35,000. For 1987-88 season. 1988.
Friends of Art and Preservation in Embassies, DC, $25,000. For general operations. 1988.
Georges Pompidou Art and Cultural Foundation, Houston, TX, $10,000. For general operations. 1988.
Hamilton College, Clinton, NY, $190,000. For matching grant for music center construction cost. 1988.
Houston Adventure Play Association, Houston, TX, $50,230. Toward expenses. 1988.
Houston Ballet Foundation, Houston, TX, $1,000,000. For matching grant toward endowment drive. 1988.

Houston Ballet Foundation, Houston, TX, $140,000. For support. 1988.
Houston Foto Fest, Houston, TX, $25,000. Toward general operating fund. 1988.
Houston Grand Opera Association, Houston, TX, $1,000,000. For matching grant for Wortham Move, new works and endowment. 1988.
Houston Grand Opera Association, Houston, TX, $100,000. Toward endowment campaign. 1988.
Houston Grand Opera Association, Houston, TX, $30,000. Toward general operating fund. 1988.
Houston Museum of Natural Science, Houston, TX, $250,000. To purchase Imax projection system. 1988.
Houston Museum of Natural Science, Houston, TX, $10,000. Toward annual fund for 1987. 1988.
Houston Parks Board, Houston, TX, $15,000. Toward renovation of Hildago Park. 1988.
Houston Parks Board, Houston, TX, $15,000. Toward Westchase Park Project. 1988.
Houston Parks Board, Houston, TX, $5,000. For Sparks Program. 1988.
Houston Symphony Society, Houston, TX, $141,000. For general operating fund. 1988.
Institute for Humanities at Salado, Salado, TX, $15,000. Toward program development and books. 1988.
International Council on Monuments and Sites, DC, $200,000. For restoration project. 1988.
James Dick Foundation for the Performing Arts, Round Top, TX, $5,000. For student scholarship. 1988.
John F. Kennedy Center for the Performing Arts, DC, $25,000. For new American plays. 1988.
Junior League of Corpus Christi, Corpus Christi, TX, $10,000. Toward concert expenses. 1988.
Lacoste School of Arts in France, Bloomsbury, NJ, $25,000. Toward general operating support. 1988.
Metropolitan Museum of Art, NYC, NY, $333,000. To fund decorative arts gallery. 1988.
Metropolitan Museum of Art, NYC, NY, $25,000. For general operations. 1988.
Mid-America Arts Alliance, Kansas City, MO, $5,000. For Reaching Rural Audiences Project. 1988.
Museum of Fine Arts of Houston, Houston, TX, $1,615,000. To extend matching grant 10 years. 1988.
Museum of Fine Arts of Houston, Houston, TX, $112,000. Toward museum support. 1988.
Museum of Fine Arts of Houston, Houston, TX, $52,500. For Shartle Symposium. 1988.
Museum of Fine Arts of Houston, Houston, TX, $15,000. For support of symposium. 1988.
National Trust for Historic Preservation, DC, $100,000. Toward preservation of Lindhurst Estate. 1988.
National Trust for Historic Preservation, DC, $25,000. For general operations. 1988.
Pacific Tropical Botanical Garden, Lawai, HI, $10,000. For water management and irrigation project. 1988.
San Antonio Art Institute, San Antonio, TX, $200,000. For cost of college and auditorium. 1988.
San Antonio Art Institute, San Antonio, TX, $6,000. For matching grant for landscaping and general operating fund. 1988.
School of American Ballet, NYC, NY, $140,000. To endow distinguished senior faculty chair. 1988.
Skowhegan School of Painting and Sculpture, NYC, NY, $60,000. Toward general operating fund. 1988.
Skowhegan School of Painting and Sculpture, NYC, NY, $10,000. Toward endowment for scholarship fund. 1988.
Skowhegan School of Painting and Sculpture, NYC, NY, $5,000. For general operating fund. 1988.
Society for the Performing Arts, Houston, TX, $10,000. Toward general operating fund. 1988.
Solomon R. Guggenheim Foundation, NYC, NY, $20,000. Toward works and process program. 1988.
Stages, Houston, TX, $50,000. To augment acting company salaries. 1988.
Texas Composers Forum, Dallas, TX, $9,000. Toward Meet the Composer grant program. 1988.
Texas Institute for Arts in Education, Houston, TX, $50,000. For teacher training program. 1988.
Texas State Historical Association, Austin, TX, $250,000. For support of research. 1988.
Theater Under the Stars, Houston, TX, $5,000. For summer presentation. 1988.
University of Houston, Houston, TX, $10,000. For Shakespeare Festival operating fund. 1988.
University of Houston, Houston, TX, $5,000. For Children's Theater Festival. 1988.
Whitney Museum of American Art, NYC, NY, $25,000. For general operations. 1988.

2958
William and Catherine Bryce Memorial Fund

c/o Texas American Bank/Fort Worth
P.O. Box 2050
Fort Worth 76113 (817) 884-4266

Trust established in 1944 in TX.
Financial data (yr. ended 9/30/88): Assets, $11,587,200 (M); expenditures, $621,124, including $537,250 for 25 grants (high: $50,000; low: $1,000).
Purpose and activities: Emphasis on child welfare, higher education, the aged, cultural programs, youth agencies, hospitals, and a community fund.
Limitations: Giving primarily in TX, particularly in the Fort Worth area. No grants to individuals.
Application information:
Initial approach: Letter
Copies of proposal: 1
Deadline(s): Sept. 30
Board meeting date(s): Nov.
Write: Kelly A. Bradshaw, Asst. V.P. and Trust Officer, Texas American Bank
Trustee: Texas American Bank/Fort Worth.
Employer Identification Number: 756013845

2959
Burlington Northern Foundation

3000 Continental Plaza
777 Main St.
Fort Worth 76102

Incorporated in 1953 in MN; renamed in 1970.
Donor(s): Burlington Northern, Inc.
Financial data (yr. ended 12/31/87): Assets, $20,853,733 (M); gifts received, $8,833,165; expenditures, $14,327,215, including $10,652,209 for 704 grants (high: $474,576; low: $50; average: $500-$50,000) and $470,288 for 280 employee matching gifts.
Purpose and activities: Grants primarily for higher education, cultural programs, community funds, social services, including American Red Cross, civic and recreation programs, and hospitals.
Types of support: Employee matching gifts, annual campaigns, building funds, equipment, general purposes.
Limitations: Giving primarily in areas of company operations, particularly Seattle, WA. No support for religious organizations for religious purposes, veterans' or fraternal organizations, national health organizations and programs, chambers of commerce, taxpayer associations, state railroad associations, and other bodies whose activities might benefit the company, or political organizations, campaigns, or candidates. No grants to individuals, or for operating budgets of hospitals, fundraising events, corporate memberships, endowment funds, scholarships, or fellowships; no loans.
Publications: Annual report, program policy statement, application guidelines.
Application information: Application form required.
Initial approach: Letter
Copies of proposal: 1
Deadline(s): None
Board meeting date(s): As required
Final notification: 4 to 5 months
Write: Don S. Snyder, V.P.
Officers: Christopher T. Bayley,* Chair.; Donald K. North,* Pres.; Don S. Snyder, V.P. and Controller; Danell I. Tobey, Treas.
Directors:* Ronald H. Reimann.
Trustees: Sanford C. Bernstein & Co., Inc., Ranier National Bank.
Number of staff: 1 full-time professional.
Employer Identification Number: 416022304
Recent arts and culture grants:
A Contemporary Theater, Seattle, WA, $10,000. 1987.
Allied Arts Council of the Yakima Valley, Yakima, WA, $5,000. 1987.
American Southwest Theater Company, Las Cruces, NM, $10,000. 1987.
Arizona Opera Company, Tucson, AZ, $5,000. 1987.
Arizona Theater Company, Tucson, AZ, $10,000. 1987.
Arlington Community Theater, Arlington, TX, $5,000. 1987.
Art Institute for the Permian Basin, Odessa, TX, $5,000. 1987.
Artreach, Denver, CO, $5,000. 1987.
Arts and Humanities Council of Tulsa, Tulsa, OK, $5,000. 1987.
Arts Council of Fort Worth and Tarrant County, Fort Worth, TX, $20,000. 1987.

Arts Council of Santa Clara County, San Jose, CA, $10,000. 1987.
Arvada Center for the Arts and Humanities, Arvada, CO, $5,000. 1987.
Asia Society, NYC, NY, $110,000. 1987.
Asia Society, NYC, NY, $25,000. 1987.
Asia Society, NYC, NY, $25,000. 1987.
Association of Collegiate Schools of Architecture, DC, $5,000. 1987.
Bismarck-Mandan Orchestral Association, Bismarck, ND, $5,500. 1987.
Buffalo Bill Historical Center, Cody, WY, $30,000. 1987.
California Confederation of the Arts, Sacramento, CA, $10,000. 1987.
California State Summer School Arts Foundation, Encino, CA, $80,000. 1987.
California Young Peoples Theater, San Jose, CA, $20,000. 1987.
Cheyenne Civic Center, Cheyenne, WY, $5,000. 1987.
Childrens Museum of Denver, Denver, CO, $5,000. 1987.
Childrens Theater Company and School, Minneapolis, MN, $5,000. 1987.
City Art League, Minot, ND, $5,000. 1987.
Columbia River Maritime Museum, Astoria, OR, $10,000. 1987.
Corporate Council for the Arts, Seattle, WA, $50,000. 1987.
Craft and Folk Art Museum Incorporating the Egg and the Eye, Los Angeles, CA, $5,000. 1987.
Custer County Art and Heritage Center, Miles City, MT, $5,000. 1987.
Denver Center for the Performing Arts, Denver, CO, $10,000. 1987.
Douglas County Historical Society, Omaha, NE, $5,000. 1987.
El Paso Pro-Musica, El Paso, TX, $26,000. 1987.
El Paso Symphony Orchestra Association, El Paso, TX, $25,000. 1987.
El Paso Symphony Orchestra Association, El Paso, TX, $12,000. 1987.
El Paso Zoological Society, El Paso, TX, $10,000. 1987.
Empty Space Theater, Seattle, WA, $45,000. 1987.
Fargo-Moorhead Symphony Orchestra, Fargo, ND, $5,000. 1987.
Flathead Valley Art Association, Kalispell, MT, $50,000. 1987.
Fort Worth Civic Opera Association, Fort Worth, TX, $10,000. 1987.
Fresno Arts Center and Museum, Fresno, CA, $10,000. 1987.
Friends of the Arts, San Francisco, CA, $50,000. 1987.
Galesburg Symphony Society, Galesburg, IL, $9,000. 1987.
Glacier Natural History Association, West Glacier, MT, $5,000. 1987.
Grand Peoples Company, Los Angeles, CA, $48,000. 1987.
Greater Grand Forks Community Theater, Grand Forks, ND, $5,000. 1987.
Greater Saint Louis Council for Arts and Education, Saint Louis, MO, $12,500. 1987.
Guthrie Theater Foundation, Minneapolis, MN, $10,000. 1987.
Helena Arts Council, Helena, MT, $10,000. 1987.
Henry Gallery Association, Seattle, WA, $20,000. 1987.
High Desert Museum, Bend, OR, $25,000. 1987.
Houston Ballet Foundation, Houston, TX, $5,000. 1987.
Intiman Theater, Seattle, WA, $35,000. 1987.
K Z U M Radio, Sunrise Communications, Lincoln, NE, $5,000. 1987.
Kansas City Spirit, Kansas City, MO, $5,000. 1987.
Kendall County Historical Society, Yorkville, IL, $5,000. 1987.
Kern County Museum, Bakersfield, CA, $10,000. 1987.
Los Angeles Master Chorale Association, Los Angeles, CA, $46,000. 1987.
Lyric Opera of Kansas City, Kansas City, MO, $5,000. 1987.
Mexican Museum, San Francisco, CA, $90,000. 1987.
Minneapolis Society of Fine Arts, Minneapolis, MN, $20,000. 1987.
Minnesota Opera Company, Saint Paul, MN, $10,000. 1987.
Minnesota Orchestral Association, Minneapolis, MN, $17,000. 1987.
Minnesota Public Radio, KCCM/FM, Moorhead, MN, $5,000. 1987.
Museum of Flight Foundation, Seattle, WA, $60,000. 1987.
Museum of Science and Industry, Chicago, IL, $10,000. 1987.
National Public Radio, DC, $10,000. 1987.
Nelson Gallery Foundation, Kansas City, MO, $10,000. 1987.
New Mexico Symphony Orchestra, Albuquerque, NM, $5,000. 1987.
Northern Minnesota Public Television, Bemidji, MN, $10,000. 1987.
Northwest Chamber Orchestra, Seattle, WA, $50,000. 1987.
Northwest Chamber Orchestra, Seattle, WA, $5,597. 1987.
On the Boards, Seattle, WA, $10,000. 1987.
Opera Colorado, Denver, CO, $7,500. 1987.
Opera Theater of Saint Louis, Saint Louis, MO, $7,500. 1987.
Oregon Symphony Society, Portland, OR, $12,000. 1987.
Pacific Northwest Ballet Association, Seattle, WA, $50,000. 1987.
Pacific Science Center, Seattle, WA, $50,000. 1987.
Pacific Science Center, Seattle, WA, $25,000. 1987.
Paramount Arts Center Endowment, Aurora, IL, $5,000. 1987.
Phoenix Symphony Association, Phoenix, AZ, $5,000. 1987.
Pioneer Square Theater, Seattle, WA, $5,000. 1987.
Portland Art Association, Portland, OR, $5,000. 1987.
Portland Opera Association, Portland, OR, $5,000. 1987.
Powder River Arts Council, Gillette, WY, $5,500. 1987.
Ramsey County Historical Society, Saint Paul, MN, $5,000. 1987.
Sacramento Childrens Museum, Sacramento, CA, $63,633. 1987.
Saint Louis Symphony Society, Saint Louis, MO, $12,500. 1987.
Saint Paul-Ramsey United Arts Council, Saint Paul, MN, $15,000. 1987.
San Diego Museum Association, San Diego, CA, $150,700. 1987.
Santa Fe Chamber Music Festival, Santa Fe, NM, $25,000. 1987.
Santa Fe Chamber Music Festival, Santa Fe, NM, $5,000. 1987.
Santa Fe Opera, Santa Fe, NM, $38,000. 1987.
Science Museum of Minnesota, Saint Paul, MN, $7,000. 1987.
Seattle Chamber Music Festival, Seattle, WA, $5,000. 1987.
Seattle Childrens Theater, Seattle, WA, $35,000. 1987.
Seattle Childrens Theater, Seattle, WA, $20,000. 1987.
Seattle Symphony Orchestra, Seattle, WA, $100,000. 1987.
Southwest Museum, Los Angeles, CA, $10,000. 1987.
Spokane Interplayers Ensemble, Spokane, WA, $15,000. 1987.
Springfield Symphony Association, Springfield, MO, $10,000. 1987.
Tacoma Actors Guild, Tacoma, WA, $5,000. 1987.
Tacoma Art Museum, Tacoma, WA, $10,000. 1987.
Tulare County Museum, Visalia, CA, $7,000. 1987.
Very Special Arts Wyoming, Cheyenne, WY, $5,000. 1987.
Vigilante Players, Bozeman, MT, $5,000. 1987.
Village Theater, Issaquah, WA, $18,000. 1987.
Walker Art Center, Minneapolis, MN, $10,000. 1987.
Yellowstone Art Center Foundation, Billings, MT, $15,000. 1987.

2960
The George and Anne Butler Foundation

2220 Allied Bank Plaza
1000 Louisiana
Houston 77002

Incorporated in 1956 in TX.
Donor(s): George A. Butler,† Anne G. Butler,† Houston Corp., McEvoy Co.
Financial data (yr. ended 12/31/87): Assets, $1,802,180 (M); gifts received, $16,856; expenditures, $129,716, including $115,790 for 13 grants (high: $25,000; low: $600).
Purpose and activities: Emphasis on higher and secondary education, arts and cultural programs, health, youth, and Protestant church support.
Types of support: Annual campaigns, emergency funds, lectureships.
Limitations: Giving primarily in TX.
Publications: Annual report.
Application information:
Deadline(s): None
Write: George V. Grainger, V.P.
Officers and Trustees: Anne B. Leonard, Pres.; Ida Jo B. Moran, V.P.
Number of staff: None.
Employer Identification Number: 746063429

2961
The Effie and Wofford Cain Foundation
6116 North Central Expressway, Suite 909-LB65
Dallas 75206 (214) 361-4201

Incorporated in 1952 in TX.
Donor(s): Effie Marie Cain, R. Wofford Cain.†
Financial data (yr. ended 10/31/88): Assets, $41,173,205 (M); expenditures, $1,921,613, including $1,563,335 for 78 grants (high: $250,000; low: $500; average: $2,000-$35,000).
Purpose and activities: Giving primarily for higher and secondary education, public service organizations, and cultural programs; grants also for religious organizations, aid to the handicapped, and medical services and research.
Types of support: Building funds, endowment funds, seed money, operating budgets, research, scholarship funds.
Limitations: Giving limited to TX. No grants to individuals.
Publications: Application guidelines.
Application information: Application form required.
Copies of proposal: 1
Deadline(s): Aug. 31 for Oct. meeting
Board meeting date(s): Oct. (annual); 4 to 6 interim meetings (dates vary)
Final notification: Varies
Write: Harvey L. Walker, Exec. Dir.
Officers: Effie Marie Cain,* Pres.; Frank W. Denius,* V.P.; R.J. Smith,* Secy.-Treas.; Harvey L. Walker, Exec. Dir.
Directors:* James B. Cain.
Number of staff: 2 full-time professional; 1 full-time support; 1 part-time support.
Employer Identification Number: 756030774

2962
Flora Cameron Foundation
4600 Broadway, Suite 106
San Antonio 78209 (512) 824-8301

Established in 1952 in TX.
Financial data (yr. ended 8/31/87): Assets, $1,399,873 (M); expenditures, $82,054, including $61,835 for 18 grants (high: $24,215; low: $200).
Purpose and activities: Giving for schools and cultural programs.
Types of support: General purposes.
Limitations: Giving primarily in the San Antonio, TX, area.
Application information:
Initial approach: Letter
Deadline(s): None
Write: Flora C. Atherton, Pres.
Officers: Flora C. Atherton, Pres. and Treas.; Gloria Labatt, V.P.; Holt Atherton, Secy.-Treas.
Trustee: Everitt H. Jones.
Employer Identification Number: 746038681

2963
Amon G. Carter Foundation
1212 NCNB Center
P.O. Box 1036
Fort Worth 76101 (817) 332-2783

Incorporated in 1945 in TX.
Donor(s): Amon G. Carter,† N.B. Carter,† Star-Telegram Employees Fund, Carter Foundation Production Co.
Financial data (yr. ended 12/31/88): Assets, $170,000,000 (M); expenditures, $7,772,812, including $7,574,222 for 130 grants (high: $2,479,216; low: $500; average: $10,000-$175,000).
Purpose and activities: Grants primarily for the visual and performing arts, education, health and hospitals, social service and youth agencies, programs for the aged, and civic and community endeavors that enhance the quality of life. The foundation sponsors and largely supports an art museum.
Types of support: Continuing support, annual campaigns, seed money, emergency funds, building funds, equipment, land acquisition, matching funds, professorships, research, renovation projects, capital campaigns, general purposes, special projects.
Limitations: Giving largely restricted to Fort Worth and Tarrant County, TX. No grants to individuals, or for ongoing operating budgets, deficit financing, publications, or conferences; no loans.
Publications: Program policy statement.
Application information: Grants outside local geographic area usually initiated by board.
Initial approach: Letter
Copies of proposal: 1
Deadline(s): None
Board meeting date(s): Apr., Sept., and Dec.
Final notification: Within 10 days of board meeting
Write: Bob J. Crow, Exec. Dir.
Officers and Directors:* Ruth Carter Stevenson,* Pres.; Robert W. Brown, M.D.,* V.P.; W. Patrick Harris, Secy.; Paul W. Mason,* Treas.; Bob J. Crow, Exec. Dir.; J. Lee Johnson IV, Mark L. Johnson.
Number of staff: 1 full-time professional; 2 part-time professional; 1 full-time support.
Employer Identification Number: 756000331
Recent arts and culture grants:
Amon Carter Museum, Fort Worth, TX, $3,117,075. For general support. 1987.
Art Library Society of North America, Tucson, AZ, $5,000. For special program. 1987.
Arts Council of Fort Worth, Fort Worth, TX, $75,000. For general support. 1987.
Fort Worth Chamber Foundation, Fort Worth, TX, $10,000. For Arts in the Park. 1987.
Fort Worth Symphony Orchestra, Fort Worth, TX, $25,000. For special program. 1987.
Fort Worth Zoological Society, Fort Worth, TX, $10,000. For general support. 1987.
Fort Worth, City of, Water Garden, Fort Worth, TX, $60,000. For special program. 1987.
Jubilee Players, Fort Worth, TX, $15,000. For building fund. 1987.
Modern Art Museum of Fort Worth, Fort Worth, TX, $500,000. For endowment. 1987.
National Trust for Historic Preservation, DC, $20,000. For general support. 1987.
Shakespeare in the Park, Fort Worth, TX, $25,000. For general support. 1987.
Streams and Valleys, Fort Worth, TX, $10,000. For general support. 1987.
Texas Boys Choir of Fort Worth, Fort Worth, TX, $5,000. For general support. 1987.
Texas Christian University, Department of Art, Fort Worth, TX, $10,000. For special program. 1987.
Texas State Historical Association, Austin, TX, $10,000. For special program. 1987.
University of Texas, Center for the Study of American Architecture, Arlington, TX, $28,300. For special program. 1987.
Van Cliburn Foundation, Fort Worth, TX, $25,000. For general support. 1987.

2964
Catto Foundation
110 East Crockett
San Antonio 78205 (512) 222-2161

Established in 1967 in TX.
Donor(s): Henry E. Catto, Jr., Jessica Hobby Catto, A & C Communications.
Financial data (yr. ended 12/31/87): Assets, $396,131 (M); gifts received, $250,000; expenditures, $249,719, including $243,616 for 44 grants (high: $50,000; low: $250).
Purpose and activities: Support primarily for higher education; grants also for cultural programs.
Types of support: General purposes.
Limitations: Giving primarily in Washington, DC, and San Antonio, TX. No grants to individuals.
Application information:
Initial approach: Letter
Deadline(s): None
Write: Jessica H. Catto
Officers: Jessica Hobby Catto,* Pres.; Henry E. Catto, Jr.,* V.P.; Susan R. Farrimono, Secy.-Treas.
Directors:* William P. Hobby, Heather C. Kohout.
Employer Identification Number: 746089609

2965
The Clark Foundation
6116 North Central Expressway, Suite 906
Dallas 75206 (214) 361-7498

Trust established in 1951 in TX.
Donor(s): Anson L. Clark, M.D.†
Financial data (yr. ended 12/31/87): Assets, $1,919,732 (M); expenditures, $309,236, including $275,000 for 5 grants (high: $62,500; low: $25,000).
Purpose and activities: Grants largely for higher and secondary education, including scholarships and research; support also for cultural programs and social services.
Types of support: Endowment funds.
Limitations: Giving limited to TX, with emphasis on the Dallas-Ft. Worth metropolitan area. No grants to individuals, or for operating budgets, continuing support, annual campaigns, emergency or building funds, deficit financing, land acquisition, special projects, publications, or conferences; no loans.
Application information:
Initial approach: Letter, telephone, or proposal
Copies of proposal: 1
Deadline(s): Nov. 15
Board meeting date(s): Feb., Apr., Aug., Oct., and Dec.
Final notification: 45 days
Write: Robert H. Middleton, Trustee

Trustees: Ray Bell, Robert H. Middleton, DeWitt T. Weaver.
Number of staff: 1 part-time professional.
Employer Identification Number: 756015614

2966
The Clayton Fund
Five Post Oak Park, Suite 1980
Houston 77027 (713) 623-0113

Trust established in 1952 in TX.
Donor(s): William L. Clayton,† Susan V. Clayton.†
Financial data (yr. ended 12/31/88): Assets, $22,823,209 (M); expenditures, $829,578 for 84 grants (high: $100,000; low: $300; average: $5,000-$25,000).
Purpose and activities: Support largely for higher education, including medical education and scholarships; grants also for hospitals, medical research, social services, population control, and cultural programs.
Types of support: Scholarship funds, continuing support, operating budgets, program-related investments, employee-related scholarships.
Limitations: Giving primarily in TX.
Application information: Request application guidelines for scholarship program.
Copies of proposal: 1
Write: S.M. McAshan, Jr., Trustee
Trustees: W.L. Garwood, Jr., S.M. McAshan, Jr., Burdine Venghiattis.
Number of staff: 1 full-time professional; 1 full-time support.
Employer Identification Number: 746042331

2967
Clements Foundation
1901 North Akard
Dallas 75201
Application address: c/o Office of the Governor, State Capitol, Austin, TX 78701; Tel.: (512) 463-2000

Established in 1968 in TX.
Financial data (yr. ended 12/31/87): Assets, $3,608,713 (M); gifts received, $172,500; expenditures, $267,144, including $189,333 for 21 grants (high: $70,000; low: $500).
Purpose and activities: Support primarily for youth groups, education, the arts, and medicine.
Types of support: General purposes.
Limitations: Giving primarily in the Dallas, TX, area.
Application information:
Write: Janie Harris
Officers: William P. Clements, Jr., Pres.; Nancy Clements, V.P. and Treas.; B. Gill Clements, V.P.
Employer Identification Number: 756065076

2968
Coastal Bend Community Foundation
860 First City Bank Tower - FCB 276
Corpus Christi 78477 (512) 882-9745

Established in 1980 in TX.
Financial data (yr. ended 12/31/88): Assets, $2,852,499 (M); gifts received, $910,220; expenditures, $765,748, including $705,962 for 82 grants (high: $326,978; low: $125; average: $1,000-$2,000) and $4,101 for 10 grants to individuals.
Purpose and activities: Giving primarily for social services, higher education, including scholarship funds, and culture.
Types of support: Seed money, scholarship funds, equipment, general purposes, special projects, student aid, fellowships.
Limitations: Giving limited to Aransas, Bee, Jim Wells, Kleberg, Nueces, Refugio, and San Patricio counties, TX.
Publications: Grants list, newsletter, informational brochure (including application guidelines).
Application information:
Initial approach: Letter
Copies of proposal: 1
Deadline(s): Oct. 1
Board meeting date(s): Feb. May, Aug. and Nov.
Final notification: Nov.
Write: Dana Williams, Exec. V.P.
Officer: Dana Williams, Exec. V.P.
Number of staff: 1 full-time professional; 1 full-time support.
Employer Identification Number: 742190039

2969
Cockrell Foundation
1600 Smith, Suite 4600
Houston 77002-7348 (713) 651-1271

Trust established in 1957 in TX; incorporated in 1966.
Donor(s): Mrs. Dula Cockrell,† E. Cockrell, Jr.,† Virginia H. Cockrell.†
Financial data (yr. ended 12/31/87): Assets, $45,857,647 (M); gifts received, $4,684,818; expenditures, $2,192,398, including $1,932,243 for 35 grants (high: $666,000; low: $500).
Purpose and activities: Giving for higher education; support also for cultural programs, social services, youth, religion, and hospitals.
Types of support: Annual campaigns, building funds, capital campaigns, endowment funds, fellowships, general purposes, matching funds, operating budgets, professorships, research, scholarship funds, special projects.
Limitations: Giving primarily in Houston, TX. No grants to individuals.
Publications: Annual report, 990-PF.
Application information:
Initial approach: Proposal
Copies of proposal: 1
Deadline(s): None
Board meeting date(s): Mar. and Oct.
Final notification: 6 weeks
Write: Mary McIntier, Exec. V.P.
Officers: Alf Roark,* Pres.; Mary McIntier, Exec. V.P.; Ernest H. Cockrell,* V.P.; W.F. Wright, Jr., Secy.-Treas.
Directors:* Janet S. Cockrell, Carol Cockrell Curran, Richard B. Curran.
Number of staff: None.
Employer Identification Number: 746076993

2970
Carr P. Collins Foundation, Inc.
P.O. Box 1330
Lewisville 75067 (214) 221-6202

Incorporated in 1962 in TX.
Donor(s): Carr P. Collins.
Financial data (yr. ended 12/31/86): Assets, $24,377,242 (M); expenditures, $1,553,286, including $1,310,000 for 9 grants (high: $1,085,000; low: $5,000; average: $10,000-$100,000).
Purpose and activities: Support for social services, cultural programs, and youth programs.
Limitations: Giving primarily in TX. No grants to individuals.
Application information: Funds presently committed. Applications currently not accepted.
Board meeting date(s): Annually
Write: Connie G. Romans, Treas.
Officers: Ruth Collins Sharp,* Pres.; Michael J. Collins,* V.P.; R. Hubbard Hardy, Secy.; Connie G. Romans, Treas.
Directors:* J.C. Cantrell, Calvert Collins, James M. Collins, Lynn Craft, W. Dewey Presley, Robert H. Stewart III.
Number of staff: 1 full-time professional.
Employer Identification Number: 756011615

2971
Communities Foundation of Texas, Inc.
4605 Live Oak St.
Dallas 75204 (214) 826-5231

Community foundation established in 1953 in TX; incorporated in 1960.
Financial data (yr. ended 6/30/88): Assets, $139,774,498 (M); gifts received, $11,023,922; expenditures, $45,537,440, including $44,123,835 for 2,672 grants (high: $15,000,000; low: $25; average: $500-$25,000).
Purpose and activities: Grants from unrestricted funds are generally for education, health and hospitals, social services, youth, and cultural programs.
Types of support: Seed money, emergency funds, building funds, equipment, land acquisition, matching funds, technical assistance, special projects, research, capital campaigns.
Limitations: Giving primarily in the Dallas, TX, area. No support for religious purposes from general fund, media projects, publications, or organizations which redistribute funds to other organizations. No grants to individuals, or for continuing support, deficit financing, endowment funds, scholarships, or fellowships.
Publications: Program policy statement, application guidelines, financial statement, newsletter, annual report.
Application information:
Initial approach: Letter
Copies of proposal: 1
Deadline(s): 1st day of month prior to meetings
Board meeting date(s): Distribution Committee for unrestricted funds meets in Mar., Aug., and Nov.
Final notification: 1 week after Distribution Committee meeting
Write: Edward M. Fjordbak, Pres.

Officers: Edward M. Fjordbak, Pres.; Joe D. Denton,* Treas.; Kimberly Floyd, Grant Admin.; Pamela Dees, Financial Officer.
Trustees:* Ruth Collins Sharp, Vice-Chair.; Ebby Halliday Acers, Louis A. Beecherl, Jr., Durwood Chalker, Thomas C. Unis.
Number of staff: 7 full-time professional; 10 full-time support.
Employer Identification Number: 750964565
Recent arts and culture grants:
American Federation of Arts, NYC, NY, $115,750. 1987.
American Friends of Bermuda, Bermuda, $12,000. 1987.
American Friends of the Israel Museum, NYC, NY, $5,750. 1987.
Anderson Ranch Arts Center, Aspen, CO, $10,000. 1987.
Arts for People, Dallas, TX, $7,125. 1987.
Committee for the Preservation of the Treasury Building, DC, $10,000. 1987.
Dallas Arboretum and Botanical Society, Dallas, TX, $2,050,315. 1987.
Dallas Ballet, Dallas, TX, $58,282. 1987.
Dallas Black Dance Theater, Dallas, TX, $11,000. 1987.
Dallas County Heritage Society, Dallas, TX, $7,800. 1987.
Dallas Historical Society, Dallas, TX, $16,660. 1987.
Dallas Institute of Humanities and Culture, Dallas, TX, $19,350. 1987.
Dallas Museum of Art, Dallas, TX, $616,062. 1987.
Dallas Opera, Dallas, TX, $104,090. 1987.
Dallas Summer Musicals, Dallas, TX, $5,000. 1987.
Dallas Symphony Association, Dallas, TX, $117,591. 1987.
Dallas Theater Center, Dallas, TX, $20,802. 1987.
Dallas Zoological Society, Dallas, TX, $27,250. 1987.
Eastland Fine Arts Association, Eastland, TX, $5,000. 1987.
For The People, Dallas, TX, $86,016. 1987.
Fort Worth Museum of Science and History, Fort Worth, TX, $12,300. 1987.
Fort Worth Symphony Orchestra, Fort Worth, TX, $6,000. 1987.
Friends of Channel 13, Dallas, TX, $6,400. 1987.
Historic Preservation League, Dallas, TX, $11,000. 1987.
Houston Symphony Society, Houston, TX, $8,500. 1987.
International Center of Photography, NYC, NY, $33,500. 1987.
Midland Community Theater, Midland, TX, $6,000. 1987.
Millards Crossing, Nacogdoches, TX, $12,992. 1987.
Motion Picture and Television Fund, Woodland Hills, CA, $10,000. 1987.
National Corporate Theater Fund, NYC, NY, $56,000. 1987.
North Texas Public Broadcasting, Dallas, TX, $15,400. 1987.
Princess Grace Foundation - USA, NYC, NY, $21,100. 1987.
Public Communication Foundation for North Texas, Dallas, TX, $24,480. 1987.
Solomon R. Guggenheim Museum, NYC, NY, $92,000. 1987.
Taca, Dallas, TX, $9,050. 1987.
Texas Business Hall of Fame, Dallas, TX, $10,500. 1987.
Turtle Creek Center for the Arts, Dallas, TX, $15,000. 1987.
Van Cliburn Foundation, Fort Worth, TX, $5,000. 1987.
Versailles Foundation, NYC, NY, $5,000. 1987.
Whitney Museum of American Art, NYC, NY, $201,000. 1987.
Wichita Falls Museum and Art Center, Wichita Falls, TX, $51,000. 1987.

2972
Compaq Computer Foundation
P.O. Box 692000
Houston 77269-2000 (713) 374-4625

Established in 1989 in TX.
Purpose and activities: Supports health and human services, arts and culture, civic affairs, crime and law enforcement, and welfare; also makes in-kind gifts.
Types of support: In-kind gifts.
Limitations: Giving limited to Houston, TX.
Application information: Application form required.
Write: Lou Ann Champ, Corp. Contribs. Admin.

2973
The Constantin Foundation
3811 Turtle Creek Blvd., Suite 900-LB 39
Dallas 75219 (214) 760-6950

Trust established in 1947 in TX.
Donor(s): E. Constantin, Jr.,† Mrs. E. Constantin, Jr.†
Financial data (yr. ended 12/31/88): Assets, $25,874,439 (M); expenditures, $1,687,619, including $1,524,395 for 17 grants (high: $1,000,000; low: $2,000).
Purpose and activities: Emphasis on higher education; some support for social service and youth agencies, and hospitals.
Types of support: Building funds, matching funds, general purposes, land acquisition, equipment, capital campaigns, continuing support, renovation projects.
Limitations: Giving limited to the Dallas, TX, metropolitan area. No support for state schools, theater, or for churches. No grants to individuals, or for research; no loans.
Publications: Application guidelines.
Application information:
Initial approach: Proposal
Copies of proposal: 6
Deadline(s): Oct. 31; grants considered only at Dec. meeting
Board meeting date(s): Mar., June, Sept., and Dec.
Final notification: Jan.
Write: Betty S. Hillin, Exec. Dir.
Officer: Betty S. Hillin, Exec. Dir.
Trustees: Henry C. Beck, Jr., Gene H. Bishop, Walter L. Fleming, Jr., Paul A. Lockhart, Jr., Joel T. Williams, Jr.
Number of staff: 1 full-time professional; 1 full-time support.
Employer Identification Number: 756011289

2974
Loring Cook Foundation
P.O. Box 1060
McAllen 78502
Scholarship application address: Counselor, McAllen Memorial High School, McAllen, TX 78502

Incorporated in 1953 in TX.
Financial data (yr. ended 3/31/87): Assets, $1,764,020 (M); expenditures, $70,384, including $54,145 for 34 grants (high: $21,320; low: $100) and $6,250 for grants to individuals.
Purpose and activities: Emphasis on Protestant church support, cancer and heart disease research, higher education, youth and social service agencies, and cultural programs; also awards scholarships to students graduating from a local high school.
Types of support: Student aid.
Limitations: Giving primarily in TX.
Application information: Application form required for scholarships.
Deadline(s): Mar. 1 for scholarships
Officers and Directors:* Vannie E. Cook, Jr.,* Pres.; Clarence Johnstone,* V.P.; Mrs. Vannie E. Cook, Jr., Secy.-Treas.
Employer Identification Number: 746050063

2975
Cooper Industries Corporate Giving Program
First City Tower
1001 Fannin, 40th Fl.
Houston 77002 (713) 739-5400
Mailing Address: P.O. Box 4446, Houston, TX 77210

Financial data (yr. ended 12/31/88): Total giving, $750,000, including $700,000 for grants (high: $80,000; low: $500; average: $1,000-$10,000) and $50,000 for in-kind gifts.
Purpose and activities: Supports United Funds, education, cultural, civic and community and some limited health and welfare programs in communities where the company's operations are located. Local gifts of over $1,000 are made through the foundation; local operating units make funding decisions for their communities and submit a budget to the foundation. Gifts of less than $1,000 are made directly from the operating units, as are in-kind gifts. Foundation approval is required for in-kind gifts worth more than $1,500.
Types of support: In-kind gifts, employee matching gifts, matching funds, equipment, annual campaigns, building funds, capital campaigns, emergency funds, employee-related scholarships, seed money.
Limitations: Giving primarily in headquarters city and all operating locations in the U.S.: GA, IL, IN, MI, MO, MS, NC, NJ, NY, OH, PA, SC, TX, VA, and WI.
Publications: Application guidelines.
Application information: Include description of project, proposed budget, financial statement, 501(c)(3) status letter, and list of board members and major donors.
Initial approach: Local requests to the nearest operating unit; local requests sent to the foundation will be referred to nearest local operation for recommendation
Copies of proposal: 1

Deadline(s): Applications accepted throughout the year; requests considered quarterly
Board meeting date(s): Quarterly
Final notification: Within 90 days

2976
Cooper Industries Foundation
First City Tower, Suite 4000
P.O. Box 4446
Houston 77210 (713) 739-5615

Incorporated in 1964; absorbed Crouse-Hinds Foundation in 1982; absorbed McGraw-Edison Foundation in 1985.
Donor(s): Cooper Industries, Inc.
Financial data (yr. ended 12/31/88): Assets, $2,385,651 (M); expenditures, $2,186,558, including $1,910,341 for 508 grants (high: $65,000; low: $250; average: $1,000-$5,000) and $272,000 for 1,991 employee matching gifts.
Purpose and activities: Functions solely as a conduit through which Cooper Industries, Inc. and its operating units throughout the country make contributions to local charities, United Funds, education, civic and community affairs and limited health and welfare programs where company's operations are located; emergency funds are for local organizations only.
Types of support: Operating budgets, continuing support, annual campaigns, seed money, emergency funds, matching funds, employee matching gifts, employee-related scholarships, special projects, building funds, capital campaigns, general purposes.
Limitations: Giving primarily in Houston, TX, and other communities of company operations in AL, CA, CT, GA, IL, IN, ME, MI, MO, MS, NJ, NY, NC, OH, OK, PA, SC, TN, TX, and VA,. No support for religious, fraternal, veterans', or lobbying organizations. No grants to individuals (except for scholarships to children of company employees), or for endowment funds, publications, or conferences; no loans.
Publications: Application guidelines.
Application information: Requests that are local in nature will be referred to the nearest local operation for recommendation.
Initial approach: Letter of inquiry
Copies of proposal: 1
Deadline(s): None
Board meeting date(s): Feb.; distribution committee meets quarterly
Final notification: Within 90 days
Write: Patricia B. Mottram, Secy.
Officers and Trustees:* Robert Cizik,* Chair.; Thomas W. Campbell,* Pres.; Alan E. Riedel,* V.P.; Patricia B. Mottram, Secy.; Dewain K. Cross,* Treas.
Number of staff: 2 part-time professional; 1 full-time support.
Employer Identification Number: 316060698

2977
Coral Reef Foundation
1001 Fannin, Suite 4368
First City Tower
Houston 77002

Established in 1978 in TX.
Donor(s): Jayne L. Wrightsman, Charles B. Wrightsman.†
Financial data (yr. ended 12/31/87): Assets, $9,899,554 (M); expenditures, $765,826, including $736,000 for 7 grants (high: $340,000; low: $1,000).
Purpose and activities: Giving to cultural organizations, including museums and libraries.
Limitations: Giving primarily in New York, NY. No grants to individuals.
Application information: Contributes only to pre-selected organizations. Applications not accepted.
Board meeting date(s): Nov.
Write: Larry A. Lenz, Treas.
Officers: Jayne L. Wrightsman,* Pres.; James F. Dolan,* Secy.; Larry A. Lenz, Treas.
Directors:* Taggart Whipple.
Number of staff: None.
Employer Identification Number: 741969035

2978
Aubrey M. Costa Foundation
5580 LBJ Fwy, Suite 530
Dallas 75240

Established in 1968 in TX.
Donor(s): Aubrey M. Costa.†
Financial data (yr. ended 3/1/89): Assets, $1,326,933 (M); expenditures, $171,521, including $137,500 for 24 grants (high: $30,000; low: $300).
Purpose and activities: Emphasis on education; support also for health agencies, culture, community funds, Jewish welfare, and religious support.
Limitations: Giving primarily in TX. No grants to individuals.
Application information: Contributes only to pre-selected organizations. Applications not accepted.
Copies of proposal: 1
Board meeting date(s): As required
Final notification: 2 weeks
Trustees: Edward C. Greene, M.J. Greene.
Number of staff: None.
Employer Identification Number: 756085394

2979
Una Chapman Cox Foundation
P.O. Box 749
Corpus Christi 78403 (512) 883-3621
Application address: 1800 M St., N.W., Suite 3505, Washington, D.C. 20016; Tel.: (202) 223-0887

Established in 1980 in TX.
Donor(s): Una Chapman Cox.†
Financial data (yr. ended 11/30/87): Assets, $10,102,798 (M); expenditures, $340,548, including $211,548 for 9 grants (high: $80,000; low: $3,000).
Purpose and activities: Support for the U.S. Foreign Service through grants to finance leaves of absence of State Dept. personnel, and for films and other projects.
Types of support: Conferences and seminars, special projects.
Publications: Informational brochure, application guidelines.
Application information: See information brochure.
Deadline(s): None
Write: Alfred L. Atherton, Jr., Exec. Dir.
Officers: Harvie Branscomb, Jr., Pres.; Alfred L. Atherton, Jr., Secy. and Exec. Dir.
Trustees: George S. Vest, Jane C. Owen.
Number of staff: 1 part-time professional.
Employer Identification Number: 742150104

2980
The Cullen Foundation
601 Jefferson, 40th Fl.
Houston 77002 (713) 651-8600
Mailing address: P.O. Box 1600, Houston, TX 77251

Trust established in 1947 in TX.
Donor(s): Hugh Roy Cullen,† Lillie Cullen.†
Financial data (yr. ended 12/31/87): Assets, $125,634,558 (M); expenditures, $6,735,549, including $4,869,700 for 23 grants (high: $1,500,000; low: $5,000; average: $50,000-$300,000).
Purpose and activities: Giving for charitable, educational, medical, and other eleemosynary purposes; grants for hospitals, medical, including eye, research, and higher education; support also for music, the performing arts, social services, drug abuse prevention, and community funds.
Types of support: Annual campaigns, deficit financing, building funds, equipment, land acquisition, general purposes, matching funds, professorships, research, renovation projects.
Limitations: Giving limited to TX, with emphasis on Houston. No grants to individuals; no loans.
Publications: 990-PF, application guidelines.
Application information:
Initial approach: Proposal, letter, or telephone
Copies of proposal: 1
Deadline(s): None
Board meeting date(s): Usually in Jan., Apr., July, Oct., and as required
Final notification: Varies
Write: Joseph C. Graf, Exec. Secy.
Officers: Wilhelmina Cullen Robertson,* Pres.; Roy Henry Cullen,* V.P.; Isaac Arnold, Jr.,* Secy.-Treas.; Joseph C. Graf, Exec. Secy.
Trustees:* Douglas B. Marshall, Jr.
Number of staff: 1 full-time professional; 1 full-time support.
Employer Identification Number: 746048769

2981
The Dallas Foundation
8333 Douglas Ave., Suite 1555
Dallas 75248 (214) 373-6080

Community foundation established in 1929 in TX.
Financial data (yr. ended 12/31/87): Assets, $12,343,816 (M); gifts received, $121,086; expenditures, $2,641,358, including $2,424,687 for 30 grants (high: $100,000; low: $3,500; average: $20,000-$75,000).
Purpose and activities: Giving to promote charitable, educational, cultural, recreational, and health programs through grants to community organizations and agencies, principally for capital purposes.

Types of support: Building funds, land acquisition, capital campaigns, equipment, general purposes, special projects.
Limitations: Giving limited to the City and County of Dallas, TX. No grants to individuals, or for endowment funds, operating budgets, research, scholarships, or fellowships; no loans.
Publications: Newsletter, program policy statement, application guidelines, informational brochure.
Application information:
Initial approach: 1-page proposal
Deadline(s): None
Board meeting date(s): Usually in Feb., May, Sept. and Nov.
Final notification: Following Nov. board meeting
Write: Mary M. Jalonick, Exec. Dir.
Officer: Mary M. Jalonick, Exec. Dir.
Governors: George Schrader, Chair.; Robert W. Decherd, James R. Erwin, Harriet Miers, J. Fulton Murray, Jr., Joseph R. Musolino, John Field Scovell, Joel T. Williams, Jr.
Trustee Banks: Allied Bank of Dallas, BancTexas Dallas, First City Bank of Dallas, First RepublicBank Dallas, N.A., First RepublicBank Greenville Avenue, First RepublicBank Oak Cliffs, MBank Preston, North Dallas Bank & Trust Co., Texas American Bank/Dallas.
Number of staff: 1 full-time professional; 1 full-time support.
Employer Identification Number: 756038529

2982
The Dallas Morning News - WFAA Foundation
c/o A.H. Belo Corp.
Communications Center
Dallas 75265 (214) 977-6600

Trust established in 1952 in TX.
Donor(s): A.H. Belo Corp.
Financial data (yr. ended 12/31/88): Assets, $3,643,179 (M); expenditures, $210,000 for 13 grants.
Purpose and activities: Giving for journalism education, civic improvement programs, cultural programs, and health and social service organizations.
Types of support: Building funds, endowment funds, capital campaigns.
Limitations: Giving primarily in Dallas, TX, and in cities where Belo has operating companies. No grants to individuals.
Application information: Application form required.
Initial approach: Letter or proposal; no visits
Copies of proposal: 1
Board meeting date(s): Once a year
Write: Secy.
Trustees: Joe M. Dealey, Robert W. Decherd, Reece A. Overcash, Jr., James M. Moroney, Jr., Thomas B. Walker, Jr.
Number of staff: None.
Employer Identification Number: 756012569

2983
Dallas Rehabilitation Foundation
8828 Stemmons Freewy., Suite 106, LB-39
Dallas 75247 (214) 630-6181

Established in 1981 in TX; corpus derived from sale of Dallas Rehabilitation Institute to National Medical Enterprises, Inc.
Financial data (yr. ended 10/31/87): Assets, $6,455,484 (M); gifts received, $460,000; expenditures, $1,045,240, including $646,045 for 10 grants (high: $43,000; low: $15,000; average: $25,000-$40,000) and $399,195 for 4 foundation-administered programs.
Purpose and activities: Giving for projects that advance the science and art of rehabilitation of severely physically handicapped individuals, primarily through research activities; some support also for educational projects, such as educational conferences, and film production.
Types of support: Equipment, special projects, research, seed money, matching funds, scholarship funds, professorships, internships, fellowships, publications, conferences and seminars.
Limitations: Giving primarily in TX. No grants to individuals, operating budgets, continuing support, annual campaigns, emergency funds, deficit financing, building funds, land acquisition, renovation projects, endowments, program-related investments, or exchange programs; no loans.
Publications: Program policy statement, application guidelines, newsletter, informational brochure.
Application information:
Initial approach: Proposal or letter
Copies of proposal: 1
Deadline(s): Sept. 15
Board meeting date(s): Feb., May, Aug., and Nov. or Dec.
Final notification: Dec.
Officers and Trustees: Jack W. Hawkins, V.P.; Mark Sinclair, Treas.; Linda Alesi-Miller, Manuel Avila, Robert O. Helberg, Hilton Hemphill, Randolph B. Marston, Mrs. Paul W. Phy, Francis W. Thayer, George W. Wharton, Robert J. Wright.
Number of staff: 2 full-time professional; 1 full-time support.
Employer Identification Number: 751783741

2984
The James R. Dougherty, Jr., Foundation
P.O. Box 640
Beeville 78104-0640 (512) 358-3560

Trust established in 1950 in TX.
Donor(s): James R. Dougherty,† Mrs. James R. Dougherty.†
Financial data (yr. ended 11/30/87): Assets, $8,410,678 (M); expenditures, $745,020, including $633,308 for 127 grants (high: $35,000; low: $500; average: $1,000-$5,000).
Purpose and activities: Support for Roman Catholic church-related institutions, including higher, secondary, and other education, cultural programs, health and hospitals, and youth and social service agencies.
Types of support: Operating budgets, land acquisition, research, endowment funds, building funds, scholarship funds, equipment, annual campaigns, capital campaigns, conferences and seminars, general purposes, renovation projects.
Limitations: Giving primarily in TX. No grants to individuals; no loans.
Application information:
Initial approach: Proposal
Copies of proposal: 1
Deadline(s): 10 days prior to board meeting
Board meeting date(s): Semiannually
Final notification: 6 months or less
Write: Hugh Grove, Jr., Asst. Secy.
Officers and Trustees: May Dougherty King, Chair.; Mary Patricia Dougherty, Secy.-Treas.; F. William Carr, Jr., James R. Dougherty III, Ben F. Vaughan III, Genevieve Vaughan.
Number of staff: 3
Employer Identification Number: 746039858

2985
Dr. Pepper Corporate Giving Program
P.O. Box 655086
Dallas 75265-5086 (214) 824-0331

Financial data (yr. ended 12/31/88): $100,000 for grants.
Purpose and activities: Supports civic programs, education, environmental issues, arts and culture, hospitals, minority programs, science, United Way and urban problems. Other non-monetary assistance includes volunteer recruitment, donations of equipment and furniture, employee matching fund for welfare programs and building funds.
Types of support: Employee matching gifts, building funds, in-kind gifts.
Limitations: Giving primarily in headquarters city, headquarters state, entire U.S. and international locations.
Application information: Include project description, proposed budget, annual report, financial report, 501(c)(3), board list, and donor list.
Initial approach: Letter of inquiry
Final notification: If rejected, will send notification
Write: Ira M. Rosenstein, V.P., Administration

2986
Dresser Foundation, Inc.
P.O. Box 718
Dallas 75221 (214) 740-6078
Harbison-Walker scholarship program application address: Scholarship Committee, One Gateway Ctr., Pittsburgh, PA 15222; Dresser Harbison Fdn. scholarship program application address: c/o Assoc. of Universities and Colleges of Canada, 151 Slater St., Ottawa, Canada KIP 5N1

Trust established in 1953 in TX.
Donor(s): Dresser Industries, Inc.
Financial data (yr. ended 10/31/88): Assets, $9,842,000 (M); expenditures, $1,581,670, including $1,360,000 for 250 grants (high: $100,000; low: $50; average: $1,000-$50,000) and $186,670 for 350 employee matching gifts.
Purpose and activities: Emphasis on community funds and higher education, including employee-related scholarships through National Merit Scholarship Corporation and through two foundation programs; support also for hospitals, youth agencies, and cultural

programs; provides minor welfare assistance to retired employees.
Types of support: General purposes, employee matching gifts, building funds, employee-related scholarships, grants to individuals.
Limitations: Giving primarily in areas of company operations, particularly Pittsburgh, PA, Waukesha, WI, Marion, OH, and Houston and Dallas, TX. No grants to individuals (except for employee-related scholarships and old age assistance payments), or for endowment funds; no loans.
Publications: Application guidelines.
Application information: Completion of application forms required for all employee-related scholarship programs but not for other programs.
Initial approach: Proposal
Copies of proposal: 1
Deadline(s): None for general grants; Feb. 14 for Harbison-Walker employee scholarships, and June 1 for Dresser Canada, Inc. employee scholarships
Board meeting date(s): As required
Final notification: 2 months
Write: Richard E. Hauslein, Chair. of Contrib. Comm.
Officers and Directors:* John J. Murphy,* Chair.; J.J. Corboy,* Pres.; R.E. Hauslein,* V.P.; Bill D. St. John,* V.P.; M.S. Nickson, Secy.; Paul W. Willey, Treas.
Trustees: NCNB Texas, Merrill Lynch Asset Management, Inc.
Number of staff: 1 full-time support.
Employer Identification Number: 237309548

2987
Early Foundation, Inc.
6319 Mimosa Lane
Dallas 75230 (214) 361-5625

Established in 1963 in TX.
Financial data (yr. ended 5/31/87): Assets, $1,940,941 (M); expenditures, $65,229, including $64,245 for 44 grants (high: $12,600; low: $50).
Purpose and activities: Emphasis on education, particularly higher education, and culture; some support also for the aged, and for Protestant giving.
Limitations: Giving primarily in Dallas, TX.
Application information:
Write: Jeannette B. Early, Pres.
Officer: Jeannette B. Early, Pres.
Employer Identification Number: 756011853

2988
El Paso Community Foundation
Texas Commerce Bank Bldg., Suite 1616
El Paso 79901 (915) 533-4020

Community foundation incorporated in 1977 in TX.
Financial data (yr. ended 12/31/88): Assets, $11,000,910 (M); gifts received, $439,750; expenditures, $2,192,293, including $1,549,301 for 334 grants.
Purpose and activities: Giving for education, social service and youth agencies, health, arts and humanities, environment, and community development.
Types of support: Operating budgets, seed money, emergency funds, land acquisition, matching funds, special projects, student aid, equipment, renovation projects, continuing support, publications, consulting services, technical assistance, capital campaigns, program-related investments.
Limitations: Giving limited to the El Paso, TX, area. No grants to individuals (except for scholarships), or for deficit financing or research.
Publications: Annual report, application guidelines, 990-PF.
Application information: Include 16 copies of summary sheet with 5 proposal copies. Application form required.
Initial approach: Proposal with 16 copies of summary sheet
Copies of proposal: 5
Deadline(s): Feb. 1
Board meeting date(s): May
Final notification: Following May meeting
Write: Janice W. Windle, Exec. Dir.
Officers: John Kelley, Pres.; Frances Roderick Smith, 1st V.P.; Guillermo Licon, 2nd V.P.; Carl E. Ryan,* Secy.; Joe Kidd,* Treas.; Janice W. Windle, Exec. Dir.
Trustees:* H.M. Daugherty, Jr., Bernice Dittmer, Richard H. Feuille, Hugh K. Frederick, Jr., Morris Galatzan, Richard Hickson, Hector Holguin, Betty M. MacGuire, Mary Lou Moreno, Guillermo Ochoa, Jim Phillips, Patricia Rogers, Mary Carmen Saucedo.
Trustee Banks: First City National Bank, MBank-El Paso, NCNB-Texas, Sunwest El Paso, Texas Commerce Bank.
Number of staff: 3 full-time professional; 2 full-time support.
Employer Identification Number: 741839536
Recent arts and culture grants:
El Paso Cultural Planning Council, El Paso, TX, $5,000. For project support. 1987.
El Paso Pro-Musica, El Paso, TX, $5,000. For operating support. 1987.
K X C R 89.5 FM, El Paso, TX, $5,000. For general support for cultural and arts programming. 1987.
Plaza Theater, El Paso, TX, $100,000. For capital support. 1987.

2989
Electronic Data Systems Corporate Giving Program
7171 Forest Ln., A340
Dallas 75230 (214) 604-6000

Purpose and activities: Supports fine arts institutes, general education and private colleges, civic affairs, and programs for the disabled and handicapped.
Limitations: Giving primarily in headquarters city and major operating locations.
Application information: Include background information, financial statement, use of funds, board listing.
Initial approach: Letter and proposal
Write: Mgr. Community Relations/Corp. Contribs.

2990
Margaret & James A. Elkins, Jr. Foundation
713 River Oaks Bank Tower
2001 Kirby Dr.
Houston 77019 (713) 526-6374

Established in 1956 in TX.
Financial data (yr. ended 10/31/88): Assets, $3,318,421 (M); expenditures, $177,257, including $158,600 for 7 grants (high: $60,000; low: $2,500).
Purpose and activities: Support primarily for education, social services, religion, cultural programs and science.
Limitations: Giving primarily in Houston, TX.
Application information:
Initial approach: Letter
Deadline(s): None
Write: Howard Sides, Pres.
Officers: Howard Sides, Pres.; W.C. Menasco, V.P.; R.A. Seale, Jr., Secy.-Treas.
Employer Identification Number: 746051746

2991
Enron Foundation
(Formerly The Enron Foundation - Omaha)
1400 Smith
P.O. Box 1188
Houston 77251 (713) 853-5400

Established in 1979 in NE as InterNorth Foundation; in 1986 name changed to Enron Foundation - Omaha; in 1988 absorbed Enron Foundation - Houston (name changed from HNG Foundation) and name changed to Enron Foundation.
Donor(s): Enron Corp.
Financial data (yr. ended 12/31/87): Assets, $9,538,739 (M); gifts received, $2,455,527; expenditures, $4,479,438, including $3,958,268 for 424 grants (high: $200,000; low: $100; average: $5,000-$10,000) and $277,921 for 865 employee matching gifts.
Purpose and activities: Support primarily for higher education, arts and culture, community funds and civic organizations, and social service and youth agencies.
Types of support: General purposes, operating budgets, continuing support, annual campaigns, seed money, emergency funds, building funds, matching funds, employee matching gifts, capital campaigns, equipment, renovation projects, research.
Limitations: Giving limited to areas of company operations, with preference given to the Midwest and the Houston, TX, area; giving also in Omaha, NE, and Winter Park, FL. No support for non-educational religious organizations. No grants to individuals, or for fellowships; generally no grants for endowment funds or advertising for benefit purposes; no loans.
Publications: Informational brochure (including application guidelines).
Application information:
Initial approach: Letter
Copies of proposal: 1
Deadline(s): 30 days before board meeting
Board meeting date(s): May, Aug., Nov., and Feb.
Final notification: Generally, within 30 days; grants for over $10,000 are considered at

quarterly board meetings and may require a longer response period
Write: Deborah Christie, Exec. Dir.
Officers and Directors: Kenneth L. Lay, Chair.; Rich Kinder, Vice-Chair.; Larry DeRoin, Sr. V.P.; Peggy Menchaca, V.P. and Secy.; Elizabeth Labanowski, V.P.; Edward Segner, V.P.; Ross Workman, V.P.; Deborah Christie, Exec. Dir.
Number of staff: 2 full-time professional; 1 full-time support; 1 part-time support.
Employer Identification Number: 470615943

2992
Enserch Corporate Contributions Program
Enserch Center
300 South St. Paul St.
Dallas 75201 (214) 651-8700

Purpose and activities: Supports education, social welfare, public health, and the arts.
Limitations: No grants for religious activities, individuals, or scholarships administered solely through institutions.
Application information:
Initial approach: Brief letter
Deadline(s): None
Write: Richard B. Williams, Sr. V.P., Administration

2993
Exxon Company, U.S.A. Corporate Contributions Program
P.O. Box 2180
Houston 77252 (713) 656-9199

Purpose and activities: Supports community and civic affairs, culture and the arts, minority education, environmental issues, equal rights, federated campaigns, general health care, international groups, legal services, medical research, science, urban problems, public policy, social services, volunteerism, wildlife, rehabilitation, leadership development, homeless, drug abuse, economics, welfare organizations, youth service, and women's programs. Support of education is through the Exxon Education Foundation. Also available are volunteer recruitment, employee volunteer programs, use of company in-house services, use of company facilities, and donations of company's primary goods or services.
Types of support: In-kind gifts, employee matching gifts, equipment, capital campaigns, emergency funds, program-related investments, research, special projects.
Limitations: Giving primarily in locations where company has operations, employees, and retirees.
Publications: Corporate giving report.
Application information: Include proof of tax-exempt status and other sources of funding.
Initial approach: Letter of inquiry
Copies of proposal: 1
Deadline(s): Applications accepted throughout the year
Write: Arthur G. Randol III, Coord., Public Affairs

2994
Fain Foundation
500 City National Bldg.
Wichita Falls 76301

Established in 1942 in TX.
Donor(s): Minnie Rhea Wood.
Financial data (yr. ended 12/31/87): Assets, $1,383,477 (M); gifts received, $50,000; expenditures, $166,949, including $159,200 for 18 grants (high: $100,000; low: $500).
Purpose and activities: Giving for health and social services, youth agencies, and Protestant organizations.
Types of support: Operating budgets, special projects.
Limitations: Giving primarily in TX.
Application information: Application form required.
Officers and Directors: Minnie Rhea Wood, Pres. and Treas.; Martha Fain White, V.P.; Herbert B. Story, Secy.; Jerry C. Helfenstine.
Employer Identification Number: 756016679

2995
The R. W. Fair Foundation
P.O. Box 689
Tyler 75710 (214) 592-3811

Trust established in 1936; incorporated in 1959 in TX.
Donor(s): R.W. Fair,† Mattie Allen Fair.†
Financial data (yr. ended 12/31/87): Assets, $15,192,264 (M); expenditures, $1,695,762, including $1,084,372 for 114 grants (high: $197,500; low: $200; average: $1,000-$20,000).
Purpose and activities: Grants largely for Protestant church support and church-related programs and for secondary and higher education, including legal education; some support for hospitals, youth and social service agencies, libraries, and cultural activities.
Types of support: Seed money, building funds, equipment, general purposes, endowment funds, research, special projects, scholarship funds, matching funds.
Limitations: Giving primarily in the Southwest, with emphasis on TX. No grants to individuals, or for operating budgets.
Publications: Application guidelines.
Application information: Application form required.
Initial approach: Letter
Copies of proposal: 1
Deadline(s): Mar. 1, June 1, Sept. 1, and Dec. 1
Board meeting date(s): Mar., June, Sept., and Dec.
Final notification: 3 months
Write: Wilton H. Fair, Pres.
Officers and Directors: Wilton H. Fair, Pres.; James W. Fair, Sr. V.P.; Sam Bright, V.P.; Marvin N. Wilson, Secy.-Treas.; Calvin N. Clyde, Sr., Will Knight, B.B. Palmore, C.E. Peeples, Richard L. Ray.
Number of staff: 2 part-time professional.
Employer Identification Number: 756015270

2996
I.D. & Marguerite Fairchild Foundation
P.O. Box 150143
Lufkin 75915-0143

Established in 1977 in TX.
Donor(s): Marguerite Fairchild.†
Financial data (yr. ended 6/30/88): Assets, $1,673,480 (M); expenditures, $131,613, including $123,086 for 6 grants (high: $53,461; low: $1,625).
Purpose and activities: Support primarily for a higher education scholarship foundation; support also for a library, museum and a zoo.
Types of support: Building funds, capital campaigns, scholarship funds, special projects.
Limitations: Giving limited to Angelina County, TX.
Application information:
Initial approach: Letter
Deadline(s): May 1
Board meeting date(s): June
Officers: Virginia R. Allen, Pres.; Hilda Mitchell, V.P.; Mary Duncan, Secy.
Employer Identification Number: 751572514

2997
The William Stamps Farish Fund
1100 Louisiana, Suite 1200
Houston 77002 (713) 757-7313

Incorporated in 1951 in TX.
Donor(s): Libbie Rice Farish.
Financial data (yr. ended 6/30/88): Assets, $75,789,394 (M); expenditures, $3,915,736, including $3,615,000 for 110 grants (high: $200,000; low: $1,200; average: $10,000-$60,000).
Purpose and activities: Giving primarily for higher and secondary education, the humanities, hospitals and medical research, and social services.
Types of support: Research, general purposes.
Limitations: Giving primarily in TX. No grants to individuals, or for annual campaigns, deficit financing, operating budgets, exchange programs, or consulting services; no loans.
Publications: Application guidelines.
Application information:
Initial approach: Proposal
Copies of proposal: 1
Deadline(s): Mar. 30
Board meeting date(s): Semiannually
Write: W.S. Farish, Pres.
Officers: W.S. Farish,* Pres.; Martha Farish Gerry,* V.P.; J.O. Winston, Jr.,* V.P.; Caroline Rotan, Secy.; Terry W. Ward, Treas.
Trustees:* Myrtle M. Camp, Cornelia G. Corbett, Dan R. Japhet.
Number of staff: 1 full-time professional.
Employer Identification Number: 746043019

2998
The Favrot Fund
909 Wirt Rd., No. 101
Houston 77024-3444 (713) 956-4009

Incorporated in 1952 in TX.
Donor(s): Laurence H. Favrot,† Johanna A. Favrot, George B. Strong.
Financial data (yr. ended 12/31/87): Assets, $6,738,467 (M); expenditures, $378,629,

including $310,000 for 24 grants (high: $25,000; low: $2,000).
Purpose and activities: Emphasis on community-based programs directed toward health, support of the needy, and the arts, including the performing arts; grants for education and for social agencies, including family planning and youth agencies.
Types of support: Operating budgets, building funds, equipment, general purposes.
Limitations: Giving primarily in TX, CA, NY, and DC.
Application information:
Initial approach: Letter
Copies of proposal: 1
Deadline(s): None
Board meeting date(s): Oct. or Nov.
Write: Mrs. Carol Parker
Officers and Trustees: Johanna A. Favrot, Pres.; Lenoir M. Josey, V.P. and Mgr.; Celestine Favrot Arndt, Laurence de Kanter Favrot, Leo Mortimer Favrot, Marcia Favrot-Anderson, Romelia Favrot, Jeanette Favrot Peterson.
Employer Identification Number: 746045648

2999
The Feldman Foundation
7800 Stemmons Freeway
P.O. Box 1046
Dallas 75221 (214) 689-4337

Trust established in 1946 in TX.
Donor(s): Commercial Metals Co. Subsidiaries.
Financial data (yr. ended 12/31/87): Assets, $10,138,977 (M); gifts received, $637,877; expenditures, $776,781, including $753,500 for 20 grants (high: $200,000; low: $500; average: $1,000-$100,000).
Purpose and activities: Giving primarily for Jewish welfare funds; some support for cultural programs, medical research, hospitals, higher education, and social service agencies.
Types of support: Research, building funds, general purposes, scholarship funds, special projects.
Limitations: Giving primarily in TX and NY.
Application information:
Initial approach: Proposal
Copies of proposal: 1
Deadline(s): None
Board meeting date(s): As needed
Final notification: Upon receipt of proposal
Write: Jacob Feldman, Trustee
Trustees: Daniel E. Feldman, Jacob Feldman, Moses Feldman, Robert L. Feldman, M.B. Zale.
Number of staff: 1 full-time support.
Employer Identification Number: 756011578

3000
Fifth Avenue Foundation
801 Cherry St., Suite 1200
Fort Worth 76102 (817) 877-2800

Established in 1979 in TX.
Donor(s): Pauline G. Evans.†
Financial data (yr. ended 12/31/87): Assets, $1,520,169 (M); expenditures, $113,266, including $100,500 for 62 grants (high: $15,000; low: $300; average: $1,000-$5,000).
Purpose and activities: Support primarily for cultural programs, hospitals and health associations, and social service agencies.
Types of support: Annual campaigns, capital campaigns, continuing support, emergency funds, renovation projects.
Limitations: Giving limited to local organizations in the Dallas-Ft. Worth, TX, area and national organizations. No grants for scholarships.
Application information:
Initial approach: Letter
Deadline(s): None
Write: Whitfield J. Collins, Pres.
Officers: Whitfield J. Collins, Pres.; Marie Harper, V.P.
Employer Identification Number: 751659424

3001
Leland Fikes Foundation, Inc.
325 North St. Paul, Suite 3206
Dallas 75201 (214) 754-0144

Incorporated in 1952 in DE.
Donor(s): Leland Fikes,† Catherine W. Fikes.
Financial data (yr. ended 12/31/87): Assets, $54,764,254 (M); gifts received, $25,000; expenditures, $5,706,670, including $4,995,541 for 135 grants (high: $300,000; low: $25).
Purpose and activities: Giving primarily for medical research, health, youth, and social services, public interest groups, and education; grants also for population research and control, and cultural programs.
Types of support: Annual campaigns, seed money, emergency funds, building funds, equipment, land acquisition, endowment funds, research, scholarship funds, matching funds, continuing support, capital campaigns, general purposes, operating budgets, professorships, special projects.
Limitations: Giving primarily in the Dallas, TX, area. No grants to individuals; no loans.
Publications: Application guidelines.
Application information: Submit proposal upon request.
Initial approach: Letter
Copies of proposal: 1
Deadline(s): None
Board meeting date(s): Bimonthly
Write: Nancy Solana, Research and Grant Administration
Officers: Catherine W. Fikes,* Chair.; Lee Fikes,* Pres. and Treas.; Nancy Solana, Secy.; Amy L. Fikes.
Number of staff: 1 full-time professional; 3 part-time professional; 1 full-time support; 1 part-time support.
Employer Identification Number: 756035984

3002
First City Bancorporation of Texas Corporate Giving Program
P.O. Box 2557
Houston 77252 (713) 658-5293

Financial data (yr. ended 12/31/88): $713,000 for grants (high: $50,000; low: $350; average: $10,000-$15,000).
Purpose and activities: Supports arts and culture, health and welfare, education and civic programs. Other support through employee volunteer programs, use of company in-house services, use of company facilities and donations of company's primary goods or services.
Types of support: In-kind gifts, capital campaigns, operating budgets, special projects.
Limitations: Giving primarily in headquarters city and state, and in Sioux Falls, SD. No support for political, fraternal, or religious groups. No grants to individuals.
Application information: Proposal including description of organization, amount requested, purpose for which funds are sought, recently audited financial statement, lists of board members and major donors, application form and proof of 501 (c)(3) status.
Initial approach: Letter and proposal
Deadline(s): None
Final notification: 3-4 weeks
Write: Maureen G. MacAuley, Contribs. Coord.

3003
First Interstate Foundation
(Formerly Allied Banks Foundation, Inc.)
815 Walker
P.O. Box 1515
Houston 77253-3326

Incorporated in 1979 in TX.
Donor(s): Allied Bank of Texas, First Interstate Bank of Texas.
Financial data (yr. ended 12/31/87): Assets, $195,323 (M); expenditures, $233,930, including $228,072 for 59 grants (high: $30,000; low: $50).
Purpose and activities: Emphasis on cultural programs, including the performing arts, community funds, and social agencies; support also for civic affairs, youth agencies, health, and education.
Limitations: Giving primarily in TX.
Trustees: Thomas C. Clausen, Walter E. Johnson, Bob D. Ward.
Employer Identification Number: 742066478

3004
Ray C. Fish Foundation
2001 Kirby Dr., Suite 1005
Houston 77019 (713) 522-0741

Incorporated in 1957 in TX.
Donor(s): Raymond Clinton Fish,† Mirtha G. Fish.†
Financial data (yr. ended 6/30/86): Assets, $19,039,025 (M); gifts received, $83,571; expenditures, $936,469, including $675,500 for 67 grants (high: $300,000; low: $500).
Purpose and activities: Emphasis on educational institutions, hospitals, medical research, youth and social service agencies, and cultural organizations, including the performing arts.
Types of support: General purposes.
Limitations: Giving primarily in TX, with emphasis on Houston.
Application information:
Initial approach: Letter
Deadline(s): None
Officers: Barbara F. Daniel, Pres.; Robert J. Cruikshank, V.P.; James L. Daniel, Jr., V.P.; Maxine Costello, Secy.; Christopher J. Daniel, Treas.
Number of staff: 1
Employer Identification Number: 746043047

3005
The Fleming Foundation
1007 Interfirst Fort Worth Bldg.
Fort Worth 76102 (817) 335-3741

Incorporated in 1936 in TX.
Donor(s): William Fleming.†
Financial data (yr. ended 12/31/86): Assets, $13,660,491 (M); expenditures, $883,230, including $669,810 for 46 grants (high: $228,000; low: $250; average: $1,000-$10,000).
Purpose and activities: Emphasis on cultural programs and Protestant church support and church-related activities; support also for higher education and youth and social service agencies.
Types of support: Operating budgets, continuing support, annual campaigns, emergency funds, professorships, research, special projects.
Limitations: Giving primarily in TX, with emphasis on Fort Worth. No grants to individuals, or for deficit financing, building or endowment funds, land acquisition, matching gifts, scholarships, fellowships, exchange programs, publications, or conferences; single-year grants only; no loans.
Application information:
Initial approach: Proposal
Copies of proposal: 1
Deadline(s): None
Board meeting date(s): Jan., Apr., July, and Sept.
Final notification: 2 months
Write: G. Malcolm Louden, Asst. Secy.
Officers and Directors: Mary D. Walsh, Pres.; F. Howard Walsh, V.P.; F. Howard Walsh, Jr., Secy.-Treas.; G. Malcolm Louden.
Number of staff: 2
Employer Identification Number: 756022736

3006
The Florence Foundation
c/o NCNB Texas, Trust Dept.
P.O. Box 830241
Dallas 75283-0241 (214) 922-6267
Additional tel.: (214) 922-5181

Established in 1956.
Donor(s): The Fred F. Florence Trust.
Financial data (yr. ended 11/30/88): Assets, $1,850,000 (M); expenditures, $87,250, including $75,030 for 23 grants (high: $5,000; low: $500).
Purpose and activities: Giving for social services, hospitals, higher education, and cultural programs.
Types of support: General purposes, matching funds, equipment, building funds, special projects.
Limitations: Giving primarily in TX. No grants for scholarships; no loans.
Application information:
Initial approach: Letter
Copies of proposal: 1
Deadline(s): Feb. 15 and Aug. 15
Board meeting date(s): Spring and fall
Write: Carol A. Cook, Secy.
Trustee: NCNB Texas.
Members: Cecile Cook, Chair.; Carol Cook, Jr., Secy.; James Aston, David Florence, Paul Harris, John T. Stuart.
Employer Identification Number: 756008029

3007
The Fondren Foundation
7 TCT 37
P.O. Box 2558
Houston 77252-8037 (713) 236-4403

Trust established in 1948 in TX.
Donor(s): Mrs. W.W. Fondren, Sr.,† and others.
Financial data (yr. ended 10/31/88): Assets, $77,845,407 (M); expenditures, $3,392,020, including $3,386,825 for 69 grants (high: $500,000; low: $1,500; average: $5,000-$50,000).
Purpose and activities: Emphasis on higher and secondary education, social service and youth agencies, cultural organizations, and health.
Limitations: Giving primarily in TX, with emphasis on Houston, and in the Southwest. No grants to individuals, or for annual or operating fund drives.
Application information:
Initial approach: Letter
Copies of proposal: 1
Deadline(s): None
Board meeting date(s): Quarterly
Write: Melanie A. Boone, Asst. Secy.
Officers and Trustees: Sue Trammel Whitfield, Chair.; Linda Knapp Underwood, Vice-Chair.; Walter W. Fondren III, Secy.-Treas.; Doris Fondren Bertron, Melanie A. Boone, Ellanor Ann Fondren, Ann Gordon Trummell, David M. Underwood, William F. Whitfield, Sr.
Number of staff: None.
Employer Identification Number: 746042565

3008
The Fuller Foundation, Inc.
2020 Texas American Bank Bldg.
Fort Worth 76102 (817) 336-2020

Incorporated in 1951 in TX and in DE.
Financial data (yr. ended 12/31/87): Assets, $4,020,862 (M); expenditures, $233,153, including $203,679 for 36 grants (high: $25,000; low: $250).
Purpose and activities: Giving for hospitals, secondary and higher education, art, and music; grants also for Protestant church support, and youth agencies.
Application information:
Initial approach: Proposal
Deadline(s): None
Write: William M. Fuller, V.P.
Officers and Directors: Andrew P. Fuller, Pres.; William M. Fuller, V.P.; R.L. Bowen, Treas.
Employer Identification Number: 756015942

3009
Garvey Texas Foundation, Inc.
P.O. Box 9600
Fort Worth 76107-0600

Incorporated in 1962 in TX.
Donor(s): James S. Garvey, Shirley F. Garvey, Garvey Foundation.
Financial data (yr. ended 12/31/86): Assets, $4,366,590 (M); gifts received, $205,423; expenditures, $179,731, including $170,201 for 72 grants (high: $25,860; low: $50).
Purpose and activities: Support primarily for youth agencies, education, cultural activities, community funds, and hospitals.
Limitations: Giving primarily in TX.
Officers: Shirley F. Garvey,* Pres.; James S. Garvey,* V.P.; Jeffrey L. Ault, Secy.; C.B. Felts, Jr., Treas.
Trustees:* Richard F. Garvey, Janet G. Sawyer, Carol G. Sweat.
Employer Identification Number: 756031547

3010
Robert and Ruth Glaze Foundation
2001 Bryan Tower, Suite 3131
Dallas 75201 (214) 969-5595

Established in 1986 in TX.
Donor(s): Robert E. Glaze, Ruth T. Glaze.
Financial data (yr. ended 12/31/87): Assets, $2,864,382 (M); expenditures, $317,777, including $213,874 for 20 grants (high: $108,500; low: $100).
Purpose and activities: Primarily for religious organizations, particularly a Baptist church and groups promoting Christian ministry. Some support also for a symphonic association.
Limitations: Giving primarily in Dallas, TX.
Application information:
Initial approach: Letter
Deadline(s): None
Write: Robert E. Glaze, Pres.
Officers and Directors: Robert E. Glaze, Pres. and Treas.; Ruth T. Glaze, Secy.; Maryanne Romano.
Employer Identification Number: 752102493

3011
The Green Foundation
3300 First City Center
Dallas 75201

Trust established in 1958 in TX.
Donor(s): Cecil H. Green, Ida M. Green.
Financial data (yr. ended 12/31/87): Assets, $5,660,440 (M); gifts received, $4,554,469; expenditures, $105,983, including $93,250 for 26 grants (high: $25,000; low: $200).
Purpose and activities: Emphasis on cultural programs, higher education, a secondary school and a community fund.
Types of support: Operating budgets.
Limitations: Giving primarily in the Dallas, TX, area.
Application information:
Deadline(s): None
Write: William E. Collins, Trustee
Trustees: William E. Collins, Cecil H. Green, Bryan Smith.
Employer Identification Number: 756015446

3012
Morris Greenspun Foundation
3717 Maplewood Ave.
Dallas 75205-2826 (214) 871-8600

Established in 1964 in TX.
Financial data (yr. ended 12/31/87): Assets, $1,103,424 (M); expenditures, $61,153, including $52,990 for 119 grants (high: $3,000; low: $20).

Purpose and activities: Giving primarily for cultural programs, museums, and higher education.
Application information:
Initial approach: Letter
Deadline(s): None
Write: Theodore S. Hochstim, Dir.
Directors: Iva G. Hochstim, Raymond Marcus, Theodore S. Hochstim.
Employer Identification Number: 756019227

3013
Paul and Mary Haas Foundation
P.O. Box 2928
Corpus Christi 78403 (512) 888-9301

Trust established in 1954 in TX.
Donor(s): Paul R. Haas, Mary F. Haas.
Financial data (yr. ended 12/31/87): Assets, $1,147,872 (M); gifts received, $200,000; expenditures, $571,292, including $458,230 for 112 grants (high: $51,000; low: $80; average: $3,500) and $57,361 for 70 grants to individuals.
Purpose and activities: Grants for social service and youth agencies, church support, higher education, and cultural programs; scholarships only to undergraduates and vocational school students; limited medical support.
Types of support: Special projects, student aid, annual campaigns, building funds, capital campaigns, emergency funds, equipment, general purposes, renovation projects, seed money, operating budgets.
Limitations: Giving primarily in the Corpus Christi, TX, area. No grants to individuals (except for student aid); no support for graduate students.
Publications: Annual report (including application guidelines), application guidelines.
Application information: Application form provided for scholarship applicants.
Initial approach: Proposal
Copies of proposal: 1
Deadline(s): For scholarships preference is 3 months before the semester; none for other grants
Board meeting date(s): As needed
Final notification: Within a few weeks of receipt of proposal
Write: Nancy Wise Somers, Fdn. Dir.
Trustees: Mary F. Haas, Paul R. Haas, Raymond P. Haas, Rene Haas, Rheta Haas Page.
Number of staff: 1 part-time professional; 1 part-time support.
Employer Identification Number: 746031614
Recent arts and culture grants:
Corpus Christi Arts Council, Corpus Christi, TX, $5,650. 1987.
Foundation for Sciences and Arts, Corpus Christi, TX, $20,000. For Watergarden. 1987.
South Texas Public Broadcasting System, Corpus Christi, TX, $18,527. For Sesame Street. 1987.
Texas Institute for Arts in Education, Houston, TX, $5,400. 1987.

3014
The Haggar Foundation
6113 Lemmon Ave.
Dallas 75209
Scholarship application address: Haggar Scholarship Program, The University of North Texas, P.O. Box 13707, Denton, TX 76203-3707

Trust established in 1950 in TX.
Donor(s): Joseph M. Haggar, Rose M. Haggar, Haggar Co., and others.
Financial data (yr. ended 6/30/88): Assets, $19,354,689 (M); expenditures, $2,198,855, including $2,004,246 for 269 grants (high: $250,000; low: $100).
Purpose and activities: Emphasis on higher and secondary education, including a scholarship program for children of company employees, and hospitals; contributions also for youth agencies, cultural programs, and Catholic church support.
Types of support: Employee-related scholarships, building funds.
Limitations: Giving primarily in southern TX, and in OK, in areas of company operations.
Publications: Application guidelines.
Application information: Application guidelines available for employee-related scholarship program. Application form required.
Deadline(s): Submit scholarship application on or before Apr. 30; deadline Mar. 31
Write: Rosemary Haggar Vaughan, Exec. Dir.
Trustees: Edmond R. Haggar, Sr., Joseph M. Haggar, Jr., Joseph M. Haggar III, Robert C. Qualls, Rosemary Haggar Vaughan.
Employer Identification Number: 756019237

3015
The Ewing Halsell Foundation
711 Navarro St.
San Antonio Bank and Trust Bldg., Suite 537
San Antonio 78205 (512) 223-2640

Trust established in 1957 in TX.
Donor(s): Ewing Halsell,† Mrs. Ewing Halsell,† Grace F. Rider.†
Financial data (yr. ended 6/30/85): Assets, $33,570,115 (M); expenditures, $6,161,048, including $531,913 for 27 grants (high: $150,000; low: $100; average: $1,000-$20,000).
Purpose and activities: Grants for educational and charitable purposes; giving for cultural programs, health organizations, and youth agencies.
Types of support: Operating budgets, continuing support, annual campaigns, building funds, equipment, land acquisition, research, publications, technical assistance, seed money.
Limitations: Giving limited to TX, with emphasis on southwestern TX, and particularly San Antonio. No grants to individuals, or for deficit financing, emergency funds, general endowments, matching gifts, scholarships, fellowships, demonstration projects, or conferences; no loans.
Publications: Biennial report (including application guidelines), program policy statement.
Application information:
Initial approach: Letter or proposal
Copies of proposal: 1
Deadline(s): None
Board meeting date(s): Quarterly
Final notification: 3 months
Officers and Trustees: Gilbert M. Denman, Jr., Chair.; Helen Campbell, Secy.-Treas.; Leroy G. Denman, Jr., Hugh Fitzsimmons, Jean Holmes McDonald.
Number of staff: 1 full-time professional; 2 part-time support.
Employer Identification Number: 746063016

3016
George and Mary Josephine Hamman Foundation
1000 Louisiana, Suite 820
Houston 77002 (713) 658-8345

Incorporated in 1954 in TX.
Donor(s): Mary Josephine Hamman,† George Hamman.
Financial data (yr. ended 4/30/87): Assets, $22,954,383 (M); expenditures, $1,753,611, including $600,130 for 82 grants (high: $120,130; low: $500; average: $1,000-$10,000) and $168,750 for 94 grants to individuals.
Purpose and activities: Giving for construction and operation of hospitals, and medical treatment and research organizations and programs; grants to churches and affiliated religious organizations (nondenominational); individual scholarship program for local high school students; grants to building programs or special educational projects at colleges and universities, mostly local; contributions also to cultural programs, social services, and youth agencies.
Types of support: Annual campaigns, emergency funds, building funds, equipment, research, professorships, scholarship funds, continuing support, matching funds, student aid.
Limitations: Giving limited to TX, primarily the Houston area. No support for post-graduate education. No grants to individuals (except for scholarships), or for deficit financing, maintenance of buildings, or endowment funds.
Publications: Application guidelines, financial statement.
Application information: Application form required for scholarships.
Initial approach: Letter
Copies of proposal: 1
Deadline(s): Mar. 31 for scholarships, none for other grants
Board meeting date(s): Monthly
Final notification: 60 days
Write: Stephen I. Gelsey, Admin.
Officers and Directors: Charles D. Milby, Pres.; Henry R. Hamman, Secy.; Louise Milby Feagin.
Number of staff: 2 full-time professional.
Employer Identification Number: 746061447

3017
The Don and Sybil Harrington Foundation
700 First National Place I, Suite 700
801 South Fillmore
Amarillo 79101 (806) 373-8353

Trust established in 1951 in TX; incorporated in 1971.
Donor(s): Donald D. Harrington,† Mrs. Sybil B. Harrington.
Financial data (yr. ended 12/31/88): Assets, $72,129,862 (M); expenditures, $7,405,194, including $5,166,690 for 43 grants (high: $1,646,284; low: $5,000; average: $10,000-$100,000).
Purpose and activities: Interests include hospitals and health agencies, cultural programs, higher education, including scholarship funds, youth agencies, social services, and civic affairs.
Types of support: Scholarship funds.
Limitations: Giving primarily in limited to the 26 northernmost counties of the Texas Panhandle. No grants to individuals, or for operating budgets.
Application information:
Initial approach: Letter
Copies of proposal: 1
Deadline(s): At least 1 month prior to board meeting
Board meeting date(s): Quarterly
Final notification: 2 months
Write: Jim Allison, Pres. or Patricia M. Smith, Grants Coord.
Officers and Directors:* Wales Madden, Jr.,* Chair.; Jim Allison, Pres. and Exec. Dir.; Gene Edwards,* V.P.; Patricia M. Smith, Secy.-Treas.
Number of staff: 2 full-time professional.
Employer Identification Number: 751336604

3018
S. T. & Margaret D. Harris Foundation
3428 St. John's Dr.
Dallas 75205

Established in 1961 in TX.
Financial data (yr. ended 10/31/87): Assets, $529,899 (M); gifts received, $19,997; expenditures, $122,412, including $120,100 for 18 grants (high: $48,500; low: $100).
Purpose and activities: Support primarily for museums and higher education.
Officers: S.T. Harris, Pres.; A.R. Harris, V.P.; Margaret D. Harris, Secy.-Treas.
Employer Identification Number: 237118609

3019
Hawn Foundation, Inc.
1540 Republic Bank Bldg.
Dallas 75201 (214) 220-2828

Incorporated in 1962 in TX.
Donor(s): Mildred Hawn.†
Financial data (yr. ended 8/31/87): Assets, $18,950,355 (M); expenditures, $1,158,658, including $905,850 for 54 grants (high: $100,000; low: $500; average: $3,500-$30,000).
Purpose and activities: Emphasis on medical research, health agencies, hospitals, higher education, social services, and cultural programs.
Limitations: Giving primarily in TX, with emphasis on Dallas.
Application information:
Initial approach: Letter
Deadline(s): None
Board meeting date(s): Aug. and as necessary
Final notification: Between 30 and 90 days
Write: E.S. Blythe, Secy.
Officers and Directors: William Russell Hawn, Pres.; E.S. Blythe, Secy.-Treas.; Joe V. Hawn, Jr., W.A. Hawn, Jr., William Russell Hawn, Jr., R.S. Strauss, I.N. Taylor.
Number of staff: None.
Employer Identification Number: 756036761

3020
Earl Hayes Foundation, Inc.
511 East John Carpenter Freeway, Suite 400
Irving 75039 (214) 869-2400

Incorporated in 1949 in DE.
Donor(s): Frue Alline Hayes, Robert T. Hayes, Bob Hayes Chevrolet, Inc.
Financial data (yr. ended 11/30/86): Assets, $129,540 (M); gifts received, $190,000; expenditures, $193,132, including $182,590 for 44 grants (high: $45,000; low: $50).
Purpose and activities: Emphasis on culture, particularly dance and music, and hospitals.
Limitations: Giving primarily in the Dallas, TX, area.
Application information:
Initial approach: Proposal
Deadline(s): None
Write: Frue Alline Hayes, Dir.
Officer: Margaret Robbins, Pres.
Directors: Douglas Dunlap, Frue Alline Hayes, Robert T. Hayes.
Employer Identification Number: 756011537

3021
Hobby Foundation
3050 Post Oak Blvd., Suite 1330
Houston 77056 (713) 993-2580

Incorporated in 1945 in TX.
Donor(s): W.P. Hobby,† Mrs. Oveta Culp Hobby, The Houston Post Co.
Financial data (yr. ended 12/31/86): Assets, $15,613,911 (M); gifts received, $523,460; expenditures, $642,126, including $536,224 for 128 grants (high: $150,000; low: $100).
Purpose and activities: Giving for higher and secondary education, museums, cultural programs, and hospitals.
Limitations: Giving primarily in TX.
Publications: Application guidelines.
Application information:
Deadline(s): None
Write: Oveta Culp Hobby, Pres.
Officers: Oveta Culp Hobby,* Pres.; William P. Hobby, Jr.,* V.P.; Audrey Horn, Secy.; Peggy C. Buchanan, Treas.
Trustees:* Jessica Hobby Catto, Diana P. Hobby.
Employer Identification Number: 746026606

3022
Hoblitzelle Foundation
1410 Tower I
NCNB Center
Dallas 75201 (214) 979-0321

Trust established in 1942 in TX; incorporated in 1953.
Donor(s): Karl St. John Hoblitzelle,† Esther T. Hoblitzelle.†
Financial data (yr. ended 4/30/88): Assets, $66,345,789 (M); expenditures, $4,334,334, including $2,736,234 for 55 grants (high: $150,000; low: $750; average: $10,000-$100,000).
Purpose and activities: Grants for higher and secondary education, hospitals and health services, youth agencies, cultural programs, social services, and community development.
Types of support: Seed money, building funds, equipment, land acquisition, matching funds, general purposes, renovation projects, capital campaigns, special projects.
Limitations: Giving limited to TX, primarily Dallas. No support for religious organizations for sectarian purposes. No grants to individuals; only occasional board-initiated support for operating budgets, debt reduction, research, scholarships, or endowments; no loans.
Publications: Annual report, program policy statement, application guidelines, newsletter.
Application information:
Initial approach: Letter
Copies of proposal: 1
Deadline(s): Apr. 15, Aug. 15, and Dec. 15
Board meeting date(s): Latter part of May, Sept., and Jan.
Final notification: After next board meeting
Write: Paul W. Harris, Exec. V.P.
Officers: James W. Aston,* C.E.O. and Chair.; James W. Keay,* Pres.; Paul W. Harris, Exec. V.P.; Mary Stacy, Secy.; John M. Stemmons,* Treas.
Directors:* James D. Berry, Lillian M. Bradshaw, Dorothy R. Cullum, Gerald W. Fronterhouse, Robert Lynn Harris, Van Alen Hollomon, George L. MacGregor, Charles C. Sprague, M.D.
Number of staff: 1 full-time professional; 1 full-time support.
Employer Identification Number: 756003984
Recent arts and culture grants:
Dallas Museum of Art, Dallas, TX, $1,761,660. For contibution of Antique English Silver Collection. 1987.
Dallas Museum of Art, Dallas, TX, $906,800. For contribution of paintings. 1987.
Dallas Museum of Art, Dallas, TX, $6,450. For contribution of 43 copies of Hoblitzelle Silver Book. 1987.
Vive Les Arts Societe, Killeen, TX, $10,000. Toward fine arts center. 1987.

3023
Irene Cafcalas Hofheinz Foundation
c/o InterFirst Bank Houston
P.O. Box 2555
Houston 77001 (713) 652-6515

Established about 1984 in TX.
Donor(s): Roy M. Hofheinz Charitable Foundation.
Financial data (yr. ended 12/31/87): Assets, $2,658,115 (M); expenditures, $377,876, including $284,357 for 24 grants (high: $187,824; low: $100) and $216,667 for loans.
Purpose and activities: Giving primarily for higher education, the arts, with emphasis on museums and a music organization, and civic affairs and social service agencies.
Types of support: Loans, program-related investments.

Limitations: Giving primarily in Houston, TX. No grants to individuals.
Application information:
Initial approach: Letter
Deadline(s): None
Write: Fred Hofheinz, Trustee
Trustees: Fred Hofheinz, InterFirst Bank, N.A.
Employer Identification Number: 760083597

3024
Houston Endowment, Inc.
P.O. Box 52338
Houston 77052 (713) 223-4043

Incorporated in 1937 in TX.
Donor(s): Jesse H. Jones,† Mrs. Jesse H. Jones.†
Financial data (yr. ended 12/31/87): Assets, $595,723,714 (M); expenditures, $20,606,195, including $10,874,517 for 278 grants (high: $1,000,000; low: $1,000; average: $1,000-$1,000,000).
Purpose and activities: For "the support of any charitable, educational or religious undertaking." Grants largely for higher education and hospitals, and social service agencies.
Types of support: Building funds, equipment, scholarship funds, special projects, fellowships, professorships, continuing support.
Limitations: Giving primarily in TX; no grants outside the continental U.S. No grants to individuals, or for permanent endowment funds; no loans.
Publications: Biennial report (including application guidelines).
Application information:
Initial approach: Letter
Copies of proposal: 1
Deadline(s): None
Board meeting date(s): Monthly
Final notification: 1 to 2 months
Write: J.H. Creekmore, Pres.
Officers and Trustees: J.H. Creekmore, Pres. and Treas.; Jo Murphy, V.P.; Alvin R. Thigpen, Secy.; Audrey Jones Beck, H.J. Nelson III, Philip G. Warner.
Coordinator of Grants: Marshall F. Wells.
Number of staff: 3 full-time professional; 4 part-time professional.
Employer Identification Number: 746013920
Recent arts and culture grants:
Fort Bend County Museum Association, Richmond, TX, $10,000. For operating support. 1987.
Galveston Historical Foundation, Galveston, TX, $50,000. For preservation of ELISSA. 1987.
Houston Ballet Foundation, Houston, TX, $37,500. For operating support. 1987.
Houston Grand Opera Association, Houston, TX, $50,000. For maintenance funds. 1987.
Houston Pops Orchestra, Houston, TX, $20,000. Toward free concerts in public parks. 1987.
Houston Symphony Society, Houston, TX, $100,000. Toward maintenance fund. 1987.
Midland-Odessa Symphony and Chorale, Midland, TX, $25,000. For operating support. 1987.
Museum of Fine Arts of Houston, Houston, TX, $1,000,000. Toward addition to house Beck Collection. 1987.
Museum of Fine Arts of Houston, Houston, TX, $75,000. For maintenance funds. 1987.
Prairie View A & M University, Prairie View, TX, $6,000. For JHJ and MGJ scholarships in fine arts and music. 1987.
Texas Architectural Foundation, Houston, TX, $9,000. For scholarships in architecture. 1987.
Texas Institute of Letters, Waco, TX, $9,000. Toward Dobie Paisano Fellowships. 1987.
Texas Institute of Letters, Waco, TX, $6,000. For prize for Best Texas Novel by a Texan or about Texas. 1987.
Texas Womans University, Denton, TX, $7,500. For MGJ scholarships in home economics or music. 1987.
University of Texas, Austin, TX, $15,000. For JHJ and MGJ scholarships in fine arts. 1987.

3025
Howell Corporate Giving Program
1010 Lamar Building, Suite 1800
Houston 77002 (713) 658-4000

Financial data (yr. ended 12/31/87): $30,500 for 22 grants (high: $5,000; low: $100).
Purpose and activities: Supports arts and culture, health and welfare, education, and civic affairs.
Types of support: Continuing support, general purposes, operating budgets.
Limitations: Giving primarily in Houston and San Antonio, TX; also consider applications from other states/areas where company operates.
Application information: Include narrative/letter, board list, and audited financial statement.
Initial approach: Letter of inquiry
Copies of proposal: 1
Deadline(s): Applications accepted throughout the year
Board meeting date(s): Quarterly
Final notification: 6 weeks
Write: Steven K. Howell, Pres.

3026
The Humphreys Foundation
1915 Trinity St.
Box 1139
Liberty 77575 (409) 336-3321

Incorporated in 1957 in TX.
Donor(s): Geraldine Davis Humphreys.†
Financial data (yr. ended 9/30/88): Assets, $5,331,535 (M); expenditures, $360,287, including $253,770 for 17 grants (high: $92,000; low: $1,000).
Purpose and activities: Giving largely for local theater and opera programs, and performing arts college scholarships.
Types of support: Scholarship funds, special projects.
Limitations: Giving limited to TX. No grants to individuals, or for building funds; no loans.
Publications: Application guidelines.
Application information: Application form required.
Initial approach: Letter or proposal
Copies of proposal: 4
Deadline(s): Submit proposal preferably in Aug.; deadline Aug. 25
Board meeting date(s): Sept. and as required
Write: L.Q. Van Deventer, Jr., Mgr.
Officers and Trustees: John S. Boles, Pres.; Claude C. Roberts, V.P. and Secy.; Mrs. J.G. Bertman, V.P. and Treas.
Number of staff: 1 part-time professional; 1 full-time support.
Employer Identification Number: 746061381

3027
Huthsteiner Fine Arts Trust
c/o Texas Commerce Bank-El Paso
P.O. Drawer 140
El Paso 79980 (915) 546-6515

Established in 1980.
Donor(s): Robert and Pauline Huthsteiner Trust.
Financial data (yr. ended 7/31/88): Assets, $1,530,907 (M); expenditures, $117,144, including $94,660 for 17 grants (high: $13,500; low: $500).
Purpose and activities: Support for the arts, especially music.
Types of support: Continuing support, emergency funds, endowment funds, equipment, general purposes, matching funds, operating budgets, publications.
Limitations: Giving primarily in West TX.
Application information:
Initial approach: Letter
Copies of proposal: 1
Deadline(s): None
Write: Terry Crenshaw, Charitable Services Officer, Texas Commerce Bank-El Paso
Trustees: Texas Commerce Bank-El Paso.
Number of staff: 1 full-time professional; 1 part-time professional.
Employer Identification Number: 746308412

3028
The Burdine Johnson Foundation
760 Southpark One Bldg.
1701 Directors Blvd.
Austin 78744-1066 (512) 441-1588

Trust established in 1960 in TX.
Donor(s): Burdine C. Johnson, J.M. Johnson.
Financial data (yr. ended 12/31/87): Assets, $11,196,886 (M); gifts received, $6,250; expenditures, $393,039, including $348,000 for 13 grants (high: $250,000; low: $1,000).
Purpose and activities: Giving for cultural programs, including a performing arts organization, and for education and social services.
Limitations: Giving primarily in TX.
Application information:
Initial approach: Proposal
Deadline(s): None
Trustees: Thomas James Barlow, Burdine C. Johnson, William T. Johnson.
Employer Identification Number: 746036669

3029
The Jonsson Foundation
3300 NCNB Tower II
Dallas 75201 (214) 969-5535

Incorporated in 1954 in TX.
Donor(s): J.E. Jonsson, Margaret E. Jonsson.†

Financial data (yr. ended 12/31/88): Assets, $3,402,098 (M); expenditures, $329,978, including $280,579 for 20 grants (high: $100,000; low: $500; average: $5,000-$10,000).
Purpose and activities: Giving in areas of health, education, culture, and general community interests.
Types of support: General purposes, building funds, equipment, matching funds, capital campaigns.
Limitations: Giving primarily in the Dallas, TX, area. No grants to individuals, or for endowment funds, scholarships, or fellowships; no loans.
Publications: Application guidelines.
Application information: Funds largely committed.
Initial approach: Letter
Copies of proposal: 1
Deadline(s): None
Board meeting date(s): Feb., May, and Sept.
Final notification: At next meeting
Write: Nelle C. Johnston, Secy.
Officers: Philip R. Jonsson,* Pres. and Treas.; Kenneth A. Jonsson,* V.P. and Treas.; Margaret J. Rogers,* V.P.; Nelle C. Johnston, Secy.
Trustees:* J.E. Jonsson.
Number of staff: 4
Employer Identification Number: 756012565

3030
Philip R. Jonsson Foundation
14951 Dallas Parkway, Suite 1030
Dallas 75240 (214) 458-8400

Established in 1954 in TX.
Financial data (yr. ended 12/31/87): Assets, $1,092,522 (M); expenditures, $68,988, including $35,500 for 13 grants (high: $20,000; low: $500).
Purpose and activities: Support for the arts, education, environment, and social services; grants also for health agencies and for public policy organizations.
Types of support: Operating budgets, building funds.
Limitations: Giving primarily in the Dallas, TX, area. No grants to individuals.
Application information:
Initial approach: Proposal not exceeding 2 pages
Write: Janet W. Hill, Exec. Secy.
Officers and Directors: Philip R. Jonsson, Pres.; Eileen J. Lewis, 1st V.P.; Kenneth B. Jonsson, 2nd V.P.; Christina A. Jonsson, Secy.; Steven W. Jonsson, Treas.
Employer Identification Number: 751552642

3031
Kaneb Services Corporate Giving Program
2400 Lakeside Blvd.
Richardson 75081 (214) 699-4000
Mailing Address: P.O. Box 650283, Dallas, TX 75265-0283

Purpose and activities: Supports fine arts institutes, general education, and private colleges.
Limitations: Giving primarily in headquarters city and major operating locations.
Application information:
Write: Jack D. Strube, V.P., Corp. Communs.

3032
Ben E. Keith Foundation Trust
c/o Texas American Bank, Fort Worth
P.O. Box 2050
Fort Worth 76113 (817) 884-4161

Trust established in 1951 in TX.
Financial data (yr. ended 6/30/87): Assets, $8,800,000 (M); expenditures, $500,000, including $450,000 for 200 grants (high: $15,000; low: $500).
Purpose and activities: Giving for higher education and social service agencies; some support also for cultural programs and hospitals.
Types of support: General purposes, operating budgets, continuing support, annual campaigns, seed money, emergency funds, deficit financing, building funds, equipment, land acquisition, endowment funds, matching funds, capital campaigns.
Limitations: Giving limited to TX. No grants to individuals, or for scholarships or fellowships; no loans.
Publications: 990-PF.
Application information:
Initial approach: Letter
Board meeting date(s): Jan., Mar., June, and Oct.
Write: Richard L. Mitchell, Secy.
Officers and Directors: John Beauchamp, Chair.; Richard L. Mitchell, Secy.; Howard Hallam, Robert Hallam, Troy LaGrone, Ronnie Wallace, Hugh Watson.
Advisory Board: Texas American Bank/Fort Worth.
Number of staff: None.
Employer Identification Number: 756013955

3033
The M. W. Kellogg Corporate Giving Program
Three Greenway Plaza
Houston 77046 (713) 960-2160

Purpose and activities: Giving program run by pubic relations department in conjunction with Human Resources and Administration. The ad-hoc Philanthropic Committee is cross-representative of all staff. Support for social services, the arts and culture.
Application information:
Write: Raymond P. Waters, Manager, Public Relations and Advertising

3034
Harris and Eliza Kempner Fund
P.O. Box 119
Galveston 77553 (409) 765-6671
Application address: P.O. Box 119, Galveston, TX 77553-0119

Trust established in 1946 in TX.
Donor(s): Various Kempner interests and members of the Kempner family.
Financial data (yr. ended 12/31/88): Assets, $16,514,116 (M); gifts received, $20,750; expenditures, $942,114, including $777,077 for 141 grants (high: $125,000; low: $500; average: $1,000-$5,000).
Purpose and activities: Emphasis on higher education, including scholarship funds, student loans, a matching gifts program, community funds, welfare funds, community projects, and cultural programs, including historic preservation.
Types of support: General purposes, operating budgets, continuing support, annual campaigns, seed money, emergency funds, deficit financing, building funds, equipment, land acquisition, endowment funds, scholarship funds, professorships, special projects, research, publications, conferences and seminars, student loans, capital campaigns.
Limitations: Giving primarily in Galveston, TX. No grants to individuals.
Publications: 990-PF, annual report (including application guidelines).
Application information:
Initial approach: Letter requesting guidelines
Copies of proposal: 1
Deadline(s): For grant program: Mar. 1, Aug. 1 and Nov. 1
Board meeting date(s): Usually in Apr., Sept., Dec., and as required
Final notification: 2 weeks
Write: Elaine Perachio, Grants Administrator
Officers and Trustees: Leonora K. Thompson, Chair.; Harris K. Weston, Vice-Chair.; Lyda Ann Q. Thomas, Secy.-Treas.; Arthur M. Alpert, Jack T. Currie, Anna O. Hamilton, Hetta T. Kempner, Robert K. Lynch, Barbara Weston Sasser.
Number of staff: 1 part-time professional; 2 part-time support.
Employer Identification Number: 746042458
Recent arts and culture grants:
Galveston Arts and Galveston Historical Foundation, Galveston, TX, $20,000. For capital fund drive. 1987.
Galveston Arts Center, Galveston, TX, $26,500. For support of programs. 1987.
Galveston Historical Foundation, Galveston, TX, $16,500. For general operating funds. 1987.
Galveston Historical Foundation, Galveston, TX, $7,500. For Kemper Park fund development plans. 1987.
Galveston Historical Foundation, Galveston, TX, $6,000. For residential program operating funds. 1987.
Grand 1894 Opera House, Galveston, TX, $16,500. For operating funds. 1987.
Ohio Humanities Council, Columbus, OH, $5,000. For Cincinnati Experience film. 1987.
Satori, Galveston, TX, $5,000. For Artist-In-Residence Program. 1987.
Strand Street Theater, Galveston, TX, $10,000. For operating funds. 1987.

3035
The John G. and Marie Stella Kenedy Memorial Foundation
First City Tower II, Suite 1020
Corpus Christi 78478 (512) 887-6565

Incorporated in 1960 in TX.
Donor(s): Sarita Kenedy East.†
Financial data (yr. ended 6/30/88): Assets, $126,841,099 (M); gifts received, $1,024;

expenditures, $11,022,356, including $9,062,497 for 168 grants (high: $500,000; low: $1,000; average: $10,000-$100,000).
Purpose and activities: A private operating foundation; ninety percent of grants issued are restricted to sectarian, primarily Roman Catholic activities; ten percent must be given to non-sectarian activities in TX. Support for education, arts and humanities, social services, youth, and health agencies.
Types of support: Building funds, equipment, land acquisition, matching funds, special projects.
Limitations: Giving limited to TX. No grants to individuals, or for operating budgets, annual fund drives, deficit financing, or scholarships; no support generally for endowments or requests in excess of $500,000.
Publications: Application guidelines, informational brochure, program policy statement.
Application information: Application form required.
Copies of proposal: 1
Deadline(s): Mar. 31, June 30, Sept. 30, and Dec. 31 for Catholic organizations
Board meeting date(s): Feb. 28 for non-sectarian giving; quarterly for Catholic giving
Write: James R. McCown, General Mgr.
Officers and Directors: Rene H. Gracida, Pres.; Lee H. Lytton, Jr., V.P.; E.B. Groner, Secy.; Daniel Meaney, Treas.; Sister Bernard Marie Borgmeyer, Ronald W. Bradley.
Number of staff: 3 full-time professional; 5 full-time support.
Employer Identification Number: 746040701

3036
William S. & Lora Jean Kilroy Foundation
1021 Main St., Suite 1900
Houston 77002-6662 (713) 651-0101

Established in 1985 in TX.
Donor(s): William S. Kilroy, Lora Jean Kilroy.
Financial data (yr. ended 12/31/88): Assets, $2,935,802 (M); gifts received, $1,455,000; expenditures, $68,386, including $60,255 for 17 grants (high: $15,000; low: $100).
Purpose and activities: Support primarily for higher education, museums, and community funds.
Types of support: Operating budgets, annual campaigns, capital campaigns.
Application information:
Initial approach: Letter
Deadline(s): None
Write: William S. Kilroy, Trustee
Trustee: William S. Kilroy.
Number of staff: None.
Employer Identification Number: 760169904

3037
Kimberly-Clark Corporate Giving Program
P.O. Box 619100
Dallas 75261 (214) 830-1200
Mailing Address: P.O. Box 619100, DFW Airport Station, Dallas, TX 75261
Purpose and activities: Supports civic and community affairs, all levels of education, environmental issues, arts and culture, health care, hospitals, legal advocacy, legal services, medical research, minority programs, urban problems, organizations for senior citizens, youth, women, and job development. Also, employee volunteer programs, use of company's facilities, building funds and donations of company's primary goods or services.
Types of support: In-kind gifts, building funds, scholarship funds.
Application information: Include proposed budget, financial statement, proof of 501(c)(3) status, board members list and list of donors.
Write: Colleen B. Manno, V.P.

3038
Kimberly-Clark Foundation, Inc.
P.O. Box 619100
Dallas 75261 (214) 830-1200

Incorporated in 1952 in WI.
Donor(s): Kimberly-Clark Corp.
Financial data (yr. ended 12/31/87): Assets, $5,311,348 (M); expenditures, $2,302,450, including $2,302,440 for 101 grants (high: $354,715; low: $40; average: $1,000-$20,000).
Purpose and activities: Emphasis on higher education, including National Merit and achievement scholarship funds, community funds, community development, social services, and cultural programs. The employee matching gift program was discontinued in 1988.
Types of support: Annual campaigns, building funds, continuing support, emergency funds, equipment, land acquisition, operating budgets, seed money, scholarship funds, general purposes, capital campaigns.
Limitations: Giving primarily in communities where the company has operations. No support for preschool, elementary, or secondary education, state-supported institutions, denominational religious organizations, or sports or athletics. No grants to individuals; no loans.
Publications: Annual report.
Application information:
Initial approach: Proposal
Copies of proposal: 1
Deadline(s): None
Board meeting date(s): Apr.
Final notification: By year end
Write: Colleen B. Berman, V.P.
Officers: Colleen B. Berman, V.P.; Donald M. Crook, Secy.; W. Anthony Gamron, Treas.
Number of staff: 1 full-time professional; 1 full-time support.
Employer Identification Number: 396044304

3039
Carl B. and Florence E. King Foundation
5956 Sherry Lane, Suite 620
Dallas 75225

Incorporated in 1966 in TX.
Donor(s): Carl B. King,† Florence E. King,† Dorothy E. King.
Financial data (yr. ended 12/31/87): Assets, $26,472,034 (M); expenditures, $1,614,673, including $569,767 for 32 grants (high: $100,000; low: $250; average: $2,000-$15,000) and $210,000 for 141 grants to individuals.
Purpose and activities: Emphasis on higher and secondary education, youth and social service agencies, and cultural programs; scholarships and student loans limited to TX high school students; some support for hospitals and health agencies.
Types of support: Scholarship funds, special projects, student aid, student loans.
Limitations: Giving primarily in the Dallas, TX, area. No support for religious purposes.
Publications: Program policy statement, application guidelines.
Application information: Application forms required for scholarships only and available from the foundation and the Texas Interscholastic League; scholarships limited to TX high school students.
Initial approach: Letter
Copies of proposal: 1
Deadline(s): None for organizations; students should contact Texas Interscholastic League
Board meeting date(s): Quarterly
Final notification: 6 weeks
Write: Carl Yeckel, V.P.
Officers and Directors: Dorothy E. King, Pres.; Carl Yeckel, V.P.; Thomas W. Vett, Secy.-Treas.; M.E. Childs, Jack Phipps, Sam G. Winstead.
Number of staff: 4 full-time professional.
Employer Identification Number: 756052203

3040
Robert J. Kleberg, Jr. and Helen C. Kleberg Foundation
700 North St. Mary's St., Suite 1200
San Antonio 78205 (512) 271-3691

Incorporated in 1950 in TX.
Donor(s): Helen C. Kleberg,† Robert J. Kleberg, Jr.†
Financial data (yr. ended 12/31/86): Assets, $75,255,479 (M); expenditures, $3,375,742, including $2,331,400 for 28 grants (high: $750,000; low: $1,000; average: $5,000-$200,000).
Purpose and activities: Giving on a national basis for medical research, veterinary science, wildlife, and related activities; support also for local community organizations.
Types of support: Building funds, equipment, research, conferences and seminars, matching funds, renovation projects.
Limitations: No support for community organizations outside TX, for non-tax-exempt organizations, or for organizations limited by race or religion. No grants to individuals, or for general purposes, endowments, deficit financing, ongoing operating expenses, overhead or indirect costs, scholarships, or fellowships; no loans.
Publications: Annual report, application guidelines.
Application information:
Initial approach: Letter
Copies of proposal: 1
Deadline(s): None
Board meeting date(s): Usually in June and Dec.
Final notification: 6 months
Write: Robert L. Washington, Grants Coord.

Officers and Directors: Helen K. Groves, Pres.; John D. Alexander, Jr., V.P. and Secy.; Emory G. Alexander, V.P. and Treas.; Helen C. Alexander, V.P.; Caroline R. Alexander, Dorothy D. Alexander, Henrietta K. Alexander.
Number of staff: 1 full-time professional.
Employer Identification Number: 746044810
Recent arts and culture grants:
Brandywine Conservancy, Chadds Ford, PA, $30,000. For environmental management programs. 1987.
San Antonio Festival, San Antonio, TX, $25,000. For performing arts sponsorship. 1987.
San Antonio Museum Association, San Antonio, TX, $65,000. For art collection expansion. 1987.
Texas State Aquarium, Corpus Christi, TX, $25,000. For exhibit design and construction. 1987.

3041
Robert W. Knox, Sr. and Pearl Wallis Knox Charitable Foundation
c/o First RepublicBank Houston
P.O. Box 2518
Houston 77252-2518

Established in 1964 in TX.
Donor(s): Robert W. Knox, Jr.†
Financial data (yr. ended 8/31/87): Assets, $3,828,336 (M); expenditures, $263,956, including $233,481 for 31 grants (high: $45,000; low: $60).
Purpose and activities: Emphasis on cultural programs, youth activities, parks and recreation, and religious organizations.
Limitations: Giving primarily in Houston, TX.
Application information:
Initial approach: Letter
Deadline(s): None
Write: Carl Schumacher, V.P. and Trust Officer, First RepublicBank Houston
Trustee: First RepublicBank Houston.
Employer Identification Number: 746064974

3042
Marcia & Otto Koehler Foundation
P.O. Drawer 121
San Antonio 78291

Established in 1980 in TX.
Donor(s): Marcia Koehler.†
Financial data (yr. ended 7/31/87): Assets, $6,292,648 (M); expenditures, $391,514, including $356,255 for grants (high: $25,000; low: $1,000).
Purpose and activities: Support for culture, higher education, youth, and social services.
Types of support: Operating budgets, renovation projects, building funds, research.
Limitations: Giving primarily in Bexar County, TX.
Application information:
Write: Patricia M. Myers, Trust Officer, NBC Bank-San Antonio, N.A.
Trustee: NBC Bank-San Antonio, N.A.
Employer Identification Number: 742131195

3043
Mary Potishman Lard Trust
c/o University Center
1320 South University Dr., Suite 1014
Fort Worth 76107 (817) 332-7559

Trust established in 1968 in TX.
Donor(s): Mary P. Lard.†
Financial data (yr. ended 12/31/86): Assets, $8,494,762 (M); expenditures, $646,938, including $282,900 for 50 grants (high: $20,000; low: $1,000).
Purpose and activities: Emphasis on education, including higher education; support also for social services, youth agencies, hospitals, medical research, and cultural organizations.
Limitations: Giving primarily in TX, with emphasis on Fort Worth. No grants to individuals.
Application information:
Initial approach: Letter
Deadline(s): None
Board meeting date(s): Generally in June or July, and Dec.
Final notification: Within 2 weeks of meeting
Write: Bayard H. Friedman, Trustee
Trustees: Bayard H. Friedman, Mayme Friedman, Walker C. Friedman.
Number of staff: 1 full-time professional.
Employer Identification Number: 756210697

3044
LBJ Family Foundation
Tenth and Brazos Sts.
P.O. Box 1209
Austin 78767 (512) 472-4993

Trust established in 1957 in TX.
Donor(s): Lyndon B. Johnson,† Mrs. Lyndon B. Johnson, Texas Broadcasting Corp.
Financial data (yr. ended 12/31/86): Assets, $3,000,000 (M); expenditures, $142,000, including $140,000 for 80 grants (high: $1,500; low: $200; average: $500).
Purpose and activities: Emphasis on conservation and recreation; some support for higher and secondary education, educational television, hospitals, and cultural programs, including support of presidential libraries.
Types of support: Continuing support, general purposes, scholarship funds, special projects.
Limitations: Giving primarily in Austin, TX. No grants to individuals or for endowment funds; no loans.
Application information:
Initial approach: Letter
Copies of proposal: 1
Deadline(s): None
Board meeting date(s): June and Dec.
Write: John M. Barr, Mgr.
Trustees: Claudia T. Johnson, Luci B. Johnson, Charles S. Robb, Lynda J. Robb.
Number of staff: None.
Employer Identification Number: 746045768

3045
Lightner Sams Foundation, Inc.
11811 Preston Rd., Suite 200
Dallas 75230 (214) 458-8811

Established in 1980.
Financial data (yr. ended 12/31/87): Assets, $1,545,417 (M); expenditures, $916,842, including $681,928 for 70 grants (high: $100,000; low: $250; average: $5,000-$10,000).
Purpose and activities: Giving for cultural programs, including museums and the performing arts, and education; some support also for hospitals, youth organizations, Protestant religious organizations, community development, and social services; grants to a zoo and a playhouse.
Types of support: Annual campaigns, building funds, capital campaigns, equipment, operating budgets, renovation projects, research.
Limitations: Giving primarily in TX and WY. No grants to individuals.
Application information:
Initial approach: Letter
Copies of proposal: 1
Deadline(s): Submit proposal 2-3 weeks prior to board meetings
Board meeting date(s): Feb. 15, May 15, Aug. 15, and Nov. 15
Final notification: As soon as possible after meetings
Write: Larry Lightner, Trustee
Trustees: Earl Sams Lightner, Larry Lightner, Robin Lightner, Sue B. Lightner.
Number of staff: 1 full-time professional.
Employer Identification Number: 742139849

3046
The LTV Foundation
c/o The LTV Corporation
P.O. Box 655003
Dallas 75265-5003 (214) 979-7726

Trust established in 1950 in OH.
Donor(s): Republic Steel Corp.
Financial data (yr. ended 12/31/88): Assets, $10,000,000 (M); expenditures, $1,162,109 for 429 grants (high: $30,000; low: $100; average: $1,000-$5,000) and $27,737 for 10 grants to individuals.
Purpose and activities: Giving largely for community funds, hospitals, higher and other education, youth agencies, health agencies, urban renewal, arts and cultural programs; employee-related scholarships through the National Merit Scholarship Corp.
Types of support: Operating budgets, annual campaigns, building funds, equipment, endowment funds, special projects, research, matching funds, capital campaigns, emergency funds, employee-related scholarships.
Limitations: Giving limited to areas of company operations, with emphasis on OH, TX, IL, IN, and NY. No support for religious or political purposes, fraternal or veterans' organizations, government agencies, or athletic teams. No grants to individuals, or for seed money, deficit financing, land acquisition, publications, conferences, or courtesy advertising; no loans.
Publications: Informational brochure (including application guidelines).

Application information:
Initial approach: Proposal
Copies of proposal: 1
Deadline(s): None
Board meeting date(s): Quarterly
Final notification: 2 to 4 months
Write: Brent Berryman, Exec. Dir.
Officers: Brent Berryman, Exec. Dir.
Trust Committee: Raymond A. Hay, David H. Hoag, James F. Powers.
Trustee: AmeriTrust Co.
Number of staff: 1 part-time professional; 1 part-time support.
Employer Identification Number: 346505330

3047
Sharon Lee MacDonald Charitable Trust
c/o Texas Commerce Bank
P.O. Box 2558
Houston 77252

Established in 1974 in TX.
Financial data (yr. ended 12/31/87): Assets, $1,273,412 (M); expenditures, $104,173, including $63,277 for 14 grants (high: $21,100; low: $1,000).
Purpose and activities: Support for social service and youth agencies and cultural programs.
Limitations: Giving primarily in Austin and Houston, TX.
Application information: Contributes only to pre-selected organizations. Applications not accepted.
Trustees: William S. Arendale, Texas Commerce Bank.
Employer Identification Number: 746203857

3048
Elizabeth Huth Maddux Foundation
P.O. Box 171717
San Antonio 78217

Established in 1968 in TX.
Donor(s): Elizabeth Huth Maddux.
Financial data (yr. ended 12/31/86): Assets, $2,202,687 (M); gifts received, $130,000; expenditures, $350,811, including $346,782 for 5 grants (high: $245,182; low: $1,000).
Purpose and activities: Giving for cultural programs; support also for general charitable purposes.
Limitations: Giving primarily in TX.
Application information: Contributes only to pre-selected organizations. Applications not accepted.
Trustees: Elizabeth Stieren Kelso, Elizabeth Huth Maddux, Arthur T. Stieren.
Employer Identification Number: 742212693

3049
The Edward and Betty Marcus Foundation
One Preston Center
8222 Douglas, Suite 360
Dallas 75225
Application address: 3111 F. Windsor Rd., Austin, TX 78703

Established about 1984 in TX.
Donor(s): Betty B. Marcus.†
Financial data (yr. ended 12/31/87): Assets, $4,549,296 (M); gifts received, $2,370,660; expenditures, $61,055, including $1,300 for 1 grant.
Purpose and activities: Emphasis on the arts, particularly architecture, and elementary and secondary education.
Application information:
Initial approach: Letter
Deadline(s): None
Write: Melba Davis Whatley, Chair.
Officers: Melba Davis Whatley, Chair.; Richard C. Marcus, Vice-Chair.; Mary O'Boyle English, Secy.; Carolyn Levy Clark, Treas.
Trustees: Peter J. Blum, Theodore S. Hochstim, Cary Shel Marcus.
Employer Identification Number: 751989529

3050
Maxus Energy Corporate Contributions Program
717 North Harwood St.
Dallas 75201 (214) 954-2833

Financial data (yr. ended 12/31/88): Total giving, $400,000, including $335,000 for grants (high: $75,000; low: $100), $55,000 for employee matching gifts and $10,000 for in-kind gifts.
Purpose and activities: Supports education, health and welfare, civic affairs, culture and the arts, and programs for women, youth, the homeless, and the disadvantaged.
Types of support: General purposes, matching funds, scholarship funds, annual campaigns, employee matching gifts, employee-related scholarships, special projects, capital campaigns.
Limitations: Giving primarily in operating locations in Dallas and Amarillo, TX.
Publications: Program policy statement, application guidelines.
Application information: Include description of organization, amount requested, purpose for funds, recently audited financial statement, and proof of tax-exempt status.
Copies of proposal: 1
Board meeting date(s): Varies
Write: Carol Carter, Dir., Public Affairs
Number of staff: 1 part-time professional; 1 part-time support.

3051
McAshan Educational and Charitable Trust
Five Post Oak Park, Suite 1980
Houston 77027

Trust established in 1952 in TX.
Donor(s): Susan C. McAshan, Susan Vaughn Clayton Trust No. 1.
Financial data (yr. ended 12/31/86): Assets, $35,895,505 (M); gifts received, $3,872,980; expenditures, $572,309, including $515,308 for 60 grants (high: $150,000; low: $50).
Purpose and activities: Emphasis on education, including the handicapped, population control, conservation, medical research, and the arts and music.
Limitations: Giving primarily in TX, with emphasis on Houston.
Application information:
Initial approach: Proposal
Trustees: Lucy Johnson Hadac, Susan C. McAshan, S.M. McAshan, Jr.
Employer Identification Number: 746042210

3052
McCombs Foundation, Inc.
9000 Tesoro, Suite 122
San Antonio 78217

Established in 1981 in TX.
Donor(s): Gary V. Woods, and members of the McCombs family.
Financial data (yr. ended 12/31/87): Assets, $233,412 (M); gifts received, $300,000; expenditures, $244,655, including $244,630 for 51 grants (high: $100,000; low: $100).
Purpose and activities: Giving for higher education, medical research, religious organizations, cultural and civic affairs, and social services.
Application information:
Initial approach: Letter
Deadline(s): None
Write: Billy J. McCombs, Pres.
Officers: Billy J. McCombs, Pres.; Charline McCombs, V.P.; Gary V. Woods, Secy.-Treas.
Employer Identification Number: 742204217

3053
The Eugene McDermott Foundation
3808 Euclid
Dallas 75205 (214) 521-2924

Incorporated in 1972 in TX; The McDermott Foundation merged into above in 1977.
Donor(s): Eugene McDermott,† Margaret McDermott.
Financial data (yr. ended 8/31/87): Assets, $54,796,602 (M); expenditures, $2,138,532, including $1,996,850 for 97 grants (high: $425,000; low: $1,000; average: $1,000-$25,000).
Purpose and activities: Support primarily for museums and other cultural programs, higher and secondary education, health, and general community interests.
Types of support: Building funds, equipment, operating budgets.
Limitations: Giving primarily in Dallas, TX. No grants to individuals.
Application information:
Initial approach: Letter
Copies of proposal: 1
Deadline(s): None
Board meeting date(s): Quarterly
Final notification: Prior to Aug. 31
Write: Margaret McDermott, Pres.
Officers and Trustees: Margaret McDermott, Pres.; J.E. Johnson, V.P.; Mary McDermott Cook, Secy.-Treas.; C.J. Thomsen.
Number of staff: 1
Employer Identification Number: 237237919

3054
Amy Shelton McNutt Charitable Trust
1777 Northeast Loop 410, Suite 1512
San Antonio 78217

Established about 1983 in TX.

Financial data (yr. ended 9/30/86): Assets, $5,005,479 (M); expenditures, $231,804, including $204,590 for 6 grants (high: $80,000; low: $1,400).
Purpose and activities: Giving for higher education, the arts, and research in the sciences.
Application information:
Initial approach: Proposal
Deadline(s): None
Write: Jack Guenther, Trustee
Trustees: R.B. Cutlip, Jack Guenther, Ruth Johnson, Edward D. Muir.
Employer Identification Number: 742298675

3055
Meadows Foundation, Inc.
Wilson Historic Block
2922 Swiss Ave.
Dallas 75204-5928 (214) 826-9431

Incorporated in 1948 in TX.
Donor(s): Algur Hurtle Meadows,† Mrs. Virginia Meadows.†
Financial data (yr. ended 12/31/87): Assets, $405,917,715 (M); gifts received, $3,503,319; expenditures, $26,227,799, including $21,022,977 for 285 grants (high: $1,675,000; low: $1,000; average: $25,000-$50,000).
Purpose and activities: Support for the arts, social services, health, education, and civic and cultural programs. Operates a historic preservation investment-related program using a cluster of Victorian homes as offices for non-profit agencies.
Types of support: Operating budgets, continuing support, seed money, emergency funds, deficit financing, building funds, equipment, land acquisition, matching funds, scholarship funds, professorships, internships, fellowships, special projects, research, publications, conferences and seminars, program-related investments, technical assistance, consulting services, renovation projects.
Limitations: Giving limited to TX. No grants to individuals, or for annual campaigns; no loans. Generally no grants for church construction, media projects in planning stages, or for general endowment funds.
Publications: Annual report (including application guidelines).
Application information:
Initial approach: Proposal
Copies of proposal: 1
Deadline(s): None
Board meeting date(s): Grants Review Committee meets monthly; full board meets 2 or 3 times a year to act on major grants
Final notification: 3 to 4 months
Write: Dr. Sally R. Lancaster, Exec. V.P.
Officers: Curtis W. Meadows, Jr.,* Pres.; Sally R. Lancaster,* Exec. V.P.; Robert A. Meadows,* V.P. and Chair.; G. Tomas Rhodus, V.P. and Secy.; Robert E. Wise, V.P. and Treas.; Judy B. Culbertson, V.P.; Linda S. Perryman,* V.P.; Eloise Meadows Rouse,* V.P.
Directors:* Evelyn Meadows Acton, John W. Broadfoot, Vela Meadows Broadfoot, J.W. Bullion, Eudine Meadows Cheney, John A. Hammack, John H. Murrell, Evy Kay Ritzen, Dorothy C. Wilson.
Number of staff: 12 full-time professional; 2 part-time professional; 18 full-time support; 1 part-time support.
Employer Identification Number: 756015322
Recent arts and culture grants:
Afro-American Artists Alliance, Dallas, TX, $15,000. Toward cooperative production of Death and the King's Horseman with Addison Center Theater. 8/23/88.
Archaeological Conservancy, Santa Fe, NM, $20,000. For assistance in acquiring and preserving Caddo Indian Mounds in East Texas. 3/16/88.
Art Community Center of Corpus Christi, Corpus Christi, TX, $100,000. Toward renovation of new center facility. 6/21/88.
Art Institute for the Permian Basin, Odessa, TX, $25,000. Toward compensation of Executive Director. 12/10/87.
Artreach Dallas, Dallas, TX, $28,700. For purchase of computer system to expand program capabilities in providing tickets to cultural events to disadvantaged and handicapped groups. 10/8/87.
Arts District Friends, Dallas, TX, $10,000. For Latin Music and Jazz Festival and other 1988 programs. 1/25/88.
Association for Community Television, Houston, TX, $44,545. Toward production of film documentary on arts education. 11/16/87.
Black Arts Alliance, Austin, TX, $15,000. For community performances of Theater in Black and other productions. 12/10/87.
City Ballet of Houston, Houston, TX, $10,000. Toward production of Nutcracker with and for inner-city children. 7/14/88.
Dallas Bach Society, Dallas, TX, $8,500. For matching support season ticket marketing campaign. 3/16/88.
Dallas Childrens Theater, Dallas, TX, $50,000. For priority equipment and technical supervision services at Crescent Theater. 5/20/88.
Dallas Historical Society, Dallas, TX, $150,000. To establish operating reserve fund. 11/16/87.
Dallas Historical Society, Dallas, TX, $31,500. For joint publication of semi-annual journal of North Central Texas history, Dallas Heritage, by Dallas County Heritage Society and Dallas Historical Society. 7/14/88.
Dallas Museum of Art, Dallas, TX, $125,000. Toward production of catalog and installation of Images of Mexico: The Contribution of Mexico to 20th Century Art. 7/14/88.
Dallas Museum of Art, Dallas, TX, $18,000. For gift of ten piece Copeland porcelain dining room ensemble. 12/10/87.
Dallas Museum of Art, Dallas, TX, $16,000. For gift of seventeen-piece epergne/candelabrum ensemble. 6/21/88.
Dallas Museum of Art, Dallas, TX, $10,000. To renew Corporate Director membership. 6/21/88.
Dallas Museum of Natural History, Dallas, TX, $350,000. Toward expenses of Ramses II exhibit. 4/19/88.
Dallas Summer Musicals, Dallas, TX, $5,000. For 1988 locally produced shows, and underwriting for broad community participation on governing board without regard for economic circumstances. 12/10/87.
Dallas Theater Center, Dallas, TX, $55,000. Toward expansion of Project Discovery enabling Dallas Independent School District students to attend productions free of charge. 10/8/87.
Dallas Womans Forum, Dallas, TX, $49,427. Toward restoration of historic Forum headquarters. 11/16/87.
Devine, City of, Devine Sesquicentennial Committee, Devine, TX, $80,000. To complete renovation of historic lumber warehouse for library/community center to be named Meadows Auditorium. 1/25/88.
Ellis County Art Association, Fine Arts Gallery, Waxahachie, TX, $11,455. Toward rewiring of historic headquarters building. 7/14/88.
Friends of the Summer Musical, Austin, TX, $10,000. For matching grant for summer productions. 4/6/88.
Friona, City of, Friona, TX, $25,000. Toward renovation of old Santa Fe Depot for community center. 4/6/88.
Galveston Historical Foundation, Galveston, TX, $100,000. Toward maintenance endowment fund for historical properties which Foundation operates. 10/8/87.
Garland Civic Theater, Garland, TX, $30,000. For matching grant for general operating support. 2/22/88.
Gaslight Theater, Shiner, TX, $25,887. To rewire and replace roof of 1895 Shiner Opera House. 2/22/88.
Greenhills Foundation, Dallas, TX, $20,000. For capital repairs, additions, and equipment for Dallas Nature Center. 3/16/88.
Hidalgo County Historical Museum, Edinburg, TX, $87,500. Toward renovation of additional Museum facility. 8/23/88.
Historic Fort Worth, Fort Worth, TX, $100,000. Toward stabilization and reconstruction of exterior foundations of historic Eddleman-McFarland home. 8/23/88.
Houston Ballet Foundation, Houston, TX, $25,000. For Miller Outdoor Theater free summer performances with $10,000 for multilingual and ethnic marketing. 5/20/88.
Houston Museum of Natural Science, Houston, TX, $100,000. Toward capital campaign for facility expansion, renovation, and endowment. 2/22/88.
Institute of Nautical Archaeology, College Station, TX, $97,256. For continuing support for projects to locate and preserve Ships of Discovery. 4/19/88.
InterCultura, Fort Worth, TX, $250,000. Toward costs of U.S./U.S.S.R. art exchanges, specifically to enable exhibitions in Texas. 8/23/88.
Kilgore Junior College District, Kilgore, TX, $10,000. For underwriting summer 1988 Texas Shakespeare Festival. 3/16/88.
Lamp-Lite Players, Nacogdoches, TX, $6,980. To construct storage building. 2/22/88.
Museum of the Southwest, Midland, TX, $100,000. Toward construction of Fredda Turner Durham Children's Museum. 7/14/88.
National Museum of Communications, Irving, TX, $35,000. For general operating support. 7/14/88.
North Texas Public Broadcasting, Dallas, TX, $25,000. To produce two films on Black Men: An Endangered Species. 5/20/88.
Panhandle Plains Historical Museum, Canyon, TX, $25,000. For general operating support

to help offset loss in state appropriation. 8/23/88.
Pegasus Foundation, Dallas Institute of Humanities and Culture, Dallas, TX, $185,000. Toward principal payment on first-lien mortgage. 7/14/88.
Public Films, Houston, TX, $12,500. For general operating support. 11/16/87.
R G V Educational Broadcasting, Harlingen, TX, $63,000. Toward expansion of physical plant and replacement of transmitter parts. 8/23/88.
Raymondville Independent School District, Raymondville, TX, $75,000. For repairs and refurbishing of school building housing Raymondville Historical Center. 1/25/88.
Saint Francis Episcopal Day School, Houston, TX, $20,000. Toward costs of developing model visual arts education curriculum. 8/23/88.
Sam Houston State University, Sam Houston Memorial Museum, Huntsville, TX, $50,000. For matching grant for advance funding for East Texas Folk Festival to benefit Museum, and general operating support to help replace withdrawn state appropriation. 2/22/88.
San Antonio Community Radio Corporation, San Antonio, TX, $25,000. Toward construction of 100,000 watt public radio station for San Antonio and South Texas. 3/16/88.
Sherman Historical Museum, Sherman, TX, $7,000. To finish out storage areas in future museum building. 3/16/88.
Society for Theatrical Artists, Guidance and Enhancement (STAGE), Dallas, TX, $9,955. To purchase Macintosh II computer system to produce agency publications and for administrative uses. 4/6/88.
South Dallas Cultural Center, Advisory Council, Dallas, TX, $8,500. Toward production costs of Joplin. 6/21/88.
South Texas Public Broadcasting System, K E D T - TV, Corpus Christi, TX, $13,700. For distribution of school adaptation of Lone Star series on Texas history at no charge, to all Regional Education Resource Centers in Texas. 6/21/88.
Southern Methodist University, Meadows School of Arts, Dallas, TX, $3,500,000. For matching grant to renovate space in Unphrey Lee Center for communication arts, toward construction of new arts library, and for Meadows Museum development. 4/19/88.
Southern Methodist University, Meadows School of the Arts, Dallas, TX, $86,000. Toward costs of events and programs associated with 1987 Algur H. Meadows Award for Excellence in the Arts. 10/8/87.
Southwest Science Museum Foundation, Dallas, TX, $150,000. Toward capital campaign. 12/10/87.
Stephens County Historical Committee, Breckenridge, TX, $15,000. For necessary repairs on Swenson Memorial Museum of Stephens County. 8/16/88.
Texas Fine Arts Society, Odessa, TX, $15,849. For furnishings and equipment for Meadows Library and adjacent stairwell and workroom. 2/22/88.
Texas Opera Theater, Houston, TX, $30,000. Toward 1988 and 1989 Residency Troup performances in Texas communities. 5/20/88.
Texas Tech University, Museum of Texas Tech University, Lubbock, TX, $50,000. For matching grant for emergency operating funds to bridge gap caused by loss of direct state appropriation. 2/22/88.
University of Houston, Victoria, TX, $150,000. Toward implementation of South Texas Union Catalog on optical disc, integrating holdings of three major regional library consortia. 7/14/88.
USA Film Festival, Dallas, TX, $25,000. For matching grant toward debt retirement. 3/16/88.
Waco Performing Arts Company, Waco, TX, $54,000. For holiday production of It's a Wonderful Life and assistance toward debt reduction. 8/23/88.
Waxahachie Symphony Association, Waxahachie, TX, $6,470. Toward support of professional orchestra series. 11/16/87.
Wichita Falls Museum and Art Center, Wichita Falls, TX, $100,000. Toward facility renovations additions, and endowment. 12/10/87.
Young Artist Program and Art Center, Dallas, TX, $5,000. Toward continuation of Senior Art-Salute program. 1/25/88.

3056
Mechia Foundation
P.O. Box 1310
Beaumont 77704

Established in 1978.
Donor(s): Ben J. Rogers.
Financial data (yr. ended 12/31/87): Assets, $1,172,573 (M); gifts received, $20,000; expenditures, $90,504, including $88,790 for 74 grants (high: $9,200; low: $100).
Purpose and activities: Giving for cultural programs, higher education, health associations and hospitals, and Jewish welfare organizations and Jewish temples.
Limitations: Giving primarily in Beaumont and Houston, TX.
Application information: Contributes only to pre-selected organizations. Applications not accepted.
Officers: Ben J. Rogers, Pres.; Julie Rogers, V.P.; Regina Rogers, Secy.-Treas.
Employer Identification Number: 741948840

3057
Menil Foundation, Inc.
1427 Branard St.
Houston 77006 (713) 524-9028

Incorporated in 1953 in TX.
Donor(s): John de Menil,† Dominique de Menil.
Financial data (yr. ended 12/31/87): Assets, $95,209,634 (M); gifts received, $2,202,099; expenditures, $7,431,150, including $545,847 for 23 grants (high: $200,000; low: $500) and $5,358,347 for 7 foundation-administered programs.
Purpose and activities: A private operating foundation primarily exhibiting its art collection at Rice University in Houston and museums throughout the world; currently building museum at Houston to permanently house and exhibit its collection; supports art centers at Rice University; conducts research projects on black iconography, Magritte and Max Ernst, and colloquiums at the Rothko Chapel.
Application information: Contributes only to pre-selected organizations. Applications not accepted.
Board meeting date(s): Annually
Officers: Dominique de Menil,* Pres.; Miles Glaser,* V.P.
Directors:* Walter Hopps, Paul Winkler.
Employer Identification Number: 746045327

3058
Meredith Foundation
P.O. Box 117
Mineola 75773

Trust established in 1958 in TX.
Donor(s): Harry W. Meredith.†
Financial data (yr. ended 12/31/86): Assets, $6,837,689 (M); expenditures, $371,618, including $255,611 for 8 grants (high: $100,110; low: $2,000).
Purpose and activities: Emphasis on civic and cultural projects.
Limitations: Giving limited to Mineola, TX, and its environs.
Publications: Program policy statement.
Application information: Contributes only to pre-selected organizations. Applications not accepted.
Board meeting date(s): Monthly
Trustees: James Dear, Chair.; Sid Cox, Vice-Chair.; Ray Williams, Secy.-Treas.; T.W. Benham, Everett Smith, Coulter Templeton.
Employer Identification Number: 756024469

3059
Alice Kleberg Reynolds Meyer Foundation
P.O. Box 6985
San Antonio 78209 (512) 820-0552

Established in 1978 in TX.
Donor(s): Alice K. Meyer.
Financial data (yr. ended 12/31/87): Assets, $2,698,092 (M); gifts received, $250,000; expenditures, $152,128, including $142,795 for 16 grants (high: $78,000; low: $100; average: $100-$2,000).
Purpose and activities: Grants primarily for cultural organizations and medical research; support also for education.
Types of support: General purposes.
Limitations: Giving primarily in TX.
Application information:
Initial approach: Proposal
Copies of proposal: 1
Deadline(s): None
Write: Alice K. Meyer, Pres.
Officers: Alice K. Meyer, Pres. and Treas.; Vaughan B. Meyer, V.P. and Secy.
Number of staff: None.
Employer Identification Number: 742020227

3060
Mitchell Energy and Development Corporate Contributions Program
2001 Timberloch Place
The Woodlands 77380 (713) 363-5500
Mailing address: P.O. Box 4000, The Woodlands, TX 77387

Purpose and activities: Supports education, including colleges, universities, engineering and business programs; health, welfare, social services, drug rehabilitation, historic preservation, literacy, medical research, museums, arts and humanities, youth services, and civic affairs.
Types of support: Annual campaigns, capital campaigns, research, employee-related scholarships, scholarship funds, special projects.
Limitations: Giving primarily in major operating locations. No grants to individuals, political organizations, mass mailed form letters, or telephone solicitations.
Application information: Include narrative/letter, description of organization and project, complete budget, goals for the project, IRS letter, list of contributors and an audited statement.
Initial approach: Submit letter and complete proposal including budget
Deadline(s): Applications accepted throughout the year but best time to apply is after Feb. 1.
Write: Minnie Adams, Corp. V.P.

3061
The Moody Foundation
704 Moody National Bank Bldg.
Galveston 77550 (409) 763-5333

Trust established in 1942 in TX.
Donor(s): William Lewis Moody, Jr.,† Libbie Shearn Moody.†
Financial data (yr. ended 12/31/87): Assets, $357,004,726 (M); gifts received, $161,271; expenditures, $21,046,248, including $18,701,670 for 56 grants (high: $9,800,779; low: $500; average: $10,000-$150,000).
Purpose and activities: Funds to be used for historic restoration projects, performing arts organizations, and cultural programs; for promotion of health, science, and education; for community and social services; and in the field of religion.
Types of support: Seed money, emergency funds, building funds, equipment, consulting services, technical assistance, matching funds, professorships, special projects, research, publications, conferences and seminars, capital campaigns, land acquisition, renovation projects, student aid.
Limitations: Giving limited to TX. No grants to individuals (except for students covered by one scholarship program in Galveston County), or for operating budgets, except for start-up purposes, continuing support, annual campaigns, or deficit financing; no loans.
Publications: Annual report, application guidelines, 990-PF, financial statement.
Application information: Application format as outlined in guidelines required.
Initial approach: Letter or telephone
Copies of proposal: 1
Deadline(s): 6 weeks prior to board meetings
Board meeting date(s): Quarterly
Final notification: 2 weeks after board meetings
Write: Peter M. Moore, Grants Officer
Officer: Robert E. Baker, Exec. Admin. and Secy.
Trustees: Frances Moody Newman, Chair.; Robert L. Moody, Ross R. Moody.
Number of staff: 7 full-time professional; 6 full-time support.
Employer Identification Number: 741403105

3062
The Rotan Mosle Foundation
c/o Rotan Mosle, Inc.
P.O. Box 3226
Houston 77253-3226 (713) 236-3325

Established in 1972.
Donor(s): Rotan Mosle, Inc.
Financial data (yr. ended 9/30/88): Assets, $22,927 (M); gifts received, $50,000; expenditures, $77,666, including $76,500 for 91 grants (high: $10,000; low: $100; average: $1,000).
Purpose and activities: Support primarily for charities in which company employees are actively involved, with emphasis on youth programs, community funds, higher education, cultural programs, and social services.
Types of support: Operating budgets, research, annual campaigns, building funds, capital campaigns, special projects.
Limitations: Giving primarily in TX. No grants to individuals.
Application information: Foundation supports primarily those institutions where Rotan Mosle employees serve as volunteers.
Initial approach: Letter
Copies of proposal: 1
Deadline(s): None
Write: Stuart Hellmann, Trustee
Officer: Susan Martin, Secy.
Trustee: Stuart Hellmann.
Number of staff: None.
Employer Identification Number: 237200336

3063
Harry S. Moss Foundation
2121 San Jacinto St.
Dallas 75210 (214) 747-8184

Incorporated in 1952 in TX.
Donor(s): Harry S. Moss, Florence M. Moss, Moss Petroleum Co.
Financial data (yr. ended 11/30/86): Assets, $2,826,256 (M); expenditures, $116,087, including $105,696 for 39 grants (high: $30,000; low: $350).
Purpose and activities: Emphasis on arts and cultural programs, youth agencies, and education.
Types of support: General purposes.
Limitations: Giving primarily in Dallas, TX.
Application information:
Deadline(s): None
Officers: Frank S. Ryburn, Pres.; John M. Little, Jr., V.P.; Frank M. Ryburn, Jr., V.P.; Mary Jane Ryburn, V.P.; F. Kenneth Travis, Treas.
Employer Identification Number: 756036333

3064
W. B. Munson Foundation
c/o Texas American Bank-Denison
P.O. Box 341
Denison 75020 (214) 465-3030

Trust established in 1943 in TX.
Financial data (yr. ended 12/31/86): Assets, $4,141,684 (M); expenditures, $80,222, including $43,909 for 12 grants (high: $10,000; low: $200; average: $3,024) and $7,025 for 17 grants to individuals.
Purpose and activities: Support for a hospital, an agricultural project, the arts, and scholarships for local high school graduates; applications not accepted for scholarships.
Types of support: Student aid, building funds, endowment funds, equipment, operating budgets, renovation projects.
Limitations: Giving limited to Grayson County, TX.
Application information: Applications not accepted for scholarships.
Initial approach: Letter
Deadline(s): None
Board meeting date(s): No set dates
Write: J. Brent Reed, Sr. V.P. & Trust Officer, Texas American Bank-Denison
Officer and Governors: Joseph W. Gay, Pres.; Roy L. McKinney III, W.B. Munson III.
Trustee: Texas American Bank/Denison.
Employer Identification Number: 756015068

3065
Kathryn Murfee Endowment
2200 Post Oak Blvd., Suite 320
Houston 77056

Established in 1981 in TX.
Financial data (yr. ended 8/31/87): Assets, $4,156,430 (M); expenditures, $302,213, including $175,000 for 8 grants (high: $75,000; low: $5,000).
Purpose and activities: Support primarily for research, education, religious organizations, and the arts.
Types of support: General purposes, research.
Limitations: Giving primarily in the Houston, TX, area.
Application information:
Deadline(s): 3 months prior to the commencement of the school term for which aid is requested
Write: June R. Nabb, Trustee
Trustees: Dan R. Japhet, June R. Nabb, James V. Walzel.
Employer Identification Number: 760007237

3066
Navarro Community Foundation
512 Interfirst Bank Bldg.
P.O. Box 1035
Corsicana 75110 (214) 874-4301

Community foundation established in 1938 in TX.
Financial data (yr. ended 12/31/87): Assets, $7,053,094 (M); expenditures, $182,629, including $62,850 for 10 grants (high: $20,750; low: $500).
Purpose and activities: Support largely for public schools, higher education, community

development, and a community fund; grants also for Protestant church support, child welfare, youth agencies, a hospital, a library, and cultural programs.
Types of support: Annual campaigns, seed money, building funds, scholarship funds, matching funds, general purposes.
Limitations: Giving limited to Navarro County, TX. No grants to individuals, or for research, conferences, endowment funds, publications, or special projects; no loans.
Application information:
Initial approach: Proposal
Copies of proposal: 2
Deadline(s): Jan. 1, Apr. 1, July 1, or Oct. 1
Board meeting date(s): Jan., Apr., July, and Oct.
Write: David M. Brown, Exec. Secy.
Officers and Trustees: C.E. Middleton, 2nd Vice-Chair.; David M. Brown, Exec. Secy.-Treas.; O.L. Albritton, Jr., C. David Campbell, M.D., William Clarkson III, Tom Eady, Embry Ferguson, Mrs. Jack McFerran, H.R. Stroube, Jr.
Trustee Banks: The Corsicana National Bank, The First National Bank, The State National Bank.
Number of staff: 1 full-time professional; 1 part-time professional.
Employer Identification Number: 750800663

3067
Oshman Foundation
P.O. Box 230234
Houston 77223-8234

Donor(s): Oshman Sporting Goods.
Financial data (yr. ended 11/30/88): Assets, $1,885,827 (M); gifts received, $25,000; expenditures, $86,628, including $80,803 for 7 grants (high: $35,000; low: $300).
Purpose and activities: Support for the aged, culture, and higher education.
Application information: Applications not accepted.
Officers and Directors Jeanette Oshman Efron, Pres.; Marilyn O. Lubetkin, V.P.; Judy O. Margolis, V.P.; Marvin Aronowitz, Alvin Lubetkin.
Employer Identification Number: 746039864

3068
Overlake Foundation, Inc.
700 Preston Commons West
8117 Preston Road
Dallas 75225-6306 (214) 750-0722

Incorporated in 1981 in TX.
Donor(s): Mary Alice Fitzpatrick.
Financial data (yr. ended 11/30/88): Assets, $3,108,161 (M); gifts received, $200,000; expenditures, $234,428, including $203,000 for 26 grants (high: $100,000; low: $500; average: $1,000-$10,000).
Purpose and activities: Grants for social services, education, health associations, and cultural programs.
Limitations: Giving primarily in TX.
Application information:
Write: Donald J. Malouf, V.P.
Officers: Rayford L. Keller, Pres. and Treas.; Donald J. Malouf, V.P. and Secy.; Michael Scott Anderson, Steve Craig Anderson.
Employer Identification Number: 751793068

3069
Alvin and Lucy Owsley Foundation
3000 One Shell Plaza
Houston 77002 (713) 229-1271

Trust established in 1950 in TX.
Donor(s): Alvin M. Owsley,† Lucy B. Owsley.
Financial data (yr. ended 12/31/86): Assets, $5,100,410 (M); expenditures, $239,821, including $199,660 for 113 grants (high: $20,000; low: $25; average: $1,000-$2,000).
Purpose and activities: Support for education, medicine, cultural activities, civic affairs, and social services.
Types of support: Operating budgets, continuing support, annual campaigns, seed money, emergency funds, building funds, endowment funds, matching funds, scholarship funds.
Limitations: Giving limited to TX. No grants to individuals, or for endowment funds; no loans.
Application information:
Initial approach: Letter
Copies of proposal: 1
Deadline(s): Submit proposal preferably in months when board meets; no set deadline
Board meeting date(s): Mar., June, Sept., and Dec.
Final notification: 2 months
Write: Alvin M. Owsley, Jr., General Mgr.
Officer and Trustees: Alvin M. Owsley, Jr., General Mgr.; Constance Owsley Garrett, David T. Owsley, Lucy B. Owsley.
Number of staff: None.
Employer Identification Number: 756047221

3070
The Pangburn Foundation
c/o Texas American Bank, Fort Worth
500 Throckmorton St., P.O. Box 2050
Fort Worth 76113 (817) 884-4266

Established in 1962 in TX.
Financial data (yr. ended 3/31/88): Assets, $4,649,864 (M); expenditures, $304,313, including $259,805 for 18 grants (high: $55,000; low: $1,505).
Purpose and activities: Emphasis on cultural programs, especially music and the performing arts; grants also for education, social services and youth agencies.
Limitations: Giving limited to the Fort Worth, TX. No grants to individuals.
Application information:
Initial approach: Letter
Copies of proposal: 1
Deadline(s): Sept. 30
Board meeting date(s): Oct. or Nov.
Write: Kelly Bradshaw
Trustee: Texas American Bank/Fort Worth.
Employer Identification Number: 756042630

3071
Panhandle Eastern Pipe Line Corporate Giving Program
5400 Westheimer Court
Houston 77056 (713) 627-4900
Application address: P.O. Box 1642, Houston, Texas 77251-1642

Purpose and activities: Giving for civic affairs, culture, education, health care, the handicapped/disabled and minority groups, legal advocacy and services, public broadcasting, United Way, welfare, and youth services.
Types of support: Annual campaigns, building funds, capital campaigns, research.
Limitations: Giving primarily in Houston, Harris, and Fort Bend counties, TX.
Application information: Include description of project, proposed budget, financial statement, list of board members and donors and proof of 501 (c)(3) status.
Deadline(s): Oct. 1 for inclusion in following year's budget
Board meeting date(s): Not formalized
Write: James W. Hart, Jr., V.P., Public Affairs
Number of staff: 1 part-time professional; 1 part-time support.

3072
The Parker Foundation
1111 Alamo Bldg.
San Antonio 78205 (512) 227-3128

Incorporated in 1957 in TX.
Donor(s): Members of the Parker family.
Financial data (yr. ended 3/31/88): Assets, $1,442,732 (M); expenditures, $34,371, including $23,500 for 21 grants (high: $4,620; low: $110).
Purpose and activities: Emphasis on secondary and higher education, social service agencies, cultural programs, hospitals, and Christian religious associations.
Limitations: Giving primarily in the San Antonio, TX, area.
Application information: Contributes only to pre-selected organizations. Applications not accepted.
Write: George Parker, Jr.
Officers and Directors: Mary H. Parker, Pres.; Camilla M. Parker, V.P.; Joseph B. Parker, V.P.; John M. Parker, Secy.-Treas.; Patricia H. Parker, William A. Parker.
Employer Identification Number: 746040454

3073
J. C. Penney Corporate Giving Program
P.O. Box 659000
Dallas 75265-9000

Financial data (yr. ended 1/31/87): $18,400,000 for grants.
Purpose and activities: Support for health and welfare, education, from preschool to college, civic betterment, and the arts. Health and welfare programs receive the largest portion of grants, with the United Way being a major recipient. Arts are the lowest priority.
Limitations: Giving limited to the fifty states of the U.S.A.
Application information:
Initial approach: Letter
Deadline(s): None
Write: David Lenz, V.P., J.C. Penney Company Fund and Mgr., Corp. Public Affairs

3074
The Pineywoods Foundation
P.O. Box 1731
Lufkin 75901 (409) 634-7444

Established in 1984 in TX.
Donor(s): The Southland Foundation.
Financial data (yr. ended 12/31/87): Assets, $1,739,643 (M); expenditures, $92,316, including $61,279 for 15 grants (high: $10,000; low: $500).
Purpose and activities: Giving primarily for social and civic affairs.
Types of support: General purposes, equipment, building funds, matching funds, seed money, special projects.
Limitations: Giving limited to Angelina, Cherokee, Houston, Jasper, Nacogdoches, Panola, Polk, Sabine, San Augustine, San Jacinto, Shelby, Trinity, and Tyler counties, TX. No support for governmental agencies, state colleges, universities, churches, or other religious organizations. No grants to individuals, or for salaries or annual operating budgets.
Publications: Informational brochure, application guidelines.
Application information: Application form required.
Initial approach: Proposal
Copies of proposal: 7
Deadline(s): None
Board meeting date(s): Quarterly, at will
Write: Bob Bowman, Secy.
Officers and Trustees: John F. Anderson, Chair.; Bob Bowman, Secy.; George Henderson, Treas.; Jack McMullen, Jr., E.G. Pittman, Claude Smithhart.
Number of staff: 1 part-time professional.
Employer Identification Number: 751922533

3075
Pollock Foundation
2310 Cockrell Ave.
Dallas 75215
Application address: P.O. Box 660005, Dallas, TX 75266-0005; Tel.: (214) 428-7441

Established in 1955 in TX.
Donor(s): Lawrence S. Pollock, Sr.
Financial data (yr. ended 12/31/87): Assets, $831,137 (M); expenditures, $166,178, including $165,600 for 29 grants (high: $70,000; low: $500).
Purpose and activities: Giving primarily for culture and the arts; support for a museum.
Limitations: Giving primarily in TX.
Application information:
Deadline(s): None
Write: Lawrence S. Pollock, Jr., Trustee
Trustees: Lawrence S. Pollock, Jr., Robert G. Pollock.
Employer Identification Number: 756011985

3076
Potts and Sibley Foundation
P.O. Box 8907
Midland 79708
Application address: Ten Cambridge Ct., Midland, TX 79705; Tel.: (915) 694-0694

Established in 1967.
Donor(s): Effie Potts Sibley Irrevocable Trust.
Financial data (yr. ended 7/31/87): Assets, $1,599,015 (M); expenditures, $176,718, including $100,800 for 29 grants (high: $13,300; low: $500).
Purpose and activities: Emphasis on higher education, cultural programs, and ecology programs.
Limitations: Giving primarily in TX.
Application information: Application form required.
Deadline(s): None
Write: Robert W. Bechtel, Trustee
Directors: Robert W. Bechtel, D.J. Sibley, Jr.
Trustees: M.R. Bullock, First RepublicBank.
Employer Identification Number: 756081070

3077
Sid W. Richardson Foundation
309 Main St.
Fort Worth 76102 (817) 336-0494

Established in 1947 in TX.
Donor(s): Sid W. Richardson,† and associated companies.
Financial data (yr. ended 12/31/87): Assets, $206,125,000 (M); expenditures, $11,560,580, including $10,078,581 for 100 grants (high: $5,500,000; low: $1,000; average: $1,000-$350,000).
Purpose and activities: Giving primarily for education, health, the arts, and social service programs.
Types of support: Operating budgets, seed money, building funds, equipment, land acquisition, endowment funds, research, publications, conferences and seminars, matching funds, special projects, renovation projects, continuing support, general purposes.
Limitations: Giving limited to TX, with emphasis on Fort Worth for the arts and human services, and statewide for health and education. No support for religious organizations. No grants to individuals, or for scholarships or fellowships; no loans.
Publications: Annual report (including application guidelines).
Application information: Application form required.
Initial approach: Letter
Copies of proposal: 1
Deadline(s): Mar. 1, June 1, and Sept. 1
Board meeting date(s): Spring, Summer, and Fall
Final notification: Varies
Write: Valleau Wilkie, Jr., Exec. Dir.
Officers and Directors:* Perry R. Bass,* Pres.; Lee M. Bass,* V.P.; Nancy Lee Bass,* V.P.; Sid R. Bass,* V.P.; Jo Helen Rosacker, Secy.; M.E. Chappell,* Treas.; Valleau Wilkie, Jr., Exec. Dir.
Number of staff: 4 full-time professional; 2 full-time support; 4 part-time support.
Employer Identification Number: 756015828
Recent arts and culture grants:
Amon Carter Museum, Fort Worth, TX, $5,400. Toward meeting additional costs of graduate students and Independent School District program related to American Frontier Life: Early Western Painting and Prints. 1987.
Arts Council of Fort Worth and Tarrant County, Fort Worth, TX, $10,000. For general support. 1987.
Fort Worth Art Association, Fort Worth, TX, $5,100,000. To establish endowment fund for purpose of acquiring works of fine art for display at Modern Art Museum of Fort Worth and for general operating expenses of Museum. 1987.
Fort Worth Ballet, Fort Worth, TX, $100,000. For matching grant for general support. 1987.
Fort Worth Cultural District Committee, Fort Worth, TX, $104,000. Toward development of Master Plan for cultural district. 1987.
Fort Worth Museum of Science and History, Fort Worth, TX, $25,000. For general support for Museum's education program. 1987.
Fort Worth Opera, Fort Worth, TX, $28,800. For general support. 1987.
Fort Worth Symphony Orchestra, Fort Worth, TX, $345,050. For matching funds for bringing Philadelphia Symphony to Fort Worth and underwriting for Kiri Te Kanawa performance with Orchestra. 1987.
InterCultura, Fort Worth, TX, $30,000. For program of high quality, scholarly exhibitions on art of world cultures. 1987.
Kimbell Art Museum, Fort Worth, TX, $1,000,000. For current acquistion fund. 1987.
Tarrant, County of, Fort Worth, TX, $1,500,000. For exterior renovation of Civil Courts Building. 1987.
Texas Association of Museums, Austin, TX, $6,000. Toward expenses related to annual meeting held in Fort Worth. 1987.
Youth Orchestra of Greater Fort Worth, Fort Worth, TX, $5,000. For general support. 1987.

3078
Rienzi Foundation, Inc.
2001 Kirby Dr., Suite 714
Houston 77019

Established in 1958 in TX.
Financial data (yr. ended 12/31/87): Assets, $2,252,353 (M); gifts received, $3,200; expenditures, $101,012, including $91,675 for 106 grants (high: $10,000; low: $50).
Purpose and activities: Giving for cultural programs, social services, higher education, and hospitals.
Limitations: Giving primarily in TX.
Officer: Evangeline Thomas, Secy.-Treas.
Directors: Carroll S. Masterson, Harris Masterson, Isla C. Reckling, Randa R. Roach, Bert F. Winston, Lynn David Winston.
Employer Identification Number: 741484331

3079
Rockwell Fund, Inc.
910 Travis St., Suite 1921
Houston 77002 (713) 659-7204

Trust established in 1931; incorporated in 1949 in TX; absorbed Rockwell Brothers Endowment, Inc. in 1981.
Donor(s): Members of the James M. Rockwell family, Rockwell Bros. & Co., Rockwell Lumber Co.
Financial data (yr. ended 12/31/87): Assets, $45,885,187 (M); expenditures, $2,863,086,

including $2,412,500 for 178 grants (high: $60,000; low: $500; average: $5,000-$25,000).
Purpose and activities: Giving to causes of interest to the founders and donors, with emphasis on higher education, religious programs, hospitals, cultural programs, municipalities, and general welfare.
Types of support: Annual campaigns, seed money, general purposes, building funds, equipment, land acquisition, scholarship funds, lectureships, operating budgets, professorships, renovation projects, research.
Limitations: Giving primarily in TX, with emphasis on Houston. No grants to individuals; no loans; grants awarded on a year-to-year basis only; no future commitments.
Application information: Application form required.
Initial approach: Letter
Copies of proposal: 1
Deadline(s): Nov. 1
Board meeting date(s): Quarterly
Final notification: December 15
Write: Joe M. Green, Jr., Pres., or Mary Jo Loyd, Grants Coord.
Officers and Trustees: Joe M. Green, Jr., Pres.; R. Terry Bell, V.P.; Helen N. Sterling, Secy.-Treas.
Number of staff: 2 full-time professional; 1 part-time professional; 2 full-time support.
Employer Identification Number: 746040258

3080
Roderick Foundation, Inc.
Texas Commerce Bank
201 E. Main
El Paso 72201 (915) 546-6501

Incorporated in 1953 in TX.
Donor(s): Dorrance Roderick, Olga B. Roderick, El Paso Times, Inc.
Financial data (yr. ended 12/31/88): Assets, $2,270,733 (M); expenditures, $64,687, including $16,200 for 5 grants (high: $10,000; low: $200).
Purpose and activities: Giving for higher and other education, including a military institute and a parish school, cultural programs, including a symphony association, and social service and youth agencies; support also for health associations, health services, and hospitals.
Limitations: Giving primarily in El Paso, TX.
Application information:
Write: Terry Crenshaw
Officers and Directors:* Olga B. Roderick,* Pres.; Frances R. Smith,* V.P.; K.B. Clark,* Secy.; Robert E. Sympson, Treas.
Employer Identification Number: 746044969

3081
Ralph B. Rogers Foundation
8100 Carpenter Freeway
Dallas 75247 (214) 637-3100

Trust established in 1953 in TX.
Donor(s): Ralph B. Rogers.
Financial data (yr. ended 12/31/87): Assets, $993,468 (M); gifts received, $66,679; expenditures, $353,745, including $325,750 for 24 grants (high: $267,640; low: $10; average: $1,000-$5,000).
Purpose and activities: Support for cultural programs, health education, medical research, and an independent school.
Types of support: Research.
Limitations: Giving primarily in TX.
Application information:
Initial approach: Letter
Deadline(s): None
Board meeting date(s): Dec.
Write: Ralph B. Rogers, Trustee
Trustees: Robert Alpert, Ralph B. Rogers, Robert D. Rogers, Frances B. Conroy.
Number of staff: None.
Employer Identification Number: 136153567

3082
C. L. Rowan Charitable & Educational Fund, Inc.
1918 Commerce Bldg.
Fort Worth 76102 (817) 332-2327

Established in 1954 in TX.
Donor(s): Merle M. Rowan.
Financial data (yr. ended 10/31/87): Assets, $801,188 (M); expenditures, $180,749, including $87,400 for 49 grants (high: $25,000; low: $100) and $42,260 for 3 grants to individuals.
Purpose and activities: Giving primarily for higher and other education, particularly the University of Texas Law School Foundation; support also for cultural programs, scholarships to individuals and to institutions, and grants to individuals.
Types of support: Student aid, scholarship funds, grants to individuals.
Limitations: Giving primarily in Fort Worth, TX.
Application information:
Initial approach: Letter
Deadline(s): None
Write: Elton M. Hyder, Jr., Pres.
Officers and Directors:* Elton M. Hyder, Jr., Pres.; Nita Gothard, Secy.-Treas.
Employer Identification Number: 756009661

3083
San Antonio Area Foundation
808 Travis Bldg.
405 North St. Mary's
San Antonio 78205 (512) 225-2243

Community foundation incorporated in 1964 in TX.
Financial data (yr. ended 9/30/88): Assets, $14,682,892 (M); gifts received, $2,077,591; expenditures, $1,698,830, including $1,300,062 for 256 grants and $88,775 for 101 grants to individuals.
Purpose and activities: To provide an effective channel for private giving to meet educational, cultural, medical, research, social, religious, and civic needs at all levels of society.
Types of support: Operating budgets, continuing support, annual campaigns, seed money, emergency funds, building funds, equipment, land acquisition, endowment funds, matching funds, scholarship funds, special projects, research, publications, conferences and seminars, student aid, general purposes, lectureships, professorships, renovation projects.
Limitations: Giving limited to TX, with emphasis on the Bexar County and San Antonio areas, except when otherwise specified by donor. No support for political or lobbying programs. No grants to individuals; or for deficit financing; no loans.
Publications: Annual report, program policy statement, application guidelines.
Application information: Application form required.
Copies of proposal: 15
Deadline(s): Feb. 15
Board meeting date(s): Apr. and Nov., and as required
Final notification: 8 weeks
Write: Katherine Netting Folbre, Exec. Dir.
Officer: Katherine Netting Folbre, Secy.-Treas. and Exec. Dir.
Distribution Committee: Jerome Weynand, Chair.; Gaines Voigt, Vice-Chair.; John E. Banks, Sr., Clifton J. Bolner, John H. Foster, Richard E. Goldsmith, Pete Martinez, Edith McAllister, Al J. Notzon, William Reddell, L. John Streiber, Jr., Dale A. Wood, M.D.
Trustee Banks: Broadway National Bank, First City Bank-Central Bank, First RepublicBank San Antonio, Frost National Bank, Groos Bank, Kelly Field National Bank, MBank Alamo, NBC of San Antonio, N.A.
Number of staff: 1 full-time professional; 1 part-time professional.
Employer Identification Number: 746065414
Recent arts and culture grants:
Daughters of the Republic of Texas, San Antonio, TX, $5,000. For scholarships. 1987.
Orchestra San Antonio, San Antonio, TX, $5,000. For program support. 1987.
San Antonio Art Institute, San Antonio, TX, $12,650. For building fund and general support. 1987.
San Antonio Botanical Center Society, San Antonio, TX, $20,000. For acquisition, removal and adaptive restoration of Sullivan Carriage House. 1987.
San Antonio Festival, San Antonio, TX, $76,100. For presentations of St. Cecilia's Mass and Berlioz' Childhood of Christ, debt retirement, toward Meadows Foundation matching grant and general support. 1987.
San Antonio Festival, San Antonio, TX, $7,500. For program support. 1987.
San Antonio Museum Association, San Antonio, TX, $66,063. For exhibition of Monstrance of Santa Clara from Colombia; Folk Art Program; Ancient Art Program; Greek and Roman Antiquities Department; purchase automobile for Museum use; and general support. 1987.
San Antonio Symphony, San Antonio, TX, $18,050. Toward Maddux challenge grant and general support. 1987.
San Antonio Symphony, San Antonio, TX, $12,000. For Concert for Kids featuring Bob McGrath of Sesame Street. 1987.
San Antonio Zoological Society, San Antonio, TX, $46,100. To construct deck adjacent to Lion's Pride Restaurant and general support. 1987.
Southwest Craft Center, San Antonio, TX, $6,000. For Visiting Artists Program. 1987.
Very Special Arts, San Antonio, TX, $5,000. For Margaret Putnam Theme Piece Project. 1987.

3084
Scaler Foundation, Inc.
2200 Post Oak Blvd., Suite 707
Houston 77056 (713) 627-2440

Incorporated in 1954 in TX.
Financial data (yr. ended 12/31/87): Assets, $7,502,026 (M); gifts received, $60,380; expenditures, $360,807, including $298,958 for 10 grants (high: $118,470; low: $1,000; average: $10,000-$30,000).
Purpose and activities: Grants for major national art museums to aid in acquiring objects of contemporary art from young talent.
Types of support: Operating budgets, seed money, special projects, general purposes, continuing support.
Limitations: Giving primarily in the U.S. and France. No grants to individuals, or for building and endowment funds, research, scholarships, fellowships, or matching gifts; no loans.
Application information: Contributes only to pre-selected organizations. Applications not accepted.
Officers and Directors: Eric Boissonnas, Pres.; Sylvie Boissonnas, V.P.; Elliott A. Johnson, Secy.-Treas.
Number of staff: None.
Employer Identification Number: 746036684

3085
William E. Scott Foundation
3200 Continental Plaza
Fort Worth 76102 (817) 336-0361

Incorporated in 1960 in TX.
Donor(s): William E. Scott.†
Financial data (yr. ended 5/31/88): Assets, $3,194,719 (M); expenditures, $248,284, including $151,400 for 17 grants (high: $34,000; low: $500; average: $5,000).
Purpose and activities: Giving primarily for programs in the arts; some grants for elementary and higher education, youth agencies, and community funds.
Types of support: Annual campaigns, capital campaigns, general purposes, special projects.
Limitations: Giving limited to TX, with emphasis on the Fort Worth-Tarrant County area, and in LA, OK, and NM. No grants to individuals.
Publications: Application guidelines.
Application information: Application form required.
Initial approach: Letter
Copies of proposal: 1
Deadline(s): None
Board meeting date(s): As required
Write: Robert W. Decker, Pres.
Officers and Directors: Robert W. Decker, Pres.; Raymond B. Kelly III, V.P.
Number of staff: 1 part-time support.
Employer Identification Number: 756024661

3086
Scurlock Foundation
700 Louisiana, Suite 3920
Houston 77002 (713) 222-2041

Incorporated in 1954 in TX.
Donor(s): E.C. Scurlock, Scurlock Oil Co., D.E. Farnsworth,† W.C. Scurlock,† J.S. Blanton, and other members of the Blanton family.
Financial data (yr. ended 12/31/87): Assets, $7,308,912 (M); gifts received, $41,205; expenditures, $649,492, including $622,976 for 114 grants (high: $42,120; low: $50).
Purpose and activities: Emphasis on hospitals and secondary and higher education; support also for health agencies, Protestant churches, social service and youth agencies, cultural programs, and public interest groups.
Types of support: Building funds, general purposes, annual campaigns, emergency funds, land acquisition, endowment funds, research, matching funds, continuing support.
Limitations: Giving primarily in TX. No grants to individuals, or for scholarships or fellowships; no loans.
Application information: Funds committed for approximately the next two years.
Initial approach: Letter
Copies of proposal: 1
Deadline(s): None
Board meeting date(s): Dec. and as required
Write: J.S. Blanton, Pres.
Officers and Directors: J.S. Blanton, Pres.; Ben Love, V.P.; Kenneth Fisher, Secy.-Treas.; Eddy S. Blanton, Jack S. Blanton, Jr., Laura Lee Blanton, Elizabeth B. Wareing.
Number of staff: None.
Employer Identification Number: 741488953

3087
Sarah M. & Charles E. Seay Charitable Trust
2014 MBank Bldg.
1704 Main St.
Dallas 75201 (214) 742-4251

Established in 1983 in TX.
Donor(s): Charles E. Seay, Sarah M. Seay.
Financial data (yr. ended 5/31/87): Assets, $1,820,549 (M); gifts received, $236,828; expenditures, $73,430, including $63,449 for 45 grants (high: $10,583; low: $50).
Purpose and activities: Giving for higher and other education, religious organizations, cultural programs, social service and youth agencies, and community affairs.
Limitations: Giving primarily in TX, with emphasis on Dallas.
Application information:
Initial approach: Letter
Write: Charles E. Seay, Trustee
Trustees: Charles E. Seay, Sarah M. Seay.
Employer Identification Number: 751894505

3088
Harold Simmons Foundation
Three Lincoln Centre
5430 LBJ Fwy., Suite 1700
Dallas 75240

Incorporated in 1988 in TX.
Donor(s): NL Industries, Inc., Contran Corp.
Financial data (yr. ended 12/31/88): Assets, $2,700,000 (M); expenditures, $1,662,000 for 194 grants (high: $100,000; low: $100; average: $1,000-$5,000) and $52,013 for 223 employee matching gifts.
Purpose and activities: Grants for community programs and projects, including United Way, and for health and welfare agencies, culture and art, youth, and education.
Types of support: Annual campaigns, building funds, continuing support, emergency funds, employee matching gifts, operating budgets, renovation projects, research, seed money, special projects.
Limitations: Giving limited to Dallas, TX, area. No grants to individuals, or for deficit financing, land acquisitions, endowment funds, publications, or conferences; no loans.
Publications: Application guidelines.
Application information:
Initial approach: Proposal
Copies of proposal: 1
Deadline(s): None
Board meeting date(s): As needed
Final notification: 3 months
Write: Lisa K. Simmons, Pres.
Officers: Harold Simmons,* Chair.; Lisa K. Simmons,* Pres.; Steven L. Watson,* Secy.; James F. Kauffman, Treas.
Directors:* J. Landis Martin.
Number of staff: 1 full-time professional.
Employer Identification Number: 752222091

3089
Clara Blackford Smith and W. Aubrey Smith Charitable Foundation
c/o NCNB
300 West Main St.
Denison 75020 (214) 465-2131

Established in 1985 in TX.
Donor(s): Clara Blackford Smith.†
Financial data (yr. ended 6/30/88): Assets, $13,159,550 (M); expenditures, $827,425, including $737,248 for 15 grants (high: $400,000; low: $972).
Purpose and activities: Giving primarily for a medical center building fund, higher education, social services and cultural organizations.
Types of support: Building funds.
Limitations: Giving primarily in Denison, TX.
Application information: Application form required.
Deadline(s): None
Officers: Charles H. Green, Chair.; Jane Ayres, Trust Officer.
Directors: Jack G. Berry, Wayne E. Delaney, Jerdy Gary, Roy L. McKinney III.
Trustee: NCNB.
Employer Identification Number: 756314114

3090
Vivian L. Smith Foundation
2000 West Loop S., Suite 1900
Houston 77027 (713) 622-8611

Established in 1981 in TX.
Donor(s): Vivian L. Smith.
Financial data (yr. ended 12/31/87): Assets, $3,265,991 (M); expenditures, $163,956, including $162,318 for 20 grants (high: $71,000; low: $1,000).
Purpose and activities: Giving primarily for cultural programs; some support for education.
Types of support: General purposes.
Limitations: Giving primarily in Houston, TX. No grants to individuals.

Application information:
Initial approach: Letter or proposal
Deadline(s): None
Write: W.N. Finnegan
Officers and Trustees: Vivian L. Smith, Pres. and Treas.; R.A. Seale, Jr., V.P. and Secy.; Richard H. Skinner, Jack T. Trotter.
Employer Identification Number: 760101380

3091
Southland Corporate Giving Program
2828 North Haskell
Dallas 75204 (214) 828-7255
Additional tel.: (214) 828-7277

Financial data (yr. ended 12/31/88): Total giving, $885,133, including $843,596 for 295 grants (high: $71,110; low: $25) and $41,537 for 241 employee matching gifts.
Purpose and activities: Supports federated campaigns, arts and culture, libraries, human rights, crime and law enforcement, public affairs, health, medical research, United Way, youth services, drug abuse programs, family services, and programs for the handicapped. Also supports education, including international studies and business education. Also available is employee gift matching for education.
Types of support: Annual campaigns, building funds, general purposes, matching funds, research, special projects, employee matching gifts.
Limitations: Giving primarily in headquarters city and where 7-Eleven stores are located.
Publications: Corporate report.
Application information:
Initial approach: Letter of inquiry
Copies of proposal: 1
Board meeting date(s): Donations Committee meets quarterly in Mar., June, Sept., and Dec.
Final notification: After applicable meeting or as otherwise determined by Donations Committee
Write: John H. Rodgers, Sr. V.P. and Secy. or Cathy Franklin, Mgr., Corp. Secretarial Services
Administrator: John H. Rodgers, Sr. V.P. and Secy.
Number of staff: 2 full-time professional; 1 full-time support.

3092
Southland Foundation
P.O. Box 619208, DFW Station
Dallas 75261-9208 (214) 556-0500

Established in 1974 in TX.
Donor(s): Southland Life Insurance Co., Southland Financial Corp., Las Colinas Corp., Southland Corporate Services, Inc., Southland Investment Properties.
Financial data (yr. ended 12/31/87): Assets, $234,470 (M); gifts received, $5,000; expenditures, $10,291, including $10,250 for 3 grants.
Purpose and activities: Giving primarily for health, community funds, higher and business education, social service agencies, and cultural programs.
Types of support: Building funds, operating budgets, general purposes, research, continuing support.
Limitations: Giving primarily in TX. No grants to individuals.
Application information:
Initial approach: Letter
Copies of proposal: 1
Deadline(s): None
Write: J. Michael Lewis, Secy.
Officers: Ben H. Carpenter, Pres.; Dan C. Williams, V.P.; J. Michael Lewis, Secy.
Employer Identification Number: 237337606

3093
Nelda C. and H. J. Lutcher Stark Foundation
602 West Main St.
P.O. Box 909
Orange 77631-0909 (409) 883-3513

Incorporated in 1961 in TX.
Donor(s): H.J. Lutcher Stark,† Nelda C. Stark.
Financial data (yr. ended 2/28/88): Assets, $73,655,532 (M); gifts received, $950,000; expenditures, $1,946,037, including $145,850 for 6 grants (high: $105,850; low: $3,000), $1,250 for 3 grants to individuals and $1,386,149 for 2 foundation-administered programs.
Purpose and activities: Grants primarily for education, historical restoration, and the performing arts; operating programs include the construction, operation, and maintenance of a museum to house and exhibit an extensive art collection owned by the foundation and to underwrite performances of a theater for the performing arts.
Types of support: Student aid.
Limitations: Giving limited to TX and southwest LA. No grants to individuals (except limited scholarships), or for endowment funds or operating budgets.
Application information:
Initial approach: Brief letter
Deadline(s): None
Board meeting date(s): Monthly
Final notification: 1 month
Write: Clyde V. McKee, Jr., Secy.
Officers and Trustees: Nelda C. Stark, Chair.; Eunice R. Benckenstein, Vice-Chair.; Clyde V. McKee, Jr., Secy.-Treas.; William J. Butler, Sidney H. Phillips, W.G. Riedel III, John C. Sargent, Homer B.H. Stark.
Number of staff: 6 full-time professional; 34 full-time support.
Employer Identification Number: 746047440

3094
Dorothy Richard Starling Foundation
P.O. Box 66527
Houston 77266 (713) 651-9102

Foundation established in 1969 in TX.
Donor(s): Frank M. Starling.†
Financial data (yr. ended 12/31/87): Assets, $11,349,564 (M); expenditures, $510,407, including $430,000 for 6 grants (high: $232,000; low: $15,000).
Purpose and activities: Support for institutions offering instruction in classical violin performance and study arts.
Types of support: Endowment funds.
Application information:
Initial approach: Letter
Deadline(s): None
Final notification: Within 60 days
Write: Any of the trustees
Trustees: Robert K. Jewett, A.C. Speyer, Jr., H. Allen Weatherby.
Employer Identification Number: 746121656

3095
Stemmons Foundation
1200 Tower East
2700 Stemmons Freeway
Dallas 75207 (214) 631-7910

Established in 1963 in TX.
Financial data (yr. ended 12/31/87): Assets, $3,011,571 (M); gifts received, $95,127; expenditures, $326,126, including $309,950 for 73 grants (high: $50,000; low: $100).
Purpose and activities: Giving for cultural programs, youth agencies, social services, health agencies, and education.
Types of support: Scholarship funds.
Limitations: Giving primarily in Dallas, TX.
Application information:
Initial approach: Proposal
Write: Ann M. Roberts, V.P.
Officers: Heinz K. Simon, Pres.; Ann M. Roberts, V.P.; John M. Stemmons, Jr., V.P.; John M. Stemmons, Sr., V.P.; Ruth T. Stemmons, Secy.; Allison S. Simon, Treas.
Employer Identification Number: 756039966

3096
Ann Bradshaw Stokes Foundation
3204 Beverly Dr.
Dallas 75205 (214) 528-1924

Established in 1982 in TX.
Donor(s): Ann Bradshaw Stokes.†
Financial data (yr. ended 12/31/87): Assets, $1,804,693 (M); expenditures, $125,814, including $94,145 for 19 grants (high: $8,889; low: $1,408).
Purpose and activities: Grants limited to drama departments of TX colleges and universities for scholarship aid and department projects.
Types of support: Student aid, equipment, special projects.
Limitations: Giving limited to TX.
Publications: Informational brochure (including application guidelines).
Application information: Contact school's Drama Dept. Application form required.
Copies of proposal: 1
Trustee: William N. Stokes, Jr.
Number of staff: None.
Employer Identification Number: 751866981

3097
Strake Foundation
712 Main St., Suite 3300
Houston 77002-3210 (713) 546-2400

Trust established in 1952 in TX; incorporated in 1983.

Donor(s): George W. Strake, Sr.,† Susan K. Strake,† George W. Strake, Jr., Susan S. Dilworth, Georganna S. Parsley.
Financial data (yr. ended 12/31/87): Assets, $17,076,687 (M); expenditures, $1,024,295, including $863,130 for 193 grants (high: $40,000; low: $500; average: $1,000-$10,000).
Purpose and activities: Giving primarily to Roman Catholic-affiliated associations, including hospitals and higher and secondary educational institutions.
Types of support: Building funds, operating budgets, continuing support, annual campaigns, seed money, emergency funds, equipment, endowment funds, special projects, research, matching funds, capital campaigns.
Limitations: Giving primarily in TX, especially Houston; no grants outside the U.S. No support for elementary schools. No grants to individuals, or for deficit financing, consulting services, technical assistance, or publications; no loans.
Publications: Annual report (including application guidelines).
Application information:
Initial approach: Brief proposal
Copies of proposal: 1
Deadline(s): Submit proposal preferably in Mar. or Sept.; deadline 1 month prior to board meetings
Board meeting date(s): May or June, and Nov. or Dec.
Final notification: 1 month after board meetings
Write: George W. Strake, Jr., Pres.
Officers and Trustees:* George W. Strake, Jr.,* Pres. and Treas.; Georganna S. Parsley,* V.P. and Secy.; Thomas B. Brennan, Sharon McNearney, Burke M. O'Rourke, Joseph A. Reich, Jr., Stephen D. Strake, Linda D. Walsh.
Number of staff: 1 part-time professional; 2 part-time support.
Employer Identification Number: 760041524

3098
Roy and Christine Sturgis Charitable and Educational Trust

c/o NCNB Texas National Bank, Trust Division
P.O. Box 830241
Dallas 75283-0241

Established in 1981 in AR.
Financial data (yr. ended 9/30/87): Assets, $30,229,798 (M); gifts received, $556,589; expenditures, $2,112,753, including $1,695,000 for 22 grants (high: $400,000; low: $1,000).
Purpose and activities: Support primarily for religious, charitable, scientific, literary, and educational organizations.
Types of support: Building funds, capital campaigns, endowment funds, general purposes, matching funds, operating budgets, research, special projects.
Limitations: Giving primarily in AR and TX. No grants to individuals; no loans.
Publications: Application guidelines.
Application information: Requests are considered only once every two years. No personal interviews granted.
Initial approach: Letter or proposal
Copies of proposal: 2
Deadline(s): Mar. 1
Board meeting date(s): Apr.
Final notification: May
Trustee: NCNB Texas National Bank.
Employer Identification Number: 756331832

3099
Anne Burnett and Charles D. Tandy Foundation

801 Cherry St., Suite 1577
Fort Worth 76102 (817) 877-3344

Established in 1978 in TX.
Donor(s): Anne Burnett Tandy,† Charles D. Tandy,† Ben Bird.
Financial data (yr. ended 12/31/88): Assets, $173,397,180 (M); expenditures, $11,693,024, including $10,372,757 for 42 grants (low: $5,000).
Purpose and activities: Support for health care and cultural organizations, including major museum projects; support also for social service and youth agencies, community affairs, and education.
Types of support: General purposes, capital campaigns, special projects, technical assistance, seed money.
Limitations: Giving primarily in the Fort Worth, TX, area. No grants to individuals, or for scholarships or fellowships.
Publications: Program policy statement, application guidelines, annual report (including application guidelines).
Application information: Application form required.
Initial approach: Letter
Copies of proposal: 1
Deadline(s): None
Board meeting date(s): Generally in Mar., June, and Nov.
Final notification: 90 days
Write: Thomas F. Beech, Exec. V.P.
Officers: Anne W. Marion,* Pres.; Thomas F. Beech, Exec. V.P.; Edward R. Hudson, Jr.,* V.P. and Secy.-Treas.; Perry R. Bass,* V.P.
Trustees:* Benjamin J. Fortson.
Number of staff: 1 full-time professional; 1 full-time support.
Employer Identification Number: 751638517
Recent arts and culture grants:
Amon Carter Museum, Fort Worth, TX, $100,000. For support of staff expenses of Cultural District Committee. 1987.
Arts Council of Fort Worth and Tarrant County, Fort Worth, TX, $50,000. For evaluation of role and purposes of Arts Council and production of long range plan. 1987.
Fort Worth Art Association, Modern Art Museum of Fort Worth, Fort Worth, TX, $2,500,000. Toward creation of permanent endowment. 1987.
Fort Worth Art Association, Modern Art Museum of Fort Worth, Fort Worth, TX, $321,000. For acquistion of works of art by Jackson Pollock. 1987.
Fort Worth Art Association, Modern Art Museum of Fort Worth, Fort Worth, TX, $300,000. For general operting support. 1987.
Fort Worth Art Association, Modern Art Museum of Fort Worth, Fort Worth, TX, $250,000. For acquisition of works of art by Morris Louis. 1987.
Fort Worth Ballet, Fort Worth, TX, $75,000. Toward underwriting of cost of Fort Worth Symphony for Ballet performances. 1987.
Fort Worth Chamber Foundation, Arts in the Park, Fort Worth, TX, $20,000. Toward underwriting for Fourth of July Concert. 1987.
Fort Worth Civic Opera Association, Fort Worth, TX, $100,000. For general operating support. 1987.
National Cowboy Hall of Fame and Western Heritage Center, Oklahoma City, OK, $200,000. For capital campaign. 1987.
National Trust for Historic Preservation, DC, $20,000. For general operating support for Texas/New Mexico field office. 1987.
North Texas Public Broadcasting, Dallas, TX, $125,000. Toward expenses to bring Channel 2 on the air. 1987.
Texas and Southwestern Cattle Raisers Foundation, Fort Worth, TX, $25,000. For renovation and expansion of Cattlemen's Museum. 1987.
Texas Boys Choir of Fort Worth, Fort Worth, TX, $20,000. For scholarships. 1987.
Texas Heritage, Thistle Hill, Fort Worth, TX, $18,000. For renovation costs. 1987.
Van Cliburn Foundation, Fort Worth, TX, $57,280. Toward underwriting of collaborative production involving Van Cliburn Foundation, Fort Worth Ballet, Fort Worth Symphony, Fort Worth Theatre, Modern Art Museum, and Stage West. 1987.

3100
David L. Tandy Foundation

8937 Random Rd.
Fort Worth 76179 (817) 236-7908

Established in 1968 in TX.
Financial data (yr. ended 5/31/88): Assets, $2,902,387 (M); expenditures, $143,872, including $126,000 for 30 grants (high: $20,000; low: $1,000).
Purpose and activities: Giving for educational and cultural programs and social services.
Limitations: Giving primarily in TX.
Application information: Applications not accepted.
Board meeting date(s): 2nd Monday in July
Write: William H. Michero, V.P. and Secy.
Officers and Directors:* Emmett Duemke,* Pres.; A.R. Tandy, Jr., V.P.; E.C. Whitney, V.P.; William H. Michero,* V.P. and Secy.; B.R. Roland,* V.P. and Treas.
Number of staff: None.
Employer Identification Number: 756083140

3101
The Community Trust of Metropolitan Tarrant County

210 East Ninth St.
Fort Worth 76102 (817) 335-3473

Community foundation established in 1980 in TX.
Financial data (yr. ended 12/31/87): Assets, $14,807,855 (M); gifts received, $890,450; expenditures, $622,509, including $515,583 for 28 grants (high: $72,451; low: $1,500; average: $5,000-$10,000).
Purpose and activities: Support for community development, social services,

education, health, and cultural programs; emphasis on one-time grants to new and innovative programs.
Types of support: General purposes, seed money, matching funds, emergency funds, special projects, technical assistance.
Limitations: Giving primarily in Tarrant County, TX. No support for secular, religious, or political organizations. No grants to individuals, or for annual campaigns, deficit financing, or endowment funds.
Publications: Application guidelines, annual report, informational brochure.
Application information:
Initial approach: Letter to request guidelines
Copies of proposal: 1
Deadline(s): None
Board meeting date(s): Quarterly
Write: Stewart W. Stearns, Exec. Dir.
Staff: Stewart W. Stearns, Exec. Dir.
Officer: Robert W. Decker, Chair.
Executive Committee: Louise Appleman, Alann Bedford, Paul Brandt, Marcus Ginsberg, Leland Hodges, Marty Leonard, Robert S. Patterson, Bruce Petty, Lynda Roodhouse, Earle A. Shields, Lloyd J. Weaver.
Number of staff: 1 part-time professional; 1 part-time support.
Employer Identification Number: 750858360

3102
T. L. L. Temple Foundation
109 Temple Blvd.
Lufkin 75901 (409) 639-5197

Trust established in 1962 in TX.
Donor(s): Georgie T. Munz,† Katherine S. Temple.†
Financial data (yr. ended 11/30/87): Assets, $170,371,934 (M); gifts received, $100,000; expenditures, $8,405,632, including $8,111,884 for 110 grants (high: $1,585,215; low: $700; average: $1,000-$50,000).
Purpose and activities: Support for education, hospitals, and social services; support also for civic affairs and cultural programs.
Types of support: Operating budgets, seed money, emergency funds, building funds, equipment, land acquisition, matching funds, scholarship funds, special projects, research, conferences and seminars.
Limitations: Giving primarily in counties in TX constituting the East Texas Pine Timber Belt. No support for private foundations, or religious organizations for religious purposes. No grants to individuals, or for continuing support, annual campaigns, deficit financing, or endowment funds; no loans.
Publications: Application guidelines, program policy statement.
Application information:
Initial approach: Letter
Deadline(s): None
Board meeting date(s): Monthly
Final notification: 2 months
Write: Ward R. Burke, Exec. Secy.
Officers and Trustees: Arthur Temple, Chair.; Ward R. Burke, Exec. Secy.; Phillip M. Leach, Arthur Temple III, W. Temple Webber, Jr.
Number of staff: 1 full-time professional; 1 full-time support.
Employer Identification Number: 756037406

3103
Temple-Inland Foundation
303 South Temple Drive
P.O. Drawer 338
Diboll 75941 (409) 829-1313

Established in 1985 in TX.
Donor(s): Temple-Inland, Inc.
Financial data (yr. ended 6/30/88): Assets, $5,699,565 (M); gifts received, $650,000; expenditures, $677,805, including $379,864 for 34 grants (high: $106,081; low: $200), $52,625 for 24 grants to individuals and $227,647 for 263 employee matching gifts.
Purpose and activities: Gives employee-matching contributions for various fields, including culture and higher and secondary education; contributes to preselected charitable organizations; and supports a scholarship program for children of employees of Temple-Inland.
Types of support: Employee matching gifts, general purposes, research, employee-related scholarships.
Limitations: No grants to individuals (other than employee-related scholarships).
Publications: 990-PF.
Application information: Contributes only to preselected charitable organizations; application forms required for scholarships.
Initial approach: Letter
Copies of proposal: 1
Deadline(s): Mar. 15 for scholarships
Board meeting date(s): Varies
Final notification: June 1 for new scholarship applications; Aug. 15 for renewals
Write: Richard Warner, Pres.
Officers: M. Richard Warner, Pres.; Roger D. Ericson,* V.P.; James R. Wash, Secy.-Treas.
Directors:* Clifford J. Grum, W. Wayne McDonald.
Number of staff: None.
Employer Identification Number: 751977109

3104
Tenneco Corporate Contributions Program
P.O. Box 2511
Houston 77252-2511 (713) 757-3930

Financial data (yr. ended 12/31/87): Total giving, $6,539,939, including $5,764,939 for grants (high: $50,000; low: $500; average: $1,000-$10,000), $275,000 for 1,232 employee matching gifts and $500,000 for in-kind gifts.
Purpose and activities: Supports education, colleges, universities, health, welfare, united funds, youth groups, law and justice, urban affairs, hospitals, programs for the elderly, civic and public services, environmental issues, arts and humanities, museums, women's groups, libraries, performing arts, historic preservation and medical research. Other support includes in-kind donations, use of company facilities, and technical assistance.
Types of support: Building funds, capital campaigns, professorships, renovation projects, matching funds, fellowships, scholarship funds, employee matching gifts, in-kind gifts.
Limitations: Giving primarily in headquarters cities of New York, NY, and Washington, D.C. No grants to individuals, or for political, religious, fraternal or veterans' organizations.
Application information: Include narrative/letter, complete budget, IRS letter, list of contributors and board members, description of organization and project and a financial statement.
Initial approach: Initial contact by letter on letterhead stationery
Copies of proposal: 1
Deadline(s): Prior to Aug. 15 for consideration in next calendar year's budget
Board meeting date(s): 2nd Tuesday in Jan. each year
Final notification: 4 weeks after submission of application
Write: Jo Ann Swinney, Dir., Community Affairs
Administrators: Connie Griffith, Sr. Contribs. Asst.; Ethel Samuels, Sr. Contribs. Coord.
Number of staff: 1 full-time professional; 1 full-time support.

3105
Texas Commerce Bank Foundation of Texas Commerce Bank - Houston, Inc.
c/o Texas Commerce Bank-Houston
P.O. Box 2558
Houston 77252-8050

Incorporated in 1952 in TX.
Donor(s): Texas Commerce Bank-Houston.
Financial data (yr. ended 12/31/87): Assets, $294,250 (M); gifts received, $795,000; expenditures, $714,963, including $713,333 for grants.
Purpose and activities: Giving for a community fund, cultural programs, higher education, and health and medical research organizations; some support for social service agencies.
Types of support: Annual campaigns, building funds, continuing support, employee matching gifts, research, capital campaigns.
Limitations: Giving limited to the Houston, TX, area. No grants to individuals or for endowment funds; no loans.
Application information:
Initial approach: Letter
Copies of proposal: 1
Officers: Marc J. Shapiro, Chair. and Pres.; Shelby R. Rogers, Secy.; Beverly McCaskill, Treas.
Employer Identification Number: 746036696

3106
Texas Instruments Foundation
13500 North Central Expwy.
P.O. Box 655474, Mail Station 232
Dallas 75265 (214) 995-3172

Trust established in 1951 in TX; incorporated in 1964.
Donor(s): Texas Instruments, Inc., and wholly-owned subsidiaries.
Financial data (yr. ended 12/31/88): Assets, $12,472,395 (M); expenditures, $872,960 for 69 grants (high: $30,000; low: $500; average: $1,000-$10,000) and $424,041 for employee matching gifts.

Purpose and activities: Giving largely for community funds; grants also for higher and secondary education, including employee matching gifts, hospitals, youth agencies, and cultural programs; Founders Prize awarded for outstanding achievement in the physical, health, or management sciences, or mathematics.
Types of support: Employee matching gifts, building funds, scholarship funds, research, continuing support, capital campaigns, renovation projects.
Limitations: No grants to individuals, or for company products or advertising; no loans.
Application information: Application for Founders Prize by nomination only; application forms available from L.M. Rice, Jr., Pres.
Initial approach: Letter
Copies of proposal: 1
Deadline(s): Jan., Apr., July, and Nov.; Dec. 31 for Founders Prize
Board meeting date(s): Feb., May, Aug., and Dec.
Final notification: 3 weeks after board meetings
Write: Liston M. Rice, Jr., Pres.
Officers: Liston M. Rice, Jr.,* Pres.; William P. Weber,* V.P.; Joe Richardson, Secy.; William A. Aylesworth, Treas.
Directors:* Gerald W. Fronterhouse, J.E. Jonsson, Jerry R. Junkins, Mark Shepherd, Jr., S.T. Harris, William P. Weber.
Number of staff: 1 full-time support.
Employer Identification Number: 756038519

3107
Texas Non-Profit Corporation
(also known as Strake Foundation Charitable Trust)
3300 Texas Commerce Bank Bldg.
712 Main St., Suite 3300
Houston 77002 (713) 546-2400

Established in 1952 in TX.
Donor(s): George W. Strake, Sr.,† Susan K. Strake.†
Financial data (yr. ended 12/31/88): Assets, $19,507,171 (M); expenditures, $1,173,589, including $1,072,900 for 197 grants (high: $100,000; low: $500; average: $5,000).
Purpose and activities: Support for higher and secondary education, cultural programs, youth activities, civic affairs, hospitals and health organizations, community funds, social services, including programs for children and the elderly, and Catholic organizations, including welfare services and schools.
Types of support: General purposes, building funds, special projects.
Limitations: Giving primarily in TX. No support for elementary schools. No grants to individuals.
Application information:
Initial approach: Letter
Copies of proposal: 1
Deadline(s): 1 month before semiannual meeting
Board meeting date(s): May or June and Nov. or Dec.
Write: George W. Strake, Jr., Pres.
Officers and Trustees: George W. Strake, Jr., Pres. and Treas.; Georganna S. Parsley, V.P. and Secy.; Thomas B. Brennan, Sharon McNearney, Burke M. O'Rourke, Joseph A. Reich, Jr., Stephen D. Strake, Colleen D. Stroup, Linda D. Walsh.
Number of staff: 1 part-time professional; 2 part-time support.
Employer Identification Number: 746031399

3108
Texas Utilities Corporate Giving Program
2001 Bryan Tower
Dallas 75201 (214) 653-4600

Purpose and activities: Supports economic development, environmental issues, fine arts institutes, general education, private colleges and United Way.
Limitations: Giving primarily in headquarters city and major operating locations.
Application information:
Write: E.L. Watson, Sr. V.P.

3109
The Tobin Foundation
P.O. Box 2101
San Antonio 78297 (512) 223-6203

Incorporated in 1951 in TX.
Donor(s): Edgar G. Tobin,† Margaret Batts Tobin.
Financial data (yr. ended 12/31/86): Assets, $2,059,261 (M); expenditures, $188,017, including $173,660 for 22 grants (high: $71,615; low: $120).
Purpose and activities: Giving to cultural programs, community funds, and education; support also for a church.
Limitations: Giving primarily in TX. No grants to individuals.
Application information:
Initial approach: Letter
Deadline(s): None
Write: Arnold Swartz, Trustee
Officers: Margaret Batts Tobin, Pres.; R.L.B. Tobin, V.P. and Treas.; Harold Gasnell, Secy.
Trustees: James T. Hart, Arnold Swartz.
Employer Identification Number: 746035718

3110
Tracor Corporate Giving Program
6500 Tracor Lane
Austin 78725-2006 (512) 926-2800

Financial data (yr. ended 12/31/87): Total giving, $65,000, including $35,000 for 200 employee matching gifts and $30,000 for 15 in-kind gifts.
Purpose and activities: Supports arts and culture, health, welfare, public broadcasting, education and civic affairs. Also available are employee gift matching for education, in-kind services, and technical assistance.
Types of support: Technical assistance, employee matching gifts, annual campaigns, building funds, capital campaigns, operating budgets, scholarship funds, in-kind gifts.
Limitations: Giving primarily in headquarters city and major operating locations.
Publications: Informational brochure (including application guidelines).
Application information: Proposal including narrative/letter, complete budget, IRS letter, lists of board members and major donors, audited statement and city solicitation permit.
Initial approach: Initial contact by letter of inquiry describing project
Copies of proposal: 1
Deadline(s): Best time to apply is Aug.
Final notification: 4 weeks. All requests will be answered
Write: Judith Newby, V.P., Public Relations
Number of staff: 1 full-time professional; 1 full-time support.

3111
Transco Energy Corporate Giving Program
2800 Post Oak Boulevard
P.O. Box 1396
Houston 77251 (713) 439-2000

Financial data (yr. ended 12/31/87): Total giving, $1,281,432, including $1,188,244 for 234 grants (high: $100,000; low: $500; average: $3,000), $21,550 for 17 grants to individuals and $71,638 for employee matching gifts.
Purpose and activities: Supports colleges and universities, and economic, elementary, minority, and business education, child welfare, engineering, heart disease, homeless, literacy, drug abuse programs, welfare, arts and culture, civic affairs, youth services, United Way and programs for the handicapped. Also gives in-kind donations.
Types of support: Building funds, capital campaigns, employee matching gifts, general purposes, research, operating budgets, special projects, employee-related scholarships, scholarship funds, in-kind gifts.
Limitations: Giving primarily in headquarters city and major operating areas in Houston and other parts of AL, and LA, NC, NJ, PA, SC, and TX. No support for secondary education, religious or veterans' organizations. No grants to individuals.
Publications: Informational brochure.
Application information: Include purpose statements of organization and project, requested amount, recently audited financial statement, other sources of funding, donors list, benefits of the organization or project.
Initial approach: Initial contact by letter of inquiry
Copies of proposal: 1
Deadline(s): Applications accepted throughout the year but best times are the first of Dec., Mar., June, and Sept.
Board meeting date(s): Dec. 15, Mar. 15, June 15, and Sept. 15
Write: Beth Anne Clay, Mgr., Corp. Contribs.
Contributions Committee: G.L. Bellinger, R.M. Chiste, B.A. Clay, J.H. Collar, D.F. Mackie, G.E. Sims, George S. Slocum, T.W. Spencer, D.E. Varne, J.P. Wise.
Number of staff: 1 full-time professional; 1 part-time professional; 1 part-time support.

3112
Turner Charitable Foundation
811 Rusk, Suite 205
Houston 77002 (713) 237-1117

Incorporated in 1960 in TX.
Donor(s): Isla Carroll Turner,† P.E. Turner.†
Financial data (yr. ended 12/31/87): Assets, $9,315,489 (M); expenditures, $426,835, including $353,750 for 44 grants (high: $45,000; low: $500; average: $5,000-$10,000).
Purpose and activities: Giving for higher, secondary and elementary education; social service and youth agencies; fine and performing arts groups and other cultural programs; Catholic, Jewish, and Protestant church support and religious programs; hospitals and health services; urban and community development; and conservation programs.
Types of support: Annual campaigns, building funds, capital campaigns, conferences and seminars, continuing support, emergency funds, endowment funds, equipment, fellowships, general purposes, land acquisition, lectureships, operating budgets, professorships, renovation projects, research.
Limitations: Giving limited to TX. No grants to individuals.
Application information:
Initial approach: Written request
Copies of proposal: 1
Deadline(s): Mar. 15
Board meeting date(s): Apr.
Final notification: None unless grant approved
Write: Eyvonne Moser, Asst. Secy.
Officers and Trustees: T.R. Reckling III, Pres.; Bert F. Winston, Jr., V.P.; Clyde J. Verheyden, Secy.; Isla S. Reckling, Treas.; Thomas E. Berry, Chaille W. Hawkins, Christiana R. McConn, T.R. "Cliffe" Reckling.
Number of staff: 1 full-time professional.
Employer Identification Number: 741460482

3113
The Tyler Foundation
3200 San Jacinto Tower
Dallas 75201 (214) 754-7800

Established in 1971 in TX.
Donor(s): Tyler Corp.
Financial data (yr. ended 12/31/86): Assets, $1,354,092 (M); expenditures, $402,730, including $401,325 for 72 grants (high: $200,000; low: $100; average: $500-$5,000).
Purpose and activities: Giving for welfare, the arts, youth agencies, and recreation.
Limitations: Giving primarily in TX. No grants to individuals, or for scholarships, fellowships, or matching gifts; no loans.
Application information:
Initial approach: Proposal
Copies of proposal: 1
Board meeting date(s): As required
Final notification: 3 to 4 weeks
Write: Rick Margerison, Pres.
Officers: Rick Margerison,* Pres.; W. Michael Kipphut, Secy.; D.L. Smart,* Treas.
Trustees:* Joseph F. McKinney, Chair.
Number of staff: None.
Employer Identification Number: 237140526

3114
U. S. Home Corporate Giving Program
1800 West Loop South
Houston 77027 (713) 877-2311

Financial data (yr. ended 12/31/88): $10,000 for 8 grants (high: $5,000; low: $100).
Purpose and activities: Supports public colleges, health associations, and theater.
Types of support: Capital campaigns.
Limitations: Giving primarily in headquarters city and major operating locations; emphasis on Houston, TX.
Application information: Applications not accepted.
Write: Isaac Heimbinder, Pres. and C.O.O.

3115
United Gas Pipe Line Corporate Giving Program
600 Travis
Houston 77002 (713) 229-4082
Special address for applications: P.O. Box 1478, Houston, TX 77251-1478

Financial data (yr. ended 12/31/88): Total giving, $435,852, including $312,662 for grants and $123,190 for employee matching gifts.
Purpose and activities: Supports education, health and human services, the arts, including music and theatre, higher education, and civic activities.
Types of support: Employee matching gifts, general purposes, scholarship funds.
Limitations: Giving primarily in the Gulf Coast states: AL, FL, LA, MI and TX.
Application information: A formal proposal is required for major projects but a simple request is sufficient for requests under $500.
Deadline(s): Best time to apply is June
Write: Jerrold Packler, Mgr. Project Analysis and Control
Number of staff: 3 part-time support.

3116
Vale-Asche Foundation
910 River Oaks Bank Bldg.
2001 Kirby Dr.
Houston 77019 (713) 520-7334

Incorporated in 1956 in DE.
Donor(s): Ruby Vale,† Mrs. Ruby Vale,† Fred B. Asche.
Financial data (yr. ended 11/30/87): Assets, $4,133,729 (M); expenditures, $200,298, including $187,317 for 18 grants (high: $25,000; low: $1,000).
Purpose and activities: Grants for medical research, health care, child welfare, and aid to the aged and the handicapped; support also for secondary education and cultural programs, and projects that benefit the homeless.
Types of support: Equipment, research, special projects.
Limitations: Giving primarily in Houston, TX. No grants to individuals.
Application information: Request reviewed Sept.-Oct.
Initial approach: Letter
Deadline(s): None
Write: Mrs. Vale Asche Ackerman, Pres.
Officers and Trustees: Mrs. Vale Asche Ackerman, Pres.; Bettyann Asche Murray, V.P.; Harry H. Hudson, Secy.-Treas.; Asche Ackerman.
Employer Identification Number: 516015320

3117
Rachael & Ben Vaughan Foundation
P.O. Box 1579
Corpus Christi 78403 (512) 883-9266

Established in 1952 in TX.
Donor(s): Ben F. Vaughan, Jr.,† Edgar H. Vaughan.†
Financial data (yr. ended 11/30/88): Assets, $2,227,916 (M); expenditures, $108,603, including $105,051 for 35 grants (high: $15,000; low: $700).
Purpose and activities: Support for educational, cultural and religious development of Central and South Texas; support for the needy and disadvantaged in this area.
Types of support: Annual campaigns, building funds, capital campaigns, conferences and seminars, consulting services, continuing support, emergency funds, employee matching gifts, endowment funds, equipment, exchange programs, fellowships, general purposes, internships, land acquisition, lectureships, matching funds, operating budgets, professorships, program-related investments, publications, renovation projects, research, seed money, special projects, technical assistance.
Limitations: Giving limited to south and central TX. No grants to individuals; no loans.
Publications: Application guidelines, 990-PF.
Application information:
Initial approach: Letter
Copies of proposal: 1
Deadline(s): Sept. 1
Board meeting date(s): Nov.
Final notification: End of first week in Dec.
Write: Ben F. Vaughan III, Pres.
Officers and Trustees: Ben F. Vaughan III, Pres.; Kleberg Eckhardt, V.P.; Ben F. Vaughan IV, V.P.; Genevieve Vaughan, V.P.; Daphne duPont Vaughan, Secy.-Treas.
Employer Identification Number: 746040479

3118
James M. Vaughn, Jr. Foundation Fund
c/o MBank of Austin, Trust Dept.
P.O. Box 2266
Austin 78780

Established about 1971 in TX.
Financial data (yr. ended 12/31/86): Assets, $3,074,912 (M); expenditures, $552,130, including $298,777 for 26 grants (high: $33,818; low: $347) and $87,960 for 9 grants to individuals.
Purpose and activities: Support for cultural programs, including museums and a library, and for higher education; fellowships for mathematical research in format conjecture.
Types of support: Fellowships, research.
Application information: Application forms obtained through the American Mathematical Association; interviews required. Application form required.
Deadline(s): None

Officers: James M. Vaughn, Jr., Pres.; Bonna B. Vaughn, V.P.; Sally Vaughn, V.P.; Jan Werner, Secy.-Treas.
Employer Identification Number: 237166546

3119
Crystelle Waggoner Charitable Trust
c/o NCNB-Texas
P.O. Box 1317
Fort Worth 76101 (817) 390-6114

Established in 1982 in TX.
Donor(s): Crystelle Waggoner.†
Financial data (yr. ended 6/30/88): Assets, $3,986,279 (M); expenditures, $346,625, including $250,920 for 46 grants (high: $25,000; low: $500; average: $2,000-$4,000).
Purpose and activities: Giving to charitable organizations in existence before Jan. 24, 1982.
Types of support: General purposes, operating budgets, continuing support, annual campaigns, seed money, emergency funds, professorships, scholarship funds, building funds, capital campaigns, endowment funds, equipment, lectureships, publications, renovation projects, research, special projects.
Limitations: Giving limited to TX, especially Fort Worth and Decatur. No grants to individuals, or for challenge grants, consulting services, deficit financing, or conferences; no loans.
Publications: Annual report (including application guidelines).
Application information:
Initial approach: Letter
Copies of proposal: 1
Deadline(s): Mar. 31, June 30, Sept. 30, Dec. 31
Board meeting date(s): Jan., Apr., July, and Oct.
Final notification: 6 months
Write: Darlene Mann, V.P., NCNB-Texas
Trustee: NCNB-Texas.
Number of staff: None.
Employer Identification Number: 751881219

3120
Walsh Foundation
1007 InterFirst Fort Worth Bldg.
Fort Worth 76102

Established in 1956 in TX.
Donor(s): Mary D. Walsh, F. Howard Walsh, Sr.
Financial data (yr. ended 12/31/86): Assets, $1,693,551 (M); gifts received, $409,962; expenditures, $402,418, including $394,750 for 30 grants (high: $70,000; low: $100).
Purpose and activities: Emphasis on elementary and higher education, support also for cultural programs, including those for youth.
Types of support: Annual campaigns, continuing support, equipment, operating budgets, special projects.
Officers: F. Howard Walsh, Sr., Pres.; Mary D. Walsh, V.P.; G. Malcolm Louden, Secy.-Treas.
Employer Identification Number: 756021726

3121
Marjorie T. Walthall Perpetual Charitable Trust
12500 San Pedro, Suite 600
San Antonio 78216
Application address: 185 Terrell Rd., Suite 502, San Antonio, TX 78209

Trust established in 1976 in TX.
Donor(s): Marjorie T. Walthall.
Financial data (yr. ended 12/31/86): Assets, $1,907,190 (M); expenditures, $88,557, including $76,200 for 21 grants (high: $7,000; low: $1,000).
Purpose and activities: Emphasis on health, medical and nursing education, scientific research and similar activities; support also for cultural programs.
Limitations: Giving primarily in south Texas.
Application information:
Initial approach: Letter
Deadline(s): Oct. 1
Write: John W. Pancoast, Trustee
Trustees: Thomas W. Folbre, John W. Pancoast, Marjorie T. Walthall.
Employer Identification Number: 510170313

3122
Joe L. Ward Company, Ltd. Charitable Trust
P.O. Box 1310
Waco 76703-1310

Financial data (yr. ended 12/31/87): Assets, $22,959 (M); gifts received, $7,100; expenditures, $4,800, including $4,800 for 7 grants (high: $2,200; low: $100; average: $100-$500).
Purpose and activities: Support for religious giving, education, arts and culture, social services, and the United Way.
Application information:
Initial approach: Letter
Deadline(s): None
Write: Joe L. Ward, Jr., Trustee
Trustee: Joe L. Ward, Jr.
Employer Identification Number: 746047138

3123
Mamie McFaddin Ward Heritage Foundation
P.O. Box 3391
Beaumont 77704 (409) 838-9398

Established in 1976 in TX.
Donor(s): Mamie McFaddin Ward.†
Financial data (yr. ended 12/31/87): Assets, $15,040,036 (M); gifts received, $12,840,714; expenditures, $1,514,287, including $553,467 for 11 grants (high: $200,000; low: $800; average: $5,000-$7,500).
Purpose and activities: Support for the Mamie McFaddin Ward Heritage Museum and other cultural programs; some support for hospitals.
Limitations: Giving limited to Jefferson County, TX. No grants to individuals.
Application information:
Write: Ann Knupple, V.P. and Trust Officer, First City National Bank of Beaumont
Trustees: Eugene H.B. McFaddin, James L.C. McFaddin, Jr., Ida M. Pyle, Rosine M. Wilson, First City National Bank of Beaumont.
Employer Identification Number: 746260525

3124
James L. and Eunice West Charitable Trust
c/o Shannon, Gracey, Ratliff, & Miller
2200 First City Bank Tower - 201 Main St.
Fort Worth 76102-3191

Established in 1980.
Donor(s): James L. West,† Eunice West.
Financial data (yr. ended 12/31/86): Assets, $23,744,571 (M); expenditures, $1,243,172, including $1,209,800 for 38 grants (high: $340,000; low: $50; average: $100-$100,000).
Purpose and activities: Giving primarily for youth and child welfare organizations, cultural programs, hospitals, higher education, social services, church support, and a community fund.
Types of support: General purposes, operating budgets, equipment, building funds, endowment funds.
Limitations: Giving primarily in Fort Worth, TX.
Application information:
Initial approach: Letter
Deadline(s): None
Board meeting date(s): 3 or 4 times a year
Write: Loren Q. Hanson, Trustee
Trustees: Billy R. Roland, Managing Trustee; Loren Q. Hanson, Dean Lawrence, Eunice West, Herschel Winn.
Number of staff: None.
Employer Identification Number: 751724903

3125
J. M. West Texas Corporation
P.O. Box 491
Houston 77001

Incorporated in 1957 in TX.
Financial data (yr. ended 2/29/88): Assets, $5,092,698 (M); expenditures, $268,252, including $229,663 for 17 grants (high: $30,000; low: $1,000).
Purpose and activities: Emphasis on higher education and medical research; support also for youth agencies and cultural programs.
Limitations: Giving primarily in TX.
Application information:
Initial approach: Letter
Deadline(s): None
Write: Coordinator of Grants
Officers: William R. Lloyd, Jr.,* Pres.; William B. Blakemore II,* V.P.; James A. Reichert, V.P.; Jack T. Trotter,* V.P.; Robert H. Parsley,* Secy.-Treas.
Trustees:* Margene West Lloyd.
Employer Identification Number: 746040389

3126
Erle and Emma White Foundation
P.O. Box 4669
Wichita Falls 76308

Established in 1981 in TX.
Financial data (yr. ended 12/31/87): Assets, $3,706,301 (M); expenditures, $357,749, including $302,730 for 42 grants (high: $60,000; low: $500).
Purpose and activities: Support for hospitals, health organizations, social services, and cultural programs.

Limitations: Giving primarily in the Wichita Falls, TX, area.
Application information: Contributes only to pre-selected organizations. Applications not accepted.
Officers: Emma White, Chair.; Marilyn Onstott, Secy.-Treas.
Trustee: Carolyn Brown.
Employer Identification Number: 751781596

3127
Ralph Wilson Public Trust
c/o Don Keen
600 South General Bruce Dr.
Temple 76501

Established in 1974.
Donor(s): Ralph Wilson.†
Financial data (yr. ended 12/31/87): Assets, $2,559,740 (M); expenditures, $181,957, including $180,000 for 5 grants (high: $125,000; low: $10,000).
Purpose and activities: Support mainly for the Ralph Wilson Youth Clubs; support also for cultural programs and child welfare.
Limitations: Giving primarily in TX.
Officers and Trustees: Jim Bowmer, Pres.; Ralph Wilson, Jr., V.P.; Betty Prescott, Secy.; Donald Keen, Treas.; and 9 additional trustees.
Employer Identification Number: 237351606

3128
The Wiseda Foundation
P.O. Box 122269
Fort Worth 76121-2269 (817) 737-6678

Established in 1976 in TX.
Donor(s): William S. Davis, Davoil, Inc.
Financial data (yr. ended 9/30/88): Assets, $1,139 (M); gifts received, $116,000; expenditures, $115,767, including $114,645 for 21 grants (high: $35,000; low: $100).
Purpose and activities: Emphasis on social service agencies, health, cultural programs, and historic preservation; substantial support for a local garden club.
Limitations: Giving primarily in TX. No grants for indivduals.
Application information:
Initial approach: Letter or proposal
Deadline(s): None
Write: William S. Davis, Trustee
Trustee: William S. Davis.
Employer Identification Number: 751533548

3129
The Wortham Foundation
2727 Allen Pkwy., Suite 2000
Houston 77019 (713) 526-8849

Trust established in 1958 in TX.
Donor(s): Gus S. Wortham,† Lyndall F. Wortham.
Financial data (yr. ended 9/30/88): Assets, $129,879,370 (M); expenditures, $7,932,876, including $7,148,308 for 40 grants (high: $1,499,890; low: $500; average: $5,000-$100,000).
Purpose and activities: Support primarily for the performing arts, museums, and community improvement, including civic beautification projects.
Types of support: Annual campaigns, seed money, emergency funds, deficit financing, general purposes, matching funds, continuing support.
Limitations: Giving limited to Houston and Harris County, TX. Generally no grants to colleges, universities, or hospitals. No grants to individuals, or for building funds.
Publications: 990-PF, informational brochure.
Application information: Application form required.
Initial approach: Letter
Copies of proposal: 1
Deadline(s): Submit proposal preferably by the first week of Nov., Feb., May, or Aug.
Board meeting date(s): 3rd week of deadline months
Final notification: 1 month
Write: Allen H. Carruth, Pres.
Officer and Trustees: Allen H. Carruth, Pres.; H. Charles Boswell, Fred C. Burns, Brady F. Carruth, E.A. Stumpf III, R.W. Wortham III.
Number of staff: 2 full-time support.
Employer Identification Number: 741334356
Recent arts and culture grants:
AD Players, Houston, TX, $5,000. For general funding. 1987.
Alley Theater, Houston, TX, $100,000. For general funding. 1987.
Armand Bayou Nature Center, Houston, TX, $25,000. For park improvements. 1987.
Concert Chorale of Houston, Houston, TX, $20,000. 1987.
Council for the Visual and Performing Arts, Houston, TX, $5,000. For general funding. 1987.
Daughters of the Republic of Texas, Houston, TX, $30,000. For general funding for Texas Heritage Garden. 1987.
Galveston Historical Foundation, Galveston Arts, Galveston, TX, $7,500. For general funding. 1987.
Houston Arboretum, Houston, TX, $10,000. For park improvements. 1987.
Houston Foto Fest, Houston, TX, $12,000. For general funding. 1987.
Houston Grand Opera, Houston, TX, $250,000. For contribution to Annual Operating Fund. 1987.
Houston Grand Opera, Houston, TX, $200,000. For special performance. 1987.
Houston Oratorio Society, Houston, TX, $6,000. For general funding. 1987.
Houston Pops Orchestra, Houston, TX, $25,000. For general funding. 1987.
Houston Symphony Society, Houston, TX, $312,500. For Financial Stabilization Fund. 1987.
Houston Symphony Society, Houston, TX, $300,000. For operations. 1987.
Houston Symphony Society, Houston, TX, $294,042. For contribution to Special Matching Fund. 1987.
Lyric Theater of Houston Foundation, Houston, TX, $5,000,000. For construction of Lyric Theater. 1987.
Museum of Art of the American West, Houston, TX, $15,000. For general funding. 1987.
Museum of Medical Science, Houston, TX, $15,000. For general funding. 1987.
Society for the Performing Arts, Houston, TX, $75,000. For general funding. 1987.
Stages, Houston, TX, $10,000. For general funding. 1987.
Texas and Southwestern Cattle Raisers Foundation, Fort Worth, TX, $25,000. For general funding for Cattlemens Museum. 1987.
University of Houston, Drama Department, Houston, TX, $5,000. For Shakespeare Outreach. 1987.
Young Audiences of Houston, Houston, TX, $5,000. For general funding. 1987.

3130
Lola Wright Foundation, Inc.
P.O. Box 1138
Georgetown 78627-1138 (512) 255-3067

Incorporated in 1954 in TX.
Donor(s): Miss Johnie E. Wright.†
Financial data (yr. ended 12/31/86): Assets, $6,900,000 (M); expenditures, $483,000, including $395,000 for 43 grants (high: $50,000; low: $1,500; average: $1,500-$25,000).
Purpose and activities: Emphasis on social services, health, hospitals, cultural programs, youth development, and higher education.
Types of support: Matching funds, building funds, equipment, endowment funds, continuing support, scholarship funds, renovation projects, research, special projects.
Limitations: Giving limited to TX, primarily the Austin area. No grants to individuals, or for operating budgets.
Publications: Application guidelines.
Application information:
Initial approach: Letter
Copies of proposal: 6
Deadline(s): Apr. 1 and Oct. 1
Board meeting date(s): Semiannually
Final notification: May 15 and Nov. 15
Write: Patrick H. O'Donnell, Pres.
Officers and Directors: Patrick H. O'Donnell, Pres.; William Hilgers, V.P.; Vivian E. Todd, Secy.-Treas; Martha Greenhill, James Meyers, Carole Rylander.
Number of staff: 1 part-time professional; 1 part-time support.
Employer Identification Number: 746054717

3131
The Zachry Foundation
2500 Tower Life Bldg.
San Antonio 78205 (512) 554-4666

Incorporated in 1960 in TX.
Donor(s): H.B. Zachry Co. International, H.B. Zachry Co.
Financial data (yr. ended 12/31/87): Assets, $1,365,000 (M); gifts received, $523,698; expenditures, $428,443, including $403,575 for 26 grants.
Purpose and activities: Emphasis on higher education, music, and public television.
Types of support: Capital campaigns, annual campaigns, continuing support, endowment funds, internships, research, scholarship funds, special projects.
Limitations: Giving primarily in the San Antonio, TX, area.

Application information:
Initial approach: Telephone or letter
Copies of proposal: 1
Write: Dorothy G. Martin, Admin. and Trustee
Officers and Trustees: H.B. Zachry, Jr., Pres.; Emma Leigh Carter, V.P.; Murray L. Johnston, Jr., Secy.; Charles Ebrom, Treas.; Dorothy G. Martin, Mollie S. Zachry.
Number of staff: 1 part-time support.
Employer Identification Number: 741485544

UTAH

3132
Val A. Browning Charitable Foundation
P.O. Box 9936
Ogden 84409
Application address: 1528 28th St., Ogden, UT 84401

Established in 1975 in UT.
Donor(s): Val A. Browning.
Financial data (yr. ended 12/31/87): Assets, $2,911,278 (M); gifts received, $420,000; expenditures, $475,392, including $462,020 for 15 grants (high: $300,000; low: $200).
Purpose and activities: Support primarily for a hospital and a secondary school; some support for health associations, social services, and cultural programs.
Limitations: Giving primarily in Ogden and Salt Lake City, UT.
Application information:
Initial approach: Letter
Deadline(s): Preferably by Sept. 30
Write: Val A. Browning, Chair.
Directors: Val A. Browning, Chair.; John Val Browning, Judith B. Jones.
Trustee: First Security Bank of Utah, N.A.
Employer Identification Number: 876167851

3133
Marie Eccles Caine Charitable Foundation
324 North 500 East
Brigham City 84302 (801) 723-2770

Established in 1981 in UT.
Donor(s): Marie Eccles Caine.†
Financial data (yr. ended 5/31/87): Assets, $5,511,645 (M); gifts received, $165,259; expenditures, $280,845, including $254,937 for 48 grants (high: $19,000; low: $610).
Purpose and activities: Giving for the advancement of the fine arts, particularly at Utah State University, for other programs at that university which were of interest to the donor, and for other charitable purposes as determined by the committee from time to time.
Limitations: Giving primarily in Logan County, UT.
Application information:
Initial approach: Proposal
Copies of proposal: 4
Deadline(s): None
Write: Manon C. Russell or Dan C. Russell
Trustee: First Security Bank of Utah, N.A.
Committee members: Dan C. Russell, Manon C. Russell, George R. Wanlass, Kathryn C. Wanlass.
Employer Identification Number: 942764258

3134
Castle Foundation
c/o Moore Trust Co.
200 South Main St.
Salt Lake City 84101 (801) 531-6075

Established in 1953.
Financial data (yr. ended 6/30/88): Assets, $1,963,897 (M); expenditures, $91,730, including $67,672 for 31 grants (high: $5,000; low: $1,000).
Purpose and activities: Giving for the arts, child welfare and social service agencies, higher and secondary education, and hospitals.
Types of support: Scholarship funds, special projects, equipment, operating budgets.
Limitations: Giving primarily in UT.
Application information: Application form required.
Initial approach: Letter
Deadline(s): None
Write: Gilbert M. Bean, Trust Officer, Moore Trust Co.
Trustee: Moore Trust Co.
Employer Identification Number: 876117177

3135
Annie Taylor Dee Foundation
3939 Harrison Blvd.
Ogden 84403

Trust established in 1961 in UT.
Donor(s): Maude Dee Porter.†
Financial data (yr. ended 12/31/86): Assets, $1,582,182 (M); expenditures, $103,159, including $93,000 for 11 grants (high: $50,000; low: $1,000).
Purpose and activities: Support primarily for the McKay-Dee Hospital; some support for higher and secondary education, cultural programs, religious purposes, and conservation.
Limitations: Giving primarily in UT. No grants to individuals; no loans.
Application information:
Initial approach: Letter
Copies of proposal: 1
Deadline(s): Submit proposal preferably by Sept. 30
Board meeting date(s): Apr. and Oct.
Write: Thomas D. Dee II, Chair.
Distribution Committee: Thomas D. Dee II, Chair.; Thomas D. Dee III, Vice-Chair.; Geary Pehrson.
Trustee: First Security Bank of Utah, N.A.
Employer Identification Number: 876116380

3136
Lawrence T. and Janet T. Dee Foundation
First Security Bank Bldg., No. 1214
2404 Washington Blvd.
Ogden 84401 (801) 621-4863

Established in 1971 in UT.
Donor(s): L.T. Dee,† Janet T. Dee.†
Financial data (yr. ended 12/31/87): Assets, $4,360,360 (M); expenditures, $249,033, including $212,000 for grants.
Purpose and activities: Emphasis on hospitals, particularly the McKay-Dee Hospital; support also for higher education, cultural programs, and social service agencies.
Types of support: Annual campaigns, emergency funds, building funds, equipment, endowment funds, research, scholarship funds, matching funds.
Limitations: Giving primarily in UT. No grants to individuals; no loans.
Application information:
Initial approach: Letter
Copies of proposal: 1
Deadline(s): Submit proposal preferably by Sept. 30
Board meeting date(s): Mar. and Sept.
Write: Thomas D. Dee II, Chair.
Managers: Thomas D. Dee II, Chair.; Thomas D. Dee III, Vice-Chair.; David L. Dee.
Trustee: First Security Bank of Utah, N.A.
Employer Identification Number: 876150803

3137
Dr. Ezekiel R. and Edna Wattis Dumke Foundation
600 Crandall Bldg.
Ten West First South
Salt Lake City 84101 (801) 363-7863

Incorporated in 1959 in UT.
Financial data (yr. ended 12/31/88): Assets, $4,638,955 (M); expenditures, $291,525, including $262,113 for 27 grants (high: $40,000; low: $1,000).
Purpose and activities: Grants largely for higher education, cultural programs, medical and hospital services, and youth agencies.
Types of support: Building funds, technical assistance, research, general purposes, equipment.
Limitations: Giving primarily in UT and ID. No grants to individuals.
Application information: Application form required.
Deadline(s): Feb. 1 and July 1
Write: Max B. Lewis, Secy.
Officers and Directors: Ezekiel R. Dumke, Jr., Pres.; Martha Ann Dumke Healy, V.P.; Max B. Lewis, Secy. and Mgr.; Edmund E. Dumke, Treas.; Valerie Rork, Claire Dumke Ryberg, Nancy Healy Schwanfelder.
Employer Identification Number: 876119783

3138
The George S. and Dolores Dore Eccles Foundation
Desert Bldg.
79 South Main St., 12th Fl.
Salt Lake City 84111 (801) 350-5336

Incorporated in 1958 in UT; absorbed Lillian Ethel Dufton Charitable Trust in 1981.
Donor(s): George S. Eccles.†
Financial data (yr. ended 12/31/87): Assets, $87,612,100 (M); gifts received, $40,000,000; expenditures, $3,376,084, including

$2,813,331 for 63 grants (high: $660,026; low: $1,000; average: $2,500-$100,000).
Purpose and activities: Emphasis on higher education, hospitals and medical research, the performing and visual arts, and social services and youth agencies.
Types of support: Annual campaigns, building funds, capital campaigns, equipment, general purposes, matching funds, professorships, program-related investments, research, scholarship funds.
Limitations: Giving limited to UT. No grants to individuals, or for endowment funds; no loans.
Application information: Application form required.
Initial approach: Letter
Copies of proposal: 3
Deadline(s): None
Board meeting date(s): Quarterly
Final notification: Following meeting
Write: Karen Gardner, Exec. Asst.
Officers and Directors: David P. Gardner, Chair; Spencer F. Eccles, Pres.; Alonzo W. Watson, Secy.; Robert Graham, Treas.; Dolores Dore Eccles.
Number of staff: 1
Employer Identification Number: 876118245

3139
Marriner S. Eccles Foundation
701 Deseret Bldg.
79 South Main St.
Salt Lake City 84111 (801) 322-0116

Established in 1973.
Financial data (yr. ended 3/31/87): Assets, $16,695,558 (M); expenditures, $1,177,615, including $1,035,703 for 77 grants (high: $90,000; low: $1,000; average: $5,000-$25,000).
Purpose and activities: Giving primarily for higher education, hospitals, the performing arts, fine arts, museums, and social services.
Types of support: Equipment, seed money, operating budgets, general purposes, scholarship funds, research.
Limitations: Giving limited to UT. No grants to individuals, or for capital expenditures for construction of buildings.
Application information:
Initial approach: Proposal
Copies of proposal: 7
Deadline(s): None
Board meeting date(s): Quarterly, usually beginning in July
Final notification: Within a week after meeting
Write: Erma E. Hogan, Mgr.
Officers and Committee Members: Sara M. Eccles, Chair.; Alonzo W. Watson, Jr., Secy.; John D. Eccles, Spencer F. Eccles, Harold J. Steele, Elmer D. Tucker.
Trustee: First Security Bank of Utah, N.A.
Number of staff: 1 full-time professional.
Employer Identification Number: 237185855

3140
Financial Foundation
185 South State St., Suite 202
Salt Lake City 84111

Established in 1979 in UT.
Donor(s): Various local banks.
Financial data (yr. ended 12/31/87): Assets, $191 (M); gifts received, $121,331; expenditures, $121,454, including $121,331 for 21 grants (high: $22,632; low: $10).
Purpose and activities: Emphasis on civic affairs, cultural programs, including the performing arts, and social and youth agencies.
Limitations: Giving primarily in UT. No grants to individuals.
Publications: 990-PF.
Application information:
Initial approach: Proposal
Copies of proposal: 8
Deadline(s): 2nd Wednesday of each month
Board meeting date(s): Monthly
Final notification: 2 months
Officer: Melanie R. Harris, Secy.-Treas.; Gaylen C. Larsen, Don Rocha.
Trustees: Bruce Baird, Marvin J. Hammond, Richard W. Kieffer, Brent Milne.
Number of staff: 2
Employer Identification Number: 942662971

3141
The William H. and Mattie Wattis Harris Foundation
Crandall Bldg., Suite 600
10 West First South St.
Salt Lake City 84101 (801) 363-7863

Trust established in 1960 in UT.
Donor(s): Mattie Wattis Harris,† William H. Harris.
Financial data (yr. ended 12/31/87): Assets, $4,074,891 (M); expenditures, $384,945, including $278,300 for 66 grants (high: $24,500; low: $1,000).
Purpose and activities: Emphasis on arts, education, social service programs, conservation, and science.
Limitations: Giving primarily in the western U.S., with emphasis on UT. No support for religious or tax-supported organizations. No grants to individuals, or for scholarships; no loans.
Publications: Program policy statement, application guidelines.
Application information: Application form required.
Initial approach: Letter or proposal
Copies of proposal: 4
Deadline(s): Feb. 1 and Aug. 1
Board meeting date(s): Apr. and Oct.
Write: Max B. Lewis, Pres.
Officer and Trustees: Max B. Lewis, Pres. and Fdn. Mgr.; Marguerite Heydt, Exec. V.P.; James W. Hite, V.P.; Marilyn H. Hite, Secy.
Employer Identification Number: 870405724

3142
Herbert I. and Elsa B. Michael Foundation
c/o Moore Trust Co.
P.O. Box 30177
Salt Lake City 84130

Application address: Continental Bank and Trust Co., Trust Dept., P.O. Box 30177, Salt Lake City, UT 84130

Established in 1950 in UT.
Donor(s): Elsa B. Michael.†
Financial data (yr. ended 9/30/88): Assets, $3,836,788 (M); expenditures, $285,266, including $233,600 for 38 grants (high: $100,000; low: $1,000).
Purpose and activities: Emphasis on cultural programs and higher and secondary education; support also for hospitals and social service agencies.
Limitations: Giving primarily in UT. No support for sectarian religious activities.
Application information: Application form required.
Deadline(s): None
Write: Gilbert Bean
Trustees: Albert J. Colton, K. Jay Holdsworth, Continental Bank and Trust Co.
Advisory Committee: Francis W. Douglas, Gordon Hall, Chase N. Peterson.
Employer Identification Number: 876122556

3143
Questar Corporate Giving Program
180 East First South St.
P.O. Box 11150
Salt Lake City 84147 (801) 534-5435

Financial data (yr. ended 12/31/88): Total giving, $350,000, including $330,000 for grants and $20,000 for 15 in-kind gifts.
Purpose and activities: Support for the aged, the disadvantaged, the handicapped, and the homeless; the arts and culture, including fine and performing arts, and museums, child welfare and family services, education, hospitals and hospital building funds, community development, health and health services, the humanities, and volunteerism.
Types of support: Building funds, endowment funds, scholarship funds, special projects.
Limitations: Giving primarily in service and operating locations in UT. No support for religious or fraternal organizations. No grants for group trips, exhibitions, or operating expenses.
Application information:
Initial approach: Letter
Copies of proposal: 1
Board meeting date(s): Every 6-8 weeks
Write: Janice Bates, Dir. Community Affairs
Number of staff: 1 part-time professional; 1 part-time support.

3144
S. J. and Jessie E. Quinney Foundation
P.O. Box 45385
Salt Lake City 84145-0385 (801) 532-1500

Established about 1982 in UT.
Donor(s): S.J. Quinney.†
Financial data (yr. ended 12/31/86): Assets, $12,604,612 (M); gifts received, $3,815,625; expenditures, $292,627, including $248,965 for 40 grants (high: $10,900; low: $500).
Purpose and activities: Support for the arts, health associations, and higher education, a ballet, a museum, and a university.

Types of support: General purposes.
Limitations: Giving limited to UT.
Application information:
Deadline(s): June 30th of each year
Write: Herbert C. Livsey, Trustee
Trustees: Clark P. Giles, Janet Q. Lawson, Herbert C. Livsey, David E. Quinney, Jr.
Directors: James W. Freed, Frederick Q. Lawson, Peter Q. Lawson, Stephen B. Nobeker, JoAnne L. Shrontz, Alonzo W. Watson, Jr., Gene Q. Wilder.
Employer Identification Number: 870389312

3145
Charles Redd Foundation
La Sal 84530

Established in 1971 in UT.
Financial data (yr. ended 12/31/87): Assets, $1,587,969 (M); expenditures, $138,760, including $106,595 for 20 grants (high: $50,000; low: $60).
Purpose and activities: Support for agricultural, econmic and historical research at public and private universities in UT.
Types of support: Research, equipment, conferences and seminars, fellowships, land acquisition.
Limitations: Giving primarily in southeastern UT and southwestern CO.
Application information:
Copies of proposal: 8
Deadline(s): Nov. 30
Board meeting date(s): Jan.
Trustee: Charles Hardy Redd.
Number of staff: None.
Employer Identification Number: 876148176

3146
Junior E. & Blanche B. Rich Foundation
2826 Pierce Ave.
Ogden 84409

Established in 1975 in UT.
Financial data (yr. ended 12/31/87): Assets, $1,112,096 (M); expenditures, $65,903, including $53,950 for 8 grants (high: $6,000; low: $100).
Purpose and activities: Support primarily for higher education; support also for youth and arts organizations.
Types of support: Building funds, general purposes.
Limitations: Giving primarily in UT.
Application information:
Initial approach: Letter
Deadline(s): Sept. 30
Write: Sharon Rich Lewis, Chair.
Directors: Sharon Rich Lewis, Chair.; Blanche B. Rich, Edward B. Rich.
Trustee: First Security Bank of Utah, N.A.
Employer Identification Number: 876173654

3147
Steiner Foundation, Inc.
505 East South Temple St.
Salt Lake City 84102-1061 (801) 328-8831
Application address: P.O. Box 2317, Salt Lake City, UT 84102

Established in 1959 in UT.
Donor(s): Steiner Corp.
Financial data (yr. ended 06/30/88): Assets, $1,906,379 (M); expenditures, $111,289, including $97,867 for 35 grants (high: $30,000; low: $500).
Purpose and activities: Support for culture and the arts, youth and community organizations, and social services.
Limitations: Giving primarily in UT.
Application information: Proposal.
Write: Kevin K. Steiner, Pres.
Officers: Kevin K. Steiner, Pres.; Timothy L. Weiler, Secy.
Employer Identification Number: 876119190

3148
Tanner Charitable Trust
1930 South State St.
Salt Lake City 84115

Incorporated in 1965 in UT.
Donor(s): Obert C. Tanner.
Financial data (yr. ended 12/31/87): Assets, $203,496 (M); gifts received, $265,000; expenditures, $264,940, including $241,807 for 20 grants (high: $50,000; low: $100) and $10,500 for 2 grants to individuals.
Purpose and activities: Grants for higher education and cultural programs including music.
Types of support: Student aid.
Limitations: Giving primarily in UT.
Application information: Contributes only to pre-selected organizations. Applications not accepted.
Trustees: Carolyn T. Irish, Chair.; O. Don Ostler, Grace A. Tanner, Obert C. Tanner.
Employer Identification Number: 876125059

VERMONT

3149
Howfirma Foundation
14 Central St.
Woodstock 05091 (802) 457-1370

Established about 1983 in VT.
Financial data (yr. ended 12/31/87): Assets, $23,533 (M); gifts received, $30,000; expenditures, $173,467, including $161,509 for 365 grants (high: $25,000; low: $25).
Purpose and activities: Support for youth and social services, health associations, medical education, conservation, and cultural organizations.
Limitations: Giving primarily in the Woodstock, VT, area.
Application information: Application form required.
Deadline(s): None
Write: Gary R. Brown, Trustee
Trustees: Gary R. Brown, Frank H. Teagle, Jr., AmeriTrust Company.
Employer Identification Number: 222495072

3150
National Life Insurance Corporate Contributions Program
National Life Dr.
Montpelier 05604 (802) 229-3333

Financial data (yr. ended 12/31/88): Total giving, $171,000, including $161,000 for 150 grants (high: $15,000; low: $50) and $10,000 for 23 in-kind gifts.
Purpose and activities: Giving primarily for health, including AIDS programs, and safety, education and higher education, arts and culture and civic and community affairs; in-kind contributions.
Types of support: Annual campaigns, continuing support, special projects, general purposes, capital campaigns, operating budgets, in-kind gifts.
Limitations: Giving primarily in central VT and Chittenden County; low priority for programs outside of VT. No support for political candidates, officeholders or parties, fraternal, veterans', labor, or international organizations, churches or religious groups, groups on either side of controversial community issues, and United Way member organizations unless project is beyond the bounds of United Way funding and meets other National Life criteria. No grants to individuals.
Publications: Informational brochure (including application guidelines).
Application information:
Initial approach: Letter
Copies of proposal: 1
Final notification: 2-3 weeks
Write: Jane W. Robb, Communications Assoc.
Number of staff: 2 part-time professional; 1 part-time support.

3151
The Windham Foundation, Inc.
P.O. Box 70
Grafton 05146 (802) 843-2211

Incorporated in 1963 in VT.
Donor(s): The Bunbury Co., Inc., Dean Mathey.†
Financial data (yr. ended 10/31/88): Assets, $32,113,146 (M); expenditures, $2,013,406, including $195,289 for 86 grants (high: $25,000; low: $100; average: $100-$5,000) and $153,502 for 402 grants to individuals.
Purpose and activities: A private operating foundation; eighty-five percent of adjusted net income applied to operating programs of foundation, including civic improvement and historic preservation; primary activity is preservation of properties in rural areas of VT to maintain their charm and historic, native, or unusual features, with emphasis on restoration of houses in Grafton; remaining fifteen percent of income for general charitable giving, primarily confined to the disadvantaged, youth activities, aid to students and to educational institutions, and organizations assisting the disabled.
Types of support: Operating budgets, seed money, building funds, matching funds, continuing support, student aid, special projects, equipment, general purposes.

Limitations: Giving limited to VT, with emphasis on Windham County. No grants to individuals (except for college scholarship program), or for endowment funds; no loans.
Publications: Annual report (including application guidelines), informational brochure, newsletter.
Application information:
Initial approach: Letter
Copies of proposal: 1
Deadline(s): 1 month prior to board meeting
Board meeting date(s): Feb., May, July, and Oct.
Final notification: Following the board meeting
Write: Stephan A. Morse, Exec. Dir.
Officers: James R. Cogan,* Pres. and C.E.O.; Charles B. Atwater,* V.P., Secy., and Dir. of Scholarships; William B. Wright,* V.P. and Treas.; Stephan A. Morse, Exec. Dir.
Trustees:* Samuel W. Lambert III, Edward J. Toohey.
Number of staff: 5 full-time professional; 1 full-time support.
Employer Identification Number: 136142024

VIRGINIA

3152
Atlantic Research Corporate Giving Program
5390 Cherokee Ave.
Alexandria 22312 (703) 642-4000

Purpose and activities: Support for the aged, culture and the arts, child and family services, education, community development, health, medical research, science and technology, social services, volunteerism, general welfare, women, youth, minorities, law and justice, civic affairs, and the homeless; includes in-kind giving.
Types of support: In-kind gifts, continuing support, emergency funds, employee matching gifts, fellowships, general purposes, operating budgets, professorships, publications, research, scholarship funds, special projects.
Limitations: Giving primarily in areas where company facilities are located and/or company employees live.
Application information:
Initial approach: No discussion on telephone. All applications in writing; include 501(c)(3); analysis of percentage of funds that go to program
Copies of proposal: 1
Deadline(s): Sept. 1 for following year's grants
Board meeting date(s): Varies
Final notification: Check sent if award made; no notification if rejected
Write: Corp. Commun. Office
Administrators: Theda A. Parrish, Corp. Commun. Mgr.

3153
BDM International Corporate Giving Program
7915 Jones Branch Dr.
McLean 22102 (703) 848-5000

Financial data (yr. ended 12/31/87): $432,405 for 172 grants (high: $25,000; low: $100).
Purpose and activities: Support for culture, the humanities, music, education, business education, engineering, and science and technology.
Types of support: Annual campaigns, conferences and seminars, continuing support, general purposes, operating budgets, scholarship funds, special projects, seed money.
Limitations: No grants for denominational or sectarian organizations.
Application information:
Copies of proposal: 1
Deadline(s): None
Board meeting date(s): Periodic
Write: Earle C. Williams, Pres. and C.E.O.
Administrator: George S. Newman, V.P., Government and Public Affairs.
Number of staff: 1 full-time professional.

3154
Best Products Foundation
P.O. Box 26303
Richmond 23260
Application address: 1616 P St., N.W., Suite 100, Washington, DC 20036; Tel.: (202) 328-5188

Established in 1967 in VA.
Donor(s): Best Products Co.
Financial data (yr. ended 1/31/87): Assets, $3,460,544 (M); expenditures, $1,342,855, including $1,049,151 for 629 grants (high: $57,290; low: $35; average: $100-$10,000) and $21,129 for 148 employee matching gifts.
Purpose and activities: Support primarily for higher education, including an employee matching gift program, museums and cultural programs, community and social welfare organizations, including youth agencies, and projects concerning reproductive rights.
Types of support: Matching funds, special projects, employee matching gifts, seed money, emergency funds, scholarship funds.
Limitations: Giving primarily in areas of company operations. No support for religious institutions, government-supported organizations, or secondary or elementary schools. No grants to individuals, or for publications, conferences, seminars, research, or building or endowment funds; no loans.
Publications: Annual report (including application guidelines), 990-PF, informational brochure.
Application information: Information brochures available for general policies and employee matching gift program.
Initial approach: Letter
Copies of proposal: 1
Deadline(s): 2 months before board meetings
Board meeting date(s): Usually in Jan., Mar., June, Sept., and Nov.
Final notification: 45 days after completion of screening process
Write: Susan L. Butler, Exec. Dir.
Officers and Directors: Frances A. Lewis, Chair.; Sydney Lewis, Pres.; Robert L. Burrus, Jr., Secy.; Susan L. Butler, Treas. and Exec. Dir.
Number of staff: 1 full-time professional; 1 full-time support.
Employer Identification Number: 237139981

3155
The Robert G. Cabell III and Maude Morgan Cabell Foundation
P.O. Box 1377
Richmond 23211 (804) 780-2050

Incorporated in 1957 in VA.
Donor(s): Robert G. Cabell III,† Maude Morgan Cabell.†
Financial data (yr. ended 12/31/87): Assets, $17,229,620 (M); expenditures, $315,384, including $176,251 for 6 grants (high: $100,000; low: $25,000; average: $25,000-$100,000).
Purpose and activities: Grants primarily for higher and secondary education, health care, historic preservation, the arts, and cultural projects.
Types of support: Building funds, capital campaigns, equipment, renovation projects, special projects.
Limitations: Giving primarily in VA. No support for political organizations or special interest groups. No grants to individuals, or for endowment funds, or operating programs, or research projects.
Publications: Financial statement.
Application information:
Initial approach: Letter
Copies of proposal: 1
Deadline(s): None
Board meeting date(s): Mar., May, and Nov.
Final notification: Before end of calendar year
Write: B. Walton Turnbull, Exec. Dir.
Officers: J. Read Branch,* Pres.; Robert G. Cabell, V.P.; Royal E. Cabell, Jr.,* Secy.; B. Walton Turnbull, Exec. Dir.
Directors:* Joseph L. Antrim III, J. Read Branch, Jr., Patteson Branch, Jr., Charles Cabell, Edmund A. Rennolds, Jr., John K.B. Rennolds.
Number of staff: 1 part-time professional; 2 part-time support.
Employer Identification Number: 546039157

3156
Camp Foundation
P.O. Box 813
Franklin 23851 (804) 562-3439

Incorporated in 1942 in VA.
Donor(s): James L. Camp, P.D. Camp, and their families.
Financial data (yr. ended 12/31/88): Assets, $9,316,990 (M); expenditures, $503,330, including $410,950 for 45 grants (high: $31,850; low: $500; average: $1,000-$20,000) and $64,000 for 28 grants to individuals.
Purpose and activities: "To provide or aid in providing in or near the town of Franklin, Virginia, ... parks, playgrounds, recreational facilities, libraries, hospitals, clinics, homes for the aged or needy, refuges for delinquent, dependent or neglected children, training schools, or other like institutions or activities."

Grants also to select organizations statewide, with emphasis on youth agencies, hospitals, higher and secondary education, including scholarships filed through high school principals, recreation, historic preservation, and cultural programs.
Types of support: Annual campaigns, seed money, emergency funds, building funds, equipment, land acquisition, matching funds, scholarship funds, student aid.
Limitations: Giving primarily in Franklin, Southampton County, Isle of Wight County, and Tidewater, VA, and northeastern NC.
Publications: Informational brochure, 990-PF.
Application information:
Initial approach: Proposal
Copies of proposal: 7
Deadline(s): Submit proposal between June and Aug.; deadline Sept. 1; scholarship application deadlines Feb. 26 for filing with high school principals; Mar. 15 for principals to file with foundation
Board meeting date(s): May and Dec.
Final notification: 3 months
Write: Harold S. Atkinson, Exec. Dir.
Officers and Directors: Robert C. Ray, Chair.; Sol W. Rawls, Jr., Pres.; James L. Camp, V.P.; John M. Camp, Jr., Treas.; Harold S. Atkinson, Exec. Dir.; John M. Camp III, W.M. Camp, Jr., Clifford A. Cutchins III, William W. Cutchins, Mills E. Godwin, Jr., Paul Camp Marks, J. Edward Moyler, Jr., John D. Munford, S. Waite Rawls, Jr., J.E. Ray III, Richard E. Ray, Toy D. Savage, Jr., W.H. Story.
Number of staff: 1 part-time professional; 1 full-time support; 1 part-time support.
Employer Identification Number: 546052488

3157
J. L. Camp Foundation, Inc.
University Station
P.O. Box 3816
Charlottesville 22903 (804) 293-7004

Incorporated in 1946 in VA.
Donor(s): J.L. Camp, Jr.,† Mrs. J.L. Camp, Jr., James L. Camp III.
Financial data (yr. ended 12/31/87): Assets, $2,600,144 (M); expenditures, $132,504, including $119,410 for 22 grants (high: $25,920; low: $500).
Purpose and activities: Emphasis on higher and secondary education, a student aid fund, the arts, and religion.
Types of support: Continuing support, scholarship funds.
Limitations: Giving primarily in VA. No grants for scholarships, propaganda, or voter registration drives.
Application information:
Initial approach: Proposal
Deadline(s): None
Write: James L. Camp III, Pres.
Officer and Directors: James L. Camp III, Pres.; Jane G. Camp, V.P. and Treas.; Toy D. Savage, Jr., V.P.; Douglas B. Ellis, Secy.
Employer Identification Number: 540742940

3158
The Beirne Carter Foundation
P.O. Box 3096
Salem 24153

Established in 1986 in VA.
Donor(s): Beirne B. Carter.
Financial data (yr. ended 12/31/87): Assets, $3,178,367 (M); gifts received, $999,953; expenditures, $17,840, including $8,100 for 17 grants (high: $1,000; low: $25).
Purpose and activities: Giving primarily for cultural and youth organizations.
Application information: Contributes only to pre-selected organizations. Applications not accepted.
Officers and Directors:* Beirne B. Carter,* Pres.; Mary Ross Carter,* V.P.; John F. Carroll, Jr., Secy.-Treas.
Employer Identification Number: 541397827

3159
Central Fidelity Banks, Inc. Foundation
c/o Central Fidelity Bank
P.O. Box 27602
Richmond 23261

Established in 1980.
Financial data (yr. ended 12/31/87): Assets, $41,453 (M); expenditures, $896,796, including $895,530 for 381 grants (high: $50,000; low: $25).
Purpose and activities: Giving for higher education, community funds, and cultural programs; support also for health and hospitals, youth agencies, and social services.
Limitations: Giving primarily in VA.
Application information:
Initial approach: Letter
Deadline(s): None
Write: Charles Tysinger, Mgr.
Directors: Charles Tysinger, Mgr.; Lewis N. Miller, Jr., Carroll L. Saine, William F. Shumadine, Jr.
Employer Identification Number: 546173939

3160
Chesapeake Corporation Foundation
1021 East Cary St.
P.O. Box 2350
Richmond 23218-2350 (804) 697-1000

Established in 1955 in VA.
Donor(s): Chesapeake Corp.
Financial data (yr. ended 12/31/88): Assets, $965,218 (M); gifts received, $510,000; expenditures, $403,322 for 87 grants (high: $50,421; low: $1,000) and $16,378 for 87 employee matching gifts.
Purpose and activities: Giving primarily for higher and other education, including an employee matching gift program for higher education, and scholarships for children of company employees; support also for community development, civic affairs, cultural programs, and health.
Types of support: Employee matching gifts, employee-related scholarships, matching funds, capital campaigns.
Limitations: Giving primarily in areas of company operations. No grants to individuals.
Application information:
Initial approach: Letter
Board meeting date(s): Feb., June, and Oct.
Write: Alvah H. Eubank, Jr., Secy.
Officer: A.H. Eubank, Jr., Secy.-Treas.
Trustees: O.D. Dennis, T.G. Harris, G.P. Mueller, S.G. Olsson, W.T. Robinson.
Employer Identification Number: 540605823

3161
The Clisby Charitable Trust
(Formerly The Flager Foundation)
P.O. Box 1515
Richmond 23212-1515 (804) 648-5033

Incorporated in 1963 in VA.
Donor(s): Jessie Kenan Wise.†
Financial data (yr. ended 12/31/86): Assets, $14,983,402 (M); expenditures, $931,191, including $848,312 for 59 grants (high: $262,302; low: $500; average: $500-$25,000).
Purpose and activities: Support largely for higher and secondary education, historic restoration and preservation, and cultural programs.
Limitations: Giving primarily in VA, with emphasis on Richmond, and in FL, with emphasis on St. Augustine. No grants for capital programs or long-range projects.
Application information:
Initial approach: Proposal
Deadline(s): None
Board meeting date(s): Irregularly
Final notification: None
Write: Lawrence Lewis, Jr., Pres.
Officers and Directors: Lawrence Lewis, Jr., Pres. and Treas.; Mary L.F. Wiley, V.P.; Janet P. Lewis, Secy.
Number of staff: 1
Employer Identification Number: 546051282

3162
Quincy Cole Trust
c/o Sovran Bank, N.A.
P.O. Box 26903
Richmond 23261
Grant application address: c/o Sovran Ctr., Richmond, VA 23261; Tel.: (804) 788-2143

Established in VA in 1969.
Donor(s): Quincy Cole.†
Financial data (yr. ended 6/30/87): Assets, $5,591,431 (M); gifts received, $2,300; expenditures, $261,936, including $237,735 for 11 grants (high: $61,948; low: $3,500).
Purpose and activities: Support for cultural programs, including the performing arts, museums, and historic preservation, and for higher education.
Limitations: Giving limited to the Richmond, VA, metropolitan area.
Application information:
Initial approach: Letter
Deadline(s): Apr. 20
Board meeting date(s): June
Write: Rita Smith
Trustee: Sovran Bank, N.A.
Employer Identification Number: 546086247

3163
Crestar Bank Charitable Trust
(Formerly United Virginia Charitable Trust)
c/o Crestar Bank, N.A.
P.O. Box 27385
Richmond 23261
Application address: 919 East Main St., Richmond, VA 23219; Tel.: (804) 782-7906

Established in 1964.
Donor(s): Crestar Bank, N.A.
Financial data (yr. ended 12/31/87): Assets, $978,995 (M); expenditures, $418,865, including $376,633 for 48 grants (high: $50,000; low: $100).
Purpose and activities: Giving for higher education, hospitals, and cultural programs.
Types of support: General purposes, continuing support, annual campaigns, building funds, equipment, land acquisition, endowment funds, matching funds.
Limitations: Giving primarily in VA. No support for government-supported organizations, or for religious or national health agencies. No grants to individuals, or for scholarships, or fellowships; no loans.
Publications: Informational brochure, program policy statement, application guidelines.
Application information:
Initial approach: Proposal
Copies of proposal: 1
Deadline(s): Large grant requests should be made by Oct. for consideration for the following year
Board meeting date(s): Semiannually and as required
Final notification: 1 to 6 months
Write: J. Thomas Vaushan
Trustee: Crestar Bank, N.A.
Number of staff: 3
Employer Identification Number: 546054608

3164
Crestar Foundation
(Formerly UVB Foundation)
919 East Main St.
Richmond 23219 (804) 782-7907

Established in 1973 in VA.
Donor(s): Crestar Bank, N.A., and other affiliates of United Virginia Bankshares.
Financial data (yr. ended 12/31/87): Assets, $116,409 (M); gifts received, $1,200,000; expenditures, $1,200,246, including $1,107,494 for 175 grants () and $92,496 for 563 employee matching gifts.
Purpose and activities: Priority given to community funds and established educational and cultural organizations in the communities served by bank affiliates; support also for capital campaigns of private colleges and universities in VA.
Types of support: Building funds, employee matching gifts.
Limitations: Giving limited to VA and communities served by bank affiliates. No support for government-supported, religious, or national health agencies. No grants to individuals, or for research, scholarships, or fellowships; no loans.
Publications: Informational brochure, program policy statement, application guidelines.
Application information:
Initial approach: Letter or proposal
Copies of proposal: 1
Deadline(s): Submit proposal before Oct.
Board meeting date(s): Semiannually as required
Write: J. Thomas Vaughan, Pres.
Officers: J. Thomas Vaughan, Pres.; Shirley Swarthout, Secy.-Treas.
Employer Identification Number: 237336418

3165
Dan River Foundation
P.O. Box 261
Danville 24541
Scholarship application address: Chair., Scholarship Comm., P.O. Box 2178, Danville, VA 24541; Tel.: (804) 799-7384

Incorporated in 1957 in VA.
Donor(s): Dan River, Inc.
Financial data (yr. ended 12/31/87): Assets, $1,934,916 (M); expenditures, $207,586, including $189,475 for 72 grants (high: $60,000; low: $100) and $3,945 for 3 grants to individuals.
Purpose and activities: Grants largely for community funds, higher education, including educational associations, scholarships to company employees and their children, and welfare organizations; some support for cultural programs, youth agencies, health agencies and hospitals.
Types of support: Employee-related scholarships.
Limitations: Giving primarily in areas of company operations, particularly Danville, VA, Greenville, SC, and New York, NY. No grants to individuals, except for employee-related scholarships.
Application information: Application form required.
Initial approach: Letter
Copies of proposal: 1
Deadline(s): Last day of Feb.
Board meeting date(s): Apr. and Dec.
Write: Grover S. Elliot, Pres.
Officers: Grover S. Elliot,* Pres. and Treas.; L.W. Van de Visser,* V.P.; H.H. Huntley, Secy.
Directors:* R.C. Crawford, Lester A. Hudson, Jr., David W. Johnston, Jr., W.J. Mika, R.S. Vigholo.
Employer Identification Number: 546036112

3166
Dominion Bankshares Charitable Trusts
213 South Jefferson St.
Roanoke 24040 (703) 563-7000

Financial data (yr. ended 12/31/88): Expenditures, $525,000 for grants.
Purpose and activities: Support for the arts, business education, civic affairs, and health and welfare.
Application information: Application form required.
Initial approach: Proposal
Write: Warner N. Dalhouse, Pres. and C.E.O., Dominion Bankshares Corp.

3167
Dominion Bankshares Corporate Giving Program
213 S. Jefferson St.
Roanoke 24040 (703) 563-7000

Financial data (yr. ended 12/31/88): Total giving, $641,000, including $578,658 for grants and $62,342 for 222 employee matching gifts.
Purpose and activities: Supports arts and culture, including fine arts, museums, and dance, health and hospitals, education, including business education and higher education, community development, civic affairs, and general welfare.
Types of support: Employee matching gifts, equipment, special projects.
Limitations: Giving primarily in headquarters city and all operating locations in VA, MD, TN, and DC.
Application information: Include description of the project, project budget, a financial report, 501(c)(3) status letter, board member list and donor list. Application form required.
Initial approach: Proposal
Copies of proposal: 1
Final notification: If turned down the company will send a rejection notice
Write: Warner N. Dalhouse, Pres. and C.E.O.
Administrator: James W. Harkness, Exec. V.P.

3168
Doyle Foundation, Inc.
P.O. Box 2157
Martinsville 24113 (703) 957-2221

Donor(s): Doyle Lumber, Inc.
Financial data (yr. ended 12/31/87): Assets, $79,601 (M); gifts received, $20,000; expenditures, $11,805, including $11,450 for 5 grants (high: $5,000; low: $100) and $2,500 for 1 loan to an individual.
Purpose and activities: Support for education, the arts, health services, and student loans in Martinsville.
Types of support: Student loans.
Limitations: Giving primarily in Martinsville, VA.
Application information: Application form and personal interview required for loans.
Write: Wilbur S. Doyle
Officers: Wilbur S. Doyle, Pres.; Lillie T. Doyle, Secy.
Employer Identification Number: 546056454

3169
Andrew H. & Anne O. Easley Trust
(also known as The Easley Foundation)
c/o Trust Dept., Central Fidelity Bank
P.O. Box 700
Lynchburg 24505

Established in 1968 in VA.
Donor(s): Andrew H. Easley.†
Financial data (yr. ended 6/30/88): Assets, $5,011,491 (M); expenditures, $239,725, including $195,399 for 11 grants (high: $50,000; low: $5,000).
Purpose and activities: Giving to youth organizations, education, health care, social

services, and cultural programs, including historic preservation.
Limitations: Giving limited to the Lynchburg, VA, area. No support for religious organizations. No grants to individuals, or for research, deficit financing, seed money, annual campaigns, or conferences and seminars; no loans.
Publications: Application guidelines.
Application information:
Initial approach: Proposal not exceeding 2 pages
Copies of proposal: 6
Deadline(s): Apr. 1 and Oct. 1
Board meeting date(s): June and Dec.
Write: Secy., The Easley Foundation
Trustee: Central Fidelity Bank.
Number of staff: None.
Employer Identification Number: 546074720

3170
Ethyl Corporate Giving Program
330 South Fourth Street
P.O. Box 2189
Richmond 23217 (804) 788-5598

Financial data (yr. ended 12/31/88): Total giving, $3,201,509, including $3,019,189 for grants (average: $5,000-$10,000), $37,320 for grants to individuals and $145,000 for 475 employee matching gifts.
Purpose and activities: Supports a wide variety of educational, cultural and charitable organizations. Company "believes in demonstrating responsible corporate citizenship by its active participation in local, state and national concerns which relate to the success of its business." Each operating division or department determines involvement on local level in accordance with policies and practices in effect at headquarters and other major company locations. Supports federated campaigns.
Types of support: Employee matching gifts, general purposes, capital campaigns, endowment funds, scholarship funds, special projects, employee-related scholarships.
Limitations: Giving primarily in company headquarters and major operating areas. No support for fraternal, religious or community organizations located where company has no significant investments in terms of facilities or employees. No grants to individuals or for telephone or mass solicitations.
Publications: Application guidelines.
Application information: Proposal including brief history of organization and statement of purpose; project description and budget; list of board members; current financial report; and proof of 501(c)(3) status.
Initial approach: Letter; proposal
Copies of proposal: 1
Deadline(s): Applications accepted throughout the year, but should be in by Sept. 1 for consideration
Board meeting date(s): Executive committee meets annually to review consolidated budget proposals of company locations
Final notification: Minimum 4 weeks required for full review and decision
Write: V.P., Corp. Communications
Contributions Manager: Floyd D. Gottwald, Chair. and C.E.O.
Number of staff: 2 part-time professional; 1 part-time support.

3171
Fairchild Industries Foundation, Inc.
P.O. Box 10803
Chantilly 22021-9998

Incorporated in 1953 in MD.
Donor(s): Fairchild Industries, Inc.
Financial data (yr. ended 12/31/88): Assets, $460,000 (M); gifts received, $300,000; expenditures, $217,000, including $193,000 for 78 grants (high: $10,000; low: $100), $26,000 for 23 grants to individuals and $19,180 for 144 employee matching gifts.
Purpose and activities: Giving primarily for higher education, including employee matching gifts, community funds, and civic affairs; support also for scholarships to children of employees and aid to needy employees or retired employees.
Types of support: Operating budgets, continuing support, annual campaigns, emergency funds, general purposes, equipment, endowment funds, matching funds, scholarship funds, special projects, employee-related scholarships, research, fellowships, employee matching gifts.
Limitations: Giving primarily in areas of company operations. No grants to individuals (except to aid needy employees or retirees), or for deficit financing; no loans.
Application information:
Initial approach: Letter
Copies of proposal: 1
Deadline(s): None
Board meeting date(s): Jan. or as required
Write: John D. Jackson, Pres.
Officers: John D. Jackson,* Pres.; Hazel S. Chilcote, V.P. and Secy.; Karen L. Schneckenburger, Treas.
Trustees:* T.H. Moorer, R. James Woolsey.
Number of staff: 1 part-time professional.
Employer Identification Number: 526043638

3172
Gannett Foundation
1101 Wilson Blvd.
Arlington 22209

Incorporated in 1935 in NY.
Donor(s): Frank E. Gannett.†
Financial data (yr. ended 12/31/88): Assets, $547,540,276 (M); expenditures, $33,382,883, including $23,301,011 for 2,687 grants (high: $686,613; low: $20), $767,300 for 194 grants to individuals, $800,807 for 1,683 employee matching gifts and $2,939,036 for 2 foundation-administered programs.
Purpose and activities: Grants to nonprofit educational, charitable, civic, cultural, health, and social service institutions and organizations in areas served by daily newspapers, broadcast stations, outdoor advertising companies, and other properties of Gannett Company, Inc. in the U.S. and Canada. Primary national interests are support of journalism-related programs and the advancement of philanthropy, volunteerism, and the promotion of adult literacy. The foundation also operates the Gannett Center for Media Studies, the nation's first institute for the advanced study of mass communication and technological change, located at Columbia University in New York, and the Paul Miller Washington Reporting Fellowships in Washington, DC.
Types of support: Operating budgets, continuing support, seed money, emergency funds, deficit financing, building funds, equipment, land acquisition, scholarship funds, employee-related scholarships, special projects, publications, conferences and seminars, general purposes, capital campaigns, matching funds, renovation projects, technical assistance, fellowships, employee matching gifts.
Limitations: Giving primarily in areas of Gannett Co., Inc. operations in the U.S. and Canada. No support for national or regional organizations, medical or other research unrelated to journalism, literacy, philanthropy or volunteerism; religious purposes; political; fraternal and similar organizations; or for primary or secondary school programs, except for those helping exceptional or disadvantaged children and youth. No grants to individuals (except for employee-related scholarships, fellowships and journalism-related research), or for annual campaigns (other than United Ways), or endowment funds; no loans.
Publications: Annual report, informational brochure (including application guidelines), newsletter.
Application information: Grant proposals from organizations in communities served by Gannett properties should be directed to the chief executive of the local property; executive committee of board approves grants monthly or as required. Journalism proposals should be directed to Gerald M. Sass, V.P./Education. Application form required.
Initial approach: Letter or proposal
Copies of proposal: 1
Deadline(s): None
Board meeting date(s): 3 to 4 times a year, and as required; annual meeting in Apr. or May
Final notification: 2 to 4 months for positive responses
Write: Eugene C. Dorsey, Pres.; or local Gannett Co., Inc. chief executives or publishers, for requests originating in areas served by Gannett Co., Inc.
Officers: Eugene C. Dorsey,* Pres. and C.E.O.; Charles L. Overby, Sr. V.P.; Christy C. Bulkeley, V.P.; Harvey S. Cotter, V.P.; Calvin Mayne, V.P. - Grants Administration; Gerald M. Sass, V.P. - Education; Tracy A. Quinn, V.P. - Communications; Thomas L. Chapple, Secy.; Jimmy L. Thomas, Treas.
Trustees:* Allen H. Neuharth, Chair.; Martin F. Birmingham, Bernard B. Brody, M.D., Harry W. Brooks, Jr., John Curley, John E. Heselden, Madelyn P. Jennings, Douglas H. McCorkindale, Dillard Munford, John C. Quinn, Frank H.T. Rhodes, Carl Rowan, Carrie Rozelle, Josefina A. Salas-Porras.
Number of staff: 14 full-time professional; 2 part-time professional; 24 full-time support; 14 part-time support.
Employer Identification Number: 166027020
Recent arts and culture grants:

A Special Place, San Bernardino, CA, $5,000. Toward campaign to establish children's hands-on arts and science museum. 7/15/88.
American Indian Services, Sioux Falls, SD, $5,000. To produce program booklet for Tribal Art '88, September juried art show organized by Northern Plains Tribal Arts Advisory Committee. 8/15/88.
Appalshop, Louisville, KY, $5,000. To help community radio station in Whitesburg, Kentucky, to buy equipment to serve more people in isolated Appalachian towns. 8/15/88.
Arizona Museum for Youth, Phoenix, AZ, $5,000. To buy furnishings for hands-on museum for children. 10/15/87.
Arizona Theater Company, Phoenix, AZ, $5,000. Toward campaign for new facilities in Tucson and Phoenix. 7/15/88.
Arizona Theater Company, Tucson, AZ, $25,000. Toward new facilities in Tucson and Phoenix. 4/15/88.
Arizona Zoological Society, Phoenix, AZ, $5,000. Toward cost to build exhibit at Phoenix Zoo on roadrunner, Arizona's most popular bird. 7/15/88.
Arkansas Opera Theater, Little Rock, AR, $9,681. To buy sound system for opera's touring program. 3/15/88.
Art in the Stations, Detroit, MI, $12,500. For renewed support to help complete mural in Financial Station as part of art project in downtown Detroit. 1/15/88.
Artsbridge, Marietta, OH, $50,000. To continue program to spur local economic development by linking cultural attractions and promoting tourism in Mid-Ohio Valley from Marietta to Parkersburg, West Virginia. ARTSBRIDGE aims also to attract businesses to move to area by increasing their awareness of area's cultural resources. 12/7/87.
Austin Childrens Museum, Austin, TX, $5,085. To help underwrite Smithsonian visiting exhibit, Getting the Picture: The Growth of Television in America. 3/15/88.
Austin Lyric Opera, Austin, TX, $5,500. To fund supertitles for production of La Traviata to enable audiences to read English lyrics of opera on special screen. 7/15/88.
Bedford Historical Society, Bedford, NY, $5,000. To restore historic Bedford Free Library building. 11/16/87.
Belle Isle, Friends of, Detroit, MI, $5,000. Toward campaign to restore statuary on historic island serving as public park. 4/15/88.
Boys and Girls Club of Green Bay, Green Bay, WI, $5,000. Toward start-up costs of music program at East and West Side clubs. 10/15/87.
Brevard Art Center and Museum, Melbourne, FL, $5,000. To sponsor competition for commemorative poster for organization's tenth anniversary celebration. 8/15/88.
Brevard Community College Foundation, Cocoa, FL, $50,000. To help equip new Performing Arts Center. 11/16/87.
Brevard Community College Foundation, Cocoa, FL, $25,000. For renewed support to help equip college's new performing arts center. 2/15/88.
Brooklyn Music School, Brooklyn, NY, $7,000. To fund school's Intergenerational Chorus program for 1988-89. 6/15/88.
Broome County Arts Council, Binghamton, NY, $20,000. For renewed support for annual United Cultural Fund Drive. 4/15/88.
Camden County Cultural and Heritage Commission, Camden, NJ, $7,000. For in-home chamber music concerts for critically ill and homebound residents. 9/15/88.
Central Business District Foundation, Detroit, MI, $15,000. For renewed support to improve lighting of landmark buildings and statues throughout downtown Detroit. 2/15/88.
Central City Opera House Association, Denver, CO, $10,000. Toward opera performance during 1988 Summer Festival. 4/15/88.
Channel 5 Public Broadcasting, Reno, NV, $8,000. Toward digital video effects generator. 4/15/88.
Charlotte County Art Guild, Fort Myers, FL, $6,500. Toward campaign to build arts center in Punta Gorda, Florida. 11/16/87.
Chemeketa Community College, Salem, OR, $10,000. Toward cost of video projector for Cinema-360 films and improved presentations of other planetarium programs. 11/16/87.
Childrens Museum, Boston, MA, $10,000. For Children-at-Risk Program providing job training and counseling to troubled adolescents. 4/15/88.
Cincinnati Ballet Company, Cincinnati, OH, $12,000. Toward Nutcracker production. 10/15/87.
Cincinnati Historical Society, Cincinnati, OH, $5,000. To help publish special issue of society's quarterly journal as part of city's bicentennial celebrations. 7/15/88.
Cincinnati Institute of Fine Arts, Cincinnati, OH, $10,000. To help fund Cincinnati Playhouse's INTERACT Program introducing students to theater. 2/15/88.
Cincinnati Museum Association, Cincinnati, OH, $5,000. To buy computer and related equipment for communications/graphic-design department at Art Academy of Cincinnati. 7/15/88.
Cincinnati Music Hall Association, Cincinnati, OH, $25,000. Toward campaign to renovate 110-year-old music hall. 7/15/88.
Cincinnati Symphony Orchestra, Cincinnati, OH, $15,000. For audiotapes for students in grades k-8 to introduce classical music through 1988 Young People's Concert Series. 2/15/88.
Colorado State University, Denver, CO, $5,000. For university's library to sort, arrange and index films, videotapes and papers of Carl Akers, retired veteran anchorman and news executive for KUSA-TV. 10/15/87.
Community Arts Council of Arlington, Arlington, VA, $6,000. To expand activities at Arlington Arts Center. 4/15/88.
Community Circle Players, Lansing, MI, $10,000. To renovate warehouse in downtown Lansing into Riverwalk Theater. 6/15/88.
Como Conservatory Restoration Fund, Minneapolis, MN, $5,000. Toward renovation campaign. 5/13/88.
Contemporary Arts Center of Hawaii, Honolulu, HI, $5,000. To help move center's headquarters to Makiki Heights. 11/16/87.
Council for Public Television, Channel 6, Denver, CO, $5,000. For Super Six School News program, written, produced and aired five times week by fifth and sixth graders from 58 schools. 11/16/87.
Council for the Arts in Westchester, White Plains, NY, $50,000. Toward start-up costs of Performing Arts Trust to underwrite arts and cultural programs at Westchester County Center in White Plains. 2/15/88.
Council for the Arts in Westchester, White Plains, NY, $45,000. For renewed support of annual joint-appeal for funding to assist more than 70 nonprofit arts organizations. 6/15/88.
Davis Planetarium Foundation, Jackson, MS, $5,000. For renewed support of program to construct and operate Student Space Station adjacent to planetarium for simulated 14-day space-education sessions. 7/15/88.
Denver Symphony Association, Denver, CO, $5,000. To assist Grade School Concert Program. 8/15/88.
Des Moines Ballet Association, Des Moines, IA, $10,000. Toward debt-retirement campaign. 5/13/88.
Des Moines Botanical Center, Des Moines, IA, $5,000. For renewed support for science-curriculum enhancement program for elementary schools. 4/15/88.
Des Moines Metro Opera, Indianola, IA, $10,000. For OPERA Iowa, comprehensive opera-education program for schools throughout Iowa. 5/13/88.
Detroit Educational Television Foundation, Detroit, MI, $8,000. For national telecast of Lionel Hampton: Back to Paradise in Orchestra Hall to provide positive cultural image for Detroit. 6/15/88.
Detroit Institute of Arts, Founders Society, Detroit, MI, $15,000. To sponsor 51st Annual Detroit Public Schools Student Exhibition. 1/15/88.
Detroit Public Schools, Detroit, MI, $5,000. To fund students program of short skits discouraging dropping out of school, using drugs and teen pregnancy. 6/15/88.
Detroit Symphony Orchestra, Detroit, MI, $25,000. To sponsor Vladimir Ashkenazy/Lynn Harrel concert. 4/15/88.
Detroit Zoological Society, Detroit, MI, $12,500. For renewed support for campaign to build new chimpanzee exhibit as part of renovation project at the zoo. 1/15/88.
Detroit, City of, Recreation Department, Detroit, MI, $6,000. For renewed support for performing arts summer day camp for children ages 8-12 at historic Fort Wayne. 8/15/88.
Dinsmore Homestead Foundation, Cincinnati, OH, $7,000. Toward microfilming papers of Dinsmore family that has owned same 30-acre site in Northern Kentucky since 1839. Grant will also equip Burlington, Ky., living history museum, developed at site, to use microfilm. 11/16/87.
Dinsmore Homestead Foundation, Cincinnati, OH, $5,000. Toward campaign to buy historic Dinsmore House and property in Burlington, Kentucky. 5/13/88.

Downtown Development Corporation of Tucson, Tucson, AZ, $20,000. To help fund study to develop Arts District to enhance downtown's role as incubator for artistic activity and small business. 2/15/88.
Drury College, Springfield, MO, $7,500. To buy computers for Language and Literature Department. 4/15/88.
Dutchess County Arts Council, Poughkeepsie, NY, $10,000. For renewed support of united-funding campaign for cultural agencies. 3/15/88.
Dutchess County Historical Society, Poughkeepsie, NY, $7,000. To help publish Justice on Main and Market Street, history of Dutchess County Court House. 5/13/88.
East Coast Zoological Society of Florida, Melbourne, FL, $5,000. Toward new fence around Melbourne zoo. 11/16/87.
Edmundson Art Foundation, Des Moines, IA, $12,000. To expand Des Moines Art Center's Art Enrichment Program for third grade students. 9/15/88.
Elizabeth Seton College, Yonkers, NY, $15,000. Toward funds needed to complete historic restoration of Alder, national landmark building on College's campus. 9/15/88.
Ethan Allen Homestead Trust, Burlington, VT, $5,000. To develop educational materials for teachers bringing students to visit this historic site. 5/13/88.
Fairmount Historical Museum, Fairmount, IN, $5,000. Toward restoration of museum. 11/16/87.
Florida History Associates, Tallahassee, FL, $5,000. For Arts Day Activities at capital in Tallahassee. 4/15/88.
Flynn Theater for Performing Arts, Burlington, VT, $10,000. Toward restoration campaign. 5/13/88.
Genesee Country Museum, Mumford, NY, $5,000. To help produce three new brochures. 2/15/88.
Genesee Valley Arts Foundation, Rochester, NY, $50,000. Toward campaign to complete renovation of GeVa's professional theater in downtown Rochester and to retire debt remaining after shortfall in 1982-84 campaign. 3/15/88.
Gilbert House Childrens Museum, Salem, OR, $10,000. To complete design and engineering of exhibits for new children's museum. 4/15/88.
Greater Huntington Park and Recreation District, Huntington, WV, $10,000. Toward renovation and operating costs of floating stage in downtown park on Ohio River. 3/15/88.
Greater Louisville Fund for the Arts, Louisville, KY, $57,000. For renewed support of annual campaign to support area arts organizations. 11/16/87.
Greater Washington Educational Television Association, DC, $5,000. To assist Independent Minority Producers Laboratory. 4/15/88.
Hattiesburg, City of, Hattiesburg, MS, $10,000. Toward campaign to renovate and upgrade Kamper Park Zoo. 12/87.
Hawaii Public Radio, Honolulu, HI, $10,000. For renewed support of capital improvement campaign. 8/15/88.
Hawaii Theater Center, Honolulu, HI, $10,000. Toward restoration campaign for historic theater in Chinatown area. 4/15/88.
Historic Pensacola, Pensacola, FL, $5,000. To help build T.T. Wentworth Jr. Museum at Historic Pensacola Village. 7/15/88.
Hole in the Sock Productions, Boston, MA, $5,000. To help sponsor Parenting Project, call-in show on W G B H public radio for parents of children ages 9-14. 5/13/88.
Huntington Galleries, Huntington, WV, $11,000. To help fund ArtReach, museum's traveling exhibition program that introduces art to communities throughout tri-state area. 6/15/88.
Inland Empire Symphony, San Bernardino, CA, $7,500. To help sponsor annual Sinfonia Mexicana, special concert of Mexican classical music, and to support Music in the Schools program. 7/15/88.
Inland Empire Symphony Association, San Bernardino, CA, $9,000. For general support and to help sponsor annual Sinfonia Mexicana, special concert of Mexican classical music. 11/16/87.
Interlochen Center for the Arts, Interlochen, MI, $10,000. To fund 1988 scholarships for low-income minority stuents at nationally known center for music and arts education. 1/15/88.
International Museum of Photography at George Eastman House, Rochester, NY, $10,000. To help publish issue of Image magazine. 8/15/88.
Invest in Neighborhoods, Cincinnati, OH, $5,000. For renewed support of A Day in Eden, neighborhood summer program by cultural organizations in Eden Park. 7/15/88.
Jackson Arts Alliance, Jackson, MS, $5,000. For renewed support for Jubilee Jam, arts and music festival in downtown Jackson. 5/13/88.
Jackson, City of, Davis Planetarium, Jackson, MS, $6,000. For start-up expenses of program to construct and operate Student Space Station for simulated 14-day space-education experiences. Student Space Station may be part of national network of local space-simulation projects associated with Challenger Center for Space Science Education. 11/16/87.
Junior League of Detroit, Detroit, MI, $5,000. Toward cost of restoring historic Sibley House. 2/15/88.
Junior Museum and Planetarium of Lee County, Fort Myers, FL, $26,000. Toward cost of laser projection equipment for new Nature Center Planetarium to enhance educational and entertainment qualities of presentations. 11/16/87.
Kirkland Art Center, Utica, NY, $5,000. To help build fire escape at Clinton, NY community center. 6/15/88.
Lansing Symphony Association, East Lansing, MI, $5,000. For renewed support for annual Pops Concert. 3/15/88.
LuckyRides, New Haven, CT, $5,000. To add music keyboards to life-size, mobile merry-go-round sculpture that will provide educational experience for elementary school children. 4/15/88.
Marietta Bicentennial Committee, Marietta, OH, $5,000. For performance of Cincinnati Symphony. 3/15/88.
Martin Luther King Jr. Center for Nonviolent Social Change, Atlanta, GA, $5,000. To help fund KINGFEST, annual summer arts festival. 10/15/87.
Martin Luther King Jr. Center for Nonviolent Social Change, Atlanta, GA, $5,000. For renewed support to help fund KINGFEST, annual summer arts festival. 6/15/88.
Mary McLeod Bethune Memorial Museum and Archives, DC, $5,000. Toward start-up costs of planned 1990 exhibition, conference and documentary on Black Women in Civil Rights Movement, 1954-1965. 2/15/88.
Michigan Hispanic Scholarship Fund, Lansing, MI, $8,750. To fund one-day workshops at five higher education institutions in five Michigan cities for Hispanic students interested in pursuing writing careers. 12/87.
Michigan Opera Theater, Detroit, MI, $7,000. To help sponsor production of La Boheme. 1/15/88.
Michigan State University, Wharton Center, Lansing, MI, $5,000. For support for ACT ONE, a program offering theater experiences for youth. 3/15/88.
Monroe, City of, Monroe Beautification Board, Monroe, LA, $5,000. To help print 1988 calender depicting city's landmarks as drawn by schoolchildren. 10/15/87.
Monterey County Cultural Council, Salinas, CA, $5,000. To fund Professional Artists in Schools Program at four school districts in Salinas. 7/15/88.
Music Center of Los Angeles County, Los Angeles, CA, $5,000. For education-division activities. 4/15/88.
Muskogee Performing Arts, Muskogee, OK, $5,000. To repair Roxy theater sign and marquee as part of restoration of theater. 3/15/88.
National Ballet of Canada, Toronto, Canada, $7,310. To buy sound equipment for Toronto agency. 5/13/88.
National Symphony Orchestra Association of Washington, D.C., DC, $10,000. For renewed support toward 1987-1988 guide for students attending symphony's Young People's Concerts. 2/15/88.
National Warplane Museum of Geneseo, Rochester, NY, $15,000. Toward expansion of museum into year-round educational facility. 11/16/87.
Naval Aviation Museum Foundation, Pensacola, FL, $15,000. To help fund symposium, The Battle of Midway and Its Implications, co-sponsored by United States Naval Institute. 3/15/88.
New York Landmarks Preservation Foundation, NYC, NY, $112,500. To help produce historic markers to be hung in 51 historic districts of city's five boroughs. 10/20/87.
Northeast Louisiana Arts Council, Monroe, LA, $10,000. For Southwest Regional Ballet Association Festival and Council's Arts-In-Education program. 9/15/88.
Oakland University, Detroit, MI, $5,000. To help preserve historic Meadow Brook Hall. 4/15/88.
Oklahoma City Arts Council, Oklahoma City, OK, $5,000. Toward renovating studio/rehearsal hall for Dance Enrichment Program for Hearing Impaired. 9/15/88.
Oklahoma Museum of Art, Oklahoma City, OK, $5,000. To help fund exhibition, Hidden

Heritage: Afro-American Art, 1800-1950. 10/15/87.
Pensacola Historical Society, Pensacola, FL, $10,000. To help publish pictorial history book of Pensacola. 7/15/88.
Phoenix Symphony Association, Phoenix, AZ, $10,000. For two educational programs, Symphony for the Schools and Musicians in the Schools. 3/15/88.
Playmakers, Tampa, FL, $5,000. For summer production of Jazz, Jive, and Jam, providing theatrical training and employment for minority students. 4/15/88.
Punta Gorda, City of, Punta Gorda, FL, $5,035. To construct old-fashioned newsstand and street-vending area in historic Herald Courtyard as part of city's downtown revitalization. 5/13/88.
Red Earth, Oklahoma City, OK, $5,000. To help fund annual Native American arts festival. 9/15/88.
Roberson Center for the Arts and Sciences, Binghamton, NY, $7,500. For visits to Broome County History Gallery by elementary and high-school students. 4/15/88.
Robert W. Woodruff Arts Center, Atlanta, GA, $17,000. For new participative video exhibit for Junior Gallery, where schoolchildren participate in arts projects. 4/15/88.
Rochester Philharmonic Orchestra, Rochester, NY, $15,000. To sponsor opening performances of new season. 2/15/88.
Rockford Museum Association, Rockford, IL, $35,000. For renewed support to reconstruct print shop in museum's turn-of-the-century Midway Village. 4/15/88.
Saint Georges Historical Society, Wilmington, DE, $5,000. Toward restoration of town landmark into community center. 11/16/87.
San Bernardino Valley Concert Association, San Bernardino, CA, $5,000. To help sponsor concert in commemoration of organization's 50th anniversary. 7/15/88.
Save Orchestra Hall, Detroit, MI, $12,500. For renewed support toward campaign to restore and modernize Orchestra Hall. 4/15/88.
Scarab Club, Detroit, MI, $5,000. Toward campaign to restore 1928 clubhouse and cultural center located behind Detroit Institute of the Arts. 6/15/88.
Science and Technology Museum of Atlanta, Atlanta, GA, $6,000. Toward museum completion. 10/15/87.
Shelburne Museum, Shelburne, VT, $5,258. To expand museum's services to two inner-city elementary schools predominantly serving low-income families. 5/13/88.
Sidell Community Historical Society, Danville, IL, $5,500. To renovate century-old Lane Printing Office to house Sidell Museum. 5/13/88.
Smithsonian Institution, DC, $10,000. For Discovery Theater and Discover Graphics programs serving high school students interested in performing arts and printmaking. 4/15/88.
Smithsonian Institution, DC, $5,000. Toward symposium, Afro-Americans and Evolution of Living Constitution. 2/15/88.
Snug Harbor Cultural Center, Staten Island, NY, $5,000. To help establish program providing free tickets and transportation to cultural center for agencies serving elderly and disabled people. 6/15/88.
Southwest Florida Symphony Orchestra and Chorus Association, Fort Myers, FL, $10,000. To assist musical outreach program for fourth- and fifth-grade students in Lee County. 5/13/88.
Springfield Art Museum, Springfield, MO, $6,120. Toward summer program teaching educators how to include visual arts in their curricula. 4/15/88.
Summer Music Festival, Binghamton, NY, $10,085. To buy Infrared Hearing Assistance System for Anderson Center for the Performing Arts. Technology amplifies music to higher frequencies than standard hearing aids, producing high-fidelity sound for people with impaired hearing. 10/15/87.
Tennessee Repertory Theater Trust, Nashville, TN, $15,000. For expanded marketing campaign. 5/13/88.
Toronto, City of, Toronto, Canada, $8,046. To display Dennis Adams' Bus Shelter VII at Toronto's City Hall. 6/15/88.
Tucson Museum of Art, Tucson, AZ, $9,740. To expand program integrating deaf and blind children with non-handicapped children in art classes. 2/15/88.
United Arts Fund of the Mohawk Valley, Utica, NY, $5,000. For renewed support of annual campaign for 16 art and cultural organizations in Utica area. 6/15/88.
United Fund for the Arts, Jackson, MS, $6,000. For renewed support for annual campaign for five major Mississippi arts organizations. 8/15/88.
United Okinawan Association of Hawaii, Honolulu, HI, $5,000. Toward campaign for cultural center in Waipio, Oahu, celebrating the contributions of Okinawans to Hawaii. 5/13/88.
University Cultural Center Association, Detroit, MI, $10,000. Toward development of 43-acre site in heart of Detroit's cultural center. 2/15/88.
University of Rochester, Memorial Art Gallery, Rochester, NY, $17,500. For renewed support of free admission to gallery on Tuesday evenings and Saturday mornings. 7/15/88.
University of South Florida Foundation, Fort Myers, FL, $5,000. For Suncoast Young Authors' Conference for students from kindergarten through eighth grade. 8/15/88.
Vermont Council on the Arts, Burlington, VT, $5,000. For five one-month artists' residencies in public schools. 4/15/88.
W E T A Greater Washington Educational Television Association, DC, $5,000. Toward Public Broadcasting Service special on role of media in civil rights movement. 10/15/87.
W H Y Y-TV, Wilmington, DE, $10,000. Toward campaign to build new facility for Delaware Valley's public broadcasting services. 3/15/88.
Washington Drama Society, DC, $5,000. To support Living Stage Theater Company, Arena Stage's program providing free performances for disadvantaged people. 10/15/87.
Washington Project for the Arts (WPA), DC, $25,000. Toward campaign to renovate space in downtown building as headquarters of organization that promotes new and experimental art. 6/15/88.
Wilmington Institute Free Library, Wilmington, DE, $10,000. To microfilm Delaware newspapers from 1790-1880 and to buy computer and related equipment. 2/15/88.

3173
Gottwald Foundation
c/o Floyd D. Gottwald, Jr.
P.O. Box 2189
Richmond 23217

Established in 1957.
Donor(s): Floyd D. Gottwald, Sr.†
Financial data (yr. ended 12/31/87): Assets, $7,172,627 (M); gifts received, $168,437; expenditures, $484,048, including $475,500 for 21 grants (high: $228,000; low: $100).
Purpose and activities: Emphasis on education, hospitals, cultural programs, and youth agencies; support also for a foundation benefiting a military institute.
Limitations: Giving primarily in VA.
Application information: Contributes only to pre-selected organizations. Applications not accepted.
Officers: Floyd D. Gottwald, Jr., Pres.; Anne C. Gottwald, V.P.; Bruce C. Gottwald, Secy.-Treas.
Employer Identification Number: 546040560

3174
Richard and Caroline T. Gwathmey Memorial Trust
c/o Sovran Bank
P.O. Box 26903
Richmond 23261 (804) 788-2964

Established in 1981 in VA.
Donor(s): Elizabeth G. Jeffress.†
Financial data (yr. ended 6/30/88): Assets, $7,542,327 (M); expenditures, $467,790, including $416,662 for 23 grants (high: $50,000; low: $3,000).
Purpose and activities: Support for a variety of charitable, cultural, and educational activities.
Types of support: General purposes.
Limitations: Giving primarily in VA. No grants to individuals.
Publications: Informational brochure (including application guidelines).
Application information:
Initial approach: Letter requesting guidelines
Deadline(s): Mar. 1 and Sept. 1
Final notification: Immediately following meeting at which proposal was considered
Write: Dr. J. Samuel Gillespie, Jr., Trust Advisor
Trustee: Sovran Bank, N.A.
Number of staff: 2
Employer Identification Number: 546191586

3175
Eugene Holt Foundation
300 Massey Bldg.
Fourth & Main Sts.
Richmond 23219 (804) 649-9394

Financial data (yr. ended 8/31/87): Assets, $1,445,621 (M); gifts received, $0;

expenditures, $74,567, including $70,171 for 29 grants (high: $38,053; low: $10).
Purpose and activities: Support primarily for wildlife and ecological organizations; support also for historical societies and historical preservation associations, and museums.
Application information:
Initial approach: Letter
Deadline(s): July 31
Write: Ivor Massey, Secy.
Officers: Anne Holt Massey, Pres.; Ivor Massey Jr., V.P.; Ivor Massey, Secy.-Treas.
Employer Identification Number: 540802044

3176
The John Jay Hopkins Foundation
1199 North Fairfax St.
P.O. Box 25047
Alexandria 22313

Trust established in 1954 in DC.
Donor(s): John J. Hopkins.†
Financial data (yr. ended 12/31/87): Assets, $1,934,770 (M); expenditures, $180,060, including $131,405 for 65 grants.
Purpose and activities: Giving for Protestant church support and church-related schools, and higher education; support also for cultural programs.
Types of support: Continuing support, annual campaigns, building funds, fellowships, general purposes.
Limitations: Giving primarily in VA and the Washington, DC, metropolitan area. No grants to individuals, or for endowment funds, operating budgets, seed money, emergency funds, deficit financing, land acquisition, matching gifts, special projects, research, publications, or conferences; no loans.
Publications: 990-PF.
Application information: Contributes only to pre-selected organizations. Applications not accepted.
Board meeting date(s): Oct. or Nov. and as required
Write: Lianne H. Conger, Pres., or Philip Tierney, Secy.
Officers and Trustees: Lianne H. Conger, Pres.; Philip Tierney, Secy.; Clement E. Conger, Treas.; Jay A. Conger, Shelley Conger, Harry Teter.
Number of staff: None.
Employer Identification Number: 526036649

3177
James River Corporation Public Affairs Department
Tredegar Street
P.O. Box 2218
Richmond 23217 (804) 644-5411

Financial data (yr. ended 4/30/88): $2,800,000 for grants.
Purpose and activities: James River's first social responsibility is "jobs first: the corporation can make the most effective social contribution by creating and maintaining secure, safe and productive jobs. The wealth these jobs create permeates the communities by way of the supplies and services purchased by the company and its employees, taxes paid and the enlightenment and philanthropy made possible. The second social responsibility of the company is to prosper and grow, and to contribute to the health of society and provide a reasonable environment in which business can be conducted. As resources (cash and human) allow, it is James River's intent to demonstrate its civic responsibility through charitable contributions, business and professional memberships, community involvement and employee volunteerism in the communities where our employees live and work." Company supports education, economic development, health, the arts, and community development.
Types of support: Capital campaigns, employee matching gifts, general purposes, equipment, special projects, endowment funds, internships.
Limitations: Giving primarily in company operating areas; national organizations are generally not considered for support. No support for religious, fraternal, veterans', political, labor, or athletic organizations. No grants to individuals, or for telephone or mass mail solicitations.
Publications: Application guidelines.
Application information: Include narrative/letter, 501(c)(3), board list, donor list and audited financial statement.
Initial approach: Initial contact by query letter describing project
Copies of proposal: 1
Deadline(s): Applications accepted throughout the year; best time to apply is Mar.-Oct.
Final notification: 6-12 weeks
Write: Stephen H. Garnett, V.P., Public Affairs
Administrator: Tyler Bird Paul, Mgr., Corp. Relations; Tracey Beard, Matching Gifts Program Admin.
Number of staff: 1 part-time professional; 1 part-time support.

3178
W. Alton Jones Foundation, Inc.
433 Park St.
Charlottesville 22901 (804) 295-2134

Incorporated in 1944 in NY.
Donor(s): W. Alton Jones.†
Financial data (yr. ended 12/31/88): Assets, $171,469,847 (M); expenditures, $12,759,945, including $10,508,233 for grants (high: $2,500,000; average: $5,000-$100,000).
Purpose and activities: The foundation limits most of its grantmaking to two subject areas: environmental protection, with emphasis on conservation of biological diversity worldwide and protection of land, air, and water from pollution and toxic contamination; and prevention of nuclear war.
Types of support: General purposes, special projects, research, conferences and seminars, seed money, matching funds, exchange programs, land acquisition, loans, operating budgets, publications, program-related investments.
Limitations: No support for conduit organizations. No grants to individuals, or for building or endowment funds, deficit financing, scholarships, or fellowships.
Publications: Annual report, application guidelines.
Application information: Applicants must wait 1 year after a grant is approved or declined before submitting another application; applications accepted only for programs in environmental protection and arms control;.
Initial approach: Proposal
Copies of proposal: 1
Deadline(s): Jan. 15, Apr. 15, July 15, and Oct. 15
Board meeting date(s): Quarterly
Final notification: 3 months
Write: R. Jeffrey Kelleher, Dir.
Officers and Directors: Mrs. W. Alton Jones,* Chair.; Patricia Jones Edgerton,* Pres.; Bradford W. Edgerton,* V.P.; Diane Edgerton Miller,* Secy.; Bernard F. Curry,* Treas.; R. Jeffrey Kelleher.
Trustees:* James S. Bennett, William A. Edgerton, Elizabeth Marie Jones, Scott McVay.
Number of staff: 4 full-time professional; 3 full-time support.
Employer Identification Number: 136034219
Recent arts and culture grants:
Aljira Arts, Newark, NJ, $5,000. For Art from the Afro-Diaspora exhibition, which traces historical and stylistic continuum of art of West Africa through Caribbean, to black and Hispanic American artists of today. 1987.
Architects/Designers/Planners for Social Responsibility, NYC, NY, $20,000. For expanding membership and for developing new chapters. 1987.
Artists Space, NYC, NY, $20,000. For Selections, exhibition in which Artists Space brings to public view cream of crop of 10 to 12 artists in its slide registry; and for outreach and publicity efforts for Artists File. 1987.
Aspen Art Museum, Aspen, CO, $25,000. To fund inauguration of Latitudes, traveling exhibition series conceived by Aspen Art Museum, and featuring works by emerging artists from regional centers nationwide. 1987.
BACA Downtown, Brooklyn, NY, $20,000. To support artists' fees and production expenses of Fringe Series, season of premiere performances of new plays, and for Performers Showcase Forum, two-month annual performance festival. 1987.
Ballet Florida, West Palm Beach, FL, $30,000. To add three dancers to company, and to commission world premiere, Salome, from choreographer Nebrada, to debut in April 1988. 1987.
Baltimore Chamber Orchestra, Baltimore, MD, $10,000. For grant, in conjunction with support from Young Audiences of Baltimore, which provided eleven performances in inner-city Baltimore schools in 1987. 1987.
Baltimore School for the Arts, Baltimore, MD, $39,720. To support school outreach program in which 20-week series of free afternoon classes in the arts will be offered to elementary and middle school children throughout city. 1987.
Center Stage, Baltimore, MD, $50,000. For support of Re: Discovery, new dimension in Center Stage's commitment to new plays. Three plays, new or undiscovered works will be presented in repertory as part of Center Stage's mainstage 1987-88 season. 1987.

Central Park Conservancy, NYC, NY, $75,000. To support SummerStage, outdoor performing arts series launched in 1986, which provides free public performances of dance and of folk, ethnic, and international music. 1987.
Chautauqua Institution, Chautauqua, NY, $150,000. For 1987-1988 Chautauqua Conferences on U.S.-Soviet Relations. 1987.
Colorado Stage Company, Denver, CO, $5,000. For general operations. 1987.
Creative Time, NYC, NY, $25,000. To support artists' and architects' fees and materials for Art on the Beach, series of creative installations that began in Battery Park in Wall Street district, and is now offered in Hunters Point, dilapidated waterfront property on East River in Queens. 1987.
Crossroads Theater Company, New Brunswick, NJ, $75,000. To support New Play Rites, program designed to nurture new and midcareer playwrights, and to enable them to sustain careers in theater. 1987.
Dance Theater Workshop, NYC, NY, $50,000. For Out-of-Towners series' offering up-and-coming artists a New York residency at Schonberg Theater; and Membership Services Program, which provides extensive range of administrative, promotional, and technical resources to over 500 independent artists and arts organizations. 1987.
Denver Chamber Orchestra, Denver, CO, $15,000. To engage up-and-coming young soloists to perform with orchestra, and to extend scope of ensemble's touring, to rural Colorado, Wymoing, and Montana. 1987.
Haddonfield Symphony Orchestra, Haddonfield, NJ, $20,000. For annual Solo Competition for Young Instrumentalists, one of largest competitive showcases of young talent in Eastern United States; and Student Internship Program, established in 1986, which offers stipends to promising young performers to spend season with symphony. 1987.
Independent Curators, NYC, NY, $40,000. To launch six new traveling exhibitions in 1987, and publish catalogues for each. 1987.
Institute for Theater Training, Jupiter, FL, $15,000. To increase scholarship aid to apprentices, and to add teaching support in voice and movement. 1987.
Los Angeles Theater Center, Los Angeles, CA, $50,000. For Young Playwrights' Lab, encouraging career development of emerging Los Angelino playwrights; and New Works Project, research and development function of Los Angeles Theater Center, offering one-year fellowships to playwrights in residency at Center, and resulting in annual New Works Festival. 1987.
Missouri Botanical Garden, Saint Louis, MO, $150,000. For extensive botanical surveys, training of Malagasy botanists, nature park in Madagascar's capital city, databanking of plant information, and efforts to establish new parks and reserves to preserve Madagascar's unique biological diversity. 1987.
Museum of Contemporary Art, Los Angeles, CA, $60,000. For Artists Project Series, which gives young artists opportunity and space to test, experiment, and grappel with new ideas; and for retrospective exhibition of prominent Los Angeles architect Frank Gehry. 1987.
Musica Sacra, NYC, NY, $25,000. To continue Musica Sacra's long-standing tradition of fostering new sacred choral music by commissioning and presenting world premiere, The Death of Moses, by leading contemporary American composer Ned Rorem. 1987.
Newark Community School of the Arts, Newark, NJ, $40,000. To offer scholarships to its most talented performing arts students to join forces with professional faculty of school in series of public performances. 1987.
Performance Space 122, NYC, NY, $25,000. To fund First Floor Events, first rung on P.S. 122 Ladder, in which emerging artists in dance, music, theater, film, and performance art are given extended runs to create their work and build audience. 1987.
Philharmonic Orchestra of Florida, Fort Lauderdale, FL, $40,000. Toward young people's concerts, and partly for Celebrity Series, which features young artists in early stages of their careers as soloists with orchestra. 1987.
Pipeline, Los Angeles, CA, $10,000. To expand production schedule at two home theaters, and to develop bold export strategy of theater downtown, around town, and out of town. 1987.
Playwrights Horizons, NYC, NY, $75,000. To support development of New Theatre Wing, providing talented newcomers and lesser-known, midcareer experimental playwrights chance of limited-run productions in intimate studio theater setting. 1987.
Power Plant Visual Arts Center, Fort Collins, CO, $10,000. To support exhibitions, to provide honoraria for artists, and to engage outside guest curators. 1987.
Res Musica Baltimore, Baltimore, MD, $5,000. To commission new works, and to build on touring schedule. 1987.
Seventeen Hundred Eight East Main, Richmond, VA, $5,000. For workshops and other services to individual artists, and for enhancing registry of artists' slides. 1987.
Theater for the New City, NYC, NY, $50,000. For commissioning and presenting of new works. 1987.
Thomas A. Edison Black Maria Film Festival and Competition, West Orange, NJ, $7,500. For general support and to increase awards and royalties to film makers. 1987.
Virginia Museum Foundation, Richmond, VA, $50,000. Fo exhibit Uncommon Ground, Virginia Artists 1988, and for Fast Forward, season of experimental music, dance, and performance art. 1987.
W G B H Educational Foundation, Boston, MA, $100,000. For 13-hour prime time documentary series and television course entitled War and Peace in the Nuclear Age, which will trace military, political, and technological developments that have dominated contemporary thought from dawn of nuclear age to present. 1987.

3179
Lafarge Corporate Giving Program

1130 Sunrise Valley Dr.
Reston 22091 (703) 264-3600
Mailing Address: P.O. Box 4600, Reston, VA 22090

Purpose and activities: Support for child welfare, the homeless, the disadvantaged, community development, culture and the arts, medical research, and Canadian issues.
Types of support: Annual campaigns.
Limitations: Giving primarily in the Washington, D.C. area, the Dallas, TX, area, and the Northeast and Midwest.
Publications: Informational brochure.
Application information:
Initial approach: Letter
Copies of proposal: 1
Write: Katrina Farrell, Dir., Corp. Communications

3180
Landmark Charitable Foundation

150 West Brambleton Ave.
Norfolk 23510 (804) 446-2030

Incorporated in 1953 in VA.
Donor(s): The Virginian-Pilot and Ledger-Star, Greensboro Daily News and Greensboro Record, The Roanoke Times and The World-News, WTAR-AM and FM, WLTY-FM, KLAS-TV, KNTV-TV.
Financial data (yr. ended 10/31/88): Assets, $13,223,119 (M); gifts received, $1,354,000; expenditures, $972,350 for 168 grants (high: $106,000; low: $500; average: $1,000-$10,000).
Purpose and activities: Grants largely for higher education, cultural organizations, and community funds in areas served by the donor newspapers and TV stations; support also for journalism associations, literacy, secondary education, and business education.
Types of support: Annual campaigns, building funds, capital campaigns, endowment funds, scholarship funds, seed money, special projects.
Limitations: Giving primarily in communities served by a Landmark company participating in the Foundation in the Hampton Roads and Roanoke, VA, areas; Greensboro, NC area; San Jose, CA; and Las Vegas, NV. No support for non-tax exempt organizations or programs. No grants to individuals.
Application information:
Initial approach: Proposal or phone call
Copies of proposal: 1
Deadline(s): By Dec. of preceding year in which grant is expected
Board meeting date(s): As required
Write: Carolyn S. Wood, Exec. Dir.
Officers: Richard F. Barry III,* Pres.; J. William Diederich,* V.P.; Jane O. Pruitt, Secy.; James D. Wagner, Treas.
Directors:* Frank Batten, Chair.; Robert D. Benson, Conrad M. Hall, Carl W. Mangum, Walter Rugaber, Louis F. Ryan, John O. Wynne.
Number of staff: None.
Employer Identification Number: 546038902

3181
Sydney & Frances Lewis Foundation
P.O. Box 26303
Richmond 23260

Established in 1966 in VA.
Donor(s): Sydney Lewis, Frances A. Lewis.
Financial data (yr. ended 6/30/88): Assets, $483,040 (M); gifts received, $333,682; expenditures, $549,899, including $547,840 for 165 grants (high: $107,000; low: $15).
Purpose and activities: A private operating foundation; support primarily for art museums and the arts; support also for Jewish organizations.
Application information: Contributes only to pre-selected organizations. Applications not accepted.
Officers and Directors: Sydney Lewis, Pres.; Susan L. Butler, V.P.; Frances A. Lewis, Secy.-Treas.; Robert L. Burrus, Jr., Robert E.P. Huntley, Andrew M. Lewis.
Employer Identification Number: 546061170

3182
The Mars Foundation
6885 Elm St.
McLean 22101 (703) 821-4900

Incorporated in 1956 in IL.
Donor(s): Forrest E. Mars.
Financial data (yr. ended 12/31/87): Assets, $4,208,189 (M); gifts received, $600,665; expenditures, $1,075,488, including $1,021,000 for 124 grants (high: $100,000; low: $1,000; average: $2,000-$15,000).
Purpose and activities: Support for higher and secondary education, wildlife preservation, health agencies, the fine arts, and medical research.
Types of support: Continuing support, annual campaigns, building funds, equipment, endowment funds, research, matching funds.
Limitations: No grants to individuals, or for scholarships; no loans.
Application information:
Initial approach: Letter
Copies of proposal: 1
Deadline(s): 6 weeks prior to meeting
Board meeting date(s): June and Dec.
Final notification: 4 to 6 weeks after meeting
Write: Roger G. Best, Secy.
Officers: Forrest E. Mars, Jr., Pres.; David H. Badger, V.P.; John F. Mars, V.P.; Roger G. Best, Secy.; William C. Turnbull, Treas.
Directors: Adrienne B. Mars, Virginia C. Mars, Jacqueline M. Vogel.
Number of staff: 2
Employer Identification Number: 546037592

3183
Massey Foundation
Four North Fourth St.
Richmond 23219 (804) 788-1800

Established in 1958 in VA.
Donor(s): A.T. Massey Coal Co., Inc.
Financial data (yr. ended 11/30/88): Assets, $28,602,610 (M); expenditures, $1,682,955, including $1,395,750 for 76 grants (high: $210,000; low: $1,000; average: $1,000-$25,000).
Purpose and activities: Giving primarily for higher and secondary education; some support for hospitals and health services, cultural programs, and social services.
Limitations: Giving primarily in VA, particularly Richmond. No grants to individuals.
Application information:
Initial approach: Letter
Board meeting date(s): Annually
Write: William E. Massey, Jr., Pres.
Officers and Directors: William E. Massey, Jr., Pres.; William Blair Massey, V.P. and Secy.; E. Morgan Massey, Treas.
Number of staff: None.
Employer Identification Number: 546049049

3184
Ruth Camp McDougall Charitable Trust
c/o Sovran Bank, N.A., Trust Tax Div.
P.O. Box 26903
Richmond 23261 (804) 788-2573

Trust established in 1976 in VA.
Donor(s): Ruth Camp McDougall.†
Financial data (yr. ended 12/31/87): Assets, $6,751,913 (M); expenditures, $436,802, including $398,800 for 76 grants (high: $75,000; low: $1,000).
Purpose and activities: Giving primarily for higher and secondary education; support also for youth agencies, and cultural programs.
Limitations: Giving primarily in VA.
Application information:
Initial approach: Letter
Deadline(s): None
Write: Donnie E. Koonce, 1st V.P., Sovran Bank, N.A.
Directors: John M. Camp, Jr., Paul D. Camp III, Paul Camp Marks, Harry W. Walker.
Trustee: Sovran Bank, N.A.
Employer Identification Number: 546162697

3185
The Media General Foundation
333 East Grace St.
Richmond 23219-1717 (804) 649-6978

Financial data (yr. ended 12/31/87): Assets, $817,863 (L); expenditures, $49,333, including $49,333 for 39 grants.
Purpose and activities: Support for general charitable giving.
Limitations: Giving primarily in VA.
Application information:
Copies of proposal: 1
Write: Edward C. Tosh
Officers: D. Tennant Bryan,* Chair.; J.S. Bryan,* Pres.; A.J. Brent,* Secy.; J. Curtis Barden, Treas.
Directors:* J.A. Evans.
Number of staff: None.
Employer Identification Number: 510235902

3186
Mobil Foundation, Inc.
3225 Gallows Rd.
Fairfax 22037 (703) 846-3381

Incorporated in 1965 in NY.
Donor(s): Mobil Oil Corp.
Financial data (yr. ended 12/31/87): Assets, $10,563,474 (M); gifts received, $10,662,000; expenditures, $15,957,781, including $9,999,699 for 1,041 grants (high: $550,000; low: $100; average: $1,000-$10,000) and $4,248,724 for 2,212 employee matching gifts.
Purpose and activities: Support for arts and cultural programs, higher education, including grants in fields relating to the petroleum and chemical industries, a scholarship program for children of employees, and an employee matching gift program; support also for community funds, civic affairs, social services, health agencies, and hospitals.
Types of support: Employee-related scholarships, employee matching gifts, research, exchange programs, general purposes.
Limitations: Giving primarily in areas of company operations in CA, CO, IL, LA, NJ, NY, TX, VA, and WA. No support for local and national organizations concerned with specific diseases, or religious or fraternal organizations. No grants to individuals, or for building or endowment funds, operating budgets, charity benefits, athletic events, or advertising; no loans.
Publications: Financial statement, application guidelines, grants list.
Application information:
Initial approach: Letter or proposal
Copies of proposal: 1
Deadline(s): None
Board meeting date(s): Monthly
Final notification: 6 to 8 weeks
Write: Richard G. Mund, Secy.
Officers: Andrew L. Gaboriault,* Pres.; Richard G. Mund, Secy. and Exec. Dir.; Anthony L. Cavaliere, Treas.
Directors:* Robert F. Amrhein, Donald J. Bolger, Douglas O. Fitzsimmons, Ellen Z. McCloy, John P. McCullough, Walter S. Piontek, Peter A. Spina, Jerome F. Trautschold, Jr.
Number of staff: 3 full-time professional; 8 full-time support.
Employer Identification Number: 136177075
Recent arts and culture grants:
Action for Childrens Television, Cambridge, MA, $5,000. 1987.
Affiliate Artists, NYC, NY, $13,000. 1987.
Aldrich Museum of Contemporary Art, Ridgefield, CT, $20,000. 1987.
American Council for the Arts, NYC, NY, $7,500. 1987.
American Council of Learned Societies, NYC, NY, $5,000. 1987.
Art Institute of Chicago, Chicago, IL, $5,000. 1987.
Asia Society, NYC, NY, $10,000. 1987.
Brooklyn Academy of Music, Brooklyn, NY, $10,000. 1987.
Brooklyn Institute of Arts and Sciences, Brooklyn Museum, Brooklyn, NY, $15,000. 1987.
Broward Community College Foundation, Fort Lauderdale, FL, $8,500. For arts and cultural programs. 1987.
Business Arts Fund, Houston, TX, $12,000. 1987.
Business Committee for the Arts, NYC, NY, $10,000. 1987.
Capital Childrens Museum, DC, $5,000. 1987.
Capital Repertory Company, Albany, NY, $5,000. 1987.

Carnegie Hall Society, NYC, NY, $35,000. 1987.
Cooper Union for the Advancement of Science and Art, NYC, NY, $5,000. 1987.
Dallas Black Dance Theater, Dallas, TX, $7,325. 1987.
Dallas Museum of Art, Dallas, TX, $40,000. 1987.
Dallas Theater Center, Dallas, TX, $11,000. 1987.
Dancers Unlimited Repertory Company, Dallas, TX, $5,000. 1987.
Fairfax County Council of the Arts, Fairfax, VA, $7,000. 1987.
Fairfax County Symphony Orchestra, McLean, VA, $10,000. 1987.
Fords Theater Society, DC, $9,000. 1987.
Fort Hays State University Endowment Association, Hays, KS, $50,000. For arts and cultural programs. 1987.
Georgetown University, DC, $12,000. For arts and cultural programs. 1987.
Glassboro State College Development Fund, Glassboro, NJ, $8,150. For arts and cultural programs. 1987.
Greater Dallas Youth Orchestra, Dallas, TX, $5,000. 1987.
Highland Park Chamber Orchestra, Dallas, TX, $5,000. 1987.
Houston Pops Orchestra, Houston, TX, $5,000. 1987.
John F. Kennedy Center for the Performing Arts, DC, $62,500. 1987.
Junior Black Academy of Arts and Letters, Dallas, TX, $5,000. 1987.
Kansas City Lyric Theater, Kansas City, MO, $6,800. 1987.
Lincoln Center for the Performing Arts, NYC, NY, $25,000. 1987.
McCarter Theater Company, Princeton, NJ, $24,000. 1987.
Metropolitan Museum of Art, NYC, NY, $7,500. 1987.
Michigan Opera Theater, Detroit, MI, $6,375. 1987.
Midland Community Theater, Midland, TX, $6,000. 1987.
National Corporate Fund for Dance, NYC, NY, $8,000. 1987.
National Corporate Theater Fund, NYC, NY, $8,000. 1987.
National Plastics Museum, Leominster, MA, $10,000. 1987.
National Symphony Orchestra Association of Washington, D.C., DC, $6,000. 1987.
New Mexico Symphony Orchestra, Albuquerque, NM, $5,000. 1987.
New Orleans Philharmonic Symphony Society, New Orleans, LA, $17,000. 1987.
New York City Opera, NYC, NY, $10,000. 1987.
New York Zoological Society, Bronx, NY, $10,000. 1987.
Original Ballets Foundation, NYC, NY, $11,000. 1987.
Performing Arts Council of the Music Center, Los Angeles, CA, $5,000. 1987.
Princeton University, Princeton, NJ, $5,000. For arts and cultural programs. 1987.
Robert W. Woodruff Arts Center, Atlanta, GA, $10,000. 1987.
Soho Center for Visual Artists, NYC, NY, $15,000. 1987.
University of California at Los Angeles Foundation, Los Angeles, CA, $7,500. For arts and cultural programs. 1987.
Washington Ballet, DC, $5,000. 1987.
Washington Opera, DC, $9,000. 1987.
Will County Metropolitan Exposition and Auditorium Authority, Joliet, IL, $5,000. 1987.
Wolf Trap Foundation for the Performing Arts, Vienna, VA, $15,000. 1987.
Young Audiences, NYC, NY, $7,500. 1987.

3187
Noland Company Foundation
2700 Warwick Blvd.
Newport News 23607

Established in 1962 in VA.
Donor(s): Noland Co.
Financial data (yr. ended 12/31/87): Assets, $611,723 (M); gifts received, $5,000; expenditures, $102,984, including $101,859 for 57 grants (high: $10,674; low: $100).
Purpose and activities: Giving for cultural programs, particularly museums and performing arts groups, social service and youth agencies, and higher education.
Limitations: Giving primarily in VA.
Application information: Contributes only to preselected organizations. Applications not accepted.
Officers: Lloyd U. Noland, Jr., Pres.; Arthur P. Henderson, Jr., V.P.; J.E. Gullett, Secy.-Treas.
Employer Identification Number: 540754191

3188
The Norfolk Foundation
1410 Sovran Center
Norfolk 23510 (804) 622-7951

Community foundation established in 1950 in VA by resolution and declaration of trust.
Financial data (yr. ended 12/31/88): Assets, $26,815,407 (M); gifts received, $610,195; expenditures, $1,428,448, including $1,052,966 for 41 grants (high: $169,000; low: $666; average: $4,000-$75,000) and $238,970 for 192 grants to individuals.
Purpose and activities: Support for hospitals, educational institutions, family and child welfare agencies, a community fund, and cultural and civic programs; certain donor-designated scholarships restricted by residence in nearby localities and/or area colleges, and payable directly to the school.
Types of support: Seed money, building funds, equipment, land acquisition, research, special projects, capital campaigns, student aid.
Limitations: Giving primarily in Norfolk, VA, and a 50-mile area from its boundaries. No support for national or international organizations, or religious organizations for religious purposes. No grants to individuals (except for donor-designated scholarships), or for operating budgets, endowment funds, or deficit financing; no loans.
Publications: Annual report, application guidelines, program policy statement.
Application information:
Initial approach: Letter or telephone
Copies of proposal: 1
Deadline(s): For scholarships only, Dec. 1 to Mar. 1
Board meeting date(s): 4 times a year
Final notification: 3 to 4 months
Write: Lee C. Kitchin, Exec. Dir.
Officer: Lee C. Kitchin, Exec. Dir.
Distribution Committee: Charles F. Burroughs, Jr., Chair.; Toy D. Savage, Jr., Vice-Chair.; Jean C. Bruce, Joshua P. Darden, H.P. McNeal, H.B. Price III, Kurt M. Rosenbach.
Number of staff: 1 full-time professional; 2 part-time support.
Employer Identification Number: 540722169
Recent arts and culture grants:
Business Consortium for Arts Support, Norfolk, VA, $92,500. 1987.
Chrysler Museum, Norfolk, VA, $100,000. For expansion of museum. 1987.
Virginia Wesleyan College, Norfolk, VA, $50,000. For new Humanities Center. 1987.
W H R O-FM TV, Norfolk, VA, $30,000. For capital campaign. 1987.

3189
Norfolk Shipbuilding and Drydock Corporation Charity Trust
c/o Sovran Bank
P.O. Box 3000
Norfolk 23514
Application address: Charitable Trust Comm., P.O. Box 2100, Norfolk, VA 23501

Established in 1952 in VA.
Donor(s): Norfolk Shipbuilding & Drydock Corp.
Financial data (yr. ended 12/31/87): Assets, $548,935 (M); expenditures, $76,999, including $70,000 for 24 grants (high: $11,000; low: $100).
Purpose and activities: Support for a community fund, higher education, cultural programs, hospitals and health services, and social services.
Limitations: Giving primarily in VA.
Application information:
Initial approach: Letter
Deadline(s): None
Trustee: Sovran Bank.
Employer Identification Number: 546036745

3190
Norfolk Southern Foundation
One Commercial Place
Norfolk 23510-2191 (804) 629-2650

Established in 1983 in VA.
Donor(s): Norfolk Southern Corp.
Financial data (yr. ended 12/31/87): Assets, $9,841,129 (M); gifts received, $4,918,467; expenditures, $2,749,692, including $2,076,630 for 209 grants (high: $95,000; low: $100; average: $750-$25,000) and $640,882 for employee matching gifts.
Purpose and activities: Giving primarily for cultural programs, including museums and performing arts groups, community funds, and higher education, including independent college funds. The foundation also sponsors an employee gift program to educational and cultural institutions.
Types of support: Employee matching gifts, operating budgets.

Limitations: Giving primarily in Atlanta, GA, and Hampton Roads and Roanoke, VA. No grants to individuals.
Application information:
Initial approach: Letter
Deadline(s): None
Final notification: 60 days
Write: Joseph R. Neikirk, V.P.
Officers: Arnold B. McKinnon, Chair., Pres., and C.E.O.; Joseph R. Neikirk, V.P. and Exec. Dir.; John S. Shannon, V.P.; John R. Turbyfill, V.P.; D.H. Watts, V.P.; Donald E. Middleton, Secy.; Thomas H. Kerwin, Treas.
Employer Identification Number: 521328375

3191
The Tom and Claire O'Neil Foundation, Inc.
c/o Mark O'Neil
930 Graydon Ave.
Norfolk 23507

Incorporated in 1954 in CT.
Donor(s): Thomas F. O'Neil.
Financial data (yr. ended 12/31/87): Assets, $1,102,004 (M); expenditures, $67,796, including $66,107 for 36 grants (high: $10,000; low: $100).
Purpose and activities: Emphasis on Roman Catholic church support, church-related associations, and social service and youth agencies; support for educational institutions, hospitals, and cultural programs.
Application information: Contributes only to pre-selected organizations. Applications not accepted.
Officers and Directors: Thomas F. O'Neil, Pres. and Treas.; Claire M. O'Neil, V.P.; William M. Regan, Secy.; Mark O'Neil, Principal Mgr.; Eileen O'Neil, Shane O'Neil.
Employer Identification Number: 066035099

3192
The Ohrstrom Foundation, Inc.
c/o Whitewood
The Plains 22171
Application address: 540 Madison Ave., 35th Fl., New York, NY 10022; Tel.: (212) 759-5380

Incorporated in 1953 in DE.
Donor(s): Members of the Ohrstrom family.
Financial data (yr. ended 5/31/87): Assets, $17,415,251 (M); gifts received, $1,000; expenditures, $641,677, including $611,000 for 120 grants (high: $142,000; low: $1,000; average: $1,000-$10,000).
Purpose and activities: Emphasis on elementary, secondary, and higher education; support also for civic affairs, conservation, hospitals, and museums.
Types of support: Operating budgets, continuing support, annual campaigns, seed money, emergency funds, building funds, equipment, land acquisition, endowment funds, matching funds.
Limitations: Giving primarily in VA and NY. No grants to individuals, or for deficit financing, scholarships, fellowships, research, special projects, publications, or conferences; no loans.
Application information:
Initial approach: Letter
Deadline(s): Mar. 31
Final notification: 3 to 6 months
Write: George L. Ohrstrom, Jr., V.P.
Officers: George L. Ohrstrom, Jr.,* V.P.; Ricard R. Ohrstrom, Jr.,* V.P.; Palma Cifu, Treas.
Trustees:* Magalen O. Bryant.
Number of staff: 1 part-time support.
Employer Identification Number: 546039966

3193
William G. Pannill Foundation
P.O. Box 5151
Martinsville 24115

Established in 1984 in VA.
Donor(s): William G. Pannill.
Financial data (yr. ended 12/31/87): Assets, $1,328,905 (M); expenditures, $205,606, including $192,000 for 14 grants (high: $125,000; low: $1,000).
Purpose and activities: Support for Christian religious purposes, higher education, and cultural activities.
Types of support: Operating budgets, research.
Limitations: Giving primarily in VA. No grants to individuals.
Application information: Contributes only to pre-selected organizations. Applications not accepted.
Officers and Directors: William G. Pannill, Pres. and Treas.; Catherine Stuart Pannill, V.P.; William L. Pannill, Secy.
Employer Identification Number: 541268236

3194
Richard S. Reynolds Foundation
Reynolds Metals Bldg.
P.O. Box 27003
Richmond 23261
Application address: David P. Reynolds, 6601 West Broad St., Richmond, VA 23261; Tel.: (804) 281-4801

Incorporated in 1965 in VA.
Donor(s): Julia L. Reynolds.†
Financial data (yr. ended 6/30/87): Assets, $28,427,298 (M); gifts received, $15,158; expenditures, $801,010, including $701,000 for 22 grants (high: $500,000; low: $1,000).
Purpose and activities: Support for higher and secondary education, health, hospitals, and museums.
Limitations: Giving primarily in VA.
Application information:
Initial approach: Letter
Deadline(s): None
Officers and Directors: David P. Reynolds, Pres.; Mrs. Glenn R. Martin, V.P.; Richard S. Reynolds III, Secy.; William G. Reynolds, Jr., Treas.
Number of staff: None.
Employer Identification Number: 546037003

3195
Reynolds Metals Company Foundation
P.O. Box 27003
Richmond 23261-7003 (804) 281-2222

Foundation established around 1978.
Donor(s): Reynolds Metals Co.
Financial data (yr. ended 12/31/87): Assets, $1,750,847 (M); expenditures, $726,933, including $723,890 for 169 grants (high: $150,000; low: $100; average: $200-$75,000).
Purpose and activities: Emphasis on higher education, including an employee matching gift program, and community funds; support also for cultural programs, hospitals and health associations, youth agencies, and civic affairs.
Types of support: Employee matching gifts, building funds, scholarship funds, special projects.
Limitations: Giving primarily in areas of company operations, with emphasis on Richmond, VA.
Application information: Application form required.
Initial approach: Letter
Deadline(s): None
Write: Janice H. Bailey, Admin.
Officers: William O. Bourke,* Chair. and C.E.O.; John M. Noonan, Pres.; R. Bern Crowl,* Exec. V.P. and C.F.O.; John H. Galea,* Sr. V.P.; James E. Hertz,* V.P.; Donald T. Cowles, Secy.; Julian H. Taylor, Treas.
Directors:* Richard G. Holder.
Employer Identification Number: 541084698

3196
C. E. Richardson Benevolent Foundation
74 West Main St., Rm. 211
P.O. Box 1120
Pulaski 24301 (703) 980-6628
Additional tel.: (703) 980-1704

Established in 1979.
Financial data (yr. ended 5/31/88): Assets, $2,526,963 (M); expenditures, $163,142, including $139,400 for 37 grants (high: $40,000; low: $300).
Purpose and activities: Support for programs for needy children, aged people, and indigent or handicapped persons, and for private colleges and universities; support also for cultural programs.
Limitations: Giving limited to thirty miles north and south of Interstate 81 from Lexington to Abingdon, VA. No grants to individuals.
Publications: Program policy statement, application guidelines.
Application information: Application form required.
Initial approach: Letter or telephone
Copies of proposal: 1
Deadline(s): 1 month after the date of the published public notice; is stated in the notice, usually Sept. 15
Write: Betty S. King, Secy.
Officer: Betty S. King, Secy.
Trustees: James D. Miller, Annie S. Muire, James C. Turk.
Number of staff: 1 part-time support.
Employer Identification Number: 510227549

3197
Greater Richmond Community Foundation
4001 Fitzhugh Ave.
P.O. Box 11553
Richmond 23230 (804) 353-3406

Established in 1968 in VA.

Financial data (yr. ended 12/31/87): Assets, $3,514,690 (M); gifts received, $1,326,638; expenditures, $256,583, including $195,731 for 50 grants (high: $69,000; low: $100; average: $3,500-$5,000) and $200 for 1 grant to an individual.
Purpose and activities: Giving for charitable purposes.
Types of support: Technical assistance, renovation projects, emergency funds, equipment, general purposes, matching funds, seed money, special projects.
Limitations: Giving limited to metropolitan Richmond, VA. No grants for annual campaigns, deficit financing, or land acquisition.
Publications: Annual report, application guidelines, financial statement, newsletter, informational brochure.
Application information: Application form required.
Initial approach: Telephone or proposal
Copies of proposal: 1
Deadline(s): Jan. 15, Apr. 15, July 15 and Oct. 15
Board meeting date(s): Quarterly
Final notification: 60 days
Write: Darcy S. Oman, Exec. Dir.
Officers: Paul H. Riley, Chair.; Frank G. Louthah, Vice-Chair.; Wallace Stettinius, Vice-Chair.; Frances H. Rosi, Secy.; Robert L. Thalhimer, Treas.; Darcy S. Oman, Exec. Dir.; William L.S. Rowe, General Counsel.
Number of staff: 1 full-time professional; 1 part-time support.
Employer Identification Number: 237009135

3198
Robins Foundation
1516 Coggins Point Rd.
Hopewell 23860 (804) 458-2938

Estalished in 1957 in VA.
Financial data (yr. ended 12/31/87): Assets, $1,279,361 (M); expenditures, $41,470, including $39,500 for 6 grants (high: $35,000; low: $500).
Purpose and activities: Support for hospitals, youth organizations, education, cultural programs, and social services.
Application information:
Initial approach: Letter
Write: H.C. Townes, Secy.-Treas.
Officers and Directors: E.C. Robins, Pres.; E.B. Heilman, V.P.; H.C. Townes, Secy.-Treas.; A.B. Marchant, E.R. Porter, E.C. Robins, Jr., L.M. Robins.
Employer Identification Number: 540784484

3199
Sovran Foundation, Inc.
c/o Trust Dept., Sovran Bank, N.A.
P.O. Box 26903
Richmond 23261 (804) 788-2963

Incorporated in 1966 in VA.
Donor(s): Sovran Financial Corp.
Financial data (yr. ended 12/31/87): Assets, $1,253,162 (M); gifts received, $1,198,154; expenditures, $2,135,455, including $1,464,172 for 357 grants (high: $185,000; low: $100; average: $500-$25,000) and $115,433 for employee matching gifts.
Purpose and activities: Emphasis on higher education, economic education, health, the arts and culture, civic programs, and youth activities; social services supported through the United Way.
Types of support: Employee matching gifts, continuing support, annual campaigns, building funds, equipment, land acquisition, endowment funds, matching funds.
Limitations: Giving limited to communities in which the company has facilities, with emphasis on VA. No grants to individuals, or for scholarships or fellowships; no operating funds for United Way agencies; no loans.
Publications: Program policy statement, application guidelines.
Application information:
Initial approach: Letter
Copies of proposal: 1
Deadline(s): May 15 and Oct. 15
Board meeting date(s): July and Jan.
Write: Elizabeth D. Seaman, Secy.-Treas.
Officers: Clifford A. Cutchins III, Pres.; C. Coleman McGehee, V.P.; Elizabeth D. Seaman, Secy.-Treas.
Trustee: Sovran Financial Corp.
Employer Identification Number: 546066961

3200
Charles G. Thalhimer and Family Foundation
615 East Broad St.
Richmond 23219 (804) 643-4211

Established in 1976 in VA.
Donor(s): Members of the Thalhimer family.
Financial data (yr. ended 10/31/87): Assets, $2,055,516 (M); expenditures, $186,509, including $142,360 for 41 grants (high: $80,125; low: $25).
Purpose and activities: Giving primarily for cultural activities and higher education; support also for civic affairs.
Limitations: Giving primarily in VA. No grants to individuals.
Application information:
Initial approach: Letter
Deadline(s): None
Write: Charles Thalhimer, Pres.
Officers and Directors: Charles G. Thalhimer, Pres.; Charles G. Thalhimer, Jr., V.P.; Harry R. Thalhimer, V.P.; William B. Thalhimer, Jr., V.P.; Rhoda R. Thalhimer, Secy.-Treas.; Barbara J. Thalhimer.
Employer Identification Number: 546047108

3201
Thalhimer Brothers Foundation
615 East Broad St.
Richmond 23219 (804) 643-4211

Incorporated in 1950 in VA.
Donor(s): Thalhimer Brothers, Inc., Carter Hawley Hale Stores, Inc.
Financial data (yr. ended 11/30/88): Assets, $1,177 (M); gifts received, $289,000; expenditures, $288,326, including $285,343 for 78 grants (high: $41,000; low: $250).
Purpose and activities: Emphasis on community development, higher education, environmental activities, Jewish welfare funds, cultural programs, and youth.
Limitations: Giving primarily in Richmond, VA. No grants to individuals.
Application information: Applications not accepted.
Initial approach: Letter
Copies of proposal: 1
Deadline(s): None
Write: James E. Branson, Secy.-Treas.
Officers and Directors: William B. Thalhimer, Jr., Pres.; Michael C. Weisberg, V.P.; James E. Branson, Secy.-Treas.; William B. Thalhimer III.
Number of staff: None.
Employer Identification Number: 546047107

3202
William B. Thalhimer, Jr. and Family Foundation
P.O. Box 26724
Richmond 23261 (804) 643-4211

Incorporated in 1953 in VA.
Donor(s): William B. Thalhimer, Jr., Barbara J. Thalhimer.
Financial data (yr. ended 10/31/87): Assets, $1,779,150 (M); expenditures, $174,388, including $155,750 for 49 grants (high: $37,000; low: $20).
Purpose and activities: Giving for Jewish welfare funds and temple support; grants also for cultural progams and higher education.
Limitations: Giving primarily in VA.
Application information:
Initial approach: Letter
Deadline(s): None
Write: William B. Thalhimer, Jr., Pres.
Officers and Directors: William B. Thalhimer, Jr., Pres.; Charles G. Thalhimer, V.P.; Robert L. Thalhimer, V.P.; William B. Thalhimer III, V.P.; Barbara J. Thalhimer, Secy.-Treas.; Rhoda R. Thalhimer.
Employer Identification Number: 546047110

3203
The J. Edwin Treakle Foundation, Inc.
P.O. Box 1157
Gloucester 23061 (804) 693-3101

Incorporated in 1963 in VA.
Donor(s): J. Edwin Treakle.†
Financial data (yr. ended 4/30/88): Assets, $3,449,012 (L); expenditures, $219,886, including $145,000 for grants (high: $20,500; low: $200).
Purpose and activities: Emphasis on Protestant church support, community development, youth agencies, higher education, hospitals, and cultural organizations.
Types of support: Annual campaigns, building funds, capital campaigns, continuing support, equipment, general purposes, scholarship funds.
Limitations: Giving primarily in VA. No grants to individuals.
Application information: Application form required.
Copies of proposal: 1
Deadline(s): Submit proposal between Jan. 1 and Apr. 30
Board meeting date(s): Thursday after 2nd Monday in Feb., Apr., June, Aug., Oct., and Dec.
Write: John W. Cooke, Treas.

Officers and Directors: James B. Martin, Pres.; Harry E. Dunn, V.P.; J. Kirkland Jarvis, Secy.; John W. Cooke, Treas.
Number of staff: 2 part-time support.
Employer Identification Number: 546051620

3204
The Truland Foundation
1511 North 22nd St.
Arlington 22209

Trust established in 1954 in VA.
Donor(s): Truland of Florida, Inc., and members of the Truland family.
Financial data (yr. ended 3/31/88): Assets, $2,217,871 (M); gifts received, $1,500; expenditures, $114,653, including $107,139 for 62 grants (high: $70,000; low: $10).
Purpose and activities: Emphasis on conservation; some support also for community welfare, higher education, and the arts.
Limitations: Giving primarily in VA.
Application information: Applications not accepted.
Trustees: Alice O. Truland, Robert W. Truland, Walter R. Truland.
Employer Identification Number: 546037172

3205
Universal Leaf Foundation
Hamilton St. at Broad
P.O. Box 25099
Richmond 23260 (804) 359-9311

Established in 1975 in VA.
Donor(s): Universal Leaf Tobacco Co., Inc.
Financial data (yr. ended 6/30/87): Assets, $714,381 (M); gifts received, $340,000; expenditures, $411,246, including $358,561 for 175 grants (high: $30,000; low: $75) and $49,940 for 147 employee matching gifts.
Purpose and activities: Emphasis on higher education, community funds, museums, youth agencies, health, medical research, and the arts.
Types of support: Annual campaigns, building funds, capital campaigns, emergency funds, employee matching gifts, operating budgets, renovation projects, research, technical assistance.
Limitations: Giving primarily in VA.
Publications: Annual report.
Application information:
Initial approach: Letter of inquiry
Deadline(s): None
Final notification: 3 to 4 weeks
Write: Nancy G. Powell, Mgr., Corp. Relations
Officers: T.R. Towers, Pres.; W.L. Chandler,* V.P.; F.V. Lowden III, Secy.; O. Kemp Dozier, Treas.
Directors:* Harry H. Harrell, J.M. White.
Employer Identification Number: 510162337

3206
Virginia Electric & Power Company Corporate Giving Program
P.O. Box 26666
Richmond 23261 (804) 771-4417
Special address for applications: 10 South Sixth Street, Richmond VA 23261

Financial data (yr. ended 12/31/88): Total giving, $2,381,551, including $1,564,325 for 653 grants (high: $90,000; low: $50; average: $500-$2,500), $207,326 for 2,107 employee matching gifts, $409,387 for company-administered programs and $200,513 for 77 in-kind gifts.
Purpose and activities: Supports civic affairs, child welfare, higher education, race relations programs, science, youth, United Funds, environmental issues, hospitals, music, theater, the performing arts, and museums.
Types of support: General purposes, capital campaigns, employee matching gifts, building funds, in-kind gifts.
Limitations: Giving primarily in areas where the home offices and service areas are located. No support for tax-supported organizations or national health organizations.
Publications: Informational brochure (including application guidelines).
Application information: Include narrative/letter, complete budget, 501(c)(3), application form, board list, donor list and audited financial statement. Application form required.
Initial approach: Complete proposal with budget
Copies of proposal: 1
Deadline(s): Jan. is the best time to apply
Final notification: 4 weeks
Write: Thomas M. Hogg, Contribs. Admin.
Number of staff: 8 full-time professional; 1 full-time support.

3207
Washington Forrest Foundation
2300 Ninth St. South
Arlington 22204 (703) 920-3688

Incorporated in 1968 in VA.
Donor(s): Benjamin M. Smith.†
Financial data (yr. ended 6/30/88): Assets, $6,560,751 (M); expenditures, $596,359, including $299,632 for 80 grants (high: $20,006; low: $100; average: $500-$5,000).
Purpose and activities: Emphasis on the arts and humanities, education, youth programs, health, religion, science, and welfare.
Types of support: General purposes, operating budgets, continuing support, annual campaigns, seed money, emergency funds, building funds, equipment, matching funds, special projects, capital campaigns, renovation projects, scholarship funds.
Limitations: Giving primarily in northern VA. No grants to individuals, or fellowships; no loans or multi-year pledges.
Publications: Program policy statement.
Application information: Application form required.
Initial approach: Letter or telephone
Copies of proposal: 1
Deadline(s): Contact foundation
Board meeting date(s): Contact foundation
Final notification: 2 weeks
Write: Lindsey Peete, Exec. Dir.
Officers: Margaret S. Peete, Pres.; Leslie Ariail, V.P.; Benjamin M. Smith, Jr., Secy.-Treas.; Lindsey Peete, Exec. Dir.
Members: James McKinney.
Number of staff: 1 part-time professional; 1 part-time support.
Employer Identification Number: 237002944

3208
Wheat Foundation
707 East Main St.
Richmond 23219 (804) 649-2311

Established in 1959.
Donor(s): Wheat First Securities, Inc.
Financial data (yr. ended 3/31/88): Assets, $924,941 (M); gifts received, $651,680; expenditures, $426,819, including $418,034 for 143 grants (high: $100,000; low: $500).
Purpose and activities: Support for higher and secondary education, hospitals, and health services.
Types of support: Building funds, professorships, endowment funds, capital campaigns, renovation projects, scholarship funds.
Limitations: Giving primarily in VA, WV, NC, DC, and PA. No grants to individuals or for operating funds; no loans.
Application information:
Initial approach: Letter, telephone, and/or personal visit
Copies of proposal: 1
Deadline(s): None
Board meeting date(s): Feb., May, Aug., and Nov.
Final notification: Within 30 days following board meeting
Write: William V. Daniel, V.P.
Officers and Trustees: James C. Wheat, Jr., Pres.; William V. Daniel, V.P. and Treas.; John L. McElroy, Jr., V.P.; A. Jack Brent II, Secy.; William B. Lucas, Marshall B. Wishnack.
Employer Identification Number: 546047119

WASHINGTON

3209
Norman Archibald Charitable Foundation
c/o First Interstate Bank of Washington
P.O. Box 21927
Seattle 98111 (206) 292-3543

Established in 1976 in WA.
Donor(s): Norman Archibald.†
Financial data (yr. ended 9/30/88): Assets, $5,578,480 (M); expenditures, $343,326, including $264,000 for 85 grants (high: $12,500; low: $500).
Purpose and activities: Support for youth and child development programs; support also for medical research, education, the arts, and conservation.
Types of support: General purposes, seed money, building funds, equipment, land acquisition, conferences and seminars, program-related investments, publications, renovation projects, research, special projects.
Limitations: Giving primarily in the Puget Sound region of WA. No support for government entities or private foundations. No grants to individuals, or for deficit financing,

endowment funds, scholarships, and fellowships; no loans.
Publications: Annual report, application guidelines.
Application information:
Initial approach: Letter
Copies of proposal: 3
Deadline(s): None
Write: Lawrence E. Miller, Asst. V.P. and Trust Officer, First Interstate Bank of Washington
Advisors: Durwood Alkire, Lowell P. Mickelwait, Stuart H. Prestrud.
Trustee: First Interstate Bank of Washington.
Number of staff: None.
Employer Identification Number: 911098014

3210
E. K. and Lillian F. Bishop Foundation
c/o Security Pacific Bank Washington, Charitable Srvcs.
P.O. Box 3917, T25-2
Seattle 98124 (206) 621-4445
Scholarship application address: Bishop Scholarship Committee, c/o Security Pacific Bank Washington, Grays Harbor Branch, P.O. Box 149, Aberdeen, WA 99520

Trust established in 1971 in WA.
Donor(s): E.K. Bishop,† Lillian F. Bishop.†
Financial data (yr. ended 4/30/88): Assets, $14,673,636 (M); expenditures, $1,041,766, including $815,105 for 60 grants (high: $100,000; low: $600; average: $5,000-$30,000) and $82,130 for 61 grants to individuals.
Purpose and activities: To promote the welfare of youths, ages 0 to 23, through scholarships and grants to educational, cultural, and welfare organizations.
Types of support: Seed money, building funds, equipment, matching funds, general purposes, student aid.
Limitations: Giving primarily in WA, with emphasis on Grays Harbor County; scholarship applicants must have resided in Grays Harbor County at least a year immediately before applying. No grants for endowment funds, research, or fellowships; no loans.
Publications: Program policy statement, application guidelines.
Application information: Application form provided for scholarships. Application form required.
Initial approach: Letter
Copies of proposal: 5
Deadline(s): Scholarship applications must be postmarked by June 1
Board meeting date(s): Jan., Apr., July, and Oct.
Final notification: 2 to 3 months
Write: Thomas J. Nevers
Directors: Isabelle Lamb, Gladys Phillips, Janet T. Skadon.
Trustee: Security Pacific Bank Washington.
Number of staff: None.
Employer Identification Number: 916116724

3211
The Bloedel Foundation, Inc.
7501 Northeast Dolphin Dr.
Bainbridge Island 98110

Incorporated in 1952 in DE.
Donor(s): Prentice Bloedel, J.H. Bloedel,† Eulalie Bloedel Schneider, Virginia Merrill Bloedel.
Financial data (yr. ended 6/30/87): Assets, $4,032,884 (M); expenditures, $170,977, including $140,080 for 61 grants (high: $29,916; low: $100).
Purpose and activities: Giving for museums, the performing arts, and Protestant church support; some support for secondary education, social agencies and conservation.
Limitations: Giving primarily in WA. No grants to individuals.
Application information:
Initial approach: Letter
Deadline(s): None
Write: Jack E. Gordon, Pres.
Officers and Trustees: Virginia Bloedel Wright, Chair.; John E. Gordon, Pres.; John F. Hall, Secy.; Prentice Bloedel, Virginia Merrill Bloedel, Maxwell Carlson, Solomon Katz, Eulalie Bloedel Schneider.
Employer Identification Number: 916035027

3212
The Boeing Company Charitable Trust
P.O. Box 3707, M/S 18/83
Seattle 98124 (206) 292-3543

Trust established in 1964 in WA as successor to the Boeing Airplane Company Charitable Trust, established in 1952.
Donor(s): The Boeing Co.
Financial data (yr. ended 12/31/88): Assets, $25,000,000 (M); expenditures, $15,700,000 for grants (high: $1,900,000), $800,000 for employee matching gifts and $2,600,000 for 150 in-kind gifts.
Purpose and activities: Emphasis on education at all levels, cultural programs, and human services.
Types of support: Employee matching gifts, building funds, capital campaigns, equipment, exchange programs, fellowships, matching funds, operating budgets, professorships, renovation projects, scholarship funds, seed money, special projects.
Limitations: Giving primarily in areas of company operations. No grants to individuals.
Publications: Corporate giving report.
Application information: Contributes only to preselected organizations. Applications not accepted.
Copies of proposal: 1
Deadline(s): None
Board meeting date(s): 4 to 6 weeks
Write: Joe A. Taller, Corporate Dir. Public and Community Affairs
Number of staff: 1 full-time professional.
Employer Identification Number: 916056738

3213
The Boeing Company Corporate Giving Program
P.O. Box 3707, M/S 18/83
Seattle 98124 (206) 655-6679

Purpose and activities: Supports the aged, child welfare, community funds, the handicapped, programs fighting delinquency and drug abuse, education, including early childhood, minority, and vocational education, mathematics, literacy, science and technology, business, performing arts, museums, and the humanities. Support also for law and justice and community services; also in-kind giving.
Types of support: Building funds, capital campaigns, employee matching gifts, equipment, fellowships, matching funds, professorships, renovation projects, research, scholarship funds, in-kind gifts.
Limitations: Giving primarily in Wichita, KS; Philadelphia, PA; and Seattle, WA, and other operating locations.
Publications: Corporate giving report.
Application information: Include description of project and complete proposal, with budget.
Initial approach: Query letter
Copies of proposal: 1
Deadline(s): None, but few grants approved during fourth quarter
Board meeting date(s): No regular schedule
Final notification: 2-4 weeks; will send rejection letter
Write: Joe A. Taller, Corp. Dir., Public and Community Affairs
Administrator: Joe A. Taller, Corp. Dir., Public and Community Affairs.
Number of staff: 3 full-time professional.

3214
Ben B. Cheney Foundation
First Interstate Plaza, Suite 1600
Tacoma 98402 (206) 572-2442

Incorporated in 1955 in WA.
Donor(s): Ben B. Cheney,† Marian Cheney Olrogg.†
Financial data (yr. ended 12/31/87): Assets, $16,381,843 (M); gifts received, $964,575; expenditures, $1,582,588, including $1,220,360 for 110 grants (high: $50,000; low: $1,300; average: $1,500-$20,000).
Purpose and activities: Giving primarily for education, health, social services, youth, community development, and cultural programs.
Types of support: Seed money, building funds, equipment, general purposes, scholarship funds, special projects, emergency funds.
Limitations: Giving limited to WA and OR. No support for religious organizations for sectarian purposes. No grants to individuals, or for operating budgets; no loans.
Publications: Application guidelines, informational brochure.
Application information: Application form required.
Initial approach: Letter
Copies of proposal: 4
Deadline(s): 4 weeks prior to board meetings
Board meeting date(s): May, Oct., and Dec.
Final notification: Within 3 months
Write: Elgin E. Olrogg, Exec. Dir.

Officers and Trustees: Francis I. Cheney, Pres.; R. Gene Grant, V.P.; John F. Hansler, Secy.; Elgin E. Olrogg, Treas. and Exec. Dir.
Number of staff: 2 full-time professional; 1 full-time support.
Employer Identification Number: 916053760
Recent arts and culture grants:
Centrum Foundation, Port Townsend, WA, $10,000. For festival of American Fiddle Tunes. 1987.
Eagle Point Historical Society, Eagle Point, OR, $10,000. To relocate Bridge. 1987.
Givan Park, Medford, OR, $28,200. To rehabilitate Givan home and provide for resident caretaker. 1987.
Gonzaga University, Spokane, WA, $5,000. For artwork for Jepson Center School of Business Administration. 1987.
High Desert Museum, Bend, OR, $25,000. For Overland Migration Interpretive Exhibit. 1987.
Lakewold Gardens, Tacoma, WA, $50,000. To make gardens accessible to public. 1987.
Northwest Trek Wildlife Park, Eatonville, WA, $25,000. For conversion of Cheney Pavilion into Children's Activity Area. 1987.
Pantages Center for the Performing Arts, Tacoma, WA, $12,160. For Glenn Miller performance. 1987.
Peter Britt Gardens Music and Arts Festival Association, Medford, OR, $50,000. For permanent seating at outdoor theatre. 1987.
Tacoma Actors Guild, Tacoma, WA, $10,000. For musical production for 87-88 Season. 1987.
Tacoma Symphony, Tacoma, WA, $15,000. To sponsor musical fund raising event. 1987.
Tacoma, City of, Tacoma, WA, $25,000. For Locomotive Monument Sculpture. 1987.
Tall Ships Restoration Society, Aberdeen, WA, $50,000. For construction of replica Lady Washington. 1987.
Washington State Historical Society, Tacoma, WA, $5,000. For Magnificent Voyagers. 1987.
Whale Museum, Friday Harbor, WA, $25,000. For acquisition of building. 1987.

3215
Comstock Foundation
819 Washington Trust Financial Center
Spokane 99204 (509) 747-1527

Trust established in 1950 in WA.
Donor(s): Josie Comstock Shadle.†
Financial data (yr. ended 12/31/88): Assets, $11,769,254 (M); expenditures, $1,001,478, including $937,546 for 68 grants (high: $100,000; low: $325; average: $300-$35,000).
Purpose and activities: Emphasis on capital grants to recreational facilities and other community development projects, social agencies, aid to the handicapped, child welfare, and youth agencies. Giving also for arts, civic affairs, and higher education.
Types of support: Building funds, equipment, land acquisition, scholarship funds, research, general purposes, matching funds.
Limitations: Giving limited to Spokane County, WA. No grants to individuals, or for endowment funds or operating budgets; no loans. In general, no grants payable for reserve purposes, deficit financing, publications, films, emergency funds, conferences, or travel.
Publications: Informational brochure, program policy statement, application guidelines.
Application information: Application form required.
Initial approach: Proposal
Copies of proposal: 1
Deadline(s): None
Board meeting date(s): Weekly
Final notification: 10 days
Write: Horton Herman, Trustee
Trustees: Harold W. Coffin, Horton Herman, Luke G. Williams.
Number of staff: 1 part-time support.
Employer Identification Number: 916028504

3216
Harriet Cheney Cowles Foundation, Inc.
West 999 Riverside Ave., Rm. 626
Spokane 99201

Incorporated in 1944 in WA.
Donor(s): Spokane Chronicle Co., Cowles Publishing Co., Inland Empire Paper Co.
Financial data (yr. ended 12/31/87): Assets, $5,508,857 (M); gifts received, $300,000; expenditures, $355,935, including $333,031 for 4 grants (high: $250,000; low: $5,000).
Purpose and activities: Support for a historical society, orchestra, YMCA, and a cathedral.
Types of support: Endowment funds, capital campaigns.
Limitations: Giving primarily in Spokane, WA.
Application information: Contributes only to pre-selected organizations. Applications not accepted.
Officers and Trustees: William H. Cowles III, Pres.; James P. Cowles, V.P.; M.K. Nielsen, Treas.
Employer Identification Number: 910689268

3217
Fales Foundation Trust
The Bank of California
P.O. Box 3123
Seattle 98114

Established in 1986 in WA.
Financial data (yr. ended 1/31/88): Assets, $2,458,088 (M); expenditures, $172,630, including $134,714 for 22 grants (high: $13,800; low: $500).
Purpose and activities: Support primarily for community development, health and cultural programs, and the arts.
Types of support: Operating budgets.
Limitations: Giving limited to WA.
Trustees: Ward L. Sax, The Bank of California, N.A.
Employer Identification Number: 916087669

3218
Forest Foundation
820 A St., Suite 1276
Tacoma 98402 (206) 627-1634
Application address: 820 A St., Suite 545, Tacoma, WA 98402; Tel.: (206) 627-1634

Incorporated in 1962 in WA.
Donor(s): C. Davis Weyerhaeuser, William T. Weyerhaeuser.
Financial data (yr. ended 10/31/88): Assets, $19,448,823 (M); expenditures, $993,576, including $649,099 for 71 grants (high: $87,900; low: $1,000).
Purpose and activities: Giving primarily for social services, child development and welfare, family services, the handicapped, Native Americans, health and medical research, the performing arts, and museums.
Types of support: Building funds, equipment, operating budgets, emergency funds, land acquisition.
Limitations: Giving primarily in western WA, with emphasis on Pierce County and southwest Washington. No support for religious organizations for religious purposes. No grants to individuals, or for endowment funds, research, scholarships, or fellowships; no loans.
Publications: Program policy statement, application guidelines.
Application information:
Initial approach: Letter or proposal
Copies of proposal: 5
Deadline(s): None
Board meeting date(s): At least 6 times per year
Final notification: 60 to 90 days
Write: Frank D. Underwood, Exec. Dir.
Officers: Gail T. Weyerhaeuser,* Pres. and Treas.; Annette B. Weyerhaeuser,* V.P.; J. Thomas McCully, Secy.; Frank D. Underwood, Exec. Dir.
Directors:* C. Davis Weyerhaeuser, William T. Weyerhaeuser.
Number of staff: None.
Employer Identification Number: 916020514

3219
The Foster Foundation
1111 Third Ave., Suite 2210
Seattle 98101

Established in 1984 in WA.
Donor(s): Evelyn W. Foster.
Financial data (yr. ended 12/31/87): Assets, $4,834,634 (M); gifts received, $3,789,026; expenditures, $202,614, including $198,500 for 8 grants (high: $150,000; low: $5,000).
Purpose and activities: Support for cultural programs, education, social services, health and the environment.
Types of support: Seed money, building funds, equipment, research, matching funds, special projects.
Limitations: Giving primarily in the Pacific Northwest and Alaska. No grants for fundraising, endowment funds, unrestricted operating funds; no loans.
Application information:
Initial approach: Letter
Final notification: 3 months
Write: Jill Goodsell, Admin.
Directors: Jill Goodsell Admin., Evelyn W. Foster, Michael G. Foster, Pamela Foster, Thomas B. Foster.
Employer Identification Number: 911265474

3220
Gottfried & Mary Fuchs Foundation
c/o The Bank of California
P.O. Box 1917
Tacoma 98401 (206) 591-2549

Trust established in 1960 in WA.
Donor(s): Gottfried Fuchs,† Mary Fuchs.†
Financial data (yr. ended 12/31/87): Assets, $9,150,000 (M); expenditures, $555,215, including $438,243 for 64 grants (high: $22,000; low: $500).
Purpose and activities: Priority of support for charitable, educational, scientific, literary or religious purposes not normally financed by tax funds; emphasis on child welfare and youth agencies, higher and secondary education, cultural programs, hospitals, and food programs. Prefers funding special capital or services projects rather than operating budgets.
Types of support: Continuing support, annual campaigns, emergency funds, building funds, equipment, scholarship funds, research, operating budgets, matching funds, special projects, capital campaigns.
Limitations: Giving primarily in Tacoma, Pierce County, and the lower Puget Sound area of WA. No grants to individuals.
Publications: Application guidelines.
Application information: Application form required.
Initial approach: Letter
Copies of proposal: 5
Deadline(s): 3 weeks prior to board meetings
Board meeting date(s): Apr., Aug., and Nov.
Write: Harlan Sachs, V.P. and Trust Officer, The Bank of California
Trustee: The Bank of California, N.A.
Number of staff: 1 part-time professional.
Employer Identification Number: 916022284

3221
Glaser Foundation, Inc.
P.O. Box N
Edmonds 98020 (206) 546-6149

Incorporated in 1952 in WA.
Donor(s): Paul F. Glaser.†
Financial data (yr. ended 11/30/87): Assets, $4,900,000 (M); expenditures, $235,000, including $218,000 for 50 grants (high: $12,000; low: $500; average: $3,000-$5,000).
Purpose and activities: Support for direct-line service health agencies, and agencies serving children, youth, the handicapped, the aged, and the indigent; support also for some arts organizations.
Types of support: Emergency funds, matching funds, special projects, research, seed money.
Limitations: Giving primarily in the Puget Sound area, WA. No grants to individuals, or for general purposes, building or endowment funds, scholarships, fellowships, publications, or conferences; no loans.
Publications: Program policy statement, application guidelines.
Application information: Request copy of guidelines before applying for a grant.
Initial approach: Letter
Copies of proposal: 2
Deadline(s): 3 weeks prior to next board meeting
Board meeting date(s): Jan., Mar., May, July, Sept., and Nov.
Final notification: 2 weeks after meeting
Write: R.W. Carlstrom, Exec. Dir.
Officers and Directors: R.N. Brandenburg, Pres.; Janet L. Politeo, V.P.; R. Thomas Olson, Secy.; P.F. Patrick, Treas.; R.W. Carlstrom, Exec. Dir.
Number of staff: None.
Employer Identification Number: 916028694

3222
Joshua Green Foundation, Inc.
1414 Fourth Ave.
P.O. Box 720
Seattle 98111 (206) 344-2285

Trust established in 1956 in WA.
Donor(s): Joshua Green, Mrs. Joshua Green.
Financial data (yr. ended 12/31/87): Assets, $5,075,264 (M); gifts received, $14,800; expenditures, $272,121, including $269,423 for 60 grants (high: $80,000; low: $200; average: $1,000-$3,000).
Purpose and activities: Emphasis on higher and secondary education, community funds, cultural programs, health associations and services, and church support.
Limitations: Giving primarily in the Seattle, WA, area. No grants to individuals, or for scholarships or fellowships; no loans.
Application information:
Initial approach: Proposal
Copies of proposal: 1
Board meeting date(s): Mar., July, Sept., and Dec.
Officers and Trustees:* Joshua Green III,* Pres.; Charles P. Burnett III,* V.P.; Charles E. Riley,* V.P.; Wendy Cadman, Secy.; Steven E. Carlson, Treas.
Employer Identification Number: 916050748

3223
GTE Northwest Corporate Giving Program
1800 41 St.
Everett 98206 (206) 261-5321
Special address for applications: P.O. Box 1003 (1-COM), Everett, WA 98201

Financial data (yr. ended 12/31/88): Total giving, $581,000, including $329,500 for grants, $28,000 for grants to individuals, $85,500 for employee matching gifts and $138,000 for in-kind gifts.
Purpose and activities: Support for historic preservation, museums, music, performing arts, theater, education, literacy, health and heart disease, hospitals, volunteerism, community development, homeless, disadvantaged, drug abuse, hunger, and housing.
Types of support: Annual campaigns, building funds, capital campaigns, equipment, fellowships, lectureships, matching funds, employee-related scholarships, technical assistance, employee matching gifts.
Application information: Prefer written requests for information. Do not meet one-on-one with requestors, unless special information is required. Application form required.
Initial approach: Letter
Copies of proposal: 1
Deadline(s): May 1 of this year for consideration in budget for following year
Write: Marilyn Spoerhase, Community Affairs Mgr.
Administrator: Marilyn Spoerhase, Community Affairs Mgr.
Number of staff: 1 full-time professional.

3224
The Johnston Foundation
East 627 17th Ave.
Spokane 99203 (509) 838-2108

Trust established in 1948 in WA.
Donor(s): Eric Johnston.†
Financial data (yr. ended 12/31/87): Assets, $3,685,946 (L); expenditures, $242,408, including $203,535 for 44 grants (high: $25,000; low: $235).
Purpose and activities: Giving primarily for private higher and secondary education, youth agencies, and cultural programs.
Limitations: Giving limited to Spokane, WA, with the exception of independent education. No support for publicly supported educational institutions. No grants to individuals, or for scholarships or fellowships; no loans.
Publications: 990-PF.
Application information:
Initial approach: Telephone or letter
Copies of proposal: 1
Deadline(s): None
Board meeting date(s): Usually in Apr., June, Sept., and Dec.
Final notification: 3 months
Write: Mrs. William C. Fix, Treas.
Officers and Trustees: Mrs. Eric Johnston, Pres.; Mrs. Fred Hanson, Secy.; Mrs. William C. Fix, Treas.; William C. Fix, Fred Hanson, Maage LaCounte, Scott B. Lukins.
Number of staff: 2 part-time professional.
Employer Identification Number: 910749593

3225
Kreielsheimer Foundation Trust
c/o Bogle & Gates
Bank of California Center
Seattle 98164 (206) 682-5151
Additional application address: send 1 copy of proposal to Gary E. Grina, V.P., Seattle-First National Bank, P.O. Box 3586, Seattle, WA 98124

Established in 1979 in WA.
Donor(s): Leo T. Kreielsheimer,† Greye M. Kreielsheimer.†
Financial data (yr. ended 5/31/88): Assets, $29,072,903 (M); expenditures, $1,396,663 for 19 grants (high: $375,000; low: $1,000).
Purpose and activities: Giving for cultural programs, higher education, and hospitals; support also for a civic project.
Limitations: Giving limited to the Pacific Northwest, including western AK, and with emphasis on western WA. No support for religious or youth organizations. No grants to individuals.
Publications: Application guidelines.
Application information:
Initial approach: Proposal
Board meeting date(s): Semiannually

Final notification: Grants made within 30 days of the end of each calendar quarter
Write: Charles F. Osborn, Trustee
Trustees: Charles F. Osborn, Seattle-First National Bank.
Number of staff: None.
Employer Identification Number: 916233127

3226
Leuthold Foundation, Inc.
1006 Old National Bank Bldg.
Spokane 99201 (509) 624-3944

Incorporated in 1948 in WA.
Donor(s): Members of the Leuthold family.
Financial data (yr. ended 6/30/88): Assets, $6,509,524 (M); expenditures, $416,096, including $327,006 for 74 grants (high: $60,100; low: $30; average: $100-$10,000).
Purpose and activities: Giving primarily for youth agencies, hospitals, secondary and higher education, Protestant church support, community funds, and music.
Types of support: Operating budgets, continuing support, annual campaigns, building funds, matching funds, endowment funds, equipment, general purposes, scholarship funds.
Limitations: Giving limited to Spokane County, WA. No grants to individuals; no loans.
Publications: Application guidelines, program policy statement.
Application information: Application form required.
Initial approach: Letter
Copies of proposal: 1
Deadline(s): Submit proposal preferably in May or Nov.; deadlines June 15 and Nov. 15
Board meeting date(s): May and Dec.
Final notification: 1 week after board meets
Write: John H. Leuthold, Pres.
Officers and Trustees: John H. Leuthold, Pres.; Betty B. Leuthold, V.P.; O.M. Kimmel, Jr., Secy.-Treas.; Caroline E. Leuthold, Allan H. Toole.
Number of staff: 1 part-time support.
Employer Identification Number: 916028589

3227
Byron W. and Alice L. Lockwood Foundation
c/o Paul Cressman, Short & Cressman
Interstate Center, 999 Third Ave., 30th Fl.
Seattle 98104

Established in 1968 in WA.
Financial data (yr. ended 12/31/86): Assets, $8,928,694 (M); expenditures, $547,483, including $427,030 for 50 grants (high: $100,000; low: $1,000).
Purpose and activities: Support for health, culture, youth and social service organizations, and higher education.
Limitations: Giving primarily in Seattle, WA.
Officers and Trustees: Paul R. Cressman, Pres.; James R. Palmer, Secy.-Treas.; Margaret Whiteman.
Employer Identification Number: 910833426

3228
Lozier Foundation
P.O. Box 98769
Des Moines 98198

Established in 1986 in WA.
Donor(s): Allan G. Lozier.
Financial data (yr. ended 12/31/87): Assets, $3,395,265 (M); gifts received, $590,754; expenditures, $277,183, including $270,710 for grants.
Purpose and activities: Suppport primarily to organizations providing social services, youth organizations, and cultural institutions.
Limitations: Giving primarily in Omaha, NE.
Application information: Contributes only to pre-selected organizations. Applications not accepted.
Trustees: Sheri L. Andrews, Allan G. Lozier, Lee E. Schultz.
Employer Identification Number: 943027928

3229
Matlock Foundation
1201 Third Ave., Suite 4900
Seattle 98101-3009 (206) 224-5000

Incorporated in 1954 in WA.
Donor(s): Simpson Timber Co., Simpson Paper Co., Pacific Western Extruded Plastics Co.
Financial data (yr. ended 12/31/88): Expenditures, $1,439,583, including $1,402,757 for 390 grants (high: $45,600; low: $50; average: $500-$15,000) and $36,826 for 87 employee matching gifts.
Purpose and activities: Allocates funds for giving by Simpson Fund and Simpson Reed Fund to community funds and for scholarships; giving also for arts and cultural programs, other education, social service and youth agencies, and health services and hospitals.
Types of support: Seed money, general purposes, emergency funds, building funds, equipment, land acquisition, employee matching gifts, annual campaigns, capital campaigns, operating budgets, special projects, renovation projects.
Limitations: Giving primarily in CA, MI, OH, OR, PA, TX, and WA. No grants to individuals, or for endowments; no loans.
Application information: Application form required.
Initial approach: Letter
Copies of proposal: 1
Deadline(s): Submit application preferably one month before fund committee meetings
Board meeting date(s): Apr., June and Nov.
Final notification: 1 week following fund committee meeting
Write: Lin L. Smith
Officers: Joseph L. Leitzinger,* Pres.; Betty Y. Dykstra, Secy.; J. Thurston Roach, Treas.
Directors:* John J. Fannon, Robert B. Hutchinson, T.R. Ingham, Jr., Furman C. Moseley, Susan R. Moseley, Eleanor H. Reed, William G. Reed, Jr.
Number of staff: 4 part-time professional; 4 part-time support.
Employer Identification Number: 916029303

3230
A. B. and Flavia McEachern Foundation
c/o The Bank of California, N.A.
P.O. Box 3123
Seattle 98114 (206) 587-3697

Established in 1958 in WA.
Financial data (yr. ended 12/31/87): Assets, $1,392,876 (M); expenditures, $84,230, including $60,850 for 30 grants (high: $14,000; low: $125).
Purpose and activities: Giving primarily for Christian religious organizations, and cultural activities; support also for youth programs.
Types of support: Operating budgets.
Application information:
Initial approach: Letter
Deadline(s): None
Trustee: The Bank of California, N.A.
Employer Identification Number: 916113467

3231
Medina Foundation
1300 Norton Bldg.
801 Second Ave., Fl. 13
Seattle 98104 (206) 464-5231

Incorporated in 1948 in WA.
Financial data (yr. ended 12/31/87): Assets, $28,731,281 (M); expenditures, $1,474,036, including $1,170,714 for 108 grants (high: $60,300; low: $300).
Purpose and activities: Giving for direct service delivery programs for emergency food and shelter, to aid the handicapped, and to improve the effectiveness of eleemosynary and/or governmental organizations; support also for cultural programs, youth and child welfare, community development, and education.
Types of support: Emergency funds, building funds, equipment, technical assistance, operating budgets, seed money.
Limitations: Giving limited to the greater Puget Sound, WA, area, with emphasis on Seattle. No support for public institutions. No grants to individuals, or for endowment funds, research, scholarships, or matching gifts; no loans.
Publications: Informational brochure, program policy statement, application guidelines.
Application information: Application form required.
Initial approach: Letter
Deadline(s): None
Board meeting date(s): Monthly
Final notification: 30 to 60 days
Write: Gregory P. Barlow, Exec. Dir.
Officers: Norton Clapp,* Pres.; Samuel H. Brown,* V.P.; Linda J. Henry,* V.P.; Margaret Ames, Secy.; Gary MacLeod,* Treas.; Gregory P. Barlow, Exec. Dir.
Trustees:* James N. Clapp II, K. Elizabeth Clapp, Kristina H. Clapp, Matthew N. Clapp, Jr., Marion Hand, Patricia M. Henry, Anne M. Simons.
Number of staff: 1 full-time professional; 1 full-time support.
Employer Identification Number: 910745225

3232
The R. D. Merrill Foundation
1411 Fourth Ave. Bldg., Suite 1415
Seattle 98101 (206) 682-3939

Incorporated in 1953 in WA.
Donor(s): R.D. Merrill, R.D. Merrill Co.
Financial data (yr. ended 6/30/88): Assets, $2,551,171 (M); expenditures, $165,229, including $129,333 for 58 grants (high: $20,000; low: $100).
Purpose and activities: Giving primarily to a community foundation, an art museum, health services, theatres and other cultural organizations, and the urban environment.
Limitations: Giving primarily in WA.
Application information:
Deadline(s): None
Write: Lois Hawkins, Asst. Secy.
Officers and Directors: Virginia Merrill Bloedel, Chair.; Corydon Wagner, Jr., Pres.; Virginia Bloedel Wright, V.P. and Treas.; Justin M. Martin, V.P.; Wendy Wagner Weyerhaeuser, V.P.; W.J. Wright, Secy.; Eulalie Merrill Wagner.
Employer Identification Number: 916029949

3233
M. J. Murdock Charitable Trust
703 Broadway, Suite 710
Vancouver 98660 (206) 694-8415
Mailing address: P.O. Box 1618, Vancouver, WA 98668

Trust established in 1975 in WA.
Donor(s): Melvin Jack Murdock.†
Financial data (yr. ended 12/31/87): Assets, $189,504,613 (M); expenditures, $15,560,817, including $11,362,345 for 141 grants (high: $950,000; low: $2,500; average: $20,000-$150,000).
Purpose and activities: Support primarily for special projects or programs of private, non-profit charitable organizations aimed at the solution or prevention of significant problems with implications beyond the immediate geographical area and which are able to thrive after initial funding; support also for projects which address critical problems for the Portland, OR/Vancouver, WA area. Desirable characteristics include self-help, free enterprise concepts leading to greater self-sufficiency and capability for organizations and the people they serve, a strategy for using up-front money including assistance from other supporters, and evidence that the problem-solving effort will make an important difference. Giving primarily for higher education; also provides seed money for selected medical and scientific research programs which have been identified as major priorities. Grants usually for a limited time, one or two years.
Types of support: Seed money, building funds, equipment, research, special projects.
Limitations: Giving primarily in the Pacific Northwest, (WA, OR, ID, MT, and AK); support for community projects only in the Portland, OR/Vancouver, WA, area. No support for government programs; projects common to many organizations without distinguishing merit; sectarian or religious organizations whose principal activities are for the benefit of their own members; agencies served by United Way of Columbia-Willamette, except for approved special projects; or institutes which unfairly discriminate by race, ethnic origin, sex, or creed. No grants to individuals, or for annual campaigns, general support, continuing support, deficit financing, endowment funds, operating budgets, emergency funds, scholarships, fellowships, or matching gifts; no loans.
Publications: Annual report, informational brochure (including application guidelines).
Application information: Submit original plus 3 copies of non-research proposal, original plus 9 copies of research or technical proposal.
Initial approach: Letter or telephone
Deadline(s): None
Board meeting date(s): Monthly
Final notification: 3 to 6 months
Write: Ford A. Anderson II, Exec. Dir.
Officers: Ford A. Anderson II, Exec. Dir.
Trustees: James B. Castles, Walter P. Dyke, Lynwood W. Swanson.
Number of staff: 2 full-time professional; 1 part-time professional; 4 full-time support.
Employer Identification Number: 237456468
Recent arts and culture grants:
American Indian Institute, Bozeman, MT, $15,000. For American Indian Art Collection. 5/19/88.
Bigfork Center for the Performing Arts Foundation, Bigfork, MT, $75,000. For challenge grant for building campaign. 5/19/88.
Helena Arts Council, Helena, MT, $190,000. For support, partially matching, for Holter Museum of Art. 7/26/88.
High Desert Museum, Bend, OR, $225,000. For establishment of Professional Development Department. 8/25/88.
Naval Undersea Warfare Museum Foundation, DC, $150,000. For funds, partially matching, for completion of Tower Building. 7/26/88.
Oregon Public Broadcasting Foundation, Portland, OR, $750,000. To purchase and equip new broadcasting facility, contingent upon purchase of building by 6/30/90 and naming of Radio Broadcast Center for M. J. Murdock. 5/19/88.
Portland Civic Theater, Portland, OR, $75,000. For New Professional Children's Theater Company. 3/31/88.
Washington State Capitol Historical Association, Washington State Capital Museum, Olympia, WA, $25,000. For Washington Salutes Washington: The President and the State, State Centennial Project. 7/26/88.

3234
Murray Foundation
First Interstate Plaza, Suite 1750
Tacoma 98402 (206) 383-4911

Trust established in 1952 in WA.
Donor(s): L.T. Murray Trust.
Financial data (yr. ended 12/31/86): Assets, $2,950,000 (M); expenditures, $195,000, including $180,000 for 12 grants (high: $100,000; low: $500; average: $5,000).
Purpose and activities: Giving for higher and secondary education, hospitals, cultural programs, and community funds. Priority given to capital programs in the Puget Sound area.
Types of support: Building funds, capital campaigns, endowment funds, matching funds, publications, scholarship funds, special projects.
Limitations: Giving primarily in Tacoma and Pierce County, WA. No grants to individuals, or for endowment funds, research, scholarships, or fellowships; no loans.
Publications: 990-PF.
Application information:
Initial approach: Letter
Copies of proposal: 1
Board meeting date(s): Dec. and as required (3 to 4 times a year)
Write: Lowell Anne Butson, Exec. Dir.
Officers and Directors: Anne Murray Barbey, Pres.; L.T. Murray, Jr., V.P.; Charles F. Osborn, Secy.; Amy Lou Eckstrom, Treas.; Lowell Anne Butson, Exec. Dir.
Number of staff: 1 part-time professional.
Employer Identification Number: 510163345

3235
New Horizon Foundation
820 A St., Suite 545
Tacoma 98402 (206) 627-1634

Established in 1983 in WA.
Donor(s): Sequoia Foundation.
Financial data (yr. ended 10/31/86): Assets, $5,097 (M); gifts received, $695,000; expenditures, $725,919, including $622,000 for 93 grants (high: $50,000; low: $300; average: $11,000).
Purpose and activities: Giving primarily for social services, with an emphasis on food, shelter, and emergency aid programs; support also for arts and culture, education, the environment, community improvement, and mental health programs.
Types of support: Equipment, general purposes, operating budgets, renovation projects, special projects, matching funds.
Limitations: Giving primarily in western WA, with primary emphasis on Pierce County. No support for private foundations or operating foundations, or political organizations. No grants to individuals; no support for endowments, annual campaigns, debt reduction, film, publications, conferences or travel.
Publications: Application guidelines.
Application information:
Initial approach: Summary letter or proposal
Copies of proposal: 2
Deadline(s): None
Final notification: Between 30 and 60 days after submission of complete application
Write: Frank D. Underwood, Pres.
Officers and Directors: Frank D. Underwood, Pres. and Treas.; John F. Sherwood, V.P.; Elvin J. Vandeburg.
Employer Identification Number: 911228957

3236
The Norcliffe Fund
First Interstate Center, Suite 1006
999 Third Ave.
Seattle 98104 (206) 682-4820

Incorporated in 1952 in WA.
Donor(s): Theiline M. McCone.

Financial data (yr. ended 11/30/88): Assets, $17,907,345 (M); gifts received, $714,761; expenditures, $1,296,001, including $1,266,302 for 255 grants (high: $500,000; low: $10; average: $1,000-$5,000).
Purpose and activities: Emphasis on cultural programs, Roman Catholic church support and religious associations, hospitals, higher and secondary education, and historic preservation; support also for medical research, youth agencies, the aged, and conservation.
Types of support: Operating budgets, continuing support, annual campaigns, seed money, emergency funds, building funds, equipment, land acquisition, research, special projects, capital campaigns, conferences and seminars, general purposes, lectureships, renovation projects, scholarship funds.
Limitations: Giving primarily in the Pacific Northwest, especially Seattle, WA; some grants in CA and nationally. No grants to individuals, or for deficit financing, matching gifts, scholarships, or fellowships; no loans.
Publications: Program policy statement, application guidelines.
Application information:
Initial approach: Letter
Copies of proposal: 1
Deadline(s): None
Board meeting date(s): As required
Final notification: 6 to 8 weeks
Write: Theiline P. Scheumann, Pres.
Officers and Trustees: Theiline M. McCone,* Chair.; Theiline Scheumann, Pres.; Carol R. Peterson, Secy.; Mary Ellen Hughes,* Treas.; Virginia S. Helsell, Charles M. Pigott, James C. Pigott, Susan W. Pohl, Ann P. Wyckoff.*
Number of staff: 1 part-time support.
Employer Identification Number: 916029352

3237
PACCAR Foundation
c/o PACCAR, Inc.
P.O. Box 1518
Bellevue 98009 (206) 455-7400

Incorporated in 1951 in WA.
Donor(s): PACCAR, Inc.
Financial data (yr. ended 11/30/87): Assets, $2,014,876 (M); gifts received, $750,000; expenditures, $1,430,881, including $1,402,398 for 85 grants (high: $264,850; low: $500).
Purpose and activities: Support for civic organizations, community funds, higher educational institutions, cultural programs, youth agencies, and hospitals.
Types of support: Employee matching gifts, annual campaigns, capital campaigns.
Limitations: Giving primarily in areas of company operations, particularly King County, WA. No grants to individuals, or for scholarships or fellowships.
Application information:
Initial approach: Proposal
Copies of proposal: 1
Deadline(s): None
Board meeting date(s): Quarterly; dates vary
Final notification: 2 to 3 months
Write: E.A. Carpenter, V.P.
Officers: Charles M. Pigott,* Pres.; E.A. Carpenter, V.P. and Treas.; G. Glen Morie, Secy.
Directors:* J.M. Dunn, J.M. Fluke, Jr., Harold J. Haynes, J.C. Pigott, John W. Pitts, James H. Wiborg, T.A. Wilson.
Number of staff: None.
Employer Identification Number: 916030638

3238
Pacific First Financial Corporate Giving Program
P.O. Box 1257
1145 Broadway
Tacoma 98401 (206) 383-2511

Financial data (yr. ended 12/31/88): Total giving, $560,632, including $500,207 for 246 grants (high: $25,000; low: $50) and $60,425 for 50 in-kind gifts.
Purpose and activities: Support for wide variety of programs including the aged, arts, business, business education, drug abuse, ecology and wildlife, the homeless, employment, hospices, hunger, literacy, urban development, public affairs, and religious schools.
Types of support: Annual campaigns, building funds, capital campaigns, conferences and seminars, equipment, general purposes, lectureships, loans, renovation projects, research, special projects, scholarship funds, student loans.
Limitations: Giving primarily in the Northwest, primarily OR and WA.
Application information:
Initial approach: Written application
Copies of proposal: 1
Deadline(s): Ongoing - however, 3rd quarter advantageous
Board meeting date(s): 3rd Wednesday of each month
Write: Michael K. Rogers, Sr. V.P., Corp. Communications
Administrators: Michael K. Rogers, Sr. V.P.; Kathleen N. Heric, Asst. V.P.
Number of staff: 2 full-time professional.

3239
Puget Sound Power and Light Corporate Giving Program
P.O. Box 97034
Bellevue 98009-9734 (206) 462-3799

Financial data (yr. ended 12/31/88): Total giving, $612,101, including $597,101 for 79 grants (high: $25,000; low: $50) and $15,000 for 124 employee matching gifts.
Purpose and activities: Support for higher and elementary education, arts and humanities, including museums and performing arts, engineering, enviromental programs, volunteerism, health services, hospitals, and medical research. Also giving for social services, urban development, and employee matching gifts for education.
Types of support: Capital campaigns, conferences and seminars, employee matching gifts.
Limitations: Giving primarily in headquarters city and major operating locations. No support for churches or other religious organizations, except for programs which benefit the overall community and do not support a specific religious doctrine, fraternal or labor organizations, or organizations which are themselves strictly grant making bodies. No grants to individuals, or for mass mailings, tickets, goodwill advertising, endorsements, or travel; no support for the general funds of tax-supported educational institutions.
Application information: Application form required.
Initial approach: Short letter
Copies of proposal: 1
Deadline(s): Late summer and early fall
Board meeting date(s): 3rd month of each quarter
Write: Neil L. McReynolds, Sr. V.P., Corp. Relations
Number of staff: 1

3240
Robertson Charitable & Educational Trust
c/o First Interstate Bank of Washington
P.O. Box 9728
Yakima 98909 (509) 575-7427

Established in 1972 in WA.
Donor(s): W.H. Robertson,† Ruth Robertson,† Dorothy "Bill" Robertson.
Financial data (yr. ended 12/31/86): Assets, $1,357,198 (M); expenditures, $253,851, including $242,375 for 54 grants (high: $35,000; low: $25; average: $5,000).
Purpose and activities: Grants to youth agencies and cultural programs.
Types of support: Operating budgets, continuing support, annual campaigns, seed money, emergency funds, building funds, equipment, land acquisition, endowment funds, matching funds, internships, scholarship funds, exchange programs, fellowships, capital campaigns, general purposes, renovation projects, special projects.
Limitations: Giving limited to the Yakima, WA, area. No grants to individuals, or for deficit financing.
Application information:
Board meeting date(s): As needed
Write: Shirley M. Nelson, Trust Officer, First Interstate Bank of Washington
Trustees: Dorothy "Bill" Robertson, First Interstate Bank of Washington.
Employer Identification Number: 916159252

3241
Safeco Corporate Giving Program
SAFECO Plaza
Seattle 98185 (206) 545-5015

Financial data (yr. ended 12/31/86): Total giving, $2,071,177, including $1,994,179 for 502 grants and $76,998 for 659 employee matching gifts.
Purpose and activities: Support for civic programs, culture, all levels of education, health, social services, and United Way; also has a matching gifts program and employee volunteer programs.
Types of support: Fellowships, employee matching gifts, matching funds, building funds, special projects, scholarship funds.
Limitations: Giving primarily in the Pacific Northwest in WA, CA, CO, and OR; less giving in OH, IL, TN, GA, TX, and MO. No support

for national organizations, projects or programs operating outside the U.S. or Canada, or political or religious organizations involved in partisan or sectarian programs. No grants to individuals, or for endowment funds, loans and investments, fundraising events and advertising associated with such events.
Application information:
Initial approach: Brief letter of inquiry describing organization, proposed program, amount requested, geographic area and people to be served, how project will be evaluated, and 501(c)(3)
Deadline(s): None
Board meeting date(s): All requests are evaluated either in SAFECO's Home Office or in the branch office closest to the requesting organizations
Final notification: 6 weeks
Write: Jill A. Ryan, Asst. V.P., Public Relations

3242
Josephine Stedem Scripps Foundation
221 First Ave. West, Suite 405
Seattle 98119
Application address: P.O. Box 1861, San Diego, CA 92112

Established in 1958 in WA.
Donor(s): Members of the Scripps family.
Financial data (yr. ended 11/30/88): Assets, $1,072,452 (M); expenditures, $69,995, including $67,500 for 24 grants (high: $20,000; low: $250).
Purpose and activities: Support for hospitals, medical and scientific research, education, agricultural and animal welfare organizations; some support for cultural programs.
Application information:
Deadline(s): None
Write: Ellen S. Davis, Treas.
Officers and Trustees:* Antonio Davis MacFarlane,* Pres.; Sally S. Weston,* V.P.; Roxanne D. Greene,* Secy.; Ellen S. Davis, Treas.
Employer Identification Number: 916053350

3243
Seafirst Foundation
P.O. Box 3586
Seattle 98124 (206) 358-3441

Established in 1979 in WA.
Donor(s): Seafirst Corp.
Financial data (yr. ended 12/31/87): Assets, $175,641 (M); expenditures, $1,299,183, including $1,295,644 for 112 grants (high: $97,978; low: $125; average: $3,000-$35,000).
Purpose and activities: Giving primarily for community development, including youth training and employment, higher and economic education, arts and culture, and to human service agencies through the United Way; multiple-year and capital grants sometimes considered but are limited in size and scope. All grants of more than one year are subject to review before funds are released for the subsequent year.
Types of support: Building funds, general purposes, seed money, special projects, capital campaigns, lectureships, operating budgets, renovation projects.
Limitations: Giving limited to WA. No support for fraternal organizations or religious organizations (unless the proposed project is non-denominational and does not promote religious advocacy), single disease organizations, or primary or secondary schools. No grants to individuals, or for research, endowment funds, travel expenses, operating deficits, fundraising events, scholarships (except for Seafirst scholarship programs), or film.
Publications: Informational brochure (including application guidelines).
Application information: Application form required.
Initial approach: Letter
Copies of proposal: 1
Deadline(s): None, but requests received after Oct. 1 will be carried forward to the following Jan.
Board meeting date(s): Quarterly
Final notification: 4 to 6 weeks
Officers and Trustees: James Williams, Pres.; Barbara Ells, Treas.; Joan Enticknap, Jeffrey Farber, Jim Kirschbaum, Larry Ogg, Pat Prout, Tim Turnpaugh.
Number of staff: 2
Employer Identification Number: 911094720

3244
The Seattle Foundation
425 Pike St., Suite 510
Seattle 98101 (206) 622-2294

Community foundation incorporated in 1946 in WA.
Financial data (yr. ended 6/30/88): Assets, $31,518,556 (M); gifts received, $3,249,000; expenditures, $4,522,000, including $4,522,000 for 300 grants (high: $75,000; low: $1,000; average: $5,000-$10,000).
Purpose and activities: To administer gifts and bequests for the benefit of charitable, cultural, educational, health, and welfare organizations.
Types of support: Building funds, equipment, renovation projects.
Limitations: Giving limited to the Seattle, WA, area. No grants to individuals, or for scholarships, fellowships, endowment funds, research, operating budgets, general purposes, matching gifts, conferences, exhibits, film production, or publications; no loans.
Publications: Annual report, informational brochure, program policy statement, application guidelines.
Application information:
Initial approach: Telephone, followed by proposal
Copies of proposal: 1
Deadline(s): Feb. 1, May 1, Aug. 1, and Nov. 1
Board meeting date(s): Mar., June, Sept., and Dec.
Final notification: 6 weeks to 2 months
Write: Anne V. Farrell, Pres.
Officers: Anne V. Farrell, Pres.; Susan Duffy, Secy.; Walter H. Crim,* Treas.
Trustees:* Samuel Stroum, Chair.; Christopher T. Bayley, Vice-Chair.; Elaine Monson, Vice-Chair.; and 22 additional trustees.
Trustee Banks: The Bank of California, N.A., Old National Bank of Washington, First Interstate Bank, Peoples National Bank of Washington, Rainier National Bank, Seattle-First National Bank, Seattle Trust and Savings Bank, Washington Mutual Savings Bank.
Number of staff: 2 full-time professional; 1 part-time professional; 1 full-time support; 1 part-time support.
Employer Identification Number: 916013536

3245
Security Pacific Bank Northwest Corporate Contributions
c/o Social Policy Dept.
P.O. Box 3966, NO5-7
Seattle 98124-3966 (206) 621-4173

Financial data (yr. ended 12/31/88): Total giving, $1,846,496, including $1,836,646 for 756 grants (high: $340,000; low: $235) and $9,850 for employee matching gifts.
Purpose and activities: Support for health, welfare, and human services to encourage and establish economic self-reliance of individuals; art and culture, including major art museums and performing arts organizations in areas of company operations; civic affairs, with emphasis on housing for low-income or disadvantaged residents; and education, to enhance the quality and general understanding of business. To that end, SPBN sponsors several professorships, scholarships and endowments, and contributes to public and private colleges, universities, and community colleges throughout the Pacific Northwest and Alaska. Six four-year full-tuition scholarships are awarded through the Merit Scholarship program to outstanding Washington or Alaska high school graduates who attend colleges or universities in those states. Recipients must plan to major or minor in business economics or finance, combined with a major or minor in liberal arts. Matching gifts to education are also made.
Types of support: Capital campaigns, operating budgets, scholarship funds, matching funds.
Limitations: Giving primarily in WA and AK; no support for national organizations. No support for individual United Way agencies; religious, political, fraternal or labor organizations. No grants to individuals.
Application information:
Initial approach: Letter
Deadline(s): Sept. 15 for capital campaigns; none for other grants
Board meeting date(s): Oct. for capital campaigns
Write: Peter Broffman, Mgr., Corp. Contribs.
Contributions Committee: Donald B. Summers, Chair. (Sr. V.P. and Mgr., Personnel Admin.); Peter Broffman, Mgr. Corp. Contribs. (Admin., Social Policy Dept.).

3246
Sequoia Foundation
820 A St., Suite 545
Tacoma 98402 (206) 627-1634

Established in 1982 in WA.

Donor(s): WBW Trust No. 1, W. John Driscoll, C. Davis Weyerhaeuser, F.T. Weyerhaeuser, William T. Weyerhaeuser.
Financial data (yr. ended 8/31/87): Assets, $15,612,077 (M); gifts received, $2,168,693; expenditures, $2,044,181, including $1,798,705 for 44 grants (high: $185,000; low: $500; average: $1,000-$75,000).
Purpose and activities: Giving primarily to serve the cultural and social needs of the world community. Grants are focused on the stimulation, encouragement, and support of established, voluntary, non-profit organizations set up to meet national and international need in the areas of cultural programs, education, environment, hunger and emergency shelter, international peace, and world crisis relief. Geographic and interest area priorities change annually.
Types of support: Special projects, building funds, general purposes.
Limitations: No support for local organizations except for foundation-initiated grants. No grants to individuals, or for annual appeals, debt retirement, endowments, long-term commitments, lobbying or political propaganda, voter registration drives, travel, publications, or film projects.
Publications: Program policy statement, application guidelines.
Application information:
Initial approach: Letter or proposal
Copies of proposal: 2
Deadline(s): None
Board meeting date(s): At least 6 times a year
Final notification: Between 30 and 60 days for complete applications
Write: Frank D. Underwood, Exec. Dir.
Officers and Directors:* William T. Weyerhaeuser,* Pres. and Treas.; Gail T. Weyerhaeuser,* V.P.; J. Thomas McCully, Secy.; Frank D. Underwood, Exec. Dir.
Members: James R. Hanson, Annette B. Weyerhaeuser.*
Employer Identification Number: 911178052

3247
Skinner Foundation
Skinner Bldg., Seventh Fl.
Seattle 98101 (206) 623-6480

Trust established in 1956 in WA.
Donor(s): Skinner Corp., Alpac Corp., NC Machinery.
Financial data (yr. ended 3/31/88): Assets, $2,869,461 (M); gifts received, $501,168; expenditures, $595,271, including $555,064 for 177 grants and $11,389 for employee matching gifts.
Purpose and activities: Grants for culture and the arts, health and human sevices, education, and civic and community affairs.
Types of support: Operating budgets, seed money, building funds, equipment, matching funds, technical assistance, professorships, fellowships, employee matching gifts, capital campaigns, endowment funds, renovation projects, general purposes, special projects.
Limitations: Giving primarily in areas of company operations in the Seattle, Tacoma, and Yakima areas of WA; and AK and HI. No support for religious organizations for religious purposes. No grants to individuals, or for continuing support, United Ways for operating funds, deficit financing, or conferences; no loans.
Publications: Annual report, informational brochure (including application guidelines).
Application information: Application form required.
Initial approach: Letter
Copies of proposal: 8
Deadline(s): Submit letter in May, Aug., Nov., or Feb.; deadline for application form 28 days before board meetings
Board meeting date(s): July, Oct., Jan., and Apr.
Final notification: 2 weeks
Write: Sandra Fry, Dir.
Trustees: Sally Skinner Behnke, Chair.; John S. Behnke, Robert J. Behnke, Shari D. Behnke, Arthur E. Nordhoff, Grace A. Nordhoff, Catherine E. Skinner.
Number of staff: 1 full-time professional.
Employer Identification Number: 916025144

3248
Spokane Inland Northwest Community Foundation
400 Paulsen Center
West 421 Riverside Ave.
Spokane 99201-0403 (509) 624-2606

Community foundation incorporated in 1974 in WA.
Financial data (yr. ended 6/30/88): Assets, $4,225,850 (M); gifts received, $1,584,397; expenditures, $997,254, including $696,229 for 349 grants (low: $25; average: $1,500) and $54,252 for 71 grants to individuals.
Purpose and activities: Giving for charitable and philanthropic purposes in the fields of music, the arts, the elderly, education and youth, civic improvement, historical restoration, rehabilitation, and social and health services; four scholarship programs for students.
Types of support: Annual campaigns, land acquisition, endowment funds, special projects, publications, seed money, consulting services, technical assistance, student aid, general purposes, scholarship funds.
Limitations: Giving limited to the inland Northwest. No support for sectarian religious purposes. No grants to individuals (except for scholarships), or for deficit financing, building funds, emergency funds, research, or matching grants; no loans.
Publications: Annual report (including application guidelines), informational brochure (including application guidelines), newsletter, application guidelines.
Application information: Application form required.
Initial approach: Letter
Copies of proposal: 7
Deadline(s): Oct. 1 (Spokane, WA); Nov. 1 (Pullman and Dayton, WA); May 1 (northern ID); Apr. 15 and Oct. 15 (ISC Fund); Apr. 1 for scholarships
Board meeting date(s): Sept. through June
Final notification: 3 months
Write: Jeanne L. Ager, Exec. Dir.
Officers and Trustees: Beverly N. Neraas, Pres.; Harold B. Gilkey, V.P.; Nancy McGregor, V.P.; Allan H. Toole, Secy.; Molly M. Philopant, Treas.; Jeanne L. Ager, Exec. Dir.; and 28 additional trustees.
Number of staff: 3 full-time professional; 1 part-time support.
Employer Identification Number: 910941053

3249
Teachers Foundation, Inc.
325 Eastlake Ave., East
Seattle 98109

Established in 1965 in WA.
Donor(s): The Handy Trust.
Financial data (yr. ended 12/31/86): Assets, $1,628,937 (M); gifts received, $75,441; expenditures, $336,417, including $333,345 for 83 grants (high: $22,000; low: $500).
Purpose and activities: Support for child welfare, social services, aid for the handicapped, environmental and higher education, and some support for culture, including museums.
Limitations: Giving primarily in WA, with emphasis on Seattle.
Officers: Lester R. Roblee, Pres.; Astrid I. Moen, V.P.; Stanley O. McNaughton, Secy.-Treas.
Employer Identification Number: 916068353

3250
Thurston Charitable Foundation
900 Fourth Ave., 38th Fl.
Seattle 98104 (206) 623-1031

Established in 1962 in WA.
Financial data (yr. ended 6/30/87): Assets, $1,231,275 (M); expenditures, $60,112, including $49,490 for 54 grants (high: $10,000; low: $25).
Purpose and activities: Giving for hospitals and health services, local and national health and welfare organizations, civic and cultural affairs, and secondary and higher education; some support for religion.
Limitations: Giving primarily in WA. No grants to individuals.
Application information:
Initial approach: Letter
Deadline(s): None
Write: Harry Henke Jr.
Officer: Harry Henke, Pres.
Employer Identification Number: 916055032

3251
U. S. Bank of Washington Giving Program
P.O. Box 720, WWH658
Seattle 98111-0720 (206) 344-2360

Financial data (yr. ended 12/31/88): Total giving, $634,000, including $594,000 for 300 grants (high: $25,000; low: $25; average: $1,000-$10,000), $10,000 for employee matching gifts and $30,000 for 33 in-kind gifts.
Purpose and activities: Support for the arts and culture, including music, theater, fine and performing arts; child development and welfare; health, including single-disease and health associations. Also supports programs for the aged, the disadvantaged, families, the handicapped, minorities, women, and youth;

capital campaign gifts are limited to 1 percent of total amount to be raised.
Types of support: Annual campaigns, capital campaigns, continuing support, emergency funds, employee matching gifts, equipment, general purposes, matching funds.
Limitations: Giving primarily in Adams, Benton, Clallam, Cowlitz, Franklin, Garfield, Grant, Grays Harbor, Island, Jefferson, King, Kitsap, Kittitas, Lincoln, Okanogan, Pierce, Skagit, Snohomish, Spokane, Thurston, Walla Walla, Whatcom, Whitman, and Yakima counties, WA. No grants to individuals, or to fund out of state travel, or to national organizations.
Application information:
Initial approach: Phone call or letter
Copies of proposal: 1
Deadline(s): None
Board meeting date(s): Every 6 to 8 weeks
Final notification: Phone call and/or letter following meeting
Write: Molly W. Reed, V.P. and Mgr., Social Responsibility
Number of staff: 2 full-time professional; 1 part-time support.

3252
Univar/VWR Foundation
1600 Norton Bldg.
Seattle 98104

Established in 1967.
Donor(s): Univar Corp., VWR Corp.
Financial data (yr. ended 2/29/88): Assets, $247,878 (M); gifts received, $154,250; expenditures, $119,688, including $119,683 for 30 grants (high: $20,000; low: $400; average: $5,000).
Purpose and activities: Giving to community funds, cultural programs, higher education, and youth agencies.
Types of support: General purposes, building funds, operating budgets, research, publications.
Limitations: Giving primarily in the Seattle, WA, area.
Application information:
Write: Robert D. O'Brien, Pres.
Officers: Robert D. O'Brien,* Pres.; Susan Schmid, Secy.; N. Stewart Rogers,* Treas.
Trustees:* M.M. Harris, James H. Wiborg, Richard E. Engebrecht, James W. Bernard.
Number of staff: None.
Employer Identification Number: 910826180

3253
Wagner Fund
2221 North 30th
Tacoma 98403 (206) 627-6667

Established in 1958 in WA.
Financial data (yr. ended 6/30/87): Assets, $930,676 (M); expenditures, $186,155, including $157,451 for 33 grants (high: $28,000; low: $100).
Purpose and activities: Giving primarily for social services, organizations concerned with conservation, especially horticulture and wildlife, and cultural programs.
Limitations: Giving primarily in Seattle and Tacoma, WA. No grants to individuals.
Application information: Funding limited for the next several years; most grants made to organizations previously supported by or known to the board members.
Deadline(s): None
Write: H.L. Everson, Secy.-Treas.
Officers: Corydon Wagner, Pres.; Merrill W. Ryman,* V.P.; Wendy Wagner Weyerhaeuser,* V.P.; Henry L. Everson, Secy.-Treas.
Directors:* Eulalie M. Wagner.
Employer Identification Number: 916029837

3254
Washington Mutual Savings Bank Foundation
c/o Washington Mutual Savings Bank
1101 Second Ave.
Seattle 98101 (206) 464-4965

Established in 1979 in WA.
Donor(s): Washington Mutual Savings Bank.
Financial data (yr. ended 12/31/87): Assets, $550,000 (M); gifts received, $1,025,000; expenditures, $634,500, including $628,319 for grants (high: $50,000; low: $500), $2,000 for employee matching gifts and $10,000 for loans.
Purpose and activities: "To provide assistance and encouragement to local communities through nonprofit organizations in the areas of health and welfare, cultural enhancement, education, and civic betterment;" in addition to making grants, the bank sponsors a variety of community and civic projects and activities.
Types of support: Operating budgets, scholarship funds, matching funds, special projects, employee matching gifts, building funds, capital campaigns, endowment funds, emergency funds, equipment, loans, renovation projects, seed money.
Limitations: Giving primarily in WA, especially Seattle, Tacoma, and Spokane. No support for religious organizations for religious purposes, or veterans' or labor organizations. No grants to individuals.
Publications: Annual report (including application guidelines).
Application information: Application form required.
Copies of proposal: 1
Deadline(s): Quarterly
Board meeting date(s): Quarterly
Write: Deloria Jones, V.P. and Mgr., Community and Public Relations, Washington Mutual Savings Bank
Officers and Directors: Sally Skinner Behnke, Pres.; Deloria Jones, Secy.; Ernest Jurdana, Treas.; Rev. Samuel B. McKinney, Lou H. Pepper, William G. Reed, Jr., Holt W. Webster.
Number of staff: 1 full-time professional; 1 part-time professional; 1 part-time support.
Employer Identification Number: 911070920

3255
Washington Trust Foundation
c/o Washington Trust Bank
P.O. Box 2127
Spokane 99210 (509) 353-3802

Established in 1981 in WA.
Donor(s): Washington Trust Bank.
Financial data (yr. ended 12/31/88): Assets, $35 (M); gifts received, $292,754; expenditures, $309,575, including $309,575 for 42 grants (high: $49,275; low: $1,000).
Purpose and activities: Support primarily for secondary and higher education, culture, and social services.
Types of support: General purposes.
Limitations: Giving primarily in Spokane, WA.
Application information:
Initial approach: Proposal
Copies of proposal: 1
Deadline(s): None
Board meeting date(s): As needed
Write: Thomas C. Garrett, Trustee
Trustees: Thomas C. Garrett, William K. Scammell, Jr., Philip H. Stanton.
Employer Identification Number: 911145506

3256
George T. Welch Testamentary Trust
c/o Baker-Boyer National Bank
P.O. Box 1796
Walla Walla 99362 (509) 525-2000

Established in 1938 in WA.
Financial data (yr. ended 9/30/87): Assets, $2,850,816 (M); expenditures, $165,247, including $38,175 for 16 grants (high: $24,300; low: $220) and $102,674 for 115 grants to individuals.
Purpose and activities: Grants to the needy, including medical assistance, and scholarships; some support also for youth agencies and cultural programs.
Types of support: Special projects, student aid, grants to individuals.
Limitations: Giving limited to Walla Walla County, WA. No grants for capital or endowment funds, general purposes, or matching gifts; no loans.
Publications: Program policy statement, application guidelines.
Application information: Application form required.
Initial approach: Proposal
Copies of proposal: 1
Deadline(s): May 1 for scholarships, July 1 for community projects, and Feb. 20, May 20, Aug. 20, and Nov. 20 for health and welfare for the needy
Board meeting date(s): Feb., May, Aug., and Nov.
Final notification: 30 days
Write: Bettie Loiacono, Asst. V.P., Baker-Boyer National Bank
Trustee: Baker-Boyer National Bank.
Number of staff: None.
Employer Identification Number: 916024318

3257
Wyman Youth Trust
304 Pioneer Bldg.
Seattle 98104

Trust established in 1951 in WA.
Donor(s): Members of the Wyman family.
Financial data (yr. ended 12/31/87): Assets, $2,713,502 (M); expenditures, $175,879, including $156,766 for 106 grants (high: $8,000; low: $50).

Purpose and activities: Support for "youth-oriented projects, civic and cultural development, and special community endeavors"; support also for schools and health services.
Limitations: Giving limited to King County, WA, and York County, NE. No grants to individuals, or for capital funds or aggregate donors.
Publications: Program policy statement, application guidelines.
Application information:
Initial approach: Proposal
Copies of proposal: 1
Deadline(s): Mar. 1, June 1, Sept. 1, and Dec. 1
Board meeting date(s): Mar., June, Sept., and Dec.
Final notification: 4 to 6 months
Write: Deehan M. Wyman, Trustee
Trustees: Ann McCall Wyman, Deehan M. Wyman, Hal Wyman.
Number of staff: None.
Employer Identification Number: 916031590

WEST VIRGINIA

3258
Beckley Area Foundation, Inc.
P.O. Box 1575
Beckley 25802-1575

Established in 1985 in WV.
Donor(s): Dr. Thomas Walker Memorial Health Foundation, and others.
Financial data (yr. ended 3/31/88): Assets, $1,865,591 (L); gifts received, $10,000; expenditures, $105,356, including $83,760 for grants.
Purpose and activities: Support primarily for education, social services, health, the arts, and recreation.
Limitations: Giving primarily in the Beckley and Raleigh County, WV, area.
Publications: Annual report.
Application information:
Initial approach: Letter
Officers and Directors: Alex D. George, Jr., Pres.; Robert B. Sayre, V.P.; Mrs. Albert M. Tieche, Secy.; Leslie C. Gates, Treas.; Charles K. Connor, Jr., Exec. Dir.; and 11 other directors.

3259
The Daywood Foundation, Inc.
1200 Charleston National Plaza
Charleston 25301 (304) 343-4841

Incorporated in 1958 in WV.
Donor(s): Ruth Woods Dayton.†
Financial data (yr. ended 12/31/88): Assets, $7,785,000 (M); expenditures, $376,300 for 48 grants (high: $48,000).
Purpose and activities: Grants restricted to local organizations (except for a few out-of-state training institutions), with emphasis on higher education; some support for welfare agencies, youth agencies, and community funds.
Types of support: Annual campaigns, building funds, capital campaigns, emergency funds, equipment, general purposes, matching funds, renovation projects, seed money.
Limitations: Giving limited to Barbour, Charleston, Greenbrier, Kanawha, and Lewisburg counties in WV. No grants to individuals, or for endowment funds, research, scholarships, or fellowships; no loans.
Publications: Application guidelines.
Application information:
Initial approach: Letter
Copies of proposal: 1
Deadline(s): Submit proposal preferably in Jan. through May; deadline May 31
Board meeting date(s): July and Dec.
Final notification: Dec.
Write: William W. Booker, Secy.-Treas.
Officers and Directors: L. Newton Thomas, Pres.; Richard E. Ford, V.P.; William W. Booker, Secy.-Treas.
Number of staff: 1 part-time support.
Employer Identification Number: 556018107

3260
The Greater Kanawha Valley Foundation
P.O. Box 3041
Charleston 25331 (304) 346-3620

Community foundation established in 1962 in WV.
Financial data (yr. ended 12/31/88): Assets, $23,605,600 (M); gifts received, $884,762; expenditures, $1,387,221, including $737,982 for 175 grants (high: $9,000; low: $500; average: $550-$5,000) and $449,589 for 350 grants to individuals.
Purpose and activities: Support for education, social services, health, the arts, and recreation.
Types of support: Operating budgets, continuing support, seed money, building funds, equipment, student aid, special projects, research, publications, conferences and seminars, technical assistance, annual campaigns, capital campaigns, general purposes, student loans.
Limitations: Giving limited to the Greater Kanawha Valley, WV, area, except scholarships which are limited to residents of WV. No grants for annual campaigns, deficit financing, or general endowments.
Publications: Annual report (including application guidelines), informational brochure, application guidelines.
Application information:
Initial approach: Proposal
Copies of proposal: 1
Deadline(s): 1st of Mar., June, Sept. and Nov.
Board meeting date(s): Usually in Apr., July, Oct., and Dec.
Final notification: Immediately after board action
Write: Betsy B. VonBlond, Exec. Dir.
Officers and Trustees: David C. Hardesty, Jr., Chair.; G. Thomas Battle, Vice Chair.; Charles W. Loeb,* Secy.; Betsy B. VonBlond, Exec. Dir.; Brooks F. McCabe, Jr., Charles R. McElwee, William O. McMillan, Jr., Margaret A. Mills, William E. Mullett, Richard C. Sinclair, Olivia R. Singleton,* Louis S. Southworth II, Martha G. Wehrle, Adeline J. Voorhees.*
Advisory Committee:* Frederick H. Belden, Jr., Bert A. Bradford, Jr., W.G. Caperton, Elizabeth E. Chilton, William M. Davis, Willard H. Erwin, Jr., J.W. Hubbard, Jr., Stanley Lowenstein, Thomas N. McJunkin, Harry Moore, James H. Nix, Mark H. Schaul, Dolly Sherwood, Charles B. Stacy, L. Newton Thomas, Jr.
Trustee Banks: One Valley Bank, United National Bank, Charleston National Bank, City National Bank of Charleston, National Bank of Commerce of Charleston.
Number of staff: 1 full-time professional; 1 full-time support.
Employer Identification Number: 556024430
Recent arts and culture grants:
Charleston Ballet, Charleston, WV, $8,781. 1987.
Charleston Symphony Orchestra, Charleston, WV, $98,959. 1987.
Film News Now Foundation, NYC, NY, $13,000. 1987.
Fund for the Arts, Charleston, WV, $27,000. 1987.
General Charles E. Yeager Statue Fund, Charleston, WV, $15,000. 1987.
Kanawha Players, Charleston, WV, $8,056. 1987.
Old Charles Town Museum, Charles Town, WV, $17,889. 1987.
Sunrise Museums, Charleston, WV, $27,101. 1987.
West Virginia Public Radio, Charleston, WV, $8,000. 1987.

3261
Sarah & Pauline Maier Foundation, Inc.
P.O. Box 6190
Charleston 25362 (304) 343-2201

Established in 1958 in WV.
Donor(s): William J. Maier, Jr.†
Financial data (yr. ended 10/31/87): Assets, $15,832,810 (M); gifts received, $6,060; expenditures, $1,782,955, including $1,018,536 for 18 grants (high: $300,000; low: $3,925; average: $10,000-$50,000).
Purpose and activities: Giving primarily for educational institutions; support also for a medical facility and the arts.
Types of support: Scholarship funds, annual campaigns, building funds, capital campaigns, endowment funds, equipment, matching funds, operating budgets, professorships, special projects.
Limitations: Giving limited to WV. No grants to individuals.
Application information:
Initial approach: Letter
Copies of proposal: 1
Deadline(s): Oct. 31
Board meeting date(s): Ist Friday in Dec.
Final notification: Dec. 31
Write: Ed Maier, Pres.
Officers: Pauline Maier, Chair.; Edward H. Maier, Pres.; W.J. Maier III, V.P.; Sara M. Rowe, Secy.-Treas.
Members: John T. Copenhaver, Elizabeth M. Culwell, Sidney P. Davis, Jr., Earl F. Morris.
Number of staff: None.
Employer Identification Number: 556023833

WISCONSIN

3262
Judd S. Alexander Foundation, Inc.
500 Third St., Suite 509
P.O. Box 2137
Wausau 54402-2137 (715) 845-4556

Incorporated in 1973 in WI.
Donor(s): Anne M. Alexander.†
Financial data (yr. ended 6/30/88): Assets, $17,873,558 (M); expenditures, $884,646, including $689,625 for 61 grants (high: $240,000; low: $200; average: $5,000-$10,000) and $12,200 for 2 loans.
Purpose and activities: Support for civic affairs, youth agencies, higher education, cultural programs, and social agencies.
Types of support: Seed money, emergency funds, building funds, equipment, land acquisition, matching funds, technical assistance, program-related investments, capital campaigns, scholarship funds.
Limitations: Giving primarily in WI, with emphasis on Marathon County. No grants to individuals, or for endowment funds, fellowships, special projects, research, publications, or conferences.
Application information:
Initial approach: Letter, proposal, or telephone
Copies of proposal: 1
Deadline(s): None
Board meeting date(s): Monthly
Final notification: 60 days
Write: Stanley F. Staples, Jr., Pres.
Officers and Directors: Stanley F. Staples, Jr., Pres.; Harry N. Heinemann, V.P.; John F. Michler, Secy.; Richard D. Dudley, Treas.
Number of staff: None.
Employer Identification Number: 237323721

3263
Walter Alexander Foundation, Inc.
500 Third St., Suite 509
P.O. Box 2137
Wausau 54402-2137 (715) 845-4556

Incorporated in 1952 in WI.
Donor(s): Ruth Alexander,† Anne M. Alexander.†
Financial data (yr. ended 11/30/87): Assets, $2,064,773 (M); gifts received, $36,000; expenditures, $113,506, including $97,830 for 25 grants (high: $15,000; low: $500; average: $1,500-$2,500) and $13,000 for 1 loan.
Purpose and activities: Support for higher and secondary education, cultural programs and social agencies.
Types of support: Capital campaigns, seed money, emergency funds, building funds, equipment, land acquisition, matching funds, program-related investments, scholarship funds.
Limitations: Giving primarily in WI. No grants to individuals, or for endowment funds, fellowships, special projects, research, or conferences.
Application information:
Initial approach: Letter, proposal, or telephone
Copies of proposal: 1
Deadline(s): None, but preferably before June
Board meeting date(s): 3 times a year or as required
Final notification: 4 months
Write: Stanley F. Staples, Jr., Secy.
Officers and Directors: Nancy Anne Cordaro, Pres.; Jean A. Koskiner, V.P.; Stanley F. Staples, Jr., Secy.; John F. Michler, Treas.
Number of staff: None.
Employer Identification Number: 396044635

3264
Frank G. Andres Charitable Trust
P.O. Box 753
Tomah 54660

Trust established in WI.
Financial data (yr. ended 6/30/87): Assets, $1,807,813 (M); expenditures, $124,442, including $111,198 for 21 grants (high: $30,159; low: $269).
Purpose and activities: Emphasis on civic affairs, a hospital, education, social agencies, and cultural programs.
Limitations: Giving primarily in Tomah, WI.
Application information: Application form required.
Deadline(s): May 15
Officer and Trustees: Roxanne O'Conner, Secy.-Treas.; R.W. Ahlstrom, Richard Baumgarten, Jeff Drew, John W. Drew, Donald Kortbein, David Myer.
Employer Identification Number: 510172405

3265
Apollo Fund, Ltd.
c/o Foley & Lardner
777 East Wisconsin Ave.
Milwaukee 53202 (414) 289-3569

Established in 1948.
Financial data (yr. ended 7/31/88): Assets, $1,677,418 (M); expenditures, $122,322, including $110,000 for grants.
Purpose and activities: Giving for higher education, youth agencies, cultural programs, health agencies, and hospitals.
Types of support: Annual campaigns, capital campaigns.
Limitations: Giving primarily in Milwaukee, WI.
Application information:
Initial approach: Letter
Deadline(s): None
Write: Orin Purintun, Secy.
Officers and Directors: F.H. Roby, Pres.; Orin Purintun, Secy.; R.J. Maier, Treas.; R.B. Bradley, James F. McKenna.
Number of staff: None.
Employer Identification Number: 396044029

3266
Appleton Papers Corporate Giving Program
825 East Wisconsin Ave.
P.O. Box 359
Appleton 54912 (414) 734-9841

Financial data (yr. ended 12/31/88): Total giving, $650,000, including $596,848 for 300 grants (high: $100,000; low: $50; average: $1,000-$5,000), $22,500 for grants to individuals, $14,652 for 112 employee matching gifts and $16,000 for 25 in-kind gifts.
Purpose and activities: Supports education, including private colleges; health, including health associations, AIDS programs, and drug abuse; civic affairs; community funds; performing arts; media and communications; and youth.
Types of support: Annual campaigns, capital campaigns, continuing support, operating budgets, employee-related scholarships, scholarship funds, special projects, employee matching gifts, in-kind gifts.
Limitations: Giving primarily in operating locations in MI, OH, PA, and WI.
Application information:
Initial approach: Phone call
Board meeting date(s): Feb. and Dec.
Write: John W. Turner, Chair. and C.E.O.
Administrator: Dennis N. Hultgren, Secy., Contribs. Comm.
Number of staff: 1 full-time professional; 1 full-time support.

3267
Applied Power Foundation
P.O. Box 325
Milwaukee 53201 (414) 781-6600

Donor(s): Applied Power, Inc.
Financial data (yr. ended 7/31/87): Assets, $626,704 (M); gifts received, $75,000; expenditures, $87,988, including $80,000 for 23 grants (high: $10,000; low: $100).
Purpose and activities: Giving to health, social services, arts, community funds, and higher education programs.
Types of support: General purposes.
Limitations: Giving primarily in WI.
Application information: Application form required.
Initial approach: Letter
Copies of proposal: 1
Deadline(s): Fiscal year ends July 31
Write: Martin E. Pschirrer, Trustee
Trustees: Marine Trust Co., N.A., Martin E. Pschirrer, Richard G. Sim.
Employer Identification Number: 396062180

3268
Badger Meter Foundation, Inc.
4545 West Brown Deer Rd.
Milwaukee 53223 (414) 355-0400

Incorporated in 1952 in WI.
Donor(s): Badger Meter, Inc.
Financial data (yr. ended 12/31/87): Assets, $2,525,270 (M); gifts received, $50,000; expenditures, $313,535, including $286,200 for 119 grants (high: $20,000; low: $25; average: $100-$10,000).
Purpose and activities: Grants largely for community funds, higher education, the arts, health care, and programs for the disabled.
Types of support: Operating budgets, continuing support, annual campaigns, seed money, emergency funds, deficit financing,

building funds, equipment, land acquisition, endowment funds, research, special projects.
Limitations: Giving limited to WI, almost exclusively in the greater Milwaukee area. No grants to individuals, or for matching gifts, scholarships, fellowships, publications, or conferences; no loans.
Application information:
Initial approach: Letter
Copies of proposal: 1
Deadline(s): Aug. 31
Final notification: 3 to 4 months
Write: Mary George, Secy.
Officers: James O. Wright,* Pres.; R. Robert Howard,* V.P.; Mary George, Secy.; Rebecca Rush, Treas.
Directors:* Ronald H. Dix, Richard S. Gallagher, E.G. Smith, Barbara M. Wiley.
Number of staff: 1 part-time professional.
Employer Identification Number: 396043635

3269
Robert W. Baird and Company Foundation, Inc.
777 East Wisconsin Ave.
Milwaukee 53202

Established in 1967 in WI.
Donor(s): Robert W. Baird & Co., Inc.
Financial data (yr. ended 12/31/87): Assets, $1,630,171 (M); gifts received, $100,000; expenditures, $159,914, including $142,047 for 122 grants (high: $22,330; low: $50).
Purpose and activities: Giving primarily for higher education, community funds, cultural programs, civic affairs, and community development.
Limitations: Giving primarily in WI.
Application information: Contributes only to preselected organizations. Applications not accepted.
Trustees: G. Frederick Kasten, Jr., Arthur J. Laskin, Brenton H. Rupple.
Employer Identification Number: 396107937

3270
Banc One Wisconsin Foundation
(Formerly The Marine Foundation, Inc.)
111 East Wisconsin Ave.
P.O. Box 481
Milwaukee 53201 (414) 765-2624

Incorporated in 1958 in WI.
Donor(s): Marine Midland Bank, N.A., and other Marine banks in WI.
Financial data (yr. ended 12/31/87): Assets, $9,019 (L); gifts received, $360,905; expenditures, $356,170, including $311,725 for 50 grants (high: $115,500; low: $100; average: $6,235) and $44,417 for 559 employee matching gifts.
Purpose and activities: Emphasis on a community fund, cultural programs, higher education, and youth agencies.
Types of support: General purposes, operating budgets, continuing support, annual campaigns, seed money, emergency funds, deficit financing, building funds, equipment, employee matching gifts, special projects, research, conferences and seminars.
Limitations: Giving limited to WI; except for employee matching gifts to education. No grants to individuals, or for land acquisition, endowment funds, scholarships, fellowships, or publications; no loans.
Application information:
Initial approach: Proposal
Copies of proposal: 1
Deadline(s): 15 days before board meetings
Board meeting date(s): Jan., May, Aug., and Dec.
Final notification: 2 to 3 months
Write: Frances G. Smyth, Secy.
Officers and Directors:* George R. Slater,* Pres.; Ronald C. Baldwin,* V.P.; Frederick L. Cullen,* V.P.; Leila Fraser,* V.P.; Richard D. Headley,* V.P.; David J. Kunbert,* V.P.; James C. LaVelle,* V.P.; Jon R. Schumacher,* V.P.; Jon H. Stowe,* V.P.; Frances G. Smyth, Secy.; Clem F. Maslowski, Treas.
Number of staff: None.
Employer Identification Number: 396050680

3271
Banta Company Foundation, Inc.
P.O. Box 8003
100 Main St.
Menasha 54952-8003 (414) 722-7771

Incorporated in 1953 in WI.
Donor(s): George Banta Co., Inc.
Financial data (yr. ended 12/31/87): Assets, $271 (M); gifts received, $250,000; expenditures, $286,258, including $270,760 for 98 grants (high: $50,000; low: $100; average: $2,000-$3,000) and $15,465 for 40 employee matching gifts.
Purpose and activities: Emphasis on higher education and youth agencies; support also for cultural programs, including an historical society, and hospitals.
Types of support: Operating budgets, continuing support, annual campaigns, seed money, emergency funds, deficit financing, building funds, equipment, land acquisition, employee matching gifts, matching funds, special projects.
Limitations: Giving limited to areas of company operations including CA, IL, MN, MO, NC, NY, VA, and WI. No grants to individuals, or for scholarships, fellowships, or endowment funds; no loans.
Application information:
Initial approach: Letter
Copies of proposal: 1
Deadline(s): Nov. 1
Board meeting date(s): Apr., June, Sept., and Dec.
Write: Dean E. Bergstrom, V.P.
Officers: Gerald A. Henseler, V.P.; Harry W. Earle, Pres.; Dean E. Bergstrom, V.P. and Secy.-Treas.; Margaret Banta Humleker, V.P.; Donald S. Koskinen, V.P.
Number of staff: None.
Employer Identification Number: 396050779

3272
Norman Bassett Foundation - Wisconsin
7601 Ganser Way
Madison 53719
Application address: 201 Waubesa St., Madison, WI 53704

Established in 1954 in WI.
Financial data (yr. ended 3/31/87): Assets, $3,023,701 (M); expenditures, $676,793, including $651,314 for 35 grants (high: $350,000; low: $500).
Purpose and activities: Giving primarily for cultural programs, including performing arts groups, social service agencies, and education.
Limitations: Giving primarily in Madison and Dane County, WI.
Application information:
Initial approach: Letter
Deadline(s): None
Write: J. Reed Coleman
Officers: J. Reed Coleman, Pres.; F. Chandler Young, V.P.; Thomas R. Ragatz, Secy.; Robert W. Taplick, Treas.
Employer Identification Number: 396043890

3273
Becor Western Foundation, Inc.
1100 Milwaukee Ave.
South Milwaukee 53172 (414) 768-4350
Application address: P.O. Box 500, South Milwaukee, WI 53172

Incorporated in 1951 in WI.
Donor(s): Bucyrus-Erie Co.
Financial data (yr. ended 12/31/87): Assets, $10,025,858 (M); expenditures, $921,176, including $811,342 for 198 grants (high: $135,000; low: $25).
Purpose and activities: Grants for higher education, the arts, hospitals, and community funds; support also for social services and youth agencies.
Types of support: Operating budgets, continuing support, annual campaigns, building funds, equipment, endowment funds, employee matching gifts, employee-related scholarships, capital campaigns.
Limitations: Giving primarily in metropolitan Milwaukee, WI. No grants to individuals (except scholarships for children of employees), or for research, special projects, seed money, emergency funds, deficit financing, land acquisition, matching gifts, publications, or conferences; no loans.
Application information: Application form required for scholarships for children of employees.
Initial approach: Letter
Deadline(s): Dec. for scholarships
Board meeting date(s): Feb. and Oct.
Final notification: At the latest, after next board meeting
Write: D.L. Strawderman, Mgr.
Officers and Directors: N.K. Ekstrom, Pres.; D.M. Goelzer, Secy.; N.J. Verville, Treas.; D.L. Strawderman, Mgr.; P.W. Cotter, D.E. Porter, Brenton H. Rupple.
Number of staff: 2 part-time support.
Employer Identification Number: 396075537

3274
Alvin and Marion Birnschein Foundation, Inc.
740 North Plankinton Ave., Suite 510
Milwaukee 53203 (414) 276-3400

Established in 1968 in WI.
Financial data (yr. ended 12/31/87): Assets, $2,432,302 (M); expenditures, $236,914,

including $179,538 for 26 grants (high: $20,000; low: $1,000).
Purpose and activities: Giving for social service and child welfare agencies, higher education, cultural programs, and hospitals.
Types of support: General purposes.
Limitations: Giving primarily in Milwaukee, WI.
Application information: Contributes only to pre-selected organizations. Applications not accepted.
Write: Peter C. Haensel, Pres.
Officers and Directors: Peter C. Haensel, Pres.; Loraine E. Schuffler, Secy.; Fred A. Erchul II.
Employer Identification Number: 396126798

3275
Eugenie Mayer Bolz Family Foundation
P.O. Box 8100
Madison 53708

Established in 1976 in WI and IL.
Donor(s): Eugenie M. Bolz.
Financial data (yr. ended 12/31/86): Assets, $2,814,035 (M); gifts received, $200,000; expenditures, $162,505, including $131,750 for 38 grants (high: $14,000; low: $500).
Purpose and activities: Giving primarily for social services and the arts.
Types of support: General purposes.
Application information:
Deadline(s): None
Write: Ronald Mattox, Dir.
Officers: Robert M. Bolz, Pres.; Marjorie B. Allen, V.P.; John A. Bolz, Secy.-Treas.
Director: Ronald Mattox.
Employer Identification Number: 237428561

3276
The Bradley Family Foundation, Inc.
c/o Arthur Andersen & Co.
P.O. Box 1215
Milwaukee 53201

Incorporated in 1967 in WI.
Donor(s): Margaret B. Bradley,† Jane Bradley Pettit.
Financial data (yr. ended 9/30/87): Assets, $2,698,318 (M); gifts received, $14,014; expenditures, $2,320,095, including $798,025 for grants.
Purpose and activities: Support primarily for a sculpture garden operated by the foundation; grants also for arts and cultural organizations, with emphasis on music.
Limitations: Giving primarily in WI and FL. No grants to individuals, or for building or endowment funds, or operating budgets.
Application information: Contributes only to pre-selected organizations. Applications not accepted.
Board meeting date(s): Annually
Officers and Directors: Jane Bradley Pettit, Pres.; Lloyd H. Pettit, V.P.; Lynde V. Uihlein, Secy.; David V. Uihlein, Jr., Treas.
Employer Identification Number: 396105450

3277
The Lynde and Harry Bradley Foundation, Inc.
777 East Wisconsin Ave., Suite 2285
Milwaukee 53202 (414) 291-9915

Incorporated in 1942 in WI as the Allen-Bradley Foundation, Inc.; adopted present name in 1985.
Donor(s): Harry L. Bradley,† Caroline D. Bradley,† Margaret B. Bradley,† Margaret Loock Trust, Allen-Bradley Co.
Financial data (yr. ended 7/31/88): Assets, $339,775,000 (M); expenditures, $25,897,105, including $22,749,105 for 270 grants (high: $1,000,000; low: $2,080; average: $25,000-$200,000) and $291,188 for foundation-administered programs.
Purpose and activities: Support locally for cultural programs, education, social services, medical programs, health agencies, and public policy. National support for research and education in domestic, international, and strategic public policy; grants also for higher education; in particular, activities that investigate and nurture the moral, cultural, intellectual, and economic institutions which form a free society.
Types of support: Annual campaigns, capital campaigns, conferences and seminars, continuing support, equipment, fellowships, internships, lectureships, matching funds, operating budgets, professorships, publications, renovation projects, research, scholarship funds, special projects.
Limitations: No support for strictly denominational projects. No grants to individuals, or for endowment funds.
Publications: Annual report, informational brochure (including application guidelines).
Application information:
Initial approach: Letter of inquiry
Copies of proposal: 1
Deadline(s): Mar. 15, July 15, Sept. 15, and Dec. 15
Board meeting date(s): Feb., May, Sept., and Nov.
Final notification: 3 to 5 months
Write: Michael S. Joyce, Pres.
Officers: I. Andrew Rader,* Chair.; Michael S. Joyce,* Pres.; Hillel G. Fradkin, V.P. for Prog.; Richard H. Lillie, M.D.,* V.P.; Wayne J. Roper,* Secy.; James D. Ericson,* Treas.
Directors:* Sarah D. Barder, William J. Bennett, Urban T. Kuechle, J. Clayburn LaForce, George J. Stigler, Allen M. Taylor, David V. Uihlein, Jr.
Number of staff: 4 full-time professional; 1 part-time professional; 5 full-time support; 1 part-time support.
Employer Identification Number: 396037928
Recent arts and culture grants:
Discovery World Museum of Science, Economics and Technology, Milwaukee, WI, $100,000. To support education programs. 1987.
EAA Aviation Foundation, Sheboygan, WI, $5,000. To support general programming. 1987.
ETV Endowment of South Carolina, Blackwell Corporation, Spartanburg, SC, $250,000. To support 1987/88 season of the television series, American Interests. 1987.
Foundation for Cultural Review, NYC, NY, $100,000. To support its publication of The New Criterion. 1987.
Great Lakes Shipwreck Historical Society, Sault Sainte Marie, MI, $10,000. To support museum development. 1987.
Historic Sites Foundation, Milwaukee, WI, $100,000. To support 1987 Circus Parade. 1987.
Lakeland College, Sheboygan, WI, $300,000. To support development of Margaret B. Bradley Fine Arts Center. 1987.
Milwaukee Art Museum, Milwaukee, WI, $500,000. For challenge grant to support general programming. 1987.
Milwaukee Art Museum, Milwaukee, WI, $100,000. To support annual operating campaign. 1987.
Milwaukee Jazz Experience, Milwaukee, WI, $10,000. To support jazz festival/educational seminar held at University of Wisconsin-Milwaukee. 1987.
Milwaukee Symphony Orchestra, Milwaukee, WI, $56,000. To support the 1986 Leonard Bernstein Festival. 1987.
National Endowment for the Humanities, DC, $10,000. To support Jefferson Lecture. 1987.
Performing Arts Center, Milwaukee, WI, $50,000. To support children's theater program. 1987.
Radio Free Europe, Radio Liberty, DC, $30,000. To support 1987 summer intern program and book project on free speech by direct dial. 1987.
Smith College, Center for the Study of Social and Political Change, Northampton, MA, $45,000. To support study of history and civics textbooks. 1987.
Statue of Liberty-Ellis Island Foundation, NYC, NY, $20,000. To support restoration and preservation of the Statue of Liberty and Ellis Island. 1987.
United Performing Arts Fund, Milwaukee, WI, $25,000. To support benefit dinner/auction. 1987.
University of Wisconsin, School of Architecture and Urban Planning, Milwaukee, WI, $100,000. To support World Cities of the Future Design Competition. 1987.

3278
Victor F. Braun Foundation, Inc.
7154 South 76th St.
Franklin 53132

Established in 1956.
Financial data (yr. ended 11/30/86): Assets, $1,577,413 (M); expenditures, $126,835, including $117,000 for 57 grants (high: $4,000; low: $1,000).
Purpose and activities: Emphasis on medical research, hospitals, higher, secondary, and vocational education, social service and youth agencies, and cultural programs.
Limitations: Giving primarily in WI, with emphasis on Milwaukee; also in KY, MI, AR, and CT.
Application information: Contributes only to pre-selected organizations. Applications not accepted.
Officers and Directors:* Victor F. Braun, Pres.; James V. Braun,* V.P.; Roger Myers, Secy.; John H. Ladish,* Treas.
Employer Identification Number: 396043684

3279
Briggs & Stratton Corporation Foundation, Inc.

12301 West Wirth St.
Wauwatosa 53222 (414) 259-5333
Mailing address: P.O. Box 702, Milwaukee, WI 53201

Incorporated in 1954 in WI.
Donor(s): Briggs & Stratton Corp.
Financial data (yr. ended 11/30/88): Assets, $4,507,523 (M); expenditures, $641,495, including $605,520 for 50 grants (high: $198,000; low: $100; average: $500-$20,000) and $33,000 for 33 grants to individuals.
Purpose and activities: Support primarily for higher and vocational education, health, rural issues, community funds, and cultural programs; scholarship program is open to the sons and daughters of company employees.
Types of support: Operating budgets, special projects, employee-related scholarships, capital campaigns.
Limitations: Giving limited to WI, with emphasis on Milwaukee. No support for religious organizations. No grants to individuals (except employee-related scholarships).
Application information:
Initial approach: Proposal
Copies of proposal: 1
Deadline(s): Jan. 31 for employee scholarship program; none for public charity grants
Board meeting date(s): June and Nov.
Final notification: Nov. 30
Write: Kasandra K. Preston, Secy.-Treas.
Officers and Directors: Frederick P. Stratton, Jr., Pres.; L.G. Regner, V.P.; Kasandra K. Preston, Secy.-Treas.
Number of staff: None.
Employer Identification Number: 396040377

3280
Frank G. Brotz Family Foundation, Inc.

3518 Lakeshore Rd.
P.O. Box 551
Sheboygan 53081 (414) 458-2121

Incorporated in 1953 in WI.
Donor(s): Plastics Engineering Co.
Financial data (yr. ended 9/30/88): Assets, $9,329,758 (M); gifts received, $700,000; expenditures, $412,973, including $398,175 for 66 grants (high: $50,000; low: $100).
Purpose and activities: Emphasis on hospitals, higher education, youth agencies, religious giving, and cultural programs.
Types of support: Building funds.
Limitations: Giving primarily in WI. No grants to individuals.
Application information:
Initial approach: Letter
Deadline(s): None
Board meeting date(s): Periodically
Write: Grants Comm.
Officers: Ralph T. Brotz,* Pres.; Stuart W. Brotz,* V.P. and Treas.; Ralph R. Brotz, Secy.
Trustees:* Roland M. Neumann.
Employer Identification Number: 396060552

3281
M. G. Bush-D. D. Nusbaum Foundation, Inc.

c/o Schreiber Foods Inc., 425 Pine St.
P.O. Box 19010
Green Bay 54301 (414) 437-7601

Donor(s): Schreiber Foods.
Financial data (yr. ended 12/31/87): Assets, $58,686 (M); gifts received, $10,000; expenditures, $3,300, including $3,000 for 2 grants of $1,500 each.
Purpose and activities: The foundation intends to focus on its support in the areas of health and welfare, education, culture and the arts, and civic betterment.
Limitations: Giving primarily in areas of company operations. No support for tax supported institutions, to religious interests, or to political parties or candidates. No grants to individuals.
Application information:
Initial approach: Letter
Write: Robert J. Pruess
Officers and Directors: Robert H. Bush, Pres.; R.J. Preuss, V.P. and Secy.-Treas.; D.D. Nusbaum.
Employer Identification Number: 391537768

3282
Carrie Foundation

One East Milwaukee St.
Janesville 53545 (608) 756-4141

Established in 1984 in WI.
Financial data (yr. ended 11/30/87): Assets, $308,674 (M); expenditures, $173,449, including $172,300 for 13 grants (high: $55,000; low: $200).
Purpose and activities: Primarily supports higher education, Catholic institutions and cultural programs.
Application information:
Initial approach: Letter
Deadline(s): None
Write: George K. Steil, Sr., Trustee
Trustees: James Fitzgerald, Marilyn Fitzgerald, George K. Steil, Sr.
Employer Identification Number: 391503227

3283
Chapman Foundation

777 East Wisconsin Ave., Suite 3090
Milwaukee 53202 (414) 276-6955

Established in 1944 in NY.
Donor(s): Laura Isabelle Miller,† and other donors.
Financial data (yr. ended 12/31/86): Assets, $1,300,000 (M); gifts received, $600,000; expenditures, $445,000, including $442,000 for 110 grants (high: $83,000; low: $25; average: $500).
Purpose and activities: Grants for education, health services, conservation, and culture; support also for the United Way.
Types of support: Capital campaigns, general purposes.
Limitations: Giving primarily in Milwaukee, WI. No grants to individuals.
Application information: At present, contributes primarily to pre-selected organizations.
Initial approach: Letter or proposal
Deadline(s): None
Write: George M. Chester, Pres.
Officers and Directors:* George M. Chester,* Pres.; Marion C. Read, V.P.; Verne C. Read, V.P.; William M. Chester, Jr.,* Secy.-Treas.
Employer Identification Number: 396059569

3284
Consolidated Papers Foundation, Inc.

231 First Ave. North
P.O. Box 8050
Wisconsin Rapids 54495-8050 (715) 422-3368

Incorporated in 1951 in WI.
Donor(s): Consolidated Papers, Inc., Hotel Mead Corp.
Financial data (yr. ended 12/31/88): Assets, $7,988,634 (M); gifts received, $750,100; expenditures, $1,201,730, including $1,195,374 for 109 grants (high: $266,500; low: $100; average: $5,000-$8,000) and $35,731 for 441 employee matching gifts.
Purpose and activities: Giving for local community funds, and youth and social service agencies in communities where Consolidated Papers, Inc. conducts operations; higher education grants generally limited to those in WI; support also for the fine and performing arts and other cultural programs.
Types of support: Operating budgets, continuing support, annual campaigns, seed money, emergency funds, building funds, equipment, endowment funds, employee matching gifts, scholarship funds, employee-related scholarships, capital campaigns, renovation projects, professorships.
Limitations: Giving primarily in WI, usually near areas of company operations. No grants to individuals (except scholarships), or for deficit financing, research, or conferences; no loans.
Application information:
Initial approach: Proposal
Copies of proposal: 1
Deadline(s): Mar. 31 and Sept. 30
Board meeting date(s): May or June, and Nov. or Dec.
Final notification: 3 months
Write: Daniel P. Meyer, Pres.
Officers: Daniel P. Meyer,* Pres.; Mrs. Howard J. Bell,* V.P.; Carl R. Lemke, Secy.; Lamont O. Jaeger, Treas.
Directors:* I.F. Boyce, Patrick F. Brennan, L.A. Engelhardt, George W. Mead, D.L. Stein.
Number of staff: None.
Employer Identification Number: 396040071

3285
Patrick and Anna M. Cudahy Fund

P.O. Box 11978
Milwaukee 53211 (414) 962-6820

Incorporated in 1949 in WI.
Donor(s): Michael F. Cudahy.†
Financial data (yr. ended 12/31/87): Assets, $17,701,756 (M); expenditures, $1,288,338, including $1,110,200 for 102 grants (high: $69,200; low: $400; average: $5,000-$10,000).

Purpose and activities: Support primarily for social services, youth agencies, and education; support also for national programs concerned with environmental and public interest issues, and cultural and civic affairs programs.
Types of support: General purposes, operating budgets, continuing support, annual campaigns, seed money, emergency funds, deficit financing, building funds, equipment, land acquisition, matching funds, consulting services, technical assistance, scholarship funds, special projects, research, fellowships, renovation projects, capital campaigns.
Limitations: Giving primarily in Milwaukee, WI, and Chicago, IL, and for national programs. No grants to individuals, or for endowments; no loans.
Publications: Annual report, application guidelines.
Application information:
Initial approach: Letter
Copies of proposal: 1
Deadline(s): 1 month prior to board meetings
Board meeting date(s): Usually in Mar., June, Sept., and Dec.
Final notification: 1 week after meetings
Write: Richard W. Yeo, Admin.
Officers: Janet S. Cudahy,* Pres.; Louise A. McMenamin, Secy.-Treas.; Richard W. Yeo, Admin.
Directors:* Richard D. Cudahy, Chair.; James Bailey, Kit Cudahy, Richard D. Cudahy, Jr., Dudley J. Godfrey, Jr., Jean Holtz, Philip Lerman, Wesley Scott.
Number of staff: 1 part-time professional.
Employer Identification Number: 390991972

3286
CUNA Mutual Insurance Group Charitable Foundation, Inc.
5910 Mineral Point Rd.
Madison 53705 (608) 231-7314

Incorporated in 1967 in WI.
Financial data (yr. ended 12/31/87): Assets, $200,592 (M); gifts received, $498,573; expenditures, $439,419, including $439,010 for 174 grants (high: $135,000; low: $15; average: $500).
Purpose and activities: Giving for community funds, health promotion, higher and secondary education, cultural programs, and urban and civic affairs.
Types of support: Operating budgets, continuing support, annual campaigns, seed money, emergency funds, employee matching gifts, scholarship funds, fellowships, special projects, research, capital campaigns, matching funds.
Limitations: Giving primarily in WI. No grants to individuals, or for deficit financing, land acquisition, endowment funds, or publications; no loans.
Publications: Informational brochure (including application guidelines).
Application information: Application form required for requests of over $500.
Initial approach: Proposal, letter, or telephone
Copies of proposal: 1
Board meeting date(s): Feb., May, and Sept.
Final notification: 4 to 6 weeks
Write: Richard C. Radtke, Asst. Secy.-Treas.
Officers and Directors: James C. Barbe, Pres.; Rosemarie Shultz, V.P.; Robert L. Curry, Secy.-Treas. and Exec. Officer; Gerald J. Ping.
Number of staff: None.
Employer Identification Number: 396105418

3287
Gretchen & Andrew Dawes Endowment, Inc.
c/o Foley & Lardner
777 East Wisconsin Ave.
Milwaukee 53202-5373

Established in 1983 in WI.
Financial data (yr. ended 12/31/87): Assets, $9,809 (M); gifts received, $140,000; expenditures, $139,243, including $136,000 for 6 grants (high: $100,000; low: $1,000).
Purpose and activities: Support primarily for an exhibition and for the endowment of a staff position at a zoological society; support also for capital acquisitions for a public museum and a symphony orchestra.
Types of support: Endowment funds, capital campaigns.
Limitations: Giving primarily in Milwaukee, WI.
Application information:
Deadline(s): None
Write: Stephen M. Fisher, Secy.-Treas.
Officers and Directors: Gretchen N. Dawes, Pres.; Allen M. Taylor, V.P.; Stephen M. Fisher, Secy.-Treas.
Employer Identification Number: 391455825

3288
DEC International-Albrecht Foundation
P.O. Box 8050
Madison 53708

Financial data (yr. ended 12/31/87): Assets, $1,402 (M); gifts received, $29,257; expenditures, $29,866, including $29,857 for 56 grants (high: $12,000; low: $40).
Purpose and activities: Giving for civic affairs, health associations, youth, United Way, arts, and religious giving.
Limitations: Giving primarily in the midwest area.
Application information:
Initial approach: Letter
Officers: Pat Burchard, Pres. and Treas.; Randal Albrecht, Secy.
Employer Identification Number: 396075225

3289
Edward U. Demmer Foundation
c/o The Marine Trust Co.
P.O. Box 1308
Milwaukee 53201 (414) 765-2800

Trust established in 1963 in WI.
Donor(s): Edward U. Demmer.†
Financial data (yr. ended 12/31/87): Assets, $2,121,290 (M); expenditures, $306,390, including $274,000 for 38 grants (high: $73,500; low: $1,000).
Purpose and activities: Giving restricted to Protestant or non-sectarian institutions, with emphasis on projects related to children; support also for cultural institutions, health agencies, and hospitals.
Limitations: Giving primarily in WI. No grants to individuals.
Application information:
Initial approach: Proposal
Copies of proposal: 4
Deadline(s): None
Board meeting date(s): Mar., June, Sept., and Dec.
Write: Robert L. Hanley, Sr. V.P. - The Marine Trust Co.
Trustees: Lawrence Demmer, Harrold J. McComas, Carl N. Otjen, The Marine Trust Co.
Employer Identification Number: 396064898

3290
Mathilde U. & Albert Elser Foundation, Inc.
c/o Foley & Lardner
777 East Wisconsin Ave., Suite 3800
Milwaukee 53202-5366 (414) 289-3613

Established in 1955 in WI.
Donor(s): Marianne E. Markham, Gertrude E. Schroeder.
Financial data (yr. ended 12/31/87): Assets, $152,784 (M); gifts received, $82,623; expenditures, $124,672, including $120,530 for 98 grants (high: $16,000; low: $15).
Purpose and activities: Support primarily for culture and conservation; giving also to health associations.
Limitations: No grants to Individuals.
Application information:
Initial approach: Handwritten letter
Deadline(s): None
Write: Richard H. Miller, Secy.
Officers and Directors:* Marianne E. Markham,* Pres. and Treas.; Gertrude E. Schroeder,* V.P.; Richard H. Miller, Secy.
Employer Identification Number: 396044395

3291
Ralph Evinrude Foundation, Inc.
c/o Quarles and Brady
411 East Wisconsin Ave.
Milwaukee 53202-4497 (414) 277-5000

Incorporated in 1959 in WI.
Donor(s): Ralph Evinrude.†
Financial data (yr. ended 7/31/87): Assets, $2,359,842 (M); expenditures, $125,336, including $84,750 for 18 grants (high: $25,000; low: $250).
Purpose and activities: Emphasis on education, hospitals, health agencies, cultural programs, youth agencies, and community funds.
Types of support: Annual campaigns, building funds, capital campaigns, equipment, general purposes, matching funds, operating budgets, renovation projects, research, scholarship funds, seed money, special projects.
Limitations: Giving primarily in Milwaukee, WI, and Stuart, FL. No grants to individuals; no loans.
Application information:
Initial approach: Proposal or letter
Copies of proposal: 1
Deadline(s): Submit proposal preferably in Jan., Apr., July, or Oct.
Board meeting date(s): Quarterly in Feb., May, Aug., and Nov.

Final notification: Within 2 weeks after meeting
Write: Patrick W. Cotter, V.P.
Officers and Directors: Thomas J. Donnelly, Pres.; Patrick W. Cotter, V.P. and Treas.; Theodore F. Zimmer, Secy.
Number of staff: 1 part-time professional.
Employer Identification Number: 396040256

3292
The Evjue Foundation, Inc.
1901 Fish Hatchery Rd.
P.O. Box 8060
Madison 53708 (608) 252-6401

Incorporated in 1958 in WI.
Donor(s): William T. Evjue.†
Financial data (yr. ended 2/28/88): Assets, $1,529,736 (M); gifts received, $788,093; expenditures, $653,801, including $590,319 for 113 grants (high: $50,000; low: $195; average: $1,000-$5,000).
Purpose and activities: Support for mental health, higher education, cultural programs, and youth and social service agencies.
Types of support: Continuing support, annual campaigns, seed money, emergency funds, special projects, scholarship funds, professorships, internships, publications, conferences and seminars, endowment funds.
Limitations: Giving primarily in Dane County, WI. No support for medical or scientific research. No grants to individuals, or for building funds, equipment, land acquisition, renovation projects, or operating expenses; no loans.
Publications: Program policy statement, application guidelines.
Application information:
Initial approach: Letter
Copies of proposal: 7
Deadline(s): Submit proposal preferably in Oct. or Nov.
Board meeting date(s): Jan., Mar., June, and Sept., and as required
Final notification: 3 months
Write: Frederick W. Miller, Treas.
Officers and Directors: John H. Lussier, Pres.; Mrs. Frederick W. Miller, V.P.; Frederick H. Gage, Secy.; Frederick W. Miller, Treas.; Nancy Brooke Gage, James D. Lussier, Gordon Sinykin.
Number of staff: 1 part-time support.
Employer Identification Number: 396073981

3293
First Wisconsin Foundation, Inc.
777 East Wisconsin Ave.
Milwaukee 53202 (414) 765-4933

Incorporated in 1954 in WI.
Donor(s): First Wisconsin Bankshares Corp., and affiliates.
Financial data (yr. ended 12/31/87): Assets, $4,441,474 (M); expenditures, $764,965, including $754,311 for 165 grants (high: $310,000; low: $25; average: $1,000-$25,000).
Purpose and activities: Emphasis on a community fund, cultural programs, secondary and higher education, youth and social service agencies, and health; also supports Jewish organizations.
Types of support: Annual campaigns, building funds, continuing support, deficit financing, equipment, general purposes.
Limitations: Giving primarily in the Milwaukee, WI, area. No grants to individuals, or for endowment funds, research, or matching gifts; no loans.
Publications: Program policy statement, application guidelines.
Application information:
Initial approach: Letter
Copies of proposal: 1
Deadline(s): None
Board meeting date(s): Monthly
Final notification: 60 days
Write: Dennis R. Fredrickson
Officers and Directors:* Roger L. Fitzsimonds,* John H. Hendee, Jr.,* Chair.; John A. Becker,* Pres.; William H. Bergner, V.P.; William H. Risch, V.P.; Charles P. Hoke, Secy.-Treas.; and 15 additional directors.
Number of staff: 3
Employer Identification Number: 396042050

3294
Fort Howard Paper Foundation, Inc.
P.O. Box 11325
Green Bay 54307-1325 (414) 435-8821
Illinois office: 7575 South Kostner Ave., Chicago, IL 60652

Incorporated in 1953 in WI.
Donor(s): Fort Howard Paper Co.
Financial data (yr. ended 12/31/87): Assets, $13,227,704 (M); expenditures, $1,544,121, including $1,290,013 for 29 grants (high: $200,000; low: $700; average: $16,000-$125,000) and $15,364 for 5 grants to individuals.
Purpose and activities: Emphasis on education, cultural programs, and social service and youth agencies; support also for health-care facilities, and a competitive college scholarship award.
Types of support: Building funds, equipment, scholarship funds, student aid.
Limitations: Giving primarily in areas of company operations and limited surrounding areas; emphasis on Green Bay, WI, and Muskogee, OK.
Application information: Application form required for scholarships; contact foundation for information on scholarships. Application form required.
Deadline(s): Nov. 1 for scholarships
Write: Bruce W. Nagel, Asst. Secy.
Officers and Directors:* Paul J. Schierl,* Pres.; Kathleen J. Hempel,* V.P.; Robert E. Manger,* V.P.; Carol A. Schierl,* V.P.; Michael J. Schierl,* V.P.; James J. Schoshinski,* V.P.; Thomas L. Shaffer,* V.P.; Cheryl A. Thomson, Secy.; Susan M. Van Schyndle, Treas.; John W. Hickey.
Number of staff: None.
Employer Identification Number: 362761910

3295
Community Foundation for the Fox Valley Region, Inc.
222 West College Ave.
P.O. Box 563
Appleton 54912 (414) 730-3773

Organized in 1986 in WI.
Financial data (yr. ended 6/30/88): Assets, $1,907,989 (M); gifts received, $68,458; expenditures, $112,529, including $37,196 for grants.
Purpose and activities: Support for social services, civic affairs, health, education, and cultural affairs.
Limitations: Giving limited to the Fox Valley, WI, area. No support for sectarian or religious purposes, or specific research or medical projects. No grants for operating expenses, annual fund drives, deficit financing, endowment funds, capital projects, or travel expenses.
Publications: Biennial report, informational brochure.
Application information:
Initial approach: Letter or telephone
Deadline(s): Jan. 15, Apr. 15, July 15, and Sept. 30
Board meeting date(s): Feb., May, Aug. and Nov.
Write: Paul H. Groth, Exec. Dir.
Officers: Walter L. Rugland, Chair.; Arthur P. Remley, Pres.; Roger A. Baird, V.P.; O.C. Boldt, V.P.; Mary Sensenbrenner, V.P.; Larry L. Kath, Secy.; Gail E. Janssen, Treas.; Paul H. Groth, Exec. Dir.
Directors: John F. Barlow, and 38 other directors.
Employer Identification Number: 391548450

3296
The Gardner Foundation
111 East Wisconsin Ave., Suite 1359
Milwaukee 53202 (414) 272-0383

Incorporated in 1947 in NY.
Donor(s): Herman Gardner.†
Financial data (yr. ended 12/31/88): Assets, $1,357,236 (M); expenditures, $110,683, including $104,150 for 42 grants (high: $10,383; low: $100; average: $1,000-$5,000).
Purpose and activities: Grants for social services, education, community development, health services, and culture.
Types of support: Operating budgets, renovation projects, capital campaigns, emergency funds, scholarship funds.
Limitations: Giving primarily in the greater Milwaukee, WI, area.
Publications: Program policy statement, application guidelines.
Application information: Application form required.
Initial approach: Letter
Copies of proposal: 1
Deadline(s): Mar., Aug., and Nov.
Board meeting date(s): Apr., Sept., and Dec.
Final notification: Within one month of meeting
Write: Theodore Friedlander, Jr., Pres.
Officers and Directors: Theodore Friedlander, Jr., Pres.; Gardner L. Friedlander, V.P.; A. William Asmuth, Jr., Secy.; Gardner L.R.

Friedlander, Jean W. Friedlander, Karen Friedlander, Louise Friedlander, Theodore Friedlander III, John C. Geilfuss, Norman Paulsen, Eleanor S. Poss.
Number of staff: None.
Employer Identification Number: 396076956

3297
Harnischfeger Foundation, Inc.
P.O. Box 554
Milwaukee 53201 (414) 784-4679

Incorporated in 1929 in WI.
Donor(s): Walter Harnischfeger,† Harnischfeger Corp.
Financial data (yr. ended 12/31/87): Assets, $2,106,222 (M); expenditures, $84,965, including $54,850 for grants (high: $10,000; low: $100).
Purpose and activities: Emphasis on hospitals and health care, a community fund, higher education, cultural activities, and youth agencies.
Limitations: No grants to individuals, or for endowment funds, research, scholarships, fellowships, or matching gifts; no loans.
Application information:
Initial approach: Letter
Copies of proposal: 1
Board meeting date(s): May and Nov.
Write: Henry Harnischfeger, Pres.
Officers and Directors:* Henry Harnischfeger,* Pres.; Elizabeth Ogden,* V.P.; George B. Knight,* Secy.; Norman O. Rieboldt, Treas.
Employer Identification Number: 396040450

3298
Evan and Marion Helfaer Foundation
735 North Water St.
Milwaukee 53202 (414) 276-3600

Established in 1971 in WI.
Donor(s): Evan P. Helfaer.†
Financial data (yr. ended 7/31/87): Assets, $15,339,527 (M); expenditures, $985,208, including $811,560 for 137 grants (high: $69,435; low: $375).
Purpose and activities: Support for higher education, cultural programs, youth and social service agencies, and health.
Types of support: Lectureships, professorships, building funds, research.
Limitations: Giving limited to WI. No grants to individuals.
Application information: Application form available, but not required or preferred.
Initial approach: Letter
Deadline(s): None
Board meeting date(s): Periodically
Final notification: Within 90 days after end of fiscal year
Write: Thomas L. Smallwood, Trustee
Trustees: Thomas L. Smallwood, Admin.; Jack F. Kellner, Marshall & Ilsley Trust Co.
Number of staff: 1
Employer Identification Number: 396238856

3299
Margaret Banta Humleker Charitable Foundation, Inc.
735 North Water St.
Milwaukee 53202

Established in 1982 in WI.
Donor(s): Margaret Banta Humleker.
Financial data (yr. ended 11/30/87): Assets, $87,936 (M); gifts received, $209,992; expenditures, $121,833, including $115,817 for 212 grants (high: $13,500; low: $5).
Purpose and activities: Support primarily for higher education and cultural organizations.
Application information: Contributes only to pre-selected organizations. Applications not accepted.
Trustees: John Hein, Margaret Banta Humleker, Peter D. Humleker III.
Employer Identification Number: 391427005

3300
Thomas H. Jacob Foundation, Inc.
P.O. Box 8010
Wausau 54402-8010 (715) 845-3111

Financial data (yr. ended 9/30/87): Assets, $735,814 (M); expenditures, $139,693, including $117,663 for 101 grants (high: $40,774; low: $25).
Purpose and activities: Support primarily for youth organizations, community development, and cultural organizations and institutions.
Types of support: Scholarship funds.
Limitations: Giving primarily in the Wausau and northern WI, area.
Application information:
Initial approach: Letter
Deadline(s): None
Write: John W. Ullrich, Pres.
Officers and Directors: John W. Ullrich, Pres.; V.J. Travis, V.P.; Elizabeth S. Peters, Secy.; Clifford Vander Wall, Treas.
Employer Identification Number: 396044815

3301
Janesville Foundation, Inc.
121 North Parker Dr.
P.O. Box 1492
Janesville 53547 (608) 752-1032

Incorporated in 1944 in WI.
Donor(s): Merchants and Savings Bank, The Parker Brothers Pen Company, and others.
Financial data (yr. ended 12/31/88): Assets, $7,456,545 (M); gifts received, $4,650; expenditures, $671,636, including $497,704 for 30 grants (high: $158,035; low: $100; average: $5,000-$10,000) and $30,425 for 37 grants to individuals.
Purpose and activities: Support for the purpose of equipping individuals to help themselves and to aid the community; emphasis on higher and secondary education, scholarships for local high school graduates, youth and child welfare agencies, community funds, and historic restoration.
Types of support: Continuing support, seed money, building funds, equipment, land acquisition, matching funds, student aid, special projects, conferences and seminars.
Limitations: Giving limited to Janesville, WI. No support for political projects. No grants to individuals (except for scholarships), or for operating budgets or endowment funds; no loans.
Publications: Informational brochure (including application guidelines).
Application information:
Initial approach: Letter with brief outline of proposal, or by telephone
Copies of proposal: 5
Deadline(s): 15th of month prior to each board meeting
Board meeting date(s): Feb., May, Aug., and Nov.
Final notification: As soon as possible after board meetings
Write: Alan W. Dunwiddie, Jr., Exec. Dir.
Officers: Alan W. Dunwiddie, Jr.,* Pres. and Exec. Dir.; Roger E. Axtell, V.P.; Alfred P. Diotte,* V.P.; Phyllis Saevre, Secy.-Treas.
Directors:* George S. Parker, Chair.; Rowland J. McClellan.
Number of staff: 1 full-time professional; 2 part-time support.
Employer Identification Number: 396034645
Recent arts and culture grants:
Janesville, City of, Historic Commission, Janesville, WI, $21,500. For matching grant for identification and nomination of Historic Districts in City of Janesville. 11/23/87.
Wisconsin Public Radio Foundation, Madison, WI, $5,000. For matching grant to encourage increased listener support in Rock County area. 11/23/87.

3302
S. C. Johnson & Son Corporate Contributions Program
1525 Howe St.
Racine 53403 (414) 631-2000

Purpose and activities: Support by the company is directed to worthy recipients who do not fall within the established giving guidelines of The Johnson's Wax Fund, Inc. Direct company contributions support educational institutions, including a private secondary school, a medical school, a summer work program for youth, community development, health care programs for children, public television, a zoological society, and civic groups. The company also provides in-kind donations of equipment, products, and services, and administers the H.F. Johnson Community Service Awards and an employee volunteer program, "People Who Care." The awards program recognizes employee volunteers by contributing to charities in the name of the award winner.
Types of support: In-kind gifts, endowment funds, building funds, continuing support.
Limitations: No support for political causes, religious institutions for denominational purposes, or fraternal, labor, and veterans' organizations.

3303
Johnson Controls Foundation
5757 North Green Bay Ave.
P.O. Box 591
Milwaukee 53201 (414) 228-2219

Trust established in 1952 in WI.
Donor(s): Johnson Controls, Inc.
Financial data (yr. ended 12/31/88): Assets, $17,026,046 (M); gifts received, $3,500,000; expenditures, $3,388,046, including $3,013,091 for 1,753 grants (low: $25), $84,500 for grants to individuals and $177,900 for 1,230 employee matching gifts.
Purpose and activities: Grants for higher education; health and hospitals; community funds; social services, including aid to the handicapped, care of children, and the aged; and civic, arts, and cultural organizations.
Types of support: Operating budgets, continuing support, annual campaigns, seed money, emergency funds, building funds, endowment funds, matching funds, employee-related scholarships, employee matching gifts.
Limitations: No support for political or religious purposes; public or private pre-schools; elementary or secondary schools; industrial groups or trade associations supported by industrial groups; foreign-based institutions; or fraternal, veterans', or labor groups. No grants to individuals (except employee-related scholarships), or for fundraising events, courtesy advertising, deficit financing, equipment, land acquisition, special projects, research, publications, conferences, or seminars; no loans.
Publications: Application guidelines.
Application information: Employee-related scholarship awards are paid directly to institutions and not to individuals.
Initial approach: Letter
Copies of proposal: 1
Deadline(s): None
Board meeting date(s): Usually Mar., June, and Sept.
Final notification: Up to 120 days
Write: Florence R. Klatt, Member, Advisory Board
Advisory Board: Fred L. Brengel, James H. Keyes, Florence R. Klatt, Philip R. Smith, R. Douglas Ziegler.
Trustee: First Wisconsin Trust Co.
Number of staff: 1 full-time professional; 1 part-time professional; 4 part-time support.
Employer Identification Number: 396036639
Recent arts and culture grants:
Detroit Symphony Orchestra, Detroit, MI, $5,000. 1987.
Madison Art Center, Madison, WI, $5,000. 1987.
Milwaukee Art Museum, Milwaukee, WI, $63,500. 1987.
Milwaukee Art Museum, Milwaukee, WI, $6,708. For matching support. 1987.
Milwaukee Institute of Art and Design, Milwaukee, WI, $5,000. 1987.
Milwaukee Public Museum, Milwaukee, WI, $20,000. 1987.
Milwaukee Symphony Orchestra, Milwaukee, WI, $7,193. For matching support. 1987.
Museum of Science, Economics and Technology, Discovery World, Milwaukee, WI, $6,000. 1987.
United Performing Arts Fund, Milwaukee, WI, $200,000. 1987.
United Performing Arts Fund, Milwaukee, WI, $7,906. For matching support. 1987.
University of Michigan, Museum of Art, Ann Arbor, MI, $9,500. 1987.
University of Wisconsin, School of Fine Arts, Milwaukee, WI, $5,000. 1987.
W M V S/W M V T Public Television, Milwaukee, WI, $7,318. For matching support. 1987.
W M V S/W M V T Public Television, Channel 10/36, Milwaukee, WI, $20,000. 1987.
Wisconsin Conservatory of Music, Milwaukee, WI, $5,000. 1987.
Zoological Society of Milwaukee County, Milwaukee, WI, $50,000. 1987.
Zoological Society of Milwaukee County, Milwaukee, WI, $6,850. For matching support. 1987.

3304
The Johnson Foundation, Inc.
P.O. Box 547
Racine 53401-0547 (414) 639-3211

Incorporated in 1958 in NY.
Donor(s): S.C. Johnson & Son, Inc., and descendants of the late H.F. Johnson.
Financial data (yr. ended 6/30/88): Assets, $11,739,812 (M); gifts received, $1,820,255; expenditures, $2,781,506, including $27,654 for 7 grants (high: $7,500; low: $1,500) and $2,447,000 for foundation-administered programs.
Purpose and activities: A private operating foundation; supports four broad areas of activity: international understanding, educational excellence, intellectual and cultural growth, and improvement of the human environment; support also for family services, welfare, and the arts. The foundation's principal activity is planning and carrying out conferences at Wingspread, its educational conference center in Racine. Grants limited to activities directly related to Wingspread programs. Publications based on Wingspread conferences available on request.
Types of support: Conferences and seminars, publications.
Limitations: No grants to individuals.
Publications: Annual report (including application guidelines).
Application information:
Initial approach: Letter
Copies of proposal: 1
Board meeting date(s): June and Dec.
Final notification: Approximately 8 weeks
Write: Lovice M. Becker, Asst. Secy.
Officers: Samuel C. Johnson,* Chair.; Charles W. Bray,* Pres.; Catherine B. Cleary,* V.P. and Secy.; M. Jon Vondracek, V.P., Programs and Public Communication; Harold F. Greiveldinger, Treas.
Trustees:* Robben W. Fleming, Patricia Albjerg Graham, Robert S. Ingersoll, Donald F. McHenry, Robert M. O'Neil, William J. Raspberry.
Number of staff: 6 full-time professional; 12 full-time support.
Employer Identification Number: 390958255

3305
The Johnson Foundation Trust
1525 Howe St.
Racine 53403

Established in 1937.
Financial data (yr. ended 6/30/88): Assets, $1,373,295 (M); expenditures, $38,729, including $28,200 for 8 grants (high: $10,000; low: $1,000).
Purpose and activities: Giving primarily for higher education, cultural programs, conservation, and recreation programs.
Application information: Most grants are pre-selected by trustees.
Write: Robert C. Hart, Secy.
Officers: Samuel C. Johnson, Chair.; Robert C. Hart, Secy.
Trustees: John M. Schroeder, M & I Marshall & Ilsley Bank.
Employer Identification Number: 396052073

3306
The Johnson's Wax Fund, Inc.
1525 Howe St.
Racine 53403 (414) 631-2267

Incorporated in 1959 in WI.
Donor(s): S.C. Johnson & Son, Inc.
Financial data (yr. ended 6/30/88): Assets, $2,060,159 (M); gifts received, $2,622,142; expenditures, $2,117,623, including $1,247,898 for 112 grants (high: $195,350; low: $500; average: $1,000-$40,000) and $771,522 for 3,209 employee matching gifts.
Purpose and activities: Scholarships for children of company employees through the Citizen's Scholarship Foundation of America and the National Merit Scholarship Corp.; scholarships and fellowships in specific areas of interest, i.e., chemistry, biology, marketing, and business; grants to local colleges; support for local welfare, cultural, and civic organizations; grants also for environmental protection, health, and education.
Types of support: Seed money, building funds, equipment, scholarship funds, exchange programs, fellowships, research, employee matching gifts, employee-related scholarships, capital campaigns.
Limitations: Giving primarily in WI and the Midwest in areas of company operations. No support for national health organizations or religious and social groups, organizations receiving support from the United Way, or veterans', labor, or fraternal organizations. No grants to individuals, or for operating budgets, emergency funds, deficit financing, demonstration projects, or conferences; no loans.
Publications: Informational brochure (including application guidelines), corporate giving report.
Application information:
Initial approach: Letter and proposal
Copies of proposal: 1
Deadline(s): None
Board meeting date(s): Mar., June, Sept., and Dec.
Final notification: 3 to 4 months
Write: Reva A. Holmes, V.P. and Secy.
Officers: Samuel C. Johnson,* Chair. and Pres.; David H. Cool,* Vice-Chair.; Reva A. Holmes, V.P. and Secy.; John M. Schroeder, Treas.

Trustees:* Richard A. Baradic, Wesley A. Coleman, Raymond F. Farley, Jane M. Hutterly, Serge E. Logan, Robert G. McCurdy.
Number of staff: 1 part-time professional; 1 part-time support.
Employer Identification Number: 396052089
Recent arts and culture grants:
American Craft Council, NYC, NY, $12,000. For continued support. 1987.
John F. Kennedy Center for the Performing Arts, DC, $5,500. 1987.
Lac Du Flambeau Historical and Cultural Center, Lac Du Flambeau, WI, $5,000. 1987.
Manitowoc Maritime Museum, Manitowoc, WI, $10,000. To help underwrite Wooden Ship Era exhibit. 1987.
Milwaukee Art Museum, Milwaukee, WI, $6,000. 1987.
Milwaukee Repertory Theater, Milwaukee, WI, $5,000. To support development of Theater's new quarters. 1987.
Racine Theater Guild, Racine, WI, $30,000. For capital funds campaign. 1987.
Racine United Arts Fund, Racine, WI, $12,500. To support Racine Symphony Orchestra, Racine Theater Guild, Wustum Museum, and Racine Arts Council. 1987.
United Performing Arts Fund, Milwaukee, WI, $20,000. For continued support. 1987.

3307
Journal Communications Corporate Giving Program
333 West State St.
P.O. Box 661
Milwaukee 53201 (414) 224-2000

Purpose and activities: Support for the arts.
Limitations: Giving primarily in areas of company operations; national charities not considered.
Application information:
Write: Thomas J. McCollow, Chair.

3308
Kearney & Trecker Foundation, Inc.
11000 Theodore Trecker Way
West Allis 53214 (414) 476-8300

Incorporated in 1945 in WI.
Donor(s): Kearney and Trecker Corp.
Financial data (yr. ended 9/30/88): Assets, $1,684,216 (M); expenditures, $191,280, including $132,462 for 91 grants (high: $50,412; low: $25) and $51,645 for 34 employee matching gifts.
Purpose and activities: Support for 1)Education: any museum accredited by the American Association of Museums. Also any technical institution, graduate or professional school, two-year junior or community college, or four-year college or university which is listed in the Education Directory of the U.S. Department of Health, Education, and Welfare. Donations wholly or partially in lieu of tuition, or for tuition, will not be matched. Also support for any radio or television station affiliated with a technical institution, school, college or university. 2)Health and Welfare: any hospital accredited by the American Association, and any member of a United Way or equivalent community welfare fund, to which Kearney and Trecker Foundation made a contribution in its preceding fiscal year. 3)Arts: any United Performing Arts or equivalent community arts fund to which the foundation made a contribution in its preceding year.
Types of support: Employee matching gifts, capital campaigns, matching funds.
Limitations: Giving primarily in WI, with emphasis on the Milwaukee area. No support for government agencies. No grants to individuals, or for endowment funds; no loans.
Application information:
Initial approach: Proposal
Copies of proposal: 1
Board meeting date(s): Jan., May, and Sept.
Write: Donald P. Muench, Treas.
Officers: Richard T. Lindgren,* Pres.; Donald P. Muench, V.P. and Treas.; Donald E. Porter, Secy.
Directors:* Russell A. Hedden, Chair.; Patrick W. Cotter, William J. Fife, Hebert W. Pohle, Brenton H. Rupple, Robert R. Spitzer, Francis J. Trecker.
Employer Identification Number: 396044253

3309
Kohler Corporate Giving Program
Public Affairs Dept. 019
444 Highland Dr.
Kohler 53044 (414) 457-4441

Purpose and activities: Supports arts and culture, public broadcasting, civic and community programs, conservation, law and justice, drug abuse programs, and education, including private colleges, economic education, business education, economic development and environmental programs. Types of support include employee volunteer programs, use of company facilities, and donations of company's primary goods and services. In 1988 the company made in-kind grants to 850 organizations, cash grants to 215 organizations, and awarded 35 scholarships.
Types of support: In-kind gifts, scholarship funds, seed money, matching funds, equipment, endowment funds, building funds, employee-related scholarships.
Limitations: Giving primarily in headquarters city, and communities surrounding Brownwood, TX, Kohler, WI, and Spartanburg, WV from which Kohler Co. draws its employees.
Publications: Informational brochure.
Application information: Include project description, budget, financial report, 501(c)(3) and list of donors and board members.
Initial approach: Letter of inquiry/proposal
Copies of proposal: 1
Deadline(s): Aug. 31
Board meeting date(s): Decisions are made as needed
Final notification: Contributions are made before Dec. 31
Write: Peter J. Fetterer, Mgr., Media and Civic Services
Administrator: Peter J. Fetterer, Mgr., Media and Civic Services.
Number of staff: 1 full-time professional; 1 part-time support.

3310
Kohler Foundation, Inc.
104 Orchard Rd.
Kohler 53044 (414) 458-1972

Incorporated in 1940 in WI.
Donor(s): Herbert V. Kohler,† Marie C. Kohler,† Evangeline Kohler,† Lillie B. Kohler,† O.A. Kroos.†
Financial data (yr. ended 12/31/86): Assets, $21,419,657 (M); expenditures, $1,100,350, including $734,077 for 31 grants (high: $125,000; low: $185) and $67,600 for 79 grants to individuals.
Purpose and activities: Supports education and the arts in WI. Grants are made for seed money, capital expenses or special one-time projects. No gifts for operating or annual fund raising drives. Annual program funds provide scholarships for students graduating from Sheboygen County high schools and to establish a Scholarship Endowment at private colleges in WI. All scholarship recipients are chosen by their schools.
Types of support: General purposes, seed money, building funds, equipment, land acquisition, endowment funds, publications, conferences and seminars, scholarship funds, fellowships, matching funds, special projects, student aid, program-related investments, capital campaigns.
Limitations: Giving limited to WI. No support for health care or medical programs. No grants to individuals (except for scholarships in Sheboygan County), or for operating budgets; no loans.
Publications: Application guidelines.
Application information:
Initial approach: Letter
Copies of proposal: 1
Deadline(s): Submit proposal preferably between Sept. and Nov. or Jan. and Apr.; deadlines Apr. 15 and Nov. 1
Board meeting date(s): May and Dec. and as required
Final notification: 1 week after contributions meetings
Write: Eleanor A. Jung, Exec. Dir.
Officers: Herbert V. Kohler, Jr.,* Chair.; Ruth DeYoung Kohler II, Pres.; Paul Tenpas,* Secy.; Eugene P. Seifert, Treas.; Eleanor A. Jung, Exec. Dir.
Directors:* Sam H. Davis, Frank C. Jacobson.
Number of staff: 2 part-time professional; 1 part-time support.
Employer Identification Number: 390810536

3311
Charles A. Krause Foundation
c/o Krause Consultants, Ltd.
330 East Kilbourne Ave., Two Plaza East 570
Milwaukee 53202 (414) 273-2733

Incorporated in 1952 in WI.
Financial data (yr. ended 12/31/88): Assets, $2,716,412 (M); expenditures, $188,635, including $176,750 for 36 grants (high: $31,000; low: $100) and $6,000 for 2 grants to individuals.
Purpose and activities: Giving primarily for higher and secondary education, conservation, museums, and cultural programs.

Types of support: Capital campaigns, continuing support, general purposes.
Limitations: Giving primarily in WI. No grants to individuals.
Publications: 990-PF.
Application information: Employee-related scholarship program has been discontinued. Previous commitments honored; no new awards to individuals.
Copies of proposal: 1
Deadline(s): Nov. 1
Board meeting date(s): mid - Dec.
Write: Charles A. Krause III, Secy.
Officers: Carol Krause Wythes, Pres.; E.A. Longenecker, V.P.; Charles A. Krause III, Secy.-Treas.; Eleanor T. Sullivan.
Number of staff: None.
Employer Identification Number: 396044820

3312
La Crosse Foundation
P.O. Box 489
La Crosse 54602-0489 (608) 782-1148

Community foundation established in 1930 in WI.
Financial data (yr. ended 12/31/88): Assets, $4,146,206 (M); gifts received, $128,024; expenditures, $358,614, including $291,468 for 169 grants (high: $35,000; low: $150).
Purpose and activities: Support for social programs, higher education, the arts, civic affairs, and youth.
Types of support: Operating budgets, continuing support, annual campaigns, seed money, emergency funds, building funds, equipment, matching funds, scholarship funds, research, conferences and seminars, grants to individuals, program-related investments, publications, employee matching gifts, capital campaigns, general purposes, renovation projects, special projects.
Limitations: Giving limited to La Crosse County, WI. No grants for deficit financing, land acquisition, consulting services, or technical assistance; grants to individuals for scholarships only, with payment made directly to the institution; no loans.
Publications: Annual report (including application guidelines), application guidelines.
Application information: Application form required.
Initial approach: Letter
Copies of proposal: 7
Deadline(s): Submit proposal by the 15th of Feb., May, Aug., and Nov.
Board meeting date(s): Mar., June, Sept., and Dec.
Final notification: Within 1 month of committee meetings
Write: Carol B. Popelka, Prog. Dir.
Directors: Louis F. Robinson, Jr., Chair.; Signe G. Schroeder, Secy.; David D. Baptie, Ruth M. Dalton, M.D., Jack H. Glendenning.
Trustee: La Crosse Trust Company.
Number of staff: 1 part-time professional.
Employer Identification Number: 396037996

3313
Herman W. Ladish Family Foundation, Inc.
c/o Ladish Malting Co.
790 North Jackson St., 2nd Fl.
Milwaukee 53202 (414) 271-4763
Additional address: P.O. Box 2044, Milwaukee, WI 53201

Incorporated in 1956 in WI.
Donor(s): Herman W. Ladish.†
Financial data (yr. ended 6/30/88): Assets, $16,805,541 (M); expenditures, $760,359, including $729,500 for 41 grants (high: $100,000; low: $2,000).
Purpose and activities: Emphasis on higher and secondary education, hospitals and health agencies, youth organizations, and cultural programs.
Limitations: Giving primarily in WI.
Application information:
Deadline(s): None
Board meeting date(s): Twice a year
Write: John H. Ladish, Pres.
Officers: John H. Ladish,* Pres.; Victor F. Braun,* V.P.; Robert T. Stollenwerk, Secy.-Treas.
Directors:* Elwin J. Zarwell.
Number of staff: None.
Employer Identification Number: 396063602

3314
Camille A. Lonstorf Trust
c/o Foley & Lardner
777 East Wisconsin Ave.
Milwaukee 53202 (414) 289-3528

Established in 1985 in WI.
Donor(s): Marge Long.†
Financial data (yr. ended 12/31/87): Assets, $1,248,082 (M); expenditures, $94,254, including $76,000 for 10 grants (high: $10,000; low: $1,000).
Purpose and activities: Support for higher education, social service agencies, cultural programs, and a community fund.
Limitations: Giving primarily in Milwaukee, WI.
Application information:
Initial approach: In writing
Deadline(s): None
Write: Harrold J. McComas, Trustee
Trustee: Harrold J. McComas.
Employer Identification Number: 391509343

3315
The Lubar Family Foundation, Inc.
777 East Wisconsin Ave., Suite 3380
Milwaukee 53202

Established in 1968 in WI.
Donor(s): Members of the Lubar family.
Financial data (yr. ended 12/31/87): Assets, $887,264 (M); expenditures, $280,971, including $250,551 for 69 grants (high: $140,000; low: $20).
Purpose and activities: Grants for higher education, Jewish organizations, and culture.
Types of support: Endowment funds, capital campaigns.
Limitations: Giving primarily in WI.
Application information: Contributes only to pre-selected organizations. Applications not accepted.
Officers and Directors: Marianne S. Lubar, Pres.; Sheldon B. Lubar, V.P. and Secy.; James C. Rowe, Treas.; Kristine L. Thompson.
Employer Identification Number: 391098690

3316
Madison Community Foundation
(Formerly United Madison Community Foundation)
615 East Washington Ave.
Madison 53703 (608) 255-0503
Application address: P.O. Box 71, Madison, WI 53701

Established as a trust in 1979 in WI.
Financial data (yr. ended 4/30/88): Assets, $3,858,302 (M); gifts received, $1,141,739; expenditures, $268,885, including $164,188 for 40 grants (high: $20,000; low: $1,000).
Purpose and activities: To address emerging needs of the community in the areas of health and human services, youth, arts and culture, and economic development.
Types of support: Operating budgets, seed money, emergency funds, matching funds, continuing support, technical assistance, special projects, conferences and seminars, consulting services.
Limitations: Giving limited to Dane County, WI. No grants to individuals, or for annual campaigns, deficit financing, scholarships, or fellowships.
Publications: Annual report, application guidelines, informational brochure.
Application information:
Initial approach: Letter followed by proposal
Copies of proposal: 6
Deadline(s): Mar. 15
Board meeting date(s): Quarterly
Final notification: May 1
Write: Jane Taylor Coleman, Exec. Dir.
Board of Governors: W. Robert Koch, Chair.; and 14 other members.
Number of staff: 2 full-time professional; 1 part-time support.
Employer Identification Number: 396038248

3317
Manpower Foundation, Inc.
5301 North Ironwood Rd.
Milwaukee 53201 (414) 961-1000

Established in 1953 in WI.
Donor(s): Manpower, Inc.
Financial data (yr. ended 12/31/87): Assets, $468,668 (M); gifts received, $466,664; expenditures, $128,034, including $124,350 for 20 grants (high: $86,040; low: $200) and $3,000 for 3 grants to individuals.
Purpose and activities: Support for higher education, United Way, arts and culture, and social services; also awards college scholarships for children of employees.
Types of support: Employee-related scholarships.
Application information:
Initial approach: Letter; for scholarships, write to Scholarship Program Coord.
Deadline(s): May 31 for scholarships

Write: Scholarship Program Coord.
Officers and Directors:* Mitchell S. Fromstein, Pres.; Milton B. Berland, V.P.; Gil Palay,* V.P.; Dudley J. Godfrey, Jr.,* Secy.; Robert Krikorian,* Treas.
Employer Identification Number: 396052810

3318
Marcus Corporation Foundation, Inc.
212 West Wisconsin Ave.
Milwaukee 53203 (414) 272-6020

Established in 1961 in WI.
Donor(s): Marcus Corp.
Financial data (yr. ended 12/31/87): Assets, $229,027 (M); gifts received, $246,249; expenditures, $383,892.
Purpose and activities: Grants for cultural programs, medical research, higher and secondary education, and social services.
Types of support: Building funds, research.
Application information:
Initial approach: Letter
Write: Ben Marcus, Pres., or Stephen Marcus, Treas.
Officers and Directors: Ben Marcus, Pres.; Robin Irwin, Secy.; Stephen Marcus, Treas.; C.E. Stevens.
Employer Identification Number: 396046268

3319
Marshall & Ilsley Foundation, Inc.
(Formerly Marshall & Ilsley Bank Foundation, Inc.)
770 North Water St.
Milwaukee 53202

Incorporated in 1958 in WI.
Donor(s): Marshall & Ilsley Bank.
Financial data (yr. ended 12/31/86): Assets, $2,785,531 (M); gifts received, $1,227,927; expenditures, $801,018, including $783,525 for 93 grants (high: $105,000; low: $100; average: $1,000-$21,500) and $16,000 for 11 grants to individuals.
Purpose and activities: Emphasis on higher education, social services, the arts, hospitals, and youth agencies.
Types of support: Student aid.
Limitations: Giving primarily in WI.
Application information:
Initial approach: Letter
Deadline(s): None
Board meeting date(s): As necessary
Final notification: Varies
Write: Diane Sebion, Secy.
Officers: John A. Puelicher,* Pres.; James B. Wigdale,* V.P.; Diane L. Sebion, Secy.
Directors:* Wendell F. Bueche, Burleigh E. Jacobs, Jack F. Kellner, James O. Wright.
Number of staff: None.
Employer Identification Number: 396043185

3320
Faye McBeath Foundation
1020 North Broadway
Milwaukee 53202 (414) 272-5805

Trust established in 1964 in WI.
Donor(s): Faye McBeath.†
Financial data (yr. ended 12/31/88): Assets, $12,417,150 (M); expenditures, $1,195,517, including $1,027,535 for 43 grants (high: $65,000; low: $500).
Purpose and activities: To benefit the people of WI by providing homes and care for elderly persons; promoting education in medical science and public health; providing medical, nursing, and hospital care for the sick and disabled; promoting the welfare of children; promoting research in civics and government directed towards improvement in the efficiency of local government.
Types of support: Seed money, building funds, equipment, special projects, matching funds, renovation projects, capital campaigns, continuing support, technical assistance.
Limitations: Giving limited to WI, with emphasis on the greater Milwaukee area. No support for specific medical or scientific research projects. No grants to individuals, or for annual campaigns, endowment funds, scholarships, or fellowships; grants rarely for emergency funds; no loans.
Publications: Annual report, program policy statement, application guidelines.
Application information:
Initial approach: Letter or telephone
Copies of proposal: 1
Deadline(s): 1 month prior to board meetings
Board meeting date(s): At least bimonthly, beginning in Jan.
Final notification: 2 weeks after meetings
Write: Sarah M. Dean, Exec. Dir.
Officer: Sarah M. Dean, Exec. Dir.
Trustees: Charles A. Krause, Chair.; Bonnie R. Weigell, Vice-Chair.; William L. Randall, Secy.; Joan Handy, Thomas J. McCollow, First Wisconsin Trust Co.
Number of staff: 1 part-time professional.
Employer Identification Number: 396074450
Recent arts and culture grants:
Friends Mime Theater, Milwaukee, WI, $15,000. Toward support of in-school residency programs in five school districts. 12/17/87.
Friends of Boerner Botanical Gardens in Whitnall Park, Milwaukee, WI, $42,000. Toward Children's Horticultural Education Project, which will provide horticultural concepts and gardening skills to Milwaukee area children, from kindergarten through 5th grade. 9/14/87.
Theater School, Milwaukee, WI, $24,500. For support of Theater Express Project during 1987-88 school year, to present multi-arts and educational programming in Milwaukee Public Museum, with goal of expanding understanding of Museum's cultural, historic and scientific exhibits and programs. 9/14/87.

3321
Menasha Corporation Foundation
P.O. Box 367
Neenah 54956 (414) 751-1000

Established in 1953 in WI.
Donor(s): Menasha Corp.
Financial data (yr. ended 12/31/87): Assets, $637,835 (M); gifts received, $354,000; expenditures, $251,322, including $188,862 for 121 grants (high: $5,000; low: $100), $44,300 for 54 grants to individuals and $16,410 for 41 employee matching gifts.
Purpose and activities: Grants primarily for health, welfare, cultural, and higher educational organizations in areas of company operations; giving also for employee-related scholarships and an employee matching gift program.
Types of support: Employee matching gifts, employee-related scholarships.
Limitations: Giving primarily in areas of company operations.
Application information:
Initial approach: Proposal
Deadline(s): None
Write: Oliver C. Smith, Pres.
Officers: Oliver C. Smith, Pres.; D.C. Shepard, V.P.; Steven S. Kromholz, Secy.-Treas.
Employer Identification Number: 396047384

3322
Mielke Family Foundation, Inc.
P.O. Box 2575
Appleton 54913 (414) 734-3416
Application address: Ten Sunnyslope Ct., Appleton, WI, 54911

Established in 1963 in WI.
Financial data (yr. ended 12/31/87): Assets, $3,467,418 (M); gifts received, $427,532; expenditures, $162,186, including $147,811 for 10 grants (high: $75,000; low: $3,000).
Purpose and activities: Support primarily for education, the arts, and health programs.
Limitations: Giving limited to the Appleton and Shawano, WI, areas.
Application information:
Initial approach: Letter
Deadline(s): Apr. 15 and Oct. 15
Board meeting date(s): May and Nov.
Write: Paul Groth, Dir.
Officers and Directors: Jeffrey Riester, Pres.; Philip Keller, V.P.; Warren Parsons, Secy.-Treas.; Harold C. Adams, M.D., Paul H. Groth, John E. Mielke, Marion Nemetz.
Employer Identification Number: 396074258

3323
The Steve J. Miller Foundation
15 North Central Ave.
Marshfield 54449

Trust established about 1946 in WI.
Donor(s): Central Cheese Co., Inc., Steve J. Miller.†
Financial data (yr. ended 12/31/87): Assets, $2,982,367 (M); expenditures, $288,388, including $255,800 for 40 grants (high: $27,100; low: $200).
Purpose and activities: Grants largely for higher education, health agencies, community development, and cultural programs.
Limitations: Giving primarily in WI and Tucson, AZ.
Application information:
Initial approach: Letter
Deadline(s): None
Write: Harvey D. TeStrake, Secy.
Officers: Elizabeth Black Miller, Chair.; Norman C. Miller, Pres.; Isabell E. Black, V.P.; Marbeth M. Spreyer, Asst. V.P.; Harvey D. TeStrake, Secy. and Mgr.; William T. Gaus, Treas.
Employer Identification Number: 396051879

3324
Milwaukee Foundation
1020 North Broadway
Milwaukee 53202 (414) 272-5805

Community foundation established in 1915 in WI by declaration of trust.

Financial data (yr. ended 12/31/87): Assets, $61,736,572 (M); gifts received, $2,379,886; expenditures, $5,192,728, including $4,144,371 for grants (average: $10,000-$20,000).

Purpose and activities: Present funds include many discretionary and some funds designated by the donors to benefit specific institutions or for special purposes, including educational institutions, the arts and cultural programs, social services, health care and hospitals; support also for community development, and conservation and historic preservation.

Types of support: Seed money, building funds, equipment, matching funds, scholarship funds, special projects, renovation projects.

Limitations: Giving primarily in the Milwaukee, WI, area. No support for the general use of churches or for sectarian religious purposes, or for specific medical or scientific projects except from components of the foundation established for such purposes. No grants to individuals (except for established awards), or for operating budgets, continuing support, annual campaigns, endowment funds, or deficit financing.

Publications: Annual report, informational brochure (including application guidelines), grants list, newsletter, program policy statement.

Application information: Capital requests such as construction and renovation for hospitals and health-related agencies are reviewed at June and Dec. board meetings. Application form required.

Initial approach: Proposal, telephone, or letter
Copies of proposal: 1
Deadline(s): Submit proposal preferably 8 weeks before board meetings; deadlines Jan. 1, Apr. 1, July 1, and Oct. 1
Board meeting date(s): Mar., June, Sept., Dec., and as needed
Final notification: 2 weeks after board meetings
Write: David M.G. Huntington, Exec. Dir.

Officer: David M.G. Huntington, Secy. and Exec. Dir.

Foundation Board: Charles W. Parker, Jr., Chair.; Gwen T. Jackson, Vice-Chair.; Orren J. Bradley, Doris H. Chortek, Harry F. Franke, John Galanis, Richard A. Gallun, Dennis Purtell, Brenton H. Rupple.

Trustees: Bank One Wisconsin Trust Co., N.A., First Bank Milwaukee, First Wisconsin Trust Co., N.A., Marshall & Ilsley Trust Co.

Number of staff: 3 full-time professional; 1 part-time professional; 3 full-time support.

Employer Identification Number: 396036407

Recent arts and culture grants:

American Civil Liberties Union of Wisconsin Foundation, Milwaukee, WI, $6,000. To develop theatrical production to be performed throughout state of Wisconsin in celebration of bicentennial of United States Constitution. 9/87.

Artreach Milwaukee, Milwaukee, WI, $8,000. For interim operating support. 6/88.

Ballet Foundation of Milwaukee, Milwaukee, WI, $50,000. For Dance Factory project, new second-stage and experimental choreography center. 12/87.

Bauer Contemporary Ballet, Milwaukee, WI, $6,000. Toward radio and television adaptation of company's earlier multi-media production, The Mind Parasites. 12/87.

Clavis Theater, Milwaukee, WI, $5,700. For joint hiring of part-time advertising manager to sell playbill advertising for all three companies. Grant shared with Milwaukee Chamber Theater and Theater Tesseract. 6/88.

Community Art Centers, Milwaukee, WI, $7,500. For further development of program to provide disabled persons with creative opportunities for artistic expression. 4/8/88.

Friends Mime Theater, Milwaukee, WI, $5,000. For 1988 Cream City Semi-Circus production, outdoor theatrical variety show presented during summer in variety of public settings. 4/8/88.

Greater Milwaukee Committee, Milwaukee, WI, $5,000. Toward cost of preliminary planning for lighting exteriors of seven landmark buildings in downtown Milwaukee. 9/87.

Historic Sites Foundation, Baraboo, WI, $5,000. Toward construction of new exhibit hall and visitors center at Circus World Museum in Baraboo. 12/87.

International Institute of Wisconsin, Milwaukee, WI, $10,000. For feasibility study of multi-ethnic center that could potentially serve more than 100 ethnic groups which are currently members of Institute. 6/88.

Milwaukee Art Museum, Milwaukee, WI, $15,000. For audio-visual presentation to be shown at Museum's centennial exhibition and as introduction to Frederick Layton collection, part of Museum's permanent collection. 12/87.

Milwaukee Artists Foundation, Milwaukee, WI, $10,000. Toward development of central ticket marketing facility (joint box office) for Milwaukee area art and entertainment events. 4/8/88.

Milwaukee Chamber Theater, Milwaukee, WI, $5,600. For joint development and production with WUWM Milwaukee Public Radio of short continuous radio programs written and performed by Milwaukee Chamber Theater and produced and broadcast by WUWM. 6/88.

Milwaukee Chamber Theater, Milwaukee, WI, $5,000. To arrange for guest director for 1988 Shaw Festival. 12/87.

Milwaukee Music Ensemble, Milwaukee, WI, $7,000. For development of full-time music director position. 4/8/88.

Milwaukee Opera Company, Milwaukee, WI, $5,000. For development of apprentice training program for young Milwaukee artists pursuing operatic careers. 12/87.

Peoples Theater, Milwaukee, WI, $7,500. For Community Arts Cavalcade project, series of musical and dramatic productions featuring black experience. 4/8/88.

Skylight Comic Opera, Milwaukee, WI, $10,000. To strengthen management and development staff capacity. 12/87.

Theater X, Milwaukee, WI, $15,000. Toward renovation of new facility. 4/8/88.

United Performing Arts Fund, Milwaukee, WI, $12,500. Toward development of strategic fund raising and marketing plan for 1990s. 6/88.

United Performing Arts Fund, Milwaukee, WI, $9,700. For annual campaign. 9/87.

United Performing Arts Fund, Milwaukee, WI, $6,000. For annual campaign. 6/88.

University of Wisconsin Foundation, School of Fine Arts, Milwaukee, WI, $10,000. Toward support of exhibition of Edward Steichen photography organized for display in Art Museum in conjunction with School's 25th anniversary. 9/87.

Wauwatosa Historical Society, Wauwatosa, WI, $10,000. To develop administrative staff services for Kneeland-Walker Museum and Preservation Center. 4/8/88.

Wisconsin Black Historical Society, Milwaukee, WI, $25,000. Toward establishment of museum in Milwaukee to provide focal point for study and appreciation of black history in state. 6/88.

Wisconsin Conservatory of Music, Milwaukee, WI, $10,000. For sustaining support. 6/88.

Wisconsin Heritages, Milwaukee, WI, $10,000. Toward restoration and repairs of Pabst Mansion. 12/87.

3325
Mosinee Paper Corporation Foundation, Inc.
1244 Kronenwetter Dr.
Mosinee 54455-9099 (715) 693-4470
Special address for scholarship applications: Principal, Mosinee High School, 100 High St., Mosinee, WI 54455; Tel.: (715) 593-3200

Established in 1956 in WI.

Financial data (yr. ended 12/31/87): Assets, $25,585 (M); expenditures, $51,309, including $47,500 for 26 grants (high: $11,000; low: $50) and $3,175 for grants to individuals.

Purpose and activities: Support for arts and culture, higher and other education, social services and youth, health and rehabilitation, conservation, and community funds; support for scholarships for local Mosinee High School students only.

Types of support: Scholarship funds, annual campaigns, building funds, capital campaigns, special projects, employee-related scholarships.

Limitations: Giving primarily in WI.

Application information: The Norman S. Stone Memorial Scholarship is limited to the study of pulp and paper technology or paper science. The Norman S. Stone Memorial Scholarship, the University of Wisconsin-Marathon Center Scholarship, and the North Central Technical Institute Scholarship are limited to the graduating students of Mosinee High School only.

Initial approach: Application for scholarships may be in letter form, and must include what college prep courses have been completed, rank in class, and grade point average
Copies of proposal: 1
Deadline(s): At least 2 weeks prior to board meeting; Mar. 10 for Norman S. Stone Memorial Scholarship

Board meeting date(s): In 1989: Feb. 16, Apr. 20, June 22, Aug. 17, Oct. 19, and Dec. 14
Write: Theresa M. Legner, Asst. Secy. or Richard L. Radt, Pres.
Officers: Richard L. Radt, Pres.; San W. Orr, Jr.,* V.P.; Daniel G. Briner, Secy.; Stanley F. Staples, Jr.,* Treas.
Directors:* Richard Jacobus, Clarence Scholtens.
Employer Identification Number: 396074298

3326
North Shore Bank Foundation
(Formerly First Interstate Bank Foundation)
735 West Wisconsin Ave.
Milwaukee 53233 (414) 783-6505

Financial data (yr. ended 12/31/87): Assets, $58 (M); gifts received, $10,449; expenditures, $10,391, including $10,373 for 26 grants (high: $5,000; low: $15).
Purpose and activities: Support for community funds, youth, religion, health services, and the arts.
Limitations: Giving primarily in WI.
Application information:
Initial approach: Letter
Write: Harlow Fuhr, Trustee
Trustees: Harlow Fuhr, Herbert Hafemann, Kathleen Spitzer.
Employer Identification Number: 396076215

3327
Northwestern National Insurance Foundation
(Formerly ARMCO Insurance Group Foundation)
18650 West Corporate Dr.
Brookfield 53005

Established in 1967 in WI.
Donor(s): Armco Insurance Group, Inc.
Financial data (yr. ended 12/31/87): Assets, $1,694,545 (M); expenditures, $147,573, including $139,851 for 69 grants (high: $65,000; low: $50).
Purpose and activities: Emphasis on community funds, higher education, including employee matching gifts, cultural programs, and hospitals.
Types of support: Employee matching gifts.
Limitations: Giving primarily in areas of company operations.
Application information:
Deadline(s): None
Final notification: Within 6 months
Write: Robert C. Whitaker, V.P. and Secy.
Officers and Trustees: C. Robert Snyder, Chair.; Robert C. Whitaker, V.P. and Secy.; Howard Miller, Treas.
Number of staff: None.
Employer Identification Number: 396102416

3328
Oshkosh Foundation
c/o First Wisconsin National Bank of Oshkosh
P.O. Box 2448
Oshkosh 54903 (414) 424-4283

Community foundation established in 1928 in WI by declaration of trust.
Donor(s): Combs Trust.
Financial data (yr. ended 2/29/88): Assets, $5,732,860 (M); gifts received, $41,615; expenditures, $400,532, including $174,683 for 18 grants (high: $121,250; low: $43) and $141,608 for 224 grants to individuals.
Purpose and activities: Emphasis on scholarships, hospitals, medical care of the indigent, community funds, and cultural programs. Scholarships awarded for graduating Oshkosh high school seniors for a 4-year term only.
Types of support: Continuing support, annual campaigns, emergency funds, building funds, equipment, student aid, operating budgets, grants to individuals.
Limitations: Giving limited to Oshkosh, WI. No grants for endowments, matching gifts, seed money, deficit financing, special projects, research, publications, or conferences; no loans.
Publications: Annual report, application guidelines.
Application information: Applications not accepted unless residency requirements are met.
Initial approach: Proposal
Copies of proposal: 1
Deadline(s): Submit proposal preferably in Apr.; no set deadline
Board meeting date(s): Usually in Apr. and as required
Final notification: 6 weeks
Write: Sandra A. Noe, Trust Officer
Officers and Foundation Committee: Marie Hoyer, Pres.; Edith Collins, V.P.; Virginia Nelson, Secy.; Hibbard H. Engler, Fred Leist, Edward Leyhe, Lewis C. Magnusen.
Trustee: First Wisconsin National Bank of Oshkosh.
Number of staff: 1 full-time professional; 1 full-time support.
Employer Identification Number: 396041638

3329
Parker Foundation
c/o Valley Trust Co.
P.O. Box 5000
Janesville 53547 (608) 755-4249

Established in 1953 in WI.
Financial data (yr. ended 12/31/87): Assets, $1,435,408 (M); expenditures, $85,592, including $53,100 for 29 grants (high: $10,000; low: $100).
Purpose and activities: Giving primarily for higher education; support also for cultural programs and international affairs.
Types of support: General purposes, building funds.
Application information:
Initial approach: Letter
Deadline(s): None
Officers and Directors: Daniel Parker, Pres.; Robert E. Collins, V.P. and Secy.-Treas.; Peter C. Jacobs.
Employer Identification Number: 396074582

3330
Milton and Lillian Peck Foundation, Inc.
P.O. Box 441
Milwaukee 53201

Established in 1958.
Donor(s): Peck Meat Packing Corp., Emmber Brands, Inc., Gibbon Packing, Inc., Moo-Battue, Inc.
Financial data (yr. ended 12/31/87): Assets, $2,235,649 (M); gifts received, $56,000; expenditures, $219,668, including $200,000 for 2 grants of $100,000 each.
Purpose and activities: Grants primarily for hospitals and health associations, Jewish welfare funds and temple support, and cultural organizations. In addition, in 1985, the foundation awarded endowment grants of $200,000 each to three new private foundations related to the Peck family.
Application information: Contributes only to pre-selected organizations. Applications not accepted.
Write: Irving Lowe, Secy.
Officers and Directors:* Milton Peck, Pres. and Treas.; Bernard Peck,* V.P.; Lillian Peck,* V.P.; Irving Lowe,* Secy.
Employer Identification Number: 396051782

3331
Fred J. Peterson Foundation, Inc.
101 Pennsylvania St.
Sturgeon Bay 54235 (414) 743-5574

Incorporated in 1962 in WI.
Donor(s): Peterson Builders, Inc., Fred J. Peterson, Irene Peterson,† Ellsworth L. Peterson.
Financial data (yr. ended 9/30/87): Assets, $2,621,511 (M); gifts received, $106,343; expenditures, $125,334, including $121,450 for 89 grants (high: $10,000; low: $50; average: $100-$500).
Purpose and activities: Giving to organizations working to improve the quality of life for WI citizens; grants for higher education, including scholarships through Rotary International, and various colleges, cultural programs, and community development.
Types of support: Annual campaigns, building funds, capital campaigns, continuing support, equipment, general purposes, operating budgets, scholarship funds, special projects.
Limitations: Giving primarily in Door County, WI. No grants to individuals.
Application information: All scholarship decisions made by Rotary International or individual colleges.
Initial approach: Letter only
Copies of proposal: 1
Deadline(s): Sept. 1
Board meeting date(s): As needed
Final notification: Sept. 10
Write: Marsha L. Kerley, Secy.
Officers and Directors: Ellsworth L. Peterson, Pres.; Fred J. Peterson II, V.P.; Marsha L. Kerley, Secy.-Treas.; Fred J. Peterson.
Number of staff: 1
Employer Identification Number: 396075901

3332
Pfister & Vogel Tanning Company, Inc. Foundation
1531 North Water St.
Milwaukee 53201 (414) 765-5077

Financial data (yr. ended 5/31/87): Assets, $265,768 (M); expenditures, $17,609, including $8,600 for 6 grants (high: $2,000; low: $1,000) and $5,625 for 4 grants to individuals.
Purpose and activities: Support for youth training, guidance, and recreation; higher education, community service and cultural areas, and scholarships for employees' children.
Types of support: Employee-related scholarships, operating budgets.
Limitations: Giving primarily in Milwaukee, WI.
Application information:
Initial approach: Proposal
Trustee: First Wisconsin Trust Co.
Committee Members: John H. Hendee, Terrell C. Horne, Anthony M. Rood, Daniel J. Yahil.
Employer Identification Number: 396036556

3333
Melitta S. Pick Charitable Trust
c/o Foley and Lardner
777 East Wisconsin Ave., Suite 3800
Milwaukee 53202 (414) 289-3528

Trust established in 1972 in WI.
Donor(s): Melitta S. Pick.†
Financial data (yr. ended 1/31/87): Assets, $12,884,869 (M); expenditures, $596,168, including $518,000 for 49 grants (high: $80,000; low: $1,000).
Purpose and activities: Giving primarily to charities of interest to the trustees, with emphasis on the arts, youth agencies, and a community development fund.
Limitations: Giving primarily in southeastern WI. No grants to individuals.
Application information: The foundation's present plans preclude extensive consideration of unsolicited requests.
Initial approach: Letter
Deadline(s): None
Board meeting date(s): As required, usually quarterly
Write: Harrold J. McComas, Trustee
Trustees: Harrold J. McComas, Joan M. Pick.
Employer Identification Number: 237243490

3334
Pollybill Foundation, Inc.
735 North Water St., Suite 1328
Milwaukee 53202 (414) 273-4390

Incorporated in 1960 in WI.
Donor(s): William D. Van Dyke, Polly H. Van Dyke.
Financial data (yr. ended 12/31/87): Assets, $799,089 (M); gifts received, $421,300; expenditures, $417,963, including $400,000 for 30 grants (high: $100,000; low: $500).
Purpose and activities: Emphasis on private secondary education, higher education, the arts, conservation, health and social services.
Limitations: Giving primarily in WI, especially Milwaukee.
Application information:
Deadline(s): None
Write: Paul F. Meissner, Dir.
Officers and Directors: Polly H. Van Dyke, Pres. and Treas.; William D. Van Dyke III, Secy.; Leonard G. Campbell, Jr., Paul F. Meissner.
Employer Identification Number: 396078550

3335
H. C. Prange Company Fund, Inc.
2314 Kohler Memorial Dr.
Sheboygan 53081

Incorporated in 1944 in WI.
Donor(s): H.C. Prange Co.
Financial data (yr. ended 1/31/88): Assets, $119,848 (M); gifts received, $50,000; expenditures, $75,411, including $75,224 for grants.
Purpose and activities: Support for community funds, higher education, youth agencies, hospitals, and a museum.
Limitations: Giving primarily in Sheboygan, Green Bay, Appleton, and Sturgeon Bay, WI.
Officers and Directors: Henry C. Prange, Pres.; John M. Sieracke, Secy.-Treas.
Employer Identification Number: 396048083

3336
Racine County Area Foundation, Inc.
818 Sixth St.
Racine 53403 (414) 632-8474

Incorporated in 1975 in WI.
Financial data (yr. ended 12/31/87): Assets, $1,920,336 (M); gifts received, $94,479; expenditures, $160,048, including $110,416 for 53 grants (high: $8,666; low: $200; average: $2,083) and $5,833 for 17 grants to individuals.
Purpose and activities: Giving primarily for health, community services and affairs, cultural activities, and education, including scholarships for individuals.
Types of support: Seed money, emergency funds, equipment, matching funds, student aid, conferences and seminars, operating budgets.
Limitations: Giving limited to Racine County, WI. No support for church or missionary groups unless for entire community benefit. No grants for capital expenditures, including building funds, endowment funds, research, travel, publications; no continuing support after three years.
Publications: Annual report, application guidelines.
Application information: Application form required.
Initial approach: Phone or letter
Copies of proposal: 10
Deadline(s): Jan. 15, Apr. 15, July 15, and Oct. 15
Board meeting date(s): Mar., June, Sept., and Dec.
Final notification: By letter after meeting in which proposal was discussed
Write: Helen M. Underwood, Exec. Secy.
Officers: Lloyd C. Meier, Pres.; Harry Mussie, V.P. and Treas.; Glenn R. Coates, V.P.; Deanna Parrish, V.P.; Roy J. Josten, Secy.
Number of staff: 1 part-time professional; 1 full-time support; 1 part-time support.
Employer Identification Number: 510188377

3337
Rahr Foundation
P.O. Box 130
Manitowoc 54221-0130 (414) 682-6571

Incorporated in 1942 in WI.
Donor(s): Rahr Malting Co.
Financial data (yr. ended 12/31/88): Assets, $2,902,309 (M); expenditures, $199,950, including $162,358 for 83 grants (high: $11,500; low: $40; average: $1,000) and $26,750 for 14 grants to individuals.
Purpose and activities: Support for charitable and educational institutions and public welfare, higher and secondary education, youth agencies, social services, cultural programs, and a scholarship program for children of company employees.
Types of support: Employee-related scholarships, annual campaigns, capital campaigns.
Limitations: Giving primarily in MN. No grants for endowment funds or research programs; no loans.
Application information:
Initial approach: Letter
Copies of proposal: 1
Deadline(s): None
Board meeting date(s): Annually
Write: JoAnn Weyenberg
Officers: Guido R. Rahr, Jr., Pres.; Frederick W. Rahr, V.P.; George D. Gackle, Secy.-Treas.
Directors: Jack D. Gage, Elizabeth B. Rahr.
Number of staff: None.
Employer Identification Number: 396046046

3338
Rexnord Foundation Inc.
350 North Sunny Slope
Brookfield 53008-0033 (414) 797-5669

Incorporated in 1953 in WI.
Donor(s): Rexnord, Inc.
Financial data (yr. ended 10/31/87): Assets, $3,590,567 (M); expenditures, $946,161, including $624,400 for 104 grants (high: $60,000; low: $200; average: $1,000-$10,000), $30,000 for grants to individuals and $289,175 for employee matching gifts.
Purpose and activities: Grants primarily for community funds, higher education (including an employee matching gift program), hospitals, cultural programs, and youth agencies.
Types of support: Building funds, special projects, employee-related scholarships, employee matching gifts.
Limitations: Giving primarily in areas of company operations, with some emphasis on Milwaukee, WI. No support for political or religious organizations. No grants to individuals (except for employee-related scholarships), or for endowment funds.
Publications: Application guidelines.
Application information:
Initial approach: Letter or proposal

Copies of proposal: 1
Deadline(s): Submit grant proposals preferably in Feb.-Mar. or June-July; deadline mid-May for scholarship applications only
Board meeting date(s): 3 or 4 times a year
Final notification: 3 months
Write: Irene Kopisch, Foundation Admin.; Barb Alcorn for employee-related scholarships
Officers: Donald Taylor,* Pres.; John P. Calhoun,* V.P.; Charles R. Roy, Secy.; W.E. Schauer, Jr.,* Treas.
Directors:* F. Brengel, R.V. Krikorian, William C. Messinger, Gustave H. Moede, Jr., J. Swenson.
Number of staff: None.
Employer Identification Number: 396042029

3339
Rite-Hite Corporation Foundation, Inc.
9019 North Deerwood Drive
Milwaukee 53223-2437

Financial data (yr. ended 12/31/87): Assets, $184,317 (M); expenditures, $34,571, including $34,276 for 54 grants (high: $5,000; low: $20).
Purpose and activities: Support for civic affairs, child welfare, youth, health, culture, and anti-alcohol and drug abuse programs.
Application information:
Initial approach: Letter
Deadline(s): None
Write: Arthur K. White
Officers and Directors: Michael H. White, Pres.; Thomas J. Semran, Secy.-Treas.; Arthur K. White, Morgan P. White.
Employer Identification Number: 391522057

3340
Hamilton Roddis Foundation, Inc.
c/o Augusta D. Roddis
1108 East Fourth St.
Marshfield 54449

Incorporated in 1953 in WI.
Donor(s): Hamilton Roddis,† Augusta D. Roddis, Catherine P. Roddis, Roddis Plywood Corp.
Financial data (yr. ended 12/31/87): Assets, $3,087,094 (M); expenditures, $166,864, including $143,100 for 47 grants (high: $17,500; low: $100).
Purpose and activities: Emphasis on Episcopal church support and religious education, social services, medical research, educational organizations, historic preservation, and local associations.
Limitations: No grants to individuals.
Application information: Grants only to pre-selected organizations. Applications not accepted.
Officers and Directors: William H. Roddis II, Pres.; Mrs. Gordon R. Connor, V.P.; Augusta D. Roddis, Secy.-Treas.
Employer Identification Number: 396077001

3341
Thomas J. Rolfs Foundation, Inc.
c/o Arthur P. Hoberg
735 South Main St.
West Bend 53095 (414) 338-6601

Established in 1959 in WI.
Donor(s): Amity Leather Products Co.
Financial data (yr. ended 9/30/87): Assets, $1,977,096 (M); gifts received, $250,000; expenditures, $65,637, including $51,450 for 14 grants (high: $15,000; low: $100) and $10,000 for 6 grants to individuals.
Purpose and activities: Support primarily for social services, education, and the performing arts.
Types of support: Student aid.
Limitations: Giving primarily in WI.
Application information:
Initial approach: Letter
Deadline(s): None
Write: Arthur P. Hoberg, V.P.
Officers: Thomas J. Rolfs, Pres.; Arthur P. Hoberg, V.P.; John F. Rozek, Secy.-Treas.
Employer Identification Number: 396043350

3342
Will Ross Memorial Foundation
c/o Bank One Wisconsin Trust Co., N.A.
P.O. Box 1308
Milwaukee 53201 (414) 765-2800

Financial data (yr. ended 12/31/88): Assets, $2,678,813 (M); gifts received, $1,584,000; expenditures, $192,761, including $161,900 for 31 grants (high: $25,000; low: $500).
Purpose and activities: Support primarily for the arts, social services, higher education, and health.
Limitations: Giving primarily in Milwaukee, WI.
Application information:
Initial approach: Letter
Deadline(s): None
Write: Mary Ann Whalen, V.P.
Officers and Directors: Edmond C. Young, Pres. and Treas.; Richard R. Teschner, V.P.; John D. Bryson, Jr., Secy.; David L. Kinnamon, Mary Ann Whalen laBahn.
Employer Identification Number: 396044673

3343
Schoenleber Foundation, Inc.
740 North Plankinton Ave., Suite 510
Milwaukee 53203-2403 (414) 276-3400

Established in 1965 in WI.
Donor(s): Marie Schoenleber,† Louise Schoenleber.†
Financial data (yr. ended 12/31/87): Assets, $3,734,529 (M); gifts received, $2,976,795; expenditures, $51,350, including $32,045 for 6 grants (high: $10,000; low: $1,000).
Purpose and activities: Support in the following areas: Education - including scholastic institutions, the library systems and museums and historical societies; Social Welfare - with emphasis on the underpriviledged and handicapped; and the Arts - including music, theatre, and visual arts.
Limitations: Giving primarily in the greater Milwaukee, WI, area.
Application information: Application form required.
Initial approach: Letter
Copies of proposal: 1
Write: Peter C. Haensel, Pres.
Officers and Directors: Peter C. Haensel, Pres.; Frank W. Bastian, Secy.; Walter Schorrak.
Employer Identification Number: 391049364

3344
Segel Family Foundation, Inc.
4700 North 132nd St.
Butler 53007
Application address: P.O. Box 1357, Milwaukee, WI 53201; Tel.: (414) 781-2400

Established in 1955 in WI.
Donor(s): Wis-Pac Foods, Inc.
Financial data (yr. ended 11/30/87): Assets, $1,239,258 (M); gifts received, $5,000; expenditures, $119,742, including $113,005 for 39 grants (high: $50,150; low: $25).
Purpose and activities: Giving primarily to Jewish organizations; support also for higher education, and culture.
Limitations: Giving primarily in Milwaukee, WI.
Application information:
Deadline(s): None
Write: Justin N. Segel, Pres.
Officers: Floyd A. Segel, V.P. and Secy.; Justin N. Segel, Pres. and Treas.
Employer Identification Number: 396040274

3345
Siebert Lutheran Foundation, Inc.
2600 North Mayfair Rd., Suite 390
Wauwatosa 53226 (414) 257-2656

Incorporated in 1952 in WI.
Donor(s): A.F. Siebert,† Reginald L. Siebert,† Milwaukee Electric Tool Corp.
Financial data (yr. ended 12/31/87): Assets, $43,743,066 (M); gifts received, $22,062; expenditures, $1,966,753, including $1,966,753 for 239 grants (high: $200,000; low: $100; average: $2,500-$10,000).
Purpose and activities: Support limited to Lutheran churches and other Lutheran institutions, including colleges, schools, programs for the aged, and other religious welfare agencies.
Types of support: Operating budgets, seed money, emergency funds, building funds, equipment, special projects, conferences and seminars, matching funds, consulting services, renovation projects.
Limitations: Giving primarily in WI. No grants to individuals, or for endowment funds, scholarships, or fellowships; no loans.
Publications: Program policy statement, application guidelines.
Application information:
Initial approach: Letter or telephone
Copies of proposal: 1
Deadline(s): Mar. 15, June 15, Sept. 15, and Dec. 15
Board meeting date(s): Jan., Apr., July, and Oct.
Final notification: 1 week after board meeting
Write: Jack S. Harris, Pres.
Officers: Jack S. Harris, Pres.; John E. Koenitzer,* Secy.

Directors:* Richard C. Barkow, Chair.; Neil A. Turnbull, Vice-Chair.; Glenn W. Buzzard, Edward A. Grede, Jack R. Jaeger, Raymond J. Perry, Russell M. Rutter.
Number of staff: 1 full-time professional; 1 full-time support.
Employer Identification Number: 396050046
Recent arts and culture grants:
Bethany Lutheran College, Mankato, MN, $5,000. Toward construction of fine arts center. 10/25/88.

3346
A. O. Smith Foundation, Inc.
P.O. Box 23965
Milwaukee 53223-0965 (414) 359-4100

Incorporated in 1951 in WI.
Donor(s): A.O. Smith Corp.
Financial data (yr. ended 6/30/87): Assets, $242,869 (M); gifts received, $850,000; expenditures, $687,880, including $667,825 for 89 grants (high: $328,500; low: $150) and $19,780 for 72 employee matching gifts.
Purpose and activities: Support for community funds, civic and cultural affairs, social welfare, higher education, hospitals, and health services.
Types of support: Continuing support, annual campaigns, building funds, scholarship funds, employee matching gifts.
Limitations: Giving primarily in areas of company operations in CA, IL, KY, NC, OH, SC, TN, WA, and WI. No grants to individuals.
Publications: Annual report, application guidelines.
Application information:
Initial approach: Letter, telephone, or proposal
Copies of proposal: 1
Deadline(s): None
Board meeting date(s): June and as required
Final notification: 3 months
Write: E.J. O'Connor, Secy.
Officers and Directors:* L.B. Smith,* Pres.; Thomas I. Dolan,* V.P.; A.O. Smith,* V.P.; E.J. O'Connor,* Secy.; T.W. Ryan, Treas.
Employer Identification Number: 396076924

3347
Stackner Family Foundation, Inc.
411 East Wisconsin Ave.
Milwaukee 53202-4497 (414) 277-5000

Incorporated in 1966 in WI.
Donor(s): John S. Stackner,† Irene M. Stackner.†
Financial data (yr. ended 8/31/87): Assets, $12,709,442 (M); gifts received, $35,523; expenditures, $1,253,998, including $1,128,900 for 140 grants (high: $150,000; low: $200).
Purpose and activities: Grants largely for education, social service and youth agencies, arts and humanities, health agencies, including those serving the mentally ill and the handicapped, environmental protection, and historic preservation.
Types of support: Operating budgets, continuing support, annual campaigns, seed money, building funds, equipment, land acquisition, matching funds, special projects, research, publications, conferences and seminars, scholarship funds, capital campaigns.
Limitations: Giving limited to the greater Milwaukee, WI, area. No grants to individuals, or for deficit financing, or fellowships; no loans.
Application information:
Initial approach: Proposal or letter
Copies of proposal: 1
Deadline(s): Mar. 31 and Aug. 31
Board meeting date(s): Apr. and Sept.
Final notification: 3 weeks after board meetings
Write: Patrick W. Cotter, Exec. Dir.
Officers and Directors:* Patricia S. Treiber,* Pres.; John A. Treiber,* V.P.; Phillip A. Treiber,* V.P.; David L. MacGregor,* Secy.-Treas.; Patrick W. Cotter, Exec. Dir.
Number of staff: 1 part-time professional.
Employer Identification Number: 396097597

3348
Universal Foods Foundation, Inc.
433 East Michigan St.
Milwaukee 53202 (414) 271-6755

Incorporated in 1958 in WI.
Donor(s): Universal Foods Corp.
Financial data (yr. ended 9/30/88): Assets, $6,143,201 (M); gifts received, $100,000; expenditures, $503,884, including $452,778 for 128 grants (high: $55,000; low: $50) and $11,598 for 77 employee matching gifts.
Purpose and activities: Giving largely for community funds, social services and youth, arts and culture, hospitals, food-related research, higher education, and civic organizations.
Types of support: Employee matching gifts.
Limitations: No support for political organizations or sectarian religious organizations. No grants to individuals.
Application information: Contributes only to pre-selected organizations. Applications not accepted.
Write: John Heinrich, V.P., Admin.
Officers: John L. Murray, Pres.; Darrell E. Wilde, Sr. V.P.; John E. Heinrich, V.P.; Guy A. Osborn, V.P.; Dan E. McMullen, Secy.-Treas.
Number of staff: 1 part-time professional; 1 part-time support.
Employer Identification Number: 396044488

3349
Vollrath Company Foundation, Inc.
1236 North 18th St.
Sheboygan 53081 (414) 457-4851

Donor(s): Vollrath Co.
Financial data (yr. ended 9/30/88): Assets, $126,353 (M); gifts received, $183,856; expenditures, $180,486, including $178,165 for 63 grants (high: $29,487; low: $200) and $1,000 for 1 grant to an individual.
Purpose and activities: Support primarily for youth and social service organizations, higher education, and culture.
Limitations: Giving primarily in WI.
Application information:
Initial approach: Letter
Deadline(s): None
Write: Terry J. Kohler, Pres.
Officers and Directors: Terry J. Kohler, Pres.; Charlotte M. Kohler, V.P.; Mary S. Kohler, V.P.; Mary L. Ten Haken, Secy.; Roland M. Neumann, Jr., Treas.
Trustee: First Wisconsin National Bank of Sheboygan.
Employer Identification Number: 396046987

3350
Wausau Insurance Companies Corporate Giving Program
2000 Westwood Dr.
Box 8017
Wausau 54402-8017 (715) 845-5211

Financial data (yr. ended 12/31/88): $500,000 for grants.
Purpose and activities: "Approved contributions should complement company objectives and provide potential benefit to the company, its employees, policyholders or the public." Support for education; health and welfare; civic and community organizations; culture and the arts, through community arts, literature, performing arts, music, theater, public TV/radio and museums. Also supports the United Way.
Types of support: Employee matching gifts, general purposes.
Limitations: Giving primarily in the city of Wausau, Marathon County, WI, and major operating locations. No support for religious, political or labor organizations, or organizations receiving funds from a local community fund. No grants for advertising, "token" contributions or administrative support.
Publications: Corporate giving report.
Application information: Include organization description, amount and purpose of request, recently audited financial statement and 501(c)(3) status.
Initial approach: Letter or proposal
Deadline(s): None
Final notification: 6 weeks
Write: Roger Drayna, Dir. Public Relations
Directors: John A. Schoneman, T.A. Duckworth, Gerald Delmar Viste, C.C. Chamberlain.

3351
Wausau Paper Mills Foundation, Inc.
One Clarks Island
P.O. Box 1408
Wausau 54402-1408

Donor(s): Wausau Paper Mills Co., Rhinelander Paper Mills Co.
Financial data (yr. ended 8/31/88): Assets, $11,749 (M); gifts received, $80,000; expenditures, $88,851, including $88,800 for 57 grants (high: $30,000; low: $25).
Purpose and activities: Supports higher education, cultural activities and the arts, youth programs, secondary education, and civic affairs.
Types of support: General purposes.
Limitations: Giving primarily in Wausau, WI.
Application information:
Initial approach: Letter
Deadline(s): None
Write: Larry A. Baker, V.P., Administration, Wausau Paper Mills Co.

Officers: William L. Goggins, Pres. and C.E.O.; Daniel R. Olvey, V.P. and Secy.-Treas.; Larry A. Baker, V.P., Administration.
Directors: John E. Forester, Sam W. Orr, Jr., David B. Smith, Stanley F. Staples, Jr.
Employer Identification Number: 396080502

3352
Wauwatosa Savings and Loan Foundation
7500 West State St.
Wauwatosa 53213 (414) 258-5880

Established in 1985 in WI.
Donor(s): Wauwatosa Savings and Loan Association.
Financial data (yr. ended 12/31/87): Assets, $1,564,199 (M); gifts received, $400,000; expenditures, $68,355, including $60,008 for 57 grants (high: $6,000; low: $25; average: $250-$1,500) and $5,000 for 3 employee matching gifts.
Purpose and activities: Support for historical societies and social services.
Types of support: Employee matching gifts, general purposes, matching funds, program-related investments, employee-related scholarships, scholarship funds, seed money, special projects.
Limitations: Giving primarily in areas of company facilities.
Application information:
Initial approach: Proposal
Deadline(s): None
Write: Raymond J. Perry, Trustee
Trustees: Charles A. Perry, Raymond J. Perry.
Number of staff: None.
Employer Identification Number: 391548588

3353
Frank L. Weyenberg Charitable Trust
c/o Quarles & Brady
411 East Wisconsin Ave.
Milwaukee 53202 (414) 277-5000

Established in 1983 in WI.
Financial data (yr. ended 7/31/88): Assets, $2,935,896 (M); expenditures, $213,891, including $191,050 for 23 grants (high: $50,000; low: $400).
Purpose and activities: Support primarily for cultural programs, education, and social services.
Application information: Contributes only to pre-selected organizations. Applications not accepted.
Write: Henry J. Loos, Trustee
Trustees: Henry J. Loos, First National Bank in Palm Beach.
Employer Identification Number: 391461670

3354
WICOR Foundation, Inc.
777 East Wisconsin Ave.
Milwaukee 53202 (414) 291-7026

Established in 1984 in WI.
Donor(s): WICOR, Inc.
Financial data (yr. ended 12/31/87): Assets, $133,807 (M); gifts received, $150,000; expenditures, $345,055, including $344,590 for 76 grants (high: $35,000; low: $100).
Purpose and activities: Emphasis on the arts, youth organizations, and health associations.
Limitations: Giving limited to areas of company operations; support primarily in Milwaukee, WI, area.
Application information:
Initial approach: In writing
Deadline(s): None
Write: B.W. Kostecke, Secy.
Officers and Directors: R.M. Hoffer, Pres.; J.A. Brady, V.P.; W.W. Tisdale, V.P.; B.W. Kostecke, Secy.-Treas.
Employer Identification Number: 391522073

3355
Wisconsin Electric System Foundation, Inc.
231 West Michigan St.
Milwaukee 53201 (414) 221-2105

Incorporated in 1982 in WI.
Donor(s): Wisconsin Electric Power Co., Wisconsin Natural Gas Co.
Financial data (yr. ended 12/31/86): Assets, $11,738,459 (M); gifts received, $4,000,000; expenditures, $1,544,410, including $1,500,503 for 333 grants (high: $375,000; low: $10; average: $75-$10,000) and $30,439 for 139 employee matching gifts.
Purpose and activities: Giving primarily for community funds, higher education, youth and social service agencies, cultural programs, hospitals and health organizations, community development, and civic affairs.
Types of support: Employee matching gifts.
Limitations: Giving primarily in service territories in southeastern WI.
Application information:
Initial approach: Letter
Deadline(s): None
Board meeting date(s): As required
Final notification: Usually 2 weeks
Write: Jerry C. Remmel, Treas.
Officers: Charles S. McNeer, Pres.; Russell W. Britt, V.P.; John H. Goetsch, Secy.; Gerlad C. Remmel, Treas.
Number of staff: None.
Employer Identification Number: 391433726

3356
Wisconsin Power and Light Foundation, Inc.
222 West Washington Ave.
Madison 53703 (608) 252-3181
Additional address: P.O. Box 192, Madison, WI 53701

Established in 1984 in WI.
Donor(s): Wisconsin Power and Light Co.
Financial data (yr. ended 12/31/88): Assets, $4,123,557 (M); gifts received, $600,000; expenditures, $782,054, including $694,846 for grants, $32,000 for 32 grants to individuals and $15,517 for 123 employee matching gifts.
Purpose and activities: Support primarily for health, social services, education, cultural programs, and civic affairs.
Types of support: Annual campaigns, building funds, capital campaigns, continuing support, employee matching gifts, equipment, fellowships, operating budgets, scholarship funds, employee-related scholarships, seed money, renovation projects.
Limitations: Giving primarily in central and south-central WI, areas of company operations. No support for political or religious organizations. No grants to individuals.
Publications: Annual report, informational brochure (including application guidelines).
Application information:
Initial approach: Proposal
Copies of proposal: 1
Deadline(s): None
Board meeting date(s): Quarterly
Write: Donald R. Piepenburg, V.P.
Officers: Robert A. Carlsen,* Pres.; Donald R. Piepenburg, V.P.; Edward M. Gleason, Secy.-Treas.
Directors:* Roger L. Baumann, Elizabeth Benson, Willie Collins, Edward F. Killeen, Duaine Mossman, Suzette M. Mullooly.
Number of staff: 1 part-time professional; 1 part-time support.
Employer Identification Number: 391444065

3357
Wisconsin Public Service Foundation, Inc.
700 North Adams St.
P.O. Box 19001
Green Bay 54307 (414) 433-1465
Scholarship application address: Wisconsin Public Service Foundation, Inc. Scholarship Program, College Scholarship Service, Sponsored Scholarships Program, CN 6730, Princeton, NJ 08541

Incorporated in 1964 in WI.
Donor(s): Wisconsin Public Service Corp.
Financial data (yr. ended 12/31/86): Assets, $6,545,131 (M); expenditures, $603,799, including $526,679 for 117 grants (high: $50,000; low: $15) and $53,075 for grants to individuals.
Purpose and activities: Grants largely for higher education and community services, with emphasis on health, arts and culture, and conservation.
Types of support: Operating budgets, building funds, equipment, student aid, employee-related scholarships.
Limitations: Giving limited to WI and upper MI. No grants for endowment funds.
Application information: Application form required for scholarships.
Initial approach: Letter
Copies of proposal: 1
Deadline(s): None
Board meeting date(s): May and as required
Write: Mr. P.D. Ziemer, Pres.
Officers and Directors: P.D. Ziemer, Pres.; L.M. Stoll, V.P.; J.H. Liethen, Secy.-Treas.
Employer Identification Number: 396075016

WYOMING

3358
William E. Weiss Foundation, Inc.
P.O. Box 2930
Cody 82414 (307) 587-4973

Incorporated in 1955 in NY.

Donor(s): William E. Weiss, Jr.,† Helene K. Brown.†
Financial data (yr. ended 3/31/88): Assets, $4,037,444 (M); expenditures, $205,744, including $161,700 for 36 grants.
Purpose and activities: Grants largely for higher and secondary education, historic preservation, hospitals, and Protestant church support.
Types of support: Building funds, special projects, continuing support.
Limitations: Giving primarily in NY, WV, and WY. No grants to individuals.
Publications: Program policy statement, application guidelines.
Application information:
Initial approach: Proposal
Copies of proposal: 4
Deadline(s): Submit proposal preferably in Nov.
Board meeting date(s): Jan.
Final notification: Mar.
Write: Ann E. Zatkos, Secy.
Officers and Directors: William D. Weiss, Pres.; Daryl B. Uber, V.P.; Ann E. Zatkos, Secy.; P.W.T. Brown, Treas.; Mary K. Weiss.
Number of staff: 1 part-time support.
Employer Identification Number: 556016633

INDEXES

INDEX TO DONORS, OFFICERS, TRUSTEES

GEOGRAPHIC INDEX

Foundations and corporate giving programs in bold face type make grants on a national or regional basis; the others generally limit giving to the city or state in which they are located.

COLORADO

CONNECTICUT

DELAWARE

DISTRICT OF COLUMBIA

FLORIDA

GEORGIA

HAWAII

IDAHO

ILLINOIS

INDIANA

IOWA

KANSAS

KENTUCKY

LOUISIANA

MAINE

MARYLAND

NEBRASKA

NEVADA

NEW HAMPSHIRE

NEW JERSEY

NEW MEXICO

NEW YORK

NORTH CAROLINA

NORTH DAKOTA

OHIO

UTAH

VERMONT

VIRGINIA

WASHINGTON

WEST VIRGINIA

WISCONSIN

WYOMING

TYPES OF SUPPORT INDEX

Foundations and corporate giving programs in bold face type make grants on a national or regional basis; the others generally limit giving to the city or state in which they are located.

Annual campaigns: any organized effort by a nonprofit to secure gifts on an annual basis; also called annual appeals.

Building funds: money raised for construction of buildings; may be part of an organization's capital campaign.

Capital campaigns: a campaign, usually extending over a period of years, to raise substantial funds for enduring purposes, such as building or endowment funds.

Conferences and seminars: a grant to cover the expenses of holding a conference.

Consulting services: professional staff support provided by the foundation to a nonprofit to consult on a project of mutual interest or to evaluate services (not a cash grant).

Continuing support: a grant that is renewed on a regular basis.

Deficit financing: also known as debt reduction. A grant to reduce the recipient organization's indebtedness; frequently refers to mortgage payments.

Emergency funds: a one-time grant to cover immediate short-term funding needs on an emergency basis.

Employee matching gifts: a contribution to a charitable organization by a corporate employee which is matched by a similar contribution from the employer. Many corporations support employee matching gift programs in higher education to stimulate their employees to give to the college or university of their choice.

Employee-related scholarships: a scholarship program funded by a company-sponsored foundation usually for children of employees; programs are frequently administered by the National Merit Scholarship Corporation which is responsible for selection of scholars.

Endowment funds: a bequest or gift intended to be kept permanently and invested to provide income for continued support of an organization.

Equipment: a grant to purchase equipment, furnishings, or other materials.

Exchange programs: usually refers to funds for educational exchange programs for foreign students.

Fellowships: usually indicates funds awarded to educational institutions to support fellowship programs. A few foundations award fellowships directly to individuals.

General purposes: a grant made to further the general purpose or work of an organization, rather than for a specific purpose or project; also called unrestricted grants.

Grants to individuals: awards made directly by the foundation to individuals rather than to nonprofit organizations; includes aid to the needy. (See also 'Fellowships' and 'Student aid.')

Internships: usually indicates funds awarded to an institution or organization to support an internship program rather than a grant to an individual.

Land acquisition: a grant to purchase real estate property.

Loans: temporary award of funds which usually must be repaid. (See also 'Program-related investments' and 'Student loans.')

Matching funds: a grant which is made to match funds provided by another donor. (See also 'Employee matching gifts.')

Operating budgets: a grant to cover the day-to-day personnel, administrative, and other expenses for an existing program or organization.

Professorships: usually indicates a grant to an educational institution to endow a professorship or chair.

Program-related investments: a loan made by a private foundation to profit-making or nonprofit organizations for a project related to the foundation's stated purpose and interests. Program-related investments are often made from a revolving fund; the foundation generally expects to receive its money back with interest which will then provide additional funds for loans to other organizations.

Publications: a grant to fund reports or other publications issued by a nonprofit resulting from research or projects of interest to the foundation.

Renovation projects: grants for renovating, remodeling, or rehabilitating property.

Research: usually indicates funds awarded to institutions to cover costs of investigations and clinical trials. Research grants for individuals are usually referred to as fellowships.

Scholarship funds: usually indicates a grant to an educational institution or organization to support a scholarship program, mainly for students at the undergraduate level. (See also 'Employee-related scholarships'; for scholarships paid to individuals, see 'Student aid.')

Seed money: a grant or contribution used to start a new project or organization. Seed grants may cover salaries and other operating expenses of a new project. Also known as 'start-up funds.'

Special projects: grants to support specific projects or programs as opposed to general purpose grants.

Student aid: assistance awarded directly to individuals in the form of educational grants or scholarships. (See also 'Employee-related scholarships.')

Student loans: assistance awarded directly to individuals in the form of educational loans.

Technical assistance: operational or management assistance given to nonprofit organizations; may include fundraising assistance, budgeting and financial planning, program planning, legal advice, marketing, and other aids to management. Assistance may be offered directly by a foundation staff member or in the form of a grant to pay for the services of an outside consultant.

Annual campaigns

Building funds

Capital campaigns

Conferences and seminars

Consulting services

Continuing support

Deficit financing

Emergency funds

Employee matching gifts

Employee-related scholarships

Endowment funds

Equipment

Exchange programs

Fellowships

General purposes

Grants to individuals

In-kind gifts

Internships

Land acquisition

Lectureships

Loans

Matching funds

Operating budgets

Professorships

Program-related investments

Publications

Renovation projects

Research

Scholarship funds

Seed money

Special projects

Student aid

Student loans

Technical assistance

SUBJECT INDEX

Foundations and corporate giving programs in bold face type make grants on a national or regional basis; the others generally limit giving to the city or state in which they are located.

Archaeology

Architecture

Arts

Cultural programs

Dance

Film

Fine arts

Historic preservation

Humanities

Language and literature

Media and communications

Museums

Music

Performing arts

Theater

INDEX OF FOUNDATIONS AND CORPORATE GIVING PROGRAMS